W9-AMA-761

CRITICAL SURVEY
OF
DRAMA

CRITICAL SURVEY

OF

DRAMA

Second Revised Edition

Volume 3

Maria Irene Fornes - Tina Howe

Editor, Second Revised Edition
Carl Rollyson
Baruch College, City University of New York

Editor, First Editions, English and Foreign Language Series
Frank N. Magill

SALEM PRESS, INC.
Pasadena, California   Hackensack, New Jersey

Editor in Chief: Dawn P. Dawson
Managing Editor: Christina J. Moose
Developmental Editor: R. Kent Rasmussen
Project Editor: Rowena Wildin
Research Supervisor: Jeffry Jensen
Research Assistant: Michelle Murphy

Acquisitions Editor: Mark Rehn
Photograph Editor: Philip Bader
Manuscript Editor: Sarah Hilbert
Assistant Editor: Andrea E. Miller
Production Editor: Cynthia Beres
Layout: Eddie Murillo and William Zimmerman

Copyright © 2003, by Salem Press, Inc.

All rights in this book are reserved. No part of this work may be used or reproduced in any manner whatsoever or transmitted in any form or by any means, electronic or mechanical, including photocopy, recording, or any information storage and retrieval system, without written permission from the copyright owners except in the case of brief quotations embodied in critical articles and reviews. For information, address the publisher, Salem Press, Inc., P.O. Box 50062, Pasadena, California 91115.

∞ The paper used in these volumes conforms to the American National Standard for Permanence of Paper for Printed Library Materials, Z39.48-1992(R1997).

Library of Congress Cataloging-in-Publication Data

Critical survey of drama / edited by Carl Rollyson.-- 2nd rev. ed.

    p. cm.

Previous edition edited by Frank Northen Magill in 1994.

"Combines, updates, and expands two earlier Salem Press reference sets: Critical survey of drama, revised edition, English language series, published in 1994, and Critical survey of drama, foreign language series, published in 1986"--Pref.

Includes bibliographical references and index.

    ISBN 1-58765-102-5 (set : alk. paper) -- ISBN 1-58765-105-X (vol. 3 : alk. paper) --

    1. Drama--Dictionaries. 2. Drama--History and criticism--Dictionaries. 3. Drama--Bio-bibliography. 4. English drama--Dictionaries. 5. American drama--Dictionaries. 6. Commonwealth drama (English)--Dictionaries. 7. English drama--Bio-bibliography. 8. American drama--Bio-bibliography. 9. Commonwealth drama (English)--Bio-bibliography. I. Rollyson, Carl E. (Carl Edmund) II. Magill, Frank Northen, 1907-1997.

PN1625 .C68 2003

809.2'003—dc21

2003002190

RENFRO LIBRARY
MARS HILL UNIVERSITY
MARS HILL, NC 28754

SEP 0 7 2015

R
809.2003
C9348m
v.3

Fourth Printing

PRINTED IN THE UNITED STATES OF AMERICA

CONTENTS

VOLUME 3

COMPLETE LIST OF CONTENTS

VOLUME 1

VOLUME 2

VOLUME 3

VOLUME 4

VOLUME 5

VOLUME 6

VOLUME 7

AMERICAN DRAMA

VOLUME 8

CRITICAL SURVEY
OF
DRAMA

MARIA IRENE FORNES

Born: Havana, Cuba; May 14, 1930

PRINCIPAL DRAMA

The Widow, pr., pb. 1961

There, You Died!, pr. 1963, revised pr. 1964, pb. 1971 (as *Tango Palace*)

The Successful Life of Three, pr. 1965, pb. 1971

Promenade, pr. 1965, pb. 1971 (music by Al Carmines)

The Office, pr. 1966

A Vietnamese Wedding, pr. 1967, pb. 1971

The Annunciation, pr. 1967

Dr. Kheal, pr. 1968, pb. 1971

The Red Burning Light: Or, Mission XQ3, pr. 1968, pb. 1971

Molly's Dream, pr. 1968, pb. 1971

The Curse of the Langston House, pr. 1972

Aurora, pr. 1974

Cap-a-Pie, pr. 1975

Fefu and Her Friends, pr. 1977, pb. 1980

Lolita in the Garden, pr. 1977

In Service, pr. 1978

Eyes on the Harem, pr. 1979

Evelyn Brown: A Diary, pr. 1980

Blood Wedding, pr. 1980 (adaptation of Federico García Lorca's play)

Life Is a Dream, pr. 1981 (adaptation of Pedro Calderón de la Barca's play)

A Visit, pr. 1981

The Danube, pr. 1982

Mud, pr. 1983, pb. 1986

Abingdon Square, pr. 1984, pb. 1988

Sarita, pr. 1984, pb. 1986

No Time, pr. 1984

The Conduct of Life, pr. 1985, pb. 1986

Lovers and Keepers, pr. 1986, pb. 1987 (music by Tito Puente)

Drowning, pr. 1986, pb. 1987 (adaptation of Anton Chekhov's story)

And What of the Night?, pr. 1989

Oscar and Bertha, pr. 1991

Enter the Night, pr. 1993, pb. 1996

Balseros, pr. 1996

Summer in Gossensass, pr. 1998

Letters from Cuba, pr. 2000

OTHER LITERARY FORMS

Maria Irene Fornes began as a painter, but after the early 1960's, she became almost exclusively a playwright. She has worked in a variety of styles, from musicals with people such as Tito Puente and John Fitz Gibbon to avant-garde works with the Judson Poets Theatre and other companies.

ACHIEVEMENTS

Maria Irene Fornes has been recognized and honored by the Guggenheim Memorial Foundation, the Rockefeller Foundation, and The National Endowment of the Arts. In addition, she has been an active and vital force in the Off-Broadway theater scene. She won Obie awards in 1965, 1977, 1979, 1982, 1984, 1985, 1988, and 2000. Her 1982 award was the Obie for Sustained Achievement in the Theater, and her 2000 Obie was for her play *Letters from Cuba*. She has also been honored with a Whitney Fellowship, a Yale University Fellowship, and the Cintas Foundation fellowship and has received a Distinguished Artists Award, an American Academy Award, and a New York State Governor's Arts Award. Most recently, New York's Signature Theatre Company devoted its entire 2000 season to Fornes's works.

Fornes has been a major force in the avant-garde and feminist theaters. Her writing has a unique style that blends elements of the avant-grade, modernism, and Magical Realism. Fornes's work has always been difficult to classify as she is constantly experimenting with both the form of drama as well as the text. Fornes writes with a clear sense of the theatrical in her works.

In addition to her work as a playwright, Fornes has served as a director and designer for many of her own works. Some critics have attributed her theatricality in her works to her involvement in the production process. She has also been heavily involved with the teaching and development of new playwrights, especially new Hispanic playwrights.

BIOGRAPHY

Maria Irene Fornes was born in Havana, Cuba, in 1930. She immigrated with her family to the United States in 1945 and was naturalized in 1951. From 1954 to 1957, she studied painting in Europe, where she saw Roger Blin's famous production of Samuel Beckett's *En attendant Godot* (pb. 1952, pr. 1953; *Waiting for Godot*, 1954). Fornes returned to the United States in 1957 and worked in New York as a textile designer. During this time, she read plays and began to think about moving into theater. In 1960, she created *The Widow*, which was first performed in New York in 1961 and then moved to Mexico in September of that year. In 1963 she joined the playwrights unit of the Actors Studio to further develop her writing skills. In the late 1960's, she served as a costume designer for several avant-garde theater companies including the New Dramatists Committee and the Judson Poets Theatre. Fornes also wrote during this period and had some success with plays such as *The Successful Life of Three* and *A Vietnamese Wedding*. She won her first Obie award for playwriting in 1965, the same year *Successful Life of Three* was produced. In 1966 she had a brief experience with Broadway when *The Office*, a play she had written, had several previews at the Henry Miller but never opened.

Fornes continued to work in Off-Broadway and regional American theaters throughout the 1960's and early 1970's. In 1972 she helped found and run the New York Theater Strategy, an organization dedicated to the development of avant-garde theater artists. *Fefu and Her Friends* premiered in 1977 and earned an Obie award. Fornes received another Obie for direction in 1979. Fornes continued to write, producing some of her most popular works, including *Mud*, *The Conduct of Life*, and *Abingdon Square*.

Fornes has also been a major force in the development of young playwrights, especially those of Hispanic descent. She has spent a great deal of her time conducting workshops, classes, and projects on playwriting with a variety of students to bring new voices into the theater.

ANALYSIS

Maria Irene Fornes is a unique voice in American theater. Defying categorizations, she refuses to allow her work to be defined by either who she is or by any specific genre. She instead creates stunning and powerfully visual works of theater. In general, her writing attempts to blend nonrealistic staging with psychologically based dialogue. Fornes is not trapped by plot, however. In many of her plays, major plot moments are referred to obliquely through the use of dialogue and through throwaway references made during scenes. She writes with a clear poetic sense and creates strong verbal and visual imagery both with her words and the stage pictures that she paints. In addition, she is not afraid to break theatrical convention by making the audience aware of the theatrical frame with which she is working. She considers the audience to be an active participant in her plays, whether actually following the action throughout the theater (such as in *Fefu and Her Friends*) or forcing them to piece together the interlocking relationships of her characters (such as in *Abingdon Square*).

Her strong desire to create theatrical compositions onstage has been linked to her background as a painter, although her directing experience may also play a part. In all of her plays, she pays a great deal of attention to staging and stage directions. She provides detailed set descriptions as well as evocation descriptions of the movement in her plays. Yet her emphasis on theatricality in her works in no way diminishes the depth of her characterization. Fornes has a great ability to create fully realized and tremendously complex characters in all of her works. Even the minor characters in her plays are given their full due; one has only to look at the eight individual women she created in *Fefu and Her Friends* to realize how complex her characters are.

FEFU AND HER FRIENDS

In 1935 New England, eight women gather at Fefu's house to discuss their upcoming presentation on education. Fefu greets the women, a collection of new acquaintances and old friends. Most notable among the old friends is Julia, a friend of Fefu's who has been paralyzed ever since witnessing a deer being shot. Fefu shocks the newcomers by being "outrageous," specifically by fixing toilets and playing a game with her husband wherein she fires a blank at him. After all the women are together, Fornes breaks the audience into four groups. The groups then proceed to four different areas, each within hearing/visual distance from the others. The cast then performs four separate scenes, and the audience shifts from scene to scene. For the third act the audience returns to their seats and the actors go back to the main living room set. The women plan their presentation, and then, as the other women participate in a water fight in the kitchen, Julia is encouraged by Fefu to fight against her paralysis. In an attempt to cheer her friend up, Fefu goes offstage to "shoot" her husband again. The shot is fired, and spot of blood appears on Julia's forehead as Fefu comes in holding the dead body of a rabbit she accidentally killed.

With *Fefu and Her Friends*, Fornes uses the gathering of women to demonstrate the transformation of roles of women and the advantage men have over them. Fefu is considered "outrageous" because her behavior is seen as too masculine, whereas Julia is seen as too helpless and empathetic to survive the new modern age. Some critics have suggested that the playwright's disruption of the stage space and the traditional actor/audience relationship in the second act forces the audience to question the dominant (masculine) theater paradigm.

MUD

Mud was another major triumph for Fornes. Set in a wooden room on top of an earth promontory, *Mud* tells of the interrelationship among Lloyd, Mae, and Henry. Lloyd and Mae are undereducated and in their mid-twenties, while Henry is slightly more educated but very philosophical. Henry is also much older than Mae. When Henry falls in love with Mae, she allows him to move into her and Lloyd's world. When Henry moves in, Lloyd is very resentful and encourages Mae to leave him. Mae convinces Lloyd to become more educated and to cure himself of his illness. As Lloyd becomes more independent of Mae, Henry becomes more dependent, eventually having a stroke and needing to be spoon-fed. At the end of the play, as the two men are fighting, Mae leaves but is shot by Lloyd and dies.

In *Mud*, Fornes requires the actors to freeze in place for five seconds after each scene. Through the ever-present mud on the stage, she seems to be commenting on people's desire to evolve out of the muck and to reinvent the self. Indeed, this is the theme that Mae constantly evokes, and when she dies, she dies "as a starfish," having finally reinvented herself into something beautiful.

THE CONDUCT OF LIFE

Perhaps Fornes's best-known play, *The Conduct of Life* partners violence against women with political violence. The play centers on the figure of Orlando, who is the head of his household and also an army officer involved in state-sponsored torture. Orlando mocks his wife, Leticia, and dominates his household, including Olympia, his housekeeper. He also beats and rapes Nena, a twelve-year-old girl whom he keeps in the basement for his sexual pleasures. As the action progresses, Fornes shows how violence breeds more violence: Leticia finally rebels and kills Orlando. She then gives the gun to Nena, and the play ends with her asking Nena to shoot her as well.

The Conduct of Life shows Fornes's continuing concern with the intersections of gender, power, and violence. Olympia survives because she is able to dismiss Orlando despite his threats, and Nena survives her brutal ordeal through a Christ-like acceptance of others' pain. Orlando is only able to perform sexually if violence is involved. He rapes Nena and forces himself on his wife at the end of the play. Leticia, who tries to endure this world, finally resorts to violence. With these characters, Fornes explores many different ways in which power and gender interact and shows the potential danger of how oppression breeds violence and hatred.

ABINGDON SQUARE

Fornes returns to the themes of sexuality, gender, and repression in *Abingdon Square*. Set in early twentieth century New York, the play tells the story of Marion, a young woman of fifteen married to Juster, a successful fifty-year-old widower who has fallen in love with her. As the play continues, the audience learns that Marion merely admires Juster and does not love him. As she defies convention and has an affair, Fornes shows the effects her scandalous behavior has on all members of the family. At the end, Juster suffers a stroke after debating whether to kill Marion or himself, and Marion leaves her lover to fulfill her obligation to her husband.

In many ways, *Abingdon Square* can be seen as an extension of many of the themes dealt with in Fornes's earlier plays. She sets up the conflict between desire and duty, age and youth, and freedom and repression. She shows the emotional and psychic damage these issues cause all members of the family with the tense, emotion-loaded, staccato scenes of dialogue that she uses to construct the play.

BIBLIOGRAPHY

Kent, Assunta Bartolomucci. *Maria Irene Fornes and Her Critics*. Westport, Conn.: Greenwood Press, 1996. Kent traces Fornes's work from the point of view of feminist criticism and explores how this criticism can and cannot be applied to her work. This book has a large section on feminist theory, as well as detailed sections on the plays and their reception, particularly *Fefu and Her Friends* and *And What of the Night?*

Moroff, Dianne Lynn. *Fornes: Theatre in the Present Tense*. Ann Arbor: University of Michigan Press, 1996. This work examines several of Fornes's better-known plays (*Fefu and Her Friends, Mud, The Conduct of Life*, and *Sarita*) from a theatrical as well as a literary perspective. Moroff is primarily concerned with how the plays work as theatrical metaphor and how they illustrate the interrelationships between the genders. It also includes a detailed chronology of plays and publications.

Robinson, Marc. *The Other American Drama*. Baltimore, Md.: The Johns Hopkins University Press, 1994. Robinson places Fornes in a new genealogy of American drama, which regarded plot as less important than other elements of the theater such as "language, gesture, and presence." According to Robinson, Fornes's plays have been underappreciated, and he sets out to rediscover how she uses the power of language to discover moments of individual truth.

Robinson, Marc, ed. *The Theatre of Maria Irene Fornes*. Baltimore, Md.: PAJ Books, 1999. Robinson has edited this excellent collection by a variety of theater artists and scholars. The result is a comprehensive and fascinating look at her career from a variety of viewpoints. The book includes essays on style and performance, several reviews of her plays, and a long section entitled "Fornes on Fornes," in which the playwright describes some of her own work and her writing process.

David Jortner

MICHAEL FRAYN

Born: London, England; September 8, 1933

PRINCIPAL DRAMA

The Two of Us, pr., pb. 1970
The Sandboy, pr. 1971
Alphabetical Order, pr. 1975, pb. 1977
Donkeys' Years, pr. 1976, pb. 1977
Clouds, pr. 1976, pb. 1977
Liberty Hall, pr. 1980
Make and Break, pr., pb. 1980
Noises Off, pr. 1982
Benefactors, pr., pb. 1984

Plays: One, pb. 1985
Balmoral, pr., pb. 1987 (revised version of *Liberty Hall*)
Look Look, pr., pb. 1990
Audience, pb. 1991
Plays: Two, pb. 1991
Here, pr., pb. 1993
Now You Know, pr., pb. 1995 (adaptation of his novel)
Alarms and Excursions: More Plays than One, pb. 1998
Copenhagen, pr., pb. 1998
Plays: Three, pb. 2000

OTHER LITERARY FORMS

Michael Frayn began his career as a reporter and columnist for the *Manchester Guardian* (1957-1962) and *The Observer* (1962-1968). Frayn has published several collections of these largely satirical newspaper columns and returned briefly to writing a column in 1994. Frayn has also written several novels. He has translated and adapted several plays by Leo Tolstoy, Jean Anouilh, and Anton Chekhov. Frayn's 1983 adaptation of Chekhov's *Tri sestry* (pr., pb. 1901, rev. pb. 1904; *The Three Sisters*, 1920) received especially favorable notice. Frayn has written numerous documentaries and original scripts for television and became a motion picture screenwriter with *Clockwise* in 1986. In 2001 Frayn published *The Copenhagen Papers: An Intrigue*, a short nonfiction work concerning a mysterious bundle of papers he received during the production of *Copenhagen* that may have resolved the mysteries at the play's core.

ACHIEVEMENTS

Already established as a respected journalist and novelist, in middle age Michael Frayn won even greater acclaim as a playwright. His first plays, amusing and well-crafted comedies, suggested that yet another clever farceur, someone akin to the early Alan Ayckbourn, had arrived on the scene. More discerning viewers, however, began to note that Frayn was a serious writer employing comedy to explore philosophical themes: the relationship of language and perception, of order and misrule, of human beings' illusory control of self and environment. Soon after arriving on the theatrical scene, Frayn was winning awards as author of the best comedy of the year (for *Alphabetical Order*, *Donkeys' Years*, and *Noises Off*). In 1980, *Make and Break*, more reflective than his previous plays, won awards as both the year's best comedy and the year's best play. In 1984, *Benefactors*, his darkest comedy, not only won awards as the year's best play but also afforded Frayn a place among such contemporary British dramatists of the first rank as Harold Pinter and Tom Stoppard. His subsequent work for the stage, however, fell off in quality and quantity, achieving neither the popular success of *Noises Off* nor the critical acclaim of *Benefactors*. *Look Look* in

Michael Frayn (Hulton Archive by Getty Images)

1990 and *Here* in 1993 fared poorly with audiences and critics alike. In the late 1990's Frayn's reputation soared again when his play *Copenhagen* (1998) won three Tony Awards including Best Play, and his novel *Headlong* (1999) was listed as a finalist for the Booker Prize.

BIOGRAPHY

Michael Frayn's family lived in Mill Hill in northwest London but moved to Holloway soon after his birth and then to Ewell, a southwest suburb, where he was reared. His father was an asbestos salesperson who occasionally took Michael and his sister to the nearby Kingston Empire, a music hall, as a special treat. Frayn remembers borrowing music-hall routines for the home entertainments—puppet shows and conjuring acts—that he devised for an audience of three—father, mother, and sister. At Christmastime, the elder Frayn became the star performer in comic sketches that he himself wrote. Michael and his sister were relegated to supporting roles, and Mrs. Frayn formed an audience of one. Michael Frayn's mother, who had earlier worked as a shop assistant and occasional model in Harrods, London's grandest department store, died when he was twelve, a disorienting experience for the boy. At that time, his father removed him from private day school, which the boy hated, and enrolled him in the state-run Kingston Grammar School, where he was far more comfortable.

Frayn got along with his chums by playing the fool and cleverly mimicking his teachers while doing a minimum of schoolwork. That changed when an English master, aware of the boy's incipient talent for writing, challenged him to produce even better work. These were the years in which Frayn discovered poetry, music, religion, and politics. He and his friends declared themselves atheists and formed a model communist cell in the school. Although his interest in communism soon waned, it led him to study the Russian language. He subsequently traveled to the Soviet Union, employing it as the setting of his spy novel *The Russian Interpreter* (1966). In addition, he has become Great Britain's foremost translator of Russian drama, specifically the plays of Chekhov, which are peopled with characters as bewildered, troubled, and comic as Frayn's own.

Frayn perfected his Russian when he was drafted into the army in 1952 and sent to language school at Cambridge University. He returned to Cambridge as an undergraduate after completing his national service in 1954. In addition to studying philosophy, he dabbled in university theatricals, collaborating on a musical revue and playing a servant in a production of Nikolai Gogol's *Revizor* (1836; *The Inspector General*, 1890). Trapped onstage in Gogol's play for what seemed an eternity when a door refused to open and the audience started a slow handclap, he vowed never again to tread the boards, an experience that may have provided an inspiration for *Noises Off*, a play about theatrical mishaps.

After graduating from Cambridge in 1957, Frayn worked for *The Guardian* (Manchester) and two years later began a satirical humor column, which he has likened to the work of American columnists Russell Baker and Art Buchwald. Like Joseph Addison and Richard Steele in *The Spectator* (1711-1712),

Frayn invented a cast of characters, among them two couples reappearing with great frequency: Christopher and Lavinia Crumble, who knew everything, and Horace and Doris Morris, who knew nothing at all. The relationship of two other contrasting couples, the fortunate Kitzingers and the unfortunate Molyneuxs, would become the basis of his most acclaimed work, *Benefactors*.

After further newspaper work on *The Observer*, Frayn decided that the novel would allow him greater latitude for the exploration of character and ideas. Between 1965 and 1973, he published five novels to generally favorable reviews, the most effective among them *Towards the End of the Morning* (1967; U.S. edition, *Against Entropy*, 1967), a comic exploration of Frayn's familiar newspaper world. A television script brought him to the attention of theatrical producer Michael Codron, who urged him to write a play. Frayn's first attempt was *The Two of Us*, a collection of four one-acts, with all the characters played by two actors and ending in a farcical disaster of a dinner party. Although it entertained audiences for half a year, the play did not amuse the critics. Intrigued, nevertheless, by the possibilities of dramatic presentation, Frayn believed that he could do better. His subsequent plays have proved him right.

Frayn married Gillian Palmer in 1969 and has three daughters with whom he enjoys a close relationship, but he and his wife separated in 1981 and divorced in 1990. In 1993 Frayn married Claire Tomalin, literary editor of the London *Sunday Times*.

After the relative failure of *Here*, Frayn briefly resumed writing his newspaper column, focusing on communication in the modern world. These columns were published as a collection in *Speak After the Beep: Studies in the Art of Communicating with Inanimate and Semi-animate Objects* (1995). He adapted his novel *Now You Know* (1992) into a play produced in 1995 and also published an additional collection of early newspaper columns; a novel, *Headlong* (1999); two television scripts; and a motion picture screenplay. In 1998 Frayn's play *Alarms and Excursions* premiered to mixed reviews, while the same year *Copenhagen* received critical acclaim.

ANALYSIS

Like Chekhov, his inspirational mentor, Michael Frayn is at his best when he allows his audience an intimate glimpse of characters attempting to make order out of the routine chaos of their mundane existence. There are no grand confrontations, no melodramatic plot twists, merely bursts of wasted energy frequently followed by a deepening frustration as his characters—reporters, salespeople, actors, and architects—perceive a world that ought to be changed, but one on which their ineffectual efforts and plans make no impression. Only the characters change, surrendering to the inevitable, as, comically, a disordered world continues its mad spin.

ALPHABETICAL ORDER

Frayn's third play and first critical success, *Alphabetical Order*, locates what would become his abiding concerns. In the library of a provincial newspaper office, several middle-aged reporters, who resemble little boys lost, take refuge amid the office debris. Their daily routine dictates that they enlighten the surrounding world, yet they would rather run and hide from the world, mothered by the head librarian, Lucy, who indulges their whims just as she allows a haphazard filing system to take care of itself. Their personal lives are in as much disarray as the room itself, cluttered with baskets and boxes of news items, even a broken chair. Lucy lives with John, is interested in Wally, and offers sympathy to Arnold, whose unloved wife, Megan, is in the hospital.

When Lucy hires a young woman, Leslie, as her assistant, the newcomer immediately takes control. When a reporter cuts his hand and Lucy cannot find the key to the first-aid kit, Leslie's first act is to break open the kit with a smartly delivered blow with a leg from the broken chair. Leslie not only rearranges the furniture but also manages to have all the clutter neatly filed away. More significant, Leslie imposes order on chaos by rearranging relationships as well. She enters into an affair with John, freeing Lucy for Wally; Lucy resists the neat arrangement, however, and takes Arnold into her home instead, thus dashing the hopes of Nora, the features editor.

The newly imposed order is short-lived. A seemingly more efficient library has no effect on a news-

paper that is failing. When the paper's closing is announced, the library's habitués, with Leslie out of the room, revolt. Throwing caution to the wind, grown men reduced to little boys convert folders and clippings into missiles to pelt one another. Chaos has dictated order, which in turn has dictated chaos. When Leslie, the youngest and most recent employee, enters to announce that she is in the vanguard of those who will take over the paper to run it themselves, she reasserts the notion that order will rule once more, but to what purpose? Her fellow employees' lives are as messy as ever, and Leslie's failing relationship with John further suggests that her compulsion for efficiency does not extend to that area of her life that really matters.

Critics have viewed Leslie as the villain of the piece, seeing her as the symbol of arid organization in confrontation with the confused humanity of Lucy, the heroine. Frayn himself takes a different view. Perhaps, he suggests, *Alphabetical Order* demonstrates that order and disorder are interdependent, that any extreme provokes its opposite. Lucy's inefficiency is only a perception; her library functions. Leslie's order, too, is only a perception. She is hardly responsible for the paper's failure, but as she rules her roost, the paper grinds to a halt. A semblance of change occurs, but the essentials remain the same.

NOISES OFF

In an essay entitled "Business Worries," originally written for *The Observer* and collected in *At Bay in Gear Street* (1967), Frayn offers a reason for not going to the theater: An audience sits in fear—a fear of something going wrong onstage. A carefully rehearsed play represents an ordered world that should comfort an audience that lives in an uncertain world in flux. Actors, however, can trip and fall, cigarette lighters can fail to light, cues can be missed. In *Noises Off*, Frayn takes theatrical accidents to their extreme, but an audience can view it all happily, knowing that the disorder onstage is, in fact, the order of art. Frayn's award-winning farce presents a predetermined world in which accidents are programmed to occur. First produced in 1982, *Noises Off*, a play in which an actual unforeseen mishap occurring to an actor is accepted by the viewer as yet one more comic disaster planned by the author, so delighted audiences that it achieved a four-and-a-half-year run, breaking all records at London's Savoy Theatre, and has afforded Frayn financial independence. In addition to its nearly two-year Broadway run, *Noises Off* has been translated into thirty-six languages including Russian, the language that Frayn has so frequently translated into English. Despite the failure of an Americanized film adaptation in 1992, *Noises Off* is one of the most successful stage farces of the last quarter of the twentieth century. What has, however, surprised its author is that the laughter has obscured, for most audiences, who may consider it mindless entertainment, the fact that the play has a general application even for them. It is about, Frayn insists, what everyone does in life: keep a performance going.

Noises Off, whose title derives from a British stage term for offstage sound effects, parodies the innocuous sex farces, such as Anthony Marriott and Alistair Foot's *No Sex Please, We're British* (1973), which have become a staple of London's commercial theater. In act 1, the audience witnesses the combination technical dress rehearsal of the first act of a farce called "Nothing On," performed by third-rate actors whose careers have been limited to barely professional companies that play middle-class seaside resorts such as Weston-Super-Mare. Whatever can possibly go wrong does, but only mildly in act 1. In act 2, Frayn changes the perspective. The audience witnesses the performance of "Nothing On" again, but this time from a backstage view. The actors are seen directly behind their set preparing to make their entrances. In act 1, an inept company at least attempted to work together to put on a play. Four weeks later, the inevitably developing professional jealousies and personal entanglements have turned the backstage area into a battlefield. As a result, "Nothing On" is falling apart. In act 3, the perspective is reversed again. Four more weeks have gone by, and the audience witnesses that first act yet again from an audience's usual point of view. By then, however, "Nothing On," the play-within-the-play, has totally collapsed as *Noises Off*'s actual audience, perceiving the changes brought to the performance by the realities of human involvements, reels from laughter.

Perhaps in repeating the first act of "Nothing On" three times with variations within the framework of *Noises Off*, Frayn had in mind the repetition of the two acts of Samuel Beckett's *En attendant Godot* (pb. 1952, pr. 1953; *Waiting for Godot*, 1954), another play about actors of sorts keeping a performance going. In *Waiting for Godot*, too, the essential does not change, but the characters' despair—and the audience's—deepens. What keeps the audience happy at *Noises Off* is that, as the characters fail to find solace in the rehearsed world of performance, the audience knows that for once everything has gone right. Here, chaos represents order.

BENEFACTORS

Frayn's view of *Noises Off* being about the necessity of keeping life going provides a key to his darkest comedy, *Benefactors*, whose subtleties took playgoers by surprise following, as it did, a knockabout farce. For the author, it is the petty jealousies and pique, the link to *Noises Off*, that is at the root of what he considers to be, within the context of a thought-provoking domestic comedy, society's "progressive collapse." The bleakest aspect of *Benefactors* is that, in wrecking their own lives, the two couples who constitute its cast—four friends who are white, middle-class, reasonably comfortable, basically good, and committed to helping others—unwittingly destroy the hopes of a better, more comfortable life for a class of people further down the social and economic scale, the residents, some white, more of them black, of a public housing enclave in southeast London. The real victims, who never come onstage in the play, are the inhabitants of a slum area, euphemistically referred to by the local housing authority as a "twilight area," who pay for the casual bickering and increasingly strained relationships between the two couples in the foreground of the play and provide *Benefactors* with its too-easily ignored "noises off."

Like the self-deluded architect-protagonist of Frayn's failed second play, *The Sandboy*, liberal-minded David Kitzinger believes he is helping others by designing high-rise local housing. When his wife, Jane, brings their hapless neighbor Sheila into their home as general factotum, Sheila's husband, Colin, an unemployed journalist, is upset by the growing relationship between Sheila and David, supposedly his best friend. He takes action by turning public sentiment against David's housing scheme. The relationships among the four persons who had thought of themselves as two friendly couples undergo obvious and subtle shifts that end with the collapse of one marriage and a total change in dependency in the other. No one by the end, as the four characters relate their own perceptions of what took place some years earlier, is quite sure just what did happen, but people, David finally understands, have a way of wrecking any possibility of meaningful change. The Kitzingers had played at being benefactors for the Molyneuxs, but if Sheila's marriage is destroyed, she has at least achieved a measure of independence she had never known before. Colin, too, is a benefactor. Whatever his motive for opposing David's plan, he has, he convinces himself, actually saved the inhabitants of the area undergoing redevelopment from the dehumanizing conditions that David's efficient scheme would have imposed on them. Colin even provides Jane a new career working for another housing trust that plans to rehabilitate rather than rebuild.

What adds impact to the play is Frayn's choice of names for the streets bounding the area for which David has been designing the new housing—"Basuto Road, Bechuana Road, Matebele Road, Mashona Road, and Barotse Road." "Basuto Road" becomes an evermore despairing refrain as the architect's plans undergo extensive modifications until they are at last rejected. By evoking, through the dispossessed people of the Basuto Road enclave, an echo of Basutoland, once an outpost of the British Empire, now the independent enclave of Lesotho surrounded by a hostile South Africa, Frayn suggests that Great Britain's privileged class has not only failed itself but also, ultimately, betrayed its responsibilities to those who had come there from the far reaches of the empire in search of a better life. In like manner, South Africa has exploited the Basutos, who must leave their infertile land to search for a livelihood among a people who oppress them. In *Benefactors*, chaos breeds chaos, and the need for order is implied by the discipline of the dramatist's art. Basuto Road, for Frayn,

becomes a ruined Eden. Lured by false hopes, desperately in need of help, the dispossessed are betrayed even by their so-called benefactors, who are too involved in their own petty concerns to comprehend the damage that their well-intentioned works can do.

Benefactors concludes ambiguously with the audience only certain that David, Jane, Colin, and Sheila—each one pitted against the others in a quest for self-fulfillment—have been involved in "progressive collapse." By the end of the play, the phrase has become not merely an architectural term but a dramatist's diagnosis of an unhealthy society's desperate need for change while it perpetuates, in a frantic flurry of compromise and accommodation, the desperation of stasis. Possessing wider implications than any of his other plays, *Benefactors*, still within a comic framework, reinforces Frayn's pessimistic view of the human search for order, sanity, and compassion.

COPENHAGEN

The highly acclaimed *Copenhagen* dramatizes a 1941 meeting between the physicists Werner Heisenberg and Niels Bohr. Heisenberg led the failed Nazi effort to build an atomic bomb. Historically, Heisenberg and his Danish mentor Bohr gave differing accounts of their meeting: Bohr said Heisenberg had claimed the Germans might build an atomic bomb, while Heisenberg insisted he had told Bohr he opposed the development of nuclear weapons.

Frayn's dramatization explores whether the Nazis' atomic bomb program failed because Heisenberg was unwilling to provide Hitler with the world's most powerful weapon or because he simply did not understand how to build a nuclear bomb. Frayn's complex dialogue requires audiences to wrestle with nuclear fission, quantum physics, and the uncertainty principle, while the two physicists, and Bohr's wife, Margarethe, look back on the meeting and examine it from their very different perspectives. Ultimately, Heisenberg's uncertainty principle applies in the futile human struggle to determine scientific truth—the search for truth is colored by each individual's point of view.

Frayn returned to farcical material with *Alarms and Excursions*, eight short plays in which hapless businesspeople and middle-class couples are tormented by their own answering machines, smoke alarms, corkscrews, and other assorted gadgets of everyday life.

OTHER MAJOR WORKS

LONG FICTION: *The Tin Men*, 1965; *The Russian Interpreter*, 1966; *Towards the End of the Morning*, 1967 (published in U.S. as *Against Entropy*, 1967); *A Very Private Life*, 1968; *Sweet Dreams*, 1973; *The Trick of It*, 1989; *A Landing on the Sun*, 1991; *Now You Know*, 1992; *Headlong*, 1999; *Spies*, 2002.

SCREENPLAYS: *Clockwise*, 1986; *First and Last*, 1989.

NONFICTION: *The Day of the Dog*, 1962; *The Book of Fub*, 1963 (published in U.S. as *Never Put Off to Gomorrah*, 1964); *On the Outskirts*, 1964; *At Bay in Gear Street*, 1967; *Constructions*, 1974; *The Original Michael Frayn: Columns from the "Guardian" and "Observer,"* 1983; *Speak After the Beep: Studies in the Art of Communicating with Inanimate and Semi-animate Objects*, 1995; *The Additional Michael Frayn*, 2000; *Celia's Secret: The Copenhagen Papers*, 2000 (published in U.S. as *The Copenhagen Papers: An Intrigue*, 2001).

TRANSLATIONS: *The Cherry Orchard*, 1978 (of Anton Chekhov's *Vishnyovy sad*); *The Fruits of Enlightenment*, 1979 (of Leo Tolstoy's *Plody prosveshcheniya*); *The Three Sisters*, 1983 (of Chekhov's *Tri sestry*); *Number One*, 1984 (of Jean Anouilh's *Le Nombril*); *Wild Honey*, 1984 (of an untitled play by Chekhov); *The Seagull*, 1986 (of Chekhov's *Chayka*); *Uncle Vanya*, 1987 (of Chekhov's *Dyadya Vanya*); *Plays*, 1988 (a selection of Chekhov's plays); *The Sneeze*, 1989 (an adaptation of several of Chekhov's one-act plays and short stories).

BIBLIOGRAPHY

Cushman, Robert. "Michael Frayn and Farce Go Hand in Hand." *The New York Times*, December 11, 1983, p. B1, 4. Cushman introduces *Noises Off* to the Broadway audience before its New York premiere, pointing to its genesis in an essay, "Business Worries," which Frayn wrote for *The Guardian*. The key sentence of the essay about a theater audience's apprehensions is, "All the time one is waiting aghast for some embarrassing disaster to occur." Cushman offers evidence that comic events in Frayn's plays and novels stem from Frayn's own experience.

Glanz, James. "Of Physics, Friendship, and the Atomic Bomb." *The New York Times*, March 21, 2000, p. F1. Discusses the ongoing debate surrounding events dramatized in Frayn's play *Copenhagen*. Provides historical background, comments from scientists, and a brief bibliography.

Gussow, Mel. "Echoes of Chekhov Haunt Frayn's *Benefactors*." Review of *Benefactors*, by Michael Frayn. *The New York Times*, January 5, 1986, p. B3, 15. Gussow suggests that a quotation from Anton Chekhov's notebooks in Frayn's introduction to his translation of *The Three Sisters* could serve as an epigraph to *Benefactors*: "We struggle to change life so that those who come after us might be happy, but those who come after us will say as usual: It was better before, life now is worse than it used to be."

Henry, William A., III. "Tugging at the Old School Ties." *Time*, January 27, 1986, 66. Henry underscores the relationship of Frayn's life to his work—both plays and novels—in what is primarily a review of the Broadway production of *Benefactors*, which Frayn apparently preferred to the original London production. Henry suggests that "one traditional measure of a superior play is that it can sustain widely varying interpretations." *Benefactors*, according to Henry, "meets that test."

Kaufman, David. "The Frayn Refrain." *Horizon* 29 (January/February, 1986): 33-36. Written soon after the American premiere of *Benefactors*, this article suggests that Broadway is in need of such serious yet entertaining plays. He notes that Frayn finds American critics, especially John Simon, to be more perceptive about the play than were the British critics. Frayn confesses that he himself learned what his play is about from reading sound critical analyses. The article, biographical in part, is illustrated with a photograph of Frayn and scenes from the Broadway production of *Benefactors*.

"Michael Frayn, *Copenhagen* (1998) ; Michael Blakemore." In *Making Plays: Interviews with Contemporary British Dramatists and Their Directors*, edited by Duncan Wu. New York: St. Martin's Press, 2000. A brief overview of the play and interviews with Frayn and director Blakemore, who discuss the ideas at the heart of the play and the challenges of producing it for the stage.

Simon, John. "Frayn and Refrayn." Review of *Benefactors* and *Wild Honey*. *New York* 17 (September 3, 1984): 62-63. One year before the American premiere of *Benefactors*, Simon, an American critic, reviewing the London production, was overwhelmed by the play's intelligence and haunting power. Disturbed by the performance, he read the text: "Creepingly, imperceptibly," he writes, "it overpowers you." Simon reveals the play's complexity by suggesting that it is about change as "the ultimate changelessness" and concludes, "*Benefactors*, finally, is a play about everything."

Weber, Bruce. "Critic's Notebook: Science Finding a Home Onstage." *The New York Times*, June 2, 2000, p. E1. Looks at several plays from the 2000 season, including Frayn's *Copenhagen*, that take as their themes science and the search for scientific truth.

Albert E. Kalson,
updated by Maureen Puffer-Rothenberg

ALEKSANDER FREDRO

Born: Surochów, Galicia (now in Poland); June 20, 1793

Died: Lwów, Austrian Galicia (now Lviv, Ukraine); July 15, 1876

PRINCIPAL DRAMA

Intryga na prędce, pr. 1817
Pan Geldhab, pr. 1821, pb. 1826
Mąż i żona, pr. 1822, pb. 1826 (*Husband and Wife*, 1969)
Damy i huzary, pr. 1825, pb. 1826 (*Ladies and Hussars*, 1925, 1969)
Śluby panieńskie, czyli Magnetyszm serca, wr. 1827, revised pr. 1833, pb. 1834 (*Maidens' Vows: Or, The Magnetism of the Heart*, 1940, 1969)
Pan Jowialski, pr. 1832, pb. 1838
Zemsta, pr. 1834, pb. 1838 (*The Vengeance*, 1957, 1969)
Dożywocie, pr. 1835, pb. 1838 (*The Life Annuity*, 1969)
Wielki człowiek do małych interesów, wr. 1852 or 1854, pr., pb. 1877
Wychowanka, wr. 1855 or 1856, pr., pb. 1877
Ożenić się nie mogę, wr. 1859, pr., pb. 1877
Rewolwer, wr. 1861, pr., pb. 1877
Godzien litości, wr. 1862, pr., pb. 1877
The Major Comedies of Alexander Fredro, pb. 1969

OTHER LITERARY FORMS

Aleksander Fredro wrote autobiographical and patriotic poetry intermittently throughout his adult life. These poems, however, are not of major importance. Also of modest literary merit is Fredro's only novel, *Nieszczęścia najszczęśliwego męża* (1841; the misfortunes of the happiest husband). On the other hand, his posthumously published book of reminiscences, *Trzy po trzy* (1880; topsy-turvy talk), has been acclaimed as one of the masterworks of Polish prose. This work, apparently written in the late 1840's, is composed in a style similar to the one employed in Laurence Sterne's *A Sentimental Journey Through France and Italy* (1768). Fredro's *Trzy po trzy*, moreover, is highly esteemed by Polish historians as a firsthand account of the nation's military participation in the Napoleonic Wars. Another noteworthy work of nonfiction is the collection of sardonic aphorisms posthumously printed under the title *Zapiski starucha* (1880; notes of an old man).

ACHIEVEMENTS

The most productive phase in Aleksander Fredro's literary career as a writer of comedy coincided with the Romantic epoch in Polish literature. Yet Fredro was relatively unaffected by its literary tenets. In the period following the suppression of the November Insurrection of 1831, moreover, the most prominent Polish writers—men such as Adam Mickiewicz, Juliusz Słowacki, and Zygmunt Krasiński—believed that those who engage in literary activity are morally obliged to act as adjuncts to the cause of national restoration. Owing to the lack of any overt political content in his comedies, Fredro's achievements in this genre tended to be underrated by a literary establishment that had been seduced by the siren song of Romanticism. It was not until after the debacle of the January Insurrection of 1863 that the Polish intelligentsia appeared to wash its collective hands of the doctrines of Romanticism and abandoned the quixotic quest for national independence by means of political conspiracy and armed rebellion. This change in the climate of opinion permitted an objective reappraisal of Fredro's merits as a playwright, and he was henceforth duly recognized as the foremost writer of comedy in the annals of Polish theatrical history.

BIOGRAPHY

The entire territory of the Polish Commonwealth was divided up by its neighbors in a series of partitions that occurred in 1772, 1793, and 1795. As a result of the first partition, the southern area of Poland that is commonly designated as Galicia came under Austrian rule, and it was in the eastern part of this region that Aleksander Fredro was born on June 20, 1793. His birth took place in a manor house of a country estate belonging to his family that was located at Surochów, near Jarosław. His parents, Jacek and Maria Fredro, had a total of nine offspring, six of whom were boys. Among these were two older brothers, Maksymilian and Seweryn, who were to exert a strong influence on their younger sibling. Aleksander's father, for his part, was a prosperous member of the landowning gentry, who managed to obtain the hereditary title of count from the Austrian

regime, chiefly by virtue of a talent for business that enabled him to accumulate a vast personal fortune through the purchase of other estates. Aleksander received the conventional education befitting the son of a country squire on the family estate of Beńkowa Wisznia near Lwów, a city of forty thousand inhabitants that served as the capital of Galicia. On the death of his mother in 1806, Aleksander's family took up residence in Lwów proper. The fourteen-year-old boy was also concurrently deprived of the company of both older brothers, for it was decided to enhance their education by having them serve at the court of a powerful Galician magnate named Adam Czartoryski.

When Fredro was coming of age, the greater part of the Polish gentry came to believe that Napoleon Bonaparte represented the best hope for the restoration of Poland's independence. All three occupying powers—Russia, Prussia, and Austria—were united in a continental coalition whose aim it was to thwart the political ambitions of the French emperor. In order to exploit Polish money and manpower on behalf of his military ventures, Napoleon held out the prospect of national restoration as a reward for services rendered to his cause. Shortly after inflicting a crushing defeat on the Prussians at Jena in 1806, Napoleon set up a modest political entity known as the Duchy of Warsaw, consisting of those areas that Prussia had annexed during the partitions of 1793 and 1795. The Polish army itself was then reconstituted under the command of Prince Józef Poniatowski, a nephew of the last king of Poland. Owing to another overwhelming French victory over Austrian forces at Wagram in 1809, the territory of the Duchy was subsequently expanded to include the area that was occupied by Austria in 1795. As soon as Poniatowski's men marched into Galicia in support of the French, both Maksymilian and Seweryn decided to enlist. Fredro, though only a teenager, was quick to follow the example set by his older brothers and he, too, became a member of Poniatowski's army. Within a few months, Fredro was promoted to the rank of lieutenant in an elite cavalry unit. After two further years of service, moreover, he rose to the rank of captain. During this same period, he also led an active social life and cut a gallant figure in many a fashionable salon in the district of Lublin, where he was stationed.

The course of Fredro's life altered abruptly when, in the spring of 1812, Napoleon launched a grandiose military operation against Russia for the purpose of coercing Czar Alexander to join a continental alliance in opposition to England. The move to attack the czar met with enthusiastic approbation from a majority of the Polish gentry, for they envisioned the recovery of the Russian-occupied eastern provinces in the aftermath of a French victory. Poland contributed 100,000 men to the multinational army of 500,000 men that crossed the Russian frontier: All but 20,000 of the Poles were destined to perish during the ill-fated campaign against the forces of the czar. Although most Polish soldiers were assigned to multinational units of the invasion force, Prince Poniatowski was given command of an exclusively national contingent of 35,000 men that was designated as the Fifth Army Corps. Fredro and his older brothers served in this Polish Corps, and it therefore fell to their lot to be in the vanguard of the initial attack and in the rearguard of the subsequent retreat. Despite such hazards, each of the three brothers came through the campaign without permanent injury. Owing to a case of typhus, which he contracted during the retreat, however, Fredro was captured by the Russians and imprisoned in a military hospital located near Wilno. Shortly after recovering, he managed to escape and eventually rejoined Poniatowski's forces in time to participate in the last desperate battles that the Grande Armée fought against a reactivated anti-French coalition consisting of Russia, Prussia, and Austria. Poniatowski, notwithstanding several offers of amnesty on the part of the czar, proved steadfast in his commitment to Napoleon and died heroically in the savage three-day struggle known as the Battle of Nations, which was fought near Leipzig during the autumn of 1813. Further defeats of his forces on French soil led to the emperor's abdication at Fontainebleau on April 6, 1814.

The remnant of the Polish Corps—then under the command of General Wincenty Krasiński—was subsequently repatriated to its homeland, where it was to form the nucleus of the armed forces of the czarist protectorate that was established by the Congress of Vienna in 1815 and officially designated as the Kingdom of Poland. Fredro and Seweryn chose to be discharged in June, 1814, so as to assist their father in the management of his properties, and Maksymilian decided to remain in military service. In addition to receiving high honors from France in recognition of his valorous service in the emperor's cause, Fredro was also awarded his own country's highest military decoration, the Order of the Virtuti Militari.

After his discharge from the army, Fredro returned to Austrian-occupied Galicia by way of Vienna. There he made the acquaintance of Countess Zofia Skarbek (née Jabłonowska), a young woman trapped in an unhappy marriage to a powerful magnate. The attraction that he felt for Zofia proved to be mutual, and they maintained contact with each other once back in Galicia. Fredro took up residence in a village near the estate of Beńkowa Wisznia, whose management had been entrusted to his brother Seweryn. More than a decade later, Fredro moved into Beńkowa Wisznia when his father's health deteriorated abruptly, and he continued to reside there from that time onward. His father died in 1828, and in the same year Fredro was finally able to wed Zofia. They had formed a permanent relationship in 1819, but their wedding had to be deferred until her marriage to Count Skarbek was formally annulled. They subsequently had a son, Jan Aleksander, in 1829, and a daughter, Zofia, in 1837.

Fredro, while still a member of the Polish Corps in France, took the opportunity to attend the theaters in Paris and thereby familiarized himself with the plays of Molière as well as those of more recent French writers of comedy. His own literary career began in earnest a few years after his discharge from military service. He achieved a modest success with a comedy in one act entitled *Intryga na prędce* (intrigue in a hurry) when it was staged in Lwów in March of 1817. This work was soon followed by a number of full-length plays, as well as an occasional one-act play, which met with increasing approbation on the part of the public. These literary activities were temporarily interrupted by the terminal illness of his father and later by the outbreak of the November Insurrection in 1830. Even though this uprising was confined to the Russian-occupied region of Poland, Fredro feared that it might spread to Galicia. For safety's sake, he thought it best to move to Vienna along with his wife and infant son until the cessation of hostilities. Soon after the capitulation of Warsaw on September 8, 1831, Fredro and his family returned to Galicia, and he once again resumed the career of dramatist with great zeal. In 1835, however, the Romantic poet Seweryn Goszczyński published an article in which he dismissed Fredro's plays as second-rate imitations of foreign models whose content did nothing to foster the cause of Polish independence. Emotionally devastated by these charges, as well as by other critics' attacks against him, Fredro did not find the courage to write another play until the early 1850's. He did, however, continue to work intermittently on other literary projects, including the preparation of a new and expanded edition of his collected writings.

Throughout this period, Fredro also managed to play an active role in the political life of Galicia. His efforts to promote sorely needed social and political reforms in his native province were, however, seriously compromised by his son's decision to join the Polish legions, under the command of General Józef Bem, which had gone to the aid of the Hungarian insurgents engaged in a struggle against the forces of the Habsburg emperor during the Revolution of 1848. After the Hungarian revolt was crushed, Fredro's son found himself banished from all territory under the control of Austria, and he eventually took up residence in Paris. In subsequent years, his parents spent more time in the French capital than they did in Galicia. On one of his visits to his homeland, Fredro compounded his political difficulties by delivering a seditious speech to the members of a Polish patriotic organization and was subjected to a lengthy legal inquiry that ended with his formal acquittal on March 8, 1854. Three years later, his son was also politically rehabilitated and permitted to return home. In the 1850's, Fredro resumed writing plays; none of these late works, however, was produced or published during his lifetime. With his family in attendance, Fredro died on July 15, 1876, in Lwów, the city where the majority of his earlier plays had received their premiere performances. Lwów today is called L'vov and is located within the Ukraine.

ANALYSIS

Before 1835, the year when he was unjustly vilified in Goszczyński's article "Nowa epoka poezji polskiej" (the new epoch of Polish poetry), Aleksander Fredro had already written some twenty plays for the theater. Fredro's reputation as Poland's greatest writer of comedy still rests on those works that were written and produced prior to 1835.

PAN GELDHAB

His first full-length play was called *Pan Geldhab* (a title that may be literally rendered as "Mister Has Money" or more colloquially as "Mister Moneybags"). The theme of this three-act comedy in verse manifests a strong affinity with Molière's *Le Bourgeois Gentilhomme* (pr. 1670; *The Would-Be Gentleman*, 1675). Pan Geldhab is a rich merchant who seeks to enhance his own social status by marrying his daughter to a titled aristocrat who is desperately in need of money. Even though the daughter is already engaged to an impoverished member of the gentry who genuinely loves her, she readily acquiesces to her father's plans. To forestall this scheme from being implemented, her fiancé challenges the aristocrat to a duel. The aristocrat, who has in the meantime come into a sizable inheritance from his late aunt, has no desire to risk his life over a woman whom he does not really love and promptly withdraws his offer of marriage. In the light of these events, the merchant is now willing to allow his daughter to marry her fiancé. The young man is, however, thoroughly disgusted with the antics of both father and daughter and therefore decides to have nothing further to do with either of them. While the play is not overtly didactic, it fully reflects Molière's dictum that "the purpose of comedy is to correct men by entertaining them."

HUSBAND AND WIFE

Plots involving marital infidelity have been used with great frequency by writers of comedy throughout the ages, and it may seem that there is little room for novelty in works of this type. Fredro, however, takes a strikingly new approach to this theme in the play entitled *Husband and Wife*. Here, four persons who are both young and attractive engage in multiple breaches of trust. The scene is set in the town residence of Count Wacław, the husband of a woman named Elwira. Finding his marital relationship with Elwira to be routine and unexciting, he attempts to find amorous titillation by engaging in a romantic dalliance with his wife's servant, Justysia. His closest personal friend, Alfred, decides to take advantage of the disarray that prevails within the Count's household and proceeds to seduce Elwira. Before long, however, Alfred himself comes to find his relationship with Elwira somewhat tiresome and therefore enters into an amatory liaison with Justysia as well. This soubrette manages deftly to balance the needs of her two lovers, but her duplicity is finally uncovered and she is forced to enter a convent against her will. Count Wacław proves to be far more charitable toward Elwira and Alfred, however, and readily forgives both of them in view of their apparent repentance. The play ends with the Count, Elwira, and Alfred pledging to observe mutual fidelity in their future relations. In addition to the novelty of the plot, *Husband and Wife* is noteworthy for its metrical virtuosity. Whereas convention dictated the use of a thirteen-syllable line with a caesura after the seventh syllable for all lines of dialogue, Fredro composed lines of varying length so as to achieve greater expressiveness by having the number of syllables in a line match the mood of the speaker.

LADIES AND HUSSARS

As a lighthearted comedy, *Ladies and Hussars* is generally considered to be at least equal, if not superior, to *Husband and Wife*. *Ladies and Hussars* is also noteworthy for being one of the few plays that Fredro composed in prose before 1835, when the first phase of his career as a writer of comedy came to an abrupt end. Being in prose, the dialogue in *Ladies and Hussars* presents few obstacles to the process of translation and suffers very little when recast into another tongue. The play takes place during the period when the army of Prince Józef Poniatowski seized the province of Galicia in 1809 and is set on a country estate belonging to a character designated as the Major.

While on official leave, the Major plays host to a captain and a lieutenant from his own regiment, as well as to a pair of older hussars. Suddenly, this exclusively masculine domain is invaded by the Major's three sisters. Of these sisters, two are married and the third is a spinster. Also members of the party are three vivacious maids in their employ and a pretty young woman named Zofia, who is the Major's niece. The sole purpose of the sisters' visit is to persuade their old bachelor brother to marry his niece. Before long, the Major accedes to their wishes and agrees to marry Zofia. Things get a bit out of hand, however, when his spinster sister gets herself engaged to the captain and one of the maids becomes betrothed to one of the old hussars. The Major is the first to recognize the folly of the situation and cancels his nuptial plans. The other males are quick to follow suit. Once all of these mismatches have been eliminated, the way is clear for a marital union between a true pair of lovers: Zofia and the young lieutenant. Although lacking in seriousness of purpose, *Ladies and Hussars* has proved itself to be a favorite among Polish theatergoers.

MAIDENS' VOWS

Maidens' Vows is, on one level, a comedy that aims at contravening the tragic view of love that pervades the writings of the Romanticists. The dramatic embodiment of Fredro's anti-Romantic sentiments is the central figure of Gustaw, whose attitude toward life in general is a combination of both realism and optimism. With intentional irony, Fredro selected the name of Gustaw, because it had previously been used by Adam Mickiewicz to designate the arch-Romantic protagonist in part 3 of his projected poetic tetralogy titled *Dziady* (1823, 1832; *Forefathers' Eve*, 1925, 1944-1946). By calling attention to the disparity between their respective heroes in this odd way, Fredro hoped to underscore the anti-Romantic aspect of *Maidens' Vows*.

As the play opens, Gustaw's uncle, Radost, is attempting to promote a marriage between his nephew and a young lady named Aniela. Her mother also favors the match, but Aniela's cousin, Klara, has talked her into making a vow that neither of them is ever to marry. Accordingly, Aniela refuses Gustaw's offer and Klara rejects her own suitor, Albin. Gustaw, however, is determined to get Aniela to break her vow and devises a clever stratagem to activate the magnetism of the heart. He makes Aniela into his confidante and pretends to be in love with another woman who bears the same name as she does. She soon finds her resolve to remain immune to the passions of the heart weakening when Gustaw, feigning an injury to his hand, dictates a letter to her that is addressed to the imaginary Aniela. Shortly thereafter, Gustaw reveals the true state of affairs to Aniela, and she is quick to accept his offer of marriage. Gustaw also takes revenge on Klara by tricking her into believing that her father will disinherit her if she does not marry Radost. To circumvent this eventuality, Klara decides to enter into marriage with Albin as the lesser of two evils. Except for *The Vengeance*, no other play of Fredro's ranks as high as *Maidens' Vows* in terms of both critical and popular esteem.

THE VENGEANCE

There can be little doubt that *The Vengeance* represents the high point of Fredro's career as a writer of comedy. Many critics also consider it to be the finest of all Polish comedies irrespective of period. The plot of the play is extremely complex and revolves around a quarrel between two neighbors over the boundaries dividing their estates. One of them is an elderly nobleman who bears the archaic hereditary title of "royal cupbearer" (*czesnik*) and the other is a petty lawyer who is proud to hold the rank of "notary" (*rejent*). When the lawyer takes it on himself to hire masons to erect a wall that will separate the two properties, the nobleman instructs his own servants to drive away the masons. To even the score, the lawyer pressures his son, Wacław, into making a marriage proposal to a rich widow who is the object of the nobleman's affections. Wacław finds the prospect of marrying the widow most distasteful, for he is secretly in love with the nobleman's niece, Klara. Furious at the impending marriage between Wacław and the widow, the nobleman has the young man seized and brought to his home. There he forces Wacław to wed Klara. Both the bride and the groom are delighted by this turn of events. The nobleman and the lawyer, for their part, promptly resolve their dispute in the light of the new relationship that now exists between them. Much of the humor in this play stems from the grandiloquent speech of a soldier-braggart named Papkin. While not directly involved in the main events of the play, this impoverished hanger-on is always on hand to add a touch of drollery to the happenings. The other major characters are depicted more realistically, and the play as a whole presents a vivid tableau of the traditional Polish manners and customs that prevailed among the gentry with whom Fredro spent his entire life.

PAN JOWIALSKI AND THE LIFE ANNUITY

Two other plays written before 1835 are worthy of mention: *Pan Jowialski* and *The Life Annuity*. The former, a work written in prose, may be weak from a dramatic point of view, but it contains innumerable jokes, proverbs, and versified fables that are related by the eponymous hero of the play, whose name is best translated as Mister Joviality. The latter was the last play of Fredro to be produced or published during his own lifetime. In this work, a young rake sells his life annuity to a usurer. As the annuity will lose its value once its official beneficiary dies, the usurer attempts to coerce the young rake into altering his dissolute lifestyle. While this premise is highly amusing, Fredro chooses to focus most of the action on the competition between the young rake and the usurer to win the hand of the same woman.

LATE WORKS

Fredro resumed writing plays in the 1850's and eventually added another sixteen comedies to his dramatic œuvre. (Most of these works, it should be noted, were written in prose.) Despite a few successful contemporary revivals, none of these late plays has become a permanent part of the classical repertory of the Polish theater.

OTHER MAJOR WORKS

LONG FICTION: *Nieszczęścia najszczęśliwego męża*, 1841.

NONFICTION: *Trzy po trzy*, 1880; *Zapiski starucha*, 1880.

MISCELLANEOUS: *Pisma wszystkie*, 1955-1968 (13 volumes).

BIBLIOGRAPHY

Gustavsson, Sven, ed. *Polish Theatre and Dramatic Technique: Proceedings of a Symposium Held at the University of Uppsala on 23 April 1982*. Uppsala, Sweden: Uppsala University, 1983. A collection of papers on the history of Polish drama. Bibliography and index.

Krzyżanowski, Julian. *A History of Polish Literature*. Rev. ed. Warsaw: Pwn-Plish Scientific Publishers, 1978. This history of Polish literature covers the development of Polish literature, including drama, thereby providing background to understanding Fredro. Bibliography and index.

Miłosz, Czesław. *The History of Polish Literature*. 2d ed. Berkeley: University of California, 1983. A general overview of Polish literature that creates a framework for interpreting the role Fredro played in the development of Polish drama. Bibliography and index.

Segel, Harold B. Introduction to *The Major Comedies of Alexander Fredro*. Princeton, N.J.: Princeton University Press, 1969. Segel's introduction to his translation of several of Fredro's works provides both biographical information and literary criticism. Bibliography.

Victor Anthony Rudowski

BRIAN FRIEL

Born: Killyclogher, near Omagh, Northern Ireland; January 9, 1929

PRINCIPAL DRAMA

A Doubtful Paradise, pr. 1959 (also pr. as *The Francophile*)
The Enemy Within, pr. 1962, pb. 1979
The Blind Mice, pr. 1963
Philadelphia, Here I Come!, pr. 1964, pb. 1965
The Loves of Cass Maguire, pr. 1966, pb. 1967
Lovers, pr. 1967, pb. 1968
Crystal and Fox, pr. 1968, pb. 1970
The Mundy Scheme, pr. 1969, pb. 1970
The Gentle Island, pr. 1971, pb. 1973
The Freedom of the City, pr. 1973, pb. 1974
Volunteers, pr. 1975, pb. 1979
Living Quarters, pr. 1977, pb. 1978
Faith Healer, pr. 1979, pb. 1980
Aristocrats, pr. 1979, pb. 1980
Translations, pr. 1980, pb. 1981
Three Sisters, pr., pb. 1981 (adaptation of Anton Chekhov's play)
The Communication Cord, pr. 1982, pb. 1983
Selected Plays of Brian Friel, pb. 1984
Fathers and Sons, pr., pb. 1987
Making History, pr. 1988, pb. 1989

Dancing at Lughnasa, pr., pb. 1990
The London Vertigo, pb. 1990, pr. 1992 (adaptation of Charles Macklin's play *The True Born Irishman*)
A Month in the Country: After Turgenev, pr., pb. 1992
Wonderful Tennessee, pr., pb. 1993
Molly Sweeney, pr., pb. 1994
Plays, pb. 1996-1999 (2 volumes)
Give Me Your Answer, Do!, pr., pb. 1997
Uncle Vanya, pr., pb. 1998 (adaptation of Chekhov's play)
The Yalta Game, pr., pb. 2001 (adaptation of Chekhov's short story "The Lady with the Lapdog")
Afterplay, pr., pb. 2002
The Bear, pr., pb. 2002 (adaptation of Chekhov's play)
Three Plays After, pb. 2002 (includes *The Yalta Game*, *The Bear*, and *Afterplay*)

OTHER LITERARY FORMS

Brian Friel has published two collections of short stories, *The Saucer of Larks* (1962) and *The Gold in the Sea* (1966). Two selections from these works have appeared: *The Saucer of Larks: Stories of Ireland* (1969) and *Selected Stories* (1979), reprinted as *The*

Diviner (1982). The short stories in these collections are gentle, well-turned tales of ordinary people caught, largely, in the coils of personal circumstances. They belong firmly in the tradition of pastoral frustration, to which the majority of modern Irish short stories belong. The narrative tone of Friel's stories is genial, quizzical, and often humorous, and it anticipates the affection and dignity that Friel's plays typically accord the common person.

ACHIEVEMENTS

After a modest but assured beginning as short-story writer, Brian Friel has grown, thanks to his plays, into one of the most important figures in the cultural phenomenon that will surely come to be known as the Ulster Renaissance. Like many other artists from the North of Ireland, Friel has had his work deepened and darkened by the history of his native province, yet it is also true that his willingness to face that history and its web of cultural subtexts has thrown into bolder relief the innate humanity of all of his work, rendering it all the more estimable.

Throughout his plays, Friel has persistently exposed stereotype, cliché, and narrowness of various kinds. In their place, he has substituted joy, openness, and individuality, qualities that enhance the human lot and for which his birthplace has not been noted. A deep sense of division informs both his characters and his dramatic practice, yet acknowledgment of division is an avenue to sympathy, not a recipe for impairment. Emphasizing with increasing vigor, range, and sophistication the value of spontaneity and the necessity of love, Friel's work is a moving—and stirring—statement of human solidarity in a dark time.

This statement is constantly renewed by the author's formal innovations. Friel's technical brilliance, however, does not permit him to break faith with the heritage of twentieth century Irish drama: its attachment to a sense of locale, its concern for the common lot, and its resistance to institutionalized modes of thought. In fact, Friel makes these elements interrelate fruitfully and unexpectedly by subjecting them to the clear, unblinking light of his moral intelligence.

Historically and artistically, Friel's place as Ulster's most important dramatist ever and as one of Ireland's most significant dramatists in the twentieth century is secure. Friel's achievements have been acknowledged with numerous drama awards on both sides of the Atlantic, and in 1981, *Translations* received the Ewart Biggs Memorial Prize, instituted to recognize outstanding contributions to Anglo-Irish understanding. In 1992, Friel's play *Dancing at Lughnasa* won a New York Drama Critics Circle Award for best play of the 1991-1992 theater season. Also in 1992, *Dancing at Lughnasa* received a Tony Award for best play in addition to two other Tony Awards: for featured actress (Brid Brennan) and for director (Patrick Mason).

The American staging of *Molly Sweeney* in 1996 received both the Outer Critics Circle Award and the Lucille Lortel Award for outstanding Off-Broadway play of the season.

Friel was elected to Aosdana, a national association of Irish artists, in 1982. He received an Honorary Doctorate of Literature from the National University of Ireland in 1983 and was elected to the Irish senate in 1987. The *Irish Times* awarded him its Lifetime Achievement Award in 1999 for his contributions Irish literature and theater. He is a member of the Irish Academy of Letters.

BIOGRAPHY

Order, industry, fixity, and quiet are the hallmarks of Brian Friel's life. He was born in Killyclogher, near Omagh, County Tyrone, Northern Ireland, on January 9, 1929, the son of a teacher. The family lived in Omagh for ten more years before moving to Derry, the second city of Ulster and the place that, along with its County Donegal hinterland, may be properly considered to be Friel's homeland.

Friel was educated at St. Columb's College, Derry, and at Maynooth, the Irish national seminary, where he was graduated in 1948, though it was not his intention to study for the priesthood. He attended St. Joseph's Teacher Training College, Belfast, from 1949 to 1950, and for the next ten years taught in various schools in Derry. In 1954, he married Anne Morrison, with whom he would have four daughters and a son.

During this period, Friel began to write in his spare time, and from the mid-1950's, he was a regular contributor of short stories to *The New Yorker*. During this period, he also turned to drama as a form, beginning with two radio plays, which were broadcast in 1958, and at the end of the 1950's, he branched out into staged drama.

In 1960, Friel resigned from teaching to devote himself to writing. The wisdom of that decision has been confirmed by the continuing string of international successes that has ensued. English and, particularly, American audiences have greeted his plays at least as enthusiastically as have Irish ones. Friel's rapid development as a playwright was decisively influenced by the celebrated director Tyrone Guthrie, at whose theater in Minneapolis Friel spent some months in 1968, in his words, "hanging around."

Beginning in 1980, a more public Friel has been in evidence as the moving spirit behind Field Day Productions, a theater company formed in collaboration, chiefly, with the actor Stephen Rea. Based in Derry, the company's objective is to renew the theatrical life of provincial Ireland by means of touring productions. Friel has also been instrumental in establishing Field Day Publications. This imprint has issued, most notably, an important series of pamphlets on Irish cultural matters by leading contemporary Irish poets and critics.

In 1991, the three-volume *The Field Day Anthology of Irish Writing*, edited by Seamus Deane, was published, extending and consolidating much of the range and interest of the Field Day pamphlet series and creating a landmark in the development of Ireland's conception of its literary culture. This publication coincided with the international success of Friel's play *Dancing at Lughnasa*, which played to packed theaters not only in Dublin but also in London's West End and on Broadway, and which brought its author a large number of theater awards. Friel resigned from Field Day in 1994. That same, year he debuted as a director with the premiere of *Molly Sweeney* at the Gate Theater in Dublin.

Since 1998, his work for the theater has been dominated by his treatments and interpretations of the stories and plays of Anton Chekhov, with whose

work his own has been favorably compared. *AfterPlay*, which debuted at the Gate Theatre in Dublin in 2002, is an original play based on an imagined meeting between characters from Chekhov's plays *Dyadya Vanya* (pb. 1897, pr. 1899; *Uncle Vanya*, 1914) and *Tri sestry* (pr., pb. 1901, revised pb. 1904; *The Three Sisters*, 1920), both of which Friel adapted.

ANALYSIS

Brian Friel's dramatic output, wide-ranging in subject matter though it is, possesses a notable consistency of theme, tone, and attitude to the stage. Whether a Friel play's pretext is the mission of St. Columbia, Derry's patron saint, to the island of Iona in the sixth century (*The Enemy Within*), or the living room of decaying gentlefolk (*Aristocrats*), a hedge school in nineteenth century rural Ireland (*Translations*), or the encampment of a traveling show (*Crystal and Fox* or rather differently, *Faith Healer*), familiar themes recur. Their recurrence, however, is invariably fresh, given new life by the author's unfailing sympathy and the suppleness with which he shapes unexpected cultural nuances. Such flexibility and control may be seen as an expression of the author's essential good nature. In his plays, one can also see, however, one of his œuvre's most consistent traits, his daring use of theater itself. Friel's work shows a marked flair for dramaturgical experimentation, but the experiments themselves are exclusively in the service of broader human concerns, revealing how hollow yet how inevitable ritualized behavior can be, for example, or economically contrasting characters' public and private spaces. A consummate orchestrator of theatrical space and (as is increasingly evident from his later work) the possessor of a light, though commanding, touch with ensemble work, Friel's is preeminently a writer's theater rather than a director's or a star's.

Foremost among Friel's broad human preoccupations is love—its persistence, its betrayal, its challenge. Few of Friel's characters manage to rise fully to the challenge of loving adequately. Their inadequacy is transmitted from one play to another, like a cynosure of frailty. What is significant, however, is not success but the apparent inevitability of exposure to a sense of human limitation and imperfection. Love generates many other important Friel themes. The affection for common people—uneducated, shrewd street-folk—which is unsentimentally present in all of his plays, has a sympathetic loving kindness in it that his characters themselves generally decline to embody. The destructiveness of family life, particularly the unhappy effects that parents may have on children—in Friel's world an unredeemable original sin—is also a feature of the author's preoccupation with love. Love likewise informs such concerns as fidelity to place and to cultural inheritance. A marked sharpness in attitude toward behavior that is determined by cultural institutions rather than by the vigor of the individual psyche is, again, motivated by Friel's concern with love. In fact, love has developed in Friel's work from being, in early plays, a matter of impossible romance, family bitterness, or sexual buoyancy to being the finely calibrated optic of a worldview. Friel's manipulation of the optic in later plays reveals love as a saving grace, not only personally but also culturally—and usually both, interdependently, offering at once the tolerance of charity and the zest of passion, a healing ethic and a moral force.

PHILADELPHIA, HERE I COME!

Yet division, symptomatic of love's failure, is very much in evidence in Friel's work. In *Philadelphia, Here I Come!*—his first and major international success—the dichotomy between self and world is given novel dramaturgical embodiment through the device of having two actors play different aspects of the protagonist, Gar O'Donnell: Public Gar and his alter ego, Private Gar. The world sees only the former, while the audience readily perceives that it is the latter who has the greater authenticity, by virtue of his ability to satirize Public's gaucherie and emotional timidity. (Gar O'Donnell is the most winning representative of the naïve, ardent youth, a type beloved of Friel, first seen as the novice in *The Enemy Within*.)

The action takes place on the night before, and early morning of, Gar's emigration to the United States, and consists less of a plot than of a tissue of what Friel in later plays calls "episodes." In effect, Gar's past life passes before him. The passage takes place in two dimensions—the public, by means of

farewells, and the private, by means of Private's somewhat manic and mordantly witty analysis of that life's nugatory achievements. The only thing which will relieve life at home in Ballybeg of his abiding sense of depletion, as far as Gar is concerned, is an expression of affection by his father. It is never made; Gar is obliged to carry his incompleteness with him. In that case, staying or going becomes moot.

As in *The Enemy Within*, the conclusion is inconclusive. The difference is that in the earlier play, inconclusiveness was enacted in a condition; here, rather more satisfyingly, it is embodied in a character. *Philadelphia, Here I Come!* also benefits from having its cultural resonances localized, as well as having its treatment of division given clever dramatic form. This play launched Friel's mature playwriting career. It contains an affectionately critical characterization of restlessness and brio, as well as failed love and a lament for it, and longings for a fuller life and a fear of it.

CRYSTAL AND FOX

Friel's preoccupation with love, familial relations, and romance is offered in a delicate, bittersweet blend in *Crystal and Fox*, one of his most effective works. Crystal and Fox, a man-and-wife team, own a traveling show of no particular distinction. At first, audience response is poor, and Fox, in a typical fit of recklessness, fires some of the players. The company is now reduced to four, one of whom is Crystal's ailing and incompetent father, who is soon hospitalized. The traveling show, for so long an expression of Fox's restlessness, now attains a stasis, a condition that makes Fox mean and destructive. All that can save the situation is the unwavering romantic attachment, tantamount to worship, that Crystal and Fox have for each other. Into their impoverished encampment comes Gabriel, their son. Gabriel has spent years in England, like Cass in *The Loves of Cass Maguire*, the victim of a family row. Now, however, all is forgiven, and Gabriel is seen as an embodiment of renewal. He soon tells Fox that he is on the run from the English police, having, in desperation, committed robbery with violence. This information is kept from Crystal until Gabriel is arrested before her eyes. As a result, Crystal and Fox sell the show's remaining properties to help Gabriel, but en route to Gabriel's trial, Fox lies, telling Crystal that he informed on his son for the sake of the police reward. A demented Crystal leaves her husband, allowing the play to conclude with a statement from Fox about the motivation for his destructiveness. He wanted the whole of life to be reduced to one ardent form—namely, his romantic love of Crystal. Such a love, he believes, expresses the best in him. Everything else is tainted with contingency, incompleteness, and mortality. Yet the finality and totality of his love for Crystal is what prompts treachery and ruin.

The play is satisfying on a number of levels. Its spare language complements its essentially violent action. Friel's metaphoric use of playing and roles is deeply ingrained in the piece's fundamental texture. Bleakness and joy are communicated with great clarity and economy. The need for romance—the desire that there be something more to life than the mere role one plays in it—is boldly established and subjected to an impressively unsentimental critique. In all, *Crystal and Fox* is a fitting culmination of Friel's early phase. From this point onward, his work, while not forsaking love as a theme or the family setting as its representative focus, has engaged more public issues and has placed less emphasis on individual destiny than on collective experience, a departure that has meant the virtual elimination of the often stereotyped minor characters present in his early work.

THE FREEDOM OF THE CITY

With *The Freedom of the City*, Friel began his major phase. Innovative dramaturgy, a marriage of private and public themes, and a major renovation of the part played by love in human affairs, all make this play a work of notable theatrical events.

The city in question is Derry, and the play is inspired by, though it does not mimic, the events of Bloody Sunday, January 30, 1972, when British forces killed thirteen civil rights demonstrators. Friel opens the play's action by having his three protagonists flee from the violent disruption by army and police of a banned civil rights demonstration. They seek refuge successfully in the Mayor's parlor of the Guildhall (the ease with which they do so being one of the play's many ironies about "security"), and with nothing better to do, they have a party. They drink the Mayor's liquor, smoke his cigars, dress up in ceremonial robes, and parody official ceremonies, including the conferring of the freedom of the city. Skinner, the most restless, deprived, and anarchistically inclined of the threesome, does a minimal amount of damage to property, stabbing a city father's portrait with a ceremonial sword. His opposite is Michael, a clean-cut embodiment of civil rights aspirations, who, without skepticism, wants nothing more than a fair chance to better himself. Between them stands Lilly, a blowsy mother of eleven, who approves of Michael's respectability yet is stimulated by Skinner's vitality. Eventually, summoned by military bullhorn to emerge, the three (now thought of, thanks to rumor, as forty) emerge from the circumscribed freedom of their refuge, to be shot in cold blood on the Guildhall steps.

The play's action, however, is only one of its levels. It is surrounded by frameworks of judicial and intellectual evaluation. Thus, from the outset, the audience is privy to the findings of the court of inquiry, which examines and distorts the protagonists' actions and characters. The audience is also periodically subjected to an analysis of the culture of poverty voiced by an American sociologist. These two framing devices—sophisticated revisions of an ironic use of omniscience, introduced in *Lovers* and used most tellingly in *Living Quarters*—help the audience appreciate the informal, living texture of the trio's activities, as it is that very quality that the processes of evaluation and formal discourse are unable to admit.

Perhaps the play is overloaded with framing devices. In addition to the two central ones mentioned, there are also two that derive from the trio's own cultural constituency, represented by the Catholic Church and by a ballad singer. These two also distort what the characters embody. The aim to be comprehensive is no doubt laudable, and the resultant verbal range is an impressive feature of the play, but the ensuing emphasis on the distorting effects of objectification is overdone. At the same time, however, such an emphasis also draws attention to *The Freedom of the City* as a hymn to the theater, both in the value it implicitly locates in the spontaneous antics of the three victims and in the sense that the stage is large enough for spontaneity and formality to play opposite each other.

Volunteers

In *Volunteers*, Friel also uses an event and a set of issues from contemporary Irish history. The matter in question is the Wood Quay, Dublin, excavation, where, during groundbreaking for a new office block, invaluable remains of Viking Dublin were unearthed. Efforts to preserve the site on the part of local *bien-pensants* led to ugly clashes with the developers, the law, and Dublin's city fathers and also, ultimately, to frustrating defeat for the preservationists.

Out of this volatile material, Friel fashioned a marvelous play. His volunteers are jailed social activists of a not very well-defined variety; inasmuch as they have a social philosophy, it generally seems to speak in favor of a more abundant life. (The play's one ideologue, a student radical who is one of the supervisors, in the end lets down the volunteers rather seriously.) The play is set in a hole in the ground, and the action takes place on the last day of the dig, a closing date that has been peremptorily hurried forward and that will leave the work unfinished. When this state of affairs is brought to the attention of Keeney and his fellow volunteers, it increases the audience's appreciation of the magnitude of their contribution as well as exposing the sterility of orthodox socially instituted planning. Indeed, the spontaneous gesture of volunteering has placed Keeney and his mates in danger of their narrow-minded fellow prisoners. Those who give freely, it seems, will be regarded with the most suspicion.

This conclusion is reinforced by the attitude of George the foreman. Superior to the volunteers in social status alone, his inability to have anything other than a master-servant relationship with them expresses insufferable moral smugness on the part of one who watches but does not dirty his hands. The only figure with whom the volunteers can feel kinship is the skeleton they have disinterred and named Lief, and who seems to have been the victim of a ritual execution. Lief is the authentic representative of a past common to all in the play, a past that is only properly visible to the volunteers. Thus, Lief is to be cherished much more than the vase that George has assembled out of fragments rescued by the volunteers, and when one of them deliberately breaks the vase, the symbolic resonance is as great as that provided by their ceremonial reburial of Lief.

The volunteers, then, are those who come in closest contact with the texture of the past, its earthbound treasures and human blemishes—and this contact is all the more estimable for being freely given. Prisoners of the state, menaced by their own kind and by their masters, the volunteers give unlikely expression to *pietas*, which is in cultural terms what love is in personal affairs. Yet all this is communicated in anything but solemn terms; the breezy satire of *The Mundy Scheme* is here deepened and tightened almost beyond recognition. Finally, in Keeney, Friel has created a character who is in total command of himself and prepared to face whatever comes, a character whose abundant energies, verbal pyrotechnics, and keen mind equip him superbly to be the onstage director of what Seamus Heaney has memorably called "a masque of anarchy."

Translations

Friel's *Translations* is among his finest achievements, as well as being, both intellectually and culturally speaking, his most ambitious. Set in the 1830's among the Irish peasantry, it discourses wittily, economically, and profoundly on the clash between the English and the Irish cultures, on language and its imprecision, on violence and its distortions.

The play opens with young adult peasants entering the hedge school of Hugh O'Donnell for their evening class in Latin, Greek, and arithmetic. In itself, such a scene is replete with noteworthy cultural resonances, being both a far cry from the stage Irishman and a vivid introduction to contemporary peasant life, down to the aging "infant prodigy" in the background who relishes Homer in the original. Hugh's son, Manus, takes the class this particular evening, because of his father's inebriation. One of the students is Manus's sweetheart, ambitious Maire, who is anxious for a fuller life for both of them. She plans to emigrate to the United States, while Manus, to some extent his father's prisoner, possesses a fierce loyalty to the local native life he loves so well.

In a sense, Maire resembles Manus's brother, Owen. He, too, desires a wider arena for himself, as is clear from his entry into the schoolroom with two well-disposed British soldiers, Captain Lancey and Lieutenant Yolland. These two are members of a detachment of troops engaged in an ordinance survey of Ireland, an enterprise that has as one of its features the translation of Irish place names into English. Owen is employed in this work, under Yolland's supervision, and he is painfully aware of the offense against *pietas* constituted by the effective divorce of native tongue from native place that will inevitably result. His awareness is ironically contrasted with Yolland's onset of a vague, fashionable, romantic attachment to the locals, and Owen's situation is further underlined by the deft trick of showing that when the native characters speak among themselves, the soldiers do not understand them. In other words, at certain points, the audience must accept English to be Irish.

In the hope that the cultural conflict will not come to a head, Owen arranges for Yolland to attend a local dance. There, Yolland meets Maire, and despite linguistic barriers, hilarious at the time (Friel's flair for representing gaucherie is brilliantly displayed here), she seduces him. Having seen Maire home, however, Yolland is never seen again, and the play ends with peasant hegemony broken beyond repair by the threat of dire reprisal by Lancy, and by Manus's flight from the place whose main hope he was. The situation is left in the hands of Hugh, who is impotently eloquent about its linguistic implications, and Jimmy, the "infant prodigy," whom language has deluded to the extent of his announcing his impending marriage to Homer's *glaukopis Athene*.

The play's effectiveness is not solely derived from the novelty and richness of its cultural scenario: In addition, this scenario enabled Friel to marshal areas of interest that had hitherto existed separately in his works. Here one finds the intersection of public and personal history, the suffocation of love by unpromising family circumstances, the destructiveness and inevitability of passion, the author's devotion to the common people and to that sense of Ireland that Ballybeg connotes. The coalescence of these themes certainly makes *Translations*, in the words of the review in *The Times* of London, "a national classic." The play also sets the seal on Friel's reputation as the most resourceful, most engaging, and most serious voice in postwar Irish drama.

DANCING AT LUGHNASA

Friel's plays in the 1990's mark a return to the more intimate dramas of personal lives in conflict and private emotional turmoil that distinguish his early career. Political and social issues are not absent but usually appear as components of a backdrop that includes small-town life, extended families, occupational ambitions, and other ordinary influences on the personalities of his characters. Dominating the foregrounds of these plays are characters challenged by the circumstances of their lives, and ennobled by their ability to meets those challenges with courage and grace, if not success.

Dancing at Lughnasa is a quiet memory play set in 1936 in the home of the Mundy family two miles outside of the town of Ballybeg. Michael, its narrator, recalls a summer when he was seven years old, at home with his mother (who bore him out of wedlock), his three maiden aunts, and his uncle Jack, a clergyman recently returned home from missionary work in Africa for apparent health reasons. Virtually plotless, the play unfolds through exchanges and interactions between the Mundy sisters, each of whom plays a role in sustaining the family and endures the deprivations and hardships of life with stoic good nature. The sympathy and gentle bemusement Friel shows for common people is tinged with pathos because, as Michael reveals, within a year of the time of the play's events, the household will be irreparably sundered: His uncle will die, two of his aunts will seek employment in the city and become lost in its hopeless underclass, and he will never again see his loving but irresponsible father, who periodically returns to visit his mother. Unknown to any of the characters, this moment, no matter how bittersweet, is the last happy moment the Mundys will know as a complete family.

Dance is a recurring theme in the play, and Friel uses it as a central metaphor to give structure and significance to the play's events. The play takes place during the feast of the pagan god Lugh, which is celebrated in modern times with a harvest dance that the Mundy sisters used to attend but are now unable to because of their strained finances. In one of the play's most memorable moments, the women break into spirited spontaneous dancing to a traditional Celtic song on the radio, briefly expressing a passion and freedom that rarely manifests in the household. Michael's father is a dance teacher, and Michael sees the dance steps he and his mother share when they meet clandestinely as a ritual tantamount to a marriage ceremony. Dance even plays a role in Jack's missionary experiences: Recalling dance-based rituals he participated in during his years in Uganda, he arouses very strong suspicions that he was sent home because he had begun to "go native." No matter what form it takes in the play, dance evokes a simple, natural order that the characters are drawn to but allowed to enjoy only momentarily. The dance of their lives, as choreographed by Friel, is unpredictable and erratic, and puts them out of step with their world and each other.

WONDERFUL TENNESSEE

An implicit subtext of *Dancing at Lughnasa*—that happiness is either transient or ephemeral and must be lived in for the moment—is made explicit in *Wonderful Tennessee*. Like *Dancing at Lughnasa*, it is a nearly plotless play, centered around the interactions and relationships between six characters in a brief twenty-four-hour period. Also like *Dancing at Lughnasa*, it evokes a paradisiacal realm, compared with which the world the characters inhabit is fallen and compromised.

The six characters are three married couples celebrating the birthday of small-time entrepreneur Terry Martin, who has brought them to Ballybeg Pier to be ferried across to the island of Oelian Draiochta (which translates roughly as "island of mystery"). The island has a mystical history: It was a spectral island that appeared only once every seven years until sailors landed on it and dispelled its enchantment. Terry tells his party that he has bought the island sight unseen, based on cherished memories he has of it from a story his father told him in childhood. However, once their bus has departed, the six are unable to

rouse the ferryman to take them across the water, and they are left to spend their time stranded on the shore, looking across at an island they cannot reach and can barely even see.

Typical of Friel's plays, the island symbolizes an ideal the characters live in hope for but cannot attain. The reality of their lives supports this. Private and group conversations reveal that each is wrestling with unhappiness. Terry's wife Berna knows that Terry preferred her sister Angela, and she feels guilty that she has not been able to bear him children. Angela's husband Frank is desperate to publish a book that he hopes will succeed financially and free him from his tedious job as a clerk. Terry's sister Trish is married to George, who is dying of cancer. Despite their hardships and disappointments, they manage to stay friends and muddle through, bearing out Berna's contention that "Maybe that's how most people manage to carry on—'about to be happy'; the real thing almost within grasp, just a step away . . . but there are periods—occasions—when just being alive is unbearable. . . ." The island is thus emblematic of their very lives, its idyllic aspect fleeting and intangible.

Although a work of theatrical realism, *Wonderful Tennessee* verges at some points on allegory. The ferryman is named Carlin, surely a play on Charon, who ferries souls to Hades in Greek mythology, and in the closing moments, the characters enact a farewell ritual that symbolically parallels pagan ceremonies rumored to have taken place on the island. Furthermore, the play calls for an intentionally ceremonial staging. It is punctuated at many points with snatches of popular song that the characters sing as a natural part of the festivities and also to express their feelings of the moment. The blending of song and dialogue, somewhat in the manner of classic Greek drama, suggest Friel's attempt to create a unique vocabulary for expressing the otherwise inarticulable, much as he did with dance in *Dancing at Lughnasa*. The challenging staging this requires did not meet with universal approval, however, and may have contributed to the play's premature closing on Broadway after a successful run in London. Nevertheless, *New York Times* theater critic Frank Rich praised the play as that rare theatrical experience that transported the audience, "however briefly, to that terrifying and hallowed place beyond words."

MOLLY SWEENEY

In *Molly Sweeney*, Friel approaches the theme of fleeting happiness from a different angle. The title character is a woman who lives in as close to a state of joy as any of Friel's characters do. Molly has been blind since shortly after her birth, yet she does not feel handicapped or disabled. Her inability to see has sharpened her other senses to the point where she apprehends much of the world around her, albeit in a way vastly different from sighted people. An excellent swimmer, she feels pity for sighted people, because she thinks that seeing somehow qualifies the sense of total immersion in the activity that she experiences. Molly is drawn very much in the spirit of idealized characters evoked in Friel's other plays, who are vessels for a kind of mystic wisdom that transcends normal routes of expression.

All of this is stripped away from her when her husband Frank, a man whose zeal for self-improvement and noble causes exceeds his common sense, makes it his mission to restore Molly's sight. At his urging, Molly has eye surgery. The operation is a success, but the results are devastating. Wrenched from her familiar world into one of new and alien perceptions, she finds herself cut off from the comfort and peace she knew. Unable to return to the world of blindness, she retreats into "blindsight," a psychological blindness that leaves her in a world her physician describes as "neither sighted nor unsighted, somewhere she hoped was beyond disappointment; somewhere, she hoped, without expectation."

The play is very much about the difference between "seeing and understanding," as one character describes it, and it is staged with its the three characters—Molly, Frank, and the ophthalmologist, Mr. Rice—posed at different spaces onstage, reciting their parts in monologues that intersect though they themselves never interact with one another. This novel approach to staging reinforces the sense that the characters talk without communicating, and see without understanding one another. It is yet another example of Friel's continuing efforts to experiment and seek inventive dramaturgic vehicles suitable to both the form and content of his plays.

Molly Sweeney's blend of introspective drama, compassionate characterization, and provocative staging is characteristic of Friel's plays throughout the 1990's, which treat the personal struggles of characters in emotionally challenging situations with the same gravity and grace as his more politically conscious stage work of the 1970's and 1980's. Though Friel continues to evolve as a playwright, he remains a champion of the common person who bears up with dignity under the burden of a world indifferent to his or her right to happiness.

OTHER MAJOR WORKS

SHORT FICTION: *The Saucer of Larks*, 1962; *The Gold in the Sea*, 1966; *The Saucer of Larks: Stories of Ireland*, 1969; *Selected Stories*, 1979 (reprinted as *The Diviner*, 1982).

RADIO PLAYS: *A Sort of Freedom*, 1958; *To This Hard House*, 1958.

NONFICTION: *Brian Friel: Essays, Diaries, Interviews, 1964-1999*, 1999 (Christopher Murray, editor); *Brian Friel in Conversation*, 2000 (Paul Delaney, editor).

BIBLIOGRAPHY

Dantanus, Ulf. *Brian Friel: A Study*. London: Faber and Faber, 1988. A condensation and updating of the author's *Brian Friel: The Growth of an Irish Dramatist* (1985), which discusses Friel's career up to, and including, the production of *Fathers and Sons*. Through close readings of Friel's work, Dantanus focuses on the broad cultural and social issues that arise from it.

Kerwin, William, ed. *Brian Friel: A Casebook*. New York: Garland, 1997. A selection of essays by leading critics covering most of Friel's major plays, providing a variety of critical perspectives on themes that range from Friel's use of history, myth, religion, comedy, and language to his depiction of women.

McGrath, F. C. *Brian Friel's (Post)Colonial Drama: Language, Illusion, and Politics*. Syracuse, N.Y.: Syracuse University Press, 1999. An accessible study by one of Friel's more ambitious critics that views him working in the same tradition as Oscar Wilde, William Butler Yeats, Sean O'Casey, and other authors who blend historical and factual and personal memoir to a create a new national mythology that breaks with that of Ireland's colonial past.

Murray, Christopher. *Brian Friel: Essays, Diaries, Interviews, 1964-1999*. London: Faber and Faber, 1999. Chronologically ordered culling of Friel's own thoughts on the playwright's craft and specific works. Includes his seminal autobiographical essay, "The Theatre of Hope and Despair."

O'Brien, George. *Brian Friel*. Boston: Twayne, 1989. An introductory survey of Friel's stories and plays up to *Making History*. The primary emphasis is on the character and quality of Friel's artistic vision. Surveys the whole of the Friel canon, including the early, unpublished stage and radio plays. Contains an extensive bibliography.

O'Connor, Ulick. *Brian Friel: Crisis and Commitment*. Dublin: Elo, 1989. A pamphlet by a well-known playwright and biographer. Addresses the problems of the writer's social and cultural responsibilities in times of civic crisis, using as its focus the work of Friel in the context of the crisis of authority in Northern Ireland.

Pine, Richard. *Brian Friel and Ireland's Drama*. London: Routledge, 1990. The most comprehensive, intellectually sophisticated, and theoretically ambitious reading of Friel's output up to and including *Dancing at Lughnasa*. Numerous stimulating and challenging connections are made between Friel and other Irish and international dramatists, and Friel is used as a means of focusing on the status and significance of drama in contemporary Irish culture.

George O'Brien,
updated by Stefan Dziemianowicz

MAX FRISCH

Born: Zurich, Switzerland; May 15, 1911
Died: Zurich, Switzerland; April 4, 1991

PRINCIPAL DRAMA

Nun singen sie wieder: Versuch eines Requiems, pr. 1945, pb. 1946 (*Now They Sing Again*, 1972)

Santa Cruz, pr. 1946, pb. 1947

Die chinesische Mauer, pr. 1946, pb. 1947, second version pr., pb. 1955, third version pr. 1965, fourth version pr. 1972 (*The Chinese Wall*, 1961)

Als der Krieg zu Ende war, pr., pb. 1949 (*When the War Was Over*, 1967)

Graf Öderland, pr., pb. 1951, second version pr. 1956, third version pr. 1961 (*Count Oederland*, 1962)

Don Juan: Oder, Die Liebe zur Geometrie, pr., pb. 1953 (*Don Juan: Or, The Love of Geometry*, 1967)

Biedermann und die Brandstifter, pr. 1953 (radio play), pr., pb. 1958 (staged; *The Firebugs*, 1959, also as *The Fire Raisers*, 1962)

Die grosse Wut des Philipp Hotz, pr., pb. 1958 (*The Great Fury of Philip Hotz*, 1962)

Andorra, pr., pb. 1961 (English translation, 1963)

Three Plays, pb. 1962

Biografie, pb. 1967, pr. 1968 (*Biography*, 1969)

Three Plays, pb. 1967

Four Plays, pb. 1969

Triptychon: Drei szenische Bilder, pb. 1978, pr. 1979 in French, pr. 1981 in German (*Triptych*, 1981)

Jonas und sein Veteran, pr., pb. 1989

Three Plays, pb. 1992

OTHER LITERARY FORMS

Max Frisch was a versatile writer whose reputation was founded on both his dramas and his novels. He also wrote diaries, radio plays, short stories, film scenarios, and essays. His essays include discussions of literature, drama, society, architecture, town planning, and travel. There is a six-volume German edition of his works up to 1976, published by Suhrkamp in Frankfurt.

ACHIEVEMENTS

In West Germany, Austria, and Switzerland, Max Frisch's dramas are consistently among the most frequently performed works by German-language playwrights. They are also regularly performed in other European countries and in the United States. Frisch's international reputation was established in 1954 with the publication of the novel *Stiller* (*I'm Not Stiller*, 1958), which is still considered his most important work. In 1951, Frisch received a Rockefeller grant to study in the United States. He was awarded numerous prizes for his works. These include the Georg Büchner Prize, the literature prize of the city of Zurich in 1958, and the prize of the city of Jerusalem and the Schiller Prize in 1965. His works have been translated into most European languages and are often best-sellers.

BIOGRAPHY

Max Frisch was born in Zurich on May 15, 1911, the son of a self-made architect. After attending gymnasium in Zurich between 1924 and 1930, he began studying German literature at the university of Zurich in 1931, at which time he also heard lectures on art history, philosophy, law, and theology. When his father died in 1933, Frisch had to leave the university to earn a living. He became a freelance journalist and wrote for such newspapers as the *Neue Zürcher Zeitung*. In 1933, Frisch traveled to Prague, Budapest, Dalmatia, Istanbul, and Greece, experiences that he used in his first novel, *Jürg Reinhart* (1934). In 1936, thanks to the financial support of a friend, Frisch began studying architecture at the Institute of Technology in Zurich; he was awarded his diploma in 1941. Between 1939 and 1945, Frisch had to serve periodi-

cally in the Swiss army. In 1942, Frisch opened his own architect's office in Zurich. The highlight of his architectural career was winning a competition to build an open-air swimming pool in the Zurich suburb of Letzigraben, a project that was completed in 1949. In 1948, Frisch became acquainted with Bertolt Brecht, whose theories were to have an important impact on his dramas. Frisch, an inveterate traveler, wrote in *Tagebuch, 1946-1949* (1950; *Sketchbook, 1946-1949*, 1977) that a man travels for two reasons: to meet people who do not think that they know him once and for all, and to experience once again what is possible in life. Frisch traveled extensively in Europe and the United States and visited the Middle East, Mexico, Cuba, the Soviet Union, Japan, and China. His experiences in the United States were reflected especially in the novels *I'm Not Stiller* and *Homo Faber* (1957), and in the novella *Montauk* (1975). After 1954, when he gave up his architect's office, Frisch earned his living as a writer. After living in Rome between 1960 and 1965, Frisch returned to live in Tessin, Switzerland.

Max Frisch in 1973. (AP/Wide World Photos)

ANALYSIS

Max Frisch's admiration for the playwright Bertolt Brecht was an important stimulus in formulating his own dramatic theories. Frisch disagreed with Brecht's theories in several ways. Unlike Brecht, Frisch was skeptical that the theater can bring about social and political change, but he did believe that it can change a person's relationship to the world—it can make him more aware of himself and of the society in which he lives. Frisch was convinced of the power of the theater. In *Sketchbook, 1946-1949*, Frisch related how he was once sitting unobserved in an empty theater. He saw a workman come onto the stage and grumble. Then an actress walked across the stage and greeted the workman briefly. Because this very humdrum scene took place on the stage, its impact was greater than it would have been in ordinary life. To illustrate how the theater functions, Frisch used the analogy of an empty picture frame. If it is hung on the wall, it focuses a person's attention on the wall for the first time and forces him to see it. Like the picture frame, the box stage focuses a person's attention; it points out and demonstrates. Ordinary events are turned into exemplary ones on the stage.

Unlike Brecht, Frisch did not believe that the real world can be portrayed effectively on the stage; the stage can only show models of experience. In an early essay titled "Theater ohne Illusion" (1948; theater without illusion), Frisch praises Thornton Wilder for discarding realistic theater and stressing the theatrical again. According to Frisch, the theater should never try to create the illusion that it is real life on the stage. For this reason, Frisch used many alienation effects to break the suspense and to prevent the audience from thinking that it is seeing a "slice of life."

In addition, Frisch, unlike Brecht, had no ideology to impart to his audience. His function as a dramatist, he said, is to raise questions, not provide answers. Frisch wanted to make people more aware, to provoke them into finding their own solutions to the problems that he depicted. An example of such provocation can be found in *The Firebugs* when Biedermann steps out of his role and addresses the members of the audience directly, asking them what they would have done in his place. Although Frisch was not convinced that the theater can bring about social change, he nevertheless thought that the author has a responsibility to address social and political questions. In an interview with Horst Bienek in 1961, Frisch criticized the Theater of the Absurd. If he were a dictator, he said, he would allow only the plays of Eugène Ionesco to be performed. Because such plays are fun to watch, they make the audience forget political conditions in the real world outside the theater. Frisch's dramas focus mostly on personal questions, but some address social problems such as anti-Semitism and prejudice (*Andorra*) and the moral weakness of the middle class (*The Firebugs*). Yet even in those works that deal mostly with the individual, Frisch still criticizes modern society, especially for its hypocrisy and for the limits it places on the individual.

In most of Frisch's dramas, the quest for identity is a central theme. Frisch believed that most people either invent roles for themselves or else have roles imposed on them by others. Such role-playing prevents people from growing and realizing their potential as human beings—the role reduces them to fixed and known entities, a theme that Frisch develops in particular in *Andorra* and *Don Juan: Or, the Love of Geometry*. Frisch shows how difficult it is to escape from roles. Because society wants to preserve the status quo, it is hostile to any notion of change; it expects people to conform to certain socially acceptable roles that consist for the most part of deadening routine. Frisch portrays those who conform to society without any struggle as smug and self-righteous (a good example of such a character is Biedermann in *The Firebugs*). Most of Frisch's protagonists fight for the freedom to be themselves, but the social restrictions they confront are often so overwhelming that they are forced to capitulate.

DON JUAN

Don Juan had its premiere on May 5, 1953, at the Zurich Schauspielhaus and at the Berlin Schillertheater. Don Juan appears in Frisch's works for the first time in the play *The Chinese Wall*, where he protests against his literary portrayal as a seducer. In the play named for him, Don Juan is the polar opposite of the legendary Don Juan. Far from being the seducer, he is actually the seduced. The first three acts show how Don Juan is forced into the role of seducer; the last two, how, like Stiller in the novel *I'm Not Stiller*, he tries to escape from the image that people have formed of him.

To those familiar with the legend, the picture of Don Juan as the play opens is startling. Don Juan's father, Tenorio, is worried about his son because, at the age of twenty, he avoids women. To try to remedy this, Tenorio sends Don Juan to a brothel; while there, however, Don Juan plays chess. Frisch's Don Juan is an intellectual who loves geometry because it is clear, exact, and "manly." Like Walter Faber in the novel *Homo Faber*, he distrusts feelings because they are too unpredictable and chaotic. Don Juan's love of geometry is, however, responsible for his present involvement with Donna Anna. When he is sent to measure the walls of the enemy stronghold in Córdoba, he returns unharmed with the information, is named hero of Córdoba, and is given Donna Anna as his bride. Don Gonzalo, the commander, does not realize that Don Juan has used simple geometry to arrive at the measurements and has not exposed himself to danger.

The play opens on the night before Don Juan is to marry Donna Anna. The erotic festivities of this night stem from a pagan custom that the Christians have adopted. In the original custom, everyone was supposed to wear a mask. Through the power of love, the bride and groom could find each other despite the masks they were wearing. Because there were so many instances of mistaken identity, the custom was changed. Now the bride and groom do not wear masks because love can obviously err. Don Juan is drawn into the stifling eroticism of this night and sleeps with Donna Anna. He does not know that she is his bride because he has not met her before.

Don Juan's experiences on this night make him suspicious of love. When he suddenly realizes at the wedding ceremony that he has slept with Donna Anna, he refuses to marry her. He cannot promise to be faithful to her because he thinks that people are interchangeable when the biological urge to mate is aroused. The cries of the peacock seeking a mate,

which are a motif in the first part, stress this biological nature of love. Like most of Frisch's intellectuals, Don Juan is basically self-centered. In fact, he holds a grudge against heaven for separating people into two sexes; he protests that the individual alone lacks wholeness.

It is not surprising that Don Juan repudiates love, because the society that surrounds him treats love cynically. Celestina, the brothel owner, turns the prostitute Miranda away because she has fallen in love with Don Juan: Such "sentimentality," Celestina believes, is bad for business. Don Gonzalo and Donna Elvira, the parents of Donna Anna, supposedly have a model marriage, yet Donna Elvira thinks nothing of deceiving her husband by sleeping with Don Juan. When the captured Arab prince tells Don Gonzalo to take and enjoy his harem, Don Gonzalo curses the seventeen years of faithful marriage that prevent him from enjoying the proffered sensual delights. The only positive concept of love is held, ironically, by the prostitute Miranda, whose love for Don Juan remains constant.

Don Juan's refusal to marry Donna Anna and the subsequent events give rise to his reputation as a seducer. To help him escape from the family that is thirsting for revenge, Donna Elvira gives Don Juan refuge in her room, where she seduces him. From her, Don Juan goes to Donna Inez. He is curious to see whether she will sleep with him even though she is engaged to his friend Don Roderigo. When she does, this seems to confirm his belief that love is indiscriminate and merely biological. At the end of act 3, Don Juan is surrounded by people whose deaths he has unwittingly caused: His father dies of a heart attack because of his son's behavior, Donna Anna drowns herself because of Don Juan's rejection, Don Roderigo kills himself because Don Juan has slept with his fiancé, and Don Juan unintentionally kills Don Gonzalo with his sword.

The fourth act takes place thirteen years later and depicts Don Juan's descent into Hell, famous from the legend—but with a new twist. It is no longer an example of divine retribution but is actually staged by Don Juan himself to escape from his role as a seducer and from his financial problems. Don Juan seeks to persuade the bishop that his "descent into Hell" will provide the Church with proof of divine justice; the husbands of the seduced wives will have their revenge; and finally, youth will not be corrupted by following Don Juan's example as a seducer. In return, Don Juan wants the Church to give him a cell in a monastery in which he can devote his time to his beloved geometry. Don Juan invites thirteen of the women he has seduced to witness the event, and arranges for Celestina to play the part of Don Gonzalo's statue, which comes to life to punish him. Before the company arrives, Miranda, now the widow of the Duke of Ronda, offers Don Juan refuge in her castle, which he abruptly refuses. Don Juan's plan goes awry because the bishop turns out to be a disguised husband in search of revenge. Even though he reveals Don Juan's deception, the legend proves stronger than the truth—nobody believes that Don Juan has not been taken off to Hell. In the intermezzo that follows this act, Celestina tries to tell Donna Elvira (who is now a nun) about the role she played in the "descent into Hell," but Donna Elvira prefers to believe in "miracles."

In the last act, Don Juan has been forced to accept Miranda's offer of refuge and has married her. He is sitting at the table, waiting for her to come. Outside the castle, his literary legend is being created on the stage. He is a virtual prisoner in the castle because, after his spectacular "descent into Hell," he cannot return to the world. To return as a husband would also make him the laughingstock of everyone. Yet the intellectual Don Juan who despised love is beginning to love Miranda (he confesses that he misses her when she is away). Before, Don Juan could not reconcile love and intellectual pursuits. When he was drawn into erotic adventures, he felt as if he were a piece of nature while he wanted to be an intellectual; he thought that heaven scorned him as a man of the spirit. He had not treated women as individuals but as members of the female sex; his affairs with them were unimportant episodes. At the end of the play, he is beginning to grasp that a relationship with a woman can be meaningful and through it he can gain the wholeness that, as an individual, he lacks. When Miranda breaks the news to him that she is expecting his child, she tells him that she does not expect him to be pleased at first, but she is convinced that he will be pleased about it in the future. The play ends with a question mark: It is not clear whether the relationship will continue to grow or whether it will deteriorate into the dullness of everyday routine that Don Juan fears.

Throughout the play, Frisch shows how damaging preconceived images are to the individual. In contrast to the legend in which Don Juan appears as a fixed entity, Frisch shows him evolving from a naïve twenty-year-old, to a bored seducer, to a husband, and finally to a father-to-be (in the legend, Don Juan is never a father). Don Juan fights against his reputation, which does not fit him in the least. In the notes that follow the play, Frisch claims that Don Juan is more related to Icarus and Faust than to Casanova; despite his reputation, Don Juan, like Icarus and Faust, is a man of the spirit who thirsts for knowledge.

THE FIREBUGS

The Firebugs had its premiere on March 29, 1958, at the Zurich Schauspielhaus. A prose sketch titled "Burlesque" that appears in *Sketchbook, 1946-1949*, right after Frisch has mentioned the fall of the Beneš government in Czechoslovakia in 1948, forms the basic plot for the later play. The sketch tells how a stranger comes to a man's house. The man wants to win the stranger's friendship to demonstrate how humane he is. He gives the stranger shelter, storage for his gasoline, and even the matches with which the stranger and his friend incinerate him. Frisch developed this into a radio play in 1953 and finally into *The Firebugs*, in which the satire is sharper. The play was intended to share a theatrical evening with a companion play that Friedrich Dürrenmatt was to write. Later, Frisch added an epilogue to fill out the theatrical evening, but the epilogue does not add anything important to the play.

Frisch is sharply critical of the middle class and capitalism in this play. The protagonist, Biedermann, is an Everyman of the middle class (the name implies a philistine; a respectable, unimaginative bourgeois). Biedermann has become rich by manufacturing a worthless hair tonic—as he tells his wife Babette, his customers might just as well put their own urine on their scalps for all the good his hair tonic does. Unlike most of Frisch's protagonists, Biedermann does not question his identity but is smugly satisfied with himself. Above all, he wants to enjoy his rest and well-being. His appearance of bonhomie, however, serves to mask an inner ruthlessness.

As the play opens, Biedermann is sitting comfortably at home reading about arsonists in the newspapers. He proclaims that they should all be hanged. Although he has been forewarned, he still lets Schmitz stay in his attic because he wants to appear humane. His humaneness is, however, a facade, as his treatment of his former employee Knechtling demonstrates. Because Knechtling (who has invented the hair tonic) wants to share in its profits, Biedermann fires him. When Knechtling comes to ask for help for his sick wife and three children, Biedermann refuses to see him and callously says that he should put his head in the gas oven—which he subsequently does. Biedermann is morally responsible for Knechtling's death because he has driven him to suicide.

The reign of terror in Biedermann's house grows. Because Biedermann is afraid of Schmitz, he asks his wife to turn him out the next morning. Schmitz's accomplice, the former waiter Eisenring, arrives, and together they bring barrels of gasoline into the attic at night. Biedermann again is too cowardly to throw them out. In fact, when the policeman arrives with the news of Knechtling's suicide, Biedermann tells him that the barrels contain hair tonic—he is afraid to tell the truth because Schmitz has heard him say that Knechtling should gas himself. To win the friendship of the arsonists—and thus (he hopes) be spared—Biedermann prepares a festive meal for them. He even gives them the matches with which they start the fire. Although he knows that they are arsonists, he deliberately closes his eyes because he is afraid of them.

The arsonists are adept at manipulating Biedermann. When Schmitz, a former heavyweight wrestler, arrives, he first alludes to his strength, in that way intimidating Biedermann. Then he flatters him by telling him how humane he is. Schmitz later manipulates Babette by telling her stories of his disadvantaged childhood. In this way, he arouses her compassion so that she will not have the heart to throw him out. Later, Eisenring describes how the arsonists use language to disguise their intentions. One disguise is joking about their intentions; another is using sentimentality (for example, when Schmitz describes his childhood); but the best disguise of all is telling the truth because nobody believes it. The arsonists do not hide the fact that they are arsonists. They tell Biedermann that the barrels contain gasoline and that they have chosen his house because of its strategic location—when his house burns, the whole town will go up in flames. Yet Biedermann insists on thinking that they are joking. It is not exactly clear why the arsonists want to burn down the town. Their accomplice, Dr. Phil, who has joined them because he wants a revolution, claims that they set fires merely for the love of setting fires, and he leaves them because they do not have a political reason for their actions. They could represent anarchy or the principle of evil (in the epilogue, the arsonists are the devils in Hell). Yet they also administer justice by punishing Biedermann for Knechtling's death.

On one level, the play seems to allude to certain political events in the twentieth century. The original prose sketch could allude to the takeover of the Beneš government by the Communists because it appears in *Sketchbook, 1946-1949* right after Frisch has mentioned this. There are also allusions to the rise of Nazism—like the arsonists, Adolf Hitler never concealed his intentions, as is shown in his autobiography *Mein Kampf* (1925-1926). Yet, it is a mistake to think that the play applies to a specific event. Frisch was concerned about the vulnerability of middle-class democracy to terrorism because of its inner weakness and moral corruption.

Frisch himself noted that this play in particular was influenced by Bertolt Brecht, an influence that is most evident in the form. The six scenes are broken up by a chorus of firemen that comments on the situation, interprets the action, and warns of danger. The chorus is, however, helpless to avert the catastrophe—firemen can only put out fires, not prevent them. Another Brechtian device is the lack of suspense. From the outset, it is clear to everyone (except Biedermann) that the strangers are arsonists. The attention of the audience is thus focused not on how the play will end but on how Biedermann causes his own destruction. In the play, Frisch parodies the dramas of fate; what happens to Biedermann is not fate (as he would like to believe) but could have been avoided.

Frisch called his parable a "morality play without a moral," an indication of Frisch's belief that people cannot be taught. Like Brecht's *Mother Courage*, Biedermann does not learn from his experiences. This is especially evident in the epilogue, which takes place in Hell. Hell here is on strike because Heaven has pardoned too many criminals, in particular those who have obeyed orders to kill while they were in uniform (an allusion to the Nazi war trials). Biedermann refuses to believe that he is in Hell. He protests that he has always obeyed the Ten Commandments. To the end, Biedermann is convinced that his only failing was that he was too good-natured; he refuses to see that he acted wrongly. He even demands restitution for his damaged property. Because of the strike in Hell, Biedermann and Babette are saved. As the play closes, there is a vision of a new town arising out of the ashes of the old, but the chorus suggests that people have already forgotten the lesson of how the old town burned. Like Biedermann, people do not learn from their experiences, a pessimistic conclusion about the middle class.

ANDORRA

Andorra had its premiere in November, 1961, at the Zurich Schauspielhaus. Like *The Firebugs*, the plot is derived from a prose sketch, written in 1946, in *Sketchbook, 1946-1949*. The sketch, titled "The Andorran Jew," tells of a young man who everyone thinks is Jewish. Some criticize him for his supposedly Jewish traits, while others admire him for these same qualities. When he is killed, it turns out that he was an Andorran like the others. After this sketch, Frisch quotes the commandment "Thou shalt make no graven image." In *Andorra*, Frisch shows how the protagonist Andri becomes a Jew simply by being told that he is Jewish.

The action takes place in the fictional country of Andorra (Frisch stated emphatically that he was not alluding to the tiny country in the Pyrenees). Frisch intended the play to be a model: Such events, he be-

lieved, could happen anywhere. The characters are two-dimensional because Frisch was not interested in them as people but only in their attitudes to Andri. The Andorrans are convinced that their country is a model of all human virtues—it is a haven of peace, freedom, and human rights. To be an Andorran, they think, means to be moral and humane. As the image of whitewashing shows, their moral superiority is only a facade. When there is a storm, the whitewash is washed off the church, showing the red earth beneath. As the soldier comments, this makes the church look as if a pig has been slaughtered close by, an image that indicates that the virtuous appearance of the Andorrans masks brutality.

Although nobody knows it, Andri is in fact an Andorran, the illegitimate son of the teacher Can and a woman from the neighboring country of the Blacks. Instead of telling the truth, Can told everyone that he had rescued a Jewish child from the savage anti-Semitism of the Blacks, and wins praise for this "courageous" act. The Andorrans' treatment of Andri shows, however, that they cannot tolerate anyone who they think is different. The cabinetmaker is unwilling to take Andri as an apprentice; he thinks Andri should become a salesperson instead because he cares only for money. Later, the cabinetmaker assumes that the faulty chair is Andri's, and the other apprentice (whose chair it is) lets Andri take the blame. The soldier accuses Andri of cowardice, a supposedly Jewish trait. The doctor criticizes the Jews because they are ambitious. Yet these are traits of the Andorrans themselves. The cabinetmaker demands an exorbitant price for Andri's apprenticeship; the doctor is overly ambitious; and when the Blacks invade, the soldier gives up without a fight.

At first, Andri desperately tries to be an Andorran, but when this fails, the priest persuades him to accept the fact that he is different. When Can finally tells Andri the truth about his origins, Andri refuses to believe him; he thinks that it is only a pretext to prevent him from marrying Barblin, Can's daughter (his half-sister), whom he loves. When Andri's mother, who inexplicably comes to see him for the first time, is killed, the innkeeper, himself the culprit, accuses Andri of the crime. Because he is different, he is made the scapegoat. Andri's acceptance of his "Jew-ishness" causes his death. When the Blacks invade, everyone has to walk barefoot over the square, their heads covered by black cloths—a grotesque scene. Although Andri is in no way different from the oth-ers, the Jew Inspector selects him as a Jew, and Andri is taken away and murdered. Can, who belatedly has tried to tell the truth about Andri, hangs himself in re-morse. As the play ends, Barblin is whitewashing—a futile gesture because the guilt of the community can only be covered up, not erased.

Like Biedermann, most of the characters do not learn from their experiences. After some of the scenes, the characters who are responsible for Andri's fate step forward to the witness box and try to justify their behavior. With the exception of the priest, no one ac-cepts any responsibility for Andri's death; each pro-claims his innocence and no one feels remorse. De-spite Andri's death, the Andorrans' prejudice against people who are different is as strong as ever.

These plays (which are among his most success-ful) are typical of Frisch's concerns. Frisch protested against the roles that people assume, either by choice or because they are forced into assuming them because such roles limit people's potential to lead fulfilling lives. In most of his works, Frisch examined the con-sequences to the individual of such role-playing. In *Andorra*, however, he shows that people form precon-ceived images not only of individuals but also of dif-ferent groups of people and of nationalities, which leads to prejudice and racism. Frisch pessimistically concludes that most people do not learn from their experiences. In a society consisting of conformists, Frisch's protagonists vainly try to free themselves from their imprisoning roles. Such failure causes their progressive alienation from society, family, and friends—and ultimately from themselves.

OTHER MAJOR WORKS

LONG FICTION: *Jürg Reinhart*, 1934; *J'adore ce qui me brûle: Oder, Die Schwierigen*, 1943; *Stiller*, 1954 (*I'm Not Stiller*, 1958); *Homo Faber*, 1957 (*Homo Faber: A Report*, 1959); *Mein Name sei Gantenbein*, 1964 (*A Wilderness of Mirrors*, 1965); *Montauk*, 1975 (English translation, 1976); *Der Mensch erscheint im*

Holozän, 1979 (*Man in the Holocene*, 1980); *Blau-bart*, 1982 (*Bluebeard*, 1983).

SHORT FICTION: *Bin: Oder, Die Reise nach Peking*, 1945; *Wilhelm Tell für die Schule*, 1971.

NONFICTION: *Tagebuch, 1946-1949*, 1950 (*Sketch-book, 1946-1949*, 1977); *Tagebuch, 1966-1971*, 1972 (*Sketchbook, 1966-1971*, 1974); *Dienstbüchlein*, 1974; *Der Briefwechsel: Max Frisch, Uwe Johnson, 1964-1983*, 1999; *Die Briefwechsel mit Carl Jacob Burckhardt und Max Frisch*, 2000.

MISCELLANEOUS: *Gesammelte Werke in zeitlicher Folge*, 1976 (6 volumes); *Novels, Plays, Essays*, 1989.

BIBLIOGRAPHY

Butler, Michael. *The Novels of Max Frisch*. London: Macmillan, 1985. Provides criticism and interpre-tations of Frisch's works up to the mid-1970's. In-dex and bibliography.

Köpke, Wulf. *Understanding Max Frisch*. Under-standing Modern European and Latin American Literature series. Columbia: University of South Carolina Press, 1991. Explores the themes and dramatic approaches of Frisch. Bibliography and index

Lob, Ladislaus. "'Insanity in the Darkness': Anti-Semitic Stereotypes and Jewish Identity in Max Frisch's *Andorra* and Arthur Miller's *Focus*." *Mod-ern Language Review* 92 (July, 1997): 545-558. Compares the depiction of the plight of Jews in a hostile environment in both playwrights' works.

Pickar, Gertrud Bauer. *The Dramatic Works of Max Frisch*. New York: Peter Lang, 1977. Explores themes and approaches of Frisch's plays. Bibliog-raphy.

Probst, Gerhard F., and Jay F. Bodine, eds. *Perspec-tives on Max Frisch*. Lexington: University Press of Kentucky, 1982. Offers criticism and interpre-tations of Frisch's life and works. Bibliography.

Reschke, Claus. *Life as a Man: Contemporary Male-Female Relationships in the Novels of Max Frisch*. New York: Peter Lang, 1990. Examines the psy-chology of gender roles in Frisch's works.

Weisstein, Ulrich. *Max Frisch*. New York: Twayne, 1967. Provides biographical discussion of Frisch and interpretations of his works.

White, Alfred D. *Max Frisch, the Reluctant Modernist*. Lewiston, N.Y.: Edwin Mellen Press, 1995. Offers a biography and criticism of Frisch's life and works.

Yang, Peter. *Play is Play: Theatrical Illusion in "The Chinese Wall" by Frisch and Other "Epic" Plays by Brecht, Wilder, Hazelton, and Li*. Lanham, Md.: University Press of America, 2000. Discusses dramatic techniques of Frisch and his contemporaries. Bibliography and index.

Jennifer Michaels

CHRISTOPHER FRY
Christopher Fry Harris

Born: Bristol, England; December 18, 1907

PRINCIPAL DRAMA

The Boy with a Cart, pr. 1938, pb. 1939
Thursday's Child, pr., pb. 1939
The Firstborn, pb. 1946, pr. 1948, revised pb. 1952
A Phoenix Too Frequent, pr., pb. 1946
The Lady's Not for Burning, pr. 1948, pb. 1949
Thor, with Angels, pr., pb. 1948
Venus Observed, pr., pb. 1950
A Sleep of Prisoners, pr., pb. 1951
The Dark Is Light Enough, pr., pb. 1954
Three Plays, pb. 1960
Curtmantle, pr., pb. 1961
Plays, pb. 1969-1971
A Yard of Sun, pr., pb. 1970
Paradise Lost, pr., pb. 1978 (adaptation of John Milton's poem)
Selected Plays, pb. 1985
One Thing More: Or, Caedmon Construed, pb. 1985, pr. 1986

OTHER LITERARY FORMS

Christopher Fry is well known for his many translations of plays into English verse, which have had successful productions both for the stage and, in some cases, for the cinema. His first published translation was of Jean Anouilh's *L'Invitation au Château* as *Ring Round the Moon* (pr., pb. 1950), Fry's only effort in prose. He followed it with several translations, including *The Lark* (pr., pb. 1955; of Anouilh's *L'Alouette*), *Tiger at the Gates* (pr., pb. 1955; of Jean Giraudoux's *La Guerre de Troie n'aura pas lieu*), *Duel of Angels* (pr., pb. 1958; of Giraudoux's *Pour Lucrèce*), *Judith* (pr., pb. 1962; of Giraudoux's *Judith*), and *Cyrano de Bergerac* (pr., pb. 1975; of Edmond Rostand's *Cyrano de Bergerac*). Fry also published critical prose, including *An Experience of Critics* (1952) and several important essays on the use of verse in drama. He has worked on television productions and screenplays, and his work for the British Broadcasting Corporation, *The Brontës of Haworth*, was published in 1975. His screenplay credits include *Ben Hur* (1959) and *The Bible: In the Beginning* (1966). A family history, *Can You Find Me*, was published in 1978.

ACHIEVEMENTS

Christopher Fry is one of the most popular and prolific of twentieth century English verse playwrights; only T. S. Eliot and William Butler Yeats exercised a greater influence on the development of twentieth century verse drama. Fry differs from Eliot and Yeats, however, in that he did not establish a reputation as a poet before turning to the stage. Fry began with an early and practical interest in the theater as an actor and director.

With the exception of his translation of Anouilh's *L'Invitation au Château*, all of Fry's plays are in verse in a century that has provided primarily a theater of realistic prose—a prose that Fry claims has lost all contact with anything other than surface reality. Fry insists that his use of verse is in the service of reality, that verse provides a medium for his attempt to shake the world alert again to the deeper reality of every human being's ability to experience afresh the eternal miracle of life—a reality at present obscured and staled by custom. In Fry's view, humankind has domesticated the enormous miracle of life and become deadened to the wonder that is everywhere available. Fry attempts to give voice to his sense of the miracle of life with the language of poetry. He derisively identifies prose on the stage with the tinkle of breakfast cups. In a 1951 article in *Saturday Review*, Fry makes it clear that "poetry is the language in which man explores his own amazement."

This worldview probably accounts for much of the adverse criticism Fry's plays have received, for his work sometimes rings false or hollow, irresponsibly separated from the world the theatergoer accepts as real. Sometimes the reader or viewer senses that Fry protests too much for a man firmly grounded in the

Christopher Fry in 1950, making corrections to the script of a new play.
(Hulton Archive by Getty Images)

"enormous miracle" of the world, and the atmosphere of his plays often has the unfortunate effect of sheer fantasy. The use of distant times and scenes adds to a sense of unreality, and it would seem particularly unfortunate that, if Fry's aim is to reestablish wonder in modern man, he should feel the necessity for setting his dramas in a world removed from the present by time and distance. *A Sleep of Prisoners* and *A Yard of Sun* are exceptions, and *Venus Observed* and even *The Dark Is Light Enough* can be viewed as fairly direct comments on the contemporary dilemma, but Fry's plays are never "modern" in the same sense as are those of Eliot, W. H. Auden, Christopher Isherwood, and Stephen Spender.

Fry seldom seeks to come to grips with the modern world by taking it as the arena of his explorations. Rather, he works by indirection, indicating in the world of his plays the importance of the individual, the meaning of humanity, the futility and needless cruelty of wars, and the possibilities for redeeming life through love. Having demonstrated the vitality latent in the world, Fry believes that he has made sufficient comment on the modern situation. This approach is misleading in view of Fry's claim to be interested in the problems of his own time, for the emphasis in his work appears to be not on modern human beings, but on humankind, as if Fry thought he could best restore human life to its proper heritage not by showing the paltry thing it has become in the twentieth century, but by showing what it has been and yet may be. Thus, Fry's dramaturgy stems from his romanticism, which expresses itself in an undaunted humanism and draws its vocabulary from natural and biblical sources. In Fry, there is little of the peculiarly modern vocabulary that one finds in other contemporary playwrights; as a general rule, the science Fry draws on for his images is that of alchemy or astronomy; his psychology is that of the theory of humors; his textbook, Robert Burton's *The Anatomy of Melancholy* (1621). It is not surprising, then, to find the charge of romantic escapism leveled against Fry: The dangers inherent in his approach are obvious.

Given his orientation, the problem Fry faces in terms of language is perhaps clearer when one considers that the mainstream of poetic idiom for the modern verse play is that established by Eliot and manipulated by Auden and others. This is an idiom, on the whole, expressive of the modern world as it has appeared to these poets, and such a language can be of little use to Fry. He needs a language not to embody the dreary failure and, at best, partially reclaimed successes of the modern world, but a language to carry as much as possible the wonder, the miracle, the exuberance of a world that, most likely, never was. Against Eliot's habitual understatement, Fry's project demands a language of overstatement, resulting in excesses: the riot of images that often impede the dramatic progress of a passage, the wit or whimsy that sometimes seems to exist for the sake of its own good nature, and the verbal coinages that can be effective theater for a time but begin to pall before the end of the third act.

Fry's linguistic debts have been traced to various and varying sources, and if all of the critics are right in their assumptions about sources, his verse has an impressive (but impossible) cosmopolitan paternity. Fry's work has been linked to that of the Georgians, but the Elizabethan playwrights as well as the Jacobeans, Francis Beaumont and John Fletcher, are most often named as his literary ancestors. Fry's desire to recapture a sense of life and wonder does suggest certain early seventeenth century parallels, as do specific literary borrowings from William Shakespeare's comedies. In this respect also, Fry's dominant rhythmic pattern is usually blank verse, although he makes extensive use of variations involving a four-stress line and the anapestic foot, which give his verse its characteristic speed.

Clearly, Fry's verse drama has taken a direction quite opposite from Eliot's, and one need only compare Eliot's *The Cocktail Party* (pr. 1949) and Fry's *Venus Observed*, both published in 1950 and both dealing thematically with the acceptance of limitations and the discovery of identity, to discern the differences in verse and treatment. In the Eliot play, the verse is submerged, approximating in general the common speech of modern people, rising to poetry only in moments of emotional intensity. In the Fry play, the verse is insistent throughout the play. Although both playwrights are concerned with the human being in his social context, the verse of *The Cocktail Party* seems much more solid, genuinely grounded in an action, which in itself has a depth that the action in the Fry play lacks.

Fry, as a dramatist, has not consistently mastered the third voice of poetry identified by Eliot in "The Three Voices of Poetry" as "the voice of the poet when he attempts to create a dramatic character speaking in verse: when he is saying, not what he would say in his own person, but only what he can say within the limits of one imaginary character addressing another imaginary character." Fry's characters, no matter how exorbitant their humors, generally reveal in their speech the voice of the poet, slightly academic and a little self-conscious, and it is for this reason that so many of Fry's characters sound alike.

BIOGRAPHY

Christopher Fry's work was virtually unknown to playgoers or readers until the success of *The Lady's Not for Burning* in 1949, although he seems to have been on his way to the creation of this play throughout most of his life. Born Christopher Fry Harris, the son of an architect, Charles Harris, Fry was reared in an intensely religious home. His father had been a lay missionary in the Bristol slums and his mother was a devout Quaker. Fry was still young at the time of his father's death, and his mother took in boarders in order to send her only son to the Bedford Modern School. She also did much to encourage his natural musical talents, translated, in his later writing career, into an appreciation for the music of language. His early performances as a solo musician may also have given him a taste for the more multi-faceted world of the professional stage, toward which he aimed his life. Fry did not pursue a university education but left school at age eighteen to become a teacher, around this time beginning to use his mother's maiden name, Fry—the name by which he has since been known.

Between periods of teaching, Fry joined the Bath Repertory Company. His next experience with the theater was eight difficult years during which he stubbornly tried to make a living with repertory troupes, performing in plays by William Shakespeare, George Bernard Shaw, Oscar Wilde, Sir James Barrie, and Noël Coward. When he moved to London in search of a career at the center of England's dramatic activities, he found that economic necessity once again forced him to try other work—as an editor, cartoonist, secretary, writer of children's plays, and even songwriter. From 1934 until its demise, he was director of the Wells Repertory Players at Tunbridge Wells. According to Fry, through all of this time his desire to write plays in verse never faltered.

Two years after his 1936 marriage, Fry received a small legacy from a cousin, which enabled him to begin sustained work on his plays. Shortly thereafter, his first published play, *The Boy with a Cart*, was conceived and first performed as a pageant play for the fiftieth anniversary of a village church, and *Thursday's Child* was produced in Albert Hall, London, with the attendance of the queen at one performance. In 1939, Fry became director of the Oxford Playhouse, but as a conscientious objector, he spent the war years in civilian service, fighting fires and clearing bomb damage in various parts of England.

In 1946, *A Phoenix Too Frequent*, the first of Fry's mature achievements in verse drama, was performed in London's private Arts Theatre Club, followed by sixty-four performances in a West End theater. The play, despite its success, drew critical reviews that saw it as too facile in its verse and too lightweight in its philosophical implications, in spite of the fact that Fry's original source was a tale from Petronius. The play, the first of Fry's to cross the Atlantic for a commercial performance, closed after only five nights in New York in April of 1950. New York critics almost unanimously condemned the play for being overwritten and too slight with regard to dramatic conception.

The Lady's Not for Burning was championed by John Gielgud for London production in 1948, a production in which Gielgud also had a hand in staging and a major character role in performance. This first of Fry's "seasonal comedies" brought him recognition and success on both sides of the Atlantic, and the play won the prestigious Shaw Prize as the best play of the year. *Venus Observed*, the "autumnal" play, followed the "spring" mood of *The Lady's Not for Burning* two years later when Sir Laurence Olivier successfully staged and acted in it. The "seasonal" round of Fry's intentions was interrupted by *A Sleep of Prisoners* published the year following, which was a religious festival play like *The Boy with a Cart* and *The Firstborn*. Published in 1955, *The Dark Is Light Enough* provided the "winter" comedy, and finally, in 1970, after slightly more than twenty years and the publication of *Curtmantle* in 1961, his Samuel Beckett play, Fry completed his expressed intention to write a play for each season of the year with *A Yard of Sun*, displacing *A Phoenix Too Frequent*, which some impatient critics had tried to take for the "summer" comedy needed for the cycle of the seasons.

As early as 1953, Fry wrote a script for a film of John Gay's *The Beggar's Opera*, followed by *Ben Hur* and *Barabbas* (1962). British television later saw his adaptation of Anne Brontë's *The Tenant of Wildfell Hall* (1968), a series of four plays on the Brontës (1973), a television play called *Sister Dora* (1977), and other mass media work.

After a gap of several years, Fry agreed to write a play about Caedmon, the unlettered peasant poet whose story is told in the Venerable Bede's *Ecclesiastical History of the English People* (731), titled *One Thing More*, on commission from the Chelmsford Cathedral. In 1987, in honor of Fry's eightieth birthday, *The Lady's Not for Burning* was televised by the British Broadcasting Corporation (BBC).

ANALYSIS

All of Christopher Fry's plays reflect his serious commitment to humanist and pacifist values and express the determined democracy of the individual spirit that is a legacy of Fry's Quaker heritage. Fry's insistence on the wonder of human life and the capacities of human beings, individually and collectively, for the growth of soul and conscience, has led him to some of the excesses of language and plotting for which he has been both disparaged and celebrated. Fry's career seems, ironically, almost a mirror of the effect of his best plays: a relatively brief and dazzling burst of light on the generally dark horizon of modern drama. He has persisted stubbornly through his original efforts and his translations of French playwrights to bring to what he sees as the contemporary theater's dreary realism a sense of delight and celebration that is nowhere else to be found and to wed this hopefully awakened sense of wonder to verse, a fit medium to oppose the dullness of the prevailing dialogue of contemporary realism. Fry's final reputation in the history of twentieth century drama may be that of one of the stubborn eccentrics he so loves to portray on the stage, but he will be respected for his desire to suggest a healthy—and very serious—alternative for his time.

A SLEEP OF PRISONERS

A Phoenix Too Frequent and *A Sleep of Prisoners* are Christopher Fry's two most successful one-act plays, a length that Fry easily mastered. Of the two, *A Sleep of Prisoners* is the more interesting because it is one of the few plays in which Fry tries to deal with a contemporary setting, and it is, formally, the most experimental of Fry's plays.

In many ways his most complex undertaking, *A Sleep of Prisoners* can be described as one of the most immediately modern of Fry's plays, not simply because it has as its characters four prisoners of war and as its setting an interlude in World War II, but also because, in this play, Fry draws on the experimental formal techniques of the modern theater. The scene of the play is a church converted into a temporary prison for four captured soldiers who, under the pressure of their surroundings, reenact biblical scenes in their dreams. Within this framework, Fry describes his intent and his design in the play's prefatory letter to Robert Gittings: "I have tried to make a more simple statement though in a complicated design where each of four men is seen through the sleeping thoughts of the others, and each, in his own dream, speaks as at heart he is, not as he believes himself to be."

This structure achieves a welding together of the spiritual history of humankind and the dreams of the four sleepers in an expressionistic fantasy that reveals the theme of the play. The dreams are made up of significant moments in the growth of vision Fry hopes to express, and the treatment of the material (the weaving of the patterns of the dreams and the final dream shared in common) suggests that the technique of the play owes more than a little to the Jungian idea of a racial memory, or perhaps to the tendency in modern poetry to suggest a composite experience and protagonist, as in Eliot's *The Waste Land* (1922) and in William Carlos Williams's *Paterson* (1946-1958).

The dreams of the four soldiers involve moments of passion, of suffering, of sacrifice, and the dream lives of the men are determined by their temperaments, which are established in the brief exchange that opens the play. Peter Abel, outwardly easygoing, uncommitted, and even-tempered, is attacked by his friend, David King, whose nerves are frayed by the whole experience and by his concern for Peter's apparent untroubled acceptance of the situation in which they find themselves. In their subsequent dreams, these two reenact the conflict in the roles that their names and natures suggest—Abel and Cain, Absalom and David, Isaac and Abraham—until they finally join Corporal Adams in his dream, and the three of them become Shadrac, Meshac, and Abednego in the fiery furnace, the crucible of humankind's experience.

The creation of their dreams in terms of army life gives the whole play a sense of immediacy while underwriting the repetitive nature of history and the cumulative meaning of human experience. The mixing of biblical situations and military terminology provides a very effective vocabulary for the verse of the play, creating the same kind of tensions that the larger design of the play encompasses.

The fourth character, Meadows, a man beyond the maximum age for enlistment, has accepted his involvement with humankind by the symbolic act of voluntary enlistment, and he provides the structural links between the waking and sleeping worlds. For the most part, as the other dreamers act out their passions, Meadows lies awake in his bunk; the others wake fitfully from time to time, and the waking men interact on the edge of their dreams. For example, after Adams, as Joab, has cut down Absalom with his tommy gun, David (no longer the king) awakens, and in the anxiety of his guilt, which had been objectified by his dream, asks Meadows, who has been awake, if he has heard a shout (the cry of the dying Absalom). Meadows's reply, "Nobody shouted," indicates the complexity of the formal convention of the dream, which is to be compared to the interior monologue technique in the sense that the world of the dream creates its own significant content and form although its larger setting is the external world.

There is a progression in the dreams that David and Peter enact, moving from the wrathful killing by Cain when Abel wins at dice to the meaningful but averted sacrifice of Isaac by Abraham. In the final experience of the furnace, when all three join in a single dream, Meadows appears as Man, who undergoes with the others the purgatorial fires in which humankind is tried. The fourth figure, the role which Meadows takes, is present in the biblical story and is traditionally identified with Christ; yet only if Christ is to be seen as a type of Everyman—not God but first of all Man, sharing the experiences of humankind—does this reading of the figure do no violence to accomplishment of the play.

In *A Sleep of Prisoners*, Fry deals more directly with the state of human beings in the modern world than in any of his other plays. David, for example, has the obsession Auden expressed in the 1930's, that the world is divided into "we's" and "they's," "ours" and "theirs"; "I've got to know which side I'm on./ I've got to be on a side." The intent of the play is to suggest, however, that sides and the wars and hatreds they represent offer no solutions, for no person is an island: "Whatever happens on the farthest pitch,/ To the sandman in the desert or the island-man in the sea,/ Concerns us very soon." The involvement of humankind in its history is a purifying experience, just as the flames in the biblical furnace suggest the purgatorial nature of the dreams the men have endured. The flames in the furnace become human figures, the unquenchable fire of breath and blood, which "can only transform."

Fry comes closer in *A Sleep of Prisoners* to achieving a totally realized verse drama than in any of his other attempts. Fry's problem in moving toward longer plays was to find a form in which to put his particular kind of language into a sustainable relationship to the whole. The most critical problem encountered in the longer play, the three-act or the five-act play, appears to be that of a structure in which verse can play an integral part and which will, in turn, justify the use of verse, for the problems of verse drama appear to be intensified and complicated by the necessities of the longer play. In the "seasonal comedies" and in *Curtmantle*, Fry stubbornly attacks the problem of the longer play in verse, only partially succeeding.

THE LADY'S NOT FOR BURNING

Fry's idea of a comedy for each season of the year is not a gimmick, but rather it belongs to the aesthetic notion that the "comedy of mood" or "comedy of seasons" can provide a unity of setting, time, and mood that will create the wholeness symbolized by the year itself.

Mood is everything in *The Lady's Not for Burning*. Two charming, young eccentrics—the rationalistic accused witch and the disenchanted soldier who wants to die—are pitted against two antagonists, one of which represents spring and all the forces of life and the other the petty world of a society that claims that "The standard soul/ Must mercilessly be maintained. No/ Two ways of life. One God, one point of view./ A general acquiescence to the mean."

All in all, this spring comedy is determined to prove that April is *not* the cruelest month, that human beings can survive the birth pangs of self-knowledge, accepting finally even the burden of an unreasonable future and an imperfect world. Typically, love reclaims the characters for life and an intuitive recognition of the wonder of the universe. In the course of their reclamation, however, there is a good deal of sheer "talk" for its own sake of the kind that weakens rather than strengthens Fry's comedies. Even the eccentricity of the characters cannot excuse a language often so circuitously poetic that the most notable thing about it is its derivative quality. The verbal high jinks, the excesses of language and imagery are as obvious as the literary derivations, and although Fry intentionally does this sort of thing at times in a scheme of romantic mockery, the device does not always work, since he is quite capable of creating a passage bearing the same verbal characteristics when his intention is entirely otherwise.

VENUS OBSERVED

Venus Observed, the autumnal comedy, is set in the declining season of the year, and its hero, the Duke of Altair, is well past the green age of youth. He has a grown son who becomes his rival in love and teaches him that he must accept the encroachments of age. At the beginning of the play, the Duke thinks that he has accepted the limitations imposed by his age, and he has gathered three of his former mistresses in his bedroom observatory to watch an eclipse of the sun through his beloved telescope. The Duke's son, Edgar, is to perform the Judgment of Paris for his father and present one of the three women with the symbolic apple, also appropriate to the day of the year, All Hallow's Eve, and to the autumn harvest. The apple is further to be identified with the legendary apple of the Fall of Man, so that through symbol and image, the scene of the play is extended to include the whole ruined Eden of the contemporary world, although there is no emphasis in the play on the modern situation.

The memory of Eden, of his first, unspoiled love, remains in the Duke, in spite of his autumnal resolves. When the eclipse has passed and the first renewed light of the sun reveals Perpetua Reedbeck standing in its rays, the Duke forgets that "'mellow'/ Is the keynote of the hour," and takes the apple to offer it to her youth and beauty. It is not until one of the Duke's aging mistresses destroys his observatory, which she sees as symbolic of the Duke's isolation and his invulnerability, that the Duke is brought to realize that so much he had "delighted in is all of ash." Out of the ash finally arises the Duke's acceptance of a love befitting his declining years. The action of the play brings the Duke into harmony with its autumnal mood—a mood that, like that of *The Cocktail Party*, leads all the characters to an examination of their limitations and to the adjustments necessary to make the best of the fading world in which they find themselves. In this respect, the play is close to the traditional function of comedy as a revelation of the follies and foibles of humankind, which brings human beings into an acceptable balance with society. As a part of this function, the speeches of certain characters (particularly of the Duke as Age pursuing lost Youth) are self-mocking, like those in *A Phoenix Too Frequent*, although Fry has achieved on the whole a quieter and less high-pitched verse.

A PHOENIX TOO FREQUENT

The verse in this play shows, in general, a certain flexibility not achieved in the earlier comedies, and it is a verse that wears for three acts with much less friction than the verse of *The Lady's Not for Burning*. The language itself is closer to the contemporary idiom, and it is "poetic" in unobtrusive ways, which involve concealed end-rhymes, internal rhymes, and alliteration. This is, on the whole, a more mature play than the earlier three-act comedy, and the language reflects this maturity. The verse almost entirely avoids the nondramatic philosophizing one ordinarily expects in a Fry play, and when such general comments do occur, they are part and parcel of the action or mood of the play.

THE DARK IS LIGHT ENOUGH

The Dark Is Light Enough is a "winter comedy" presumably because it involves the physical decline and death (but spiritual victory) of its heroine, who triumphs in death as in life, not so much through her own action as through her influence on those around her. This is a comedy, not of manners, but of the spiritual fiber that informs the world of manners, even in a no-man's-land between two warring forces. As in *The Firstborn*, the play is held together by a single, commanding character, that of the Countess, and her sphere of influence is the area of the play, even in the final moments after she has suffered death and yet controls the action about to be performed. The language, as befits a winter comedy, is sober in comparison with that of the other comedies, but on the whole, it is undistinguished either by Fry's excesses or by his achievements. At its worst, the language of the play suffers from the same sentimentality that mars the whole work. At its best, it is a language that rises out of the situation to catch and hold the mood of the play, as when the dying Countess descends the stairs for a final Thursday evening with her devoted group of admirers and tells them, "We must value this evening as the one/ Thursday in the universe, for the rest/ Have gone, and no more may come,/ And we should be on our most immortal behaviour."

A YARD OF SUN

A Yard of Sun is set in an Italian summer during the first Palio to be celebrated following the conclusion of World War II. This ancient contest, with its religious and civic affirmations, becomes the fitting occasion for the trial of individual identity, which is a central action of all of Fry's plays. It is also the occasion to bring the characters into an acceptance of the flawed universe, the world that will not bend itself to their own conceptions and desires, but which is, in spite of this fact (or, more likely, because of it), worthy of acceptance and affirmation. In fact, Ernst Cassirer's definition of comedy in "An Essay on Man" seems to have been made for Fry. Cassirer sees comic art as possessing "in the highest degree that faculty shared by all art, sympathetic vision. By virtue of this faculty it can accept human life with all its defects and foibles, its follies and vices. . . . We live in this restricted world, but we are no longer imprisoned by it."

A Yard of Sun is set in the courtyard of an ancient Siena palazzo, and the scene is never varied, for in a technique reminiscent of John Millington Synge's *The Playboy of the Western World* (pr., pb. 1907), the news of the various stages of the running of the traditional horse race comes to the audience only by report. The contest, an occasion for family reunions, provides the heightened moment which unlocks the potentiality for the real challenges of the play.

The sun in this summer comedy seems to suggest to Fry the light before which the inner shadows of the characters must yield and modify themselves. The "heat of the day" (the original title of the play) is a time for clarity, and into the yard of the palazzo come nine characters, representing a variety of modern views and problems, each related to the others in ways that must be clarified before they can accept the ambiguities of their own experiences. Winning turns out, in the end, not at all to mean what the characters had thought it would.

The verse of *A Yard of Sun* is much more controlled and unobtrusive than in any of Fry's other plays. The people are more nearly people talking to one another than they are characters making poems on the stage, and the action of this play seems to fit its meaning with an ease never before achieved. There is nothing very original in the play itself, but it is original within the Fry canon in the sense that it does not strain toward either the condition of verse or the condition of drama.

OTHER MAJOR WORKS

POETRY: *Root and Sky: Verse from the Plays of Christopher Fry*, 1975.

SCREENPLAYS: *The Beggar's Opera*, 1953 (with Denis Cannan); *Ben Hur*, 1959; *Barabbas*, 1962; *The Bible: In the Beginning*, 1966.

TELEPLAYS: *The Canary*, 1950; *The Tenant of Wildfell Hall*, 1968; *The Brontës of Haworth*, 1973 (4 teleplays); *The Best of Enemies*, 1976; *Sister Dora*, 1977 (adaptation of Jo Manton's book).

NONFICTION: *An Experience of Critics*, 1952; *Can You Find Me: A Family History*, 1978; *Death Is a Kind of Love*, 1979 (lecture); *Genius, Talent, and Failure*, 1987 (lecture).

TRANSLATIONS: *Ring Round the Moon*, 1950 (of Jean Anouilh's play *L'Invitation au Château*); *The Lark*, 1955 (of Anouilh's play *L'Alouette*); *Tiger at the Gates*, 1955 (of Jean Giraudoux's play *La Guerre de Troie n'aura pas lieu*); *Duel of Angels*, 1958 (of Giraudoux's play *Pour Lucrèce*); *Judith*, 1962 (of Giraudoux's play); *Cyrano de Bergerac*, 1975 (of Edmond Rostand's play).

CHILDREN'S LITERATURE: *The Boat That Mooed*, 1966.

BIBLIOGRAPHY

Fry, Phyl. *A Sprinkle of Nutmeg: Letters to Christopher Fry, 1943-1945*. Foreword by Christopher Fry. Chester Springs, Pa.: Dufour Editions, 1992. A selection of letters from Fry's wife, Phyl, to her husband during the last three years of the period in which he was away on war service. They give a glimpse of life in rural Oxfordshire during the war and the relationship between the playwright and his wife.

Leeming, Glenda. *Christopher Fry*. Boston: Twayne, 1990. After a brief chapter on Fry's life, the work offers a play-per-chapter discussion of the canon. It is much more a literary study of the drama than a performance study of the pieces as theater. Contains the first discussion of *One Thing More: Or, Caedmon Construed*, commissioned in 1986 by Chelmsford Cathedral and the BBC. Supplemented by a select bibliography, a chronology, and a brief index.

_____. *Poetic Drama*. New York: St. Martin's Press, 1989. Includes a long chapter on Fry's poetic drama, "in conventional setting." The work traces the language from early dramas ("assertive manifestation of the characters' thought") to later work ("the positive assertiveness of his language provokes critics to regard his work as like plum cake, too rich and too sweet"). Complemented by an index.

Roy, Emil. *Christopher Fry*. Carbondale: Southern Illinois University Press, 1968. From his success in 1948 ("A contemporary Shakespeare" said the press) to the inevitable comparisons to T. S. Eliot, Fry is examined up to his 1961 play *Curtmantle*, one play per chapter. Attention is paid to the seasonal arrangement of his plays and to the religious view, dramatized in *A Sleep of Prisoners*, "that man can grasp hope through an endurance of suffering." Includes a bibliography, an index, a chapter on Fry's imagery, and an overview.

Salmon, Eric. *Is the Theatre Still Dying?* Westport, Conn.: Greenwood Press, 1985. *Curtmantle* and *A Phoenix Too Frequent* are treated in separate discussions around Salmon's thesis that the theater is in fact alive and well if people take "some aspects of the English-speaking theatre of the last eighty years and examine them for signs of life." Sees *Curtmantle* as "surely and safely theatrical" and laments its disappearance from the repertory. Bibliographical essay and index.

Spanos, William V. *The Christian Tradition in Modern British Verse Drama: The Poetics of Sacramental Time*. New Brunswick, N.J.: Rutgers University Press, 1967. A discussion of *A Sleep of Prisoners*, demonstrating its debt to Charles Williams's "sacramental doctrine of the Way of the Affirmation of Images." Cites Fry's "conception of human action as a figured dance that traces the outline of the mystery." Select bibliography and index.

Donna Gerstenberger,
updated by Thomas J. Taylor

ATHOL FUGARD

Born: Middelburg, South Africa; June 11, 1932

PRINCIPAL DRAMA

No-Good Friday, pr. 1958, pb. 1977

Nongogo, pr. 1959, pb. 1977

The Blood Knot, pr. 1961, pb. 1963

People Are Living There, wr. 1962, pr. 1968, pb. 1969

Hello and Goodbye, pr. 1965, pb. 1966

The Coat: An Acting Exercise from Serpent Players of New Brighton, pr., pb. 1967 (with Serpent Players)

The Occupation, pb. 1968 (one act)

Ten One-Act Plays, pb. 1968 (Cosmo Pieterse, editor)

Boesman and Lena, pr., pb. 1969

Friday's Bread on Monday, pr. 1970 (with Serpent Players)

Orestes: An Experiment in Theatre as Described in a Letter to an American Friend, pr. 1971, pb. 1978

Statements After an Arrest Under the Immorality Act, pr. 1972, pb. 1974

Sizwe Bansi Is Dead, pr. 1972, pb. 1973 (with John Kani and Winston Ntshona)

The Island, pr. 1973, pb. 1974 (with Kani and Ntshona)

Three Port Elizabeth Plays, pb. 1974 (includes *The Blood Knot*, *Hello and Goodbye*, and *Boesman*

and *Lena*; revised pb. 2000 includes *"MASTER
HAROLD" . . . and the Boys*)
Dimetos, pr. 1975, pb. 1977
A Lesson from Aloes, pr. 1978, pb. 1981
The Drummer, pr. 1980 (improvisation)
"MASTER HAROLD" . . . and the Boys, pr., pb.
1982
The Road to Mecca, pr. 1984, pb. 1985
A Place with the Pigs, pr. 1987, pb. 1988
My Children! My Africa!, pr., pb. 1990
Blood Knot and Other Plays, pb. 1991
Playland, pr., pb. 1992
My Life, pr. 1994, pb. 1996
Valley Song, pr. 1995, pb. 1996
The Captain's Tiger, pr., pb. 1997
Plays: One, pb. 1998
Sorrows and Rejoicings, pr., pb. 2001

OTHER LITERARY FORMS

Although Athol Fugard has written in a variety of
literary forms, he is known primarily for his plays.
Tsotsi, a long-lost novel written between 1959 and
1960 and abandoned until its publication in 1979,
displays characterization, graphic language, and sardonic humor that foreshadow much in Fugard's later
drama. Of Fugard's screenplays—*The Occupation*
(1964), *Boesman and Lena* (1973), *The Guest* (1977),
and *Marigolds in August* (1982)—the last three, under the superb direction of Ross Devenish, have been
filmed and released. A post-apartheid version of
Boesman and Lena starring Danny Glover and Angela Bassett was released in 2000. Fugard also wrote
Mille Miglia (1968), a television script for the British
Broadcasting Corporation, which explores in flashback the relationship between race drivers Stirling
Moss and Denis Jenkinson, who won the last Italian
one-thousand-mile race in 1955, and their preparations for the race.

Fugard's *Notebooks, 1960-1977* (1983) testify to
the breadth of the influences on him and his influence
on others. The notebook entries reflect his political
engagement as well as his practical concerns as a dramatist. His *Cousins: A Memoir* (1994) relates the
playwright's early-life experiences with two influential relatives: his older cousins Johnnie and Garth.

Johnnie's love of music and performance and Garth's
adventurous wanderlust were important elements in
shaping Fugard's personality.

ACHIEVEMENTS

Athol Fugard—playwright, director, and actor—
is South Africa's most widely produced dramatist
abroad. His plays, though rooted in one nation, have
earned international acclaim. Fugard meticulously details life in a remote corner of the globe yet raises
compelling issues of general interest. Using social realism, linear plot development, and naturalistic language graced by metaphor and symbol, Fugard has
forged an impressive body of work for the theater,
ranging from full-length plays to improvisational exercises. Theatrically sparse, with small casts and little, if any, reliance on elaborate sets, costumes, or
props, Fugard's plays have been read easily on radio and adapted frequently for television and film.
On December 4, 1984, Fugard received the Commonwealth Award for Distinction in Dramatic Arts, an
award which he shared with Stephen Sondheim.

Fugard's distinction as a playwright is inseparable
from his contributions to and influences on South African theater, as well as on the Yale Repertory Theatre. He has radically affected both the practice and
purpose of serious drama in his native land. His interpretation of his world, his use of "poor theater" for its
maximum effect, and his dedication to his actors,
both black and white, have earned for him a critical
respect accorded few modern playwrights. Early in
his career, he chose to be a witness against what he
called a "conspiracy of silence" about South Africa's
apartheid legislation. Fugard considers theater to be
no more—and no less—than a civilizing influence,
one that may sensitize, provoke, or anger. He de-
plores the label "political playwright." He believes
that if a playwright tells a story, a good one, the larger
implications will take care of themselves. Because
they are set in South Africa, Fugard's plays cannot ignore apartheid, but Fugard's plays are not agitprop.
Critics and actors alike commend Fugard's craft, especially his attention to what he calls "carnal reality"
and his ability to develop resonant images that merit
repeated readings or performances.

Athol Fugard (Richard Corman)

Fugard's plays—and his actors—have been honored often. *The New York Times* voted *The Blood Knot* Best Play of the 1964 season. Fugard was elected Man of the Year in the Arts in South Africa in 1969. *Boesman and Lena* received an Obie Award for Distinguished Foreign Play from the *Village Voice* in 1971. Janet Suzman won the London *Evening Standard* Award for Best Actress in 1973 for her portrayal of Hester Smit in Fugard's *Hello and Goodbye*. *Sizwe Bansi Is Dead*, devised by Fugard with actors John Kani and Winston Ntshona, was chosen Play of the Year in 1974 by the London Theatre Critics. Kani and Ntshona went on to share Tony Awards for Best Acting in the 1974-1975 New York season for *The Island*, another Fugard play devised with their help. In 1975, Fugard was commissioned by the Edinburgh Festival to write a new play, *Dimetos*, and in 1980 the Actors Theatre of Louisville (Kentucky) commissioned an improvisational work, *The Drummer*. (These works, along with *Mille Miglia*, a 1968 British Broadcasting Corporation television play, are not set in South Africa.) *A Lesson from Aloes* was awarded the New York Drama Critics Circle Award for Best New Play of the 1980-1981 season, while *"MASTER HAROLD" . . . and the Boys* won both the Drama Desk Award and the Outer Critics Circle Award for Best Play of 1982, as well as a Tony Award for Zakes Mokae as Outstanding Featured Actor and the *Evening Standard* Award for Best Play of 1983. The play also won South Africa's largest cash award for theater: the AA Mutual Life/Vita Award for Best New South African Play, 1983-1984. In 1986, Fugard was also the recipient of the Drama League Award, and the New York Drama Critics Circle Award and Helen Hayes Award for Direction followed in 1988 and 1990, respectively.

Fugard has been given honorary doctorates by three South African universities: the University of Natal, Durban, in 1981; Rhodes University, Grahamstown, 1983; and the University of Cape Town, in 1984. Yale University in 1983 and Georgetown University in 1984 also honored Fugard with doctorates.

Fugard is also a gifted director who exhibited a wide range of his interests through the plays he chose to direct at The Rehearsal Room in Johannesburg in the late 1950's and to stage with the Serpent Players in New Brighton from 1963 to 1973, including Harold Pinter's *The Dumb Waiter* (pr. 1960) in Johannesburg and Niccolò Machiavelli's *La mandragola* (pr. c. 1519; *The Mandrake*, 1911), Sophocles' *Antigonē* (441 B.C.E.; *Antigone*, 1729), and August Strindberg's *Fadren* (pr., pb. 1887; *The Father*, 1899) in New Brighton. Fugard's talents as an actor have enabled him to perform in many of his own plays when they were first staged.

BIOGRAPHY

Harold Athol Lannigan Fugard (pronounced *few-gard*) was born June 11, 1932, in Middelburg, a town in the Great Karoo, a semidesert region of Cape Province, South Africa. The son of an Anglo-Irish father and an Afrikaner mother, Fugard is an ethnic hybrid. English is his first language, but because of his mother's dominant personality, Afrikaner culture profoundly affected him. Fugard simultaneously honors and excoriates his Afrikaner roots. The two major abstractions of Fugard's work—love and truth—he saw fleshed out as he grew up in Port Elizabeth, a multiracial, industrial, windswept town on the eastern Cape to which his family moved when he was three.

Fugard's father lost a leg in a shipboard accident as a child, and in spite of successfully leading a series of jazz bands, he retired early, when Fugard was young, to a life of unemployment and alcoholism. Fugard's ambivalent feelings about his father color much of his work, especially *Hello and Goodbye* and *"MASTER HAROLD" . . . and the Boys*. His mother supported the family, first by running a boardinghouse, the Jubilee Hotel, and then by operating the St. George's Park Tea Room, the scene of *"MASTER HAROLD" . . . and the Boys*. Early in life, Fugard thus learned about failed expectations, a major theme in his work, and about hard times.

As a schoolboy, Fugard, then known as Hally, shunned his peers and spent his free time with his mother's waiters, Sam Semela and Willie Malopo. (These men appear in *"MASTER HAROLD" . . . and the Boys* under their real names.) Sam, in particular, though middle-aged, became Fugard's friend and the most influential adult in his life. Fugard looked up to Sam as a man in the fullest sense of that word; while Sam taught Fugard about being a man, Fugard shared his schoolroom experiences and books with him. For some inexplicable reason, one day Fugard insulted Sam; he did not expiate his guilt for this act until he wrote *"MASTER HAROLD" . . . and the Boys*. In real life, Sam Semela forgave Fugard almost immediately, and they remained friends until Sam died in 1983, shortly before the play in his honor opened in Johannesburg.

Fugard studied philosophy at the University of Cape Town from 1950 to 1953, but he quit immediately before his final examinations to hitchhike up Africa with a poet friend, deciding that the academic life was not for him. From 1953 to 1955, he traveled around the world on a merchant ship on which he was the only white crew member. He was married in 1956 to Sheila Meiring, who introduced him to the theater. When they moved to Johannesburg in 1958, Fugard was employed for three months as a clerk in the Fords-

burg Native Commissioner's Court; then he began working with amateur black actors in Sophiatown, then Johannesburg's black ghetto. He also worked as a stage manager for the National Theatre Organization before he and his wife went to England and Europe in 1959.

The Fugards returned to South Africa in 1960, and the initial production of *The Blood Knot* in 1961 and its six-month tour around South Africa were crucial to Fugard's development as a playwright. In 1962, Fugard instigated a boycott of South Africa's segregated theaters by British playwrights, but by 1967 he had decided that even in such compromising circumstances, voices were preferable to silence. Fugard visited the United States briefly in 1964 and returned to England in 1966; both trips involved productions of *The Blood Knot*. His government withdrew his passport from 1967 to 1971. From 1963 to 1974, he directed and produced European plays as well as collaborating on indigenous South African material with the New Brighton actors known as the Serpent Players; many of these actors were arrested between 1965 and 1967. Since 1977, Fugard's reputation has been such that he divides his time between South Africa and the rest of the globe: the United States, Europe, Asia, and India. The United States, however, is the only place he could live, he claims, if he could not live in South Africa.

Fugard has singled out several early incidents in his life as being of particular importance. For example, he says that his experience as a sailor cured him of any racial prejudice he might have had. His wife's prodding him into helping her establish a theater workshop in Cape Town, the Circle Players, in 1956 and 1957 led to the evolution of his lean, one-room dramaturgy. The move to Johannesburg and his work in the Commissioner's Court caused him to see the worst of apartheid legislation; there, an African was sent to jail every two minutes. Fugard turned this ugly nightmare to dramatic use when he devised *Sizwe Bansi Is Dead* with actors John Kani and Winston Ntshona in 1972; the play is an exposé of the passbook law, which required every African over sixteen to carry an identity book that restricted both his employment opportunities and his movements inside South Africa.

The rejection of Fugard's scripts by the Royal Court Theatre in London in 1960, the hand-to-mouth existence the Fugards shared there, and Fugard's sense of isolation from his roots convinced him that he was a regional writer. Before the Fugards' return to South Africa in 1960, in response to the Sharpeville Massacre, they helped form—with Tone Brulin, David Herbert, and Clive Farrell—the short-lived New Africa Group, dedicated to the staging of original South African plays in Europe. Fugard played Okkie, the Greek who tries to pass for white, in Herbert's *A Kakamas Greek* (pr. 1960), which was set in the Karoo, Fugard's birthplace. This production won the Best Entry Award at the Festival of Avant-garde Theatre in Brussels in 1960 and toured thereafter in the Flemish part of Belgium, Holland, and Germany—performed in English. The question of racial identify in *A Kakamas Greek* also haunts Fugard's first critical success, *The Blood Knot*.

While he was writing, in solitude, *The Blood Knot*, *People Are Living There*, *Hello and Goodbye*, and *Boesman and Lena*, which detail claustrophobic relationships, Fugard was also experimenting with adapting European plays to South African life and with improvising from the raw material of his actors' lives. *The Coat* in 1967 and *Orestes* in 1971, which actress Yvonne Bryceland considers "the most important single thing" in Fugard's career, are examples of improvisations from life.

The "Statements" plays (*Statements After an Arrest Under the Immorality Act*, *Sizwe Bansi Is Dead*, and *The Island*), which secured Fugard's reputation outside South Africa, also evolved from collaborative theater. These plays together constitute Fugard's most outspoken indictment of apartheid. An early version of *Statements After an Arrest Under the Immorality Act* was the inaugural production in 1972 of The Space, an "open" theater in Cape Town that evaded audience segregation rulings. *Sizwe Bansi Is Dead* was next, followed by an early version of *The Island* in 1973. These two plays did not exist in written form until Fugard and actors Kani and Ntshona were safely in London, later in 1973, for the South African Season at the Royal Court Theatre. In 1977 and 1978, Kani and Ntshona performed *Sizwe Bansi Is Dead* and *The Island* in Johannesburg at the Market Theatre, an "open" venue.

In 1974, after Fugard's success in London, *Three Port Elizabeth Plays*—including *The Blood Knot*, *Hello and Goodbye*, and *Boesman and Lena*—was published by Oxford University Press, with a detailed introduction by Fugard of excerpts from his notebooks. This introduction, combined with that to *Statements After an Arrest Under the Immorality Act*, constituted the clearest summary of Fugard's aesthetics—as well as a biographical gloss on his plays—before 1984, when *Notebooks, 1960-1977* appeared. In 1978, the "Statements" plays were performed and published in German; in 1979, *The Island* was translated and performed in French, and *Boesman and Lena* was translated and presented in Afrikaans in Cape Town.

Fugard returned to solo composition when *Dimetos* was commissioned by the Edinburgh Festival in 1975, but in spite of rewriting and a cast headed by Paul Scofield for the London West End run in 1976, *Dimetos* failed with critics and audiences alike. Its poetic allegory and nonregional setting are atypical of Fugard, yet the play remains one of his favorites. Like *Statements After an Arrest Under the Immorality Act*, another play that Fugard cherishes, *Dimetos* attempts to use prose musically and frequently becomes too elliptical and ambiguous.

Between 1978 and 1984, Fugard produced three major plays: *A Lesson from Aloes*, *"MASTER HAROLD" . . . and the Boys*, and *The Road to Mecca*. Fugard's tenure at Yale, with which these plays are associated, began in January, 1980, and he later bought a house in rural New York State so that he could continue his hobby of birdwatching when he was not at the Yale Repertory Theatre.

Fugard's plays have constantly been revived and produced and have become staples of nonprofit professional theater in the United States and Great Britain. Fugard has continued to direct his own plays, both in the commercial British and in the nonprofit professional American theaters, such as his production of *My Children! My Africa!*, which enjoyed several venues, including the Lyttelton Theatre in London, the Perry Street Theatre in New York, the Yale

Repertory Theatre in New Haven, Connecticut, and the La Jolla Playhouse in California. He also continued to act in his own plays on occasion, starring in *A Lesson from Aloes* in Los Angeles in 1991. Throughout the 1990's Fugard continued his multifarious participation in live theatre through acting and directing as well as writing. After *Playland* in 1992, Fugard directed and acted in the 1995 and 1996 productions of *Valley Song*. Most extraordinarily, Fugard played two characters in *Valley Song*, the white Author and black grandfather (Jonkers), and specified that in future productions only one actor could continue to play both parts. In 2001 and 2002 Fugard directed his *Sorrows and Rejoicings*, first at the McCarter Theatre in Princeton, New Jersey, then in Cape Town, South Africa, and finally Off-Broadway.

ANALYSIS

Athol Fugard's plays satisfy a major criterion of good drama: the creation of vivid, lifelike characters. His characterization is immature in his early plays, *No-Good Friday* and *Nongogo*—with their black-ghetto gangsters, hustlers, musicians, whores, pimps, dreamers, and even a white priest—but these stereotypes foreshadow such fully developed characters in the 1960's plays as the half brothers in *The Blood Knot*, the landlady in *People Are Living There*, the siblings in *Hello and Goodbye*, and the destitute couple Boesman and Lena, in the play of that title. In the 1970's, Fugard created such powerful characters as the miscegenational lovers in *Statements After an Arrest Under the Immorality Act*, the urban and country blacks in *Sizwe Bansi Is Dead*, the prisoners in *The Island*, and the isolated Anglo-Afrikaner couple and their "colored" friend in *A Lesson from Aloes*. In his later plays, Fugard presents two black waiters and a teenage schoolboy (*"MASTER HAROLD" . . . and the Boys*) and an elderly, reclusive sculptor, her young friend, and a local pastor (*The Road to Mecca*). Fugard's characters, who seem so specific and concrete as to personify South Africa, are at the same time universal in their humanity.

Most of these characters do little or nothing except validate their existence through words that cry out to be heard. Their language ranges from the harshly naturalistic to the eloquently poetic; their rhythms are acutely South African, yet they cross linguistic barriers. Fugard's *Notebooks, 1960-1977* records the South African images from which his plays come: two brothers in a shack; a landlady who stays in her nightclothes for a whole day; a woman arriving with a suitcase and a man on crutches; a couple with their worldly possessions on their backs; six police photographs of two naked lovers; a self-confident black with a cigarette in one hand, a pipe in the other; two prisoners putting sand into wheelbarrows; and a lonely man studying an aloe plant. Program notes for *"MASTER HAROLD" . . . and the Boys* and *The Road to Mecca* provide images of ballroom dancing and a magical room of light and color. From such images, Fugard has crafted works of art as solid as steel, as fragile as china. Sturdy yet delicate, his plays wear well—the ultimate tribute to a master artist.

Fugard has long acknowledged his debt to Albert Camus and Samuel Beckett. In Camus, he found a kindred spirit for his worldview and his role as an artist; in Beckett, he found a dramaturgy of maximum import with minimum theatrical outlay. Confined to one room or space, two or three characters recollect, recriminate, role-play, and resign themselves to their existence in a world without meaning and with little hope for change. They delude themselves with false hopes and dreams, amuse themselves with games to pass the time; such nobility as they possess comes in the fleeting, lucid moments when they acknowledge their condition—and their dependence on each other. As does Camus, Fugard opts for a "courageous pessimism" born of the clear-sighted recognition of modern human beings' plight—trapped in a world as capricious as Ariadne's web and as mazelike as the Cretan Minotaur's labyrinth.

In his 1957 Nobel address at the University of Uppsala, Camus said, "To create today is to live dangerously"; he continued, "The suffering of mankind is such a vast subject that it seems no one could touch it unless he was like Keats so sensitive . . . that he could have touched pain itself with his hands." In an interview with Barrie Hough in 1977, prompted by *The Guest*, Fugard's film about Eugène Marais, Fugard commented that "one of the major Marais statements was that all living, survival, is grounded on pain. . . . It's really a theme that has gone through all my work; it's the string that holds all the beads together to make a necklace." Fugard has touched pain in his plays, as much as he has touched love and truth. He revels in the palpable, the tangible. In the realities of daily living—sore feet, tired bodies, arthritic hands, mounting stress, and cruel insults—Fugard reminds people that they are the sum of their pain. The whole is greater than the sum of its parts, but their interdependence is undeniable. Fugard forces us to recognize this interdependence preeminently in *The Blood Knot*, *Boesman and Lena*, *The Island*, *A Lesson from Aloes*, and *"MASTER HAROLD" . . . and the Boys*, the most representative of his plays, as well as in *The Road to Mecca*.

THE BLOOD KNOT AND BOESMAN AND LENA

The two plays that began and ended Fugard's work in the 1960's, *The Blood Knot* and *Boesman and Lena*, illustrate his talent for full-bodied characterization, as well as his progression toward structural sparseness and multileveled, resonant language. The half brothers of *The Blood Knot*, bound inextricably in a union of opposites, reveal themselves completely in a long play of seven scenes that builds to a harrowing climax. The Nomadic outcasts and mixed breeds, or "Coloreds," Boesman and Lena, hover on the edge of life and death in what appears to be a cyclic pattern of eviction, of breaking and making camp, of Boesman's beating Lena, and of Lena's manic search for her identity, in two acts that are half as long as *The Blood Knot*. However, unlike Beckett's tramps in *En attendant Godot* (pb. 1952, pr. 1953; *Waiting for Godot*, 1954), whose essence is not to change, Fugard's characters do change in the course of the play. Superficially, more happens in *The Blood Knot*'s shanty over a much longer period of time than the one cold evening under the stars of *Boesman and Lena*, but the latter's reduction in plot and stage business results in a thematic and symbolic complexity that allows for greater character revelation as well as greater character development.

In both plays, two characters diametrically opposite in temperament and goals explode in words and acts when confined in a small space. Such conflicts

are the heart of Fugard's drama, beginning with *The Blood Knot*. Morris, the light-skinned brother, suffers from agoraphobia—fear of open spaces—after wandering ten years trying to pass for white, while Zach, the dark-skinned brother, has suffered from claustrophobia ever since Morris returned to minister to him by ordering his life. In his notebook entry on the brothers, Fugard said, "Morris, if anything, hates himself. Zach hates the world that has decided his blackness must be punished. . . . Morris is the better equipped mentally for this last fight—also, weakened by thought and sympathy. Zach has the physical strength and impetus of hate. Zach wins." The tyrannical alarm clock that regulates the brothers' lives rings just in time to keep Zach's violence at bay. When Zach asks Morris for an explanation of why their game of black-white domination has gone awry, Morris responds, "I'll keep the clock winded, don't worry. One thing I'm certain is sure, it's a good thing we got the game. It will pass the time. Because we got a lot left, you know! Almost a whole life . . . stretching ahead. . . . I'm not too worried at all. . . . I mean, other men get by without a future. In fact, I think there's quite a lot of people getting by without futures these days."

Condemned at birth to have no future, the brothers reconstructed a brief childhood reprieve in which they took an imaginary, wild, car ride—stopped only by a flock of butterflies—chased donkeys in the veld, climbed trees, teased girls, stole fruit, and caught birds. In contrast, the humor of their adult games is sardonic and menacing, their laughter double-edged. They are two particular South African brothers, yet avatars of Cain and Abel.

Like Morris and Zach, Boesman and Lena are locked in an intimate love-hate relationship as mates—one they have fallen into years before the play opens, and one that Lena chooses to reassert as the play ends, in spite of her open rebellion throughout. Motifs that recall *The Blood Knot*'s birds, donkeys, and aimless walking recur in the later play, while staccato, contrapuntal speeches are interleaved with poetic monologues in both. Lena's frenzied songs and dances on the mud flats parallel the brothers' childhood games, but the violence talked about in

The Blood Knot actually happens in *Boesman and Lena*. Lena's bruises are real, and the old African whom she befriends dies before dawn. He literally becomes the white man's refuse that Boesman has said he and Lena are, and because they cannot dispose of him, they must resume walking. Though she threatens to remain behind, Lena prepares to follow Boesman; in response, he tells her the correct sequence of their journeys, which she had so desperately tried to get straight throughout the play—as if that knowledge would explain how she got where she is. "It doesn't explain anything," she says, but her parting shot, "I'm alive, Boesman. There's daylights left in me," is believable because she has demonstrated repeatedly her will to live.

Suicide is out of the question for Boesman and Lena. As absurd as their existence is, they endure it; they even tried to perpetuate it, but only one of Lena's babies was born alive, and it lived only six months. In recounting her past to the old African, who cannot understand her language any more than Boesman and Lena can understand his, Lena defines pain: "Pain? Yes! . . . One night it was longer than a small piece of candle and then as big as darkness. Somewhere else a donkey looked at it. . . . Pain is a candle *entjie* [end] and a donkey's face." Such metaphoric language typifies Fugard, as it does Beckett. Moreover, both have been accused of writing plays of despair or bitter comedy. Fugard defends Beckett against such charges, as many critics defend Fugard. Fugard finds Beckett's humor, combined with his love and compassion for humanity's "absurd and bruised carnality," positive and life-affirming; describing Beckett's humor to his wife, Fugard once said, "Smile, and then wipe the blood off your mouth." *Boesman and Lena* is Fugard's most pessimistic play, in mood and theme, but it is not morbid or maudlin; it is his most profound response to the world as he sees it, a world in which endurance and survival alone may be the only card human beings hold in a stacked deck.

THE ISLAND

In *The Island*, collaborative and improvisational in origin, Fugard experimented with the theories of Polish director Jerzy Grotowski, as he did in the unpublished *Friday's Bread on Monday*, in 1970, and

Orestes, whose 1971 performance is described only in a letter. *The Island* is a tribute to actors' theater, but once written, it has stood on its own merits as a strong play for actors other than John Kani and Winston Ntshona, Fugard's original performers and collaborators. It reads as well as it plays. Unified structurally and centrally focused, it demonstrates Fugard's mastery of the one-act form. Its companion piece, *Sizwe Bansi Is Dead*, another virtuoso play for actors, comes closer to a stream-of-consciousness novella than to a drama built on the classical unities of time, space, and action that Fugard observes in *Boesman and Lena* and his three subsequent critical successes. Yet Fugard has always practiced what he calls "actors' theater."

As early as 1962, Fugard defined the pure theater experience: "the actor and the stage, the actor *on* the stage. Around him is space, to be filled and defined by movement and gesture; around him is also a silence to be filled with meaning. . . ." The actor, space, and silence—Fugard continued exploring these dramatic requisites after a reading of Grotowski's *Towards a Poor Theatre* (1969) that validated the use of the actor as a creator, not simply as an interpreter. *The Island* could not have been written without Kani and Ntshona's experiences as South African blacks or without what they and Fugard knew of the Serpent Players, who had been sent to Robben Island, South Africa's hard-labor, maximum-security prison primarily as political prisoners; some returned to tell their stories. (Kani and Ntshona were never imprisoned on Robben Island, though they were arrested in 1976 before a performance of *Sizwe Bansi Is Dead* and imprisoned briefly until an international actors' protest secured their release.) Fugard credits Grotowski with giving him the courage to "write directly into . . . space and silence via the actor," using the basic device of "challenge and response"; he also credits Brian Astbury, the founder of The Space in Cape Town, for his "vision and tenacity of purpose" in providing the venue for the "Statements" plays.

The Island, like *The Blood Knot* and *Boesman and Lena*, features two characters who are polar opposites in every sense. John and Winston (both the actors' actual names and the names of the characters) wrestle with fundamental questions of identity and purpose.

The play opens and closes with the two convicts miming the futile labor of putting sand into wheelbarrows, pushing a barrow to where the other has been digging, and emptying the sand into that hole; the piles of sand therefore remain the same. A whistle blows, and the prisoners mime being handcuffed together and shackled at the ankles before the whistle blows again to send them off on a torturous three-legged run. They do not run fast enough to avoid being beaten. Bruised and bleeding, they collapse in their cell before uttering a word. After they nurse their wounds and curse their sadistic warder, John gives a news broadcast and weather report: "Black domination was chased by White domination. . . . Conditions locally remain unchanged—thunderstorms with the possibility of cold showers and rain. Elsewhere, fine and warm!" Soon, John begins to rehearse *Antigone* for a prison show. Winston does not want to play a woman, and his reluctance to appear as such is comic until the very end, when his identification with Antigone becomes complete. Condemned to life in prison, he faces the audience and cries, "Brothers and Sisters of the Land! I go now to my last journey"; he tears off his wig and confronts them with, "I go now to my living death, because I honoured those things to which honour belongs." (John had been sentenced for burning his passbook in front of a police station.)

The Island is more, however, than an anguished cry of defiance. Like all of Fugard's plays, it focuses on close human relationships; John and Winston are linked in a bond almost as indissoluble as that of Morris and Zach or Boesman and Lena—almost, because midway through the play, John discovers that he will be free in three months, while Winston must remain for life. Before receiving that news, they talked on an imaginary telephone to their friends in New Brighton, another funny game of the many that Fugard's characters play; after John's news, Winston re-creates John's release and welcome home. Ultimately, Winston recovers from his agony and, like Antigone, comes to terms with his fate. *The Island* is as compelling as Fugard's earlier plays because, once again, its particulars are transcended in a work of universal significance, a study of humanity's inhumanity to humanity and people's capacity to endure entrap-

ment through a joy in embracing ideals—regardless of their consequences.

A LESSON FROM ALOES

In *A Lesson from Aloes*, isolation, neurosis, and exile are the cost that Fugard's characters must pay for their fidelity to the ideals of love and friendship; there is little laughter here. The three characters are Fugard's first attempt to portray his own kind: literate, well-meaning South Africans caught in their government's crackdown on dissent in 1963, which led many to flee the country. Every Fugard play can be seen as an exploration of the effects of public policy on individual lives, but *A Lesson from Aloes* is Fugard's most quietly anguished portrait of this phenomenon.

Aloes are thorny, spiky, succulents that survive without much water in very harsh environments. Piet Bezuidenhout, a middle-aged Afrikaner, once an active member of an antiapartheid group that was silenced by the police, grows aloes in his back garden. Identifying them by name is his chief pleasure, other than reciting English poetry. Piet's English-speaking wife, back home after a stay in the Fort English mental home, and his "colored" friend and former comrade, Steve Daniels—preparing to leave South Africa on a one-way exit permit and just out of jail for breaking his banning order—are the other characters in this subtle but searing study of personal desolation. All three characters have internalized the shocks their world has given them.

The first act opens with Piet trying to identify a rare aloe; this leads to a revelation of the bitterness that mars his relationship with Gladys. For her part, Gladys cannot forget the police seizure of her personal diaries during a raid prompted by Piet's political involvement; Piet broodingly wonders why his old friends suspect him of being an informer. Tension builds as Piet and Gladys await the arrival of the Daniels' family for a farewell celebration. When Steve does arrive, in the second act—without his family and a bit drunk—the party fails miserably. Playing a very nasty game, Gladys tells Steve that Piet had informed on him, but then she withdraws the charge. Piet refuses, however, to say anything: "Hell, Steve, you know why. If you could have believed it, there was no point in denying it." Apparently reconciled with Piet, Steve leaves. Gladys decides to return to the hospital, and Piet is left alone with his unidentified aloe. In spite of its explicit title and insistent metaphor, *A Lesson from Aloes* is not didactic. There are no clear-cut answers and few, if any, happy endings in Fugard's plays. Like Piet, Fugard cultivates a private garden with unidentifiable species.

"MASTER HAROLD" . . . AND THE BOYS

In *"MASTER HAROLD" . . . and the Boys*, Fugard returned to the humor associated with his earlier plays to underscore the point that personal choice and action define a life worth living. Set still further back in Fugard's past than *A Lesson from Aloes*, and his most autobiographical play, *"MASTER HAROLD" . . . and the Boys* takes place in a Port Elizabeth tearoom one rainy afternoon in 1950. A long one-act play—too long perhaps—it opens with two black waiters, Sam and Willie, joking and practicing ballroom dancing for a contest two weeks away. Both men will compete if Willie can appease the partner whom he has recently beaten for not getting the quickstep right. Sam hits on an ingenious solution for Willie's future practice sessions: "Give her a handicap. . . . Give her a ten-second start and then let Count Basie go. Then I put my money on her. Hot favorite in the Ballroom Stakes: Hilda Samuels ridden by Willie Malopo." As Sam demonstrates his superior skills, Hally, the teenage son of the tearoom owner, enters and applauds. Hally's long friendship with the waiters—especially with Sam—is soon apparent, but Hally is tense because of his father's imminent release from the hospital. Hally loves but is ashamed of his crippled, bigoted, alcoholic father and looks to Sam as a role model instead. Fugard lovingly re-creates Hally's camaraderie with the waiters; he focuses particularly on a kite that Sam made for Hally from scrap materials—a kite that miraculously flew. Nevertheless, Hally's "second family" cannot stand up against the demons of his first. These malign forces are unleashed in the play's climax, when Hally insists that the "boys" call him "Master Harold," tells them a crude racial joke, and, when Sam responds, spits in his face. Sam almost literally turns the other cheek, but Hally is too wracked

with guilt to apologize. He leaves, and the curtain falls on the two waiters dancing once again—after Willie has used what was to be his bus fare home to start up the jukebox.

A play about growing up and the real meaning of family as much as it is about racism, *"MASTER HAROLD" . . . and the Boys* is at once exhilarating, sobering, exuberant, and wrenching. Like all of Fugard's plays, it relies on resonant language; here, the governing metaphor is that of life as a ballroom dance, which leads Sam to dream of a world without accidents or collisions if people and nations can only get the steps right. The game that Hally and Sam play to identify "men of magnitude" who have benefited all humankind leads to some provocative choices by Hally—Charles Darwin, Leo Tolstoy, Socrates, Karl Marx, and Friedrich Nietzsche among others; Sam's choices are Abraham Lincoln, William Shakespeare, Jesus Christ, and Sir Alexander Fleming. Sam's poor-looking kite becomes the most splendid thing Hally has ever seen aloft, and the bench to which Sam ties it when he has to return to work becomes the "Whites Only" bench of Sam's final words to Hally: "If you're not careful . . . Master Harold . . . you're going to be sitting up there by yourself for a long time to come, and there won't be a kite up in the sky. . . . I reckon there's one thing you know. You don't have to sit up there by yourself. You know what that bench means now, and you can leave it any time you choose. All you've got to do is stand up and walk away from it." Avoiding sentimentality in a play that revels in sentiment is Fugard's rare achievement here; *"MASTER HAROLD" . . . and the Boys* is a masterwork from a master craftsperson.

THE ROAD TO MECCA

Fugard's experiments as a dramatist have been within the confines of social naturalism or realism. His modes are representational rather than expressionist or surreal; his plots are convincing; his language is often poetic but rarely abstruse, colloquial but rarely vulgar. In short, Fugard is not an innovator but a conservator: He emulates the best of his predecessors, but he translates their voices and techniques into his own uniquely South African vision. Over the years—a quarter of a century—he has become inimitable, and no more so than in *The Road to Mecca*. A three-character play, like *"MASTER HAROLD"* . . . *and the Boys*, *The Road to Mecca* is one of Fugard's most daring experiments.

The play is set in the autumn of 1974, and all three of its characters are white: two proud Afrikaners who live in New Bethesda (a village in the Great Karoo) and an equally proud young English-speaking school-teacher from Cape Town. The plot is essentially un-complicated. The young woman, Elsa Barlow, drives eight hundred miles for an overnight visit with her old friend, Miss Helen—a reclusive sculptor whom the local pastor, Marius Byleveld, wants to put in a nursing home for her own security. In the first act, the two women slowly reestablish their long-standing friendship, but Marius arrives at the opening of the second act and begins to undermine Miss Helen's confidence in her ability to cope and to create. Elsa briefly adopts Marius's point of view when he tells her that Miss Helen almost set her house on fire ear-lier. Finally, in a moving reverie about the purpose of her Mecca, Miss Helen becomes courageous enough to dismiss Marius and assert her right to live with the danger of her creative impulses. Disheartened by his failure to convert Helen—and to make her love him—Marius leaves. The play ends with the women trusting each other once again.

Although this plot is fairly conventional, Fugard's choice of characters, the importance of the set, and the focus on the self-realization of the artist mark this play as a genuine advance for Fugard, a widening of his range. Although women and their concerns crop up obliquely in other Fugard plays—especially in *People Are Living There* and *Boesman and Lena*—*The Road to Mecca* is Fugard's first attempt to fill space with two women talking, arguing, and nurtur-ing each other. It is also the first time Fugard has dra-matized the necessary isolation of the artist. Fugard's epigraph for *The Road to Mecca* is an Emily Dick-inson poem: "The soul selects her own society/ Then shuts the door./ On her divine majority/ Obtrude no more." An extended metaphor for the artist's vision—its genesis and its consequences—*The Road to Mecca* may also be read as a parable about pain, the pain of loving and not being loved. Apartheid is only

the subtext of the play, but Fugard's initial title was "My English Name Is Patience." These are the words of the young, barefoot Afrikaner woman whom Elsa befriends en route to Helen's house. This absent char-acter pervades *The Road to Mecca* from beginning to end—like so many of Fugard's striking offstage presences, whose silences become virtually audible. What all of these silent characters share is a need for love.

Near the end of *The Road to Mecca*, candles flicker in mirrors and cast light on the walls—a stun-ning witness to Fugard's belief that the "candle burns brighter because the night is dark" and an answer to his question, "Would the making of meaning be so moving without the eternal threat of chaos and noth-ingness?" Miss Helen's laboriously crafted garden of statues—all manner of animals, camels, wise men, mermaids, and earth goddesses pointing East—did exist, at the home of the real Helen, Helen Niemand, in New Bethesda, South Africa. Created over a re-markable twenty years of Helen's life, from age fifty to seventy, by a small, slight woman using broken bits of glass and hand-mixed cement, the statues are mute witnesses to her courage, integrity, and imagi-nation. Thought mad by her myopic neighbors, she persevered alone. In her life and work, Fugard found the perfect fusion of symbol and referent, fiction and fact. All artists try to give meaning to matter, form to the formless, but only rarely does an artist give mean-ing to beauty, truth, love, and trust in so magical a form as *The Road to Mecca*.

PLAYLAND

The first play Fugard wrote after the fall of apart-heid takes place one month before the fall. Ironi-cally titled, *Playland* concerns a dramatic encounter between a black night watchman (Martinus) and a white South African (Gideon) at an itinerant carni-val on New Years Eve, 1989. Gideon's drunken brag-ging about killing blacks in a border war motivates Martinus's confession to killing a white man who was trying to rape a servant, Martinus's fiancé.

The difficulty of forgiveness is a major theme in *Playland*. Lurking beneath their stunning confessions are two angry, guilt-ridden characters both on the verge of violence and in search of expiation for their sins. In fact, Gideon's fear and self-loathing almost provoke Martinus into retributive violence against him, culminating in Gideon's exhortation, "Forgive me or kill me." Also Martinus's search to exorcise his own guilt is magnified because he would have to forgive the rapist that he killed as well as himself. The play-land itself is an ironic symbol not of "play" but of escape from reality and denial of truth. Also the non-working carnival ride, flickering lights, and Gideon's broken car are all emblems of national disrepair. Like South Africa's Truth and Reconciliation Commission to follow, Gideon and Martinus are microcosmic representations of two factions of a country that must listen to each other, rage, forgive, and choose to work together for the good of all, a reflection of Fugard's optimism about his new country's future.

MY LIFE

My Life, Fugard's next work, is more a performance piece than a scripted play. Fugard chose diary entries from five different South African young women and wove the threads into performance art. His intent was to share the varied and similar hopes, dreams, and perceptions of the younger generation. *My Life* celebrates racial diversity, uniformity of visions, and South Africa's future.

VALLEY SONG

Another play that blurs color lines is *Valley Song*. Here the main character is the Author, who speaks directly to the audience; even more unusual is that Fugard stipulates in the printed script that the same actor who plays the Author also play the role of a black farmer, Abraam Jonkers. This positive, forward-thinking play celebrates the limitless possibilities for South Africa's youth. For *Valley Song*, Fugard returns to the setting of *The Road to Mecca*, the fertile valley of the Karoo, which is ripe for the rebirth of a country and its peoples. In *Valley Song*, the classic generation gap is typified by seventeen-year-old Veronica's dreams of leaving the rural area for the big city while her seventy-year-old *oupa* (grandfather) is afraid of youthful rebellion and wants Veronica to continue to stay with him. The image of pumpkin seeds permeates the play—the celebration of nurtured growth. The play ends happily on a note of salvation, survival, and harmony.

THE CAPTAIN'S TIGER

In *The Captain's Tiger*, the young writer protagonist is running from a miserable childhood, trying to find his authorial voice while heading from Africa to Japan on a tramp steamer in 1952. The young author deals with his conflicted feelings for his mother by striving, in vain, to rewrite his mother's painful life into the happier life she should have had. *The Captain's Tiger* revealed a new post-apartheid Fugard who clearly feels free to explore more personal issues.

SORROWS AND REJOICINGS

The Off-Broadway production of Fugard's *Sorrows and Rejoicings* opened in February, 2002. When the play begins, South African writer Dawid Olivier is already dead. In flashback we discover that Dawid had chosen the creative suicide of political exile to England when threatened with jail for his activist views. Present at the funeral are Dawid's white British wife and angry eighteen-year-old daughter, his black former lover, and his own spirit. Fugard has said of this aptly titled play, "It is both a sorrowing for the pain of my country and the rejoicings of what it is becoming."

OTHER MAJOR WORKS

LONG FICTION: *Tsotsi*, 1979.

SCREENPLAYS: *The Occupation*, 1964; *Boesman and Lena*, 1973; *The Guest*, 1977; *Marigolds in August*, 1982.

TELEPLAY: *Mille Miglia*, 1968.

NONFICTION: "The Gift of Freedom," in *At the Royal Court: Twenty-five Years of the English Stage Company*, 1981 (Richard Findlater, editor); *Notebooks, 1960-1977*, 1983; *Cousins: A Memoir*, 1994.

BIBLIOGRAPHY

Benson, Mary. *Athol Fugard and Barney Simon: Bare Stage, a Few Props, Great Theatre*. Randburg, South Africa: Ravan Press, 1997. Benson relates her friendship with South Africa's two major playwrights and extraordinary insights into their lives and works

_____. "Keeping an Appointment with the Future: The Theatre of Athol Fugard." *Theatre Quarterly*

7, no. 28 (1977): 77-86. A personal biography regarding Fugard's wife and daughter, his early career struggles, and his aesthetic debts to Jerzy Grotowski, Albert Camus, and others. Benson's interview is followed by some comments on acting by and about Fugard. The entire issue is devoted to South African theater.

Fugard, Athol. "Athol Fugard's South Africa: The Playwright Reveals Himself to a Fellow Writer." Interview by André Brink. *World Press Review* 37 (July, 1990): 36-39. Excerpted from the Cape Town periodical *Leadership*, Brink discusses Fugard's "commitment to the search for meaning" in a warm interview following the opening of *My Children! My Africa!* Fugard states that he regrets the time he must spend away from Africa, where his energies belong.

Gray, Stephen. *Southern African Literature: An Introduction.* New York: Barnes and Noble Books, 1979. A strong discussion of *Boesman and Lena,* "seen by more South African audiences than any other South African play," in its stage or film versions. Gray interprets the play as a "rewording of the myth" of Hottentot Eve: "The play is ultimately more about the strains of the marriage bond between her and her husband than the colour problem which aggravates it."

Vandenbroucke, Russell. *Truths the Hand Can Touch: The Theatre of Athol Fugard.* New York: Theatre Communications Group, 1985. A full study of the playwright's life, work, and philosophies. Contains introductory material on South Africa and a concluding chapter on influences, crosscurrents, language, style, and critical reputation. Appendices offer the full text of *The Drummer,* an essay on *Dimetos,* and a production chronology. Bibliography and index.

Walder, Dennis. *Athol Fugard.* New York: Grove Press, 1985. A general survey and appreciation of Fugard's work up to *"MASTER HAROLD" . . . and the Boys.* Walder says, Fugard's plays speak "not only of the South African dimension of man's inhumanity to man, but also of the secret pain we all inflict upon each other in the private recesses of our closest relationships." Plates and index, but no chronology.

Wetheim, Albert. *The Dramatic Art of Athol Fugard: From South Africa to the World.* Bloomington: Indiana University Press, 2000. Wertheim explores Fugard's life and work in such great detail as to make this a vital resource.

Nancy Kearns,
updated by Thomas J. Taylor
and Howard A. Kerner

CHARLES FULLER

Born: Philadelphia, Pennsylvania; March 5, 1939

PRINCIPAL DRAMA
Sun Flowers, The Rise, pr. 1968 (one-acts)
The Village: A Party, pr. 1968, pr. 1969 (as *The Perfect Party*)
In My Many Names and Days, pr. 1972
The Candidate, pr. 1974
First Love, pr. 1974
In the Deepest Part of Sleep, pr. 1974
The Lay Out Letter, pr. 1975
The Brownsville Raid, pr. 1976

Sparrow in Flight, pr. 1978
Zooman and the Sign, pr. 1979, pb. 1982
A Soldier's Play, pr., pb. 1981
Sally, pr. 1988
Prince, pr. 1988
Eliot's Coming, pr. 1988 (pr. as part of the musical revue *Urban Blight*)
We, pr. 1989 (combined performance of *Sally* and *Prince;* parts 1 and 2 of five-part play series)
Jonquil, pr. 1990 (part 3 of *We* play series)
Burner's Frolic, pr. 1990 (part 4 of *We* play series)

OTHER LITERARY FORMS

Charles Fuller is known primarily for his plays. He adapted his screenplay *A Soldier's Story* (1984) from his drama *A Soldier's Play*.

ACHIEVEMENTS

Charles Fuller is one of a growing number of African American playwrights who have entered the mainstream of American drama. Previously, plays dealing with the black experience, such as Louis Peterson's *Take a Giant Step* (pr. 1954), Lorraine Hansberry's *A Raisin in the Sun* (pr., pb. 1959), and Ossie Davis's *Purlie Victorious* (pr. 1961), were rueful reproaches of white intolerance. Probably because of the period during which they were written (the late 1950's and early 1960's), they did not seek to stir up violent passions but rather to nudge the audience's sensibilities; as a result, they could enjoy a modest run in a commercial theater on Broadway. By the end of the 1960's, however, the Off-Broadway theater, which was always more daring (and less expensive), encouraged plays such as *Dutchman* (pr., pb. 1964) by Amiri Baraka (LeRoi Jones), *Ceremonies in Dark Old Men* (pr. 1965) by Lonne Elder III, and *No Place to Be Somebody* (pr. 1967) by Charles Gordone, the first black playwright to win a Pulitzer Prize, in 1970; these works paved the way for a more aggressive theater reflecting more militant times. As a result, when Fuller appeared on the scene, while he was able to dramatize the plight of African Americans for audiences that were more receptive than they had been in the past, he differed from his fellow playwrights in that he examined the effect of violence *among* black people as resulting from their environment.

Several of Fuller's plays deal with black-on-black murder and are constructed as mysteries; the hunt is on to discover not only the killer's identity but also the cause of the crime. His plays are less traditional in structure, freely moving back and forth in time. His characters often break the illusion of the fourth wall by actively engaging the audience in soliloquies, so that although his subject matter is realistic, his technique is expressionistic. In addition to his own screen adaptation of his drama *A Soldier's Play* (the film version is entitled *A Soldier's Story* and was a

Charles Fuller in 1977. (AP/Wide World Photos)

great success), he has contributed an adaptation of an Ernest J. Gaines story to public television and an original script to network television. He has also taught at Temple and Toronto universities. Fuller has been the recipient of two Obie Awards, of Rockefeller and National Endowment for the Arts grants in 1976, of a Guggenheim Fellowship in 1977, and in 1982 of a New York Drama Critics Circle Award, an Outer Critics Circle Award, and a Pulitzer Prize—the second awarded to an African American playwright.

BIOGRAPHY

Charles Henry Fuller, Jr., was born in Philadelphia, Pennsylvania, on March 5, 1939. In the course of time, his parents housed twenty foster children, eventually adopting two of them. The family lived in a Philadelphia housing project until Fuller's father, a printer, went into business for himself and became one of the first African Americans admitted to the local printer's union. Soon, the family moved to a racially mixed neighborhood in North Philadelphia, where the Fullers, devout Roman Catholics, sent their children to integrated parochial schools.

As a young boy, Fuller became interested in books through helping his father correct galley proofs;

when he was thirteen and had gone to the theater for the first time in his life to see Molly Picon performing in Yiddish (a language he did not even understand), he was so exhilarated that he was convinced he wanted to do nothing but write plays. In high school, he formed a lifelong friendship with Larry Neal, to whom he later dedicated *A Soldier's Play* and after whom he modeled its leading character, Captain Richard Davenport. Because Neal also was devoted to literature, eventually becoming a published poet and critic, the two young men buoyed up each other's ambitions. After graduation from high school in 1956, Fuller, an English major, attended Villanova University, where he was discouraged from writing because of his race. He left in 1959 to enlist in the army in Japan and South Korea, an experience he prefers not to discuss although it must have served as material for his plays. Returning to civilian life in 1962, he registered at La Salle College, studying at night while supporting himself by working as a bank loan collector in a loan company, as a student counselor at Temple University, and later as a housing inspector for the city. During this time, he kept alive his love for drama by helping to found and run the Afro-American Art Theater in Philadelphia, creating a kind of street theater for ghetto inhabitants. After his first play was produced at Princeton's McCarter Theater in 1968, Fuller left La Salle College without graduating and devoted himself full-time to his literary career. His plans included work on a musical and a cycle of plays concerning the African American experience from 1866 to 1900. Drawing from that experience, he created a series of five plays set during the American Civil War and post-bellum America, produced by the Negro Ensemble Company between 1988 and 1990.

Analysis

While the plays of Charles Fuller, like those of other African American dramatists, explore the tensions in a society in which the African American minority is constantly exploited and repressed by the white majority, Fuller has set his sights on changing the way Western civilization perceives black people. At the same time, he attempts to avoid stereotyping whites, insisting that groups are formed of individuals, and all are different, some good, some bad. As a consequence, his characters have greater depth and complexity, and he avoids the clichéd situations that afflict so many problem plays. He is also deeply interested in telling a story, which is the point at which he usually begins his plays. First, what happened; then, to whom; and finally, why? Even after these questions appear to be answered, the results often raise greater issues that lead to even more perplexing questions. Ambiguity, not resolution, is at the heart of Fuller's work.

Fuller's major concern is not only the violence in today's universe and the way it erodes character but also the violence that black people employ against one another. Although they occupy a world originally shaped by whites who enslaved and abused them, African Americans continue to prey on one another while accepting the role of victim at the hands of their oppressors. The cycle is always the same: sullen passivity that erupts into armed rebellion, followed by chaos, before subjugation and a relapse into bitter acceptance. All of his plays possess this cycle, regardless of the difference in subject matter; artistically, they are a poignant echo of real life, of the race riots that have burned American cities since the 1960's. Yet, though Fuller's canvas is large, his use of the personalized grief of his characters gives the plays a human scale; he is never didactic.

Early Plays

In his first full-length play, *The Village: A Party*, he builds the story around a community composed of five interracial couples. When the black leader falls in love with a black woman, against all the rules of their society, disaster occurs. What is original here is the way Fuller turns accepted convention upside down: In real life, obstacles to marriage confront people of different races. If the play, however, is taken as a metaphor for the barriers encountered by slaves who were forbidden to marry, it becomes clear that Fuller is condemning any law that arbitrarily decides what is right or wrong without considering its effect on human beings. Another early work, *In My Many Names and Days*, consists of six one-act plays about a black family, a structure he would adopt again when planning his five-play cycle of full-length dramas. *The Candidate* represents his study of a black man's campaign to become mayor of his city and the struggles this entails, revealing Fuller's growing attraction to political themes.

THE BROWNSVILLE RAID

Fuller, who was becoming increasingly engrossed by the Civil War (he dates the African American relation to the United States from the Emancipation Proclamation), blended politics with history in his greatest success to date, *The Brownsville Raid*. While working in New York with the Negro Ensemble Company, which had previously staged his first play for the group (*In the Deepest Part of Sleep*), Fuller showed the direction that his future plays would take. Using a historical event as its basis, *The Brownsville Raid* dramatizes the story of a company of black soldiers who, in 1906, were wrongfully accused of causing a riot in Texas and shooting a man. In the play, Fuller also explores the relationship between President Theodore Roosevelt and Booker T. Washington, who asks his black editors to play down the "incident" to preserve the peace. The soldiers are dishonorably discharged, and only sixty years later are they vindicated when the truth is discovered. For all of them, however, it is too late.

ZOOMAN AND THE SIGN

Although Fuller returned to a smaller-scale play with *Zooman and the Sign*, he again used the device of a murder investigation, which had already appeared in *The Brownsville Raid*, to propel the story. In addition, he began experimenting with the title character's soliloquies, which alternated with the general action, giving the play an abrupt, stop-start rhythm. The situation in *Zooman and the Sign* is one all too recognizable today: A twelve-year-old girl is accidentally killed in a fight between two street gangs, and the play charts the efforts of her anguished parents to discover the killer. Equally harrowing is the underlying theme: The father, in despair that none of his neighbors will come forward to identify the killer (because they are afraid that as witnesses they will have to deal with the police, though they themselves are innocent), puts up a sign outside his house

proclaiming that his daughter's killers are free because of the community's indifference. The neighbors, in turn, are so incensed by the accusation that they threaten his life and attempt to tear down the sign. Their rage, in short, is turned against one of their own people; they have lost their sense of responsibility to one another because it has been destroyed by the very institution that should be protecting them: the law. Here, Fuller has touched on a universal theme, for in just such a way were Nazi concentration-camp monitors, though prisoners themselves, wont to ally themselves against their fellow captives because of their own brutalization. Meanwhile, the killer, Zooman, has proclaimed himself to the audience and in his soliloquies explains his way of life, noting that if a black man kills a black man and is not caught immediately, the authorities forget about it. In an ironic twist, the dead girl's uncle, unaware of the murderer's identity, accidentally shoots him, just as the niece was accidentally killed. When the parents look at the dead face of the "perpetrator," it is that of a teenage boy who, in his mind, has made virility synonymous with violence.

A SOLDIER'S PLAY

In his finest and most successful work, *A Soldier's Play*, which Fuller says was inspired by Herman Melville's *Billy Budd, Foretopman* (1924), he combines and perfects the themes and technique of his two previous dramas. Calling on audience imagination, he sets his story in a space almost Elizabethan in its use: minimal scenery, few props, and areas that could be transformed from outdoors to indoors or from an office to a soldier's bunk. In addition, as one character is narrating an event in the present moment, by crossing from one side of the stage to the other, he moves into time past.

The play is a mixture of fact and fiction. It depicts an actual unit of black soldiers in the 1940's, stationed in a small southern town while awaiting transfer to Europe. One of the ironies of the situation is the fact that while they are fighting for freedom abroad, they are still segregated at home. The play opens with true Elizabethan violence: A black sergeant is murdered by someone unseen, and he cries out in his death agony, "They still hate you," the sense of which is obscure until the pieces fall into place. The murder worries the white officer in charge of the group because of the suspicion that it was committed by the Ku Klux Klan, resentful that black soldiers had been quartered in the Klan's vicinity. A black officer, Captain Richard Davenport, who is also a lawyer, is sent to investigate; his presence disconcerts the white officers, one of whom confesses that he cannot accustom himself to the sight of an African American in charge. The black soldiers, who are pathetically proud of Davenport's status, are nevertheless unresponsive to his questions because, like the uncooperative neighbors of *Zooman and the Sign*, they are fearful that anything they reveal will cause trouble for them with the white authorities.

What finally emerges is the portrait of the murdered: He is the sadistic Sergeant Waters who, ashamed of being black, drove his men unmercifully, particularly one private, C. J. Memphis. Waters was infuriated by the good-natured, slow-moving, guitar-strumming C. J., who, he believed, prevented ambitious African Americans from moving ahead because he seemed to represent the traditional "nigguh" as seen by whites. Waters harassed C. J., first accusing him of a shooting in town, of which he was innocent, and then provoking him into a fight so that he could be arrested for attacking his superior. Unable to endure being imprisoned like a caged bird, C. J. killed himself; in revenge for what Waters has done, Private Peterson, the most intelligent and, therefore, the most rebellious man in the unit, shot Waters and fled, accompanied by his friend, Private Wilkie, who had witnessed the murder.

When the two are caught, Davenport asks why Wilkie stood by and did nothing while one African American murdered another; all Wilkie can stammer is that he was afraid. Before his death, Waters had gone on a drunken binge to erase the memory of what had happened to C. J.; encountering two white officers, Waters had found in alcohol the courage to speak disrespectfully to them. They, in turn, had beaten him brutally and left him on the road at the moment when Peterson found him, began an argument with him, and finally shot him. In Peterson's eyes, Waters is the real villain, not because he drove

C. J. to suicide but because he was so full of hatred for his own blackness. The scene dissolves to the beginning, and suddenly, it becomes clear what Waters meant as he was dying: There is no use in struggling because no matter what black people do, white people will always hate them. At that moment, Waters becomes not a villain but the product of a society that has used him, first to destroy his fellow African Americans and then to turn his rage on himself. At the end, the unit is transferred to Europe, where, Davenport tells the audience, it was wiped out by a German advance. Grudgingly, the white captain admits that he will have to get used to the idea of African Americans in positions of authority.

Some black critics believe that Fuller softened the conclusion to make the play palatable to white audiences: The truth triumphs, the innocents are exonerated, the white captain apologizes, and the black captain has proved himself worthy of his assignment. This play, however, has no happier ending than a Shakespearean tragedy. There are resolutions, but they leave a bitter taste because there are no real winners, only an overwhelming sense of wasted lives.

WE

Once more, Fuller moved back to American history. After watching the classic film *One Third of a Nation* (1939), with its infamous depiction of black-white relationships, Fuller decided to counter with his own perspective and planned his five-part opus, *We*.

Directed by Douglas Turner Ward of the Negro Ensemble Company in 1989, *Sally* and *Prince*, the first two plays in Fuller's projected cycle, provide a panoramic view of the American Civil War and its aftermath from an African American perspective. The mood of both plays is that of trust betrayed. *Sally*, set in South Carolina in the middle of the war, has a title character who is a recently freed slave and widow with a teenage son; she wishes for her son's safety, some land, and a man of her own. In one of several episodes dealing with freed slaves at loose ends or serving as Union soldiers, the black soldiers, resentful at being paid less than their white counterparts, bring about a strike and a betrayal. A black sergeant named Prince, who gains Sally's attention but has no wish to settle down, has the same kinds of ambitions and dreams common to white men. Forced to be an intermediary between the strikers and the sympathetic but firm-minded white general in charge, he is persuaded by the latter—who sees the strike as a rebellion against his authority—to identify the ringleaders, who are then shot. Prince faces a moral dilemma; he must choose whether to betray his fellow black soldiers or the army system of which he approves and in which he flourishes.

Recalling some of the same characters and more focused than the first play, *Prince* deals with the protagonist, a Union prison guard in Virginia, who fatally shoots a ruthlessly taunting Southern captive and runs off. Other characters include former slaves on a farm, who have long waited to be paid for picking cotton for the North. One worker named Burner (the title character of *Burner's Frolic*, the fourth play in the cycle) objects to the delay and is imprisoned by the well-meaning but benighted Northerner running the plantation. Burner's lover is a tough black businesswoman who makes a living selling sweetcakes and wants to have her own store. When Prince, ready to pursue his dream of heading west, refuses her request to free Burner, she stabs him, but he survives and continues on his way.

The third play in the cycle, *Jonquil*, reveals Sally with other freed women slaves being abused and raped by Klu Klux Klan members. Sally's rapist, she discovers from the blind Jonquil who recognizes him from his voice, is a judge known for his benevolence toward slaves and malignance toward those freed. Sally persuades her reluctant husband to form a black militia to fight against thuggish whites, but the results have sad consequences.

The plays received mixed but not largely positive reviews, owing to problems of focus and structure. In Fuller's plays, the focus is on the injury that blacks do to blacks, which always results ultimately from the racist infrastructure in which they find themselves. Fuller does not focus on problems between blacks and whites but rather the experiences of blacks among themselves. "I wanted," he said, "to put blacks and whites on stage as people. I didn't want to do the usual black and white confrontation piece."

OTHER MAJOR WORKS

SCREENPLAYS: *A Soldier's Story*, 1984 (adaptation of his play); *Zooman*, 1995 (adaptation of his play).

TELEPLAYS: *Roots, Resistance, and Renaissance*, 1967 (series); *Mitchell*, 1968; *Black America*, 1970-1971 (series); *The Sky Is Gray*, 1980 (from the story by Ernest J. Gaines); *A Gathering of Old Men*, 1987 (adaptation of the novel by Ernest J. Gaines); *Love Songs*, 1999.

BIBLIOGRAPHY

Banham, Martin, ed. *The Cambridge Guide to World Theatre*. New York: Cambridge University Press, 1988. Errol Hill, a black writer and educator, contributes an article on African American theater, its history and development, which are important factors in the career of Fuller. Hill also discusses the playwright's two best-known plays in terms of their favorable reception by white critics and the more reserved attitude of black critics.

Boardman, Gerald. *The Oxford Companion to American Theatre*. New York: Oxford University Press, 1984. Contains a long and useful discussion of black playwrights in American theater, giving invaluable insights into the struggle of African American artists, particularly playwrights, to find a place for themselves. How Fuller emerged from such a background is amply documented.

Draper, James P., ed. *Black Literature Criticism*, Vol. 4. Detroit, Mich.: Gale, 1992. Contains an informative article on Fuller with a biographical/critical introduction including an interview, chronology, and five excerpted critical reports in chronological order by Harold Clurman, Amiri Baraka, Richard Gilman, William Demastes, and Richard Hornby. Baraka clearly states his reserved attitude toward Fuller's depiction of black characters, as white critics present more positive reactions.

Fuller, Charles. "Pushing Beyond the Pulitzer." Interview by Frank White. *Ebony* 38 (March, 1983): 116. In this interview, Fuller appraises what the Pulitzer Prize has meant to him and discusses the kind of plays he wishes to write—broader in scope, freer in style. He offers some illuminating details about his association with the Negro Ensemble Company and his method of work with its director and playwright, Douglas Turner Ward.

_____. "When Southern Blacks Went North." Interview by Helen Dudar. *The New York Times*, December 18, 1988, p. C5. This interview was conducted with Fuller after the two plays in his cycle, *We*, opened at the Negro Ensemble Company's theater. Fuller explains his plan to dramatize the lives of men and women as they moved North to escape slavery in the South. Fuller's goal has been to give literary permanence to black history that has been handed down largely through oral tradition.

Harriot, Esther. "Charles Fuller: The Quest for Justice." In *American Voices: Five Contemporary Playwrights in Essays and Interviews*. Jefferson, N.C.: McFarland, 1988. Harriot's critical essay places Fuller as one of five Pulitzer Prize playwrights of the same generation who have provided an image of the United States as a violent and unstable society. The other writers are Sam Shepard, Lanford Wilson, David Mamet, and Marsha Norman. Fuller is identified as a writer consistently focusing attention on social issues; his major plays' leading characters are cogently discussed. Harriot's interview reveals Fuller's motivations, aspirations, working methods, and his attitude on racism.

Moritz, Charles, ed. *Current Biography, 1989*. New York: H. W. Wilson, 1989. The article on Fuller deals with his early career in the theater that he ran in Philadelphia. It also emphasizes his conviction that black-white relationships must be seen in all their complexity if they are ever to be understood.

Savran, David. *In Their Own Words: Contemporary American Playwrights*. New York: Theater Communications Group, 1988. Includes one of the best and most comprehensive articles on Fuller. It offers a brief critique of his major plays and then records an interview held between Fuller and Savran in the former's apartment on November 28, 1986. In this free-ranging discussion, Fuller touches on everything from his taste in literature (Franz Kafka, Jean-Paul Sartre) to his experiments in dramatic technique and his experience in adapting *A Soldier's Play* for the screen. Photograph.

Mildred C. Kuner,
updated by Christian H. Moe

G

JOHN GALSWORTHY

Born: Kingston Hill, England; August 14, 1867
Died: London, England; January 31, 1933

PRINCIPAL DRAMA

The Silver Box, pr. 1906, pb. 1909
Joy, pr. 1907, pb. 1909
Strife, pr., pb. 1909
Justice, pr., pb. 1910
The Little Dream, pr., pb. 1911
The Eldest Son, pr., pb. 1912
The Pigeon, pr., pb. 1912
The Fugitive, pr., pb. 1913
The Mob, pr., pb. 1915
A Bit o' Love, pr., pb. 1915
The Little Man, pr. 1915, pb. 1921
The Foundations, pr. 1917, pb. 1919
Defeat, pr. 1920, pb. 1921
The Skin Game, pr., pb. 1920
A Family Man, pr. 1921, pb. 1922
The First and the Last, pr., pb. 1921
Hall-marked, pb. 1921
Punch and Go, pb. 1921, pr. 1924
The Sun, pb. 1921, pr. 1922
Loyalties, pr., pb. 1922
Windows, pr., pb. 1922
The Forest, pr., pb. 1924
Old English, pr., pb. 1924
The Show, pr., pb. 1925
Escape, pr., pb. 1926
Exiled, pr., pb. 1929
The Roof, pr., pb. 1929

OTHER LITERARY FORMS

There are six multivolume editions of John Galsworthy's collected works; the most important and comprehensive is the thirty-volume Manaton edition (1922-1936). Galsworthy wrote prolifically, composing many novels, poems, stories, addresses, sketches, and essays.

ACHIEVEMENTS

Galsworthy's literary reputation rests soundly on his fiction, especially the novels and stories collected in *The Forsyte Saga* (1922). Adapted for television by the British Broadcasting Corporation, *The Forsyte Saga* appeared in Great Britain, Canada, the United States, and other countries during the late 1960's and early 1970's, reviving interest in his fiction.

Several of Galsworthy's plays gained critical and popular approval at the time of their first production or early revival in England, Europe, and the United States. They were translated into many languages, and their popularity in the 1920's contributed to the recognition that culminated with the Nobel Prize in 1932. Galsworthy wrote realistic, often almost documentary problem plays, which focused on social problems far more impartially than was usual in contemporary social melodrama. Social issues such as labor unrest, prison reform, and anti-Semitism, all of which Galsworthy addressed dramatically, continue to be of great concern, but Galsworthy's plays, however much they spurred reform in attitudes or legislation in their own day, are now out of date. Their topicality and their uneasy tension between didactic moralizing and melodramatic theatricality have ensured that there is little interest in reviving his plays.

BIOGRAPHY

John Galsworthy was born August 14, 1867, at Kingston Hill, Surrey, to John Galsworthy, a kind, charming, and prosperous London lawyer and company director whom his son idolized, and Blanche Bartleet, an unimaginative, fussy, and religious woman to whom Galsworthy was never close. The Gals-

John Galsworthy (© The Nobel Foundation)

worthys were a newly rich, upper-middle-class family; their wealth came from house and shop rentals and from speculations and investments in real estate that were begun by Galsworthy's grandfather, a merchant who came from Devon to settle in London.

Because of the family's wealth, Galsworthy enjoyed a childhood of privilege and luxury; his family could afford the kind of education his father had not had, so Galsworthy was privately tutored before being sent at age nine to a preparatory school at Bournemouth. He went on to Harrow, where he distinguished himself as an athlete, and then entered New College, Oxford, where he seemed more interested in behaving like a gentleman of leisure, dressing well, and gambling on the horses than in studying. He was graduated in 1889 with a second-class degree in jurisprudence and continued to study law

until 1894 at Lincoln's Inn in London; apparently, he wanted to please his father by following in his footsteps. He found the study and work boring and completed only one law case; he preferred hunting, shooting, and the company of a young singing teacher. His father disapproved of the infatuation and sent Galsworthy on several trips abroad to cure him of it. Sailing home from the South Pacific islands and Australia in 1893, Galsworthy met Joseph Conrad, then second mate on the *Torrens*; Conrad afterward became Galsworthy's lifelong friend. Galsworthy had undertaken the trip partly in the hope of meeting Robert Louis Stevenson, whose fiction he admired, but he showed no serious interest in becoming a writer himself for two more years.

In 1895, Galsworthy's acquaintance with his cousin Arthur's wife, Ada Nemesis Pearson Cooper Galsworthy, turned into an adulterous affair. Ada, the illegitimate daughter of Anna Pearson of Norwich, had been adopted by a Norwich physician, Emanuel Cooper, who provided for her and her brother in his will. Ada married unwisely; her escape from the unhappy marriage to Arthur had a profound emotional effect on her and on John Galsworthy, who transformed the episode into fiction several times, most notably into the marriage of Soames and Irene Forsyte in *The Man of Property* (1906). With Ada's advice and encouragement, and with support from a private income provided by his father, Galsworthy abandoned his abortive career at law and began writing fiction; his first stories appeared pseudonymously in 1897. Between 1895 and 1905, Galsworthy and Ada continued their affair, living separately in London but traveling together on vacations abroad. Galsworthy published three novels and two books of stories before his marriage to Ada in 1905 and made friends with a group of writers that included Conrad, Ford Madox Ford, Constance Garnett, and Edward Garnett, all of whom provided encouraging criticism of his work.

In 1906, Galsworthy scored a double success, publishing *The Man of Property* (the first and best novel of the Forsyte series) and producing *The Silver Box*, his first play. Staged at the Royal Court Theatre by the Barker-Vedrenne management, the play attracted favorable attention for its unsparing portrayal of one law for the rich and another for the poor. Its concern for issues of social importance set the tone for Galsworthy's best plays, *Strife*, *Justice*, *Loyalties*, and *Escape*. Galsworthy was soon spoken of, together with George Bernard Shaw, Sir James Barrie, and Harley Granville-Barker, as part of a new renaissance in English drama.

Galsworthy's new literary prominence coincided with the social respectability he enjoyed by being married, and he soon felt able to speak out and to write pamphlets, letters, and essays on a number of subjects, such as humane slaughtering of animals, prison reform, and censorship in the theater. He told Ada that after coming down from Oxford to London and being sent to collect rents on some of his family's properties in poor neighborhoods, his social conscience had been awakened, and throughout the remainder of his life, he showed sympathy and concern for those less fortunate than he. He not only wrote on their behalf but also provided charitable assistance in the manner of his character Wellwyn in *The Pigeon*. Not a religious man, Galsworthy was disgusted with people who claimed to be Christians yet would not act charitably toward those in need. His novel *The Island Pharisees* (1904) portrays the rebellion of a young gentleman against upper-class social and religious hypocrisy. Particularly during his ten-year affair with Ada, during which he was ostracized from polite society, he seems to have felt strongly a sense of identity with social outsiders such as prisoners (he visited Dartmoor Prison to study conditions of servitude) and the poor.

After their marriage, the Galsworthys lived comfortably and pleasantly in London and in the countryside. Ada, plagued by illnesses during the English winters, liked to travel to warmer countries, and the Galsworthys made frequent and extensive trips abroad. Galsworthy seemed to be able to write copiously wherever they traveled. Yet success and comfort had their penalties: Though his books usually sold quite well, the quality of Galsworthy's writing did not improve significantly, and the onset of World War I severely shook his optimistic belief in the possibility of humanity's progress toward a better world.

After the war, Galsworthy's reputation grew with the publication of *The Forsyte Saga* and with the popular success of three plays, *The Skin Game*, *Loyalties*, and *Escape*. Galsworthy refused a knighthood but accepted many honorary degrees, the Order of Merit (1929), and the 1932 Nobel Prize in Literature. He was an active member of PEN, the international writers' association, from 1921 until his death, probably caused by a brain tumor, on January 31, 1933.

ANALYSIS

Both John Galsworthy's strengths and weaknesses as a dramatist derive from his commitment to the ideas and methods of realistic drama. He was neither a religious man nor a political activist, and his plays spoke for no specific ideology or orthodoxy, but he believed that "every grouping of life and character has its inherent moral; and the business of the dramatist is so to pose the group as to bring that moral poignantly to the light of day." This meant, as he said in "Some Platitudes Concerning Drama," that "a drama must be shaped so as to have a spire of meaning."

Such a theory of drama attempts two mutually contradictory tasks: first, the objective, balanced, impartial depiction of reality, and second, the embodiment of the playwright's subjective, ethical, emotional response in the posing or shaping of a moral spire of meaning. Galsworthy's plays are secular morality plays. His gentlemanly didacticism issues in dramatic sermons that attempt to evoke sympathy and understanding for the human condition and that teach the humanistic creeds of civility, compromise, and fair play. In Galsworthy's plays, the sentimental or melodramatic pointing of a moral frequently undercuts the attempt to depict faithfully the problems of individual characters or social groups.

The realistic problem play was not a new form when Galsworthy took it up; its development in England can be traced back to the middle of the nineteenth century, when Tom Taylor and Thomas William Robertson attempted to leaven their melodramas with realistic settings and restrained social comment. (Robertson's *Caste*, produced in 1867 and notable for dramatizing a marriage across class lines, was Galsworthy's favorite play when he was at Oxford.) In the late nineteenth century, this English tradition drew strength from the influence of Henrik Ibsen's realistic social dramas, which were championed in England by William Archer and also by Shaw, who published *The Quintessence of Ibsenism* during this period (1891, 1913). Following Ibsen's example but lacking his genius, Henry A. Jones and Arthur Wing Pinero combined upper-middle-class marriage problems with the form of the well-made play; the result was a rejuvenation of English drama. Though he wrote comedy in the paradoxical mode pioneered by W. S. Gilbert and Oscar Wilde, Shaw's challenging and idiosyncratic variety of dramatic realism was also inspired by Ibsen. Shaw's plays and polemics helped to create an atmosphere of critical acceptance in England for the realistic theater of ideas and social problems. Shaw's *Candida: A Mystery* (pr. 1897) appeared in 1904 at the Royal Court Theatre as part of the Barker-Vedrenne management's effort to raise the level of English drama. When Galsworthy sent the manuscript of *The Silver Box* to Harley Granville-Barker, it arrived on a Saturday, was read by Barker and Shaw on Sunday, and was accepted for production at Shaw's urging on Monday.

Throughout Galsworthy's dramatic works, there is a tension between oppressive moralism and melodramatic theatricality. As critic Allardyce Nicoll has observed, "Galsworthian realism and Socialist Realism tend to suffer from the same pathetic complaint—deplorable and even tawdry sentimentalism." In plays such as *Strife, Loyalties*, and *Escape*, however, Galsworthy successfully combined realistic representation with dramatic presentation of theme. His plays remain historically interesting because they embody his perceptions of English social and ethical attitudes in the early twentieth century. As examples of realistic drama, his plays have merit as the works of a sincere and careful craftsperson who wrote in a tradition made great by the true artists who made it their own: Henrik Ibsen, August Strindberg, Anton Chekhov, and George Bernard Shaw.

THE SILVER BOX

In a letter, Galsworthy remarked that the "main idea" of *The Silver Box* was "that 'one law for the rich, another for the poor' is true, but not because society wills it so, rather, in spite of society's good intentions, through the mere mechanical wide-branching power of money." Galsworthy's play contrasts the unprincipled, propertied, and pragmatic upper-middle-class characters with their lower-class victims in the manipulation of the judicial system. The audience knows from the beginning who the culprits are in two related cases of petty thievery, but Galsworthy creates suspense through gradual revelation of their guilt to their families. The first thief is young Jack Barthwick, down from Oxford on vacation, who, while out drinking with a female companion, steals her purse containing seven pounds. The play opens as Jack returns to the Barthwick home with Jones, a drunken, unemployed groom. When Jack passes out, Jones steals the purse and a silver cigarette box. Jack's theft is revealed to his family but is concealed in court at Jones's trial until after Jones's sentencing, when he can only cry out in helpless frustration, thus giving the audience the "main idea" of the play: "It's 'is money got 'im off—*Justice!*"

The Barthwicks' cowardly hypocrisy is illustrated throughout the play, especially in one scene at the end of act 2. Jack's father, John Barthwick, a Liberal Member of Parliament, is so concerned that the scandal of a trial will damage his political and social reputation that he betrays his "Liberal" sympathy for the poor. One of the Jones children is heard sobbing outside the Barthwicks' window because the child cannot find Mrs. Jones, his mother and the Barthwicks' housekeeper (she has been wrongly accused, arrested, and imprisoned with her husband, even though he has admitted his guilt). The sound of the child's suffering moves Mrs. Barthwick to suggest that the case be dropped, but Mr. Barthwick says the matter is out of their hands and refuses to help. The curtain drops on a melodramatic tableau, as Mrs. Barthwick turns her back on the crying, Mr. Barthwick covers his ears, and a servant closes the window to shut out the noise of suffering.

Galsworthy also teaches his dramatic lesson through contrasts and parallels. To illustrate further the disparity between the lives of rich and poor, he sets one scene in the Joneses' lodgings during their meager meal of potatoes and onions and contrasts it with the following scene of the Barthwicks' elaborate dinner. In act 3, the trial for theft is preceded by a hearing to remand the children of an out-of-work father to court custody. The court-ordered breakup of a family arouses Barthwick's liberal sentiments, but Galsworthy shows that liberal zeal for social reform is quickly sacrificed to self-interest as Barthwick seeks to suppress all evidence of Jack's involvement in Jones's case.

In *The Silver Box*, Galsworthy attempts to portray realistically a serious issue of injustice without resorting to the heroics of melodrama. He imagines the characters as social types and describes their "keynotes" in a letter to Granville-Barker; the play has no hero, and if there is a villain, it is a social class rather than an individual. The drawback of this method was once its virtue, but the sense of recognition to be gained from its topical documentary realism has been lost, and one is left with a double overdose of obvious didacticism and melodramatic attempts to arouse pathos, as in the crying child scene.

STRIFE

The rise to real power of the English labor movement early in the twentieth century provided a subject suited to Galsworthy's realistic method: *Strife* comes closest, among his plays, to a work of lasting value. Through the careful dramatic opposition of ideas, characters, metaphors, and structural elements, the play presents the tragedy of two fanatically iron-willed leaders who battle against each other at great cost to themselves and their followers. The play takes place during six hours on a February afternoon and evening at the Trenartha Tin Plate Works on the English-Welsh border, where a strike has lasted for five months, crippling the company and bringing suffering, hunger, and a winter without heat to the laborers. The deadlock results from the conflict between the leaders of the opposing sides, David Roberts of the strikers and John Anthony of the company directors.

Galsworthy constructed the play so that its spire of meaning would arise from the dialectic of opposing concepts represented by Anthony and Roberts. In a letter to a director who wanted to revive the play

in 1931, Galsworthy insisted that "the play's real theme" was not the battle between capital and labor but rather "hubris, or violence; *Strife* is, indeed, a play on extremism or fanaticism." Both Anthony and Roberts refuse to compromise their principles by giving in to the other side; their rigidity of purpose shows a kind of heroic intellectual vainglory, producing bitterness, suffering, waste, and death. Galsworthy once more created "type" characters, but Anthony and Roberts are types as extremists, not as members of any social class—such men may be found in any class.

Galsworthy imposes structural balance on the action to achieve the resonant effect of contrast and parallelism of idea, character, and situation. The confrontations of labor and management in the first and third acts balance each other, as do the separate meetings of directors and strikers in the second and third acts, in which each side rejects its leader's plan for action and decides to accept instead the terms for compromise proposed by the union representative. Galsworthy handles his large cast of characters with an almost schematic balancing of psychological and social types. He also uses settings, properties, and dramatic language appropriate to the theme of *Strife*: In several scenes, he contrasts the excesses of cold and heat, hunger and plenty, luxury and deprivation. Metaphoric language carries the idea that if Anthony and Roberts are like gods in their power over men, they are also like devils in the way they use power to cause suffering for the sake of their principles. The play has its melodramatic moments, such as the fight among the workers at the end of the second act, but overall, it is much less encumbered by the sentimentality and overly theatrical scenes that spoil many of Galsworthy's plays.

Strife, in an understated and bitter conclusion, neither celebrates nor condemns the opposing sides in the struggle of labor versus capital; instead, it portrays the need for civility and compromise in human affairs. The plan proposed by the union representative at the beginning of the play finally is adopted; Anthony and Roberts have a moment of mutual recognition after their followers have rejected the inhumanity of blind, proud adherence to principle. The theme of hubris is, if anything, too carefully and obviously portrayed in Galsworthy's systematic balancing of scenes, characters, and metaphors, and in the working out of a metaphoric dialectic of opposed ideas. *Strife*, nevertheless, remains Galsworthy's best problem play and the best realization of his theory of drama.

LOYALTIES

Galsworthy wrote in his diary for 1921: "During the summer *Loyalties* was written. . . . This was the only play of mine of which I was able to say when I finished it: 'No manager will refuse this.'" The play's popular success proved Galsworthy to be correct; he had adapted his realistic techniques to his audience's preference for entertainment instead of sermons. As in *The Silver Box*, he used a crime plot but spent far more effort creating a suspenseful modern melodrama that, along with his peek into the lives of the postwar, aristocratic, horse-racing set, includes a critique of upper-class anti-Semitism, hypocrisy, and misplaced loyalty to its own members. For the first time since *The Silver Box*, Galsworthy employed neither a pattern of recurrent imagery nor a central emblematic property or setting to underline his theme. The ideas in the play emerge in short speeches closely related to the action; the closest Galsworthy comes to a debate in *Loyalties* is the exchange between Ferdinand De Levis, a young, rich, Jewish social outsider, and General Canynge, the patrician elder statesman of Establishment values and taste. De Levis has (rightly) accused Captain Ronald Dancy, "a soldier and a gentleman," of stealing one thousand pounds. Canynge regards De Levis as an arrogant, insolent bounder and makes no secret of his distaste for De Levis's disregard of "the *esprit de corps* that exists among gentlemen." Other significant words or phrases, such as "unwritten code," "duty," and "honour," occur infrequently and unobtrusively; in context, they are appropriate to the plot and are not overly obvious guideposts to Galsworthy's moral. Just as Galsworthy does not unduly underline the theme of intolerance, neither does he follow his usual practice of overtly pointing up the merit of charity and unselfishness. Instead, the action embodies his theme of uncharitable Christians versus charitable non-Christians in implicit and understated ways.

The play's three acts emphasize three different kinds of loyalties in three appropriate settings. In the first act, at a country estate near Newmarket, De Levis's accusations against Dancy are attacked by Canynge and Charles Winsor out of personal loyalty, the code of the gentleman. In the second act, at a London club, social loyalty is the subject: Canynge and Winsor fear for the reputation of the club and the army; De Levis's loyalty to his race motivates him to refuse to sign an apology. In act 3, at the law office, loyalty to an institution, the profession of law, is emphasized. Finally, in the last scene, the Inspector embodies loyalty to a similar but more abstract institution, the Law itself.

ESCAPE

Galsworthy appropriately structures the plot to carry the dramatic presentation of these types of loyalty and their conflicts. The controlled balancing of plot, character, and language that made *Loyalties* not only a popular success but also Galsworthy's best postwar social drama served him well again in *Escape*, which also places less importance on ideas than on action. In a series of ten episodes organized almost cinematically, an escaped prisoner evades capture, meets a variety of characters from all social classes, and eventually, acting out of conscience, gives himself up, having come to terms with the gentleman's code that Barthwick and Dancy betray in *The Silver Box* and *Loyalties*, respectively.

OTHER MAJOR WORKS

LONG FICTION: *Jocelyn*, 1898 (as John Sinjohn); *Villa Rubein*, 1900 (as Sinjohn); *The Island Pharisees*, 1904; *The Man of Property*, 1906; *The Country House*, 1907; *Fraternity*, 1909; *The Patrician*, 1911; *The Dark Flower*, 1913; *The Freelands*, 1915; *Beyond*, 1917; *The Burning Spear*, 1919, 1923; *Saint's Progress*, 1919; *In Chancery*, 1920; *To Let*, 1921; *The Forsyte Saga*, 1922 (includes *The Man of Property*, "Indian Summer of a Forsyte," "Awakening," *In Chancery*, and *To Let*); *The White Monkey*, 1924; *The Silver Spoon*, 1926; *Swan Song*, 1928; *A Modern Comedy*, 1929 (includes *The White Monkey, The Sil-*

ver Spoon, *Two Forsyte Interludes*, and *Swan Song*); *Maid in Waiting*, 1931; *Flowering Wilderness*, 1932; *Over the River*, 1933; *End of the Chapter*, 1934 (includes *Maid in Waiting*, *Flowering Wilderness*, and *Over the River*).

SHORT FICTION: *From the Four Winds*, 1897 (as John Sinjohn); *A Man of Devon*, 1901 (as Sinjohn); *A Commentary*, 1908; *A Motley*, 1910; *The Inn of Tranquility*, 1912; *Five Tales*, 1918; *Tatterdemalion*, 1920; *Captures*, 1923; *Caravan: The Assembled Tales of John Galsworthy*, 1925; *Two Forsyte Interludes*, 1927; *On Forsyte 'Change*, 1930; *Soames and the Flag*, 1930; *Forsytes, Pendyces, and Others*, 1935.

POETRY: *The Collected Poems of John Galsworthy*, 1934 (Ada Galsworthy, editor).

NONFICTION: *A Sheaf*, 1916; *Another Sheaf*, 1919; *Castles in Spain*, 1927; *Candelabra: Selected Essays and Addresses*, 1932; *Letters from John Galsworthy, 1900-1932*, 1934 (Edward Garnett, editor).

MISCELLANEOUS: *The Little Man and Other Satires*, 1915; *The Works of John Galsworthy*, 1922-1936 (30 volumes).

BIBLIOGRAPHY

Fréchet, Alec. *John Galsworthy: A Reassessment*. Totowa, N.J.: Barnes and Noble Books, 1982. A biography of Galsworthy that provides information on his life and works. Bibliography and index.

Gindin, James Jack. *John Galsworthy's Life and Art: An Alien's Fortress*. Ann Arbor: University of Michigan Press, 1987. A biography of the life and literary works of Galsworthy. Bibliography and index.

McDonald, Jan. *The New Drama, 1900-1914: Harley Granville Barker, John Galsworthy, St. John Hankin, John Masefield*. New York: Grove, 1986. McDonald examines the drama of Galsworthy along with that of several other dramatists writing in the early twentieth century. Bibliography and index.

Radhamani Gopalakrishnan, M. *Galsworthy's Plays: A Thematic Study*. Madras, India: New Era, 1982. A study of the plays written by Galsworthy. Bibliography and index.

Rønning, Anne Holden. *Hidden and Visible Suffrage: Emancipation and the Edwardian Woman in Galsworthy, Wells, and Forster*. New York: Peter Lang, 1995. An analysis of the role of women in the works of Galsworthy, H. G. Wells, and E. M. Forster. Bibliography and index.

Sternlicht, Sanford V. *John Galsworthy*. Boston: Twayne, 1987. A basic biography of Galsworthy, covering his life and works. Bibliography and index.

Stevens, Earl E., and H. Ray Stevens, eds. *John Galsworthy*. De Kalb: Northern Illinois University Press, 1980. An annotated bibliography of writings, with contributions by Pierre Coustillas and others. A later, exhaustive bibliography of the author.

Philip E. Smith II,
updated by Mildred C. Kuner

GRISELDA GAMBARO

Born: Buenos Aires, Argentina; July 28, 1928

PRINCIPAL DRAMA

Las paredes, pr. 1964, pb. 1979 (English translation, 1992)

El desatino, pr., pb. 1965

Matrimonio, pr. 1965

Los siameses, pr., pb. 1967 (*The Siamese Twins*, 1967)

El campo, pb. 1967, pr. 1968 (*The Camp*, 1970)

Información para extranjeros, wr. 1971, pb. 1987 (*Information for Foreigners*, 1992)

Nada que ver, pr. 1972, pb. 1983

Solo un aspecto, pb. 1973, pr. 1974

Sucede lo que pasa, pr. 1976, pb. 1983

Decir sí, pb. 1978, pr. 1981

El despojamiento, pr., pb. 1981

La malasangre, pr. 1982, pb. 1984 (*Bad Blood*, 1994)

Real envido, pr. 1983, pb. 1984

Del sol naciente, pr., pb. 1984

Teatro, pb. 1984-1996 (6 volumes)

OTHER LITERARY FORMS

Although Griselda Gambaro is known primarily for her plays, she has also written short stories and novels that have received literary prizes. A number of her most successful plays have been derived from prose pieces, including *Las paredes* (the walls), *El desatino* (the blunder), and *The Camp*, which were first short stories, while *Nada que ver* is related to the novel *Nada que ver con otra historia* (1972; nothing to do with another story).

ACHIEVEMENTS

Of the many successful Argentine dramatists, Griselda Gambaro is consistently named among the top playwrights of her country and of Latin America in general. Despite working within a confined sociopolitical context, she has been successful in creating a theatrical experience that relates to the particular problems of her country yet is couched in a universal theatrical idiom. In 1963 Gambaro received the Prize of the Argentine Fondo Nacional de las Artes for *Madrigal en ciudad* (1963; madrigal in the city) while her play *Las paredes* won the Premio de la Asociacion de Teatros and the Fondo Nacional de las Artes in 1964. In 1965 she was awarded the Premio Emece for her short story collection *El desatino*. She won the Argentores Prize from the Society of Argentinian Authors first in 1968 for *The Camp* and in 1976 for *Sucede lo que pasa*. *The Camp* also earned her awards from the Municipality of Buenos Aires, *Talia* magazine, and "Theatrical Broadcast News" of Municipal Radio of Buenos Aires. In 1982 she was granted a Guggenheim Fellowship.

Because her view of the human condition transcends national boundaries and her plays are richly textured in terms of theme and technique, Gambaro's work has been the focus of an increasing number of articles and dissertations in the United States, Canada, and Europe. In general, her work may be characterized as having a contemporary sociopolitical message that is conveyed with intense visual images of compelling dramatic interest that work well onstage.

BIOGRAPHY

Griselda Gambaro was born in Buenos Aires, Argentina, and has spent her life there, aside from a year in Rome in 1970 and almost three years in Barcelona (1977-1980). She is the daughter of a postal worker, and because she came from a family with limited economic means, after she finished high school in 1943 she went to work in the business office of a publishing company. Through her writing and its successes, she has enjoyed greater financial security. She is married to the sculptor Juan Carlos Distefano and is the mother of two children, Andrea, born in 1961, and Lucas, born in 1965. Many of the critics who meet Gambaro in Argentina or during one of her trips abroad are struck by her gentle manner and gracious demeanor, which belie the brutality, vigor, and cruelty expressed in her texts. Although she once called herself "a cowardly person," any reader or spectator of her work soon realizes that the texts also disprove this evaluation, for the writer of these plays must be brave indeed to face the types of bleak and cruel situations that are portrayed. The expectation is implied, however, that the works will bring forth the kind of participation needed to correct the real problems of today's sociopolitical environment.

According to her recollections, she was always writing; that is, from the moment she learned to read she also began to write. She threw away many pieces of work until she was sufficiently satisfied to offer as her first effort worthy of publishing *Madrigal en ciudad*, a collection of three short novellas that won the Prize of the Argentine Fondo Nacional de las Artes for narrative in 1963. Soon after, she received the Premio Emece in 1965 for the collection *El desatino* (1965), also containing novellas and short stories. At the same time, two plays emerged from the prose pieces, *Las paredes* and *El desatino*, each winning theatrical prizes: for *Las paredes*, the Premio de la Asociacion de Teatros and the Fondo Nacional de las Artes in 1964, and for *El desatino*, the Prize of the Revista Teatro XX in 1965. One of the characteristics of her writing production that emerged from the beginning was her development of some of the prose pieces as dramatic works almost at the same time that she was writing the prose pieces. She continued this practice until 1972, the year in which she completed work on the novel *Nada que ver con otra historia* and the play *Nada que ver*. She no longer works in that almost parallel fashion in the two genres, finding that she now writes either a play or a piece of fiction independent of one or the other; the plays, however, have become more famous than her fiction and have been translated into several languages and staged around the world. In Argentina, she was closely associated with the experimental art group located at the Centro de Experimentacion audiovisual del Instituto Torcuato Di Tella, a foundation formed in 1958 to patronize the fine arts and foster sociological investigations. The Institute, which unfortunately closed in 1971, worked in part as a theatrical laboratory for young writers who were able to experiment with techniques and representation by adapting audiovisual phenomena to the stage. As part of its promotion of vanguardist and creative talents, the Institute published as well as produced a number of her plays. Jorge Petraglia, a noted Argentine director and actor, has also been associated with Gambaro's work in both of his talented capacities.

As a woman who writes in Latin America, Gambaro is often asked about her role as a woman writer, with questions ranging from the problematics of a feminine discourse to extraliterary problems concerning whether she has faced discrimination in her career because of gender. Her response is usually to present her own specific experiences rather than offer observations applicable to women in Latin America. Argentina, for example, has a long tradition of women writers, and there are many well-established women in literary circles. She sees any difficulties she may have in promoting her as related more to social class than to gender; all the successful women in Argentina have been from the upper class and appear to act with an inborn sense of security absent in a person from the lower classes. In regard to feminine discourse, she was asked to present a paper on the question, "¿Es posible y deseable una dramaturgia especificamente femenina?" (1980; is it possible or desirable to have a specifically feminine dramaturgy?), and her answer is that one writes naturally, without thinking of gender, and the result is the particular view of the writer, showing his or her particular characteristics. The women characters in her own work fit no particular pattern and seem to reflect the greater division Gambaro has perceived in human behavior: Some people are victims of the oppressive acts of others, but at any one moment, anyone can become a victim.

Gambaro has been invited to many international theater conferences. Her first visit to the United States in 1968 was as the guest of the International Exchange Program; she has returned to the United States frequently as an invited speaker at various conferences and university programs, such as the First International Drama Festival in San Francisco in 1972 and the symposium on Latin American theater at Florida International University in 1979. She has also made frequent trips to France, Italy, and Spain, countries in which her work is well known and well received critically.

ANALYSIS

Griselda Gambaro is one of the Argentine dramatists who has maintained steady theatrical activity since 1964, when her first produced play, *Las paredes*, also won theatrical prizes. Since then, her productions have consistently been well received in national and international theatrical circles. Critics often compare her plays with European currents, especially the Theater of the Absurd and the Theater of Cruelty, because of the obvious similarities in tone, techniques, and themes. In particular, it is possible to see the relationship between Antonin Artaud's theories for a Theater of Cruelty and Gambaro's skillful use of nonrhetorical language integrated with gestures and movements and her manipulation of the space of the stage to create a physical environment that first moves deeply the emotions of the audience before its intellect is engaged. In the manner Artaud envisioned for his theater, she makes good use of violent physical images as a potent means to express her own vision of the cruelty of existence.

In response to comments associating her work with international movements, Gambaro generally stresses the importance of the Argentine context in the formation of her dramatic vocabulary. While the plays of the 1960's, which formed the basis of her dramatic reputation, utilize a general Spanish-language expression, her later plays, from the 1970's onward, are written with the more specific Argentine language form of the *voseo* (the use of the familiar singular form of *vos* instead of the more generalized *tu* form), openly marking the language of the plays with a particularly national flavor. She prefers to see the effect of the Argentine dramatic tradition called the *grotescocriollo*, as well as the real absurdities of the Argentine political situation, as the true inspiration for her tone of black humor and her treatment of humankind's inhumanity, of that paradox in human nature—the capacity of ordinary human beings to participate in atrocities. Although she may deal with real facts and situations in the real world, all of Gambaro's plays may be considered tragicomedies based on variations of the grotesque rather than on realistic conventions.

In form, Gambaro's plays are generally structured with two parallel acts or one act with many fast-moving scenes. Despite anecdotal differences, a recurring pattern of action is found in most of the plays: An average person finds himself in a not unusual setting that soon becomes transformed into a threatening environment because of the inexplicable, menacing actions of adversaries who are often from his intimate circle of family and friends. The relationships among the characters are generally that of oppressor to oppressed; the authority figure may be an unsuspected type, as the mother of *El desatino*, who belies her traditional role as a positive nurturing figure, or an obvious dictatorial character, such as Franco in *The Camp*, or the neighborhood barber, as in *Decir sí*. The victim is generally an unassuming individual who does not rise to the challenge of the situation with heroism, but sinks into an abyss of passive cowardice.

It also should be noted that in Gambaro's plays dialogue functions differently from both the traditional presentation and the innovations of the Theater of the Absurd. Traditionally, dramatic action progressed by means of the dialogic exchanges, a rational sequencing that the absurdists parodied when their characters would speak alternatively without communicating an intellectually viable argument, as in Eugène Ionesco's *La Cantatrice chauve* (pr. 1950; *The Bald Soprano*, 1956). In Gambaro's plays, on the other hand, there is an attempt by the victim to communicate, but he is generally deliberately deceived by his tormentors. When the Youth of *Las paredes* remarks that the walls of his room seem to be growing smaller or that he hears pitiful screams from his invisible neighbors, these real observations are noticed, too, by the spectators; the Custodian ignores or denigrates the observations with the effect that the Youth soon distrusts his own senses and resignedly accedes to whatever the Custodian claims, no matter how "absurd," or out of harmony with the real world. This pattern is found in most of Gambaro's plays written in the 1960's and 1970's: The victim's observations are verified by the spectators, but the oppressor figures purposely question and discredit the veracity of the real observations in an attempt to undermine the individual's sense of integrity and well-being. The individual is gradually deprived of his ability to discern for himself between real events and the deceptive interpretations offered by the authorities. His attempts to communicate and to make sense of his universe are overwhelmed, and he is rendered passive, a victim prepared to accept whatever the authorities decide or demand. Gambaro presents this extreme picture of victimization in order to shock her spectators out of their own passivity.

EL DESATINO

In *El desatino*, the contrast between dialogue and actions is especially menacing because the unidentified Youth and the tormentors of *Las paredes* are replaced by a circle of family and friends. When Alfonso attempts to extricate himself from the iron object attached to his foot, his mother, Doña Viola, is too preoccupied with her own needs to pay attention to the problems of her son. She gives all of her attention to Luís, Alfonso's best friend, although Luís acts the opposite of the caring companion. Luís verbalizes the typical solicitations of a friend, but by his actions he actively threatens Alfonso with physical injury. "I'll warm you, I'll protect you," says Luís as he ties a scarf around Alfonso's neck, and in the process nearly strangles him. None of Alfonso's closest companions tries to help him, and only one character in the play appears to take his problem seriously. El muchacho (the boy), identified only as a road-construction worker, offers to do whatever possible to help Alfonso, but his aid is rejected because of his social class. His goodness and concern for others are contrasted with the selfishness of Alfonso's group and Alfonso's own cowardice. The play has been read as an allegory of the problems of the middle class in contemporary Argentina and Latin America, Alfonso representing the middle class, which is dominated by tradition and arrogantly scornful of the efforts of the well-meaning working class.

THE SIAMESE TWINS

The contrast between words and actions typical of Gambaro's dramatic images is graphically demonstrated in *The Siamese Twins*. The play develops as a series of encounters in which Lorenzo, the dominant member of the pair alluded to in the title, is driven by envy to cause the destruction of Ignacio. This relationship re-creates the Cain and Abel motif, yet the play never makes explicit that the two are blood brothers; their fraternal relationship seems to be a myth exploited by Lorenzo or, if true, a fact not willingly accepted by Ignacio. Lorenzo's attempt at domination is dramatically expressed in the scene in which he forces Ignacio to walk with him as if the two were real Siamese twins, attached physically. This theatrical gesture contradicts the verbal messages that indicate that the two are physically separate and psychologically different as well. Lorenzo is cunning, envious, and treacherous while Ignacio is ingenuous, compassionate, and good-natured. The docile character Ignacio is the victim of Lorenzo's various dirty tricks and destructive behavior. Lorenzo's need to rid himself of Ignacio is predicated on the erroneous belief that without Ignacio he will somehow be more whole, more independent. By the end of

the play, Lorenzo has finally succeeded in implicating Ignacio in some deed for which the police torture and kill him. In the final scene, Lorenzo realizes too late that his destruction of Ignacio has not left him whole but deficient, and has caused his own victimization.

The impact of the final scene is strengthened by its power to recall the final moments of Samuel Beckett's *En attendant Godot* (pb. 1952, pr. 1953; *Waiting for Godot*, 1954). Lorenzo is alone on an empty stage, ironically assuming the identity of Ignacio by re-creating the latter's fetal position as a dead man. Like Estragon's famous *allons*, which brings no action, Lorenzo, too, announces his imminent departure but goes nowhere. His inability to act contradicts his words and his very existence; the completion of his goal has brought his own destruction.

THE CAMP

Although Gambaro's use of visual images and stage space is not to be underestimated, neither should the importance of her explorations of language be ignored. Gambaro's choice of words is meant to point out the multiplicity of meanings inherent in any sign. Her titles are an obvious indication of this play with language, with *The Camp* offering a particularly rich demonstration of her technique. In Spanish, *el campo* refers to the countryside and carries connotations of peace and tranquillity, fresh air, open skies, and physical freedom from constraints. In the play with that title, Martin comes to the *campo* to work, yet the place soon becomes transformed from its traditional reference to assume the particular twentieth century meaning of a *campo de concentración*, a concentration camp. The central character, Martin, freely enters the camp on assignment as a bookkeeper. He is directed in his duties by Franco, who is dressed in a Gestapo uniform and armed with a whip. Franco's outfit, the prison garb of the character Emma, and the presence of guards and inmates all suggest that the camp is a prison. Yet Franco claims to see and hear children and farmers singing at work to support the illusion of the first, more harmless, meaning of camp. Franco treats Emma as a great lady and a renowned pianist despite her obvious prison attire. His true relationship to Emma is dramatized when he repeatedly strikes the ground with his whip and Emma gestures in agony as if she has been physically hit.

Martin never finds peace or freedom at the camp; the menacing treatment of the armed guards, the smell of charred flesh and screams of torture, and his own victimization become the reality of his environment. Like Emma, whose wounds and prison markings aroused his sympathy and stimulated him to become involved in her predicament, Martin ends up as another victim in the camp. The trajectory of his experiences, from innocent worker to prisoner, from positive to negative, was first suggested by the ambiguous meaning of the play's title.

NADA QUE VER

Nada que ver is another equivocal title that anticipates a play based on actions of irony and counterpoint. Literally it means "nothing to see," an irony in a play that is a spectacle meant to be seen. In addition, the phrase is part of a Spanish idiom that conveys the idea that something has nothing to do with another thing, as in *esto no tiene nada que ver con eso* (this has nothing to do with that). The title implies that the play has nothing to do with anything else, yet this implication is seen to be patently false once the action begins. Unlike the brief allusion to *Waiting for Godot* at the end of *The Siamese Twins*, *Nada que ver* clearly wishes to elaborate on its relationship with another well-known text, Mary Wollstonecraft Shelley's *Frankenstein* (1818). The two-act play offers some interesting new aspects not only to Shelley's story but also to the basic patterns of Gambaro's dramaturgy. Gambaro offers a parody of the earlier work in order to comment on sociopolitical events relevant to her own time. With ironic humor, in contrast to the serious tone and anguished characters of Shelley's work, Gambaro relates the story of Manolo, an Argentine version of Shelley's scientist-inventor Frankenstein, who speaks with the typical Argentine *voseo* and mannerisms. Manolo is a poor veterinary student who works within a cockroach-infested room that serves as home and laboratory. From whatever castoffs he could find, he creates his own monster, Toni, a Boris Karloff spin-off in appearance only. Toni acts like the cruel and threatening creature on which he is based; as he gains in expe-

riences and interacts with human beings, he slowly becomes more human in appearance and behavior. Whereas Shelley's monster kills Dr. Frankenstein's betrothed, Toni falls in love with Brigita María, Manolo's girlfriend. She overcomes her initial repugnance to his appearance and reciprocates his amorous feelings.

Although Toni learns to respect and cherish other human beings, he lives in a society that acts in a monstrous way, that is, indiscriminately attacking people and causing senseless deaths. Brigita María becomes the victim of one of these gratuitous acts, and her violent death is deeply mourned by both Manolo and Toni; creator and creature become equal through their shared grief. As a birthday present for Toni, Manolo fabricates another monster in the image of Brigita María, a tasteless simulacrum of the dead woman. Toni and Manolo both learn, however, that human beings are not easily replaceable, and the injustices are not easily corrected. Although Toni has witnessed actions that can be classified only as monstrous, the progression of his own behavior has proceeded from monsterdom to humanity; to carry the analogy to its logical conclusion, one sees by means of the play's actions that the true monsters are not made but are defined by their actions. In a subtle manner, the typical Argentine linguistic expressions employed in the play and the references to political acts of violence recall Argentine political history of the 1970's, during which time a military junta ruled the country almost as a monster gone wild, creating many victims by its inhumane treatment of dissenters. *Nada que ver* purposely offers no clear reference, however, to any specific political system; as the title indicates, it has nothing to do with specifics. In a typical ironic movement that has been a constant of her technique, Gambaro recalls Shelley's text in order to reinterpret the general nature of monsterdom in terms of twentieth century events. Her farces *Real envido* (royal bidding) and *Del sol naciente* (from the rising sun) can also be read as political allegories that offer critiques of totalitarian regimes.

INFORMATION FOR FOREIGNERS

Gambaro's *Information for Foreigners* is another political allegory that was written in the early 1970's but not published then because of its obvious political content. Unconventional in its dramatic structure, it is a multi-focused work composed of a collage of vignettes, episodes, and spectacles. The physical structuring of the stage space is also unconventional as it is envisioned by the stage directions: either a house of empty rooms with stairs and corridors or a theater where the seats have been removed and replaced by numerous enclosed spaces and narrow hallways. The spectators are expected to move about the alternately darkened and illuminated spaces, interspersed with actors, a situation that creates a dynamic space that corresponds to the dynamic events surrounding the spectators. No story is developed, and the sequence of events is variable; only the last scene takes place at a specified point in the performance, when both spectators and actors are brought together. A guide leads the audience through a series of violent spectacles characterized by black humor, abusive and vulgar language, nudity, and incongruous childish games. Some scenes portray kidnappings, murders, bombings, and the trials of political activists.

Because the spectators are positioned in the midst of the events enacted, they are forced to be more than passive witnesses to the scenes. The boundary between stage and life becomes blurred as the guides ask the spectators to comment on the acting they have just seen as well as on the reality of the events enacted. To the spectators, the guide does not seem to be an actor, but rather the link between the actors and the spectators; the guide functions as an authoritarian figure in his relationship to both actors and audience, telling them what to do, where to go, how to behave. The political implications of the content become evident, then, for the spectators cannot act on their own and their well-being is threatened since they cannot escape their proximity to people who are being tortured and persecuted. *Information for Foreigners* becomes more than an interesting theatrical experiment, as it forces the spectators to recognize their general passivity and requires them to question and respond more fully to the nature of events in their environment. In the earlier plays, only the actors were involved with trying to determine the nature of the reality presented to them by the authority figures, but in *Information for Foreigners* the spectator is made a part of the process as well. Because of its dramatic self-consciousness, the work can be seen as a metaplay, transforming the world into a stage, the stage into the world.

BAD BLOOD

The spatial and formal innovations of *Information for Foreigners* were not developed further in Gambaro's later plays. The play that has been her most successful and has caused the greatest impact on the Argentine public is *Bad Blood*. It is set in the 1840's, during the time of the dictator Juan Manuel de Rosas, whose cruelty and barbarous excesses were being repeated by the military dictatorship under which Gambaro presented the play. As is common in her dramatic technique, Gambaro creates a provocative visual text that relates to the Argentine present and to universal issues dealing with power and the abuses of authority.

For the first time she creates a historical drama that develops a naturalistic plot that is a love story. All the action takes place in one room of a castle ruled by a father who acts the stereotype of the patriarch—a domineering, cruel, and insensitive figure. The room is covered with deep, blood-red tapestries, and all the clothes worn by the characters are in shades of red, echoing the allusion to blood in the title and foreshadowing the bloody acts to follow. The father, never given a proper name, acts brutally toward his wife and daughter and brooks no opposing will to his own. He has apparently killed the daughter Dolores's last tutor because of supposed moral improprieties between the two, and he is about to hire a new tutor, Rafael, who is a hunchback. The father believes that Rafael's deformity will be an obstacle to any sexual contact between his daughter and the tutor. While the characters interact onstage, the noise of a wagon is heard outside; from the comments made, it becomes clear that the wagoneer is not selling melons, as is first suggested, but rather is transporting the severed heads of the father's victims. At the outset, Dolores appears insensitive to her father's cruelty, but through her experiences with Rafael, she is taught not only to treat others with respect but also to rebel against the authority of her evil father.

Rafael represents a new character in Gambaro's dramatic world, for he is not a passive person and he recognizes the dangers of the system in which authority is not challenged. That he becomes another of the victims of the father's wrath does not obviate the success he has in converting the daughter of the dictator to a new state of consciousness. After the death of Rafael, Dolores continues his challenge to authority by rebelling against her father. Just as Rafael, as one individual, was unable to overwhelm the power of the dictator, Dolores, too, is unable to topple him. Yet the dictator is shown to be powerless to destroy the courage and dignity of those individuals who are willing to stand up and cry out. The repression of the individual voices will not go on forever, suggests Gambaro, as more people speak up. Gambaro's characters have come a long way from the automaton-like figure of the Youth of *Las paredes*, who lost his dignity and power to act by his cowardly compliance with the authorities.

EVOLUTION OF FEMALE CHARACTERS

In the same way that Rafael stands out for his willingness to challenge the system, Dolores is a new type of character for Gambaro, appearing as a decisive and assertive rebel. Previously, Gambaro developed relatively few women on her stage, and those who appeared seemed to fit well the stereotypes of the patriarchal woman. Doña Viola of *El desatino*, for example, is typical of the domineering woman corrupted by the patriarchal society of Latin America, while Lily, Alfonso's wife, is merely a figment of his imagination and another stereotype of the sexy female. Emma of *The Camp* is also a victim of patriarchy. The woman monologuist of *El despojamiento* is the most pathetic female figure of Gambaro's theater, for in her outpouring of words she reveals that she has been physically abused and psychologically dominated by family, friends, and strangers, to the point that she readily submits to subjugation at the slightest provocation. She has no reserves of strength or dignity left, and by her own actions she divests herself of her clothes and her emotional protective covering. Brigita María of *Nada que ver*, in contrast, is active and politically engaged, but she, too, ends up a victim of a senseless society.

Dolores is never passive and leaves the stage fighting and shouting her defiance to authority. Perhaps the image of Dolores is a fitting image of Gambaro's entire production, for she has also challenged the imposition of silence of a dictatorial system and succeeded in creating lasting images of intense dramatic power.

OTHER MAJOR WORKS

LONG FICTION: *Una felicidad con menos pena*, 1967; *Nada que ver con otra historia*, 1972; *Ganarse la muerte*, 1976; *Dios no nos quiere contentos*, 1979; *Lo impenetrable*, 1984 (*The Impenetrable Madame X*, 1991); *Déspues del día de fiesta*, 1994; *El mar que nos trajo*, 2001.

SHORT FICTION: *Madrigal en ciudad*, 1963; *El desatino*, 1965; *Lo mejor que se tiene*, 1998.

NONFICTION: *Escritos inocentes*, 1999.

MISCELLANEOUS: *Conversaciónes con chicos*, 1966.

BIBLIOGRAPHY

Cypress, Sandra Messinger. "Physical Imagery in the Plays of Griselda Gambaro," *Modern Drama* 18, no. 4 (1975): 357-364. Explores the use of space and imagery of Gambaro's plays.

_____. "The Plays of Griselda Gambaro." In *Dramatists in Revolt: The New Latin American Theater*, edited by George W. Woodyard and Leon F. Lyday. Austin: University of Texas Press, 1976. Examines political trends in theater as a "new" development in the 1970's.

Foster, David William. "The Texture of Dramatic Action in the Plays of Griselda Gambaro." *Hispanic Journal* 1, no. 2 (1979): 57-66. An exploration of the dramatic techniques of Gambaro.

Holzapfel, Tamara. "Griselda Gambaro's Theatre of the Absurd." *Latin American Theatre Review* 4, no. 1 (1970): 5-12. Discusses the techniques and themes used by Gambaro and common to the Theater of the Absurd movement.

Jehenson, Myriam Yvonne. "Staging Cultural Violence: Griselda Gambaro and Argentina's 'Dirty War.'" *Mosaic: A Journal for the Interdisciplinary Study of Literature* 32, no. 1 (March, 1999): 85-104. Examines Gambaro's play *Information for*

Foreigners and its link between politics and art, drawing parallels to the mechanisms of Argentina's repressive regime in the 1970's.

Magnarelli, Sharon. "Acting/Seeing Women: Griselda Gambaro's *El despojamiento.*" In *Latin American Women's Writing: Feminist Readings in Theory and Crisis*, edited by Anny Brooksbank Jones and Catherine Davies. New York: Clarendon Press, 1996. Focuses on Gambaro's use of the theatrical element as a thematic thread in *El despojamiento*, itself an allegory for Argentina's military regime.

Mendez-Faith, Teresa. "Sobre el uso y abuso de poder en la producción dramatica de Griselda Gambaro." *Revista Iberoamericana* 51 (1985): 831-841. Explores Gambaro's depictions of the use and abuse of power in her plays.

Reinelt, Janice, ed. *Crucibles of Crisis: Performing Social Change.* Ann Arbor: University of Michigan Press, 1996. Essay by Diane Taylor uses *Information for Foreigners* to explore the intersection of theater and terror, examining especially the theater's ability to prevent or conceal violence.

Witte, Ann. *Guiding the Plot: Politics and Feminism in the Work of Women Playwrights from Spain and Argentina.* New York: Peter Lang, 1996. Focuses on the theater in Argentina and Spain between 1960 to 1990, a period of important sociopolitical change in both countries. Examines the way in which playwrights can provide an oppositional stance to those in power and work within the confines of an oppressive environment.

Sandra Messinger Cypess

GAO MING
Gao Zecheng

Born: Rui-an, Wenzhou, China; c. 1303
Died: Ning-hai, China; c. 1370

PRINCIPAL DRAMA
Pipa ji, pr., pb. c. 1367 (*The Lute*, 1980)

OTHER LITERARY FORMS

A scholar and an official who served, somewhat reluctantly, in the Mongol government of China for about a decade, Gao Ming retired to devote himself to writing. Although he is known principally as a playwright, Gao was also a specialist in the *Chunqiu* (*Spring and Autumn Annals*, 1872), the first Chinese chronological history, and a poet who wrote in both the *ci* and the *shi* forms, the former being particularly prized. Some of his poems and miscellaneous writings have been preserved in various anthologies. Although only one of his *ci* is extant, some fifty of his poems in the *shi* form survive.

ACHIEVEMENTS

One of the first southern plays in the new genre later termed *chuanqi*, Gao Ming's *The Lute* became immensely popular with its first performance around 1367. Zhu Yuanzhang, who commanded the rebel armies that drove the Mongols from China and founded the Ming Dynasty in 1368 to become Emperor Hong Wu, is said to have witnessed this performance with enthusiastic admiration. Shortly after he ascended the throne, Zhu Yuanzhang summoned Gao to court to serve on the commission being assembled to compile the official history of the Yuan Dynasty. The literatus, however, excused himself on account of age and ill health—although legend has it that he feigned madness. In any case, he escaped from this task, much to the disappointment, it is said, of the new monarch.

Later, when someone presented a copy of *The Lute* to the emperor, it is reported that he smiled and commented: "The Five Classics and Four Books are cloth, silk, meal, and millet—something every household has. Gao's *The Lute* is like some splendid, delicious delicacy, and no truly noble household should be without it." Indeed, the emperor so admired Gao's play that he required his theatrical troupe to perform it (or, more likely, selected parts of it), almost daily. Eventually growing discontented by the lack of stringed instrumental accompaniment in the performances, he ordered the officials of the Music Academy to set the southern songs to northern tunes so that the performances could be accompanied by the *pipa*, or lute, and the *zheng*, or zither.

A play may be immensely popular yet possess little artistic merit. If *The Lute* maintained its popularity with the general public, its artistic qualities were formidable enough to retain the interest and the appreciation of sophisticated, learned, and literary people. Indeed, it was regarded as a model of its kind by playwrights working in the same genre. Although Gao had made use of the conventional theme of filial piety, *The Lute* presents this theme in a new way by showing the strong role that circumstance and chance play in human affairs. Further, the conflicts that the characters experience over the issues of the meaning of filial piety are left ambiguous. Another new approach on Gao's part was his presenting of Cai Bojie, the traditional villain of earlier plays and stories, as a good and well-meaning man who is a victim of the machinations of others who are equally good and well-meaning. All are victims of chance and circumstance, as well as of the Chinese cultural code. No human villain appears in *The Lute*.

Only a few *nanxi*, or southern plays, have been preserved. *The Lute*, however, is the only *nanxi* that was preserved by being widely anthologized because of its popularity and literary merits. Three *nanxi* that predate *The Lute* have survived by having been buried in the imperial encyclopedia, *Yongle dadian* (1403-1408; grand repository of eternal joy), remnants of which were discovered in a London bookstall in 1920. A comparison of these earlier *nanxi* with *The Lute* reveals that in a lesser way they anticipate the later style that Gao brought near perfection.

If he did not invent the style later termed *chuanqi*, he certainly brought it to full flower. Gao's contributions involved innovations, elaborations, organization, and style.

The prologue of *The Lute* was an innovation. It gives an outline of the plot, states its theme, and lays down the philosophical principle that a story without a moral teaching is useless, no matter how well written. These features, which enabled the audience to comprehend at once what was at hand and created suspense as to what to expect in the future, became standard fare in the *chuanqi* plays. In contrast to the Yuan *zaju*, or northern play, the number of acts in the *nanxi* was not set, and they were of varying length. The *zaju* used solo singing only, whereas the *nanxi* used songs arranged in song sets. Southern singing was mellifluous and sinuous instead of clashing and strident, like northern music. In *The Lute*, Gao's lofty and exquisite poetry avoided entirely those vulgarities that had marked earlier drama. His language ranges from the simplicity of folk speech to the elegance of classical rhetoric, combining colloquial naturalism with the marks of sophisticated, literary education. Furthermore, he manages to encompass a variety of moods and sentiments: inner conflict, quiet humor, a tragic sense of life, satire, and irony.

Gao's *The Lute* is important in the history of the Western appreciation of Chinese literature because a complete translation into French appeared as early as 1838. Translated by A. P. L. Bazin and given the title *Le Pi-pa-ki: Ou, L'Histoire du Luth*, the volume was issued in Paris by Imprimerie Royale. Another complete translation, this one into German by Vincenz Hundhausen, appeared in 1930, with the title *Die Laute, von Gau Ming*, published in Leipzig by Pekinger Verlag. A complete English translation, excellently rendered by Jean Mulligan, appeared in 1980, under the title *The Lute: Kao Ming's P'i-p'a chi*, published in New York by Columbia University Press. The play appeared on Broadway in 1946, starring Yul Brynner as Cai Bojie and Mary Martin as his wife. This performance was based on an adaptation done by playwrights Will Irwin and Sidney Howard in 1925, later published in Chicago.

BIOGRAPHY

Gao Ming (whose *zi*, or "courtesy name," was Zecheng) was born around 1303 into a highly literate family living in Rui-an, Wenzhou Prefecture, Zhejiang Province. His paternal grandfather, his uncle on his father's side, and three of his grandmother's brothers were all writers in verse and prose.

Little is known of Gao's early years. He seems to have followed the usual course of study that would lead to an official career, poring over the Four Books and the Five Classics and learning to compose the *wenzhang*, the type of essay required in the civil service examinations. Under Mongol rule, the Chinese civil service examinations had been abolished, and this system was not reintroduced until 1313, when Gao was about ten years of age. Success in the examinations now did not guarantee an official career, however, as those under the Song had done. The Mongols required the Chinese to show their complete mastery of the curriculum, whereas Mongols and other foreigners could get away with mediocre performances. At any rate, Gao did not achieve his *juren*, or master's degree, until 1344, when he was in his early forties. The following year, he took his doctor's degree, or *jinshi*, the prerequisite for an official appointment in the government.

Gao soon received an appointment as district judicial officer in Quzhou, Zhejiang. In 1348, he was assigned adviser to the government naval forces in the effort to subdue the recalcitrant freebooter and pirate Fang Guozhen. Fang was a masterful man who maintained practically an independent regime in the east-coast Jiangzhe from 1348 to 1367. At the same time, he was, at least nominally, an official either under the Yuan Dynasty or under the rebel leader Zhu Yuanzhang when he did not serve under both at the same time. Fang supported himself partly from revenue from the cities under his control and partly by raids directed against coastal towns and piracy launched against public or private shipping. Gao's assignment did not fare well. He and the naval officers clashed; he and they did not see eye-to-eye. In disgust, Gao soon resigned his post. Because of Fang's rebellion in eastern Zhejiang, other officials had fled to other parts of the country. Fang, however, suc-

ceeded in detaining Gao, whom he required to enter his service. When, in 1352, Gao managed to regain his freedom, he hurried to Hangzhou, determined never again to serve the Yuan.

One of the principal cities of the lower Yangtze Plain, Hangzhou was the southern terminus of the Grand Canal and the capital of Zhejiang Province. It had been the imperial capital of the Southern Song Dynasty (1127-1279 C.E.), when it had been the home of many famous poets and painters, who had immortalized its scenery, such as its beautiful West Lake. In Hangzhou, Gao met his friend Zhao Fang, to whom he expressed his discontent regarding official life. Zhao, however, succeeded in persuading Gao to serve the Yuan once more. Thus, from 1352 to 1356, Gao acted as a censor in Kiangnan (then a province comprising Anhui and Jiangsu) and in Fuzhou, the capital of Fujian Province. In 1356, Gao permanently retired to the district city of Yin, Ningbo Prefecture, in the Ningshaotai circuit, Zhejiang Province.

Sometime during his retirement, Gao began work on the composition of *The Lute*, probably in the early 1360's. In Yin (Ningbo), it is said, he lived in the home of a family named Shen; it is also said that during the writing of *The Lute*, he lived in a tower for three years. It is thought that the first performance of *The Lute* took place in 1367. Its publication must have followed not long afterward because its title was included with the pre-Ming *nanxi* listed in the *Yongle dadian*, which was put together in the years 1403-1408. Gao probably wrote the play mainly for his own amusement, but there also appear to have been some serious motivations of a personal nature. He resented the depiction of the Han scholar-official Cai Yong as a villain in popular stories and plays and wished to remove the unjust stigma that had been placed on the high-principled official, who from his youth had been distinguished by his filial piety and his love of study. Skeptical of certain traditional ideals, Gao wished to examine the meaning of "filial piety" and to suggest that the meaning depended on interpretation and was ambiguous. He wanted to puncture the romantic ideal of the perfect match supposed to obtain between the "brilliant scholar" and the "beautiful lady." Finally, distrustful of official service on the basis of personal experience, Gao wished to examine the realities of official life and to show that it was not always glamorous but instead had stresses, strains, corruption, injustices, falls from grace, and other sorts of disadvantages—realities that made official life, at best, a mixed blessing.

Called to serve on the commission to write the official history of the Yuan by Zhu Yuanzhang after his enthronement in 1368, Gao excused himself. His official career began late and concluded early, and for him it had its discontents, but it must be considered that he was a Chinese trying to serve a Mongol government that manifested a decided prejudice against Gao's people. After having been summoned to court, Gao returned to Ninghai, a district city in Taizhou Prefecture, Zhejiang Province, about forty miles south of Ningbo. There he apparently died about 1370, his fame dependent on his one masterpiece, *The Lute*.

ANALYSIS

Gao Ming's *The Lute* belongs to the southern style of Yuan drama, or to *nanxi* (also termed *xiwen*). As such, it differs in its formal properties, particularly in its musical as well as its dramatic structures, from the stricter, less "pop" form of the northern style, or *zaju*. The dramatic and musical forms of the *nanxi* were not fixed but were relatively free, allowing for more intricacy, more elaboration—one might say, permitting the "baroque." Like all Chinese plays, *The Lute* is "musical drama," or "Chinese opera," although not in any Western sense. As such, its musical structure is its most important element.

The musical structure of *nanxi*, unlike *zaju*, permitted multiple singing roles, and sometimes the singing was done in unison. The role categories were more expansive in *nanxi* than in *zaju*, and the singing could be assigned to any character and to any number of characters. The music of southern drama stuck to the traditional Chinese scale, a pentatonic scale, in contrast to the northern drama, whose music employed the Mongol scale (modified by Kublai Khan), a heptatonic scale. Furthermore, southern music was fitted to the *gu* (drum) and the *paiban* (wooden clappers), whereas northern music was fitted to the *pipa*

("balloon guitar," or lute) and the *dizi* (horizontal flute). Emperor Hong Wu, dissatisfied with performances of Gao's *The Lute* because the music was not fitted to such stringed instruments as the *pipa* and the *zheng* (zither), ordered his Music Academy to have the southern songs set to northern tunes. The *nanxi* took more tunes from Tang and Song *ci* than did the *zaju*, because the latter favored folk tunes from Central Asia. Although there were "modes" in southern as well as in northern music, "mode" as such was not a measure of the aria melodies in *nanxi* drama. Instead of being organized on the basis of mode, the songs in *nanxi* were arranged on the principle of a sequence of different tunes or a sequence based on transposition or ornamental variation without regard to any modal relationship.

THE LUTE

The dramatic structure of *nanxi* was large, having as many as forty or fifty scenes (*chu*). Gao's *The Lute* consists of forty-two scenes. The acts or scenes could vary in length from short to long. The first scene of a *nanxi* presents the important division of the prologue. The prologue of *The Lute* was, as noted above, innovative in its time, setting forth a moral principle as well as an aesthetic principle on which the play is based and an outline of the action to come, together with a listing of the agents of this action. Four main role categories appear in the *nanxi*: *sheng*, *dan*, *jing*, and *chou*. The *sheng* is the leading male character, the *dan* the leading female. The *mo* is the secondary male role, and the *wai* may be either a secondary male or a secondary female role. In *The Lute*, Cai Bojie, the poor scholar who became the Top Graduate in the imperial *jinshi* examinations and married the prime minister's beautiful daughter, is played by the *sheng* actor. His first wife, Zhao Wuniang, is played by the *dan* actor. Father Cai and Mother Cai are played by the *wai* and *jing* actors respectively. Mistress Niu, the prime minister's daughter who became young Cai's second wife, is played by the *tie-dan* actor. Her father, Prime Minister Niu, is played by the *wai* actor. The *mo*, the *jing*, and the *chou* actors play a variety of subordinate roles. It is the *mo* actor who presents the important prologue in scene 1, in this case playing the part of a "master of ceremonies."

Later he plays (among other roles) the steward in the mansion of Prime Minister Niu; young Cai's neighbor Zhang Dagong, who helps Mistress Zhao look after her in-laws during the famine; a traveler; a prefectural supervisor; and a eunuch. Although the prologue precedes the main action of the play, it is an integral part of the whole. In the *nanxi*, there was neither "wedge" nor epilogue. The theme of *The Lute* is brought out in the prologue—the duty of "filial piety" (*xiao*) and how that duty is to be interpreted. Chinese plays were presented on practically a bare stage, with no scenery and a minimum of props. The audience's attention was focused on the performance of the actors; on their costumes and makeup, which ranged from plain to richly exotic; on their singing voices accompanied by instruments (the orchestra being visible to the audience on the side of the stage); and on their symbolic gestures and movements (their whole performance "an elaborate and stylized presentation of emotions and actions"). The actors performed their parts, then, within specific role categories, with which the audience was familiar and which it could immediately recognize. These were, with slight variations, common to all styles of drama in old China.

The plot of *The Lute* is intricately woven, with two lines of developing action in which conflict and contrast are emphasized. These strands of action operate more or less simultaneously in time over a period of years (seven or eight) and at a considerable distance in space (several hundred miles) until they come together and merge harmoniously at the conclusion of the total action. The story concerns a young scholar, Cai Bojie, the only son of aged parents, with whom he and his recent bride, Zhao Wuniang, live in Chenliu, a district in Kaifeng Fu, Henan. The time is the first century C.E., during the Eastern Han Dynasty. A strongly filial son, the young man has declined to take the imperial examination for the *jinshi*, or doctor's degree, whose acquisition would make him eligible for an official appointment in the government service, because he believes that it is his filial obligation to remain at home to care for his old parents. Spring having arrived again, however, it is announced in Cai's district that the imperial ex-

aminations are soon to be given at Luoyang, the capital of the Eastern Han Empire. To the young man's surprise—indeed to his chagrin—he finds his parents, particularly his father, urging him to leave home to visit the capital and compete in the civil service examinations. They insist that his true filial duty to them is not staying at home to care for them but to earn the *jinshi* degree and receive an official appointment, for these achievements will bring both honor to the family name and financial prosperity to the parents in their declining years. The young man accedes to their request, despite his doubts and his mother's forebodings. He journeys to the capital to take the examinations, leaving his parents to be cared for by his young wife, Wuniang, and a neighbor, Mr. Zhang.

When young Cai takes the examinations, he is declared the "First Winner" or "Top Graduate," a rank that naturally entitles him to a high government post. He is admired and respected by all, including particularly the emperor and Prime Minister Niu. Because the prime minister has a beautiful unmarried daughter, the emperor suggests that the brilliant young scholar would make an ideal husband for the beautiful young lady. To young Cai's complete dismay, he is required to marry Mistress Niu despite the fact that he is already married to Mistress Zhao. Although Cai is distressed by this second marriage, he is not a bigamist, because plural marriage was given full approval by ancient Chinese society. Living at the prime minister's splendid mansion with his new bride and her father, Cai is unhappy and grieves about his separation from his first wife, his parents, and his home.

Meanwhile, back in Chenliu, Cai's parents and Wuniang are suffering from a famine that has struck the area. They are living in dire poverty. Mother Cai blames her husband for sending their son away, thus leaving them helpless in a time of calamity. Although bitter about her husband's desertion of her, Wuniang does everything possible to help her parents-in-law. She sells her jewelry to get money to buy food; she begs for grain for her in-laws at the public granary; and she secretly eats only the husks of rice, saving the rice itself for her aged charges. Mother Cai suspects

Wuniang of buying food for herself to eat in private, but Father Cai maintains his confidence in Wuniang's integrity. When they spy on her, they learn that Mother Cai's suspicions are groundless. Both old people are so appalled and humiliated by the evil thoughts they had harbored that they fall down in a faint. Although Father Cai soon recovers, Mother Cai dies. Later, Father Cai falls ill and before long also dies. Before his death, he blames himself for urging his son to leave home to compete for worldly success; at the same time, however, he condemns his son for causing so much hardship for Wuniang. Wuniang is also bitter about her husband's desertion of his family. Because she has no money to bury Father Cai, she cuts her hair and attempts to sell it in the streets. Unable to hire someone to dig the grave, she attempts to dig it herself. Weary from her efforts, she falls asleep. Out of pity for her and in admiration for her filial piety, the Jade Emperor sends spirits to help her. They finish the grave, and then they appear to her in a dream. They advise her to go to the capital in search of her husband.

Wuniang sets out to find her lost husband. As she travels to Luoyang, she carries with her a *pipa*, or four-stringed lute, which she plays while begging. She also has in her possession funeral portraits of her parents-in-law which she painted herself at their graveside. On the road, dressed as a nun, Wuniang stops at a monastery, which Cai visits to pray for the safety of his family. Leaving behind the portraits, Wuniang removes herself so that Cai does not see her. He takes the portraits with him when he leaves, not recognizing that they are of his parents, and carries them to the prime minister's mansion in the capital.

Anxious and depressed, Cai displays a lack of warmth toward his beautiful second wife. As a result, she becomes angry and demands an explanation of his odd behavior. Although he refuses to comply with her wishes, she learns the truth when she overhears him grieving over the separation from his family at Chenliu. She upbraids him for deserting his wife and parents and insists that they go together to visit them. When they broach this idea to the prime minister, he decides to bring Cai's folks to the capital.

Mistress Niu hires Wuniang as a maid without knowing her true identity. Eventually, however, she learns who Wuniang is and is very sympathetic toward her. Indeed, both women feel a special kinship with each other, since each has suffered on account of Cai's desertion of his family, and each expresses her resentment of him—granting, however, that he was a victim of circumstance. Wuniang writes Cai a note and leaves it in his study to prepare him for her appearance. She finds the portraits of her parents-in-law hanging there and writes an allusive poem on the back of the painting in which she complains against him for his desertion of his family. She does not sign the poem.

When he inspects the portraits, Cai is very moved, thinking that in some ways they resemble his parents. Finding the anonymous poem on the back of the painting, he sees that it has been written only a short while ago, for the ink of the characters is not yet dry. Angered, he calls Mistress Niu to learn who has been in his study. She questions him and ascertains that he really is a man of high moral principle who would never divorce his first wife because she is poor and unattractive in appearance. Hence, Mistress Niu calls in Wuniang and reunites her with Cai. He now learns that his parents are dead and that Wuniang has proven a filial daughter and a loyal and virtuous wife. The trio make plans to travel to Chenliu to observe the proper mourning period, and Prime Minister Niu reluctantly consents to allow his daughter to be at the graveside with Cai and Wuniang.

When they arrive at Chenliu, Cai and his two wives mourn at the grave of his deceased parents. At the end of the period of mourning, Cai and his wives pay another visit to the graves. This time they find the grave site surrounded with auspicious signs, such as trees which are joined together by intertwining branches and tame white rabbits hopping about the area. Now Prime Minister Niu arrives bringing with him imperial commendations for Cai and his two wives and posthumous titles for Cai's parents. The prime minister even brings a gift of money to reward good neighbor Zhang, who had done everything in his power to help Cai's parents and Wuniang during the terrible period of their adversity. At the end of the ceremony, the prime minister and Cai and his two wives make ready to return to the capital, where Cai will resume his official career, this time happy and in complete harmony with the cosmos.

This plot synopsis fails to convey any real idea of the power of the text to move readers, much less give the remotest hint of the power of the play in performance—with its painted faces and colorful costumes, its nasal singing and sing-song speech, and the sounds of the accompanying musical instruments as well as those of an active theater audience—to move spectators. Finally, neither the refined poetry of certain scenes nor the crude comedy of others is at all apparent in the above synopsis. At any rate, there is at least some inkling that, as has been aptly remarked, "the play erects a monument to virtue and to tears, its readers or spectators alternately fortified by pious [sayings] or drenched in pathetic sentiment." The whole play is done with such an artful hand and with such a sensibility and range of feeling that *The Lute* has been admired for nearly five centuries throughout China and has become firmly established in the literature of the Chinese theater.

In respect to language, a play is primarily *speech*. It is a dramatic discourse *to be listened to*. Secondarily, it is spectacle—a picture of motion, gesture, and act—to be viewed, seen. Hearing takes priority, however, and the sounds of speech, voice, and music are paramount. In these matters, *The Lute* displays a wide range of styles—from *baihua*, or "easily understood talk," to *pianwen*, or "parallel prose," a rather florid style characterized by the use of four- and six-word parallel phrases and using most of the devices employed in poetry. Poetry is an important aspect of *The Lute*. Two traditional forms, the *shi* (which uses lines of equal numbers of syllables) and the *ci* (a poem written to existing music, in lines of unequal length), are used throughout the play. The songs of the *nanxi* do not form a "suite" (*taoshu*) as they do in the *zaju*, nor is the text of the play divided into "acts" (*zhe*) as is that of the *zaju*, for the unit of structure for what became the *chuanqi* is the "scene" (*chu*), and *The Lute* has forty-two such scenes. A scene commonly ends with a four-line poem in the *shi* form, and scenes often begin with either a *shi* or a *ci* poem.

The speech of *The Lute* is rendered in Southern pronunciation, in contrast to the Northern pronunciation of the *zaju*. Because Southern pronunciation was used in the singing and recitation parts of *xiawen*, its melodic structure differed from that of the *zaju*, in which Northern pronunciation was used. After the reunification of China, some critics, notably Zhou Deqing (c. 1270-c. 1325), objected strongly to what they regarded as stylistic "faults" in the Southern plays, and these critics championed the "purity" of Northern speech. They urged the Southern playwrights to adopt the Beijing dialect as the standard language of the theater.

In the introduction to her English translation of Gao's *The Lute*, Jean Mulligan cites the author's "attention to unity" as the play's most unusual characteristic, since the very length of the *chuanqi* form "encouraged discursiveness" and structural looseness. The unity Gao achieved began with the basic structure of the play—"a pattern of alternating scenes that contrast the life of Cai in the capital with that of his family in Chenliu." In this pattern, scenes of Gao's parents and first wife "suffering in hunger and fear" are juxtaposed and contrasted with others showing Cai feasting in abundance and generally living a life of comfort and luxury. It is "this contrasting pattern," Mulligan affirms, which "provides a structure for the long play and underscores its emotional force—Cai's abandonment of his family to ever increasing suffering." Indeed, Mulligan notes much of the power of the play stems from "the author's use of dominant symbols and images that reoccur throughout the play to express the bitter gulf between life in the capital and at home." Particularly effective, in Mulligan's opinion, is Gao's use of "concrete symbols of food and clothing and images that relate to rise and fall of heights and depths." Altogether, Mulligan thinks that the unity of *The Lute* "is one of its unique strengths as an innovative work in its genre"; at the same time, however, she cautions, "the author's attention to variety of effect should also be noted."

To understand (or to make) a discourse, one must have a knowledge of the cultural coding in it. This coding consists of the thinking, the attitudes, the behavior, the presumptions, the etiquette, the rules, the expectations, the taboos, and the hopes of those persons born, reared, and educated in the specific cultural setting and social order responsible for the cultural code found in the discourse. To understand (or to make) a discourse requires more than simply "linguistic competence"—a lexicon and a grammar. It also requires a knowledge of the generic codes and of the stylistic conventions which govern such a discourse. All these factors pertain to a modern understanding of Gao's *The Lute*, whether in its original Chinese or in English translation. Even the English translation must retain certain characteristics inherent in the Chinese language itself. Hence, such literary devices as images, symbols, signs, tropes, set or symbolic descriptions, antithesis, allusions, quotations, derivations, puns, jokes, parodies, satires, and ironies in *The Lute* need to be referenced and interpreted relative to Chinese history and culture.

Two examples selected from *The Lute* may serve to demonstrate the wisdom and the validity of such an approach. In scene 18, Cai (singing to the tune *Hua-mei xi*) expresses himself in the following manner: "To pluck the cassia I climbed to the Moon Palace,/ Never knowing that vines would wind round the tall tree./ They rejoice that on this day I have found in books/ A woman with a face like jade." Here Chinese linguistic elements have been transposed into English but still require a purely Chinese interpretation: The original Chinese for "To pluck the cassia" (*zhe kuang*) means "to gain the third, or *jinshi*, degree in the imperial civil service examinations." "I climbed to the Moon Palace" (*pan yuefu*) means "I competed in the imperial examinations." "Never knowing that vines would wind round the tall tree" (*Bu zhi pu wan gaoshu*) means "Not knowing that as a worthy man I would be married to a second wife." "They rejoice that on this day I have found in books/ A woman with a face like jade" refers to the belief that the study of the Chinese Classics would lead to official appointment and hence the acquisition of wealth and beautiful women. "A woman with a face like jade" (that is, a *yumianren*, or "jade-faced person") refers to "a lovely lady" or "a beautiful woman." It can be easily

seen here how Cai's utterance is entrenched in the Chinese linguistic and cultural tradition.

The other example from *The Lute* is taken from scene 21, in that section in which Cai discusses his marital dilemma with Mistress Niu. On entering the room, she finds him playing the *qin*, a zither indigenous to China that became the favorite instrument for private use by scholars and officials. When they engage in discourse, the situation turns into dramatic irony because when he refers to "string" she thinks he is talking about a "string" on his zither, when in fact he is talking about his two wives. Part of the dialogue goes like this:

> MISTRESS NIU: Have you gone mad? I know that you're a good player. There's no need for you to show off your versatility.
> CAI: I'm not! The problem is, I can't play this string.
> MISTRESS NIU: What's wrong with the string?
> CAI: I was used to playing the old one; this one is new, and I'm not used to it.
> MISTRESS NIU: Where is the old string?
> CAI: I threw it away a long time ago.
> MISTRESS NIU: Why did you throw it away?
> CAI: I got this new string, so I threw away the old.

The discourse continues, but this much should be sufficient to show its irony hinges on the Chinese symbolic conception that a "broken string" (*duan xian*) refers to a "lost wife." The term "old string" (*lao xian*) refers to a "discarded wife," and the term "new string" (*xin xian*) refers to a "second wife." The presence of the *qin* in Cai's hands serves to divert Mistress Niu's attention from the Chinese symbolism of the string in reference to marriage, which, undoubtedly, is of masculine origin. Mulligan's annotations to many of these Chinese features of her translated text are extremely helpful to the Western reader.

BIBLIOGRAPHY

Birch, Cyril. "Some Concerns and Methods of the Ming *Ch'uan-ch'i* Drama." In *Studies in Chinese Literary Genres*, edited by Cyrill Birch. Berkeley: University of California Press, 1974. A background essay on the Southern drama of the Ming Dynasty.

_____. "Tragedy and Melodrama in Early *Ch'uan-ch'i* Plays: *Lute Song* and *Thorn Hairpin* Compared." *Bulletin of the School of Oriental Studies* 36 (1973): 228-247. An examination of the *chuanqi* plays.

Dolby, William. *History of Chinese Drama*. London: Paul Elek, 1976. This overview of Chinese history contains an English translation of one of the scenes from *The Lute*.

Johnson, Dale R. *A Glossary of Words and Phrases in the Oral Performing and Dramatic Literatures of the Jin, Yuan, and Ming*. Ann Arbor: Center for Chinese Studies, University of Michigan, 2000. A glossary that explains some of the terms used in a discussion of Chinese drama during the Yuan period.

Mulligan, Jean, trans. Introduction to *The Lute: Kao Ming's P'i-p'a chi*. New York: Columbia University Press, 1980. In the introduction to her translation of the Chinese classic, Mulligan provides valuable information on the presentation of the work and of the times in which it was created.

Wang, Chien P'ing. *P'i p'a chi: The Story of the Lute*. Pei-ching: Hsin Shih Chieh Chu Pan She, 1999. A parallel text edition of the famous classic featuring a new English translation and the text of the original.

Richard P. Benton

FEDERICO GARCÍA LORCA

Born: Fuentevaqueros, Spain; June 5, 1898
Died: Víznar, Spain; August 19, 1936

PRINCIPAL DRAMA

El maleficio de la mariposa, pr. 1920, pb. 1957 (*The Butterfly's Evil Spell*, 1963)

Mariana Pineda, pr. 1927, pb. 1928 (English translation, 1950)

Los títeres de Cachiporra: La tragicomedia de don Cristóbal y la señá Rosita, wr. 1928, pr. 1937, pb. 1949 (*The Tragicomedy of Don Cristóbal and Doña Rosita*, 1955)

El paseo de Buster Keaton, pb. 1928 (*Buster Keaton's Promenade*, 1957)

La doncella, el marinero y el estudiante, pb. 1928 (*The Virgin, the Sailor, and the Student*, 1957)

Quimera, wr. 1928, pb. 1938 (*Chimera*, 1944)

El público, wr. 1930, pb. 1976 (fragment; *The Audience*, 1958)

La zapatera prodigiosa, pr. 1930, pb. 1938 (*The Shoemaker's Prodigious Wife*, 1941)

Así que pasen cinco años, wr. 1931, pb. 1937, pr. in English 1945, pr. in Spanish 1954 (*When Five Years Pass*, 1941)

El amor de don Perlimplín con Belisa en su jardín, pr. 1933, pb. 1938 (*The Love of Don Perlimplín for Belisa in His Garden*, 1941)

Bodas de sangre, pr. 1933, pb. 1935 (*Blood Wedding*, 1939)

Yerma, pr. 1934, pb. 1937 (English translation, 1941)

Doña Rosita la soltera: O, El lenguaje de las flores, pr. 1935, pb. 1938 (*Doña Rosita the Spinster: Or, The Language of the Flowers*, 1941)

El retablillo de don Cristóbal, pr. 1935, pb. 1938 (*In the Frame of Don Cristóbal*, 1944)

La casa de Bernarda Alba, wr. 1936, pr., pb. 1945 (*The House of Bernarda Alba*, 1947)

OTHER LITERARY FORMS

It may be argued with some justification that Federico García Lorca is best remembered as a poet. Although recognition for his poetry came first, García Lorca did divide his creative energies almost equally between the two genres, concentrating on poetry during the 1920's and devoting himself more single-mindedly in the 1930's to the theater. His first collection, *Libro de poemas*, appeared in 1921, and between 1921 and 1924 García Lorca continued work on *Poema del cante jondo* (1931; *Poem of the Gypsy Seguidilla*, 1967), *Primeras canciones* (1936), and *Canciones, 1921-1924* (1927; *Songs*, 1976)—all of which attest his considerable knowledge of Andalusian folklore and a genuine musical flair. García Lorca's reputation soared, however, with the publication in 1928 of *Romancero gitano, 1924-1927* (*The Gypsy Ballads of García Lorca*, 1951, 1953), an ambitious attempt at recapturing tradition to express it in a modern idiom. The Gypsy is cast as a contemporary victim, a natural being at odds with an inflexible, repressive society, in powerful and compelling images of frustration, loss, and death. García Lorca's fusion of personal and universal symbolism was almost too successful; critics disseminated rather too freely the facile "myth of the Gypsy" with García Lorca as its poet. This brought the angry riposte that the Gypsy was only one manifestation of the persecution of minorities; other victims included the black and the ho-

Federico García Lorca (AP/Wide World Photos)

mosexual, and both figured prominently in García Lorca's next collection, *Poeta en Nueva York* (*Poet in New York*, 1940, 1955), written in 1929-1930 but published posthumously in 1940. Visiting the United States in 1929, García Lorca had been appalled by what he saw of the New York of the Depression, finding there an anonymous, transient, and brutally violent society with no unifying mythology or collective dream. His denunciations of the alienation, pain, and spiritual desolation inflicted by the ruthless inhumanity of modern technology found expression in nightmarish, surrealistic images of the entrapment and destruction of natural forces. If García Lorca wrote less poetry after *Poet in New York*, anguish and inner torment characterize the difficult and often obscure metaphors of the poems of *Diván del Tamarit*, (*The Divan at the Tamarit*, 1944), posthumously collected and published in 1940. A notable exception is the elegy of 1935, *Llanto por Ignacio Sánchez Mejías* (*Lament for the Death of a Bullfighter*, 1937, 1939), which, classical in form, moves in four parts from shock and horror by way of ritualized lament and tranquil meditation to a philosophical funeral oration. Less important than either his poetry or drama, but often a more explicit source of many recurring themes and images, is García Lorca's prose, particularly *Impresiones y paisajes* (1918). The most complete collection of his poetic prose and other more ephemeral writings, such as letters, lectures, and interviews, may be found in *Obras completas* (1973). Throughout his life, García Lorca displayed remarkable talents for music and drawing, and the piano arrangements of his own and traditional poetry and the sketches which accompany, and sometimes explain, his poems and letters are well worth consulting.

ACHIEVEMENTS

In the decades since his death, Federico García Lorca has become something of a cult figure (particularly outside his native country, where the stylized image of Spain found in his poetry and plays has romantic appeal). His work has been widely translated, inspiring writers, composers, choreographers, painters, and filmmakers; critical studies, moreover, abound, and as a result, García Lorca's name is now probably as familiar as that of Miguel de Cervantes. Much of this fame comes from a personal myth inspired equally by memories of García Lorca's undeniably charismatic presence and the tragic circumstances of his untimely death. Proper assessment is therefore not easy.

At odds with the myth of García Lorca's quintessential Spanishness is the degree to which his stagecraft, both as dramatist and as director, belongs to broader European cultural currents. His constantly reiterated goal of the renovation of the Spanish theater was a vision entirely harmonious with the technical advances of luminaries such as Edward Gordon Craig, Max Reinhardt, and Konstantin Stanislavsky. Unlike them, he undertook the enterprise at a time when his national theater was sunk in the stagnation of unrelieved superficiality, and his achievement of a modern style is all the more creditable. In collaboration with stage-director Rivas Cherif and actress Margarita Xirgu, García Lorca brought new techniques from Paris to the staging of his own plays. Not content with winning over the theatergoing public of the capital, García Lorca's five-year stint as codirector with Eduardo Ugarte of the "university theater," La Barraca, brought the same modern techniques to the Spanish classics performed throughout Spain. His energy, ingenuity, and experience revolutionized theatrical style in the 1930's, redeeming, albeit only briefly, the national theater from a creaking nineteenth century realism.

As a dramatist, García Lorca promised much; his death cut off a brilliant future. Plays such as *The Audience* and *When Five Years Pass* are truly innovative, with elements that foreshadow the experimental theater of Samuel Beckett, Jean Genet, and Eugène Ionesco. Even García Lorca's dramas firmly rooted in the Spanish context have a universal quality. By baring the human soul, he communicated the many facets of humanity's contact with the primitive, instinctual forces of the natural work in dynamic dramatic language stripped of all superficiality. The culmination comes in *The House of Bernarda Alba*, García Lorca's revival of the idea of tragedy for modern times. What new challenges and experiments he had

in mind are, unfortunately, lost forever. Bernarda Alba's final imposition of silence was all too prophetic. Only since the 1970's, some forty years after García Lorca's death, have Spanish dramatists begun to grapple with the many innovations he envisioned so clearly.

BIOGRAPHY

Federico García Lorca was born in 1898 in a small Andalusian village about fifteen miles from Granada. His father was a prosperous landowner and his mother a sometime teacher. All four of their children grew up in comfortable circumstances with the advantages of a good formal education and the prolonged leisure to pursue the delights of music and literature. Indeed, García Lorca's interest in the theater was apparent from a very early age in the puppet-theater shows that he designed and directed to entertain the household. In 1909, the family moved to Granada, where García Lorca went to school and attended university. The move was significant: The rich and varied cultural life there fired the young García Lorca's ambition to write, while the city itself provided him with the subject matter of some of his most important works. Moreover, at the conservatory in Granada, García Lorca's considerable musical ability brought him to the attention of Manuel de Falla. Their long friendship and occasional professional collaboration was based on a mutual interest in traditional Spanish music and folklore. In 1919, García Lorca left for Madrid and began a ten-year stay at the Residencia de Estudiantes that proved of great consequence to his artistic career. There, García Lorca kept company with the senior Spanish residents, Juan Ramón Jiménez, Gregorio Martínez Sierra, Antonio Machado; made friends with Salvador Dalí and Luis Buñuel; and enjoyed the frequent visits of famous European contemporaries of the stature of H. G. Wells, François Mauriac, Igor Stravinsky, Paul Valéry, and Albert Einstein. Above all, García Lorca found at the Residencia an audience that listened with intellectual acuity and sensitive appreciation to recitals of his poetry, plays, and music in what was, for him, a period of steady output and growing recognition.

About this time, however, he fell prey to deep depression, and, by the summer of 1929, either sentimental or psychological reasons connected with his homosexuality led García Lorca to leave Spain for the United States. He registered at Columbia University to study English but soon abandoned the course. His difficulties with the language and sense of isolation in an alien culture only increased his depression, and it was with great relief that he left New York in the spring of 1930 for Cuba. García Lorca's visit to Havana brought him fame and a sense of well-being, and when he returned to Spain later that year, he embarked on the most creative and productive period of his life.

The political climate in Spain had changed radically with the fall of the dictatorship of Primo de Rivera in 1930 and the election to power of a Republican government in 1931. In this liberal atmosphere, the arts flourished, and it is no coincidence that during these years García Lorca directed with such signal success the traveling-student theater group known as La Barraca. In the performance of plays of the Golden Age in the towns and villages of Spain, García Lorca set about the renovation of the Spanish theater that he would carry through into his own work. This fame as director, playwright, and poet led to a highly successful visit, in 1935, to Buenos Aires, which marked the high point of his career as the most celebrated dramatist in the Hispanic world.

By July, 1936, civil war was inevitable. As the hostilities began, García Lorca returned to Granada—ill-advisedly, as it happened, since the city came under military rule almost immediately and, worse still, suffered an ensuing reign of terror in which political opponents and innocent victims alike were assassinated. García Lorca's well-known friendships with pro-Republican supporters and his involvement with the Republican-funded La Barraca made him an obvious political target; his reputation as a homosexual and his flamboyant success as a writer made him an easy mark for prejudice and envy. In constant fear for his life, García Lorca finally took refuge in the home of Luis Rosales, a fellow poet whose family's political sympathies were with the Nationalist cause. García Lorca was, nevertheless, arrested

there on August 16, held for a short time, and then shot either late on the night of August 18 or early the next morning.

ANALYSIS

Most of Federico García Lorca's dramas were written when the poet-playwright was in growing command of his art. Intense creativity, however, meant little time for literary theorizing, and García Lorca's views on his own work and its part in the projected renovation of the Spanish theater must be sought in the plays themselves and the various interviews he gave. His vision was at once lucid and surprisingly socialist for an otherwise apolitical writer: "I have given myself over to drama which permits more direct contact with the masses." He saw the theater as a vocation requiring personal sacrifice from the dramatist to ensure not commercial success but a real identification with his people. Only half-jokingly "speaking as a true socialist" did García Lorca think the theater should be a "barometer," marking the moral ascendancy or decadence of a nation. Thus finely attuned, the theater would act as a natural conscience, and its themes in Spain of the twentieth century would inevitably treat "a religious and socioeconomic problem." Far from seeking out the exotic, García Lorca advocated a return to the classical norms of tragedy. If he also insisted that poetry and theater were inextricably linked, his poetic drama was to be neither cultish nor middlebrow ersatz, but would live naturally onstage, since "the theater is poetry taken from books and made human." In less than ten years, García Lorca's own dramatic style moved from a quasiromantic sensitivity to a classical starkness. He utilized his poetic talent to develop symbols and re-create popular traditions that effectively emphasized his view of the omnipresence of the tragic in human life.

There is a tendency to restrict critical analysis of García Lorca's theater to the elaboration of the monolithic themes that recur throughout his works. Those most frequently identified are impossible love, frustrated love, separation, and the opposition between desire and reality. Such an approach, however, tends to fragment and compartmentalize without doing justice to the superb theatricality of García Lorca's dramas. By peopling his plays with characters who are "horribly tragic and bound to our life and times," García Lorca managed to communicate to his audience the true passions of men and women, facilitating catharsis in the best tradition of the theater. Francisco Ruiz Ramón rightly argues that García Lorca's canon derives from a basic "dramatic situation" rather than from any single theme, that his dramatic universe springs from the essential conflict between the principles of authority and freedom. This conflict is repeated and elaborated in every play and provides the dramatic structure that in every case has a concatenation of poetic symbols or themes (such as earth, water, moon, horse, bull, blood, and knife) and dramatic incarnations (examples of order, tradition, reality, and collective conscience that oppose those of instinct, desire, imagination, and individuality). Quite deliberately, García Lorca chose to present poetic drama on the modern Spanish stage; coincidentally, his is very much according to the theories of William Butler Yeats and T. S. Eliot, though with more conspicuous success in the practice than either of those two. Any exploration of the range of moral, socioeconomic, telluric, sentimental, or psychological problems encompassed by his poetic theater must take into account this radical decision. With García Lorca, nineteenth century realism in Spanish stagecraft gives way to a more fluid and dynamic concept of dramatic action to which dialogue, language, song, dance, movement, and scenery all make vital contributions.

García Lorca's theater was experimental and controversial, in keeping with his purpose of putting onstage "themes and problems that people are afraid to face." In his chosen context of the dramatic conflict between authority and personal freedom, his own untimely death was the greatest tragedy of all.

THE BUTTERFLY'S EVIL SPELL

There is an obvious thematic connection between García Lorca's first play, *The Butterfly's Evil Spell*, and, notably, poems such as "Los encuentros de un caracol aventurero," "Canción otoñal," and "Balada triste," from his first collection, *Libro de poemas*. Romantic in theme but influenced by the subtle symbolism of the early poetry of Juan Ramón Jiménez, both the poems and the play tell of love, illusion, frustration, and death; a new force breaks through the tranquillity of the old order, leaving senses and soul perturbed. The play dramatizes in lyric form the confusion caused in the daily life of a community of insects by the eruption of love which is mortal. The hero of this miniature tragedy, the cockroach poet Curianito, breaks with the logic, conventions, and strictures of his codified world by falling in love with "a vision which was far removed from his life," a dying butterfly that has fallen to the ground. Precisely his atypical condition of poet makes Curianito seek union with the butterfly, which is at once the incarnation of an unrealizable ideal and the victim of the desire to attain that ideal. Through the impossible love between Curianito and the butterfly, García Lorca dramatizes the subtle relationship between aspiration and goal and the inevitable frustration of both as deviance in an otherwise ordered world.

The essential dramatic situation of all García Lorca's theater is present even in this early effort. The dramatic structure derives from the clash between the norm and the ideal worked out onstage by archetypal characters (who will reappear in the later plays) such as the mother (Doña Curiana), the spinster (Curianita Silvia), the doomed lovers (Curianito and the butterfly), and the tyrannical voice of public opinion emanating from the chorus of neighbors and onlookers (beetles and worms).

With encouragement from Gregorio Martínez Sierra, *The Butterfly's Evil Spell* was performed at the Teatro Eslava, in Madrid, on March 22, 1920. Despite García Lorca's pious hope, expressed in the prologue, that his audience would appreciate this lesson from the natural world, the public had little interest in a play ostensibly about beetles and worms. Accustomed to the drawing-room plays of the commercial theater, they booed it mercilessly off the stage. Bitterly disillusioned, García Lorca learned the hard way that the Spanish theatergoing public still needed to be educated in the modern techniques so successful in Prague and Paris.

MARIANA PINEDA

Seven years elapsed before García Lorca ventured back to the commercial stage, and to a resounding triumph. *Mariana Pineda* was performed in June, 1927, at the Teatro Goya, in Barcelona, by Margarita Xirgu's company, with scenery designed by Salvador Dalí and under García Lorca's own direction. It premiered that October at the Teatro Fontalba, in Madrid.

In part, García Lorca's success was a matter of felicitous timing. Mariana Pineda was a legendary figure of Granada, and her contribution to the republican opposition to Ferdinand VII had contemporary relevance for a twentieth century audience living under Primo de Rivera's dictatorship. Probably this currency was rather more political than García Lorca intended; he had seized on the poetic possibilities of the historical facts. Certainly, García Lorca's second dramatic production was less esoteric than the first. His starting point was the ballad about Mariana Pineda sung in Granada's streets; this was developed into a total spectacle by expert staging and intuitive choreography. Such a combination, with the added appeal of topicality, assured the play a successful run.

On its simplest level, the play is a romantic love story full of passion and sacrifice. Mariana's association with the liberals of Granada is explained by her love for one of them, Pedro de Sotomayor, but both her love and the cause are doomed. Pedro escapes, leaving Mariana to face Pedrosa, the king's representative, and certain death. The play moves through moments of great lyricism, notably the meeting between Mariana and Pedro in act 2, and Mariana's tragic view of love in the final moments of the play. Good use is made of poetic symbolism both in a traditional visual fashion (for example, the red lettering on the banner and the children's game, which combine to suggest spilled blood and death, or the conflict between good and evil reflected in the use of white and black in the scene sets and costumes) and in novel poetic interludes or portents of disaster when García Lorca interjects a *romance* extraneous to the plot but integral to the play's thematic unity (for example, Amparo's retelling of the bullfight in act 1 or Mariana's lullaby of the tragic fate of Duke Lucena in act 2).

From the first, love dominates the scene, and there is a growing sense of individuals caught helplessly in their own passion and in the affairs of others: Mariana in her love for Pedro, Fernando in his love for Mariana, Mariana and Pedro in their hatred for Pedrosa, who himself hates Pedro and desires Mariana.

Mariana, the first fully realized character in García Lorca's theater, is also the first in a long succession of society's victims, but she never acts from purely political motives. This realization leads the spectator or reader to the second level of the play's action: a dramatic situation in which love and liberty become identical. García Lorca's heroine learns that individual liberty and society are mutually exclusive, that any attempt at personal freedom is doomed to failure and death.

THE TRAGICOMEDY OF DON CRISTÓBAL AND DOÑA ROSITA

García Lorca's early romanticism was one reaction against realism onstage; a return to the puppet theater of his youth, with its frantic pace, cross-purposes, and knockabout action, was another. His two puppet plays, *The Tragicomedy of Don Cristóbal and Doña Rosita* and *In the Frame of Don Cristóbal*, are, in effect, two versions of the same story, the second version being the more stylized.

In *The Tragicomedy of Don Cristóbal and Doña Rosita*, the theme of love in conflict with parental obligation is treated with dramatic vigor: The father sells his daughter Rosita to Don Cristóbal, a rich man known for his lechery and cruelty. In this broadly comic farce, however, the fact that Rosita and her true love Cocoliche kiss in front of the cuckolded husband is enough to make Don Cristóbal fume and die, literally, *ha estallado*. Again, the dramatic situation exposes the power that feeds on fear, lies, and covetousness and argues in favor of the authenticity of the individual who escapes societal conventions.

IN THE FRAME OF DON CRISTÓBAL

In his *In the Frame of Don Cristóbal*, García Lorca shows some of the innovative technique that distinguishes the more ambitious *The Audience* by beginning the farce with a *prólogo hablado* in which Director and Poet turn the original story inside out. Don Cristóbal, by definition evil, now turns out to be good at the heart and forced by society to play an evil role, and Rosita has the truly insatiable sexual appetite. By replacing the lyric with the grotesque, García Lorca followed closely the *esperpentos* of Ramón María del Valle-Inclán and, as the Director notes, a whole tradition from "the Gallician 'Bululu,' Monsieur Guignol from Paris, and Bergamo's Signor Harlequin." How significant was this return to "the very essence of the theater" in order to give the theater new life is better seen in García Lorca's two farces for people, *The Shoemaker's Prodigious Wife* and *The Love of Don Perlimplín for Belisa in His Garden.*

THE SHOEMAKER'S PRODIGIOUS WIFE

García Lorca started work on *The Shoemaker's Prodigious Wife* in 1926, but he did not finish the play until 1930. It was performed publicly first on December 24, 1930, at the Teatro Español with Margarita Xirgu in the leading role, Rivas Cherif as director, and costumes designed by Pablo Picasso; García Lorca subsequently revised and expanded the play into the version known today, which was premiered by Lola Membrives and her company on November 30, 1933, in Buenos Aires and on March 18, 1935, at the Teatro Coliseo in Madrid. The play was a huge success; its similarities to the highly stylized forms of ballet and operetta were noted and parallels were drawn with Manuel de Falla's adaptation of *El sombrero de tres picos* (1874). Theater critics appreciated García Lorca's blend of dialogue, poetry, and song, pointing out how he had captured the essence of Andalusian speech rhythms. The protagonist was considered a tour de force; a modern version of the unhappily married wife who, however unhappy her condition, consistently rejects all suitors, she is one more in a distinguished literary lineage that dates back to the earliest Spanish ballads.

García Lorca, himself, however, insisted on the universality of the Shoemaker's Wife and increasingly emphasized the poetic element of her struggle. In interviews held in 1932, he explained that "the Shoemaker's Wife is not any woman in particular but all women" and, moreover, that "every spectator has a Shoemaker's Wife beating in his breast." He conceived this "poetic example of the human soul" to portray the violence of the clash between fantasy and reality:

The poetic creature which the author has dressed as a shoemaker's wife with the grace of a refrain or simple ballad, lives and sparkles everywhere, and the public should not be surprised if she appears violent or assumes a bitter tone, for she is continually in conflict, she struggles against the reality which surrounds her and she struggles against fantasy when this becomes visible reality.

Violence is certainly the main characteristic of the Shoemaker's Wife; the play opens and closes with her sharp retorts: "Be silent, tattle tongue" and "Be quiet, chinwags." The whole of act 1 is rooted in violent antipathy: that of the Shoemaker's Wife toward her neighbors and toward her husband, which never diminishes. Although García Lorca provides some details about the conditions of this mismarriage (its basis in her poverty and his loneliness, the considerable differences in age and outlook) and its difficult circumstances (the harmful gossip and ill will of the neighbors), these motivations are not sufficient in themselves to account for such a violent attitude. In a novel interpretation somewhat out of line with usual criticism, Ruiz Ramón makes much of García Lorca's own avowed intention to dramatize "a myth of our pure unsatisfied illusion." Thus, the anger of the Shoemaker's Wife derives from frustration at the extent to which reality limits not only her individual dreams or desires but also her whole way of being. Her husband's physical presence confines her very self; absent, he is absorbed into that fanciful self and so remembered with nostalgic affection; on his return, as he discloses his true identity, he again triggers her angry verbal abuse.

In *Mariana Pineda*, García Lorca depicts the incarnation of liberty as an ideal; in contrast, *The Shoemaker's Prodigious Wife* shows much more directly how personal liberty is attacked and endangered on a daily basis. The only nonthreatening presence is that of the child, "a compendium of tenderness and a symbol of that which is germinating and yet has long before it blossoms"; otherwise, the alienation of the Shoemaker's Wife is complete. This violence done to the self by the other takes on tragic proportions in *Yerma*. Here (in *The Shoemaker's Prodigious Wife*), humor and the comic spirit are ascendant. Act 2 is a particularly good example of the comic treatment of integrity as reputation and public opinion and integrity as the self inviolate. The Shoemaker's Wife repulses Don Mirlo, the mayor, and others but is subject to increased vilification by the neighbors; she pursues her own dream reality, but this is shattered on the return of her husband. Hence, the gap widens between individual honor and societal norms. Precisely those forces that overwhelm the characters in the later play are at least superficially contained here: The couple agree on a modus vivendi in order to confront, together, the villagers' malicious tongues. The self joins with the other, but one may well ask oneself at what cost.

THE LOVE OF DON PERLIMPLÍN FOR BELISA IN HIS GARDEN

This pattern of the antagonistic couple as protagonists appears once more in farce in *The Love of Don Perlimplín for Belisa in His Garden*, in which a marriage is contracted between two incompatible partners: the fifty-year-old Perlimplín, inexperienced in love, and the young and nubile Belisa, who dreams, half naked on her balcony, of her lovers. The characterization goes beyond caricature; in this farcical treatment of the juxtaposition of youth and age, sensuality and frustration, there is a certain element of pathos. The comic action of the wedding night that brings the discovery of the delights of love to Perlimplín (and makes him a five-time cuckold) turns to tragedy as he plans the conquest of his wife by becoming the embodiment of her vision of love, an illusion brilliant and alluring, but one whose death is implicit in its creation. In such a paradox, García Lorca strips certain elements of farce (disguise and mistaken identity) of their comic effect and moves nearer to the innovative cryptodramas *The Audience* and *When Five Years Pass*, in which the techniques of farce are used for different and more subtle ends.

INNOVATIVE PLAYS

During his stay at the Residencia de Estudiantes, García Lorca enjoyed close friendships with Dalí and Buñuel, which were to have an obvious effect on his work. Increasingly as the 1920's wore on, García Lorca's theater became more experimental; Surrealism, cinematic techniques, and E. Gordon Craig's theories of stagecraft permeated this most avant-garde phase of his drama, which belongs roughly to the years from 1929 to 1931 and has much in common with his contemporaneous New York poems.

García Lorca, wise from his initial bad experience with the commercial theater, had few illusions about his more innovative plays, calling them "irrepresentables." *The Audience* and *When Five Years Pass* were coldly received even by García Lorca's most intimate friends. Quite rightly, García Lorca considered that the frank treatment of homosexuality and the violence in *The Audience* placed it far beyond the grasp of the average audience of its time. Only the minority experimental theater clubs might have been persuaded to stage this kind of drama, and in 1936 there were plans (which came to nothing) for a performance of *When Five Years Pass* by Pura Ucelay's group, the Club Anfistora. If public taste and attitudes were not then ready, García Lorca knew that "the impossible plays contain my true intention." Time would confirm his opinion: In 1972, students at the University of Texas claimed *The Audience* for their own with great excitement, while in 1978, when *When Five Years Pass* finally reached the Spanish stage, it was hailed as García Lorca's most original contribution to the national theater.

THE AUDIENCE

The Spanish title of *The Audience*, *El público*, stark and clinical, is, like its sets and most of its dialogue, a mystery designed to make one reflect on the meaning of love and life. As spectators, the audience observes the stage action, but, just as the play is the image of life, so the audience recognizes the masks and attitudes assumed by the actors as its own. There is, finally, no separation between actors and audience, between the episodes and incidents onstage and in life. R. Martínez Nadal's reconstruction of the incomplete text (1978) includes perhaps the most powerful and direct statement by García Lorca on the function of the theater: "My characters . . . burn the curtain and die in the presence of the public. . . . One must destroy the theatre or live in it!"

The audience of *The Audience* witnesses the process of self-discovery by the stage characters, who put on and take off their masks in a frenzied search for identity. They discuss the nature of the drama and participate in their own drama. By the offstage performance of *Romeo and Juliet*, the play-within-the-play, life is brought to the issues of homosexual love, the frustration of love by death, the treachery of appearances, and the shifting nature of all reality. For the spectators of this action onstage, the issues assume a living form; the characters are reflections of the public, and the audience of them. Boundaries and demarcations are dissolved and become, instead, an infinity of mirror images. In its intellectual range and daring use of technique and dialogue, *The Audience* is a startlingly "modern" play, certainly of the caliber of the experimental theater of Samuel Beckett, Jean Genet, or Eugène Ionesco written some twenty years later.

WHEN FIVE YEARS PASS

When Five Years Pass was completed in 1931, barely a year after *The Audience*. Despite its difficulty, which stems from the same arbitrary radicalism and almost perversely individual symbolism of all experimental theater, it is less obscure and less shocking in theme and dialogue. Unambiguously, the title and subtitle, "A Legend of Time Passing in Three Acts and Five Scenes," point to the central issue, but the composition is a musical one whereby García Lorca has dramatized in a series of fugues the tragedy of time passing for people, who are always at counterpoint, desiring the impossible and destroying what they have. Once again the characters are facets of the individual or the personification of differing attitudes toward a certain fact. El Amigo, Amigo 2° and El Viejo correspond to different facets of El Joven; their varying opinions on time passing are his at different moments in his life. They reflect the opinions and experience of the audience as well, for the play is an image which projects man's common concerns with time, love, and death.

BLOOD WEDDING

The Audience and *When Five Years Pass* are García Lorca's dramas on the lives of men; too frank and disturbing for their time, they never enjoyed the acclaim given to his dramas on the lives of women. The premiere of *Blood Wedding* on March 8, 1933, at the Teatro Beatriz in Madrid, with García Lorca di-

recting Josefina Díaz de Artigas and her company, and its enthusiastic reception by both critics and public, marked the beginning of the final and most successful phase of García Lorca's dramatic career both within Spain and abroad. The play was translated into French by Marcel Auclair and Jean Provost and was performed in English in New York in 1935; most important, its run in Buenos Aires, with Lola Membrives in the leading role, led to García Lorca's wildly successful tour of the River Plate Republics and the beginning of the myth that continues to this day. *Blood Wedding* and Lola Membrives' revivals of *Mariana Pineda* and *The Shoemaker's Prodigious Wife* made García Lorca famous, financially independent, and sure of his ability as dramatist and director. From a technical point of view, *Blood Wedding* reflects García Lorca's decision to set aside experimental theater in favor of another kind of experiment, equally audacious in its way: "We must go back to writing tragedy. We are compelled to do so by our theatrical tradition. There will be time later for comedies and farces. Meanwhile I want to give the theater tragedies."

Not conceived as a single offering, *Blood Wedding* was to be the first part of "a dramatic trilogy of the Spanish land." In 1933, García Lorca admitted that, if he was working hard on the second with its theme of the barren wife, "the third is maturing deep inside me. It will be called *La destrucción de Sodoma*"; despite García Lorca's assurances early in 1935 that this tragedy, also known as *Las hijas de Loth*, was "almost finished" and "very advanced," no version survives. Martínez Nadal again provides the only details available concerning the "magnificent theme" whose very title García Lorca conceded was "grave and compromising": "Jehovah destroys the city because of the sin of Sodom and the result is the sin of incest. What a lesson against the decrees of Justice! And the two sins, what a manifestation of the power of sex!" While it is difficult to talk of structural unity when one of the three parts is missing, García Lorca did insist, first, that he was writing a trilogy and, second, that his tragedies were according to the classical model, "with four principal characters and chorus, as tragedies are meant to be." García Lorca probably intended a modern version of the ancient Greek trilogies; the common theme was the illustration of the power of sexual energy in conflict with established societal norms and conventions. In *Blood Wedding*, in an attempt to circumvent the passionate love between Leonardo and the Novia, a marriage is arranged that ends in the death of the only two surviving male members of the feuding families; in *Yerma*, the passionate desire for maternity destroys its only hope of fulfillment. All tragedies in the trilogy were to present a struggle to the death between the two opposing principles of authority and personal freedom. The conflict is a constant in García Lorca's work, but his revival of the classical form converts it into a spectacle of great theatricality.

Much has been made of the Aristotelian pattern of *Blood Wedding*. Catharsis is possible because the characters who suffer are closely related. The catastrophe that overtakes both the Mother and the Bride may be attributed to their error, the Mother's in her unforgiving hatred of the Félix family, which results in the death of her own son, and the Bride's in marrying a man she does not love. Because the Mother brings about her son's death, thereby thwarting her own desire to see her family grow and prosper, there is reversal of intention and, because she finally listens to the Bride's story, recognition. The final solitude and pain of both the Mother and the Bride awaken pity and terror in the audience. The figures of Moon and Death provide the supernatural intervention in human life, and woodcutters and neighbors supply the chorus.

The classical pattern gives style to the original source of the play, a short newspaper account in *El defensor de Granada*. The real incident and the play's action are identical, but García Lorca removed the concrete beings to an unreal world, converting them into forces whose incentives are beyond human control. This conversion of the personal to the generic is marked by the integration of poetry and drama.

With great dramatic economy, García Lorca built a logical construct: On the axis of action, the Novia and Leonardo are placed in jealous rivalry for family and personal reasons, while on the axis of passivity the respective parents arrange a marriage in which

economic factors (money and land to be joined) and animal-like sexuality ("My son will cover her well. He's of good seed" and "My daughter is wide-hipped and your son is strong") outweigh any consideration of the Novia. The dramatic situation takes shape in the theme of passion first repressed and then triumphant: The Novia cannot resist Leonardo, the "pull of the sea," "the head toss of a mule," or force, which drives her to destruction. The power of sexual passion overthrows the proposed order (the marriage designed to lead to economic and moral prosperity) and justice, in that society demands retribution (persecution of the lovers), which leads to death: "On their appointed day, between two and three,/ these two men killed each other for love." The Luna-(Muerte)-Mendiga scene thus symbolizes the fatal relationship between the tragedy's two themes.

YERMA

This same conflict may be seen in *Yerma*, if one accepts García Lorca's own definition of the tragedy's theme: "*Yerma* will be the tragedy of the sterile woman." It is the only theme worked out in a *poema trágico* that deals with one character's continuous development. As the action begins, Yerma has been married for two years and twenty days; by the end of act 1, three years; and from act 2 until the end of the drama, five years. This concept of time passing is fundamental; it marks the movement from anxiety to desperation as Yerma suffers a gamut of emotions until she finally accepts her sterility. The entire action centers on Yerma because the other characters—Juan, Victor, Dolores, and the Vieja—derive their dramatic life from interaction with Yerma, and the chorus of washerwomen and neighbors merely provides a dramatic representation of conflicting views (her sterility or her husband's).

As Yerma begins the process of indicting her husband in order not to accept the truth about herself, the opposition between Yerma and Juan increases: He becomes the symbol of society's values, she a humiliated exception to nature's rule of fecundity. Again, as in *Blood Wedding*, at the height of the action, realism is displaced by poetic fantasy. As Yerma resists the truth, so the real world loses its reality for her until, in desperation, she seeks fecundity in magic.

When Yerma does accept her sterility during the *romería*, the dramatic situation is again conflictive. By killing Juan, Yerma takes possession of her inner life, but, like the Novia, she is "dead" to society; by her act of will, she is the author of her own sterility rather than the victim society would make of her. By engineering her own destiny, she destroys forever her own dream. The principle of authority is again set against that of personal freedom; sexual power is manifest in the overthrow of the natural order. The fecundity for which Yerma yearns but which she is denied becomes a destructive, not a creative, force, truly a "scandal" worthy of García Lorca's proposed trilogy.

DOÑA ROSITA THE SPINSTER

Yerma followed *Blood Wedding* in quick succession: The premiere took place at the Teatro Español, Madrid, on December 29, 1934, performed by Margarita Xirgu and her company and directed by Rivas Cherif. García Lorca did not, however, capitalize on its success and finish the trilogy. Instead, on December 13, 1935, he offered *Doña Rosita the Spinster: Or, The Language of the Flowers*, with Xirgu again in the leading role and again under Cherif's direction, to the Teatro Palacio Principal in Barcelona.

According to García Lorca, *Doña Rosita the Spinster* was conceived in 1924, when José Moreno Villa told him of the *rosa mutabile*. This became the central image for the passing of time in a play in which costumes, scenery, and dialogue change in minute detail with each act in order to recapture "the life, peaceful on the outside yet seething within, of a Granadine virgin who gradually becomes that being at once grotesque and moving which is the spinster in Spain." Gradually a difference is made between "real" time and the "inner" time of Rosita, who waits without hope for her fiancé's return. Like the Shoemaker's Wife, her self stays inviolate only while separate from the others. In act 2, Rosita explains to her aunt how easily she could divorce herself from the aging process, which occurs only through the eyes of others. Her tragedy is not the betrayal of her love but the destruction of her personal dream that she is loved.

In García Lorca's dramatic universe, other people, by their presence and their comments, pose a grave threat to the individual self's inner life. At first sight, Rosita is a banal heroine, one whose fussy gentility makes her pathetic self-sacrifice slightly ridiculous; she is, in fact, an excellent study in repression, revealing "the drama of Spanish vulgarity, of Spanish prurience, of the desire for enjoyment that women must suppress deep down in their febrile beings."

THE HOUSE OF BERNARDA ALBA

García Lorca never completed his projected trilogy, but shortly before his death he gave a private reading of *The House of Bernarda Alba*, the synthesis of his Spanish rural tragedies. His best work, it was an exciting shift away from poetic drama in favor of social realism. Its first public performance was by Xirgu and her company in Buenos Aires in 1945; it was not performed in Spain until January 10, 1964.

Like *Blood Wedding*, the play's inspiration was real enough: The original Doña Bernarda kept a tyrannical watch over her unmarried daughters in the house next door to that owned by García Lorca's parents in the small village of Valderrubio. Indeed, nothing is invented here except the story in García Lorca's attempt at *un documental fotográfico* on women's lives in rural Spain. The most violent conflict in García Lorca's theater between the principles of authority and personal freedom unfolds in a closed space whose dimensions are physical (Bernarda's house is variously described as a barracks, a prison, and a convent) and metaphorical (Bernarda's first and last words impose silence). Authority here is the exercise of power to further a moral and social order based on public opinion, the *qué diran*. From the first, Bernarda, defined as cruel, cold, and tyrannical, is seen as the incarnation of that authority. Her instinct for absolute power denies anyone personal liberty and, finally, negates reality itself. In opposition to this instinct for power, personal freedom translates into an equally basic instinct: sex. In a conflict lacking human or rational moments, Bernarda and the members of her household are isolated from the world and from one another. The only solution is the destruction of one or another of the conflicting forces. Madness or suicide provides the only way out of this closed world; both are extreme, neither is successful. María Josefa eludes Bernarda's locks and bolts only in her fanciful ramblings; Adela's final rebellion questions Bernarda's authority, but Bernarda's word is final: "The youngest daughter of Bernarda Alba died a virgin. Did you hear me? Silence, silence, I said. Silence!"

OTHER MAJOR WORKS

POETRY: *Libro de poemas*, 1921; *Canciones, 1921-1924*, 1927 (*Songs*, 1976); *Romancero gitano, 1924-1927*, 1928 (*The Gypsy Ballads of García Lorca*, 1951, 1953); *Poema del cante jondo*, 1931 (*Poem of the Gypsy Seguidilla*, 1967); *Llanto por Ignacio Sánchez Mejías*, 1935 (*Lament for the Death of a Bullfighter*, 1937, 1939); *Primeras canciones*, 1936; *Poeta en Nueva York*, 1940 (*Poet in New York*, 1940, 1955); *Diván del Tamarit*, 1940 (*The Divan at the Tamarit*, 1944).

NONFICTION: *Impresiones y paisajes*, 1918.

MISCELLANEOUS: *Obras completas*, 1938-1946 (8 volumes); *Obras completas*, 1954, 1960; *Obras completas*, 1973.

BIBLIOGRAPHY

Cueto, Ronald. *Souls in Anguish: Religion and Spirituality in Lorca's Theatre*. Leeds, England: Trinity and All Saints, 1994. A look at the function of religion and spirituality in the plays of García Lorca. Bibliography.

Kiosses, James T. *The Dynamics of the Imagery in the Theater of Federico García Lorca*. Lanham, Md.: University Press of America, 1999. Kiosses examines the symbolism and imagery in the dramatic works of García Lorca. Bibliography and index.

Newton, Candelas. *Understanding Federico García Lorca*. Columbia: University of South Carolina Press, 1995. Newton's analysis of the life and works of García Lorca contains chapters on his major plays and his lesser-known plays. Bibliography and index.

Smith, Paul Julian. *The Theatre of García Lorca: Text, Performance, Psychoanalysis*. New York: Cambridge University Press, 1998. A critical analysis of the works of García Lorca that focuses on his plays, particularly their stage history. Bibliography and index.

Soufas, C. Christopher. *Audience and Authority in the Modernist Theater of Federico García Lorca*. Tuscaloosa: University of Alabama Press, 1996. Soufas examines García Lorca's dramatic works with reference to audience and authority. Bibliography and index.

Stainton, Leslie. *Lorca: A Dream of Life*. New York: Farrar, Straus, Giroux, 1999. A basic biography of García Lorca that examines his life and works. Bibliography and index.

Wright, Sarah. *The Trickster-Function in the Theatre of García Lorca*. Rochester, N.Y.: Tamesis, 2000. An examination of the role of the trickster in the dramatic works of García Lorca. Bibliography and index.

K. M. Sibbald

ROBERT GARNIER

Born: La Ferté-Bernard, France; 1544?
Died: Le Mans, France; September 20, 1590

PRINCIPAL DRAMA

Porcie, pb. 1568 (verse play)
Hippolyte, pb. 1573 (verse play)
Cornélie, pb. 1574 (verse play; *Cornelia*, 1594)

Marc-Antoine, pr., pb. 1578 (verse play; *Antonius*, 1592)
La Troade, pb. 1579, pr. 1581
Antigone: Ou, La Piété, pb. 1580 (verse play)
Bradamante, pb. 1582 (verse play)
Sédécie: Ou, Les Juives, pb. 1583 (verse play)
Les Tragédies, pb. 1585

OTHER LITERARY FORMS

Robert Garnier's reputation rests solely on his plays. His first published work, however, was a collection of love poems, *Plaintes amoureuses de Robert Garnier* (amorous laments), which appeared in 1565. A longer poem of royalist propaganda in praise of Charles IX followed: the "Hymne de la Monarchie." Both works are no longer extant. There exist contemporary references to other poems by Garnier, yet only two detached pieces survive, an "Épître au Roi" (epistle to the king) in honor of Henri III and "Élégie sur la mort de Ronsard" (elegy on the death of Ronsard) in honor of the French Renaissance "prince of poets."

ACHIEVEMENTS

During his life and into the first part of the seventeenth century, Robert Garnier's plays were staged and reedited more often than those of any other contemporary playwright. His influence extended not only to other dramatists but also to the genre of oratory prose so popular at the time. Contemporaneous treatises of rhetoric often cite Garnier as a model in their explanations of rhetorical figures.

French criticism has looked on Garnier as a precursor of the classical theater inaugurated in the 1630's. At the end of the sixteenth century, most French dramatists and many English and Dutch writers imitated his dramatic techniques; there is even evidence that William Shakespeare drew from Garnier's *Antonius* (translated into English in 1592) certain scenes for his *Julius Caesar* (c. 1599-1600). Garnier eschewed somewhat the seventeenth century classicists' aim to please and instruct; yet his plays do attempt for the most part to impart a patriotic, moral, and religious lesson to his audience. Written during a period of civil war between Catholics and Protestants, his plays contain general meditations on the tragic events of the period. In several of his dedicatory prefaces, Garnier referred to the subjects of his tragedies as reflections of the "misfortunes of our time." The subject of the Roman play *Cornelia*, for example, "concerns a great Republic torn apart by the ambitious discord of its citizens." His political message is simple: The French must unite against the threat of foreign enemies if France is to survive.

Garnier's work owes a large debt to the Roman playwright Seneca, who greatly influenced all French Renaissance tragedy. Deriving from principles inherited from the ancients, Garnier's plays contain five acts, each concluding with a chorus (the sole exception is *Bradamante*). Usually, a limited number of characters engage in long monologues and spirited dialogues that are primarily didactic, destined to provide food for thought to audience and reader. Rendered largely through an aphoristic rhetorical style, this didacticism allows Garnier to focus on the power of the word—there is little true dramatic action in his work. His plays usually open with misfortune already a fact, which allows the playwright in the succeeding acts to deal with the various political, moral, and religious lessons drawn from this misfortune. Unlike seventeenth century classical theater, which is predicated on an evolving plot structure, in Garnier's plays, the plot does not develop in the course of the representation. His work has traditionally been condemned as "irregular" by classically biased French critics. Such criticism is invalid because Garnier's conception of tragedy was quite different from the theories prevalent in the seventeenth century. Today, Garnier's plays stand as the ultimate expression of French Renaissance tragedy.

BIOGRAPHY

Born in the French village of La Ferté-Bernard, Robert Garnier attended law school from 1564 to 1566 at Toulouse, then considered the finest school of law in France. His literary career apparently began in Toulouse, for he won prizes in various poetry competitions (called *jeux floraux*) and composed a number of occasional poems (one in honor of Charles IX's visit to Toulouse in 1565). In late 1566, Garnier moved to Paris. As a young lawyer, he continued his literary avocation: He became the friend and companion of such poets as Pierre de Ronsard and Jean-Antoine de Baif, and in 1568, he published his first tragedy, *Porcie*. Pursuing a successful career as a magistrate, Garnier left Paris in 1569 to settle in Le Mans, in his native province of Maine.

Very little is known of Garnier's personal life. In 1575, he married a witty and intelligent woman, Françoise Hubert, with whom he had two daughters, baptized in 1579 and 1582. His life apparently ended in tragedy. In 1583, his servants attempted to poison his entire family in order to loot the household. The attempt failed, but Garnier's wife, her health ruined, died from the effects of the poison in 1588. Contemporary observers state that the catastrophe contributed greatly to Garnier's death in 1590.

Despite his renown during his life as France's foremost tragic poet, Garnier led a quiet and relatively obscure life. He apparently made very little effort to curry the favor of the court. He was never rewarded for his literary talents with royal pensions or gifts.

ANALYSIS

An examination of Robert Garnier's œuvre discloses a marked progression: Of his first four plays, three (*Porcie*, *Cornelia*, and *Antonius*) treat the history of the collapse of the Roman Republic as recorded by Plutarch in his *Bioi paralleloi* (c. 105-115 C.E.; *Parallel Lives*, 1579).

CORNELIA

Cornelia, published in 1574, is typical. Centering on Pompey the Great's defeat in 48 B.C.E., the play presents Cornelia's lamentations over the death of her husband two years earlier. Imitating very closely the Senecan model, *Cornelia* is structurally very similar to *Porcie* and to *Antonius*. The first act consists of a long monologue that serves as prologue: Ciceron sets the scene, moralizing on the continuing civil discord in Rome, which he interprets both as an inevitable turn of Fortune's wheel and as Jupiter's punishment for Rome's overweening pride. A chorus summarizes Ciceron's speech. In act 2, Cornelia and Ciceron engage in a long dialogue in which Cornelia laments the death of Pompey; ever the philosopher, Ciceron attempts to soothe Cornelia's deepening despair. Composed of long speeches interspersed with stichomythic passages, this conversation concludes with the chorus's meditation on the world as a scene of perpetual transformation and on the transitory nature of Caesar's tyranny over Rome. Act 3 again focuses

on Cornelia's grief; in a dialogue with the chorus, she expresses her fear that her father and son may meet the same fate as Pompey. Ciceron follows with a commentary of Caesar's present success and questions why fate has delivered the virtuous Romans over to a dictator. He foresees a day when the now-enslaved Romans will revolt against their master. After Ciceron's exit, Philippes, a former servant of Pompey, brings to Cornelia an urn containing his master's ashes. The prudent Philippes exhorts Cornelia to moderate her violent imprecations against a vengeful and watchful Caesar. She retorts that she has nothing to fear; she welcomes death as a means to end her torment. As in the other acts, the chorus concludes act 3 with reflections on that "inconstant Goddess," all-powerful Fortune.

Whereas acts 2 and 3 consist solely of anti-Caesar sentiments, his appearance at the end of act 4 belies the hatred directed toward him. Act 4 encapsulates opposing political viewpoints. It opens with a debate between Cassie and Decime Brute in which the impetuous Cassie expresses his desire to assassinate the tyrannical Caesar, while Decime Brute, like Philippes in act 3, emphasizes Caesar's admirable qualities and counsels moderation. Neither character convinces the other, yet Caesar's future assassination appears more and more probable. The entrance of the chorus prevents Antoine and Caesar himself from seeing their political adversaries Cassie and Decime Brute. In conversation with Antoine, Caesar emerges as a proud yet compassionate and patriotic leader. Despite Antoine's warnings, Caesar, trusting in Fortune, refuses to crush those who would kill him. The last act actualizes one of Cornelia's fears: A messenger from Africa recounts the death of her father in an epic description (202 lines) of the battle of Thapsus. Cornelia ends the play as it opened: She grieves bitterly over Pompey, her father, and Rome.

As this summary indicates, *Cornelia* contains very little dramatic action. Aside from the news of the death of Cornelia's father, nothing really "happens." Although this catastrophe confirms her worst fears, the depth of Cornelia's despair in preceding acts makes it difficult to accept further lamentations. The audience cannot sympathize with Cornelia as she grieves for two absent—and therefore unknown—characters. It is curious that the titular heroine is never mentioned by other, important characters in the play. In act 4, Cassie and Decime Brute, and Caesar and Marc Antoine argue diverse political viewpoints, yet they never refer to the anguished Cornelia, an obvious victim of the conflicts of which they speak. Garnier's dramaturgy is clearly quite removed from the seventeenth century's concept of linear plot and structural unity. The play appears to be largely didactic, as Garnier himself suggests in the preface. The example of civil discord in Rome and its effect on an individual reflects the tragedy of France's civil war between Catholics and Protestants in the second half of the sixteenth century. Garnier does not, however, present the political antagonism in simplistic terms. The audience is led to expect a cruel and inhuman Caesar; however, the reasonable and forgiving Caesar who appears in act 4 affirms that human conflict cannot be reduced to black-and-white formulas. This notion constitutes the fundamental tragic sense of the play. Which side is ultimately right? Can savage brutality for any cause ever be justified?

BRADAMANTE

The plays composed between *Cornelia* and the later *Bradamante* and *Sédécie: Ou, Les Juives* reveal a greater economy and tension than do the first plays. A more discernible sense of unity in the characters' relationships and a heightened awareness of characterization and coherent dramatic structure mark the evolution of Garnier's art. In *Bradamante*, Garnier moves decidedly away from his earlier work. Whereas the first six plays were drawn from Greek or Roman subjects, Garnier used a new source for French theater—Ludovico Ariosto's immensely popular *Orlando furioso* (1516, 1521, 1532; English translation, 1591), the French translation of which first appeared in 1543. Garnier laid aside the genre of tragedy so common in the period and took up the relatively new genre of tragicomedy, in which grandiose characters engage in serious actions combined with incidents and characters belonging to comedy; the denouement is invariably happy. The success of *Bradamante* lasted well into the seventeenth century. Two seventeenth century dramatists (Gauthier de Costes La Calprenède

in 1637, and Pierre Corneille's brother Thomas, in 1656) wrote imitations of Garnier's *Bradamante* bearing the same title.

The Romanesque plot focuses on Bradamante, the daughter of Aymon and Beatrix, who loves the heroic Roger, a converted Saracen, who loves her in return. Her parents, however, wish to marry her to Leon, prince of Greece, who has come to the court of Charlemagne to ask for her hand. Charlemagne, who would prefer to bestow her on the absent Roger as a reward for his valor against the infidels, has decreed that he who vanquishes Bradamante in single combat shall earn the right to marry her. This plan gives the advantage to Roger, reputed the most valiant knight in Europe, over the relatively weak (Bradamante calls him "effeminate") Leon. Rather than engage in this combat himself, Leon has brought with him a proxy, a knight whom he had saved from prison and certain death. This knight, however, is Roger, whose gratitude to his deliverer prevents him from rejecting Leon's request. The despairing Roger, disguised as Leon, conquers Bradamante, thus preventing both of them from marrying happily. In act 5, however, the arrival of Bulgarian ambassadors, who wish to offer the throne of Bulgaria to Roger as reward for his valor in their war against the Greeks, resolves the problem. Because of his newly acquired status of royalty, Bradamante's parents no longer object to him as a son-in-law. Leon, who confesses that Roger, not he, had fought Bradamante, accepts the hand of Charlemagne's daughter as consolation. Joy and harmony reign at the play's close.

Providing a balance of tragic and comic scenes, the play presents a range of human types not to be seen in Garnier's other works. Following the conventions of the tragicomic genre, the piece contains fewer monologues (Garnier makes ample use of confidants in *Bradamante*), has no choruses, and is devoid of the moralistic aphorisms so common in the tragedies. The admirable character of Charlemagne, whose wise and humane words and actions both open and close the play, as well as passages in praise of monarchy, have been interpreted as evidence of Garnier's royalist and Catholic politics; however, the heavy didacticism of his earlier plays is absent in *Bradamante*.

SÉDÉCIE

Having moved away from Greek and Latin sources in *Bradamante*, Garnier in his last play, *Sédécie: Ou, Les Juives*, commonly referred to as *Les Juives*, drew his inspiration from II Kings 25, which recounts the tragedy of Zedekiah (Sédécie in the play). Considered by many critics to be Garnier's masterpiece, *Les Juives* presents a story reminiscent of Greek tragedy: Sédécie, after his failed rebellion against Nabuchodonosor, must witness the slaughter of his children, after which his eyes are put out. The destruction of Jerusalem and the anguish and captivity of the Hebrews under the cruel and vengeful Nabuchodonosor, divine punishments for their unfaithfulness, furnish Garnier with an intrinsically tragic subject matter and with many opportunities for touching and pathetic effects.

As in Garnier's other tragedies, the play opens with the monologue of the "Prophète," who laments the past, present, and future sufferings of the Jews and asks God when his just wrath shall be appeased. The chorus, composed of Jewish women, then reflects on humankind's fallen condition. Act 2 introduces the terrible king of Babylon, Nabuchodonosor, who in a dialogue with his general, Nabuzandan, refuses to show mercy; he intends to punish the rebellious Sédécie and his people. Amital, the mother of Sédécie, begs the queen to intercede with her husband and to plead for clemency. Nabuchodonosor apparently grants his wife's request and declares that Sédécie will not die. The king then reveals his decision to Amital, who receives this news with joy and gratitude. The sadistic irony of Nabuchodonosor's feigned forgiveness and his true intent—to kill Sédécie's sons and then blind him—is clear when he says in act 3 that Sédécie will never *see* chains of servitude again, nor will his sons suffer a life of slavery. Act 4 represents the confrontation between Sédécie and his antagonist, who, not to be moved, discloses to Sédécie his refined vengeance. Nabuchodonosor has recourse to a cruel ruse to lay hands on Sédécie's sons: Their mothers are told that he wishes to raise them as princes in his palace. Sensing that this is a lie, the mothers bid mournful and touching goodbyes to the innocent victims. Act 5 consists for the most part of the prophet's detailed account of the executions and Sédécie's punishment. While Amital and the wives bemoan this fate, the blind Sédécie appears. The prophet invokes the will of God in all things, and announces the downfall of Babylon, the reconstruction of Jerusalem, and the coming of the Messiah. Despite Sédécie's tragedy and despair, the play thus ends in triumph for those who serve God and defeat for those who shun Him.

Les Juives was the most popular and imitated play in the French sixteenth century. When this play is compared with earlier ones such as *Cornelia*, Garnier's evolution as playwright is clear. Garnier had turned away from his period's penchant for moralistic sentences in *Bradamante*, and the break is definite with *Les Juives*. Although the opening monologue is reminiscent of his earlier work, the rest of the play contains essential and memorable confrontational dialogues, such as the climactic clash between Nabuchodonosor and Sédécie in act 4, which penetrate and reveal fundamental human emotions. Although the flatness of characterization in Garnier's earlier efforts makes the characters appear to be simply reciters of verse, in *Les Juives* he creates full-fleshed personalities. The most impressive is perhaps the proud and tyrannical Nabuchodonosor, whose determined, cruel, yet unerringly logical lust for vengeance suggests an unbalanced mind: He equates himself with God, the Old Testament Deity who will not tolerate any other gods. The basic drama of the play centers on his ultimate decision: Will he persevere in his ruthlessness, or will he temper his anger and yield to pity? Nabuchodonosor's counterpart, Sédécie, retains a nobility, accepting without humility his punishment as expiation for his sins against God. Often compared to Jean Racine's great biblical tragedies *Esther* (1689; English translation, 1715) and *Athalie* (1691; *Athaliah*, 1722), *Les Juives* has occasionally been presented on the French stage in modern times.

As with Garnier's other works, critics have persisted in viewing *Les Juives*—in part at least—as a reflection of the author's troubled and violent times. This notion sees the tribulations of Zion as representative of those of France; The sufferings of Sédécie,

Amital, and Sédécie's wives are those of Garnier's own countrymen. The "political" interpretation of Garnier, although perhaps valid in some plays, has distorted to some extent a clearer picture of his work. A critical method that would focus on the text itself rather than on external historical circumstances is needed to rejuvenate Garnier criticism.

OTHER MAJOR WORK

POETRY: *Plaintes amoureuses de Robert Garnier*, 1565.

BIBLIOGRAPHY

Holyoake, John. *A Critical Study of the Tragedies of Robert Garnier*. New York: P. Lang, 1987. Holy-

oake presents a critical examination and interpretation of the tragedies written by Garnier. Includes bibliography.

Jondorf, Gillian. *Robert Garnier and the Themes of Political Tragedy in the Sixteenth Century*, 1969. Jondorf examines the political and social views of Garnier, as expressed in his dramatic works. Contains bibliography.

Witherspoon, A. M. *The Influence of Robert Garnier on Elizabethan Drama*. 1924. Reprint. New York: Phaeton Press, 1968. Witherspoon looks at the influence that Garnier had on drama in Elizabethan England. Bibliography included.

Robert T. Corum, Jr.

GEORGE GASCOIGNE

Born: Cardington, England; c. 1539
Died: Stamford, England; October 7, 1577

PRINCIPAL DRAMA

Jocasta, pr. 1566, pb. 1573 (with Francis Kinwelmershe; translation of Lodovico Dolce's play *Giocasta*)

Supposes, pr. 1566, pb. 1573 (translation of Ludovico Ariosto's *I suppositi*)

A Devise of a Maske for the Right Honorable Viscount Mountacute, pr. 1572, pb. 1573

The Glasse of Governement, pb. 1575

The Princely Pleasures at Kenelworth Castle, pr. 1575, pb. 1576 (with others)

The Tale of Hemetes the Heremyte, pr. 1575, pb. 1579

OTHER LITERARY FORMS

In addition to his masques and plays, George Gascoigne wrote in a number of genres in verse and prose. Whatever the genre, his style is generally direct, lucid, and idiomatic. Several of his works were the first of their kind in English literature.

Gascoigne's later moralistic writings, however, lack interest for most students of literature. In prose, these works include *The Droomme of Doomes Day* (1576) and *A Delicate Diet, for Daintiemouthde Droonkardes* (1576), and, in rhyme royal, *The Grief of Joye* (1576).

Two expository works in prose have special importance. Gascoigne's eyewitness account *The Spoyle of Antwerpe* (1576), originally written as a government report, is perhaps the best journalistic writing of the Elizabethan period, while his "Certayne Notes of Instruction Concerning the Making of Verse," included in *The Posies of George Gascoigne Esquire* (1575), is the earliest extant treatise on poetry in the English language.

Also included in that collection, and of even greater interest, is the prose narrative *The Discourse of the Adventures Passed by Master F. J.* (1573), revised and reissued as *The Pleasant Fable of Ferdinando Jeronimi and Leonora de Valasco* (1575). With lyric poems spaced throughout the prose, the experimental narrative tells the story of a young man's disillusioning love affair with a more experienced woman who is also having adulterous relations with her male secretary. The narrative, lacking in event, nevertheless deals slyly, often humorously, with courtly love conventions as they might apply in real life.

Gascoigne's best original compositions are his poems, numbering more than one hundred. Among the longer poems, two deserve to be singled out, for they share the skepticism toward life and society that is characteristic of much of his best writing: The part of *The Fruites of Warre* (1575) dealing with his own military experiences is lively reading, while *The Steele Glas, a Satyre* (1576) uses the device of a mirror to expose what the poet saw as the decline of social and moral responsibility in the Elizabethan world.

Gascoigne's finest poems, however, are to be found among the shorter poems in various forms published in *A Hundreth Sundrie Flowres Bounde Up in One Small Poesie* (1573), later revised as *The Posies of George Gascoigne Esquire*. Some of this volume's poems that are preferred by critics are "The Lullabie of a Lover," in which an aging lover sings to sleep his fading powers; "Gascoigne's Woodmanship," in which the poet likens his bad marksmanship to his other failures in life; and "The Praise of Phillip Sparrowe," a light celebration of the poet's pet bird. These and other of the poems may still delight and instruct a reader.

ACHIEVEMENTS

George Gascoigne died in 1577, when a new generation of writers such as John Lyly, Sir Philip Sidney, and Edmund Spenser were beginning an outburst of literary creativity that lasted from 1578 to the start of the Commonwealth period in 1642. Comparison of Gascoigne's works to the great literature that followed shortly afterward causes Gascoigne to be considered, and perhaps correctly, a minor writer, but his literary achievements won recognition during his own time and strongly influenced the development of English poetry and drama. At least some of his pieces may still be read with enjoyment.

That Gascoigne achieved stature as a writer during his own time is shown by his dealings between 1572 and 1577 with some of the great nobility. He seems to have enjoyed at least some patronage from Lord Grey

George Gascoigne (Hulton Archive by Getty Images)

of Wilton, later a patron to Spenser. Recognition of his ability is implied by Gascoigne's having been asked by the family of Viscount Montague to provide the masque for the Montague-Dormer wedding, and even more by his being chosen by the earl of Leicester to provide entertainment for the queen's visit to Kenilworth. The poet's appointment to government service very likely resulted from favorable notice by the queen herself.

Modern scholars continue to be interested in Gascoigne primarily because of his contributions to the development of English poetry and drama. During his lifetime, serious English writers, confronted by native and foreign traditions that differed radically, experimented in order to discover the means by which literature might best be created in the vernacular. "Certayne Notes of Instruction Concerning the Making of Verse," a pioneer work in literary criticism, provides insight both into the state of poetics at the time and into Gascoigne's own aims and methods. Consistent with his literary theory, most of his poetry uses plain English words directly and lucidly, maintaining in poetry a native English tradition bridging the gap between Sir Thomas Wyatt and such later poets as John Donne and Ben Jonson. In addition, *The Steele Glas, a Satyre* has historical interest both because it may be the first satire of the era and because it was the first original poem in English written in blank verse.

Literary historians have long recognized the importance of Gascoigne's contributions to the development of Elizabethan drama. As an example of the prodigal-son play, *The Glasse of Governement* has some historical interest but exercised little influence on later plays. Of greater significance was *Jocasta*, which was produced in 1566 and which Gascoigne, in collaboration with Francis Kinwelmershe, had translated from Lodovico Dolce's *Giocasta* (wr. 1549, an adaptation of a Latin translation of Euripides' *Phoinissai*, c. 410 B.C.E.; *The Phoenician Women*, 1781). *Jocasta* was the first Greek tragedy produced on the English stage, though the text was not translated directly from the Greek. Using blank verse, a five-act structure, and dumb shows before each act, the tragedy reinforced the tendency toward the classical mode in tragedy established in 1561 by the production of Thomas Norton and Thomas Sackville's *Gorboduc*, also at the Inns of Court. *Supposes*, Gascoigne's translation of Ludovico Ariosto's *I suppositi* of 1509, exercised an even greater influence on English drama: It not only provided William Shakespeare with the idea for the Bianca subplot in *The Taming of the Shrew* (pr. c. 1593-1594) but also helped to establish prose as the medium for comic drama and introduced Italian comedy to the English stage.

BIOGRAPHY

The life of George Gascoigne, probably the greatest writer of the early years of Queen Elizabeth's reign, illustrates some of the worst and some of the best aspects of the life of the Renaissance gentleman. An elder son of prosperous parents, young Gascoigne first undertook the study of law but then chose to pursue life at court. As presented and popularized by the Italian Count Baldassare Castiglione in *The Courtier* (1528), the ideal courtier was to be gracious, attractive, witty, intelligent, learned, wise, and skilled in warfare and in the arts and sciences; such a servant of

the king was worthy of fame and fortune. In reality, few people had the character or ability even to approach such an ideal, and the extravagance and intrigue associated with life at court were not often conducive to strength of character. Gascoigne's adult life was characterized by legal difficulties, many of which were caused by his own financial excesses and strained personal relationships. His literary accomplishments, however, were extraordinary: He did much to prepare the way for the greater writers who followed him, and he earned a solid reputation as a lyric and satiric poet.

Relatively little is known about Gascoigne's early life, the period before his admission to Gray's Inn in 1555. His father, Sir John Gascoigne, had inherited a considerable estate at Cardington and had married Margaret Scargill, coheir to the estate of her father, Sir Robert Scargill of Yorkshire. Although Sir John served as a public official in his shire, legal records indicate that he and his men became violent with a neighbor over hunting rights, that Sir John was taken in adultery with a female servant, and that he could be unscrupulous in financial dealings. None of the father's failings, however, seems to have seriously damaged the family's fortune. The family could well afford the sort of education necessary to a young gentleman of prosperous family. Sometime between 1547 and 1555, George Gascoigne entered Trinity College, Cambridge. In 1555, he was admitted to Gray's Inn, to study and practice law. Probably while still pursuing a legal career, Gascoigne entered Parliament on January 20, 1558, and was probably present to hear announced the death of Queen Mary and the succession of Elizabeth. As a substitute for his father, Gascoigne assisted as almoner in the coronation proceedings. Soon afterward, he gave up the idea of a law career in order to take up life at court.

Apparently sharing some of his father's tendencies, Gascoigne seems to have spent money extravagantly and to have earned a reputation as a ruffian. In any case, he did not soon gain preferment at court, and his financial dealings led to expensive legal actions. His marriage to Elizabeth Bretton Boyes, the widowed mother of later poet Nicholas Bretton, did little to repair Gascoigne's finances, though she had inherited substantial wealth from her first husband. When she married Gascoigne she was still, at least in the eyes of the law, the wife of an Edward Boyes, who had in his possession property and money belonging to Elizabeth and her children by Bretton. Gascoigne became involved in even more conflict, both in and out of court. In 1562, as the legal actions multiplied, Gascoigne and Boyes and their retainers came to blows in Redcross Street in London. Probably needing to live more frugally, George and Elizabeth resided in Willington in 1563 and 1564, after which George returned to Gray's Inn, evidently to resume legal training. During this sojourn at Gray's Inn, however, he seems to have written much. In *A Hundreth Sundrie Flowres Bounde Up in One Small Poesie*, he published five poems written on themes provided by friends from this period. Both *Supposes* and *Jocasta* were staged at Gray's Inn in 1566. Soon, however, Gascoigne abandoned Gray's Inn again, to try his hand at farming at Cardington during 1567-1568, the latter the year of his father's death. Although Sir John seems on his deathbed to have considered disinheriting his elder son, George did receive a legacy, but it was not, evidently, sufficient to meet his obligations, for by April of 1570, he was in Bedford jail for debt.

At this low point in his life, Gascoigne redoubled his efforts and applied them in new ways: to win fame and fortune by volunteering to fight for William of Orange in the Low Countries and to gain patronage by exhibiting his writing in print. His military experience was disillusioning, though it provided material for his poetry, particularly *The Fruites of Warre*. In May, 1572, he departed from Greenwich with the first group of English volunteers but returned to England in the fall, after a disappointing campaign. His poetry at this point seems to have gained favorable notice from Lord Grey of Wilton, and Gascoigne was engaged to provide a masque for the Montague-Dormer wedding in October, 1572. He began preparing for the press *A Hundreth Sundrie Flowres Bounde Up in One Small Poesie*, which may include some lyric poems by other writers. The last material for the book was sent from the Low Countries because he departed on March 19, 1573, for a second attempt in the wars.

Worse than the first campaign, his second venture at war ended with his being imprisoned for four months by the Spaniards and abandoning the soldier's life. On his return to England in October, 1574, he discovered that *A Hundreth Sundrie Flowres Bounde Up in One Small Poesie* had created a scandal and had been seized by the authorities.

During the last three years of his life, Gascoigne did much writing, most of it repenting the sins of his earlier life. Almost immediately he began revising *A Hundreth Sundrie Flowres Bounde Up in One Small Poesie*; the revised version was published as *The Posies of George Gascoigne Esquire*, some copies of which were also seized by the authorities. Shortly afterward, he published *The Glasse of Governement*, an original play, and for the entertainment of Queen Elizabeth at Kenilworth in July, 1575, he provided most of the literary tribute later published as *The Princely Pleasures at Kenelworth Castle*. While performing the role of Sylvanus in one of his compositions for this entertainment, Gascoigne seems to have received favorable notice from the queen.

Even as Gascoigne was winning favor, his writing continued at a brisk pace. Shortly after April, 1576, he published in a single volume *The Steele Glas* and *The Complaynt of Phylomene*. In the same year, he published *The Droomme of Doomes Day*, a long repentance tract; *A Delicate Diet, for Daintiemouthde Droonkardes*, a temperance tract very like a sermon; and *The Grief of Joye*, a group of elegies that he presented to the queen as a New Year's gift. Also in 1576, he was appointed to government service by Sir Francis Walsingham and sent to Antwerp, where he witnessed and reported on the sacking of the city by the Spanish. *The Spoyle of Antwerpe* was originally written as a government report addressed to Lord Burleigh.

Ironically, Gascoigne did not live long enough to enjoy the success that his writing had brought him. During 1576, he had referred to his own ill health. On October 7, 1577, he died at Stamford, England.

ANALYSIS

Both the state of development of drama during the 1560's and 1570's and the nature of George Gascoigne's dramatic efforts, including the masques and plays, mitigated against Gascoigne's achieving a level of art in drama equal to that in his better poems. His mastery of style may have been sufficient, if the lively prose dialogue of *Supposes* and the verse of his better poems are accepted as evidence, but the court masque, even at its best in the early 1600's, has generally been considered a minor form of art, existing primarily to grace a particular occasion and to honor powerful people. As for the plays, when *Supposes* and *Jocasta* were first produced in 1566, English playwrights had not yet learned how to combine native and classical traditions in order to create great drama. Indeed, much of the impetus behind the production of plays at the Inns of Court during the 1560's probably came from the desire of persons educated in the classical tradition to influence the development of English drama. Translations such as *Jocasta* and *Supposes* seem to have exerted a timely and beneficial influence, but the lesser art of translation, no matter how well done, does not evoke the sort of praise given creators of good original works of art. Gascoigne's one original play, *The Glasse of Governement*, has artful touches but lacks theatricality. An examination of the masques and plays may help to explain how Gascoigne's contributions to drama have earned for him a permanent place in literary history even though he is not regarded as a great playwright.

A Devise of a Maske for the Right Honorable Viscount Mountacute

Performed in October, 1572, Gascoigne's first known attempt at the masque omits many of the conventional elements of the form, which usually included mumming, music, dance, verse spoken by more than one character, spectacular costumes and properties, and mythological characters. Of all of these elements, Gascoigne's *A Devise of a Maske for the Right Honorable Viscount Mountacute* uses only spectacular costumes and verse spoken by a single character.

The writer's preface suggests a cause for the masque's peculiarities. Eight men of the Montague family had decided to provide a masque for the Montague-Dormer wedding and had already purchased Venetian costumes. They asked Gascoigne to write something to be spoken by a professional actor

that would give a pretext for the Venetian costumes. From the Montague coat of arms he gained information that served his purpose: There was an Italian branch of the Montague family.

In the masque, a boy actor, an imaginary descendant of the English Montagues, tells of his father's death and his own capture by Turks at the siege of Famagusta and of his rescue by Venetians, who are members of the Italian branch of Montagues. On the way to Venice their ship was driven ashore in England by a storm. After using 348 lines of poulter's measure to explain the presence of the Venetians, the boy presents them to the wedding party in ten lines, praises the newly married couples in eighteen lines, and speaks a two-line farewell that ends the masque.

It is true, as Ronald C. Johnson points out in *George Gascoigne* (1972), that the narrative moves well in *A Devise of a Maske for the Right Honorable Viscount Mountacute*, but except for its flattery of the Montagues, the boy's tale has little connection with the wedding. Further, the poet has relied too much on words, neglecting the dialogue, physical motion, and spectacle innate in drama, even in a form of drama as static as the masque.

The Princely Pleasures at Kenelworth Castle

By July 9, 1575, Gascoigne had learned more about courtly shows. The entertainment of Elizabeth commissioned by the earl of Leicester and later published as *The Princely Pleasures at Kenelworth Castle* was a series of presentations written by Gascoigne and five other men, each of whose compositions was identified as such in the published text. At least two of the five, as Charles T. Prouty observes, had some experience with similar entertainments at court and therefore may have given Gascoigne valuable information.

Gascoigne himself spoke the first section he had written. As a savage man draped in ivy, he met the queen in the forest as she returned from hunting and spoke poetry expressing the natural man's admiration of the great people gathered at Kenilworth, especially flattering the queen and, fairly subtly, calling her attention to the earl of Leicester, her suitor. Although this performance still relied primarily on recitation of poetry, Gascoigne made clever use of the character Echo, presumably hidden in the woods, to produce a special effect by repetition of endings of lines spoken by the savage man.

The second section composed by Gascoigne is a full-scale masque. It employs spectacular costumes, music, song, elaborate stage effects, and mythological characters that express a meaning. Diana, goddess of chastity, and four of her nymphs are passing through the forest when Diana remembers Zabeta, a favorite nymph who has abandoned her. Fearing that Juno has won Zabeta away from chastity, Diana sends her nymphs to find the lost follower. Through the help of Mercury, Diana learns that Zabeta is not yet committed to Juno. After Diana leaves, content to allow Zabeta to use her own judgment, Iris descends to earth and ends the masque by urging Zabeta to wed. The masque was never performed, perhaps because its meaning was too clear: Zabeta was Queen Elizabeth, and she was being urged to marry the earl of Leicester.

By order of the earl, Gascoigne also wrote a performance bidding the queen farewell. Again Gascoigne relied primarily on recitation, this time a prose tale spoken extemporaneously. As Sylvanus, god of the woods, Gascoigne met the queen as she went out to hunt and told her the story as he walked beside her horse. Sylvanus's tale concerns the gods' sorrow at her departure and the good things they will shower on Kenilworth if she remains. An abrupt shift to the subject of a goddess who changes her followers into trees and shrubs leads to a holly bush from which Deep Desire speaks verse entreating the queen to stay, concluding the performance with a song lamenting her determination to leave. The end of the presentation thus incorporates elements other than recitation, but Gascoigne as Sylvanus has depended on words to the point of excluding other desirable elements of the masque or pageant.

JOCASTA

Gascoigne's place in the history of drama, however, was earned roughly nine years before the entertainment of Kenilworth, in 1566, when the translations *Jocasta* and *Supposes* were produced at Gray's Inn. The title pages of the plays, first published in *A Hundreth Sundrie Flowres Bounde Up in One Small*

Poesie, provide the year and location of production, but there is no indication of precisely when the translations were done or of the order in which the plays were staged.

The tragedy *Jocasta*—its second, third, and fifth acts translated by Gascoigne, the first and fourth by Kinwelmershe—has much historical importance. Even though the title page states that the play is a tragedy written in Greek by Euripides "translated and digested into Acte," the translators actually worked from Lodovico Dolce's *Giocasta*. Still, *Jocasta* was the first Greek tragedy presented in England. By following the earlier *Gorboduc* in the use of five-act structure, blank verse, dumb shows before each act, and Senecan emphases, the play reinforced modes in tragedy that later served playwrights such as Thomas Kyd (1558-1594) and Christopher Marlowe.

The translation of the particular play may have had bad as well as good effects on Gascoigne's development as a dramatist. As Johnson comments, *Jocasta* appealed to Elizabethans for several reasons, some of which are its concern with strife over succession to the throne, its use of dumb shows and long set speeches, and its dwelling on accounts of violence and horror. There is no shortage of subject matter: The tragedy covers almost all the events in Sophocles' trilogy on the Oedipus myth. Scene by scene, the play shifts the focus from one major character to another, emphasis falling at different times on Jocasta, Servus, Antigone, Polynices, Eteocles, Creon, Tyresias, Meneceus, and Oedipus. The shifting causes a lack of focus; moreover, the play's use of long speeches may have encouraged a similar tendency in Gascoigne, primarily a maker of poems. The play, true to its origins in classical tragedy, persistently narrates action instead of showing it onstage.

SUPPOSES

Ariosto's *I suppositi* was a much better choice for translation than was Dolce's tragedy, and Gascoigne's treatment of the play reflects much skill with language. Carefully unified, Ariosto's comedy imitates Plautus's *Captivi* (*The Captives*, 1767) and Terence's *Eunuchus* (161 B.C.E.; *The Eunuch*, 1598) by having a master and slave exchange identities so that the master can enter the house of an attractive girl as a household servant. The young master (really Erostrato) comes to Ferrara from his home in Sicily in order to study at the university, bringing his servant Dulypo with him. Seeing the beautiful Polynesta, Erostrato exchanges roles with his servant and enters service in the house of Damon, Polynesta's father. Using the nurse Balia as an intermediary, Erostrato secretly becomes intimate with Polynesta and wishes to marry her, but her father is inclined to give her hand to Cleander, a rich but miserly old lawyer who offers a large marriage settlement. In order to delay the marriage, Erostrato has his slave pretend to court Polynesta, outbidding Cleander for her hand, but Damon demands that the younger suitor's father guarantee the arrangements. The crafty slave contrives to have a Sienese traveler pose as Philogano, the father of Erostrato. Just as the real Philogano arrives in Ferrara to pay a surprise visit to his son, the real Erostrato has been caught in intimacy with Polynesta and has been imprisoned. Through Pasiphilo, the parasite, the confusion about the father's and the son's identities is resolved, and Cleander discovers his lost son in Dulypo, the crafty slave. No longer needing a marriage to beget an heir, Cleander is happy at the end of the comedy when Philogano and Damon agree on a marriage between Erostrato and Polynesta. The comic resolution is complete and satisfying.

Unlike the masques and *Jocasta*, *Supposes* has sufficient action to appeal to a large audience, and Gascoigne's translation is in light, idiomatic style. He had access to both prose and verse versions in Italian but had the good judgment to opt for prose in English, influencing large numbers of later comedies. In addition, *Supposes* brought the first Italian adaptation of Roman comedy to the English stage, which would make use of many of Roman comedy's type characters and of such devices as disguise, mistaken identity, and love intrigue. If *Supposes* had been Gascoigne's original creation, the play would have earned for him literary immortality as a playwright.

THE GLASSE OF GOVERNEMENT

Unfortunately, Gascoigne's one original play, *The Glasse of Governement*, lacks theatrical appeal even though it has interesting touches in characterization and structure. The first of Gascoigne's moralistic

writings, the play is written in the tradition of the prodigal-son plays popularized by Dutch Humanists, a tradition to which Gascoigne was probably exposed during his military service in the Low Countries.

Structured in five acts, the story line is clear. Two rich citizens and neighbors of Antwerp, Phylopaes and Philocalus, have two sons each, paired by age with the sons of the other. Anxious for their sons to go to the university but wanting the boys to be prepared both morally and academically, the fathers entrust their sons to the teacher Gnomaticus, who teaches in accordance with the ideals of Christian Humanists. The two elder sons learn very quickly but are soon bored. They are easily lured to the house of Lamia the harlot by the parasite Echo. The two younger sons are slower to learn but eager to understand their morally based instruction.

Learning that their elder sons have been seen in bad company, the fathers consult Gnomaticus, who agrees that the four sons should be sent to the University of Douai so that the elder boys will be separated from evil company. Accompanied by the evil servant Ambidexter, the boys go to Douai. Quickly the elder sons neglect their studies and, with Ambidexter, frequent taverns and brothels. The younger sons study. Hearing news of the elder sons' conduct, the fathers send the good servant Fidus to help them, but Fidus arrives too late. He returns with news that one elder son has been executed for robbery at the Palsgrave's court in the presence of his successful younger brother, who is now secretary to the Palsgrave. Another elder son has been publicly whipped and banished from Geneva for fornication, even though his younger brother, now a famous preacher there, tried to intercede on his brother's behalf. Thoroughgoing in its use of poetic justice, the play ends after all the evil characters have been punished by the law and the virtue of the two younger sons has been rewarded by social advancement.

For a play of its time, *The Glasse of Governement* has many good features. It is well organized by five-act structure, and the dialogue is in clear prose. Its greatest strength, however, lies in its characterization, which avoids mere stereotypes. The fathers are concerned and sympathetic; Gnomaticus is a kind and tolerant teacher with little practical knowledge of human nature; Severus is an officer of the law who refuses to punish offenders without firm evidence against them; and Lamia is a girl from a prosperous family who drifted into prostitution because she rejected her society's stifling restrictions on the conduct of proper young ladies.

Despite its virtues, the play seems not to have been produced, perhaps because of its untheatrical qualities. Its use of paired characters—fathers, sons, and servants—offers theatrical possibilities through comparison and contrast, but there is little differentiation between the individuals in the sets of pairs. The play's heavy-handed didacticism poses more serious problems: It creates a mood more appropriate to a pulpit than to the stage, leads to the oversimplified morality of poetic justice, and results in static scenes in which Gnomaticus and, less frequently, the good sons recite extremely long and moral speeches. Finally, the focus of the action depicted onstage is misdirected. The elder sons' wild behavior and the younger sons' triumphs are merely narrated, whereas the lectures of Gnomaticus take place onstage. This misdirected focus prevents the conflict between good and evil from coming alive in the play.

Gascoigne's tendency to rely on long recitations in drama may suggest a weakness in his sense of the dramatic, or more likely may reflect the immature state of English drama during his time. In any event, George Gascoigne created no original work of lasting fame, but through his translations, particularly his *Supposes*, he did help to make possible the greatest age of English drama.

OTHER MAJOR WORKS

LONG FICTION: *The Discourse of the Adventures Passed by Master F. J.*, 1573 (revised as *The Pleasant Fable of Ferdinando Jeronimi and Leonora de Valasco*, 1575).

POETRY: *The Fruites of Warre*, 1575; *The Steele Glas, a Satyre*, 1576; *The Complaynt of Phylomene*, 1576 (a companion piece to *The Steele Glas, a Satyre*); *The Grief of Joye*, 1576.

NONFICTION: "Certayne Notes of Instruction Concerning the Making of Verse," 1575; *A Delicate Diet, for Daintiemouthde Droonkardes*, 1576; *The Droomme of Doomes Day*, 1576; *The Spoyle of Antwerpe*, 1576.

MISCELLANEOUS: *A Hundreth Sundrie Flowres Bounde Up in One Small Poesie*, 1573 (poetry and prose; revised as *The Posies of George Gascoigne Esquire*, 1575).

BIBLIOGRAPHY

Helgerson, Richard. *The Elizabethan Prodigals*. Berkeley: University of California Press, 1976. This look at the prodigal son and repentance in early Elizabethan literature touches on Gascoigne's *The Glasse of Governement*. Bibliography and index.

Johnson, Ronald C. *George Gascoigne*. New York: Twayne, 1972. An ample discussion of Petrarch and Gascoigne precedes separate chapters on the love lyrics and the other poems. *The Steele Glas* is discussed for its satire, *The Discourse of the Adventures Passed by Master F. J.* for its variety of narrative devices, and the three plays for their relationship to dramatic traditions. Includes a brief biography and a short annotated bibliography.

Orr, David. *Italian Renaissance Drama in England Before 1625: The Influence of Erudita Tragedy, Comedy, and Pastoral on Elizabethan and Jacobean Drama*. Chapel Hill: University of North Carolina Press, 1970. Orr compliments Gascoigne's skill in *Supposes* and finds the two plots neatly joined together, with "racy and readable prose." Recognizes the play's popularity and comments on Shakespeare's use of the comedy. Sees Gascoigne's tragedy *Jocasta* as neither skillful nor popular.

Sanders, Norman, et al. *The Revels History of Drama in English, 1500-1576*. Vol. 2. New York: Methuen, 1980. Considers three Gascoigne plays in connection with other English and continental plays in the dramatic traditions that they represent. Discusses *The Glasse of Governement*, for example, in the section on prodigal son plays. Contains compliments to Gascoigne's verse, a record of performances, and a valuable index.

Millard T. Jones,
updated by Howard L. Ford

JOHN GAY

Born: Barnstaple, England; June 30, 1685
Died: London, England; December 4, 1732

PRINCIPAL DRAMA

The Mohocks, pb. 1712
The Wife of Bath, pr., pb. 1713, revised pb. 1730
The What D'ye Call It, pr., pb. 1715
Three Hours After Morning, pr., pb. 1717 (with
  Alexander Pope and John Arbuthnot)
Dione, pb. 1720 (verse tragedy)
The Captives, pr., pb. 1724 (verse tragedy)
The Beggar's Opera, pr., pb. 1728 (ballad opera)
Polly, pb. 1729, pr. 1777 (ballad opera)
Acis and Galatea, pr. 1731, pb. 1732 (libretto;
  music by George Frederick Handel)
Achilles, pr., pb. 1733 (ballad opera)
The Distress'd Wife, pr. 1734, pb. 1743
The Rehearsal at Goatham, pb. 1754
Plays, pb. 1760
The Plays of John Gay, pb. 1923 (2 volumes)

OTHER LITERARY FORMS

In addition to his plays, John Gay is well known for his poetry, principally *Trivia: Or, The Art of Walking the Streets of London* (1716), the two series of *Fables* (1727 and 1738), and numerous songs and ballads. All of these writings are available in the 1926 edition of Gay's poetic works, edited by G. C. Faber, which also includes most of the plays, or in the two-volume *John Gay: Poetry and Prose* (1974), edited by Vinton A. Dearing with the assistance of Charles E. Beckwith. The entire canon, including all of Gay's dramatic works, is contained in the six-volume *Poetical, Dramatic, and Miscellaneous Works of John Gay* (1795, reprinted 1970). The poet's correspondence is collected in *The Letters of John Gay*, edited by C. F. Burgess (1966).

ACHIEVEMENTS

John Gay's abilities and significance as a dramatist have often been underestimated. Overshadowed by his more famous friends and sometime collabora-

tors Alexander Pope and Jonathan Swift, Gay has generally been designated, as he was by Samuel Johnson, a poet of a "lower order." Although his dramatic work may be uneven, it is generally well crafted and interesting. At its best, it displays originality, dramatic power, and a serious social concern. Gay's central theme is the corruption of English society, but while his criticism is often severe, his satire is more gentle and good-humored than that of his more famous literary friends. His work is also marked by a willingness to explore and reevaluate traditional forms, a practice that results sometimes in literary satire and burlesque and other times in experimentation and innovation. His experiments with mixed forms led him to the creation of a new dramatic type, the balled opera, of which his masterpiece, *The Beggar's Opera*, is the first and finest example. Although Gay's reputation rests principally on this unique work, his other plays abound with the same original-

John Gay (Library of Congress)

ity, good-natured satire, gifted lyric expression, and genuine comic spirit that have made *The Beggar's Opera* one of the few plays outside the Shakespearean canon to find a permanent place in the English theatrical repertory.

BIOGRAPHY

John Gay was born on June 30, 1685, at Barnstaple, in Devonshire. Apprenticed from 1702 to 1706 to a London silk mercer, Gay left the business world to make his living as a writer. For most of his life, he was plagued with financial problems, in part because of poor investments and in part because of difficulties in finding a long-standing patron. In 1712, he became secretary to the duchess of Monmouth, and in 1714, he joined the household of Lord Clarendon, a position he kept less than a year. During these years, he became an active and well-liked member of the circle surrounding Alexander Pope and Jonathan Swift and remained close friends with both men all of his life.

In 1723, Gay received a government appointment that, along with an offer of lodgings at Whitehall, gave him a measure of financial security. His friendships with the royal circle, however, always made him hope for more substantial support, a hope that was perhaps unrealistic, since most of Gay's friends were Tories, and the Whigs, led by Prime Minister Robert Walpole, were in control of the government. Gay may have become concerned that the acceptance of a government post would mean the loss of his literary freedom, for in 1727, he turned down the offer of the position of Gentleman Usher to the two-year-old Princess Louisa.

Although Gay is consistently described as honest and congenial, and his works reflect his basically good-humored disposition, his struggles to achieve recognition and support left him somewhat disillusioned and disappointed. His dissatisfaction with the ruling party and with Walpole, whom he believed was responsible for blocking his own hopes, resulted in the strong vein of political satire that runs through his works. Walpole's displeasure with the satire in *The Beggar's Opera*, Gay's most financially successful play, led to the Lord Chamberlain's prohi-

bition of its sequel, *Polly*, in 1728. The resulting squabble cost Gay his lodgings at Whitehall, and he spent the last years of his life, increasingly bothered by a chronic ailment, with his patrons, the duke and duchess of Queensberry. Gay died suddenly in London on December 4, 1732; he is buried in Westminster Abbey.

ANALYSIS

John Gay's reputation rests primarily on *The Beggar's Opera*, to the extent that the rest of his work has gone largely unappreciated. Although none of his plays is as successful as *The Beggar's Opera*, a number of them show, in experimental form, the same characteristics that give Gay's masterpiece its unique form and spirit. Throughout his work, Gay is concerned with the emptiness and corruption of society, and his plays are distinguished by the innovative strategies he developed to present this theme: the use of pastoral forms to achieve a comparison between high and low classes, the inclusion of songs set to popular tunes, the use of literary satire and burlesque side by side with scenes of sincere feeling, the grafting of heroic qualities onto low characters, the use of carefully observed realistic detail, and the blending of several literary forms into a cohesive work. In those plays, principally the later ones, in which Gay is less innovative and more single-minded in purpose, there is a considerable loss of power. Gay's best plays—*The Beggar's Opera* and some of the earlier works—are characterized by a complex and original use of multiple dramatic forms that gives them a unique power and a surprisingly modern flavor.

Gay's greatest achievement lies in his experimentation with traditional forms. This formal exploration, which gives even his less successful plays great complexity and vitality, led to the creation of a new dramatic form, the ballad opera, and one brilliant play which has had an important place in the English theatrical repertory for more than two hundred years.

THE MOHOCKS AND THE WIFE OF BATH

Gay's interest in experimentation can be seen in his first two plays, *The Mohocks* and *The Wife of Bath*. Both plays have a clear literary ancestry, the first from Shakespearean comedy and the second from Geoffrey Chaucer's *The Canterbury Tales* (1387-1400). Described as a "tragi-comical farce," *The Mohocks* satirizes a group of bullies who roam London at night terrorizing the citizens. The aristocratic men of the gang are confronted by a group of watchmen strongly reminiscent of Dogberry's crew in William Shakespeare's *Much Ado About Nothing* (pr. c. 1598-1599). *The Wife of Bath* imagines the further adventures of Chaucer and some of the Canterbury pilgrims at a stop along their route. Both plays are essentially comic in form, ending in reconciliation and appropriate marriages. *The Mohocks* contains a great deal of literary burlesque, while *The Wife of Bath* gently mocks both Chaucer and the eighteenth century society from which its characters are drawn by a process of deflation, a technique Gay used in a more serious and sophisticated way in *The Beggar's Opera*. Both plays, with their combination of literary burlesque, topical satire, and farce and with their use of songs set to popular music, show Gay experimenting with techniques he later blended more effectively in *The Beggar's Opera*.

THE WHAT D'YE CALL IT

Perhaps the most complex and interesting of Gay's early plays is *The What D'ye Call It*. The play mystified its audience at first but eventually became a success. Its title, which recalls Shakespeare's *As You Like It* (pr. c. 1599-1600) or *Twelfth Night: Or, What You Will* (pr. c. 1600-1602), leads one to expect literary parody, but that is only a part of the play's complex effect. Gay works here with the technique, also reminiscent of Shakespeare, of the play-within-a-play. A group of rustics are performing a tragedy, especially created for the occasion, before a country lord and his friends. The couplet verse and excessive sentiment of the tragedy are deflated by being delivered by the simple rustics. At the same time, the real problems and emotions of the lower-class characters are given a measure of dignity through their expression in poetic form. Gay uses the exaggeration of farce to create a blend of laughter and sympathy, an effect not unlike that of modern tragicomedy or Theater of the Absurd. This complex combination disorients the audience and destroys any idea it may

have about the proper hierarchy or use of dramatic forms. At the same time, Gay resolves both inner and outer plays through a marriage that cuts across class lines and fittingly caps the play's social comment. With its combination of social satire and literary burlesque, its use of ballads, and its ability to contain and evoke genuine feelings, *The What D'ye Call It* was a major step on Gay's path toward *The Beggar's Opera*.

DIONE AND THE CAPTIVES

In his two verse tragedies, *Dione* and *The Captives*, Gay abandoned his experiments with literary form to work in a single literary mode without questioning its conventions. Both plays are concerned with fidelity in love, a theme that also appears in *The Beggar's Opera*. They also examine the social conditions that affect fidelity and independence. In *Dione*, the shallowness and infidelity of Evander and the unhappiness of court life are contrasted to the fidelity of Dione and the simple goodness of the pastoral life. This contrast is developed more fully in *The Captives*, in which the imprisoned prince and princess, who have lost all wealth and power, remain faithful to each other and to those who have befriended them in the midst of a court characterized by lust, bribery, and political intrigue. The scheming queen, who uses the king's devotion and wealth to maintain her power, is not far removed from those characters in *The Beggar's Opera* who thrive on a system of bribes and payoffs.

THE BEGGAR'S OPERA

In *The Beggar's Opera*, Gay brought to fulfillment both his experiments with dramatic form and his increasingly serious criticism of society. Although it may be true that the initial idea for *The Beggar's Opera* lay in Swift's often quoted suggestion that Gay write a "Newgate pastoral," the actual work that Gay produced has a much more complex genesis. Certainly his central theme, the sameness of all men whatever their social position, was a logical development from his earlier works, especially *The What D'ye Call It*. The unorthodox form, a combination of pastoral, burlesque, satire, tragedy, and opera, was also a logical extension of his experiments with mixed form. The realistic detail of the criminal world and the inspiration for some of the major characters came from recent publicity surrounding the capture and execution of several notorious London criminals. In addition, *The Beggar's Opera* was designed as a response to the Italian opera, which, with its artificiality, unbelievable plots, and foreign music, was becoming increasingly popular in England. The innovative form of the ballad opera allowed Gay both to satirize the extravagance of the foreign opera and to offer a native entertainment as a replacement.

A final ingredient in Gay's dramatic mixture was political satire. Gay had criticized the corruption of city life previously, but before *The Beggar's Opera*, most of his criticism had been general. In *The Beggar's Opera*, he turned his wit directly on English politics through a sustained comparison between the London underworld and the British political system. Gay's turn to more specific and more biting political satire was probably a result of his gradual disillusionment with English society and his immediate disappointment over his own lack of recognition.

The Beggar's Opera, like most of Gay's plays, has its roots in the pastoral tradition. An essential element of pastoral is the comparison of upper and lower classes, a comparison Gay used in his earlier plays primarily to ridicule the upper class. In *The Beggar's Opera*, however, it is the similarities rather than the differences between the two classes that are stressed. The lower class is dignified by being portrayed as just as good as the upper. At the same time, the aristocrats are described as no better than the thieves and prostitutes of Newgate. In *The Beggar's Opera*, Gay pictures a society that is corrupt on all levels.

Gay's thesis is established in the opening scene of the play, a scene that also establishes the central organizing principle of both high and low societies. The inhabitants of this world are motivated solely by self-interest. Peachum protects the thieves as long as it is profitable to do so; when they are no longer useful, he turns them in for the reward money. Lockit similarly turns his charges over to the justices, or, if the criminals can offer a better deal, arranges for their release. When Polly announces that she has married Macheath, her parents' primary concern is for their own

safety. Even Polly's attachment to Macheath is motivated in part by self-interest.

The one exception to this dedication to self-interest is Macheath, who displays a greater moral integrity than anyone else in the play. He is open and generous with his comrades, polite and considerate with women, and aloof from the vices of the gentlemen with whom he must associate. He is more than once referred to as a great man and is often given phrases reminiscent of Shakespearean heroes. His struggle for independence from the system controlled by Peachum gives him a kind of tragic stature; his dangerous attraction to women may be seen as his tragic flaw. He is genuinely surprised and disappointed by betrayal, first by Jenny and then by Jemmy Twitcher. The second betrayal is particularly disheartening, for it shows that there is no honor even among his comrades.

As engaging as Macheath's character is, Gay does not allow him to remain unblemished. His lack of courage as he faces death and the improbable appearance of four more wives with a child apiece seriously undermine the character's attractiveness. The deflation of Macheath's character also reduces Polly's stature somewhat, although her loyalty remains admirable. As Macheath approaches death, the author's and the audience's attitude toward him and Polly is ambiguous.

Macheath's execution is interrupted by the Beggar and Player, whose opening conversation introduced the play. The Player, voicing the audience's lingering sympathies for Macheath and Polly, protests Macheath's death. The Beggar, supposedly the author of the opera, points to the perfect poetic justice of his intended ending but agrees to a reprieve because an opera must end happily, "no matter how absurdly these things are brought about." Thus, the "taste of the town" dictates not only an absurd ending, a thrust at the conventions of Italian opera, but also an immoral one, for none of the characters is punished. The way of the world will not allow Macheath a heroic end, but insists that he be drawn back into society and reduced to its level. The playwright cannot afford to take a moral stand; his integrity, like everything in the play, can be had for a price. Gay's final attack is not only against society but also, in a sense, against himself.

The Beggar's Opera was an instant critical and popular success; it has also had considerable influence on the English theater. Gay's attack on Italian opera is generally considered responsible for the decline in that genre's popularity during the next few years. Gay's innovative form, the ballad opera—a play including ballads sung to the tunes of popular songs—continued to be popular for many years and is one of the ancestors of the modern musical comedy. The success of the political satire in *The Beggar's Opera* encouraged other writers to attack the ruling party from the stage, leading eventually to the closing of the theaters and the Licensing Act of 1737. *The Beggar's Opera* remained popular during the eighteenth and nineteenth centuries and found new life in the twentieth century through Bertolt Brecht's adaptation of it, *Die Dreigroschenoper* (pr. 1928; *The Threepenny Opera*, 1949). While the play's initial success was partially the result of its treatment of contemporary art and politics, its lasting popularity attests both Gay's originality and his exploration of permanent and universal problems of human experience.

POLLY

Perhaps to capitalize on the success of *The Beggar's Opera* and perhaps to answer criticism of the play's moral stance, Gay quickly produced a sequel, *Polly*, also a ballad opera. In it, Macheath, stripped of all heroic qualities, has been transported to the West Indies, where he lives with Jenny Diver as head of a band of pirates. Polly travels there to find him, but her quest is interrupted by a war between the pirates and the European planters and native Indians. Disguised as a boy, Polly captures Macheath, who is disguised as a black, and unknowingly sends him to his death. The play is more melodramatic and sentimental than *The Beggar's Opera*, but it contains some biting satire and clever literary burlesque. The contrast between high and low classes becomes a contrast between civilized and natural people, suggesting that the faults Gay finds in society are cultural, not part of people's nature. Unfortunately, Gay labors his moral point too heavily, and *Polly* never

reaches the emotional or satiric heights of *The Beggar's Opera*.

ACHILLES

Gay's final ballad opera, *Achilles*, is even more single-minded and less satisfying than *Polly*. To prevent her son from going to the Trojan War, Achilles' mother hides him, dressed as a girl, among the daughters of King Lycomedes. Gay exploits the farcical elements of the situation, but the characters never become fully human, and the play lacks the dramatic tension and ambiguities of Gay's more complex and experimental works. The same can be said of the comedy of manners *The Distress'd Wife*, another variation on the city-country comparison, but with little new to offer.

THE REHEARSAL AT GOATHAM

The short satire *The Rehearsal at Goatham* is more interesting and seems to refer more directly to Gay's own experiences with *The Beggar's Opera* and *Polly*; the Lord Chamberlain had prohibited the production of *Polly* without what Gay and his friends considered to be a fair hearing. Inspired by a scene in Miguel de Cervantes' *El ingenioso hidalgo don Quixote de la Mancha* (1605, 1615; *Don Quixote de la Mancha*, 1612-1620), *The Rehearsal at Goatham* portrays a performance of the puppet show *Melisandra*. The performance is prohibited by the town aldermen because it supposedly contains material offensive to the local citizens. The townsmen agree to watch a rehearsal of the piece to see if it is acceptable and proceed to find scandalous references to themselves in the most innocent phrases of the play, thus exposing their own foolishness and misconduct. *The Rehearsal at Goatham* has some of the complexity of Gay's early works, with literary and social satire developed simultaneously, but it lacks the human characters and ability to evoke a full emotional response that characterizes *The Beggar's Opera*.

OTHER MAJOR WORKS

POETRY: *Rural Sports*, 1713; *The Fan*, 1714; *The Shepherd's Week*, 1714; *Trivia: Or, The Art of Walking the Streets of London*, 1716; *Poems on Several Occasions*, 1720, 1731; *To a Lady on Her Passion for Old China*, 1725; *Fables*, 1727, 1738; *Gay's Chair: Poems*

Never Before Printed, 1820; *The Poetical Works of John Gay*, 1926 (G. C. Faber, editor; includes plays).

NONFICTION: *A Letter to a Lady*, 1714; *The Letters of John Gay*, 1966 (C. F. Burgess, editor).

MISCELLANEOUS: *Poetical, Dramatic, and Miscellaneous Works of John Gay*, 1795, 1970 (6 volumes); *John Gay: Poetry and Prose*, 1974 (2 volumes; Vinton A. Dearing, with Charles E. Beckwith, editors).

BIBLIOGRAPHY

Dugaw, Dianne. *"Deep Play": John Gay and the Invention of Modernity*. Newark: University of Delaware Press, 2001. A survey of Gay's poetry, plays, and other works.

Gaye, Phoebe Fenwick. *John Gay: His Place in the Eighteenth Century*. 1938. Reprint. Freeport, N.Y.: Books for Libraries Press, 1972. Gaye provides a historical and literary context for the life and works of John Gay. This biography presents Gay's intellectual development simultaneously with his literary one.

Lewis, Peter, and Nigel Wood, eds. *John Gay and the Scriblerians*. New York: St. Martin's Press, 1988. These ten essays, the result of the tercentenary of Gay's birth, are important in presenting later trends in the analysis and criticism of Gay's work. They focus on the dichotomies found in Gay's life and writings, the perplexing contradictions that now seem to have been purposefully and carefully constructed. Notes and index.

Noble, Yvonne, ed. *Twentieth Century Interpretations of "The Beggar's Opera."* Englewood Cliffs, N.J.: Prentice-Hall, 1975. This collection of nine essays provides an excellent introduction to Gay's most important play and its relevance in the twentieth century in terms of its literary, musical, and theatrical contributions. In addition, the introduction places the play into its political and artistic contexts. Bibliography and side-by-side chronologies of Gay's life and times.

Nokes, David. *John Gay: A Profession of Friendship*. New York: Oxford University Press, 1995. A biography of Gay that covers his life and works. Bibliography and index.

Winton, Calhoun. *John Gay and the London Theatre*. Lexington: University Press of Kentucky, 1993. This study focuses on Gay's *The Beggar's Opera*, examining its stage history and the English theater during Gay's time. Bibliography and index.

Kathleen Latimer,
updated by Gerald S. Argetsinger

JACK GELBER

Born: Chicago, Illinois; April 12, 1932

PRINCIPAL DRAMA

The Connection, pr. 1959, pb. 1960
The Apple, pr., pb. 1961
Square in the Eye, pr. 1965, pb. 1966
The Cuban Thing, pr. 1968, pb. 1969
Sleep, pr., pb. 1972
Barbary Shore, pr. 1974 (adaptation of Norman Mailer's novel)
Jack Gelber's New Play: Rehearsal, pr. 1976
Starters, pr. 1980

OTHER LITERARY FORMS

In addition to writing plays, Jack Gelber translated Franz Xaver Kroetz's play *Farmyard*, with Michael Roloff. The work was produced at the Yale Theatre in New Haven, Connecticut, on January 22, 1975, and published by Urizen the following year. In addition, the film version of *The Connection*, released in 1962, was based on Gelber's screenplay adaptation. The movie, directed by Shirley Clarke, was screened at the Cannes Festival (1961) and banned as obscene by New York state, though the New York State Supreme Court later found the language in the

Jack Gelber, left, is interviewed by author Ben Gussow, center, at the Last Frontier Theatre Conference in Valdez, Alaska, in 2002. (AP/Wide World Photos)

movie not to be obscene. Gelber's only nontheatrical literary endeavor has been a novel, *On Ice* (1964). Some of the concepts that he deals with in this prose work reappear in *Sleep*.

ACHIEVEMENTS

Whether fairly or not, Jack Gelber is primarily known for *The Connection*. The drama was popular enough to be made into a motion picture, and it achieved critical success as well, bringing the playwright the Obie, the Vernon Rice Award, and the New York Drama Critics Poll Award for most promising playwright of the 1959-1960 season. There were three reasons for the startling success of the dramatist's first play. First, and most obvious, are the nontraditional characters, setting, subject matter, and plot line. Gelber did in the American theater what John Osborne had done in the British theater with *Look Back in Anger* three years earlier; he exposed the theatergoing public to a new world, in this case,

that of skid-row junkies waiting for their heroin connection to arrive with a fix. Second, the play's thematic content is important; it goes far beyond the dreary, desolate, frustrated life of the characters portrayed, for the addicts are really metaphors for modern humankind, much as Vladimir and Estragon are in Samuel Beckett's *En attendant Godot* (pb. 1952, pr. 1953; *Waiting for Godot*, 1954). Finally, Gelber's emphasis on improvisation has had a major impact on contemporary drama. Just as free verse has a special appeal to bad poets and is easily misused by them, this approach to playwriting can lead to horrendous results, but when used by someone with Gelber's ability, the improvisational ingredient reinforces one of the theater's basic strengths, its immediacy, and enhances the participatory nature of drama, involving the audience in a way that recalls, indeed reincarnates, the origins of the genre in public ceremonies.

Much of Gelber's writing since *The Connection* has been intended to broaden the theater's possibilities even further; it should never be forgotten that drama, even when based on a text and literary conventions, is essentially rooted in performance. Some of Gelber's subsequent efforts have extended the innovative strategies of *The Connection*, and others have moved in new directions. The dramatist continues to progress, but he has yet to equal the success, either popularly or critically, of *The Connection*.

BIOGRAPHY

Jack Gelber was born in Chicago, Illinois, on April 12, 1932, the son of Harold and Molly (née Singer) Gelber. The playwright has said that as a high school student, he passed the time playing the tuba and attending movies and burlesque shows, but he never went to the legitimate theater, that he did not even know the theater existed until he went to college. Even today, he mentions with respect the Russian novelists—Ivan Turgenev, Maxim Gorky, and Nikolai Gogol—who originally attracted him as well as Rainer Maria Rilke and the German expressionists. He has also expressed an interest in Buddhism and in "religious states of being."

During the summers of his undergraduate years at the University of Illinois, Urbana, Gelber followed his father's trade as a sheet-metal worker; he has also been a shipfitter's helper in San Francisco and a mimeograph operator for the United Nations. Gelber was graduated from the university with a B.S. in journalism in 1953, and he wrote poetry before turning to dramaturgy. He became involved in Julian Beck and Judith Malina's Living Theatre, an experimental theater group, which mounted *The Connection* under Malina's direction for a run of 768 performances. *The Apple* was also written to be performed by the Living Theatre (64 performances). These first two plays have been performed in a number of foreign countries, including Brazil, England, France, Germany, and Italy. *Square in the Eye* (31 performances) was also intended to be staged by the Living Theatre, though by 1965, the group was no longer based in the United States. Meanwhile, Gelber visited Cuba in 1963 and again in 1967, and *The Cuban Thing* (1 performance) grew out of his experience in that country under Fidel Castro's rule. *Sleep* (32 performances)

followed in 1972, and *Jack Gelber's New Play: Rehearsal* was mounted in 1976.

In addition to writing for the theater, Gelber also has been active as a director. Besides his *The Cuban Thing*, *Jack Gelber's New Play: Rehearsal*, and his adaptation of Norman Mailer's *Barbary Shore*, the dramatist has directed Arnold Wesker's *The Kitchen* (in 1966), Arthur Kopit's *Indians* (for the Royal Shakespeare Company at the Aldwych Theatre, in London, in 1968), Merle Molofsky's *Kool Aid* (in 1971), Frank Chin's *The Chickencoop Chinaman* (in 1972), Robert Coover's *The Kid* (in 1972), Tennessee Williams's *A Streetcar Named Desire* (in 1976), Miguel Rinero's *Eulogy for a Small-Time Thief* (in 1977), and Sam Shepard's *Seduced* (in 1979). In 1973, he received an Obie Award for his direction of *The Kid* the previous year. Gelber's experience as a director establishes him as a theater person in the fullest sense. More important, working as a director provides him with a wider perspective on the potentials and limitations of drama that he can apply in his writing.

In 1963, Gelber began alternating between fellowships and teaching to support his writing. In 1963, he received a Guggenheim Fellowship for creative writing for the theater, and he was a writer-in-residence at the City College of New York from 1965 to 1966. He received a second Guggenheim Fellowship in 1966, and from 1967 to 1972, he was employed as an adjunct professor of drama at Columbia University. In 1972, he was awarded a Rockefeller grant as playwright-in-residence at the American Place Theatre, and that same year he became a professor of drama at Brooklyn College of the City University of New York. In 1974, Gelber was the recipient of a Columbia Broadcasting System-Yale University Fellowship, and the following year he received a National Endowment for the Arts Fellowship. Gelber has lectured and organized workshops on the new play development circuit, notably at the 1983 Aspen New Play Festival in Colorado.

ANALYSIS

Like John Osborne, Jack Gelber burst on the theatrical scene with a startling, innovative first play. In the years since, he has not written much, and he has suffered several failures. However, he has also constantly tried to expand theatrical boundaries, and even his failures in this area have been important. When he has been successful, he has altered the nature of contemporary American drama.

THE CONNECTION

In *The Connection*, his first, most famous, and best play, Gelber established himself as an innovative force in the American theater. His experimental approach to his themes wedded form and content far more successfully than would have been possible in a conventionally constructed drama.

The Connection is an exploration of universal human need, metaphorically expressed as a heroin fix. Gelber's play contains little action in any traditional dramatic sense. There is essentially no movement in the plot of this two-act play because the characters are so desperate in their need that they remain in Teach's room, the only setting in the play, afraid to leave for fear that Cowboy, their dope supplier, might come while they are gone. This is not to say that nothing happens in the play or that no dramatic tension is created. Tension evolves out of the relationships between the room's inhabitants, the question of whether Cowboy will ever come, and the question of what will happen when he arrives. This atmosphere is reinforced by the emotions and physical discomfort displayed by the characters. More traditional plays have dealt with similar themes—Clifford Odets' *Waiting for Lefty* (pr., pb. 1935), Eugene O'Neill's *The Iceman Cometh* (wr. 1939, pr., pb. 1946), and even O'Neill's *Long Day's Journey into Night* (wr. 1941, pb. 1955, pr. 1956)—and invariably plays of this nature are condemned by imperceptive critics who demand constant action onstage. In this play, Gelber's form and content come together with an unexpected result. Following the approach of the Theater of the Absurd, the plot does not appear to be carefully and logically structured. Events that do not seem related (in an Aristotelian sense) occur one after another. Things simply happen onstage, and the feeling of improvisation that Gelber so carefully cultivates is very frustrating to those members of the audience who expect, or need, to have everything carefully spelled out in a strict format as the play progresses.

For other members of the audience, the mood of improvisation is intellectually stimulating; a sophisticated audience soon realizes that the supposedly random happenings and the tedious waiting reflect the drama's theme. If the audience feels frustrated by Cowboy's not coming, they can better imagine how the characters onstage feel (much as film director Michelangelo Antonioni bored the audience of his 1964 film *The Red Desert* for nearly three hours to demonstrate how boring life is for a certain class of Italians). The way jazz music is used here also serves to emphasize the playwright's theme: The essential character of jazz is improvisational, and the music in the play varies according to the musicians' moods rather than corresponding to events transpiring onstage, as would be expected in a musical. At the same time, the music itself provides some movement and a feeling of transition (though, again, in a nontraditional way, frequently increasing the audience's frustration and anxiety as the changes that appear to be signaled by the musical breaks often remain unrealized).

In accordance with the stage directions, *The Connection* begins with the players coming onstage and arranging themselves around the set, giving the appearance of fourth-wall realism, which maintains the fiction of characters acting out their lives with no interaction between spectator and actor. As the actors move about, they are unhurried and seem to have no plans; they merely walk onstage and stand or sit randomly. Gelber emphasizes the spontaneity of the situation by indicating in the stage directions that "perhaps" there is a sign on the wall, or "perhaps" a painting or an orange-crate bookcase is in the room.

Two actors stroll down the theater aisle, and act 1 has begun. The first words are spoken by Jim Dunn, who introduces himself and Jaybird to the audience as the producer and author of *The Connection*, respectively. Those who feel that the play is about heroin should be alerted by these statements that Gelber wants the audience to be aware that they are watching a play, and that they should not take what happens onstage to be literally true. Throughout the play, one character or another directs his dialogue at the audience to make sure that they do not exercise a willing suspension of disbelief and accept the action onstage as real, even momentarily. Gelber does not want his audience to become absorbed in what is happening in the play; instead, he wants them to be constantly drawing analogies between what is transpiring in front of them and other areas in their lives. Moreover, to make sure that the audience understands exactly what the author intends, these asides clearly state the point that he wants to make. For example, Dunn announces that most recent studies of drug addiction, an "anti-social habit," have not had much to do with the subject of narcotics, per se.

As soon as the dialogue directed at the audience is completed, the Fourth Musician asks if Cowboy has come back yet, thereby immediately establishing the concept of waiting. Within a few moments, Jaybird interrupts the action to lecture the audience, reminding them that they are watching an art form, improvised theater, and noting that if they perceive a relationship between jazz and narcotics they are making their own "connection," not his.

Suspense is generated when there is a knock at the door of Teach's room, but it is not Cowboy who enters. Soon after this, two more characters enter, the First and Second Photographers. One is a black man dressed in a white suit, who is swift and agile; the other is a white man in a black suit, who moves slowly, "clodlike." During the course of the play, these two exchange their personalities and their clothing, piece by piece, as Gelber underscores the artificiality of his play so that his themes will receive more attention than the context in which they are presented.

The various characters are introduced by Dunn (Ernie is a "dope-addict psychopath," Sam is an "expert in folk lore," and so on), and the question about Cowboy's whereabouts is continually rephrased. Gelber continually reminds his audience that dope is not his subject, as when Sam, in a tirade attacking society, asserts that people who work and worry about money and new clothes are addicts ("chlorophyll . . . aspirin . . . vitamin") who are hooked worse than he

is. Solly, the intellectual, agrees, commenting that everybody is looking for a fix, a fix of "hope"—to forget, to remember, to be sad, to be happy, to be. Later, he says that everyone is his own connection. At one point, Solly theorizes about Jaybird's intentions in writing the play. Sam ironically undercuts Solly's pronouncements, noting that Solly may be educated and know a lot, but that he is in the room waiting just as everybody else is. As the play progresses, a bit is revealed about the background and nature of most of the characters, yet when act 1 ends, Cowboy has still not appeared and everyone is still waiting for him.

Act 2 opens with a jazz break, and then Cowboy enters. Ironically, as Cowboy takes each of the characters into the bathroom to give them a fix, Sister Salvation visits with those remaining in the room, preaching religious salvation to them, unaware of what is going on about her. The men, including the Second Photographer and Jaybird, get stoned and begin telling stories, and again they turn to Jaybird intermittently to see if they have discovered the meaning that he is trying to convey. Teach takes an overdose, and this leads the characters to discuss why narcotics, particularly marijuana, are illegal. The play ends with Jaybird distressed that he has failed to get his characters to kick their habit, presumably because the actors have actually taken drugs onstage in their play-within-a-play. He has learned one lesson from this evening's experience: "It all fits together," and it fits together on the stage, he tells Dunn. By way of the final exchange in the play, Gelber has reiterated his two major themes—all people need a connection, and innovative theater is an excellent medium for expressing this message.

Besides these devices, Gelber extends the traditional boundaries of the stage in other ways. For example, during the intermission between the two acts, several of the actors mingle with the audience members in the lobby, panhandling, and later, an actor who is pretending to be a member of the audience engages an actor onstage in conversation. At first glance, the drama is chaotic. Underneath, however, it is a carefully structured work, much in the style of the early plays of Luigi Pirandello.

THE APPLE

In Gelber's second play, *The Apple*, several of the devices employed in *The Connection* are extended to further blur the boundary between art and reality, as when the actors use their real names onstage, and when the painting that has been created onstage during the performance is auctioned off at the end of the show. Based on an incident involving cast members that took place in a nearby coffee shop during the time that *The Connection* was in rehearsal, this three-act drama is set in a "restaurant or coffee shop." Like *The Connection*, *The Apple* has no formal beginning. There is no curtain, and the actors and actresses move from the audience to the stage and begin to deliver their lines. Similarly, throughout the performance, the actors remind the audience that they are watching a play: Anna announces that she is in charge of the box office; Jabez comments on "control," stating that "art is precision."

Gelber purposely confuses and misleads his audience as to the significance of the play's title; the audience tries to determine how apples operate symbolically in the play, but the numerous clues that the dramatist presents appear to be unrelated. In act 1, Anna enters with a bowl of apples, and Iris starts to eat one (which Ajax takes from her); in act 2, Iris tells Jabez that she is his apple; in act 3, Tom pulls a rotten, half-eaten apple out of Jabez's mouth and throws it at the mannequin that has been onstage for most of the play. The characters talk about acting the Adam and Eve story, and Ace concludes the play with the revelation that the apple "is a golden Chinese apple and stands for knowledge." It is likely that this is, indeed, what Gelber means for the fruit to symbolize, and this makes some sense within the various contexts in which apples are represented, but ultimately, the play is so disjointed that it does not seem to matter whether any meaning can be affixed to or drawn from the apples. The multiple possibilities of interpretation engender confusion, to the point that the audience becomes bored rather than gaining any insight.

The premise for *The Apple* is simple, even though its realization is muddled. In a coffee shop during rehearsals for a play, one of the actors goes mad. In act 1, the audience observes the madman; in act 2, the presentation is from the point of view of the madman; and act 3 again puts the audience in the observing position, with Ace trying to tie everything together. Gelber has said that the title of the play originally referred to New York City, but "now I just say it's a satire on death." Perhaps the death of individuality, art, society, and intellectuality, killed by prejudice and lack of understanding and human sympathy, is implied in the play, but none of this holds together very well.

Gelber is to be admired for trying to extend the limits of theater even further than he did in *The Connection*, through a combination of straight dramatic techniques, Theater of the Absurd devices, mime, blackouts, parody, slapstick, and masks, with frequent outright social commentary and philosophizing about the nature of art and the artist. Unfortunately, *The Apple* has neither the intensity nor the underlying structural stability of *The Connection*, and ultimately it fails, both as an intellectual statement and as a piece of theater.

SQUARE IN THE EYE

Gelber's next play, *Square in the Eye* (which originally had the working title *Let's Face It*), is more conventional and more successful, up to a point. The play covers a multitude of subjects: life, death, sex, art, and relationships between husbands and wives, friends, lovers, parents and children, and teachers and students. It begins with traditional dramatic exposition, in which Ed tells the audience about his life, family, and work, but the exposition is delivered in an unconventional manner, because the actor enters from the auditorium and delivers his speech like a stand-up comedian. There are devices throughout the play that are reminiscent of experimental techniques used by Bertolt Brecht, Thornton Wilder, and Tennessee Williams—including movies and still photographs.

Gelber has called *Square in the Eye* "a tale and instant replay, about art and artists, marriage and death." To make his point, the dramatist uses flashbacks, a technique that presents the plot out of chronological order. Act 1, scene 1 takes place before Sandy's death, scene 2 is in the hospital immediately after her death, and scene 3 records Ed's second marriage, six weeks later. Act 2, scene 1 flashes back to a time before Sandy's death, and scene 2 occurs on the day before her death. This play contains more humor than does Gelber's earlier work, and despite occasional confusion because of flashbacks, the narrative is basically straightforward. Unlike *The Apple, Square in the Eye* is about real people with whom an audience can sympathize, although some of the techniques used in it can be disturbing.

THE CUBAN THING

Some critics claim that Gelber's next work, *The Cuban Thing*, is not really a play but a political "happening." The production shows the effects of Castro's revolution on an upper-middle-class Cuban family from 1958 to 1964, as their alliance changes from Fulgencio Batista to Castro. On the night before the actual premiere of the play, the fifth of a series of preview performances was marred by the explosion of five powder bombs. The play was considered pro-Castro by many, and poor reviews, claims that the dramatist had researched his material poorly, threats to the actors, active opposition by Spanish-language television and newspapers, and audience fears about physical violence led to the drama's closing after a run of only one night. An example of the "theater of commitment" or the "theater of revolution," *The Cuban Thing* was presented as a happening, a freeform event popular in the early and mid-1960's. As part of a Cuban Action Night, the play was mounted during an evening of Cuban music, Cuban food, and various other activities centering on all aspects of Cuban culture (including politics). By all accounts, however, *The Cuban Thing* was antitheater at its worst—bad writing that could not be salvaged by Gelber's own directing.

SLEEP

Square in the Eye was written during the playwright's first term as a Guggenheim Fellow; *Sleep* was written while the playwright held a Rockefeller Foundation grant as playwright-in-residence at the American Place Theatre. Like *Square in the Eye, Sleep* is more conventional in form and content than those works that immediately preceded it. The play revolves around experiments into the nature of sleep conducted by two scientists and one of the subjects of

their experimentation, a young man named Gil. The play features a simple plot line and a good deal of humor as well as commentary on mind control (supposedly induced by means of sleep deprivation) and the role of the scientist in society. There are also dream sequences (the play-within-a-play technique) simulated within the framework of the experiment. Several of the sequences bear some resemblance to *Interview* (pr. 1964), a revue sketch by Harold Pinter. For the first time, Gelber focuses on character rather than on events or abstract concepts, an extension of certain lines begun in *Square in the Eye*. In his novel *On Ice*, Gelber's protagonist has dreams that sometimes prove to be realities. In *Sleep*, Gil's dreams may not be identical to reality, but they reflect his reality outside the sleep laboratory more accurately than he perceives the reality that he experiences within the lab. Replacing the blackouts used to separate sketches in *The Apple* (particularly in act 2, the madman's act) are interruptions by the scientists as they check their subject between dream sequences. To some extent, the theme of appearance versus reality runs through all of Gelber's works, but in *Sleep* it is dealt with on a conscious level and in an imaginative though relatively traditional way. The result is one of his most conventional and, ironically, most successful works.

JACK GELBER'S NEW PLAY

Jack Gelber's New Play: Rehearsal depicts the casting, rehearsal, and, finally, the cancellation of a play about prison life (the stage author and one of the actors are convicts). Whereas *Sleep* was patently not about art and the theater, this play's subject is expressly the theater. The convicts are present merely as theatrical counters, not to provide a means to comment on convicts and prison life.

OTHER MAJOR WORKS

LONG FICTION: *On Ice*, 1964.

SCREENPLAY: *The Connection*, 1962.

TRANSLATION: *Farmyard*, 1976 (with Michael Roloff; of Franz Xaver Kroetz's play *Stallerhof*).

BIBLIOGRAPHY

Cohn, Ruby. *New American Dramatists, 1960-1990.* 2d ed. New York: St. Martin's Press, 1991. A good reprise of Gelber's association with the Living Theatre, the pivotal place of *The Connection* in subsequent theater experiments ("the trumpet of the Off-Off Broadway movement"), and his place alongside Israel Horovitz, Jean-Claude van Itallie, Megan Terry, and María Irene Fornés, in "actor-activated" theater.

Cutler, Bruce. *Two Plays of the Living Theater: The Difficult Wisdom of Nothing.* Wichita, Kan.: Wichita State University, 1977. Cutler examines Gelber's *The Apple* along with another Living Theater work, Arnold Weinstein's *Red Eye of Love.* Contains bibliography.

Gelber, Jack. "Jack Gelber Talks About Surviving in the Theater." Interview by Albert Bermel. *Theater* 9 (Spring, 1978): 46-58. A long, penetrating interview, touching on Gelber's views on staged readings, the finances of playwriting, and the idea behind *Square in the Eye.*

Gilman, Richard. *Common and Uncommon Masks: Writings on Theatre, 1961-1970.* New York: Random House, 1971. "Bad Connection" is Gilman's opinion regarding the "disappointment" of *The Apple,* which he contrasts with *The Connection:* "Like *The Connection,* the play's cast is an abstract community" but "all that selling of coffee that's brewed on stage and the nightly auctioning off of the painter's work" were embarrassing.

Marwick, Arthur. "Experimental Theatre in the 1960's." *History Today* 44, no. 10 (October, 1994): 34. Marwick discusses experimental theater, touching on the Living Theatre and Gelber.

Shank, Theodore. *American Alternative Theater.* New York: Grove Press, 1982. Describes *The Connection* in a chapter on the beginnings of the Living Theatre and the desire of Julian Beck "not merely to entertain but to affect the audience so deeply that it had a cleansing effect." Beck eventually thought of the play, however, as "deluding the audience." Bibliography and index.

Tytell, John. *The Living Theatre: Art, Exile, and Outrage.* New York: Grove Press, 1998. Tytell tells the story of the Living Theatre, including Gelber's role.

Steven H. Gale,
updated by Thomas J. Taylor

JEAN GENET

Born: Paris, France; December 19, 1910
Died: Paris, France; April 15, 1986

PRINCIPAL DRAMA

Les Bonnes, pr. 1947, pb. 1948, revised pr., pb. 1954 (*The Maids,* 1954)

Splendid's, wr. 1948, pb. 1993 (English translation, 1995)

Haute Surveillance, pr., pb. 1949, definitive edition pb. 1963 (*Deathwatch,* 1954)

Le Balcon, pb. 1956, pr. 1957 (in English), pr. 1960 (in French), revised pb. 1962 (*The Balcony,* 1957)

Les Nègres: Clownerie, pb. 1958, pr. 1959 (*The Blacks: A Clown Show,* 1960)

Les Paravents, pr., pb. 1961 (*The Screens,* 1962)

OTHER LITERARY FORMS

Jean Genet's literary career began with a small group of lyric poems, highly personal in subject matter, the first of which was the 1942 work "Le Condamné à mort" ("The Man Condemned to Death"). Collected in *Poèmes* (1948), their quality has been a matter of much debate. Genet has written four novels, *Notre-Dame des Fleurs* (1944, 1951; *Our Lady of the Flowers,* 1949), *Miracle de la rose* (1946, 1951; *Miracle of the Rose,* 1966), *Pompes funèbres* (1947, 1953; *Funeral Rites,* 1968), and *Querelle de Brest* (1947, 1953; *Querelle of Brest,* 1966). His autobiographical work, *Journal du voleur* (*The Thief's Journal,* 1954) appeared in its original version in 1948 (only four hundred copies were printed), with a revised and expurgated version appearing in 1949. This so-called autobiography is perhaps more allegorical than factual, yet it remains the only available source on Genet's early adult years. Genet's ballet scenario, *Adame miroir*, with music by Darius Milhaud, was performed by the Ballets Roland Petit in 1946. His nonfiction includes essays on the philosophy of art, the most important being the 1957 "L'Atelier d'Alberto Giacometti" ("Giacometti's Studio") and the 1958 "Le Funambule" ("The Funambulists"); essays on dramatic theory, the most important of these being "Lettre à Pauvert sur les Bonnes," an open letter to the publisher Jean-Jacques Pauvert in 1954 concerning *The Maids* and including the letters to Roger Blin concerning the production of *The Screens* (collected as *Letters to Roger Blin*, 1969); and a series of sociopolitical broadsheets, including pamphlets in defense of the Black Panthers and the Palestinian liberation movement. His four-volume *Œuvres complètes* appeared in 1952.

ACHIEVEMENTS

Despite Jean Genet's comparatively small output of only five published plays, which includes two one-act plays, he, along with Samuel Beckett and Eugène Ionesco, ranks as one of the major innovators in the French theater during that period (between 1945 and 1965) that witnessed the triumph of "the absurd" and led to the transformation of the whole concept of drama in the West.

The drama of this period, which includes that of Jean Tardieu and the earlier works of Fernando Arrabal and of Armand Gatti, is frequently defined as "absurdist" or as "neo-Surrealist." Neither term can be applied strictly to Genet, whose ancestry is to be sought much more profitably among the Symbolists of the beginning of the century and who appears to have been as unfamiliar with Antonin Artaud as with Bertolt Brecht until about 1954. Setting aside a precise debt to Jean-Paul Sartre, Genet seems to have evolved most of his fundamental dramatic theories, as opposed to his theatrical techniques, quite independently of his contemporaries. Thus, his drama is far more original than the works of, for example, Arthur Adamov or Jean Vauthier.

Genet was reared as a Catholic, and behind his theater lies a mystic's vision of the world. Everything that exists, exists simultaneously in two dimensions: that of "pure materiality," which is purposeless, meaningless, and in the fullest sense absurd, and that of an ideal transcendence, which is the domain of "purified significance," independent of any need to be confined by reality, the domain of absolutes, of "angels" and of "miracles."

Neither of these dimensions, experienced alone, is tolerable. Pure materiality is existentially nauseating in its unjustifiable and arbitrary contingency; pure transcendence is unbearable, in that it is quite literally inhuman. Miracles are "unclean" (*immonde*, a key pun in Genet's philosophy, meaning both "not of this world" and "unspeakably filthy"). Truth, or "poetry," begins at the meeting point at which pure materiality is enhanced by the apprehension of a significance beyond and at which transcendence is humanized by being chained to some aspect of brutal and sordid reality.

Abstruse as this may sound, this theory constitutes the basis of Genet's theater. At the root of all theater, Genet declared in his letter to the publisher Pauvert,

Jean Genet in 1963. (Library of Congress)

lies the ceremony, or ritual, of the Mass. In this ritual celebration, the real and the transcendental coincide absolutely. The celebrant priest is both an ordinary human being and the officiating Servant of God. The Blessed Host is both a nondescript and rather tasteless bit of wafer and the Body of Christ. No disguise, no illusion, no sleight of hand is necessary. It is the strength of faith in the communicant that will bring about the transformation of one dimension into another. To Genet, in this fundamental sense, all theater is religious: It is, or should be, an experience as intense as that of a personal communication with the beyond.

Because audiences in this century are rarely imbued with that degree of fervor in their religious beliefs sufficient to transmute reality into symbol, Genet had to find alternative sources of emotional commitment capable of effecting the transformation. He made use of three sources: sexuality (deviant in particular), politics of the extremist variety, and racial confrontation, together with a minor but effective adjunct (in *The Balcony*), which is blasphemy. None of these is used for its own sake, but rather for its efficiency as a theatrical device—for the sake of its effect on the emotions and the psyche of the audience. Genet's theater is a theater of hatred, summoned up for its pure emotional intensity, its ability to involve an audience so immediately and personally in the issues concerned that they will transmute the actors into symbols, with no need of illusion, costume, or any of the props of a naturalistic theater. If the supreme poetic experience is that which transmutes "real" into "*sur*-real" without abandoning the plane of everyday reality, then a play that commits the audience to a hatred of the actors that is so intense that they forget that they are in a theater is the supreme poetic experience.

Thus, by a roundabout route, Genet comes to link hands with the absurdists, with the neo-Surrealists, and with all the other leaders of the revolt against naturalism in the theater. His characters are never stable with the stability of day-to-day existence. They exchange identities, as in *The Maids*, they wear masks, as in *The Blacks*—yet the masks are invariably ill-fitting, half-revealing the "real" actor hidden behind them. They work out their Utopian fantasies in looking-glass brothels beneath the menace of a looking-glass revolution, as in *The Balcony*. On the other hand, they engender an atmosphere of violence and of commitment totally foreign to the politically tranquil metaphysical despair of Beckett or Ionesco. In this, they herald the later confrontationist theater of the 1970's and 1980's, that of Roger Planchon and of Ariane Mnouchkine. To write a play, *The Screens*, at the time he did, about the war in Algeria, with the Algerian revolutionaries as heroes and the French occupying forces as obscenely ludicrous, was an act of supreme political courage or one of senseless foolhardiness, or else of calculated nihilism. Or, perhaps it was an act that embodied Genet's dramatic philosophy in its most perfect form: a play calculated to raise the emotions of its Parisian audience to such a pitch that the transmutation of reality into symbol would operate of its own accord, and the supreme poetic communication between dramatist and audience would be achieved with the barest minimum of naturalistic subterfuge.

A final constituent of Genet's achievement lies in his dramatic language. In translation, this is difficult to recapture because it involves dramatic poetry of the highest order; yet its subjects and situations, even given the most liberal interpretation, must be classed as unpoetic. In early reviews of his plays, the epithet "hysterical" recurred constantly. Like Paul Claudel, Genet is a master of a certain kind of impassioned rhetoric that is rare in the French tradition; however, he applies it to situations where it is, to put it mildly, unexpected. His black prostitutes and his destitute Arab riffraff "speak with the tongues of men and of angels"; his squashed-cabbage-leaf domestics have inherited the poetry of Juliet and Cordelia. It is shocking and yet it is right, this "sudden gift of tongues," as Tardieu expressed it, "loaned unexpectedly to the eternally tongue-tied." As with all truly great dramatists, Genet's ultimate achievement lies in the fact that he is a poet.

BIOGRAPHY

Jean Genet has often been compared to his late-medieval predecessor, the thief and poet François

Villon. That Genet was a thief is undeniable; the interest and the mystery lie in how he became transmuted into a poet.

Little is known with certainty about Genet's early life because for both literary and personal reasons, he took pains to transmute the events of his life into his "legend." Born on December 19, 1910, in a public maternity ward in the rue d'Assas in Paris, the child of a prostitute, Gabrielle Genet, and an unknown father, Genet was adopted by the Assistance Publique (the national foundling society) and sent off to foster parents in the hill country of Le Morvan, between Dijon and Nevers. There, he took to petty thievery and, by the age of ten, was branded irrevocably as a thief. By his early teens, he was confined to a reformatory for juvenile criminals at Mettray, a few miles north of Tours, where he was subjected to homosexual seductions and assaults. Details about the next ten years of his life are scarce; one way or another, he became a male prostitute, a pickpocket, a shoplifter, and a remarkably unskilled burglar. He traveled from place to place, eventually making his way to Spain and then to North Africa, where he developed a sense of kinship with the Arab victims of colonization that would later emerge in *The Screens*. Yet he also, during this period, had become an assiduous autodidact who, when once arrested for stealing a volume of the poetry of Paul Verlaine, was more concerned with the quality of the verse than with the commercial value of the book.

In Genet's life, these two strains, criminality and poetry, seem to have run together in comfortable harness for twelve years or more. When he was sixteen, according to one source, he worked as guide and companion to a blind poet, René de Buxeuil, from whom he learned at least the rudiments of French prosody (and perhaps the principles of Maurrassian Fascism). Some years later, in 1936 or 1937, Genet deserted the Bataillons d'Afrique (the notorious Bat' d'Af'—the punitive division of the French Army in North Africa) after striking an officer and stealing his suitcases, illegally crossing frontiers in Central Europe, and running a racket in questionable currency. During the same period, however, he also taught French literature to the daughter of a leading gyne-

cologist in Brno, Moravia, and wrote her long letters in which explications of Arthur Rimbaud's "Le Bateau ivre" ("The Drunken Boat") alternate with laments for the fall of Léon Blum's Front Populaire in June, 1937.

It is unknown which arrest and what cause led him to the prison of Fresnes in 1942. It is certain that it was during this detention that he wrote his first published poem, "The Man Condemned to Death," and drafted his first novel, *Our Lady of the Flowers*. According to the legend, he wrote the work on stolen sugar bags. When the first version was discovered and confiscated by a warder, he simply began all over again. In prison, Genet met a visitor, Olga Barbezat, whose husband, Marc Barbezat, a publisher, could count among his friends Jean Cocteau and Simone de Beauvoir. Genet's manuscripts began to circulate, and Cocteau pronounced them works of genius. A year later, Genet had been released and arrested yet again. On this occasion, among the witnesses in court for the defense appeared Cocteau himself, who declared publicly that he considered Genet to be "the greatest writer in France."

Genet, for his part, continued his dual career as brilliant writer (poet, novelist, and, later, dramatist) and incompetent burglar. By the end of World War II, Genet had met Jean-Paul Sartre and members of his circle. In 1946, he had met theater director Louis Jouvet, a close friend of Sartre, and had shown him the manuscript of a four-act tragedy, *The Maids*. On Jouvet's advice, Genet condensed it to a one-act version. In April, 1947, Jouvet staged it at the Théâtre de l'Athénée, in an ironically conceived double bill with Jean Giraudoux's *L'Apollon de Bellac* (1942; *The Apollo of Bellac*, 1954).

In 1948, Genet was arrested again and on this occasion was menaced with "perpetual preventive detention." The circumstances surrounding this final appearance of Genet the criminal are, as usual, obscure. In all events, Genet now had powerful friends. On July 16, 1948, the influential newspaper *Combat* addressed an open letter, signed by Sartre, Cocteau, and the literary editors of the paper, Maurice Nadeau and Maurice Saillet, to the president of the Republic, "imploring his clemency on behalf of a very great poet."

The president, Vincent Auriol, was persuaded, and he granted a pardon. Thereafter, Genet was merely a writer. "I don't steal the way I used to," he told an interviewer for *Playboy* in April, 1964, nearly two decades later, "but I continue to steal, in the sense that I continue to be dishonest with regard to society, which pretends that I am not."

This comment reflects how Genet saw the situation at the time of *The Screens*, his clearest gesture of defiance against all that is held most sacred in the French bourgeois tradition. Since that time, society has triumphed. It is the supreme irony of Genet's career that the poet who used his poetry to defy society is condemned, not to be outlawed, but to be adulated by that very society he had sought to challenge and to offend. It would seem to have been in reaction to this adulation that, during the 1960's and 1970's, Genet publicly allied himself with those whose defiance of society was much more effective than his own: the Black Panthers and the Palestinian terrorists. During the latter part of his career, he occasionally sought to prevent the production of his own plays; yet, at the same time, he continued to oversee the publication of his complete works. Something of this paradox, and this dilemma, can be intuited from the closing scenes of *The Screens*: Except for a small scattering of short political diatribes, Genet was silent following the writing of that play. In him, the romantic archetype of the "poet misunderstood" has been transformed into a new, but nevertheless tragic equivalent: the subversive poet who is understood only too well by those whom he did not credit with the intelligence or the goodwill to understand him.

On April 15, 1986, Genet died alone in the Paris hotel room that had been his residence for several years.

ANALYSIS

Although Jean Genet's productive period as a dramatist covers a comparatively short period, his inspiration ranges much more widely. His aestheticism, his concept of the drama as a quasi-mystical experience relating the human to the transcendental by way of the ambiguity of symbols, his uncompromising anarchism, his richly exuberant sensuality—all these

link him directly with the enthusiasms of the *fin de siècle*, and clearly he would have felt as much spiritual affinity with Oscar Wilde and Aubrey Beardsley as with Joris-Karl Huysmans and Joséphin Péladan. His subject matter, however, is rigorously contemporary. The problems he explores are those of the post-Hiroshima world, a world of tormented consciences and inverted values, of racism and revolution, of flamboyant sexuality and puritanical indoctrination. At the same time, recalling that he was creating his drama in the comparatively calm epoch of "the absurd," with its emphasis on the ludicrous condition of humankind as viewed by the cold, ironic eye of indifferent eternity, his drama, in the violence of its revolt against the status quo, clearly anticipates that of the younger generation, a generation that still lay ahead of him. Genet was writing his drama in the decade of the Angry Young Men; however, while the causes of their anger are largely forgotten, those of Genet—a man who had much more to be angry about—are beginning only now to be appreciated.

Genet's five published plays fall into two distinct groups. The two earlier one-act dramas, *The Maids* and *Deathwatch*, have the economy of means, the tautness of construction, the close interdependence of characters, and the concentration within the rigid discipline of the three unities (time, place, and action) that are characteristic of all that is best in French classical and neoclassical theater. Their model and inspiration is almost certainly Sartre's most effective play, *Huis clos* (1944; *No Exit*, 1946). Both, moreover, are fundamentally addressed to the intellect of the spectator. By contrast, the three later plays, *The Balcony*, *The Blacks*, and *The Screens*, depend at least as much on visual effects as on language. The three are broad, flamboyant canvases of loosely related episodes, panoramic rather than conventionally dramatic in structure, or rather (to use the term favored by Brecht, whose influence can be detected at every point), "epic."

DEATHWATCH

Deathwatch was the first play that Genet wrote, although not the first to be produced; it is also the most directly autobiographical. The character of Lefranc is clearly a self-portrait of the playwright, representing an alternative direction that his life might have taken. The play evokes the prison world of Fresnes and Fontevrault, as they are described in his novel *Miracle of the Rose*. Dominating this world by the aura of his invisible presence is Snowball, a condemned murderer incarcerated somewhere in his death cell on some remote upper story. The French title for the play, *Haute Surveillance*, is one of Genet's more ingenious ambiguities, resuming in itself the significance of the action on three different levels. If *haute surveillance* is the technical name for the peculiarly sadistic form of detention that French criminal law had prescribed for its condemned prisoners awaiting execution, the term also suggests the watch kept from above by Snowball, in his transcendental state of "death in life," over the rest of the prison and all its myriad inmates. At the same time, and most important of all, it suggests the watch kept by God, who, from the high mansions of Heaven, looks down on the tragedies of humankind and makes or mars (generally mars in Genet's world) his destiny.

Onstage, three men are confined in a cell that is open to the audience: Lefranc, a burglar, shortly due to be released; Maurice, a delinquent who, had he been only a few months younger, would probably have been packed off to Mettray; and Green-Eyes, another murderer, but one who, unlike Snowball, is awaiting trial and is still not condemned. Between these three men, with only rare interruptions from a warder, the entire action takes place in one cell and in the course of a single afternoon.

In the "normal" world, there is a hierarchy of virtue having, at its summit, the saint, the man or woman who, having pushed the totality of human experience beyond the limits of endurance, has come face to face with God. In the prison, there is a similar hierarchy, not so much of evil, as of its metaphysical equivalent, transgression. He who has transgressed beyond this limit is imbued with the same mystic aura of sanctity; he sheds the same brilliant transcendental light (or darkness) over more common mortals, as does the saint. Just as the seeker after virtue may calculate by what act of self-destroying asceticism and sacrifice he may aspire to sanctity, and yet, by the very fact of having calculated, forever exclude himself from the ranks of the elect, so may a sneak thief ponder the steps that would lead to the ineffable summit of transgression, and yet, by having pondered, condemn himself for all eternity to the lowly status of failed transgressor.

This is the theme, and the action, of *Deathwatch*. At the very bottom of the hierarchy is Lefranc, the most insignificant of criminals, because, while he has violated the manmade laws of bourgeois society, he has left intact the major taboos of the race. Next comes Maurice, who, although still young, already possesses the flintiness, the inhumanity that promises great crimes in the future. Then comes Green-Eyes, the murderer, who has violated the most sacred of all taboos, that which decrees the sanctity of human life. Finally, at the summit, stands Snowball, in whom the cycle of crime and punishment (Genet at this stage owes much to Fyodor Dostoevski), of transgression and retribution, is complete. The range extends from petty lawbreaking to absolute evil. The immediate problem of the play is whether an essentially passive character, such as Lefranc (or such as Genet himself), having accepted the fact that the absolute, in his own case, can never be an absolute good and therefore must necessarily be an absolute evil, is capable of achieving this negative transcendence. The outcome is failure. Deliberately and gratuitously, Lefranc strangles the helpless Maurice, while Green-Eyes looks on, smiling sardonically; Lefranc then turns to Green-Eyes, believing that at last he has escaped his ignominious destiny and has earned his place among the elite. Green-Eyes, however, rejects him out of hand, and Lefranc discovers that it is not sufficient merely to be a murderer to shatter the walls that guard the transcendence of the spirit. His gratuitous crime is but one more failure added to the list of failures that constitute his life. He achieves his solitude, but it is Genet's own solitude of degradation, not Snowball's solitude of glory. The other path is closed to him forever.

Alone among the critics who saw the play at its first performance, François Mauriac grasped the work's implications; Mauriac described *Deathwatch* as a modern reevocation of the doctrines of Calvinism (or, in a French context, of Jansenism): a statement of the futility of the individual against the pre-destined patterns ordained by God since the moment of the Creation. The Grace of God alone, and not the will of humankind, however well intentioned, determines the ultimate value of the act. From Lefranc, the Gift of Efficient Grace was withheld, and so, in the end, his only reward is a contemptuous "Bastard!" from Green-Eyes. All appearances to the contrary, *Deathwatch* embodies a theological proposition in a modern context.

THE MAIDS

Genet's second play, *The Maids* (his first play to be performed), is based on a real-life murder trial of 1933, in which two sisters, Christine and Léa Papin, were convicted of having murdered their mistress. *The Maids* contributed almost as much as Beckett's *En attendant Godot* (pb. 1952, pr. 1953; *Waiting for Godot*, 1954) to exciting an international interest in the new French theater.

The sisters Christine and Léa have become the sisters Claire and Solange; their names alone, with suggestions of light and darkness, of sun and of angels, suffice to lift them out of the domain of sordid reality and to elevate them to the very center of Genet's mythology. From the very first line of the dialogue, however, this secondary symbolism is supplemented by another, which is rooted in the nature of the drama itself: The simultaneous awareness, for the audience, of illusion and reality is presented so that the two opposites, far from either merging or canceling each other, subsist together in all their irreconcilable hostility, each a dynamic and irreducible force in its own right. As the curtain rises, Claire and Solange, within the general context of dramatic illusion, possess a degree of reality as maids. Within this general context, however, they create a domain of secondary illusion, a play within a play. Claire plays the part of Madame, a deliberately faulty illusion in her grotesque and borrowed dresses, with her gruesomely padded body that parodies Madame's sexual attributes, whereas Solange, perfectly disguised as Solange, plays the part of Claire.

Thus, all reality is reduced to appearance, and all appearance to the status of a game. In terms of Genet's dualist metaphysic, the confrontation of two incompatible dimensions, the two symbols play an essential part: that of the mirror and that of the double. The "real" is both itself as well as its transcendental reflection. Therefore, when Solange plays the part and takes on the character of Claire, the real Claire addresses the pseudo-Claire as "Claire," even when she herself has temporarily slipped back out of her stage character as Madame and resumed her own reality as herself. The complexity of this doubling is further increased by Solange, who also slips back and forth from her role as Claire (in which case she is the maid, insulting and working herself up to a fury of hatred and vengeance against the mistress) to her reality as Solange. "In reality," Solange is jealous of her sister and accuses her of having alienated the affections of her (Solange's) lover, the Milkman. On both levels, reality and game, the hatred alone remains identical, but the transition from one level to another frequently takes place within a single speech, so that the dualities Claire/Solange and real-Claire/pseudo-Claire merge into each other and produce the fourfold mirror reflection of a single identity.

Nightly, in their ritual-sacrificial game of exchanged identities, Claire and Solange ceremonially enact the murder of Madame. As always in Genet's work, the contents of the dream spill over into waking life, for there is a real Madame, and the maids have planned her real murder, with a poison dissolved into her evening potion of lime tea. The plan, however, goes wrong. Madame has a lover, Monsieur, whom Claire has denounced to the police for some nameless felony, having first manufactured sufficient evidence to ensure that he will be convicted. The police are hesitant, and, just before Madame returns home, a telephone call informs the maids that Monsieur has been released on bail. Certain now that their treachery will be discovered, the maids realize not only that their dream of murdering Madame must become a reality if they are to escape the consequences of their denunciation but also that it must be realized immediately. Madame returns, the poison is ready, but then Claire and Solange, human beings who have betrayed another human being, are in their turn betrayed by the active malevolence of the inanimate world. The whole of the ritual is on the point of discovery when Claire reveals that it was Monsieur who had telephoned. Delirious with excitement, Madame rushes off to meet him, leaving her lime tea untasted; Claire and Solange remain alone once more, their dream of murder having evaporated, with one final sacrificial ritual for their only consolation.

For the last time, they go through their exchange of identities. This time, Solange dresses as Madame but, by her words and gestures, acts the part of Claire the maid, while Claire remains dressed as Claire (or perhaps Solange), but acts the part of Madame. As the curtain falls, it is Claire/Madame who shifts even this "reality" out of time into eternity by herself drinking the lime tea. Thus, truth and falsehood become forever indistinguishable in the wordlessness of death. The poison was intended for Madame; Claire is Madame and, now that she can no longer speak her name, will remain so for all eternity.

This extraordinary play, with its perfect one-act structure, its overwhelming dramatic tension, and its density of thought and symbolism, is rightly considered one of the masterpieces of the contemporary theater. It is a play about masks and doubles, about the evanescence of identity. It is also, marginally, a play about social injustice. In the plays that follow, this secondary preoccupation emerges ever more menacingly.

THE BALCONY

The Balcony, the first of Genet's plays in the Brechtian-epic (as opposed to the Sartrian-classical) tradition, was perhaps the most controversial of those that he had so far published. The very term "Brechtian" implies a degree of social commitment, and indeed the play shows the symbolic representatives of a threatened bourgeoisie (a Bishop, a General, a Judge, a Chief of Police) acting out in merciless caricature their erotic-masochistic fantasies in a luxurious Second-Empire brothel ("The Balcony"), while the hostile forces of the Revolution are actively engaged in occupying every point of vantage in the city. Yet in Genet's own introduction to the play, he denied most emphatically that it represents a satire or a parody of anything, calling it merely "the glorification of the Image and the Reflection." He was furious when,

in the world premiere of the play at the Arts Theatre Club in London, the director, Peter Zadek, portrayed the Queen as a caricature of the British monarchy. In an interview granted only a few days later, however, he declared that "my starting-point was Spain, Franco's Spain; and the revolutionary who castrated himself was the symbol of all Republicans who have acknowledged their defeat."

The Balcony epitomizes the problems of interpretation arising when a dramatist uses social or political themes for both asocial and apolitical purposes. On the realistic level, both reactionaries and revolutionaries are equally unacceptable to Genet's ideal of "pure poetry," for both represent the disciplined forces of anti-individualism that are repugnant to him. The difference is that the first group represents a society that has already excluded him, whereas the second group represents a movement from which he would rather exclude himself. He is strongly attracted by the archaic mysticism of reaction yet is repelled by the individuals who incarnate it. On the other hand, he is on the whole attracted by individual revolutionaries yet disgusted by their materialistic ambitions and disciplinarian methods.

In *The Balcony*, Genet reveals himself as an anarchist of the most classical variety. He has defined his own intrinsic attitude again and again. He is not in revolt against any particular society; he has simply opted out of all societies, which position, in the long run, presents him with a far more difficult attitude to sustain. Genet diligently abstracts his heroes from their social context, shows them as negative, individualistic, and concerned only with sanctity and with transcendental absolutes. With equal diligence, the audience replaces them where they came from and persists in interpreting them as positive heroes or victims in a relative social or political setting. The essence of Genet's dilemma as a dramatist consists in that although he refuses to create a socialist theater, inevitably his negative revolt will be interpreted as some sort of socialism.

These are the ambiguities that plague *The Balcony* and that make of it at once the most successful and at the same time the least convincing of Genet's dramas. *The Balcony* is another of his symbolic-suggestive titles. As the throne (Heaven, altar, or condemned cell) from which an isolated consciousness looks down on humanity and bears away the weight of its sins, the Balcony is a brothel of a special type. It is a microcosm, a mirror reflection of the real world, in which all appearances become reality. It provides costumes, props, accessories, and endless mirrors; each customer acts out, in an erotic ritual of pure appearances, the part in which he or she would like to see himself. Inside the elaborate decor of these tiny closed worlds of absolute illusion, prostitutes and customers together enact the rituals of make-believe.

Two realities lie behind all this aesthetic sublimation: the Revolution and, less obtrusive but more significant, a "theory of functions." In the last analysis (this is the essence of the play), both establishment and revolution emerge as "functions" of each other. If a judge exists, he exists only as a function of a potential criminal: Were there no criminals, there would be no judges. Similarly, were there no bourgeoisie, there would be no revolution. The proletariat depends on the bourgeoisie for its very definition, its very existence. The one is the mirror reflection of the other; as always in Genet, the reflection is more real than the image. (Once the Queen is dead, and Madame Irma, the "Madame" of the Brothel, "plays" the Queen, the "real" revolution is crushed immediately.) By destroying the establishment, the Revolution destroys its own identity, which was defined and given existence by its function, which was that of opposing the establishment. Similarly, the Chief of Police (the most enigmatic figure in the play) is defined as the opponent of the Revolution. In annihilating the Revolution, he destroys his own function and thus annihilates himself, leaving himself only the brothel as an ultimate refuge, with his quest for his own mausoleum, whereby he might perpetuate his own nonfunctional existence as a myth.

The Balcony is the most complex of Genet's plays, the most ambiguous, and yet one of the most impressive. In a social situation, a person is what he or she is seen to be by others. This other-created self is given substance by the individual's appearance—his or her uniform, robes, vestments. These props are the power symbols that constitute the person's essence, yet power is defined by the object over which that power may be exercised. Remove that object, and both the power and the symbol of power, hence the identity, evaporate into nothingness. A "function" must function; where there is no context in which functioning is possible, the power is thrown back on itself. To be, the image can only contemplate its own reflection in the mirror. Therefore, in a sense, the first four mirror scenes of *The Balcony* should also recur at the end. Had the play been written by Beckett, this might have happened. As it is, there are suggestions: "In a little while, I'll have to start all over again," says Madame Irma in her concluding monologue, "put all the lights on again . . . dress up . . . distribute roles again . . . assume my own." Basically, the structure of Genet's later plays is too Brechtian-linear to allow this type of cyclical conclusion to be fully developed. *The Balcony* is a transitional play, and the experimental audacities of its form are not quite adequate to express the sophistication of its content.

If Genet, together with many of his contemporaries, refused absolutely to commit himself to any ideology of the Left, this was for literary as well as for political reasons. To the poet, the most repulsive feature of the established Left was its reliance on platitudes and slogans. It needed the freakish genius of a Vladimir Mayakovsky to transmute slogans into poetry. For the rest, it is the seemingly irrevocable mission of the Left to crush poetry into slogans.

THE BLACKS

Genet's reply to this, both in *The Blacks* and in *The Screens*, was to reverse the accepted order of moral values accorded to either side in his confrontation of ideological opposites, thus giving the conventional platitudes a startling and shocking originality when bestowed on the right side for the wrong reason or on the wrong side for the right reason. In the drama of the political platitude (as in the melodrama, from which such drama springs), there are heroes and villains; the revolutionary heroes are good, while the reactionary villains are bad. In Genet's variant, the revolutionary "heroes" are bad (degraded, murderous, and treacherous), while the reactionary "villains" are good (beautiful, idealistic, and constructive).

The structure of *The Blacks* is that of a total theater—that is, of a theater employing all the media that contribute to the dramatic impact of the spectacle. It uses music, dance, rhythm, and ritual; contrasts masks and faces, illusion and reality; and employs different levels, exploiting a multiplicity of stage dimensions (Antonin Artaud's "poetry in space"). It borrows its techniques from the jazz band and the jam session, from the church service and from the music hall, from the circus, and even, in the episodes of orchestrated laughter, from the stylized, cadenced mockery of the Aristophanic chorus. In such a context, the chief function and dramatic value of language is realized as a medium of incantation. This play has more in common with music than with normal drama, wherein representation has given way to abstraction. The aim of convincing an audience, assumed to be intellectual, has been replaced by that of rousing it to a state of mystical or hysterical delirium, using means that the high priest shares with the demagogue and the jazz trumpeter, with the snake charmer. The final effectiveness of the piece lies in the fact that it is by no means devoid of ideas. The dialectic is there, but it is conveyed by implication rather than by statement.

The Blacks has little or no coherent story. Rather, it has a theme (the theme of black and white) and a structure that gradually reveals itself as having significance on different and unsuspected levels. The actors are black actors. They are introduced as a group of blacks with ordinary, everyday backgrounds—cook, sewing maid, medical student, prostitute—but have now come together to produce an entertainment, a "clown-show." Meanwhile, entombed on the stage in a white-draped, flower-covered catafalque lies the corpse of a murdered white woman. Around this, a further dimension of illusion is developed: the rhythms, rituals, and ceremonies of hatred and violence. Observing this, high up in their gallery, sit five blacks masked as whites: the Queen, the Missionary, the Governor, the Judge, and the Valet, providing yet a further dimension, an audience for the clownery of the others. What precisely is this audience? For the actors below them on the stage, the court both is and is not an audience. It watches them, listens to them,

applauds them, yet it is composed of actors acting as an audience, an unreal mirror reflection of the "real" audience in the pit and stalls facing them. It is also a chorus and, in symbolic form, the enemy. So the play develops for more than half its length, working out permutations and combinations with the elusive material of dimensions, of plays within plays and audiences within audiences, until suddenly, with the dramatic entry of Ville-de-Saint-Nazaire, the whole delicate structure collapses with the revelation of still another dimension: a play outside the play. Ville-de-Saint-Nazaire is not concerned with any dream of village love or of ritually murdered whites. He is a real political agitator (but what, at this point, is "real"?) who has been attending a secret meeting "just up the street outside the theater," at which not a white but another black has been condemned to execution for having betrayed the clandestine Society for Black Rights.

Meanwhile, all the others—actors, audience, true or false, black whites, and white blacks—disintegrate into dreams. The whole evening's clownery was merely a deliberate diversion (as Archibald warned from the beginning), a smoke screen to keep the audience's attention fixed while the executive committee got on with its job. The white court strips off its masks, the others strip off their personalities, and for an instant, they are any group of real blacks having an urgent political discussion. The former Valet, that erstwhile masked caricature of the bourgeois intellectual or artist in capitalist society, is now revealed as the cell leader, whose orders are obeyed instantly and without question. Eventually, he commands his combat section to take up their parts again and to resume the act; thus the audience is back in the dimensions of illusion. The victory, however, lies with Genet. In the closing scenes, when the audience knows that all is merely a "clown-show," the hard, political play outside the play moves even further from reality than the actors portraying actors of the play itself. In yet another dimension, there is more reality—immediate political reality this time—in the notion of an armed and organized Direct Action Committee for Negro Rights than there is in ritualistic dances about the imaginary catafalque of an imaginary murdered white.

Which is real and which is illusion? Compared with *The Blacks*, Luigi Pirandello's experiments with the same problem seem almost childish. Ultimately, since there must be an end, the whole masked court of whites makes its way reluctantly toward the "infernal regions," enveloped in a rain of muddled colonialistic platitudes. There is neither triumph nor fear on either side. What must be, must be. For the blacks, their victory over the whites is scarcely worth a comment; it is all in the day's work. Their real problems lie elsewhere.

In this play, masks reveal even more than they hide of the reality beneath. Among these, for the blacks, the most disquieting is the mask of language. These blacks, for all their blackness, are speaking with the language of the whites, not even Creole or *petit-nègre* (pidgin French), but the purest, most classical language of the Princesse de Clèves. The face masks can be removed easily enough, the language mask, never. Thus, when Village makes love to Vertu, he makes love to her in white language, and his black love for a black girl is transmuted into a white love for a white girl and thus becomes, even in its purest poetry, a pure falsehood. The Judge, the Governor, and the Missionary are gone, but the language remains: the irremovable trace of servitude imposed by a benevolent paternalism. In the final analysis, the black imitates more than the white: He imitates the very language that condemns his imitation. Such is the conclusion of *The Blacks* and the ultimate tragedy of colonialism.

THE SCREENS

Written in 1959-1960, at the climax of France's catastrophic conflict with Algerian nationalism, it was inconceivable that *The Screens*, a play that ridiculed French patriotism and that caricatured as ludicrous buffoons conscript members of the French Army on active service, should be performed in Paris—or indeed anywhere within metropolitan France. Fragmented versions in translation were presented in Berlin and in London; the true world premiere was given in Stockholm in Swedish. Only some four years after the war had concluded had the accompanying emotions subsided sufficiently to allow a tentative, carefully spaced run at the Théâtre National de l'Odéon in Paris; even then, there were "incidents."

Insofar as Brecht must be considered a major influence on Genet's later drama, *The Screens* is the most purely Brechtian of all his plays. Explicit argument is reduced to a minimum, and traditional psychology has dwindled to the vanishing point. Instead, the dramatic effect is created by a series of brilliant visual images, stylized and simplified almost to the point of primitivism, by violence, slogans, caricature, deliberate vulgarity, and by the overwhelming impression of hatred that remains in the atmosphere long after the actors of each individual scene have vanished. Most of the more obsessive themes and problems of Genet's earlier dramas are present but are now reduced to their visual equivalent, acted out in front of the four levels of screens on the stage, on which the performers roughly chalk in a symbolic decor as required (a technique derived from cabaret shows of the period). Beneath this camouflage of primitivism, parody, and purely dramatic spectacle, traces of ideas reveal that Genet's complex vision of the world has by no means ceased to evolve.

The "hero" of the drama is Saïd, the most abject, cowardly, debased, and unlovable of all the *fellahin*, and the "heroines" are Warda and Malika, the ritualistically costumed and painted whores of the brothel. The "villains" are, on the one hand, the European colonists and the French Army of Occupation; on the other hand, and rather more ambiguously, they are the Arab militant insurgents, armed and disciplined, the very mirror reflection of the European occupiers whom they are driving back into the sea. In this respect, but only in this respect, *The Screens* recapitulates the argument of *The Blacks*; to maintain their identity in the face of the power of the white peoples, the oppressed of the Third World must assimilate the technology and master the efficiency of the Europeans and, in so doing, destroy forever the authentic heritage of those whom they are seeking to defend. It is a dilemma from which there is no escape, one of the profoundest tragedies of the modern world.

Beneath the conflict of French and Arabs that forms the obvious subject of the play lies a much profounder and, for Genet, more immediately relevant conflict: that between anarchy and organization. If the main division of the characters is into white and brown, there is also a secondary division that cuts right across the first. On the one hand are anarchists, the reversers of conventional values so dear to Genet's heart—Saïd; his mother; Leïla, his wife; Kadidja; and Ommu—and on the other, the orthodox forces of political reality. These include not only the colonials and the *Légionnaires* but also the disciplined Arab combatants themselves, who, in the final moments of the play, execute Saïd and, in so doing, relegate Genet's dreams to where they belong: to the world of poetry, which, in political terms, is the world of acquiescent nonfunction, the world of death.

When the audience first meets Saïd, he is on his way to his wedding, accompanied by his mother. Like that of Genet himself, Saïd's authenticity resides in his abjection. He plunges downward into "sanctity" through his experiences of degradation and of evil. Leïla, his bride (the Arabic word means "night"), has only one outstanding individual characteristic: her ugliness. She is "the ugliest woman in the next town and all the towns around." Progressively her ugliness becomes, for herself, for Saïd, and for his mother, the symbol of a total negativity, a total rejection of "accepted" values, aesthetic or otherwise. Meanwhile, Saïd progresses through ever more categoric stages of negation. From an outcast he becomes a thief; from a thief, a jailbird; from a jailbird, a traitor. His treachery is his final negation of positive values because he is betraying not only his own but also his creator's committed cause; however, it is all so useless. As had happened with the prostitute Chantal in *The Balcony*, the Revolution seizes on his image and elevates it into that of a hero. It transforms him into a symbol of himself, thus condemning him to the dimension of death and of unreality, even while he is yet alive. Just as Genet himself had been transformed from a criminal into the Poet (and thus transmuted from an ignominious life into a glorious death while alive), so Saïd is transmuted from his rebellious and abject self into a Glorious Cause. Death, after that, is a relief.

The death of Saïd, however, is no solution to Genet's own problem; it merely places Genet himself in the position of having to abandon either politics or poetry, having failed successively, through *The Balcony*, *The Blacks*, and *The Screens*, in his attempt to reconcile the two. "Certain truths are not applicable, otherwise they'd die," says Ommu toward the end of *The Screens*. "They mustn't die, but live through the songs they've become." Poetry, in fact, is one thing, and politics, another. One is life, and the other is death. The only question is, which is which? Such is the insoluble problem left hanging in the air at the end of *The Screens*. "It's dead we want you, *dead*," says Ommu to Saïd. "That's leaving me dead alive," replies Saïd. After the writing of *The Screens*, Genet, caught finally in the trap of politics, would appear to have existed "dead alive."

OTHER MAJOR WORKS

LONG FICTION: *Notre-Dame des Fleurs*, 1944, 1951 (*Our Lady of the Flowers*, 1949); *Miracle de la rose*, 1946, 1951 (*Miracle of the Rose*, 1966); *Pompes funèbres*, 1947, 1953 (*Funeral Rites*, 1968); *Querelle de Brest*, 1947, 1953 (*Querelle of Brest*, 1966).

POETRY: *Poèmes*, 1948; *Treasures of the Night: The Collected Poems of Jean Genet*, 1980.

NONFICTION: *Journal du voleur*, 1948, 1949 (*The Thief's Journal*, 1954); *Lettres à Roger Blin*, 1966 (*Letters to Roger Blin*, 1969).

MISCELLANEOUS: *Œuvres complètes*, 1952 (4 volumes).

BIBLIOGRAPHY

Dobrez, L. A. C. *The Existential and Its Exits: Literary and Philosophical Perspectives on the Works of Beckett, Ionesco, Genet, and Pinter.* New York: St. Martin's Press, 1986. Dobrez examines existentialism in the works of Genet as well as those of Samuel Beckett, Eugène Ionesco, and Harold Pinter. Contains index.

Hauptman, Robert. *The Pathological Vision: Jean Genet, Louis-Ferdinand Céline, and Tennessee Williams.* American University Studies series. New York: Peter Lang, 1984. Hauptman examines ethics, specifically the presence of evil, in the works of Genet, Céline, and Williams. Contains bibliography.

Knapp, Bettina Liebowitz. *Jean Genet*. Boston: Twayne, 1989. Knapp looks at Genet's life and analyzes and interprets his works. Includes bibliography and index.

Plunka, Gene A. *The Rites of Passage of Jean Genet: The Art and Aesthetics of Risk Taking*. London: Associated University Presses, 1992. This analysis of Genet and his works focuses on the psychology of risk taking. Includes bibliography and index.

Read, Barbara and Ian Birchall, eds. *Fowers and Revolution: A Collection of Writings on Jean Genet*. London: Middlesex University Press, 1997. This collection of essays examines the life and criticizes and interprets the works of Genet. Includes index.

Sartre, Jean-Paul. *Saint-Genet, Actor and Martyr*. 1963. Reprint. New York: Pantheon Books, 1983. The French writer Sartre's biography of Genet. Includes bibliography.

Stewart, Harry E., and Rob Roy McGregor. *Jean Genet: From Fascism to Nihilism*. New York: P. Lang, 1993. The authors examine how fascism, nihilism, and other political currents affected the writings of Genet.

White, Edmund. *Genet: A Biography*. New York: Random House, 1994. A look at the life of the French writer. Includes bibliography and index.

Richard N. Coe

MICHEL DE GHELDERODE
Adémar-Adolphe-Louis Martens

Born: Ixelles, Belgium; April 3, 1898
Died: Scharbeek, Belgium; April 1, 1962

PRINCIPAL DRAMA

Piet Bouteille, wr. 1919, pr., pb. 1925 (as *Oude Piet*; English translation, 1964)

La Mort du docteur, pb. 1926, pr. 1928 (*The Death of Doctor Faust*, 1964)

Christophe Columb, pb. 1928, pr. 1929 (*Christopher Columbus*, 1964)

Escurial, pb. 1928, pr. 1929 (English translation, 1957)

Fastes d'enfer, wr. 1929, pb. 1943, pr. 1949 (*Chronicles of Hell*, 1960)

Barabbas, pr. in Flemish 1929, pb. 1932, pr. in French 1934 (English translation, 1960)

Pantagleize, pr. in Flemish 1930, pr. in French 1934, pb. 1934 (English translation 1960)

Sortie de l'acteur, wr. 1930, pb. 1942, pr. in Flemish 1961, pr. in French 1962 (*The Actor Makes His Exit*, 1990)

Magie rouge, pr. 1934, pb. 1935 (*Red Magic*, 1964)

Mademoiselle Jaïre, wr. 1934, pb. 1942, pr. 1949 (*Miss Jairus*, 1964)

La Balade du grand macabre, pb. 1935, pr. 1953

L'École des bouffons, wr. 1937, pb. 1942, pr. 1953 (*School of Jesters*, 1968)

Sire Halewyn, pr. 1938, pb. 1943 (*Lord Halewyn*, 1960)

Hop, Signor!, pb. 1938, pr. 1942 (English translation, 1964)

Théâtre, pb. 1950-1957 (5 volumes)

Marie la misérable, pr. 1952, pb. 1955

Seven Plays, pb. 1960, 1964 (2 volumes)

The Strange Rider and Seven Other Plays, pb. 1967

Ghelderode, pb. 1990

OTHER LITERARY FORMS

Michel de Ghelderode is known and remembered primarily for his singular, often highly unconventional approach to drama. During the course of his career, however, he also produced several volumes of essays and short stories as well as poetry, most of the latter supposedly written by a fictitious undertaker named Philostène Costenoble.

ACHIEVEMENTS

Described by one drama critic as "our man in the sixteenth century," Michel de Ghelderode worked for years in solitude and near-isolation toward the perfection of his intensely personal dramatic art. Only after World War II, with the author approaching fifty years of age, did the assembled corpus of his plays even begin to attract critical attention outside his native Belgium, in part as a result of developments in world drama that had rendered Ghelderode's work suddenly "fashionable." The now famous "Ostend Interviews" (1951), broadcast first in Belgium, then in France, and later published, brought belated but well-deserved recognition to a highly original practitioner and theoretician of the drama. Even so, Ghelderode died at the age of sixty-three in relative obscurity, achieving only after death the full measure of esteem that had somehow eluded him in life. A final posthumous irony came with the revelation that, had Ghelderode survived until the fall of 1962, he would in all likelihood have received that year's Nobel Prize in Literature.

More heavily influenced by the plastic arts than by the work of other playwrights past or present, Ghelderode's dramaturgy nevertheless closely approaches the goal of "total theater" long sought by Antonin Artaud and others. Ghelderode's plays, set for the most part in late medieval or early Renaissance Flanders, combine evocative poetic language with the scenic powers of Pieter Brueghel, Jan Vermeer, or Ghelderode's older contemporary James Ensor. Drawing as well on the long and honored tradition of puppetry, Ghelderode bodies forth in his work a resolutely antinaturalistic, often grotesque, yet ultimately realistic personal vision of human nature that has much in common with the later deformations wrought by Samuel Beckett, Arthur Adamov, and Eugène Ionesco. It would be misleading, however, to consider Ghelderode as a simple precursor of absurdist drama; his work remains essentially unique, with few visible models and even fewer followers.

Deeply rooted in the folklore and traditions of his native Flanders, Ghelderode's dramaturgy is both elemental and spectacular, peopled with gross characters and overshadowed by the prospect or proximity of death. Often satiric, with near-caricatures of rulers, bureaucrats, and clergymen, his plays ultimately portray the futility of all human endeavor, meanwhile highlighting humanity's heroic efforts to prevail against the inevitable. Rich in sound as well as in color, and frequently specifying musical instruments and sound effects, Ghelderode's better efforts create and sustain a mood that threatens to envelop the spectator within the author's vision, establishing for the duration of the play a substitute world with its own rules and patterns, postures and masks. Long a devotee of marionette theater, Ghelderode proved quite skillful at adapting the techniques of puppetry to the live stage, thus underscoring the helplessness of his characters' attitudes.

During some thirty years of sustained dramatic activity, Ghelderode wrote more than fifty plays, some of them little more than fragments and a good number intended for broadcast production rather than for staging. Writing always in French, he authorized Flemish translations for many of his works, thereby lending considerable support to the Flemish Popular Theater (Vlamsche Volkstonneel), which in turn contributed heavily to his early reputation. Scarcely influenced by the requirements of fashion, Ghelderode freely ignored the accepted standards of structure, playability, or length. Few, if any, of his plays last longer than one hour in performance, and fewer still are divided into acts and scenes. His intensely poetic style, often bordering on grandiloquence in his efforts toward characterization, frequently produces soliloquies that suffice to tax the memory of any actor. Still, the best of Ghelderode's plays have managed to survive him and will doubtless continue to hold interest for audiences.

In English-speaking countries, Ghelderode's dramatic reputation owes much to the work of David Grossvogel, whose study *Twentieth Century French Drama* (1967) included a substantial chapter devoted to the previously neglected Belgian playwright. Mindful of Ghelderode's eccentricities and limitations as a dramatist, Grossvogel nevertheless hailed him as a highly original writer of no mean achievement, worthy of inclusion alongside such major figures as Paul Claudel, Jean Giraudoux, and Jean-Paul Sartre. During the years to follow, both before and after Ghelderode's death, his work found considerable favor with university drama groups throughout the United States and Canada, aided by two volumes of his collected plays in English translation by George Hauger. Today, Ghelderode's singular reputation as a valued "playwright's playwright" remains secure, both in Europe and abroad.

BIOGRAPHY

The reclusive eccentric who would style himself Michel de Ghelderode (a pseudonym eventually legalized by royal decree) was born Adémar-Adolphe-Louis Martens on Palm Sunday, April 3, 1898, in Ixelles, Belgium, a suburb of Brussels frequented by artists and writers. His father, Henri-Louis Martens, was employed as a royal archivist, a line of work later to be pursued by young Ghelderode. The author's mother, née Jeanne-Marie Rans, was a former postulant for holy orders; even after bearing four children, of whom Ghelderode was the youngest, she retained evident traces of her erstwhile vocation that would strongly influence the mature Ghelderode's dramatic work: One of Mme Martens's remembered "spiritual tales," concerning a child mistakenly buried alive who remained strangely marked by death even after her rescue, inspired most of the plot and characters of Ghelderode's *Miss Jairus*, not written until the author was in his mid-thirties.

Throughout his life, Ghelderode, like Jaïre's daughter Blandine, remained oddly touched by intimations of mortality. Around the age of sixteen, while pursuing his studies at the Institut St.-Louis in Brussels, he fell gravely ill with typhus and would retain for the rest of his life the vision of "a Lady" who materialized at his bedside to utter the words, "not now, sixty-three." (Chronically ill with asthma from his late thirties onward, Ghelderode in fact died in 1962, two days short of what would have been his sixty-fourth birthday.) Amid the double disruptions of illness and World War I, he drifted increasingly into literary and artistic circles, sharpening his visual perceptions and even—however briefly—trying his hand at music. Thanks in part to his acquaintance with the novelist Georges Eekhoud, whose views helped to shape his developing vision, Ghelderode became actively interested in both regional and marionette theater; it was during his period, moreover, that the first of his writings—already signed Ghelderode—began to appear in the "little" magazines.

In order to support himself, Ghelderode first worked as a clerk in a bookstore and later followed in his father's bureaucratic footsteps at the Royal Archives. In 1924, already a recognized playwright, Ghelderode married Jeanne-Françoise Gérard, a secretary some three years his senior whom he had met during his employment at the bookstore. They were to remain married, and together, until the author's death. By the mid-1920's, Ghelderode, although still employed as an archivist, was well known in literary circles both as a writer and as an editor. His plays, translated into Flemish from their original French, soon became the staple of the Vlamsche Volkstonneel, or Flemish Popular Theater, with new works furnished regularly on demand. The author's health, meanwhile, remained precarious at best, shading his dramatic work with forebodings of decrepitude and death.

Shortly after World War II, with most of his work already behind him, Ghelderode began at last to attract the critical attention that he had long deserved. The "Ostend Interviews," recorded in 1951, brought even more widespread interest in his work, and by 1953 the best of his plays were in production all over the world, from Eastern Europe to North and South America. The habits of a lifetime, however, are often difficult to break, and Ghelderode continued to think of himself as an isolated and neglected author. Increasingly ill and infirm, he remained with his wife in the modest apartment that they had shared throughout most of their marriage, surrounded by the "playthings" of his choice—marionettes both whole and disembodied, tailor's dummies, and wooden horses long since retired from service in carnivals. In life as in art, Ghelderode truly inhabited a world largely of his own invention, overshadowed by the hovering presence of death. When death finally came to the playwright, pretty much in keeping with the feverish dream or vision of his youth, his singular universe remained quite intact, providing the world stage with a permanent and irreplaceable contribution.

ANALYSIS

Aptly described by David Grossvogel as essentially Romantic in spirit, the plays of Michel de Ghelderode are perhaps closer to the nineteenth century ideals of heroism and grotesquerie than are those of any other twentieth century writer. They are very much of their own time, however, in the deliberate irony of their conception and in the author's careful use of shifting moods and perspectives. The exchange of roles between king and jester in *Escurial*, for example, bears witness to a distinctly modern sensibility, as does the emotional predicament of Christopher Columbus in the play that bears his name. For Ghelderode, as for many other modern French playwrights, history serves less as context than as pretext, providing the author with a suitable forum for the expression of his personal vision; thus does Columbus undertake his journeys out of sheer boredom, only to finish the play as a statue unveiled by Buffalo Bill. A strong anticlerical streak runs through most of Ghelderode's plays, somewhat mitigated by a spirituality that nevertheless stops short of true belief; throughout Ghelderode's theatrical universe, religion is more often honored in the breach than in the observance, as in the emergence of Barabbas as something closely resembling a popular hero. Sensuality, another dominant characteristic, is prominent in nearly all Ghelderode's plays, most often in its least attractive forms: Gluttony and heavy drinking loom large, as does lust, often incarnated in haglike female characters with such suggestive names as Salivaine, Visquosine, and Vénéranda. Bearing witness to the author's abiding interest in the plastic arts and in puppetry, the best of his plays are rich both in sound and in spectacle, providing a truly unforgettable experience for actors and spectator alike.

ESCURIAL

Perhaps the best known and most frequently performed of Ghelderode's early plays, *Escurial* produces a memorable theatrical experience quite out of proportion to its brevity. Set in early renaissance Spain, *Escurial* fully exploits the available resources of sight and sound as an unseen Queen lies on her deathbed, mourned by the impotent, decrepit King and his jester, Folial. Only gradually, against a sonorous background of howling guard dogs, does the spectator come to understand that Folial has been the Queen's lover and that the King has poisoned her himself. In a tour de force of poetic dialogue that both recalls and transcends the best efforts of Luigi Pirandello, Ghelderode reveals each man as the other's customarily hidden double, a revelation visually realized as they don each other's costumes in a paroxysm of mourning and attempted gallows humor, observed only by a silent monk and a suitably ominous headsman. Predictably, the jester will pay with his life for his part in the grim charade, leaving behind him a visibly depleted and still frustrated monarch. Distinguished by the economy of its expression as well as by its highly original style, *Escurial* is widely recognized as one of Ghelderode's finest achievements.

PANTAGLEIZE

Described by its author as "a farce to make you sad in three acts, nine scenes and an epilogue," *Pantagleize* differs from most of Ghelderode's other work not only in its length but also in the author's unaccustomed choice of modern setting and characters. Of all Ghelderode's plays, *Pantagleize* is, moreover, the most unabashedly modern in form as well as in content, recalling German expressionism even as it hovers close to Symbolism.

Written expressly for the Flemish comedian Renaat Verheyen, who died at twenty-six, soon after appearing in the title role, *Pantagleize* depicts the troubled life and times of a nearly archetypal antihero, a "professional philosopher" whose sustained thought processes have undermined his ability "to understand anything." Employed as a fashion writer, Pantagleize is also the author—under the pseudonym Machinski—of a well-known anticapitalist pamphlet. In truth, however, Pantagleize cares little about fashion, even less about revolution, and wants more than anything else to be left alone with his increasingly inconsequential thoughts. More or less in self-defense, he has taken to expressing himself in platitudes, of which the most famous—and most characteristic—is "What a lovely day!"

Set "in a city of Europe, on the morrow of one war and the eve of another," *Pantagleize* catches and portrays with antic satire the political instability and ferment of Europe in the 1920's, with both Right and Left held up to ridicule. *Pantagleize*, anticipating by some twenty years the best efforts of Adamov and Ionesco, is indeed a remarkable and prescient work, marred for modern audiences only by Ghelderode's use of ethnic stereotypes in the creation of such characters as the jive-talking black manservant Bam-Boulah and the alluring Jewess Rachel Silberschatz. Like Ionesco in *Tueur sans gages* (pr., pb. 1958; *The Killer*, 1960) or Adamov in *Tous contre tous* (pr., pb. 1953), Ghelderode in *Pantagleize* adamantly refuses to take sides, calling attention instead to the haplessness of the individual caught between political extremes.

Unknown to Pantagleize, the butler Bam-Boulah is a political activist who has identified Pantagleize to his leftist colleagues as the man whose words will set off the coming revolution. No sooner has Pantagleize remarked, as usual, on the lovely day than shots are heard in the streets. Quite unaware of what is going on, he soon thereafter receives a revolutionary hero's welcome into the arms and bed of Rachel, a charming coconspirator of Bam-Boulah and his cronies at the Objective Bar and Grill. Thereafter, each of Pantagleize's platitudinous statements will add new ferment and momentum to the revolution, culminating in his own arrest and eventual execution before a firing squad. Still oblivious, he expires after once again remarking, "What a lovely day!"

THE ACTOR MAKES HIS EXIT

Following the premature death of Verheyen, Ghelderode severed most of his connections with the Flemish Popular Theater, preferring to work in solitude toward the perfection of his art. Judging from the nature and tone of his work written after that time, Ghelderode turned increasingly inward in his search for inspiration and material, almost completely turning his back on the rich vein of sociopolitical satire that he had mined so successfully in *Pantagleize*. *The Actor Makes His Exit*, presumably inspired by Renaat Verheyen's death, marked a return to the exploration of illusion versus reality exemplified by *Escurial*; for the most part, Ghelderode's subsequent efforts shun the social in favor of the psychological, all the while resisting the obvious, fashionable theories of Sigmund Freud, Carl Gustav Jung, and their followers. Returning almost with a vengeance to the timeless and proverbial past, Ghelderode in his later efforts concentrates most of his energies on the evocation of such basic human appetites as avarice, gluttony, and lust, finding even in these a potential affirmation of life against the eventuality of death.

RED MAGIC

Written for an unspecified audience rather than explicitly for the socially conscious Popular Theater, *Red Magic* is perhaps the strongest and most characteristic play of Ghelderode's maturity, combining most of his major themes and concerns in a memorable torrent of images and words. Containing some of the longest soliloquies in contemporary drama, *Red Magic* nevertheless involves the audience in the grotesquely comic thought processes of the archetypal miser Hieronymus, in whose presence even Molière's Harpagon would appear pale by comparison. One of the most frequently quoted scenes in all of Ghelderode's theater is that in which Hieronymus, contemplating his hoard with lip-smacking delight, makes plans to "breed" his male and female coins toward the production of innumerable shiny offspring. Ironically, however, Hieronymus's lasciviousness extends no further than his treasure; he is so avaricious, in fact, as to have withheld from his nubile wife Sybilla the pleasure of the marriage bed. Given such proclivities, Hieronymus easily falls prey to a conspiracy woven about him by Sybilla, her lover, and the neighborhood beggar Romulus. It is Romulus who persuades Hieronymus to shelter under his roof the lover, Armador, presumably fleeing persecution because of his talents as an alchemist. Blinded by greed at the prospect of a houseguest who can transmute baser metals into gold, Hieronymus gladly offers his wife as the "virgin" whose blood will be needed for the "red magic" of Armador's experiments. Thanks to Ghelderode's careful if unobtrusive plotting, matters eventually escalate to the point where Hieronymus is sentenced to death for a murder that he did not commit, unjustly charged also with the offense of counterfeiting. Sybilla, meanwhile, elopes in the company of a corrupt monk with whom Armador has been sharing her affections.

In the view of such critics as Roland Beyen and the novelist-playwright Félicien Marceau, Hieronymus is doomed from the start not by his avarice but by a deeper maladjustment of which his greed is never more than a symptom. For Beyen, Hieronymus's miserliness is at bottom a refusal to accept his own humanity or to share it with his fellow mortals: Equating money with power, Hieronymus would rather be feared and envied from afar than to accept the responsibilities of love or friendship. Significantly, Hieronymus's sexual contact is limited only to prostitutes, with intimacy neatly defined within the limits of a simple cash transaction. At a somewhat deeper level, suggests Beyen, Hieronymus's evident fear of life reflects an even stronger fear of death, from which he irrationally imagines that his riches might protect him: So great has his self-delusion become that as he prepares to meet his executioner, Hieronymus honestly believes himself to be immortal. In *Red Magic*, the latent pessimism of *Pantagleize* has grown both sharper and deeper, sparing neither characters nor audience. Whereas the self-delusion of Pantagleize is at first humorous, later pathetic, that of Hieronymus is neither. Although quite innocent of the charges leveled against him, Hieronymus nevertheless is clearly portrayed by the author as richly deserving of his fate. A similar pessimism pervades the subsequent *Hop, Signor!* in which the resolutely virginal Marguerite Harstein sensually offers her neck to the headsman's ax after obtaining the murder by torture of her husband Juréal.

CHRONICLES OF HELL

By far the most controversial—indeed, notorious—of all Ghelderode's plays, *Chronicles of Hell* created a considerable stir when it was first performed in Paris during the fall of 1949, some twenty years after it was initially conceived and written. Indeed, much of the belated circulation and celebrity that came to Ghelderode in his fifties can be traced

directly to the *succès de scandale* of *Chronicles of Hell* at the Théâtre Marigny. So little was known about Ghelderode at the time that wild rumors swept through Paris and France concerning the author's age, occupation, and beliefs. Subsequently, after matters had cooled down, aficionados of the theater began to discover Ghelderode's other works.

Set, like many other Ghelderode plays, "in bygone Flanders," *Chronicles of Hell* evokes the assassination and bizarre "resurrection" of the heretical bishop Jan in Eremo, who rises from his deathbed to seek vengeance on the corrupt clerics who have poisoned him and who are currently celebrating his demise. Diverted from his plan by the sudden apparition of his grotesquely aged mother, Vénéranda, the bishop instead coughs up the poisoned communion wafer that has served his opponents as a weapon; having pardoned his assassins, he is then free to die in peace, watched over by his mother. The feuding monks and priests, meanwhile, create among themselves a riotous spectacle of venality that sufficed, in 1949, to drive a number of otherwise receptive spectators from the theater. Particularly biting is Ghelderode's portrayal of the auxiliary bishop Simon Laquedeem, who ends the play in a paroxysm of scatology. Laquedeem, moreover, is presented throughout the play as a convert from Judaism, recalling Ghelderode's earlier questionable portrayal of the radical Rachel Silberschatz in *Pantagleize*. In form and presentation, however, *Chronicles of Hell* compares quite favorably with the best of Ghelderode's earlier efforts, rich in color, sound, and spectacle.

MARIE LA MISÉRABLE

Ironically, Ghelderode had in all likelihood exhausted his talent, or at least his inner supply of material, by the time his work began to attract worldwide attention; the last of his efforts, *Marie la misérable*, is also generally agreed to be among the least. In any case, Ghelderode had already written enough, both in quality and in quantity, to keep actors and directors profitably occupied for several more decades to come. The "Ostend Interviews," moreover, contain some of the finest observations that a playwright has ever made concerning his own work, extending outward to embrace dramatic art in general.

OTHER MAJOR WORKS

SHORT FICTION: *L'Histoire comique de Keizer Karel*, 1922; *Kwiebe-Kwiebus*, 1926; *Chronique de Noël*, 1934; *Sortilèges*, 1941.

POETRY: *La Corne d'Abondance*, 1925; *Ixelles, mes amours*, 1928.

NONFICTION: *Choses et gens de chez nous*, 1943; *Mes Statues*, 1943; *La Flandre est un songe*, 1953; *À propos de Franz Hellens*, 1964.

BIBLIOGRAPHY

Cardy, Michael, and Derek Connon, eds. *Aspects of Twentieth Century Theatre in French*. New York: Peter Lang, 2000. Provides background of developments in French language theater in the twentieth century. Bibliography and index.

Drake, Sylvie. "Good-Natured Fun with *Columbus*: Michel de Ghelderode's Little-known Version of the Explorer's Vision Portrays a Gentle Creature Who Is 'Haunted by the Horizon.'" Review of *Christopher Columbus* by Ghelderode. *Los Angeles Times*, October 23, 1992, p. 21. This review of a performance at Stages Theatre Center in Hollywood, California, directed by Florinel Fatulescu, provides an interesting perspective on this play.

Grossvogel, David. *Twentieth Century French Drama*. 1958. Reprint. New York: Gordian Press, 1967. Contains a chapter on Ghelderode that served to introduce the dramatist to English-speaking audiences.

Parsell, David B. *Michel de Ghelderode*. New York: Twayne, 1993. A basic biography of Ghelderode that covers his life and works. Bibliography and index.

Willinger, David, and Jeanine Parisier Plottel, eds. *Theatrical Gestures: From the Belgium Avant-garde*. New York: New York Literary Forum, 1987. This look at avant-garde drama in Belgium contains a discussion of Ghelderode.

David B. Parsell

GIUSEPPE GIACOSA

Born: Colleretto Parella, Piedmont (now in Italy); October 21, 1847
Died: Colleretto Parella, Italy; September 1, 1906

PRINCIPAL DRAMA

Una partita a scacchi, pb. 1872, pr. 1873 (verse play; *The Wager*, 1914)
Il trionfo d'amore, pr., pb. 1875 (verse play)
Acquazzoni in montagna, pr. 1876, pb. 1877
Il marito amante della moglie, pr. 1877, pb. 1878 (verse play)
Il fratello d'armi, pr. 1877, pb. 1878 (verse play)
Luisa, pr., pb. 1879 (verse play)
Il conte rosso, pr., pb. 1880 (verse play)
L'onorevole Ercole Mallardi, pr., pb. 1885
Tristi amori, pr. 1887, pb. 1889 (*Unhappy Love*, 1916)
Resa a discrezione, pr., pb. 1888
La Signora di Challant, pr., pb. in Italian 1891, pr., pb. in French 1891 as *La Dame de Challant* (*The Lady of Challant*, 1891)
Diritti dell'anima, pr., pb. 1894 (*The Rights of the Soul*, 1913)
La Bohème, pr., pb. 1896 (libretto with Luigi Illica, music by Giacomo Puccini, based on Victorien Sardou's play *La Vie de Bohème*; English translation, 1897)
Tosca, pb. 1899, pr. 1900 (libretto with Illica, music by Puccini, based on Sardou's play; English translation, 1899)
Come le foglie, pr., pb. 1900 (*Like Falling Leaves*, 1904)
Madama Butterfly, pr., pb. 1904 (libretto with Luigi Illica, music by Puccini, based on John L. Long's story; *Madame Butterfly*, 1905)
Il più forte, pr. 1904, pb. 1905 (*The Stronger*, 1913)

OTHER LITERARY FORMS

Although Giuseppe Giacosa owes his reputation to his dramatic repertoire, his other accomplishments are well worth mentioning because of their exceptional literary value. A collection of short stories, *Novelle e paesi valdostani* (1886), portrays the daily struggle of the mountaineers in Valdaosta against the natural forces that shape their destiny and condition their ability to make a living. *Impressioni d'America* (1891), a series of travel sketches occasioned by a trip to New York, reveals Giacosa's remarkable talent for accurate observation. *Castelli valdostani e canavesani* (1897) is a series of popularized chronicles of castles in the Canavese region.

Giacosa also collaborated with several newspapers and literary magazines and was the founder of *Lettura*, a monthly literary review. In collaboration with Luigi Illica, he wrote librettos for Giacomo Puccini's most famous operas: *La Bohème*, *Tosca*, and *Madame Butterfly*.

ACHIEVEMENTS

In the extensive dramatic production that followed the success of *The Wager*, Giuseppe Giacosa alternated romances in Martellian verse with comedies in contemporary prose, seemingly unconcerned with criteria of stylistic development. Thus, *The Wager* and *Il fratello d'armi*, both romances in verse, were followed by *Unhappy Love*, a naturalist drama in prose, with a return to verse in *Il conte rosso*, a realistic historical drama adversely affected by the artificial verse scheme, once more followed by prose in *Like Falling Leaves*, Giacosa's most famous *commedia borghese*, and by *The Stronger*, an attack on the double standards of the bourgeoisie, also in prose. What struck some critics as lack of direction in Giacosa's constant stylistic shifts made him popular with the public. Giacosa's perennial wavering between past and present reflected only too well the unsettled tastes of the bourgeoisie, fascinated by French naturalism and Giovanni Verga's *Verismo*, or Verism, yet unwilling to give up the nostalgic charm of Romantic drama, and increasingly enticed by the idealistic aspirations that were gaining in popularity in the late nineteenth century.

Following World War I, Giacosa's popularity suffered a steady decline from which it never recovered. Giacosa's insistence on using topical references and fashion symbols of his day to characterize the world of the rich—knickerbockers, portable bathtubs, plaid *tout de même*—dates his comedies and greatly reduces their attractiveness to a contemporary audience. As for his medieval romances, their charm cannot withstand the test of time. They are peculiar period pieces no longer in demand, sharing in this the fate of most nineteenth century Romantic drama. The critics, who at first had been very favorable to Giacosa, reversed their verdict and claimed that his dramatic production lacked a coherent aesthetic growth. The most severe among them charged Giacosa with *dilettantismo*, Benedetto Croce's favorite epithet for mediocrity, dealing the last blow to Giacosa's already faltering reputation. Today, a more balanced critical perspective praises Giacosa's talent for brilliant dialogue, which portrays the irresponsible rituals of the rich, dedicated solely to preserving their privileged position unchanged. In the history of the Italian theater, Giacosa unquestionably remains one of the most eloquent and versatile exponents of the *teatro borghese* (bourgeois theater).

BIOGRAPHY

Giuseppe Giacosa can best be understood as man and as writer when placed in the natural setting that gives significance to his life and to his work: the breathtaking beauty of the Alps which surround Colleretto Parella, the Piemontese village where he was born on October 21, 1847, and where he died on September 1, 1906. The rugged life of the mountaineers and their courageous struggle against enormous odds transformed Giacosa's admiration into a mythic celebration of their will to survive, lyrically expressed in his collection of short stories *Novelle e paesi valdostani*. The mountaineers' brave acceptance of a cruel fate convinced Giacosa that a person at his or her best is "l'eroe del bisogno," the hero of need, and that moral strength generates from a realistic appraisal of life. This view shapes the tragic flaw of several of his protagonists, who lack the ability to face financial ruin simply because they lack the moral strength to recognize the role of the will in overcoming misfortune.

Although Giacosa revealed his penchant for literary studies early in life, his father, a successful lawyer, convinced him to get a degree in law at the University of Turin. Giacosa complied, but without enthusiasm, and his first appearance in court was a disaster. Fortunately, his literary tendencies came to his rescue and enabled him to leave the bench forever. In March, 1872, *Nuova Antologia* published his dramatic legend *The Wager*, which attracted exceptionally favorable critical reviews. Although not intended for the stage, the play was presented on April 30, 1873, in Naples, under the direction of Achille Torelli. It was an unprecedented success, and the name of Giacosa became guarantee enough for Italian *capocomici* always searching for new talent to satisfy their public.

In December, 1891, Giacosa, who was very popular by then, traveled to New York to assist Sarah Bernhardt rehearse in *The Lady of Challant*, a historical drama he had purposely written in French for her. The Italian version of the drama was presented in Turin, in October of 1891, with Eleconora Duse as the protagonist. During the last sixteen years of his life, Giacosa moved from Turin to Milan, where he founded *Lettura*, a literary journal responsible for effecting the transition from *scapigliatura* (an aesthetic movement founded by Giuseppe Rovani and concerned with protecting artistic freedom from Utilitarian attacks) to *Verismo*, the Italian version of French naturalism. While in Milan, Giacosa taught at the Accademia dei Filodrammatici and actively participated in city government. A capable actor with excellent diction, Giacosa gave public readings of his plays both in Italy and in other European countries, where he was much in demand. As already noted, Giacosa died in Colleretto Parella, his native village in Piemonte, where he spent his summers. Piemonte still celebrates Giacosa as one of the greatest writers of the region.

ANALYSIS

Because eclecticism is the dominant note in Giuseppe Giacosa's dramatic production, the follow-ing discussion proposes to consider the most important plays from each genre: *The Wager*, a dramatic legend in Martellian verse; *Unhappy Love*, a naturalist drama; *Like Falling Leaves*, by far his most brilliant *commedia borghese*; and *The Stronger*, also a *commedia borghese*, and his last play.

THE WAGER

The Wager opens with a prologue in which the author informs the audience that this *leggenda drammatica* is based on a Provençal romance that he read by chance and found enticing because of its melodious Martellian verse. It is autumn, and like leaves that before succumbing to their seasonal doom burst into multicolored hues, the mind of the poet finds new associations by reading material doomed by long neglect. Aware of the role that reminiscences play in the creative process, the author takes the opportunity to revive the legend and to offer his own interpretation to the reader.

The Wager is divided into two scenes. Both scenes take place in the great hall of a medieval castle in the Alps, decorated with flags, a huge fireplace, and a gothic window. The first scene opens with Renato, the lord of the castle, and Iolanda, his comely daughter, sharing premonitions of the merciless winter ahead. Their isolation would be hardly tolerable if it were not for the love they have for each other. Moved by tenderness for his daughter, Renato declares that while at one time he had wished for a son, Iolanda has fulfilled his every wish so completely that his heart would have no room for anyone else. Teasingly, Iolanda objects that his heart will have to make room for her bridegroom. The old man expresses his desire to hear the laughter of Iolanda's children. Made bold by this admission, Iolanda shares with him her maiden fantasies of a handsome suitor who might brighten her days with passionate words of love. Renato reminds her of the suitors she has already refused, but Iolanda insists that the one who will win her heart must be handsome. Beauty is first to capture the beloved—the rules of love must not be disregarded. While conversing, Renato praises Iolanda for her great skill in playing chess; even he, her teacher, is no longer a worthy competitor. Iolanda, filled with love and gratitude for her father, surrenders her will in his hands: He will be the one to choose her future husband. As Renato thanks her for her absolute confidence in his wisdom, the sentinel in the tower signals the arrival of a vassal accompanied by his retinue.

In scene 2, Count Oliviero, an old comrade-in-arms of Renato, arrives with his page Fernando and other knights. Oliviero proudly introduces Fernando, who, single-handedly, has saved him from the ambush of ten highwaymen. Renato is touched by the prowess of the young man, who is an orphan and thus must rely exclusively on his ability to make his way in the world. Fernando's excessive self-assurance, however, brings a fatherly reprimand from Renato, who admires his bravery but regrets what he considers an overdose of conceit. His lack of humility defies fate: His only excuse is his youth. Fernando replies that an orphan is never young, and that his earlier experiences in war and in love have instilled in him tremendous self-assurance and an unshakable faith in his skill to overcome all obstacles. Torn between admiration and anger, Renato challenges Fernando, who claims to be an expert at chess, to test his infallibility by playing a game with Iolanda. If he wins, he will marry her; if he loses, he will die. Fernando accepts, and the game begins. Conquered by Iolanda's beauty, Fernando makes several wrong moves and loses control of the game. The melodious love duet of the players finds an effective counterpoint in the conversation between Renato and Oliviero, the former expressing his regret and his eagerness to renege on the horrible pact that he has made with Fernando. Actually, Iolanda, much more attentive to the game than the page, is winning without much competition. Renato almost begs Fernando to call off the bet, but Fernando, knowing that his honor is at stake, refuses. Iolanda, unaware of the deal between her father and the page, becomes suspicious, but Fernando is adamant.

In a lovely poetic passage, Fernando describes his native Provence and contrasts the blue-eyed, blonde charm of Iolanda to the passionate, bold looks of the women of his land. No longer capable of keeping his secret, Fernando tells Iolanda of the pact he has made with her father, and Iolanda confesses her love for him. Once she has admitted her love, Fernando

is in control of the game, and Renato, caught in his own web, offers Fernando a castle if he will give up the prize. Unwilling to displease Renato, Fernando almost yields to his demands, but Iolanda takes his hand and leads him in the final move proclaiming his victory. Quickly appeased, Renato thanks heaven for giving him a son, and the play ends with the leitmotif of the lovers that became one of Italy's favorite refrains: "*E ancor, paggio Fernando, mi affissi e non favelli? Io ti guardo negli occhi che son tanto belli.*" ("Page Fernando, why do you glance at me without a sigh? I gaze into your eyes that are so bright.") The facile ditty made Giacosa the uncontested ruler of romantic theatergoers, until changing times relegated his melodious game of chess to literary history.

UNHAPPY LOVE

In dedicating *Unhappy Love* to Piero Costa, a sculptor from his native Piemonte, Giacosa signaled a shift from the Martellian verse of his previous romances to prose. The shift, however, is not merely in metrics. Giacosa displays the influence of the French naturalist theater. Émile Augier and Henry Becque were his favorite playwrights, and Alexandre Dumas, *fils*'s *La Question d'argent* (pr., pb. 1857; *The Money-Question*, 1915) considerably influenced *Unhappy Love*. In this play, Giacosa explores the established theme of *ménage à trois* with stark realism, enhanced by a faithful adherence to the Aristotelian unities of time and place.

The action of this three-act comedy is confined to one room in the home of Giulio Scarli, a provincial lawyer whose wife, Emma—Emma Bovary comes unavoidably to mind—is having an affair with his best friend, Fabrizio Arcieri. The closely knitted plot, which culminates in the inevitable discovery of adultery, is forwarded by a terse, compelling dialogue, completely devoid of the romantic commonplaces typical of Giacosa's earlier plays. The fundamental uprightness of the protagonists and their obvious reciprocal respect save the play from the hopeless fatalism present in so many *tranche de vie* dramas and allow genuine empathy for the predicament of each character. Although a future reconciliation between Giulio and Emma seems unlikely, family ties prove stronger than personal revenge. Thus Fabrizio leaves town without Emma, who accepts a grim, lonely future to remain at the side of her only daughter, Gemma. Giulio accepts her presence for the sake of Gemma and finds solace—and, in a sense, annihilation—in the ascetic loneliness of his studio, where he will dedicate his life to increasing his fortune, thus making Gemma an heiress capable of marrying a man of considerable wealth. Relieved of pecuniary pressures, Gemma's husband will be able to dedicate the largest share of his time to making her happy. A wife's faithfulness, Giacosa seems to imply, is largely subordinate to her husband's ability to dedicate his time to her need for affection.

Ironically, the problem of conjugal love remains unsolved. Giulio's stress on the importance that material prosperity plays in the relationship between husband and wife seems to subordinate love to affluence, a notion that clearly points to Giacosa's most unsuccessful *commedia borghese*, *Like Falling Leaves*, in which the theme of *Unhappy Love* is further explored.

LIKE FALLING LEAVES

In *Like Falling Leaves*, through a reversal of fortune, the immense wealth amassed by Giovanni Rosani through the hard work of a lifetime is irremediably lost, leaving the spoiled family members completely unprepared for poverty and bitterly unwilling to cope with it.

Like Falling Leaves focuses on two themes increasingly central to Giacosa's philosophical development; financial bankruptcy and moral disintegration. The coexistence of the two evils points to the inability of the wealthy members of society to adjust to reduced financial circumstances with dignity and with a mature acceptance of their new station in life. Like leaves in autumn, beautiful but doomed, pampered individuals must perforce be crushed by unexpected reversals, for they lack the will to overcome adversity through personal labor and effective moral choices. The title *Like Falling Leaves* is an allusion to Dante's famous description of the damned seeking to board Charon's bark to reach their eternal perdition: "*Come d'autunno si levan le foglie,/ l'una appresso dell'altra fin che'l ramo/ rende a la terra tutte le sue*

spogli." ("Like leaves in Fall, one after another,/ fall to the ground till the bough/ gives back to the earth all its spoils.")

Act 1 of *Like Falling Leaves* is carefully calculated to test the reaction of every character to the specter of poverty. Fifty-six-year-old Giovanni Rosani has lost his considerable fortune through ill-advised stock investments. Conscientious to a fault, he proposes to repay his debtors by awarding them the full amount from the sale of his elegant villa and other personal effects. His second wife, Giulia, who is only thirty-four, has tried to persuade him to cheat his creditors by selling some of the valuables of the villa without their knowledge. Tommy, the charming, spoiled son of his deceased first wife, has tacitly assumed that Giovanni has agreed to go through with the deal proposed by his stepmother, and that his father will still be able to provide him with the money he needs to maintain his gambling and other dissolute habits. The Rosani family is preparing to abandon its luxurious Italian villa and move to Switzerland, where Massimo, a relative they hardly know, hearing of their financial predicament, has volunteered his help by offering Giovanni a modest but adequate position.

The play opens as Nennele, Tommy's sister and also the daughter of Giovanni's first wife, supervises the movers as they carry out the family's luggage. Nennele's efforts to keep some order in the frantic household are effectively contrasted to Tommy's and Giulia's futile attempts to ignore their new situation in life. Tommy laments the absence of the servant who usually helps him dress in the morning, while Giulia argues with the dressmaker who refuses to leave the dress that Giulia has ordered unless she receives full payment. Innuendos of shady financial deals between Giulia and Tommy, who has recently won a large sum at the gaming table, become the play's leitmotif. Meanwhile, Massimo arrives from Budapest, where he has been for a few days to complete a business transaction. He is to escort the family to Switzerland, where he has rented an unpretentious but comfortable house in the country. With the exception of Giovanni, who appreciates Massimo's efforts in their behalf, the Rosani family unanimously despises Massimo, a dedicated worker who has earned a large fortune solely through his efforts. Giovanni, whose sedentary work habits have made him a stranger to the family, realizes only too well the huge gap that divides Massimo's industrious dedication to duty from the fatuous indolence of Tommy and the irresponsible behavior of Giulia, who plans to supplement the meager family income by becoming a professional painter. Nennele's motherly love for Tommy is complemented by her devotion to Giovanni. She seems to sense the situation better than the rest, and to be willing to face the future without too many regrets.

The theme of money again opens act 2. The family is now settled in Switzerland and is struggling to make Giovanni's modest income suffice. Nennele refuses to accept from her father the entire sum needed for the month's housekeeping. She is concerned, since some of the money has been disappearing, and she begs Giovanni to give her small amounts that she can easily control. A series of vivid short scenes dramatizes the circumstances of the Rosanis' new ménage. Reluctantly, Nennele has started giving lessons in English to the son of a widow. Giulia is painting Mont Blanc, assisted by Helmer Strile, a Swedish painter who obviously is more interested in her charm than in the mountain's majestic beauty.

A master of sparkling dialogue, Giacosa adroitly employs witty skirmishes to emphasize the superficiality of his characters. The conversation moves as rapidly and as intuitively as do the short scenes. Tommy's brilliant defense of his own immorality, Nennele's plaintive satire of the widow and her son, and Giulia's phony artistic claims are brought into perspective by Massimo's stringent logic, which effectively deflates the Rosanis' rose-colored escapism. Tommy has lasted one day on the job that Massimo has found for him and is now deeply involved, financially and emotionally, with a Russian adventuress, Madame Orloff, who allows her wealthy friends to gamble in her palatial home. As he forces the Rosani family to face reality, Massimo increasingly takes on the role of *raisonneur*, and in a heated conversation with Tommy about Madame Orloff's questionable virtue, he insists that all Tommy has to do to discon-

tinue his relationship with the lady is to exercise his freedom of choice. In a moment of candid self-assessment, Tommy admits that in the past his choices had always been easy. Affluence had made them for him: He was never obliged to turn anything down. Things are different now, but he does not know how to enforce his freedom of choice. Moved by his sincerity, Massimo suggests that Tommy seek the help of Nennele, as undoubtedly she will help him strengthen his purpose and find new meaning in life. Realizing that Massimo is in love with Nennele, Tommy becomes sarcastic and replies that if Massimo were to ask her to marry him and she refused, all the freedom of choice in the world would not help him alter her decision. Offended but still self-possessed, Massimo retorts that to overcome all his problems, Tommy should marry Madame Orloff, who, to his knowledge, is looking for a husband. Act 2 ends in confusion: Giulia wants to go to a concert at the Artists' Club and take Nennele with her. Tommy does not want Nennele to go and become involved in Giulia's schemes. Giovanni comes out of his office for a brief respite, only to find the family in an uproar. Typically, he cannot understand what is wrong, and Nennele begs him to impose his authority on the quarreling family, at least this once. Giovanni, who feels guilty for depriving the family of the wealth to which it is accustomed, pleads for forgiveness and a momentary truce. Touched by Giovanni's sorrow, Tommy tries to overcome his indolence and promises to take a second job proposed by Massimo. As the act closes, repentance seems to dominate the scene: Giulia renounces her outing to the club, and Nennele decides to resume giving English lessons to the hapless son of the widow.

As act 3 opens, money is again the issue. Frustrated by what she considers to be Giovanni's lack of appreciation for her artistic talents, Giulia demands to be placed in charge of the family budget. Giovanni timidly tries to dissuade her, but to no avail. To avoid a scene, Giovanni asks Nennele, who by now is missing valuable personal articles, to allow Giulia to control the family's household expenses. Nennele agrees reluctantly, and Giovanni, guessing the truth but too weak to face it, begs her to keep an eye on Giulia.

With the pretext of having found a buyer for Giulia's paintings, but in reality to make Giulia an easier prey for his amorous advances, Helmer Strile pays a visit and is introduced to Massimo and Nennele. Giacosa capitalizes on the occasion to satirize realism and Symbolism in art through an exchange that exposes the pretentious claims of the "Maestro," as Giulia admiringly calls Helmer. Unnoticed by the others, Giulia hands Helmer her photograph, framed in a silver frame she has stolen from Nennele. As he leaves, he inadvertently drops it, and Nennele, amused by her stepmother's duplicity, breaks into spiteful laughter. Once they are alone, Massimo patiently listens as Nennele laments Tommy's gambling losses and Giulia's adulterous proclivities. Their irresponsible flirting with danger reminds him of the colorful saraband of leaves in autumn: Their graceful dance will continue until they disappear without leaving even a trace of their presence in the world.

Deeply concerned for her brother's welfare, Nennele has a confrontation with Tommy, who, after failing to pursue the job Massimo had suggested, is back in the gambling salon of Madame Orloff. He confesses to Nennele that he is deeply indebted to the Russian woman, and his position is such that he has no options left. Terrified, Nennele thinks that he is contemplating suicide, but Tommy, amused by her fear, assures her that suicide is not for people like him. He cannot summon enough courage to do away with his life. Actually he has found a better solution: He will marry Madame Orloff, who has offered to trade all his debts for his name. As Tommy leaves to fulfill his destiny, Massimo asks Nennele to marry him. Convinced that his proposal is prompted solely by compassion, Nennele refuses. Disappointed, Massimo goes away. Act 4 consists of a single scene between Giovanni and Nennele, who has decided to drown herself in the river that flows past the house. Massimo's presence in the garden saves Nennele from committing the ultimate act of weakness and allows the audience to go home with a premonition of wedding bells as Nennele's joyous voice invites Massimo to join her in Giovanni's studio. Thus the family nucleus is reconstituted by the members best able to face life with courage, and with faith

in the future. Although the denouement of the play comes as an anticlimax—Nennele's projected suicide finds no justification in the preceding acts—*Like Falling Leaves* remains one of Italy's most effective *commedie borghesi*. Giacosa unmasks the brilliant superficiality of his characters, combining satire with tragic implications in a manner that anticipates the mixing of genres characteristic of modern theater.

THE STRONGER

The Stronger, Giacosa's last play, relinquishes the love motif to concentrate on the role played by money in corroding family and social values. This three-act comedy deals with Darwinian principles in the world of high finance, where survival means the ability to capitalize on someone else's misfortune. As Cesare Nalli, the protagonist of the play, a dedicated family man who is ruthless in business, explains, "Wealth is like the water of the sea: No one recognizes the rivers that flow into it." That is to say, success is its own proof of honesty—no one cares to analyze questionable business practices as long as they are legally acceptable. As the title implies, in the world of finance "the strongest one" is the man fearless enough to prevent the moves of his adversary. Therefore, in a Machiavellian sense, the end justifies the means.

A serious condemnation of double standards, the comedy dwells on the discovery made by Silvio Nalli, Cesare's only son, of his father's heartless handling of a business deal in which he knowingly ruins a former partner to strengthen his own financial holdings. Silvio, a painter who has received an excellent liberal education through Cesare's generosity, worships his father and thinks him perfect. One evening, at the club where he is dining, he hears Fausto, the son of Cesare's former partner, call Cesare a thief. Blind with rage, Silvio wants to avenge the insult with a duel. The duel eventually is averted because Silvio's cousin Edoardo Falcieri, a pragmatist who benefits from Cesare's munificence, manages to replace him by slapping Fausto and claiming his right to fight. The sudden act of violence deprives Silvio of the privilege of defending his father's honor, and, outraged by what he considers Edoardo's attempt to strip him of a sacred duty, he prepares to go back to Rome. Before leaving, however, while speaking with Don Paolo, a friend who was to be his second, Silvio discovers that Fausto was right after all. Fausto's father's financial crisis had been hastened by Cesare's refusal to go through with a deal that they had planned for some time. In a bitter confrontation with his father, Silvio renounces his wealth, while Cesare angrily denounces his son's betrayal of the sacrifices that Cesare has made on Silvio's behalf. Cesare has become a recluse to build a fortune for his son, who is now repudiating the very money that Cesare has spent to give him an education free from practical problems and necessary compromises.

The end of the play is inconclusive. Silvio leaves Cesare's villa with a parting thrust at his cousin Edoardo, who is on his way to fight with Fausto to defend the family honor—or, more likely, to defend the monthly income generously bestowed by Cesare, who wants him to share in the family fortune. In *The Stronger*, Giacosa returns to the Aristotelian unities of time and place that he had adopted in *Unhappy Love* and uses the Nallis' living room as the central locale in which the comedy evolves. Even though the comedy is primarily a drama *a tesi* (a thesis play), and though the theme of honor, tied exclusively to a duel, weakens the impact of the moral issues, the play retains important features quite original with Giacosa. His treatment of the conflict between father and son, for example, offers a solution based on reason and love. As Silvio renounces his father's wealth, his love for his father is strong enough to make him wish to see him again, and he promises to come back occasionally and spend some time with him. Even though a reconciliation does not seem likely—the denouement is reminiscent of *Unhappy Love*—the door remains open to favorable developments.

The Stronger was presented in Turin's Teatro Alfieri, on November 25, 1904, by the theatrical company Grammatica-Talli-Calabresi, at the time one of Italy's most successful companies. In spite of the expectations raised by Giacosa's reputation, the play was a flop. The public, still elated by the brilliant dialogue of *Like Falling Leaves*, and by the comedy's unquestionable stage appeal, was disappointed by the polemical, somber tone of the play. Whatever went wrong, Giacosa can hardly be blamed for inconsistency. When he left the stage, Giacosa was still exploring the issues that had become central to the development of his *teatro borghese:* the role played by money in shaping, altering, and ultimately destroying the fragile balance of family affections.

OTHER MAJOR WORKS

SHORT FICTION: *Novelle e paesi valdostani*, 1886.

NONFICTION: *Impressioni d'America*, 1891; *Castelli valdostani e canavesani*, 1897.

BIBLIOGRAPHY

Doroni, Stefano. *Dall'androne medievale al tinello borghese: Il teatro di Giuseppe Giacosa*. Rome: Bulzoni, 1998. A critical analysis of the works of Giacosa. In Italian. Bibliography and index.

Groos, Arthur. "The Lady Vanishes." *Opera News* 59, no. 8 (January 7, 1995): 16-20. A discussion of the last act of the opera *Madame Butterfly*, comparing Luigi Illica and Giacosa's versions and Puccini's alterations.

O'Grady, Deidre. *Piave, Boito, Pirandello: From Romantic Realism to Modernism*. Lewiston, N.Y.: Edwin Mellen, 2000. An overview of Italian drama during the time in which Giacosa was active. Bibliography and index.

Corinna del Greco Lobner

WILLIAM GIBSON

Born: New York, New York; November 13, 1914

PRINCIPAL DRAMA

I Lay in Zion, pr. 1943, pb. 1947

A Cry of Players, pr. 1948, pb. 1969

Dinny and the Witches: A Frolic on Grave Matters, pr. 1948, pb. 1960

The Ruby, pb. 1955, pr. 1957

The Miracle Worker, pr. 1957 (televised), pb. 1957, pr. 1959 (staged), pb. 1959

Two for the Seesaw, pr. 1958, pb. 1959

Golden Boy, pr. 1964, pb. 1965 (musical; adaptation of Clifford Odets's play, music by Charles Strouse, lyrics by Lee Adams)

John and Abigail, pr. 1969

American Primitive, pr. 1971, pb. 1972 (revision of *John and Abigail*)

The Body and the Wheel: A Play Made from the Gospels, pr. 1974, pb. 1975

The Butterfingers Angel, Mary and Joseph, Herod the Nut, and the Slaughter of Twelve Hit Carols in a Pear Tree, pr. 1974, pb. 1975

Golda, pr. 1977, pb. 1978

Goodly Creatures, pr. 1980, pb. 1986

Monday After the Miracle, pr. 1982, pb. 1983

Handy Dandy, pr. 1984, pb. 1986

Raggedy Ann and Andy, pr. 1984 (also as *Rag Dolly* and *Raggedy Ann*; music and lyrics by Joe Raposo)

OTHER LITERARY FORMS

Although William Gibson is primarily a dramatist, his initial successes were as a poet and novelist. His first poetry book, *Winter Crook* (1948), is a collection of his early verse, which is marked by complex use of nature imagery and metaphor to explore highly personal concerns. The novel *The Cobweb* (1954), a best-seller, introduced many of the themes important in his drama: the isolation of the individual, the potentially redeeming capacity of love to form bonds, and the power of language to define the self and its world. Set in a mental institution, the novel explores the relationships that develop among the psychiatric staff, members of their families, and the patients. As the image of the cobweb suggests, these relationships, while not always healthy, connect the characters in complex ways.

Gibson has also written several nonfiction "chronicles." The first of these, *The Seesaw Log*, an account of the writing and producing of his first successful play, *Two for the Seesaw*, was published in 1959 with the text of the play. By chronicling the complexities of producing a play in mid-twentieth century America, Gibson demonstrates that a play, unlike a poem or novel, is a collaborative effort that both tests and invigorates the playwright, who has to work with producer, director, and actors, all of whom can truthfully call the play theirs.

Gibson's second chronicle, *A Mass for the Dead* (1968), is one of his most moving works. A mixture of poetry and prose loosely organized along the lines of the Catholic Mass for the Dead, the book recounts the lives of members of Gibson's family, especially his grandparents and their relatives as well as his mother and father. The book is Gibson's attempt to make sense of his ancestors' lives, tracing their progress from working-class roots to middle-class respectability.

In *Shakespeare's Game* (1978), Gibson turns his attention to practical drama criticism and critical theory. The book grew out of his experience in teaching a university course on playwriting—an experience that forced him to review all the basics of drama. As a result, he developed a terminology with which to discuss the craft and art of playwriting, and in *Shakespeare's Game* Gibson applies this terminology to the work of the greatest English-language dramatist. At the book's end, Gibson reveals the essentially psychological nature of his theory of drama, which has its roots in cognitive psychology. A play's structure, Gibson argues, like the human mind, works to achieve equilibrium; when in the uncomfortable state of disequilibrium, the play moves toward an object that promises relief. This movement dashes against barri-

William Gibson (Courtesy of the D.C. Public Library)

centering on her discovery of the power of language under the tutelage of Annie Sullivan, a master teacher who transformed Keller from a wild animal into a human being. Part of the play's power derives from Gibson's ability to dramatize a historical event. Gibson continued developing this genre in later works, such as *American Primitive*, based on the letters of John and Abigail Adams, and *Golda*, based on the autobiography of Golda Meir, one of Israel's most famous prime ministers. While Gibson's subject matter in these plays is limited by his historical sources—in *American Primitive* the dialogue, except for some verse commentary that Gibson added, comes directly from the Adamses' letters—he uses modern stagecraft to make these lives significant.

Gibson will also be remembered for his creation of strong women characters in a period when such roles were the exception. In *Two for the Seesaw*, one of his most successful Broadway plays, the character of Gittel Mosca, the Jewish girl from the Bronx, overpowers that of Jerry Ryan, the lawyer from Nebraska. As Gibson recounts in *The Seesaw Log*, Henry Fonda, who originally played Ryan, never felt comfortable in the role, partly because of Ryan's paleness compared to Gittel's fullness. *The Miracle Worker*, as well as its sequel, *Monday After the Miracle*, also developed strong women characters, as did *Golda*.

Finally, one of Gibson's most important contributions to the history of the theater is *The Seesaw Log*. By chronicling the composition and production of his play, he details how the mid-twentieth century American theater functioned, from the writing through the selling to the production of a Broadway play. Even though the chronicle is admittedly limited to Gibson's perspective, it re-creates for future audiences the texture and development of a work in progress as the producer, director, and actors, all with their own expertise, transform the playwright's initial creation into their own. Gibson has published other logs

ers that prevent the easy relief of tension in the play and its characters. Using this theory, Gibson demonstrates how a single structure underlies all of William Shakespeare's best plays.

ACHIEVEMENTS

William Gibson will be remembered for his development of the popular biographical play; for his creation of strong women characters, many of whom have been portrayed by actress Anne Bancroft; and for his commentary on mid-twentieth century drama.

Gibson's most successful play, *The Miracle Worker*, was originally written for *Playhouse 90* and in 1957 won the Sylvania Award for the year's best television drama and, three years later, won the 1960 Tony Award for best play. This play pioneered the contemporary biographical drama. In it, Gibson exploited the dramatic qualities in Helen Keller's autobiography,

("Preface: A Momento" with *Golden Boy* and "Notes on How to Turn a Phoenix into Ashes" with *Golda*), but none as detailed or as intriguing as *The Seesaw Log*.

Along with the recognition Gibson received for *The Miracle Worker*, Gibson also was awarded the Harriet Monroe Memorial Prize in 1945 for a group of his poems published in *Poetry*. In 1947 he won a Topeka Civic Theatre Award for *A Cry of Players*, while in 1958 he received a Tony nomination for best play for *Two for the Seesaw*.

BIOGRAPHY

William Gibson was born in New York on November 13, 1914, the son of lower-middle-class parents. The families of both parents were musical. Several of Gibson's maternal uncles belonged to the most famous banjo band of the early 1900's, and his mother's family operated a music school, where Gibson's mother had met his father, a talented popular pianist. Gibson himself mastered the piano and, in his late teens and early twenties, he tried to become a professional musician. This background explains his lifelong attraction to music, an interest reflected in his writing of pieces such as the libretto for the operetta *The Ruby* (which he wrote under the name of William Mass) and the text for the 1964 musical *Golden Boy*, a project that he finished for Clifford Odets, who died before it was completed.

Although Gibson was graduated at age sixteen from Townsend Harris Hall, a high school for academically talented boys that was affiliated with the City College of New York, he found college stultifying. He took his most rewarding classes at City College of New York from English professor Theodore Goodman, who encouraged his writing. After attending college sporadically for about two years, Gibson dropped out to educate himself, to become a musician, and to launch his writing career. During his years in college and immediately after, he became a Depression-era communist and lectured on street corners to support this cause.

In 1940, Gibson married Margaret Brenman, a psychoanalyst, whom he had followed first to her graduate school and then to her psychiatric positions in Topeka, Kansas (where they married), and later in Stockbridge, Massachusetts. His first literary success came with the recognition he gained from his 1945 Harriet Monroe Memorial Prize. In 1954, he published a best-selling novel, *The Cobweb*, which he sold to Hollywood. The movie of the same name starred Lauren Bacall, Charles Boyer, and Richard Widmark and appeared in 1955 after Gibson helped rewrite the screenplay.

Gibson became interested in drama early in his career. After dropping out of college, he acted at the Barter Theatre in Abingdon, Virginia, where he wrote several unproduced plays. While in Topeka, Kansas, he acted in the community theater and wrote his first produced play, *I Lay in Zion*, which was staged at the Topeka Civic Theatre in 1943. His next play, *A Cry of Players*, a three-act drama about the young Shakespeare, won the Topeka Civic Theatre Award in 1947 and was staged in 1948. In the fall of 1950, Gibson met Clifford Odets, one of America's most important leftist playwrights, who admitted him to a playwright's seminar organized at the Actors Studio. During this seminar, Gibson "learned more from him than I believed was possible from any man." After the course, while working at a psychiatric institution, Gibson directed Odets' *Rocket to the Moon* (pr. 1938) with a cast of mental patients. Odets saw this production and became a lifelong family friend.

Gibson's first national successes as a playwright were spectacular. In July of 1958, after an agonizing process (recounted in *The Seesaw Log*), *Two for the Seesaw*, which starred Henry Fonda and Anne Bancroft, opened at Broadway's Booth Theatre to enthusiastic reviews. The play ran for 750 performances and became one of the most successful plays of its era. It was also produced as a movie in 1962 starring Robert Mitchum and Shirley MacLaine. At about the same time, *The Miracle Worker*, which was originally written for television, became a Broadway hit in 1959, starring Anne Bancroft as Annie Sullivan and Patty Duke Astin as Helen Keller. These actresses recreated their roles in the popular 1962 film.

With the money he made selling *The Cobweb* to Hollywood, Gibson bought a house in Stockbridge, Massachusetts. In 1969, he cofounded and became the first executive officer of the Berkshire Theatre Festival in Stockbridge. There, *John and Abigail*, which he later revised as *American Primitive*, was first produced.

In 1971, Gibson almost died of a bleeding ulcer, an ailment from which he had suffered for years. This experience prompted him to reevaluate his life, and, during Christmas of 1972, he went to the Maharishi International University in La Antilla, Spain, to visit his son, who had enrolled in the University. There, Gibson studied under Maharishi Mahesh Yogi and was trained in the theory and practice of transcendental meditation. His interest in religion rekindled, he returned to the Catholic Church, in which he had been reared. He proceeded to write three liturgical dramas: *The Body and the Wheel*, a Passion play; *The Butterfingers Angel*, performed in Lennox, Massachusetts, in 1974; and *Goodly Creatures*, performed in 1980 at the Roadhouse Theatre in Silver Spring, Maryland.

Two major Broadway plays by Gibson that have been neither as critically nor as financially successful as his earlier works are *Golda* and *Monday After the Miracle*. In 1977, *Golda* was plagued by problems and closed after several months. In 1982, a similar fate befell *Monday After the Miracle*, the sequel to *The Miracle Worker*.

Handy Dandy, a two-person play, originally produced unsuccessfully in 1984, was revived in 1990 to slightly better reviews, with James Whitmore and Audra Lindley in the roles. Gibson's Christmas comic/tragic pageant, *The Butterfingers Angel*, which was first performed in 1974, has received several productions, notably at the Olney in Washington, D.C., in 1988, where it returned in 1989 because of popular demand. "A chronicle of hope . . . [which] poses some existential questions," was David Richards's assessment. He also noted that the play's full title, *The Butterfingers Angel, Mary and Joseph, Herod the Nut, and the Slaughter of Twelve Hit Carols in a Pear Tree*, is "a measure of the show's refreshingly antic spirit."

ANALYSIS

William Gibson's plays are marked by impressive literary as well as dramatic qualities. Like much con-

temporary drama, they deal with existential themes, particularly the social and psychological isolation of the individual. To explore these themes, Gibson uses a variety of approaches, including a mixture of comedic and serious elements and an array of innovative production techniques, most notably the split stage to emphasize the psychological isolation of characters. Despite his emphasis on themes of isolation and loneliness, Gibson is not ultimately pessimistic: He shows that love has the potential to unite lonely individuals and that language sheds light on the human condition. Indeed, the consistent weakness in his plays is his tendency toward the sentimental.

Gibson is a popular Broadway playwright whose considerable dramatic talent allows him to fuse comic and tragic elements in a satisfying whole. While not always complete artistic and formal successes, his plays explore significant aspects of the human condition, especially the dangers and joys of love and the need humans have to connect with their fellows.

TWO FOR THE SEESAW

Gibson's first major Broadway play was *Two for the Seesaw*, produced in 1958 and directed by Arthur Penn. Set in New York City, the play explores the relationship between Jerry Ryan, a Nebraska lawyer who is being divorced by his wife, and Gittel Mosca, a Jewish girl from the Bronx. Although much of the play's humor results from the cultural differences between the characters, the true conflict grows from the contrasts in their psychological makeup. Because of this psychological emphasis, *Two for the Seesaw* shares more similarities with Gibson's novel, *The Cobweb*, than with his later biographical drama.

Gibson uses *Two for the Seesaw* to explore one of his most important themes, the isolation of the individual and the need people have for human contact. The stage setting emphasizes this by creating two spaces. One is Jerry's apartment, the other Gittel's. The lighting serves to isolate and emphasize one or the other, and the set registers the passing of time and changes in Jerry and Gittel's relationship. At the play's beginning, for example, Jerry's cheap apartment is bare and impoverished. As their relationship develops, the rooms begin to take on life because of Gittel's womanly touch. When Jerry moves into Gittel's apartment, his clothes and legal papers pile up in corners and on the table. Throughout much of the play, the two characters in their isolated areas are connected only by the telephone, which symbolizes the emotional distance between them.

The central problem of the play grows from the different needs that Gittel and Jerry have for each other, and this makes the play too clichéd to be completely successful. Gittel is a giving woman who allows herself to be used by men. Jerry, on the other hand, is used to taking from the people in his life. His career in Nebraska was successful largely because his father-in-law made him a law partner and bought him a fashionable home. Part of his reason for going to New York was his desire to escape from this kind of support. Because Gittel appears weak and vulnerable, she brings out in him for the first time the need to assist and care for others, and these nurturing feelings are intensified in Jerry when her stomach ulcer hemorrhages and he has to nurse her.

From the start, the play's problem is the unsympathetic nature of Jerry, which is heightened by the basic likability and charm of Gittel. Gibson's dialogue captures her character perfectly and infuses her with humor and spirit. Jerry, on the other hand, is too self-absorbed and self-centered to be likable. Henry Fonda, who originally played Jerry on Broadway, objected to the character's self-centered behavior, arguing that Gittel would have kicked him out rather than put up with his meanness. Although Fonda can be faulted for not understanding Jerry's psychological motivation—his attachment to his Nebraskan wife conflicts with his need for Gittel's support and love—Gibson was guilty of not infusing the male character with the lifelike qualities that Gittel possesses.

The play's ending exposes the imperfections of its characters and structure. Jerry decides to return to his wife, a wiser man because of Gittel's love. Although this desertion is believable, it makes Jerry distasteful, because it is clear that Gittel is left alone and pathetic. Gibson has her claim that she, too, has learned from the experience—she gives up her illusions of

being a dancer, for example—but the audience has little hope that she will find a meaningful relationship. This bleak ending suggests that Gibson was uncertain whether *Two for the Seesaw* was to be comic or tragic, and the mixture of Gittel's comic antics and Jerry's morose irony further confuses the audience about the play's intentions.

THE MIRACLE WORKER

Gibson's reputation rests on his second major Broadway play, *The Miracle Worker*, originally a television play. It opened on Broadway in 1959 under the direction of Arthur Penn and starring Anne Bancroft and Patty Duke. In 1962, after a long run, it was made into a United Artists motion picture starring Bancroft and Duke. Gibson's first major biographical play, *The Miracle Worker* is based on the lives of Helen Keller and her teacher, Anne Sullivan.

The characters and situation are perfect vehicles for two of Gibson's major themes, the isolation of the individual and the power of love to do good and harm. Because of Helen's afflictions—an early illness has left her blind and deaf—she has been cut off from all meaningful human contact. Because of her family's misguided love, she has been pampered and allowed to run wild like an untrained animal. It is only when Annie (as Sullivan is known in the play), herself partially blind, comes to live with the family and insists on disciplining Helen that progress is made.

Two major conflicts arise in the play. The first is between Helen and Annie. When forced to behave in a civilized manner, Helen rebels by attacking Annie, throwing food, and playing for sympathy from her parents. Eradicating this behavior is Annie's first job. The second conflict is between Annie and Helen's parents, Captain and Kate Keller. Captain Keller is an Alabama autocrat who expects Annie, a young Bostonian, to obey without question. His major concern is that she control Helen rather than educate her. Kate Keller feels guilty for Helen's condition and pampers the child. Annie, on the other hand, is a forceful woman who has grown up in terrible circumstances. After her mother's early death and the desertion of her alcoholic father, she was reared in a Massachusetts almshouse and blinded by trachoma. By strength of character and determination, she talked her way into an expensive Boston school for the blind, where she underwent nine eye operations in six years. She consequently has little patience with the Kellers coddling Helen.

One of the central symbols of the play is the water pump that stands outside the Kellers' home. It is there, after months of work, that Annie manages to make Helen recognize the connection between words and things, when she signs the word "water" on the girl's palm as actual water flows across it. It is language that allows Helen to become fully human, and this development is Annie's major triumph in the play. By sticking with her demanding teaching methods, by insisting that Helen learn the importance of language despite her parents' conviction that their daughter could never do so, Annie becomes, in Gibson's eyes, the perfect teacher.

One important theme that the play does not handle well concerns Annie's reactions to Helen's miraculous progress. Because of her horrible childhood, Annie, Gibson implies, has not learned to love, only to fight. At the end of the play, when she clutches Helen to her and proclaims her love for the child, the audience is not prepared for such a transformation in character. The ending does not grow out of the play and seems added to give television viewers the warm glow they have come to expect.

Like many television dramas, *The Miracle Worker*'s answers to complex questions are too pat. At the play's end, all problems are resolved, even though in actuality Captain Keller later tried to charge the public an admission fee to view his "freakish" daughter. Nevertheless, the play remains a profound statement on the importance of faith and hard work and, in part for this reason, has become one of the twentieth century's best-known dramas.

Monday After the Miracle

Gibson takes up a darker strain in *Monday After the Miracle*, the sequel to *The Miracle Worker*. Unlike the earlier play, which is comic in structure because of its happy ending, *Monday After the Miracle* explores Annie's and Helen's personal discontentments as Helen becomes internationally famous, first as a writer and then as a lecturer. Gibson continues ex-

ploring the nature of love, but in this play he examines the gloomier side of that feeling.

The conflict in the play develops among its three major characters: Annie, Helen, and John Macy. When the play opens, Helen, now in her twenties, and Annie, now in her late thirties, have established a unique bond. As "Teacher," Annie has created Helen much as an artist creates a work of art. This project, her lifework, has both invigorated and limited her: She has functioned as Helen's eyes and ears for almost two decades. The love the two women feel for each other is powerful, but it also has become a burden on Annie, who now longs for freedom. Macy complicates matters when he completes the emotional triangle. He comes to help Helen write, and he edits her first major work, her autobiography (Keller published her autobiography, *The Story of My Life*, in 1902), which includes selections from Annie's letters describing her teaching techniques. Both Helen (who is closer to Macy's age) and Annie fall in love with him, and this competition tests the women's relationship.

When Macy falls in love with and marries Annie, other conflicts develop. First, Helen fears that Annie will desert her. This fear is confused by Helen's certainty that Macy had been falling in love with her, not the older Annie. Annie, on the other hand, must struggle with her feelings of guilt about letting someone other than Helen into her life; at the same time, she yearns for marriage, love, and children. After their marriage, Annie and Macy must resolve the conflicts that arise when he becomes sexually drawn to Helen. This situation develops not only because Macy and Helen live in the same household and work closely together but also because Macy feels neglected by his wife, whose major interest in life remains Helen. By the end of the play, Macy's character has disintegrated because of heavy drinking and his humiliating financial dependence on Helen's income from writing and speaking.

If *The Miracle Worker* glorifies the power of love to connect people, *Monday After the Miracle*, like *Two for the Seesaw*, exposes its power to harm and destroy people, especially those who are weak, such as Macy. The relationship between Annie and Helen survives all the pain and conflict, but that between

Macy and Annie does not. Indeed, the failure of the marriage results in part from the intensity of Annie and Helen's love, which began with Annie's need to mold Helen into a full human being and which has become, for better or worse, the central passion of Annie's life.

OTHER MAJOR WORKS

LONG FICTION: *The Cobweb*, 1954.

POETRY: *Winter Crook*, 1948.

SCREENPLAY: *The Cobweb*, 1954 (based on his novel).

NONFICTION: *The Seesaw Log*, 1959; *A Mass for the Dead*, 1968; *A Season in Heaven*, 1974; *Shakespeare's Game*, 1978.

BIBLIOGRAPHY

Atkinson, Brooks. "The Theatre: *Two for the Seesaw*." Review of *Two for the Seesaw*, by William Gibson. *The New York Times*, January 17, 1958, p. 15. A glowing review among many good ones (only Walter Kerr has reservations). Atkinson states that Gibson has "a tender style of writing and a beautiful little story to tell" in this play, which starred Henry Fonda and Anne Bancroft. Concludes that Gibson "has looked inside the hearts of two admirable people" and thanks Gibson for his "thoughtful writing."

Gibson, William. "On the See-Saw." *The New Yorker* 33 (February 15, 1958): 23-24. A chatty interview with Gibson at home with his wife, Margaret Brenman. Contains much personal information in anecdotal style. Informative on unproduced plays and Gibson's offhanded attitude toward them, other thwarted projects, and his early theatrical experiences at the Barter Theatre in Virginia.

Richards, David. "Holiday Pageantry." Review of *The Butterfingers Angel* by William Gibson. *The Washington Post*, December 2, 1989, p. C2. A review of the holiday play *The Butterfingers Angel*, with a few comments on Gibson's ability to "depict the dark side of those long-ago events . . . a show for very nearly the whole family." Describes the "stumblefoot angel," jealous Joseph, and the feeble donkey, and says of Mary, "You may detect a faint radiance dancing about her head."

Simon, John. *Uneasy Stages*. New York: Random House, 1975. In these chronicles, Simon reviews his theater experiences in a conversational tone. Has something to say on the musical version of *Two for the Seesaw*, shortened to *Seesaw*, in the 1972-1973 season. The reader must know what year to look into because Simon offers only seasons in the table of contents. Index.

Michael G. Moran,
updated by Thomas J. Taylor

W. S. GILBERT

Born: London, England; November 18, 1836
Died: Harrow Weald, England; May 29, 1911

PRINCIPAL DRAMA

Ruy Blas, pb. 1866 (in *Warne's Christmas Annual*)

Dulcamara: Or, The Little Duck and the Great Quack, pr., pb. 1866 (based on Gaetano Donizetti's opera *L'elisir d'amore*)

Allow Me to Explain, pr. 1867

Highly Improbable, pr. 1867

Harlequin Cock Robin and Jenny Wren: Or, Fortunatus and the Water of Life, the Three Bears, the Three Gifts, the Three Wishes, and the Little Man Who Woo'd the Little Maid, pr., pb. 1867

The Merry Zingara: Or, The Tipsy Gipsy and the Pipsy Wipsy, pr., pb. 1868

Robert the Devil: Or, The Nun, the Dun, and the Son of a Gun, pr., pb. 1868

No Cards, pr. 1869, pb. 1901 (libretto; music by
   Lionel Elliott)
*The Pretty Druidess: Or, The Mother, the Maid,
   and the Mistletoe Bough*, pr., pb. 1869
An Old Score, pr., pb. 1869
Ages Ago: A Ghost Story, pr., pb. 1869 (libretto;
   music by Frederick Clay)
The Princess, pr., pb. 1870
The Gentleman in Black, pr. 1870 (libretto; music
   by Frederick Clay)
The Palace of Truth, pr., pb. 1870
A Medical Man, pb. 1870, pr. 1872
Randall's Thumb, pr. 1871, pb. 1872
A Sensation Novel, pr. 1871, pb. 1912 (libretto;
   music by Florian Pascal)
Pygmalion and Galatea, pr. 1871, pb. 1872
Thespis: Or, The Gods Grown Old, pr., pb. 1871
   (libretto; music by Sir Arthur Sullivan)
The Brigands, pb. 1871, pr. 1889 (libretto; music
   by Jacques Offenbach)
On Guard, pr., pb. 1872
Happy Arcadia, pr., pb. 1872 (libretto; music by
   Frederick Clay)
The Wicked World, pr., pb. 1873
The Happy Land, pr., pb. 1873 (as F. Tomline, with
   Gilbert A' Beckett)
The Realm of Joy, pr. 1873
The Wedding March, pr. 1873, pb. 1879 (adaptation of
   Eugène Labiche's *Le Chapeau de paille d'Italie*)
Charity, pr. 1874
Ought We to Visit Her?, pr. 1874 (with Annie
   Edwards)
Committed for Trial, pr. 1874, pb. 1930 (adaptation
   of Henri Meilhac and Ludovic Halévy's *Le
   Réveillon*, later revised as *On Bail*)
Topsy Turveydom, pr. 1874, pb. 1931
Sweethearts, pr. 1874, pb. 1878
Trial by Jury, pr., pb. 1875 (libretto; music by
   Sullivan)
Tom Cobb: Or, Fortune's Toy, pr. 1875, pb. 1880
Eyes and No Eyes: Or, The Art of Seeing, pr. 1875,
   pb. 1896 (libretto; music by Pascal)
Broken Hearts, pr. 1875, pb. 1881
Princess Toto, pr., pb. 1876 (libretto; music by
   Frederick Clay)

Dan'l Bruce, Blacksmith, pr., pb. 1876
Original Plays, pb. 1876-1911 (4 volumes)
On Bail, pr. 1877, pb. 1881 (revision of *Committed
   for Trial*)
Engaged, pr., pb. 1877
The Sorcerer, pr., pb. 1877 (libretto; music by
   Sullivan)
The Ne'er-do-Weel, pr., pb. 1878
H.M.S. Pinafore: Or, The Lass That Loved a Sailor,
   pr., pb. 1878 (libretto; music by Sullivan)
Gretchen, pr., pb. 1879
The Pirates of Penzance: Or, The Slave of Duty,
   pr. 1879, pb. 1880 (libretto; music by Sullivan)
Patience: Or Bunthorne's Bride, pr., pb. 1881
   (libretto; music by Sullivan)
Foggerty's Fairy, pr., pb. 1881
Iolanthe: Or, The Peer and the Peri, pr., pb. 1882
   (libretto; music by Sullivan)
Comedy and Tragedy, pr. 1884, pb. 1896
Princess Ida: Or, Castle Adamant, pr., pb. 1884
   (libretto; music by Sullivan)
The Mikado: Or, The Town of Titipu, pr., pb. 1885
   (libretto; music by Sullivan)
Ruddigore: Or, The Witch's Curse, pr., pb. 1887
   (libretto; music by Sullivan)
*The Yeomen of the Guard: Or, The Merryman and
   His Maid*, pr., pb. 1888 (libretto; music by
   Sullivan)
Brantinghame Hall, pr., pb. 1888
The Gondoliers: Or, The King of Barataria, pr.,
   pb. 1889 (libretto; music by Sullivan)
Rosencrantz and Guildenstern, pr. 1891, pb. 1893
The Mountebanks, pr., pb. 1892 (libretto; music by
   Alfred Cellier)
Haste to the Wedding, pr., pb. 1892 (libretto; music
   by George Grossmith)
Utopia, Limited: Or, The Flowers of Progress, pr.,
   pb. 1893 (libretto; music by Sullivan)
His Excellency, pr., pb. 1894 (libretto; music by
   Osmond Carr)
The Grand Duke: Or, The Statutory Duel, pr., pb.
   1896 (libretto; music by Sullivan)
The Fortune Hunter, pr., pb. 1897
Fallen Fairies, pr., pb. 1909 (with Edward
   German)

The Hooligan, pr., pb. 1911
Gilbert Before Sullivan: Six Comic Plays, pb. 1967
   (Jane Stedman, editor)
Plays, pb. 1982 (George Rowell, editor)

OTHER LITERARY FORMS

Apart from his writing for the theater, W. S. Gilbert's principal literary accomplishment is *The Bab Ballads* (1869), whimsical verses that he illustrated himself. Originally published in comic journals such as *Fun* and *Punch*, they are generally regarded as the well from which Gilbert drew many of the songs and situations of his comic operas.

ACHIEVEMENTS

The comic operas of W. S. Gilbert and Sir Arthur Sullivan are the product of one of the most successful collaborations in theatrical history, for while other teams of librettist and composer have achieved comparable distinction, in no other pair have the talents so complemented each other. Both chafed at the fact that their more serious accomplishments were less well regarded, and both tried, without great success, to work with other collaborators. Gilbert's whimsy and legalistic paradoxes would have been little more than quaint if they had not been humanized by Sullivan's melodies, and Sullivan's choral and orchestral virtuosity and his propensity to parody found their focus in Gilbert's preposterous plots. Their initial collaborations took place over a span of six years, during which they were engaged in other artistic enterprises as well. With the composition of *H.M.S. Pinafore*, however, they began a decade of enormous popularity, with virtually one new opera a year, each with a measure of uniqueness yet all derived from a recognizable formula. Although the later operas are somewhat more musically complex and more extravagantly plotted, these advances are less the consequence of artistic maturity than of technical confidence. Gilbert's not too serious social criticism, his tongue-twisting lyrics, and his gentle spoofs of romantic conventions appealed to a middle-class audience that had only recently been persuaded that the theater might be a respectable institution after all. The two operas Gilbert and Sullivan produced after

the great breach that lasted from 1889 to 1893 are not sufficiently inferior to the others as to account for their unpopularity. The vogue of Gilbert and Sullivan had not ended, for the earlier operas continued to be revived. It is more likely that the collaborators had

W. S. Gilbert (Library of Congress)

produced enough operas to keep their public happy. For almost a century, these operas have remained favorites on both sides of the Atlantic, kept alive largely by the D'Oyly Carte Opera Company, holders of the copyright, from whose elaborately stylized and insistently Victorian productions other professional and amateur renditions have been derived. Although changes in the company's finances forced its closure in 1982, interest in the operas was not noticeably diminished, with both Joseph Papp's 1980 revival and the 1983 film version of *The Pirates of Penzance* being well received. Continued interest in Gilbert and Sullivan is evidenced by the release of *Topsy-Turvy*, a 1999 feature film on their collaboration by British filmmaker Mike Leigh.

BIOGRAPHY

William Schwenck Gilbert was born at 17 Southampton Street, Strand, London, on November 18, 1836, the son of a fairly well-to-do naval surgeon, who turned to a literary career at about the same time as young William did. At the age of two, while on holiday with his parents in Italy, Gilbert was kidnapped from his nurse and ransomed for twenty-five pounds. He later claimed to have a perfect recollection of the incident. At any rate, his plots frequently hinge on the removal of infants from their real parents.

Educated at Boulogne, France, and Great Ealing School, he then attended King's College, London, hoping to obtain a commission in the Royal Artillery. The sudden end of the Crimean War made a military career less appealing, and he obtained, by competitive examination, a clerkship in the Education Department of the Privy Council Office, a post he occupied from 1857 to 1862. Coming into an unexpected sum of money, Gilbert was able to free himself from that "ill-organised and ill-governed office." Having already entered the Inner Temple, Gilbert was called to the Bar in 1863. He did not thrive as a barrister, however, earning no more than seventy-five pounds in his first two years of practice. He never wholly abandoned either his military or his legal aspirations, for he held a commission in the Fifth West Yorkshire Militia, the Royal Aberdeen Highlanders, and, from

1893, was a justice of the peace for the county of Middlesex.

Gilbert's career as a writer had been launched as early as 1857, when he accepted a commission to translate a French song for a theater program. His first play to be produced, *Dulcamara*, a travesty based on Gaetano Donizetti's opera *L'elisir d'amore* (1832), was followed in succeeding years by similar treatments of operas by Donizetti, Vincenzo Bellini, Giacomo Meyerbeer, and others. In 1867, Gilbert was confident enough of his abilities to marry Lucy Blois Turner, a woman fourteen years his junior. Despite the example of the tempestuous marriage of Gilberts' parents, his own irascibility, and his almost total absorption in his work, the union appears to have been a happy one. The 1860's were also the years of the composition of *The Bab Ballads*. In 1869, he became a contributor of short comic plays for the German Reed's Royal Gallery of Illustration, which provided a kind of family entertainment mixing song with improbable fable, presented without the elaborate trappings of the stage. He also began writing full-length comedies, such as *The Palace of Truth*, *Pygmalion and Galatea*, and *Broken Hearts*, whose plots involve the intervention of fairies or other supernatural agencies in human affairs.

The first meeting of Gilbert and Sullivan took place at the Gallery of Illustration and was brought about through a common friend. Though each knew the work of the other, it was another two years before Gilbert proposed that Sullivan set to music the draft of *Thespis* (the musical score has since been lost). Neither appears to have taken this first collaboration very seriously, and four years were to elapse before they worked together on another opera, a curtain raiser prodded into being by Richard D'Oyly Carte, then the manager of the Royalty Theatre, in the Soho district of London. The extraordinary success of this piece, *Trial by Jury*, prompted D'Oyly Carte to lease the Opéra Comique as the home of the Comedy Opera Company and to commission a third opera, *The Sorcerer*.

One success followed another. To frustrate theatrical piracy, a continuing problem as the popularity of their work increased, the premiere of *The Pirates of Penzance* took place in New York. By 1881, the trio of Gilbert, Sullivan, and D'Oyly Carte had opened their own theater, the Savoy, the first in the world to be illuminated by electric light. All their subsequent operas were produced here. That two men so temperamentally different—Gilbert, robust and litigious, and Sullivan, frail and affable—should have collaborated at all is more remarkable than that their association became strained during the decade of their greatest artistic and commercial success. Each considered that he was being asked to yield too much to the other. These differences were precipitated by the famous "carpet breach." Believing that D'Oyly Carte had wrongly charged the theater's new carpeting as a cost of production of *The Gondoliers*, rather than as one of building maintenance, and that Sullivan and he were thereby aggrieved, Gilbert insisted on an immediate renegotiation of the agreement among them. When D'Oyly Carte demurred and Sullivan proved insufficiently vigorous in his support of Gilbert's demands, Gilbert became furious and actually took legal action against both of them. Although a compromise was eventually worked out, and two more operas followed the reconciliation, the heyday of the team of Gilbert and Sullivan was over.

Gilbert continued to be active with other collaborators in the 1890's, and he reverted as well to the fairy comedies of his pre-Sullivan days. Gout and other ailments, however, compelled him to lead a life of greater retirement. In 1907, some twenty-four years after Sullivan had received a similar honor, Gilbert was knighted for services to the theater—as a playwright rather than with the more prestigious designation he had craved, that of dramatist. Though rancor figured significantly in Gilbert's life, his death was gallant. Diving to rescue a young woman swimming in the lake on his estate, Sir William suffered a fatal heart attack on May 29, 1911.

ANALYSIS

Alone among the comic versifiers of his age—Lewis Carroll, Edward Lear, C. S. Calverley, Richard Barham, and others—W. S. Gilbert succeeded in converting comic verse to comic song, thereby transcending whimsy. For this, he certainly owes much to Sullivan. Yet in how many operas, comic or grand, does the work of the lyricist or librettist count for much? Gilbert has earned classic status not because he is timeless and universal, but because even after a century, he can impose a Victorian sensibility on his audience.

Gilbert has occasionally been called "the English Aristophanes"; however extravagant that designation, it may serve as a useful point of departure. Assuredly Aristophanic is Gilbert's capacity to create in his plays worlds in which recognizable institutions—the legal system, the military, the rigid caste system of Victorian society—are transformed into absurdities. In *Trial by Jury*, the legal wrangling between the counsels of the jilted Angelina and the flirtatious defendant are resolved by the judgment of the judge—to marry Angelina himself. In *The Pirates of Penzance*, a pirate must first serve an apprenticeship, as though he were an artisan or skilled mechanic; furthermore, the pirate gang is pardoned of all their offenses because "they are all noblemen who have gone wrong." Also Aristophanic, though functioning in a different way, to be sure, are Gilbert's choruses—the sisters, cousins, and aunts of Sir Joseph Porter in *H.M.S. Pinafore*, the giggling schoolgirls of *The Mikado*, or the professional bridesmaids in *Ruddigore*—which serve to accentuate the ludicrousness of the situations.

The essential distinction, however, between the absurdities of Aristophanes and those of Gilbert is that for the Greek dramatist, the source of the comedy lay in some social or political aberration that he meant to expose, if not to correct. For Gilbert, on the other hand, though his plays are not devoid of social or political implications, the source of the comedy lies in the pursuit of some intellectual crotchet or paradox to its ultimate conclusion. The topsy-turviness of Gilbert's plays originates in legalisms and logic-chopping. As a slave of duty, Frederic, the hero of *The Pirates of Penzance*, feels that he cannot betray his pirate comrades, loathsome though their trade is to him, until he is discharged of his indentures on his twenty-first birthday. Having been born on the last day of February in a leap year, however, he discovers that he is, in terms of birthdays celebrated, only a little boy of five. Similarly, through an ancestral curse, each baronet of Ruddigore must commit a crime daily or perish in unutterable agony. Failure to commit a crime is thus tantamount to committing suicide, which is itself a crime. Not only are the dilemmas of the characters resolved by similar sophistry, but also it appears that the complications have been conceived with no other purpose in mind.

One Gilbert and Sullivan work that does not quite fit this description is *Princess Ida*. This opera, however, is essentially a reworking of an earlier Gilbert play, *The Princess*, a "respectful perversion" of Alfred, Lord Tennyson's poem of the same name (1847), that odd composition whose central subject is the education of women. Even here, however, Gilbert treats the topic not as a timely social issue but as an occasion to explore the comic implications of the attempted isolation of one sex from the other. To say that Gilbert's plays take place in artificial environments hardly accounts for the intense intellectual pressure that has gone into their formation. The clash between the fairies and noblemen in *Iolanthe*, for example, originates in the play on the words "peri" and "peer." The officers of the dragoon guards in *Patience* readily abandon their military garb and their military bearing to become aesthetic poets, because only in that guise can they successfully woo the chorus of rapturous maidens.

Each opera enunciates a topsy-turvy premise, which is then examined. In *H.M.S. Pinafore*, it is the notion that "love can level ranks"; in *Patience*, it is that true love is disinterested; and in *Iolanthe*, it is that a race of immortal and insubstantial beings can exhibit all the characteristics of human beings. All these, it should be noted, are romantic notions derived very largely from literature. Gilbert's fancies are drawn as well from some of his own early works, particularly his parodies and *The Bab Ballads*. Very little seems to come from direct observation of life or reflection on personal experience, except for the minutiae, the little personal quirks and foibles that make a caricature. The result is a series of plays often quite rich in references or allusions to contemporary life but as remote from that life as animated cartoons are from the life of animals. The characters and plots have been reduced to formula.

Although some of the variations on them are quite subtle, the character types encountered in Gilbert's plays are almost as rigid as those in classical New Comedy. In addition to the fresh and innocent heroine and her equally ingenuous hero, there is the fastidious and querulous authoritarian (who usually gets to sing the patter song)—Sir Joseph in *H.M.S. Pinafore*, Major-General Stanley in *The Pirates of Penzance*, the Lord Chancellor in *Iolanthe*, King Gama in *Princess Ida*, Ko-Ko in *The Mikado*, and the Duke of Plaza Toro in *The Gondoliers*—as well as the elderly, decayed contralto, who is physically repulsive yet longing for affection—Buttercup in *H.M.S. Pinafore*, Ruth in *The Pirates of Penzance*, Lady Jane in *Patience*, Katisha in *The Mikado*, Dame Carruthers in *The Yeomen of the Guard*, and the Duchess in *The Gondoliers*. The easy classification of roles in these operas makes them particularly attractive to repertory companies.

For all the variety of locales in Gilbert's works, the most frequent form of action involves what has been called the invasion plot. That is, the territory of a more or less settled group is overrun by another, the situation demanding some kind of compromise, if not retreat. Sir Joseph Porter and his female relations board *H.M.S Pinafore*; Major-General Stanley's daughters innocently decide to picnic in the pirates' lair; the procession of peers invades the Arcadian landscape in act 1 of *Iolanthe*, only to have the fairies troop in force to Westminster in act 2. There is actual combat between military units in *Princess Ida*, and in *The Mikado*, the imperial retinue sweeps into Titipu, demanding of its inhabitants the appearance of conformity to decrees from on high.

This reduction of character and plot to a formula, although it is more commercially palatable (thanks to Sullivan's music) than the insipid paradoxes of Gilbert's earlier straight plays, does not initially seem conducive to the generation of enduring art. Yet in at least two ways, it has secured Gilbert's place in the theater, even if not as a dramaturge. First, it provided a vehicle for some of the most versatile metrical and verbal extravagances in the English language. As a lyricist, Gilbert is unsurpassed in his ability to provide both singable *and* memorable words not only to arias, ballads, duets, and choruses but also to part-songs of considerable complexity and to patter songs for single and multiple voices. (Patter songs, which sound like tongue twisters sung at top speed, include "I am the very model of a modern Major-General," from *The Pirates of Penzance*.) The challenge produced the tuneful and rollicking songs familiar to almost everyone, such as "Faint Heart Never Won Fair Lady," from *Iolanthe*, or "For He Is an Englishman," from *H.M.S. Pinafore*. Yet it also produced tender and haunting songs, such as Ko-Ko's "The Titwillow Song" in *The Mikado* (which must surely have originated as a parody of Desdemona's "Willow Song" in William Shakespeare's *Othello, the Moor of Venice* (pr. 1604) and Jack Point's "I Have a Song to Sing, O" in *The Yeomen of the Guard*.

Moreover, it is in these lyrics, rather than in the large themes or preposterous situations of the operas, that Gilbert executes his greatest satiric thrusts. On the whole, like the audience for whom he wrote, Gilbert felt enormously pleased with the general state of things in the world around him and was vexed only by ideas, such as socialism or evolution, that threatened to rend society or by fads, such as aestheticism, that tended to distract it. Yet for all his conservatism, he did not wholly succumb to philistine complacency. In his songs, he frequently targets time-honored objects of satire: the abuse of privilege, the vanity in pride of ancestry, or the posturings of the *nouveau riche*. At the beginning of the second act of *The Mikado*, for example, Yum-Yum is adorning herself in preparation for her wedding day. She sings a song ingenuously identifying her with the world of nature, a song whose operation, like that of Alexander Pope's description of Belinda at the beginning of *The Rape of the Lock* (1712, 1714), simultaneously elicits wonder and censure at the fair creature. As in this song, Gilbert's satire is often ironically self-deprecating, requiring a good deal of attention to be understood.

This demand for attentiveness constitutes Gilbert's second significant contribution to the English theater. He educated a generation of middle-class theatergoers to listen carefully to what was being said onstage and to expect paradox at every turn. Though himself unwilling or unable to use the stage for seri-ous mockery of social institutions, he made it possible for others to do so. He prepared audiences to receive the witty comedies of Oscar Wilde and the more intellectually provocative plays of George Bernard Shaw.

H.M.S. PINAFORE

Trial by Jury demonstrated that Gilbertian humor could successfully be translated to the operatic stage; *The Sorcerer*, that Sullivan could actually compose for Gilbert. In *H.M.S. Pinafore*, the collaboration attained its full flowering. The first and least complicated of their more popular operas, it is also the most familiar. The plot hinges on two threadbare conventions of comedy, a pair of lovers whose union is thwarted by their being of different social classes and a pair of babies, also of different classes, who have been switched in infancy. The discovery of the second circumstance conveniently resolves the difficulty of the first. Gilbert apparently believed in a fluid class structure: Josephine may marry up (although not too far up) but not down the social ladder, and Sir Joseph Porter, while his rise from office boy to First Lord of the Admiralty is a source of some amusement, is not repudiated, either as a cad or as a snob, for rejecting Josephine when she proves to be the daughter of a common seaman. His behavior is seen as quite understandable and serves to refute the absurd egalitarian sentiments he has uttered earlier, sentiments overwhelmed by the jingoistic sailors' chorus and glee. As is usual in Gilbert, the satire against the ruling class is mild. It manifests itself through the self-revelation of an authority figure who is on the whole rather likable, however pompous. In the final analysis, such satire is seen as secondary to the larger purpose of amusement. Sir Joseph and his retinue of sisters, cousins, and aunts are there to provide a complication and a chorus.

THE PIRATES OF PENZANCE

The Pirates of Penzance is, as many have observed, *H.M.S. Pinafore* brought to land. All the color of the nautical talk and the costuming has been preserved in the pirates, the female chorus of Sir Joseph's relations has become that of Major-General Stanley's daughters, and there is even an additional male chorus of policemen. Buttercup, who had been responsible for the mixup of babies in *H.M.S. Pinafore*, has metamorphosed into Ruth, whose blunder is to confuse words, apprenticing the young Frederic to a pirate instead of a pilot. There are distant echoes here of Shakespeare's *The Tempest* (pr. 1611) as Frederic, who has grown up knowing no women other than his nurse, Ruth, discovers the true nature of female beauty in Mabel. The complication is that, as a pirate, he is a sworn foe of legitimate authority, as represented by Mabel's father. Once again, the comic resolution undercuts any serious social criticism: Because they are really renegade noblemen, who owe fealty to Queen Victoria, the pirates surrender in her name and become suitable mates for the Major-General's daughters. There is far less occasion for criticism of social institutions in this opera, however, than in *H.M.S. Pinafore*. Rather, Gilbert takes delight in puncturing romantic myths. Instead of a band of lawless Byronic outcasts, Gilbert's pirates are a guild of credulous, tenderhearted incompetents, whose evil purposes dissolve at once if their intended victim claims to be an orphan (a weakness that Major-General Stanley is quick to exploit). Their antagonists, the local constabulary, prove to be as unheroic as the pirates are unvillainous. Major-General Stanley, like Sir Joseph Porter, is a mere functionary. In the modern world, Gilbert seems to be saying, romantic idealization is no longer tenable, and the conflict between good and evil dwindles into banality.

PATIENCE

Although *Patience* appears to be one of the most topical of Gilbert's works, taking aim at the whole aesthetic movement, the play's origins belie that contention. The central situation derives from "The Rival Curates," one of *The Bab Ballads*, in which two provincial clergymen compete for a title in abnegation or, in Gilbert's term, "mildness." Unlike the opera, the twenty-three-stanza ballad presents no motive for the eccentricity beyond that of a desire for reputation. The essential topsy-turvy premise of the opera, then, is that an affected mannerism extended to one's whole demeanor will excite admiration. Gilbert confessed that he had difficulty sustaining the conceit through the two acts of the opera without falling into bad taste or blasphemy, and this may account for the transformation of the rival curates into poets. The emergence of the young Oscar Wilde as a flamboyant exponent of aestheticism made him appear to be a perfect prototype of Bunthorne, the fleshly poet, an association that proved profitable both for Wilde and the three partners of the D'Oyly Carte Opera Company. Love interest in the opera is supplied by Patience, a dairymaid sensible enough not to be attracted by bizarre behavior yet sufficiently innocent of passion to believe that love must be totally disinterested. It is through the characterizations of the fleshly and idyllic poets, however, that *Patience* achieved its popularity and has maintained its interest. Gilbert's attack was timely, to be sure, but somewhat off the mark. The eccentricity and languor of his poets are fair enough targets of satire, but he invests them as well with a kind of puritanism more appropriate to his curates. Elsewhere, Gilbert administers occasional mild jolts to middle-class complacency; in *Patience*, however, by portraying his poets not merely as fools but also as conscious hypocrites, he panders to philistine anti-intellectualism.

IOLANTHE

Iolanthe brings together the world of Gilbert's earlier fairy plays and the world of reality, particularly legal and political reality. As in *The Pirates of Penzance*, Gilbert insists on looking at romantic matter in a matter-of-fact way. Like the Greek satirist Lucian, Gilbert endows his supernatural creatures not only with immortality, discretionary corporeality, and magical powers, but also with human emotions. The opening chorus of dancing fairies complains of boredom since the exile of Iolanthe for having married a mortal (Iolanthe is subsequently forgiven). The offspring of that union, the shepherd Strephon (a fairy from the waist up), is in love with Phyllis, the ward of the Lord Chancellor, who intends to marry her himself. Needless to say, both the young and the middle-aged lovers are properly sorted out by the end of the opera, but not before several clashes have taken place between the romantic and pragmatic worlds. Phyllis, seeing Strephon in the company of his very youthful-looking mother, is driven to jealousy; he, backed by the powerful influence of the fairies, takes over Parliament, where he proceeds to confound the whole political system by instituting competitive examinations for admission to the peerage and by eliciting assent to all his proposals. *Iolanthe* is quite remarkable for the good-naturedness of its critical observations on parliamentary democracy. At the beginning of act 2, Private Willis's song ponders the division of people into parties, by which they relinquish their private intellects and submit to the discipline of a leader on entering the House of Commons. Two songs later, Lord Mountararat extols the House of Lords for doing precisely nothing and doing it "very well": Britain's glory is contingent on the assurance that "noble statesmen do not itch/ To interfere with matters which/ They do not understand." Taken together, the two songs seem to express Gilbert's belief that, however riddled with anomalies, the British system of government works very well indeed.

The Mikado

The Mikado signaled a change of direction for Gilbert and Sullivan. With the exception of *Thespis*, whose setting is Olympus, and *Princess Ida*, which, like Tennyson's poem, is laid in a legendary atmosphere, all their operas up to *The Mikado* had been contemporary. However outlandish the premises or exaggerated the manners, they could be seen as obvious extrapolations of the familiar. Whether Gilbert felt that he had exhausted this vein or whether the possibility for more elaborate productions was the inducement, *The Mikado* initiated a movement away from the familiar. Though topical allusions abound, the last six operas all take place either in a locale definitely not English or at a time decidedly not the present. They are also characterized by more complicated plots. The simple invasion formula gives way to more intricate maneuverings, and the songs are made to carry a greater burden of exposition and development. Though *The Mikado* may be no less popular than *H.M.S. Pinafore* or *The Pirates of Penzance*, it is more difficult to unravel and its satire is more oblique. Most obviously, in its portrayal of excessive ceremony and politeness masking bloodthirstiness and tyranny, *The Mikado* sardonically congratulates Englishmen for choosing not to belong to any other nation and laughs at the Victorian fascination for things Oriental. It is equally obvious, however, that

Gilbert's Japanese have no more authenticity than his fairies: The opening choruses of *Iolanthe* and *The Mikado* are strikingly similar. In both, the singers proclaim themselves creatures of artistic convention, doomed to perform antics they know to be meaningless. The world of *The Mikado*, then, is one of stylized behavior, in which the law no longer serves society but enslaves it. The Lord Chancellor in *Iolanthe* had proclaimed, "The Law is the true embodiment/ Of everything that's excellent," but it remains for Ko-Ko, the Lord High Executioner, to have "a little list" of society's offenders who can be dispatched whenever a victim must be found, and for the Mikado himself to invent cruel and unusual punishments to "fit the crime." The plight of the thwarted lovers, Nanki-Poo and Yum-Yum, is central; what is topsy-turvy is their entire milieu, in which forms are preserved at the expense of substance.

The Yeomen of the Guard

The Yeomen of the Guard was Gilbert's response to Sullivan's repeated requests for more human situations, for characters less eccentric, and for songs whose sentiments were not continually undercut by irony. Though rich in comic turns, it aspires to the condition of grand, rather than comic, opera. It is quite likely that the setting—the Tower of London in the sixteenth century—with its potential for costuming and design, may have first suggested itself to Gilbert, and that only then did he begin to work on a plot. Sergeant Meryll, a yeoman of the guard, and his son, Leonard, and daughter, Phoebe, plan to effect the escape of Colonel Fairfax, who is destined to be executed on trumped-up charges of sorcery. Meanwhile, Fairfax, knowing nothing of their scheme, is resigned to dying, but desires to marry first and thus thwart the plan of his kinsman, who concocted the charges in order to inherit Fairfax's estate. A hasty marriage is concluded with Elsie Maynard, a strolling singer. Fairfax, disguised as young Meryll, disappears from his cell, and his jailer, Wilfred Shadbolt, who in his love for Phoebe Meryll has unwittingly assisted the plot, is in danger of suffering the penalty in his stead. Shadbolt allies himself with the jester Jack Point, who, as Elsie's lover, has also been discomfited by Fairfax's disappearance, and together, they concoct a tale. Like that of Ko-Ko and Pooh-Bah in *The Mikado*, the explanation given for Fairfax's absence is filled with "corroborative detail, intended to give artistic verisimilitude to an otherwise bald and unconvincing narrative," maintaining that Shadbolt shot Fairfax dead as he tried to escape. Phoebe, in love with Fairfax and in distress at seeing him woo Elsie in the guise of her brother, reveals his true identity to Shadbolt. As Phoebe and Shadbolt are now in possession of each other's secret, they agree to marry in order to purchase each other's silence. Fairfax, who has actually been reprieved, is genuinely attracted to the wife he has acquired out of convenience, Sergeant Meryll pairs off with Dame Carruthers, the housekeeper to the Tower, and only Jack Point is left pathetically without a mate at the opera's conclusion. The substitution of intrigue for topsy-turviness obviously distances *The Yeomen of the Guard* from *H.M.S. Pinafore*, yet the work is recognizably Gilbertian; for all their melodramatic pretensions, the characters have affinities with those of the other operas. Even Jack Point, who falls insensible as the curtain descends, is cousin to the Lord Chancellor and Ko-Ko. The plight of these characters, however, has been more poignantly imagined.

THE GONDOLIERS

Composed in the midst of mounting strife between Gilbert and Sullivan, *The Gondoliers* is their last major theatrical success. In many ways it is the most colorful and lyric of the whole series. The richness of its foreign setting may be rivaled by that of *The Mikado*, but musically, it is unequaled; for this opera, Sullivan added to his usual array of arias, duets, part songs, and choruses the rhythms of Spain and Italy. Gilbert worked what must be the ultimate variation on the baby-swapping convention: Throughout the opera, the audience waits to find out which of the two gondoliers is the rightful king of Barataria, only to discover what may have already been guessed—that neither is. During the last few minutes of the opera, an even earlier switch is announced as having taken place, conveniently preventing the marriage of royalty with the lower orders. Indeed, it often appears that Gilbert is engaging in self-parody in *The Gondoliers*, for the situations of the earlier operas are

here piled on one another. Topsy-turviness is present not merely in the mixup of the infants but also in the joint rule of the two gondoliers while they await the determination of their status and in their ludicrous attempts to introduce republican monarchy. In the antics of the Duke and Duchess of Plaza Toro, Gilbert is not repudiating the aristocratic ideal—the Grand Inquisitor sings persuasively of the need for degree in a stable society. Rather, Gilbert portrays in them examples of a decayed and venal aristocracy. Like Pooh-Bah in *The Mikado*, they have pride but no honor. For all its sprightliness, however, *The Gondoliers* lacks the integrity of the earlier operas: Themes and characters are introduced capriciously because they have worked before.

OTHER MAJOR WORKS

SHORT FICTION: *The Lost Stories of W. S. Gilbert*, 1982.

POETRY: *The Bab Ballads*, 1869; *More Bab Ballads*, 1873; *Songs of a Savoyard*, 1898.

BIBLIOGRAPHY

Crowther, Andrew. *Contradiction Contradicted: The Plays of W. S. Gilbert*. Cranbury, N. J.: Associated University Presses, 2000. Criticism and interpretation of the plays of Gilbert. Bibliography and index.

Finch, Michael. *Gilbert and Sullivan*. London: Weidenfeld and Nicolson, 1993. A look at the collaboration between Gilbert and Sir Arthur Sullivan. Bibliography and index.

Fischler, Alan. *Modified Rapture: Comedy in W. S. Gilbert's Savoy Operas*. Charlottesville: University Press of Virginia, 1991. Fischler begins his analysis with Gilbert's fiftieth theatrical work, *H.M.S. Pinafore*, because it both separated him from other Victorian playwrights and was the turning point in his comic dramaturgy. Gilbert's new approach to comedy appealed to bourgeois prejudices and provided his greatest popularity. Extensive notes and index.

Joseph, Tony. *The D'Oyly Carte Opera Company, 1875-1982: An Unofficial History*. Bristol, England: Bunthorne, 1994. A history of the opera company at which most of the Gilbert and Sullivan works were performed. Bibliography and index.

Orel, Harold, ed. *Gilbert and Sullivan: Interview and Recollections*. Iowa City: University of Iowa Press, 1994. A collections of interviews and essays remembering Gilbert and Sir Arthur Sullivan. Bibliography and index.

Stedman, Jane W. *W. S. Gilbert: A Classical Victorian and His Theatre*. New York: Oxford University Press, 1996. A look at Gilbert's life and works, including his collaborations with Sir Arthur Sullivan. Bibliography and index.

_____. *W. S. Gilbert's Theatrical Criticism*. London: Society for Theatre Research, 2000. A close examination of the criticism around Gilbert. Bibliography and index.

Wilson, Robin, and Frederic K. Lloyd. *Gilbert and Sullivan: The Official D'Oyly Carte Picture History*. New York: Alfred A. Knopf, 1984. Hundreds of photographs and designs from the 107-year history of the D'Oyly Carte Opera Company trace the evolution of the Savoy operas onstage in both England and the United States. Brief introductions to each section include biographical and critical information on Gilbert as it pertains to the opera company. Illustrations, bibliography, and index.

Ira Grushow,
updated by Gerald S. Argetsinger

REBECCA GILMAN

Born: Trussville, Alabama; 1964

PRINCIPAL DRAMA

The Land of Little Horses, pr. 1989, pb. 1998
The Glory of Living, pr. 1996, pb. 2001
My Sin and Nothing More, pr., 1996, pb. 1997
Spinning into Butter, pr. 1999, pb. 2000
Boy Gets Girl, pr., pb. 2000
Crime of the Century, pr. 2000
The American in Me, pr. 2001
The Great Baseball Strike of 1994, pr. 2001
Blue Surge, pr., pb. 2002

OTHER LITERARY FORMS

Rebecca Gilman, who considers herself exclusively a playwright, has written only works for the stage, though she has considered writing for the screen.

ACHIEVEMENTS

Since the opening of *The Glory of Living* at the Circle Theater outside of Chicago in 1996, Rebecca Gilman has enjoyed immense popularity among American dramatists. Her work was immediately recognized as important by critics and audiences and has been produced at various theaters in the United States. *The Glory of Living* received several awards for playwriting, including the American Theatre Critics Association's M. Elizabeth Osborn Award and London's *Evening Standard* Theatre Award for most promising playwright—an award Gilman was the first American playwright to win. *Spinning into Butter* appeared on Broadway and was directed by Tony-winning director Daniel Sullivan. It also received the Robert L. Stevens Award from the Kennedy Center Fund for New American Plays. Her work has also been featured at the Actors Theatre of Louisville's annual Humana festival. She has received several commissions for new work from the Goodman Theatre in Chicago as well as a Guggenheim Fellowship for writing.

Gilman has been positively received around the country for her ability to address unafraid the darker side of human nature. She has tackled such hard-to-stage issues as child abuse, racism, violence, and obsession and done so in a brutal fashion that often defies the politically correct environment of modern theater. Gilman has a strong following, along with the support of the Goodman Theatre.

BIOGRAPHY

Rebecca Gilman was born in 1964 in Trussville, Alabama, where she enjoyed a quiet southern upbringing—a childhood that is evidenced in her mild demeanor and soft southern drawl. After experiencing an unremarkable upbringing, Gilman left home at seventeen to attend college on the East Coast. A restless student, she attended four schools on her way to receiving two degrees. She dropped out of Middlebury College—an experience that would later inspire a play—before receiving her B.A. in English from Birmingham-Southern University in Alabama. Subsequently, she dropped out of graduate studies at the University of Virginia before receiving an M.F.A. in playwriting from the University of Iowa. She had been writing plays since the age of eighteen—her first play was about a Krispy Kreme doughnut shop—and some of them were produced either nonprofessionally or as student productions at Birmingham-Southern and later the University of Iowa. Many of these early works were children's plays, with titles such as *Hansel and Goosel*, and bear little resemblance to the gritty body of work for which she is now known.

After Gilman was graduated from the University of Iowa, she took a hiatus from her writing career. She got married, moved to Iowa City, and began working for a standardized testing agency to earn money. After three years and a divorce, Gilman moved to Chicago and worked as a temporary office worker while reexamining herself as a writer and shopping her work to theaters around the country. During this period, her plays were rejected by many theaters, which considered them to be too rough or daring to stage.

Gilman was thirty-two years old when she had her breakthrough production. Her agent convinced a small theater outside of Chicago, the Circle Theater in Forest Park, Illinois, to produce *The Glory of Living*, Gilman's play about a child bride turned serial killer. Though the theater was small, as was the pro-

duction, it was strong enough to garner positive feedback from Chicago critics as well as attention from Chicago's Goodman Theatre, which immediately offered Gilman a five-thousand-dollar commission for her next work.

Despite the pressure of her sudden popularity, Gilman lived up to expectations by producing *Spinning into Butter*, based on her experiences at Middlebury College. Gilman, who never felt as if she fit in with the East Coast students, whom she found somewhat pretentious, created the character of Sarah, who echoes these fish-out-of-water sentiments. *Spinning into Butter*, an exploration of hidden racism among liberal school administrators, was shocking to many audiences because of its no-holds-barred approach to tackling racism and because of its harsh and decidedly nonpolitically correct language. The Goodman Theatre was impressed enough with the positive critical response to this play to offer Gilman a standing commission. *Spinning into Butter* then went to Broadway, where the playwright's reputation would become national.

The Goodman Theatre also commissioned Gilman's next work, *Boy Gets Girl*. *Boy Gets Girl* was well received and is considered by some critics to be her strongest work. After the success of *Spinning into Butter*, *Boy Gets Girl* easily found a production in New York's Manhattan Theater Club, as did *The Glory of Living*. Gilman married literature professor Charles Harmon and moved to Columbus, Ohio. Though she considers herself a writer for the stage, she has begun exploring screenwriting.

ANALYSIS

Rebecca Gilman is remarkable because she gained almost instantaneous popularity in what is essentially the middle of her career. The same reasons that many theaters gave for rejecting her work earlier in her career—that her writing was too harsh or risky and that it risked offending or alienating the audience—are largely what have made her so popular. Gilman's risk taking has paid off and has allowed her to explore some of the more difficult issues of modern society on the theater stage. Audiences have come to expect that her writing will shock or repel them, and she has made a point of making her characters both thoughtful and brutal as well as both violent and sympathetic. Perhaps her strongest asset is her attention to realism in language, as well as her ability to develop her characters honestly in exploration of a particular issue. Her plays advocate this kind of attention to the real individual.

Gilman, in her treatment of issues as diverse as racism and the objectification of women, always keeps at the forefront her premise that individual crimes cannot be considered apart from the forces of society. Her work indicts the human tendency to make the individual into an object—something that is done whether an individual is being vilified or glorified. In the world of Gilman's characters, a young girl is capable of assisting in the serial murder of other young girls solely because she was not taught to value herself. Similarly, a seemingly ordinary blind date becomes obsessive and violent as a result of societal forces that put a price tag on the female form. Her ability to make these connections between society and the individual has enabled her to put a human face on seemingly insurmountable issues such as racism.

Gilman's villains often do not appear onstage but take shape in the audience's mind through their reported interactions with the other characters. In *Spinning into Butter*, the central character of Simon Brick—an African American student who essentially persecutes himself—is never seen onstage, but an image of his character is formed through the dialogue of those who deal with him. In *Boy Gets Girl*, the obsessive stalker is seen only in a brief and awkward opening scene before disappearing into the elusive oblivion of Theresa's retelling. This method of bringing the audience into her storytelling has allowed Gilman to bring a play about racism to audiences reluctant to talk about it and to create a widely popular feminist-leaning play about stalking.

THE GLORY OF LIVING

The Glory of Living is considered to be Gilman's professional breakthrough because it was her first work to gain recognition from the Chicago theater scene and is the work that earned her the Goodman Theatre's Scott McPherson Award. It never became as widely performed as her later plays, probably because of its graphic subject matter. *The Glory of Living* is based on a true-crime story that took place in Gilman's native Alabama. It features a neglected trailer-park teenager, who is abused and manipulated by an older husband. The two go on a murderous spree in which the wife, Lisa, lures young girls to motels for her husband's pleasure before killing them at his behest.

Gilman does not pull punches with the sexuality or violence of this setup, and its bitter slice-of-life quality characterizes her style. The style has been praised by some critics for being unflinching and dismissed by others for being needlessly brutal. *The Glory of Living* uses Lisa's childlike willingness to kill as a springboard to ask questions about youth and responsibility. Gilman asks her audience: To what extent is society responsible for the demons it produces? At what point do we become responsible for our own actions? What happens to a society when its children are neglected? In an approach that would become typical of Gilman, these question are not answered, but rather asked firmly and with a careful eye on personal consequences.

SPINNING INTO BUTTER

This Gilman play is her most commercially successful as well as her most produced. Responsible for launching her national popularity, the play is an examination of hidden racism amidst the liberal white environment of a private East Coast college campus. Her inspiration in writing this play came mostly from her own experiences as a student at Middlebury College in Vermont. The plot of *Spinning into Butter*, which involves racist threats being made at a mostly white campus and the revelation that the target of the threats and the person making them are the same African American student, is based on an actual incident that took place while Gilman was attending Middlebury. Like Gilman herself, the central character of Sarah, a school official transplanted to the East Coast from Chicago, experiences difficulty fitting in at Middlebury.

The play, in a sort of bait-and-switch fashion, establishes Sarah as a clearly sympathetic character before suddenly exposing her hidden racism. Sarah and her colleagues at the predominantly white Belmont find themselves at the center of a debate about race when an African American student—Simon Brick—becomes the victim of racist threats. At the outset of the play, Brick brings to school officials some threatening notes that he found taped to his door and a brick that was thrown through his window. The incident creates an uproar among Belmont's liberal administration, who systematically and bureaucratically proceed to deal with the problem. By the end of the play, Brick has admitted to writing the notes himself, but not before the administration has managed to alienate the school's minority population in their series of public forums.

The title reference is to the children's story "Little Black Sambo," in which a boy baits a group of prowling tigers until they fall into a frenzy and spin themselves into butter. The story resonates with the play in that, though the original threat of racism turned out to be imaginary, the frenzied efforts of the members of the administration to cover up or correct the problem eventually reveal their misunderstanding of their own feelings. A gripping monologue in the second act reveals Sarah's reluctant racism, feelings she developed while working at a minority school before moving to Belmont.

The play focused on reaching an audience of seemingly enlightened white liberals, and perhaps because of this, many African American theatergoers found it difficult to watch. Critical responses either lauded Gilman for not backing down from difficult realities or derided her for not including a single African American character in a play about racism. The play seems to suggest that public dialogue about racism is rarely truthful or productive; however, when *Spinning into Butter* premiered, the theater group held a post-play discussion on racism with the audience.

BOY GETS GIRL

Influenced by Gilman's feminist sensibility, this exploration of the social forces behind stalkers is recognized as one of her finest pieces of narrative playwriting. Centered around magazine executive Theresa and a blind date that goes from awkward to pushy to downright violent, *Boy Gets Girl* resembles the 1987 film *Fatal Attraction*, which brought attention to this form of stalking. *Boy Gets Girl*, unlike most of its counterparts on the screen, goes deeper into the social forces at work in violent male obsession. Gilman's play does not place the blame in obvious hands; rather, it explores the habits of the criminal, the habits of the victim, and the habits of those around her in its comprehensive look at female objectification.

In the world of *Boy Gets Girl*, stalking, obsession, and violence are not simply the crazed acts of a lone criminal; rather, they are the unfortunate combination of a variety of social shortcomings. Gilman embodies her indictment of objectified female beauty in the character of Les Kennkat—a Russ Meyer-style filmmaker and connoisseur of the female breast. Although Kennkat claims to be celebrating the female form, the play argues that this type of glorification is as much a form of dehumanization as anything else and is therefore to be abhorred as objectification.

Rather than portray women as the helpless victims of crimes beyond their control, Gilman explores Theresa's role in the situation as co-conspirator and product of social conditioning. The play focuses on Theresa's initial reluctance to go on the blind date and her desire to please others. Eager to avoid offense, Theresa initially ignores or even caters to Tony's bizarre behavior, until the roller coaster has gained too much momentum. The play does not so much blame the victim as analyze her role in the odd social dance of stalker and victim. Ultimately, Gilman advocates an absolute truthfulness in human interaction. All parties—Tony, Theresa, her boss, and her secretary—are eventually guilty of dehumanizing themselves and one another and of hedging the truth to preserve the status quo.

BIBLIOGRAPHY

Boehm, Mike. "Willing to Say What Others Won't." *Los Angeles Times*, September 2, 2001, p. F40. Boehm examines audience reactions to *Spinning into Butter* and Gilman's sudden popularity. He interviews Gilman as well as Goodman Theater executive director Roche Schulfer, who compares Gilman to David Mamet.

Jones, Chris. "The Beginner's Guide to Rebecca Gilman." *American Theatre* 17, no. 4 (April, 2000): 26-29. Jones presents a short biography of Gilman before delving into an analysis of her work. He emphasizes Gilman's obsession with crime, as well as her ability to connect individual deviants with social forces.

Smith, Sid. "The Solution Is the Hard Part: Playwright Puts a Provocative Spin on America's Hidden Racism." *Chicago Tribune*, May 28, 1999, p. C1. Smith interviews Gilman about the success of *Spinning into Butter*. Gilman talks about racism and the role of her play in its dialogue.

Leah Green

FRANK D. GILROY

Born: New York, New York; October 13, 1925

PRINCIPAL DRAMA

Who'll Save the Plowboy?, wr. 1957, pr., pb. 1962
The Subject Was Roses, pb. 1962, pr. 1964
That Summer—That Fall, pr., pb. 1967 (includes his teleplay *Far Rockaway*)
The Only Game in Town, pr., pb. 1968
Present Tense, pr. 1972, pb. 1973 (4 one-act plays: *So Please Be Kind, 'Twas Brillig, Come Next Tuesday, Present Tense*)
The Viewing, pr. 1976, pb. 2000
The Next Contestant, pr. 1978, pb. 1979 (one act)
Dreams of Glory, pr. 1979, pb. 1980 (one act)
Last Licks, pr. 1979, pb. 2000 (also as *The Housekeeper*, pr. 1982)
Real to Reel, pr. 1987, pb. 1993
A Way with Words, pr. 1991, pb. 1993 (one act; pr. as part of Ensemble Studio Theatre's Marathon '91)
Any Given Day, pr. 1993, pb. 1994
A Way with Words: Five One Act Plays, pb. 1993 (includes *A Way with Words, Match Point, Fore!, Real to Reel*, and *Give the Bishop My Faint Regards*)
Getting In, pr. 1997, pb. 2000
The Golf Ball, pr. 1997, pb. 2000
Contact with the Enemy, pr. 1999, pb. 2000
Frank D. Gilroy, pb. 2000 (vol. 1: *Complete Full-Length Plays: 1962-1999*, vol. 2: *Fifteen One-Act Plays*)

OTHER LITERARY FORMS

Frank D. Gilroy's career as a writer has been devoted primarily to drama, although he collaborated with his wife, Ruth G. Gilroy, on a children's book, *Little Ego* (1970), and he is also the author of two novels: *Private* (1970), a fictionalized account of his experiences in the army, and *From Noon Till Three: The Possibly True and Certainly Tragic Story of an Outlaw and a Lady Whose Love Knew No Bounds* (1973), a Western with a comic twist.

In addition, Gilroy has had an active career as a television scriptwriter and as a screenwriter. During the 1950's, he was a contributor to many of the television programs that stimulated a new interest in drama in the United States: *Studio One, Kraft Theatre, U.S. Steel Hour, Playhouse 90, Omnibus, Lux Video Theater*, the *Armstrong Theater*, and *The Dick Powell Show*. Gilroy's screenwriting career developed initially out of his work for television. *The Last Notch* (1954), a Western drama he wrote for television, became the source of his first screenplay, *The Fastest Gun Alive* (1956). In the 1960's, he adapted two of his own plays for the screen, *The Subject Was Roses* (1968) and *The Only Game in Town* (1969). In the 1970's, Gilroy was the director as well as the writer of *Desperate Characters* (1971), *Once in Paris* (1978), and the film version of *From Noon Till Three* (1976). In 1998, Gilroy's *Money Plays* won a Writers' Guild Association Award for best original comic film script of that year.

ACHIEVEMENTS

Frank D. Gilroy's most impressive accomplishment has been his ability to master the techniques of three genres of drama, television, film, and the theater, and to gain recognition for his writings in each field. He not only wrote for television during its golden age; he was one of the playwrights who made it golden. In addition to his national reputation as a playwright, Gilroy became nationally known as a screenwriter when he adapted his play *The Subject Was Roses* for film. Patricia Neal was nominated for an Academy Award for her role as Nettie Cleary, and Jack Albertson won the Academy Award for Best Supporting Actor in the role of John Cleary. In 1971, Gilroy received international attention as writer, director, and producer of *Desperate Characters*, which won a Silver Bear Award at the Berlin Film Festival.

Gilroy's achievements and contributions as a stage writer form the basis for his place in American literature. His reputation as a dramatist is assured by the literary and theatrical merits of *Who'll Save the Plowboy?* and *The Subject Was Roses*. Not only have his first two plays been more highly regarded by critics and audiences than his later works, but also they continue to be produced. *Who'll Save the Plowboy?* won the Obie Award for the best American play produced Off-Broadway during the 1961-1962 season. *The Subject Was Roses* was the choice of many as the best play of 1964-1965; it won the Outer Circle Award (1964), the New York Drama Critics Circle Award (1964), the New York Theatre Club Award (1964-1965), the Tony Award (1965), and the Pulitzer Prize in Drama (1965). Gilroy received an honorary doctor of letters degree from Dartmouth College in 1966.

Frank D. Gilroy holds up his Drama Critics Circle Award in New York City in 1965. (AP/Wide World Photos)

Gilroy has also been recognized by his fellow dramatists as a spokesperson and advocate for the writing profession. His well-publicized campaign to get and keep *The Subject Was Roses* on the stage set an example for other playwrights in challenging the play-financing establishment and in having drama produced on the playwright's own terms. In 1965, he filed suit against two publishers, a television network, and two television production companies for misappropriating his property as a writer. When Gilroy won his case eleven years later (1976), his lawyer, Robert Ehrenbard, was quoted in *Publishers Weekly* as saying, "It is a very important victory for writers and supports their rights in a way that the law hasn't done before." It is evidently for efforts such as these that Gilroy was chosen to be a member of the Council of the Dramatists Guild and then its president (1969-1971).

BIOGRAPHY

Frank Daniel Gilroy was born and grew up in New York City. He was the only child of Bettina and Frank B. Gilroy. His father, like John Cleary in *The Subject Was Roses*, was in the coffee business. The family lived in an apartment in the West Bronx. Memories of his early family life and his relationship with his parents eventually provided material for *The Subject Was Roses* as well as for *Last Licks* and *Any Given Day*. By the time Gilroy was graduated from DeWitt Clinton High School in 1943, he had shown an interest in writing but little promise as a student; his father was evidently willing to send him to college, but his grades were not good enough. Gilroy's autobiographical novel *Private* opens with an account of a visit to New Haven and the humiliating return trip to New York after Yale University had rejected his application. Gilroy uses this event as the basis for his play *Getting In*.

Gilroy was drafted into the United States Army ten months after his high school graduation. He would say later that during his tour in the army his life underwent "some good and productive changes." In Europe, however, attached to the Eighty-ninth Infantry Division Reconnaissance Troop, he saw degradation, the threat of death, and witnessed the depravity of the final days of the war. *Private* records the indelible impression of his army experiences; war memories both trivial and serious also surface in *Who'll Save the Plowboy?* and *The Subject Was Roses*.

In 1946, Gilroy came out of the army with a desire to write and the determination to go to college. He applied to forty colleges and was accepted by only two of them—Davis and Elkins, and Dartmouth. He chose Dartmouth and was graduated magna cum laude with a bachelor of arts degree in 1950. In college, he wrote stories and was an editor of the paper, but a playwriting course convinced him that drama was the form best suited to his talents. During his junior and senior years, he wrote and was accorded productions of two full-length plays and six one-act plays. In both years, he won the Frost Playwriting Award. Following his graduation, Gilroy attended the Yale School of Drama with the help of a scholarship, but his funds ran out after six months.

The growing popularity of television provided a new market for playwrights, and Gilroy began writing scripts for television in the early 1950's. To support himself during this period, he held a series of jobs—including messenger, trumpet player, and cabana salesman—but by the mid-1950's he was making a good living from television. He wrote regularly for two popular Western series, *The Rifleman* and *Have Gun, Will Travel*, in addition to having plays produced by the leading network drama programs. He wrote at least three plays for *Studio One: A Likely Story* (1955), *Uncle Ed and Circumstances* (1955; adaptation of a story by Jackie Gleason), and *The Last Summer* (1958). Two of his plays appeared on *Kraft Theater: Run for the Money* (1954) and *Ten Grapefruit to Lisbon* (1956). *A Matter of Pride* (1957; adaptation of John Langdon's story "The Blue Serge Suit") was shown on the *U.S. Steel Hour*. For *Playhouse 90* he adapted two works by John P. Marquand, *Sincerely, Willis Wayde* (in 1956) and *Point of No Return* (in 1958).

In 1954, Gilroy married Ruth Gaydos, and by the time *The Subject Was Roses* was produced, ten years later, they had three sons and lived in upstate New York. For several years at the end of the 1950's, however, while Gilroy was employed as a studio screen-writer, California was his home. This experience was evidently the inspiration for *'Twas Brillig*, a one-act comedy about a writer's first day on a studio lot. In 1960, Gilroy collaborated with Beirne Lay, Jr., on *The Gallant Hours*, a biographical film about Admiral William Halsey, starring James Cagney. Gilroy's work for television and films gave him enough time and income to write for the stage and enabled him to complete *Who'll Save the Plowboy?* in 1957.

Gilroy moved his family back to New York in 1961, and in 1962, he found a producer for *Who'll Save the Plowboy?* Although its reviews were generally favorable and it won an Obie Award, the play did not enjoy a long run—a month at the Phoenix Theatre and another month at the Orpheum Theatre. Its production at the Haymarket Theatre in the spring of 1963 introduced Gilroy's work to London audiences. On May 25, 1964, *The Subject Was Roses* opened at the Royale Theatre on Broadway, then moved to the Winthrop Ames Theatre on September 7, 1964. Although it ended up being Gilroy's longest-running drama and greatest achievement, he worked steadily for two years to get it produced and then faced the threat of an early closing. The play not only survived but also received 832 performances in New York, toured the United States, and was produced in a number of other countries. *The Subject Was Roses* won almost every award given for the best play of 1964-1965. In *About Those Roses: Or, How Not to Do a Play and Succeed* (1965), Gilroy gives a diary account of his struggles for the play from its completion in the spring of 1962 to its opening night in the spring of 1964. In a 1966 interview with Joseph Blank in *Reader's Digest*, Gilroy summed up the meaning of the experience for him: "It's amazing how much *can* be accomplished if you believe in what you want to do. The strength of your belief makes others believe."

In a story in *Life* three months after the opening of *The Subject Was Roses*, Tom Prideaux reported that Gilroy had become a "hot property" and had received offers "to adapt sixteen books into movies, to write four musicals and six TV pilot films." Gilroy may never have committed himself to any of these proj-

ects, but the decade between 1965 and 1975 was to become the most active period of Gilroy's writing career. In 1965, *Far Rockaway*, a very brief expressionistic play in thirteen scenes, was presented on National Educational Television. When it was printed with the Random House edition of *That Summer— That Fall*, Gilroy claimed that the little drama demonstrated that he was not exclusively dedicated to the "real." *That Summer—That Fall*, Gilroy's updated dramatization of the Phaedra story, opened on March 16, 1967, at the Helen Hayes Theatre in New York, and closed on March 25. The film of *The Subject Was Roses* was released in 1968, and on May 23, 1968, Gilroy's Las Vegas love comedy, *The Only Game in Town*, opened at New York's Broadhurst Theatre, only to close on June 1. The film of the comedy, for which Gilroy wrote the screenplay, was released a year later with Elizabeth Taylor and Warren Beatty as the lovers. *Little Ego*, the children's book that Gilroy wrote with his wife, Ruth, was published in 1970; the same year saw the publication of *Private*, Gilroy's autobiographical war novel. The novel is written in an impressionistic style, resembling in its form and its evocative power the interchapter vignettes of Ernest Hemingway's *In Our Time* (1924, 1925). Gilroy produced, directed, and wrote the screenplay for *Desperate Characters* in 1971; the film was adapted from a novel by Paula Fox and starred Shirley MacLaine. A program of four of his one-act plays—*Come Next Tuesday, 'Twas Brillig, So Please Be Kind*, and *Present Tense*, opened at the Sheridan Square Playhouse on July 8, 1972, and closed July 23. Gilroy's Western novel, *From Noon Till Three*, was published in 1973. Its comic irony develops from two versions of a frontier romance told first by a lady and then by her outlaw lover. Gilroy adapted the story for the screen and produced and directed the film, which was released in 1976 and featured Charles Bronson and Jill Ireland in the leading roles. In the same year, Gilroy returned briefly to television to adapt stories by John O'Hara for *Gibbsville*, a short-lived series that he directed.

In 1976, Gilroy also realized a great profit, however indirectly, from another television play, *Who Killed Julie Greer?* (1961), which he had written for

The Dick Powell Show fifteen years earlier. In the play, he created the character of Amos Burke, a wealthy detective, who became the main character in the television series *Burke's Law* two years later (1963). In 1965, Gilroy filed suit against two publishers, a television network, and two television production companies for the misappropriation of his Burke character, and after eleven years of litigation a jury awarded Gilroy one million dollars in compensation and interest.

After that, Gilroy wrote the screenplay for *Once in Paris*, which he also produced and directed. His full-length play *Last Licks* focuses on the relationship between father and son and reveals an unhappy marriage and a family triangle in their past. With its autobiographical roots, the comedy is a sequel to *The Subject Was Roses*. *Last Licks* opened at the Longacre Theatre on November 20, 1979, and closed December 1. The plays that Gilroy wrote after 1964 have closed after disappointingly short runs, yet Gilroy has retained a dramatist's interest in the theater and in theater groups devoted to developing and showcasing new plays. Two of his one-act plays, *The Next Contestant* and *Dreams of Glory*, were produced by the Ensemble Studio Theatre in its annual play festivals.

In addition to pursuing a successful television and screenwriting career, Gilroy continued to write for the stage. His plays are frequently produced in regional and community theaters. The one-act play *A Way with Words* was produced by the Ensemble Studio Theatre in May, 1991, as part of a short-play marathon; *The Subject Was Roses* was revived on Broadway in June of 1991 and continued to be revived throughout the 1990's. Unfortunately, critical opinions of that decade found the play to be outdated and overly sentimental. Generally, critics thought that the play failed to hold up for 1990's audiences

Gilroy's legacy to writing extends far beyond Monroe, New York, where he was residing at the start of the twenty-first century. Two of his sons are highly regarded screenwriters and attribute their successes to what they learned from their father. Gilroy's third son is also a part of the film industry. In 2000, Smith and Kraus publishers issued Gilroy's collected works in two volumes as a part of their Contemporary Dramatists series, demonstrating the value and appeal his plays hold for theater intellectuals and enthusiasts. As a realistic playwright in the 1960's and 1970's, Gilroy often faced the hostility or indifference of critics who were embracing the absurdists and who dismissed realistic drama as dull and outmoded. He also found himself challenging the values of producers who dismissed as a bad investment any play that was serious and had no music or lyrics. He succeeded in overcoming the opposition of both groups by the sheer power of his writing in *Who'll Save the Plowboy?* and *The Subject Was Roses*. In these plays and occasionally in his later works, Gilroy has contributed to an evolving tradition in the best modern American drama, which refines and applies the techniques of psychological realism to a focus on the family and marriage.

ANALYSIS

Most of Frank D. Gilroy's plays—both comic and serious, full-length and one-act—may be identified by their development of themes and situations that are related to marriage or family problems and by their ironic style. Unhappy or failed marriages are directly or indirectly responsible for complications in *Who'll Save the Plowboy?*, *The Subject Was Roses*, *That Summer—That Fall*, *The Only Game in Town*, *Last Licks*, *So Please Be Kind*, and *Come Next Tuesday*. Family problems centering on the relationship between father and son or on an Oedipal triangle are sources of conflict in *The Subject Was Roses*, *That Summer—That Fall*, *Last Licks*, and *Present Tense*. Gilroy's realistic drama, like Henrik Ibsen's, is distinguished not so much by its verisimilitude in dramatizing these problems as by its mastery of irony. In each of his full-length plays, in the manner of Ibsen's *Hedda Gabler* (pb. 1890, pr. 1891; English translation, 1891), Gilroy creates patterns of irony through triangular character relationships: in *Who'll Save the Plowboy?*, Albert and Helen Cobb and Larry Doyle; in *The Subject Was Roses*, John and Nettie Cleary and their son, Timmy; in *That Summer—That Fall*, Angelina and Victor Capuano and Victor's son, Steve; in *The Only Game in Town*, Fran Walker, Joe Grady, and Thomas Lockwood; and in *Last Licks*,

Matt and Dennis Quinlan and Fiona (but also Matt and Dennis Quinlan and Margaret Quinlan, the dead mother). This triangular design allows for developments, in the relationship and dialogue between two characters, that are concealed from the third character but revealed to the audience. The complexities of the pattern may be expanded by shifts in the balance of the triangle that give each character a turn as the victim of irony.

WHO'LL SAVE THE PLOWBOY?

The inciting action in *Who'll Save the Plowboy?* is deceptively simple, because only two of the characters who will form the ironic triangle are onstage when the play opens. An unhappily married couple, Albert and Helen Cobb, argue as they await the visit of Larry Doyle, Albert's buddy during the war. Larry risked his own life and was wounded in carrying out a miraculous battlefield rescue that saved Albert's life. Helen suspects that Larry is coming to ask for something, and, in an ironic way, he is. Albert, who considers Larry to be the best friend he ever had, anticipates an opportunity of some kind, perhaps a job offer. A bitter quarrel erupts when Helen balks at Albert's plan that they act like a loving couple and welcome Larry into a happy home. They exchange insults and threats, and Albert slaps his wife when she makes fun of the "Plowboy" image he is reviving for Larry's sake. Before Larry arrives, Albert warns Helen not to mention the "farm" or the "boy."

Albert and Larry have not seen each other for fifteen years, but the joy of their reunion is quickly dissipated. Each man is surprised and disappointed by the changes in the other. Albert is made increasingly uncomfortable by Larry's questions about the "boy," the son who was named after Larry and is supposedly visiting relatives. Larry is evasive in speaking about his own life and work. Both men are disturbed by Helen's cutting remarks. The first scene ends in a violent argument between the two men after Albert reveals to Larry the sordidness of his life—the failure of the farm he bought after the war, his drinking problem, and his unfaithfulness to his wife. As Albert pleads with him to save the Plowboy again, Larry, disgusted, leaves the apartment but collapses on the stairs.

The first scene provides the exposition necessary to understand the relationships among the three central characters and the basic situation in the play, yet the scene is even more important in setting up the ironies that develop in the second scene of act 1 and in act 2. Before Larry arrives, the dramatic interest is created and sustained not by irony but by the strident verbal exchanges between Albert and Helen and particularly by Helen's sarcasm and ridicule of Albert. In her self-hatred ("Every night before I go to bed I hope I won't wake up in the morning") and in the destructive power of her words, she resembles Martha of *Who's Afraid of Virginia Woolf?*, the Edward Albee play that opened eight months after Gilroy's drama. After Larry enters, the first pattern of irony is introduced in the reversal of the two friends' expectations. Albert remembers Larry as a joking, hell-raising, hard-drinking woman-chaser, and he finds that Larry is serious, single, and no longer drinks. Larry discovers that Albert, who never took a drink, now drinks heavily. He finds it even harder to believe that the young man whom he had nicknamed the "Plowboy" and who had talked constantly about owning a farm is living in a run-down apartment in New York City and reading meters for a living.

In the second scene of act 1, Gilroy introduces the first of a series of discoveries that contribute to the ironic design that gives focus and dramatic force to the play. Mrs. Doyle, Larry's mother, reveals to the Cobbs her son's secret and his purpose in visiting them. Mrs. Doyle tells them that Larry has been in and out of hospitals for years and does not have long to live. He is dying of cancer that developed from the wound he sustained in saving Albert. Shortly after the war, when Larry discovered that his condition was terminal, he dropped out of medical school, where he was the top student, and broke off his engagement to spare the girl he loved. Mrs. Doyle lets Albert know that she blames and hates him for ruining her son's life. She also suggests that Larry has come to the Cobbs in the hope of proving before his death that Albert's life and family were worth the life and happiness he gave up. The scene ends with Albert, tormented by guilt, vowing to convince Larry that he is happy in his life and marriage. Helen agrees to join him in the masquerade and to pretend that Mrs. Doyle never called or told her story.

Although the irony at the end of act 1 depends on the Cobbs's discovery of Larry's secret, the irony in act 2 is created by Larry's discovery of the Cobbs's secret, which provides both the climax and the resolution of the play. Larry's first discovery on the morning after his illness, however, merely develops the incidental irony that Helen has been just as unfaithful as Albert. After Albert has left the apartment to meet his boss, Larry tries to get Helen to tell him why she hates him. She breaks down, and when Larry plays the piano to get her to stop crying, she becomes even more upset. The trumpet player who lives upstairs appears at the door, and Larry deduces that Helen uses her piano as a signal for her lover. Promising not to reveal her secret yet unable to learn the reason for her hatred, Larry tells Helen that he intends to stay in New York until he meets the "boy" who bears his name. The "boy" is Larry's last hope of giving meaning to the life he sacrificed by saving Albert. Realizing that Larry will not heed her warning to spare himself by leaving, and "sick of lies," Helen reveals the secret about the "boy" that became a psychological cancer for her and Albert and destroyed their marriage: "I gave birth to a monster. . . . Not boy. Not girl. Not anything. . . . It took something in him and something in me. Something bad in the both of us to produce this thing." Helen's confession and the irony of its grotesque response to Larry's hope form the climax of the play. The monster child and its malignant effects on Helen, Albert, and their marriage are comparable to the imaginary child and its effects on George and Martha in *Who's Afraid of Virginia Woolf?* The monster would never have been born if Larry had not saved Albert, and that is why Helen has hated Larry. She suggests that Albert also regrets that he was not left to die.

In releasing her pent-up feelings, Helen inadvertently reveals that she and Albert know that Larry is dying. What follows this disclosure is one of the two moments of warmth and compassion in the play. After Larry tells Helen that the truth has drained away her hatred of him, she takes his head in her hands and kisses him on both cheeks and the forehead. The se-

crets that Helen and Larry now share and keep from Albert create the final ironies of the play's resolution. Albert returns with a boy whom he has picked up on the street and passes him off as his son. Although Larry is almost disgusted enough to spoil Albert's plan, he creates the second compassionate moment by accepting the boy as his namesake and, in effect, saving the Plowboy again. It is possible to interpret the close of the play as an act of compassion on Helen's part, as she answers "Yes" when Albert asks her if she thinks Larry believed the boy was their own. What makes the ending ambiguous and contributes the final irony is the sound of the trumpet in the background as Albert says, "Well, it was worth it. . . . He believed me. . . . I owed him that."

THE SUBJECT WAS ROSES

The Subject Was Roses is a more appealing play than *Who'll Save the Plowboy?*, and its three characters are more fully realized and more intrinsically interesting than Larry Doyle or the Cobbs. The irony, too, is more subtle and sympathetic and develops more directly from the characterizations of John, Nettie, and Timmy Cleary and from their relationships with one another. Although *The Subject Was Roses* is a "comedy drama," Gilroy's Cleary family may be compared with the Tyrones of Eugene O'Neill's *Long Day's Journey into Night* (pb. 1955). Like Edmund Tyrone, Timmy Cleary overcomes his resentment of his father and his blind loyalty to his mother and achieves a better understanding of both parents. Like Mary Tyrone, Nettie Cleary was devoted to her father as a girl and feels that her marriage was a mistake—a comedown in class and something of a fall from innocence. She will not forgive John his past infidelities. John Cleary, like James Tyrone, grew up in abject poverty and is tightfisted with his money. Vital and gregarious as a young man, in his middle years, he has trouble expressing his emotions and seems to be much more unfeeling than he actually is. Yet the form and substance of Gilroy's play has more to do with character relationships than with individual characterizations. A triangle is formed by the conflict between Nettie and John over Timmy, as each attempts to secure his love and allegiance. The shape of the triangle changes during the play as Timmy feels more strongly the pull of ties first to one parent and then to the other. It is only in the end that, in Timmy's eyes, all sides of the triangle are equal and the family relationships are balanced.

The first act of the play focuses on the realignment of family loyalties that begins when Timmy returns home after three years in the army. It is clear from conversations between Nettie and John and from Timmy's own remarks that in the years before he left home, he was much closer to his mother than to his father. In the exchange between Nettie and John that begins the play, John voices the hope that his relationship with his son will improve now that his son is a man, and everything that happens in the first act seems to support his hope, as Timmy displays not only a new understanding of his father but also similar personality traits. They drink together, take in a ballgame, and team up for an impromptu vaudeville routine after a night on the town. More important, they talk together, and for the first time Timmy is able to form his own impressions of his father. As a boy, he saw his father through his mother's eyes and accepted her judgments of him. Timmy gains a new appreciation of his father's humor, his fighting spirit, and his successful struggle out of poverty.

In the first act, as Timmy draws closer to his father, he pulls back gently, but firmly, from his mother. It is not that Timmy loves his mother less but that he realizes better his position at the center of his parents' conflict with each other. He is also aware that his identity is no longer defined solely by his role as a son and that he must claim his independence. Timmy's withdrawal from his mother's hold on him is dramatized in an emotionally intense moment in the first scene. When Nettie says she cannot believe he is home again, Timmy extends his hand and tells her to pinch him. His mother takes his hand, holds on, and will not let go until Timmy becomes agitated and "jerks" his hand free. Much of the irony in the first act comes as Timmy pulls away from his mother's grip on his life, and there is a reversal in her expectations of continuing their past relationship. Nettie is surprised and upset not only because Timmy is doing things with John instead of with her, but also because he shows signs of taking after his father—telling

jokes, repeating John's favorite expressions, and drinking too much.

Act 1 concludes with a bitter argument between Nettie and John following the family's evening in New York. After Timmy has gone to his room, John grows amorous, and Nettie resists. Their struggle becomes ugly when John resorts to force; it ends with Nettie smashing the vase of roses she has been led to believe were a present from John. She has been moved by the roses, but she will not forgive his unfaithfulness—his "hotel lobby whores"—and refuses to renew their sexual relationship. In his frustration at the end of the scene, John tells her that the roses were Timmy's idea. Although the friction over their son is a serious problem between them, it is only the visual symptom of other dire problems underlying and undermining their marriage.

Nettie tells John that "what's wrong" between them "has nothing to do" with Timmy, but it does. The second act opens the morning after, and John, still smarting from Nettie's rejection, vents his anger on Timmy as well as Nettie. The scene suggests the tone of John's relationships with his wife and son before Timmy left home. His petulance gives way to outraged disbelief when Timmy declines to attend Mass with him because he no longer considers himself to be a Catholic. When Nettie defends Timmy's right as a man to choose for himself, John speaks bitterly of the "familiar alliance" between mother and son. Ironically, after John leaves the house, Timmy stands up for his father and tries to get his mother to admit that it was "always us against him." It is evidently the first time Timmy has ever argued seriously with his mother or sided with his father: "You, and him, and me, and what's been going on here for twenty years. . . . *We've* got to stop ganging up on him." Timmy also accuses Nettie of bolstering the alliance against John by maintaining close ties and daily contact with her mother and sister. The irony is doubled at the end of the scene when Nettie, angered by Timmy's accusations, thanks him for the roses and stalks out of the apartment with fifty dollars in coins that she has saved.

Irony is created in the second scene of act 2 in its reversal of one of the more melodramatic scenes of the Cleary's prewar family life. It is ten o'clock on a Sunday night, and it is Nettie, not John, who has not returned home. As the father and son wait and seek news of her, it is John who is frantic and Timmy who is drunk—but well aware of the irony of his father's position. He recalls for his father the dreaded ritual that was repeated throughout his childhood of lying awake listening for his father's return from a late-night adventure and for the argument between his parents that inevitably followed. The irony of the scene is complete when Nettie comes home but refuses to respond to John's angry demands for an explanation. Instead, she uses John's favorite alibi of having been to a movie. Finally, as John presses her for an answer, Nettie insinuates that she has been with another man. She never reveals the truth of her absence to husband or son and will say only that her twelve hours away from them gave her the only "real freedom" she has ever known. Regardless of whether Nettie walked out with the intention of teaching her son a lesson, her rebellious act has that effect. Timmy's memories of his father's irresponsible behavior bring a further adjustment in his relationship with both parents.

The proof of a new evenness in Timmy's attachments to his parents is provided in the scene that follows. At two in the morning, Timmy and Nettie, who have been unable to sleep, talk together in the living room. Timmy tells his mother that he must leave home, and she accepts his decision. Nettie then tells Timmy the story of how she met and married John. Like Mary Tyrone, she describes her marriage in a litany of regret as the inevitable tragic turning point of her life. It is at this point that Timmy speaks of the shifts in his loyalties and of his new and more balanced view of his parents: "When I left this house three years ago, I blamed *him* for everything that was wrong here. . . . When I came home, I blamed *you*. . . . Now I suspect that no one's to blame. . . . Not even me."

The play ends as it began, by focusing on John and Timmy and on the final adjustment that ensures Timmy's balanced relationship with his parents and his own independence. Unsuccessful in his appeal to Nettie to persuade Timmy to stay, John himself tries to talk Timmy out of going. He tells him that he is willing to let him do as he pleases in the house, and, confessing that he was wrong in his treatment of Timmy in the past, he promises to change. Timmy insists that he must leave, but he gives his father an assurance of his love that makes his leaving bearable for both. Timmy tells his father of a childhood dream that he had dreamed again the night before—that his father would die without ever saying he loved him. Then, Timmy says, "It's true you've never said you love me. But it's also true I've never said those words to you. . . . I say them now—I love you, Pop." Timmy's declaration and what follows—the father and son in tears and embracing each other—provide the emotional climax of the play and a happy ending for Timmy, but there is no happy resolution of his parents' marital problems. Gilroy spoke openly of the play's roots in his own family life. In his interview for *Reader's Digest*, he explained that the play had been written several years after his parents' deaths as his "way of saying how [he] came to love them." By including unpleasant recollections as well as happy memories and by treating them honestly, Gilroy avoided the sentimentality that would have spoiled the play.

THAT SUMMER—THAT FALL

That Summer—That Fall, Gilroy's most ambitious drama, fails because it neglects the proven strengths of his first two plays—psychological realism and irony. Gilroy may also have made a mistake in taking the material for his play from a classical tragedy, turning away from his own experience. In another sense, however, the Phaedra story, with its unhappy marriage and its father-son conflict, was a logical choice for the author of *The Subject Was Roses*.

The play is given a contemporary setting in a rundown Italian neighborhood of New York City; with the exception of the opening and closing scenes in a playground, the action takes place in the apartment of Victor and Angelina Capuano. In his delineation of his characters and their relationships, Gilroy shows the influence of Jean Racine's *Phèdre* (pr., pb. 1677; *Phaedra*, 1701) as well as Euripides' *Hippolytos* (428 B.C.E.; *Hippolytus*, 1781). Victor, whose role is comparable to that of Theseus in the original story, is a successful restaurant owner in his mid-fifties. His wife, Angelina, who is thirty-six, is Gilroy's modern

Phaedra and, like Racine's heroine, is the dominant character in the play. Angelina falls in love with Steve Flynn before Victor brings him home and identifies him as his illegitimate son. Steve resembles Racine's Hippolytus more closely than he does Euripides' chaste woman-hater. By the end of the play, he is dating Josie, a teenage neighbor girl who has fallen in love with him. Zia Filomena, Angelina's aunt, plays the part of go-between that Euripides assigned to Phaedra's nurse and Racine expanded for Oenone, the nurse and lady-in-waiting of his Phaedra.

The plot of *That Summer—That Fall* follows Euripides' tragedy more closely than Racine's. When the play opens, Angelina is already tormented by her secret passion for Steve. From papers his mother left after her death, Steve has discovered that Victor is his father, and he has hitchhiked from California to meet him. Victor accepts Steve as his son, all the more eagerly because he and Angelina are childless. A close, trusting relationship grows quickly between father and son, and they are soon working together as partners. At the same time, Angelina's desire and frustration are intensified by living with Steve under the same roof.

The turning point of the play comes on a night on which Josie and Steve have gone to a dance. Angelina attempts to dull her pain with wine, and in an inebriated stupor, she confesses to Zia her love for Steve. The following morning, after Victor has told her that Steve will be staying, Angelina's thoughts turn to suicide. Zia realizes what Angelina plans to do and promises to help her. With the idea of bringing Angelina and Steve together to save her niece's life, Zia sends the young man to Angelina's bedroom.

The climax and resolution follow very quickly. Mistaking Steve's intentions in visiting her room, Angelina kisses him passionately and confesses her love. Steve is repulsed by her passion and tells her to go back to the playground and find another boy. When Steve returns to the apartment late that night, he finds Victor sitting alone in the dark. Angelina has killed herself, leaving a letter accusing Steve of raping her. Steve tells his father that the letter is a lie, but Victor will not believe him. After Steve runs out of the apartment, Victor confronts Zia with Steve's

denial, and she finally confesses the truth—that Angelina loved Steve, "was dying for him," but that nothing happened between them. A hysterical Josie rushes in to tell Victor that Steve has crashed his car and is dying. The play ends with Steve, who lies dying in his father's arms, saying, "Raise me up," and Victor replying, "To heaven if I could."

Gilroy was upset by the hostile reception his play received and by its failure, and he offered his defense in a foreword to the Random House edition: "It was my intention that *That Summer—That Fall* should work both realistically and as ritual. Unfortunately, the latter element has, so far, escaped detection." The problems with *That Summer—That Fall*, however, have nothing to do with realism or ritual: The play lacks adequate plot development and convincing motivation for Angelina and Steve. At the end of the play, each crucial scene—from the moment that Steve enters Angelina's bedroom to the moment of his death—is unusually brief and is developed in dialogue that is monosyllabic and frequently stichomythic. As a consequence, there is little opportunity for the development of irony. Angelina's attraction to Steve comes across as lust, not love, since she registers her feelings most strongly whenever she sees Steve bare-chested. Unrequited lust is not a believable motive for suicide or revenge, and because nothing happens, Angelina has no reason to feel guilty or sinful. Steve has even less motive for suicide, if indeed that is the way his automobile wreck is to be taken. He has no reason to blame himself for Angelina's death, and his father's wrongheaded rejection hardly seems motive enough to take his own life. Indeed, the best explanation of the motives of Angelina and Steve would seem to be that they behave as they do because that is the way Phaedra and Hippolytus behave.

THE ONLY GAME IN TOWN

The Only Game in Town is worth mentioning because it is Gilroy's only full-length comedy, and Gilroy is a talented comic writer—as is evident in *The Subject Was Roses* and *Last Licks*, as well as in the short comedies *'Twas Brillig*, *So Please Be Kind*, and *Dreams of Glory*. The plot complications in *The Only Game in Town* may be contrived, but the humor of the dialogue is as sharply honed and as quickly paced as Neil Simon's. The play also makes good use of comic irony to develop an idea that is treated seriously in Gilroy's other full-length plays: that marriage is a gamble at long odds. Appropriately enough, the comedy is set in Las Vegas, the action taking place in Fran Walker's apartment over a period of two years. Fran, one of the players in the love game, is a nightclub dancer who has not yet had the courage to bet on matrimony. It is revealed at the end of the play that she has feared and avoided marriage because her father deserted the family when she was ten years old. The other player is Joe Grady, a piano player who is also a compulsive gambler and a two-time loser at marriage. The first act traces the development of the relationship between Fran and Joe from a casual sexual liaison into a love that each feels but conceals from the other. In the second act, having lived together for almost two years, Fran and Joe remove the obstacles to their marriage and reluctantly agree to wed. Joe licks his gambling problem, and Fran, although she is still "scared," finally takes a chance. The theme of the comedy and its underlying attitude toward marriage are expressed by Joe in proposing to Fran: "Granted that marriage is a most faulty, pitiful, and wheezing institution, right now it's the only game in town and *we're* going to play it."

LATER WORK

Gilroy's first and, some would have it, finest work was done with small-cast plays. Writing in the 1960's when costs of commercial theater productions were soaring, Gilroy used small casts and one-set plays to stem the tide of rising production expenses and was able to do so without sacrificing the quality of his scripts. Although Gilroy was known for his strong writing and sense of comedy, in his later works, he was unable to strike the chord that had made successes of his earlier works. During the 1993-1994 television season, he attempted, unsuccessfully, to revive his earlier hit series *Burke's Law*. During 1993, Gilroy also saw his film script for *The Gig* (1985) revised into a musical script for theater by Douglas Cohen. The play went through a series of workshops, including the Eugene O'Neill National Music Theatre Conference, and has been performed in regional the-

aters across the country. In 1998, Gilroy wrote the screenplay for *Money Plays*, a film about a Las Vegas casino worker pulled into a gambling scheme by a call girl he has been dating. Although the film was not a huge box-office draw, it won a best original comedy script award by the Writers' Guild, demonstrating the respect that others in the writing profession hold for Gilroy.

During the latter part of the 1990's, Gilroy's output for the stage remained at a high level. Closely associated with the Ensemble Studio Theatre in New York, Gilroy contributed scripts to the theater's Marathon one-act play series. Gilroy's preoccupation with autobiographical material (dysfunctional family life and the aftereffects of military service during wartime) became more and more obvious through these later scripts. In 1997, *Getting In*, a one-act play, arose from Gilroy's own struggle to be accepted in a college after the war. Described as a comic view of postwar optimism, critics found the play to be fully rounded and satisfying, In 1999, the Marathon series featured *The Golf Ball*, Gilroy's play about retirement and the extremes to which retirees will go in order to fill their time.

CONTACT WITH THE ENEMY

Gilroy's greatest theatrical achievement during the 1990's may well be *Contact with the Enemy*, produced for a limited run by the Ensemble Studio Theatre in 1999. During World War II, Gilroy was a member of the liberation force at Ohrduf-Nord concentration camp, and the images he found there have remained with him all his life. Drawing on that experience, he created an hourlong drama about two members of that liberation force who happen to meet while visiting the United States Holocaust Museum in Washington, D.C. The guide, discovering this fact, asks them to commit their memories to tape. In the course of doing so, some other memories emerge, such as the mistreatment of a German soldier who had become a prisoner of war. The issue here is whether others, far removed from Nazism, are capable of participating in the brutality associated with the Holocaust. Critical and personal responses to this play were more positive than any others since *The Subject Was Roses*.

OTHER MAJOR WORKS

LONG FICTION: *Private*, 1970; *From Noon Till Three: The Possibly True and Certainly Tragic Story of an Outlaw and a Lady Whose Love Knew No Bounds*, 1973 (also as *For Want of a Horse*, 1975).

SCREENPLAYS: *The Fastest Gun Alive*, 1956; *The Gallant Hours*, 1960 (with Beirne Lay, Jr.); *The Subject Was Roses*, 1968 (adaptation of his play); *The Only Game in Town*, 1969 (adaptation of his play); *Desperate Characters*, 1971 (adaptation of Paula Fox's novel); *From Noon Till Three*, 1976 (adaptation of his novel); *Once in Paris*, 1978; *The Gig*, 1985; *The Luckiest Man in the World*, 1989; *Money Plays*, 1998.

TELEPLAYS: *The Last Notch*, 1954; *Run for the Money*, 1954; *A Likely Story*, 1955; *Uncle Ed and Circumstances*, 1955; *Sincerely, Willis Wayde*, 1956 (adaptation of John P. Marquand's play); *Ten Grapefruit to Lisbon*, 1956; *A Matter of Pride*, 1957 (adaptation of John Langdon's story "The Blue Serge Suit"); *The Last Summer*, 1958; *Point of No Return*, 1958 (adaptation of Marquand's play); *Who Killed Julie Greer?*, 1961; *Far Rockaway*, 1965.

NONFICTION: *About Those Roses: Or, How Not to Do a Play and Succeed*, 1965; *I Wake Up Screening! Everything You Need to Know About Making Independent Films Including a Thousand Reasons Not To*, 1993.

CHILDREN'S LITERATURE: *Little Ego*, 1970 (with Ruth G. Gilroy).

BIBLIOGRAPHY

Guernsey, Otis. *Burns Mantle Theatre Yearbook: The Best Plays of 1993-1994*. New York: Limelight Editions, 1994. The volume contains information and facts about *Any Given Day*, which is a "prequel" to *The Subject Was Roses*. John, Nettie, and Timmy Cleary are presented as younger selves.

Hischak, Thomas S. *American Theatre: A Chronicle of Comedy and Drama, 1969-2000*. New York: Oxford University Press, 2001. This survey of the commercial theater in New York gives an insight into Gilroy's place and contribution to the contemporary theater.

Kerr, Walter. "Play: Gilroy Drama of Age, *Last Licks*." Review of *Last Licks*, by Frank D. Gilroy. *The New York Times*, November 21, 1979, p. C11. This review of *Last Licks* provides an interesting examination of the genre problem caused by the incongruities of the first and second acts. Kerr questions whether the play is a comedy or "a deeply serious psychological snarl." In the second act, Kerr says. "[Gilroy] has . . . put an abrupt end to the pleasures that popped out of him while he was feeling his way."

Simon, John. *Uneasy Stages*. New York: Random House, 1975. A homage to Gilroy, whose *The Subject Was Roses* disappointed Simon. The ending, Simon remarks, "depended on a sudden and ephemeral paternal embrace, insufficiently motivated and unable to carry its load of hope—it was unearned." Simon describes Gilroy as "a product of television's Golden Age" and believes that Gilroy's plays belong on television, minus the sexual boldness.

Taubman, Howard. "Play by Frank Gilroy at the Royale Theater." Review of *The Subject Was Roses*, by Frank D. Gilroy. *The New York Times*, May 26, 1964, p. 45. Judges *The Subject Was Roses* to be "an impressive stride forward" from *Who'll Save the Plowboy?*, which Taubman says showed promise. Gilroy "knows the difference between sentiment and sentimentality and he is not betrayed into the latter." Martin Sheen, an unknown at the time, played the returning soldier in this production.

Weales, Gerald. *The Jumping-Off Place: American Drama in the 1960's*. New York: Macmillan, 1969. Weales treats Gilroy in a chapter entitled "Front Runners, Some Fading" and criticizes his work as suggesting television material rather than work for the stage: "It was neither the many scenes nor the suspicious length [of *That Summer—That Fall*] that suggested television; it was the tone of the play." Good comments on the artificially happy endings, especially in *The Only Game in Town*.

Ted R. Ellis III,
updated by Thomas J. Taylor and H. Alan Pickrell

GIAMBATTISTA GIRALDI CINTHIO

Born: Ferrara (now in Italy); November, 1504
Died: Ferrara (now in Italy); December, 1573

PRINCIPAL DRAMA

Orbecche, pr. 1541, pb. 1545 (verse play)
Didone, public reading 1541, pb. 1583 (verse play)
Cleopatra, wr. before 1543, pr. 1555, pb. 1583
    (verse play)
Altile, wr. before 1543, pr. before 1545, pb. 1583
Egle, pr., pb. 1545
Gli antivalomeni, pr. 1548, pb. 1583 (verse play)
Eudemoni, pr. 1549, pb. 1877
Selene, wr. c. 1554, pr. before 1560 (verse play)
Euphimia, pr. 1554, pb. 1583
Arrenopia, pr. 1563, pb. 1583
Epitia, pb. 1583
Le tragedie di Giambattista Cinthio, pb. 1583

OTHER LITERARY FORMS

Giambattista Giraldi Cinthio is best known today for his critical theory on drama and epic and for his short-story collection *Hecatommithi* (1565), though in his time he was an important and influential playwright and theatrical producer as well. His *Discorso intorno dei romanzi, delle commedie e delle tragedie e di altre maniere di poesia* (1554) contains a treatise on epic and chivalric poetry, *Discorso intorno al comporre dei romanzi* (*On Romances*, 1968), and two treatises on theater, one on comedy and tragedy, *Discorso intorno al comporre delle commedie e delle tragedie*, and another on satyr plays, *Discorso sopra il comporre le satire atte alla scena*. He was probably the author of the anonymous *Giuditio sopra la tragedia di Canace et Macario* (1550), which attacked Sperone Speroni's tragedy *Canace* (1542). He experimented in many other literary genres, writing Italian and Latin verse, an epic poem, and a manual of courtly deportment.

ACHIEVEMENTS

Giambattista Giraldi Cinthio was an inventive, though not a great dramatist who made a unique and often determining mark on sixteenth century tragic theater, pastoral drama, and literary theory. His major dramatic success, the tragedy *Orbecche*, which had at least eleven editions in the sixteenth century, became the model for the tragic theater that followed. Giraldi Cinthio did not approve of pastoral drama, and with his *Egle* he sought to recover the ancient Greek satyr play for the contemporary stage. Although *Egle* had no direct following, certain of its features reappeared in the later masterpieces of pastoral drama, and despite its author's intentions, it seems to have been an important precedent for the development of the genre. Finally, Giraldi Cinthio was one of the first to write a commentary on Aristotle's *De poetica* (c. 334-323 B.C.E.; *Poetics*, 1705) and, among Italian critics, the first to question some of its central precepts, though he did so by claiming to be in agreement with them. His critical writing on theater and epic proved to be even more influential than his theater, both in Italy and throughout Europe.

The appearance of Giraldi Cinthio's first tragedy, *Orbecche*, was an important moment in the history of the tragic genre in Italy, which is largely the history of the reception of Aristotle's *Poetics*, and it was a decisive one for the fortunes of Seneca in the Renaissance. Senecan tragedy had long been the model of Italian tragic theater, but Giraldi Cinthio accommodated it where necessary to Aristotle's views, adapted it for the stage, and popularized many of its specific features.

Orbecche in general follows Roman models rather than the Greek ones proposed by Giangiorgio Trissino, Giovanni Rucellai, and Alessandro de' Pazzi. While taking from the Greek certain elements such as the dialoguing chorus and the messenger who recounts offstage events, Giraldi Cinthio used the Roman five-act division rather than an episodic organization of the plot, a separate Terentian prologue as well as a Senecan prologue in the first act, Senecan themes and especially horrors. His particular composite imitation was guided by an interest in the pleasure and the moral improvement of his audience as well as by his desire to please fellow literati with an ingenious act of imitation.

Giraldi Cinthio purported to follow the *Poetics* while accommodating it to his modern audience, claiming that Aristotle too had had the audiences of his times in mind. His interpretations were often imaginative innovations. For example, Giraldi Cinthio did not share Aristotle's view that costumes and scenery were relatively unimportant; he used costume to suggest an exotic setting, and his productions were lavish. The 1541 production of *Orbecche* had sets designed by the important Ferrarese artist Girolamo da Carpi and music by one of the musicians of the ducal court, Alfonso della Viola, calculated to satisfy a public enamored of spectacle. Giraldi Cinthio followed the model of the popular Italian comedies in using musical *intermezzi* in addition to choruses between acts. His characters were not always noble, and his women often exhibited "masculine" virtues. His tragic plots were generally fictitious, not historical as Aristotle preferred, and he employed the sort of double ending and double plot that Aristotle disparaged. Finally, in perhaps his most creative misreading, Giraldi Cinthio understood catharsis to bring about, through fear and compassion, the moral improvement of the audience.

Orbecche was an immediate success. Following its first performance in 1541, there were several others the same year, and after its first edition in 1545, it was frequently reprinted in the sixteenth century. Its acclaim cannot be attributed to its poetic merits, which, at least to modern critics, have seemed scant, but must lie in its appeal both to literati, as a classical imitation that satisfied Aristotelian requirements and that used a popular vernacular model, Giovanni Boccaccio, as well, and to the spectators generally for the magnificence of the production and the excellence of the acting. Giraldi Cinthio, himself, in his *Discorso intorno al comporre delle commedie e delle tragedie*, repeatedly praises the moving performance in the role of Oronte of the famous actor Sebastiano Clarignano da Montefalco. Moreover, the Senecan elements were well received; the spectacular deaths onstage and even the so-called precious gift, the offering to the heroine on silver platters of the head and hands of her murdered husband and the bodies of

their sons, were thereafter frequently imitated. Later Italian sixteenth century tragedy followed the example of *Orbecche* and was measured against it. Giraldi Cinthio wrote eight more tragedies, the plots of which were quite inventive and varied, but only *Orbecche* left such a legacy.

Giraldi Cinthio's critical theory was, as noted above, even more influential than his theater, both in Italy and abroad. In Italy, it was attacked by more orthodox Aristotelians, and at the same time, its insistence on the moralizing role of literature was well received in the years of the Council of Trent and its aftermath. His views remained at the center of the literary debates that continued throughout the century, and his "mixed" tragedy with a happy ending contributed to the controversy over the mixed genre of tragicomedy. Outside Italy, Lope de Vega Carpio and Miguel de Cervantes in Spain, Sir Philip Sidney in England, and Jacques Pelletier and François Ogier in France were among the leading cultural figures who were influenced by Giraldi Cinthio's critical doctrines. Finally, his short story collection, *Hecatommithi*, provided subjects for dramatists such as Lope de Vega (*El piadoso veneciano*, 1618; *Servir a señor discreto*, 1618; *La cortesía de España*, 1619; and others) and William Shakespeare (*Othello*, 1604; *Measure for Measure*, 1604).

Although no one argues that Giraldi Cinthio was a poet (Carlo Dionisotti has remarked that the boring lines of Trissino's *Italia liberata dai Goti*, 1547-1548, are a *festa di poesia*, a festival of poetry, when compared with Giraldi Cinthio's epic poem, *Hercole*, 1864), he was indisputably an innovator and perhaps the most important Italian critic of his age.

BIOGRAPHY

Giambattista Giraldi Cinthio was born in Ferrara in November, 1504. He received a humanistic education and studied medicine and philosophy at the University of Ferrara, where he received his degree in 1531. In that year, he became a lecturer in philosophy at the university, and in 1534, he was given a chair of philosophy. He published a book of Latin verse in 1537, and it was then that he first used his pen name Cinthio. He belonged to the Ferrarese Academy of the Elevati, and he succeeded its most illustrious academician, Celio Calcagnini, in the chair of rhetoric at the university when the latter died in 1541. Giraldi Cinthio was also a member of the Academy of the Filareti, which was founded in 1554, some years after the closing of the Elevati.

The years between 1541 and 1563, which roughly coincide with those of the Council of Trent, were the years of Giraldi Cinthio's greatest literary activity. At the university, he taught the poetics of Horace and Aristotle and at the same time wrote and produced his first tragedy, *Orbecche*, in 1541. The play was performed in Giraldi Cinthio's house on a special stage constructed for this purpose. It was sponsored by, among others, law students at the university and was attended by Giraldi Cinthio's patron, Duke Ercole II d'Este, courtiers, and literati. The play was repeated at least twice that same year and soon was performed in other Italian cities and, in French translation, for the king of France. Following the success of Giraldi Cinthio's first tragedy, Duke Ercole commissioned him to write two plays on historical themes, *Didone*, which had a public reading in 1541, and *Cleopatra*, which was finished by 1543 and performed in June of 1555, if not before. After this experience, Giraldi Cinthio returned to fictitious plots, the most famous of which, after *Orbecche*, was *Altile*, written to be performed on the occasion of the visit of Pope Paul III to Ferrara in April, 1543, but canceled because of the death, the morning of the scheduled performance, of Flaminio Ariosti, the young actor who was to have played the part of the heroine. With *Altile*, which had been performed by 1545, Giraldi Cinthio departed definitively from traditional tragedy with an unhappy ending. *Altile* is what Giraldi Cinthio in his critical writing calls "mixed" tragedy, or tragicomedy: It is characterized by a plot that ends negatively for the evil characters and positively for the good.

In 1545, Giraldi Cinthio produced and published his satyr play *Egle*, with which he intended to reinvent the genre know to him through Euripides' *Kyklōps* (c. 421 B.C.E.; *Cyclops*, 1782) and its Italian translation by Alessandro de' Pazzi. It was staged in February and then again in March in Giraldi Cinthio's house, with Montefalco acting and the duke

and his brother Cardinal Ippolito d'Este in the audience. It seems that Giraldi Cinthio experimented with all the traditional genres about the same time by writing his only comedy, *Eudemoni*. This play is known to have been written after Giraldi Cinthio's first four tragedies, after, that is, 1543, and the manuscript bears the date 1549, either the date of composition or of a production. *Gli antivalomeni* was presented for the wedding of Anna d'Este to Francis of Lorraine, Duc de Guise, which took place on July 29, 1548, and it was revived for a performance in November, 1549. *Selene* was written by 1554 and was produced before mid-1560. *Euphimia* was probably written after 1554, since its theme of ingratitude suggests that it followed his dispute with Giambattista Nicolucci, the former student whom he accused of that failing, and P. R. Horne, on the basis of internal evidence, thinks that it was written after the departure of Reneé of France, Duchess of Ferrara, from Ferrara in August, 1560. *Arrenopia* was staged shortly before Giraldi Cinthio left Ferrara in 1563, and in its prologue Giraldi Cinthio bids his city farewell. Celso Giraldi, the playwright's son, claimed that *Epitia* was the last tragedy that his father wrote; it was probably not performed during the author's lifetime. Giraldi Cinthio was the most important and active playwright at the Ferrara court after the death of Ludovico Ariosto.

Giraldi Cinthio wrote nine tragedies, perhaps because he thought that Seneca had done so. His entire literary production seems to have been carefully scheduled. Indeed, he even wrote, or began to write, a pastoral drama, despite the objection he voiced to this genre in his treatise on the satyr play; two autograph fragments of it have survived.

Literary theory went hand in hand with Giraldi Cinthio's dramatic work. In 1543, as he began to compose tragedies, he also wrote *Discorso intorno al comporre delle commedie e delle tragedie*. In 1549, he wrote *Discorso intorno al comporre dei romanzi*, his famous defense of Ariosto's *Orlando furioso* (1516, 1521, 1532; English translation, 1591) from the objections of Aristotelians who faulted the poem's lack of unity. His dispute with his former pupil Giovambattista Nicolucci, known as Pigna, was over this defense of Ariosto, to which both writers claimed priority. *Discorso sopra il comporre le satire atte alla scena*, a discussion of the satyr play, was published together with the other *discorsi* in 1554. The anonymous *Guiditio sopra la tragedia di Canace et Macario*, an attack on Speroni's tragedy *Canace* for not following Aristotle, was probably written by Giraldi Cinthio and was certainly written between 1540, two years before the date of *Canace*, and 1550, the date of the publication of *Giuditio sopra la tragedia di Canace et Macario*. These works, together with the prologues and dedications to Giraldi Cinthio's plays, constitute an important body of sixteenth century literary theory and criticism.

During his Ferrara period, Giraldi Cinthio also published a collection of his Italian lyrics, entitled *Fiamme*, in 1548, a heroic poem, *Hercole*, dedicated to his patron, in 1557, and he probably began to write the short stories that he would later include, very likely rewriting them, in his collection *Hecatommithi*, published during his stay in Mondoví in 1565.

Giraldi Cinthio did not stay in Ferrara long after the death of his patron Ercole II in 1559 because he did not have good relations with Ercole's son and successor, Alfonso II. He left Ferrara in March of 1563 for Mondoví, where he had been called by the duke of Savoy to teach classics at the university. After three years, when the university was transferred to Turin, he followed and remained there until 1568. In that year, he accepted an invitation to teach at the University of Pavia, and there he joined the Academy of the Affidati. However, he suffered from gout, and the climate aggravated his condition, so in 1573, he returned to Ferrara, where he died that year.

ANALYSIS

Scholars of Giambattista Giraldi Cinthio's work have long argued about his position in literary history. His major literary activity came at mid-century, at the time of the Council of Trent. Some see him as a classicist who continues the humanism of the beginning of the century; others find in the religious, moralizing element of his writing a reflection of the post-Tridentine program and in his theory of mixed genres and his modern reinterpretations of the ancients an anticipation of the Baroque.

ORBECCHE

The tragedy *Orbecche*, which launched Giraldi Cinthio's career as a dramatist, established the formal model to which he returned in all of his tragedies, even those with happy endings. It stands alone, however, as a horror drama, for none of the plays that followed it depended as it did on horror to produce catharsis.

The action of *Orbecche* is close to the plot of one of Giraldi Cinthio's short stories, which is in turn a version of Boccaccio's tragic tale of Ghismonda and Tancredi, in *Decameron: O, Prencipe Galetto* (1349-1351; *The Decameron*, 1620). A background story of incest and murder is told in the first act by Nemesis, the Furies, and the ghost of Selina, the slain wife of Sulmone. Selena, executed by the king for incest with their eldest son, had been unwittingly denounced by their very young daughter Orbecche and now wants revenge. With the second act, the action proper begins. Orbecche has married Oronte secretly for love. They have had two children, but Sulmone has been told nothing of it, since Oronte, who is of noble origin, is thought to be a commoner and, therefore, an inappropriate match for the princess. Sulmone arranges a political marriage for his daughter, and the couple is forced to act. Orbecche is fearful because she knows her father's character, but Oronte believes the king will forgive them, and they decide to confess. Sulmone pretends to pardon them but, outraged by the affront, plans a terrible revenge. He mutilates Oronte, kills the children, then the father, and finally presents the "precious gift" of their mutilated bodies to Orbecche—Oronte's severed head and hands and the bodies of the children, with knives in the chest of one, and knives in the throat of the other. Orbecche too feigns, asks for forgiveness, and seizes the opportunity to kill the unsuspecting Sulmone. Then she kills herself. The slaughter of Oronte and his sons is recounted by a messenger, but their mutilated bodies are brought onstage. Onstage Orbecche fondles the head of her dead husband, and then proceeds with the rest of the bloody slaughter; the murder of Sulmone is hidden from the audience's view, but it is narrated by a semi-chorus, and Orbecche's suicide is in full view. Such gruesome events, which in Seneca were recounted, are staged by Giraldi Cinthio, who intended the horror of them to elicit compassion in the audience and thereby bring about the catharsis.

The action of this, and of all Giraldi Cinthio's plays, transpires during the course of a single day. He did not concern himself with unity of place, and in some of his plays, the action moves around widely (from battlefield, for example, to private chamber). He believed that if the plot were good, it had the important kind of unity of action imparted to it by the artist's conception; this departure from Aristotle allowed him to defend the episodic narration of Ariosto's romance and to justify the double plot for tragedy.

Not the story but certain aspects of its presentation are modeled on Seneca's *Thyestes* (c. 40-55 C.E.; English translation, 1581): the prologue spoken by divinities and a ghost in act 1, the horrors of the final act, and the use of a messenger to narrate offstage events. A discussion between Sulmone and his counselor Malecche, in which the latter tries to persuade the king of clemency, derives from a similar scene between Seneca and Nero in *Octavia*. The lyric choruses at the close of each act are also Senecan, as is the theme of tyranny versus clemency, while nobility of lineage is a theme of the *dolce stil nuovo* that is central to Boccaccio's short story. The first prologue, detached from the play, which serves to present the views of the author and the circumstances of the play, was taken from the prologues of Terence and his Italian imitators. The text is full of moral apothegms of Senecan inspiration, which seem perfectly congenial to Giraldi Cinthio's moralizing.

The dramatic tension of the play is not provided by suspense because the horrible ending is foreseen in act 1, but it is rather created by rhetorical means, through discussions in which characters argue opposite views and through the elaborate and sensational accounts of offstage events. The buildup in the final two acts proceeds from the progressive revelation of horrors.

Plot, spectacle, and rhetorical virtuosity are of central interest, although characters are one-sided, and language is often awkward. A cruel tyrant punishes innocent victims; there are evil counselors and their good counterparts, but few characters are more complex. The language is awkward, offering repetition, exaggeration, conventional expressions of emotion in the place of persuasive argumentation or representation. Literary echoes, especially of Dante and Petrarch, are often inappropriate in tone for the tragic context. It is easy to agree with Guiseppe Toffanin, who says that as a poet Giraldi Cinthio "doesn't count." Giraldi Cinthio did, however, understand plotting and dramatic effects, and he employed the best actors of the time, making it easy to understand the success he had with a viewing if not a reading public.

DIDONE AND CLEOPATRA

Following *Orbecche*, Giraldi Cinthio wrote only two other "regular" tragedies, *Didone* and *Cleopatra*. The subjects were given to him by Duke Ercole, and he turned to the obvious sources for guidance, to Vergil's *Aeneid* (c. 29-19 B.C.E.; English translation, 1553) for his Dido and to Plutarch's *Bioi paralleloi* (c. 105-115 C.E.; *Parallel Lives*, 1579) as well as the *Romaika* (probably c. 202 C.E.; *Roman History*, 1914-1927) of Dio Cassius for *Cleopatra*. He stays very close to his sources, so much so that often his *Didone* seems to be an excuse for staging Vergil. In *Cleopatra*, he suppresses sensuality in the interest of what he considered "decency" and creates a dull heroine who is only a humiliated queen.

ALTILE

With *Altile*, Giraldi Cinthio began to write a different kind of tragedy, which he called "mixed" tragedy because it included one of the elements of comedy, the happy ending. He knew that his audiences preferred a happy ending, and he believed that such an outcome would arouse their compassion. He no longer needed horror to produce the catharsis. In other respects, *Altile* is quite like *Orbecche*, and its plot, similar to that of one of his short stories, is also greatly dependent on Boccaccio's tragic tales. The triangle is different: brother, sister, lover, the former the tyrant, the latter two his victims. There is also a jealous suitor who serves as evil counselor. In this play, as in all the other "mixed" tragedies, there is an atmosphere of impending doom interrupted only by the happy conclusion, which in this play is brought about by divine intervention (the marvelous remains an important element in Giraldi Cinthio's plays). Venus alerts Norrino's father, the King of Tunis, to his son's peril, and he arrives in time to save the lovers and bring about a happy conclusion for everyone save the evil suitor Astano, whose political ambition has caused all the fuss. Astano commits suicide offstage, allowing Giraldi Cinthio to use one of his favorite devices, that of the messenger who relates the details of the event.

The heroine Altile is better developed than her predecessor Orbecche, and she defends her choice of a husband with dignity and conviction. Giraldi Cinthio's heroines belong to a modern Italian tradition, that of Boccaccio, of Matteo Boiardo, and of Ariosto. They fall into two types, the active, aggressive heroines and the passive, long-suffering ones. The first are enterprising and determined, like most of Boccaccio's female characters, and they are sometimes even capable of leading armies, for example, the lady warriors of Ariosto's and Boiardo's chivalric romances. The others are of the patient, long-suffering type. Altile and Orbecche belong to the first category, as do Epitia, Arrenopia, and Philene (in *Gli antivalomeni*; she is the only heroine who does not give her name to the play). Selene and Euphimia, of plays of the same names, belong to the second category, and the latter seems as unreal as Boccaccio's Griselda, on whom she is modeled. Giraldi Cinthio's female characters such as Altile, who choose their own husbands and defend their rights, were characteristic of the Italian tradition and are another aspect of Giraldi Cinthio's modernization of tragedy.

TRAGICOMEDIES

Each of Giraldi Cinthio's tragicomedies varies the basic story of victim and villain. The same variety that exists in the victims can be found in the villains: Some are cunning, some quite mediocre, and some have been demoted to the position of secondary characters in the plot. The actions have different structures that are either love triangles or parallel stories. *Gli antivalomeni* has a double plot, and, with its two sets of siblings, cross-dressing, and mistaken identi-

ties, it owes more to the comic than to the tragic tradition. Horrors are not generally a part of these later plays, only of *Selene* and *Epitia*, and in these, while bloody bodies and body parts are brought onstage, it is a hoax that is revealed in a final reversal and happy ending.

EGLE AND EUDEMONI

Most of Giraldi Cinthio's plays are tragicomedies, and that is the genre he preferred and that he made the greatest effort to defend in his theoretical writings. Apart from these and his "regular" tragedies, his work in other dramatic forms seems to have been only experimentation. He wrote or attempted to write one of each kind of genre. *Egle*, his satyr play, was produced, as was his comedy, *Eudemoni*, but it is not even clear that the pastoral play was finished. Both *Egle* and *Eudemoni*, like the tragicomedies, or "mixed" comedies, are unique with respect to the traditions to which they belong. The comedy, for reasons of propriety, has none of the risqué humor of the sixteenth century Italian genre. The satyr play, which was not intended to be pastoral, includes an element of that genre, the love theme, which was not a part of the only surviving satyr play, Euripides' *Cyclops*. Although the definition of genre is such a large part of Giraldi Cinthio's theoretical writing, the blurring of genre distinctions characterizes his theatrical production.

OTHER MAJOR WORKS

SHORT FICTION: *Hecatommithi*, 1565.

POETRY: *Poemata*, 1540; *Fiamme*, 1548; *Hercole*, wr. 1557, pb. 1864.

NONFICTION: *Giuditio sopra la tragedia di Canace et Macario*, 1550; *Discorso intorno dei romanzi, delle commedie e delle tragedie e di altre maniere di poesia*, 1554 (includes *Discorso intorno al comporre dei romanzi* [*On Romances*, 1968], *Discorso intorno al comporre delle commedie e delle tragedie*, and *Discorso sopra il comporre le satire atte alla scena*).

BIBLIOGRAPHY

Di Maria, Salvatore. *The Italian Tragedy in the Renaissance: Cultural Realities and Theatrical In-*

novations. Lewisburg, Pa.: Bucknell University Press, 2002. Di Maria examines the development of drama, particularly tragedy, in Italy. Includes bibliography and index.

Horne, P. R. *The Tragedies of Giambattista Giraldi Cinthio*. London: Oxford University Press, 1962. Horne examines the tragic drama of Giraldi Cinthio. Includes bibliography.

Morrison, Mary. *The Tragedies of G. B. Giraldi Cinthio: The Transformation of Narrative Source into Stage Play*. Lewiston, N.Y.: Edwin Mellen Press, 1997. This scholarly study focuses on how Giraldi Cinthio adapted narratives and made them dramas for the stage.

Elissa B. Weaver

JEAN GIRAUDOUX

Born: Bellac, France; October 29, 1882
Died: Paris, France; January 31, 1944

PRINCIPAL DRAMA

Siegfried, pr., pb. 1928 (adaptation of his novel *Siegfried et le Limousin*; English translation, 1930)

Amphitryon 38, pr., pb. 1929 (English translation, 1938)

Judith, pr., pb. 1931 (English translation, 1955)

Intermezzo, pr., pb. 1933 (*The Enchanted*, 1950)

Tessa, pr., pb. 1934 (adaptation of Margaret Kennedy's *The Constant Nymph*)

La Guerre de Troie n'aura pas lieu, pr., pb. 1935 (*Tiger at the Gates*, 1955)

Un Supplément au voyage de Cook, pr. 1935, pb. 1937 (adaptation of Denis Diderot's *Supplément au voyage de Bougainville*; *The Virtuous Island*, 1956)

Électre, pr., pb. 1937 (*Electra*, 1952)

L'Impromptu de Paris, pr., pb. 1937 (*The Impromptu of Paris*, 1938)

La Cantique des cantiques, pr., pb. 1938 (*Song of Songs*, 1961)

Ondine, pr., pb. 1939 (English translation, 1954)

L'Apollon de Bellac, pr. 1942, pb. 1946 (*The Apollo of Bellac*, 1954)

Sodome et Gomorrhe, pr., pb. 1943 (*Sodom and Gomorrah*, 1961)

Pour Lucrèce, wr. 1944, pr., pb. 1953 (*Duel of Angels*, 1958)

La Folle de Chaillot, pr., pb. 1945 (*The Madwoman of Chaillot*, 1947)

Théâtre complet, pb. 1945-1953 (16 volumes)

Four Plays, pb. 1958

Plays, pb. 1963, 1967 (2 volumes)

Three Plays, pb. 1964

OTHER LITERARY FORMS

Trained as a diplomat, Jean Giraudoux first attracted critical attention as the author of essays such as *Amica America* (1919) and *Adorable Clio* (1920) and highly intellectualized, rather esoteric novels, such as *Simon le pathétique* (1918), *Suzanne et le Pacifique* (1921; *Suzanne and the Pacific*, 1923), and *Juliette au pays des hommes* (1924). True fame and success did not come to him, however, until after he began writing for the stage with *Siegfried,* adapted from his 1922 novel *Siegfried et le Limousin* (*My Friend from Limousin*, 1923) at the urging of director Louis Jouvet. The novels and essays of Giraudoux are of interest primarily as sources of the themes that are better expressed in his dramatic works.

ACHIEVEMENTS

Owing in large measure to his long, close, and fruitful artistic partnership with the gifted *metteur en scène* Louis Jouvet, Jean Giraudoux rose to a position of prominence, indeed preeminence, during one of France's richest periods of dramatic activity since the seventeenth century. Nearly fifty years of age by the time he discovered the theater, or it discovered him, Giraudoux lost little time in establishing himself in an already crowded field of extremely gifted and talented dramatists. To a large extent, his reputation has managed to survive him, although his lesser works now seem dated, and even his finest plays are, to the modern taste, extremely mannered, daring the most dedicated efforts of actors and director to bring them alive on the stage. More than that of anyone else, the dramatic work of Jean Giraudoux has come to symbolize the literate, exuberant spirit of the Paris stage during the years between the two world wars.

Giraudioux's theater is, above all, a theater of language—frequently witty, at times intolerably smug, yet invariably triumphant in its implied declaration that human beings alone, of all the animals, are capable of speech. Scholarly and learned, with a regrettable tendency toward academic in-jokes, Giraudoux's singular style has nevertheless been known to soar when confided to the proper hands—those of Jouvet in particular—reaching hitherto undiscovered heights of eloquence and expressiveness in the theater.

In the decades following Giraudoux's death at the age of sixty-two, critics have discerned beneath the playwright's stylized, elegant language a solid, well-developed philosophical attitude that no doubt accounts for the continued popularity and viability of certain of his plays. Although not plays of ideas in the sense of those later brought to fruition by Jean-Paul Sartre or attempted by Albert Camus, Giraudoux's dramatic efforts bear witness to an informed and reflective intelligence. Indeed, Giraudoux clearly anticipated the militant humanism later expressed in the drama of Sartre, Camus, and Jean Anouilh, among others.

To the contemporary audience, Giraudoux's plays often seem more like courtroom debate than theater, with a maximum of speech and a minimum of movement. In English-speaking countries, his works are known primarily through adaptations by such estab-

lished authors as S. N. Behrman and Christopher Fry, in which, the better to serve the demands of the stage, many truly Giraudouxian touches have been altered or eliminated. Even in English, Giraudoux's plays tend toward a talkiness that has caused them to lose favor with many actors and directors. Nevertheless, the best of his efforts remain in the repertory, representing a high-water mark of taste, wit, and literacy in the modern theater.

BIOGRAPHY

Hippolyte-Jean Giraudoux was born October 29, 1882, in Bellac, France, not far from Limoges. His father, Léger, trained as an engineer, was a career civil servant based in the Limousin region; the boy grew up in a number of neighboring towns and villages, retaining a fondness for the area that he would later express frequently in his work. A gifted and diligent student, often the winner of scholarship prizes, young Jean was attracted early in life to the study of international law and diplomacy. On completion of studies at the prestigious École Normale Supérieure in Paris, Giraudoux crossed the Atlantic to pursue graduate study at Harvard University before embarking on his diplomatic career. Mobilized briefly during World War I, Giraudoux later assumed an active role in negotiations leading to the Treaty of Versailles and continued, in his spare time, to build his reputation as a writer. A dedicated civil servant like his father before him, Giraudoux remained active in diplomacy and government service throughout his adult life, even after his successes as a playwright had brought him fame and material success.

The outbreak of World War II found Giraudoux in charge of press relations for the French diplomatic corps, a position he had first occupied some fifteen years earlier. From the fall of France in 1940 until his death some four years later, Giraudoux spent much of his time, energy, and influence attempting to ensure an influential and prominent role for France in the eventual postwar world. His international reputation somewhat hampered by an acknowledged fondness for Germany and things German, his basic patriotism tempered by a hard-earned practical knowledge of diplomacy and politics, Giraudoux nevertheless clearly foresaw the threat posed to France (and to French national pride) by a coming world order divided between the United States and the Soviet Union. Within months after his death, a number of his plans for the reinstitution of local and regional government in France were in fact put into effect, allowing a more orderly flow of power than might otherwise have been possible. Giraudoux died in Paris on January 31, 1944, survived by his children and his widow, Suzanne.

ANALYSIS

As the saying goes, all is fair in love and war. Almost without exception, the plays of Jean Giraudoux concern either love or war, frequently with both at once, and few if any holds are barred. Resolutely antinaturalistic in style and presentation, Giraudoux's plays address themselves nevertheless to the basic realities and polarities of life in the so-called civilized world, especially as exemplified in the institutions of marriage and politics. No matter what the institution, implies Giraudoux, it is at odds with humankind's most natural, indeed most human, tendencies.

Significantly, the first of Giraudoux's plays to be written and performed was quite frankly political in subject matter, theme, and message, dealing not with war but with its aftermath. *Siegfried*, derived from a novel written and published by Giraudoux within four years of the Armistice, seeks to discover the true identity of an amnesiac French soldier who has been mistakenly repatriated as a German and has since ascended to a position of some power and responsibility in the government of his native country's erstwhile adversary. Already, the debatelike structure that will come to characterize Giraudoux's theatrical expression is very much in evidence, with a wide range of articulate characters to present their views in elegant, truly literary language.

From the witty speculation of *Siegfried*, Giraudoux moved increasingly in the direction of fantasy: *Amphitryon 38*, his second play and his first reworking of material drawn from classical mythology, entertainingly explores the relationship between destiny and humanity through Jupiter's planned seduction of Amphitryon's wife, Alcmene. Equally within the realm of fantasy, yet drawn wholly from the author's own imagination, is *The Enchanted*, perhaps the most widely known of Giraudoux's major plays. In *The Enchanted*, an entire town lies under the spell of a ghost who continues to upset the normal chain of events, communicating only with a substitute schoolteacher and competing for the young woman's affections against an utterly sensible but personable bureaucrat. A similar strain of fantasy pervades *Ondine*, drawn from Germanic folklore, in which a young man abandons his fiancée in order to marry a mermaid.

With his *Judith*, written and performed between *Amphitryon 38* and *The Enchanted*, Giraudoux had produced an impressive, if unsuccessful, attempt at tragedy featuring many of his characteristic themes. Unlike her counterpart in the *Apocrypha* and various prior dramatic versions, Giraudoux's Judith remains highly ambiguous in character and motivation, stabbing Holofernes in an excess of lust rather than of patriotism. Typifying a growing line of Giraudoux heroines of remarkable character and force, Judith foreshadows such later protagonists as Andromache in *Tiger at the Gates* and the title character of his *Electra*. True tragedy, however, continued to hover just beyond Giraudoux's reach, undercut by the ironic, playful spirit implicit in his dialogue and characters.

Tiger at the Gates, translated into English some twenty years later by Christopher Fry, is considered by many to be Giraudoux's worthiest play, with characterizations and dialogue that nearly compensate for the length and lofty tone of many individual speeches. The thoughts reflected in the French title, *La Guerre de Troie n'aura pas lieu*, are those of Hector himself, who finds no justification for a possible war with the Greeks and does all that he can to prevent one, with the results well known in advance. Witty and not infrequently humorous, *Tiger at the Gates* nevertheless comes closer to genuine tragedy than does *Judith*; *Electra*, written and performed some two years later, is a somewhat less successful effort in the same vein.

Hailed for *The Enchanted* and for his later political plays, Giraudoux during the 1930's also continued to explore the battle of the sexes first investigated in *Judith*. Initially with the brief *Song of Songs*, later with *Sodom and Gomorrah* (the last of Giraudoux's plays to be mounted during his lifetime), the author of *Judith* portrayed communication between the sexes as metaphysically impossible. Despite Giraudoux's continued use of titles and allusions drawn from the Old Testament, the latter two plays are set in the modern world and have only a tenuous connection to Scripture. A fourth, and related play, performed posthumously, takes its inspiration instead from Roman legend by way of William Shakespeare: In *Duel of Angels*, the encounter of Tarquin and Lucretia is recreated in nineteenth century provincial France, with the names changed accordingly.

Without question, Giraudoux's greatest posthumous success came with *The Madwoman of Chaillot*, resolutely antitragic yet closely related in theme to *Tiger at the Gates* and *Electra*. Undeniably a precursor to modern black comedy and perhaps the so-called Theater of the Absurd as well, *The Madwoman of Chaillot* achieved nearly equal success in English translation and in the original French and is frequently revived, the title role of Madame Aurélie having provided an irresistible showcase for the talents of several celebrated actresses. *The Apollo of Bellac*, a brief curtain-raiser composed around the same time and also released posthumously, compresses many of Giraudoux's characteristic themes into a single, brilliant act that is still frequently performed worldwide, offering many spectators their first taste of the author's singular, and never successfully imitated, theater.

AMPHITRYON 38

That distinctive blend of dramatic talent is immediately apparent in *Amphitryon 38*. Waggishly indicating, through his choice of title, that his is the thirty-eighth play to be based on the legend of Alcmene and Amphitryon, Giraudoux proceeds to offer a fresh, thought-provoking, and highly entertaining speculation on the nature of love, destiny, and marital fidelity. Considerably lighter in tone—and message—than such later efforts as *Judith* and *Sodom and Gomor-*

rah, *Amphitryon 38* offers an Alcmene so thoroughly devoted to her somewhat cloddish soldier-husband as to render Jupiter's planned seduction quite difficult indeed: Ignoring the blandishments of a flighty, flirty Leda—who, recalling a most pleasant evening with the Swan, tells her that she would be a fool to pass up the chance of a lifetime—Alcmene persists in her fidelity, unwittingly daring an increasingly frustrated Jupiter to adopt the form, shape, and even personality of her beloved Amphitryon. Beneath the diverting sexual innuendo, however, there lies a serious, thoughtful inquiry into the relationship between man and his destiny, the latter here represented by a world-weary Jupiter and his humorous, voyeuristic messenger Mercury.

Fully confident of his absolute powers, Jupiter knows that he can have Alcmene's body any time he chooses; what he demands, however, is her consent as well, and this she steadfastly refuses to give him. Even after the seduction has in fact taken place, and Alcmene herself has begun to suspect as much, she continues to withhold her consent, symbolically defending "humanity" as manifest in the person of her limited but oddly endearing mate. Despite the tone of light comedy that reigns throughout the play, it is difficult to ignore the author's implication that mere mortals are powerless against destiny, much as they might choose to pretend otherwise. Hercules, fruit of Jupiter's union with Alcmene, will in fact be born.

THE ENCHANTED

Set nostalgically in the provincial France of the author's own childhood, *The Enchanted* opposes humankind not to a Greco-Roman deity but to a simple Ghost, presumably representing the eventual destiny of death. Surely the most original and perhaps the most charming of Giraudoux's fantasies, *The Enchanted* exhibits for the spectator a town where, for the first time in memory, life has stopped functioning as usual. In the words of critic Robert Cohen, "the values of truth, justice, beauty and magic have suddenly overruled the social structure of politeness, circumspection and adjustment." Battered children, for example, run successfully away from home, and prizes, for once, are awarded to people who really need them. Clearly, such a state of poetic delirium is nearly enough to drive a self-respecting bureaucrat straight out of his mind, and it is not long before the Authorities prepare to take Draconian measures in order to set matters back as they should be.

The peculiar state of affairs in *The Enchanted*, it seems, results from the continued presence of a Ghost, that of a young man recently deceased, which adamantly refuses to go off and join its fellow shades wherever shades belong. Aided by the gossip of two elderly, half-deaf spinster sisters, the Authorities soon discover the cause of the Ghost's continued residence: He has formed some kind of attachment to the young substitute teacher Isabelle, who meets with him secretly "and perhaps even feeds him dessert."

The prototype of Giraudoux's strong-willed, metaphysically "available" female characters (generally known as "*les jeunes filles*"), Isabelle finds herself drawn to the Ghost by her own instinctive yearning for knowledge, experience, and the otherworldly. So long as the Ghost finds his attentions thus requited, he will refuse to move on. Isabelle, meanwhile, numbers among her human suitors an affable, Amphitryonesque fellow who is himself a bureaucrat and is known throughout the play only by his title, the Superintendent (of Weights and Measures). Unable to compete with the Ghost on the latter's own terms, the Superintendent offers Isabelle the small charms and simple poetry of everyday life, touchingly explaining in his matter-of-fact way that the life of a bureaucrat's wife is not without its pleasures. As the action proceeds, man and ghost continue their tug-of-war debate for the mind and heart of Isabelle, who eventually falls into a comatose state closely simulating death. Amid considerable suspense, the debate continues over Isabelle's unconscious form until she is finally resuscitated and restored to the Superintendent by a rousing chorus of townsfolk, including the two querulous spinsters. As Isabelle begins to revive, the victory of humanity is underscored by the news that the local millionaire has as usual won the lottery and the raffled motorcycle has been awarded to a legless orphan. The Ghost has moved on, "the interlude is over," and life is back on track, as meaningless as ever.

As Robert Cohen points out, Giraudoux could at any point have turned *The Enchanted* into a tragedy by allowing Isabelle to die. Light and diverting though it may seem, *The Enchanted* is haunted at its center by the proximity of death, as well as by the implication that "normal" human life is of necessity "absurd" in the sense of the term later coined by Albert Camus. Its original French title, *Intermezzo*, a multiple play on words (Isabelle is herself an "intermediary" between life and death just as the Ghost's visit has been an "interlude"), *The Enchanted* remains in its very ambiguity one of its author's best-realized speculative achievements as well as a highly entertaining, timeless piece of theater.

TIGER AT THE GATES

Wry and witty in its presentation of human nature and the human condition, *Tiger at the Gates* achieves high entertainment value despite the profound pessimism implicit in its premise. With a lightness of touch retained from *Amphitryon 38* and *The Enchanted*, Giraudoux moves even closer to full-bodied social satire in his portrayal of Paris, Helen, and such invented characters as the warmongering poet and publicist Demokos. As in *The Enchanted*, the bureaucratic class known and loved by Giraudoux bears most of the brunt of his satire, as when an "eminent jurist" explains the fine points of international law: Citing the example of a small city-state that, observing the letter of the law, declared war on the Greeks and was subsequently wiped off the map, Busiris maintains that the now extinct Orpheans were "right" to declare war; the annihilation of a country, he explains, does nothing "to alter its superior moral position." Similar absurdities abound throughout the play, with the main proponents of war being those who are either too young or too old to be involved in any impending action.

As elsewhere in Giraudoux's theater, much of the peripheral action is concerned with love, sex, and marriage. Paris's abduction of Helen, cited in Homer's *Iliad* (c. 750 B.C.E.; English translation, 1614) as the immediate cause of the Trojan War, falls under considerable witty scrutiny, with Hector plausibly dismissing their mutual attraction as little more than passing fancy and in any case, insufficient grounds for war. Giraudoux's Helen is a flighty creature who claims to recall "in color" the things and people that really matter to her, the rest she recalls in black-and-white. Hector's wife, Andromache, a clear descendant of Amphitryon's Alcmene, is a model wife and mother who declares at one point that she would mutilate her own son if need be, cutting off an arm or leg to prevent his going off to war as an adult. Wasted effort, she is told: Assuming that all mothers came to think as she did, wars would soon be waged by entire regiments of one-armed or one-legged men. Such is human nature.

Erroneously classified by some observers as a pacifist play, *Tiger at the Gates* is in fact both less and more than that. Deeply grounded in Giraudoux's informed and pessimistic view of the human condition, *Tiger at the Gates* examines the root causes of war in dispassionate if witty terms. Viewed by most critics as a prophetic forecast of World War II, the play is even more than that a reexamination of the previous world war, with which the author was well acquainted both as soldier and as diplomat.

Indeed, the political situation at the start of *Tiger at the Gates* is remarkably similar to that which obtained in Western Europe during 1914: Having reached a certain state of economic and political sophistication (or preparedness), both Greece and Troy are in effect waiting for something to happen. As Ulysses explains to the younger, idealistic Hector, war breaks out most often not between sworn enemies but between peoples that "Destiny" has "shined, prepared and polished" for a confrontation. Nations, he continues, are doomed to fight not by their great crimes but by their petty mistakes. "Apparently," he concludes, "you must have bungled Helen's abduction."

In a scene evoking the popular notion that differences between nations could be resolved peaceably if only the people of the respective countries were given the opportunity to know one another as human beings, Giraudoux brings Ulysses and Hector together for a friendly resolution of their differences. Recalling the "debate" between the Superintendent and the Ghost in *The Enchanted*, the meeting between Hector and Ulysses goes one step further to establish

true communication: Ulysses, it seems, is no more anxious to wage war than is Hector. Their encounter, rich in poetic and evocative phrasing, contains some of the finest lines that Giraudoux ever wrote. At the end, Ulysses agrees to rescind his grievance, not because Hector has won the debate but in simple recognition of their shared humanity: Andromache, it seems, bats her eyelashes in the same way that his wife, Penelope, does. Unfortunately (but predictably), matters by then have progressed beyond even the leaders' control, thanks mainly to the jingoistic speeches of the Trojan poet and propagandist Demokos.

A pivotal, although minor character, Demokos ranks as one of Giraudoux's most masterful creations. No less dangerous for being patently ridiculous, Demokos is the supposed author of some of the worst poetry ever declaimed from the French stage; notwithstanding, it is he whose reactionary patriotism paves the way for war and whose death, in Giraudoux's version, serves as the war's immediate cause. As Ulysses prepares to board his ship, having withdrawn the grounds for war, a frustrated Demokos begins inciting the people to riot. Hector, still hoping to keep the peace at all costs, strikes the man with what turns out to be a fatal blow merely in order to silence him. Demokos, knowing that he is mortally wounded, falsely (and deliberately) identifies the Greek warrior Ajax as his assassin, and the war is joined. "The Trojan poet is dead," observes the prophetess Cassandra, "so now the Greek one [Homer] can take his turn."

Frequently revived in production, both in France and in Fry's generally admirable English version, *Tiger at the Gates* will continue to reach audiences so long as wars continue to be waged.

THE MADWOMAN OF CHAILLOT

After the questionable success of his *Electra*, interpreted by most observers as Giraudoux's ultimate acceptance of the need for another world war, the author forsook political themes for a while, devoting most of his spare time and energy to theatrical explorations of the "couple." Eventually, however, he returned to political satire with the masterful *The Madwoman of Chaillot*, a broad but deep farce that, had he lived, might well have pointed toward a new direction in his dramaturgy. Interpreted by Robert Cohen and others as an allegory of World War II, during which it was composed, *The Madwoman of Chaillot* is doubtless that but also more, a satire of big business and technocracy with particular resonance and relevance for audiences as yet unborn when it was written.

Madame Aurélie, the "madwoman" of the Chaillot *quartier* in Paris's Sixteenth *arrondissement* (each neighborhood, the audience is told, has its own madwoman, and they frequently meet as a group), is in effect a one-woman counterculture bent on saving the world (or at least Paris) from the corrupting effects of big business. To that end, she puts together a loose confederacy of eccentrics like herself—ragpickers, itinerant musicians, "historical antivivisectionists" and, most important, the "sewer king," whose familiarity with his habitual residence provides the play with its most significant plot device.

Throughout the play, big business is equated quite openly with prostitution, and its practitioners, with pimps. As Robert Cohen observes, Giraudoux was no doubt inspired at least in part by the Parisian black market, many of whose instantly prosperous wartime tycoons had no doubt migrated upward from white slavery. The analogy, however, is one that has surely withstood the test of time, applicable with equal irony several decades later in an age of increasing automation, technocracy, and corporate takeovers. Throughout the play, there hovers a lingering suspicion that modern capitalism may indeed have got its start when the world's oldest profession was first organized.

The "property-pimps" of *The Madwoman of Chaillot* have begun to take over Paris through proliferation, elbowing aside the quaint customs and manners that, for Aurélie and her confederates, make life truly worth living. As portrayed on the stage, the impeccably dressed tycoons move like robots, their precise speech riddled with jargon and having mainly to do with oil. While Robert Cohen is quite correct in seeing close comparisons between the pimps and the hordes of goose-stepping Nazi soldiers then to be seen around Paris and heard speaking a strange language, the thrust of the play goes even deeper: The

true appeal of *The Madwoman of Chaillot*, then as now, lies in Aurélie's impassioned defense of humanity against the threat of dehumanization.

Paradoxically, yet predictably in Giraudoux's theatrical universe, Aurélie's defense involves, in Cohen's words, "an act of genocide which only an extreme degree of stylization makes palatable." Eventually persuaded by the eccentrics that there is oil to be found beneath the streets of Paris, the property pimps follow one another into the sewers, death, and oblivion, like lemmings swimming out to sea. Arguably, the tycoons are by then so drained of all humanity as to be already dead; still, the closest thing to a "happy ending" in all of Giraudoux's theater remains oddly stained by intimations of mortality—and murder.

OTHER MAJOR WORKS

LONG FICTION: *Provinciales*, 1909 (novellas); *L'Ecole des indifférents*, 1910 (novellas); *Simon le pathétique*, 1918; *Suzanne et le Pacifique*, 1921 (*Suzanne and the Pacific*, 1923); *Siegfried et le Limousin*, 1922 (*My Friend from Limousin*, 1923); *Juliette au pays des hommes*, 1924; *Bella*, 1926 (English translation, 1927); *Eglantine*, 1927.

NONFICTION: *Lectures pour une ombre*, 1917 (*Campaigns and Intervals*, 1918); *Amica America*, 1919; *Adorable Clio*, 1920; *Pleines Pouvoirs*, 1939.

BIBLIOGRAPHY

Body, Jacques. *Jean Giraudoux: The Legend and the Secret.* Cranbury, N.J.: Associated University Presses, 1991. A biography of Giraudoux that covers his life and works. Bibliography and index.

Buck, Arthur C. *Jean Giraudoux and Oriental Thought: A Study of Affinities.* New York: Peter Lang, 1984. This study examines the philosophy of Giraudoux, including his attitudes toward war, and compares his ideas with those of Asian philosophy. Bibliography and index.

Nagel, Susan. *The Influence of the Novels of Jean Giraudoux on the Hispanic Vanguard Novels of the 1920's-1930's.* Lewisburg, Pa.: Bucknell University Press, 1991. A look at how Giraudoux's work influenced Hispanic writers in the 1920's and 1930's. Bibliography and index.

Powell, Brenda J. *The Metaphysical Quality of the Tragic: A Study of Sophocles, Giraudoux, and Sartre.* New York: Peter Lang, 1990. A comparison of Giraudoux's *Electra* with works of Sophocles and Jean-Paul Sartre. Bibliography.

Reilly, John H. *Jean Giraudoux.* Boston: Twayne, 1978. A basic biography of Giraudoux that examines his life and work. Bibliography and index.

David B. Parsell

SUSAN GLASPELL

Born: Davenport, Iowa; July 1, 1876
Died: Provincetown, Massachusetts; July 27, 1948

PRINCIPAL DRAMA

Suppressed Desires, pr. 1915, pb. 1917 (one act; with George Cram Cook)
Trifles, pr. 1916, pb. 1917 (one act)
The People, pr. 1917, pb. 1918 (one act)
Close the Book, pr. 1917, pb. 1918 (one act)
The Outside, pr. 1917, pb. 1920 (one act)
Woman's Honor, pr. 1918, pb. 1920 (one act)
Tickless Time, pr. 1918, pb. 1920 (one act; with Cook)
Bernice, pr. 1919, pb. 1920
Plays, pb. 1920 (includes *Suppressed Desires*, *Trifles*, *Close the Book*, *The Outside*, *The People*, *Woman's Honor*, *Tickless Time*, and *Bernice*)
Inheritors, pr., pb. 1921
The Verge, pr. 1921, pb. 1922
The Chains of Dew, pr. 1922
The Comic Artist, pb. 1927, pr. 1928 (with Norman Matson)
Alison's House, pr., pb. 1930
Plays by Susan Glaspell, pb. 1987 (C. W. E. Bigsby, editor; includes *Trifles*, *The Outside*, *The Verge*, and *Inheritors*)

OTHER LITERARY FORMS

Susan Glaspell began her long career, which lasted almost four decades, writing short stories that appeared in such popular magazines as *Harper's Monthly*, *Good Housekeeping*, *American Magazine*, and *Woman's Home Companion*. The short stories, in the tradition of local-color writing, generally romanticized the Midwest and its people. Thirteen of her forty-three stories have been collected in *Lifted Masks* (1912). Although she enjoyed success as a short-fiction writer and a playwright, Glaspell regarded herself primarily as a novelist. Her nine novels include *The Visioning* (1911), *Ambrose Holt and Family* (1931), *Norma Ashe* (1942), and *Judd Rankin's Daughter* (1945). In addition, she is the author of a children's book, *Cherished and Shared of Old* (1940), several essays, and a biography of her first husband, George Cram "Jig" Cook, entitled *The Road to the Temple* (1926).

ACHIEVEMENTS

Susan Glaspell received recognition in three of the genres that she employed. Several of her short stories were selected for E. J. O'Brien's yearly anthology, *Best Short Stories*: "Jury of Her Peers" in 1918, "Government Goat" in 1920, and "His Smile" in 1922. Her novel *The Morning Is Near Us* (1940) was a Literary Guild selection, and another novel, *Brook Evans* (1928), was made into the film *The Right to Love* by Paramount Pictures. In addition, she won in 1931 a Pulitzer Prize for her play *Alison's House*. Her greatest achievement, however, was the work that she did with the Provincetown Players, a group that she helped found. The Provincetown Players, whose stated purpose was to produce new plays by American playwrights, was extremely influential and changed the direction of modern American drama, providing a forum where none had existed. From its inception to 1922,

Susan Glaspell (Library of Congress)

the group's theater produced ninety-three new American plays by forty-seven playwrights. All but two of these playwrights had their first plays produced by the theater. Glaspell, who wrote eleven of her fourteen plays for the group, was, after Eugene O'Neill, the group's most important playwright.

BIOGRAPHY

Born July 1, 1876, to Elmer S. and Alice Keating Glaspell, descendants of pioneer settlers, Susan Glaspell grew up in Davenport, Iowa, and attended public schools. She went to Drake University in Des Moines, receiving her B.A. in 1899. While in college, she began writing stories and published her first one in the *Davenport Weekly Outlook* in 1896. After graduation, she spent two years working for *The Des Moines Daily News* and other newspapers as a reporter covering the court and legislative beats. She returned in 1901 to Davenport determined to become a writer. Her early stories, published in popular magazines, and her first novel, the best-selling *The Glory of the*

Conquered: The Story of a Great Love (1909), were escapist, romantic, and conventional in form.

In 1907, Glaspell met Floyd Dell, future writer and social critic; George Cram Cook, a socialist writer; and Cook's feminist wife, Mollie. Cook and Dell established the Monist Society, a discussion group formulated to expose provincialism and to introduce avant-grade ideas to Davenport. Glaspell fell in love with Cook and encountered the disapproval of her friends and family. In 1909, in an attempt to end the affair, she traveled to Europe, using the royalties earned from her first novel.

On returning to the United States, she spent time in Colorado, Davenport, Chicago, and Greenwich Village. She also finished her second novel, *The Visioning*, which shows Cook's influence in the seriousness of the issues it introduced—trade unions, evolution, and divorce, to name a few—and began a third, *Fidelity* (1915), which explores small-town life in the Midwest and examines the limits placed on women by traditional gender roles. In 1912, she published *Lifted Masks*, a collection of short stories based on her experiences as a reporter. She and Cook, who had divorced his second wife, were married on April 14, 1913, in Weehawken, New Jersey. As a result of being exposed to his ideas, she grew more radical and less conventional in her fiction. Her writing moved away from the sentimental and began to focus on more contemporary themes: the conflict between morality and individual freedom, the hypocrisy of small towns, and the evolution of the "new woman."

Glaspell spent the summer of 1914 writing and acting in plays with friends in Provincetown, and the following summer the Provincetown Players was formed. Thus began a period of playwriting that lasted about fifteen years, from 1915 to 1931. She and Cook, who had a strong interest in drama, collaborated on the first play, *Suppressed Desires*, a satire on Sigmund Freud's ideas. Unable to get the play produced by the Washington Square Players, the first little theater in New York City, and encouraged by friends, Glaspell and Cook formed the Provincetown Players in 1915 as an outlet for American plays. In 1916, the group moved to Greenwich Village and, through its emphasis on new ideas and techniques and its support of new American playwrights, strongly influenced American drama. Cook became president and remained so until 1922, and Glaspell supported the endeavor primarily through writing plays but also through acting and directing, for the time being giving up her career as a novelist. She first wrote one-act plays; then in 1919, her first full-length play, *Bernice*, was produced, Glaspell performing the role of Abbie. As the Provincetown Players became more commercial, Glaspell and Cook grew disillusioned, and in 1922, they moved to Greece, fulfilling a lifetime desire of Cook, who wanted to live in the land where great drama began. There, in 1924 in the ancient town of Delphi, Cook died. During the years Glaspell spent with Cook, she wrote one novel, seven one-act plays, four full-length ones, and twenty short stories, the stories written to achieve some financial security. After her husband's death, she returned to Provincetown.

Later, traveling in Europe, Glaspell met Norman Matson, a writer, whom she married in 1925. In 1928, she returned to writing novels: *Brook Evans*, *Fugitive's Return* (1929), and *Ambrose Holt and Family*, the latter adapted from *The Chains of Dew*, the last play she wrote for the Provincetown Players. She also wrote *The Road to the Temple*, a biography of Cook, in which she allowed, as much as possible, Cook's own words, garnered from letters, diaries, and other sources, to speak for him. She collaborated with Matson on a play, *The Comic Artist*, and wrote *Alison's House*, which received a Pulitzer Prize. In 1932, Glaspell was divorced from Matson. Her last play, "The Big Bozo," was not produced or published, and no copies are known to exist.

Glaspell did not see herself as a playwright and, without the Provincetown Players' demand for new plays and without Cook's encouragement, she ceased writing plays, although she retained an interest in the theater. In 1936, she went to Chicago to direct the Midwest Play Bureau of the Federal Theatre Project, where she selected plays and organized productions. Returning to Provincetown in 1938, she wrote three more novels: *The Morning Is Near Us*, *Norma Ashe*, and *Judd Rankin's Daughter*. She died on July 27, 1948, in Provincetown, of viral pneumonia.

ANALYSIS

Although Susan Glaspell considered herself a novelist, she is best known for her plays. Her playwriting period lasted fifteen years, seven of which were during the time of her association with the Provincetown Players. In only one season, that of 1919-1920, did Glaspell not present at least one new play. Although her work in short fiction and the novel is somewhat conventional, her work in the theater is not. She experimented, taking risks with her plays. She was an early advocate of expressionism, the use of nonrealistic devices to objectify inner experience. She experimented with language, sometimes incorporating poetry into the dialogue, and her plays are more often about ideas—feminism and socialism— than they are about characters and plot. The general critical response of her contemporaries to her plays was praise for her realistic ones and a reaction of confusion to her more experimental ones.

Her plays have a range of themes, but most concern the individual and the individual's need to find self-fulfillment. Specifically, she focuses on women who attempt to go beyond societal roles, searching for independence and autonomy. Often, however, these women pay a price: in love or acceptance by family and friends, in money, or, in the case of Claire Archer in *The Verge*, in mental health. Sometimes the search is for the "otherness" of life, that which makes life worth living and takes one beyond the trivial and the commonplace. This search is often aided by a guide or mentor who, some critics argue, is patterned after Cook.

TRIFLES

Glaspell's best-known and most anthologized play is the one-act *Trifles*, written for the Provincetown Players' second season, 1916-1917, to fill out a bill with Eugene O'Neill's play *Bound East for Cardiff* (wr. 1913-1914, pr. 1916, pb. 1919) and later rewritten as the short story "A Jury of Her Peers" (1917). In *The Road to the Temple*, Glaspell describes the origin of the play, writing that she sat in the empty theater until the image of a Midwest farm kitchen with its occupants appeared before her. *Trifles*, based on an event that Glaspell covered as a reporter in Des Moines, takes place in the kitchen of Minnie Wright, a woman accused of murdering her husband. Minnie Wright, in jail, remains offstage for the entire play. *Trifles* marked Glaspell's first use of the device of the absent protagonist, which would be employed again in other plays, most notably in *Bernice* and *Alison's House*. The play, with its grounding in realism and regionalism, is not representative of her later, more experimental plays, but it is said to be the best structured of her plays, and it is certainly the most often performed.

Trifles opens as five people enter a farmhouse kitchen. The three men—the sheriff (Mr. Peters), the county attorney (Mr. Henderson), and a neighbor (Mr. Hale)—are there to uncover evidence to link Minnie to the murder of her husband, John Wright, who was choked to death with a rope while he slept. The two women—the sheriff's wife and the neighbor's wife—are there to gather a few items to take to Minnie. As the men examine the kitchen, the bedroom, and the barn, the women remain in the kitchen. They notice the preserves Minnie had canned, the quilt she was sewing, things that the men belittle, but through their observations, the women solve the murder. The uneven stitching of the quilt indicates Minnie's anxiety, and when the women discover a canary with a broken neck, they know the motive. Minnie, who loved to sing as a young woman, was, in a sense, caged by John, cut off from her interests and isolated. She was figuratively strangled by John as the bird had literally been. After he killed what she loved, the only thing that gave her joy, she responded by choking him. Although the women have information that could convict Minnie, they remain silent. Mrs. Hale, the neighbor, had already failed Minnie by not visiting her when she knew that Minnie's life was bleak, and she will not fail her again. Mrs. Peters, the sheriff's wife, understands from her own experience—she had lost her firstborn—what loneliness is, and she, too, will support Minnie. In a sense, they are the jury of her peers, peers because only they can understand her loneliness and desperation. They try and acquit her. The play, thus, is about sisterhood and the importance of women's sustaining one another in a culture that is dominated by patriarchal attitudes, attitudes that trivialize women and the work—canning, quilting, baking—that they may do.

THE VERGE

A more experimental play but one that also explores the limits placed on women is *The Verge*, a full-length play, produced in 1921 by the Provincetown Players. The play had a successful run at the New York MacDougal Street theater, but when it moved uptown to the Garrick Theatre, the audiences became more conventional and less receptive to the experimental and expressionistic play.

Claire Archer, a Faust-like figure, wants to create new life-forms, plants that transcend the boundaries of reality, reaching for "otherness." Claire has spent years in her laboratory developing her plants, but when one of them, the Edge Vine, regresses, she destroys it because it "doesn't want to be—what hasn't been." Similarly, when Claire's daughter Elizabeth accepts conventional attitudes, Claire rejects her, as she does with her sister Adelaide, who urges her to "be the woman you were meant to be." Tom Edgeworthy, one of Glaspell's mentors or guide figures, also fails Claire when he cannot commit to a complete relationship that would include both the spiritual and the physical. He does not reach for the "otherness" but instead attempts to restrain Claire: "I'm here to hold you from where I know you cannot go. You're trying what we can't do." She disagrees, "What else is there worth trying?" Because he refuses to accept the "otherness," she strangles him, destroying him as she did the Edge Vine. The play has strong feminist appeal in the character of Claire, who desires to go beyond the limits set by culture. She does succeed with her plant, the Breath of Life, but the price she pays is her sanity.

ALISON'S HOUSE

Glaspell's last produced play, *Alison's House*, presented by the Civic Repertory Theater in 1930, received a Pulitzer Prize. As she had in earlier plays—for example, *The Comic Artist*—Glaspell developed the theme of the artist and his or her obligation to society. Alison Stanhope, whose story is loosely based on the life of Emily Dickinson, has died eighteen years earlier, but some of her poems, which obviously deal with a love affair, have recently surfaced. Her relatives are torn between destroying them because they would reflect negatively on the family—

the love affair was with a married man—and publishing them because of the public's right to have access to them. The conflict is dramatized by the poet's brother, who wants the poems to remain unpublished, and his daughter Elsa Stanhope, who argues for publication. Elsa, who also had an affair with a married man, is forgiven by her father as they reach the decision that the publication of the poems should not be denied because of small-town morality and hypocrisy. In addition to these themes, the play exhibits other features common to Glaspell's plays: the absent main character and the setting of the small midwestern town.

OTHER MAJOR WORKS

LONG FICTION: *The Glory of the Conquered: The Story of a Great Love*, 1909; *The Visioning*, 1911; *Fidelity*, 1915; *Brook Evans*, 1928; *Fugitive's Return*, 1929; *Ambrose Holt and Family*, 1931; *The Morning Is Near Us*, 1940; *Norma Ashe*, 1942; *Judd Rankin's Daughter*, 1945.

SHORT FICTION: *Lifted Masks*, 1912.

NONFICTION: *The Road to the Temple*, 1926.

CHILDREN'S LITERATURE: *Cherished and Shared of Old*, 1940.

BIBLIOGRAPHY

Ben-Zvi, Linda. "Susan Glaspell's Contributions to Contemporary Women Playwrights." In *Feminine Focus: The New Women Playwrights*, edited by Enoch Brater. New York: Oxford University Press, 1989. Argues that Glaspell's plays represent the female experience and that through their structure, characters, and language, the plays help to create a woman-centered drama.

Bigsby, C. W. E. Introduction to *Plays by Susan Glaspell*. Cambridge, England: Cambridge University Press, 1987. Contains good biographical information and focuses on Glaspell's development as a playwright. Provides insightful critical comments on four of Glaspell's plays: *Trifles*, *The Outside*, *The Verge*, and *Inheritors*.

Ozieblo, Barbara. "Rebellion and Rejection: The Plays of Susan Glaspell." In *Modern American Drama: The Female Canon*, edited by June Schlueter. London: Associated University Presses, 1990. Explores why a playwright as influential as Glaspell had been to her contemporaries is excluded from many studies of drama and concludes that Glaspell was ignored because of her challenge to patriarchal attitudes.

_____. *Susan Glaspell: A Critical Biography*. Chapel Hill: University of North Carolina Press, 2000. A biography of the playwright.

Sarlós, Robert Károly. *Jig Cook and the Provincetown Players: Theatre in Ferment*. Amherst: University of Massachusetts Press, 1982. Although the focus of this book is on George Cram Cook, the author presents much useful biographical material about Glaspell. Good discussion of the influence of the Provincetown Players.

Waterman, Arthur E. *Susan Glaspell*. New York: Twayne, 1966. Primarily a critical-analytical study of Glaspell's novels and plays but also contains relevant biographical information. A chapter on the Provincetown Players describes the importance of the group and Glaspell's contribution to it. A bibliography contains both primary and secondary sources.

Barbara Wiedeman

JOHANN WOLFGANG VON GOETHE

Born: Frankfurt am Main (now in Germany); August 28, 1749

Died: Weimar, Saxe-Weimar-Eisenach (now in Germany); March 22, 1832

PRINCIPAL DRAMA

Die Laune des Verliebten, wr. 1767, pr. 1779, pb. 1806 (*The Wayward Lover*, 1879)

Die Mitschuldigen, first version wr. 1768, pr. 1780,

pb. 1787, second version wr. 1769, pr. 1777
(*The Fellow-Culprits*, 1879)

Götz von Berlichingen mit der eisernen Hand, pb.
1773, pr. 1774 (*Götz von Berlichingen with the
Iron Hand*, 1799)

Götter, Helden und Wieland, pb. 1774

Clavigo, pr., pb. 1774 (English translation, 1798,
1897)

Erwin und Elmire, pr., pb. 1775 (libretto; music
by Duchess Anna Amalia of Saxe-Weimar)

Stella, first version pr., pb. 1776, second
version pr. 1806, pb. 1816 (English translation,
1798)

Claudine von Villa Bella, first version pb. 1776,
pr. 1779, second version pb. 1788, pr. 1789
(libretto)

Die Geschwister, pr. 1776, pb. 1778

Iphigenie auf Tauris, first version pr. 1779, pb.
1854, second version pb. 1787, pr. 1800
(*Iphigenia in Tauris*, 1793)

Jery und Bätely, pr. 1780, pb. 1790 (libretto)

Die Fischerin, pr., pb. 1782 (libretto; music by
Corona Schröter; *The Fisherwoman*, 1899)

Scherz, List und Rache, pr. 1784, pb. 1790
(libretto)

Der Triumph der Empfindsamkeit, pb. 1787

Egmont, pb. 1788, pr. 1789 (English translation,
1837)

Torquato Tasso, pb. 1790, pr. 1807 (English
translation, 1827)

Faust: Ein Fragment, pb. 1790 (*Faust: A
Fragment*, 1980)

Der Gross-Cophta, pr., pb. 1792

Der Bürgergeneral, pr., pb. 1793

Was wir bringen, pr., pb. 1802

Die natürliche Tochter, pr. 1803 (*The Natural
Daughter*, 1885)

Faust: Eine Tragödie, pb. 1808, pr. 1829 (*The
Tragedy of Faust*, 1823)

Pandora, pb. 1808

Die Wette, wr. 1812, pb. 1837

Des Epimenides Erwachen, pb. 1814, pr. 1815

Faust: Eine Tragödie, zweiter Teil, pb. 1833,
pr. 1854 (*The Tragedy of Faust, Part Two*,
1838)

OTHER LITERARY FORMS

Johann Wolfgang von Goethe made substantial
contributions to German letters in almost every
genre. He is generally recognized as one of the
world's greatest lyric poets. Especially important in a
vast array of powerful and diverse poems styled in
many meters and forms are his *Römische Elegien*
(1793; *Roman Elegies*, 1876), the exuberant love lyrics of *Westöstlicher Divan* (1819; *West-Eastern Divan*, 1877), and the magnificent ballads that he created during his association with Friedrich Schiller.
With *Die Leiden des jungen Werthers* (1774; *The Sorrows of Young Werther*, 1779), Goethe achieved international fame as a novelist. His most important later
narratives, *Wilhelm Meisters Lehrjahre* (1795-1796;
Wilhelm Meister's Apprenticeship, 1825) and *Wilhelm Meisters Wanderjahre: Oder, Die Entsagenden*
(1821, 1829; *Wilhelm Meister's Travels*, 1827), became models for the development of the *Bildungs-
roman*. In addition to fiction, Goethe wrote nonfiction throughout his life, and many of his nonfiction
works became landmarks of German thought and intellectual expression. The early essay *Von deutscher
Baukunst* (1773; *On German Architecture*, 1921) is a
key theoretical document of the Sturm und Drang
movement. His autobiography, *Aus meinem Leben:
Dichtung und Wahrheit* (1811-1814; *The Autobiography of Goethe*, 1824), has special significance in the
history of letters for what it reveals of the creative literary process. Among his writings, several volumes of
scientific and technical treatises, including *Versuch
die Metamorphose der Pflanzen zu erklären* (1790; *Essays on the Metamorphosis of Plants*, 1863), *Beyträge
zur Optik* (1791, 1792; contributions to optics), and
Zur Farbenlehre (1810; *Theory of Colors*, 1840), were
of particular import to Goethe himself. In later life
he often regarded them as more meaningful than his
literary œuvre. The extensive correspondence with
Schiller is only one of many revealing volumes of letters collected and published both during his lifetime
and after his death.

ACHIEVEMENTS

From the beginning, Johann Wolfgang von Goethe's success as a playwright depended not on his

skill in creating drama per se, but rather on the manner in which his works communicated to the audience a sense of history and human experience that emphasized the special individuality of characters and the times in which they lived. The key to his artistic greatness was an unprecedented mastery of language. It gave his writings an intensity, a dynamic power of expression, and a new insight into life that set a pattern for psychological and social plays from Goethe's time forward. Lines and scenes notable for their renewal of the language of antiquity with lightness, grace, naturalness, and eloquently blended rhythms earned for his mature works recognition as pinnacles of musically poetic dramatic literature. Goethe's ability to cast in language timeless universal symbols for the diversity of human experience, achieved especially in his famous masterpiece *The Tragedy of Faust*, elevated him to the stature of a giant of world letters.

The instant overwhelming acclaim for Goethe's *Götz von Berlichingen with the Iron Hand* advanced him to the forefront of the Sturm und Drang (literally, "storm and stress") movement and made him its standard-bearer. The propagators of the Sturm und Drang movement, in reaction to the rationalism of the Enlightenment, placed high value on the individual and his power to take moral action despite—and often against—repressive society. Under the tutelage of Johann Gottfried Herder, who was the chief theoretician of Sturm und Drang, Goethe created models that exerted powerful influence on works written for the German stage throughout the nineteenth century.

Despite the attractiveness and intellectual power of their content, characterization, language, and ideas, Goethe's dramas were not immediately successful as theater. They were difficult to stage, and deviations from norms of dramaturgy left weaknesses that stimulated negative response from critics. Nevertheless, guided by Schiller during the decade of their collaboration in Weimar, Goethe eventually rendered his most important works sufficiently playable to win for them a place in the standard repertory of the German stage.

By 1808, Goethe was still most recognized by theatergoers for *Götz von Berlichingen with the Iron*

Johann Wolfgang von Goethe (Library of Congress)

Hand. The publication of the first part of *The Tragedy of Faust* together with the production of works revivified by Schiller reestablished Goethe's image with the public. In later years, he enjoyed the status of an internationally renowned figure and received visits from influential people from all over the world. It was not until many years after his death, however, that he surpassed Schiller in popular estimation to assume his position as the man most representative of German literature.

BIOGRAPHY

The early life of Johann Wolfgang von Goethe was shaped by cultivated middle-class and patrician surroundings. An emotionally complex relationship with his sister Cornelia had significant impact on many of his creative works, while the contrasts in temperament and worldview of his parents fostered a rapidly developing awareness of German cultural polarities: northern intellectual and moral intensity and southern artistic sensuousness and sensitivity.

From the autumn of 1765 until serious illness forced him to return home in 1768, Goethe studied law in Leipzig. Stimulated by encounters with popular rococo culture, a love affair with the daughter of an innkeeper, and university exposure to the ideas of Christian Fürchtegott Gellert, Johann Christoph Gottsched, Adam Friedrich Oeser, and Christoph Martin Wieland, he began creating poetry and light pastoral plays that were intended only to be socially entertaining. The poems of *Neue Lieder* (1770; *New Poems*, 1853) are his most important literary accomplishment of this period.

After a slow convalescence in Frankfurt, during which he studied the writings of Susanne von Klettenburg and the natural philosophers Paracelsus von Hohenheim and Emanuel Swedenborg, Goethe entered the university at Strasbourg. Under the influence of Herder, whom he met during the winter of 1770-1771, and other Sturm und Drang figures, the young poet turned away from the cosmopolitan tendencies of Leipzig and declared allegiance to a German gothic ideal. Homer, William Shakespeare, and the Ossian poems of James Macpherson provided the literary models for changes in creative approach that mark Goethe's subsequent writings. On the level of personal experience, his love for the pastor's daughter Friederike Brion informed his best lyrics of the time.

On completion of his studies, Goethe practiced law in Frankfurt. While at the Imperial Chancelry in Wetzlar during the summer of 1772, he fell in love with the fiancée of a friend—a situation that provided the basis for *The Sorrows of Young Werther*. In Frankfurt cultural circles, he became acquainted with Karl August, duke of Weimar; their ensuing friendship shaped the rest of Goethe's life.

The unbearable restrictions of an engagement to a wealthy banker's daughter, Lili Schönemann, caused Goethe to flee to Weimar, where he established his permanent home in 1776. During the next decade two major influences molded his personal and creative existence. Charlotte von Stein, the wife of a court official, taught him social graces, organized his daily routine, and provided him with intellectual stimulation during the course of a lengthy, frustratingly platonic love affair. The continual burden of a variety of official duties in the service of Karl August broadened Goethe's public experience but severely limited his artistic productivity. Neither a patent of nobility, which he received in 1782, nor his scientific studies provided him with the personal fulfillment that his nature demanded.

A hasty departure to Italy in 1786 was in part an escape from the pressures of life in Weimar, in part a search for renewal and rejuvenation as a writer. The two years that Goethe spent in Italy gave him the peace, freedom, and inspiration necessary to complete three of his most important plays, *Iphigenia in Tauris*, *Egmont*, and *Torquato Tasso*, and to make substantial progress in the writing of *The Tragedy of Faust*. His experiences also yielded substance for significant works of poetry, especially *Roman Elegies* and *Epigramme: Venedig 1790* (1796; *Venetian Epigrams*, 1853). The former collection, however, was also informed by his love for Christiane Vulpius. After his return to Weimar from Italy, she lived with him for many years and bore him several children before he finally married her during the French invasion of 1806.

Goethe's affirmative response to Schiller's invitation to assist him in editing a new journal led to the most productive artistic friendship in the history of German letters. It is impossible to measure the full impact of reciprocal influence of ideas on the development of their poetry, dramas, and prose writings during the decade of their association. In the case of Goethe, neither *The Tragedy of Faust* nor the Wilhelm Meister novels would have attained their ultimate form and stature without Schiller's influence.

After Schiller's death, experience of many kinds contributed substance and essence to Goethe's mature works. The German Romantics stimulated him to a wider view of literature as a world phenomenon. His insatiable curiosity about life abroad led him to new friendships. Late love affairs with Marianne von Willemer and Ulrike von Levetzow moved him to write the most profoundly beautiful love lyrics of his career. In the completion of the second part of *The Tragedy of Faust* during his final years, he culminated his existence in the creation of a grand symbol for a life that saw him become, in the words of Thomas Carlyle, "the universal man."

ANALYSIS

Like his poetry and prose narratives, Johann Wolfgang von Goethe's dramas are powerful documents of personal introspection, evaluation, and interpretation of experience. Even the plays that are based on historical and earlier literary models derive their special character from their reflection of intimate feelings, concerns, passions, and perceptions that informed the author's being. In defining the relationship between his works and his life, Goethe said that everything that he wrote was part of a grand confession. Examination of his creative growth and development, especially as mirrored in his dramatic writings, uncovers the rich and colorful panorama of his personal response to stimuli from people, both contemporaries and influential personalities of the past, directly and vicariously experienced events, traditions, issues, philosophies, cultural and social heritage, ideals, science, and confrontations with self.

The basic characteristics of Goethe's dramaturgy include episodic form, focus on cultural and existential polarities, emphasis on strong and careful characterization more than on the traditional external dramatic conflict and action, treatment of problems related to social and human ideals, and externalization of psychologically complex tensions arising from encounters between the individual and the surrounding world. Well defined in Goethe's earliest successful plays, these features mark especially his theatrical masterpieces and set them apart from works by other playwrights of the time.

Goethe's successful career as a serious creator of dramatic literature did not actually begin until he came under the influence of Herder in Strasbourg. Before then he had experimented with light, undemanding plays written in the popular anacreontic style of the day and comedy in the manner of the classical French theater, but the results had not been very impressive. *The Wayward Lover*, his first pastoral work, is interesting for its revelation of an early command of sensitive, natural, graceful lyricism, yet has little to recommend it as stageworthy. *The Fellow-Culprits*, a comedy reflecting Goethe's intense study of Molière, is a more demanding product of concrete observation of middle-class society, but a certain harshness in the portrayal of acts against law caused it to be rejected in the German theater.

Involvement with Herder and the Sturm und Drang movement in Strasbourg was the first of three major intellectually formative experiences that triggered and gave direction to the most important stages in Goethe's evolution as an internationally known dramatist. Herder introduced him to Shakespeare as a representative of a natural ideal that was preferable to the artificiality of French classicism as a literary model. Shakespeare's approach to history, the realistic content and tragic nature of his art, and his emphasis on situations centered on the personalities of powerful individuals became patterns whose lasting impression is clearly visible in Goethe's most famous plays, from *Götz von Berlichingen with the Iron Hand* through the final version of the second part of *The Tragedy of Faust*.

Goethe's special interpretation of Shakespeare's motives and intentions provided him with the timeless dramatic situation that is central, in one guise or another, to all of his best-remembered plays: the conflict between the particular nature of the individual—his specific needs, freedom of will, natural ideals, creative genius—with the demands of the social establishment. In *Götz von Berlichingen with the Iron Hand* and the original fragmentary version of *The Tragedy of Faust*, the most significant dramatic products of the Strasbourg influences, a strong element of subjectivity prevails, in that the treatment of this problem of individual freedom corresponds to Goethe's perception of his own struggle between an inner law of creativity and the external order of society's institutions.

By introducing in his Sturm und Drang plays a previously unattained richness and depth of individuality combined with a picture of life as organized around a definite focus, Goethe created a pattern that allowed his subsequent dramas to mature as symbolic and general statements about life. These artistic utterances are at once powerful in what they communicate and weak in traditional theatrical impact. Their great strengths are vivid characters who are alive in language and psychological presence; substantial, captivating situations; colorful scenes with intense representational quality; and effective dramatization of conflicting attitudes and worldviews. In his best plays, these factors outweigh significant weaknesses of plot and a persistent failure to develop dramatic situations to the full.

For more than a decade after the appearance of *Götz von Berlichingen with the Iron Hand*, Goethe was unsuccessful in completing any new play of comparable artistic merit. In some cases, potentially powerful projects were left incomplete because of the struggling playwright's inability to master the chosen substance; still other works foundered on their internal weaknesses or on general mediocrity. As Goethe turned away from the influences of Sturm und Drang, he attempted to emulate Gotthold Ephraim Lessing in the development of middle-class tragedy as a viable stage form. In *Clavigo*, he achieved a strong depiction of contemporary bourgeois society, its moods and spiritual attitudes, but could not compete with Lessing in dramatic technique or proper organization and orientation of plot. Like *Clavigo*, *Stella*, with its elegiac tone and its emphasis on the problems of the inner man, remained a secondary accomplishment in which the author captured social reality without attaining the literary power and originality that made *Götz von Berlichingen with the Iron Hand* dynamically appealing. Only in specific manifestations of the writer's facility with language, especially his lyric virtuosity, do any of the completed plays of this period display substantial literary artistry.

The second upswing in Goethe's advancement as a dramatist occurred as a direct consequence of the process of rebirth and reorientation that he experienced in Italy between 1786 and 1788. Specific renewal of his creative approach featured a return to the elaboration of individual characters for their own sake, combined with expansion of the dramatic framework to give it the breadth and reality of history. At the same time, new awareness of models provided by the art of classical antiquity moved him toward strictness of form and organization, simplicity of plot and action, and pure, refined, stylized language. In the resulting completed works, including *Iphigenia in Tauris*, *Egmont*, and *Torquato Tasso*, the external conflict between individual will and the dominant order of the social whole is subordinated to the ideals of harmonious self-education and self-fulfillment governed by the principles of pure humanism. Action and plot are minimized in favor of portraiture, psychological penetration, and revelation of the central character's internal dilemma in a situation that forces him to confront his own nature.

Following the appearance of a fragmentary version of the first part of *The Tragedy of Faust* in 1790, the quality of Goethe's completed productions again waned. Although the association with Schiller was fruitful in its impact on the technical aspects of his dramaturgy, it did not immediately stimulate the creation of new plays of lasting import. Among the writings completed before Schiller's death, only *The Natural Daughter*—the first part of a planned, unfinished trilogy and the last of four plays in which Goethe came to grips with the phenomenon of the French Revolution—exhibits elements of potential greatness. These are visible especially in its cool, formal perfection; its carefully formed, elevated language; and the richness of its disputation.

Finally, however, Schiller's influence *was* the formative impulse that moved Goethe into his last and greatest period of dramatic-literary achievement. It was Schiller who encouraged him to complete *The Tragedy of Faust*, providing him with ideas and direction that in part enabled him to master seemingly insurmountable problems that had troubled him since he began the project during his Sturm und Drang years.

The two parts of *The Tragedy of Faust*, which Goethe finished in 1808 and 1831 respectively, represent a summation, a synthesis, and a culmination in the development of the most representative characteristics of Goethe's dramatic œuvre. The episodic form that dominates *Götz von Berlichingen with the Iron Hand* and *Egmont* is carried to its greatest extreme in *The Tragedy of Faust*. Lyric language and portraiture, the major strengths of earlier works, attain new heights. The standard conflict of the great individual at odds with his social context finds logical resolution in Faust's transformation from a seeker of experience into a man who accepts limited fulfillment in constructive human service.

GÖTZ VON BERLICHINGEN WITH THE IRON HAND

Exposure to the Sturm und Drang enthusiasm for Shakespeare in Strasbourg caused Goethe to seek out identifiably German material for his plays, comparable to the English national material used by Shakespeare. In the autobiography of Gottfried von Berlichingen, a robber baron of the sixteenth century, Goethe found suitable subject matter which he adapted to his own purposes in *Götz von Berlichingen with the Iron Hand*, his first truly successful drama.

The portrayal of Götz in his role as Sturm und Drang hero—a man of natural genius, a great, free, creative personality—established the pattern for a completely new kind of dramatic literature. *Götz von Berlichingen with the Iron Hand* is not a play centered on a tension-filled situation. It is the dramatized chronicle of an entire life. In its abandonment of the traditional unities of time, place, and action; its panorama of disjointed yet often strikingly original scenes; its varied, colorful, vital dialogue; and its natural, vigorous tone, it shattered the barriers of the French classical theatrical heritage and anticipated the ultimate course of Goethe's dramaturgical development.

Central to the play's exposition of Götz's existence is the confrontation and inevitably destructive conflict between an old, natural, free human order and the artificial institutions of a changing, ever more restrictive society—the opposition between individual will and the unrelenting progress of history. This conflict—couched in the story of Götz's feud with the bishop of Bamberg, his betrayal by a childhood friend, Weislingen, and his disastrous involvement in the historical backdrop of the peasant wars—serves to convey the tragedy of a man who has outlived his times. He can no longer be the free knight that he once was, because the impersonal political configurations of the dawning era make it impossible. Faced with the necessity to choose between inner collapse resulting from the resignation of freedom, and external destruction as a consequence of maintaining his integrity, Götz stays true to himself and perishes.

Goethe's major achievement in the writing of *Götz von Berlichingen with the Iron Hand* was his success in creating the totality and fullness of a life that is its own reason for being. The lack of an organized thread of action and a uniform plot, often cited as the play's most significant weakness, is more than balanced by the powerful authenticity of the characters, the successful portrayal of a complete social-historical reality, and the new and vital language that changed German theater forever.

IPHIGENIA IN TAURIS

During his early Weimar period, Goethe became concerned with the creation of drama on the highest possible artistic level. Proceeding from the perception that only in the patterns and spirit of antiquity can aesthetic perfection be achieved, he sought to create a literary unity that combined beauty of form with a thematic content advocating humanistic idealism. The most important result of this endeavor was *Iphigenia in Tauris*. A prose version of the play was completed and performed in 1779, with Goethe himself playing the role of Orest, but the ultimate recasting in blank verse was not accomplished until 1786, when he went to Italy.

Although based on Euripides' model, *Iphigenia in Tauris* treats the existing elements of legend with a free hand, creating a synthesis of the classical and the modern. Goethe developed the tragic situation of antiquity from the perspective of the eighteenth century, replacing the ancient pagan religious motif with the concept of pure humane action. The central issue is expanded from the limited, localized situation of Euripides' play to the entire history of the family of Tantalus, presented as a symbol for the historical progress of humankind. All the harshness and terror of her ancestors' fate is brought to focus in Iphigenia, who must reexperience and suffer everything, not physically but psychologically.

Like Götz von Berlichingen, Iphigenia is faced with a moral dilemma. She matures through having to choose between lying, and thereby betraying the trust of Thoas, and telling the truth, thus placing the lives of herself, her brother, and his companion in jeopardy. Her victory over the tragic situation is a direct result of having exercised her own free will to maintain her personal integrity—a choice consistent with Goethe's belief in the inherent goodness of humanity.

Iphigenia in Tauris, like most of Goethe's major dramatic works, is lacking in external action. Its artistic success derives, rather, from masterful lyric language, as well as a penetrating portraiture that reveals the title figure as the focus of a variety of complex themes. The latter include feminine ambition, isolation, evil and guilt, virtue, and humanity as a preserving and exalting force. The play is especially significant for a moral idealism that combines Christian and classical values in glorifying the possibility of absolute human goodness.

EGMONT

Although the final version of *Egmont* was completed and first published after *Iphigenia in Tauris*, making it at least technically a product of Goethe's visit to Italy, it is primarily a document of transition from Sturm und Drang to classicism. In many respects it is the least satisfying of the major plays, exhibiting a lack of unity that is partly the result of the fact that it was written piecemeal, in the course of four distinct attempts made in the years 1775, 1778-1779, 1782, and 1787. Unsuccessful integration of surviving Sturm und Drang elements with new elements of classicism renders the presentation spotty and unconvincing, and the extreme emphasis placed on portraiture gives the work a static quality that caused even Schiller to criticize its lack of action. One result of this intensity of characterization is that secondary figures, especially Margaret of Parma, William of Orange, and the duke of Alba, are ironically more realistic, more vividly alive, than the central character.

The main dramatic concerns of *Egmont* are quite similar to those of *Götz von Berlichingen with the Iron Hand*. In Egmont, as in Götz, Goethe intended to present a powerful figure with a will to maintain his personal liberty. Set against the historical background of Spain's tightening political and religious hold on the Netherlands, the conflict is again a confrontation between the individual and a repressive social establishment—in this instance an environment dominated by fanaticism and mistrust of any freedom. To some extent, Egmont is also a Sturm und Drang hero whose behavior is governed by instinct and impulse. The problem is—and this is the critical point—he appears passive because his character is illuminated primarily from outside. The spectator is told of Egmont's achievements, virtues, strengths, and successes, but they are not confirmed directly in what Egmont does within the movement of the play. He fails to act to avert destruction and therefore perishes because of a blind, heedless confidence in himself. For that reason, he comes across as shallow, ordinary, and unworthy of sympathy.

Despite the obvious weaknesses of *Egmont*, the work is important to the development of German drama for several reasons. By transforming the historical Egmont, a middle-aged husband and father, into a youthful, carefree lover, Goethe made of him an original character and broke with the tradition that the playwright could be only the dramaturgical processor of given material. At the same time, Goethe remained faithful to the spirit of the historical record, evoking the era of religious strife with telling details. Finally, by supplementing his historical sources with personal material from his daily routine—as, for example, in certain dialogues that reflect his ministerial experience—Goethe gave the play an unprecedented realism.

TORQUATO TASSO

Aside from *The Tragedy of Faust*, the most deeply personal play that Goethe wrote was *Torquato Tasso*. It is the only drama in which he attempted to come to grips directly with the polarities and dilemmas of his vocation as a writer. Like *Götz von Berlichingen with the Iron Hand* and *Egmont*, *Torquato Tasso* derives its basic substance from the life of a real, historical person, in this case a famous Italian poet of the late Renaissance. In aspects of Tasso's situation at the court of his mentor Alfons II, Goethe saw mirrored the problematic elements of his own life in Weimar—from the frustrating relationship with Charlotte von Stein to the spiritually conflicting demands of his art and his political-social responsibilities. The result was a kind of dramatic confession, a justification of the existence of the artist in which Tasso emerges as a symbol both for Goethe himself and for the poet in general.

Tasso's fate is related to that of earlier Goethean heroes in that it dramatizes the conflict between the will and nature of the individual and the demands and expectations of his or her society. Again, the play features little external action, and the dramatic tension is a function of the central figure's inner being. The title character struggles to become a whole man, one who is at home in both the imaginative world of the poet and the practical, material realm of social intercourse and commitment. His counterpart is Antonio, Alfons's state secretary, a genius of political reality with no meaningful artistic-creative dimension. They become enemies because, as one character observes, nature did not forge them into a single being. As more cultivated, refined versions of Faust and Mephistopheles, they symbolize the existential dichotomy that Goethe perceived as the very essence of his own (and modern humankind's) nature.

In its harmonious interplay of motifs and ideas relating to individual and social behavior, ideals and etiquette, freedom and self-control, *Torquato Tasso* eloquently illuminates timeless principles of moral philosophy. Yet at the same time, the play is deeply and personally human. Its treatment of life's central ethical questions—culture and wisdom, humanism and civilization, idealism and reality—is part of one of the most profoundly moving portrayals of suffering in all German literature. Tasso's final achievement of reconciliation serves to celebrate the vitality of both the physical and the moral person.

THE TRAGEDY OF FAUST

The two plays that constitute *The Tragedy of Faust* are, as a unit, universally regarded as Goethe's greatest masterpiece and one of the most important artistic accomplishments of world literature. *The Tragedy of Faust* is the poetic-dramatic summation of Goethe's career as a writer and thinker. It is also a powerful, perceptive, intricately modeled, symbolic representation of the vast spectrum of the human condition.

The legend of Faust occupied Goethe's creative attention off and on from his Sturm und Drang years through his old age. The work that finally emerged is both the drama and the product of an entire life. Its two parts are framed and joined in the metaphysical relationship of the human to the divine in a way that justifies the work's portrayal of human progress as a positive process of eternal development.

Part one of *The Tragedy of Faust* is a nontraditional, lyricized Sturm und Drang production, consisting of short, rapidly changing scenes that carry Goethe's early episodic technique to its extreme. The action's focus is Faust the seeker. A pact that the traditional Faust made with the Devil is transformed by Goethe into a wager between the protagonist and a cleverly, cynically human Mephistopheles, with Faust's eternal soul at stake. The essence of the bet is that Mephistopheles may claim Faust's soul *if* he can fully satisfy Faust's insatiable thirst for new experience. Proceeding from this agreement, the drama unfolds in two intertwined threads of plot: the tragedy of the intellectual who fails to find in knowledge true meaning for his life, and that of Gretchen, the innocent girl whom he destroys through his inability to attain lasting contentment in love.

The central concern of the plot strand that illuminates the main character in his role as scholar is the existential definition of Faust as a symbol for humanity in the modern world. In the first scene that follows the "Prologue in Heaven," the famous opening monologue communicates Faust's frustration at the lack of fulfillment provided by his one-sided search for personal meaning in the acquisition of knowledge for its own sake. Failure to find a satisfactory solution in magic, subsequent contemplation of suicide, and the reawakening of his thirst for life in an almost mystical encounter with Easter and spring are the formative elements of experience that at last generate within him an awareness of the duality of his own nature. In a profound self-assessment in the second scene, Faust acknowledges that his soul consists of two opposing parts: one that draws him unrelentingly toward the things of the real, physical world, and another that urges him upward into an ideal, spiritual domain that holds the key to boundless existence. The internal conflict created by these two forces is what motivates him to forge the agreement with Mephistopheles and is the basis for all that follows. It leads him to new avenues of sensation and learning, including sensual, emotional gratification in the love affair with Gretchen, and the attempt to penetrate the secrets of nature through scientific investigations in renewed isolation from the world.

By presenting in the character Faust the concept of polarities within the human spirit, Goethe created the basis for a general interpretation of humankind's being. With the appearance of the two plays, the Faustian man—an individual torn between his simultaneous inclinations toward the real and the ideal sides of life—immediately became a symbol for basic mortal struggle and progress. This symbol had enormous impact on German literature in the works of the most important authors of the nineteenth and twentieth centuries.

Within the first part of *The Tragedy of Faust*, the tragedy of the intellectual serves as a frame for the self-contained, linearly developed Gretchen material. The quest for new experience in the real world leads through a magical restoration of youth to a seeking of satisfaction in the universal experience of love. Faust's seduction of the innocent Gretchen; the resulting deaths of her mother, brother, and baby; Faust's betrayal of their relationship; Gretchen's final insanity; and Faust's failure to find lasting purpose in the alliance are the particulars of a timeless story that lays bare the fundamental psychological and emotional processes that govern the interaction of people.

More important for the general conception of *The Tragedy of Faust* as a whole, however, is the fact that Faust's destructive encounter with Gretchen, with all of its ramifications, has uniquely powerful symbolic value in its representation of a primary, potentially dangerous conflict that tears at the fabric of humanity's social development. Specifically, Faust is the embodiment of cultivated civilization, while Gretchen is the essence of naïve, simple, natural being. The inherent tension between the two abstracts, culture and nature, is for Goethe the nucleus on which is centered the ultimate strain that dominates the internal world of the individual. Faust's meeting with Gretchen and its attendant consequences thus become an admonitory representation of the sacrifice of natural human beings to the growing dominance of culture, and the temporal loss of elemental purity and goodness that can be regained only in the realm of divine absolutes.

The second drama, largely a product of Goethe's old age, is a highly stylized, often weighty, symbolic idea play that is connected to the first part only by the cosmic frame and occasional faint allusion to earlier events. In spite of its five-act form, part 2 is not a unified dramatic work. It, too, consists of self-contained episodes that are often only loosely related to one another. Emphasis is on the mature Faust and his search for existential consummation in the ideal realm of aesthetics, the social context of political manipulation, and the personal achievement of great deeds, symbolized respectively in his liaison with Helen of Troy, his service in the emperor's court, and his final commitment to human service in the winning of land from the sea. Although it appears that Faust loses the wager with Mephistopheles, in that he feels a degree of fulfillment in his land-reclamation project, his ultimate redemption in the final scene of the play conveys the message that as long as people never quit striving, they will in fact achieve the divine destiny of their existence.

OTHER MAJOR WORKS

LONG FICTION: *Die Leiden des jungen Werthers*, 1774 (*The Sorrows of Young Werther*, 1779); *Wilhelm Meisters Lehrjahre*, 1795-1796 (4 volumes; *Wilhelm Meister's Apprenticeship*, 1825); *Die Wahlverwandtschaften*, 1809 (*Elective Affinities*, 1849); *Wilhelm Meisters Wanderjahre: Oder, Die Entsagenden*, 1821, 1829 (2 volumes; *Wilhelm Meister's Travels*, 1827).

SHORT FICTION: *Unterhaltungen deutscher Ausgewanderten*, 1795 (*Conversations of German Emigrants*, 1854); *Novelle*, 1826 (*Novel*, 1837).

POETRY: *Neue Lieder*, 1770 (*New Poems*, 1853); *Sesenheimer Liederbuch*, 1775-1789, 1854 (*Sesenheim Songs*, 1853); *Römische Elegien*, 1793 (*Roman Elegies*, 1876); *Reinecke Fuchs*, 1794 (*Reynard the Fox*, 1855); *Epigramme: Venedig 1790*, 1796 (*Venetian Epigrams*, 1853); *Xenien*, 1796 (with Friedrich Schiller; *Epigrams*, 1853); *Hermann und Dorothea*, 1797 (*Herman and Dorothea*, 1801); *Balladen*, 1798 (with Schiller; *Ballads*, 1853); *Neueste Gedichte*, 1800 (*Newest Poems*, 1853); *Gedichte*, 1812, 1815 (2 volumes; *The Poems of Goethe*, 1853); *Sonette*, 1819 (*Sonnets*, 1853); *Westöstlicher Divan*, 1819 (*West-Eastern Divan*, 1877).

NONFICTION: *Von deutscher Baukunst*, 1773 (*On German Architecture*, 1921); *Versuch die Metamorphose der Pflanzen zu erklären*, 1790 (*Essays on the Metamorphosis of Plants*, 1863); *Beyträge zur Optik*, 1791, 1792 (2 volumes); *Winckelmann und sein Jahrhundert*, 1805; *Zur Farbenlehre*, 1810 (*Theory of Colors*, 1840); *Aus meinem Leben: Dichtung und Wahrheit*, 1811-1814 (3 volumes; *The Autobiography of Goethe*, 1824; better known as *Poetry and Truth from My Own Life*); *Italienische Reise*, 1816, 1817 (2 volumes; *Travels in Italy*, 1883); *Zur Naturwissenschaft überhaupt, besonders zur Morphologie*, 1817, 1824 (2 volumes); *Campagne in Frankreich, 1792*, 1822 (*Campaign in France in the Year 1792*, 1849); *Die Belagerung von Mainz, 1793*, 1822 (*The Siege of Mainz in the Year 1793*, 1849); *Essays on Art*, 1845; *Goethe's Literary Essays*, 1921; *Goethe on Art*, 1980.

MISCELLANEOUS: *Works*, 1848-1890 (14 volumes); *Goethes Werke*, 1887-1919 (133 volumes).

BIBLIOGRAPHY

Bishop, Paul, ed. *A Companion to Goethe's "Faust": Parts I and II.* Rochester, N.Y.: Camden House, 2001. This collection of essays covers both parts of Goethe's *The Tragedy of Faust*. Contains essays on the character of Faust and Mephistopheles and on the production of the play. Bibliography and index.

Boyle, Nicholas. *The Poetry of Desire (1749-1790).* Volume 1 in *Goethe: The Poet and the Age.* New York: Oxford University Press, 1991. The first volume of a projected three-volume biography of Goethe. A monumental scholarly work. Covers the first forty years of Goethe's life, including the writing and publication of his early works.

_____. *Revolution and Renunciation (1790-1803).* Volume 2 in *Goethe: The Poet and the Age.* New York: Oxford University Press, 2000. This second volume covers only the next thirteen years of Goethe's life. Boyle's extensive discussion of the Wilhelm Meister novels and Goethe's drama *The Tragedy of Faust* is set amid a period of radical political and social change, fallout from the French Revolution.

Boyle, Nicholas, and John Guthrie, eds. *Goethe and the English-Speaking World: Essays from the Cambridge Symposium for His 250th Anniversary.* Rochester, N.Y.: Camden House, 2002. A collection of sixteen papers presented at a September, 1999, symposium at the University of Cambridge discuss Goethe's literary and other achievements. Bibliography and index.

Brough, Neil. *New Perspectives on "Faust": Studies in the Origins and Philosophy of the Faust Theme in the Dramas of Marlowe and Goethe.* New York: Peter Lang, 1994. Brough compares and contrasts the portrayal of the Faust story in the works of Goethe and Christopher Marlowe. Bibliography and index.

Kerry, Paul E. *Enlightenment Thought in the Writings of Goethe: A Contribution to the History of Ideas.* Rochester, N.Y.: Camden House, 2001. A examination of the philosophy that filled Goethe's writings. Bibliography and index.

Swales, Martin, and Erika Swales. *Reading Goethe: A Critical Introduction to the Literary Work.* Rochester, N.Y.: Camden House, 2002. A critical analysis of Goethe's literary output. Bibliography and index.

Wagner, Irmgard. *Critical Approaches to Goethe's Classical Dramas: Iphigenie, Torquato Tasso, and Diet Natürliche Tochter.* Columbia, S.C.: Camden House, 1995. Literary criticism of Goethe's dramas, in particular *Iphigenia in Tauris*, *Torquato Tasso*, and *The Natural Daughter*. Bibliography and index.

_____. *Goethe.* New York: Twayne, 1999. A basic biography of Goethe that covers his life and works. Bibliography and index.

Williams, John R. *The Life of Goethe: A Critical Biography.* Malden, Mass.: Blackwell Publishers, 1998. A biography of Goethe that presents his life as well as critical analyses of his works. Bibliography and index.

Lowell A. Bangerter

NIKOLAI GOGOL

Born: Sorochintsy, Ukraine, Russian Empire (now
  Ukraine); March 31, 1809
Died: Moscow, Russia; March 4, 1852

PRINCIPAL DRAMA

Vladimir tretey stepeni, wr. 1832, pb. 1842
Zhenit'ba, wr. 1835, pr., pb. 1842 (*Marriage: A
  Quite Incredible Incident*, 1926)
Revizor, pr., pb. 1836 (*The Inspector General*, 1890)
Utro delovogo cheloveka, pb. 1836, pr. 1871
  (revision of *Vladimir tretey stepeni*; *An
  Official's Morning*, 1926)
Lakeyskaya, pb. 1842, pr. 1863 (revision of
  Vladimir tretey stepeni; *The Servants' Hall*,
  1926)
Tyazhba, pb. 1842, pr. 1844 (revision of *Vladimir
  tretey stepeni*; *The Lawsuit*, 1926)
Otryvok, pb. 1842, pr. 1860 (revision of *Vladimir
  tretey stepeni*; *A Fragment*, 1926)
Igroki, pb. 1842, pr. 1843 (*The Gamblers*, 1926)
The Government Inspector and Other Plays, pb.
  1926

OTHER LITERARY FORMS

In common with the other major Russian writers
of the nineteenth century, Nikolai Gogol did not restrict himself to any one genre. Indeed, with the exception of Alexander Ostrovsky, there was no nineteenth
century Russian dramatist who was exclusively a playwright. Gogol was preeminently a writer of fiction,
producing many short stories, most of which fall into
two cycles, the Ukrainian cycle and the Petersburg
cycle. His stories and novellas and part 1 of his novel
Myortvye dushi (1842, part 2, 1855; *Dead Souls*,
1887) influenced writers not only in Russia but also
throughout the world. In addition to fiction and
drama, Gogol published a small amount of poetry, a
number of essays, and a controversial didactic work,
Vybrannye mesta iz perepiski s druzyami (1847; *Selected Passages from Correspondence with Friends*,
1969), which mixed religious exhortation with a defense of the czar and of the institution of serfdom.

ACHIEVEMENTS

Nikolai Gogol laid the foundations of the school
of realism in Russian literature. His artistic vision
was rooted in the classical and romantic traditions,
which furnished him with patterns for his earliest literary experiments, but an initial lack of success disappointed him and made him search for inspiration
elsewhere. He found it ultimately in the everyday realities of contemporary Russian life, an inexhaustible
fund of material that his unique perception reworked
to produce some of the best-loved classics of Russian
literature.

Gogol brought into sharp focus types and characters that had previously made only incidental appearances in literary works. Although earlier writers had
occasionally taken people of obscure social origins as
their main characters, their plots tended to be developed along tragic, and therefore ennobling, lines.
Gogol's characters mark a departure from this norm,
for he introduces elderly boors, corrupt officials, and
downtrodden functionaries to highlight them as what
they are and to laugh at them for their failings. Like
all truly great comic writers, however, Gogol looked
beyond the surface of his characters. A person who is
the object of ridicule is often pitiable, and it is a close
step from the pitiable to the tragic. At times, Gogol
seems to understand and sympathize with the limitations of his characters, mitigating the caustic intolerance that otherwise predominates in his treatment of
them. His understanding of his characters is based on
his observance of human nature, which at times
verges on psychological study, though this focus
never develops in Gogol's writing to the extent it does
later in Fyodor Dostoevski's great novels. Of the
nineteenth century Russian realists, Dostoevski probably owes the most to Gogol; his famous remark,
"We have all come from under Gogol's 'Overcoat,'"
was an acknowledgment of the key role that Gogol's
writing played in the development of Russian realism.

Gogol's genius lies in his ability to capture the essence of the ridiculous in life, and the continued pop-

ularity and relevance of his works is proof of their universal appeal. He was innovative in shifting the focus of his writing away from the conventional literary settings of the day, the upper echelons of society and romantic wildernesses, to concentrate on the back streets of the capital and obscure provincial locales. The appeal of his work, however, is not limited by the concreteness of the historical setting that his attention to detail evokes. His characters transcend their time and place; their bizarre vitality has not become dated.

BIOGRAPHY

Born into a family of Ukrainian gentry, Nikolai Vasilyevich Gogol received his earliest education locally. Later, he attended grammar school in Nezhin, where his first literary attempts were contributions to the school magazine. In 1828, he left the Ukraine and headed for St. Petersburg to make a name for himself in the capital but was sadly disillusioned when this goal proved to be impossible without connections and money. Even more disappointing was the failure, in 1829, of his first serious literary work, "Hanz Küchelgarten," a long, sentimental narrative poem that he published at his own expense. When it was re-

Nikolai Gogol (Library of Congress)

jected by the critics, Gogol burned all the remaining copies and decided to turn his back on Russia altogether by emigrating to the United States. When he ran out of money in Lübeck, however, he was forced to return to St. Petersburg, where he found employment in the civil service. Although he later drew on his firsthand experience of poverty and bureaucracy as a source of literary inspiration, Gogol detested the civil service, and as a form of escape he began to evoke the Ukrainian village life he had known as a boy. His colorful blend of superstition, fantasy, and realistic detail made the first volume of his *Vechera na khutore bliz Dikanki* (1831; *Evenings on a Farm Near Dikanka*, 1926) an instant success (the second volume appeared the following year). Acclaim by the most influential critic of the day, Vissarion Belinsky, assured Gogol of acceptance in literary circles. He abandoned the civil service for a teaching post in a girls' school, followed by an appointment in 1834 as a reader in history at St. Petersburg University, but he was ill-prepared for the post and resigned after only one year.

The stories published in the collection *Mirgorod* in 1835 (English translation, 1928) still had the flavor of Ukrainian rural life, but their humorous themes were colored by a new and bitter note of satire. Gogol's preoccupation with the self-seeking vulgarity of much of human life was beginning to be apparent. In the collection *Arabeski* (1835; *Arabesques*, 1982), Gogol shifted from the countryside to the city, to the treadmill existence of minor civil servants. These stories, known as the Petersburg cycle, evoke the chilling inhumanity of humanity's banal existence; they are animated by elements of grotesque and macabre fantasy. Gogol's *The Inspector General* was immediately seen as a social satire and raised such a storm of protest that he decided to travel abroad. He went to Rome, where he spent the greater part of the remainder of his life. Here he wrote the first part of *Dead Souls* and worked on its sequel.

During the last decade of his life, Gogol grew increasingly concerned with his mission as a writer. He became convinced that he had a divinely appointed role to save Russia from all the evil forces at work within it. He would achieve this aim by casting the second and third parts of *Dead Souls* after the pattern of the *Purgatorio* (*Purgatory*) and *Paradiso* (*Paradise*) of Dante's *La divina commedia* (c. 1320; *The Divine Comedy*, 1802), with the *Inferno* already being represented by the first part of *Dead Souls*. An inability to create morally regenerated positive characters of the same realistic caliber as his cheats and liars slowed the progress of the work and drove him increasingly to find a solution in religious asceticism. *Selected Passages from Correspondence with Friends* was an overt attempt to persuade others of the validity of the conservative viewpoint he espoused: support for the reactionary policies of the autocracy and acceptance of serfdom. He was denounced by the liberal intellectuals, notably Belinsky, who felt betrayed by the man whom he had mistakenly hailed as a champion against social injustice. A pilgrimage to Jerusalem in 1848 only served to heighten Gogol's asceticism; it did not revitalize his creative spirit in the manner that he desired. Returning to Moscow, he fell under the influence of a fanatic priest, Matthew Konstantinovsky, who seems to have been instrumental in convincing Gogol to burn the presumably complete, or practically so, manuscript of the second part of *Dead Souls*. This he did on February 24, 1852, reenacting the physical catharsis he had achieved at the beginning of his literary career by burning the copies of his "Hanz Küchelgarten." Only a few chapters were left extant, and he had no opportunity to begin work on it again. He became ill and died, having refused all food and medical attention, on March 4, 1852.

ANALYSIS

It is characteristic of Nikolai Gogol to create a microcosm for each of his main characters, giving his works a peculiarly episodic flavor. His plots center on an incident or a motif, rather than on a complex string of interconnecting events. This is particularly noticeable in his novel *Dead Souls*, in which the unifying theme of Chichikov's fraud is no more than a device to link together the cameos of the different characters and the physical environment peculiar to each. Such an approach is especially suited to drama, where the microcosm is the illusion created on the stage, and

Gogol makes distinctive use of the interplay between fantasy and reality in his dramatic works.

Compared with his production in other genres, Gogol's output as a playwright was small. Although he worked on a number of subjects, he completed only one full-length play and two short comedies, the one-act play *The Gamblers*, written in 1832, and the two-act play *Marriage*, written in 1835 and performed unsuccessfully in 1842. The plot of *The Gamblers* turns on a cheat cheated, while *Marriage* is an account of the bachelor Podkolyosin's efforts to marry Agafya, admirably assisted by his friend Kochkarev, an erstwhile suitor of the same girl. The twist of the plot in this case is suggested by the subtitle "A Quite Incredible Incident," as the wedding never comes off. These short comedies are more overtly humorous, more farcical, more boisterous than Gogol's full-length comedy, also written in 1835, *The Inspector General*. Although the comic elements in all three works are very similar, *The Inspector General* is more fully rounded. Themes, characters, and humorous devices are all less condensed than in the shorter sketches Any assessment of Gogol's drama should be based largely on *The Inspector General*.

THE INSPECTOR GENERAL

Gogol wrote *The Inspector General* as a comedy, taking as his main theme a case of mistaken identity. He had written in October, 1835, to Alexander Pushkin, asking for suggestions for a comic plot, and the poet furnished him with a description of how he himself had been mistaken for a government official during a trip to Nizhni Novgorod (now Gorki) and Orenburg in 1833.

The plot of the play is not complicated and may be briefly summarized: The corrupt officials of a provincial town receive a warning that a government official is on his way to the town to carry out a tour of inspection, but he will be traveling incognito. The officials are aware of what the implications of such an inspection could be for them personally, so they take stock of their shortcomings and devise ways to conceal them. They get no further than discussion, however, before news comes that the government inspector has been positively identified as a young man who has been staying at the local inn for the last two weeks.

The second act acquaints the audience with the disguised "official," one Khlestakov, an indolent young man from the fringes of St. Petersburg society who is being forced by lack of funds to return to his home in the provinces. He aspires to the high life but enters the drama completely penniless, expecting at any moment to be arrested for his unpaid bill at the inn. Wondering whether he should sell his fashionable clothes for the price of a meal, he decides that on balance it is better to return home hungry but dressed in a civilized fashion.

The town notables descend on the inn, desperate to correct the bad impression that the inspector may have formed of conditions in the town. The mayor insists on accommodating the young man in his own house, to the delight of his wife and daughter, both of whom set out to captivate the visitor. Driven to desperation by the knowledge of their dereliction of duty, the officials line up to bribe the "inspector" to look the other way. News of the inspection has reached the townsfolk, too, and deputations arrive to protest about the conduct of the officials and to persuade the inspector to do something about it.

Considerably wealthier for all this flurried activity, Khlestakov quickly becomes engaged to the mayor's daughter, Marya Antonovna, a state of affairs that delights her parents and fills their friends and associates with envy. Heeding his servant's advice that the bubble may burst at any moment, Khlestakov prepares to leave, but not before he has sent off an account of his adventure to a literary friend in St. Petersburg. The mayor provides a fast carriage with excellent horses to speed the inspector on his way to Saratov, fondly anticipating a glorious future for himself and his wife once their daughter is married to this illustrious official.

The postmaster, however, appears with unwelcome news: He has intercepted and read Khlestakov's letter, and the officials now realize that they have all been duped. They scarcely have time to adjust to this change in fortune when the arrival of the real government inspector is announced. The plot has thus come full circle. Not only does the original corruption still prevail in the town, but also the guilt of the townsmen, which has already prompted them to pay out large sums to cover it up, will doubtless cause them to do so again, for disaster is imminent once more.

Throughout the play, an underlying current of motifs suggests that the visitation by the official is a kind of nemesis, the working out of an implacable fate. In the very first scene, the mayor casually mentions the dream he has had of the two strange black rats which have come, sniffed around, and gone away; when Luka Lukich asks why an inspector should be coming at all, the mayor replies that it is obvious that it must be fate.

The possibility suggested by Victor Erlich, in his 1969 study of Gogol, is that the second government inspector may also be an impostor. This interpretation lengthens the chain of purgatory for the officials, because the real inspector's visit is still to come, and both the second impostor and the real official will have to be placated before the townsmen can sink back undisturbed into their old way of life. As the play moves toward its climax, the theme of malevolent fate becomes more insistent, and the frequent references to the Devil hint at some strange force at work. The imminent arrival, and yet still nonappearance, of the "real" inspector causes the characters to freeze into a spectacle of horrified realization. In this there is an echo of the supernatural, macabre elements that characterize Gogol's short stories, particularly "The Overcoat" (1842). The grotesque dualism of the story "The Nose" (1836), where the hero's identity is usurped by his own nose, is prefigured in *The Inspector General* by the deliberate parallel between the beginning of the play and the end, between the first inspector and the second, and by the implication that future events will parallel those of the past.

Contemporary reaction to *The Inspector General* was unfavorable. It had its premiere on April 19, 1836, at the Alexsandrinsky Theatre, St. Petersburg, and the first-night audience was hostile, seeing it as a tasteless critique of the civil service, directed at the government. In fact, the play is a satiric condemnation not of civil service per se, but of certain deeply rooted, unacceptable attitudes that pervaded it at all levels. Gogol's experience of the state bureaucracy lent authority and conviction to his presentation of the peccadilloes of the leading citizens of the town. By concentrating on minor infringements of acceptable bureaucratic behavior and treating as humorous such ideas as the judge delaying his verdict on a lawsuit concerning land so that he can course for hares over the property of both plaintiffs, or the foreign doctor who cannot speak a word of Russian and only grunts onstage, the playwright suggests that the corruption revealed in the play is only the tip of the iceberg. The corruption and graft are all-pervasive and, by implication, ineradicable. The fact that the patients in the hospital die like flies is discussed on exactly the same level as the idea that it would be impressive to have their illnesses identified in Latin over their beds. Nor is it only the civil servants who are satirized: Gogol presents in an equally unfavorable light the landowners, represented by the comic fools Bobchinsky and Dobchinsky, and the merchants. The latter, in their beards and kaftans, are stylized caricatures epitomizing the conservatives that were typical of their class.

The first-night audience was wrong, however, in attributing to Gogol any antigovernment sentiment. Contrary to the assumptions of Belinsky and the other pro-Western, liberal intellectuals who erroneously believed that the object of Gogol's satire was to redress social injustice, Gogol was a conservative. Although ultimately his writing was to become merely a vehicle for his own philosophy of salvation for Russia, at the time of writing *The Inspector General*, his perception of social evil was unaffected by the impulse to gloss over anything that varied with his quasi-religious vision. As a result, the characters in the play appear very human, embodying all the idiosyncrasies and failings familiar to the audience from its own dealings with officialdom. The nineteenth century Russian audience recognized the truth of Gogol's comedy, and rejected it, because it hit too close to home. The reason for the enduring popularity of *The Inspector General* is the essentially universal comic appeal of the characters and their preoccupations: The idea of demonstrating a high level of productivity in the hospital by kicking out some of the patients is as amusing today as it was in 1836.

The dominant comic theme of the work, mistaken identity, is developed by Gogol into a rich sampler of comic techniques, including slapstick and humorous character names as well as more subtle devices.

One of Gogol's tactics is to subvert conventional dramatic themes. The exaggerated amorous attentions of the city dandy, for example, are based on sentiment so trite that when his propositioning of Marya Antonovna is interrupted by her mother, Khlestakov simply continues his gambit but directs it at another possible conquest. Here Gogol has reduced the traditional comic love theme to mere farcical essentials by portraying mother and daughter in direct competition for the same man. Apart from their opposition as rivals, there is very little difference between them as individuals. They are both the products of the provincial milieu, but they both aspire to the lifestyle that Khlestakov appears to enjoy.

Similarly, by inverting the theme of the superfluous hero, by treating it with irony and by reducing it to a very provincial level, Gogol armed himself for an attack on something for which he had a lifelong hatred—the humdrum banality of much of human existence. The object of his hatred is summed up in Russian in the single word *poshlost*, encompassing a whole range of meanings which can be conveyed in English only by a string of synonyms: vulgarity, triviality, mediocrity, banality, triteness, and pretension. His enemy is the humdrum, the banal, the *poshlost* of daily life at all levels of society, but most frequently, as in *The Inspector General*, and later in *Dead Souls*, he takes as his battleground the middle levels of society—lesser government employees in the capital, leading citizens in sleepy backwaters, provincial landowners stultified from years of vegetating in the backlands. All three types are well represented in *The Inspector General*, leavened by a sprinkling of different sorts of people: Osip the servant, the woman who was flogged, the merchants. It is by his choice of characters, by his skillful juxtapositions of different types and backgrounds that Gogol re-creates for the audience a world, real in terms of itself, a world which is familiar and recognizable because its problems are universal human problems. Because he takes comedy as his medium of expression, the audience is beguiled into feeling superior to the characters onstage. It is here that the essential quality of Gogol's "realism" becomes apparent. His technique is to create an ostensibly real world, but it is a reality within a fantasy.

The realism of Gogol's drama does not consist in his merely looking at certain social phenomena and re-creating them on the stage as a self-contained microcosm. Rather, he abstracts from his observations of human nature and everyday life certain key factors that he enlarges to grotesque proportions until they themselves become the *raison d'être* of the characters' existence. To create a realistic background against which to set the distortion of reality experienced by his characters, Gogol draws on acute observation of social mores and human behavior. From the outset, the utter provinciality of the town is readily apparent. Discussing the judge's suggestion that the inspector's visit may be connected with treason of some kind, the mayor witheringly points out that one might gallop away from the town for three years without reaching a foreign country. Later, the position of the town is fixed a little more precisely as a point somewhere on the road between St. Petersburg and Saratov. It is thus firmly established that the town is a backwater, and not merely a provincial backwater, but an inherently old-style Russian one as well. Into this unchanging setting bursts Khlestakov, fresh from the capital and full of superficial notions of refinement and urbanity. Much of the comedy in the play arises from the interaction of these opposed sets of values, those of the slow-witted, socially naïve, stolid citizens on one hand, and on the other of the feckless Khlestakov, who has not one original thought in his head.

The Inspector General fully deserves its continuing popularity and its reputation as Gogol's dramatic masterpiece. A harmonious combination of themes found in embryonic form in his earlier sketches, it surpasses these in terms of its breadth of vision and its far-reaching social satire. The continued relevance of the play after a century and a half testifies both to Gogol's understanding of human nature and to his infallible sense of the comic in life, which together have created a universally recognizable imaginary world.

OTHER MAJOR WORKS

LONG FICTION: *Taras Bulba*, 1835 (as short story), 1842 (revised as a novel; English translation, 1886); *Myortvye dushi*, part 1, 1842, part 2, 1855 (*Dead Souls*, 1887).

SHORT FICTION: *Vechera na khutore bliz Dikanki*, volume 1, 1831, volume 2, 1832 (*Evenings on a Farm Near Dikanka*, 1926); *Mirgorod*, 1835 (English translation, 1928); *Arabeski*, 1835 (includes stories and essays; *Arabesques*, 1982).

POETRY: *Hanz Kuechelgarten*, 1829.

NONFICTION: *Vybrannye mesta iz perepiski s druzyami*, 1847 (*Selected Passages from Correspondence with Friends*, 1969); *Letters of Nikolai Gogol*, 1967.

MISCELLANEOUS: *The Collected Works*, 1922-1927 (6 volumes); *Polnoe sobranie sochinenii*, 1940-1952 (14 volumes); *The Collected Tales and Plays of Nikolai Gogol*, 1964.

BIBLIOGRAPHY

Fusso, Susanne, and Priscilla Meyer, eds. *Essays on Gogol: Logos and the Russian Word*. Evanston, Ill.: Northwestern University Press, 1992. A collection of essays on Gogol from a conference at Wesleyan University. Bibliography and index.

Jenness, Rosemarie K. *Gogol's Aesthetics Compared to Major Elements of German Romanticism*. New York: Peter Lang, 1995. An examination of aesthetics in the works of Gogol and an analysis of German romanticism. Bibliography and index.

Karlinsky, Simon. *The Sexual Labyrinth of Nikolai Gogol*. 1976. Reprint. Chicago: University of Chicago Press, 1992. A look at Gogol's literature and his relations with men. Contains annotated bibliography of Gogol's works in English. Index.

Luckyj, George Stephen Nestor. *The Anguish of Mykola Hohol a.k.a. Nikolai Gogol*. Toronto: Canadian Scholar's Press, 1998. A bibliography of Gogol that examines his life and work. Bibliography and index.

Maguire, Robert A. *Exploring Gogol*. Stanford, Calif.: Stanford University Press, 1994. A critical examination of the literary works of Gogol. Bibliography and index.

Shapiro, Gavriel. *Nikolai Gogol and the Baroque Cultural Heritage.* University Park: Pennsylvania State University Press, 1993. A scholarly study of the literary style of Gogol, examining its links to Baroque literature.

Spieker, Sven, ed. *Gogol: Exploring Absence: Negativity in Nineteenth Century Russian Literature.* Bloomington, Ind.: Slavica, 1999. A collection of essays on Gogol focusing on negativity in his works and those of other Russian writers. Bibliography and index.

Zia Hasan

CARLO GOLDONI

Born: Venice (now in Italy); February 25, 1707
Died: Paris, France; February 6, 1793

PRINCIPAL DRAMA

Il buon padre, pr. 1729

La cantatrice, pr. 1729

Amalasunta, pr. 1732

Momolo cortesan: O, L'uomo di mondo, pr. 1738, pb. 1757

La donna di garbo, pr. 1743, pb. 1747

La vedova scaltra, pr. 1748, pb. 1750 (*The Artful Widow*, 1968)

La bottega del caffè, pr. 1750, pb. 1753 (*The Coffee-house*, 1925)

Pamela nubile, pr. 1750, pb. 1753 (adaptation of Samuel Richardson's novel *Pamela*)

La locandiera, pb., pr. 1753 (*The Mistress of the Inn*, 1912)

Il campiello, pr. 1756, pb. 1758 (English translation, 1976)

La casa nova, pr. 1760, pb. 1768 (*The Superior Residence*, 1968)

I rusteghi, pr. 1760, pb. 1761 (*The Boors*, 1961)

Le baruffe chizzotte, pr. 1762, pb. 1774 (*The Squabbles of Chioggia*, 1914)

Una delle ultime sere di carnovale, pr. 1762, pb. 1797

Il ventaglio, pr. in French 1763, pr. in Italian 1767, pb. in Italian 1789 (*The Fan*, 1892)

Le Bourru bienfaisant, pr., pb. 1771 (*The Beneficent Bear*, 1892)

Tutte le opera, pb. 1935-1956 (14 volumes)

Three Comedies, pb. 1961

Four Comedies, pb. 1968

OTHER LITERARY FORMS

Carlo Goldoni is remembered only for his contributions to Italian drama. The major source of information about Goldoni and his theater is his autobiography, *Mémoires de M. Goldoni pour servir à l'histoire de sa vie, et à celle de son théâtre* (1787; *Memoirs of Goldoni Written by Himself, Forming a Complete History of His Life and Writing*, 1814). Commonly known as his *Mémoires*, Goldoni's autobiography was written in Paris, where Goldoni spent the final years of his life.

ACHIEVEMENTS

During a lifetime that spanned the eighteenth century, from 1707 to 1793, Carlo Goldoni wrote prolifically for the Italian stage, producing more than 120 comedies, as well as a number of tragedies and tragicomedies and more than fifty scenarios. Through his comedies, Goldoni was largely responsible for the transformation of Italian drama from the unwritten, improvisational performances that flourished in Italy from approximately 1660 to 1800 under the name *commedia dell'arte* to the modern, written drama of contemporary European theater.

The *commedia dell'arte* was characterized by its improvised performances, its lively dialogue and plotting, and its song, dance, and acrobatics. Starting with a scenario, troupes of actors would make generous use of *lazzi*—routinely improvised stage business expressing an emotion or reaction and often featuring practical jokes, gags, and buffoonery. Each actor in the troupe portrayed a particular stock character that did not vary from one performance to another. The character was identifiable by the mask he wore, by the dialect he spoke, and by his mannerisms. The *commedia dell'arte* borrowed freely from the plots of Greek and Roman plays, and, in the seventeenth century, from the plots of Spanish dramas. The success of a performance, however, depended less on the original plot than on the ability of the actors to make the drama interesting and alive.

By the late seventeenth century, the *commedia dell'arte* had exerted considerable influence on the drama of other European countries. The troupes traveled to France and to England; William Shakespeare borrowed plot devices and characters from the *commedia dell'arte*; and Molière incorporated several stock characters into his comedies. In Italy, however, the *commedia dell'arte* was not successfully incorporated into written comedy.

By the late seventeenth century, too, the *commedia dell'arte* had begun to lose its imaginative spontaneity, in spite of a preponderance of good actors. Once, the *commedia dell'arte* had captured the everyday lives of its audience and interpreted those lives in an imaginative, highly stylized form. Yet, in an attempt to hold the interest of audiences no longer content to applaud the old *lazzi*, the actors neglected their improvisation, and the *lazzi* descended to a more vulgar, often obscene, level. The actors of the *commedia dell'arte* thus alienated the emerging middle class, which had a stricter sense of propriety than had earlier audiences.

Goldoni's middle-class background made him sensitive to the artistic tastes and moral standards of this emerging audience. Inspired by the comedies of Molière, Goldoni sought to create an Italian comedy that would keep the best elements of the *commedia dell'arte*—the fresh and earthy sense of reality, expressed by fast, witty dialogue—while once again reflecting the everyday life of its audience. Working with the actors of the *commedia dell'arte* troupe of

Guiseppe Imer, including the renowned actor Antonio Sacchi, who played the role of Harlequin, Goldoni wrote *Momolo cortesan: O, L'uomo di mondo*, which was an improvisational scenario but also contained one role—that of Harlequin—which was completely written down. Five years later, in 1743, Goldoni achieved his reform of the *commedia dell'arte* with *La donna di garbo* (the clever woman), in which all the parts were completely written out.

BIOGRAPHY

Early eighteenth century Venice provided a cradle for the playwright Carlo Goldoni, whose Venetian forebears had also interested themselves in the theater. As a child, Goldoni practiced writing short plays and improvised for his puppet theater. His family was well-to-do, and he states in his *Mémoires* that he was born in a large and fascinating palace, surrounded "by prosperous and peaceful domesticity," surroundings that fostered his happy disposition. (It should be noted that scholars have questioned the reliability of Goldoni's memoirs.) Financial difficulties caused his father, late in life, to join the medical profession. As a doctor, Giulio Goldoni traveled extensively through northern and central Italy, eventually settling in Perugia. There he was joined by Carlo Goldoni, who began his formal education in the local Jesuit school that he attended from 1717 to 1720.

The family moved again, this time to Chioggia, a small town on the Venetian lagoon, but Goldoni's father left him in Rimini at a friend's house to study philosophy under the guidance of a Dominican father. Goldoni, however, was already restless, adventurous, and enthralled by the theater. He made friends with a company of strolling players who were performing in town. Bored with his studies and missing his family, Goldoni decided to leave town and departed with the players on their boat, which sailed to Chioggia, where his family resided.

After a short stay at home, Goldoni was dispatched to Venice as an apprentice in his uncle's law office. Later, in 1723, he entered the Ghislieri College of Pavia as a law student. Here again, his passion for comic art and satire interrupted his studies. Goldoni allowed himself in 1725 to be persuaded by "perfidious friends" to write a satire, "Il Colosso," which described a monstrous statue formed with different body parts of the girls of Pavia. The pamphlet, considered libelous by the girls' parents, caused the expulsion of young Goldoni (now in his third year) from the college. He once again had to find refuge at home with his family.

After his hasty return to Chioggia, he accompanied his father on several trips through Friuli, Görz, and Graz. He also continued his law studies in Udine and then at the University of Modena. In the meantime, he pursued his interest in the theater by staging, in Udine, a comedy by Pier Jacopo Martello, *Lo starnuto di Ercole* (1717; Hercule's sneeze); he also wrote in this period two intermezzos, *Il buon padre* (the good old father) and *La cantatrice* (the singer).

When Goldoni's father died in 1731, the family found itself in even harsher financial straits, and Goldoni was urged by his mother to complete his legal studies, which he did at the University of Padua. Goldoni took his last examination "after a night spent in gambling," as he reports in his *Mémoires*. On his return to Venice, Goldoni was admitted to the bar in 1732 and began to practice law. He also had enough time to continue writing for the theater and during this year wrote his first serious play, "L'Amalasunta," a tragedy for music. Unfortunately, he could find no one to stage it. After a year, in debt and trapped in a loveless engagement, he could see no solution other than flight from Venice. After some wandering, he reached Milan, where he found a position as personal secretary with the Venetian ambassador. Repeating a pattern, Goldoni did not keep his position for long, and, after an altercation with the ambassador, he was fired. In the meantime he had made new friends in the world of the theater; he became acquainted with Imer, the director of a very important *commedia dell'arte* group. Imer quickly became fond of Goldoni and hired him as librettist for his troupe. By the end of September, 1734, Goldoni was once again in Venice, where Imer's troupe was to perform at the renowned San Samuele theater for the year's dramatic season.

When Imer's company embarked on a tour of northern Italy, Goldoni followed them, and in Genoa he met and fell in love with a young Genoese girl, Nicoletta Connio, whom he married in 1736. Nicoletta became his faithful and patient companion, sharing with him his adventurous life. She brought an element of stability to the playwright's life by curbing some of his most destructive habits: gambling, excessive generosity, and "ruinous gallantry toward women."

Goldoni returned with his wife to Venice and continued his services as a writer for Imer and for the nobleman Michele Grimani. The latter was proprietor of both the San Samuele and the San Giovanni Crisostomo theaters. It was in this capacity that Goldoni began his reform of the Italian comedy for which he was to become famous.

Despite his position as a playwright and his sporadic law practice, Goldoni's financial situation continued to be precarious. Unable to satisfy his creditors, he once again was forced to flee Venice. Goldoni and his wife spent several years away from Venice, visiting Tuscany, the dialect of which was the most widely accepted language for literary works, as well as Florence, Sienna, and Pisa. Goldoni decided to settle in Pisa and resume his law practice, but a request from Sacchi for some new scripts, followed by a visit from another famous Harlequin, Cesare D'Arbes, led Goldoni back to the theater. D'Arbes introduced Goldoni to Girolamo Medebac, one of the greatest impresarios of his time. Medebac—who was in Leghorn with his troupe for a staging of Goldoni's *La donna di garbo*, which Goldoni himself had not yet seen performed—offered Goldoni the position of playwright for his company. Goldoni accepted, and followed Medebac to Venice, where Medebac had leased for the 1748 season the Teatro Sant' Angelo, one of the finest theaters in town.

With this new engagement, Goldoni's art acquired a new rhythm. For four years, until 1752, he remained with the Medebac company, and this was the most productive and successful period of his career as a playwright. During the 1750-1751 season, in order to keep a promise made to the public the preceding season, he wrote seventeen new comedies, some of which are among his best plays, such as *Pamela nubile* and *The Coffee-house*.

By 1753, Goldoni had completed his commitment as a writer for Medebac. Realizing that the impresario was not very generous (he published Goldoni's plays but refused to share the profit with the author), Goldoni decided to work instead for Antonio and Francesco Vendramin, brothers who owned another very important theater in Venice, the San Luca.

During this new engagement, Goldoni continued to produce some of his most admirable plays: *Il campiello*, *The Superior Residence*, *The Boors*, and *The Squabbles of Chioggia*. Goldoni's success, however, attracted the fierce rivalry of Abbé Pietro Chiari and Carlo Gozzi. Chiari was a minor author who satirized Goldoni's work in his own plays to achieve notoriety. Gozzi, however, was the author of several successful *fiabe dramatiche* (dramatic fables) and a strong advocate of preserving the traditional form of the *commedia dell'arte*, the tenets of which he adapted to his fables. A bitter controversy, centering on Gozzi's desire to preserve and Goldoni's desire to reform the *commedia dell'arte*, developed around the three playwrights. This controversy adversely affected Goldoni's popularity and contributed to his decision to eave Venice when he received an attractive offer to direct the Comédie-Italienne in Paris.

In April of 1762, after concluding the theatrical season in Venice with the staging of *Una delle ultime sere di carnovale* (one of the last evenings of the carnival), Goldoni left for Paris. He was fascinated by Parisian life and enjoyed the acquaintance of the composer Jean-Philippe Rameau, the intellectual Denis Diderot, and the philosophers Jean-Jacques Rousseau and Voltaire. Yet directing the Comédie-Italienne proved to be more difficult than he had foreseen: The actors were unwilling to accept his reforms, and the audiences continued to prefer the traditional *commedia dell'arte*, which was a welcome alternative to the *comédie larmoyante* and the classical tragedy that dominated the theater in France.

Faced with these difficulties, Goldoni returned to the kind of work that he had done at the beginning of his career: He wrote scenarios for improvised comedies because that was what both the public and the artists desired. Discouraged, Goldoni was considering retirement and a return to Italy when his contract with the Comédie-Italienne expired, but in 1765, he was invited to the court as the instructor in Italian for the princesses. During his years in Paris, he continued to send Venice comedies that were favorably received by the public. Later, when he became more fluent in French, he wrote for the French theater, and one of these plays, *The Beneficent Bear*, was a great success.

When his assignment as tutor at the court ended, he was given a modest pension, and he retired to Paris, leaving Versailles, where he had lived for several years as a friend of the royal family. Goldoni had been unable to obtain any real financial benefit from his royal friendships, or, as he said, "I was at the court but I was not a courtier." In Paris, he tried without success some publishing ventures while writing the history of his life with immense enjoyment. While Goldoni wrote his memoirs, he and his wife lived in a fairly good neighborhood in Paris and were comforted by the help and company of his nephew Antonio Goldoni, who had come to Paris with him. During his last years, Goldoni was visited by the famed Italian poet and playwright Vittorio Alfieri. In 1792, as a consequence of the French Revolution, Goldoni's pension was discontinued, but Marie-Joseph Chénier, the brother of the poet André Chénier, asked the National Convention to return the pension to Goldoni because the Italian writer had with his theater greatly contributed to the cause of the revolution and freedom. The request was granted; unfortunately Goldoni had died the previous evening, at six o'clock on February 6, 1793.

ANALYSIS

Carlo Goldoni set out to reform, rather than to eradicate, the *commedia dell'arte*, and he continued to employ the traditional characters of that form, although they no longer wore their traditional masks. The cunning servant Harlequin, the elderly parent Pantalone, the pedantic Dottore, the gossip Brighella, and the servant girl Columbina all appear in a variety of guises in Goldoni's comedies. The intrigue centering on young lovers outwitting unrelenting parents, a mainstay of the *commedia dell'arte*, is also found in Goldoni's plays, yet Goldoni's chief talent was in the sympathetic and accurate portrayal of the people and milieu of contemporary Venice. In his plays, the stock characters become the merchants, fishermen, students, gondoliers, gossips, and servants of his city; the traditional romantic intrigue becomes the drama of changing mores in eighteenth century Venice. In his comedies of characters and of milieu, Goldoni achieved his highest art.

Goldoni's comedies avoid the truly dramatic predicaments of life and never really develop a complex theme or an extensively plotted story. In their essence, they are usually cordial and happy descriptions of everyday life. Therefore, his plays are not noted for a logical or precise development of the action according to any well-defined dramatic rules. Instead, his theater offers an almost impressionistic worldview that honors the petty details of daily life, glorifies ordinary places such as coffeehouses and inns, and enlivens common occurrences such as the departure for a summer vacation. With affection and irony, Goldoni observed and described the world of the lower-middle-class families of Venice in the eighteenth century—a world of small virtues and little vices. Goldoni captured the lively surfaces of those times, not their deeper significance. The conflict between old and new, between the Baroque culture that was coming to an end and the new culture of the Enlightenment, is reduced in scale to a conflict between father and son, between an innkeeper and her noble guests, between old boors and young lovers.

THE MISTRESS OF THE INN

Among Goldoni's many successful comedies of character, the critics usually award their plaudits to *The Mistress of the Inn* and *The Boors*. *The Mistress of the Inn* is exceptional for the witticisms, sharp jesting, and shrewdness of its characters and the taut linear structure of its plot. It is perhaps the only play among Goldoni's comedies of character in which the protagonist dominates the milieu rather than being dominated by it.

The play is set in an eighteenth century inn. Count Albafiorita and Marquis Forlipopoli are guests in the inn of Mirandolina, a pretty and spirited woman with whom everyone falls in love. These two clumsy noblemen awkwardly try to conquer the heart of the charming innkeeper. One of them, the count, offers money and gifts; the other, the pennyless marquis, extends pretentious offers of protection. Another sojourner at the inn is the cavalier Ripafratta, who is an obnoxious misogynist. Mirandolina's intelligence and sensitivity are offended by the attitudes and remarks of the cavalier, and, taking a kind of revenge, she causes him to fall in love with her. Her success creates all sorts of jealousies among the other guests at the inn, and matters are complicated by the arrival of two comedians, Ortensia and Dejanira. As the situation escalates dangerously because of the heightened emotions of Ripafratta, Mirandolina reveals the game. She is not at all in love with Ripafratta; her intention is only to punish his arrogance and ill manners, and she declares that she will marry instead—faithful to her father's dying wish—the loyal Fabrizio, the waiter at her inn.

Goldoni composed this comedy in 1753, while he was still in the service of the Medebac troupe, and the play was written for the soubrette of the company, Maddalena Marliani, an exceptional actress and a willful and spirited woman very similar in personality to Mirandolina. The comedy, as was usual for Goldoni, was written quickly, as if the characters were already alive to the smallest detail in Goldoni's mind. Mirandolina represents the best-accomplished development of a long series of Columbinas—delightful and dangerous women. These comediennes appear with predictable frequency in the *commedia dell'arte* and turn up as frequently in the plays of Goldoni. Mirandolina possesses an exuberant, complex vitality that is aimed at overcoming all the obstacles that will deprive her of the pleasure of being courted. Though revered by many men, she shows disregard for those who indulge in foolish foibles. She extends the stock character of the *commedia dell'arte* to depict the personality and the predicament of a feminine Don Juan, who, loved by everyone, really loves no one.

THE BOORS

The Boors, a comedy written entirely in Venetian dialect, has met through the years with unequivocal approval by public and critics alike. In this masterpiece, Goldoni merges the best of his perceptive descriptions of environment and milieu with his skilled portrayals of character. The title characters, the boors, motivate the other characters to define their environment.

The Boors presents the antics of an old merchant, Lunardo, who plans to marry his daughter Lucietta to Filippetto, the son of his good friend Maurizio. An agreement is made, according to the ancient custom, between the two fathers, and the young people are kept ignorant of the arrangement and prevented from meeting each other until their wedding day. Margherita, the wife of Lunardo and the stepmother of Lucietta, allows the two young people to meet, however, and Filippetto, masked, and with the help of Count Riccardo, a friend of the family, is able, during Carnival, to enter the house of Lunardo. He is introduced to Lucietta, and they converse; yet, unknown to the young couple, this night is the very night on which Lunardo has invited his friends—the boors—to celebrate the marriage of Lucietta and Filippetto.

When the stern, severe old men discover that the two young people have already met, they want to cancel the wedding, but Felicita, the wife of Canciano, one of the boors, courageously opposes this decision, and with her eloquent feminine wisdom she convinces the old men to be reasonable and allow the marriage to take place.

The Boors describes the close and traditional atmosphere of Old Venice, a Venice struggling against new influences knocking at her doors: Goldoni perceives with a benevolent irony the predicament of the old-fashioned merchants who represent the ruling class of the passé Venetian world, a class perhaps too severe in its judgment, too parsimonious, but also one that valued hard work, honesty, and seriousness, and which greatly contributed to the stability and glory of the ancient Republic. The old Venice, however, was vanishing during Goldoni's lifetime; the new concepts of the Enlightenment brought to Venice a different, stronger, and more serene sense of tolerance, justice, and authority. Among the common people, these new feelings and ideas were manifested with greatest vigor in the conflict between the old and new generations.

Goldoni's chief accomplishment in *The Boors* is the creation of four characters, the boors, who all share the recognizable traits of the merchant class of Venice and yet are each distinct and memorable characters. In sharp, symmetrical contrast to the four boors are their three wives and Lucietta: They are vivacious, sensible, and joyful. In *The Boors*, Goldoni succeeds more broadly than in his other plays in creating distinctive, shaded characters ranging from the ebullient women to the austere and sere fathers.

THE COFFEE-HOUSE

Among the comedies of *ambiente*, those plays mainly concerned with the description of a milieu, the best-known is *The Coffee-house*, which is one of the seventeen comedies that Goldoni wrote in the 1750-1751 season to rekindle the interest of a public that appeared to be tiring of his theater.

Set in a *campiello*, the typical small square of Venice, *The Coffee-house* captures the colors, tones, and effects of Goldoni's city, which he seldom tired of depicting. Indeed, the protagonist of this play is the milieu. It dominates the characters, who seem to be merely creatures of their environment rather than autonomous individuals. The action develops in three shops—a barbershop, a coffeehouse, and a gambling house. On the side of the barbershop, off the street, is a house where a dancer lives.

A young merchant, Eugenio, who is good-natured but weak, has a passion for gambling, which is ruining him and also causing him to neglect his wife, whom he sincerely loves. Preying on Eugenio is Flaminio, who, under the assumed name of Count Leandro, lives by cheating at cards. He also carries on a relationship with the ballerina Lisaura. The lives of these characters are complicated by the gossip and slander of Don Marzio, a loafer who is a regular customer at the coffeehouse.

Through the good offices of Ridolfo, the honest owner of the coffeehouse, all is made right in the end. Eugenio renounces gambling and returns to the affectionate arms of his wife, Vittoria; Leandro acknowledges his faults and is reconciled with his wife, Placida, from whom he had run away; and Don Marzio, the incorrigible slanderer, is put to shame.

Goldoni had already used the setting of a coffee-house in some of his intermezzos, in which, since the scene was typically Venetian, the dialogue was in dialect instead of standard Italian. This dialect, as well as masks, appeared in the first productions of *The Coffee-house*. Ridolfo, the owner of the coffeehouse, was Brighella, and his waiter, later to be known as Trappola, was then Harlequin. When Goldoni decided to publish this comedy, he translated it into Italian and deleted the masks.

As a new dramatic force in this play, Goldoni offered a little conjugal drama between Eugenio and Vittoria that has an unusual breadth for Goldoni's plays. In Vittoria, he presents a female character who offers a rare fullness in the representation of the sentimental woman in love; she endures her trials in a deeper and more sensitive manner. The true protagonist of this play, however, is the coffeehouse, of which Don Marzio, the loafer, the slanderer, the gossiper, is the dark soul.

Don Marzio reflects characteristics and vices that could be found in everyone, and Goldoni's characterization was so realistic that several playgoers threatened him physically because they believed that they had been slandered in the character of Don Marzio.

OTHER MAJOR WORKS

NONFICTION: *Mémoires de M. Goldoni pour servir à l'histoire de sa vie, et à celle de son théâtre*, 1787 (*Memoirs of Goldoni Written by Himself, Forming a Complete History of His Life and Writing*, 1814).

BIBLIOGRAPHY

Emery, Ted. *Goldoni as Librettist: Theatrical Reform and the Drammi Giocosi per Musica*. New York: Peter Lang, 1991. A look at Italian drama and theory as well as Goldoni's libretti. Bibliography.

Farrell, Joseph, ed. *Carlo Goldoni and Eighteenth Century Theatre*. Lewiston, N.Y.: Edwin Mellen, 1997. A critical look at Goldoni's drama and at the theater of his time. Bibliography.

Fido, France, and Dino S. Cervigni, eds. *Goldoni 1993*. Chapel Hill: University of North Carolina at Chapel Hill, 1993. A collection of essays in English, Italian, and French on Goldoni and his works. Bibliography.

Holme, Timothy. *A Servant of Many Masters: The Life and Times of Carlo Goldoni*. London: Jupiter, 1976. A biography of Goldoni that covers his life and works. Bibliography and index.

Pietropaolo, Domenico, ed. *Goldoni and the Musical Theatre*. New York: Legas, 1995. An examination of the works of Goldoni, particularly his libretti. Bibliography.

Steele, Eugene. *Carlo Goldoni: Life, Work, and Times*. Ravenna, Italy: Longo Editore, 1981. A biography of Goldoni examining his literary output and life. Bibliography and index.

Patrizio Rossi

OLIVER GOLDSMITH

Born: Pallas, County Longford(?), Ireland;
    November 10, 1728 or 1730
Died: London, England; April 4, 1774

PRINCIPAL DRAMA

The Good-Natured Man, pr., pb. 1768
*She Stoops to Conquer: Or, The Mistakes of a
    Night*, pr., pb. 1773

OTHER LITERARY FORMS

Although best remembered as a dramatist, Oliver Goldsmith is also known for his work in several other genres. His only novel, *The Vicar of Wakefield* (1766), the comic and sentimental tale of a village curate's attempts to guide his children through the tribulations of growing up, remains a minor classic. *The Citizen of the World* (1762), a recasting of Charles de

Montesquieu's *Lettres Persanes* (1721; *Persian Letters*, 1722), is a collection of fictitious letters, purportedly written by a Chinese philosopher who is living in London, describing English customs and English society from an outsider's point of view.

Goldsmith's poetry was often comic as well (as in his parodies of "An Elegy on the Death of a Mad Dog," of 1766, and "An Elegy on the Glory of Her Sex: Mrs. Mary Blaize," of 1759), but when his sympathies were touched, he produced some creditable serious poems, the most notable of which is *The Deserted Village* (1770), a protest against the economic and social conditions that were forcing a massive shift of the populace from small villages to cities.

Like other eighteenth century authors, Goldsmith earned his living by writing whatever publishers thought would sell: histories of Rome and England, biographical sketches, epilogues for the plays of others, translations, and introductions to the natural sciences as well as plays, novels, and poems. The best modern edition of Goldsmith's varied canon is *The Collected Works of Oliver Goldsmith* (1966), in five volumes, edited by Arthur Friedman for Oxford University Press.

ACHIEVEMENTS

Oliver Goldsmith's success rate as a dramatist is virtually unmatched: two plays written, the first very good, the second a masterpiece. Goldsmith was the preeminent English comic dramatist in the period of almost two centuries between William Congreve and Oscar Wilde. Only his contemporary Richard Brinsley Sheridan—who wrote more plays and had better theatrical connections—came close to matching Goldsmith's talent.

The qualities that make *The Good-Natured Man* and *She Stoops to Conquer* wonderful theater are the qualities that mark all Goldsmith's writings: an eye for human foibles, a knack for creating the scene or situation in which such foibles can best display themselves, and a willingness to laugh at folly rather than to be irked by it. Goldsmith expresses his comic vision of human experience in language that induces the reader's continuing attention and seduces the reader's affection.

Goldsmith was a writer who believed that it was his duty to entertain his audience. Like a stage performer, he used every device, trick, and resource that gives pleasure. No reader finds Goldsmith's prose a chore to read; no theatergoer finds his plays too long.

BIOGRAPHY

Tony Lumpkin in *She Stoops to Conquer* is one of those classic ne'er-do-wells in English literature who would rather eat, drink, and play a merry prank than work for a living. Tony may have been Oliver Goldsmith's favorite male character in the play; at the very least, he was a kindred spirit, because the playwright himself had lived a ne'er-do-well's existence before successful authorship brought him some stability and an income, however irregular it may have been.

Goldsmith began life as the second son in the large family of an Anglo-Irish clergyman. What limited wealth the family had was destined to become part of his older brother's inheritance or of the dowry for an older sister who "married above herself"; nothing much was left for Oliver. Goldsmith seems to have been equally slighted by nature: He was a sickly child, badly disfigured by smallpox contracted at age seven, and he was considered dull by his first teachers. From this inauspicious background, it took a number of years for Goldsmith to discover his niche in the world as a writer.

Goldsmith was graduated from Trinity College, Dublin, in 1749, after fitful periods of study that were punctuated by riotous parties and pranks, clashes with administrators, and attempts to run away. Two years later, he applied for ordination in the Church of England, but the red trousers he wore to the interview seem not to have made a favorable impression on the local bishop. Goldsmith's uncle, the Reverend Thomas Contarine, gave him the money to study medicine, first at the University of Edinburgh and then at the University of Leyden, but the fledgling physician preferred to spend the time and money otherwise, wandering the Continent as a tourist. In 1756, when Goldsmith returned to London, he found it hard to support himself. His casual medical knowledge was no help in obtaining a doctor's commission in the

Royal Navy (which at the time appointed as "surgeon" almost anyone who could wield a scalpel without self-mutilation). Goldsmith tried teaching, but he proved less disciplined than the young boys he was supposed to instruct.

Not until he began work as a proofreader for novelist-printer Samuel Richardson did Goldsmith find a task that focused his energies. Drawing on his Continental wanderings, the proofreader turned author in 1759 when his *An Enquiry into the Present State of Polite Learning in Europe* was published with some success. His achievement brought Goldsmith freelance assignments from other publishers, and he contributed essays, reviews, and poems to several periodicals. From these, Goldsmith gained popular applause, the recognition of fellow writers, and a modest though unsteady income. The most notable sign of his success was his admission to the Literary Club in the early 1760's. There, Goldsmith dined and conversed with the most prominent London intellectuals, among them the painter Sir Joshua Reynolds, the politician Edmund Burke, the actor David Garrick, and the writer-critic Samuel Johnson. In the Literary Club, Goldsmith found and immersed himself in a

Oliver Goldsmith (Library of Congress)

sophisticated version of the lively fellowship Tony Lumpkin enjoys at the Three Pigeons Tavern.

Club members helped channel Goldsmith's efforts in new literary directions. When Goldsmith was threatened with arrest for nonpayment of rent, Samuel Johnson sent the unfinished manuscript of *The Vicar of Wakefield* (on which Goldsmith had been working intermittently for several years) to a publisher, who bought it for sixty pounds. Because Goldsmith did not get along with David Garrick, who was manager of the Drury Lane Theatre, Reynolds wrote a letter of recommendation to Garrick on behalf of Goldsmith's recently finished first foray into drama, *The Good-Natured Man*. Though Goldsmith was no doubt eager to become a playwright, with a chance of making hundreds of pounds if his play ran until the third night (which was the performance known as the "author's benefit"), *The Good-Natured Man* was not produced until two years later. Garrick and Goldsmith had argued over revisions and payments; eventually, Goldsmith had to take the play to another theater.

The profits from his first play were enough to provide Goldsmith with new quarters, new furnishings, and several new coats; they also whetted his desire to repeat his success. By 1771, he had finished a second comedy, *She Stoops to Conquer*, which was produced by a recalcitrant theater manager who procrastinated over the production for more than a year until Johnson again intervened. Through his reasoned arguments and bearlike presence, Johnson convinced the manager to put the play into production, and from the moment it opened on March 15, 1773, it was a huge success. Goldsmith, however, would have only thirteen months left in which to enjoy these financial rewards.

Even after he turned novelist and dramatist, Goldsmith never stopped racing from literary project to literary project. He continued to write essays, biographies, and general histories as well as to compile translations and anthologies. Despite his remarkable output in the last decade of his life, he was never far out of debt. Fortunately, publishers were always eager for his services, because they knew that Goldsmith's name on the title page increased their chances of a brisk sale.

Goldsmith wrote almost until the hour of his death. His last effort was the poem "Retaliation," a verse response to Garrick's epigrammatic remark (that Goldsmith "wrote like an angel, but talk'd like poor Poll"). Goldsmith died on April 4, 1774, the victim of both a fever and the remedy prescribed to cure it.

ANALYSIS

The Good-Natured Man and *She Stoops to Conquer* were written to spite the prevailing taste in comedy. In an essay written just after he completed the second play, Oliver Goldsmith explained that the comedy of his time, which he called sentimental comedy, was a degeneration of a genre that had been clearly defined since the days of Aristotle. Comedy, Goldsmith lamented, had become a kind of tragedy that sought to influence the audience by appealing to its sympathy.

Sentimental comedy was a dramatic subgenre that developed at the beginning of the eighteenth century. The Restoration comedy of manners, which had delighted audiences with contrasting manners, sharp wordplay, and sexual innuendo, had been attacked by Jeremy Collier and others as immoral. To save drama, some writers began to make sure that every rake reformed by the fifth act and that sober, sensible lovers got as much attention as witty, scandalous ones. Sir Richard Steele, in the influential *The Conscious Lovers* (pr. 1722), had shown that lovers could be entangled in plots of parental opposition and mistaken identities so complicated that only the playwright could untie the fifth-act knots. Audiences, it seemed, would watch good people suffer through complex but manageable difficulties and would cheer when the protagonists swept all before them. Sentimental comedy was a part of Sensibility, a movement that characterized much literature after 1740. Sensibility invited readers and audiences to prove their humanity by sympathizing with the plight of fictional or dramatic heroes and heroines; it promised that their sympathy would be rewarded because all would work out in the end, leaving viewers with emotions stirred, teased, and satisfied.

In his essay on "laughing comedy," Goldsmith described the typical sentimental play

in which the virtues of private life are exhibited . . . and the distresses rather than the faults of mankind made our interest. . . . In these plays almost all the characters are good, and exceedingly generous; they are lavish enough of their *tin* money on the stage; and though they want humor, have abundance of sentiment and feeling.

Whatever claim to merit such plays have is reduced by the fact that they—like modern television situation comedies—are too easily written. Goldsmith scoffed that in sentimental comedies, it was enough

to deck out the hero with a riband, or give the heroine a title; then to put an insipid dialogue, without character or humor into their mouths, give them mighty good hearts, very fine clothes, furnish a new set of scenes, make a pathetic scene or two, with a sprinkling of tender melancholy conversation through the whole. . . .

The essay concludes with a lament on the art of making audiences laugh, an art that Goldsmith thought had disappeared with plays of Sir John Vanbrugh and Colley Cibber at the start of the eighteenth century. Determined to show that whatever delight sentimental comedies gave, laughing comedies gave better, Goldsmith submitted his own two plays as evidence.

Even without the historical interest, many readers still find Goldsmith enjoyable for his prose style and his sense of humor. He is one of the masters of the middle style; his informal, almost conversational prose and his humane and humorous observations of individuals make his work accessible and pleasurable even to those who have never met a lord or made the Grand Tour. Goldsmith's characters and comments are rooted in universal experience.

THE GOOD-NATURED MAN

The Good-Natured Man, which debuted while Hugh Kelly's latest sentimental play, *False Delicacy* (pr. 1768), was dominating theatrical London, teased contemporary taste in two ways. First, Goldsmith created scenes that are ironic, farcical, or witty enough to generate laughter. Second, he delineated—that is, in traditional terms, offered up to ridicule—the folly of a culture hero of the age, the "good-natured man." The good-natured man is the sentimental hero, the one who thinks with his heart rather than his head and who leaps to help solve life's smallest distresses. This generous instinct, Goldsmith's good-natured man discovers, has its limitations: One so inclined to sympathize with others may be in danger of losing himself. The twin purposes of the play—literary and moral—actually work together because the laughter that the play generates makes the lesson easier for the audience to accept.

The Good-Natured Man traces Sir William Honeywood's attempt to test and reform his nephew and heir, whose easy generosity (that is, good nature) has led him into extravagance and foolishness. Sir William's plan is to involve young Honeywood in enough fictitious distresses that he will be jailed for debt. Young Honeywood, then, the uncle reasons, would learn a valuable lesson by seeing which of his friends come to his assistance and which of them have only been taking advantage of his generosity. Sir William willingly admits that his nephew's universal benevolence is "a fault near allied to excellency," but as far as Sir William is concerned, it is still a fault to be corrected.

Sir William's plot is intended to demonstrate the need for the sentimental, good-natured man to be shown his follies, and most of the play's other characters reinforce the same idea. Sir William himself is a not very subtle mouthpiece for the dramatist, expostulating precisely and exactly on the hero's mistakes. Honeywood's friend Croaker is the exact opposite of Honeywood; as a man who sees everything gloomily and selfishly, he lets the audience see the defects of the other extreme. Another friend, Lofty, is a character who counterfeits benevolence (pretending to use influence at court on his friends' behalf) in order to puff himself up in the eyes of the world. Lofty is a conscious pretender, while Honeywood is sincere, but the latter comes to see that "in attempting to please all," he "fed his vanity" as much as Lofty did.

Once Honeywood has been arrested for debt, Sir William is pleased to learn, Miss Richland, a woman of independent fortune and a close friend, has secured his release. Honeywood, however, does not need his uncle's conniving to find himself in difficulties. His benevolence, good nature, and sensibility

generate other problems, one of the most knotty being his relationship with Miss Richland. Honeywood loves her deeply, but he is content to be only a friend. "Never let me harbour," he proclaims sentimentally, "a thought of making her unhappy by a connection with one so unworthy her merits as I am." In addition to being modest about his worth to her, Honeywood fears that he could never please her guardians, Mr. and Mrs. Croaker. Rather than tackle such obstacles directly, as would the witty hero of a Restoration comedy, Honeywood is content to sigh and wring his hands in distress.

Circumstances, however, refuse to let Honeywood remain uninvolved. Honeywood must watch while Croaker tries to marry his son, Leontine, to Miss Richland, despite the fact that Leontine is really in love with Olivia, an orphan whom he has brought to England from France in place of the long-absent sister he was sent to fetch. Honeywood must not only watch Croaker's matchmaking, but he must also intercede for Lofty's wooing of Miss Richland. Lofty, pretending to sentimental friendship, calls on Honeywood to court the young heiress for him. Honeywood is on an emotional rack, stretched between the desire to please a friend and the agony of speaking love in another person's name: "What shall I do! Love, friendship, a hopeless passion, a deserving friend! . . . to see her in the possession of another! . . . Insupportable! But then to betray a generous, trusting friend!—Worse, worse."

Honeywood's dilemmas are solved in the last two acts by accident and by Sir William's intercession. He lends money to Leontine and Olivia that they may elope, but when Croaker intercepts what he thinks is a blackmail letter, Honeywood accidentally sends him after the "blackmailer" to the very inn where the lovers are hiding. Catching his son and "daughter," Croaker praises Honeywood for his help and Leontine damns him for his apparent betrayal. Meanwhile, in speaking to Miss Richland on Lofty's behalf, Honeywood coaxes an admission of love from her. Not realizing that the one she confesses to loving is himself, Honeywood decides that "nothing remains henceforward for me but solitude and repentance."

As the characters gather at the inn for the last act, Sir William sets all to rights on his nephew's behalf. First, he persuades Croaker to accept Olivia as Leontine's bride: She is, Sir William testifies, the daughter of an old acquaintance, of good family, and an orphan with a fortune. Next, Sir William exposes the pretensions of Lofty so that Honeywood sees he is no friend. Now that his sentimental dilemma between love and friendship is understood to be no dilemma after all, a pleased but surprised Honeywood receives Miss Richland's hand in marriage. The events have been a lesson for the good-natured man, who closes the play with the promise that "it shall be my study to reserve pity for real distress, my friendship for true merit, and my love for her, who first taught me what it is to be happy."

Goldsmith generates "laughing comedy" in the play by several devices: a farcical scene in which a bailiff and his deputy dress as gentlemen, humorous characters such as Croaker and Lofty whose foibles are played on repeatedly, and dialogue at cross-purposes. Dialogue at cross-purposes is one of Goldsmith's favorite comedic devices, one of several dialogue strategies that had made the Restoration comedy of manners so rich in wit. When characters speak at cross-purposes, they manage to hold what appears to be a logical conversation although each is talking about a different subject. The result is confusion among the characters onstage and delight for the audience, which appreciates the ironic interplay of one attitude with another.

The best of these scenes in *The Good-Natured Man* are Leontine's marriage proposal to Miss Richland in act 1, Honeywood's plea on Lofty's behalf in act 4, and Honeywood's interview with the Croakers in act 4. In the first instance, Leontine twists himself into verbal knots as he tries simultaneously to convince his father that he is making an ardent proposal and to make it lukewarm enough to ensure that Miss Richland will reject it. In the second, Honeywood pleads so eloquently for another that Miss Richland is convinced he speaks for himself. In the third, Honeywood counsels Croaker on how to forgive the eloping lovers—counsel that the old man mistakes for advice on how to treat a blackmailer.

SHE STOOPS TO CONQUER

What Goldsmith does well in *The Good-Natured Man*, he does brilliantly in *She Stoops to Conquer*. The second play dispenses with the mouthpiece figure of Sir William, offers more entanglements more dexterously resolved, and satirizes sentimental comedy more subtly. *She Stoops to Conquer* has no thesis at all in the usual sense. It is a play that is not *about* something; instead, it is a play that *is* something: a recipe for laughing comedy.

Talking about *She Stoops to Conquer* is somewhat like trying to explain a joke. *She Stoops to Conquer* is an inventory of dramatic tricks for making comedy: juxtaposing high-class and low-class characters, creating farcical situations, putting witty dialogue in the mouths of several characters and having them converse at cross-purposes, establishing several good intriguers to initiate the action, and adding a generous helping of mistaken identities. *She Stoops to Conquer* is one of the purest pieces of entertainment ever written; it stands above its time and historical circumstances to such a degree that it has been a theatrical staple since its first production. To enjoy Goldsmith's comedy, an audience needs no special knowledge or moral perspective; it needs only a willingness to react instinctively to high spirits, confusion, and surprise. The play is a delight for actors as well as audience because all the principal characters are good roles; it is a play for an acting company rather than a vehicle for one or two stars. Although there are two plots, they are so nicely balanced that no audience wishes to see one enhanced at the expense of the other.

Goldsmith manages throughout the play to keep the audience informed of all that occurs while the characters onstage usually act under some mistaken impression. By constantly shifting who-knows-what-about-whom, Goldsmith keeps the plot throttle on "full ahead," the characters in unexpected predicaments, and the audience wide awake. Casting the whole in clever dialogue adds to the delight. In the hands of actors capable of playing the physical comedy broadly, *She Stoops to Conquer* becomes three hours of fast-paced merriment.

So much seems to be occurring simultaneously that *She Stoops to Conquer* is a difficult play to summarize. Perhaps reviewing the *dramatis personae* and sketching the action of the two plots best reveals Goldsmith's dexterity at introducing contrasting parts while keeping the whole moving forward. This dramatist is a theatrical juggler of rare skill; once set into motion, no character, action, or situation falls from his hand.

"The mistakes of a night" occur at the country residence of Mr. and Mrs. Hardcastle, a mismatched couple, each of whom is married for a second time. Mr. Hardcastle loves the country and its old-fashioned ways; Mrs. Hardcastle yearns for the city and the latest styles. Like another literary couple grown accustomed to each other's hobbyhorses, Mr. and Mrs. Bennet in Jane Austen's *Pride and Prejudice* (1813), each Hardcastle takes an independent path while poking fun at the spouse's preference.

Living at the Hardcastle residence are three young persons on the verge of independence and love. First, there is Tony Lumpkin, Mrs. Hardcastle's son by her first marriage. He is about to turn twenty-one and come into his own estate. Mr. Hardcastle regards him as a lazy and useless child, while Mrs. Hardcastle dotes on him, one minute sure he has the makings of a scholar and the next worried that he is consumptive. Tony prefers to ignore both parents and to concentrate on drinking and singing at his favorite tavern, the Three Pigeons. Here he entertains his fellows with practical jokes and lyrics that make clear his values:

> Let schoolmasters puzzle their brain
> With grammar, and nonsense, and learning;
> Good liquor, I stoutly maintain,
> Gives genius a better discerning.

Tony, the alehouse hero, is rather a bold protagonist for Goldsmith to portray to audiences accustomed to central male characters dressed in fine linen and attentive to providing themselves with life's essentials: a pretty wife and a sufficient income.

The second resident is Constance Neville, Mrs. Hardcastle's orphaned niece. Constance is treated with as much restraint as Tony is indulged. She is eager to marry George Hastings but cannot, because her dowry, a substantial sum in jewels, is closely kept by her aunt. Mrs. Hardcastle is reluctant to give the jewels into

Constance's care because she hopes to force her niece to marry Tony. Mrs. Hardcastle's matchmaking is having no luck: The sober Constance and the lighthearted Tony thoroughly dislike each other. Constance is a typical dramatic heroine of the time: pleasant but not especially bright, rich but without control of her fortune, and restless but not very disobedient.

The third person is Kate, Hardcastle's daughter by his first marriage. She and her father get along much better than do mother and son or aunt and niece. They are honestly affectionate with each other and speak frankly to each other; they care enough for each other to indulge each other's preferences. Kate, for example, who shares her stepmother's interest in fashion, moderates her indulgence by dressing for one half of the day in current styles and the other half in a plain country style that pleases her father. Mr. Hardcastle, in turn, has allowed Charles Marlow, the son of an old friend, to become Kate's suitor only after knowing that he is financially sound, handsome, and modestly spirited. As the play begins, Kate anxiously awaits her first look at this prospecting and prospective husband.

When young Marlow and Hastings (the man Constance loves) arrive at the Hardcastle house, they mistakenly believe that they are at a public inn. This false impression is entirely Tony's fault. Tony recognizes the two London beaux when they stop to ask for directions at the Three Pigeons. Irritated by their affected manners, desirous of playing a trick on his stepfather, and anticipating no consequences but a solid embarrassment, Tony directs them to his stepfather's house, telling them that he is sending them to the best inn of the neighborhood. This first mistake of the night begins a series of events that will turn the household topsy-turvy.

Expecting the modest young men described by his old friend Sir Charles Marlow, Hardcastle greets the two weary travelers generously and familiarly. Surprised at the supposed innkeeper's behavior, Marlow and Hastings react with hauteur and sarcasm. To Hardcastle's every offer of hospitality, they respond with increased demands. This scene (act 2, scene 1) is a classic instance of Goldsmith's spectacular handling of dialogue at cross-purposes.

Soon afterward, Hastings encounters Constance and learns how Tony has deceived him and Marlow. The reunited lovers plan to elope as soon as Constance can gain possession of her jewels; to protect their plot, they decide to keep Marlow in the dark about where he is. They introduce him to Miss Hardcastle as if she had just alighted at the inn. Throughout the play these two couples will maintain distinct characteristics. Constance and Hastings, whose mutual affection is a given, will struggle against external obstacles; Marlow and Kate, having just met, will try to discover what mutual affection, if any, exists between them.

Kate is eager to meet the man who has come to court her. In a complete reversal of the bold, brash character that he showed to Mr. Hardcastle, Marlow becomes shy and stuttering in Miss Hardcastle's presence. It seems that proper young ladies of rank intimidate Marlow with their genteel and sentimental conversation. He bumbles his way through a conversation, saved only by Kate's promptings:

> MISS HARDCASTLE: You were going to observe, Sir—
> MARLOW: I was observing, Madam—I protest, madam, I forget what I was going to observe.
> MISS HARDCASTLE: . . . You were observing, sir, that in this age of hypocrisy—something about hypocrisy, sir.
> MARLOW: Yes, madam. In this age of hypocrisy, there are few who upon strict inquiry do not a-a-a-
> MISS HARDCASTLE: I understand you perfectly, sir.
> MARLOW (*aside*): Egad! and that's more than I do myself.
> MISS HARDCASTLE: You mean that in this hypocritical age there are few that do not condemn in public what they practise in private, and think they pay every debt to virtue when they praise it.

While Constance enlists Tony's help to get the jewels from his mother and thus free both of them from her matchmaking, Kate and Mr. Hardcastle try to decide who is the real Marlow: the overbearing puppy who insulted his host or the tongue-tied dandy who courted the daughter? The mystery begins to clear a little when Kate, now wearing her plain country dress, meets Marlow a second time. The young man makes his second mistake of the night. Not recognizing Miss Hardcastle in what appears to be a bar-

maid's outfit, Marlow is immediately and frankly attracted to the pretty servant. He proves not shy at all in the presence of lower-class women. With them he can wittily compliment, flirt, and steal a kiss. When Mr. Hardcastle sees Kate receiving this impudent attention, he is ready to order Marlow from his house. Kate, however, having seen what a charming wooer the young man can be, protests that this is the same modest man she interviewed earlier. She asks her father for the chance to show Marlow's real character; he begins to wonder if the usually sensible Kate is not now afflicted by that same malady that makes all young people undecipherable by their elders. At a second interview, Marlow begins to fall in love with the girl he assumes to be a household servant.

For one frantic moment the two plots intertwine before going separate ways. Tony filches Constance's jewels from his mother's bureau and gives them to Hastings. To get them out of sight, Hastings hands the jewels to Marlow. Thinking that such valuable gems must not lie around unguarded, Marlow gives them to Mrs. Hardcastle for safekeeping. Mrs. Hardcastle, alerted by the odyssey of the jewels that something is afoot, is quickly suspicious when her illiterate Tony receives a letter. Neither Constance's extemporaneous excuses nor Tony's obstinacy can prevent Mrs. Hardcastle from snatching the letter and discovering instructions from Hastings about the elopement. Determined to frustrate her niece and Hastings, Mrs. Hardcastle orders her carriage made ready for a trip to London: Constance is going to be taken where she can be better watched.

Thus, by the end of act 4, Goldsmith has every character's fate up in the air. The dramatist who knotted things into such a delightful tangle, however, has enough legerdemain to unravel the confusion. Goldsmith will not have to step in to rescue the characters: Kate by her stooping and Tony by his prankstering will set all to rights.

Kate has quite a tangle to undo: first, her father's impression that Marlow is a rude guest and an inconsiderate lover; second, Sir Charles's fear that the son he thought to be honest and modest is really the lout that Hardcastle has described and an indifferent lover to his friend's daughter; third, Marlow's belief that he can be gallant in the pantry but *must act* standoffish in the parlor. She accomplishes all three ends by having the fathers witness the third interview of Kate the maid and Marlow. He professes his love for her—and learns to his shock that he has wooed the redoubtable Miss Hardcastle as well as the pliant Kate.

Meanwhile Tony has been frustrating his mother's flight to London. In the darkness, he has led her carriage on repeated rounds of the estate before driving it into a pond; Mrs. Hardcastle is convinced that she is stranded "forty miles from home." Determined to torment her further, Tony leads his mother into a gloomy thicket where even Mr. Hardcastle, out for a walk in his yard, may look like something more sinister. Although Tony's prank is soon exposed, he at least has had the pleasure of exhausting his mother.

Tony has exhausted the eloping lovers as well. Constance and Hastings decide it will be easier to talk Mrs. Hardcastle into compliance than to escape her this evening. All the cold and sore wanderers in the night return to the house and find Kate and Marlow engaged while the fathers stand beaming. When Mrs. Hardcastle threatens revenge on Tony and Constance, Mr. Hardcastle breaks another surprising bit of news: Tony has already reached the age of majority. The Hardcastles had kept this fact secret to keep the irresponsible Tony from squandering his inheritance, but Mr. Hardcastle now resents his wife's misuse of her authority. Tony's first act as an independent gentleman is to renounce any claim to Constance. George Hastings quickly grabs the marriageable hand that Tony surrenders. Everyone except Mrs. Hardcastle now sees that the mistakes of a night have turned out happily indeed.

Even this account of the play omits some of its brighter moments: Hardcastle's amusingly futile efforts to turn rough farm laborers into stylish drawing-room valets, the rousing but innocent debauchery of Tony's friends at Three Pigeons, and Kate's dumb-show wooing that quickly heals Marlow's embarrassment after his mistakes were revealed. Actually nothing but reading or viewing can give a complete idea of the brilliance of *She Stoops to Conquer*. It is a rare play, in which no situation is unexploited, no detail wrong, and no word wasted.

OTHER MAJOR WORKS

LONG FICTION: *The Vicar of Wakefield*, 1766.

SHORT FICTION: *The Citizen of the World*, 1762 (collection of fictional letters first published in *The Public Ledger*, 1760-1761).

POETRY: "An Elegy on the Glory of Her Sex: Mrs. Mary Blaize," 1759; "The Logicians Refuted," 1759; *The Traveller: Or, A Prospect of Society*, 1764; "Edwin and Angelina," 1765; "An Elegy on the Death of a Mad Dog," 1766; *The Deserted Village*, 1770; "Threnodia Augustalis," 1772; "Retaliation," 1774; "The Captivity: An Oratoria," 1820 (wr. 1764).

NONFICTION: *An Enquiry into the Present State of Polite Learning in Europe*, 1759; *The Bee*, 1759 (essays); *The Life of Richard Nash of Bath*, 1762; *A History of England in a Series of Letters from a Nobleman to His Son*, 1764 (2 volumes); *Life of Henry St. John, Lord Viscount Bolingbroke*, 1770; *Life of Thomas Parnell*, 1770; *An History of the Earth, and Animated Nature*, 1774 (8 volumes; unfinished).

MISCELLANEOUS: *The Collected Works of Oliver Goldsmith*, 1966 (5 volumes; Arthur Friedman, editor).

BIBLIOGRAPHY

Bloom, Harold, ed. *Oliver Goldsmith*. New York: Chelsea House, 1988. A collection of essays of literary criticism on Goldsmith's writings. Bibliography and index.

Dixon, Peter. *Oliver Goldsmith Revisited*. Boston: Twayne, 1991. A basic biography of Goldsmith that provides coverage of his life and critical analysis of his works. Bibliography and index.

Lucy, Seán, ed. *Goldsmith, the Gentle Master*. Cork, Ireland: Cork University Press, 1984. A group of lectures on Goldsmith that discuss his literary works. Bibliography and index.

Pathania, B. S. *Goldsmith and Sentimental Comedy*. New Delhi, India: Prestige Books, 1988. A study of Goldsmith that focuses on his plays and their relation to sentimental comedy. Bibliography.

Swarbrick, Andrew, ed. *The Art of Oliver Goldsmith*. Totowa, N.J.: Barnes and Noble Books, 1984. This insightful series of essays on Goldsmith's works attempts to restore serious critical attention to those classics created by Goldsmith as well as the certain areas of his life and work previously disregarded. Balances literary criticism with studies of more general aspects of the author, such as his political inclinations, his classical inheritance, his place within certain eighteenth century literary traditions, and his lack of originality. Chronological table.

Worth, Katharine. *Sheridan and Goldsmith*. New York: St. Martin's Press, 1992. Worth compares and contrasts the lives and works of Goldsmith and Richard Brinsley Sheridan. Bibliography and index.

Robert M. Otten,
updated by Genevieve Slomski

WITOLD GOMBROWICZ

Born: Małoszyce, Poland; August 4, 1904
Died: Vence, France; July 24, 1969

PRINCIPAL DRAMA

Iwona, księżniczka Burgunda, pr. 1938, pr. 1957, revised pb. 1958 (*Princess Iwona*, 1969; best known as *Ivona, Princess of Burgundia*)
Ślub, pb. in Spanish 1948, pb. in Polish 1953, revised pb. in Polish 1957, pr. 1963 (*The Marriage*, 1969)
Historia, wr. 1951, pb. 1975, pr. 1977
Operetka, pb. 1966, pr. 1969 (*Operetta*, 1971)

OTHER LITERARY FORMS

The preponderance of Witold Gombrowicz's literary production consists of fictional and nonfictional prose. Besides his plays, he wrote four novels, more than a dozen stories, a three-volume literary diary, a book of "conversations" about his life and art, approximately eighty book reviews, essays, travel accounts, polemical articles, minor short prose pieces, and an unfinished novel. Although he was known first and best for his prose fiction, especially his novels, he eventually won equal recognition as a playwright, and the influence of his plays rivals that of his novels and diary.

Gombrowicz made his debut with a volume of seven short stories, entitled *Pamiętnik z okresu dojrzewania* (1933; memoir from adolescence), and all but one of the remainder of his short stories were

written before World War II. Eccentric in form and content, they are masterpieces of the genre, and their style, themes, and obsessions hold the key to his later work. His novels develop inspirations from his stories with great analytical verve and comic inventiveness. His first novel, *Ferdydurke* (1937; English translation, 1961), is unusually structured, with three individual parts separated by polemical essays and mock-philosophical parables. The three parts of the main plot are unified by the device of temporal and psychosocial regression and descent into a subculture or underworld, leading backward from the hero's adulthood through adolescence—the stage of life on which the plot focuses—to childhood. His next novel, *Opetani* (1939; *Possessed: Or, The Secret of Myslotch*, 1980), an unfinished mock-gothic potboiler serialized in daily newspapers and published under a pseudonym, is intentionally aimed below the level of his other books. *Trans-Atlantyk* (1953), a comical fictional memoir of the author's adventures during his first several weeks in exile, views exile less as a misfortune than as an opportunity for a new start in a new life, and its language parodies the archaic style of a seventeenth century Polish squire. *Pornografia* (1960; English translation, 1966) treats themes and situations from *Possessed* in a more restrained and conventional manner, while parodying war stories, criminal romances, the spy thriller, the manorial novel, and pornography (there are no sex scenes). *Kosmos* (1965; *Cosmos*, 1966), a parody of the detective novel, is a metaphysical farce travestying cosmology, epistemology, and psychoanalysis. It associates the sexual obsessions of a law student on vacation with a theory of knowledge about the birth of order out of chaos, and the texture of its prose is the densest Gombrowicz ever created.

Gombrowicz's *Dziennik, 1953-1966* (1957-1967; *Diary*, 1988-1993), written for publication and appearing in monthly installments during the last sixteen years of his life, combines genres: essay, confession, autobiography, self-commentary, and fiction. Its more relaxed and accessible style was intended to attract readers by providing a more intimate portrait of the artist. Because the composition of his diary happened to coincide with the rise of his literary career, its three volumes resemble an old-fashioned success novel describing the author-hero's struggle to overcome obstacles and the simultaneous rise of his career and the biological decline of his life. Suspense is maintained by the hero's race with time and death.

Gombrowicz's "conversations," a kind of guidebook to his life and art first published as part of his diary, appeared in book form in French under the title *Entretiens avec Gombrowicz* (1968), and in Polish as *Rozmowy z Gombrowiczem* (1969; *A Kind of Testament*, 1973). The author himself wrote the entire book, which parodies the genre of conversations with famous men. His radio scripts, written between 1959 and 1961 but published only after his death under the title *Wspomnienia polskie: Wędrówki po Argentynie* (1977; Polish memoirs), represent a first draft of his "conversations" and provide some new autobiographical material as well. Aimed at an unsophisticated audience, they have a primarily documentary value.

ACHIEVEMENTS

Witold Gombrowicz's writing is indebted to and reflects his personal achievements. The greatest of these was his stubborn persistence in overcoming the formidable obstacles that relegated his provocative and unconventional books and personality to the periphery of various literary and cultural establishments. His three decades of literary activity produced a quantitatively moderate but qualitatively outstanding body of work, whose quite readable surface conceals a poetic density and compactness that a short critical survey can only begin to suggest.

Before World War II, Gombrowicz's eccentric writings and literary café persona succeeded in attracting young and independent writers, and his first novel, *Ferdydurke*, was in contention for a major literary prize, but his moderate success was short-lived because Poland was soon under German occupation and he found himself in exile in Argentina. Remaining there after the war, he continued to attract successive generations of young writers and intellectuals. With their enthusiastic collaboration, *Ferdydurke* and his second play, *The Marriage*, were translated into Spanish and published in Buenos Aires. Slighted by the Argentine and Polish émigré literary establishments, Gombrowicz won a following among the Polish émigré cultural elite as a regular contributor to the Paris-based Polish journal, *Kultura*, whose publishing house, the Institut Littéraire, issued his books.

In the mid-1950's, when culture was liberalized in Poland, his works, publicized by the critic Artur Sandauer, underwent a violent resurgence of popularity. Everything Gombrowicz had written, except his diary, was published, and his first play, *Ivona, Princess of Burgundia*, was staged with great success in Warsaw. A shift in cultural policy ended the vogue for Gombrowicz, however, and his works have not been reissued in Poland. At the same time, aided by the Polish-French critic K. A. Jeleński, Gombrowicz's international career took off with the appearance of *Ferdydurke* in French in 1958, and his books began to be translated, eventually into all the major and nearly all the minor European languages, both Western and Eastern, as well as into Hebrew and Japanese. Decisive factors were Gombrowicz's return to Europe in 1963 and his winning the prestigious International Publishers' Prize in 1967. He was a Nobel Prize candidate in 1968 and was rumored to have been the frontrunner in 1969; he died, however, before the jury met. Following another liberalization of cultural policy in Poland after 1970, republication of his works was considered but suspended indefinitely, a result of political objections to certain passages in his diary (whose publication in full Gombrowicz required as a condition for reissuing any of his works). Nevertheless, Gombrowicz criticism in Polish flourished qualitatively and quantitatively with new insights and approaches that helped change the discipline of criticism itself. In addition, all his plays, as well as dramatic adaptations of his prose works, were staged with great popular success and entered the standard repertory of Polish theaters. Outside Poland, his collected works are available in Polish (published in Paris), German, and French, and his plays, regularly performed in France and Germany, have been staged almost as widely as his books have been published.

The list of writers and other artists whom Gombrowicz has influenced is impressive. Among Poles it includes Nobel Prize-winning poet Czesław Miłosz, novelist Jerzy Kosinski, science fiction writer Stanisław Lem, playwrights Sławomir Mrożek and Tadeusz Różewicz, and theater reformers Jerzy Grotowski and Tadeusz Kantor. Other than Poles, Gombrowicz has influenced novelists Horst Bienek, Milan Kundera, Philip Roth, Julio Cortázar, and Ernesto Sábato; theater directors Jorge Lavelli and Alf Sjöberg; and film and theater director Ingmar Bergman. Gombrowicz belongs at the summit of Polish literature, and outside Poland he is regarded as a major world author. The vitality of his works assures the enduring stature of his reputation.

BIOGRAPHY

Witold Gombrowicz's life spanned the extremes of affluence and poverty, obscurity and fame. The youngest of four children in a wealthy landowning family, he was born August 4, 1904, on his parents' country estate, Małoszyce, in what is today southeastern Poland. His father was an estate manager and industrialist and his mother an educated but conventional woman of her social class. Distant from his father and brothers, the young Gombrowicz found himself in the orbit of his mother and sister, who overprotected him. He suffered from chronic respiratory illnesses, which plagued him all his life and worsened when asthmatic attacks began ten years before his death. Images of choking, strangling, and

suffocation recur in his writing. He rebelled against maternal smothering at an early age, and his youthful alienation from his family became a dominant autobiographical theme in his writing (his adult relations with his family were cordial). Balancing the pathological aspect of his biography was his indefatigable sense of humor, with which he deterrorized his psychological and physical ailments.

When Gombrowicz was seven, the family moved to Warsaw, where he received a good education, including private tutoring and attendance at an elite high school. He took a law degree at Warsaw University and, after an apprenticeship with a judge, devoted himself full time to writing. From an early age, he devoured literature, philosophy, and history. His first literary effort, at age sixteen, was a history of his family, based on the four-hundred-year-old family archives. Later, he secretly wrote fiction but achieved satisfying results only during his law apprenticeship, when his first book took shape. Its reception in 1933 was overwhelmingly positive, but a few condescending reviews led him to regard his debut as a failure. Nevertheless, his strong and eccentric personality soon established itself in Polish literary life. His polemical novel *Ferdydurke* placed him in the spotlight, winning for him zealous admirers and detractors, but his play *Ivona, Princess of Burgundia* was noticed by a single critic, and *Possessed*, his last work before emigrating, was a potboiler written for money.

In the summer of 1939, Gombrowicz took a cruise to Argentina as a journalist and was stranded abroad when the war broke out. Though speaking no Spanish and short of money, he decided to remain in Buenos Aires, where there was a Polish community. He had little in common with his émigré compatriots or the Argentine literary establishment, and despite introductions to leading writers and editors, he could not support himself through journalism. He was saved from starvation by the charity of Polish friends and a wealthy Argentine heiress, low-paying clerical jobs, a few small subsidies, and panhandling. He spent the war years mostly avoiding high culture and frequenting the slum and port districts of Buenos Aires. After the war, he began writing again. The Argentine heiress funded the publication of *Ferdydurke* and *The*

Marriage in Spanish, but the books failed to launch his career in Argentina. Weary of poverty, he took a job at a bank, but the success of his books among Spanish-speaking youth energized him, and his years at the bank (the job was a semi-sinecure) were some of his most productive.

In 1951, Gombrowicz made his debut as a Polish émigré writer by publishing excerpts of *Trans-Atlantyk* in the journal *Kultura*. As with *Ferdydurke*, the novel provoked attacks, but when his diary began appearing in April, 1953, he became a fixture in émigré culture. He left the bank in 1955 and lived modestly on his literary earnings, paid lectures on philosophy, small grants, and the hospitality of friends. He spent long periods in provincial Argentine towns, where he did much of his writing and attracted yet another generation of youth. For a decade, he had tried to have his works published and his plays staged in Poland and France, but not until the 1950's did he have any success. The enthusiastic reception of his books in Poland encouraged him, and their suppression in 1958 was a severe blow. When his works began to appear throughout Europe, the Argentine literary establishment finally began to pay him some attention, but by that time Gombrowicz had accepted a generous Ford Foundation fellowship to be a writer-in-residence in Berlin, and he left Argentina in April, 1963.

The majority of Polish émigrés were indifferent to Gombrowicz's international fame, but he found a more sympathetic audience among Western Europeans, for whom his controversial tone was refreshing. His fiction and drama rapidly conquered Europe, gaining for him literary prizes and the status of a celebrity with a devoted following, but his yearlong stay in Berlin fatally weakened his health, and he spent the last five years of his life as an invalid, barely able to taste the fruits of his late and dearly earned success. Recuperating after Berlin, he met a young French-Canadian student, Marie-Rita Labrosse, who became his companion and later his wife, with whom he settled on the French Riviera. Despite his continually deteriorating health, Gombrowicz remained active and productive until the very end, retaining his characteristic pungency and humor. He died in his sleep on July 24, 1969, and the obituaries in Poland and throughout Europe mourned his death.

ANALYSIS

Although Witold Gombrowicz wrote only three theater pieces and fragments of a fourth and had no professional connections with the theater, his plays are held in high esteem because of their union of compelling dramatic interest with intense theatricality. Like traditional dramas, his plays are carefully constructed, with well-defined plots, conflicts, and characters, and the texts—language, speech, and the human voice—are essential to their effect. The innovative aspect of his plays is found in their multidimensional theatricality. Theatricality is typical not only of his dramas but also of the rest of his writing, in which dramatic conflicts, mime, gestures, grimaces, masks, façades, role-playing, and the recurrent figure of the regisseur are prominent. Gombrowicz had some acquaintance with interwar theatrical experimentation and movements, such as expressionism and Symbolism, in Poland and abroad, but he learned his craft by reading the classics of European drama and attending performances, mainly of light, popular genres, such as operetta, vaudeville, cabaret, and film. As a boy he so thoroughly assimilated the dramas of William Shakespeare that he knew many long passages from memory, and the fruits of his reading are evident in his own dramas: for example, the main model for both *Ivona, Princess of Burgundia* and *The Marriage* is *Hamlet, Prince of Denmark* (pr. c. 1600-1601).

While spectacle, lighting, sound effects, and scenic and costume design are significant elements in Gombrowicz's dramaturgy, the core of his theater is the actor, both individually and in disciplined ensemble work. Ensemble work is important in all his plays, but it is raised to the status of a formal organizing principle in *The Marriage* and in *Operetta*, where the drama is conceived not only in theatrical but also in musico-theatrical terms. He describes *The Marriage* as a symphonic score (actors are instruments, the regisseur the conductor) and *Operetta* as a libretto. Both plays contain solos, duets, choruses, leitmotifs, and stage directions indicating tone and dynamics.

The musical appeal of his plays is reflected in the fact that they have inspired two operas (both by German composers): Boris Blacher's *Yvonne, Prinzessin von Burgund* (1972) and Volker David Kirchner's *Die Trauung* (1975; the marriage).

All of Gombrowicz's plays are tragicomedies characterized by artificiality and the grotesque. None conforms to the convention of realism, and their atmosphere resembles that of fables or dreams. The author warns, however, that stylization should never become so intense that his characters lose their recognizably human traits, and the plots concern familiar family themes and conflicts. Each play is a family drama cast as a royal or princely drama, and except for the unfinished fragment *Historia* (history), the main plot incident, reflecting the theme of ambivalent sexuality, concerns a failed attempt at marrying or mating. The main characters always include a Father, Mother, and Son who are simultaneously King, Queen, and Prince (in *Operetta*, Prince, Princess, and Count), and these royal families caricature the author and his parents (in *Historia* he audaciously casts his entire family in the main roles under their own real names with personalities caricaturing their real traits). Because the speech and behavior of the fictional royal families are often below the norms of their high social status, the result is travesty.

Theatricality and drama are essential components of Gombrowicz's vision of the world, which is based on the conflict of two core ideas, Form and Immaturity. Form is associated with order, cultural superiority, seriousness, and maturity, and its negative aspects include a tendency to rigidification, painful constriction, stagnation, and declining vitality (biological inferiority). Immaturity is associated with disorder, cultural inferiority and subculture, mockery, and vulgarity, and its positive aspects include flexibility, resilience, energy, creative potential, relaxation, and rising vitality (biological superiority). Humans are caught in a dilemma in that they desire the advantages of both Form and Immaturity without their disadvantages, but this desire can never be fulfilled. Gombrowicz offers several methods of coping with this dilemma. One is to gain distance from Form by viewing it as theater. A person always wears a mask and acts a role in a world that resembles a stage set. Yet if roles are regarded as temporary expedients, the individual can maintain his or her "immature" flexibility, resilience, and adaptability and thus avoid the main pitfall of Form. A second, more effective method of coping with the dilemma is to descend into the realm of Immaturity by engaging in subversion, degradation, and mockery of Form—in other words, through the artistic attitude and technique of parody. Parody satisfies both the need for distance and flexibility and the desire to demonstrate cultural superiority through formal mastery, and it prevents the Form, or game, from becoming an end in itself.

A particular kind of parody to which Gombrowicz was partial and which is conspicuous in all his plays is *parodia sacra* (sacred parody), a medieval tradition associated with Carnival, in which monks and clerics during special holidays were given the license of parodying any and every aspect of Church ritual and doctrine. Parodied rituals and ceremonies are important in all of Gombrowicz's works and are central to all of his plays, in which they constitute the crux of the plot. The point of sacred parody was not to destroy the objects but to relax their unrelieved solemnity and thus renew them through laughter. Similarly, Gombrowicz's parody of familiar traditional models, once thought moribund, gives them a new lease on life and endows his works with unusual creative energy.

IVONA, PRINCESS OF BURGUNDIA

Ivona, Princess of Burgundia concerns the disintegration and restoration of order, or the struggle between inferiority and superiority, Immaturity and Form. Immaturity fights from below by means of subversion, while Form retaliates from above by means of intimidation. The heroine, Ivona, represents Immaturity and inferiority; the royal court, Form and superiority. Ivona is unusual in Gombrowicz's work in that she is an almost completely negative embodiment of Immaturity. She is characterized as unappealing, apathetic, and anemic, and her subversive power is peculiar in that it is primarily passive and silent. Ivona's sluggishness "relaxes" the tension on which the social superiority of the royal court depends. Her unresponsiveness provokes the courtiers' irritability and frustration, and this negative energy is then turned against them, resulting in personal and social decomposition. Ivona also acts as a catalyst, or enzyme, causing chemical changes in others without being essentially changed herself. In addition, she produces the effect of alcoholic intoxication. The correct translation of the play's title is "Ivona, Princess of Burgundy Wine," for the Polish word *Burgund* refers to the beverage, and only as a distant pun does it allude to the Kingdom of Burgundia. The name of Prince Philip, however, recalls two famous dukes who presided at the opulent court of the Kingdom of Burgundia, where Form had taken on a Byzantine rigidity during the decline of medieval civilization. Gombrowicz's modern royal court turns out to be equally brittle beneath its self-assured exterior, reflecting an analogous decline on the eve of the collapse of interwar European order.

Prince Philip proposes marriage to Ivona, because her defects intoxicate him, but alcohol acts as a stimulant only briefly, while its long-lasting effect is that of a depressant. Thus, prolonged contact with her, like alcoholic overindulgence, is demoralizing, and the court is transformed into a brood of comic monsters. Each member of the royal family, as well as the Chamberlain, tries individually to kill Ivona while she sleeps but fails because the deed lacks formal justification. The murder succeeds only as a collective enterprise arranged by the play's regisseur, the Chamberlain, in which the entire court unites in its superiority to crush the inferior Ivona from above. At a banquet ostensibly in her honor, she is intimidated into choking to death on a fish with an unusually large number of bones, and her demise restores order at the royal court. Because Ivona takes abuse without reacting, her behavior suggests that of a martyr, and her imprisonment, persecution, and death as a scapegoat constitute a sacred parody of the familiar Gospel story (the fish on which she chokes is a Christian symbol). Ivona's silence makes her a mystery, or a blank slate, on which others project their own images, and perhaps for this reason *Ivona, Princess of Burgundia* is Gombrowicz's most frequently performed play.

THE MARRIAGE

Along with *Ferdydurke*, whose theme of humankind's conflict with Form it develops, Gombrowicz considered *The Marriage* his most important work. It is his longest, most difficult, and most demanding drama, and it is generally regarded as his masterpiece. It is also his most theatrically self-conscious play, and on one level, it may be interpreted as a drama revealing the process of its own self-creation. Although it is staged about half as frequently as *Ivona, Princess of Burgundia*, ambitious productions of *The Marriage* have become memorable theatrical events.

The Marriage is a dream play, mixing illusion and reality, dreaming and waking. In addition, the dream motif provides formal techniques, such as fluid and unexpected scenic transitions, oscillations in mood, stylistic shifts, and metamorphoses of plot and character, all of which present the actors and director with great technical difficulties. The setting, for example, contains five layers: a battlefield in northern France, a ruined church in Poland, Henry's (and Gombrowicz's) childhood home, Małoszyce, and the transformation of that home, a country estate, into both a tavern and the royal court. The play represents the hero, Henry's, dream, and its action takes place both on his internal stage and on the external stage that serves both as a projection of his internal conflict and as an objectively existing order independent of him. Because of this intimate link, when Henry's mood wavers between seriousness and farce, so does the entire structure of the drama. *The Marriage*, however, is not solely a psychodrama, for the external social reality that the dreamer-hero creates is capable of independent action and eventually thwarts his plans.

If *Ivona, Princess of Burgundia* shows the decay and restoration of a brittle order, *The Marriage* portrays the impossibility and undesirability of restoring an order that has definitively collapsed. The battle between Form and Immaturity in *The Marriage* takes place within Henry as well as within society at large. He is torn between his desire to restore the old order and regain his former status, symbolized by the Father-King (Form), and his knowledge that an absolute and permanent order is no longer possible, a state of affairs symbolized by the Drunkard (Immaturity). The battle between the Drunkard and the Father suggests a Freudian conflict between Henry's libido and superego. In Gombrowicz's view, however, the main theme of the play is the transition from the Church of God, with its fixed and stable metaphysical, political, and social hierarchies, to the Earthly Human Church, where nothing is stable, hierarchies are fluid, and humanity creates its own gods, who are other men temporarily elevated to the status and power of a divinity. In the Earthly Human Church, the author states, the object of worship is the interhuman spirit. The interhuman sphere, a new concept that Gombrowicz introduces in *The Marriage*, is an arena of unpredictable and violent change, where individuals, playing the roles of regisseurs, or "priests," of the Earthly Human Church, battle for power. Henry and the Drunkard become rival regisseurs, or "priests," who try to impose their own forms and styles. Henry, however, is carried away by the momentum of his own creation. It imprisons him in institutionalized rigidity (he becomes a tyrant), after which he opts out of the game. The action of the play recalls similar transitional historical periods, for example, from the late Middle Ages to Renaissance Humanism, and Gombrowicz's intention is to show the appropriateness of his model for the twentieth century.

The Marriage is a much more ambitious parody of *Hamlet* than *Ivona, Princess of Burgundia* is, for besides transforming Shakespeare's characters and situations, it also imitates Shakespearean soliloquies and prosody. Gombrowicz, an "antipoet" who disliked pure versified poetry, made an exception for impure forms (such as Shakespeare's) mixing prose and verse, and the re-creation of Shakespearean blank verse (which is only partially intended as travesty) combined with highly cadenced free verse successfully imitates natural colloquial speech. *The Marriage* is a triumph of the poetic use of language, and excerpts from it are included in anthologies of Polish poetry.

As an orchestrated ritual, the drama draws on a specific source, Ludwig van Beethoven's *Missa Solemnis* (1818-1823), a monumental orchestral and choral setting of the Mass. Beethoven's work reflects the transition from the divine to the human church,

for it was criticized for placing too little emphasis on God and too much on humankind. The Mass both as idea and as structure provides a model for sacred parody in *The Marriage*. A more specific ritualistic aspect of the play is contained in its title. Although its primary meaning is "marriage" or "marriage ceremony," another meaning of the Polish word *ślub* is "oath, vow, pledge." The marriage vow is the heart of the traditional ceremony, but neither this vow nor the ceremony occurs in the play. Instead, the key ritual is the suicide pact between Henry and Johnny, yet another sacred parody, in which Henry's manipulating Johnny into swearing an oath to commit suicide on his command is intended to confirm his aspirations to become a god. He sacrifices Johnny as his young rival (that is, his "son") to purify and save his debased world. Henry's fiancée, Molly (whose Polish name is a variant of Mary), is the third member of this mockholy family. Because Henry's divinity is merely self-proclaimed, Johnny's suicide does not ratify his godhood but kills his will to power. As at the end of *Ivona, Princess of Burgundia*, the marriage celebration is replaced with a parodied funeral, in which the murderer sanctifies his deed, but Henry's deed (which is individual and not collective) not only fails to restore the old order but also destroys his desire for restoration. Henry's placing himself under arrest suggests his imprisonment by Form, but his renunciation of royalty and divinity also implies his descent from the superior world of Form to the inferior world of Immaturity, as well as his acceptance of community with the human race that he so recently despised and tyrannized. These remarks provide only the barest outline, for *The Marriage* is rich enough in interpretive possibilities to remain an object of enduring fascination for literature and the theater alike.

HISTORIA

Gombrowicz's unfinished play, *Historia*, discovered only after his death, marks a transition from the recently completed *The Marriage* to his final play, *Operetta*. Despite its fragmentary nature, it is considered a viable drama, successfully performed in Germany and Poland and published in French and German translations. Its plot tells the story of a barefoot adolescent named Witold who is transformed from an object of ridicule into a hero with a historical mission. Mocked and persecuted by his family and by the institutions of his society (also played by the family members), he discovers his vocation in his attempt to prevent the outbreak of World War I and World War II. The bare foot is an emblem of freedom, health, and primitive vitality, and its defenselessness corresponds to the insecurity of adolescent life. The upper classes, by contrast, are always shod, and their shoes and boots serve both as armor and as weapons. Finally, footwear is associated with Form, maturity, and History, while bare feet belong with Immaturity and the relaxation of Form and History. Although History is a boot that crushes its random victims, and the unshod foot appears to be helpless, the barefoot Witold becomes a secret emissary to the leaders of the world and the makers of history. The historical figures who appear in the play include Czar Nicholas II, Kaiser Wilhelm II, the Polish head of state, Marshall Józef Piłsudski, and (in a projected scene) Adolf Hitler. Witold attempts to teach them the secret of barefootedness, the necessity of escaping from the imprisonment of their public roles into Immaturity, which is their single chance for survival in a changing world. The public role cramps like a tight shoe, while the bare foot is relaxed and flexible, and Gombrowicz's solution to the threat of historical brutality is the relaxation of statist absolutism and the avoidance of war.

OPERETTA

What Gombrowicz sketched out and abandoned in *Historia* comes to fruition in his last play, *Operetta*. Staged about as frequently as *The Marriage*, because of its light tone and surprisingly (for Gombrowicz) affirmative ending, *Operetta* has proved to be an accessible and attractive theater piece. A musical comedy about the brutal history of the twentieth century, *Operetta* is a libretto that, like *The Marriage*, can be fully realized only in performance. Yet if *The Marriage* is a score that can be performed by the actors, *Operetta* remains incomplete without authentic, old-fashioned Viennese operetta music, and much of the text consists of arias or choruses meant to be sung. The operetta genre parodies the pretentiousness of grand opera, and thus the musical dramas of Richard

Wagner and the musically conceived historical dramas of Polish Romantic and modernist theater that Gombrowicz used as models. Gombrowicz regards operetta as a supremely theatrical genre, and he packs *Operetta* with intrigues, plots, duels, a disguised agitator, a revolution, a storm, a trial, a fashion contest, and a masked ball. The play, however, is not simply frivolous froth, for it was the author's intention, as he states in his preface, to enclose within the "monumental idiocy" of the operetta form the "monumental pathos of history," and the third act contains pathetic and tragic scenes that Gombrowicz describes as Shakespearean. The aim of his parody is not to reject History as such—which, at any rate, is impossible—but to carnivalize its solemn and bloody pretensions and thus deprive it of its ability to mesmerize and terrorize its victims. Because History is only a particular instance of the larger problem of Form, Gombrowicz embodies it in the operetta metaphor of fashion (Form as costume). Fashion is ruled by Fior, the dictator of fashion, and the footwear and bare feet of "History" become the clothing and nakedness of *Operetta*.

If Gombrowicz's first two plays concern the success or failure to restore order, *Operetta* presents a new and changed attitude toward order itself. The new attitude corresponds to the defeat of Form by Immaturity as embodied in naked youthful beauty. The aristocratic playboys, Count Charm and Baron Firulet, want to dress the beautiful Albertinette in lavish costumes, but Albertinette, as a result of being fondled by the Pickpocket, dreams only of being nude. Nakedness possesses all the attributes of the bare foot from "History" and the added advantage of beauty, but the boot emblem is changed. The revolutionary dreams of the Lackeys, condemned to polish and lick their masters' boots ceaselessly, is not to go barefoot but to tear off their masters' legs. Only the Pickpockets are barefoot, and so they belong with the naked Albertinette at the end of the play.

As in *Historia*, the action of *Operetta* begins before World War I and ends sometime after World War II, but instead of concrete historical figures, the characters represent social classes or historical and cultural forces. Consistent with this abstraction, almost all the incidents in the play are ritualized, and the climactic ritual, on which the plot turns, occurs near the end of the play. This is the mock funeral for Albertinette, who is assumed to be dead, and it thus represents a desire that appears to be forever unattainable. Yet when the dictator of fashion, cursing people's clothing, places human nakedness itself in the coffin, his renunciation of Form resurrects Immaturity in the shapely person of young, naked Albertinette, hidden in the coffin by the barefoot Pickpockets. Albertinette's death, disappearance, and resurrection in the company of thieves is Gombrowicz's last sacred parody. Although his previous sacred parodies retained the content while negating the spirit of his sources, here he changes the content while retaining the spirit. As youth for Gombrowicz signifies life itself, Albertinette's ritual rising from the dead goes beyond parody to his affirmation of the eternally renewed vitality of the human race.

OTHER MAJOR WORKS

LONG FICTION: *Ferdydurke*, 1937 (English translation, 1961); *Opetani*, 1939 (unfinished; *Possessed: Or, The Secret of Myslotch*, 1980); *Trans-Atlantyk*, 1953 (English translation, 1994); *Pornografia*, 1960 (English translation, 1966); *Kosmos*, 1965 (*Cosmos*, 1966); *Three Novels by Witold Gombrowicz*, 1978 (includes *Ferdydurke*, *Pornografia*, and *Cosmos*).

SHORT FICTION: *Pamiętnik z okresu dojrzewania*, 1933; *Bakakaj*, 1957 (includes *Pamiętnik z okresu dojrzewania* and other stories).

NONFICTION: *Dziennik, 1953-1956*, 1957; *Dziennik, 1957-1961*, 1962; *Dziennik, 1961-1966*, 1967; *Diary*, 1988-1993 (collection and translation of 3 previous titles; Jan Kott, editor); *Sur Dante: Glose*, 1968; *Rozmowy z Gombrowiczem*, 1969 (*A Kind of Testament*, 1973); *Varia*, 1973; *Wspomnienia polskie: Wędrówki po Argentynie*, 1977.

MISCELLANEOUS: *Dzieła zebrane*, 1969-1977 (11 volumes).

BIBLIOGRAPHY

Berressem, Najo. *Lines of Desire: Reading Gombrowicz's Fiction with Lacan*. Evanston, Ill.: Northwestern University Press, 1998. Although this psychological analysis of Gombrowicz's works focuses on his fiction rather than his drama, it sheds light on his plays. Bibliography and index.

Brodsky, David. "Gombrowicz and the Theatre." *Theatre in Poland* 23 (1981): 18-23. A look at the theatrical career of Gombrowicz.

Kurczaba, Alex. *Gombrowicz and Frisch: Aspects of the Literary Diary*. Bonn: Bouvier, 1980. A comparison and contrast of the diaries of Gombrowicz and Max Frisch. Bibliography.

Thompson, Ewa M. *Witold Gombrowicz*. Boston: Twayne, 1979. A basic biography of Gombrowicz that covers his life and works. Bibliography and index.

Ziarek, Ewa Plonowska, ed. *Gombrowicz's Grimaces: Modernism, Gender, Nationality*. Albany: State University of New York Press, 1998. A critical analysis of the works of Gombrowicz. Bibliography and index.

David Brodsky

MAXIM GORKY
Aleksey Maksimovich Peshkov

Born: Nizhny-Novgorod, Russia; March 28, 1868
Died: Gorki, U.S.S.R.; June 18, 1936

PRINCIPAL DRAMA

Meshchane, pr., pb. 1902 (*Smug Citizen*, 1906)
Na dne, pr., pb. 1902 (*The Lower Depths*, 1912)
Dachniki, pr., pb. 1904 (*Summer Folk*, 1905)
Deti solntsa, pr., pb. 1905 (*Children of the Sun*, 1906)
Varvary, pr., pb. 1906 (*Barbarians*, 1906)
Vragi, pb. 1906, pr. 1933 (*Enemies*, 1945)
Posledniye, pr., pb. 1908

Chudake, pr., pb. 1910 (*Queer People*, 1945)

Vassa Zheleznova (first version), pb. 1910, pr. 1911 (English translation, 1945)

Falshivaya moneta, wr. 1913, pr., pb. 1927

Zykovy, pb. 1914, pr. 1918 (*The Zykovs*, 1945)

Starik, wr. 1915, pr. 1919, pb. 1921 (*Old Man*, 1924)

Yegor Bulychov i drugiye, pr., pb. 1932 (*Yegor Bulychov and Others*, 1937)

Dostigayev i drugiye, pr., pb. 1933 (*Dostigayev and Others*, 1937)

Vassa Zheleznova (second version), pr., pb. 1935 (English translation, 1975)

Seven Plays, pb. 1945

Five Plays, pb. 1956

Plays, pb. 1975

OTHER LITERARY FORMS

Maxim Gorky began his career as a short-story writer and originally gained renown for his works in that genre. In 1898, a two-volume collection called *Ocherki i rasskazy* (sketches and stories) appeared in St. Petersburg. A third volume came out the following year. Although Gorky is today perhaps better known for his work within other genres, he continued to write stories regularly into the 1920's, and several of his short works are among his finest achievements: "Chelkash" (1895; English translation, 1901), "Byvshye lyudi" (1897; "Creatures That Once Were Men," 1905), and "Dvadtsat' shest' i odna" (1899; "Twenty-six Men and a Girl," 1902). Gorky's first published novel was *Foma Gordeyev* (1899; English translation, 1901), which, like many of his plays and subsequent novels, describes the life and mores of the merchant class in provincial Russia. His novel *Mat* (1906; *Mother*, 1906), which was written in the United States, deals with the emerging revolutionary forces in Russia. It achieved enormous popular success and, after the Bolshevik revolution, served as a model for the definition of socialist realism. After working intensively in this genre throughout the first decade of the twentieth century, Gorky published only two more novels during the last twenty-five years of his career. Of these, *Zhizn Klima Samgina* (1927-1936; *The Life of Klim Samgin*, 1930-1938), while left unfinished at his death, is a massive four-volume work that offers virtually an encyclopedia of Russia's social and intellectual currents during the forty years that led up to the revolution.

Gorky's nonfiction is also an important part of his achievement. Indeed, many would rank his autobiographical trilogy—*Detstvo* (1913; *My Childhood*, 1915), *V lyudyakh* (1916; *In the World*, 1917), and *Moi universitety* (1923; *My Universities*, 1923)—as the crowning work of his career. Also receiving much critical acclaim are his memoirs of writers, notably those devoted to Leo Tolstoy, Anton Chekhov, and Leonid Andreyev. In each case, Gorky manages to create a powerful living portrait out of a few seemingly insignificant details. Finally, Gorky also wrote many literary reviews and essays, as well as writings on social and political topics.

ACHIEVEMENTS

Maxim Gorky was one of the most prominent figures in Russian literature from the late 1890's until his death. His importance extended well beyond his purely literary accomplishments. In 1899, he became a member of the Sreda ("Wednesday") Circle, a group of realistic writers who met to discuss their ongoing work. He rapidly emerged as the leading figure in the group, and in 1903 he began to put out the Znanie anthologies, which published the work of the group's members and achieved great popularity in subsequent years. Throughout his career, Gorky continued his efforts as editor, publisher, and organizer. After the 1917 revolution, he was instrumental in establishing projects that would give writers both outlets for publishing and an established income. To take care of their material needs, he helped set up several "houses" that provided shelter, food rations, and a place to meet. After leaving Russia in 1921, he continued his journalistic efforts abroad, and during his final years in the Soviet Union, he helped formulate the doctrine of socialist realism, which, for better or worse, became the guiding credo of Soviet literature for at least the next two decades.

Gorky was also deeply involved in politics from the start of his literary career. Although his relationship with Vladimir Ilich Lenin and other Bolshevik

Maxim Gorky (Library of Congress)

leaders was not always smooth, his early support helped give him much authority when they took power. Gorky provided editorial guidance and material aid to countless writers; for that alone his service was of immeasurable importance for Russian literature.

Gorky's plays, like much of his fiction, are notable first of all for broadening the thematic scope of Russian literature. Most famous in this regard is *The Lower Depths*. In treating tramps, thieves, and other outcasts of society (a milieu that he also described in his innovative stories of the previous decade), Gorky was moving far from the gentry families and well-off merchants who had predominated on the Russian stage until his time. In *Enemies* and *Posledniye* (the last ones), Gorky dealt directly with the political upheavals that were beginning to tear the country apart. He became one of the first to use—or attempt to use (despite some stagings in outlying areas, censorship forbade the presentation of these plays in the country's main theaters)—the stage to advocate a viewpoint sympathetic to the revolutionary cause.

Several of Gorky's plays, with *The Lower Depths* again serving as the outstanding example, are also notable for their unusual structure. Although Gorky was not averse to composing works with relatively straightforward plots and clearly defined relationships among his characters, in many of his best creations he strove for density over clarity, for chaos over order. Characters may come and go; several of the most important figures in *The Lower Depths* are completely absent from the fourth and final act. Also, as the Russian critic L. M. Farber has noted, that play is actually three plays in one: a four-act drama about the lower depths, a philosophical study in acts 1 to 3 dealing especially with questions of truth and the "consoling lie," and a political treatise in act 4. Yet in Gorky's successful works, all the disparate elements ultimately coalesce to create works whose complex form makes them all the more striking in their impact.

Perhaps Gorky's most lasting contribution to the Russian theater, though, lies in his ability to portray characters and through them entire levels of society. In some of his works, no single character dominates, but he uses a series of individuals to capture the feel of a given environment. In *Barbarians*, Gorky presents at least three different groups—educated engineers from outside the town where the play is set, the boorish leading citizens of the town, and a sprinkling of provincial nobility—and lets all three sets interact. By the end he has shown that both the local inhabitants and the outsiders are barbarians; the play's title applies to all. Most remarkable, however, are the individual portraits that Gorky has created, often in plays that are less known (or unknown) among English-speaking audiences. Yegor Bulychov is by now familiar to many outside the Soviet Union, but equally striking are such figures as Vassa Zheleznova (especially in the first version of the play), Antipa Zykov (*The Zykovs*), and Mastakov (*Old Man*). All are such powerful creations that they more than compensate for any inconsistencies in plot or structure.

BIOGRAPHY

Maxim Gorky presents the would-be biographer with a paradox. On one hand, vast amounts of information exist about certain periods in his life. Gorky himself composed, in addition to his autobiographical trilogy, numerous memoirs as well as sketches and stories that are directly based on his life. In 1930, replying to a questionnaire that had been sent to a group of prominent writers, he noted that autobiographical material served as the basis for most of his works. Further, from the late 1890's on, he lived an extremely public life. As a literary celebrity his every pronouncement was recorded, his letters saved by his correspondents, his deeds recalled and described by countless memoirists. On the other hand, not all the material is reliable. Memoirists can be self-serving. Gorky himself treated his autobiographical writings as literary rather than purely factual works, and even the correspondence sometimes reveals contradictory information. Also, several aspects of Gorky's biography—his activities just after the 1917 revolution, his life in the Soviet Union following his return, and the circumstances of his death—remain clouded by a paucity of factual records and obfuscation caused by efforts to make him a sacred figure within the Soviet literary establishment.

Aleksey Maksimovich Peshkov (Gorky, his nom de plume, means "bitter") was born in 1868 in Nizhny-Novgorod, a major trading and manufacturing center on the Volga River, famous for its annual fair. When he was three years old, the Peshkovs moved to Astrakhan, another town on the Volga. The young Aleksey contracted cholera during an epidemic. Although he recovered, his father caught the disease and died. The mother and son returned to Nizhny-Novgorod and moved in with her parents, the Kashirins. Vasily Kashirin owned a dye-works in the town and was stern with both his workers and his family. Aleksey, however, became extremely close to his grandmother, Akulina, who instilled in him a fondness for folktales that remained with him all his life and had a great influence on his work. After his mother's death in 1879, the eleven-year-old Aleksey worked as an apprentice in various shops and began his education, which consisted largely of reading works of fiction. In 1884, he went to Kazan, where he hoped to enter the university. Lacking sufficient knowledge or funds, however, he worked instead at a number of different

jobs and, in 1887, underwent a crisis that led to an attempt at suicide. He first came into contact with revolutionary movements during his Kazan period, and his growing political awareness was to determine many of his future interests. Over the next several years, he wandered about much of southern Russia, in between periods of work back in Nizhny-Novgorod. His adventures as a boy and his youthful travels provided him with much of the impetus for his fiction.

Gorky's first story, "Makar Chudra," was published in 1892. His stories began to appear regularly in various newspapers from cities along the Volga. Soon his works were also coming out in the more important literary journals, and when a two-volume collection of his short pieces appeared in 1898, his fame was instantaneous. From then on, he became an increasingly prominent literary figure as well as a spokesperson for revolutionary politics. His stories, plays, and novels all received both critical and popular acclaim; Gorky soon achieved an international reputation. His election as an honorary member of the Academy of Sciences in 1902 was annulled by the czar as a result of Gorky's political activities. Anton Chekhov and Vladimir Korolenko both resigned their honorary memberships in protest. Gorky was caught up in the revolutionary activities of 1905, was briefly arrested, and the following year left Russia. After a not entirely successful trip to the United States to raise funds for the revolutionary cause, he settled in Capri, where he had one of his most productive periods as a writer. His most intensive work as a playwright came during the years 1902-1910, when he completed nine full-length plays, including nearly all those that are best known in the West: *The Lower Depths*, *Summer Folk*, and *Enemies*. A measure of Gorky's fame was the appearance of his plays in foreign translations (and performances) virtually simultaneously with their production in Russia.

The period of upheaval that came with World War I and the October Revolution caused Gorky to turn most of his energies to publicistic writings and, after the revolution, to tireless efforts to help his fellow writers. Although a strong supporter of the Bolsheviks during the years leading up to the revolution, Gorky had many differences with Lenin and the Bolshevik leadership over the next few years. A combination of those differences and his own poor health caused him to leave the Soviet Union in 1921 and settle once again in Italy. He did not return before 1928, and from then on, he made lengthy visits before settling permanently in the Soviet Union in 1933. From about 1915 until 1930, he did very little work in the dramatic form, but over the last few years of his life, he published two new plays and a total reworking of of *Vassa Zheleznova*. In addition, he revised other works and wrote another full-length play that remained unpublished. During this last period, he was venerated within Russia as the "Father of Soviet Literature" and received numerous rewards and honors, including the renaming of his hometown as Gorki. In his public pronouncements, Gorky was a vehement supporter of the government, though it has been suggested that he was growing uncomfortable with the increasingly oppressive atmosphere. His sole surviving child, Maxim, died in an accident in 1934. Gorky's death in 1936 when he was sixty-eight was at first described as the result of pneumonia and then blamed on a Trotskyite conspiracy to murder him. Within the former Soviet Union his death is again considered to have come from natural causes, though the story of a conspiracy has left many with a suspicion that Joseph Stalin somehow had a hand in Gorky's demise.

ANALYSIS

One of the more remarkable aspects of Maxim Gorky's career as a dramatist is the rapidity with which he mastered the playwright's art. His first play, *Smug Citizen* (also known as *The Petty Bourgeois* and *The Philistines*), contains imperfections but is nevertheless very promising. *The Lower Depths*, which premiered in the same year as *Smug Citizen*, is generally regarded as his dramatic masterpiece. At the same time, Gorky did not stand still as a playwright. Indeed, his treatment of the tramp figure in *The Lower Depths* was to be the last time that he devoted a major work to these social outcasts. He goes on to describe members of Russia's intelligentsia in a minicycle of plays, to tackle political issues, and, most interestingly, to write a group of what could be called

morality plays during the 1910's. These last plays reveal a sparser set of characters than do the earlier plays, but they also contain a greater psychological and dramatic intensity.

Gorky's beginnings as a playwright owe much to his relationship with Anton Chekhov. The two began a correspondence shortly after the first collection of Gorky's stories appeared in 1898. At that time, Chekhov, well established as a brilliant short-story writer, was about to gain recognition for his equally outstanding contributions to world theater; the plays by which Chekhov is best known were staged by the Moscow Art Theater between late 1898 and 1904. Chekhov encouraged Gorky in his dramatic experiments and lent his younger colleague support when work on his first play went badly. Chekhov's influence on Gorky's early plays was considerable, even though Chekhov himself was often to find fault with specific aspects of Gorky's dramatic technique.

SMUG CITIZEN

That influence is particularly evident in Gorky's first play. The basic four-act structure of Chekhov's plays appears in *Smug Citizen* as well as in most of Gorky's other plays. Like Chekhov, Gorky sets his work in the provinces, and he focuses on a single household that is in turmoil. Gorky, too, tends to emphasize situation over plot. The play deals with the well-to-do head of the housepainters' guild and his two children, both of whom are deeply troubled, caught between the expectations of their father and a vague desire for a better life. The action of the play does not so much involve a complex intrigue as it involves the changing relationships among characters while they are undergoing a critical moment in their lives. The personal dilemmas of the characters, as well as a number of small details in the play, recall Chekhov's *Tri sestry* (pr., pb. 1901, rev. pb. 1904; *The Three Sisters*, 1920).

At the same time, even before the end of act 1, the play embraces a new, non-Chekhovian element. Gorky introduces a character, Nil, who is meant to be the play's true hero. The character is not sufficiently developed to carry as much of the play's message as Gorky desires—and Chekhov in fact criticized the play on these grounds. Yet in his rejection of bourgeois society and his scorn for the abstract philosophizing of other characters, Chekhov represents a social and political outlook that is close to Gorky's own. Chekhov is more willing to let the audience draw its own conclusions about his characters; Gorky wants to convey a specific message.

This first play, while containing many fine scenes and well-drawn portrayals, seems static. Some characters who should be more prominent—Nil, the figure of the father—remain on the periphery; too much time is spent with others who add little either to the plot or to the play's message. Still, the work marked an auspicious beginning and enjoyed some success from the time of its first performance.

THE LOWER DEPTHS

Gorky's reputation as a playwright, though, was established only with the triumphant opening of *The Lower Depths*. Like Gorky's first play and Chekhov's major works, its original staging was by Konstantin Stanislavsky. The cast for the premiere included some of Russia's finest actors; Stanislavsky himself played the role of Satin, Olga Knipper (Chekhov's wife) had one female lead, and Marie Fiodorovna Andreyeva, soon to become Gorky's companion, another.

The play's chief strength lies in its characters. Gorky presents a large group of figures who have been living "on the bottom" (the literal translation of the play's title), which in this case happens to be the dirty basement of a flophouse. Despite the large number of roles, each of the individuals is carefully delineated and distinguished from the rest. For example, the Baron is a person who has come down in life, and he mocks those who try to imagine a better life for themselves; yet he expresses pride in his supposed pedigree, and when his musings about his noble family are attacked as lies, he is not able to cope. Although most of the figures have reached the bottom by the time the play opens, the locksmith Kleshch drifts down to that level as the action unfolds. His wife, Anna, whom he had brutally mistreated, dies in the course of the play, yet he seems less malicious than simply inadequate to deal with the challenges that life sets before him. The play's main intrigue involves the efforts of a thief, Vaska Pepel, to run off with the sister-in-law of the lodging's owner and start a new life. In an altercation, Pepel kills the owner and ends up in jail.

The play's thematic concerns are expressed most directly through two figures who stand somewhat to the side of the rest: Satin, a cardsharper who has spent time in prison for killing a man, and Luka, a wanderer who comes to the lodging house for only a short time. Luka offers others consolation. He tells Anna that death is nothing to be feared, for she will have peace at last. He advises Pepel to run off to Siberia. Luka believes in lying when necessary to inspire people or at least to avoid despair. Although he acts more humanely than any of the other characters in the play, Gorky meant him to be a negative character, somebody who consoled others only to preserve his own peace and comfort. Satin, whose monologue dominates the final act after Luka has left the play, offers a ringing affirmation of truth, of a life that lacks illusions, of a humankind capable of anything. The distinction between Luka and Satin is in fact less sharp than Gorky's later interpretations would indicate. Characters such as the Baron, who believes only in a harsh truth, are indeed the opposite of Luka, whereas both Satin and Luka do ultimately want to help people better themselves. During the course of his monologue, Satin even quotes Luka's words to good effect.

The play has been criticized both for its multitude of concerns and for its seemingly lopsided structure, with the fourth act so different from the preceding ones in its set of characters and in its type of action. Yet the various themes all do build on one another, and it can be convincingly argued that the somewhat sparser final act is necessary to focus attention on Gorky's central themes. To be sure, the fourth act is in many ways redeemed dramatically by the final scene. The Actor, a habitual drunkard who has found a bit of hope in Luka's assurance that there are places where people like him can be cured, comes to realize under the taunts of his fellow lodgers that his dreams are in vain. While the other lodgers loudly carouse, he leaves, and the Baron bursts in a short while later to yell over the singing that the Actor has hanged himself. All fall silent, and only Satin's response—that the Baron has spoiled the song—can be heard as the curtain falls.

SUMMER FOLK

The play *Summer Folk*, part of the cycle that deals with the intelligentsia, concentrates on the efforts of certain members to break away from that society. Gorky divides his characters into three groups—as in *The Lower Depths*, no single figure is predominant. Some, such as the lawyer Basov and his assistant Zamyslov, seem totally at home in the corrupt society of which they are part. Others, including those who are intellectuals or at least aspire to intellectual pursuits, sense that something is wrong but are inept in every undertaking. This group includes a writer, Shalimov, and Basov's sister Kaleria. Third are those who fully understand what is wrong with their lives. A few of these characters are also too weak and indecisive to make a break, but others—notably Basov's wife and her brother, along with a woman doctor named Marias Lvovna—reject the milieu of the "summerfolk" and strike out for a new life.

Although the play never quite attains the vibrancy of *The Lower Depths*, Gorky's effective character portrayals and the occasional comic relief make it a particularly satisfying work. Appearing as well are several elements that bear witness to Gorky's growing confidence and maturity as a playwright. As part of the summertime activity, an entertainment is being planned. Actors drift past the other characters on the way to rehearsal and bring into relief the artificiality of those who live in the dachas—their life is only a game; real life is somewhere else. Gorky also makes fine use of the tension created by hints of imminent violence, which dissolve into empty threats and one almost comically inept attempt at suicide. His restraint, his not feeling the need to rely on a sudden death for dramatic effect, shows that he is willing to let the inherent tension of the situation he has set up carry the play. Also pervading the work is the shadow of Chekhov, albeit this time the play that is recalled is not *Three Sisters* but *Chayka* (pr. 1896, rev. pr. 1898; *The Seagull*, 1909): the staging of a play, the presence of both a writer (Shalimov) and a would-be writer (Kaleria), and so forth. Yet in comparison with *Smug Citizen*, the Chekhovian qualities of *Summer Folk* seem less obtrusive; in it, Gorky's own manner carries the play.

OLD MAN

Gorky's works of the 1910's were to represent a sharp departure in his playwriting. He came to concentrate on only a few characters, and his plots began to have only one or two lines, instead of the multisided relationships that predominated in his earlier plays. Previously his main characters were rarely sympathetic; now they tended to appear in a more favorable light. Social and political issues moved to the background, and Gorky shifted his attention to moral issues. At the same time he allowed representatives of the merchant class—who were often treated with scorn earlier—to take on positive features.

All these qualities are evident in *Old Man* (originally translated into English as *The Judge*). The hero, Mastakov, is a well-to-do individual who has done much good. As the play opens, he has just completed work on a school building for his town. Mastakov, it turns out, has a secret that he has withheld from everybody. He was once unjustly accused of murder and sentenced to hard labor, from which he escaped and started life anew. Now a fellow prisoner from that time, Pitirim, the "old man" of the title, has wandered into the town as a tramp. He seeks retribution from Mastakov, who did not serve out his term and whose life has been far more successful than Pitirim's. However, Pitirim cannot decide on the nature of that retribution. He apparently wants to see Mastakov suffer in such a way as to bring Mastakov down to his level. Mastakov, feeling himself more and more trapped, ultimately resorts to the only way out—suicide.

Gorky himself defined his main concern in *Old Man* when he wrote a preface for the first English translation: "I have tried to show how repulsive a man may be who becomes infatuated with his own suffering, who has come to believe that he enjoys the right to torment others for what he has suffered." On a number of occasions, Pitirim refers to himself as Mastakov's judge, but he is less a judge than he is an executioner. Pitirim's "aggressive suffering" has been seen by some critics as a response on Gorky's part to Fyodor Dostoevski's Dmitri Karamazov. Convicted of a crime that he did not commit, Dmitri implies that suffering can in some cases purify the individual. For Dostoevski, the higher goal is what is important; he did not believe in suffering for its own sake. Gorky, who admired Dostoevski's genius but quarreled with his ideas in both his essays and his fiction, claims here and in other plays of this period that suffering rarely leads to any good at all. Further, Gorky rejects the right of any individual to pass judgment on another; the attempt to assume such power leads only to disaster.

In simplifying the plot and cast, Gorky brought issues of universal concern into much sharper focus. The last few plays he wrote before the revolution are hardly less interesting than the earlier work for which he is better known; they are deserving of greater attention than they have received outside the Soviet Union.

YEGOR BULYCHOV AND OTHERS

Among Gorky's late plays, the most accomplished is *Yegor Bulychov and Others*. As in the plays of the 1910's, the central character is a merchant who is by no means totally evil, and the play's success depends strongly on the strength of that figure's portrayal. In his earlier years, Bulychov was as grasping and greedy as any of his fellow merchants, but he has accomplished his goals by dint of inner strength and hard work. In the play he is faced with a dual crisis. He discovers that he has cancer of the liver; in his futile struggle with death, he begins to question the values by which he has lived. The other aspect of the crisis is more social and political. The fateful year of 1917 arrives, and with it the upheavals that will bring down the entire order within which he has achieved success. What distinguishes Bulychov both from his fellow merchants and from the petty family intrigues that surround him is his awareness and acceptance of what has happened both to him and to his world. The clarity with which he sees the wrongs of his own life, of organized religion, and of the government under which he has lived gives him a certain grandeur.

The play, though, is more than another work about the merchant class. In the last half of the play, Gorky creates a mad, at times grotesquely comic whirlwind of strange happenings that come to symbolize the de-

cline of the old system. At the end of act 2, Bulychov is introduced to a fire fighter who is also an amateur trumpet player. The fire fighter, significantly named Gavrilo (Gabriel), believes that blasts on his instrument have curative powers; as he blows on his trumpet, Bulychov proclaims the end of the old world. In the third act, a sorceress and a "holy fool" come to help cure Bulychov but create only further disruptions. The play's contrasts in mood, from the intensely serious to the maniacally comic, as well as its range and the originality of its characters, attest that even at the end of his life Gorky's powers as a playwright had not diminished.

OTHER MAJOR WORKS

LONG FICTION: *Goremyka Pavel*, 1894 (novella; *Orphan Paul*, 1946); *Foma Gordeyev*, 1899 (English translation, 1901); *Troye*, 1901 (*Three of Them*, 1902); *Mat*, 1906 (*Mother*, 1906); *Ispoved*, 1908 (*The Confession*, 1909); *Zhizn Matveya Kozhemyakina*, 1910 (*The Life of Matvei Kozhemyakin*, 1959); *Delo Artamonovykh*, 1925 (*Decadence*, 1927; also known as *The Artamonov Business*, 1948); *Zhizn Klima Samgina*, 1927-1936 (*The Life of Klim Samgin*, 1930-1938; includes *The Bystander*, 1930, *The Magnet*, 1931, *Other Fires*, 1933, and *The Specter*, 1938).

SHORT FICTION: "Chelkash," 1895 (English translation, 1901); "Byvshye lyudi," 1897 ("Creatures That Once Were Men," 1905); *Ocherki i rasskazy*, 1898-1899 (3 volumes); "Dvadtsat' shest' i odna," 1899 ("Twenty-six Men and a Girl," 1902); *Rasskazy i p'esy*, 1901-1910 (9 volumes); *Orloff and His Wife: Tales of the Barefoot Brigade*, 1901; *Skazki ob Italii*, 1911-1913 (*Tales of Italy*, 1958?); *Tales of Two Countries*, 1914; *Po Rusi*, 1915 (*Through Russia*, 1921); *Chelkash and Other Stories*, 1915; *Stories of the Steppe*, 1918; *Zametki iz dnevnika: Vospominaniia*, 1924 (*Fragments from My Diary*, 1924); *Rasskazy 1922-1924 godov*, 1925; *Selected Short Stories*, 1959; *A Sky-Blue Life and Selected Stories*, 1964; *The Collected Short Stories of Maxim Gorky*, 1988.

NONFICTION: *Detstvo*, 1913 (*My Childhood*, 1915); *V lyudyakh*, 1916 (*In the World*, 1917); *Vozpominaniya o Lev Nikolayeviche Tolstom*, 1919 (*Reminiscences of Leo Nikolaevich Tolstoy*, 1920); *Moi universitety*,

1923 (*My Universities*, 1923); *Vladimir Ilich Lenin*, 1924 (*V. I. Lenin*, 1931); *Reminiscences of Tolstoy, Chekhov, and Andreyev*, 1949; *Untimely Thoughts: Essays on Revolution, Culture, and the Bolsheviks*, 1968.

MISCELLANEOUS: *Polnoe sobranie sochinenii*, 1949-1955 (30 volumes); *Polnoe sobranie sochinenii*, 1968-1976 (25 volumes); *Collected Works of Maxim Gorky*, 1978-1982 (10 volumes).

BIBLIOGRAPHY

Courtney, W. L. *The Development of Maurice Maeterlinck and Other Sketches of Foreign Writers*. London: G. Richards, 1994. This series of sketches on foreign writers includes one of Maxim Gorky.

Levin, Dan. *Stormy Petrel: The Life and Work of Maxim Gorky*. Rev ed. New York: Schocken Books, 1985. A biography of Gorky that covers his life and works.

Luker, Nicholas, ed. *Fifty Years On: Gorky and His Time*. Nottingham, England: Astra, 1987. A collection of essays on Gorky. Bibliography and index.

Scherr, Barry P. *Maxim Gorky*. Boston: Twayne, 1988. A basic biography of Gorky that provides critical analysis of selected works. Bibliography and index.

Terry, Garth M., comp. *Maxim Gorky in English: A Bibliography*. Rev. ed. Nottingham, England: Astra, 1992. An annotated bibliography of English translations of the works of Gorky. Index.

Troyat, Henri. *Gorky*. New York: Crown, 1989. A translation of a Russian biography of Gorky that presents his life and works. Bibliography and index.

Yedlin, Tova. *Maxim Gorky: A Political Biography*. Westport, Conn.: Praeger, 1999. A biography of the Russian writer that focuses on his political and social views. Bibliography and index.

Barry Scherr

CARLO GOZZI

Born: Venice (now in Italy); December 13, 1720
Died: Venice (now in Italy); April 4, 1806

PRINCIPAL DRAMA

Il teatro comico all'osteria del Pellegrino, pb. 1750

L'amore delle tre melarance, pr. 1761, pb. 1772 (*The Love of the Three Oranges*, 1921)

Il corvo, pr. 1761, pb. 1772 (verse play; *The Raven*, 1989)

Il re cervo, pr. 1762, pb. 1772 (verse play; *The King Stag*, 1958)

Turandot, pr. 1762, pb. 1772 (verse play; English translation, 1913)

La donna serpente, pr. 1762, pb. 1772 (verse play; *The Snake Lady*, 1988)

Zobeide, pr. 1763, pb. 1772 (verse play)

I pitocchi fortunati, pr. 1764, pb. 1772 (verse play)

Il mostro turchino, pr. 1764, pb. 1772 (verse play; *The Blue Monster*, 1951)

L'augellino belverde, pr. 1765, pb. 1772 (verse play; *The Green Bird*, 1985)

Zeim re de'geni, pr. 1765, pb. 1772

La donna vendicativa disarmata dall'obbligazione, pr. 1767 (verse play)

La caduta di donna Elvira regina di Navarra, pr. 1768 (verse play)

La donna innamorata davvero, pr. 1771 (verse play; adaptation of Miguel de Cervantes' play *Pedro de Urdemales*)

La principessa filosofa: Ossia, Il contravveleno, pr. 1772

I due fratelli nimici, pr. 1773 (adaptation of Augustín Moreto y Cabaña's play *Los hermanos encantados*)

Le droghe d'amore, pr. 1777 (adaptation of Tirso de Molina's play *Celos con celos se curan*)

Bianca contessa di melfi: Ossia, Il maritaggio per vendetta, pr. 1779

Five Tales for the Theatre, pb. 1989

OTHER LITERARY FORMS

Carlo Gozzi wrote some poetry in the satirical vein. He also wrote his memoirs in the three-volume *Memorie inutili* (1797; *Useless Memoirs*, 1890). This eight-hundred-page autobiography represents his other major contribution to Italian literature. Gozzi's attraction to, and involvement in, the Italian theater are predictably detailed in his memoirs. His recollections, however, are possibly more valuable for their depiction of the Venetian republic and its declining culture. In France, ideas and events that would shape an age were occurring, and Gozzi provides an incisive view of the disdain and fear that he and other members of the aristocracy felt toward these developments.

ACHIEVEMENTS

Perhaps no other Italian playwright has received such divergent criticism of his work as Count Carlo Gozzi. Some critics believe that Gozzi constitutes a notable example of the decadent literature that Venice produced during the latter portion of the eighteenth century; others laud him as a playwright second only to William Shakespeare in language, verse form, and dramatic impact. This controversy in the criticism of Gozzi's works seems a logical extension of several controversies that actually provoked him to write his plays and that surrounded their theatrical production. Although Gozzi was writing poetry at the age of nine, along with gift sonnets and philosophical treatises during his ensuing youthful years, his major contribution to Italian literature rests in the thirty-two plays he wrote between 1761 and 1798. The most famous of these are his *fiabe*, fairy tales that he took from a Neapolitan collection by Giambattista Basile and transformed into fantasy dramas satirizing the Venetian scene and literary circumstances of his day.

Rigidly conservative by background and nature, Gozzi wrote the *fiabe* in an effort to denigrate the realistic comedies of manners and character that his arch rivals, Abbé Pietro Chiari and Carlo Goldoni, had popularized on the Venetian stage. Gozzi wished to show that traditional, nonrealistic Italian plays, the type he so dearly loved, could be as popular, if not more so, than the "new wave" productions he despised. To achieve his purpose, Gozzi drew on the great *commedia dell'arte* form, which had made Italian actors and their productions famous throughout Europe during the sixteenth and seventeenth centuries. Even though his use of fantasy, satire, and especially written dialogue exceeded the limits of the traditional, improvisational *commedia* form, Gozzi invariably included four of the stock characters, or "masks," from that form in his *fiabe*. Later critics have seen this as a major flaw in Gozzi's works because these characters or masks, incorporated by Gozzi with strict fidelity to their *commedia dell'arte* origins, do not change from play to play, even though their station in life and geographic locations may vary drastically. On the other hand, because he did employ these masks as a standard feature in his plays, Gozzi is credited with lifting the *commedia dell'arte* form out of its moribund state in Venice and putting it back "on the boards" during the second half of the eighteenth century.

Linked to the *commedia dell'arte* form, providing Venetians a welcome escape from the problems of the declining republic, Gozzi's *fiabe* were very successful. They virtually eclipsed the realistic plays of Chiari and Goldoni, so much so that Goldoni left Italy for France, where the realistic dramas still prevailed, and Chiari retired from writing. Because Gozzi's plays contained much fantasy, high virtue, and pageantry, all encased in verse form, his works also became popular with members of the early Romantic movement. The English Romantics heralded Gozzi's use of imagination and heroic virtue as part of the emerging Romantic vision. The Germans were especially taken with the highly imaginative and phantasmagoric aspects of his plays, aspects they believed provided a sense of direction away from the eighteenth century and its "age of reason." Johann Wolfgang von Goethe and Friedrich Schiller both adapted works of Gozzi to the German idiom; Ludwig Tieck and E. T. A. Hoffmann were directly prompted by Gozzi's use of satire and caustic humor to use similar elements in their own works. Gozzi's prominence among German writers was underscored when Andrea Maffeio decided to translate the "classics" of German literature into Italian. His selections included Schiller's *Turandot*, an adaptation of

Gozzi's own piece, which was therefore being translated back into the language in which it had been originally written.

Another aspect of Gozzi's works, which the Germans developed extensively, was the musical adaptation of his pieces. In the early nineteenth century, German composers often turned Gozzi's tales into operettas, and composers from other nations also drew on this potential. Later, in the twentieth century, Sergey Prokofiev added music to Gozzi's first *fiabe*, *The Love of the Three Oranges*; Giacomo Puccini's last opera was based on Gozzi's most widely read tale, *Turnadot*.

Perhaps the greatest irony of Gozzi's career is that, even though he triumphed over Chiari and especially Goldoni in matters of the theater, later history and critics have not afforded him comparable success. Most of Gozzi's own works, when performed during the nineteenth century, were seen in the puppet theaters. Goldoni's plays, on the other hand, achieved a national prominence in Italy, where they have been produced for their dramatic qualities and studied for their literary merit, where a statue stands in honor of Goldoni, and where a theater in Venice is named for him.

Biography

Carlo Gozzi was a member of the aristocrat-burgher class of eighteenth century Venice, the sixth of eleven children born to Jacopo Antonio Gozzi and Angela Tiepolo. Although Gozzi was not of the patrician class and therefore unable to be directly involved in governing the Venetian republic, he shared the traditional values of the upper classes and championed the conservative view in all areas, especially the theater.

Gozzi's involvement with the theater began early when he and his brothers and sisters performed improvised plays at their summer home for the local, rustic audience. Apparently, Gozzi's attitude toward theater audiences was influenced in part by these activities. He held a low opinion of those who attended the theater in Venice, believing that they did not represent the higher stations or qualities of Venetian life. Some critics contend that Gozzi, therefore, chose the

fairy tale, or *fiabe*, as the basis for his plays because that was the type of puerile story the Venetian audiences could best understand and appreciate.

Gozzi had just begun a formal education when a stroke paralyzed his father, aggravating the family's already shaky financial situation and ending his formal schooling. He studied intermittently with several priests after that, but most of his education came from his own efforts and his insatiable appetite for reading. Gozzi remained, however, basically an uneducated man, a fact that critics point out is evident in his plays, in which coarse language, improper grammar, and a varying use of dialect often appear.

Family financial problems also forced Gozzi, at seventeen, to leave home for Dalmatia and a military secretarial position with the Venetian forces occupying that country. Disdaining the bawdy and licentious life his comrades led, Gozzi immersed himself in Italian literature. He also became a poet of some repute after reading a sonnet in praise of peace at a celebration for the governor general in Zara. Gozzi became even better known for his participation in the plays that were put on periodically for the governor general; he played the soubrette, the intriguing, outgoing female servant, a rendition that he claims in his memoirs was called "the wittiest and most humourous soubrette who ever trod the boards of a theatre." The improvisational aspects of the role attracted Gozzi. His memoirs reveal that he realized that the characters, whether Gozzi acted the parts or wrote them, provided an outlet for the emotionless, reclusive count, and he directed much of his energy toward their creation in his plays.

When Gozzi returned from service in Dalmatia, he was personally in debt and his family's affairs were in a state of collapse. Unwillingly, he stepped in to try to salvage what was left of the family's possessions and honor because his elder brother, Gasparo, had relinquished all such matters to his wife's inexperienced hands while he wrote plays, most of them unsuccessful. This period in Gozzi's life was not, however, without effect on his ideas about the theater. During this time of family quarrels and bitterness, Gasparo translated the French comedy *Esop at the Court* for presentation in Venice. The production was successful, and a sequel entitled *Esop in the Town* followed. To the latter, however, Gasparo added a scene that satirized and scolded Carlo and two other brothers for their meddling in family financial matters. Although not as successful as the first Esop production, the sequel helped introduce Carlo to the idea of satirizing contemporary figures, attitudes, and events in the drama, something that became a central device in his plays. After Gozzi's father's death in 1745, litigation over family finances lasted eighteen years; Gozzi ultimately received some parcels of land that provided him a small income and allowed him to devote more time to literary pursuits.

One of the few diversions Gozzi enjoyed during the years of family disputations was the Accademia Granellesca, a Venetian literary society dedicated to the traditional values in literature, especially a pure and simple use of language. As a member and informal head of this group, Gozzi entered into the first of the great controversies that occurred during his career.

The state of Venice was divided into two main factions during the eighteenth century. The liberals read Voltaire and Jean-Jacques Rousseau, envisioning an egalitarian society, while conservatives clung to traditional views and accepted social stratification. This division extended to the theater. The new plays, the "pathetic comedies," which Goldoni and Chiari had brought to the Venetian stage under the French influence, were thoroughly repugnant to Gozzi and the Accademia Granellesca. Besides their questionable use of the language (Gozzi labeled Chiari's and Goldoni's work in this regard "diarrhea"), these plays shunned accepted religious principles, mocked heroic virtue, and attacked established elements in society such as the female's role. The outrage Gozzi felt over these plays prompted him to prepare the first major salvo in his battle against them, *La tartana degli influssi* (1757). In this mock-almanac, Gozzi examined various disasters that supposedly threatened Venice, not the least of which were the plays of Goldoni and Chiari. Gozzi also tried his hand at his first play, *Il teatro comico all'osteria del Pellegrino*, which was designed to satirize and condemn the types of plays his rivals wrote. It was not, however,

until Chiari and Goldoni directly challenged Gozzi and his fellow academicians to present a play that was as popular as theirs that Gozzi began in earnest to write the plays that constitute his major literary achievement.

Despite his family's financial problems and his own frequent indebtedness, Gozzi never sold his plays. As a member of the aristocratic class in Venice, he considered taking money for his writings to be improper. Goldoni, the plebeian, could sell his works; Gozzi *gave* his to the performing troupes, in particular to the Sacchi Company, a *commedia dell'arte* company that had toured Portugal with some success but was forced by the great earthquakes of 1755 to return to Venice. The troupe, a victim of the public's thirst for the novelty of Goldoni's and Chiari's plays, was playing to meager audiences in a run-down theater in Venice when Gozzi became acquainted with them. He was especially attracted to this band of players because of their reputation for high moral standards, a striking contrast to the usual image of actors and their morals at that time. Thus Gozzi became the playwright-patron of the Sacchi Company, a position that fulfilled his desire to become a more active member of the world of the drama and that eventually brought him in contact with the one great romantic interest in his life, Teodora Ricci.

Ricci was a semitalented actress whom Antonio Sacchi had hired, along with her husband, into his company. Although Gozzi recognized that Ricci was not an actress of the first class, he wrote several plays to help establish her in the Venetian theater. The early attempts at making Ricci a "star" failed because of her limited acting ability, but Gozzi's *La principessa filosofa: Ossia, Il contravveleno*, adapted from the Spanish, proved to be a vehicle well suited to Ricci's talents, and she became established as the Sacchi Company's leading lady. Gozzi, in his fifties by this time, also became Ricci's *cavalier servente*, and he attended her publicly, as was customary in such a relationship in Venice, despite her marital status. This relationship also led to the next great controversy in which Gozzi would become involved.

Piero Antonio Gratarol was everything Gozzi was not. Rich, he lavished extravagant gifts on his friends and acquaintances; flamboyant, he was well-known about Venice for his colorful and distinctive apparel; powerful, he was secretary to the senate of the Republic. Gratarol was also an inveterate womanizer who made the mistake of ending a relationship with Catherine Tron, the brilliant and vindictive wife of the Procuratore of San Marco, to direct his attentions to Teodora Ricci. The latter luxuriated in the attention given her by both Gozzi and Gratarol, often playing them against each other for her own gain. The scandal that arose from Ricci's open alliance with Gratarol, and the humiliation it caused Gozzi, forced Gozzi to end his liaison with Ricci formally. As all this occurred, Gozzi was also preparing a new play, *Le droghe d'amore*, an adaptation of the Spanish play by Tirso de Molina. Rumors flew that Gozzi would strike back at Gratarol by mercilessly satirizing him in the play. In his memoirs, Gozzi adamantly, and apparently legitimately, denies any such intention, but on opening night, with Gratarol in the expectant audience, the actor who portrayed Don Adone displayed such an obvious and outrageous parody of Gratarol's manners and dress that the secretary left the theater furious. Various public meetings, threats, and rejoinders between Gratarol and Gozzi followed, the latter even offering to halt the play's production to cease the offense to Gratarol. The Venetian censor's office stepped in, however, and declared that the play had to be presented and to be performed as scheduled because it had been approved by that office and therefore was considered public property. This action, in part precipitated by the vengeful Signora Tron, so disgraced Gratarol that he left Venice for Stockholm, where he wrote a scathing condemnation of all those involved in the affair, which cost him his properties and status in Venice.

The Gozzi-Gratarol controversy marked the end of Gozzi's most productive literary period. After 1780, he wrote only two more plays, and the Sacchi Company disbanded. In 1798, Gozzi stopped writing for the theater entirely.

ANALYSIS

In many of Carlo Gozzi's plays, he philosophizes to his Venetian audiences. Although Gozzi initially feared that his ideas fell on deaf ears, perhaps his audiences were a bit more sophisticated than he first thought. His movement away from the extreme use of fantasy and magic in his plays and into more serious and substantial themes would seem to indicate that the playwright thought that his words, and the players' actions, would not be lost on his audiences. This progression in his plays intimates that Gozzi hoped to contribute more than merely "fairy tales" to eighteenth century Italian literature.

IL TEATRO COMICO ALL'OSTERIA DEL PELLEGRINO

Gozzi's first play, *Il teatro comico all'osteria del Pellegrino*, was notable because it unveiled his penchant for using his plays to satirize and criticize the Venetian scene—in this instance, certain literary aspects. Written during the early stages of Gozzi's feud with Chiari and Goldoni, *Il teatro comico all'osteria del Pellegrino* enacts a carnival scene at Saint Mark's Square, where the merrymakers are interrupted by a monster with four faces and four mouths. Gozzi used this monster to represent the Goldoni theater; the several mouths open to present aspects of the comedy of manners and plebeian prose that characterized Goldoni's plays. The onlookers in the play become bored with these attempts at theater, thus revealing the monster's fifth mouth, previously hidden, which confesses that the weak and objectionable aspects that came from the other mouths of the monster had been created solely for one purpose—to gratify the desires of the monster's belly. Thus, with this initial sally into the world of drama, Gozzi established his use of satire and fantasy in his plays.

THE LOVE OF THE THREE ORANGES

Gozzi's *fiabe* continued his use of these devices; the *fiabe* also evidenced a progression in the themes and components he would employ in his works. *The Love of the Three Oranges*, Gozzi's first fairy-drama, makes full use of satire, fantasy, and high romance presented in the *commedia dell'arte* form. In the play, Tartaglia, one of the characters, or masks, which the playwright adopted from the *commedia* form, portrays the son of the King of Spades, the latter appropriately dressed in giant playing cards throughout the play. The prince is dying from boredom and consumption; the only cure for this malady is to laugh, something his father and the courtiers have not been able to make the prince do. Truffaldino, however, another of the *commedia* masks, is also at court and attends the prince to see what can be done about this situation. The fairy Morgana enters the square dressed as an old woman, and Truffaldino, employing a standard *lazzo* (bit of comic "business") from the *commedia* form, trips her, sending her head over heels. This makes the long-suffering prince laugh and thus shed his ailments. In retribution for this humiliation, Morgana curses the prince and implants an undeniable desire in him to seek the mythic three oranges that have been imprisoned in a distant, fantastic castle. The remainder of the play deals with the prince's adventures, as he and Truffaldino travel to the distant land and find the oranges, which turn out to house three beautiful maidens, each of whom must be given water as soon as she is released from the orange, lest she die of thirst immediately. High drama and romance pervade the ending of the tale, as Truffaldino, unaware of the presence of the maidens in the oranges and unable to handle the situation as the first maiden emerges, breaks open the second orange to try to give a drink to the first maiden. Both maidens die, but the prince happens on the scene in time to fill his boot with water and therefore save the final maiden's life. Love between the two youthful figures develops instantaneously, and the prince vows to marry her. Some further complications by Morgana delay the wedding; nevertheless, the tale ends with the couple happily wed and the King of Spades exhorting all within the range of his voice to keep martellian verse (the form found in Chiari's and Goldoni's plays) away from his court, so that ready wit and improvised humor can flourish there and make all happy.

The great latitude that Gozzi found in the tale of the three oranges allowed him to incorporate the fantasy and satire that made his first *fiabe* a great success. Venetian audiences apparently recognized the boredom and consumption that affected the prince as a statement about the realistic, often somber plays that Chiari and Goldoni wrote. On the other hand, the inspired wit and antics of Truffaldino represented the kind of improvised comedy that Gozzi loved and his audiences expected. Actions, however, were not the only elements in this play that Gozzi used to satirize his rival playwrights. The martellian verse, which the king forbids at the end of the play, is used at one point to kill a character with boredom. Another condemnation by Gozzi appears with the king blaming the new comedies by Chiari and Goldoni for his son's disobedience when the latter defies his father and leaves to find the three oranges. Various characters also appear in this tale who represent extreme versions of characters in the Chiari and Goldoni plays. All these satiric elements, mixed with fantastic items such as the "thousand league" iron boots, which the prince and Truffaldino wear to get to the enchanted castle, various devils, a magic salve that opens the rusty gates of the castle, the baker's wife who sweeps the oven with her breasts for lack of a broom, and the overgrown oranges with their imprisoned maidens provided the Venetian audiences with some delightful theater and established Gozzi as a formidable member in the dramatic circles in Venice.

THE RAVEN

Gozzi's next two plays show his continued reliance on the fantastic and magical. *The Raven* deals with two magicians, one evil and vengeful, the other beneficent and just. These men's powers are brought into contention as Gennaro, brother of King Millo, tries to save the latter from some great suffering, which has been imposed on him by an ogre/magician whose raven the king has accidentally killed. To save him, Gennaro must find a woman with features as rare as the raven's who will marry the king and free him from the curse. Unfortunately, Gennaro abducts Armilla, who possesses the necessary features, but she is the daughter of another great magician, and he, in turn, imposes further maledictions on Gennaro and Millo. Gennaro learns that a messenger hawk he has sent to his brother will pluck out the king's eye, a dragon will attack the king in his bedchamber after he weds Armilla, and a horse he has as a gift for his brother will kill the king. To add to this, Gennaro is powerless to warn his brother of these impending misfortunes, because Gennaro is also cursed and will turn into a statue immediately should he attempt to do so. This transformation does occur when Gennaro is forced to try to save his brother; Armilla, however, selflessly takes her own life so that Gennaro can be restored his, all of which prompts her father to bring her back to life as a reward for her behavior and to round out the circle of transformations. While Gozzi's emphasis on magical and extravagant transformations remained strong in this play, *The Raven* differed perceptibly from *The Love of the Three Oranges* in certain other ways. The *lazzi* and pranks, which were very prominent in his first *fiabe*, were reduced to a lesser number and position in this play. In what he called a "lofty tragedy," Gozzi also attempted to deal with some more serious themes, such as the question of punishment for needless cruelty and the proper exercise of brotherly devotion and family obligations.

THE KING STAG

Gozzi's third *fiabe*, *The King Stag*, continues his proclivity for magic and multiple transformations, along with some political philosophy. King Deramo receives two gifts from a magician, the first one allowing him to tell when a woman is lying, therefore enabling him to find an honest wife. After several thousand maidens fail the test, one, Angela, succeeds and is to marry the king. The *commedia dell'arte* figure, Tartaglia, however—in this play the king's minister—desires Angela for himself. He learns from the king that the second gift from the magician is a verse that, if recited over a corpse, causes the reciter to become an enlivened version of the corpse. Tartaglia tricks the king into reciting the verse over the body of a dead stag. It works, thus allowing Tartaglia to repeat the verse over the king's body so he can assume that form and marry Angela. Several ensuing transformations occur, but virtue conquers as Angela uncovers Tartaglia's deception, recognizes her husband, now in the body of an old man, and Tartaglia is changed into a grotesque monster as punishment for his evil deeds. The notion that justice prevails made this one of Gozzi's "lofty" tales. He also recounts in his memoirs that many people saw this particular piece in a political light as a warning to monarchs or others in positions of power who rely too much and too easily on their ministers, a warning

about the possibilities for malfeasance that such reliance can produce.

TURANDOT

Gozzi's next play, *Turandot*, shows his movement away from the world of magic and transformations and into a world of more human drama, the world of "tragicomedy," as he labeled it. In order to counter the charge that the stage effects and fantastic elements in his plays were what made them so popular, Gozzi wrote *Turandot* and *I pitocchi fortunati* without the wondrous and special effects that characterized his earlier *fiabe*. *Turandot*, in particular, relies much less on stage effects and more on the dramatic interplay of the characters to deal with a theme that several of Gozzi's plays would pursue, the woman opposed to marriage. Although *Turandot* uses an exotic Eastern locale, which was something of the vogue in Venice at that time and which appeared periodically in Gozzi's plays, the main emphasis in the play is Turandot's character and its evolution. The haughty Princess Turandot, wishing to avoid marriage, has set forth three riddles that her suitors must solve to win her hand. All fail, and are put to death as a result, until Prince Calaf, in disguise, correctly answers the questions. Rather than submit to his demands for her hand in marriage, however, Turandot restates her hatred for men and vows to kill herself. Calaf, in the true romantic and chivalric manner, tells Turandot that if she can discover his real identity, he will kill himself instead. Because a female servant who secretly loves Calaf has unwittingly revealed his name, Turandot is in a position to eliminate Calaf. Nevertheless, love rather than hate or pride conquers the princess, and as Calaf draws his dagger to end his life, Turandot declares her love for him and her intention to marry the prince. These romantic and exotic elements made this play one of Gozzi's most popular, especially outside Italy, and his movement into character and sentiment rather than fantasy and effect has made *Turandot* one of Gozzi's best-known tales.

THE GREEN BIRD

Although not as popular as *Turandot* or *The Love of the Three Oranges*, most critics agree that *The Green Bird* represents a high point in terms of Gozzi's ability to mix elements such as tragedy, satire, philosophy, the grotesque, and comedy. The plot, fragmented but manageable, concerns the twins Renzo and Barbarina, whose mother, the queen, was hated by the wicked queen-mother and imprisoned after the twins' birth. The babies were to be killed by Pantalone, another of Gozzi's stock characters; instead, they were spared and given to a peasant couple, Truffaldino and Smeraldina, to be reared by them. The twins, however, are turned out of the house by Truffaldino in a fit of rage, and the major portion of the play deals with their wanderings as they search for a home, philosophizing, along the way, about life and their predicament. They discuss such matters as family obligations, obedience to parents who mistreat their children, respect for elders, the need for family ties, and death. Renzo is bitter because of their experiences, and he expresses his negative attitudes toward these subjects. Later, however, as the twins travel along a desert shore, they encounter a talking statue, which rebukes Renzo and sets forth the belief that selfishness does not govern all actions, that virtue and a sincere desire to act kindly toward others are what really motivate people. These views, presumably Gozzi's own (as spoken by the statue), lead to a resolution of all the disparate elements in the play. Barbarina confesses that she has been courted by a little green bird, the latter having saved the twins' mother's life by bringing her food and drink as she remained buried alive in a dungeon. The entombed mother is eventually freed and returned to her husband the king, the evildoers in the play are transformed into ugly animals, and the green bird becomes a prince and marries Barbarina.

OTHER MAJOR WORKS

POETRY: *La marfissa bizzarra*, 1772.

NONFICTION: *La tartana degli influssi*, 1757; *Memorie inutili*, 1797 (*Useless Memoirs*, 1890).

MISCELLANEOUS: *Opere*, 1801-1802 (14 volumes).

BIBLIOGRAPHY

DiGaetani, John Louis. *Carlo Gozzi: A Life in the Eighteenth Century Venetian Theater, an Afterlife in Opera*. Jefferson, N.C.: McFarland, 2000. This biography of Gozzi looks at his popularity during his lifetime and the popularity of his plays for operas after his death. Bibliography and index.

_____. Introduction to *Carlo Gozzi: Translations of "The Love of Three Oranges," "Turandot," and "The Snake Lady,"* by Carlo Gozzi. New York: Greenwood, 1988. DiGaetani provides critical analysis of Gozzi's works in his introduction to his translations. Bibliography and index.

Harvey, Dennis. Review of *The Green Bird*, by Carlo Gozzi. *Variety*, October 16-22, 2000, p. 44. Review of a performance of *The Green Bird*, adapted by Steven Epp for Theatre de la Jeune Lune. Discusses the play and its suitability for modern presentation.

Wilson, Edwin. "Gozzi's Enchanting Fable." Review of *The King Stag*, by Carlo Gozzi. *Wall Street Journal*, September 21, 1990, p. A12. This review of a production of *The King Stag* by the American Repertory Theater in Cambridge, Massachusetts, provides insights into the play as comments on the rivalry between Gozzi and Carlo Goldoni.

Kenneth A. Howe

CHRISTIAN DIETRICH GRABBE

Born: Detmold, Lippe, Westphalia (now in
　　Germany); December 11, 1801
Died: Detmold, Lippe, Westphalia (now in
　　Germany); September 12, 1836

PRINCIPAL DRAMA

Herzog Theodor von Gothland, wr. 1822, pb. 1827,
　　pr. 1892 (verse play)
Scherz, Satire, Ironie, und Teifere Bedeutung, wr.
　　1822, pb. 1827, pr. 1876 (*Jest, Satire, Irony, and
　　Deeper Significance*, 1955)

Nannette und Maria, wr. 1823, pb. 1827, pr. 1914

Marius und Sulla, pb. 1827, pr. 1938

Don Juan und Faustus, pr., pb. 1829 (verse play)

Kaiser Friedrich Barbarossa, pb. 1829, pr. 1875

Aschenbrödel, wr. 1829, pb. 1835, pr. 1937

Kaiser Heinrich VI, pb. 1830, pr. 1875

Napoleon: Oder, Die hundert Tage, pb. 1831, pr. 1869

Hannibal, pb. 1835, pr. 1918

Die Hermannschlacht, pb. 1838, pr. 1936

OTHER LITERARY FORMS

Christian Dietrich Grabbe wrote various critical articles on the theater, including reviews of his own dramatic works. A notable article, "Über die Shakespearo-Manie," written and published in 1827, marks his attempt to free himself from the dramatist who had influenced him most since his school days. It strongly opposes the William Shakespeare cult in Germany and calls for national originality on the German stage. Despite Grabbe's assertions, Heinrich Heine, among others, has identified Grabbe's strong kinship with Shakespeare.

ACHIEVEMENTS

Three-quarters of a century ahead of his time, Christian Dietrich Grabbe was a direct precursor of Friedrich Hebbel's realism, Gerhart Hauptmann's naturalism, the expressionist theater of the 1920's, and Bertolt Brecht's epic theater. In the early nineteenth century, both Georg Büchner and Hebbel studied Grabbe's dramatic techniques. It was not, however, until the vogue of naturalism in the last decades of the century that Grabbe was rediscovered for the stage. In the twentieth century, expressionism brought a second rediscovery. Technically, Grabbe's theater represented a strong move away from the rounded plot and the unities of the classical theater to an "open" form. Instead of the traditional five acts, his plays juxtaposed numerous separate scenes to light up the theme from many sides. In their general tone, his plays, like the man himself, "poured the corrosive acid of the intellect" on feelings with a relentlessness that resulted in nihilism: "My intellect is empty and feeling destroyed."

Grabbe's life was dramatized by Hans Johst in a play entitled *Der Einsame* (pr. 1917; the lonely man). Brecht's *Baal* (wr. 1918, pb. 1922; English translation, 1963) was written as an ironic reply to Johst's sentimentality and seems to reflect a dynamic *poète maudit* such as Arthur Rimbaud or Paul Verlaine rather than the more passive, shattered figure of Grabbe.

BIOGRAPHY

Christian Dietrich Grabbe was born in Detmold, the capital of Lippe, a small duchy in Westphalia (now in Germany), on December 11, 1801, the only son of a jail warden. A frail child, one of his earliest somber experiences consisted of conversations with a prisoner on death row. He always considered it his great misfortune to have been born in a provincial town in which an educated man was regarded as simply "a run-down fatted ox." At the age of sixteen, he discovered the works of Shakespeare, and the direction of his literary career was decided: "I can only write . . . what Shakespeare did: dramas." A grant from the duchy enabled him to study philosophy and history, first at the University of Leipzig, then at Berlin, where Georg Wilhelm Friedrich Hegel and Wilhelm von Humboldt were then on the faculty. In both cities, he frequented literary salons and associated with young authors of the time, including Heinrich Heine and other Sturm und Drang, Romantic, and post-Romantic celebrities. Later, Heine gave Grabbe a rather left-handed compliment, praising him as "one of the greatest German dramatists, . . . a drunken Shakespeare."

Grabbe often went to the theater, drank excessively, and visited houses of prostitution, where he probably contracted syphilis. After failing to get his first plays published or to obtain a job as an actor, the disheartened young man returned to Detmold, where, following a brief period of stagnation, he surprised everyone by passing his bar examinations. In 1826, he became a legal officer for the duchy's small military contingent, a post he held until two years before his death, when he voluntarily retired because of ill health, alcoholism, and overwork, all of which impeded his literary productivity. In 1827, four of

Grabbe's plays were finally published; only one of his plays, however, *Don Juan und Faustus*, was ever performed during his lifetime, in 1829. In 1833, Grabbe married Louise Christiane Clostermeier, daughter of a local archivist and historian who had been instrumental in his obtaining the opportunity to go to the university; the marriage proved disastrous for both. Before a year was over, Grabbe began a wandering existence, first to Frankfurt, then to Düsseldorf. Finally, a sick and penniless man and an alcoholic, he borrowed money to return home to Detmold, an unwelcome patient in his wife's house, only a few months before his death on September 12, 1836, in his mother's arms.

ANALYSIS

What puts Christian Dietrich Grabbe far ahead of his time as a historical dramatist is that he does not feel compelled to simplify history in order to meet moralistic needs—as did Schiller with his *Wilhelm Tell* (pr., pb. 1804; *William Tell*, 1841), reducing a vast politicosocial drama into one of individual morality and personal, family self-defense—or to subsume the action under a single overriding thesis-antithesis dramatic tension—as did Hebbel in *Judith* (pr. 1840; English translation, 1974), turning a religio-national heroine into an erotically fascinated super-woman. On the contrary, when Grabbe revises history, as he does in *Hannibal*, the reason is not to tighten the material within an idealistic force-counterforce dramatic scheme but to condense historical time in order to elucidate the variety of external social and material factors that constitute the dramatic situation. This awareness of complexity is at the heart of Grabbe's theater; he abandons the traditional dramatic bipolarity or positive-negative dualism in favor of multiple ethical and sociopolitical vectors, each depicted in detail according to its own specific reality and not distorted under bipolar constraints. The vehicle for this kind of drama is Grabbe's "open" form, much studied by other dramatists since his time. This form consists of no rounded plot and no classical unities, but instead numerous separate short scenes to capture the multifaceted disparity of the forces brought to bear on the central character, and no streamlining or

idealization, but instead a critical, dispassionate scrutiny of a rich and complex character and his or her cultural world. The result is greater historical accuracy and critical validity.

HERZOG THEODOR VON GOTHLAND

Grabbe's first extant play, *Herzog Theodor von Gothland*, is rich in reminiscences of Shakespearean and other dramas, especially the fate tragedies (for example, Adolf Müllner's *Die Schuld*, pr. 1813; *Guilt*, 1819), a genre that it rejects in principle in favor of a destiny ruled by chance.

The play's main character, like Karl Moor in Friedrich Schiller's *Die Räuber* (pb. 1781; *The Robbers*, 1792), is a man disillusioned by a catastrophe precipitated on him by a treacherous enemy, and who turns bitterly against God and humankind. Misled into believing that his older brother has murdered his younger one, Gothland sees it as his duty to commit fratricide to avenge the first crime. Raging with grief and remorse when he discovers his error—"I believed I was acting most justly, and I murdered my innocent brother"—Gothland revolts against God for having permitted him to sin; indeed, he regards God as an evil being who has created humankind only for the sadistic pleasure of destroying it. Tormented with guilt and hating everyone, he takes command of the enemy forces against his own nation and indulges in sadistic cruelty and destruction. After having, in an elegiac description, admired the idyllic existence of a weary farmer plodding homeward, the envious Gothland reasons: "I don't see how he deserves this beautiful destiny more than I do; if he had been tempted as I was, he would have fallen as I did," and he maliciously orders the farmer's house to be torn down and his fields trampled. Succumbing to a powerful destructive urge in a frenzy of slaughter that presages the Nazi horrors, Gothland orders the massacre of five thousand Swedish prisoners. He denies the existence of God and of any transcendental realm of objective values. He has totally lost his "faith in mankind, without which there is no love, only eternal hatred, . . . and which alone makes him humane."

This first play of Grabbe, circulated in manuscript in the literary circles of Berlin, shocked his contemporaries. Even the cultured salon hostess Rahel von

Varnhagen found its crude portrayals of vice and crime so repugnant and alarming that she wanted the manuscript removed from her house immediately, for "she could not sleep a wink as long as that atrocious work was there." In a sense, this play was an antidote and reply to the sugary, prudish Romantic fare of the German stage at the time. In Grabbe's vision, insipid idealistic love in sylvan Arcadias is replaced by perfunctory sex with a beautiful prostitute, and "sweet and glorious" patriotic death is transformed into senseless brutal slaughter described in all its gory details; one character is even locked inside a tomb and hears the worms gnawing on the corpses. The net effect is one of post-Romantic *Weltschmerz*, or disillusionment: The need for ideals is strongly felt, but the real world is now perceived as totally devoid of them, with a resulting despair and pessimism.

JEST, SATIRE, IRONY, AND DEEPER SIGNIFICANCE

Jest, Satire, Irony, and Deeper Significance, written in 1822, immediately after *Herzog Theodor von Gothland*, presents the same bleak, nihilistic world, but in the guise of a Romantic literary comedy (lampooning contemporary literature, especially that written by and for women). Rising above the genre, it directs the brunt of its irony and satire not at literature but at the world itself.

The plot is hilarious, using traditional motifs in a new ribald, ironic manner, scintillating with barbs in every direction. A drunken schoolmaster tries to present a stupid farm boy as a genius because the boy's father has promised him a vat full of brandy. Four natural scientists discover the Devil wrapped in a thick fur coat and frozen stiff on a hilltop; he has had to leave his warm home in Hell temporarily because housecleaning is taking place there. The scientists dispute the Devil's identity and decide that such an ugly face could belong only to "a German woman-writer." When revived, the Devil identifies himself as a churchman "honored with a papal order," and he is taken to the castle of Baron von Haldungen. Here the main plot begins to unreel. Liddy, the baron's intelligent, beautiful niece, is courted by three suitors: Warnthal, who is willing to sell her for money; Mordax, who lusts for her body and is willing to kill to

get it; and Mollfels (Soft-Rock), ugly but sincere, intelligent, and decent, who in the end wins the lady. The Devil makes a deal with Warnthal and Mordax, giving Liddy, who is to be abducted, to the latter. This plot is foiled when the schoolmaster, at a cabin in the forest, the romantic scene of Liddy's intended abduction, captures the Devil in an iron cage, using as bait either prophylactics or Casanova's works, depending on the version. The Devil's grandmother, a beautiful, elegant young lady ("Don't you know that we immortals remain eternally young?"), comes to his rescue and takes him home to Hell, as the housecleaning is now finished. Mordax and Warnthal escape into the audience, and author Grabbe appears before the curtain falls, carrying a lit lantern, amid the schoolmaster's jeers:

> That is the damned Grabbe, or, as he really ought to be called, the dwarf-crab, the writer of this play! He is stupid as a crowbar, criticizes all writers and is himself worthless, has bow-legs, cock-eyes and a pale monkey-face! Let's lock him out, Baron, let's lock him out.

As the play ends, Liddy rebukes him: "Schoolmaster, schoolmaster, how bitterly you scold against the man who wrote you!"

The play abounds in jokes and makes very lively stage fare, which is why, since its rediscovery, it has remained in the German repertory year after year. Much slapstick comedy is connected with the Devil. He loses a horseshoe from one of his hoofed feet and must go to the blacksmith to be reshod. More than once he absentmindedly amuses himself by sticking his finger in the candle flame, and he smashes a valuable chair to light a fire in the oven, where he is discovered lying in the fire to warm himself. All this amusing activity is in the mode of the low comedy of the medieval *Fastnachtsspiele* (carnival plays).

At times, exaggerations almost suggest the modern Theater of the Absurd. The schoolmaster draws a long ink mark across his face to give the impression of being absentmindedly devoted to his pedagogical tasks. He has a wide knowledge of contemporary literature because every other week his cousin sends him half-rotten herring "wrapped in the fresh galley-proofs of the most miserable poetic works and periodicals"—which happen to be the best literary products of the time. The poet Rattengift (Rat-Poison) explains his greatest inspiration—namely, to write a poem about his total lack of inspiration. Warnthal, the venal suitor, in a very comic scene, bargains with the Devil to sell Liddy at a price based on her attributes item by item: The Devil is willing to pay two thousand talers for her beauty; seven thousand talers for her fine, soft hand (because that will make her slaps softer); but only thirty-one cents for her innocence because that was the going rate on the streets of Berlin; and only three cents for her imagination, since that ruins the complexion, causes rings under the eyes, and spoils the soup. Liddy herself is virtually the only nongrotesque character in the whole play: the very opposite of the sentimental, clinging females of the traditional stage at that time—a beautiful yet intelligent and enlightened young woman who stands solidly on her own two feet and sees through the schemers around her.

DON JUAN UND FAUSTUS

Don Juan und Faustus is a much more streamlined play than the sprawling *Herzog Theodor von Gothland*. Its dialogues lead straight to the point, and its action moves efficiently. In a bizarre mixture of German classicism and Romantic irony, it blends together two important thematic traditions of the stage. Don Juan represents the hedonistic quest for worldly pleasure, Faust an unbounded desire for metaphysical insight. The connecting link is Donna Anna, the governor's daughter, whom they both want and whose wedding to Don Octavio they both seek to sabotage. In a pact with Faust, the Devil promises him Donna Anna, "this most beautiful woman in Rome," in return for his eternal damnation. Faust agrees in order to see intellectually how love would have made him happy but first insists on visiting the depths of Hell and the heights of the stars. On his return, the Devil makes him fall passionately in love with Donna Anna. Don Juan kills her father and her fiancé in duels, and Faust kidnaps her and takes her to his magic castle, where he tries futilely by all kinds of diabolical tricks to win her love.

In a key dialogue between the counterposed protagonists, Don Juan rejects Faust's quest for the pre-

ternatural: "Why superhuman, when you remain a man?" Faust, in reply, asserts humankind's intrinsic striving for transcendence: "Why a man, if you do not strive for the superhuman?" The two never become truly human: They are a theatrically effective counterposition of two possible extreme stances, neither of which represents an adequate ethical and human scope of feeling or responsibility. Faust, in a burst of hatred at being rejected, finally murders Donna Anna. In the end, the Devil comes to fetch both Don Juan and Faust. Faust surrenders willingly out of remorse over Donna Anna's murder, while the unrepentant Don Juan—to whom repentance would have meant the surrender of his personal identity—is dragged to Hell in the traditional manner by the governor's statue. Both Faust's absolute striving for access to the preternatural, beyond all earthly limits and without inhibitions by any ethical principles, and Don Juan's unidealistic hedonism are defeated, the result of their egotism and their lack of real love in their approach to the beautiful Donna Anna. The play never achieves tragic dimensions because its protagonists represent ideas rather than psychologically credible persons; however, as a tragicomic drama of ideas effectively intermingling burlesque and thought, this play has a very modern tone, and so, together with *Jest, Satire, Irony, and Deeper Significance*, it is one of Grabbe's works that still is performed regularly.

KAISER FRIEDRICH BARBAROSSA

Grabbe completed only two plays of a projected eight-play cycle on the Hohenstaufen dynasty, a period that marked the pinnacle of secular culture and imperial power in the high Middle Ages. The first of these, *Kaiser Friedrich Barbarossa*, depicts that emperor's struggle against the Papacy and its regionalist ally, Duke Henry the Lion, of Saxony. Both as a man and as a ruler, Barbarossa is depicted as a paragon, seeking for the nations a secularized state "free of clerical slavery." Pope Alexander III questions Barbarossa's aims: Is he not trying to impose his dynasty on the whole world? Barbarossa and Henry the Lion are initially the closest of friends, but the different temperaments and destinies of their north and south German clans lead inevitably to their conflict. There is an element of the fate tragedy in this: The two men are not free to escape such a conflict even if it goes against their personal choice. Their respective political positions as leaders of different peoples will inevitably put them at the head of opposing armies. Henry is not guilty of breach of loyalty; he breaks with Barbarossa because he cannot in good conscience support the emperor's plans for world conquest. The plays' sprawling onstage battle scenes are said to be practically unperformable.

KAISER HEINRICH VI

Kaiser Heinrich VI portrays Barbarossa's son, who has inherited his father's ambition for world conquest. Even at seventeen, he aspires to subjugate Russia and North Africa to Hohenstaufen rule. He lacks the milder qualities of his father. His personality is concentrated on the single driving force of political ambition, and he lacks all human feeling except greed for power. Irreligious, deceitful, and unscrupulous, he stops at nothing to attain his ends, yet for all his striving he is struck down by a heart attack while at the height of his power. Whereas his father and Henry the Lion had illustrated the conflict between personal desire and historical necessity, Henry VI exemplifies how all political grandeur is destined to fall. A courtly poet sums up this theme of the play: "All this glory will vanish some day! It is too great! And greatness is eternal only in the realm of fantasy." Henry's dying words are: "To die so unexpectedly, so miserably—Oh, if only I had never been born!" Death, the great leveler, leaves the mighty empty-handed.

NAPOLEON

Grabbe broke new ground in the writing of historical dramas with his *Napoleon: Oder, Die hundert Tage* (Napoleon: or, the hundred days). The traditional emphasis on a psychological or ethical flaw in the protagonist that leads to his destruction is abandoned in favor of a more objective portrayal of the social world in separate scenes that illuminate the political vectors controlling the course of events. Accurately, impartially, and with no artificial reshaping to force them into a line of plot, Grabbe depicts the conflicting persons and elements in a vast panoramic historical study. Yet the result is not a formless factu-

ality; by the self-analyses and commentaries of various characters, the vantage point is placed at a sufficient distance from the action to give a holistic picture of the historical epoch and its specific *Zeitgeist*. Thus, Grabbe presents the drama of an entire historical period rather than merely of one self-determining protagonist. A battery of vectorlike scenes traces Napoleon Bonaparte's return to power after his exile on the island of Elba and his defeat at Waterloo after one hundred days in a wide spectrum of politicosocial reality. Although, on the surface, the traditional five acts are retained, they have lost their dramatic function, which is assumed by powerful scenes depicting Napoleon's antagonists: the mobs of Paris, Louis XVII and the returned nobility, Gebhard Leberecht von Blüchner and the Prussians, the duke of Wellington and his British staff and troops. The outcome is determined by real confrontations and chance events and does not appear as merely an extrapolation of ethical principles or a conflict of ideals. Except for two former soldiers of Napoleon's "grand army," most characters, including Napoleon himself, appear in only one or two scenes. The play is justly famous for its mass scenes with the Paris rabble and for its battle scenes, perhaps more suitable for the cinema than for the stage. The overall technique of the play is a meticulous marshaling of precise objective detail, presented with vivid directness and a modicum of commentary; the audience becomes, as it were, an eyewitness of the events as they occurred.

At the time of writing, only fifteen years after Waterloo, the Restoration had clamped the repressive rule of the monarchs and nobility back on Europe, and the Biedermeier age of apolitical retreat to private happiness, comfort, and boredom seemed stagnant and degenerate compared with the enthusiasm that Napoleon, as bearer of the ideals and turmoil of the French Revolution, had aroused in many Europeans, including—though without hero worship—Grabbe himself, who once wrote: "With Napoleon's end, the world became like a book we had finished reading, and we stood before it like a reader cast back out again, reflecting on what he had read." Although Napoleon, however talented and even genial, is depicted as simply a man whose greatness was not intrinsic but borne by a multitude of fixed or chance social factors, as a man flawed by self-centered ambition and vanity, in some passages the suspicion arises that his defeat was a defeat of genuine human aspirations for justice, equality, and brotherhood, for a new era of happiness worth far more than the drab, humdrum Restoration of the *ancien régime.*

HANNIBAL

Again in *Hannibal,* the hero is destroyed not by any inner conflict or flaw but by the concerted though variegated forces at work in the social world of his time. More than any other of Grabbe's protagonists, Hannibal incarnates the author's pessimistic sense of life. Grabbe takes some liberties with history, condensing and fusing events and characters from the entire ancient world and from two different Punic wars to capture the spirit of the great conflict between the two superpowers, Rome and Carthage. The great Carthaginian general, the victorious Hannibal, faces two enemies: his military opponent Rome and the unappreciative Carthaginian politicians and businessmen, who have no concept of their country's national interests and honor. The play opens with Hannibal's decisive victory at Cannae in 216 B.C.E., which put him "at the gates of Rome," and ends with the total destruction of Carthage in 146, according to Cato's famous dictum: "Carthago delenda est" (Carthage must be destroyed).

Only about half as long as *Napoleon,* this drama similarly lights up the action from many sides, but it is far more streamlined, and only a few characters of its vast *dramatis personae* are developed with any detail. The author's anti-Carthaginian stance is suggested in the slave-market scene and in the sacrifice of children to Moloch, scenes that show the cruel mercantilism and abject inhumanity of the Carthaginian citizenry. Plotting against one another and at cross-purposes to their country's welfare, the Carthaginian leaders withhold troops and supplies needed to meet the Roman threat. Hannibal is rejected by his countrymen and wastes his career by becoming a mercenary, selling his military skills to various other countries. Finally, betrayed to the Romans by his current employer, Hannibal takes his own life with poison in order to avoid falling into the hands of the Romans. His disloyal

master, in a ritualistic gesture devoid of substance, drapes a red royal cloak over his corpse.

The disciplined Romans are contrasted with the selfish, squabbling, bourgeoisified Carthaginians, and especially in the persons of the two Scipios, they are worthy and dangerous opponents for Hannibal, but the Roman world is not idealized either. It, too, is based on slavery, war, and boundless cruelty. By a skillful anachronism, Grabbe fuses the playwright Terence with the historian Polybius to provide a cultured observer who is sickened by the horrors of war. The real world is not a comedy but a devastating tragedy in which brute power and cruel impulses destroy entire societies. Nor is Hannibal, as a man of this same ancient world, exempt from this cruelty: He ruthlessly orders scouts crucified for having misled the army. More fundamentally, he lacks vision and has no ambition to break the cycle of war and slaughter.

As in *Napoleon,* the main character is the absolute center of focus, illuminated from various perspectives, though formidable opponents are also developed. This drama, too, presents a sociopolitical and cultural portrait of an entire age. Its conflict is not the projection of one man's psychological or ethical problem. The struggles are fought out on a real plane without moral valuation. In *Hannibal,* a great man is destroyed by the limitations of the epoch that created him.

DIE HERMANNSCHLACHT

Completed in Grabbe's last months, just before his death, *Die Hermannschlacht* (the battle of Arminius, or Hermann) deals with the famous victory of the Germanic tribes in the Teutoburg Forest not far from the dramatist's own native town of Detmold. This play is not divided, even externally, into five acts. Instead, a central portion containing the long, shifting events of the battle is framed between a prologue that establishes the setting, the Roman campaign to subjugate the Germanic tribes in their own forested homeland, and an epilogue in Rome after the three Roman legions in Germany have been exterminated. This was a most crucial defeat for Rome because it prevented the Roman Empire from extending its borders to include all Central Europe and completely subjugating the Germans and forced it instead to set up a defensive perimeter along the Rhine and its tributaries. Relying on a historical work, *Wo Hermann den Varus schlug* (1822; where Hermann defeated Varus), by his father-in-law, Christian Gottlieb Clostermeier, Grabbe used the actual local place names for the various events, and he presented the Germanic tribesmen realistically, giving them the simple down-to-earth character of Lippe peasants rather than resorting to semimythical idealization as prior writers had done. Only the two commanders are developed in any detail: Hermann, who sees the need for an overarching Germanic unity but realizes that this is unattainable since the tribes have no national concept and are united only as a loose aggregate to oppose Roman oppression, and Varus, commander of the Roman troops, a brave man trapped in a disastrous situation. *Die Hermannschlacht* is not, however, a piece of propaganda for German unity; its aim is purely historical: to portray the objective factors at work in a crucial battle of world history.

BIBLIOGRAPHY

Cowen, Roy C. *Christian Dietrich Grabbe.* New York: Twayne, 1972. A basic study of Grabbe's life and works. Includes bibliography.

Nichols, Roger A. *The Dramas of Christian Dietrich Grabbe.* The Hague: Mouton, 1969. An analysis of the works of Grabbe. Bibliography included.

Sutherland, Margaret Anne. *The Reception of Grabbe's "Hannibal" in the German Theatre.* New York: Peter Lang, 1984. Sutherland examines Grabbe's *Hannibal*, paying particular attention to how it was produced and staged as well as how it was received. Contains bibliography.

David J. Parent

HARLEY GRANVILLE-BARKER

Born: London, England; November 25, 1877
Died: Paris, France; August 31, 1946

PRINCIPAL DRAMA

The Weather-Hen: Or, Invertebrata, pr. 1899 (with Berte Thomas)

The Marrying of Ann Leete, pr. 1902, pb. 1909

Prunella: Or, Love in a Dutch Garden, pr. 1904, pb. 1906 (with Laurence Housman, music by Joseph Moorat)

The Voysey Inheritance, pr. 1905, pb. 1909

A Miracle, pr. 1907

Waste, pr. 1907, pb. 1909

The Madras House, pr. 1910, pb. 1911

Rococo, pr. 1911, pb. 1917 (one act)

The Morris Dance, pr. 1913 (adaptation of Robert Louis Stevenson and Lloyd Osborne's play *The Wrong Box*)

The Harlequinade, pr. 1913, pb. 1918 (with Dion Calthrop)

The Dynasts, pr. 1914 (adaptation of Thomas Hardy's verse drama)

Vote by Ballot, pr., pb. 1917 (one act)

Farewell to the Theatre, pb., pb. 1917

Three Short Plays, pb. 1917 (3 one-acts; *Rococo*, *Vote by Ballot*, and *Farewell to the Theatre*)

Deburau, pr. 1920, pb. 1921 (adaptation of Sacha Guitry's play)

The Secret Life, pb. 1923

His Majesty, pb. 1928

The Collected Plays of Harley Granville-Barker, pb. 1967

Plays, pb. 1987 (edited by Dennis Kennedy)

OTHER LITERARY FORMS

Harley Granville-Barker's concern for a serious drama, and for a serious theater to interpret that drama, informs much, if not all, of his prose writings. With William Archer, Granville-Barker compiled *A National Theatre: Scheme and Estimates* (1907, revised by Granville-Barker in 1930), a working blueprint for a national repertory theater. *The Exemplary Theatre* (1922) presents Granville-Barker's conception of the theater from the perspective of a director-actor-playwright. His other writings on the theater, *On Dramatic Method* (1931), *The Study of Drama* (1934), *On Poetry in Drama* (1937), and *The Use of Drama* (1945), focus primarily on his conception of a theatrically viable drama. This particular concern is evident as well in his famous series *Prefaces to Shakespeare* (1927-1947) and in its predecessor, the various prefaces and introductions Granville-Barker wrote for the volumes of *The Player's Shakespeare* (1923-1927). The remainder of Granville-Barker's literary works consists of a handful of articles on drama and on the theater; six short stories, of which only three have been published; and numerous translations.

ACHIEVEMENTS

In addition to his full-length plays, Harley Granville-Barker wrote three one-act plays, *Rococo*, *Vote by Ballot*, and *Farewell to the Theatre*. "Agnes Colander" (wr. 1901) and the unfinished "The Wicked Man" (wr. 1910-1914) were never published or produced. Also never published were the four plays Granville-Barker wrote in collaboration with Berte Thomas between 1895 and 1899. Two of his other collaborations, however—*Prunella: Or, Love in a Dutch Garden*, with Laurence Housman, and *The Harlequinade*, with Dion Calthrop—were published. The remainder of Granville-Barker's dramatic writing consists of translations or adaptations, most notably a translation of Arthur Schnitzler's *Anatol* (pr. 1911) and an adaptation of Sacha Guitry's *Deburau*. He also translated plays by Jules Romains and, with his wife, Helen Huntington Barker-Granville, by Gregorio Martínez Sierra, and by Serafín Álvarez Quintero and Joaquín Álvarez Quintero.

Granville-Barker's reputation as an *homme de théâtre* began to suffer a decline after he left active theater work and became a "mere professor." His plays, already looked on with suspicion by his contemporaries, suffered an even greater decline. Although Granville-Barker's plays were lauded by such

Harley Granville-Barker in 1915. (Library of Congress)

fellow dramatists as George Bernard Shaw, John Masefield, and Gilbert Murray, external factors, such as the growing dominance of Shaw and changes in dramatic and theatrical styles, hastened the decline of his plays into obscurity. However, in the late twentieth century, a revival of interest occurred in the plays of Granville-Barker (*The Madras House*, for example, was produced for television by the British Broadcasting Corporation). This revival of interest betokens Granville-Barker's significance as a dramatist.

The Granville-Barker play is singular among plays of the Edwardian period in its use of heterosexual relationships to define the worth of human actions and to signify the larger moral concerns that are the prime concern of his plays: the necessity of what he termed "the secret life," the inner reality that puts into perspective the trivialities of everyday life. Granville-Barker was lauded by his fellow dramatists not only for the superb "actability" and polish of his plays but also for his dramatic portrayal of the real, vital dilemmas of human sensibility and of absolute morality beneath the superficialities of daily existence. Granville-Barker's greatest achievement as a dramatist, and his significance as a dramatist to our age, lies in his successful deployment of heterosexual relationships as signs of our fragile hold on our essential selves and our humanity.

BIOGRAPHY

Harley Granville-Barker was, in a manner of speaking, born into the theater in 1877. Granville-Barker's mother, Mary Elizabeth Barker, formerly Bozzi-Granville, was a professional entertainer. The family traveled around together to her engagements, and young Harley was brought up to appear and to recite poetry with her professionally. Little is known of the extent and the nature of his formal education, but, at the age of fourteen, he was enrolled in Sarah Thorne's theatrical school at the Margate Theatre. During his six-month sojourn at the school, Granville-Barker met Berte Thomas, with whom he collaborated in the writing of his first four plays. Granville-Barker's first major acting job was touring with Ben Greet's Shakespeare Company, which included Lillah McCarthy, whom he was later to marry. In 1899, at the age of twenty-two, Granville-Barker took the main role in William Poel's Elizabethan Stage Society production of William Shakespeare's *Richard II* (pr. c. 1592-1593). Poel's production led Granville-Barker to become involved in the newly founded Stage Society, for which he functioned as both an actor and a director. One of the results of his involvement with the Stage Society was his long and close friendship with George Bernard Shaw and, through his involvement with Shaw, his membership in the Fabian Society.

Another, more significant result of Granville-Barker's work with the Stage Society was the revolutionary Vedrenne-Barker management at the Court Theatre from 1904 to 1907; J. E. Vedrenne acted as business manager, and Granville-Barker directed all the plays and acted in many. The Vedrenne-Barker seasons at the Court Theatre were revolutionary not only in the plays they presented (by John Galsworthy,

Henrik Ibsen, Maurice Maeterlinck, Gerhart Hauptmann, and Shaw, to name a few) but also in their format of repertory. In 1906, Granville-Barker married Lillah McCarthy, who also had been involved in the Vedrenne-Barker productions. Following the Vedrenne-Barker management, Granville-Barker's involvement with the theater took the form of efforts to establish a repertory theater in London. Such efforts defined the nature of his management of the Duke of York Theatre in 1910 (a venture backed by the American impresario Charles Frohman), the McCarthy-Granville-Barker management of the Little Theatre in 1911, and the Granville-Barker management of the St. James Theatre in 1913. In 1912, Granville-Barker gave his last performance as an actor, preferring to devote his time and his energy to directing, to the establishment of a repertory theater, and to the writing of plays.

On a trip to America in 1914, Granville-Barker met Helen Huntington, his future second wife. On his return to England, Granville-Barker became involved in World War I, serving with the Red Cross. He later enlisted in the Royal Horse Artillery and was soon transferred to Army Intelligence. Lillah McCarthy and Harley Granville-Barker were divorced in 1917, and the following year he married Helen Huntington; it was also at this time that he hyphenated his name. Granville-Barker's second marriage marked the beginning of the end of his friendship with George Bernard Shaw. Moreover, the new Mrs. Granville-Barker's dislike of Shaw in particular and theater people in general, coupled with Granville-Barker's own disillusionment with the theater, led to his retirement from active theater work in 1921.

Beginning in 1922, Granville-Barker devoted himself entirely to the program of writing that he began with his first attempts at playwriting. In 1930, the Granville-Barkers moved to Paris, where they lived until the German invasion of France. They spent the remainder of the war years in New York, where Granville-Barker worked for the British Information Services until 1942. After the war, the Granville-Barkers returned to England and then to Paris, where Granville-Barker died in 1946, a few months before his sixty-ninth birthday, of arteriosclerosis.

ANALYSIS

Harley Granville-Barker's early dramatic efforts— his apprentice plays—reveal that from the beginning, his plays were preoccupied with, if not generated by, the question of how a heterosexual relationship delineates and nurtures that moral strength or secret life essential to confront absolute moral dilemmas. The protagonist of a Granville-Barker play (Shaw preferred "worm" to "protagonist" in his letters to Barker) is thrust into a moral dilemma through a conflict between his outer, public life and his inner, secret life. The dramatic action of the play, then, is ordered by this conflict between the inner and the outer life of the protagonist. Granville-Barker heightens this basic conflict by means of his deft interweaving of theatrical symbol, dialogue, and theme. The dialogue itself, condensed, close-textured, and elliptical to the point of appearing disjointed, further underscores the central conflict of the play. In addition, much of the power of a Granville-Barker play is generated by what is implied through theatrical symbol rather than what is verbally stated. Granville-Barker's stage directions are decidedly Shavian in their wealth, precision, and breadth of detail and description. In *The Madras House*, for example, much of Jessica Madras is revealed through the description of her as "the result—not of thirty-three years—but of three or four generations of cumulative refinement. She might be a race horse!"

The basic conflict inherent in all the plays naturally imposes a similar structural pattern on them. The protagonist is faced with a moral dilemma in which he is opposed by a figure of authority, refuses the negative examples of his close associates, and ends by accepting a mate under his own difficult conditions. The crucial point in this pattern is the protagonist's great refusal to accept the prevailing conditions and the prevailing wisdom in favor of his own conditions and his own wisdom. This great refusal invariably involves a sexual conclusion—that is, a consideration by the protagonist and his mate of how to continue in a world made difficult by the action of the inner life on the outer. The element of sex in Granville-Barker's plays is not the "farmyard world of sex" denounced by Philip Madras but the relationship that prevails between the sexes, as in the case of Ann Leete and Abud, in the new world that the protagonist strives to create.

THE MARRYING OF ANN LEETE

In *The Marrying of Ann Leete*, the conflict of the inner and the outer life takes the form of marriage. Carnaby Leete, a parliamentarian out of favor with his party, attempts to revive his career through the marriage of his daughter Ann to Lord John Carp, as he had once before salvaged his career by marrying his daughter Sarah to a member of the opposite party. Sarah's marriage, now falling apart in acrimonious mutual contempt, is a negative example for Ann. Her brother George provides another negative example of marriage; in defiance of his father, he has married a woman beneath his station who reveals herself to be little more than a vulgar social climber. Although Ann presumes that she will be married, she refuses to permit her father to sell her into marriage.

When Carp tells Ann he loves her, she responds: "It suddenly occurs to me that sounds unpleasant." For Ann, marriage is the union of male and female in the service of life; it requires no metaphysical justification. Her decision to marry John Abud, the gardener, is a manifestation of her inner life, of her need to forge a sexual relationship that is true to the fundamental moral purpose of men and women. The reference to Ann as a "new woman" and as the "new generation" underscores not only her determination not to repeat the marital mistakes of her brother and sister but also the role she forges for herself: the new Eve who will bring the future into the world. Ann's marrying, however, is left at the play's close as a frail gesture against the unlivable present. The class suspicions that emerge in the wedding scene, along with Ann's recognition of the experimental nature of her marriage, suggest that whatever the private significance of Ann's marrying, its public significance is minimal. Ann's marital experiment must bear fruit in the private life before it can be recognized by the public life.

THE VOYSEY INHERITANCE

Although *The Voysey Inheritance* also ends with a marriage, the focus of the play is not really on marriage per se. The central conflict of the play is structured in terms of capitalism and creativity. The elder Voysey, like his father before him, has placed the family's small solicitor's firm on the brink of ruin by systematically defrauding clients' accounts for personal profit through financial speculation. Moreover, the elder Voysey has managed this fraud with an artistic flair and a brilliance that ensures not only the prolongation of the game but also the temporary well-being of his clients. The elder Voysey's death pitches his son and heir, Edward Voysey, into the moral dilemma of continuing the family "practice" or turning himself in to the authorities, thereby atoning for the family's financial sins.

Edward is persuaded into accepting his inheritance by his potential wife, Alice Maitland. She encourages Edward to persist in his father's game of fraud to rectify the past and to ensure the economic future of his clients and of his firm. Although he never approaches the elder Voysey's talent for creative fiscal management, Edward's inheritance does save him from the morally flaccid existence of the "well-principled prig" and from the morally compromising positions of his brothers: the cold legality of Trenchard, the moral conventionality of Booth, and the uncontrolled creativity of Hugh. In the final scene, a new Edward, with his new fiancée, Alice, charts the implications of their new life of benevolent fraud and of mutual help. Moreover, the final scene strongly suggests that Edward Voysey's inheritance is not the moral dilemma of financial corruption but the moral resolution of an admixed creativity and capitalism, the merging of the inner life with the outer.

WASTE

Of all Granville-Barker's dramas, *Waste* is the most concerned, outwardly, with politics; its inner subject, however, is again the sexual relationship that unlocks the secret life. In fact, *Waste*'s open reference to sex—an abortion—prompted its censorship until 1936. Henry Trebell's suicide superficially results from his disappointment in the loss of a cabinet seat and in the rejection of his life's work by his party. In reality, his suicide is the direct result of his lack of a secret life. A meaningless sexual encounter with a

married woman that culminates in her death in a back-alley abortion forces Trebell to a recognition of his own back-alley act of spiritual abortion: His angry hatred of women and his powerful reason (he is described at various times as a machine) have killed his human sensibility, his secret life, before it was born.

Trebell's lack of a secret life, his incapability of loving another human being, is matched by that of his mate of the moment, Amy O'Connell, who is incapable of accepting the fact of life and of her womanhood without the placebo of love. Without a secret life and without a sexual means of engendering a secret life, Trebell is destroyed by the assumption of the void within him by his outer, political life. The motif of waste in the play achieves its final, most powerful resonance in the waste of Trebell. Without the supportive strength of the secret life, Trebell becomes the plaything of the Edwardian political oligarchy that controls government policy by Machiavellian infighting and that deliberately uses the bogey of public morality to destroy the threat posed to it by the able man with the good cause.

THE MADRAS HOUSE

Implicit in all of Granville-Barker's plays is the question of the social and moral position of women. This question is made explicit in *The Madras House*, becoming, in fact, the dominant theme of the play. The play's action proceeds in a documentary fashion that suggests the simultaneous existence of contrasting groups of women within the great Edwardian middle class. Each act shows a different kind of woman and a different perspective—familial, marital, and professional—on women's economic dependence on men. Act 1 counterpoints Mrs. Huxtable, the paragon of that respectability that inhibits all spontaneous impulses and reduces life to domestic conventions, to her six, no longer young, daughters. This particular gaggle of spinsters is indistinguishable. The Huxtable daughters have no expressive language of their own, only a code of verbal behavior imposed on them that governs them and threatens all who approach them. Act 2 presents the economic slavery of the independent woman. Most of the employees of Huxtable and Roberts and of the Madras House live on the premises under the morally vigilant eye of Miss Chancellor. When it is discovered that Miss Yates, one of Miss Chancellor's charges, is pregnant, an inquisition into her morals is held. Miss Yates's secret life, which has its source in her pregnancy, permits her to scoff at the world's equation of virtue with gainful employment. Her ability to rise above her moral dilemma throws into relief the pathos of Miss Chancellor, whose life has been stunted by the conventional morality imposed on her spirit by thirty years of economic slavery to the drapery firm of Huxtable and Roberts.

Act 3 is the antithesis of act 1, as it presents a male banquet of articulateness in a fantastic seraglio setting. The masters of the drapery trade, enthroned in the "Moorish" rotunda of the Madras House, are shown engaged in the business of reducing women to sexual automata for economic exploitation in haute couture. Mr. State, an American millinery magnate, idolator of the "woman-spirit" and admirer of the women's movement as womanly sartorial self-expression, defines the middle-class woman as "one of the greatest Money Spending Machines the world has ever seen." The only women to appear in the act are barely women at all. The grotesquely dehumanized fashion mannequins, members of the industrial seraglio, are present only because actual automata are inefficient and uneconomical in comparison to flesh-and-blood automata.

The fourth and final act of the play attempts to bring to a resolution the question of womanhood delineated in the preceding acts. Philip Madras, the play's connecting character, by rejecting a position in the Madras House, rejects the prevailing conceptions of womanhood. Rather than exploit women, and through them, men, Philip chooses to change prevailing conditions by joining the County Council. Jessica Madras, the epitome of the Edwardian middle-class lady, supports her husband provided that he, in his new world, creates a meaningful place for her by his side. More disgusted than her husband by the farmyard world of sexual games symbolized by the Madras House, Jessica yearns for a world in which men and women can be friends. The play closes with the unresolved, because it is unresolvable, discussion between Philip and Jessica as to the place of woman in this new life. Like Ann Leete and John Abud, Philip and Jessica Madras must make their marriage the testing ground for the moral dilemma represented by their redefinition of the sexual relationship and their need to realize the secret life of both man and woman.

THE SECRET LIFE

The Secret Life, written after Granville-Barker left the theater, is his finest, fullest dramatic exploration of sexual relationships and the secret life. *The Secret Life* is an exploration of the potential hazards of middle age, with its loss of purpose and of conviction, its desires that fail to come to fruition, and the extreme difficulty of bringing the inner life to bear on the outer. As in *Waste*, to which it is the natural pendant, the outer life of the play unfolds in the political arena. Evan Strowde, who left politics years ago to write a multivolume industrial history, is being wooed back into politics at the start of the play by his parliamentarian friends. Strowde himself is attempting to renew his courtship of his old love, Joan Westbury. Evan and Joan are presented throughout the play as antithetical yet complementary. Strowde, like Trebell, has a full outer life but no inner life, whereas Joan, stripped of her outer life by the deaths of her husband and her sons and by the destruction of her home, has a rich inner life. Although Strowde needs Joan to kindle his inner life and she needs him to structure her outer life, Joan refuses to commit herself to him. Such a commitment would destroy her inner life and, by extension, herself: "I couldn't have lived my love for you, Evan . . . it would have killed me." Joan's secret life is based on her love for the unattainable in Evan, and its existence depends on the sanctity of that unattainability. Union with Strowde would make external her secret life, would reduce her secret life to an everyday triviality, and would leave her an empty shell.

Because Joan, like Amy O'Connell and Trebell, refuses to risk her happiness in what is, essentially, a commitment to the absolute morality of life, she condemns herself and Strowde to death. Strowde loses himself in his renewed political career, and Joan loses herself in death. Although Joan's great refusal of life destroys both herself and Strowde, it does provide the play's youth, Oliver and Susan, with a negative example of the power of the secret life. In the play's final scene, Oliver, Strowde's illegitimate son, and Susan, Joan's alter ego, reveal the potential to make the great commitment demanded by the conflict of the inner life with the outer life.

OTHER MAJOR WORKS

NONFICTION: *A National Theatre: Scheme and Estimates*, 1907 (with William Archer), 1930 (revised by Granville-Barker); *The Exemplary Theatre*, 1922; *The Player's Shakespeare*, 1923-1927 (prefaces and introductions); *Prefaces to Shakespeare*, 1927-1947; *On Dramatic Method*, 1931; *The Study of Drama*, 1934; *On Poetry in Drama*, 1937; *The Use of Drama*, 1945; *Granville-Barker and His Correspondents*, 1986 (Eric Salmon, editor).

TRANSLATIONS: *Anatol*, pr., pb. 1911 (of Arthur Schnitzler's six playlets); *The Romantic Young Lady*, pr. 1920, pb. 1923 (with Helen Granville-Barker; of Gregorio Martínez Sierra's *Sueño de una noche de agosto*); *The Two Shepherds*, pr. 1921 (with Helen Granville-Barker; of Martínez Sierra's *Sueño de una noche de agosto*); *The Kingdom of God*, pr., pb. 1923 (with Helen Granville-Barker; of Martínez Sierra's *El reino de Dios*); *Wife to a Famous Man*, pb. 1923, pr. 1924 (with Helen Granville-Barker; of Martínez Sierra's *La mujer del héroe*); *Six Gentlemen in a Row*, pr., pb. 1927 (one act; of Jules Romains's *Amédée et les messieurs en rang*); *The Women Have Their Way*, pb. 1927, pr. 1928 (with Helen Granville-Barker; of Serafín and Joaquín Álvarez Quintero's *Pueblo de las mujeres*); *A Hundred Years Old*, pb. 1927, pr. 1928 (with Helen Granville-Barker; of the Álvarez Quintero brothers' *Papa Juan: Centenario*); *Fortunato*, pb. 1927, pr. 1928 (with Helen Granville-Barker; of the Álvarez Quintero brothers' play); *The Lady from Alfaqueque*, pb. 1927, pr. 1928 (with Helen Granville-Barker; of the Álvarez Quintero brothers' *La consulesa*); *Take Two from One*, pb. 1931 (with Helen Granville-Barker; of Martínez Sierra's play); *Love Passes By*, pb. 1932 (with Helen Granville-Barker; of the Álvarez Quintero brothers' *El amor que pasa*); *Peace and Quiet*, pb. 1932 (with Helen Granville-Barker; of the Álvarez Quintero brothers' *La escondida senda*); *Doña Clarines*, pb. 1932, pr. 1934 (with Helen Granville-Barker; of the Álvarez Quintero brothers' play).

BIBLIOGRAPHY

Kauffmann, Stanley. "Rediscovering a Self-made Giant of the British Stage." *The New York Times*, March 12, 2000, p. 5. A tribute to Granville-Barker that provides biographical information and a discussion of his plays, in particular *The Voysey Inheritance*.

Kennedy, Dennis. *Granville-Barker and the Dream of Theatre*. Cambridge, England: Cambridge University Press, 1985. A detailed examination of Granville-Barker's work as a producer and director of theater. It focuses on how he influenced drama and concludes that his dream was realized by the establishment of a national British theater, which he championed during his life. Richly illustrated. Contains a comprehensive listing of his productions and an index.

McDonald, Jan. *The New Drama, 1900-1914*. New York: Grove Press, 1986. Examines the "new drama" movement in the British theater, its theaters, and its major playwrights, Granville-Barker, John Galsworthy, and John Masefield. Provides a brief biography and extensive discussion of each of Granville-Barker's major plays. Bibliography and index.

Mehra, Monmohan. *Harley Granville-Barker: A Critical Study of the Major Plays*. Calcutta: Naya Prokash, 1981. Considers Granville-Barker's experience in theatrical production as the background to his work as a playwright. His merit lies in his ability to create vividly drawn characters while subordinating plot to political and social themes, but without preaching. Emphasizes Granville-Barker's characters who revolt against the social conventions of sex and politics. Index.

Salenius, Elmer W. *Harley Granville-Barker*. Boston: Twayne, 1982. A basic biography of Granville-Barker that covers his life and works. Bibliography and index.

Salmon, Eric. *Granville Barker: A Secret Life*. Cranbury, N.J.: Associated University Presses, 1984. Salmon examines the various aspects of Granville-Barker's life as independent entities. He concludes that Granville-Barker's greatness was in his imaginative perception. Illustrations, chronology, bibliography of works by Granville-Barker, and index.

Weiss, Rudolf. "Harvey Granville-Barker: The First English Chekhovian." *New Theatre Quarterly* 14, no. 53 (February, 1998): 53-63. A discussion of the work and writing technique of Harley Granville-Barker.

Stella Maloney,
updated by Gerald S. Argetsinger

GÜNTER GRASS

Born: Danzig (now Gdańsk, Poland); October 16, 1927

PRINCIPAL DRAMA

Hochwasser, pr. 1957, pb. 1960, revised pb. 1963 (*Flood*, 1967)

Stoffreste, pr. 1957 (ballet)

Beritten hin und zurück, pb. 1958, pr. 1959 (*Rocking Back and Forth*, 1967)

Noch zehn Minuten bis Buffalo, pb. 1958, pr. 1959 (*Only Ten Minutes to Buffalo*, 1967)

Onkel, Onkel, pr. 1958, revised pb. 1965 (*Mister, Mister*, 1967)

Fünf Köche, pr. 1959 (ballet)

Zweiunddreißig Zähne, pr. 1959 (radio play)

Die bösen Köche, pr., pb. 1961 (*The Wicked Cooks*, 1967)

Goldmäulchen, pr., pb. 1963 (radio play), pr. 1964 (staged)

Mystisch-barbarisch-gelangweilt, pr. 1963

POUM: Oder, Die Vergangenheit fliegt mit, pb. 1965

Die Plebejer proben den Aufstand, pr., pb. 1966 (*The Plebeians Rehearse the Uprising*, 1966)

Four Plays, pb. 1967 (includes *Only Ten Minutes to Buffalo*, *The Wicked Cooks*, *Flood*, and *Mister, Mister*)

Davor, pr., pb. 1969 (partial translation as *Uptight*, 1970; complete translation as *Max: A Play by Günter Grass*, 1972)

Die Vogelscheuchen, pr. 1970 (ballet)

Theaterspiele, pb. 1970 (includes *Only Ten Minutes to Buffalo*, *Flood*, *Mister, Mister*, and *The Wicked Cooks*)

OTHER LITERARY FORMS

In addition to drama, Günter Grass is best known for his novels, shorter fiction, poetry, political essays and speeches (he is an active Socialist), and ballet libretti. His first novel, *Die Blechtrommel* (1959; *The Tin Drum*, 1961), reflects its author's concern with the rehabilitation of humanity in postwar Nazi Germany in particular and in a nearly absurd postwar society in general. Grass is also an artist, having published prints and sketches, some in conjunction with his literary works. In addition to his several volumes of political essays and other writings, Grass's aesthetic writings include essays about poetry and the possibilities of literature after Auschwitz.

ACHIEVEMENTS

Günter Grass was awarded the Nobel Prize in Literature in 1999, a distinction that many felt to be long overdue. Only two other Germans, Heinrich Böll and Thomas Mann, were awarded the Nobel Prize in Literature in the twentieth century. The Swedish Academy cited Grass's "black fables" that "portray the forgotten face of history," praising his talent for "reviewing contemporary history by recalling the disavowed and the forgotten: the victims, losers, and lies that people wanted to forget because they once had believed in them all."

Grass's involvement in and dedication to Social Democratic politics and the peace movement no doubt has much to do with the vitality and social preoccupations of his writing. His works not only record the personal and societal struggles of postwar, post-Nazi Germany but also grapple—at times comically and even grotesquely—with the orientation of the individual in such an absurd world. In turn, his writings (especially *The Tin Drum*), which have enjoyed international distribution, have provided their author with an international forum for his beliefs on a wide range of issues—political, environmental, nuclear, and more. Grass withdrew from the Social Democratic Party in 1992; he had already formally left the Catholic church in 1974.

In addition to the Nobel Prize in Literature, Grass is the recipient of numerous literary awards, among them the prestigious Gruppe 47 Award in 1958, the Georg Büchner Prize in 1965, the Fontane Prize in 1968, and the Premio Internationale Mondello in 1977. He established two prizes: in 1969 one for anthologies and readers to be used as texts in German schools and in 1978 the Alfred Döblin Prize for literary achievements.

When his novel *The Tin Drum* appeared in 1959, the senate of the Hanseatic city of Bremen refused to award Grass its literary prize for which he was nominated. Grass has been awarded the Alexander Majkowski medal, Danzig (1978); International Literary Prize, Viareggio (1978); the Weinpreis for Literature, Göttingen (1980); the Feltrinelli Prize (1982); the "Plakatte" of the Free Academy of Arts, Hamburg (1992); Premio Hidalgo, Madrid (1993); Great Prize for Literature of the Bavarian Academy of Fine Arts (1994); Medal of the University of Complutense, Madrid (1994); the Karel Čapek prize, Prague (with Philip Roth, 1994); the Herman Kesten medal (1995); the Hans Fallada prize (1995); the Sonning prize, the most significant literary prize in Denmark (1996); and the Thomas Mann Prize of the City of Lübeck (1996). Additionally, Volker Schlöndorff's film of Grass's novel *The Tin Drum* earned the film prize of the Federal Republic of Germany (1979), the Golden Palm at Cannes (1979), and an Oscar for best foreign film (1980).

Grass has also been distinguished with several prizes for his political position for human rights, for example, with the Carl von Ossietzky medal, Berlin (1967) and the Premio Comites, Berlin/Italy (1992). He has been awarded honorary doctorates by Kenyon College (1965) and Harvard University (1976) in the United States and by the University of Posen (1990) and the University of Danzig (1993) in Poland. In 1993 he also became an honorary citizen of Danzig. Grass has also served his profession in notable capacities, and the acknowledgment of his peers was confirmed by his election in 1963 to the Academy of Arts, Berlin, whose president he was 1983-1986, and from which he resigned in protest in 1989 owing to its lack of solidarity with the writer Salman Rushdie. In 1970 Grass was elected to the American Academy of Arts and Sciences.

BIOGRAPHY

Günter Grass was born in Danzig (now Gdańsk, Poland) on October 16, 1927. His parents owned a

Günter Grass (Mottke Weissman)

grocery store in the suburb Langfuhr. His father's family included workers and carpenters; his mother's family was Kaschubian. Biographical elements from his working-class youth appear throughout his literary works, especially in the *Danziger Trilogie* (1980; *Danzig Trilogy*, 1987). Grass attended the Conradinum *gymnasium* in Danzig. As a teenager, he served in an antiaircraft battery during World War II, was wounded, and became an American captive. Subsequently, he worked his way from Bavaria to Düsseldorf, where he became an apprentice stonecutter (1946-1947) in order to earn money for art school. He studied both graphic design and sculpture in Düsseldorf (1948-1952) and sculpture in Berlin under Karl Hartung (1953-1956).

During these years, Grass also began to write; his initial efforts were in the area of lyric poetry. He resided in Paris from 1956 to 1959. He first read before the literary group Gruppe 47 in 1955, winning the group's prize in 1958 for excerpts from his novel *The Tin Drum*, which catapulted him to fame after its publication in 1959. Grass participated in Gruppe 47 until its last meeting in 1967.

In the elections of 1961, Grass actively took up the cause of the Social Democrats and campaigned intensively for Willy Brandt, former mayor of West Berlin and chancellor of the Federal Republic of Germany. Grass has drawn frequent criticism from both extreme left and right political groups. He openly criticized the East German government at the East Berlin Writers' Congress and wrote an open letter to the East German writer Anna Seghers after the construction of the Berlin Wall on August 13, 1961. Grass has always been a focal point of political criticism in Germany. He unfailingly reminded post-World War II Germans of their ignoble past, he argued against German reunification, and he angered many Germans with his outspoken critique of German politics in the 1990's, including German treatment of foreigners, West German treatment of East Germans, and human rights in general.

The early phase of Grass's literary career, during the mid-1950's, includes poetry, shorter prose fiction, and absurdist dramas, although it was also during these early years that he wrote *The Tin Drum*. His first

collection of poetry, *Die Vorzüge der Windhühner*, appeared in 1956. He also won third prize in a poetry contest sponsored by the South German Radio in 1954. In 1956 he first exhibited his drawings in Stuttgart; in 1957 his sculpture and drawings were exhibited in Berlin. In 1957 *Flood* had its premiere in Frankfurt, and a ballet, *Stoffreste*, also enjoyed its first performance, in Essen. Further absurdist dramatic works appeared in rapid succession: *Mister, Mister* in 1958 in Cologne, and in 1959 two plays (*Only Ten Minutes to Buffalo* and *Zweiunddreißig Zähne*), a ballet (*Fünf Köche*), and a farce (*Rocking Back and Forth*, in Frankfurt and Hamburg). A poetry collection. *Gleisdreieck*, with illustrations by the author, appeared in 1960. With the publication in 1961 of *Katz und Maus* (*Cat and Mouse*, 1963) and in 1963 of *Hundejahre* (*Dog Years*, 1965)—which together with *The Tin Drum* constitute the *Danzig Trilogy*—Grass firmly established himself as the leading German novelist since World War II. In 1961 the drama *The Wicked Cooks* premiered, while another drama *Goldmäulchen* was first performed as a radio play in 1963, premiered as a stage work in 1964 in Munich, and received a second run in 1968 in Berlin. Grass also revised *Mister, Mister* during these early 1960's before its publication in 1965.

Grass's engagement with the theater continued into the 1960's with a short play, *Mystisch-barbarisch-gelangweilt* (mystic, barbaric, and bored), a dramatization of the chapter "Inspection of Concrete" from *The Tin Drum*, which was produced in 1963 in Düsseldorf. His political drama about the 1961 campaign with Willi Brandt, *POUM: Oder, Die Vergangenheit fliegt mit* (POUM, or, the past is a fellow passenger), was published twice in 1965. Grass's play *Max* premiered in 1969 at the Schiller Theater, Berlin, while his ballet, *Die Vogelscheuchen* (the scarecrows), a dramatization from *Dog Years*, also enjoyed its premiere in Berlin in 1970.

Grass's career in the 1960's was characterized by increased political activity, reflected in such works as *The Plebeians Rehearse the Uprising*, the novel *Örtlich betäubt* (1969; *Local Anesthetic*, 1969), and poems from his collection *Ausgefragt* (1967; *New Poems*, 1968). The tale *Aus dem Tagebuch einer*

Schnecke (1972; *From the Diary of a Snail*, 1973) is a transitional work in that the author employs a relatively new narrative technique—one that anticipates subsequent works—while simultaneously drawing on themes from earlier novels. Grass discusses here the elections of 1969 that led to Willy Brandt's victory as well as the treatment of Jews during World War II and the Third Reich, both in relation to the postwar Federal Republic of Germany. After the publication of this work and until the appearance of his next long novel, *Der Butt* (1977; *The Flounder*, 1978), Grass withdrew from the public eye and concentrated on lyric poetry and graphic art. This period in the mid-1970's might be compared to the similar one during the mid-1950's before the publication of *The Tin Drum*.

The publication of *The Flounder* in 1977 reaffirmed Grass's position as the leading contemporary German novelist. In the earlier *Danzig Trilogy*, Grass used several narrators to relate different perspectives of German-speaking lands under Nazi domination. In these works the narrator looks back from the 1950's and early 1960's to the time just before, during, and after World War II. In *The Flounder*, Grass employs a radically new narrative technique: He has a single first-person narrator tell his story from the Stone Age until the 1970's. In rapid succession appeared *Das Treffen in Telgte* (1979; *The Meeting at Telgte*, 1981) and *Kopfgeburten: Oder, Die Deutschen sterben aus* (1980; *Headbirths: Or, The Germans Are Dying Out*, 1982). *The Meeting at Telgte* is the expansion from *The Flounder* of a chapter that occurs during the Thirty Years' War. The fanciful meeting of baroque poets in 1647 at Telgte is an imaginative analogue to the initial meeting of twentieth century poets in 1947 as the Gruppe 47. *Headbirths* discusses other, more contemporary political issues raised in *The Flounder*. Because *The Flounder* is formally divided into nine months from the conception of a child in October, 1973, until its birth in the summer of 1974, this birth is a physical parallel to the subsequent intellectual, or "head," birth. Grass illustrated a volume of poems, *Ach Butt, dein Märchen geht böse aus* (1983), a lyric and artistic treatment of themes from *The Flounder*. Grass's novel *Die Rätten* (1986; *The Rat*, 1987) con-

tinues and elaborates on narrative techniques and themes begun in *The Flounder*.

Grass remained a prolific writer during the 1990's with a series of works reflecting on the German past and present: *Wider das dumpfe Einheitsgebot* (1990; *Two States—One Nation?*, 1990), *Unkenrufe* (1992; *The Call of the Toad*, 1992), *Ein weites Feld* (1995; *Too Far Afield*, 2000), and *Mein Jahrhundert* (1999; *My Century*, 1999). *The Call of the Toad* takes up the possibilities offered by German reunification with its action beginning one week after November 9, 1989, the day the Berlin Wall came down. Grass explores here environmental issues, German-Polish relations (Grass was born in Danzig and his mother was a Kaschubian, a Polish minority), German national borders, emigration from beyond Europe, and the racial tensions between Europeans and non-Europeans. These modern themes are woven together with ideas and characters from earlier works, and he presents the time frames of the novel in a tripartite manner, thus embarking on yet another highly original innovation in narrative structure. In *Too Far Afield*, which is narrated by a team of archivists, Grass directly addresses the problems and issues of German reunification that he found most troubling. The novel was greeted by an intense wave of criticism and condemnation, and the novel itself soon took backseat to the debate it provoked. Grass's last major prose work of the twentieth century, *My Century*, provides a mix of autobiographical sketches with fictional memoirs in one hundred short chapters, one for each year from 1900 through 1999.

Grass has remained an active artist in other media as well, publishing poetry, nonfiction, and graphic works, including *Zeichen und Schreiben II* (1984; signs and writings), *In Kupfer, auf Stein Werkverzeichnis der Radierungen und Lithographien* (1986, in copper, on stone, catalog of the engravings and lithographs), *Zunge Zeigen* (1988; *Show Your Tongue*, 1989), *Mit Sophie in die Pilze gehen* (1988; hunting for mushrooms with Sophie), *Calcutta* (1988), *Skizzenbuch* (1989; sketchbook), and *Kahlschlag in unseren Köpfen* (1990; lithographs). He also has continued to publish essays and shorter pieces.

Together with Günter "Baby" Sommer, Grass produced, performed, and recorded *Es war einmal ein*

Land (1987; once upon a time there was a country) and *Da sagte der Butt* (1993, then the flounder said), excerpts from *The Tin Drum* and *The Rat*, for lyrics and percussion. A second collaboration between Grass and Sommer appeared on two cassettes under the title *Wer da lacht, hat gelacht* (1988, whoever is laughing, has laughed) from *The Tin Drum, Dog Years*, and *The Rat*). Grass also recorded himself reading both *Brief aus Altdöbern* ("letter from Altdöbern") and the entire *The Tin Drum*, as he read it in Göttingen in 1990, on cassette (1991). Grass's involvement with several facets of the theater and the publication of himself reading from his works involves performance on a variety of levels and is a neglected aspect of his œuvre.

His first marriage to Anna Margareta Schwarz, a Swiss ballet dancer with whom he had four children, ended in divorce; his daughter Helene with Veronika Schröter, to whom his novel *The Flounder* is dedicated and whose prenatal development and birth is outlined in that novel, was born in 1974; Grass married the musician Ute Grunert in 1979.

ANALYSIS

Few modern writers exhibit the scope, diversity, and depth of artistic production of Günter Grass. As a playwright he provides witty dialogues and clever situations as well as black humor, and his use of theatrical techniques is adept. Together with his novels, poetry, and graphics, Grass's plays constitute an œuvre that is unsurpassed in postwar German literature.

Grass's preoccupation with dramatic forms—plays and ballets—predates and partially overlaps with his early novels, which have earned him enduring literary fame. His dramatic works developed over the years, and their genesis usually predates their first production by a year or two. Therefore, like his enduring occupation with lyric poetry and the graphic arts, these plays deserve critical attention as the crucibles in which his later monumental narratives were first formed. Grass's dramas demonstrate his literary and graphic œuvre to be an organic, if often surprising, whole, in which thought patterns and ideas are reshaped, recycled, and reconstituted. The seeds of many later episodes, characters, and ideas in his nov-

els and political essays can be found first in the dramatic works.

Grass's plays were performed in important regional theaters such as Munich, Frankfurt, Cologne, Hamburg, and Bochum, and broadcast on the radio. Three of his plays, *The Wicked Cooks, The Plebeians Rehearse the Uprising*, and *Max*, and his ballet *Die Vogelscheuchen* had their premiere in Berlin. Some of his plays were considerably reworked over a long period from their first genesis to the performance version to final publication. The collected works of Grass in German (*Werkausgabe*, 1987), published in honor of his sixtieth birthday, contain eleven plays. Although almost all his major works have appeared in English translation, there is no complete English edition.

The characteristic feature of Grass's plays is the extreme lack of action. Nothing, or very little, happens, thus focusing the viewer's attention on the ideas and structures rather than the plot. Often his plays feature a play-within-a-play. Because many of Grass's plays were first published in literary magazines, much clarity about the origins, the first publications, and performance history of Grass's plays has been provided by the final volume of his German collected works with its commendable scholarly apparatus.

Grass's polyhistorical interests permeate all aspects of his artistic production, both graphic and literary. The dramas demonstrate the author's command of form as expressed in the idiom of the theater and, by comparison to his other works, the control and manipulation of content. All of his plays experiment with traditional dramatic elements, themes, and structures. Grass's plays have met with only limited success, a fact that might be attributed to the topical nature of the plays, to the dearth of any real action and the focus on verbal argument, and to their inherent tendency to be nondramatic. For example, temporal as well as geographic proximity of themes in *The Plebeians Rehearse the Uprising* and *Max*—Bertolt Brecht, the revolt of 1953, the Berlin Wall, student rebellions—may have prompted the initially mixed reception of these works.

His dramatic works are generally divided into two categories. The earlier group, which includes *Flood,*

Mister, Mister, Only Ten Minutes to Buffalo, and *The Wicked Cooks*, features the absurd or grotesque, and *The Plebeians Rehearse the Uprising* and *Max* represent the new dramaturgical impetus of dialectical theater in the Brechtian sense. The two groups are distinct in the treatment of thematic material as well as in dramatic elements and structures. In all the plays, however, there is a marked tendency to avoid dramatic situations and the resolution of the plot in a traditional manner. The author refuses to provide any answers to the many provocative questions posed in his dramatic works.

Grass himself relegated the early plays to the category of "poetic" theater, a designation that reflects the integral relationship of his early lyrics and plays. Poems that bear the same name or that treat themes similar to those of the corresponding drama exist in many instances. Grass explains his procedure in this way:

> And so the transition from poetry to drama happened like this: poems were written in dialogue form, and were then extended. That was shortly after the war. Then slowly, gradually, stage directions were added, and so, parallel with my main occupation at that time, sculpture, I evolved my first play. That is why in a relatively short time, between 1954 and 1957, I wrote four full-length and two one-act plays, which, just like my poems and my prose, contain fantastic and realistic elements; these fantastic and realistic elements rub against each other and keep each other in check.

FLOOD

The two-act play *Flood* depicts humankind's uncanny ability to deal nonchalantly with periodic catastrophe and the inability to learn anything at all from this experience. Noah, together with his sister-in-law Betty, moves his cherished collection of antique inkwells to a higher story; she, in turn, is worried about her photo collection. Noah's daughter, Jutta, and her fiancé, Henn, are listless youths, too bored to help or even to make love. The arrival of the aggressive duo, Leo (Noah's son) and Kongo (Leo's friend and an erstwhile boxer), from out of a packing crate catalyzes the situation. Leo and Kongo force Henn out on the roof, where a pair of wise rats, Strich

and Perle (their names allude to rain), observe and comment on history and human behavior. Henn is not at all perturbed by Jutta's liaison with Kongo; everyone is aware that their attraction for each other will last only as long as the flood.

Meanwhile, Noah naps and Betty sews parasols for the sunny weather ahead. What strikes the audience is that no one is worried about the rain and the rising water, no one considers the imminent peril; all are content to wait until their previous lifestyles can be resumed. The notion of rats abandoning a sinking ship receives an ironic twist: Here the wise rats, who suspect a return to normality and therefore to rattraps, embark for Hamelin as soon as the water recedes. Henn returns to Jutta, Noah sees to his inkwells, and Leo and Kongo depart for Liverpool (or maybe the North Pole), taking along Noah's grandfather clock, from which emerges an official insurance inspector, who is anxious to assess the damages incurred during the flood.

Biblical elements and their parodies abound: Noah, the dove with some "weeds" in its beak, the dove on the armband of the insurance assessor, the cyclical rain and high waters versus the biblical flood, and the moldy rainbow that whets the rats' appetite. The unusual juxtaposition of persons, objects, and animals, typical of Grass's early works, returns to "normal" after the flood. The play points to the absurdity of human behavior in the face of disaster—with a minimum amount of action. As in *Rocking Back and Forth*, there is emphasis on motion leading nowhere—back and forth, up and down the stairs to avoid the rising water.

ONLY TEN MINUTES TO BUFFALO

In *Only Ten Minutes to Buffalo*, Grass similarly flouts the tradition of forward-moving motion of the plot and action. The countdown to only ten minutes to Buffalo contrasts starkly to the immobility of the rusty locomotive in an alpine meadow. The marine terminology used by Krudewil and Pempelfort in their train, which is presumed to be speeding toward Buffalo, is further underscored by the painter Kotschenreuter's nautical scene as well as his conversation with the cowherd, Axel, in which he maintains that language is arbitrary and distinctions between "cow, ship, professor, and buttercup" must be seen as mere conventions. The nautical tone is appropriate to the title of the play, a literary spoof on Theodor Fontane's ballad *John Maynard* about a Lake Erie boat captain who, at the cost of his own life, saves his passengers. As it happens, the two men on the locomotive encounter Fregate, their former captain, a tough woman smoking three cigars, and together they row across the meadow. Axel, however, realizes the true artistic potential of the scene and climbs into the locomotive, which promptly chugs away.

ZWEIUNDDREIβIG ZÄHNE

Zweiunddreißig Zähne (thirty-two teeth), a farce in five acts, involves a main character, Ernst Friböse, who has a doppelgänger who emerges out from under his bed or from behind his back. Both Ernst and his double teach night classes, but one reads the works of the Enlightenment educator Pestalozzi and the other reads crime novels. His compulsive cleanliness is owing to an unclear connection to Nazi gas chambers. The title of the play is a reference to Friböse's neurosis about the possibility of someone else using his toothbrush.

ROCKING BACK AND FORTH

Rocking Back and Forth, which premiered in Hamburg in 1959, bears the subtitle "A Prelude on the Theater," a direct allusion to Johann Wolfgang von Goethe's *Faust: Eine Tragödie* (pb. 1808, pb. 1833; *The Tragedy of Faust*, 1823, 1828). In this static play a clown rocks back and forth on a rocking horse. Through a series of comic episodes in which a Playwright and a Critic try to bring conventional plot lines (a love interest, for example) onstage, the clown, like Oskar Matzerath of *The Tin Drum*, maintains an unwavering infantile viewpoint. By remaining on his rocking horse, the Clown demonstrates his awareness of the absurdity of the world. He can make no progress, regardless of how hard he tries; a vision of disaster abruptly ends the play.

MISTER, MISTER

Mister, Mister reflects Grass's return to a more strictly composed drama, although the theme is nevertheless absurd and grotesque. Each of the four acts is preceded by a prologue. Two tough inner-city kids, Sprotte and Jannemann, also serve to structure the

work, which concerns a serial murderer, Bollin, whom none of his intended victims takes seriously. In the first prologue, Sprotte and Jannemann accost Bollin as he sits on a park bench. Their singsong encounter with him anticipates several macabre aspects of the play. They do not accept candy from him, not because he is a stranger but because they want something else. Their mindless aggression is reminiscent of the corrupt and violent duo Leo and Kongo from *Flood*. The pair taunt Bollin: "Mister, mister, aintcha got a thing, aintcha got a thing . . . maybe in your pocket."

The play proper consists of Bollin's encounter with prospective victims. None of them is in the least perturbed by his appearance. In fact, the adults seem even flattered to be chosen by this notorious killer. In the last act, Bollin appears much older, more decrepit, and somewhat lame. Usually a loner, he has agreed to meet an accomplice to stake out a potential victim. While he lurks outside waiting for his rendezvous, Sprotte and Jannemann persuade Bollin to give them first his pen, then his watch, and finally his revolver. Jannemann inadvertently fires the gun and kills Bollin. Further associations of sex and violence become manifest, as Sprotte and Jannemann run off to have sex. Based on their sexual misinformation, it seems that they have little sexual experience.

The four prologues perform an expository function, as structural elements incorporating the Sprotte-Jannemann plot and revealing the blacker and more abstract elements of the protagonist's nature. For example, in the second prologue, Bollin twice stabs and repairs the doll Pinkie, stolen from a sick girl, one of the intended victims who unwittingly thwarted the planned molestation and murder. He then hangs the doll on a hook and shoots it. Bollin's grotesque methodology and penchant for systematic detail echo Nazi tactics. As a serial murderer, he has enjoyed numerous past successes, yet all current attempts fail. He himself is carelessly killed by two children who rely on no system. His methodological ideology dies with him.

THE WICKED COOKS

In *The Wicked Cooks*, Grass's characteristic gastronomical motifs are applied to the nature of the artist. Themes related to food and cooking occur throughout his fiction and poetry. The art of cooking is transformed into a metaphor for art itself, and the cook becomes identical with the artist. In the play, Herbert Schymanski, the Count, has learned to cook a certain gray soup. The wicked cooks—Petri, Vasco, Grün, Stach, and Benny—try to force the Count to give them the recipe. A competing band of cooks, led by one Kletterer, attempts to get the recipe first and disrupt a party that Vasco's fiancée, Martha, is forced to attend. The cooks suggest an exchange: love for the recipe. Martha goes with the Count, and he promises to give them the recipe at a later date. The situation becomes problematic when the Count's sexual encounter causes him to forget the recipe. The cooks threaten the pair; the Count and Martha commit suicide.

The recipe can be interpreted as a symbolic formula for artistic creativity that simply cannot be transferred. The Count's behavior can also be seen as active resistance to the unscrupulous methods of the cooks. At the first performance of the play, the actor portraying the Count wore a mask in the likeness of Grass, a theatrical interpretation that supports the contention that the play represents the artistic dilemma of an author.

GOLDMÄULCHEN

Goldmäulchen (little golden mouth) was first produced in 1963 as a radio play for the Hessian Radio and premiered in 1964 onstage in Munich. This absurdist play seriously reworks similar material from "The Hundredth Publicly Discussed Materniad" of *Dog Years*, in which the perfidious Walter Matern both discusses and is the object of discussion. The title refers to Matern's opposite in the novel, the young half-Jewish artist Amsel, who lost all thirty-two of his teeth in a beating by masked thugs, among them his former friend Matern. Sometime later in the novel Amsel appears in Berlin with a new passport under the name Herman Haseloff and at a dental clinic gets thirty-two gold teeth, which earns him the sobriquet "Little Golden Mouth." Grass also reworked and produced other dramatic works from his novels during this same period. *Mystisch-barbarisch-gelangweilt* (1963) is a dramatization of the chapter "Inspection

of Concrete, or Barbaric, Mystic, Bored" from book 2 of *The Tin Drum*. *Die Vogelscheuchen*, dating from 1957, is a ballet from *Dog Years* that was first produced in 1970 with music by Aribert Reimann. Grass's dramatic adaptations of themes and motifs from his novels concerning the immediate German past attest to his high level of productivity in the late 1950's and early 1960's and to his continuing preoccupation with political and social themes into the 1970's.

POUM

POUM: Oder, Die Vergangenheit fliegt mit is a political one-act play about an airplane trip by the Candidate (clearly Will Brandt) and the Writer (Grass himself). Although the Writer finds the campaign trail strenuous, he can contribute to politics by improving the speeches of his Candidate. POUM is the abbreviation for the "Partido Obrero de Unificación Marxista," a left-wing Spanish workers' party.

THE PLEBEIANS REHEARSE THE UPRISING

The Plebeians Rehearse the Uprising relates fictive events around a historical occasion, a revolt on June 17, 1953, in the Soviet sector of Berlin (formerly East Berlin). Grass takes up the theme of the politically engaged artist as the focus of this four-act drama. Many characteristics of the theater director "Boss" allude to Bertolt Brecht, who was director of the Theater am Schiffbauerdamm. As the fictitious theater ensemble rehearses the Boss's adaptation of William Shakespeare's *Coriolanus* (pr. c. 1607-1608), the plebeians, who have the function of messengers, enter the theater from the outside and report various stages of the revolt. There is little physical action in the play; the verbal arguments for and against the rebellion provide the focus of the drama, which bears the subtitle "A German Tragedy."

Early reception of the play reflected only moderate success. Many critics saw it merely as an anti-Brecht play or a documentary drama. Although Grass does attempt to assimilate the Brechtian legacy here, the Boss represents not only Brecht but also the position of many Marxist intellectuals. The fact that most of the *dramatis personae* do not have personal names but are known by their functions (Boss, Bricklayer) or by their roles in the Shakespeare play (Volumnia,

Flavis) is an indication that the play-within-the-play is meant to serve as a model. The realities of the revolt and the play, of Berlin and Rome, overlap. Only as the Shakespeare production progresses does it occur to the Boss that the actual, unrehearsed uprising, which he gives little chance for success, poses grave questions for his theater and his rehearsed revolt. With the noble intentions of a liberal intellectual, the Boss had wanted to enlighten the workers through theater, to show them how to make a revolution. As the drama closes, the Boss admits that Shakespeare cannot be adapted or changed unless people themselves change. The Boss fails, not because he does not provide the workers with a manifesto, but because he cannot give them his theoretical knowledge of revolution. The Boss, the only character who is correct in his estimation of the uprising, is morally wrong. He has failed all those who have pinned their hopes on him in the expectation that a single renowned public figure might change the historical process. The Boss abandons his production and goes to the country to write poetry. In Shakespeare's *Coriolanus*, the protagonist is not a plebeian but a friend of the patricians. Brecht's adaptation idealizes the plebeians, who triumph. In view of Grass's own literary production and growing political involvement at the time, the play emerges as a statement about the dilemma of the politically involved artist.

MAX

Max, a play in thirteen scenes, derives from Grass's novel *Local Anesthetic*, but it takes the perspective of the Dentist, a teacher named Eberhard Starusch, and his pupil Philipp "Flip" Scherbaum. The dramatic core of the play is not action itself but discourse about an action. Should Flip protest the use of napalm in Vietnam by burning his dog Max in front of the café at the Hotel Kempinski and disgust the well-heeled, overweight Berlin women, known for their love of canines and cake? Flip's Maoist girlfriend, Vero, encourages him to act. The Dentist and another teacher, Fräulein Seifert, also support his decision to burn the dog, not because they approve of or believe in his own protest but because they want him to act vicariously on their behalf. The various scenes of the drama represent Starusch's attempt to dissuade

his student. In the end Flip does not burn the dog, and he assumes the editorship of the school paper. Vero, who boycotts the first editorial meeting, vows to go to the Hotel Kempinski and eat cake in her own protest.

OTHER MAJOR WORKS

LONG FICTION: *Die Blechtrommel*, 1959 (*The Tin Drum*, 1961); *Katz und Maus*, 1961 (*Cat and Mouse*, 1963); *Hundejahre*, 1963 (*Dog Years*, 1965); *Örtlich betäubt*, 1969 (*Local Anesthetic*, 1969); *Aus dem Tagebuch einer Schnecke*, 1972 (*From the Diary of a Snail*, 1973); *Der Butt*, 1977 (*The Flounder*, 1978); *Das Treffen in Telgte*, 1979 (*The Meeting at Telgte*, 1981); *Danziger Trilogie*, 1980 (*Danzig Trilogy*, 1987; includes *The Tin Drum*, *Cat and Mouse*, and *Dog Years*); *Kopfgeburten: Oder, Die Deutschen sterben aus*, 1980 (*Headbirths: Or, The Germans Are Dying Out*, 1982); *Die Rättin*, 1986 (*The Rat*, 1987); *Unkenrufe*, 1992 (*The Call of the Toad*, 1992); *Ein weites Feld*, 1995 (*Too Far Afield*, 2000); *Mein Jahrhundert*, 1999 (*My Century*, 1999); *Im Krebsgang*, 2002 (*Crabwalk*, 2003).

POETRY: *Die Vorzüge der Windhühner*, 1956; *Gleisdreieck*, 1960; *Selected Poems*, 1966 (includes poems from *Die Vorzügie der Windhühner* and *Gleisdreieck*); *Ausgefragt*, 1967 (*New Poems*, 1968); *Poems of Günter Grass*, 1969 (includes *Selected Poems* and *New Poems*; also in a bilingual edition as *In the Egg and Other Poems*, 1977); *Gesammelte Gedichte*, 1971 (includes *Die Vorzüge der Windhühner* and *Gleisdreieck*); *Mariazuehren, Hommageàmarie, Inmarypraise*, 1973 (trilingual edition); *Liebe geprüft*, 1974 (*Love Tested*, 1975); *Die Gedichte, 1955-1986*, 1988; *Novemberland: Selected Poems, 1956-1993*, 1996 (bilingual edition).

NONFICTION: *Über das Selbstverständliche*, 1968 (partial translation *Speak Out!*, 1969); *Über meinen Lehrer Döblin und andere Vorträge*, 1968; *Der Bürger und seine Stimme*, 1974; *Denkzettel: Politische Reden und Aufsätze 1965-76*, 1978; *Aufsätze zur Literatur*, 1980; *Widerstand lernen: Politische Gegenreden, 1980-1983*, 1984; *Zunge Zeigen*, 1988 (*Show Your Tongue*, 1989); *Skizzenbuch*, 1989; *Deutscher Lastenausgleich: Wider das dumpfe Einheitsgebot*, 1990 (*Two States—One Nation?*, 1990); *Ein Schnappchen*

namens DDR: Letzte Reden vorm Glockengelaut,
1990; *Schreiben nach Auschwitz: Frankfurter Poetik-*
Vorlesung, 1990; *Totes Holz: Ein Nachruf,* 1990;
Gegen die verstreichende Zeit: Reden, Aufsätze und
Gespräche, 1989-1991, 1991; *Günter Grass, vier*
Jahrzehnte, 1991; *Rede vom Verlust: Über den Nie-*
dergang der politischen Kultur im geeinten Deutsch-
land, 1992 (*The Future of German Democracy,* 1993);
Angestiftet, Partei zu ergreifen, 1994; *Die Deutschen*
und ihre Dichter, 1995; *Gestern, vor 50 Jahren: Ein*
deutsch-japanischer Briefwechsel, 1995; *Fünf Jahr-*
zenhnte: Ein Werkstattbericht, 2001.

MISCELLANEOUS: *Werkausgabe,* 1987 (10 volumes); *Cat and Mouse and Other Writings,* 1994.

BIBLIOGRAPHY

Cunliffe, W. Gordon. *Günter Grass.* New York:
Twayne, 1969. Still provides the best introduction
to the early Grass works. The chapter "Grass and
the Theater of the Absurd" remains very useful,
treating *Rocking Back and Forth, Flood, Mister,*
Mister, Only Ten Minutes to Buffalo, and *The*
Wicked Cooks with a brief mention of *Zweiund-*
dreißig Zähne.

Hayman, Ronald. *Günter Grass.* London: Methuen,
1985. Provides a brief overview of Grass's life and
works. The first chapter, "Puppets and Ballerinas,"
is useful for understanding his dramas.

Hollington, Michael. *Günter Grass: The Writer in a*
Pluralist Society. London: Boyars, 1980. A good
introduction to Grass up to *Das Treffen in Telgte*
(1979; *The Meeting at Telgte,* 1981). Includes a
short chapter outlining the four plays that appeared in English in 1967.

Keele, Alan Frank. *Understanding Günter Grass.* Columbia: University of South Carolina Press, 1988.
A text for students and nonacademic readers that
provides a good outline of Grass's major works.
Includes a short chapter on the plays and poems.

Lawson, Richard. *Günter Grass.* New York: Unger,
1985. Contains a short chapter on the plays, which
is the best English-language introduction.

O'Neill, Patrick. *Critical Essays on Günter Grass.*
Boston: G. K. Hall, 1987. A collection in English
of nine reviews of English translations of Grass's
works and thirteen critical essays. One review and
one essay focus on a single play, *The Plebeians*
Rehearse the Uprising, and the rest center on his
novels. Includes a bibliography of works about
Grass in English.

_____. *Günter Grass Revisited.* New York: Twayne,
1999. Contains a good overview of the author's
life and works and a short chapter on the early absurdist plays *Flood, Mister, Mister,* and *The Wicked*
Cooks.

Preece, Julian. *The Life and Work of Günter Grass*
Literature, History, Politics. Basingstoke, England:
Palgrave, 2001. A scholarly monograph providing
an excellent overview of Grass's life, work (in
particular, the novels), political development, and
literary productions from the 1960's through 2000
while placing him in a social and historical context. Although there is no separate chapter devoted to the plays, most of them are discussed.

Thomas, Noel. *The Narrative Work of Günter Grass:*
A Critical Interpretation. Amsterdam/Philadelphia:
Benjamins, 1982. Eight chapters—one each on
The Tin Drum, Cat and Mouse, Dog Years, Local
Anesthetic, From the Diary of a Snail, The Floun-
der, The Meeting at Telgte, and *Headbirths*—
provide an interpretation of Grass's novels. There
is no introduction, conclusion, or index.

White, Ray Lewis. *Günter Grass in America: The*
Early Years. Hildesheim/ New York: Olms, 1981.
A collection of reviews of Grass's works, includ-
ing a short chapter of reviews of *The Plebeians*
Rehearse the Uprising from U.S. sources.

Mara R. Wade

SIMON GRAY

Born: Hayling Island, England; October 21, 1936

PRINCIPAL DRAMA

Wise Child, pr. 1967, pb. 1968

Spoiled, pr. 1968 (televised) pr. 1970 (staged), pb. 1971

Dutch Uncle, pr., pb. 1969

The Idiot, pr. 1970, pb. 1971 (adaptation of Fyodor Dostoevski's novel)

Butley, pr., pb. 1971

Dog Days, pr. 1975, pb. 1976

Otherwise Engaged, pr., pb. 1975

Molly, pr. 1977, pb. 1978 (revision of Gray's television play *Death of a Teddy Bear*)

The Rear Column, pr., pb. 1978

Close of Play, pr., pb. 1979

Stage Struck, pr., pb. 1979

Quartermaine's Terms, pr., pb. 1981

Tartuffe, pr. 1982, pb. 1990 (adaptation of Molière's play)

The Common Pursuit, pr., pb. 1984

Otherwise Engaged and Other Plays, pb. 1984

The Rear Column and Other Plays, pb. 1985

Plays: One, pb. 1986

Melon, pr., pb. 1987 (revised as *The Holy Terror*, pr. 1989 [radio play], pb. 1990, pr. 1991 [staged])

Hidden Laughter, pr. 1989, pb. 1990

The Definitive Simon Gray, pb. 1992-1994 (4 volumes)

Cell Mates, pr., pb. 1995

Simply Disconnected, pr., pb. 1996

Just the Three of Us, pr. 1997, pb. 1999

Life Support, pr., pb. 1997

The Late Middle Classes, pr., pb. 1999

Japes, pr., pb. 2000

OTHER LITERARY FORMS

Simon Gray is primarily known as a stage dramatist, but he began his playwriting career as an author of television scripts, including *The Caramel Crisis* (1966), *Death of a Teddy Bear* (1967), *A Way with the Ladies* (1967), *Sleeping Dog* (1967), *Pig in a Poke* (1969), *The Dirt on Lucy Lane* (1969), *Style of the Countess* (1970), *The Princess* (1970), and *Man in a Sidecar* (1971).

Besides being a successful dramatist, Gray has also published novels: *Colmain* (1963), *Simple People* (1965), *Little Portia* (1967), *A Comeback for Stark* (1968; under the pseudonym Hamish Reade), and *Breaking Hearts* (1997). Gray has also used the pen name James Holliday. Gray became editor of *Delta* magazine in 1964, and he coedited with Keith Walker an anthology entitled *Selected English Prose* that was published in 1967.

In 1975, the playwright wrote the screenplay version of his play for the film *Butley*, directed by Harold Pinter and starring Alan Bates, re-creating his stage role as the title character. The movie was made as part of the American Film Theatre series.

ACHIEVEMENTS

Simon Gray has received many of the highest awards for dramatists. *Death of a Teddy Bear* won a Writers Guild Award, *Butley* received the *Evening Standard* (London) Award for Best Play of the Year in 1972, and *Otherwise Engaged* was voted Best Play by the New York Drama Critics Circle. Moreover, the filming of *Butley* and the option taken to film *Death of a Teddy Bear* are indicators of the dramatist's popularity.

BIOGRAPHY

Simon Gray was born on Hayling Island, Hampshire, England, on October 21, 1936, the son of James Davidson and Barbara Celia Mary (née Holliday) Gray. The elder Gray was a pathologist and first-generation Canadian of Scottish ancestry, and when World War II began, Simon Gray was sent from Great Britain to his grandparents' home in Montreal. He returned to the United Kingdom for a while after the war and then moved back and forth between England, Canada, France, and Spain. He married Beryl Mary Kevern, a picture researcher, on August 20, 1964, and they had a son and a daughter. The couple divorced, and in 1997, Gray married Victoria Rothschild. He has had bouts with cancer and alcoholism. He has been a recovering alcoholic since 1996, when alcoholism killed his much younger brother, Piers, at the age of forty-nine. This experience shows up in his plays, most particularly in *Japes*.

Gray, a lecturer in English, taught at Trinity College, Cambridge, from 1965 through 1966 and was on the faculty at Queen Mary College of the University of London from 1965 to 1984. This experience, together with his educational background, serves as the source of many of the dramatist's subjects (and characters) and his literate style. He attended the Westminster School in London, and he received a B.A. (honors in English) from Dalhousie University in Canada in 1958, and another B.A. (again with honors in English) from Cambridge University in England in 1962. Between the awarding of his two bachelor's degrees, Gray served as a lecturer at the University in Clermont-Ferrand, France. He resided in France from 1960 to 1961 and in Spain from 1962 to 1963.

In 1987, Gray's play *Melon* was produced in London, and that same year saw the production of his screenplay *A Month in the Country*. *Hidden Laughter* was produced in Brighton in 1989, and in London a year later. *The Holy Terror*, a revision of *Melon*, was broadcast in 1989 on the British Broadcasting Corporation's radio and was published in 1990. The 1991 Arizona production was its premiere as a stage piece.

ANALYSIS

Two important elements in Simon Gray's playwriting career evolved directly from his educational background. The Cambridge experience was clearly an important one. In a sense, when Gray reports, "I went to university when I was seventeen and I never left," he is speaking metaphorically as well as literally. His postgraduate life has been spent in academia, but it is obvious that there are symbolic connections with his everyday life that reappear in his plays. During Gray's tenure at Cambridge, there was an extraordinarily gifted group of other students also in attendance. The intellectual atmosphere was stimu-

lating; a number of undergraduates wrote and acted in satiric revues on campus and then moved on to the London stage immediately afterward (and sometimes even while still pursuing their studies). Peter Cook, a contributor to the immensely successful *Beyond the Fringe* (1959), was one such. Novelist Margaret Drabble, television personality David Frost, actor Derek Jacobi, and Christopher Booker, a cofounder of *Private Eye* magazine, were among Gray's contemporaries. Furthermore, director John Barton was a don at King's College and poet Sylvia Plath lived in the town of Cambridge.

Besides the literary climate of the present and the long line of literati connected with the university in the past, Gray was also exposed to literary and dramatic traditions in his course work. Many of his characters, settings, and plot situations derive from this aspect of his life. The numerous literary allusions that are characteristic of his style are direct outgrowths of Gray's Cambridge experience. Finally, the many references to Cambridge, typically related to the concept of class distinctions, are similarly attributable to this period in his life.

The second element is Gray's experience as a teacher. A number of the aspects of his writing that can be traced to his university days extend to his professional career as well; the origins of several of Gray's dramatic works reflect the attitude of an academic mind.

Unlike many contemporary playwrights who began writing dramas while in college, Gray actually became a dramatist as a young man after he was graduated and while he was trying to write short stories and novels. He had already published two prose volumes, *Colmain* in 1963 and *Simple People* in 1965, when he adapted a short story that was primarily dialogue and sold it as a television script. The piece, entitled *The Caramel Crisis*, was televised in 1966, and within a year *Death of a Teddy Bear*, *A Way with the Ladies*, and *Sleeping Dog* were also televised. *Death of a Teddy Bear* was an award-winning script, and *Sleeping Dog* was well received for its examination of the elements of domination and submission in the British national character (represented by Sir Herbert, a retired colonial administrator, who imprisons Claud, a black homosexual, in the basement of his manor house—the theme of ambiguous sexuality is also introduced).

Gray's plays are interesting, witty, and well structured, and his characters are believably drawn. Furthermore, he uses language well, and it is clear that the use of language in his later works has been influenced by Harold Pinter's dramaturgy, improving an already good product. If Gray's plays lack profound timely significance, they nevertheless excel in stagecraft and technique, and his works have entertained audiences at home in England and abroad. He does not contend that his plays are meant to convey a message, but he does work at his writing rigorously; *Otherwise Engaged*, for example, required thirty-five drafts. Combining this attention to craftsmanship with a flair for witty dialogue, Gray has achieved both critical acclaim and popular acceptance.

Gray has had his difficulties with the theater establishment, despite the abiding commitment that director Pinter and actor Bates have invested in his work. He documents these difficulties in books such as *Fat Chance* (1995), which chronicles his exasperating experience with his play *Cell Mates* when the star actor, Stephen Fry, walked off the cast after the first week of its run in the West End and doomed the play just as it was gaining momentum. In 2001, he published *Enter a Fox*, which details the journey and problems associated with the production of his play *The Late Middle Classes*, killed in out-of-town tryouts. Gray speaks of *Japes*, produced in 2000, as perhaps his last play. He has always moved on to a new play before, but, he says, the drive seems to have gone out of him. Beyond such difficulties, Gray's commitment to a theater rich in language, realistic in style, and highly structured in linear fashion runs counter to trends of the last decades of the twentieth century. Nevertheless, his characters are stunningly spectacular. They are riveting and memorable because of their obsessions, their abuse of one another, their wit, and ultimately their own self-destructive natures.

WISE CHILD

Wise Child was written for television, too, but it was reportedly considered "too bizarre for home viewing," and it became Gray's first play to be staged in the theater (at the Wyndham on October 10, 1967). The play is usually considered Gray's best early effort, and it has been favorably compared with the work of Joe Orton. The plot revolves around a criminal who is wanted for a brutal mail robbery and is hiding from the police by disguising himself as a woman (creating a sort of black comedy version of Brandon Thomas' 1896 farce *Charley's Aunt*) while his accomplice poses as his son. After the pair murder their homosexual landlord, the older man reverts to wearing men's clothing, and the younger man dons the maid's clothes. Gray was fortunate that one of the finest actors of all time, Sir Alec Guinness, took the lead role. The "son's" part was played by Simon Ward, who would appear in later plays by Gray. Harold Hobson, drama critic for the London *Sunday Times*, was impressed by the piece.

DUTCH UNCLE

Dutch Uncle followed *Wise Child* and was considerably less successful. Mounted by the Royal Shakespeare Company at the Old Vic in London, the drama shows the academic turn of mind characteristic of Gray's later works. The play was inspired by the case of police constable Reginald Christie, a mass murderer who did away with his wife, the wife of his upstairs lodger, and several other women. (Christie walled up the corpses in his kitchen. Gray's play *Death of a Teddy Bear*, written a few years earlier, was similarly based on an actual murder case.) In *Dutch Uncle*, the main character, Mr. Godboy, tries to murder his wife to attract the attention of Inspector "Manly" Hawkins. His motivation is a homosexual obsession for the police officer. Unfortunately for Godboy, he proves ineffectual as a murderer—his wife blissfully and unknowingly avoids his trap—and when the inspector finally becomes interested in the household, it is because the upstairs tenant is the Merritt Street rapist. The play was not well received, and Gray himself described it as a failure "as witless as it was macabre. . . . [It] would goad an audience into an irritated restlessness." He goes on to claim that the London opening was "the worst night in the British theatre." Nevertheless, the husband's distaste for his role as a husband and the dramatist's exploration of the themes of domination and submission (also dealt with in *Wise Child*) mark the play as a contemporary work. It was probably these elements that attracted Harold Pinter to Gray's work.

SPOILED

Next came *Spoiled*, a realistic domestic drama that was televised in 1968 and adapted for the stage in 1970. The play, which premiered at the Close Theatre Club in Glasgow, Scotland, on February 4, moved to London's Haymarket Theatre on October 31 of the following year. It is about the relationships among a high school French instructor, his pregnant wife, and a young male student. While tutoring the teenager, the teacher seduces him, and the play evolves into a straightforward study of the "unthinking abuse of trust and power." *Spoiled* also serves as a companion piece to *Butley*; both plays involve student-teacher relationships in an academic setting as well as failed marriages and homosexual activities. There are also some parallels with *Otherwise Engaged*. In contrast with the latter play, however, in which Simon Hench is too detached to be able to maintain a human relationship, Howarth, the teacher in *Spoiled*, falls tragically because he is too emotionally involved.

BUTLEY

Butley, one of Gray's most successful dramas, premiered at the Oxford Playhouse on July 7, 1971, and then moved to the Criterion Theatre in London exactly one week later. The first of Gray's works to be directed by Pinter, it starred Alan Bates in the title role. Subsequently the play moved to the Morosco Theatre in New York City, on October 31, 1972.

All the action in the two-act play takes place in Ben Butley's office in a college of London University. Act 1 opens at ten o'clock in the morning on the first day after the midterm break, and the second act begins about two hours later, "shortly after lunch."

Butley is an English teacher at the university. He shares an office with Joseph Keyston, whom he calls Joey. Joey is also an English instructor, a former student of Butley and his current lover.

From the play's beginning, it is clear what kind of person Butley is—even the office set reflects the nature of his mind. His desk, for example, "is a chaos of papers, books, detritus" in contrast to Joey's neat, almost bare desk. Similarly, Butley's bookcase is "chaotic with old essays and mimeographed sheets scattered among the books." Butley's attitude toward his profession is certainly evident, as is the unsettled state of his mind. The photograph of T. S. Eliot indicates the kind of literature that interests Butley and is a visual reference to the source of some of the literary allusions that embellish Butley's conversations. The smeared and curled corner shows that what was once important enough to Butley that he put it on his wall no longer has his attention and has become damaged (and not repaired) as a result. The lamp that will not work for Butley is further evidence of the lack of connections in his life, the way that things no longer work for him.

Butley's egocentrism and the tactics that he uses to isolate himself from others and from his responsibilities are evident in his very first speech. He tells the head of his department, who has called him on the telephone, that he cannot talk at the moment because he is "right in the middle of a tutorial"—and all the while the audience can plainly see that Butley is sitting alone in his office. In a sense, there is dramatic irony involved here, too, and not only because the audience is aware of something that one of the characters (the caller, in this case) is not. Throughout the play, people try to get in touch with Butley, and he rejects their attempts; he constantly uses the false tutorial excuse to avoid contact. The comic touch of Butley taking a squashed banana from his pocket and throwing the peel on Joey's desk seems to lighten the effect of Butley's lie, but it soon becomes evident that this is merely another indication of Butley's sloppy habits, his lack of consideration for others, and his conscious attempts to belittle everyone. The piece of toilet paper stuck to his chin to stop the blood from a cut sustained while he was shaving is a parallel to the banana. Obviously Butley does not demonstrate much respect for himself, and he shows even less for those with whom he comes in contact.

In the first act, Gray introduces most of the rest of the characters who play major parts in the protagonist's life. In essence, there is no action and no traditional plot. Joey appears first, and through his conversation with Butley, the various levels of their relationship are exposed, as is Butley's estrangement from his wife and the possibility that Butley is about to be replaced in Joey's life by Reg Nuttall.

The word games, wit, literary allusions (often in the form of direct quotations), and cruelty that characterize Butley are also revealed. Butley emerges as a sad, lonely man who wants some sort of relationship with someone, preferably Joey, but who is unable to give enough of himself or accept enough from anyone else to allow them to penetrate his sarcasm to create a truly emotional relationship. Instead, Butley retreats behind a wall of sterile intellectualism.

Miss Heasman, a minor character, makes an appearance, serving as a bit of comic relief (and creating dramatic irony) when Butley purposely misunderstands her request and then lies about her duties (the audience already knows about his treatment of a student with a similar request previously). There is also a confrontation between Butley and his wife, who informs him that she has decided to take up with an acquaintance of theirs.

In his dealings with all of these people, Butley is consistently sarcastic and offensive, he knows where his victims are most vulnerable, and he sticks the knife in with sadistic pleasure and precision. He jokes about homosexuality, frequently by using double entendres or literary allusions. Other literary allusions (to Eliot, William Blake, Gerard Manley Hopkins, and others) provide further insight into Butley's character (unwittingly on his part), as he uses them as weapons. Butley's use of literary allusions is effective because the other characters in the play recognize their sources; this is an essential part of his game playing. Also indicated is the probability that patterns are being repeated, implying that they have all engaged in the activity before—and this is reinforced by Butley's expressed appreciation for good comebacks by his targets. One of the games that he plays revolves around Joey's constant use of the tag "in point of fact." When Joey says that Reg's family lives "in a place just outside Leeds, in point of fact," Butley pretends that he thinks that "point of fact" is the name of a suburb. This becomes a running joke in the play and serves a dual purpose by simulta-

neously drawing attention to Reg's lower-middle-class background. Butley also prepares the audience for the situation concerning Gardner.

In act 2, the only major character not met in act 1 appears when Reg comes to collect Joey (and, incidentally, to make sure that Butley does not adversely influence the younger man's decision to leave). Beyond this, about all that happens is a continuation of the lines self-destructively developed by Butley, leaving him as he was when he first came onstage—alone and ineffectually trying to turn on the lamp. Butley's nonstop allusions (to Eliot, nursery rhymes, John Donne, D. H. Lawrence, John Milton, Sir John Suckling, Richard Lovelace, and Beatrix Potter, among others), his use of a Northern dialect to denigrate Reg's social background—all of this epitomizes his hollowness.

In her essay, Sophia B. Blaydes discusses this important aspect of the writer's technique and demonstrates how the allusions may provide insight into Butley's self-image as an individual "beset by betrayal and mediocrity," a tragic figure rather than the pitiable, "irresponsible, wasted man" that the characters in the play perceive him to be. The truth probably lies somewhere between: Butley is, indeed, surrounded by foolish people, but he cannot see beyond their flaws to their common humanity.

OTHERWISE ENGAGED

Otherwise Engaged, also directed by Pinter and featuring Bates in the part of Simon Hench, was first presented at London's Queen's Theatre on July 30, 1975. In February, 1977, the production was transferred to the Plymouth Theatre in New York City, with Tom Courtenay making his long-awaited Broadway debut in the lead role.

The setting for *Otherwise Engaged* is more elegant than that of *Butley*. As in the earlier play, the action is limited to the events that transpire in one room, in this instance over a period of time equivalent to the running time of the drama. That room is Hench's living room in London. The plot has been described as the depiction of a series of events that occur during an afternoon that Hench wishes to spend listening to a newly acquired phonograph recording of Richard Wagner's opera *Parsifal* and that prevent him from accomplishing his goal; however, this is a bit like saying that *Butley* is about a teacher who is not interested in teaching.

In act 1, Hench, a book publisher, is discovered preparing to listen to his new purchase. He is interrupted by Dave, a dull polytechnic student who is renting a flat from him. This is only the first of a series of interruptions. Hench no sooner gets rid of the young man, who is seeking advice on his love life and money, than Hench's brother, Stephen, enters to expose fears and self-doubts about his professional status. Hench is witty, sociable, and somewhat supportive, but his rather obvious wish is to return to his recording. This pattern is repeated throughout the play.

The next interruption comes in the form of Jeff Golding, a dilettantish literary critic who seems not to be particularly attractive either as a critic or as a person. He confesses, for example, that he does not like literature, and his own description of how he mistreats women is damning. Next, Jeff's current mistress, Davina, appears, searching for her lover, whom she immediately dismisses. After Jeff leaves, Davina tries to seduce Hench. She is unsuccessful, but he does agree to consider for publication a book that she has written.

Hench then records a message on his telephone answering machine to inform anyone who might call that he is "otherwise engaged" for the rest of the day. Bernard Wood enters. Hench and Wood attended Wundale School at the same time, a place where both men engaged in homosexual activities. Wood accuses Hench of seducing his fiancée, Joanna, and Hench admits to the transgression as the curtain falls.

Act 2 opens where act 1 left off; in the continuation it becomes clear that Hench does not consider the seduction as a serious transgression. Wood wants to know if Hench's wife is aware of his activities; the audience soon learns that Mrs. Hench is involved in an affair and that she is considering leaving her husband. Hench finds her choice of partners tasteless but sees the affair, like his, as posing no threat to their marriage. Wood, on the other hand, has a history of being unstable, and he calls to leave a message on the telephone recorder: He is going to shoot himself in

the head because he is despondent about the Hench-Joanna affair, and he wants the act recorded so that Hench can hear it. Hench switches the machine off the instant before Wood squeezes the trigger. The play ends with Jeff returning to sit with Hench, listening to *Parsifal*.

The theme of *Otherwise Engaged* is again that of a man incapable of sustaining human relationships. Unlike Butley, however, Hench does not even seem to desire a meaningful relationship. He is comfortable in his marriage—whether he or his wife, Beth, actually have engaged in affairs is less important to him than his desire that they remain together, mainly because breaking up is a tiresome process, and staying together makes life easier, especially since he does not wish to become emotionally involved with anyone, including his wife, anyway.

There are some contradictory pieces of information provided by the dramatist. In act 1, Hench refuses to be seduced by the attractive Davina, even though she is aggressively willing and he admits that "I fancy you because of your breasts" (which she has exposed by removing her shirt). This scene is in direct contrast with Wood's claim that Hench seduced his fiancée. Additionally, in spite of Stephen's protests to the contrary, Hench does seem to have an interest in his brother's well-being. Finally, there is the ironic counterpointing between Hench's apparent attempts to remain emotionally disengaged from those intruders who surround him and his pleasure (and possibly his retreat) into Wagner's *Parsifal*. Wagner's music is lush and romantic in nature, full-bodied and emotional. If Hench enjoys this kind of music, it would indicate that he, too, has a romantic, emotional nature. His seeming lack of concern for Wood or Beth may stem either from his sense of hurt and betrayal, or from his realization that there may be little that he can do to alter the circumstances, or both. On the other hand, it may well be that he has no feelings for people and that he seeks emotional release in the safety of music—which can make no demands on him and which does not interrupt his privacy. Somewhat like the characters in *Close of Play* four years later, those in *Otherwise Engaged* are so wrapped up in their own problems that they think that all action focuses on them, and they are insensitive to and inconsiderate of others.

Stylistically, the play is entertaining. Gray is at his witty, literate best, and he handles the language masterfully. There are some echoes from Pinter's plays, particularly *The Caretaker* (pr., pb. 1960), *The Collection* (pr. 1961), and *The Homecoming* (pr., pb. 1965), and there are some amusing plot twists. The repetition of certain tags ("Not as stupid as he seems," for example) and other stylistic devices used in *Butley* reappear in *Otherwise Engaged*. Structurally, the interweaving of reappearing characters, motifs (egotism, fidelity, dominance, sexuality, and so forth), and images (drinks thrown in people's faces) all combine to give the play an operatic texture.

CLOSE OF PLAY AND STAGE STRUCK

Gray's subsequent plays did not immediately develop his earlier themes and style. In *Close of Play* (presented at the National Theatre's Lyttleton Theatre in London on May 24, 1979), Gray returned to an intellectual setting of sorts. Jasper, a retired academic, sits silently while his wife, children, grandchildren, and assorted in-laws reveal the desperate nature of their lives. *Close of Play* is a dark, mature drama, yet it breaks no new ground for the playwright. With *Stage Struck* (Vaudeville Theatre, London, November 21, 1979), the dramatist tried his hand at a stage thriller in the vein of Ira Levin's *Deathtrap* (pr. 1978) and Anthony Shaffer's *Sleuth* (pr., pb. 1970).

QUARTERMAINE'S TERMS AND
THE COMMON PURSUIT

In 1981, *Quartermaine's Terms*, his play about an ineffectual upper-class teacher who is fired by his school's new principal, opened at Queen's Theatre, London, on July 28. In New York, the Long Wharf Theatre presented the drama at Playhouse 91 in February, 1982. *Quartermaine's Terms* earned wide praise; critic John Simon noted the play's powerful mixture of laughter and melancholy and raved over its "understatedly heartbreaking ending." *The Common Pursuit* focuses on a reunion of 1960's campus rebels who have become 1980's sellouts. The play manipulates time in a fashion that reminded some

critics of Pinter's *Betrayal* (pr., pb. 1978); Gray, though, explained that his source for the technique was an older television drama.

JAPES

Among the very best of Gray's plays is *Japes*, which opened November 23, 2000, in Colchester and opened soon after the new year in the West End. It portrays the bizarre life that two brothers (Jason or Japes and Michael or Mikey) lead over a span of twenty-seven years, as they share their parents' inherited house and the woman Michael marries. It is a poignant and sad display of cruelties and missed directions, mixed with love and mutual devotion.

OTHER MAJOR WORKS

LONG FICTION: *Colmain*, 1963; *Simple People*, 1965; *Little Portia*, 1967; *A Comeback for Stark*, 1968 (as Hamish Reade); *Breaking Hearts*, 1997.

SCREENPLAYS: *Butley*, 1975; *A Month in the Country*, 1987; *Unnatural Pursuits*, 1992.

TELEPLAYS: *The Caramel Crisis*, 1966; *Death of a Teddy Bear*, 1967; *Sleeping Dog*, 1967; *A Way with the Ladies*, 1967; *Pig in a Poke*, 1969; *The Dirt on Lucy Lane*, 1969; *The Princess*, 1970; *Style of the Countess*, 1970; *Man in a Sidecar*, 1971; *Plaintiffs and Defendants*, 1975; *Two Sundays*, 1975; *After Pilkington*, 1987; *Running Late*, 1992; *Femme Fatale*, 1993.

NONFICTION: *An Unnatural Pursuit and Other Pieces*, 1985; *How's That for Telling 'Em, Fat Lady?*, 1988; *Fat Chance*, 1995; *Enter a Fox*, 2001.

EDITED TEXT: *Selected English Prose*, 1967 (with Keith Walker).

BIBLIOGRAPHY

Blaydes, Sophia B. "Literary Allusion as Satire in Simon Gray's *Butley*." *Midwest Quarterly* 18 (Summer, 1977): 374-391. Discusses the academic setting of *Butley* and concentrates on explicating some of the more obscure literary allusions. Includes an end note on the making and distribution of the film version in 1975.

Burkman, Katherine H., ed. *Simon Gray: A Casebook*. New York: Garland, 1992. An introduction and a chronology are followed by fourteen essays, a bibliography, and an index. This volume is the first book-length exploration of Gray's work, from *Wise Child* to *Hidden Laughter*. Contains single-work essays, overviews, and articles on adaptations. *The Holy Terror*, a revision of *Melon*, which was produced in Arizona in 1991, is mentioned in the chronology but is not dealt with in the essays.

Nothof, Anne. "The Pictures of Simon Gray: Dramatizing Degeneration." *Modern Drama* 43, no. 1 (2000): 56-65. The essay portrays the artist as a disillusioned idealist whose degeneration (like that of the picture of Dorian Gray) is manifested in his plays, his protagonists, and his autobiographical notes.

Rich, Frank. "Stage: Simon Gray Play, *The Common Pursuit*." *The New York Times*, October 20, 1986, p. C17. This first play since *Quartermaine's Terms* is about Cambridge "litterateurs from twenty years ago." Rich provides some history of the play's New Haven tryout and change of direc-

tors, one of whom is Gray himself. Includes a description of the play's staging.

Shafer, Yvonne. "Aristophanic and Chekhovian Structure in the Plays of Simon Gray." *Theater Studies* 31/32 (1984/1985): 32-40. Deals extensively with *Otherwise Engaged* (whose central character is "a solitary searcher for order and peace in a chaotic world") and *Quartermaine's Terms*, with a Chekhovian atmosphere and a "central character moving through a landscape of incipient disaster, unable to take any action to save himself."

Stern, Carol Simpson. "Gray, Simon." In *Contemporary Dramatists*, edited by Thomas Riggs. 6th ed. Detroit, Mich.: St. James Press, 1999. A thorough account of Gray's work and his relationship with the British theater.

Steven H. Gale,
updated by Thomas J. Taylor,
Robert McClenaghan, and Stanley Longman

SPALDING GRAY

Born: Providence, Rhode Island; June 5, 1941

PRINCIPAL DRAMA

Sakonet Point, pr. 1975 (with Elizabeth LeCompte)
Rumstick Road, pr. 1977 (with LeCompte)
Nyatt School, pr. 1978 (with LeCompte)
Three Places in Rhode Island, pr. 1979 (with LeCompte)
Point Judith, pr. 1979
Sex and Death to the Age Fourteen, pr. 1979
Booze, Cars, and College Girls, pr. 1979
India (and After), pr. 1979
A Personal History of the American Theatre, pr. 1980
Interviewing the Audience, pr. 1981
In Search of the Monkey Girl, pr. 1981, pb. 1982
Swimming to Cambodia, pr., pb. 1985

Sex and Death to the Age Fourteen (collection of monologues including: *Sex and Death to the Age Fourteen*; *Booze, Cars, and College Girls*; *Forty-seven Beds*; *Nobody Wanted to Sit Behind a Desk*; *Travels Through New England*; and *Terrors of Pleasure: The House*), pb. 1986
Travels Through New England, pr. 1986
Terrors of Pleasure, pr. 1986
Rivkala's Ring, pr., pb. 1986 (based on Anton Chekhov's story "The Witch")
Monster in a Box, pr. 1990, pb. 1992
Gray's Anatomy, pr. 1993, pb. 1994
It's a Slippery Slope, pr. 1996, pb. 1997
Morning, Noon, and Night, pr., pb. 1999

OTHER LITERARY FORMS

Spalding Gray's reputation is almost entirely based on his dramatic monologues. He has also written a collection of short stories entitled *Seven Scenes from a Family Album* (1981) and a thinly veiled autobiographical novel *Impossible Vacation* (1992).

Gray has also worked as an actor for the Performance Group and the Wooster Group, appeared onstage in a number of shows, and performed his own monologues. He has also appeared in several films including adaptations of *Swimming to Cambodia* (1987), *Monster in a Box* (1992), and *Gray's Anatomy* (1997).

ACHIEVEMENTS

Spalding Gray is considered mainly a performance artist rather than a playwright. He has received grants from the National Endowment for the Arts (1978), Rockefeller Foundation (1979), and Edward Albee Foundation (1985) as well as fellowships from the National Endowment for the Arts (1978) and the Rockefeller Foundation (1979). He was awarded the prestigious Guggenheim Fellowship in 1985. Despite Gray's identity as a performance artist, in 1985 he was awarded an Obie Award, a Special Citation for his work as an actor and writer for *Swimming to Cambodia*. He was nominated for two Independent Spirit Awards (Best Male Lead and Best Screenplay) for the film adaptation of the show.

As a performer Gray has been involved with many of the important theatrical groups of the mid- to late twentieth century. After leaving Richard Schechner's Performance Group, he helped found the Wooster Group in 1977, which would go on to be one of the most significant New York companies of the later part of the twentieth century. Despite this storied background, Gray managed to become an even more influential artist once he left the Wooster Group to become a solo artist.

Gray, along with performers such as Laurie Anderson and Eric Bogosian, has been credited with bringing a performance-based aesthetic deeper into the mainstream. Gray helped show the mass appeal of "performance art," a feat that was especially important in the mid-1980's when National Endowment for the Arts funding was coming under fire. His autobiographical, anecdotal work helped pave the way for other performance artists who explore issues of the

self in their work. Gray's success with his nonaggressive performance pieces opened up the New York downtown theater scene to audiences who might otherwise not have ventured south of Times Square.

BIOGRAPHY

Spalding Gray was born in 1941 in Rhode Island to middle-class parents. He went to Emerson College where he studied acting. After graduation he worked as an actor for summer stock companies and traveled around North America. When he returned to Rhode Island in 1967, he found out that his mother had committed suicide. Her death would play a significant role in many of his monologues as well as his novel *Impossible Vacation*.

In 1970 he joined Richard Schechner's Performance Group and remained there for five years until he and fellow group member Elizabeth LeCompte broke with Schechner to form the Wooster Group, an avant-garde performance troupe. While at the Wooster Group, he and LeCompte produced their trilogy of plays entitled *Three Places in Rhode Island* (1979), which included *Sakonnet Point*, *Rumstick Road*, and *Nyatt School*. These plays explored Gray's relationship to his family and especially his mother's suicide.

After teaming with LeCompte for *Three Places in Rhode Island*, Gray began to work individually on a series of monologues about his early life. These pieces, eventually titled *Sex and Death to the Age Fourteen* and *Booze, Cars, and College Girls*, would become the first of an ongoing series of monologues that Gray performed about his own life. These monologues made Gray famous and form what he describes as "an ongoing oral history, within which I include myself, of course, and all the others who have been a part of 'our' history along the way." In 1981 Gray performed *Interviewing the Audience*, an improvisational piece that was made up of a dialogue between him and his viewers. This piece helped Gray perfect the interview technique that he would use in creating characters for his later monologues.

Gray came to national attention in 1985 with *Swimming to Cambodia*, a monologue that he wrote about his experiences as an actor working on the film

Spalding Gray in 1991. (AP/Wide World Photos)

The Killing Fields (1984). The piece, performed at the Performance Garage in New York City, was also made into a 1987 film by Jonathan Demme, with music by Laurie Anderson. The piece would also win a special Obie award in 1985.

In the 1990's, Gray wrote a succession of successful monologues about his life. Beginning in 1992 with *Monster in a Box*, about his attempts to write a novel (which would eventually become *Impossible Vacation*, 1992), and continuing through his battle with eye problems in *Gray's Anatomy*, his marriage to and divorce from his longtime girlfriend Renée in *It's a Slippery Slope*, and his life with his new family in *Morning, Noon, and Night*.

In addition to his monologues, Gray has a successful career as an actor. He has performed in films such as *Beaches* (1988), *Beyond Rangoon* (1995), and *Diabolique* (1996). He has also appeared onstage in a variety of roles, most notably as Hoss in Sam Shepard's *Tooth of Crime* in 1973 and as the Stage Manager in the Lincoln Center Revival of Thorton Wilder's *Our Town* in 1988.

ANALYSIS

Spalding Gray's works are deeply autobiographical. He uses both his own name and the names of those with whom he has interacted in his monologues. When he performs, he does so behind a desk with a microphone, notepad, and glass of water as his only props. He makes no attempt to disguise his identity the way an actor playing a role typically would. It is this transparency that raises the most basic question about Gray's work: Is he just Spalding Gray, or is he an actor playing the role of Spalding Gray? Moreover, because he makes an effort in his daily life to observe and remember every bit of minutia that happens to him as fodder for his next monologue, does he, as an actor, ever stop performing Spalding Gray?

Gray's character is fairly easy to describe. Much like Woody Allen's persona of the nebbishy New York Jew, Gray plays the nebbishy, New England WASP (white, Anglo-Saxon Protestant) actor and docile male. It is this emasculated, paranoid persona of Spalding Gray that Gray takes on in all his monologues. It has also become the persona that he has taken on in real life.

This is not to say that Gray does not take on a variety of characters in performing his pieces. To the contrary, he often assumes the voice and subtle body movements of the characters with whom Spalding Gray interacts. It is these changes in character that further call into question whether Gray is being himself or performing a role. Unlike impressionists who rarely will interact as "themselves" with their impressions, Gray freely converses with himself as someone else. Without differentiating between how he plays others and how he plays himself, Gray further blurs the lines that separate reality from history and from performance.

Many of Gray's monologues reference his search for a "perfect moment." This longing for the perfection that he seeks in his life propels many of his stories. This moment however, is almost always difficult to achieve and, as the name "perfect moment," suggests, only lasts briefly. It is this search for perfection, no matter how brief, that drives Gray to action. The moments, when related to the audience, are almost always anticlimatic to the quest to achieve them.

Gray's work is often referred to as "sit-down" comedy, as if the only difference between his work and the storytelling of a standup comedian such as Bill Cosby is his or her presentation to the audience. There are three major distinctions that should be made between the two art forms. First, Gray's work is intimate, at times uncomfortably so. He talks freely about his sexual anxieties, conquests, and misadventures; his philandering; his mother's suicide; his paranoia; and a host of other issues that would seem to be off-limits, or at least unsavory, for a comic whose goal is simply to entertain. Gray's work, by his own admission, is a type of talk therapy for him to work out his personal demons in front of an audience. By

extension, he hopes that his audience can and will relate to his misadventures and experience a similar catharsis. Second, Gray uses his very personal stories to discuss greater issues that affect society. He expects that his very small story will shed light on a more important issue or fundamental similarity that affects everyone. Third, Gray's audience comes in expecting performance art, not standup. This may be the most significant difference between Gray and standup comedians. Expectations affect the way the audience interacts with him. These expectations also add gravity to his pieces that they may or may not deserve.

Gray's texts, as they exist in published form, are typically transcriptions of a performance. He never performs from a finished script but rather follows an outline in his notebook to cue him from one story to another.

SEX AND DEATH TO THE AGE FOURTEEN

This was Gray's first real attempt at an autobiographical monologue. Although highly entertaining, it is difficult to find any real line in the text. The monologue reveals some very intimate moments of Gray's early life, and somehow the endless parade of dying pets and masturbation stories has a certain charm.

Gray's stories here attempt to be both deeply personal and universal at the same time. Most members of his audience would be able to relate to these stories of growing up and loss. Although not yet attempting to broach some of the more global issues raised in later monologues, *Sex and Death to the Age Fourteen* as well as its sequel *Booze, Cars, and College Girls* attempts to place Gray as an archetypical child and adolescent.

SWIMMING TO CAMBODIA

Clearly Gray's most important work, *Swimming to Cambodia* offers the best of what Gray does in his monologues: a deeply personal story about his work on the film *The Killing Fields*; fantastic character sketches including Jim Bean, the cocaine-addicted sailor with his finger on the button; and a historical and political bend in his treatment of the bombings of Cambodia.

The monologue is equally funny and disturbing. Gray's insights into human nature, at every point in the piece, cut very close to the bone. No one is spared his clear eye, including, perhaps especially, himself. In his quest for the perfect moment in Thailand (where *The Killing Fields* was filmed), Gray appears paranoid, whiney, misogynistic, indecisive, and arrogant. Gray equates the U.S. military's bungling of the war in Vietnam and Cambodia with his shortsightedness in both his relationship with Renée and his search for an agent and further fame in Hollywood.

Gray raises many questions about identity in this piece. He draws attention to the different attitudes between westerners and easterners, New Yorkers and New Englanders, and men and women. More significant than his calling attention to these differences is his own embodiment of all of these personalities. In doing this, Gray suggests that all differences are performative, not essential. However, by embodying minorities in his white male body, Gray reinforces his hegemonic power. Perhaps it is Gray's embodiment of minorities that made his piece palatable to mainstream audiences when a similar piece done by a non-hegemonic performer would have been more controversial.

IT'S A SLIPPERY SLOPE

The story of Gray's relationship with Renée Shafransky runs through all of his monologues. Some have suggested that Gray's stories act like a serial radio play with Spalding and Renée as the two main characters. In this piece, Gray exposes his infidelities to Renée and describes the end of their relationship. This is Gray's most personal work since *Sex and Death to the Age Fourteen*.

Because Gray narrates his own story, his infidelity is less disturbing to the audience. This convention raises questions about the nature of love and especially calls into question the legitimacy of monogamy. The Gray character here is as unlikeable as he has ever been. Yet despite the cruelty that he showed Renée (here named Ramona for legal reasons), he expects his audience to buy into his main conceit that

love is as involuntary as skiing, the sport that Gray learns over the course of the piece.

OTHER MAJOR WORKS

LONG FICTION: *Impossible Vacation*, 1992.

SHORT FICTION: *Seven Scenes from a Family Album*, 1981.

BIBLIOGRAPHY

Auslander, Philip. *Presence and Resistance: Postmodernism and Cultural Politics in Contemporary American Performance*. Ann Arbor: University of Michigan Press, 1994. In his chapter about Gray and Laurie Anderson, Auslander explores the relationship between postmodern performance art and popular culture.

Leverett, James. "Introduction: Spalding Gray." *Extreme Exposure: An Anthology of Solo Performance Texts from the Twentieth Century*. New York: Theatre Communications Group, 2000. This book is a collection of performance pieces. In his introductions, Leverett attempts to codify the concept of performance art and how each of the individuals profiled fits in that codification.

Peterson, Michael. *Straight White Male: Performance Art Monologues*. Jackson: University Press of Mississippi, 1997. Compares the work of Gray, Eric Bogosian, and others. Peterson attempts to show the difference between standup comics and performance artists. He also questions how hegemonic men function within the performance art world, which is typically a way for underrepresented groups to have a voice.

Phelan, Peggy. "Spalding Gray's *Swimming to Cambodia*: The Article" *Critical Texts* 5, no. 1 (1988): 27-30. A feminist reading of Gray's most important work. Phelan questions the validity of the work as a self-expressive piece based on Gray's use of sarcasm as a way to protect himself.

Matthew J. Kopans

PAUL GREEN

Born: Lillington, North Carolina; March 17, 1894
Died: Chapel Hill, North Carolina; May 4, 1981

PRINCIPAL DRAMA

Surrender to the Enemy, pr. 1917

The Last of the Lowries, pr. 1920, pb. 1922

The Long Night, pb. 1920

Granny Boling, pb. 1921 (revised as *The Prayer Meeting*, pb. 1924)

The Old Man of Edenton, pr. 1921, pb. 1925

Old Wash Lucas (The Miser), pr. 1921, pb. 1924

The Lord's Will, pr., pb. 1922

Blackbeard, pr. 1922, pb. 1925 (with Elizabeth Lay Green)

White Dresses, pb. 1922, pr. 1923 (one act)

Sam Tucker, pb. 1923 (revised as *Your Fiery Furnace*, pb. 1926)

Wrack P'int, pr. 1923

Fixin's, pr. 1924, pb. 1934 (with Erma Green)

The Hot Iron, pb. 1924 (revised as *Lay This Body Down*, pb. 1959, pr. 1972)

In Aunt Mahaly's Cabin: A Negro Melodrama, pb. 1924, pr. 1925

The No 'Count Boy, pr., pb. 1924

The Lord's Will and Other Carolina Plays, pb. 1925

The Man Who Died at Twelve O'Clock, pr. 1925, pb. 1927

Quare Medicine, pr. 1925, pb. 1928

The End of the Row, pb. 1926

In Abraham's Bosom, pr., pb. 1926 (one-act version), pr. 1926, pb. 1927 (full-length version)

Lonesome Road: Six Plays for the Negro Theatre, pb. 1926

The Man on the House, pb. 1926

Supper for the Dead, pb. 1926, pr. 1954

The Field God, pr., pb. 1927

Unto Such Glory, pb. 1927, pr. 1936

Blue Thunder: Or, The Man Who Married a Snake, pb. 1928

Bread and Butter Come to Supper, pb. 1928, pr. 1954 (as *Chair Endowed*)

The Goodbye, pb. 1928

In the Valley and Other Carolina Plays, pb. 1928

Old Christmas, pb. 1928

The Picnic, pb. 1928

Saturday Night, pb. 1928

Tread the Green Grass, pb. 1929, pr. 1932 (music by Lamar Stringfield)

The House of Connelly, pr., pb. 1931

Potter's Field, pb. 1931, pr. 1934 (revised as *Roll Sweet Chariot*, pr. 1934, pb. 1935; symphonic drama; music by Dolphe Martin)

Shroud My Body Down, pr. 1934, pb. 1935 (revised as *The Honeycomb*, pb. 1972)

The Enchanted Maze, pr. 1935, pb. 1939

Hymn to the Rising Sun, pr., pb. 1936 (one act)

Johnny Johnson: The Biography of a Common Man, pr. 1936, pb. 1937 (music by Kurt Weill)

The Southern Cross, pr. 1936, pb. 1938

The Lost Colony, pr., pb. 1937 (symphonic drama)

Alma Mater, pb. 1938

The Critical Year, pb. 1939

Franklin and the King, pb. 1939

The Highland Call, pr. 1939, pb. 1941 (symphonic drama)

Out of the South: The Life of a People in Dramatic Form, pb. 1939

Native Son, pr., pb. 1941 (with Richard Wright; adaptation of Wright's novel)

A Start in Life, pr., pb. 1941 (radio play; also as *Fine Wagon*)

The Common Glory, pr. 1947, pb. 1948 (symphonic drama)

Faith of Our Fathers, pr. 1950

Peer Gynt, pr., pb. 1951 (adaptation of Henrik Ibsen's play)

Serenata, pr. 1953 (with Josefina Niggli)

The Seventeenth Star, pr. 1953 (symphonic drama)

Carmen, pr. 1954 (adaptation of the libretto of Georges Bizet's opera)

Wilderness Road, pr. 1955, pb. 1956 (symphonic drama)

The Founders, pr., pb. 1957 (symphonic drama)

The Confederacy, pr., pb. 1958 (symphonic drama)

The Stephen Foster Story, pr. 1959, pb. 1960
    (symphonic drama)

The Thirsting Heart, pb. 1959, pr. 1971

Five Plays of the South, pb. 1963

Cross and Sword, pr. 1965, pb. 1966 (symphonic
    drama)

The Sheltering Plaid, pb. 1965

Texas, pr. 1966, pb. 1967

Sing All a Green Willow, pr. 1969

Trumpet in the Land, pr. 1970, pb. 1972

Drumbeats in Georgia, pr. 1973

Louisiana Cavalier, pr. 1976

We the People, pr. 1976

The Lone Star, pr. 1977

OTHER LITERARY FORMS

An extremely prolific writer, Paul Green produced work in all the main literary genres. Related to his numerous stage plays is his work in other dramatic forms. Some of the screenplays he wrote for Hollywood include *Cabin in the Cotton* (1932; adaptation of Harry Harrison Kroll's novel of the same title), *State Fair* (1933, with Sonya Levien; adaptation of Phil Stong's novel of the same title), *Dr. Bull* (1933; adaptation of James Gould Cozzens's novel *The Last Adam*), *David Harum* (1934; adaptation of Edward Noyes Westcott's novel of the same title), *Time Out of Mind* (1947; adaptation of Rachel Field's novel of the same title), and *Black Like Me* (1963; adaptation of John Howard Griffin's novel of the same title).

Green's fiction includes two novels, *The Laughing Pioneer* (1932) and *This Body the Earth* (1935), and several collections of short stories: *Wide Fields* (1928), *Salvation on a String and Other Tales of the South* (1946), *Dog on the Sun* (1949), *Words and Ways* (1968), *Home to My Valley* (1970), and *Land of Nod and Other Stories* (1976). Green's verse appeared in *The Lost Colony Song-Book* (1938), *The Highland Call Song-Book* (1941), *Song in the Wilderness* (1947), *The Common Glory Song-Book* (1951), *Texas Song-Book* (1967), and *Texas Forever* (1967).

Nonfiction by Green includes a critical work, *Contemporary American Literature: A Study of Fourteen Outstanding American Writers* (1925, with Elizabeth Lay Green); a book about teaching, *Forever Growing: Some Notes on a Credo for Teachers* (1945); and four collections of writings on the theater, *The Hawthorn Tree* (1943), *Dramatic Heritage* (1953), *Drama and the Weather* (1958), and *Plough and Furrow* (1963).

ACHIEVEMENTS

Early in his long career as a playwright, Paul Green was hailed as the promising young Eugene O'Neill of the South. The New York drama critics were encouraging and so was a Pulitzer Prize for *In Abraham's Bosom* in 1927. Green's promise, however, was never quite fulfilled, although he continued to write for the New York stage up until World War II. Both Green's initial success and his ultimate failure in New York can be attributed to his folksy images of the South—images that, on examination, and with repetition and age, proved stereotypical, especially in comparison with the work of more substantial Southern writers, such as Thomas Wolfe and William Faulkner. Green wrote too prolifically for his work to attain consistent quality: In particular, his characters, usually meant to be realistic, tended to be one-dimensional (or, when he tried to make them complex, merely inconsistent), and, for a student and teacher of philosophy, Green's lack of philosophical depth is disappointing.

When the romance with New York waned, Green, who had a down-home lover in the Carolina Playmakers and who had flirted with German experimental drama and with Hollywood, went in other directions. These other directions constitute his main achievement. Along with such groups as the Carolina Playmakers, Green helped to expand the material, techniques, and audiences of legitimate drama in the United States. He brought in more folk and historical material, music, and stylized techniques, and his "symphonic" plays (historical plays usually with patriotic themes), performed in outdoor theaters recalling the original Greek drama, brought drama to the people, particularly in the South. Immensely popular, great tourist attractions, some of the symphonic dramas continue to be performed, including the first one, *The Lost Colony*. Unfortunately, the setting, ritual, and spectacle of the symphonic dramas do not cover up Green's tendency toward stereotypes, which became even more pronounced with the historical material.

Of Green's prodigious output, his best work includes *White Dresses* and *Hymn to the Rising Sun* among the one-act plays, *In Abraham's Bosom* and *Johnny Johnson* among the full-length plays, and *Wilderness Road* among the symphonic dramas.

BIOGRAPHY

Paul Eliot Green was a product of the Cape Fear River farming region of eastern North Carolina. His paternal grandfather, John Green, had owned a plantation and slaves before the Civil War, and his maternal grandfather, William Byrd, was a preacher, singing teacher, and composer of hymns. Green's parents were William Archibald and Betty Byrd Green (William's second wife). His father owned and operated a large farm, where, with the other Green children, Paul played, worked, and got to know the sharecrop-

Paul Green in 1941. (Library of Congress)

pers, black and white. This rural background provided a rich source of material for Green's future plays.

After attending public elementary school, Green entered Buie's Creek Academy (now Campbell College) and benefited from the teaching of the academy's dedicated founder, James Archibald Campbell. On graduation, Green earned money to attend college by working for two years as the principal of tiny Olive Branch School and as a professional baseball player for the Lillington Cats. (He was an ambidextrous pitcher—a fact in which some critics of his plays might see a symbolic fitness.) He entered the University of North Carolina, Chapel Hill, in 1916, the same year as Thomas Wolfe, but his university studies were interrupted by volunteer service (1917-1919) in the United States Army Engineers. After serving at the front during World War I and in Paris afterward, attaining the rank of second lieutenant, Green left the engineers to resume his university studies. During Green's absence, Frederick Koch had come to the University of North Carolina and established the Carolina Playmakers. Koch and the Playmakers, with their emphasis on folk drama, exercised a profound influence on Green and his subsequent career, although at the university Green majored in philosophy.

Through Green's involvement with the Carolina Playmakers, he met his future wife, Elizabeth Lay, who had written the first play produced by the Playmakers and continued to work for them after her graduation in 1919. She helped produce some of Green's early one-act plays and collaborated with him in writing *Blackbeard*. They were married in 1922, between two years of graduate study in philosophy for Green, first at North Carolina, then at Cornell. In 1923, they returned to Chapel Hill, where they made their home and reared four children and where Green taught at the university, as lecturer and then associate professor of philosophy (1923-1939), as professor of dramatic arts (1939-1944), and as professor of radio, television, and motion pictures (1962-1963).

Green's 1927 Pulitzer Prize for *In Abraham's Bosom* was followed in 1928 by a Guggenheim Fellowship allowing him to study theater for two years in Germany and England. In Berlin, Green was particularly impressed by Alexis Granowsky's stylized productions in the Yiddish Theater (including the actors' imitation of puppets) and by the "epic theater" (deliberately theatrical, didactic drama) of Bertolt Brecht. Also influential was Green's intermittent screenwriting work in Hollywood (1932-1936, 1942, 1964). Finally, in the last part of his life, Green's successful production of patriotic outdoor dramas received further stimulus when he was frequently called on to represent the United States officially and unofficially: Among other such activities, he was a United States delegate to the United Nations Educational, Scientific, and Cultural Organization (UNESCO; 1950-1952), lectured for UNESCO in Asia (1951), and attended the International Conference on the Performing Arts (Athens, 1962). He received the Freedom Foundation's George Washington Medal three times (1951, 1956, 1966).

ANALYSIS

Paul Green's playwriting career is usually divided into three phases: an early phase when he wrote one-act plays about the South; a middle phase when he advanced to full-length plays, at first traditional but then experimental in form, mostly set in the South but including other settings; and a final phase when he concentrated on historical outdoor plays, the so-called symphonic dramas, still mostly set in the South. Another division scheme is suggested by a surprising break in his career around World War II, when for five years (1942-1946) this prolific playwright produced no work for the stage (though he was writing for Hollywood). The five-year break effectively divides Green's period of concentration on indoor drama from his period of concentration on outdoor drama.

During the five-year period, Green apparently reassessed his dramatic career and emerged not only with a new form but also with new material and new attitudes. Before the break, Green relentlessly criticized social injustice in the United States, particularly the southern parts, but the born-again Green celebrated the patriotic *Faith of Our Fathers* and became a member of the United States Executive Committee and of the National Commission, UNESCO (1950-

1952). The onetime antiwar playwright filled the stage with battles. Green can be accused of inconsistency here—or at least of going for popularity by merely reflecting changes in social climate from the 1930's to the 1950's. In his defense, however, it should be noted that his development was dictated, in part, by the opportunities available to him (which perhaps, in turn, were influenced by the prevailing social climate).

More important, the gulf between *Native Son* and *The Common Glory* is not as great as it first appears. The uniting strand is Green's democratic belief in human rights, expressed in a negative, critical form before World War II and in a positive, celebratory form after the war. Green's emphasis changed, but his beliefs remained the same, as can be seen most clearly in his consistently sympathetic portrayal of African Americans. His consistent development is demonstrated by the following analysis of his best work during the various phases.

The one-act plays *White Dresses* and *Hymn to the Rising Sun* both depict brutal social conditions in the South early in the twentieth century. *White Dresses* focuses on the relationship of a white landowner and his black female tenants, while *Hymn to the Rising Sun* shows guards and convicts on a chain gang. Both plays are expository in nature, with little plot, the action serving to demonstrate a sordid condition—the cruel dominance of one party and subjection of another, as though the South knows no other pattern.

WHITE DRESSES

In *White Dresses*, the mulatto girl Mary McLean has likings for young Hugh Morgan, the white landlord's son (with whom she has apparently had sexual relations), and talks of going to New York and passing for white. Her aspirations in both directions are crushed by the landlord, Henry Morgan, who forces her to marry another black tenant, Jim Matthews; otherwise, he will evict her sickly old grandmother. Henry Morgan comes across as a Simon Legree, but as the eye-popping conclusion reveals, he has at least one good reason for preventing a liaison between Hugh and Mary—Mary is Hugh's half sister. Also, because it is Christmas Eve, Henry delivers Mary a present, apparently from Hugh: a white dress matching the one Henry gave Mary's mother to bribe her. The dress is a powerful symbol of Mary's crushed hopes and the cycle of degradation from which she had hoped to escape.

HYMN TO THE RISING SUN

Hymn to the Rising Sun, the chain-gang drama, is set on an ironic date, the Fourth of July. All the action takes place between dawn's first light and sunrise of another hot Southern day, the nearest thing to Hell in the life of the chain-gang members (black and white here are treated equally). The state legislature and judges have decreed "hard labor" for the convicts, and Captain, the head guard, is there to see that the decree is carried out. A stereotype of the Southern sheriff or "boss" (fat, sombrero-crowned, wearing a whip curled up in one boot), Captain obviously takes pleasure in his work, although he denies it. His easygoing humor loaded with sinister threats, Captain rules by intimidation and sadism. To celebrate the holiday, Captain has the guards blast off their shotguns, makes a speech to the convicts on his concept of democracy (law is of, by, and for the Establishment), and forces the convicts to sing a verse of "America." He then proceeds to routine matters: whipping Bright Boy for talking too much and releasing Runt from eleven days in the sweatbox (unfortunately, the man is dead).

Both *White Dresses* and *Hymn to the Rising Sun* have social implications beyond their immediate themes of race and penal servitude, although Green does not push these wider implications to the fore. *White Dresses* shows the paternalistic economic system by which the few control the many, and *Hymn to the Rising Sun* shows what happens to those who step out of line: They are given a few basic civics "lessons." The chain gang, hired out by the governor to build the railroad, is a microcosm of the whole system, and Captain, with his Mussolini-style harangue on "democracy," in particular suggests the system's totalitarian nature.

IN ABRAHAM'S BOSOM

Like Mary McLean in *White Dresses*, Abraham McCranie of *In Abraham's Bosom* is a mulatto who hopes to break out of the cycle of Southern degradation. Unlike Mary, Abe aspires to lift his whole race

with him. He is, therefore, a much more dangerous character than Mary; Mary only wanted to go to New York, but Abe wants to teach blacks to read and write. A heroic figure who first struggles to teach himself, Abe is feared by both blacks and whites, with the exception of Goldie, a mulatto who becomes his devoted wife, and Colonel McCranie, a white landowner and Abe's father. Although the stereotypical old Colonel whips Abe onstage (because Abe throws the Colonel's mean white son, Lonnie, into a brier patch), he genuinely likes Abe, encourages him, and eventually helps him to open a school for black children. Unfortunately, when the Colonel dies, the children stop coming, and Abe is run out of town. Eighteen years later, Abe returns and tries to open his school again, but he is beaten by a white mob and, after he kills the abusive Lonnie, he is gunned down in the doorway of his home.

One of the many depressing aspects of *In Abraham's Bosom* is the way other African Americans oppose Abe's aspirations. His sarcastic old aunt, Muh Mack, constantly derides him, and his fellow turpentine workers consider him uppity; they are convinced that blacks are hewers of pine trees and pickers of cotton, and they resent any effort to prove otherwise. Such is the heavy weight of oppression on the blacks that they have internalized white attitudes toward them. Another psychological inversion is represented by Douglass, Abe and Goldie's son, who, though named after a great black leader, turns out no-good and stirs up the white mob against his father. He embodies Abe's self-defeating anger and frustration, which boil forth occasionally (although too abruptly and awkwardly) and lead to Abe's killing of Lonnie, his white half-brother. To complete the Cain-Abel parallel, Abe sometimes thinks, in this cycle of waste and defeat, that even God is against him. In the sense that God has abandoned Abe, the play's multifaceted title seems sardonic, a theological mockery.

JOHNNY JOHNSON

Although some of Green's plays might be considered dated, such is not the case with *Johnny Johnson*, an outstanding antiwar satiric comedy. The play is as timely now as when it was written, and audiences have grown more receptive to antiwar themes. In addition, Green's technique in *Johnny Johnson* caught American audiences and critics by surprise in the 1930's; now they should be more prepared. The early critics thought they should pan *Johnny Johnson* for its rambling plot and mix of harsher material with comedy; nevertheless, they felt a strange affinity for the play. The play is in the epic theater style of Brecht (whose work Green had admired on his German theatrical tour, 1928-1929), complete with music by Brecht's partner, Kurt Weill, who had fled Adolf Hitler's Germany. Besides songs, other Brechtian features include emblematic settings and scenes, folk sayings, signs, vaudeville tricks, and stereotypical characters (here Green's penchant for stereotypes served him well).

Although Johnny Johnson is a Southern bumpkin, he has enough sense to know that peace is better than war. He would rather stay home and marry his girl than fight in the war. His girl, Minny Belle, has other ideas: Swept up by patriotic fervor, she demands his complete sacrifice. Persuaded by President Woodrow Wilson's words that this is the war to end all wars, Johnny finally enlists. Wounded on the Western Front (actually, shot in the behind), he steals a cylinder of laughing gas from the hospital and reduces the Allied High Command to silly ninnies. Having elicited from them orders to stop the fighting, he dons the American commander's cap and coat and, with the spontaneous assistance of like-minded German soldiers, halts World War I. Soon, however, the ruse is discovered, Johnny is arrested, and the war resumes. Johnny is confined in an insane asylum for ten years, during which time Minny Belle marries his rival, the prospering owner of Crystal Mineral Springs, Anguish Howington, whom the army rejected on medical grounds.

An early example of black humor, *Johnny Johnson* mixes farce and horror, but its main components are irony and satire. War is announced at a small-town ceremony to unveil a peace monument, and the populace instantly switches gears. Recruits are enticed by a phonograph blaring "Democracy March," and they are immediately introduced to military dehumanization by a brutal physical examination. The insane asylum's debating society, solving problems

and prescribing world order, sounds like Congress or the United Nations. The overriding irony is that the common man, Johnny Johnson, has better sense than his leaders but is declared insane.

As Howington's prosperity shows, war is good for some people's business. As the war hysteria shows, war also encompasses the nature of bloody ritual. War's cyclic nature is suggested by the play's ending, set in the 1930's, that shows the pacified Johnny Johnson selling homemade toys in front of a crowded stadium from which martial noises (music and shouted slogans) are issuing. Along comes Minny Belle, fat and fur-swathed, accompanied by her son, Anguish Jr., who wants to buy a toy soldier. Johnny, however, whom Minny Belle fails to recognize, does not make toy soldiers.

WILDERNESS ROAD

The theme of war as insane ritual and the Cain-Abel theme of brother against brother continue in *Wilderness Road*, Green's symphonic outdoor drama of the Civil War. Named after the road carved into Kentucky by struggling early settlers, *Wilderness Road* was commissioned by Berea College, a distinguished Kentucky college established in 1855 for poor people, black and white. The founding of Berea College (by abolitionists) is closely linked to the action of the play, set in the Kentucky hills nearby. Influenced by Berea's founders, John Freeman struggles to establish a school for mountain children. At first the community supports him, but some of his slave-owning neighbors do not like his radical notion that "God hath made of one blood all nations of men" (Berea's motto). To these fearful neighbors, led by the politician Jed Willis, education itself is a subversive idea. Against such forces, in the midst of brewing civil war, Berea's founders and John Freeman have to travel a "wilderness road," like Abraham McCranie of *In Abraham's Bosom* or like Jesus walking "that lonesome valley" (in the Appalachian hymn so prominent in the play). Eventually, the school board withdraws its support from John. He is beaten and the school vandalized by the hooded Knights of the White Star, also led by Jed Willis.

When the war comes, the divided community, like neutral Kentucky as a whole, sends men off to both sides. Both sides whoop it up, but, as the dead and wounded come home, the whoops change to lamentations. Performed on three adjacent stages and summarized by the play's narrator, the Civil War panorama unfolds in swift, emblematic scenes like movie montages, but the audience gets a taste of stunning realism from the fireworks going off all around and the sound effects of shells whizzing overhead. Altogether, Green leaves little doubt that war is hell.

A pacifist, John Freeman stays out of the action until the community is overrun by Southern forces, again led by Jed Willis, who gloats that the new social order will reflect his ideas. Willis's temporary triumph provides a shocking glimpse of the totalitarian society that might have emerged if the South had won the Civil War. Faced with this possibility, John Freeman joins the Union forces, leads a raid to destroy a key railroad bridge near his home, and is killed in action. On the railroad bridge, which supplies Southern forces, hangs the fate of Kentucky and, to some extent, the Union; thus, by his death John Freeman strikes a decisive blow for freedom. He leaves behind Elsie Sims, a girlfriend who will now marry his brother and rival, Davie (on the vast outdoor stage, the initial love interest in the play can hardly compete with the cannon fire). Also surviving, minus a leg, is Neill Sims, Elsie's brother and John's best student, who will carry on the school.

To a great extent, *Wilderness Road*, the best example of Green's work in his most successful form, represents the culmination of his development as a playwright. Here his interests in the folk, in music, and in history are integrated; so also are the influences of Brecht and the movies. *Wilderness Road*, in addition, shows the coming together of Green's various themes. Through his portrayal of civil war, of brother against brother, Green comments on the nature of all war: If God has made of one blood all nations of human beings, then all war is civil war. For purposes of persuasion, Green much preferred education to warfare, yet, as John Freeman illustrates, there are some things worth fighting for: One such thing was whether, as Lincoln said, the United States would be defined as free or slave—a very close call in American history. Green, in his life and work, was still struggling to establish the definition of freedom in the United States. A man of the South and of the folk, Green contributed more than his share to the cause.

OTHER MAJOR WORKS

LONG FICTION: *The Laughing Pioneer*, 1932; *This Body the Earth*, 1935.

SHORT FICTION: *Wide Fields*, 1928; *Salvation on a String and Other Tales of the South*, 1946; *Dog on the Sun*, 1949; *Words and Ways*, 1968; *Home to My Valley*, 1970; *Land of Nod and Other Stories*, 1976.

POETRY: *The Lost Colony Song-Book*, 1938; *The Highland Call Song-Book*, 1941; *Song in the Wilderness*, 1947; *The Common Glory Song-Book*, 1951; *Texas Forever*, 1967; *Texas Song-Book*, 1967; *This View from Above*, 1970.

SCREENPLAYS: *Cabin in the Cotton*, 1932 (adaptation of Harry Harrison Kroll's novel); *Dr. Bull*, 1933 (adaptation of James Gould Cozzens's novel *The Last Adam*); *The Rosary*, 1933; *State Fair*, 1933 (with Sonya Levien; adaptation of Phil Stong's novel); *Voltaire*, 1933 (with Maude T. Howell); *Carolina*, 1934 (adaptation of his play *The House of Connelly*); *David Harum*, 1934 (adaptation of Edward Noyes Westcott's novel); *Time Out of Mind*, 1947 (adaptation of Rachel Field's novel); *Broken Soil*, 1949; *Red Shoes Run Faster*, 1949; *Roseanna McCoy*, 1949 (adaptation of Albert Hannum's novel); *Black Like Me*, 1963 (adaptation of John Howard Griffin's novel).

NONFICTION: *Contemporary American Literature: A Study of Fourteen Outstanding American Writers*, 1925 (with Elizabeth Lay Green); *The Hawthorn Tree*, 1943; *Forever Growing: Some Notes on a Credo for Teachers*, 1945; *Dramatic Heritage*, 1953; *Drama and the Weather*, 1958; *Plough and Furrow*, 1963; *A Southern Life: Letters of Paul Green, 1916-1981*, 1994.

MISCELLANEOUS: *A Paul Green Reader*, 1998 (Laurence G. Avery, editor).

BIBLIOGRAPHY

Isaac, Dan. "A White Voice for Downtrodden Blacks." *The New York Times*, January 28, 2001, p. 6. Discusses Green's life and his works, in particular *Hymn to the Rising Sun*.

Kenny, Vincents. *Paul Green*. New York: Twayne, 1971. Kenny discusses how Green's abiding faith in human nature fuses the common person, the outdoors, and the United States into a working democracy. Green's plays are divided into three categories: white-folk literature dramatizing the bitter lot of the tenant farmer, black-folk literature dramatizing the plight of the farmer's struggles with the soil and society, and the later development of the outdoor symphonic drama. Notes, references, annotated bibliography, and index.

Lazenby, Walter S. *Paul Green*. Austin, Tex.: Steck-Vaughn, 1970. This forty-four-page monograph provides a brief commentary on the development of Green's plays simultaneously with his development as a writer. Green's early plays are motivated by compassion for the lowly and by the troubling aspects of the South. *In Abraham's Bosom, The Field God*, and *The House of Connelly* are given in-depth analysis. Lazenby then turns to the outdoor symphonic dramas, devoting primary attention to *Potter's Field* and *The Lost Colony*.

Rowley, Hazel. "Backstage and Onstage: The Drama of *Native Son*." *Mississippi Quarterly* 52, no. 2 (Spring, 1999): 215-239. Discusses the difficulties encountered when Green adapted Richard Wright's *Native Son* for the stage, including John Houseman's involvement in rewriting Green's play.

Watson, Charles S. *The History of Southern Drama*. Lexington: University Press of Kentucky, 1997. A history of drama in the South, that contains a significant discussion of Green and the role that he played in converting regional themes to drama of national interest.

Harold Branam,
updated by Gerald S. Argetsinger

GRAHAM GREENE

Born: Berkhamsted, England; October 2, 1904
Died: Vevey, Switzerland; April 3, 1991

PRINCIPAL DRAMA

The Heart of the Matter, pr. 1950 (with Basil Dean; adaptation of his novel)
The Living Room, pr., pb. 1953
The Potting Shed, pr., pb. 1957
The Complaisant Lover, pr., pb. 1959
Carving a Statue, pr., pb. 1964
The Return of A. J. Raffles: An Edwardian Comedy in Three Acts Based Somewhat Loosely on E. W. Hornung's Characters in "The Amateur Cracksman," pr., pb. 1975
For Whom the Bell Chimes, pr. 1980, pb. 1983
Yes and No, pr. 1980, pb. 1983
The Collected Plays of Graham Greene, pb. 1985

OTHER LITERARY FORMS

Graham Greene tried his hand at every literary genre. He was poet, reporter, critic, essayist, pamphleteer, dramatist, screenwriter, short-story writer, biographer, and autobiographer. His near compulsion to travel led to published accounts of his numerous journeys. His established place in literature, however, is the result of the worldwide acclaim that has greeted most of his twenty-odd novels. Critics have noted a strong autobiographical element in his fiction and have charted the development of his philosophical, religious, and political thought through his career. Certain themes recur in a recognizable pattern: human beings as aliens at home and abroad, oppressed by evil in a violent world, flirting with suicide as an answer to their despair, seeking salvation, perhaps finding it at last, through the grace of God. Since *Brighton Rock*, published in 1938, most of the novels are decidedly the work of a confirmed Roman Catholic, but Greene himself rejected the label "Catholic writer." Acknowledging his Catholicism as a point of reference, Greene, borrowing the title of one of his novels, preferred to think of himself as a writer exploring the human factor.

Graham Greene in 1954. (Hulton Archive by Getty Images)

From 1929 to the early 1960's, Greene's works, with few exceptions, were published in Great Britain by William Heinemann. From the mid-1960's, his British publisher has been the Bodley Head, a firm in which he served as a director from 1958 to 1968. In 1970, the two British publishing houses became jointly involved in issuing a uniform edition of his collected works, for which Greene wrote new introductions. In the United States, his works have been published by the Viking Press and Simon and Schuster.

ACHIEVEMENTS

Graham Greene, most highly regarded for his work as a novelist, was not a distinguished dramatist, nor was he an innovator in dramatic form. His first dramatic work was not even meant for the stage: *The Great Jowett*, a character study of Benjamin Jowett, the late nineteenth century educator and head of Balliol College, Oxford, was written as a radio play for the British Broadcasting Corporation and broad-

cast in 1939. One of Greene's early plays, for which no manuscript survives, was accepted by a theatrical firm but never reached production. Only five of his plays—*The Living Room, The Potting Shed, The Complaisant Lover, Carving a Statue*, and *The Return of A. J. Raffles*—have been produced in London. Two later plays, *Yes and No*, a curtain raiser consisting of a comic dialogue between a director and an actor, and *For Whom the Bell Chimes*, a black farce in the manner of Joe Orton, have been produced in the provinces.

Greene's major plays—*The Living Room, The Potting Shed*, and *The Complaisant Lover*—suggest the influence of the well-made play as they recall the work of Henrik Ibsen in his realist phase. As in Ibsen's work, the present dilemma in which the characters find themselves has been dictated by the irrevocable events of the past. Tradition, superstition, and religion all take their toll on characters torn between a sense of duty and the urgings of love. Despite their serviceable structure and moving content, Greene's plays generally echo his superior fiction without deepening its themes.

BIOGRAPHY

Graham Greene was born on October 2, 1904, in Berkhamsted, a small town twenty-eight miles northwest of London, and was the fourth of six children. His father, Charles Henry Greene, was a teacher, and later headmaster, at the Berkhamsted School. Being the son of the headmaster created difficulties for the sensitive youngster. He was victimized, or so he believed, by his schoolmates and made the butt of their jokes. His bouts of depression led him, at an early age, to several attempts at suicide, which, in later years, he understood to be merely disguised pleas for attention and understanding rather than serious efforts to end his own life. In his teens, he was determined to be a writer, to demonstrate to his schoolmates and to the world that there was something at which he could excel, and several of his stories were printed in the school paper, some even finding their way into the local newspaper.

When Greene was sixteen, his older brother, then studying medicine, suggested to his father that Graham needed psychiatric help. Agreeing, his father sent him to live in London for six months with an analyst, Kenneth Richmond, who helped the boy make some necessary social adjustments. During this period, Greene developed an interest in dreams and the subconscious. He also read widely and later claimed that the works that most influenced him were the melodramatic adventure stories of Anthony Hope, John Buchan, and H. Rider Haggard. Marjorie Bowen's *The Viper of Milan* (1917) enabled him to recognize evil as a force to be dealt with in his everyday life.

From 1922 to 1925, at Balliol College, Oxford, Greene involved himself in the literary life of a great university. He edited the *Oxford Outlook* and published a book of verse, *Babbling April: Poems* (1925). The depression of his early youth was replaced by a boredom that plagued him for much of his life and was the impetus for his frequent travels. His method of relieving boredom during his Oxford days was to engage in excessive drinking, even some Russian roulette, this time the result of an urge to gamble rather than a desire to kill himself. At Oxford, he met Vivien Dayrell-Browning, who wrote to him objecting to his reference in a film review to Catholics "worshiping" the Virgin Mary.

Unsure of his next move, but determined not to be a teacher, Greene applied for work with *The Times* of London but could find employment only with the Nottingham *Journal*. Interested in Vivien, whom he was still seeing, he sought out a Father Trollope in Nottingham to give him Catholic instruction in order to understand her better. As a result, in February, 1926, he converted to Catholicism, a decision that influenced all his subsequent writing but that first appeared as a thematic concern in the novel *Brighton Rock* in 1938. In 1926, he also became subeditor for *The Times*. Greene and Vivien married the next year and had two children, a son and a daughter. A few years later, the couple separated. Thereafter, Greene protected his family's privacy by maintaining silence in regard to their relationships.

After the publication of *The Man Within* in 1929, Greene expected to support himself as a novelist. The failure of his next works, *The Name of Action*

(1930) and *Rumour at Nightfall* (1931), which he later suppressed, proved a setback. In 1932, however, *Stamboul Train: An Entertainment* began a string of successes for Greene. For a time in the 1930's, he supplemented his royalties by serving as film critic for the *Spectator* and *Night and Day*. During the 1930's, he also began a series of extended journeys, such as a walking trip across Liberia that led to *Journey Without Maps: A Travel Book* (1936) and a trip to Mexico that led to both a travel book, *The Lawless Roads: A Mexican Journal* (1939), and a work of fiction, *The Power and the Glory* (1940).

In 1940, Greene became literary editor for the *Spectator* and two years later worked in Sierra Leone, Africa, for British Intelligence under the authority of Kim Philby, who later defected to the Soviet Union. In 1948 and 1949, Greene worked with director Sir Carol Reed on the films *The Fallen Idol* and *The Third Man*, gaining a sound preparation for his coming theatrical endeavors. Before seriously undertaking his own plays for the theater, in 1950 he adapted his novel *The Heart of the Matter* (1948) for the stage with director Basil Dean. Another of his novels, *The Power and the Glory*, was made into a play, but Greene had no hand in its adaptation. His three most significant plays—*The Living Room*, *The Potting Shed*, and *The Complaisant Lover*—were all produced in the 1950's.

A trip to Indochina in 1954 and 1955 bore fruit in the publication of *The Quiet American* (1955); likewise, a trip to the Belgian Congo led to the publication of *A Burnt-out Case* (1961). *The Comedians* was published in 1966 following a trip to Haiti, and later trips to Paraguay and Chile laid the foundation for *The Honorary Consul* (1973). A strain of anti-Americanism is apparent in some of these works, perhaps traceable in part to a libel suit involving Greene's references to the nine-year-old Shirley Temple as a sexual tease, a contretemps that developed while he was writing film criticism for the short-lived comic weekly *Night and Day*. He also felt harassed by the State Department when, on more than one occasion, his visas for travel to the United States were delayed. He was vociferous in his condemnation of the United States' actions in Vietnam as well.

Greene was awarded an honorary doctorate from Cambridge University in 1962, was made a fellow of Balliol College, Oxford, in 1963, and was named Companion of Honour by Queen Elizabeth in 1966.

Though he never received the Nobel Prize many expected for him, Greene remained a productive and well-regarded writer into his eighties. Such critically successful novels as *Doctor Fischer of Geneva: Or, the Bomb Party* (1980) and *Monsignor Quixote* (1982) showed that age had not blurred his literary vision. In his final years, he turned increasingly to writing a lengthy journal of his dreams. When he died in Switzerland at the age of eighty-six, he was universally regarded as one of the century's major writers.

ANALYSIS

In the introduction to the 1974 edition of his first thriller-novel, *Stamboul Train*, Graham Greene confesses to an early passion for playwriting. While his earliest attempts at that genre have never come to light, the idea of shaping scenes dramatically informed much of his work as a novelist. Greene admitted that he sometimes found it essential to escape the liquidity of the novel to play out a situation, a confrontation between two characters perhaps, within the narrow confines of a space approximating the dimensions of a stage. This dramatic method within the form of the novel reached its climax in *The Honorary Consul*, in which most of the story takes place in a hut in which the kidnapped victims are held hostage.

Whereas dramatic form has influenced Greene's novels, the theme of what may be his most popular novel, *The End of the Affair* (1951), pervades his most ambitious plays: *The Living Room*, *The Potting Shed*, and *The Complaisant Lover*. Frequently thought of as a Catholic novelist, Greene, who may have converted to Catholicism out of an intellectual need to find answers to questions ignored by the Anglican Church, makes his most explicit statements about the relationship of God and human beings in *The End of the Affair*, a first-person narrative in which a novelist, Bendrix, searches through his memories of Sarah Miles, the woman he loved and lost, to attempt some understanding of the role that God has played in his own life. Sarah, who did not remember that she

had been secretly baptized a Catholic by her mother against her father's wishes, had undergone a crisis during a London bombing. Finding her lover supposedly dead amid the debris, she had prayed to God to restore him to life. In exchange, she would believe in him. With Bendrix alive, Sarah broke off the affair and remained with her loving but dull and passionless husband Henry, a civil servant. Unable to cope with the pain of a life without passion at its center, Sarah seems to have willed her own death after a cold is aggravated by her being caught in the rain. Bendrix, who contemplates but rejects suicide, comes to understand Sarah's dilemma, her growing need for God, when he reads her diary and enters his own dilemma as he attempts, but fails, to shut God out of his life. The novel's real miracle is not Bendrix's seeming resurrection after the bombing but his finding and offering of comfort and love in a nonphysical relationship with Henry Miles, whose need for Sarah is as great as his own. God's love offers them all eventual peace.

THE LIVING ROOM

In *The Living Room*, twenty-year-old Rose Pemberton, the child of a Catholic mother and a non-Catholic father, both deceased, goes to live with her two spinster great-aunts and her great-uncle, a priest who for many years has been confined to a wheelchair as the result of a car crash. Just before coming to her new home, Rose has entered into a physical relationship on the night of her mother's funeral with a man twice her age, Michael Dennis, the executor of her mother's will and a lecturer in psychology at the University of London. Dennis still cares deeply for his neurotic wife, who has a desperate need for him, and he makes clear to Rose that he cannot marry her. When Rose sees Dennis attempting to comfort his wife, she realizes for the first time that there are different kinds of love. Rose tries to overcome her despair by submitting to God's love and mercy as she takes a fatal dose of the pills with which Dennis's wife had threatened to commit suicide herself. Rose's great-uncle, the crippled priest, must explain to Dennis, who understands the mind of man but not the ways of God, that God's realm is eternal. As a woman loves her child after the pain and suffering of bearing it, humankind finds eternal comfort in God's love. Death is the child of humankind. For that death, which leads to God's mercy, to be borne, human beings must first suffer the pain of life.

The most intriguing aspect of *The Living Room*, a play marred by its too-frequent emotionally charged confrontations, bordering on the melodramatic, is its unusual setting. Rose's elderly great-aunts, Teresa and Helen, practicing Catholics, fear death even more than they love God. Like Luigi Pirandello's character Henry IV (in his 1922 play), in an attempt to freeze time, to keep death at bay, they have made the third-floor nursery of their home its only living room. Every room in the house in which someone has died has been closed off. The dead have been forgotten; their pictures have been removed. The only room still available in the house, the living room, becomes Rose's bedroom, and it is in the living room that Rose makes her choice, reverts to childhood as she seeks God in prayer, and dies.

The sisters Helen and Teresa, the characters in *The Living Room* who undergo a believable change as a result of the play's action, force the theological issues of the play without being at its center. Helen, younger than Teresa but the stronger of the two, prevents Rose from committing the mortal sin of going off with a married man by convincing her nearly senile sister that she is ill and that Rose must stay to help nurse Teresa back to health. Helen has her daily woman, Mary, spy on Rose just as Bendrix, in *The End of the Affair*, hired Parkis, a private detective, to follow Sarah. Like Parkis, Mary comes to sympathize with her prey and regrets her involvement. After Rose's death, Teresa asserts herself by choosing to move into the living room, which Helen wants to abandon. By embracing the memory of her dead grandniece, by choosing to meet her own eventual death in the room in which Rose died, Teresa forces her sister to an acknowledgment that God's mercy could not be served by Helen's unmerciful acts toward Rose, another of God's creatures, for whom, hypocritically, Helen had only professed love. Helen's role as villain, however, is a relative matter. A Catholic audience would understand that her actions have in fact kept Rose within the Church and leave Helen's judgment to

God. That same audience would further recognize the ambiguity of the play's ending. Is Rose finally damned because of her suicide or does she achieve salvation? Greene leaves the question—which echoes that posed by Scobie's suicide in the novel *The Heart of the Matter*—unanswered.

THE POTTING SHED

Greene's next work for the theater, *The Potting Shed*, adheres to the conventional structure of the well-made play. A secret withheld from the protagonist is eventually revealed to him and to the audience as well. Benefiting from his experience as a writer of some well-plotted novels that he termed entertainments, Greene builds the suspense in what might be considered his religious thriller for the stage with a sure hand for most of the play. What makes *The Potting Shed* a sounder work than *The Living Room* is the author's ability to relax the dramatic tension with humorous dialogue and some nuances of characterization absent from the one-dimensional earlier play. Adding an extra dimension to *The Potting Shed* and contributing greatly to its success was the memorable performance by John Gielgud in its central role. First produced in New York in 1957, *The Potting Shed* was presented in London the following year with some minor changes that reflected Greene's original intentions. The most significant change was in the season of the third act—during the Christmas season in the American version, closer to Easter in the British version.

Like *The Living Room*, *The Potting Shed* is centered on death. The play's premise is the imminent death of one H. C. Callifer, author of *The Cosmic Fallacy* and founder of a rationalist movement to disprove the existence of God (a belief that aligns him with Smythe, to whom Sarah Miles turned for comfort in *The End of the Affair*). Callifer's works, which enjoyed a great vogue during the period in which twentieth century people moved from doubt to disbelief in the existence of a deity guiding their destiny, have in recent years fallen out of fashion. Faith is respectable once again, and Callifer, on his deathbed, has generally been forgotten. Indeed, in the last year, his soon-to-be-widowed wife reports, his masterwork has sold only three copies for export. Mrs. Callifer had instructed her precocious thirteen-year-old granddaughter Anne to send telegrams to absent family members informing them that Callifer is near death. With a mind of her own, Anne has taken it on herself to add the name of her uncle, James Callifer, the younger of H. C.'s two sons, to those summoned to Wild Grove, the family home, despite her grandmother's deliberate omission of his name.

James Callifer, a newspaperman in his mid-forties who lives and works in Nottingham, has not seen his father in fifteen years and has spent little time at home in the last thirty years after having been sent away to school when he was fourteen. The estrangement from his parents seems to have been their doing. In fact, as his father's death becomes imminent, his mother forbids him to enter Callifer's sickroom.

Curiously, James has no memory of anything in his life before he was fourteen, and his life from that time on has been an empty one. His marriage to Sara, who has also joined the family in the Callifer household, failed when both husband and wife became aware that he had lost interest in the relationship, or perhaps had never had any. James has no close relationships, not even with his dog Spot, who is being housed in the potting shed, where seedlings are prepared for planting and the garden tools are stored. Overcome by an unaccountable fear on the dark path to the shed, James would let his dog spend the night without water rather than go to him.

After the memorial ceremony, marred by Spot's spilling the ashes as they are about to be consigned to the river, James learns that another family member was not notified of Callifer's impending death. His Uncle William's absence, however, is understandable, for William is the family pariah. H. C.'s younger brother did not merely convert to Catholicism; he committed what was for his rationalist brother the ultimate sin: He became a priest.

On the eve of his return to Nottingham, James is informed by his niece Anne that she has heard that something shocking involving him occurred many years ago in the potting shed. In trying to learn something of his past, James has been seeing a psychiatrist in Nottingham. Despairing of a cure, however, he has hinted at suicide, even stolen some pills from his doctor. Prodded by Anne, he eventually learns the family's dark secret when he hunts down his drunken uncle, Father William, in a run-down presbytery in an East Anglian town.

Long ago, James and his uncle were close, and William attempted to teach James basic Christian precepts, which H. C. violently opposed. The confused fourteen-year-old James hanged himself in the potting shed. Finding him dead, William prayed to God for a miracle—a miracle the reverse of that in *The End of the Affair*. In the novel, on finding Bendrix dead, Sarah offered God her belief in him in exchange for her lover's life. In the play, on the other hand, William, a believer, offered God, in exchange for the boy's life, what he loved most in the world: his faith. Having forgotten the terms of the bargain, Father William has spent the intervening years in despair, with whiskey his only means of getting through an existence without meaning, without hope.

James's journey toward the light is a moving one, and the confrontation between nephew and uncle is as highly charged a scene as any that Greene has written in novel or play. That the mystery is solved at the end of the second act, however, makes an anticlimax of the third act, in which Mrs. Callifer admits to spending her life protecting her husband from an acceptance of the truth of the events in the potting shed. Having accepted God's love, loving him in return, her son James is at last enabled to love another human being and offers that love to his former wife, Sara. Despite the weakness of its final act, *The Potting Shed*, more than *The Living Room*, can, on the strength of its intriguing mystery, engage an audience uncommitted to the author's own religious beliefs.

THE COMPLAISANT LOVER

In *The Complaisant Lover*, Greene returned to that staple of so much of his fiction, the tragic triangle. The relationships of Sarah Miles and the two men in her life, her civil servant husband and her novelist lover, in *The End of the Affair*, were obviously still on his mind when he wrote this play about Mary Rhodes, her dull dentist-husband Victor, and her worldly-wise lover, Clive Root, an antiquarian bookseller. In the play, however in contrast to the novel,

Greene chose to rely on the sense of humor so evident in *The Potting Shed* but absent from *The Living Room*, a humor that should come as no surprise to readers of his fiction. Long an admirer of the comic actors J. Robertson Hare and Alfred Drayton and their Aldwych farces so beloved by London audiences of the 1920's and 1930's, in both *The Complaisant Lover* and his following play, *Carving a Statue*, Greene extended himself by exploring the relationship between farce and tragedy. In *The Complaisant Lover*, he was successful; in *Carving a Statue* he was not. Perhaps the single feature contributing to the success of the former is, surprisingly in a work by Greene, the total absence of any allusion to God. Mary loves both men, and both return that love without any of them having to come to terms first with a love for or a hatred of God.

Evident from the start of *The Complaisant Lover*, an obvious advance over his earlier work for the stage, is Greene's ability to sustain a scene in which characters reveal themselves in extended small talk rather than dramatic confrontations. In the after-dinner conversation at the Rhodeses', Victor engages in some mildly boorish behavior as he relates unamusing anecdotes and plays practical jokes on his guests. One of them, Clive Root, who is paying his first visit to the Rhodes household, is obviously unamused. He has recently entered into an affair with Victor's wife, Mary, and he is unable to surrender himself to Victor's jolly mood. Clive is also irritated by the unwelcome advances of yet another guest, a determined but inexperienced nineteen-year-old. Alone with Mary, Clive pleads with her to leave her husband and family, but Mary already understands what Rose had to learn in *The Living Room*: There are different kinds of love. The best Mary can offer Clive is a brief holiday abroad. Telling Victor that she is going to Amsterdam with an imaginary friend whom she spontaneously christens Jane Crane (the rhyming jokes about Mary's friend become the play's running gag), Mary makes plans for a trip with Clive. Her plans further call for Victor to join her after "Jane's" departure.

The comedy of manners of the opening scene becomes the pure farce of the play's second scene, set in a hotel room in Amsterdam. As Clive is about to leave, Victor appears a day earlier than planned, accompanied by a Dutch manufacturer of dental equipment who speaks no English. Entirely without guile, Victor is pleased to see Clive and has no suspicions concerning his wife. When Mary asks Clive, who still wants to marry her, to let matters stand until Victor learns the truth, Clive attempts to force the issue. He dictates to a bewildered hotel valet a letter to be posted to Victor, supposedly from the valet, informing the dentist of his wife's infidelity.

The mood changes again in the second act after Victor reads the letter, part of which the valet has got right, part of which has gone hilariously wrong. The revelation, however, plunges Victor into despair, not at the abandonment of his God but at the possibility of his abandonment by the wife without whom he cannot live. Contemplating suicide but rejecting it as a silly solution for which he is not properly dressed—tragedy requires togas, not the dinner jackets of domestic comedy—the sometime boorish dentist takes on near tragic proportions. In a moving scene with his wife, he pleads with her to stay, making clear Greene's belief that marriage has little to do with sexual satisfaction and more to do with living in a house with someone one loves. Victor had stopped making love to her only when he had become aware that he was no longer giving her physical pleasure. Mary, desirous of a future involving a physical relationship with Clive, cannot turn her back on her past sixteen years with a man who needs her, a man who has been a good husband to her and a good father to her children. With a variation on the ending of *The End of the Affair*, the establishing of a solid relationship between husband and lover after Sarah's death, Victor, eager to be a complaisant husband, suggests that his very-much-alive wife keep both of her men. Reluctantly, Clive enters into the newly formed relationship.

The accommodation at the end of *The Complaisant Lover* is by no means a conventional happy ending. Bendrix and Miles at the conclusion of *The End of the Affair* may in fact be happier in their loss than are the three characters in *The Complaisant Lover* in their resignation. None has exactly what he wants, and Clive is realistic enough to understand that the day will eventually come when he will tire of the arrangement, when Mary, recognizing Clive's pain, will end it. Greene seems unable to refrain from bringing to bear his own religious scruples, here unstated, on his characters' moral dilemma. At any rate, in *The Complaisant Lover* he has fashioned his most successful play and expertly handled its varying moods.

THE RETURN OF A. J. RAFFLES

As Ibsen moved toward mysticism in his exploration of artistic creation in *Bygmester Solness* (pb. 1892; *The Master Builder*, 1893) and *Naar vi døde vaagner* (pb. 1899; *When We Dead Awaken*, 1900), Greene, too, turned mystical in *Carving a Statue*, a play about a failed artist and his indifference toward his unhappy child, which Greene may intend as an echo of God's creation and the sacrifice of his son to redeem it. In the delightful *The Return of A. J. Raffles*, by contrast, Greene for once gave himself over wholeheartedly to the pursuit of fun. The author's subtitle tells all: *An Edwardian Comedy in Three Acts Based Somewhat Loosely on E. W. Hornung's Characters in "The Amateur Cracksman."* As Raffles helps Lord Alfred Douglas get even with his father, the marquess of Queensberry, in a plot involving the prince of Wales, Greene sends his characters scampering in and out of an established social order, the conventions of which parallel the bewildering manners and mores of the contemporary world. The play's inability to find an audience despite an elegant and accomplished production by the prestigious Royal Shakespeare Company may well have dampened Greene's enthusiasm for the theater.

OTHER MAJOR WORKS

LONG FICTION: *The Man Within*, 1929; *The Name of Action*, 1930; *Rumour at Nightfall*, 1931; *Stamboul Train: An Entertainment*, 1932 (pb. in U.S. as *Orient Express: An Entertainment*, 1933); *It's a Battlefield*, 1934; *England Made Me*, 1935; *A Gun for Sale: An Entertainment*, 1936 (pb. in U.S. as *This Gun for Hire: An Entertainment*); *Brighton Rock*, 1938; *The Confidential Agent*, 1939; *The Power and*

the Glory, 1940 (reissued as *The Labyrinthine Ways*); *The Ministry of Fear: An Entertainment*, 1943; *The Heart of the Matter*, 1948; *The Third Man: An Entertainment*, 1950; *The Third Man and The Fallen Idol*, 1950; *The End of the Affair*, 1951; *Loser Takes All: An Entertainment*, 1955; *The Quiet American*, 1955; *Our Man in Havana: An Entertainment*, 1958; *A Burnt-Out Case*, 1961; *The Comedians*, 1966; *Travels with My Aunt*, 1969; *The Honorary Consul*, 1973; *The Human Factor*, 1978; *Dr. Fischer of Geneva: Or, The Bomb Party*, 1980; *Monsignor Quixote*, 1982; *The Tenth Man*, 1985; *The Captain and the Enemy*, 1988.

SHORT FICTION: *The Basement Room and Other Stories*, 1935; *The Bear Fell Free*, 1935; *Twenty-four Stories*, 1939 (with James Laver and Sylvia Townsend Warner); *Nineteen Stories*, 1947 (revised as *Twenty-one Stories*, 1954); *A Visit to Morin*, 1959; *A Sense of Reality*, 1963; *May We Borrow Your Husband? and Other Comedies of the Sexual Life*, 1967; *Collected Stories*, 1972; *How Father Quixote Became a Monsignor*, 1980.

POETRY: *Babbling April: Poems*, 1925; *After Two Years*, 1949; *For Christmas*, 1950.

SCREENPLAYS: *Twenty-one Days*, 1937; *The New Britain*, 1940; *Brighton Rock*, 1947 (adaptation of his novel; with Terence Rattigan); *The Fallen Idol*, 1948 (adaptation of his novel; with Lesley Storm and William Templeton); *The Third Man*, 1949 (adaptation of his novel; with Carol Reed); *The Stranger's Hand*, 1954 (with Guy Elmes and Giorgino Bassani); *Loser Takes All*, 1956 (adaptation of his novel); *Saint Joan*, 1957 (adaptation of George Bernard Shaw's play); *Our Man in Havana*, 1959 (adaptation of his novel); *The Comedians*, 1967 (adaptation of his novel).

TELEPLAY: *Alas, Poor Maling*, 1975.

RADIO PLAY: *The Great Jowett*, 1939.

NONFICTION: *Journey Without Maps: A Travel Book*, 1936; *The Lawless Roads: A Mexican Journal*, 1939 (reissued as *Another Mexico*); *British Dramatists*, 1942; *Why Do I Write? An Exchange of Views Between Elizabeth Bowen, Graham Greene, and V. S. Pritchett*, 1948; *The Lost Childhood and Other Essays*, 1951; *Essais Catholiques*, 1953 (Marcelle Sibon, translator); *In Search of a Character: Two Af-*

rican Journals, 1961; *The Revenge: An Autobiographical Fragment*, 1963; *Victorian Detective Fiction*, 1966; *Collected Essays*, 1969; *A Sort of Life*, 1971; *The Pleasure Dome: The Collected Film Criticism, 1935-1940, of Graham Greene*, 1972 (John Russell-Taylor, editor; published in the U.S. as *The Pleasure-Dome: Graham Greene on Film, Collected Film Criticism, 1935-1940*); *Lord Rochester's Monkey: Being the Life of John Wilmot, Second Earl of Rochester*, 1974; *Ways of Escape*, 1980; *J'Accuse: The Dark Side of Nice*, 1982; *Getting to Know the General: The Story of an Involvement*, 1984.

CHILDREN'S LITERATURE: *The Little Train*, 1946; *The Little Fire Engine*, 1950 (also as *The Little Red Fire Engine*); *The Little Horse Bus*, 1952; *The Little Steam Roller: A Story of Mystery and Detection*, 1953.

EDITED TEXTS: *The Old School: Essays by Divers Hands*, 1934; *The Best of Saki*, 1950; *The Spy's Bedside Book: An Anthology*, 1957 (with Hugh Greene); *The Bodley Head Ford Madox Ford*, 1962, 1963 (4 volumes); *An Impossible Woman: The Memories of Dottoressa Moor of Capri*, 1975.

MISCELLANEOUS: *The Portable Graham Greene*, 1973 (Philip Stout Ford, editor).

BIBLIOGRAPHY

Haskins, Robert. *Graham Greene: A Character Index and Guide.* New York: Garland, 1991. An interesting document of "characters, historical and literary allusions, place names, and foreign phrases likely to be of special interest." This valuable information source contains a full section on the plays (eight in all), with each major character receiving a profile and each play a plot-line summary. Divided by play, from *The Living Room* to *For Whom the Bell Chimes*.

Meyers, Jeffrey, ed. *Graham Greene: A Revaluation.* New York: St. Martin's Press, 1990. These essays by eight scholars offer critical analyses of Greene's accomplishments, in the shadow of his death. Roger Sharrock contributes "Unhappy Families: The Plays of Graham Greene" and states that "Greene's stage is haunted by the ghosts of the absent." He cites a "rather superficial smoothness, a reliance on slightly forcing the strong situation—in a word, slickness" as a fault. All-article index.

Miller, R. H. *Understanding Graham Greene.* Columbia: University of South Carolina Press, 1990. Chapter 6 contains notes for understanding the plays, along with the short stories and essays. Miller notes the early "lost" plays from the 1920's and quotes Greene in an interview: "I think [the theatre is] a necessary release from the solitude of being a novelist." The style is concise yet informative and evaluative, but the author runs too quickly through the canon. Bibliography and index.

Sherry, Norman. *The Life of Graham Greene, 1904-1939.* Vol. 1. London: Jonathan Cape, 1989. This first volume does not discuss Greene's drama except in passing reference to early interest in the theater. It addresses his life and values in an exhaustive, authoritative way, and it is essential to all subsequent Greene scholarship. Greene approved Sherry as his official biographer in 1974. Fully illustrated with portraits, production shots from films, and grisly photographs of executed priests.

Wolfe, Peter, ed. *Essays in Graham Greene: An Annual Review.* Greenwood, Fla.: Penkeville, 1987. A chapter contributed by Germaine Goetz, "Greene the Dramatist," offers a good biographical summary, some quotations by Greene from prefaces and introductions, and a surprisingly informative review of theater conditions in the West End from the mid-1940's to 1960, Greene's active theater years. The notes serve as a source for continued inquiry.

Albert E. Kalson,
updated by Thomas J. Taylor
and Robert McClenaghan

ROBERT GREENE

Born: Norwich, Norfolk, England; c. July, 1558
Died: London, England; September 3, 1592

PRINCIPAL DRAMA

Alphonsus, King of Aragon, pr. c. 1587
Orlando furioso, pr. c. 1588, pb. 1594 (verse play)
A Looking Glass for London and England, pr.
    c. 1588-1589, pb. 1594 (verse play; with
    Thomas Lodge)
Friar Bacon and Friar Bungay, pr. c. 1589, pb.
    1594 (verse play)
John of Bordeaux, pr. c. 1590-1591 (fragment;
    verse play)
James IV, pr. c. 1591, pb. 1598 (verse play)
Complete Plays, pb. 1909

OTHER LITERARY FORMS

Although Robert Greene is perhaps most respected today for his contribution to English drama, it was as a writer of prose fiction that he was best known to his contemporaries. His novellas made him England's most popular writer of fiction in the 1580's. Among his early works, showing the influence of Italian writers, are *Mamillia: A Mirror or Looking Glass for the Ladies of England* (part 1, 1583; part 2, 1593), *Morando: The Tritameron of Love* (part 1, 1584; part 2, 1587), *Arbasto: The Anatomy of Fortune* (1584), and *Planetomachia* (1585). Turning to the pastoral romance in 1588, Greene published such novellas as *Alcida: Greene's Metamorphosis* (1588), *Pandosto: The Triumph of Time* (1588), *Ciceronis Amor* (1589; also known as *Tullies Love*), and *Menaphon* (1589). Pastorals featuring repentance as a major theme include *Greene's Never Too Late* (1590), *Francesco's Fortunes* (1590), *Greene's Mourning Garment* (1590), and *Greene's Farewell to Folly* (1591).

Greene created still another literary fashion in the last two years of his brief life, as he cultivated another form, the rogue, or "connycatching," pamphlet. His *A Notable Discovery of Cozenage* (1591), *A Disputation Between a Hee Conny-catcher and a Shee Conny-Catcher* (1592), and *The Black Book's Mes-*senger (1592), as well as other small books in the series, combined London street argot with satire of middle-class greed to produce a form that appealed to all levels of society.

Greene's untimely death in 1592 sparked the publication of two alleged "deathbed" pamphlets, *Greene's Groatsworth of Wit Bought with a Million of Repentance* (1592) and *The Repentance of Robert Greene* (1592), both usually attributed to him but neither closely resembling his style and thus probably spurious. The one surely authentic posthumous work, *Greene's Vision* (1592), follows the pastoral penitent style of 1590 and was probably written during that most fruitful year of his career.

ACHIEVEMENTS

Robert Greene's accomplishments as a playwright have always been greatly overshadowed by those of his younger contemporary, William Shakespeare. Still, it is accurate to say that Greene created in comedy the form on which Shakespeare worked his greater miracles, just as Thomas Kyd and Christopher Marlowe led the way for Shakespeare in tragedy. The form Greene developed, the English romantic comedy, as demonstrated most clearly in *Friar Bacon and Friar Bungay, James IV,* and the fragmentary *John of Bordeaux,* is strikingly different from its predecessors. Departing from the morality tradition still current on the London stage, Greene chose as his principal theme romantic love between princely men and beautiful women. The popularity of this approach was greatly enhanced by Greene's ability to weave the love plot into a tapestry of affairs of state—usually events from English history—and to convey in dialogue the varied atmospheres of court, city, and countryside.

Greene's most immediate influences were his own prose romances, in which his heroes and heroines become embroiled in the wars of love through their pride, only to be chastened by the disasters they occasion and thus eventually brought to repentance and reconciliation. These romances, in their lengthy, intense monologues and conversations between lovers, created in the 1580's a drama of character, as it were, well before Marlowe's *Tamburlaine the Great* lit up the stage in 1587. The vision of Greene's romances and plays differed from, even opposed, Marlowe's vision of the individual will able to dominate society and bend morality to its own consciousness. Through his thoroughly comic perspective, Greene saw individual attempts to conquer or dominate as ineluctably limited by an inherent human need to form communities and by the ideals of peace and the orderly succession of generations.

The few contemporary assessments of his work that have survived praise Greene as a "plotter of plays." Certainly, his ability to move characters across a stage and from scene to scene is unmatched before Shakespeare, who no doubt profited from Greene's example. Indeed, Shakespeare learned more from Greene than plotting: Greene was also the first English playwright to vary verse and prose significantly in order to imply differences in rank or tone; he also varied rhyme and blank verse for tonal effects. Moreover, Greene was the first to create memorable female characters in English drama (the women in his romances are usually more interesting and important characters than his men). Greene's Margaret, Dorothea, and Ida worthily precede Shakespeare's

Robert Greene (Hulton Archive by Getty Images)

Rosalind and Viola. Perhaps Greene best prepared the way for Shakespeare by peopling his plays with individuals who could also represent the various levels within a society. In this way, Greene could create for the spectators the illusion that they were witnessing the reactions of an entire nation to critical events.

Though not a satiric dramatist, Greene also influenced the comedy of Ben Jonson and Thomas Middleton through his connycatching pamphlets of London life. These works created a tremendous vogue for tales of the exploits of thieves and confidence men. In these dramatic narratives, Greene brought such figures to life through dialogue rich with the patois of the city. Shakespeare's Falstaff and Autolycus, as well as the rogues of London comedy after 1600, take much of their inspiration from Greene's connycatchers.

BIOGRAPHY

According to the best, albeit sketchy, evidence, Robert Greene was born in Norwich, Norfolk, in 1558, of a saddler and his wife. It is certain that this ambitious son of bourgeois parents went on to St. John's College, Cambridge, in 1576 on a sizar's appointment (a sort of work-study position by which scholars earned their keep, usually as valets for sons of aristocrats). Though Greene's record at St. John's appears to have been undistinguished, he did take his baccalaureate in 1580. Greene continued his studies at Cambridge and received his master of arts degree from there in 1583, the same year in which his first prose romance, *Mamillia: A Mirror or Looking Glass for the Ladies of England*, was published. A second master's, from Oxford, came in 1588; this degree was more a formality than the result of further study. There is no evidence that after 1583 Greene intensely pursued any course other than the winning of a large, eager audience in London for his romances, plays, and pamphlets.

Concerning Greene's no doubt adventurous life as a writer in London from 1583 until his death in 1592, there is much rumor and rancor but little solid fact. His publication record indicates that he was immensely popular; his title pages from 1588 onward include his name within the titles themselves, as in *Greene's Mourning Garment* and *Greene's Never Too*

Late. His friend Thomas Nashe declared that printers felt "blest to pay him dear for the very dregs of his wit." Nevertheless, since the London publishing industry, still in its infancy, provided large returns for printers but no royalties for authors, even great popularity guaranteed no security. Thus, Greene survived on the speed of his pen. Curiously, there is no indication that he seriously vied for the relative stability of noble patronage, nor does he seem to have written for the pay of either the Anglican Establishment or their Puritan opponents, as did many, including Nashe and Marlowe.

Perhaps more because of the persistent theme of repentance in his writings than because of his actual life, Greene at his death left a considerable reputation as a rakehell, albeit a penitent one. His vitriolic companion Nashe wrote that he cared only "to have a spell in his purse to conjure up a good cup of wine with the poet Gabriel"; Harvey, whom Greene had insulted in a pamphlet, called him "A rakehell, a makeshift, a scribbling fool/a famous Bayard in city and school." Gentler wits, such as the critic Francis Meres, ignored the gossip and merely noted Greene's achievement as one of the "best for comedy" among the playwrights.

Of Greene's allegedly bitter feelings toward the acting companies that bought his plays, much has been echoed through four centuries. In the posthumous tract *Greene's Groatsworth of Wit Bought with a Million of Repentance*, there is a thinly veiled attack on the players, one "Shakescene"—no doubt Shakespeare—in particular. Careful studies, however, have concluded that another, most likely Henry Chettle, the author and printer, wrote these words and passed them off as Greene's. That the playwright's dealings with the actors were not always cordial is certain; Greene himself admits, for example, that he sold the same play, *Orlando furioso*, to rival companies. Nevertheless, that at least five of his plays were produced in London between 1588 and 1591 attests largely amicable relations between the author and his clients.

ANALYSIS

The most obvious common feature of Robert Greene's two best-known plays, *Friar Bacon and Friar Bungay* and *James IV*, is the love plot, the romantic battle of strong male and female personalities. The women in both plays are particularly striking; it is no wonder that critics have focused much attention on them and that they see Greene's principal dramatic impulse as romantic. Nevertheless, what joins all five of Greene's known plays is not the love interest but rather the playwright's exploration of the individual's role within society; in those plays in which it is central, the love plot is merely one overt vehicle by which Greene asks his characters to choose between the desire to dominate others and the desire to live in harmony.

ORLANDO FURIOSO

Greene found a locus for his first known dramatic handling of this theme within Ariosto's long narrative epic, *Orlando furioso* (1516, 1521, 1532). Greene's play of the same title centers on the affection of the epic hero for Angelica, daughter of the King of Africa. In the play, Orlando, a warrior but not a king, contends with monarchs for the heroine. When he wins her, it is the victory that means everything to him; Angelica herself means nearly nothing to him. So little does he know or trust her that he eagerly believes the lies of Sacrapant, here a minor court attendant, that she has betrayed him with one Medoro. Orlando goes mad with jealousy; he runs wild through a stage forest, killing and dismembering. Symbolic of his ignorance of Angelica is his failure to recognize her when they meet in the forest; rather, he speaks his rage to a dummy (or a clown) made up to look somewhat like his beloved. Only after a woodland priestess, Melissa, is brought in to heal his madness can Orlando understand his fault and beg Angelica's forgiveness.

In *Orlando furioso*, Greene paints with bold and none too careful strokes his typical portrait of the proud hero who slights his lover, suffers disasters, and comes to repentance. The audience cannot take the ranting Orlando seriously, though he might be more likable than the unbearably pompous kings who are his rivals; before the final scene, Orlando does virtually nothing to win the audience's hearts, nor does the audience sympathize with the slighted Angelica, who (albeit in the fragmentary version of the play that has survived) shows none of the depth of Greene's later heroines. Greene's heavy hand is deliberate here, however, for *Orlando furioso* is an out-and-out parody of Marlowe's hero, Tamburlaine, the second part of whose history had appeared a few months earlier than Greene's play. Greene had attacked Marlowe's thumping verse and arrogant hero in the preface to his romance *Perimedes the Blacksmith* (1588), and here he burlesques Tamburlaine's megalomania as mere insanity. Critics have misjudged the play as Greene's failed attempt to match Marlowe as a bombastic tragedian; since Greene throughout his prose and verse shows consistent antipathy to the conqueror type, there is no reason to see *Orlando furioso* as anything other than satire.

FRIAR BACON AND FRIAR BUNGAY

If *Orlando furioso* is misjudged as a serious but inept attempt at what might be called tragicomedy, then it is difficult indeed to account for the skill and sensitivity apparent in Greene's next play, *Friar Bacon and Friar Bungay*, produced most likely in 1589. This play is still only beginning to be appreciated for its plotting, its use of verse and prose structures, and its study of ideas, though scholars have long recognized it as the prototype of English romantic comedy.

As in *Orlando furioso*, the love story is the primary vehicle for Greene's exploration of the individual's relationship to society. Here, the love intrigue has social consequences that every member of Greene's audience could easily appreciate, particularly in the year following the invasion of the Spanish Armada. Greene sets his play within the reign of Henry III (1216-1272) and focuses his plot on the prince of Wales, Edward, who must choose between honoring an arranged marriage with Eleanor, princess of Castile, and pursuing the affections of the beautiful Margaret, an English country maid. The first third of the play is devoted to Edward's strategems for securing the maid as a mistress, including his hiring the great English scientist (popularly considered a magician) Roger Bacon to use the "art" to win Margaret. When Edward fails to appear at court, his father and the royal Habsburg visitors grow nervous and set out to find him. When the prince is stymied in his illicit

suit by Margaret's falling in love with Edward's best friend, Lacy, earl of Lincoln, the tension almost provokes bloodshed. Finally, however, the deep, honest love of Margaret and Lacy cures Edward's fury. He heads back to court, once again knowing his duty to king, nation, and conscience.

Nevertheless, the play is only half over. The second half beautifully juxtaposes two stories. One is Bacon's attempt to rise at court, at first by overmatching the Habsburg magician in a test of powers, then by conjuring a wall of brass to surround England and thus ward off potential invaders (the audience would have immediately thought of Spain). The other story is Lacy's attempt to assure himself of Margaret's constancy to him despite her being ceaselessly flattered and bribed by rich suitors. Both Bacon's and Lacy's attempts are proved shameful. Not only would Bacon's wall destroy the harmony of nations promised in the marriage of Edward and Eleanor, but also, as Bacon comes to see, the conjuring requires the aid of evil powers. On Lacy's part, his test of Margaret gravely insults her; moreover, his hesitancy to ask her hand leaves her at the mercy of two boorish suitors, Lambert and Serlsby, who grow so incensed at her refusal to choose between them that they fall to swords; both are killed. The tragedy is compounded—and the two plots brought strategically together—when the sons of the combatants, both scholars at Bacon's college in Oxford, witness their fathers' duel through one of Bacon's conjurations, a "perspective glass." The sons turn enemies, and they, too, wound each other mortally. By juxtaposing these plots, Greene allows his audience to see that both Bacon and Lacy have been blinded by their desire for control, Bacon's over the power of magic, Lacy's over the power of Margaret's beauty.

When Lacy eventually gives up the stupid test and comes to claim her, Margaret forgives him heartily, even though he fails to see how much he has hurt her. Then, in the final scene, which celebrates the double wedding of Edward and Eleanor, Lacy and Margaret, this country lass, now Eleanor's attendant, offers to all the royalty present an example of humility and thanksgiving. By stating her thanks to "Jove" rather than to the favor of the court, she implicitly reawakens the awareness of all, especially Edward and Lacy, to the dangers which have providentially been averted. She places the emphasis of the closing scene where it belongs, on the sanctity of marriage rather than on the euphoria occasioned by a successful political match. Friar Bacon, now penitent, is also on hand to lend further solemnity to the celebration.

The final impact of the play is intensified by what might be called the delicate power of Greene's verse. His ability to evoke in diction and line the flavor of the English countryside has been amply noted by critics, but the varying of this accent with the equally accurate rendering of the courtly and academic atmospheres is perhaps just as remarkable. The play affirms the power of language to embody the spirit of place and person. That Greene's style shifts easily from blank verse to Skeltonics to prose, and from images of "butter and cheese, cream and fat venison" to those of "cates, rich Alexandria drugs" helps to create an environment as magical as Bacon's spells or Margaret's beauty. In such an atmosphere, rich with promise, one easily believes in the magic of love to soften hearts and heal wounds of the spirit.

A LOOKING GLASS FOR LONDON AND ENGLAND

Written in collaboration with the playwright and romance writer Thomas Lodge, *A Looking Glass for London and England* explores England's relations with other countries in a form quite different from the romantic comedy. Neither tragedy nor comedy, *A Looking Glass for London and England* is a dramatic sermon, Greene and Lodge's quite faithful retelling of the biblical story of Jonah and the Ninevites. An enduringly popular play in printed form and on the stage, it was one of the last and best of the religious dramas of the 1570's and 1580's that had developed out of the morality and mystery play traditions. Like *Friar Bacon and Friar Bungay*, *A Looking Glass for London and England* urges the audience to consider ethically its attitudes and actions toward foreign neighbors. The particular focus of the play is on the moral state of nations basking in victory over foreign foes. Though the censure is only implied in the parable of Nineveh, Greene and Lodge judged England to be on the verge of losing its ethical perspective in the

wake of its defeat of the "invincible" Armada. Reminiscent of *Orlando furioso*, the play's opening scenes ring with pompous speeches by vainglorious nobility; these court scenes are juxtaposed to scenes of the merchant and laboring classes lost in greed, drunkenness, and adultery.

One of Greene's presumed contributions to the play (it is impossible to determine each author's influence exactly) is the light touch with which much of the dissipation among the commons is handled. Greene's romances of these years show his increasing skill in creating clowns and cityfolk with whom his audience could identify, and this talent is used here to draw characters who can lull an audience into feeling that all of these dangerous excesses are mere jests and good fun. Having trapped the audience, however, Greene suddenly turns the plot so that dire consequences result; the most dramatic incident of this kind is the jovial drinking bout that leads to a brawl—which in turn leads to murder. Greene uses these scenes not only to prove the prophet Jonas's point about the perils into which the society can fall, but also to compare the typical evils of the populace with the even more dangerous behavior of the nobles, who are expected to lead society.

JAMES IV

James IV, probably written shortly after *A Looking Glass for London and England*, retains some of the former play's sermonizing tone while replacing the parabolic structure with that of a masquelike fairy tale. One of Elizabethan drama's most imaginative spectacles, *James IV* combines authentic British history with materials adapted from Italian romance and then invests the story with sweetness and light by means of fairies, clowns, and balladlike verse. As in *Friar Bacon and Friar Bungay*, Greene here uses the pleasing form to move his audience gently toward accepting a controversial political stance, in this case the rightful succession of the Scots king, James VI, to the English throne.

Greene sets his play a century back in history, to the reign of James IV, another Scots monarch who had roused English ire. With the aid of a romance on the same theme by the Italian writer Giambattista Giraldi Cinthio, he twists the chronicle to create another love story in which the hero's injury to his beloved leads his nation to the brink of disaster. James, married to Dorothea, daughter of the English king, falls in love with a young gentlewoman, Ida, a peerless beauty. Urged on in his adultery by Ateukin, a Machiavellian adviser who secretly desires the King's overthrow, James banishes Dorothea, whom Ateukin accused of plotting against her husband. When news of the banishment reaches England, King Henry leads an army against James, whose demoralized forces wither before the English. Thousands of soldiers die and many towns fall; then, just as the climactic battle is about to commence, Dorothea, who has lived like a hunted animal, appears on the battleground. She begs her husband and father to throw down their arms. James, at last overcome by his injustice, implores her forgiveness. She replies with renewed vows of obedience to him. Again, the Greene heroine sets the example of humble love.

As in *Friar Bacon and Friar Bungay*, the fairy tale works because several poetic and structural devices conspire to create a magical atmosphere. One key element is the subplot involving Ida and an English officer, Eustace, whose courtship occasions the most tender wooing scene in Greene's dramatic canon. Their love makes all the more painful the estrangement of James and Dorothea, and it also sustains the audience's faith in the potential of romantic relationships to engender love and fidelity. Also vitally important to the fairy-tale magic is Greene's poetry, particularly the frequent alternation between blank verse and ballad stanzas. The rhyme provides minstrel-like distance between the harsh events being portrayed and their poetic evocation by Greene. Particularly in the dialogue between the banished Dorothea and her trusty servant, Nano, the rhyme enhances the poignancy of the situation. Greene's technique is put to a purpose far different from that in *Friar Bacon and Friar Bungay*, in which rhyme forms had been used satirically by Miles, the clown.

In *A Looking Glass for London and England*, Greene and Lodge had used another plotting device, the frame, as a means of relating the Ninevite parable to contemporary England. In the frame plot, a second prophet, Oseas, comments on the action. In *James IV*, Greene again turns to the frame plot to focus the audience's attention on a key issue in the play. Here, two antithetical types, a dour Scots cynic, Bohan, and an immortal optimist, Oberon, king of the fairies, observe the historical pageant as a test of their opposing views of human nature. Though for them the play will merely confirm or deny a point of view, these objective onlookers become more and more emotionally involved as the action proceeds. The intent is obvious: Greene again wants to move the audience to understand how the power of compassion can affect even the most resistant spirits. If even the cynic and the fairy king can feel for these characters, the audience is supposed to ask, how can love not prevail?

Though Greene provides many devices to heighten the artifice of this pseudohistory, the patriotic appeal in *James IV* is even more obvious than that of *Friar Bacon and Friar Bungay*, with its direct references to England's defenses. The marriage of James and Dorothea would have immediately reminded the spectators of the recent marriage of James IV to Anne of Denmark, while the English-Scottish alliance in the play directly foreshadows the likely advance of James VI to the English throne on the death of Elizabeth. Greene's presentation of James's character indicates the author's sympathy for the fears of the English public toward the current king's suspected reliance on untrustworthy ministers. The romantic ambience of the play, however, and the happy resolution of the plot are meant to ease the fears of the audience. Moreover, the horrors of war depicted in the play are intended to keep spectators aware of the inevitable outcome of opposition to the succession. Thus, the political presentation is balanced, not partisan. Greene's interest, as in his earlier plays, is to encourage in the theatergoing public the same faith in the power of love that his romances tried to evoke in his readers.

POSSIBLE GREENE PLAYS

Scholars have attributed to Greene various plays otherwise anonymous because these plays bear some distinguishing marks of Greene's style. Long thought a Greene play is *Alphonsus, King of Aragon* (pr. c. 1587, pb. 1599), which bears the name "R. Green" on its 1599 edition, the only extant; the play itself, however, is little like anything Greene is known to have written, so the attribution is doubtful. A more plausible case can be made for the bitterly satiric *A Knack to Know a Knave* (pr. 1592, pb. 1594), which emphasizes a Greene-like concern for the moral health of the different levels of society and which vividly portrays some of the tricks of characters doubtless drawn from Greene's connycatching pamphlets. *A Knack to Know a Knave* gradually degenerates, however, into a brutally vengeful depiction of the punishments of wrongdoers. Certainly antithetical to Greene's philosophy of forgiveness, this play, as it exists, may be a revision by another writer, perhaps the violent-tempered Nashe, of a work left unfinished by Greene at his death.

JOHN OF BORDEAUX

The only anonymously produced play definitely of Greene's authorship is *John of Bordeaux*, a sure sequel to *Friar Bacon and Friar Bungay*. Loosely based on the chivalric romance *Duke Huon of Bordeaux*, this play features Roger Bacon, who had renounced his magic in the earlier play, here using his powers to free beggars from prison, relieve their suffering, and confound their enemies. The play seems a perfect vehicle to rehabilitate this popular character from his relative ignominy at the close of *Friar Bacon and Friar Bungay*. As one might expect, the friar shares center stage with a chaste and loyal woman, Rossalin, the wife of Bordeaux. Her warrior husband gone and feared dead, the constant Rossalin is wooed by a tyrant, then banished, penniless, when she rejects him. Eventually, her endurance, Bacon's magic, and Bordeaux's return win a happy ending.

The appeal of this play is more social than political. Rather than supporting a particular view of a specific national situation, it attempts to move the audience to identify with the poor folk portrayed onstage. In the most affecting scene of the play, Rossalin and her children beg from passersby, who probably resemble members of the audience; they scorn her pleas as the ruses of a begging thief or give her the cold comfort of pious warnings about the wages of sin. That chance can reverse the places of rich and poor is one message of the play, a message that

Greene hoped to insinuate through his characteristic appeal to the finer emotions of his audience. *John of Bordeaux* illustrates once again that Greene's way in drama, as in prose, is not to threaten or lecture his audience on their duties to one another, but to create characters of sympathy and courage, humility and humor, who might win their hearts and set examples to follow.

OTHER MAJOR WORKS

LONG FICTION: *Mamillia: A Mirror or Looking Glass for the Ladies of England*, 1583, 1593 (2 parts); *Arbasto: The Anatomy of Fortune*, 1584; *The Mirror of Modesty*, 1584; *Morando: The Tritameron of Love*, 1584, 1587 (2 parts); *Planetomachia*, 1585; *Euphues His Censure to Philautus*, 1587; *Penelope's Web*, 1587; *Alcida: Greene's Metamorphosis*, 1588; *Pandosto: The Triumph of Time*, 1588; *Perimedes the Blacksmith*, 1588; *Ciceronis Amor*, 1589 (also known as *Tullies Love*); *Menaphon*, 1589; *Francesco's Fortunes*, 1590; *Greene's Mourning Garment*, 1590; *Greene's Never Too Late*, 1590; *Greene's Farewell to Folly*, 1591; *Greene's Vision*, 1592; *Philomela: The Lady Fitzwater's Nightingale*, 1592.

POETRY: *A Maiden's Dream*, 1591.

NONFICTION: *The Spanish Masquerado*, 1589; *The Royal Exchange*, 1590; *A Notable Discovery of Cozenage*, 1591; *The Second Part of Conny-Catching*, 1591; *The Third and Last Part of Conny-Catching*, 1592; *The Defense of Conny-Catching*, 1592; *A Disputation Between a Hee Conny-Catcher and a Shee Conny-Catcher*, 1592; *The Black Book's Messenger*, 1592; *A Quip for an Upstart Courtier*, 1592; *Greene's Groatsworth of Wit Bought with a Million of Repentance*, 1592; *The Repentance of Robert Greene*, 1592.

MISCELLANEOUS: *Life and Complete Works in Prose and Verse*, 1881-1886 (15 volumes).

BIBLIOGRAPHY

Chapman, William Hall. *William Shakespeare and Robert Greene: The Evidence*. 1912. Reprint. New York: Haskell House, 1974. This work examines the relationship between Shakespeare and Greene and the question of authorship.

Crupi, Charles. *Robert Greene*. Boston: Twayne, 1986. A basic biography of Greene that covers his life and works. Bibliography and index.

Helgerson, Richard. *The Elizabethan Prodigals*. Berkeley: University of California Press, 1976. This study of the prodigal son and repentance in Elizabethan literature touches on works by Greene. Bibliography and index.

Hoster, Jay. *Tiger's Heart: What Really Happened in the Groat's-Worth of Wit Controversy of 1592*. Columbus, Ohio: Ravine Books, 1993. This work examines *Greene's Groatsworth of Wit Bought with a Million of Repentance*, looking at the facts behind it. Also examines the sixteenth century English theater. Bibliography and index.

Newcomb, Lori Humphrey. *Reading Popular Romance in Early Modern England*. New York: Columbia University Press, 2002. A look at Greene's *Pandosto: The Triumph of Time* and William Shakespeare's *A Winter's Tale* (pr. c. 1610-1611). Although *Pandosto* is a novel rather than a play, Newcomb's comments on romance shed light on Greene's plays. Bibliography and index.

Senn, Werner. *Studies in the Dramatic Construction of Robert Greene and George Peele*. Berne, Switzerland: Francke, 1973. Senn compares and contrasts the dramatic works of Greene and Peele. Bibliography.

*Christopher J. Thaiss,
updated by Frank Day*

LADY AUGUSTA GREGORY

Born: Roxborough, Ireland; March 15, 1852
Died: Coole Park, Ireland; May 22, 1932

PRINCIPAL DRAMA

Spreading the News, pr. 1904, pb. 1905
The Rising of the Moon, pb. 1905, pr. 1907
Kincora, pr., pb. 1905, pr. 1909 (revised)
The White Cockade, pr. 1905, pb. 1906
Hyacinth Halvey, pr., pb. 1906
The Canavans, pr. 1906, pr. 1907 (revised), pb. 1912
The Gaol Gate, pr. 1906, pb. 1909
Dervorgilla, pr. 1907, pb. 1908
The Jackdaw, pr. 1907, pb. 1909
The Workhouse Ward, pr. 1908, pb. 1909 (with Douglas Hyde; revision of *The Poorhouse*, pb. 1903, pr. 1907)
Seven Short Plays, pb. 1909
The Travelling Man, pb. 1909, pr. 1910
The Image, pr. 1909, pb. 1910
The Full Moon, pr. 1910, pb. 1911
Coats, pr. 1910, pb. 1913
The Deliverer, pr. 1911, pb. 1912
Grania, pb. 1912

Damer's Gold, pr. 1912, pb. 1913
The Bogie Men, pr. 1912, pb. 1913
Irish Folk-History Plays, pb. 1912
New Comedies, pb. 1913
The Wrens, pr. 1914, pb. 1922
Shanwalla, pr. 1915, pb. 1922
The Golden Apple, pb. 1916, pr. 1920
Hanrahan's Oath, pr. 1918, pb. 1922
The Jester, wr. 1918, pb. 1923
The Dragon, pr. 1919, pb. 1920
Aristotle's Bellows, pr. 1921, pb. 1923
The Story Brought by Brigit, pr., pb. 1924
Sancho's Master, pr. 1927, pb. 1928
Dave, pr. 1927, pb. 1928
Selected Plays, pb. 1962 (Elizabeth Coxhead, editor)
The Collected Plays of Lady Gregory, pb. 1970 (4 volumes; Ann Saddlemyer, editor)

OTHER LITERARY FORMS

Lady Augusta Gregory would have been a significant figure in Irish literature even if she had never written any plays. Her earliest writing centered largely on the life and correspondence of her deceased husband, Sir William Gregory. In 1894, two years after his death, she completed the editing of *An Autobiography of Sir William Gregory*, and in 1898 she published *Mr. Gregory's Letter Box*.

Lady Gregory also did a number of translations, most notably of Molière's plays. Her plays were published in various collections throughout her lifetime and were collected in 1970 in *The Collected Plays of Lady Gregory*. A selection of nine plays can be found in *Selected Plays*, edited by Elizabeth Coxhead.

Lady Gregory's most valuable work for literature and Irish culture, however, was the gathering and publishing of the myths and legends of Ireland, a love for which began early in her life and lasted until the end. Traveling from village to village and cottage to cottage (including trips to the Aran Islands at the same time as John Millington Synge), she devoted herself to the recording of an oral tradition that she felt was central to the future as well as to the past of Ireland. The first of these numerous collections appeared as *Cuchulain of Muirthemne* in 1902, and the last, as *Visions and Beliefs in the West of Ireland* in 1920.

Lady Gregory also wrote for and about the Irish Renaissance itself, particularly about the dramatic revival. In 1901, she edited a book of essays, *Ideals in Ireland*, that called for a renewal of Irish culture and criticized English domination. Her account of the rise of Irish drama and the struggles at the Abbey Theatre is given in *Our Irish Theatre* (1913).

Lady Gregory's other nondramatic writings grow largely out of her personal life. In 1921, she published *Hugh Lane's Life and Achievement*, a memorial to her beloved nephew who died with the sinking of the *Lusitania*, and in 1926 *A Case for the Return of Hugh Lane's Pictures to Dublin*, part of a futile battle to get his French Impressionist collection returned from England. Others oversaw the publication of some of her private thoughts and reminiscences in *Coole* (1931) and *Lady Gregory's Journals, 1916-1930* (1946).

ACHIEVEMENTS

The achievement of Lady Augusta Gregory is not to be found in awards and prizes given to her, but in the gift of her life, possessions, and talents to the literary and cultural awakening of modern Ireland. She would be a significant figure for any one of her contributions, but the sum of them makes her central to one of the most important movements in modern literature.

Lady Gregory's initial contribution to what has been called the Irish Renaissance (or Irish Literary Revival) was the early collecting of the myths and folktales of the Irish people. In so doing, she was participating in the discovery of the richness of so-called primitive cultures that was only beginning at the end of the nineteenth century to engage the interest of the earliest anthropologists and ethnologists. These efforts not only served an important historical function but also became a part of both her own plays and the poetry and plays of William Butler Yeats, and contributed significantly to the Irish people's rediscovery of and pride in their own past.

Lady Gregory's plays, while not greatly influential on other playwrights, were important in their contribution to what has come to be called the Irish dra-

Lady Augusta Gregory (Library of Congress)

matic movement (especially in its primary expression, the Abbey Theatre) and as works of art in their own right. They broke new ground, for example, in the mixing of the fabulous with the realistic and in the transformation of peasant speech into successful dramatic dialect. Lady Gregory perfected the one-act play; she also led the way in demonstrating that the lives and speech of peasants could be the stuff of dramatic art—and, in fact, the popular success of her plays helped sustain the Abbey Theatre during years of great struggle.

Perhaps her most important and most widely acknowledged achievement was as a motivating and sustaining force behind the Irish dramatic movement. As cofounder, with Yeats and Edward Martyn, of the Irish Literary Theatre at the turn of the century, later to become the Abbey Theatre, she worked tirelessly as director, fund-raiser, playwright, and defender in what seemed times of endless trouble.

Lady Gregory's contribution, however, extended beyond the dramatic movement itself. She also played the important role of encourager, comforter, guide, provider, and friend to fellow writers and laborers in the cultural renewal of Ireland. The symbol for this was her country estate, Coole Park, near Galway in the west of Ireland, where she graciously provided spiritual and material sustenance to many, in the best-known instance to Yeats.

Biography

Lady Augusta Gregory was born Isabella Augusta Persse on March 15, 1852, at Roxborough in County Galway, the twelfth of sixteen children. Her staunchly Protestant family was thought to have come to Ireland in the seventeenth century at the time of Oliver Cromwell's suppression of Ireland. The intellectual and aesthetic sterility of her childhood was relieved by the storytelling and quiet nationalism of her Catholic nurse, Mary Sheridan.

An avenue to the larger world of which she longed to be a part was provided by her marriage in 1880 to Sir William Gregory, a man of sixty-three who had recently resigned as governor of Ceylon and returned to his country estate at Coole Park, not far from Roxborough. As the new Lady Gregory, she found a large library, a kind and intelligent husband, and the beginning of an outlet for her incipient talents.

It was to be many years before Lady Gregory would think of herself as a writer. Her first efforts consisted largely of editing the autobiography and letters of her husband, who died in 1892. Of more importance to her career, however, was the publication in 1893 of both Douglas Hyde's *Love Songs of Connacht* and Yeats's *The Celtic Twilight*. These two books sparked her own latent interest in the tales and speech of the Irish peasant. She was drawn to their lyric beauty, imaginativeness, and rich spirituality, and she made it her task for much of the rest of her life to record this rich oral tradition.

Lady Gregory first discussed with Yeats in 1894 the possibility of launching a theater devoted to the writers and plays of Ireland. Their dream became a reality in January, 1899, with the founding of the Irish Literary Theatre. This movement was to be the central concern and accomplishment of her life.

Initially, Lady Gregory's contribution was largely practical. She was an organizer, fund-raiser, encourager, and occasional collaborating playwright; it was she who first argued that the theater should be in Dublin, not London, as Yeats proposed. Within a few years, however, she was writing plays of her own, initially, she said, to provide some brief comic relief from Yeats's more esoteric works. These one-act plays proved to be more popular with the Dublin audiences than were Yeats's, and her career as a playwright was well, if late, begun.

The early years of the literary movement also saw the publication of a series of her collections of Irish myth and folklore, beginning with *Cuchulain of Muirthemne* and followed in rapid succession by *Poets and Dreamers* (1903), *Gods and Fighting Men* (1904), *A Book of Saints and Wonders* (1907), and *The Kiltartan Wonder Book* (1910). These were important books because they offered a single coherent telling of previously scattered tales (especially of the mythic hero Cuchulain) and, in so doing, made this heritage more widely known not only in Ireland but also abroad.

The single phrase that sums up all that Lady Gregory aimed for and achieved was her own oft-repeated observation to her fellow laborers that "we work to add dignity to Ireland," and work she did. As one of the directors of the Abbey Theatre (initially with Yeats and Synge), she was involved in constant battles—artistic, political, financial, and personal—to preserve the dramatic movement. As an Anglo-Irish Protestant with strong nationalistic convictions, she was suspected and attacked by both sides in the increasingly politicized and polarized Ireland.

The symbol of all this was the famous riots early in 1907 over Synge's *The Playboy of the Western World* (pr., pb. 1907). Considered a slur against Ireland by the ardent nationalists, and immoral by some quarters of the Catholic Church, the play evoked a series of riotous confrontations within the theater and an ongoing controversy without. Lady Gregory defended the play with all her energies at the time and during a subsequent tour in the United States in the winter of 1911 to 1912, even though she personally disliked it.

Lady Gregory's skill as a dramatist grew rapidly, and her works were increasingly important to the financial solvency of the Abbey Theatre (especially since she collected no royalties for her plays). The first of a number of collections of her dramas, *Seven Short Plays*, came out in 1909, followed later by *Irish Folk-History Plays* (1912) and *New Comedies* (1913).

The beginning of World War I marks a tragic turn in the life of a remarkable woman who became a central figure in the literary life of a nation, a woman who did not write her first imaginative work until she was fifty. Lady Gregory's beloved nephew, Hugh Lane, died in the sinking of the *Lusitania*. His death left her with the task of trying to get his important collection of French Impressionist art returned from England to its rightful place in Ireland, a battle into which she futilely poured her declining energy until her death. In January, 1918, her only child, Robert Gregory, was killed while flying for the Royal Flying Corps. These personal tragedies, combined with her grief for the suffering of Ireland during the prolonged bloodshed of that nation's struggle for liberation, cast a darkness over Lady Gregory's declining years.

The 1920's were still years of effort on behalf of the Abbey Theatre, however, and they were brightened for a time by Lady Gregory's special role in the discovery and encouragement of Sean O'Casey. That undertaking also took a sad turn, as O'Casey broke relations with her and the Abbey Theatre over their rejection in 1928 of *The Silver Tassie*. Lady Gregory's last years were spent in poor health and growing loneliness, but she maintained her aristocratic dignity up until her death at Coole Park in 1932.

ANALYSIS

Lady Augusta Gregory's beginnings as a dramatist were modest. Her first efforts involved contributions of pieces of realistic dialogue and plot to Yeats's early poetic drama. Even when she began to write her own plays, she claimed that they were only to serve as brief comic relief from the more serious work of the poet. This situation, however, did not last long. Lady Gregory's plays soon became important in their own right to the Abbey Theatre and to the Irish dramatic movement, and they remain a significant part of one of the most seminal periods in modern literature.

The central motivation behind all that Lady Gregory did is found in her statement that she and others worked "to add dignity to Ireland." Some of the ways in which her plays contributed to this lofty goal are suggested in her remarks on the desired impact of her historical plays, comments that at the same time give telling clues to the nature of her own work:

> I had had from the beginning a vision of historical plays being sent by us through all the counties of Ireland. For to have a real success and to come into the life of the country, one must touch a real and eternal emotion, and history comes only next to religion in our country. And although the realism of our young writers is taking the place of fantasy and romance in the cities, I still hope to see a little season given up every year to plays on history and in sequence at the Abbey, and I think schools and colleges may ask to have them sent and played in their halls, as a part of the day's lesson.

One sees here much that finds dramatic expression in Lady Gregory's plays, including the desire to have her work both spring from and appeal to the common people of Ireland; the intention to recover and respect

Irish history, particularly as it is found in the stories and songs of the people rather than in the books of academics; the unapologetic combination of didacticism and entertainment; the wish to preserve romance, myth, and imagination in an increasingly skeptical, political, and materialistic age; and the hope that Irish drama could be a natural part of the education and life of the Irish people.

These desires find expression in each of the three categories into which Lady Gregory's plays are usually divided: comedy, tragedy and tragicomedy (including the historical plays), and plays of wonder and the supernatural. Lady Gregory's first plays were comedies. Like most of her drama, they were largely one-act works that combine a skillful command of structure, plot, and dialogue with genuine insight into human nature.

In their formal character, Lady Gregory's plays can most readily be understood, following critic Ann Saddlemyer, as classical treatments of largely Romantic subject matter. The plays demonstrate economy and balance, are very linear and simple in construction, and generally observe the classical unities of time, place, and action. The tendency to sameness and predictability in structure is relieved by her storyteller's gift for local color and suspense, and by her effective adaption to the stage of the Irish-English dialect that she called Kiltartan (after the district in which she and her peasant models lived).

Lady Gregory was not a great playwright. She was not considered so at the time, by herself or by others, and is only in recent years being rescued from the oblivion into which her reputation fell following her death. She deserves great respect, however, as one of a lesser rank who made a significant contribution at a crucial time and in so doing served both her art form and her country well.

COMEDIES

The recurring locale for Lady Gregory's comedies is the rural community of Cloon, a fictional version of the real town of Gort, near which Lady Gregory lived on her estate, Coole Park. The poor peasants and only slightly less impoverished townspeople with whom she mingled from her earliest childhood became her characters. She tried to capture not only

their speech and mannerisms but also the quality of their lives that transcended their poverty and sometime clownishness. That quality had to do with their closeness to the spiritual heart of life, to myth and legend, to a sense of the past and of community, and to other dimensions of reality that Lady Gregory feared were disappearing from Ireland and from the world.

These characters are not idealized. They are often fools, simpletons, and ne'er-do-wells. Hers are not the heroic poor of some literature, yet beneath their gullibility, love of gossip, and simplemindedness is a closeness to the core of life that Lady Gregory admired and tried to capture. This accounts for the consistent sympathy for her comic creations. Lady Gregory laughed with, not at, her characters, and she did not set herself apart from the human foibles that they portray.

One of those foibles, both a weakness and a strength, is the Irish love of talk. This very human desire to share lives manifests itself comically (and sometimes tragically) in Lady Gregory's plays in an unquenchable thirst for gossip, a penchant for exaggeration and misrepresentation, a disposition to argument for its own sake, and an irrepressible urge to know their neighbor's business. This foible is at the heart of two of her most successful works, *Spreading the News* and *The Workhouse Ward*.

SPREADING THE NEWS

The skillfully structured *Spreading the News* turns on the eagerness of a man's neighbors to hear and believe the worst about him. Poor Bartley Fallon, a man convinced that if something bad is to happen, it will happen to him, finds that his innocent attempt to do a good deed becomes the basis, through a series of outrageous misunderstandings of everyday speech, of the universally believed story that he has murdered his neighbor and plans to run off with the neighbor's wife. The humor of the situation grows exponentially as each new person who happens on the expanding story embraces it eagerly and adds to its enormity in passing it on. The comic tension builds even beyond where it seems it must be released as the appearance in good health of the supposedly murdered man only prompts the police to arrest him along with Bartley as they set off to find the body of the "real" victim, whom he is assumed to be impersonating.

THE WORKHOUSE WARD

The Workhouse Ward also turns on the Irish love of talk. Two old men in a poorhouse argue viciously with each other until the sister of one, whom he has not seen for five years, arrives to offer to take him into her home (for largely selfish reasons). He is eager to leave his pitiful surroundings until he learns that his roommate cannot come with him. After the sister leaves, the two old men resume their fighting, hurling objects as well as words at each other.

Both comedies illustrate Lady Gregory's ability to capture the rich dialect of the Irish peasant in all its color, cadence, and natural metaphor. One of the old men in *The Workhouse Ward* responds to the charge of the other in typical fashion: "To steal your eggs is it? Is that what you are saying now. . . . Isn't it a bad story for me to be wearing out my days beside you the same as a spancelled goat. Chained I am and tethered I am to a man that is ransacking his mind for lies!"

As with most of Lady Gregory's comedies, these two reveal her interest in something more than laughter. The condescending and uncomprehending attitude of the English magistrate in *Spreading the News* is a clear if commonplace indictment of Ireland's oppressor, and his repeated references to his earlier duties in the Andaman Islands indicate that Ireland too is simply another of England's exploited colonies. Both plays also reveal Lady Gregory's fondness for symbolism and near allegory. She later said she wanted the two old men in *The Workhouse Ward* to be seen as symbols of Ireland itself, suggesting that the Irish, as with any family, feel free to fight among themselves but do not desire the interference of outsiders, especially hypocritical ones whose apparent benevolence is only thinly disguised exploitation.

TRAGEDIES

Although it was her comedies that were most popular and are most likely to last, Lady Gregory herself preferred to write tragedy. Her work in this form ranges from the highly condensed power of *The Gaol Gate* to one of her most ambitious works, the three-act *Grania*. One finds in the tragedies the clearest expression of the idealism, patriotism, and respect for the noble lost cause that are so much a part of Lady Gregory's own character. The tragedies generally center on people who have refused to be the passive pawns of circumstance, and who, in insisting on acting independently, come to grief against the harsh realities of life.

THE GAOL GATE

In *The Gaol Gate*, the man who has acted independently is dead before the play begins. Refusing to inform on his friends, he is hanged for a political murder he did not commit. The action of the play centers on the discovery of his fate by his wife and mother. As they approach the prison, unaware that he has been executed, they agonize over the rumors that he has in fact informed against his friends. His wife makes excuses for him in preparation for the possibility that it may be true, but his mother, with a longer memory of the suffering of the people, will not tolerate the idea of a son who is not faithful to his neighbors. On learning that her son has died for his loyalty, the mother breaks into a shocking celebration that reveals simultaneously the strength of the code of honor of the nationalist, the woman's own selfish desire to triumph over her son's false accusers, and the mental strain of a grief too great to bear; the latter is reminiscent of Maurya's break with reality at the end of Synge's *Riders to the Sea* (pb. 1903).

GRANIA

Given the nature of Irish history, it is fitting that Lady Gregory's historical plays are found among the tragedies and tragicomedies. This is true both of plays based on Ireland's mythological history, such as *Grania*, and of those based on more verifiable history, such as *The White Cockade*, an idiosyncratic account of James II and that infamous turning point for Ireland, the Battle of the Boyne. In *Grania*, a play that Lady Gregory never allowed to be produced during her lifetime, one finds in the treatment of the legendary love triangle between Grania, Diarmuid, and Finn perhaps her most sophisticated exploration of psychological motivation. As a strong woman whose determination to live intensely rather than conventionally leads her into a lifetime of turmoil to which she never succumbs, Grania perhaps contains more elements of Lady Gregory than she herself was ready to make public on the stage.

PLAYS OF WONDER

The third major category consists of the plays of wonder and the supernatural. Here Lady Gregory explored most directly that realm of folk spirituality she loved and valued so much. It was this sense of the spiritual (in both a figurative and literal sense), underlying and giving meaning to the physical, that Lady Gregory feared was disappearing from the modern world. Her plays of wonder and the supernatural, many of them written for children, portray that world where reality is multilayered and the physical world is suffused with beings of another dimension.

THE TRAVELLING MAN

The Travelling Man, in which Lady Gregory gave the Christian tradition of entertaining angels or Christ an Irish setting, is a case in point. Lady Gregory adapted a story told her by an old peasant woman about a destitute girl who had been directed by Christ to the house of her future husband, but who herself failed years later to show charity to Christ in the guise of a traveling beggar. In the play, the woman readies the house, as she does each year on the anniversary of her rescue, for the possibility that her Saviour from long ago, the King of the World, will return as he had promised. She is so absorbed in preparing only the finest for what she assumes will be his dignified and impressive return, that she turns furiously against the poor beggar who interrupts her preparations, and who, of course, is Christ himself. In this play, as in many others, Lady Gregory demonstrated her interest in the deeper reality that infused the life of the Irish peasant with a significance that transcended physical deprivation.

This need for a spiritual sustenance to redeem the tragic physical and political burden that had long been Ireland's is the overarching theme of Lady Gregory's plays. She valued, above all, the mythmakers of Ireland, whether the anonymous poets of ancient legend, or Raftery, the blind wandering poet of the early nineteenth century, or a political mythmaker such as Charles Parnell. She wanted the Irish Renaissance to be a revival of mythmakers, herself among them. The potential for all this rested, she believed, in the Irish people themselves, particularly the peasants, with their natural mythmaking reflected in their common stories, their conception of the world about them, and their very speech.

OTHER MAJOR WORKS

NONFICTION: *Our Irish Theatre*, 1913; *Hugh Lane's Life and Achievement*, 1921; *A Case for the Return of Hugh Lane's Pictures to Dublin*, 1926; *Coole*, 1931; *Lady Gregory's Journals, 1916-1930*, 1946 (Lennox Robinson, editor); *Lady Gregory's Diaries, 1892-1902*, 1995 (James Pethica, editor).

EDITED TEXTS: *An Autobiography of Sir William Gregory*, 1894; *Mr. Gregory's Letter Box*, 1898; *Ideals in Ireland*, 1901; *Cuchulain of Muirthemne*, 1902; *Poets and Dreamers*, 1903; *Gods and Fighting Men*, 1904; *A Book of Saints and Wonders*, 1907; *The Kiltartan History Book*, 1909; *The Kiltartan Wonder Book*, 1910; *The Kiltartan Poetry Book*, 1919; *Visions and Beliefs in the West of Ireland*, 1920 (2 volumes).

BIBLIOGRAPHY

Kohfeldt, Mary Lou. *Lady Gregory: The Woman Behind the Irish Renaissance.* New York: Atheneum, 1985. A narrative biography that provides information about Lady Gregory's early personal life as well as a thorough account of her involvement with the Irish Literary Revival. While the work's main emphasis is on the literary personalities among whom Lady Gregory spent the influential part of her life, use is also made of archival material.

Kopper, Edward A., Jr. *Lady Isabella Persse Gregory.* Boston: Twayne, 1976. A basic biography of Lady Gregory that covers her private and professional life as well as her writings. Bibliography and index.

Saddlemyer, Ann, and Colin Smythe, eds. *Lady Gregory: Fifty Years After.* Totowa, N.J.: Barnes and Noble Books, 1987. A substantial collection of essays that provide a comprehensive scholarly treatment of Lady Gregory's life and times. Her playwriting and involvement with the Abbey Theatre provide the volume with its central focus. Also included is a considerable amount of material pertinent to an evaluation of the overall cultural significance of Lady Gregory's career.

Stevenson, Mary Lou Kohfeldt. *Lady Gregory: The Woman Behind the Irish Renaissance*. New York: Atheneum, 1984. A basic biography of Lady Gregory that covers her life and works. Examines at length her role in the Irish Literary Renaissance. Bibliography and index.

Tobin, Seán, and Lois Tobin, eds. *Lady Gregory Autumn Gatherings: Reflections at Coole*. Galway, Ireland: Lady Gregory Autumn Gathering, 2000. This collection of essays examines Lady Gregory, her life and friends, her professional life, and her writings. Bibliography.

Daniel Taylor,
updated by George O'Brien

ALEXANDER GRIBOYEDOV

Born: Moscow, Russia; January 15, 1795
Died: Teheran, Persia; February 11, 1829

PRINCIPAL DRAMA

Molodye suprugi, pr., pb. 1815 (adaptation of Creuze de Lesser's play *Secret de ménage*)

Student, pb. 1817, pr. 1904 (with P. A. Katenin)

Svoya sem'ya: Ili, Zamuzhnyaya nevesta, pr. 1818 (with A. A. Shakhovskoy and Nikolay Khmelnitsky)

Pritvornaya nevernost, pr., pb. 1818 (with A. A. Gendre, adaptation of Nicolas Barthe's play *Les Fausses Infidelités*)

Proba intermedii, pr. 1819

Kto brat, kto sestra: Ili, Obman za obmanom, pr. 1824 (with P. A. Vyazemsky)

Gore ot uma, wr. 1824, uncensored pr. 1831, censored pb. 1833, uncensored pb. 1861 (*The Mischief of Being Clever*, 1857)

OTHER LITERARY FORMS

In addition to his masterpiece *The Mischief of Being Clever* and a few early comedies and dramatic fragments of which he was sole or, more often, partial author, Alexander Griboyedov wrote a few lyrics, including a translation of Psalm 151, some epigrams, and a short poem addressed to the Decembrist poet Alexander Ivanovich Odoevsky. Although Griboyedov's first comedies and poems showed promise, a number of them are incomplete or appear as parts of works written jointly with other Russian playwrights.

It was only with *The Mischief of Being Clever*, his sole significant work, that he achieved the status of a major writer.

ACHIEVEMENTS

Along with such famous authors as Nikolai Gogol, Alexander Ostrovsky, and Alexander Sukhovo-Kobylin, Alexander Griboyedov is regarded as one of the great Russian playwrights of the nineteenth century. He is usually remembered as the author of a single comedy, *The Mischief of Being Clever*; his other works are generally considered to be too fragmentary and undeveloped to be regarded as masterpieces. Like his eighteenth century predecessor Denis Ivanovich Fonvizin, Griboyedov was an assimilator of Western European forms; he was able to adapt French comedy to a Russian setting. Molière's famous play *Le Misanthrope* (pr. 1666; *The Misanthrope*, 1709) served as a model for *The Mischief of Being Clever*. Both comedies are distinguished for their witty style, the tightness of their plots, and their vivid characters. Griboyedov's use of rhymed iambic lines in varying lengths probably demonstrates the impact of the famous Russian fabulist Ivan Krylov, who wrote at the end of the eighteenth and beginning of the nineteenth centuries. Like Krylov and Fonvizin, Griboyedov made extensive use of colloquial language in *The Mischief of Being Clever*, and this combination of idiomatic language with taut, tightly constructed iambs made the play memorable to readers of his time. As a result, a great number of the lines have become proverbs, especially those from the speeches of the protagonist Chatsky and of Khlyostova, a pillar of Moscow society and the aunt of Chatsky's love interest, Sofia.

Like Fonvizin, Griboyedov combined stylistic brilliance with an accurate picture of contemporary Russia. Early nineteenth century Moscow was a society in transition, based on a solidly Russian foundation, essentially rural and conservative, yet with a patina of foreign, particularly French, culture. It is because of his brilliant depiction of this conflict between the old and new in Russian life, combined with his implied criticism of the limitations of the Russian milieu and his memorable style, that Griboyedov has come to be so highly regarded by modern critics.

BIOGRAPHY

Alexander Sergeyevich Griboyedov was born in Moscow on January 15, 1795. His father, Sergey Ivanovich, was a retired captain of the dragoons. His mother, Nastasya Fyodorovna (née Griboyedova), was from a more prominent branch of the same family. Although not wealthy, the Griboyedovs were comfortable. They belonged to high society, and Alexander received a good education.

In accordance with the custom of the time, Griboyedov was taught at home by German tutors. His first tutor, Johann Petrosilius, was later the librarian at Moscow University, while a subsequent tutor, Johann Ion, had been a student at Göttingen University. Griboyedov spent several years in the University School in Moscow before entering Moscow University in 1806, when he was only eleven. He completed courses in literature and in law, studied physics and mathematics, and was ready to embark on a doctorate in 1812 when the Napoleonic invasion interrupted his studies. By this time, he was fluent in French, German, English, and Italian and was also a fine pianist.

Following limited service in the Napoleonic Wars, Griboyedov moved to St. Petersburg and entered the College of Foreign Affairs. A talented musician and a dandy, he spent considerable time with actors and playwrights, and it was at this time that he wrote, either alone or in collaboration with friends, the short comedies that were the precursors of *The Mischief of*

Being Clever. He joined the same Masonic lodge, Des Amis Réunis (the assembled friends), to which the philosopher Peter Chaadayev and the future Decembrist Pavel Pestel belonged.

Griboyedov's connections with the theatrical world and his involvement with the ballerina Istomina led to a quarrel and later a duel in which Griboyedov and Count Zavadovsky were paired against A. I. Yakubovich and A. I. Sheremetev. Zavadovsky killed Sheremetev, and the encounter between Griboyedov and Yakubovich was delayed. The surviving principals were punished; Zavadovsky was exiled, and Yakubovich was sent to the Caucasus with the Nizhny-Novgorod Dragoons. Yakubovich and Griboyedov subsequently fought in the Caucasus, and Griboyedov was wounded in the hand.

Griboyedov's facility with languages having enabled him to acquire knowledge of Persian, he was given the post of secretary in the Russian Legation in Teheran. Griboyedov spent nearly two years, from early 1819 until the end of 1821, in Persia. He intensely disliked his situation and was able to obtain the post of diplomatic secretary to the proconsul of the Caucasus, General A. P. Yermolov, serving in Tiflis, Georgia, through 1822 and the beginning of 1823. He subsequently spent most of 1823 and part of 1824 in Moscow on extended leave, followed by a stay in St. Petersburg. Because of his friendships with a number of the Decembrists, Griboyedov was suspected of complicity in the Decembrist Revolt of 1825. Lack of evidence led to his release after a four-month imprisonment, and he returned to the Caucasus in 1826.

Russia's military successes against Persia resulted in the treaty of Turkmanchai (drafted by Griboyedov), in consequence of which the province of Erivan (later the Republic of Armenia) was ceded to Russia. Griboyedov returned to Teheran to take charge of executing the treaty. Having left his Georgian bride in Tabriz, he arrived in the capital early in January, 1829.

Three Armenians—a eunuch who was comptroller of the imperial household, and two women from the harem of the shah's son-in-law—asked for asylum at the Russian legation under terms of the new treaty. The outraged Persians, whose religious and social customs had been disregarded and whose national dignity had been insulted, stormed the legation on February 11, 1829, to kill the eunuch and bring back the women. The fury of the mob was so great that everyone in the building, including Griboyedov, was slaughtered. His body was dragged through the streets and was so terribly mutilated that it could only be identified by the deformity resulting from his duel with Yakubovich. Any manuscript that he may have had in his possession perished with him. He was thirty-four.

ANALYSIS

Alexander Griboyedov's early comedies demonstrate in embryonic form the same facility with colloquial Russian, mastery of plot, and ability to create interesting characters that are a hallmark of his masterpiece, *The Mischief of Being Clever*. With the exception of the fragmentary tragedy *Gruzinskaya noch* (1859; Georgian night), his initial efforts generally involve love intrigues in which jealousy is used to arouse an insufficiently responsive spouse or suitor, as occurs in *Molodye suprugi* (young spouses) and *Pritvornaya nevernost* (feigned infidelity). These first plays are quite successful attempts to superimpose French works on a Russian setting: *Molodye suprugi* is an adaptation of *Secret de ménage* (1809; the secret of the household), by Creuze de Lesser. It is only with the appearance of *The Mischief of Being Clever* itself that Griboyedov can be considered to have written an entirely original play. The love conspiracies central to the earlier works are here employed primarily to illuminate character or to provide a means of criticizing society. Like Alexander Pushkin, Griboyedov managed to combine a ready understanding of human behavior with a witty, colloquial style to produce the sort of social analysis that would later be the hallmark of Russian literature.

THE MISCHIEF OF BEING CLEVER

Although completed in 1824, Griboyedov's *The Mischief of Being Clever* was prohibited by the censor. It circulated in manuscript and was printed with large cuts in 1833. It was not published in full until 1861, the year in which the serfs were liberated.

In *The Mischief of Being Clever*, Griboyedov observes the classical unities of time, place, and action. The play takes place within a twenty-four-hour period, is set in the Famusovs' house in Moscow, and revolves around Chatsky's attempt to rekindle the love of Sofia, only to find that, in his absence, she has bestowed her affections on someone else. The curtain rises on the Famusov household early in the morning. Sofia Famusova has spent the night playing duets with her beloved, Alexey Molchalin ("Aleksis the Reticent"), her father's secretary and a resident in the house. The anxious maid, Liza, is afraid that Sofia's father, Pavel Afanasevich, a director of a government office, will be furious when he discovers that his seventeen-year-old daughter has spent the night, however chastely, with a man. When Sofia does not heed her warning calls, Liza makes the clock strike and is apprehended by the already suspicious father. He decides that what he had assumed to be music was actually the chimes of the striking clock, and he chides Liza for making so much noise while simultaneously fondling her. Pavel Famusov's surreptitious displays of affection are discouraged only when Sofia summons Liza and finally appears with a candle in her hand, followed by Molchalin.

Scene 4 opens with Famusov and Molchalin colliding in a doorway, the sort of chance encounter that was a main component of the early comedies that Griboyedov produced. Molchalin's servility before Famusov (underscored in Russian by the suffix *s*, an abbreviation of "your excellency") stresses the awkwardness of their meeting. Famusov assumes that Sofia and Molchalin have met early that morning, never suspecting that they have spent the night together. Famusov bemoans the lot of the widowed father attempting to rear a young daughter alone, and the reader is reminded that the arrangement of an offspring's suitable marriage was of cardinal importance for the Russian nobility. An employee and a flunky, Molchalin would not be considered a proper match for Sofia. Liza confides to Sofia when they are alone in the following scene that Famusov, like all Muscovites, wants a son-in-law with medals, rank, and money, such as Colonel Skalozub ("grinner"). Sofia's scornful rejection of Skalozub prompts Liza to reminisce about the wit and charm of Alexander Sergeevich Chatsky, but Sofia, having fallen in love with Molchalin, is critical of Chatsky's rapier-sharp wit, and she is apparently hurt by his having left three years earlier. With this introduction, Chatsky makes an appearance at the beginning of the next scene.

As in Griboyedov's other comedic efforts, the arrival of Chatsky presages romantic complications, for he is Molchalin's rival for Sofia's affections. In *The Mischief of Being Clever*, however, the emphasis is on Chatsky's critique of Moscow society, not on the love intrigue. Puzzled by the cool reception from his childhood friend Sofia yet dazzled by her beauty, Chatsky launches into a critique of the superficialities and failings of people they both know. His attack seems to be twofold: He is not only trying to elicit a response from her but also delivering a stinging commentary on the aristocracy. He sarcastically comments, "What new thing will Moscow show me? Yesterday there was a ball, tomorrow there will be two . . . the same verses in albums." He mentions, in passing, Sofia's own relative who was "an enemy of books" and was against education. When Chatsky criticizes Molchalin, Sofia makes a stinging reply, and he in turn is hurt by her treatment. He declares his love. Famusov reappears, happy to see Chatsky but shocked and frightened by Chatsky's ridicule of the pretensions and inequities of contemporary Russia. Famusov considers him a *carbonari* (revolutionary) and calls him a "dangerous man." Hearing of the imminent entrance of Skalozub, a possible suitor and a powerful careerist, Famusov cautions Chatsky to watch his tongue. Famusov and Skalozub preen themselves about the glories of modern Moscow, particularly the young women who love military men because of "patriotism." After both have gloated over the new houses built since the fire of 1812, Chatsky's acid rejoinder that the "homes are new, but the prejudices are old" emphasizes the inanity of the conversation. Thereupon Famusov introduces Chatsky to Skalozub, remarking on Chatsky's inexplicable aversion to serving in a governmental agency. Clearly the mouthpiece for the playwright's views, Chatsky excoriates the excesses of the upper classes and recounts a horrible tale of a brutish aristocrat who exchanged his faithful servants for three greyhounds. (The refusal of the censors to pass the play in full until 1861, the year in which the serfs were liberated, surely stems from lines such as these.) The dense Skalozub, having missed the point, once again launches into a discussion of uniforms and of the Russian officers who speak French.

Griboyedov then abruptly shifts his emphasis back to the love interest. Molchalin's fall from a horse has left him uninjured but has terrified Sofia; her anxious reaction to his accident reveals to all her concern and arouses Chatsky's suspicions. Molchalin is anxious about the impressions others may receive and is afraid that Sofia's obvious concern will be a source of gossip. With encouragement from Liza, Sofia goes to visit Skalozub, Chatsky, and her father. Molchalin takes advantage of her absence to attempt to bestow his affections on Liza in a scene that stresses once more the vulnerability of women in the lower classes in prerevolutionary Russia and the inequities of serfdom.

Chatsky's declaration early in act 3 that he would not lose his mind if Sofia could prove Molchalin deserving of her love is Griboyedov's first mention of insanity in the play, a motif that is repeated with Chatsky later. The Russian word for madness, *sumasshestvie* (going out of one's mind), recalls the title, which translates literally as woe from the mind. It is precisely this, Chatsky's intelligence, that has caused Sofia's love for him to cool and has made him the outsider in his society. Chatsky's ensuing conversation with Molchalin stresses yet again that the mind of the former is contrasted to the mindlessness of the latter.

Chatsky's alienation from Moscow life is underscored when he meets two old friends, modeled on friends of Griboyedov, and finds that they have been married in his absence. The wife's fondness for society life and her protectiveness of her husband have caused strains in the marriage, and Chatsky deeply regrets the changes in his former companion. When an intelligent man marries and becomes part of the Muscovite milieu, is he then automatically emasculated?

The arrival of other guests at the Famusovs' ball provides Griboyedov with an opportunity to introduce typical Muscovite characters, such as the prince and princess who want to marry off their six daughters to appropriate young men. Sofia's aunt Khlyostova has also come to the party; her marvelous use of colloquial Russian (set in iambs) is the antithesis of the Frenchified jargon, typical of much of the aristocracy, that Chatsky (along with Griboyedov) criticizes.

Molchalin's ability to smooth over an awkward moment leads Chatsky to make a pointed observation about him, and Sofia angrily comments that Chatsky is not himself (literally, "not in his mind"). This remark is interpreted as "has gone out of his mind," a misunderstanding that Sofia does not attempt to correct. From this point on, Chatsky's separation from his fellows is absolute and permanent; even Sofia's chance discovery of Molchalin's true feelings at the end of the play (in typical vaudeville style) does not cause a renewal of her love for Chatsky. He calls for his carriage and flees Moscow even as he had done three years earlier, yet now without the comfort of Sofia's affection and without hope. The play ends with Famusov worrying about what "Princess Marja Aleksevna is going to say," Griboyedov thereby stressing once again the shallowness of contemporary Russian life.

Composed in iambs, with a good percentage of the lines in Alexandrines, *The Mischief of Being Clever* continues the poetic tradition of eighteenth and early nineteenth century Russian literature, for it was only in the 1830's and 1840's that prose became the accepted medium for drama. Although Griboyedov's early comedic efforts are also in verse, his employment of a stilted rhyme scheme (*aabbcc*) in these plays makes the lines flow much less smoothly than they do in *The Mischief of Being Clever*. The colloquial language and the poetic structure combine so well that the lines of the play are easy to memorize; Pushkin predicted that half the lines were bound to become proverbs, and time has indeed proven this to be true. Sixty-one phrases from the play are proverbial; it is the most quoted book in Russian.

The Mischief of Being Clever is admired as much for its keen analysis of society as for its remarkable style. In Chatsky, the outsider who has left Moscow only to return three years later, Griboyedov has the perfect social critic. Chatsky's keen sense of observation penetrates all corners. He mocks the toadying and careerism of Molchalin, blasts the Frenchified Russian adopted by the upper classes, despises the endless, meaningless socializing characteristic of life in Moscow and St. Petersburg, the "two capitals." Chatsky is particularly critical of his countrymen's attempts to acquire the veneer of Western European culture while leaving the substance untouched. Griboyedov bravely used his comedy as a vehicle to condemn some of the worst excesses of his society. The play touches now and again on the inescapable fact that all the wealth and glitter, the luxurious life of the aristocracy of his time, rested on the backs of the serfs, who could be disposed of ("traded for greyhounds") at a whim. It is a note also sounded in his potentially brilliant fragment *Gruzinskaya noch*, in which a Georgian nobleman precipitates a tragedy by trading his old nurse's son for a prized horse.

The characters in *The Mischief of Being Clever* can generally be considered as types. Famusov is the proper father who is not above squeezing Liza on the sly, a kind man who nevertheless sends two servants to Siberia at the end of the last act for not having noticed Chatsky lingering in the house. Like his sister-in-law Khlyostova, he is a decent and engaging individual who is nevertheless limited; both are very much at one with their conservative, pretentious society. Molchalin is the opportunist willing to prostitute himself to further his career, while Skalozub is the military man opposed to education and societal change.

Sofia and Chatsky are clearly the most interesting individuals in *The Mischief of Being Clever*. An intelligent, attractive young woman, one of the only people whom Chatsky admires, Sofia is enigmatic. She reacts very strongly against Chatsky's acid criticisms of Moscow society, yet she is too intelligent to be unaware of her society's flaws. Her preference for Molchalin seems to depend more on what he is not than on what he is. Molchalin never exhibits ambition, cunning, or sarcasm. He is always agreeable and silent, a cog in the workings of the state bureaucracy, while Chatsky refuses to be part of that system, preferring instead to "escape" abroad.

The obvious focal point of the play, Chatsky deserves special attention. He rails against the inanity of Moscow life and censures especially the backwardness of social institutions and customs. Chatsky is a patriot, however, or he would never have braved a trip in winter to return to a home he had previously found disagreeable (although his love for Sofia surely is an important factor in his return). His attachment to Sofia may actually be considered emblematic of the depth of his feeling for Russia, for Sofia's rejection at the end of the play is identified by him as and coincides with the ultimate rejection by his society.

The combination of Sofia-Molchalin and Chatsky-Sofia is one that recurs in nineteenth and twentieth century Russian literature, from Pushkin's *Evgeny Onegin* (1825-1833; *Eugene Onegin*, 1881) through such prose works as Ivan Turgenev's novellas and Ivan Goncharov's *Oblomov* (1859; English translation, 1915) to such Soviet masterpieces as Yuri Olesha's *Zavist* (1927; *Envy*, 1936). The strong woman is unable to form a relationship with the protagonist, who is always on the edge of society, and instead she becomes involved successfully with an uninteresting, nonindividualized man who fits in much more effectively with his fellows. While the unfortunate loser in these situations has generally and mistakenly been deemed "weak" and "superfluous," this designation is not necessarily correct. It is actually society that is flawed. So rigid are the rules, so narrow the limits within which one is permitted to function, that the thinking individual is doomed to ineffectiveness. A woman could be strong because she was not expected to take an active role, but a man had to conform or be ostracized.

It is no accident that Chatsky is rejected by his milieu. Unable to function within a system he despises, he is considered "mad" and is expelled. His fictitious "madness" symbolizes his distance from the "norm." The recurrence both of the "superfluous man" and of "madness" in Soviet literature and society is a reminder that Russian institutions are still bedeviled by the same suspicious mistrust of the new and the same superficial acquisition of Western culture that inspired the critical thrust of Griboyedov's great comedy, written nearly one hundred years before the Russian Revolution.

BIBLIOGRAPHY

Harden, Evelyn. J. *The Murder of Griboedov: New Materials*. Birmingham, Ala.: University of Birmingham, 1979. This examination of the death of Griboyedov examines his personal and literary life. Bibliography.

Karlinsky, Simon. *Russian Drama from Its Beginnings to the Age of Pushkin*. Berkeley: University of California Press, 1985. This historical overview of Russian drama provides the background in which to place Griboyedov's work. Bibliography and index.

Mirsky, D. S. *A History of Russian Literature from Its Beginnings to 1900*. 1958. Reprint. Evanston, Ill.: Northwestern University Press, 1999. This history covers Russian literature before and during the time in which Griboyedov was active.

Zinik, Zinovy. "Failing Triumphantly." Review of *The Mischief of Being Clever*, by Griboyedov. *Times Literary Supplement*, April 2, 1993, p. 18. Reviews a production of Griboyedov's most famous work.

Janet G. Tucker

FRANZ GRILLPARZER

Born: Vienna, Austria; January 15, 1791
Died: Vienna, Austro-Hungarian Empire; January 21, 1872

PRINCIPAL DRAMA

Blanca von Kastilien, wr. 1809, pb. 1912, pr. 1958
Die Ahnfrau, pr., pb. 1817 (*The Ancestress*, 1938)

Sappho, pr. 1818, pb. 1819 (English translation, 1928)

Das goldene Vliess, pr. 1821, pb. 1822 (*The Golden Fleece*, 1942; includes *Der Gastfreund* [*The Guest*], *Die Argonauten* [*The Argonauts*], and *Medea* [English translation])

König Ottokars Glück und Ende, pb. 1824, pr. 1825 (*King Otakar's Rise and Fall*, 1930)

Ein treuer Diener seines Herrn, pr. 1828, pb. 1830 (*A Faithful Servant of His Master*, 1941)

Des Meeres und der Liebe Wellen, pr. 1831, pb. 1840 (*Hero and Leander*, 1938)

Melusine, pr., pb. 1833

Der Traum ein Leben, pr. 1834, pb. 1840 (*A Dream Is Life*, 1946)

Weh' dem, der lügt, pr. 1838, pb. 1840 (*Thou Shalt Not Lie!*, 1939)

Ein Bruderzwist in Habsburg, pr., pb. 1872 (*Family Strife in Habsburg*, 1949)

Libussa, pb. 1872, pr. 1874 (English translation, 1941)

Die Jüdin von Toledo, pr. 1872, pb. 1873 (*The Jewess of Toledo*, 1913-1914)

Sämtliche Werke, pb. 1878-1880 (10 volumes)

OTHER LITERARY FORMS

Like his dramas, the works that Franz Grillparzer produced in other genres reflect probings of the human spirit that lay bare the fundamental conflicts of humankind's existence. His poetry is reserved and thoughtful with strong confessional overtones. Especially characteristic in their melancholy self-analysis are the seventeen poems of the cycle *Tristia ex Ponto* (1835; elegies from the Black Sea). In these lyrics, the author captured the torment of his personal situation as he pondered love relationships that remained unfulfilled. He also wrote pointed political verse and clever, bitter epigrams. Two novellas, *Das Kloster bei Sendomir* (1827; the monastery at Sendomir) and *Der arme Spielmann* (1847; *The Poor Fiddler*, 1946), are closely akin to his dramas in their psychological penetration of life and in their intensity of dramatic effect. *The Poor Fiddler*, a coded portrait of Grillparzer's own soul, is particularly powerful in its revelation of his passionate love for the common people.

Many significant notes about theater and literature, filled with deep insight into the nature and enduring laws of art, are contained in the fragmentary autobiography and the diaries and letters that were collected, edited, and published after his death.

ACHIEVEMENTS

Only belatedly recognized as the most important Austrian dramatist of the nineteenth century, Franz Grillparzer mediated the influence of German classicism on productions created for the Viennese stage. In so doing, he integrated a multitude of impulses from folk theater, romanticism, Baroque and Spanish tradition, and Shakespearean tragedy, introduced uniquely Austrian historical and cultural substance, gave the resulting creations elevated literary form, and established them in an appropriate relationship to the great Weimar plays of Friedrich Schiller and Johann Wolfgang von Goethe.

Throughout his career, Grillparzer experienced alternating extremes of public success and rejection. His first produced drama, *The Ancestress*, was greeted with enormous praise when it premiered in 1817, although it also caused him to be branded as a writer of fate tragedies. This circumstance gave him a degree of notoriety in Vienna even when later works were misunderstood or received with harsh criticism. Because of the controversial subject matter of some of his historical tragedies, he encountered repeated difficulties with the Austrian censors; their intervention sometimes delayed performance and publication of individual pieces for years. Grillparzer was extremely sensitive to critical opinion, and the initial failure of the comedy *Thou Shalt Not Lie!* in 1838 caused him to withdraw from open theatrical involvement for the rest of his life.

At first, the more successful plays enjoyed short-lived popularity. After Grillparzer's retirement from the stage, however, they were all but forgotten, even in Vienna. Not until Heinrich Laube began to revive the interest of theatergoers with new performances of the tragedies at the Burgtheater did these creations finally gain acceptance as standards of the Austrian stage. In contrast to the disastrous premier twenty years earlier, Laube's production of *Hero and Leander* in 1851 was an overwhelming triumph. As a result, *Hero and Leander* eventually became Grillparzer's most popular dramatic work. Because of its powerful influence on subsequent German treatments of material from Greek antiquity, the trilogy *The Golden Fleece* is now regarded as a high point of nineteenth century theatrical art, comparable to Schiller's *Wallenstein* trilogy (pr. 1798, 1799, 1799, respectively; pb. 1800), and a significant monument of world literature.

BIOGRAPHY

The external life of Franz Serafikus Grillparzer was rather quiet and lonely. Following a colorless childhood, he matriculated at the University of Vienna, where he studied law with little enthusiasm. When his father died in 1809, he was forced to go to work to help support his mother and three brothers. A close relationship with his overly sensitive mother contributed to the development of a personality that caused him to have extreme difficulty in adapting to normal public life and basic human associations. Experience as a tutor and unpaid assistant in the court library preceded his entry into a full-time civil service career in 1814. Between those beginnings and 1856, when he retired from his official duties with the title of Privy Councilor, he worked variously in the customs department, the finance ministry, and the state archives, of which he became director in 1832. In 1861, he was elected to the Herrenhaus, where he continued to participate in political affairs for a number of years.

While still a student, Grillparzer wrote his first play, *Blanca von Kastilien*. Although it was rejected when he submitted it to the Burgtheater, he continued to cultivate his interest in the stage. A turning point in his life occurred in 1816, when he became acquainted with Josef Schreyvogel, who was then director of the Burgtheater. Schreyvogel encouraged his literary efforts, giving him the stimulus that he needed to write *The Ancestress*. Embittered by the criticism of the play as a fate tragedy following its sensational premier, Grillparzer looked for less controversial substance for his next work. *Sappho*, which he completed in the summer of 1817, was well received,

Franz Grillparzer (Library of Congress)

and he was appointed theater dramatist at the Burgtheater.

A relatively intense period of creativity was interrupted in 1819, when Grillparzer's mother committed suicide. His recovery from the brink of nervous collapse was facilitated by a trip to Italy, where he was enthralled by the architectural wonders of major cultural centers. On his return home, however, a poem that he had written about Rome was interpreted as an attack on the Catholic Church, and he found himself in trouble with the imperial court. This incident set the pattern for subsequent encounters with censorship. The fact that he was out of favor also made it impossible for him to advance in the civil service as he wished to do.

On his return from Italy, Grillparzer completed the powerful trilogy *The Golden Fleece*. Its immediate failure in the theater caused Grillparzer to lose confidence in his creative ability, but within a year he had become engrossed in a new project. Performance of *King Otakar's Rise and Fall* was delayed for more than two years after he finished it. The portrayal of racial conflicts within the empire and unfavorable treatment of the Bohemians caused it to be banned until the empress read it and arranged for it to be staged.

During the next fifteen years, Grillparzer's literary endeavors met with spotty success. To relieve tensions that arose when a club to which he belonged was raided on suspicion of subversive activity, he traveled to Germany in 1826. There he met Goethe and other writers. When he returned to Vienna, he began work on *A Faithful Servant of His Master*, which enjoyed an enthusiastic reception at its premier in 1828. A period of isolation from the theater and the public in the early 1830's was followed by travel abroad to Paris and London in 1836. After *Thou Shalt Not Lie!* failed to measure up to audience expectations in 1838, Grillparzer ceased to publish his writings, although he completed three additional dramas before his death on January 21, 1872.

Personal loneliness throughout his life played an important role in Grillparzer's development of specific literary themes. He never wed, although he continued a courtship of Katharina Fröhlich for more than fifty years. His inability to commit himself to a permanent relationship was a deeply personal problem equaled only by the tragic situations in his plays. When, on his eightieth birthday, he finally asked Kathi to marry him, she turned him down, placing a final seal on his failure to find any degree of lasting happiness in a melancholy life.

ANALYSIS

Several specific features of his œuvre determine the nature of Franz Grillparzer's legacy as a dramatist. Among the most important are a strong confessional tone, intense psychological development of characters, a focus on human destiny as a product of individual personality, and a clear striving toward the creation of myth. In conscious emulation of Goethe, the Austrian author conceived plays that directly reflected his innermost concerns. As parts of a grand statement about Grillparzer's life, they are notable for their expression of resignation, weariness, lack of faith in self, and tragic sensitivity. Far removed from

Schiller's heroic idealism, they dwell on the perception that earthly fulfillment is a shadow. The result is a combination of baroque sensibility and the brooding *Weltschmerz* that spread through Europe at the beginning of the nineteenth century.

Particularly remarkable is the diversity of substance in which Grillparzer encased the exposition of his central themes and problems. Legend and mythology, Greek and Slavic sagas, European history, and models from other literatures all yielded material that he processed into drama that testifies to his unique theatrical awareness and attention to detail. From the perspective of richly varied backgrounds, he explored the human condition in all its private tensions, contradictions, burdens, and inevitabilities. His primary interest was the spectrum of circumstances that arise from and contribute to the individual's inadequacy in the social context. It is in that light that his creations emerge as documents of self-observation and self-interpretation.

BLANCA VON KASTILIEN

An almost natural mastery of theatrical technique, careful integration of impulses from a broad variety of sources, and the search for a viable personal style are the most visible characteristics of Grillparzer's early dramaturgical endeavors. Although it was rejected by the Burgtheater because of its broken form, *Blanca von Kastilien* documents the young university student's talented application of stagecraft to literary substance even before his successful public debut with *The Ancestress*. Reminiscent of Schiller's *Don Carlos, Infant von Spanien* (pr., pb. 1787; *Don Carlos, Infante of Spain*, 1798) in tone and approach, Grillparzer's first play combines Spanish subject matter with romantic constructs, presenting a wealth of dramatic motifs in artful iambic verse. His rapid mastery of technical matters in the works that followed allowed him to bring to Viennese theater a new richness of conception.

THE ANCESTRESS

The Ancestress is especially interesting for the harmonious interweaving of elements from many different origins. Among the models that influenced the mood and direction of this play were Ludwig Tieck's horror drama, the focus on the classical concept of fate as employed by Goethe and Schiller, William Shakespeare's device of the effective curse, Zacharias Werner's fatal determinism, and Adolf Müllner's adaptation of the incest theme within the context of popular fate tragedy. Grillparzer's own contribution of realistic immediacy based on internal illumination of key figures set his creation apart from those of his predecessors, anticipating trends that would become widespread in German stage productions only after his death.

The critics who dismissed *The Ancestress* as fate tragedy in the popular manner of the time failed to recognize that Grillparzer's approach to his subject matter was fundamentally new, replacing external motivation with psychological impulses shaped by the imperatives of individual character. Outwardly, it is true, the exposition of *The Ancestress* contains all the elements of a romantic horror story, including a prophetic curse, robbers, a ghost, a dagger, and the classic gothic setting of a Moravian castle. Internally, however, the calamitous course of events is determined by the specific psychological responses of three central characters to situations with which they are confronted. Ultimately, the figures themselves must bear full responsibility for their own destruction.

For each of the principal characters, perception of basic conflicts and the resulting destructive reactions are different. The premise of the story is that the ghost of an adulterous ancestress appears in times of crisis to warn later generations of impending doom. Her last known descendant, Count Borotin, accepts the woman's legendary curse at face value. Because he believes that fate is determined to destroy his line, he cannot act effectively to avert the coming catastrophe. The robber Jaromir, Borotin's missing son, who is patterned somewhat after Schiller's character Karl Moor from his play *Die Räuber* (pb. 1781; *The Robbers*, 1792), unwittingly slays his father when the latter joins in a foray against the outlaws. Jaromir's own death occurs in the arms of his ghostly forebear. His heart fails him when he must face up to the fact of his patricide and acknowledge that Bertha, with whom he is in love, is his sister. Bertha, on the other hand, whose resemblance to the ancestress intensifies the incest theme of the play, commits suicide in the face of the events that reveal her lover first as a robber, then as her brother, and finally as the murderer of her father.

The effectiveness of *The Ancestress* on the stage is a reflection of Grillparzer's certain instinct for successful theater. More substantial than the fate motif in the drama's structure, for example, is the mythical opposition of father and son, which creates the real inner tension of the work. The rapid, sometimes dreamlike action is enhanced by the quick flow of the four-foot Spanish trochaic verse pattern. Pathos saturates the substance and gives it nobility, while the directness and clarity of the lines provide an appropriate vehicle for the revelation of the agitated spiritual lives of the characters in powerful illumination of the psychology of evil.

SAPPHO

In an effort to draw closer to the dramatic ideals fostered by Weimar classicism, Grillparzer turned to material from ancient Greek tradition for the plays that immediately succeeded *The Ancestress*. Of special importance for his presentation of archetypal human problems in *Sappho* and *The Golden Fleece* is the combination of objective revelation of individual motives for action with the processing of myth as symbolic representation of mortal reality. The tragedy of the aging priestess-poetess Sappho's unrequited love for the young Phaon provides a vehicle for a theme that was of great personal significance to Grillparzer: the inability to reconcile life and art. In softly subtle, gracefully dignified lines that tenderly expose the entire spectrum of mature feminine feeling, the dramatic poet sought to blend the noble moderation of Goethe's *Iphigenie auf Tauris* (pr. 1779; *Iphigenie in Tauris*, 1793) with the unhappy artistic dilemma of *Torquato Tasso* (pb. 1790; English translation, 1827). The result was a distinctive work that underlines Grillparzer's ability to create and magnify effects that lay bare subconscious drives through peculiarly unsettling natural utterance, sound, gesture, and reflex motion, all of which communicate poetically the essence of the nature of humankind.

THE GOLDEN FLEECE

With *The Golden Fleece*, Grillparzer gave voice to a new type of tragic sensitivity in the renewal of material that had been dramatized earlier by Euripides, Seneca, Pierre Corneille, and Friedrich Maximilian Klinger. Internal intensification of the mythical object is carried to extremes through the externalization of the dramatic action in a manner that reinforces and heightens the exposure of Medea's monstrousness. The destructive circumstances of her unhappy alliance with Jason and its aftermath provide the framework for what some critics regard as Grillparzer's most powerful statement concerning subjection to a fate that has its genesis within the individual spirit. In that respect, the trilogy exhibits a kinship with traditional Austrian Jesuit drama in its depiction of unhappiness as a tragic consequence of weakness in the face of divine order.

The most consistently pessimistic of Grillparzer's dramatic creations, *The Golden Fleece* consists of *Der Gastfreund* (one act, *The Guest*), *Die Argonauten* (four acts, *The Argonauts*), and *Medea* (five acts). Despite the apparent distance from intimate reality that is inherent in the mythological substance, *The Golden Fleece* was for its author a deeply personal confessional work. The play's fearful vision of the impossibility of happy marriage, depicted in the painful relationship between Jason and Medea, was an outgrowth of Grillparzer's own failure to find fulfillment in his encounters with women. A primary focus of the entire trilogy is the ultimate isolation of man from woman.

Superficially, the three plays follow the pattern of action established in earlier dramatizations of the classical sources. *The Guest*, which serves as a prologue to the Medea plot, describes the destruction of the young Greek Phrixus, who is slain by the barbarian, King Aeetes. In violation of the sacred law of hospitality, the savage monarch kills Phrixus for the golden fleece that he wears, thereby calling down a curse on himself and his family. In *The Argonauts*, Jason, who has come to reclaim the fleece, wins the love of Medea, enlists her aid against her father and brother, thereby causing their deaths, and removes her from her raw, natural surroundings to the civilization of his homeland. The action reaches its climax in *Medea*, in which the title figure fails to bridge the abyss that separates her inner being and savage origins from the cultivated life of Jason's world. Her inability to cope with Jason's betrayal and adapt herself to the demands of the foreign culture causes her to slay both her female rival for Jason's affections and her own children.

Much of the theatrical strength of *The Golden Fleece* derives from the dramatist's use of innovative devices to heighten internal contrasts and increase the inner tension of the presentation. One obvious example is the clear differentiation between barbarians and Greeks in the poetic form of their spoken lines: The cultured Greeks speak in regular blank verse, while Medea and the other barbarians express themselves in excited, choppy free rhythms. Language determines the dramatic color of the scenes, intensifying harsh moods, underscoring personality, and fully conveying the darkness of human anguish.

In sharp deviation from the original legend, in which the golden fleece serves as an external focus for tragedy by virtue of its nature as a demoniac and destructive talisman, Grillparzer's trilogy unfolds its tragic conflicts from within the characters themselves. The fleece moves into the background, and its fateful power is replaced by the confrontation of mortal passions, the internal polarities of individual characters, and the conflict between the individual and the social environment. In this extraordinary work, Grillparzer created settings for lyric, even operatic monologues that have since become recognized as high points in classical German drama.

HERO AND LEANDER

Hero and Leander, Grillparzer's most poignant adaptation of classical source material, can be seen as refining and perfecting techniques that were established in *The Golden Fleece*. Keen psychological insight directs the portrayal of the two lovers in the welding together of classical, romantic, and baroque elements in a beautiful harmony of content and form.

Grillparzer's historical and political plays reflect a concerted attempt to achieve the directness of Shakespeare's dramatic portraits of powerful rulers. A primary focus is the grand tragedy of the soul that is guilty and doomed by reason of its very nature. The works in this group offer a fresh view of history that mixes a sensitive though often sentimental patriotism with an acute awareness of communality in the weaving together of individual, state, and people. These plays also reveal Grillparzer's vision of an Austrian tradition distinguished by its humanistic liberalism.

KING OTAKAR'S RISE AND FALL

In *King Otakar's Rise and Fall*, realistic characterization and motivation give special force to the tension that exists between the static picture of Emperor Rudolf I of Habsburg, symbol of the good and noble ruler, and the dynamic rendering of the falling monarch Otakar. A calculated glorification of the Habsburg dynasty, this play emerged not out of belief in the crown itself but out of a much broader faith in the divinely ordained mission of Austria in the world. Intended as a bridge between Baroque and classical theater, *King Otakar's Rise and Fall* is a model of carefully executed form and painstaking technical detail.

In 1823, when Grillparzer began to concern himself with the problem of the general, typical, exemplary element of human action that affects the course of history, he focused his attention on Napoleon Bonaparte. The combination of his interest in the French emperor and a newly awakened consciousness of Austria's historic destiny stimulated the creation of *King Otakar's Rise and Fall*, the most successful of his political plays. Grillparzer consciously compared the Bohemian king to Napoleon, identifying in both lives a key turning point in the separation of a first marriage and the entering of a second. Beginning from this intimate point of departure, he formulated within the drama a human personality that is psychologically developed in finest detail.

Grillparzer's primary purpose was to portray in the fall of Otakar the birth of the Habsburg dynasty. Essential to his dramatic conception of the situation is the juxtaposition of the great but ruthless tyrant, who tumbles from power as a victim of his own hubris, with the monumentality of the rising Emperor Rudolf I. Otakar, a law unto himself, who in his greed for land has lost any sense of restraint, parts from his wife Margareta, whom he had married only for her property. He then weds the Hungarian heiress Kunegunde, for whom he is too old. His betrayal of Margareta establishes the inner basis for his fall. Political and military successes that follow the new marriage lead him to believe that he is moving toward his goal, when, in fact, his willful rejection of the demands of justice causes him to lose position. Beginning in the second act, when he receives the imperial crown, Rudolf of Habsburg appears in counterpoint to Otakar as an example of the just ruler who governs in moderation. He increases in glory in direct proportion to Otakar's decline. Only in the final tragic recognition of the impropriety of his actions does Otakar regain personal dignity.

Despite the particular strength that the play obtains from Grillparzer's masterful handling of a fullness of private, intimately suggestive psychological characteristics in the projection of his central figures, the work does exhibit visible weaknesses. Specifically, artificial constructs carry greater weight than poetic elements, and the action and characterization often go in different directions. In the light of the dramatist's intention to create a patriotic celebration of the House of Habsburg, the portrayal of Rudolf is somewhat disappointing. His moral superiority is presented in such a fashion that he comes across as a schoolmaster rather than an enlightened monarch.

A FAITHFUL SERVANT OF HIS MASTER

An intense presentation of individual struggle within the context of social involvement is given in *A Faithful Servant of His Master*, perhaps the most painfully gripping of Grillparzer's histories. It explores the heroic ideal of loyalty to duty in an almost clinical study of human interrelationships. The notion that life is fatefully determined by qualities of the inner person is dramatized in this story of the moral defeat of a violently assertive, passionate power-figure who destroys the young wife of a retainer while the latter faithfully conducts the king's affairs in his absence.

A DREAM IS LIFE

Moral considerations also form the basis for the two nontragic dramatic fairy tales that Grillparzer produced in the 1830's. *A Dream Is Life* and *Thou Shalt Not Lie!*, the last plays that he himself published, employ the devices of Viennese folk theater in the presentation of cleverly framed learning experiences. Both plays share with Grillparzer's tragedies a richness of suggestively formed, inwardly motivated characters, carefully maintained dramatic tension, harmony of dialogue and gesture, and masterfully structured stage effect. *A Dream Is Life*, adapted from a play by Pedro Calderón de la Barca and a story by Voltaire, portrays the purifying effect of a dream in which the central figure encounters the destructive results of the ambition that has led him to a criminal career. When he awakens, he repents and resumes a life of quiet contentment.

THOU SHALT NOT LIE!

In an effort to employ an ethical focus in raising the literary level of the German comedy beyond that which had been achieved by the folk theater of Ferdinand Raimund, Grillparzer wrote the hilarious dramatic fairy tale *Thou Shalt Not Lie!* Unlike the tragedies, this play is an extremely light-hearted work, free of sexual confusion and weighty problems of guilt and atonement. Framed against a background of historical reality taken from a French chronicle account, *Thou Shalt Not Lie!* explores the question of whether absolute truth is a reasonable expectation, given human frailty and the complexity of life. The ambiguity of language plays a special role in conveying the piece's message. The presentation moves between drastic comic effect and smiling wisdom in a convincing in-depth revelation of humankind's essential nature.

The central character of the comedy is the kitchen boy Leon, who is given the task of obtaining the freedom of Atalus, nephew of the Bishop Gregor von Chalon. Atalus is being held hostage by the heathen Count Kattwald. Under an oath never to lie while engaged in the undertaking, Leon succeeds in his quest by telling the truth. In one instance, his progress depends on the fact that others do not believe him when he reveals his actual intentions; in another, his open truthfulness wins him an unexpected ally. Although truth is victorious, the victory is not pure, and the play ends with a modification of Chalon's demand in recognition of the mitigating circumstances of the human condition.

The dramatic tension of the play arises from the confrontation between Chalon's defense of absolute truth as a principle of God's law and the colorful disorder of mortal reality; each new situation emphasizes from a fresh perspective the complexity of the issue. In the key encounter between Leon and the ferryman, the former leaves deceptive ambiguities behind and embraces genuine truthfulness through the exercise of trust in God. The comical elements in situations, characters, and language are thus used effectively to reveal the world's weaknesses while affirming existence from the higher perspective of faith in the divine order of being. Although its subtleties were not appreciated by Grillparzer's contemporaries, *Thou Shalt Not Lie!* is one of the few truly great German comedies.

LATER WORKS

The works that remained unpublished at Grillparzer's death represent a synthesis of his inner and outer worlds. In loosely composed political tragedies that are remarkable for their beauty of vision, their musical, imagistic language, and their insight into the powerful interplay of conscious and subconscious experience, he issued a deeply pessimistic warning about the dissolution of the old humane Europe. More than anything else, the literary creations of his old age are an accounting of the writer with himself as the lonely defender of a traditional world order against a subjectively oriented materialistic civilization.

OTHER MAJOR WORKS

LONG FICTION: *Das Kloster bei Sendomir*, 1827 (novella); *Der arme Spielmann*, 1847 (novella; *The Poor Fiddler*, 1946).

POETRY: *Tristia ex Ponto*, 1835; *Gedichte*, 1872.

MISCELLANEOUS: *Sämtliche Werke: Historisch-kritische Gesamtausgabe*, 1909-1948 (42 volumes); *Sämtliche Werke, Ausgewählte Briefe, Gespräche, und Berichte*, 1960-1964 (4 volumes).

BIBLIOGRAPHY

Peck, Jeffrey M. *Hermes Disguised: Literary Hermeneutics and the Interpretation of Literature: Kleist, Grillparzer, Fontane*. Berne, Switzerland: Lang, 1983. Examines German literature in the nineteenth century, focusing on Grillparzer, Heinrich von Kleist, and Theodor Fontane. Bibliography.

Reeve, William C. *The Federfuchser, Penpusher from Lessing to Grillparzer: A Study Focused on Grillparzer's "Ein Bruderzwist in Habsburg."* Buffalo, N.Y.: McGill-Queen's University Press, 1995. An examination of Grillparzer that centers on his plays, particularly *Family Strife in Habsburg.* Bibliography and index.

_____. *Grillparzer's "Libussa": The Tragedy of Separation.* Montreal: McGill-Queen's University Press, 1999. This study of Grillparzer's drama focuses on his play *Libussa.* Bibliography and index.

Roe, Ian F. *Franz Grillparzer: A Century of Criticism.* Columbia, S.C.: Camden House, 1995. An analysis of the literary criticism that arose around Grillparzer's works over time. Bibliography and index.

_____. *An Introduction to the Major Works of Franz Grillparzer, 1791-1872: German Dramatist and Poet.* Lewiston, N.Y.: Edwin Mellen Press, 1991. A critical look at the major literary works of Grillparzer, including his drama. Bibliography and index.

Thompson, Bruce. *Franz Grillparzer.* Boston: Twayne, 1981. A basic biography of Grillparzer, covering his life and works. Bibliography and index.

Wagner, Eva. *An Analysis of Franz Grillparzer's Dramas: Fate, Guilt, and Tragedy.* Lewiston, N.Y.: Edwin Mellen Press, 1992. A study of Grillparzer's plays, focusing on his views of fate and guilt. Bibliography.

Lowell A. Bangerter

ANDREAS GRYPHIUS

Born: Glogau, Silesia (now Głogów, Poland); October 2, 1616

Died: Glogau, Silesia (now Głogów, Poland); July 16, 1664

PRINCIPAL DRAMA

Beständige Mutter: Oder, Die Heilige Felicitas, wr. c. 1634-1644, pr., pb. 1657 (translation of Nicholaus Causinus's *Tragoediae sacrae*)

Die Sieben Brueder: Oder, Die Gibeoniter, wr. c. 1640-1641, pr. 1652, pb. 1698 (translation of Joost van den Vondel's *De Gebroeders*)

Seugamme: Oder, Untreues Haussgesinde, wr. c. 1645, pb. 1663 (translation of Girolamo Razzi's *La Balia*)

Leo Armenius: Oder, Fürstenmord, wr. 1646, pb. 1650, pr. 1661

Catharina von Georgien: Oder, Bewehrete Beständigkeit, wr. 1647, pr. 1655, pb. 1657

Cardenio und Celinde: Oder, Unglücklich Verliebte, wr. c. 1647-1649, pb. 1657, pr. 1661

Horribilicribrifax Teutsch: Oder, Wählende Liebhaber, wr. c. 1647-1649, pb. 1663

Absurda Comica: Oder, Herr Peter Squentz, wr. c. 1648, pb. 1657, pr. 1672 (based on William Shakespeare's *A Midsummer Night's Dream*)

Ermordete Majestät: Oder, Carolus Stuardus, König von Gross Britannien, version A wr. c. 1649, pr. 1650, pb. 1657, version B pb. 1663, pr. 1665

Majuma: Freuden-Spiel, wr. 1653, pr. 1653, pb. 1657 (musical comedy)

Grossmüttiger Rechts-Gelehrter: Oder, Sterbernder Aemilius Paulus Papinianus, pb. 1659, pr. 1660

Piastus, Lustund Gesang-Spiel, wr. c. 1660, pr. 1660, pb. 1698 (musical)

Verliebtes Gespenste und die gelibte Dornrose, pr., pb. 1660 (*The Beloved Hedgerose*, 1928)

Der Schwermende Schäffer, wr. 1661, pr. 1661 (translation of Thomas Corneille's *Le Berger extravagant*)

OTHER LITERARY FORMS

Andreas Gryphius was one of the most important European poets of the Baroque period, comparable in power and complexity to the English Metaphysical poets. This is all the more astonishing as there was little vernacular German poetry to serve as a model other than the theoretical exhortations of Martin Opitz in his *Buch von der deutschen Poeterey* (1624) and the samples given there. Like many of his contemporaries, Gryphius cut his poetic teeth on Latin verse composition in school; as early as 1632, he wrote *Herodis furiae et Rachelis lacrymae* (1634), an epic in Latin on the story of Herod, which he followed with another one in 1635 and *Olivetum libri tres* (1646), a verse epic on the sorrows of Christ on Mount Olive. His claim to fame, however, rests on his mastery of the sonnet form, which he began to display with his first German publication, the *Lissaer Sonette* (1637), a collection that also earned for him the title of *poeta laureatus*. His command of the ode, epigram, and other poetic forms is evident in his subsequent publications of 1639 and 1657, where he not only domesticates the classical models but also manages to bend them to a powerful expression of his own worldview.

The themes of his poems are those familiar throughout Western Europe at this time, ranging from the vanity of all things, the fleeting and problematic nature of time, and the dubious nature of worldly reality all the way to an expectation of permanence, peace, and constancy in another existence constituted by love, human and divine. What makes Gryphius special is his ability to convey within the traditional tropes and topoi the genuine anguish and personal feeling about human suffering and about the destruction which the Thirty Years' War brought to Germany generally and his family in particular. His use of paradox, caesura, juxtaposition of thought, and metaphor is again commonplace. What sets him apart from others is the power of his language, the vivid metaphors, and above all the creativity he demonstrates in inventing a vocabulary quite his own, his famous *Zentnerworte*, words heavy with meaning and sound, frequently neologisms. Both scholars and general readers found Gryphius particularly congenial

after the two world wars, when his worldview and theirs seemed to be most congruent.

ACHIEVEMENTS

Experts in the field of German Baroque literature have called Andreas Gryphius the most outstanding author of the seventeenth century next to Hans Jakob Christoffel von Grimmelshausen. This assessment not only reflects the important role of Gryphius's work in the development of German literature, where he established both the sonnet and a new kind of drama in the vernacular but also indicates that, like Grimmelshausen, he is still readable today—a judgment more appropriate to his poetry than his drama, for modern expectations of drama have changed significantly more than those applied to poetry.

Gryphius has been called the first German high-culture dramatist whose plays, especially his tragedies, were highly regarded in his own time, as many editions and performances attest. His comedies proved to be no less popular over the ages, and today his mixed-form plays attract the greatest interest. In *Cardenio und Celinde*, often regarded as his most complex and fascinating drama, he broke with several norms and expectations of his age. Most notably, he used non-royal personages to act out the juxtaposition of chaste and nonchaste love, establishing in the process ambiguous and richly complex interpersonal relations. Even in his first published play, *Leo Armenius*, he speculates (in a manner very evocative of twentieth century literary theory) on the ways in which language constitutes reality. In his late work *Verliebtes Gespenste und die gelibte Dornrose*, he not only used dialect for the first time in German drama, anticipating by more than 250 years Gerhart Hauptmann's use of Silesian in his naturalist play *Die Weber* (pb. 1892; *The Weavers*, 1899), but also brought to a close, as it were, the medieval interlude by elevating it to the level of a complete and independent play. The juxtaposition of social and language levels, the broad and witty use of linguistic nuances, the structural contrasts—all combined to create a kind of play that would not be seen again on the German stage until the nineteenth century.

Gryphius is also important as a cultural mediator. Thanks to his knowledge of numerous languages (some claim that he was fluent in as many as thirteen) and his study and travel abroad, he came to know and in some cases translate congenial works from the major cultural centers of his time. In the Netherlands, particularly at the University of Leiden, where he studied and lectured from 1638 through 1644, Gryphius encountered the works of the great Dutch dramatist Joost van den Vondel, whose *De Gebroeders* (pb. 1640) he translated and later adapted into a play of his own, *Die Sieben Brueder*. During his travels through France and Italy between 1644 and 1646, Gryphius seems to have perfected his French and Italian to the point where he could render into German Girolamo Razzi's *La Balia* (pr. 1560), probably around 1645, and later Thomas Corneille's *Le Berger extravagant* (pb. 1653). A translation of Nicolas Caussin's *Tragoediae sacrae* (pb. 1620) from the Latin probably goes back to Gryphius's early days, between 1634 and 1644. These translations served several purposes for the busy student and later administrator: They provided five-finger exercises for his own dramatic productions, introduced his countrymen to contemporary theater, and sometimes became raw material for all or parts of his own plays.

Finally, Gryphius is often described as a polyhistor, a universal Renaissance man. Given the list of his lectures at Leiden, this appellation seems justified, for they ranged from mathematics, astronomy, and philosophy to a more expected collegium on poetry. Nor was he by any means a dabbler or amateur: Many of the greatest specialists of his day continued their close contacts with him, and he received invitations to become professor at Frankfurt an der Oder (for mathematics), Heidelberg, and even Uppsala in Sweden.

What makes this prodigious learning and literary output all the more impressive is the fact that it occurred against the background of the Thirty Years' War and its devastations, achieved by a boy who lost his father when he was four and his mother at the age of twelve, carried through by a man who was often sick, close to death at times, and lived to be only forty-seven years old, all the while writing in addition to his jobs as tutor, lecturer, and administrator.

BIOGRAPHY

Information about authors living through the upheavals of the seventeenth century is notoriously incomplete, but the main outlines of Andreas Gryphius's life are quite well established, even if some dates are under debate. Two years before the official outbreak of the Thirty Years' War, Gryphius was born on October 2, 1616, almost at midnight, a fact that seemed symbolically significant to him throughout his life. It is hard to argue with his perception that—from a superficial point of view—darkness seemed to dominate his era, that "brown night" he so often invokes. His hometown, Glogau, in the most northeasterly province of the Holy Roman Empire, had just been destroyed by one of the many great fires endemic to the period, and the Lutheran burghers quarreled with their Catholic imperial local official. His father was a local Lutheran pastor who died—many believe—because of the stresses of the war in 1621, and his young mother, remarried in 1622, died in 1628, leaving the boy to be reared by his stepfather, Michael Eder, and his family. Gryphius and his hometown experienced plundering soldiers, occupation, and exile, which interrupted his schooling several times but without lasting negative effect. In fact, he did very well in school, where he played lead roles in the Latin school dramas favored by progressive schools and excelled in mathematics and Latin. Indeed, in 1634, he had his first Latin verse epic published in Glogau, displaying his familiarity with the classical tradition more than his poetic talents. Still, this work and its sequel one year later anticipate some of Gryphius's stylistic peculiarities. A flair for dramatic, dialectical juxtapositions, repeated questions and imperatives, and powerful rhythms is notable, as are the descriptions of bloody scenes of cruelty that recurred in his later German tragedies.

Time and again, Gryphius had to finance his studies by tutoring the children of the well-to-do—in Danzig for the admiral of the Polish fleet, Alexander von Seton, for example, and near Freystadt on the estate of George Schönborner von Schönborn, a high imperial official then retired. Gryphius showed a remarkable ability for attracting patronage and maintaining contacts and friendships over the years. After Schönborner's death, he departed for the Netherlands with the two sons of his patron to study at Leiden (1638-1644), where he impressed many as one of the most learned men of his age. There he published another volume of his *Sonette* (1643), in which he included revised versions of his *Lissaer Sonette* (1637), while he had already brought out his *Sonn-und Feiertags-Sonette* in 1639 with the renowned publishing house of Elzevir. Although many of the poems obviously had been written earlier, the time at Leiden inspired revision on the basis of the latest theoretical requirements, revisions that did not always result in improvements in the power or liveliness of image or rhythm. The odes and epigrams included in the 1643 edition of poems show Gryphius experimenting in both Latin and German. On the whole, the shorter forms are the more successful, especially the simple strophic odes and satiric epigrams. In Leiden, as noted above, Gryphius also was exposed to Dutch dramatists such as Joost van den Vondel and Pieter C. Hooft, as well as to influential thinkers such as David Heinsius, Justus Lipsius, and Claudius Salmasius. The latter two are especially significant for an understanding of Gryphius's tragedies, which treat the Lipsian neo-Stoic theme of *constantia* as well as the conservative divine right theories of Salmasius, which had also been defended by Gryphius's earlier patron Schönborner.

Selected as companion to a group of young gentlemen on their Grand Tour, Gryphius traveled through France and Italy from 1644 through 1646. The journey included all the major stops from Paris to Rome to Venice and inspired Gryphius to write many poems and another Latin epic, *Olivetum libri tres* (1646). During this time, he must have seen *commedia dell'arte* productions, read or heard the story of Cardenio and Celinde (the basis for the tragedy of that title, written later in the decade), and begun to write his first German play, *Leo Armenius*, which he completed at Strassburg in 1647.

The time at Strassburg was fruitful despite its relatively short duration. While maintaining many friendships and participating in disputations there, he also worked on *Catharina von Georgien* and prepared a volume of his works, *Teutsche Reim-Gedichte* (1650), which included *Leo Armenius*, two books of odes, four books of sonnets, and two containing epigrams. Unfortunately, the publisher went out of business and an unauthorized version of these works appeared in Frankfurt am Main in 1650, including several poems not by Gryphius—the ultimate accolade. Returning to Silesia via the Netherlands, he arrived back at Fraustadt, in November, 1647.

That Gryphius refused calls to various European universities during the next year seems to indicate that he had already been promised a position back home. This is all the more likely because he became engaged on November 28, 1648, to Rosina Deutschländer, the daughter of an important merchant and city councillor at Fraustadt. The wedding took place on January 12, 1649. Of the seven children from this union, four died in their infancy, and one daughter—Anna Rosina—contracted what seems to have been polio and was incapacitated for the rest of her short life. Only two boys grew up to attain majority: Daniel, who died in Naples at the age of twenty-four, and Christian, the eldest, who followed in his father's footsteps as writer, lawyer, and administrator. Christian Gryphius also edited his father's works in 1698, including some previously unpublished materials.

In May of 1649 or 1650, Andreas Gryphius became syndic of Glogau, his hometown, a position he held until his death in 1664. His tasks included the legal defense of the interests and privileges of the Lutheran Silesian Estates against the encroachments of Catholic Habsburgs' absolutist centralism and led, among other things, to his compilation and publication in 1653 of a collection of legal documents concerning his clients and the territory of Glogau. That he also continued his many other interests is shown by the publication of a report on his investigation of two Egyptian mummies in Breslau, entitled *Mumiae Wratislavienses* (1662). His obligations clearly did not leave much time for new creative work. This period of his life was thus dominated by revisions of earlier work, new editions of collections in 1657 and 1663, occasional pieces such as *Majuma* and *Piastus*,

Lustund Gesang-Spiel, written for local potentates, and a translation or two. Of his original works, only *Grossmüttiger Rechts-Gelehrter* falls into this final period of his life; also during this period, he undertook a delightful partial adaption of *The Beloved Hedgerose*. Both of these are among Gryphius's best and most polished dramatic works.

On July 16, 1664, Gryphius, not quite forty-eight years old, died of a stroke suffered in the middle of a stormy session of the Estates. His contemporaries, with many of whom he had maintained continuous contact, were unanimous in praise of his achievements, and his position in the annals of German literature has remained secure. Not all of his writings are readily accessible to the modern, post-Romantic consciousness because they require a knowledge of the traditions of rhetoric, emblems, and biblical references and an ability to think and read allegorically. Yet many of his poems and some of his comedies have remained popular no matter what the shift in taste of a particular period might seem to dictate.

ANALYSIS

Although not widely known outside Germany, Andreas Gryphius is among the exemplary figures of his age. His drama, like his poetry, contributes greatly to an understanding of that complex period of European culture known as the Baroque.

There is a natural division to Gryphius's dramatic production and a remarkable consistency of themes. There are, first, his translations and adaptations from other languages; second, his tragedies; and third, his comedies and occasional pieces. They all center on the vanity of all earthly things and the need to maintain constancy of faith in the face of adversity. This central concern may be expressed either in the form of a great personage enduring hardships with magnanimity, as it appears in the tragedies, or it may manifest itself as an investigation into the nature of love and its complexities, as it often does in the comedies. Unfortunately, the available information does not allow precise dating of certain works, but there is a rough chronology that indicates that most of Gryphius's translations and adaptations were written at the beginning and toward the end of his career. The early

translations and adaptations were followed in time, more or less, by the tragedies, which in turn were followed by the comedies. It is worthy of note that Gryphius's actual dramatic production was concentrated in the relatively short time span between 1645-1646 and 1650-1652, and then again between 1659 and 1661.

BESTÄNDIGE MUTTER

The earliest translation, to start with that group, seems to have been *Beständige Mutter*, by Nicholaus Causinus, which Gryphius translated from the Latin, possibly between 1634 and 1644-1646. This translation of *Tragoediae sacrae* (1621) of Causinus, who was the Jesuit father confessor to Louis XIII of France, exemplifies the standard martyr tragedy of the Baroque and provides the basic scheme of many of Gryphius's later tragedies in the same genre. The action is set in Rome during the reign of Marcus Aurelius: The emperor tries to force Felicitas to renounce her Christian faith, only to be firmly rebuked by the steadfast paradigmatic believer. With great constancy, Felicitas endures the execution of her seven sons and rejects the advances, religious and amorous, of the tyrannical pagans, dying in prison still faithful to her Christian faith. Recalling the psychomachia of medieval theater, the basic pattern of such martyr tragedies, as employed by Gryphius and others, is a triangle consisting of the suffering but steadfast martyr and his or her family; evil counselors and Machiavellian tyrants, here including the lustful Apollonius, who is inflamed by the physical and spiritual beauty of Felicitas; and finally, a ruler torn between human impulses and evil counsel, who finally gives in and condemns the martyr to a gruesome death. This pattern is followed closely in *Catharina von Georgien*, written around 1647.

DIE SIEBEN BRUEDER

Another early translation is *Die Sieben Brueder*, based on Joost van den Vondel's *De Gebroeders* and probably undertaken around the time of Gryphius's stay in Leiden. The sources for this piece are the second book of Samuel in the Old Testament and Flavius Josephus's *Antiquitates Judaicae* (93 C.E.; *Jewish Antiquities*, 1737), book 7. The issue is the obedience of David to God's will despite the appearance of inhumanity, juxtaposed to the embittered people and priests, who demand the execution of Saul's sons to lift the curse from their land. (Of interest to scholars is the comment by Christian Gryphius that his father had composed all but the fifth and last act of an independent play concerning the same theme which, however, has been lost.)

SEUGAMME

Seugamme, probably completed around 1645, is a translation from the Italian Girolamo Razzi's *La Balia* first published in 1560. A typical *commedia* with several interlocking plots and intrigues, it displays the corruption of several families, households, and generations by lust and love, which is, however, resolved in the end despite lingering implausibilities. The attraction for Gryphius, who translates rather literally, seems to have lain in the power of lust and deception and the disruptions they can wreak in human affairs, a topic to which he returned in his *Cardenio und Celinde*, albeit in tragic garb.

The early translations not only indicate Gryphius's mastery of languages and his familiarity with contemporary and earlier European drama but also left notable traces in his own works. By contrast, the later translations and adaptations, such as *Der Schwermende Schäffer*, do not appear to have provided the playwright with a genuine learning experience.

LEO ARMENIUS

Leo Armenius was Gryphius's first independent drama. First published in 1650 and reprinted at least five times in the course of the seventeenth century, it was probably written before 1647. This historial tragedy, an exemplification of the workings of fickle fortune in human affairs, shows how easily the mighty are humbled. Based on the Greek historians Cedrenus and Zonaras, *Leo Armenius* is the story of the fall of the Byzantine emperor at the hands of his general Michael Balbus. Leo admonishes Michael to desist from his plottings against the throne and finally condemns him to die at the stake. At the intercession of his wife, the Empress Theodosia, however, he stays the execution; Michael's coconspirators use the delay to enter the palace and kill the emperor on the night before Christmas. Gryphius had probably known of the Je-

suit drama *Leo Armenius* (1646) by Joseph Simon, dealing with the very topical issue of tyrannicide. Yet where the Counter-Reformation Jesuit sees divine justice done in the fall of the heretic Leo, Gryphius condemns the killing of a prince, both as a Lutheran and as a lawyer believing in the divine right of princes and God's prerogative to judge them. This conservative tendency also informs his later depiction of the death of Charles I in England, as well as that of his jurist hero Papinian. In the highly stylized, declamatory *Leo Armenius*, little emphasis is given to establishing causal connections or psychological motivations. The interest focuses instead on the moral and spiritual significance of acts and symbols, such as the emperor's apotheosis and transformation into a Christ figure when he dies at the altar, on the eve of Christ's birth, clutching the Cross on which Christ supposedly died.

CATHARINA VON GEORGIEN

A slightly different emphasis underlies the first of the martyr tragedies, *Catharina von Georgien*, also written about 1647. Like *Leo Armenius*, this play was based on historical sources, although from contemporary history. Gryphius's subtitle, speaking of "proven constancy," indicates his theme. Reprinted four times before 1698 and frequently performed, this was one of Gryphius's most popular dramas. Catherine, queen of Georgia, has been captured by the Persian Shah Abbas after fighting him successfully in defense of her dynastic interests and her Christian faith. Now in his power, she steadfastly rejects his advances; he is torn between his lust and his love for her—between his tyrannical impulses and his human inclinations. Having given the order to have Catherine tortured and then executed, he relents too late to save her; she has demonstrated exemplary constancy and greatness to the end. The entire action takes place in the imperial palace and consists of Catherine's last day. The prologue sets the tone: It is delivered by Eternity, the ultimate measure of all acts and the source of the heroic queen's stoic fortitude. When judged *sub specie aeternitatis*, all human, changing affairs take on an aspect of relative insignificance and fleetingness. Despite such heroic dimensions, however, the play also shows considerable complexity. Catherine is by no means fearless; she fears suffering but decides to endure. Similarly, not all the play's power rests in eternity: There are also dynastic reasons for Catherine's action.

ERMORDETE MAJESTÄT

Drawing again on contemporary history, but much closer to home, is the tragedy of *Ermordete Majestät*: This play exists in two quite different versions; the first was probably written as early as 1649 and published in 1657, while the second was published in 1663, in the last edition of his works supervised by the author himself. Spurred on by personal acquaintance with relatives of England's King Charles I, Gryphius once more took up the question of the killing of a sovereign. After *Leo Armenius*, it comes as no surprise that Gryphius's play condemns the murder of a king, yet it also uses the death of the monarch to transform him into a witness to greatness, a martyr whose fall from temporal power is the occasion for attaining spiritual stature. The earthly crown is replaced by that of the martyr only to be transformed into the eternal crown of immortality (a triple structure that is reflected in the title-page print of one of Gryphius's sources). Gryphius's equation of the king with Christ has both religious and political implications, and the later version underscores this equation even more firmly: There, Charles rejects a rescue attempt in order to fulfill his destiny and role, both of which require a figural exegesis for their full understanding.

CARDENIO UND CELINDE

The other tragedy written around 1649 is *Cardenio und Celinde*. In many ways, this is an oddity among Gryphius's plays and those of his time. It presents a tragic subject through personages not of the highest rank; also, it draws heavily on stage machinery and complexities of plot and motivation that made it less than popular in its own time but which are appealing to modern interpreters. Cardenio falls in love with Olympia, who will eventually marry Lysander, who thus incurs the hate of Cardenio, while Celinde, who loves Cardenio, wants to bind him to herself with the help of magic. As Cardenio plots Lysander's death and Celinde yearns for Cardenio's enthrallment, they both have a vision of the vanity of all earthly lust that will transform them and their plans, thus assuring the victory of eternity and death over temporality and lust. Put differently, in the words of the author's introduction, the play deals with the juxtaposition of two kinds of love: one chaste and virtuous, the married love of Olympia and Lysander; the other insane, lustful, and desperate, the desires of Cardenio and Celinde. The bitter experience of temporality and the vanity of life is the pathway to moral self-awareness.

GROSSMÜTTIGER RECHTS-GELEHRTER

The last major tragedy, *Grossmüttiger Rechts-Gelehrter*, dealing with the death of Papinian, the magnanimous lawyer and imperial councillor, was published in 1659 and performed the following year. Although there is no external evidence about its time of composition, internal indications are that it is a late work, showing Gryphius in full command of his creative abilities as a dramatist. Once again Gryphius turns to history and a martyr but this time with a difference. It is not Christianity that is at stake but virtue, remaining true to one's values, in a general sense. Historically, Papinian, one of Rome's greatest jurists, refused to justify the murder of Geta by his half brother, the emperor Caracalla, and was thus executed in 212 C.E. In the play, Papinian is an imperial councillor, related to the imperial family, and subject to many calumnies. When the emperor attempts to bribe and threaten Papinian into defending the killing of Geta by Bassianus Caracalla, Papinian refuses and is forced to witness the death of his son and then suffer execution himself, having rejected the army's offer to kill the emperor and elevate him to the throne as well as the Empress Julia's hand. A subplot, centering on the courtier Laetus, highlights Papinian's integrity by contrasting his resolve with Laetus's opportunistic Machiavellianism. In the end, Gryphius's themes are the same as they were in the beginning, but they have gained depth and complexity. Not a specific moral system, that of Christianity, is at stake but the free moral decision of humankind, in the face of eternity, to adopt and maintain certain moral and political standards, no matter what the blandishments or threats. Remaining true to one's own self is as central an issue as Christian salvation. Both are by no means private but are deeply embedded in politics and history and have public dimensions. The conservative acceptance of divine kingship is predicated on the assumption that order must be opposed to the chaos of the world and that its ultimate sanction is divine, as will be the punishment for its transgression.

ABSURDA COMICA

If Gryphius's tragedies were mainly cherished in their own time, the comedies have enjoyed continued popularity and success among amateurs and schools to this day. *Absurda Comica*, probably written between 1647 and 1649 and first published in 1657, treats the well-known Piramus and Thisbe story from Ovid. Despite its obvious affinity to William Shakespeare's *A Midsummer Night's Dream* (pr. c. 1595-1596), no connection has been established. This little satire is a parody of all those dilettantes and amateurs who became the butt of many jokes, not only from the aristocracy for their social pretensions but also from literary reformers for their artistic failures. Here Gryphius uses the time-honored tricks of *commedia dell'arte* and traveling troupes—slapstick and situation comedy. The play also is a ready vehicle for wordplay and topical humor. Gryphius intended *Absurda Comica* to be performed in connection with an unnamed tragedy, possibly *Cardenio und Celinde*, which would give it an entirely different interpretive context. Without it, the death of the lovers is merely a silly consequence of a silly passion, a negative example or inversion of the positive overcoming of false love shown in *Cardenio und Celinde*. In any case, *Absurda Comica* is a brilliant example of the courtly Baroque parody of bourgeois pretensions.

HORRIBILICRIBRIFAX TEUTSCH

In his *Horribilicribrifax Teutsch*, Gryphius indulges his linguistic abilities, plays with the traditional figure of the miles gloriosus, satirizes the blowhards of the Thirty Years' War, and generally amuses himself. Two loudmouthed captains, the titular hero and his rival Daradiridatumtaridas, who woo and leave the same maiden, and a schoolmaster pedant Sepronius, who reminds one of Shakespeare's Polonius, are key comic elements in a farce that never does quite get off the ground despite all the standard ingredients. The best part remains the brilliantly presented mixture of languages, the linguistic equivalent

of the moral confusion caused by the Thirty Years' War. Once again, Gryphius is concerned with forms of love and moral corruption but chooses to present them in a lighthearted fashion, as a warning and an entertainment.

THE BELOVED HEDGEROSE

Modern readers have shown more interest in the mixed-form dual play *The Beloved Hedgerose*, written, performed, and published in 1660. The first part is a typical high-culture comedy, based on Philippe Quinault, where—once again—Cornelia loves Sulpicius who loves Chloris, Cornelia's daughter, while Levin loves Cornelia. After much confusion, showing the power of love as much as that of intrigue, a positive resolution is achieved demonstrating that humanity's best-laid plans are but delusion. The main plot is interspersed with a low-life playlet, loosely based on Joost van den Vondel's *Leeuwendalers* (pb. 1647), in which peasants speak Silesian dialect. The simple and slow-witted peasants are shown with their daily problems; their love, as in the case of Dornrose (Thorny Rose) and Kornblume (Blue Flower of the Fields) is that of kind, natural hearts, almost anticipating Romantic attitudes. Again, Gryphius shows a fine ear for the varieties of language, from the Glogau dialect to High German, from common talk to the parody of pseudo-German, laden with misused foreign words. Not until Heinrich von Kleist and Gerhart Hauptmann would such language be heard and such simple life be seen again on the German stage.

MAJUMA

Finally, in *Majuma*, an allegory in which love overcomes war, Gryphius shows himself to be a master of the standard Baroque opera. This typical occasional piece was written on the announcement of the elevation of Ferdinand III to the title of Roman king in May, 1653, and thus as emperor of the Holy Roman Empire. Like *Piastus, Lustund Gesang-Spiel*, it shows what Gryphius can do with traditional forms.

OTHER MAJOR WORKS

POETRY: *Herodis furiae et Rachelis lacrymae*, 1634; *Dei Vindicis Impetus et Herodis Interitus*, 1635;

Lissaer Sonette, 1637; *Sonn-und Feiertags-Sonette*, 1639; *Sonette*, 1643; *Olivetum libri tres*, 1646.

MISCELLANEOUS: *Teutsche Reim-Gedichte*, 1650; *Mumiae Wratislavienses*, 1662; *Gesamtausgabe de deutschprachigen Werke*, 1963-1968 (7 volumes).

BIBLIOGRAPHY

Becker, Hugo. *Andreas Gryphius: Poet Between Epochs*. Berne, Switzerland: Herbert Lang, 1973. A critical analysis of the literary work of Gryphius, with emphasis on his poetry. Bibliography.

Metzger, Erika A., and Michael M. Metzger. *Reading Andreas Gryphius: Critical Trends, 1664-1993*. Columbia, S.C.: Camden House, 1994. A look at the literary criticism pertaining to Gryphius over the years. Bibliography and index.

Schindler, Marvin S. *The Sonnets of Andreas Gryphius: Use of the Poetic World in the Seventeenth Century*. Gainesville: University of Florida Press, 1971. Although this critical analysis of Gryphius centers on his poetry, it also sheds light on his dramatic works.

Spahr, Blake Lee. *Andreas Gryphius: A Modern Perspective*. Columbia, S.C.: Camden House, 1993. An examination of the life and works of Gryphius. Bibliography and index.

Herbert A. Arnold

JOHN GUARE

Born: New York, New York; February 5, 1938

PRINCIPAL DRAMA

Universe, pr. 1949

Theatre Girl, pr. 1959

The Toadstool Boy, pr. 1960

Did You Write My Name in the Snow?, pr. 1962

The Golden Cherub, pr. 1962(?)

To Wally Pantoni, We Leave a Credenza, pr. 1964

The Loveliest Afternoon of the Year, pr. 1966, pb. 1968

Something I'll Tell You Tuesday, pr. 1966, pb. 1968

Muzeeka, pr. 1967, pb. 1969 (one act)

Cop-Out, pr. 1968, pb. 1969

Home Fires, pr. 1968, pb. 1969

A Play by Brecht, pr. 1969 (libretto; music by Leonard Bernstein; lyrics by Stephen Sondheim; based on *The Exception and the Rule* by Bertolt Brecht)

A Day for Surprises, pr., pb. 1970

The House of Blue Leaves, pr., pb. 1971

Two Gentlemen of Verona, pr. 1971, pb. 1973 (with Mel Shapiro; music by Galt MacDermot; adaptation of William Shakespeare's play)

Marco Polo Sings a Solo, pr. 1973, pb. 1977

Optimism: Or, The Misadventures of Candide, pr. 1973 (with Harold Stone; adaptation of Voltaire's novel)

Rich and Famous, pr. 1974, pb. 1977

Landscape of the Body, pr. 1977, pb. 1978

Bosoms and Neglect, pr. 1979, pb. 1980

In Fireworks Lie Secret Codes, pr. 1979, pb. 1981

A New Me, pr. 1981

Gardenia, pr., pb. 1982

Lydie Breeze, pr., pb. 1982

Women and Water, pr. 1984, pb. 1990

The Talking Dog, pr. 1986, pb. 1987 (one act; based on a story by Anton Chekhov)

Moon over Miami, pr. 1988

Six Degrees of Separation, pr., pb. 1990

Four Baboons Adoring the Sun, pr. 1992, pb. 1993

The War Against the Kitchen Sink, pb. 1996

The General of Hot Desire, pr., pb. 1999

The General of Hot Desire and Other Plays, pb. 1999 (includes title play, *Greenwich Mean*, *The Talking Dog*, and *New York Actor*)

Lake Hollywood, pr. 1999, pb. 2000

A Book of Judith, pr. 2000

Lydie Breeze, pr. 2000, pb. 2001 (revision of *Lydie Breeze* and *Gardenia*)

Chaucer in Rome, pr. 2001

Sweet Smell of Success, pr. 2001

A Few Stout Individuals, pr. 2002

OTHER LITERARY FORMS

John Guare's short teleplay *Kissing Sweet*, a satirical pastiche about pollution, appeared as part of New York's WNED-TV program *Foul!* on November 25, 1969. His 1971 screenplay for director Miloš Forman's *Taking Off* was actually a revision of a script by Forman and Jean-Claude Carrière. His screenplay *Atlantic City* (1981) was Guare's original work. The 1986 revival of *The House of Blue Leaves* resulted in a Public Broadcasting Service (PBS) televised version on the *Great Performances* series; similarly, the British Broadcasting Corporation (BBC) broadcast on radio a version of *Women and Water* in October of 1988. In 1993 Guare wrote his own screenplay for the MGM film version of *Six Degrees of Separation*.

ACHIEVEMENTS

Although John Guare has been recognized from early in his career as one of the United States' best playwrights Off-Broadway, the distinction of success on Broadway was late in coming. He has been the recipient of numerous awards and honors, among the early ones Off-Broadway's Obie Award in 1968 honoring *Muzeeka* as the Best Distinguished Play of the Year. The following year, *Variety* magazine named Guare the Most Promising Playwright of 1969. *The House of Blue Leaves* won for him another Obie Award, in 1971, as well as the New York Drama Critics Circle Award, also in 1971, for Best American Play of the Year and an Outer Critics Circle Award. In 1972, Guare was honored with Broadway's Tony Award for his triumphant musical version of *Two Gentlemen of Verona*, for which he wrote the lyrics and which was produced by Joseph Papp at the New York Shakespeare Festival. *Two Gentlemen of Verona* also earned for him a New York Drama Critics Circle Award in 1972 for Best Musical. Guare was playwright-in-residence at the New York City Shakespeare Festival in 1976 and 1977. In 1981, he received the

American Academy Award of Merit Medal, and in 1987, a New York Institute for the Humanities Fellowship. Twelve years later, Guare was the 1999 honoree of the William Inge Theatre Festival.

BIOGRAPHY

John Guare was born and reared in New York City's borough of Queens, the only child of John Edward Guare, a clerk in the Wall Street stock exchange, and Helen (Grady) Guare. The young Guare very early showed his predilection for theater. In 1949, at the age of eleven, Guare wrote a play that was performed at Atlantic Beach, Long Island; the following year, he auditioned for his uncle, the film producer Billy Grady, an incident that he dramatized in *The House of Blue Leaves*. Educated in New York City's Catholic schools (St. Joan of Arc elementary school in Queens and St. John's Preparatory School in Brooklyn), Guare matriculated at Georgetown University, receiving his A.B. in 1960. While at Georgetown, Guare wrote two plays that were produced there: *Theatre Girl* in his junior year and *The Toadstool Boy* a year later.

To avoid the draft, Guare attended the Yale School of Drama, where *The Golden Cherub* and *Did You Write My Name in the Snow?* were produced in 1962; he received his M.F.A. in 1963. Guare further forestalled being drafted by serving in the Air Force Reserves. His first Off-Broadway play, *To Wally Pantoni, We Leave a Credenza*, appeared without much notice in 1964. Travel in Rome in 1965 gave Guare the inspiration for *The House of Blue Leaves*, which appeared in a one-act version at the Eugene O'Neill Foundation Theater in Waterford, Connecticut, in 1966, with Guare playing Artie Shaughnessy. Subsequent summers at the Eugene O'Neill Foundation Theater saw the productions of his *Muzeeka*, *Cop-Out*, *Home Fires*, and *Optimism: Or, the Misadventures of Candide*. Critical praise for these plays, and Off-Broadway productions of others, led to the banner year of 1971, which saw two Obie Award-winning plays and a successful screenplay for Guare. He produced several new plays in the 1970's, but none achieved the level of success of *The House of Blue Leaves*.

Each of the following three decades would begin with watershed years for Guare. In 1981 it was his marriage to Adele Chatfield-Taylor (the New York Landmarks Foundation Director for whom Guare wrote the *Lydie Breeze* cycle of plays), and the critical success of his film script for *Atlantic City* (which won an Academy Award for Best Screenplay). In 1991 it was dual nominations, for a Pulitzer Prize and a Tony Award. In 2001 it was a pairing with composer Marvin Hamlisch in a Broadway musical version of the 1957 film *Sweet Smell of Success*, as well as being tapped to write the screenplay for a remake of Alfred Hitchcock's 1941 film *Suspicion*.

Analysis

As vastly different as John Guare's plays may be in plot, several elements are found in all of them—even though they were written over a span of several decades. The most noticeable is a central character with an overwhelming need to escape his or her present life, either through taking on a new identity or through fame. The theme of American culture's obsession with fame, in fact, is almost universal in Guare's plays. A second characteristic is an often bewildering fusion of farcical comedy and inexplicable violence. For some critics, this fusion is grotesque, leading to a breakdown in sympathy for the characters and an artistic flaw in the play. A third element is a tendency toward the metadramatic, self-reflexive technique of having characters address the audience directly, breaking out of the pretense of stage reality. Finally, the theme of alienation, so common in contemporary drama, is given a new twist in Guare's plays, as total strangers form impromptu connections with one another, connections that are presented as more vital than their existing relationships.

Something I'll Tell You Tuesday

Guare's techniques can be seen in his earliest plays to be published, the one-acts *Something I'll Tell You Tuesday* and *The Loveliest Afternoon of the Year*, which saw Off-Off-Broadway production as a double bill at Caffé Cino in New York on October 27, 1966.

John Guare, center, at the Last Frontier Theatre Conference in Valdez, Alaska, in 2002. (AP/Wide World Photos)

The first is the least experimental of Guare's early plays and the only one in which no characters address the audience directly. All the other elements, however, are present. The main characters, an elderly couple named Agnes and Andrew, desire escape to an idealized past. Yet their daughter Hildegarde and her husband, George, represent their real past: constantly bickering, with a threat of physical violence. The undertone of violence in this play is close to Guare's later style of mixing farce with violent tragedy, yet the farcical element is not present in *Something I'll Tell You Tuesday*. Nevertheless, Guare effects a reversal of audience expectations by ending with Agnes's nostalgic yearning not for peace but for argument, for her seemingly idyllic harmony with Andrew is not love but a loss of the energy to fight.

THE LOVELIEST AFTERNOON OF THE YEAR

The second play of Guare's 1966 double bill, *The Loveliest Afternoon of the Year*, is much more typical of his later works. The play consists of only two characters, a lonely man and woman, and it opens on their first meeting. He overcomes her fear of strangers, and when they kiss, they turn to the audience and tell their story. This first example of Guare's trademark direct address to the audience is representative of the way Guare would use it throughout his career. Direct audience address, however, is not a new technique. The ancient Greeks called it "parabasis," a common element of the Old Comedy of Aristophanes. Yet in Guare's plays, it is not used to give the author a platform, as in Aristophanes' work, nor as a technique of alienation, as in Bertolt Brecht's drama or in the Story Theatre popular in the 1960's. Instead, it is used to move the plot, to streamline the action: By having characters say what happened next, Guare alternates drama and narration, shifting scenes more quickly than otherwise possible.

Unlike in *Something I'll Tell You Tuesday*, Guare's combination of farce and violence is seen in *The Loveliest Afternoon of the Year*. The play ends with the man's wife (seen by the characters but not appearing onstage) shooting dead both the man and the woman. During the play, the man tells absurd stories about horrible tragedies befalling his relatives: his father falling in a steam calliope, his sister having her

arm bitten off by a polar bear. The absurdity of the details invites laughter, while the gruesomeness of the details begs for compassion. It is precisely this conflict that has led some critics to consider Guare's plays as essentially flawed.

MUZEEKA

Guare's next play, produced in Connecticut in July of 1967 and brought to New York the following spring, was another one-act, *Muzeeka*. In addition to garnering his first major award (an Obie) and major critical attention, *Muzeeka* continued Guare's experiments in theatrical form. The protagonist, Jack Argue (an anagram of "Guare"), does the same thing that the man of *The Loveliest Afternoon of the Year* did, since he also leaves his wife for a perfect stranger, Evelyn Landis. Yet unlike the man from the previous play, Argue did not meet his new love by chance: He responded to sexual graffiti (he calls it an "ad") in a men's room in a New York bar. What drives Argue to this seemingly uncharacteristic behavior is, as he tells the audience in a speech in the opening scene, a primitive erotic impulse that he saw in early Etruscan art. The speech combines several of Guare's most characteristic devices: direct address of the audience, the refrain (the first and last sentences are the same), and a yearning for fame ("If I could've been born anybody—my pick of a Kennedy or a Frank Sinatra or a Ford").

COP-OUT

Guare's *Cop-Out* and *Home Fires* followed the same production history as *Muzeeka* and met with similar critical success, *Cop-Out* winning for him the *Variety* Award for the Most Promising Playwright of 1969. The award carried somewhat of a burden, for it created pressure on Guare to live up to such promise, which the playwright later acknowledged in his play *Rich and Famous*.

Cop-Out, like *Rich and Famous*, also has an autobiographical origin. In 1968, Guare was knocked unconscious at an antiwar protest but saw as he passed out a look of terror on the face of the young police officer whose horse had kicked him. This momentary human sympathy between two people on opposite sides of the civil strife of the late 1960's was the basis for *Cop-Out* and helped make the play more interesting than most of the plays of the period on the same theme. *Cop-Out* chronicles a love relationship between a female protestor and a male police officer assigned to contain the protest. The theme of the police officer submerging his identity in a uniform escapes being a 1960's cliché by following the pattern of Guare's other characters who seek new identities. The police officer's long autobiographical speech to the audience shows how carefully constructed his persona is: He keeps correcting his natural impulse to use the impersonal word "father" by replacing it with the more folksy "pop"—but it is clearly an act of editing, of self-mythologizing.

HOME FIRES

Home Fires is Guare's first attempt at a period play, set on the night after the armistice that ended World War I. Its characters typify Guare's people yearning for a new identity: Peter Smith, who Americanizes his German name, Schmidt, to escape persecution; his daughter Nell, who changes her name back to Schmidt to reclaim her heritage; his son Rudy, who makes his name Smythe to adapt "old-money" airs; and Rudy's fiancée, Margaret Ross-Hughes, who poses as an heiress but is revealed in the end to be a housemaid. Guare identifies the play as a "farce," and it shows evidence of the theatrical conventions of the World War I era: sudden bursts of period song, melodramatic dialogue, and rags-to-riches plotting that unravels at the end.

MUSIC

Songs in the popular style were always a major part of Guare's plays. *Muzeeka* opens with a vaudeville-like sketch in which Jack Argue "Sings a Penny"—a vocal interpretation of the words on a U.S. penny. The main plot of the play turns on Argue's plan to take over the Muzeeka corporation, which pipes insipid music into businesses, and sneak in seductive Eros-and-Frenzy-inspiring music. Guare's next work, *Kissing Sweet*, gained much of its energy from the television jingle that introduced it. Originally written for television, this ten-minute piece is a parody of television commercials that prey on people's fears and encourage them to solve all their inadequacies with chemicals. The song is the first of many for which Guare wrote both words and music.

A DAY FOR SURPRISES

Returning to the Off-Off-Broadway theater Caffé Cino, Gaure produced the short one-act *A Day for Surprises* in 1970. Much like *The Loveliest Afternoon of the Year*, this play deals with two anonymous characters, A (a woman) and B (a man), furtively seeking love. As in the earlier play, however, a previous relationship comes between them. Both are librarians at the New York Public Library and are experiencing stereotypical sexual frustrations. A, like the man of *The Loveliest Afternoon of the Year*, tells manic, impossible stories. She says that she saw the stone lion from the front of the library in the ladies' room, devouring Miss Pringle, her rival. B responds in kind, telling of an affair he had with Miss Pringle, through which she conceived and gave birth to a book. A then sees the lion return to his proper place; the play ends with A and B holding each other in newfound love, A singing a Guare song. The delight of this play, which also saw a London production in 1971, is in the juxtaposition of romantic love and impossibilities: Love creates the illusion that all things are possible. Nevertheless, the undercurrent of violence is still there: The lion, after all, has devoured A's rival, though the effect in the play is comic.

TWO GENTLEMEN OF VERONA

Guare's next two plays not only were filled with his music but also were his first full-length plays. The first, *The House of Blue Leaves*, is a musical only in a qualified sense. It appears to be a comedy drama, but the main character, Artie Shaughnessy, is a songwriter who performs his compositions at the piano throughout the show. Guare's other full-length play of 1971, *Two Gentlemen of Verona*, is a full-fledged musical, with some thirty songs by Galt MacDermot for which Guare provided lyrics. The adaptation of William Shakespeare's play (by Guare and director Mel Shapiro) is more a translation into modern idiom than a rewriting: the character names and plot remain untouched. Yet in the lyrics of the songs, Guare was able to create a voice of his own, sometimes playing modern counterpoint to Shakespeare. Though an adaptation should not be measured against Guare's original plays, there is much in Shakespeare's original that resonates with Guare's work: shifting identities (implied by the very name Proteus), alienation (banishment to the forest outside Mantua), and speeches directed to the audience (though here they are soliloquies).

THE HOUSE OF BLUE LEAVES

More typical of Guare's work is *The House of Blue Leaves*, which not only assured Guare's success but also achieved the status of his masterpiece, now an important part of the American literary canon, with a revival on Broadway in 1986 (its true Broadway debut) and countless college and community theater productions. One reason *The House of Blue Leaves* has become a classic is that it combines the energy of Guare's apprentice period with the discipline that comes from reworking the play over a five-year period. Its first form was as a one-act play, in which Guare himself played the leading role of Artie Shaughnessy. By interweaving several plot strands suggested in that one-act play, Guare was able to produce his first full-length work.

The motif of American obsessions with fame, latent in Guare's earliest plays, is fully developed in *The House of Blue Leaves*. Artie, who performs in nightclubs, wants to be a popular songwriter; his son Ronnie wants to assassinate the pope and be on the eleven o'clock news; Artie's wife, Bananas, dreams of famous people; his mistress, Bunny Flingus, speaks in tabloid headlines; a group of nuns in Artie's apartment have turned their adoration for the pope into the fanaticism of pop-star groupies. Setting the play on the day of Pope Paul VI's visit to New York to address the United Nations (October 4, 1965), Guare shows the effect of the resulting media attention on the lives of various people.

The result is largely farcical, but characteristically, the plot takes sudden twists in the direction of tragedy, usually without warning. The bomb intended for the pope kills a visiting film actress. Her lover, a film director and Artie's friend (named Billy Einhorn), ends Artie's dreams of Hollywood happiness by ignoring Artie's music and stealing his girlfriend. Left alone with his hopelessly demented wife, Artie caresses her in a tender scene that unexpectedly shifts in tone when Artie's caress becomes a stranglehold. Then the tone shifts again when, having choked his wife to death, Artie goes into his nightclub act.

MARCO POLO SINGS A SOLO

The next Guare play to be produced was *Marco Polo Sings a Solo*, though it did not come to New York until 1977, heavily rewritten. Ideas explored in *The House of Blue Leaves* are pushed to the limit in this bizarre farce. Every character in it alternately seeks and avoids fame; sexual paths cross and re-cross in every possible combination; and self-obsession dominates every scene. Guare himself asserts the connection with *The House of Blue Leaves* in his author's note to the published version of *Marco Polo Sings a Solo*; as the former was "a play about limits," *Marco Polo Sings a Solo* would explore the self-absorption of "people living without traditional limits."

Unlike the Artie Shaughnessys, who coveted fame and were trapped by obscurity, the characters in *Marco Polo Sings a Solo* are smothered in fame but seek to rise above it. Tom Wintermouth is a political mover and shaker who modestly belittles his accomplishment until he accidentally becomes president. He is in love with Diane McBride, who had been the most famous concert pianist in the world until she gave up her career to marry Stony McBride, a world-famous filmmaker. The McBrides' servant, Freydis, turns out to be the wife of famous astronaut Frank Schaeffer, who wants her to go down in history as the first woman impregnated from space. Lusty McBride, Stony's stepfather, is an actor so famous that he is about to be immortalized on a postage stamp. Lusty's wife is both Stony's mother and his father: Born a man, Elliott Dempsey, he had a sex-change operation to win Lusty's affections. Receiving a womb transplant and impregnated with his own sperm, he/she gave birth to Stony.

Though Guare insists that the play is a comedy, it is imbued with violence. Its violence is not personal, as in previous plays, but a violence against nature and time. In the opening scene, Diane tells about Bob and Stephanie Shootself, the archetypal couple of the late twentieth century, who repeat their marriage vows because, after so much plastic surgery, they are no longer the same people. The fragmentation of identity is rampant: Stony thinks he is Frank Schaeffer; Frank's wife, Skippy, creates a Norwegian persona of Freydis to hide from him; Elliott becomes a woman.

The changes are effected through technology, the agent of the submerged violence in this play: Elliott's sex-change surgery, Skippy's electronic impregnation, and the prosthesis of Larry Rockwell, for whom Diane buys marvelous electronic legs after she crushes his real legs in a car accident. Promising improvements, all these operations end up hurting and alienating.

RICH AND FAMOUS

Rich and Famous, as its title suggests, continues Guare's exploration of the manifold effect of fame on culture. Like *Marco Polo Sings a Solo*, it was first produced in a regional theater, then brought to New York in a revised form a few years later (1976). Like most Guare plays, *Rich and Famous* sports autobiographical elements: The protagonist, Bing Ringling, is a writer of autobiographical plays, 843 of them unproduced. Bing is elated to have his 844th attempt actually produced, and by the great Veronica Gulpp-Vestige, who has never had anything but hits. He is crestfallen, however, when Veronica tells him that she chose his play to be her first flop so that she could have a comeback—and flop it does.

The rest of the play is Bing's vain, surrealistic attempt to understand his failure by interviewing the myriad individuals in and out of show business (all played by one actor and one actress) connected with his career. His parents are supportive until they discover that their son is a flop: They, too, want only the "Rich and Famous," and when their son is neither, they look for a surrogate son in Bing's childhood friend Tybalt Dunleavy, now a successful actor. For Tybalt, too, fame is more important than life. When his agents convince him that suicide would increase his fame, he jumps to his death—off of a billboard image of himself.

LANDSCAPE OF THE BODY

Landscape of the Body was a departure for Guare in many ways, and an indication of the future of his drama. For one thing, Guare's odd balance of tragedy and farce, both lauded and deplored by critics, is tipped in favor of tragedy. The darkness that had been an undercurrent in previous plays is now the mainstream, with only eddies of comedy here and there. The violence is now central to the plot. The pivotal event is the murder and decapitation of the only son of the protagonist, Betty Yearn. The story is told as a flashback in the police interrogation room, where Betty is trying to convince Captain Marvin Holahan that she is not the murderer.

Joining in the flashback are the ghosts of other people in Betty's life who have recently died: her sister Rosalie, who sings hauntingly inappropriate songs by Guare; her boss, Raulito, who died in a prank played by Betty's son Bert; her childhood friend Mavis, who died of cancer. As in previous plays, the plot development in *Landscape of the Body* is alternately narrative and dramatic. This time, however, the alternating technique arises naturally out of the framing scene in the interrogation: Betty is *supposed* to be telling her story. Much more of the narration, however, goes to the ghost of Rosalie. The detachment from the play that results from a direct address of the audience is all the more appropriate for mirroring Rosalie's metaphysical detachment from the world of the living.

BOSOMS AND NEGLECT

Bosoms and Neglect can be considered an updating or expansion of Guare's falling-in-love-by-chance plays such as *The Loveliest Afternoon of the Year* or *A Day for Surprises*. In *Bosoms and Neglect*, however, the plot has a more mature tone. The lyrical zaniness of young people in love develops an ugly side and is shown to be only a manifestation of an unstable personality. The lovers here are Scooper, a computer analyst, and Dierdre, who runs a mail-order used-book business. They meet because they both have the same psychiatrist. Like the characters of Guare's earlier romances, Dierdre spins ludicrous fantasies about her past and her family, and Scooper is involved with another woman when he begins the relationship. Instead of providing comedy, Dierdre's tales evoke sympathy for her need to lie; instead of heightening the drama, Scooper's infidelity is shown to be a symptom of his pervasive selfishness. The violence of the earlier plays had a whimsical side; here, it is too real, too integral a part of the characters to be slapstick. Dierdre and Scooper become vicious at the end of the first act: She stabs him, and he hits her.

Yet the background of this romance is seen in the prologue and the second act: Scooper's discovery that his mother, Henny, has been hiding cancer sores on her breast for more than two years. The "neglect" of the title is not only her neglect of cancer, allowing it to spread, but also Henny's and Scooper's mutual neglect of each other. Dierdre, it appears, has a similar relationship with her father, leading to her ridiculous stories about him, as well as her penchant for "neglected authors." Because neither Dierdre nor Scooper can deal with the other-gender parent, neither has success in relating to the opposite sex. The play ends with both of them going off together, leaving the audience purposely unsure whether that is a good idea.

LYDIE BREEZE CYCLE

The 1980's became for Guare the decade of his most ambitious project: a tetralogy of plays tracing the complex interrelationships of several characters in New England in the late nineteenth century. Known as the *Lydie Breeze* cycle, the plays were conceived as a unit, and three of the four were written and produced in the 1980's; *Women and Water*, *Gardenia*, and *Lydie Breeze*. The middle play of the series, *Bullfinch's Mythology* (revised from the 1982 *Gardenia*) was actually completed sixteen years after the end piece, in 1998 when the whole cycle was produced at the Signature Theatre in New York City. Then the whole series was revised two years later for the New York Theatre Workshop, for which Guare wrote a final Lydie Breeze play, *A Book of Judith*.

The complex story begins on the eve of the American Civil War, in 1861, and ends in 1895 with a second generation exorcising the personal violence that came out of that time. The central character is Lydie Breeze. The daughter of a ship's captain whose white crew mutinied to protest his equal treatment of black crewmen, she, too, came to embody freedom, rejecting the traditional role of wife and mother (though she became both) and starting a commune near her ancestral home in Nantucket. In the more than thirty years spanned by the plays, she becomes a nurse and privateer in the Civil War, marries a dashing young socialist named Joshua Hickman, maintains a previous relationship with another war privateer named Dan Grady, and commits suicide years after her husband is sent to prison for killing Grady.

The *Lydie Breeze* plays are ambitious in more than just scope: They are Guare's first sustained attempt at realism and his first serious historical drama (*Home Fires* is historical but not too serious). After successfully capturing the language style of his generation in the 1960's and 1970's, Guare achieved equal success in imitating the rhythms and vocabulary of the second half of the nineteenth century. By turns poetic and conversational, the plays establish the form of poetic drama that Guare seems to have been seeking in his career. The infectious comedy is gone (and missed), but the *Lydie Breeze* plays by themselves earn for Guare a major place in contemporary drama.

SIX DEGREES OF SEPARATION

Guare continued developing in new directions in the 1990's, while touching base with his traditional themes. In *Six Degrees of Separation*, the motif of fame drives the plot. The idolization of celebrity by the main characters, Flan and Ouisa Kittredge, allows a man named Paul to bilk money from them by convincing them that he is the son of famous actor Sidney Poitier. Paul's character (based on a real-life con artist who posed as "Paul Poitier" in the early 1980's) is fluid: In later scenes, he poses as Kittredge's neglected, illegitimate son.

FOUR BABOONS ADORING THE SUN

In *Four Baboons Adoring the Sun*, Guare returns to one of his ideas in *Muzeeka*: an attempt to resurrect the Dionysian spirit of the ancient Etruscans. In doing so, he reaches for the roots of Western theater, for ancient Greek drama began in revels sacred to Dionysus. The god at the center of *Four Baboons Adoring the Sun* is Eros, who provides commentary and transitions through songs in Guare's familiar style. The main characters, Penny and Philip McKenzie, are newly married anthropologists on a dig in Sicily; each has several children from previous marriages, whom they are trying to meld into a family. The eldest children, Penny's daughter and Philip's son, become closer than siblings, brought together sexually by Eros in an attempt at transcendence ending in the son's death.

Though reviewers, including those who had championed Guare's earlier work, were not kind to *Four Baboons Adoring the Sun*, and though it was not a commercial success, it served as a sign that Guare would not abandon his earlier zany style, with its sometimes uncomfortable combination of farce and tragedy, realism and fantasy. Furthermore, combining fantasy and myth added a new dimension to Guare's drama, maintaining his position as a major force in the American theater at the close of the twentieth century.

REVISIONS, RETROSPECTIVES, AND RESURRECTIONS

At first glance, the 1990's would appear to have been a look backward for John Guare as a playwright. In the process of writing his preface for the 1996 collection of his early plays, *The War Against the Kitchen Sink*, Guare had to re-read and reflect on his earliest work. One result, Guare said in a 1999 interview, was a reworking of a 1966 play that would become *Lake Hollywood* that year. Throughout the 1990's he reworked his Lydie Breeze plays, culminating in a 1998 staging of the whole cycle and a Guare retrospective at the Signature Theatre in New York City. Yet two directors involved in the retrospective offered proof that it was neither an exercise in nostalgia nor a playwright's opportunistic revision of his greenwork. First, Mel Shapiro chose to direct *Marco Polo Sings a Solo* for the retrospective, despite the fact that, when he had directed it a quarter of a century earlier, it earned Guare perhaps the worst reviews of his career. However, while he was earnestly revising other plays, Guare refused to change a line in *Marco Polo Sings a Solo*. The second indication was Nicholas Martin's revival of *Bosoms and Neglect*: Martin reported that theatergoers who were not aware that it was a revival thought that the nearly twenty-year-old play was fresh and new. Yet the only changes were directorial choices like changing "records" to "CDs."

The 1990's ended with the publication of another collection of Guare's shorter plays *The General of Hot Desire and Other Plays*, this time from the 1980's and 1990's. The title play is a deconstruction of the book of Genesis by a group of English literature stu-

dents. *Greenwich Mean*, one of the collected plays, reintroduces one of Guare's favorite early motifs: sudden and unexpected violence that acts as a climax device. In this case it is an earthquake that interrupts two characters involved in unpacking as they move in together. They had both been expressing their love for and faith in each other, but when the quake hits, one of them grabs personal belongings rather than the supposedly beloved other character, undercutting all that had been said up to that point. *New York Actor* explores the insecurities of a former stage actor returning to New York after success in a Hollywood sitcom. Guare's early theme of the packaging of fame gets a new twist as the jaded Hollywood actor yearns to return to the New York stage, while the New York stage actors around him in the bar yearn to have their experience in Hollywood.

CHAUCER IN EUROPE

The 2001 comedy *Chaucer in Europe* is a glance backward of another type: one of its characters, Ron Shaughnessy, is the son of the protagonist of Guare's 1971 play *The House of Blue Leaves*. The boy who wanted to blow up the pope in the 1971 play is now a middle-aged pilgrim visiting the pope's city, Rome. The satire against the packaging of religion is harsher in the 2001 play, though it is localized in the character of Father Shapiro, a cynically commercial priest cashing in on the influx of American pilgrims visiting Rome during the Church's Jubilee Year of 2000-2001.

A FEW STOUT INDIVIDUALS

The twin themes of Guare's 1974 *Rich and Famous* are revisited in the 2002 play *A Few Stout Individuals*. A once-wealthy man whose son dissipated his fortune can regain it with a multimillion-dollar book deal for his memoirs. For all of their novelty, Guare's plays of the early twenty-first century carry faint strains of his themes from the middle of the twentieth.

OTHER MAJOR WORKS

SCREENPLAYS: *Taking Off*, 1971 (with Miloš Forman and Jean-Claude Carrière); *Atlantic City*, 1981; *Six Degrees of Separation*, 1993.

TELEPLAY: *Kissing Sweet*, 1969.

NONFICTION: *Chuck Close: Life and Work, 1988-1995*, 1995.

BIBLIOGRAPHY

Bernstein, Samuel J. *The Strands Entwined*. Boston: Northeastern University Press, 1980. A survey of contemporary drama, this volume includes an excellent chapter on *The House of Blue Leaves*, which also touches on Guare's other plays. A particularly helpful feature of this book is the summary of, and quotation from, major reviews.

Guare, John. "The Art of Theater IX." Interview by Anne Cattaneo. *The Paris Review* 34 (Winter, 1992): 68-103. A wide-ranging interview that provides valuable insights into Guare's working methods and his conception of theater. "I love the part of playwrighting [*sic*] that is a craft to be learned continually," Guare remarks, "The *-wright* part, like *shipwright* or *wheelwright* or *cartwright*." Particularly interesting are Guare's comments on the journal he has kept for many years, a resource frequently mined for his plays.

_____. "Preface." In *The War Against the Kitchen Sink*. New York: Smith & Kraus, 1996. Guare's introduction to his early work explains that his first approach to drama was a "war" (his name sounds like the French word for war, *guerre*, as Nicholas Martin suggested) against the type of naturalistic drama known as "kitchen sink realism."

_____. "Preface to the Plume Edition." In *The House of Blue Leaves and Two Other Plays*. New York: NAL Penguin, 1987. Intended as an introduction to *The House of Blue Leaves* after its successful revival in 1986, this essay by Guare also touches on *Bosoms and Neglect* and *Landscape of the Body*.

Martin, Nicholas. "Chaos and Other Muses." *American Theatre* 16, no. 4 (1999): 26-29. A major Broadway director involved with the 1998 Guare retrospective interviews the playwright on the writing process, autobiographical elements in his plays, and his first four decades as a writer.

Savran, David. *In Their Own Words: Contemporary American Playwrights*. New York: Theatre Communications Group, 1988. This volume, consisting of a series of interviews with leading American playwrights, includes an insightful interview with Guare. In it, he discusses *The House of Blue Leaves* revival, the *Lydie Breeze* cycle of plays, and autobiographical elements in his plays.

John R. Holmes

BATTISTA GUARINI

Born: Ferrara (now in Italy); 1538
Died: Venice (now in Italy); October 7, 1612

PRINCIPAL DRAMA

Il pastor fido, pb. 1590, pr. 1596 (*The Faithful Shepherd*, 1602)
L'idropica, wr. 1583, pr. 1609, pb. 1613

OTHER LITERARY FORMS

Although Battista Guarini is primarily known as the author of a pastoral tragicomedy, he also collected his correspondence in the two-volume *Lettere* (1593-1596); among his nonfiction are *Il segretario* (1594; the secretary), a dialogue on the obligations of a secretary, and a political treatise, *Trattato della politica libertà* (1818; treatise on political freedom). He also collected his verse in a book entitled *Rime* (1598).

ACHIEVEMENTS

Battista Guarini's most famous play, *The Faithful Shepherd*, was first staged in the city of Crema during the Carnival of 1596 and later in September of the same year in Ronciglione, in the state of the Farnesi.

The numerous editions of *The Faithful Shepherd* in the seventeenth, eighteenth, and nineteenth centuries and the several translations into French, Spanish, English, German, Greek, Polish, Swedish, and Dutch are clear evidence of the great success of this work. The first translation into English was done by John Dymock in 1602. However, the translation in 1647 by Sir Richard Fanshawe, which uses heroic couplets and remains very close to the original, is still considered to be the best. The 1964 edition of that translation was republished in 1976 with an introduction by John H. Whitfield.

Much to Guarini's credit, he accompanied his painstaking work of composition and revision with a robust theoretical defense of *The Faithful Shepherd* and of a hedonistic conception of art, free of moralizing. Guarini built his work on the pastoral tradition of the fifteenth and sixteenth centuries, on the results of the critical elaboration of Italian sixteenth century drama (tragedy and comedy), and on humanist and Renaissance culture in general. His tragicomedy manifests his expertise in manipulating stage techniques, constructing a complex plot, and employing the traditional tools of tragedy. The theatricality of his work is enhanced by brilliant lyric and dramatic scenes conveyed by a language that strives for musical effects and achieves a balance between the highly stylized and the restrained manner of the *dolce stil nuovo*. He thus prepares the ground for the pastoral world to become the material for melodrama.

The Faithful Shepherd, a product of Renaissance rhetoric and ideology, has a subtle quality that makes it the vehicle of very important traits of Counter-Reformation and Baroque cultures. Guarini's pastoral world is fraught with unsuspected signs of crisis: the replacement of Renaissance optimism by a sense of human finiteness in a world of uncertainty, illusion, and disillusionment in which human actions, directions, and plans prove useless and wrong. The pastoral world that he portrays is a metaphor for the human condition, powerless if left to itself and able to reach the truth only with the help of Providence. This leitmotif, commonly found in much theater of the late Renaissance, especially in tragedy, stresses the misguided nature of human enterprises and the need to

find solace in the divine. Human error in a pastoral is less serious, and the very notion of a happy ending, unlike the catastrophe in tragedy, implies that Providence is able to achieve a proper and happy resolution of human events.

Biography

Battista Guarini was born in Ferrara in 1538, the offspring of a noble family that had brought honor to the city of Ferrara through its achievements in the literary and political arenas for more than two centuries. Guarini studied law at the University of Padua and in 1557 was professor of rhetoric and poetry at the University of Ferrara. Between 1564 and 1567, he was a member of the Accademia degli Eterei of Padua, where he met, among others, Scipione Gonzaga and Torquato Tasso.

On his return home, he accepted employment with Alfonso II d'Este, duke of Ferrara, and spent twenty-one years as secretary of the Este court. As a diplomat, he was sent on missions to other Italian courts and states (Turin, 1569-1571; Venice, 1572; Rome, 1572), and to Poland (1574, 1575-1576), where he unsuccessfully represented the rights of Alfonso II to the succession to the Polish throne.

After these diplomatic activities, he became the official court poet at Ferrara. Yet service at court, be it in Ferrara, Mantova, Florence, or Urbino, where he was employed after 1588, did not satisfy Guarini. Italian courts in the last thirty years of the sixteenth century provided a very limited role for a courtier or secretary when compared to the political importance assigned to a courtier in the Humanist age. Guarini suffered from this diminished role, in which his high self-esteem, dignity, and decorum were hardly matched by the daily chores, which he found demeaning. In 1580, Guarini began to work on *The Faithful Shepherd*, which was first published in 1590.

If for Guarini court life was a cause of dissatisfaction and ambivalence that was barely compensated for by the universal accolades received by his masterpiece, his private life as father of eight children did not provide much happiness either. His biographers have pointed out how, in dealing with his children, he proved to be avaricious, litigious, and incapable of balancing paternal sternness with parental affection. He was particularly harsh toward his son Alessandro, whom he forced to marry a rich heiress. He caused both of them much suffering, especially when they challenged his administration of that inheritance.

Guarini's feisty spirit never yielded, either in court, where he attacked enemies and defended himself against the state, his family, and private individuals, or in the literary field, as when he reacted to the criticism leveled at his *The Faithful Shepherd* even before its publication. He spent his last years much as he had his earlier life, in continuous feuds. He became ill and died in Venice on October 7, 1612.

ANALYSIS

Italian pastoral drama, generally speaking, deals with a world separated from history. It is an escape into another, more primitive world. It presents also a subworld, or a symbolic world, very much in line with the ideology of the particular culture. Although any kind of classification is somewhat arbitrary, historically one can say that the literary tradition of the pastoral spans more than two centuries, beginning with *Il ninfale d'Ameto* (1341-1342; also known as *Commedia delle ninfe*), by Giovanni Boccaccio and reaching a high point in *The Faithful Shepherd*. The pastoral covers the time from the autumn of the Middle Ages to the crisis of the Renaissance or the beginning of the Baroque age. Even a cursory look at this tradition must include a few milestones, such as Angelo Poliziano's *Orfeo* (pr. c. 1480; English translation, 1879; also known as *Orpheus*), a lyric pastoral with dramatic forms of *sacra rappresentazione*; and Jacopo Sannazaro's *Arcadia* (1504), a romance alternating pastoral eclogues with narrative prose. It was in the first half of the sixteenth century, however, that Italian pastoral drama grew through the study of Aristotle's *De poetica* (c. 334-323 B.C.E.; *Poetics*, 1705) and Greek tragedy. Giambattista Giraldi Cinthio (who also wrote a pastoral drama, *Egle*, pr. 1545), with his treatise *Discorso sopra il comporre le satire atte alla scena* (1554; on the composition of satires fit for the stage), was the first to pose the question of the mixture of tragedy and comedy. This form was perfected by Tasso's *Aminta* (pr. 1573; English trans-

lation, 1591), and by Guarini's *The Faithful Shepherd*, the crowning jewels of Italian pastoral drama.

THE FAITHFUL SHEPHERD

The setting of *The Faithful Shepherd* is Arcadia, the pastoral world par excellence, which is subject to a long-standing curse caused by an unfaithful nymph, Lucrina, who had provoked the death of her beloved shepherd, Aminta. This sin must be atoned for annually by the Arcadians through the sacrifice of a virgin to Diana. Also, the law of the land establishes that any woman who breaks her promise to a lover should be killed. The oracle has prophesied to the people:

> Your woe shall end when two of Race Divine
> Love shall combine:
> And for a faithless Nymph's apostate state
> A faithful Shepherd supererogate.

The only two people who can end the curse are Silvio and Amarilli, both of divine origin. Their nuptials are wished for by all Arcadia and are prepared by their parents. Yet, typical of pastoral situations, Silvio, who is loved by Dorinda, is not in love with Amarilli and despises love: He is a worshiper of Diana, the goddess of hunting, not of Venus. Amarilli, always a champion of honor and modesty, is secretly in love with Mirtillo, who came to Arcadia only for her and who wants to see her to confess his love. Mirtillo, however, is also loved by Corisca, a scheming, libertine nymph who does her best to destroy her rival, Amarilli. In fact, in order to disguise the real goals of her actions, Corisca brings about a meeting between Mirtillo and Amarilli. Later, however, she persuades Amarilli to enter a cave where she might catch Silvio with another woman. This would give Amarilli a chance to break her promise to Silvio and be free to love Mirtillo. Mirtillo, thanks to Corisca's machinations, also enters the cave with the intention of catching Amarilli with another man and of publicly denouncing her.

The two lovers are discovered together by the guards, and according to the law, Amarilli must be put to death for breaking her faith to Silvio. Mirtillo prevents this by offering himself in place of the virgin, and the substitution is accepted. The priest Montano is about to perform the execution when it is discovered that Mirtillo is the son of Montano and thus of divine origin, and that Mirtillo's real name is Silvio. The blind soothsayer Tirenio announces that the words spoken by the oracle have been fulfilled: By marrying Amarilli, Mirtillo-Silvio, the faithful shepherd of divine origin, will free Arcadia. The other Silvio finally falls in love with and marries Dorinda. Corisca, in the end, repents and is forgiven.

When Guarini called *The Faithful Shepherd* a pastoral tragicomedy, he wanted to stress that it is a combination of tragic and comic motifs within the framework of the pastoral genre. Even before the publication of his work, Guarini had to defend this notion against the negative criticism of sixteenth century commentators of Aristotle's *Poetics*. Beginning in 1587, the legitimacy of tragicomic poetry was questioned by Giasone De Nores, a professor of moral philosophy at the University of Padua. De Nores asserted that Aristotle never talked about tragicomedy or pastoral and called the former a monstrous composition and the latter an illicit amplification of the eclogue into a comedy or tragedy with unlikely characters: shepherds who reason like princes or philosophers. Guarini answered with *Il verato* (1588) and *Il verato secondo* (1593), two polemical treatises named after a famous actor of the day.

Later, in his *Compendio della poesia tragicomica* (1601; compendium of tragicomic poetry), Guarini became the most thorough theoretician of the pastoral as a dramatic genre. Deriving from Aristotle the justification for his work, Guarini defined tragicomedy as "a fusion of all tragic and comic parts that with likelihood and decorum can stay together under a single dramatic form." Tragicomedy borrows from tragedy "great characters and not the plot; a plausible but not a true story; deep but blunted emotions; delight, not sadness; danger, not death" and from comedy "not licentious laughter, [but rather] modest pleasantness; a complete plot, a happy reversal of fortune and, especially, a happy ending." The peripeteia, or change of fortune, with its "wonderful" reversals produces pleasure, which removes sadness in the audience. This is the tragicomic catharsis.

In reacting against the classicist notion of separation of styles according to genre, Guarini proposed a mixture of styles, more specifically a mixture of the

magnificent style, typical of heroes and of the characters of *The Faithful Shepherd* therefore, and the polished style—namely, the style of Italian lyric poetry. The polemic for or against this genre, one of the most important controversies in European literary history, continued throughout the seventeenth and into the eighteenth centuries because much more than pastoral drama was at stake. A new conception of poetry was here being defended on the basis of the popular response of the day against traditional conception backed by the recognized masterpieces of the past. For Guarini, tragicomedy, and not tragedy or comedy, was the theatrical form that best responded to contemporary taste and that realized a hedonistic conception of art, *delectare*, and not a moralistic one, *prodere*, proposed by De Nores.

The source for the *antefatto*, that is, the curse on Arcadia, is the *Ellados Periegesis* (c. 150 C.E.; *Description of Greece*, 1898), of Pausanias, a Greek historian and geographer of the second century. *The Faithful Shepherd* has similarities also with its most illustrious forerunner, *Aminta*, such as corresponding scenes (act 1, scene 1), episodes (the stolen kiss episode), and choruses (the ones in *The Faithful Shepherd* being ideological reversals of those in *Aminta*), which have been pointed out by critics. Such derivation does not take anything away from Guarini's masterpiece.

A prologue opens the work, which is divided into five acts. There is a chorus at the end of each act in the form of a poetic song. Lyric, dramatic, and narrative parts are fused within its complex structure. The traditional tragic tools of recognition and peripeteia, or reversal of fortune, are used. The play's meter consists of hendecasyllables in discursive and narrative sections, with a free alternation of hendecasyllables and septenarii in the lyric parts; rhyme is employed only to create stylistic effects. Guarini operates within the Italian Petrarchan lyric tradition, a reduction of the semantic value of language for the sake of musical qualities. His pastoral was contemporary to the appearance of the first melodrama, *La Dafne* (1594), based on a pastoral text by Ottavio Rinuccini and accompanied by music by Jacopo Peri and Giulio Caccini. The search for effects of musicality and euphony, together with the poetics of "wonder," link *The Faithful Shepherd* to the next generation of Baroque culture.

Variations on the love theme are a very important feature of *The Faithful Shepherd*: love and constancy in Mirtillo, love and honesty in Amarilli, sentimental love in Dorinda, pity and love in Silvio, love as brutish instinct in the Satyr, and love without self-restraint in Corisca. Unlike much Italian drama of the sixteenth century, which uses a narrator to relate lyric and dramatic parts, *The Faithful Shepherd* presents directly on the stage exquisite lyric and dramatic scenes: Dorinda trying her best to be kissed by Silvio, who plays with her feelings; Mirtillo revealing his love to Amarilli, who responds coldly in defense of her honesty; the following scene, in which she is left alone and confesses how much she loves him; and the dramatic confrontation between Corisca and the Satyr, who thinks that he has finally cornered her and can punish her for her infidelity but is left with her wig in his hand after falling.

Critics through the first half of the twentieth century have interpreted *The Faithful Shepherd* as a work rich in lyricism and sensuality. In the second half of the twentieth century, the studies of Nicolas T. Perella, Norbert Jonard, Louise G. Clubb, Roberto Alonge, Deanna Battaglin, and many other scholars have shed new light on this work, pointing out how it sums up Renaissance culture, directly reflects Counter-Reformation culture, and is the precursor of Baroque culture.

The Faithful Shepherd seems to contradict the Renaissance belief in humankind's control, through reason, over his environment. As has been argued convincingly by Perella, the tragicomedy shows that both senses and reason are inadequate instruments that fail humankind in its search for the truth. All characters in this pastoral, with the exception of Tirenio, the blind seer, are immersed in total darkness as to the pursuit of their immediate goals. They unconsciously follow the dictates of a superior entity that mysteriously leads them to a happy ending. Silvio, in his passion for hunting, is completely unaware of his feelings about love, which he will discover in the end through no merit of his own. Mirtillo, on the other hand, passionately in love, does not realize that the nature of the love required of him is more than sheer sensuality and will ultimately mean the delivery of Arcadia from the curse. Amarilli, in trying to remain true to her promise to Silvio and by hiding her true feelings from Mirtillo, seems to be moving in a direction contrary to the logic of a woman in love and of a happy resolution of the initial impasse. Corisca herself, so confident in her powers to manipulate reality for her own selfish ends, winds up being the cause of the union of Mirtillo and Amarilli, an end diametrically opposed to what she had set out to accomplish. Even the chorus confesses its inability to understand part of the prophecy of the oracle, clear enough in its semantic value but unclear as to its referent.

Therefore, it is important to notice how a typical situation of the pastoral, with its portrayal of a topsy-turvy human world of people pursuing unrequited loves, has been here invested with a much deeper meaning while illustrating a particular historical and cultural perception of the human condition. The stage has become the visual means by which humankind postulates the presence of a supreme truth, a reality that is above it, and the maladroit groping of the characters on the stage attests humankind's sense of its limits and of the fallacy of its conviction that people can affect and be master of their destinies. The Arcadia of *The Faithful Shepherd* is still an idyllic land of refined shepherds; however, it is also the reflection of a disenchanted culture in transition from an optimistic, humanistic notion of the universe to a less optimistic expression of a post-lapsarian state of things. This transition is made more dramatic by humankind's wanderings in a maze built on its illusory desire to control its destiny or even simply understand itself and its world. Humankind's ineffectual groping is particularly obvious in the figures of Mirtillo and Amarilli, two dynamic characters in pursuit of their goals: The former, thanks to his intelligence and cunning, has succeeded in stealing a kiss from Amarilli and, against all odds, he is able to have her in his arms; the latter, even if mindful of her maidenly honor, acts to stave off her marriage with Silvio and to realize her dream of marrying Mirtillo. Yet all of their actions are doomed to failure.

Although people are portrayed as unable to break through appearances and reach the truth, they are not totally lost in spite of their errors. The presence of a Divine Providence that acts on behalf of humankind but beyond its senses and reason, sets the record straight in a manner that, although unpredictable to the characters involved, stresses nevertheless a moral undertone and intention that correspond to the ideological climate that prevailed during the Counter-Reformation. The final happy resolution of the tragicomedy rewards the constancy in love of Mirtillo and the honor and modesty of Amarilli. These virtues are elevated to a higher level because they bring about, after all, the salvation of a whole people. *The Faithful Shepherd*, in spite of its idyllic and sensual moments, as, for example, the episode of the stolen kiss, exalts constancy and honesty through a deft contrast between the beginning and the end of the play. A world in the state of sin is transformed into a redeemed world thanks to the heroic virtues of the two protagonists. Although blind to a destiny that they cannot fathom, all characters are free to act more or less in accordance with the Divine Will. That is why the behavior of Mirtillo and Amarilli will be rewarded with their bliss, while Corisca's unabashed invitation to enjoy a life dominated by the senses will have no confirmation and will be undermined and repudiated by her failure to win Mirtillo for herself. The denial of what Corisca is and represents means the triumph of what Mirtillo and Amarilli represent.

OTHER MAJOR WORKS

POETRY: *Rime*, 1598.

NONFICTION: *Il verato*, 1588; *Il verato secondo*, 1593; *Lettere*, 1593-1596 (2 volumes); *Il segretario*, 1594; *Compendio della poesia tragicomica*, 1601; *Trattato della politica libertà*, 1818.

BIBLIOGRAPHY

Donno, Elizabeth Story, ed. *Three Renaissance Pastorals: Tasso, Guarini, Daniel*. Binghamton, N.Y.: Medieval and Renaissance Texts and Studies, 1993. Three early pastorals—Battista Guarini's *The Faithful Shepherd*, Torquato Tasso's *Aminta*, and Samuel Daniel's *Queen's Acadia*—are presented and analyzed. Contains bibliographical references.

Niccoli, Gabriel Adriano. *Cupid, Satyr, and the Golden Age: Pastoral Dramatic Scenes of the Late Renaissance*. New York: P. Lang, 1989. Niccoli examines the works of a number of pastoral dramatists from the late Renaissance, including Guarini's *The Faithful Shepherd*. Bibliography and index included.

Perella, Nicolas J. *The Critical Fortune of Battista Guarini's "Il Pastor Fido."* Florence, Italy: L. S. Olschki, 1973. Perella examines the reception of Guarini's *The Faithful Shepherd*. Bibliography included.

Franco Manca

A. R. GURNEY, JR.

Born: Buffalo, New York; November 1, 1930

PRINCIPAL DRAMA

Three People, pb. 1956
Turn of the Century, pb. 1958
Love in Buffalo, pr. 1958
The Bridal Dinner, pb. 1961, pr. 1962
The Comeback, pr. 1964, pb. 1966

The Open Meeting, pr. 1965, pb. 1968
The Rape of Bunny Stuntz, pr. 1966, pb. 1976
The David Show, pr. 1966, pb. 1968
The Golden Fleece, pb. 1967, pr. 1968
The Problem, pb. 1968, pr. 1969
The Love Course, pb. 1969, pr. 1970
Scenes from American Life, pr., pb. 1970
The Old One-Two, pb. 1971, pr. 1973

Children, pr., pb. 1974 (based on John Cheever's short story "Goodbye, My Brother")

Who Killed Richard Cory?, pr., pb. 1976

The Middle Ages, pr. 1977, pb. 1978

The Wayside Motor Inn, pr. 1977, pb. 1978

The Golden Age, pr. 1981, pb. 1984

The Dining Room, pr., pb. 1982

What I Did Last Summer, pr. 1982, pb. 1983

The Perfect Party, pr. 1985, pb. 1986

Another Antigone, pr. 1986, pb. 1988

Sweet Sue, pr. 1986, pb. 1987

The Cocktail Hour, pr. 1988, pb. 1989

Love Letters, pr. 1988, pb. 1989

The Old Boy, pr. 1991, pb. 1992

The Snow Ball, pr. 1991, pb. 1992 (adaptation of his novel)

The Fourth Wall, pr. 1992, pb. 1996

Later Life, pr. 1993, pb. 1994

A Cheever Evening, pr., pb.1994 (based on the stories of Cheever)

Collected Works, pb. 1995-2000 (4 volumes)

Sylvia, pr. 1995, pb. 1996

Overtime, pr. 1995

Far East, pr. 1998, pb. 1999

Darlene, pr. 1998, pb. 1999

The Guest Lecturer, pr. 1998, pb. 1999

Labor Day, pr. 1998, pb. 1999

Ancestral Voices, pr. 1999, pb. 2000

Strawberry Fields, pr. 1999 (libretto)

Buffalo Gal, pr. 2001

Human Events, pr. 2001

OTHER LITERARY FORMS

A. R. Gurney, Jr., has written for television and film as well as for the stage; in addition, he has published the novels *The Gospel According to Joe* (1974), *Entertaining Strangers* (1977), and *The Snow Ball* (1984).

ACHIEVEMENTS

A. J. Gurney, Jr., is often labeled the dramatist of the WASP (white Anglo-Saxon Protestant) enclave. He laughs at, ridicules, even satirizes WASPs but at the same time understands them and in some ways sympathizes with them. Being born and reared a WASP, he knows his material. His characters live and breathe. They vividly represent a passing culture. Their motivations are clearly depicted, along with their frustrations and emotional tensions. Never really damnable, they are bored, fenced in, and stifled. They crave freedom and self-realization. Gurney's mastery of concise form reflects his classical bent. His plays are brief and to the point. They exemplify glories of artistic structure similar to those of the sonnet or sonata form. No excesses mar their impact. They abound with thrilling resonance of offstage events.

Gurney is in like manner a master of dramatic dialogue. The clichés and literary reflections of his characters are consonant with their status and emotions. Like Henrik Ibsen's plays, Gurney's are well wrought. Stage settings, props, and costumes are carefully detailed. Following in the tradition of such American innovators of drama as Eugene O'Neill, Arthur Miller, Tennessee Williams, and Edward Albee, Gurney loosens space, opening up the stage. Hamlet-like, his characters address the audience, who at times even become participants in the play. The rueful humor of Gurney's highly polished, smoothly crafted plays makes for entertaining theater, despite the underlying pessimism of his work.

Gurney's formal awards early in his career include a New York Drama Desk Award (1971), Rockefeller Playwright Award (1977), and National Endowment for the Arts Playwrighting award (1981-1982). Gurney was cited with the McDermott Award for the Arts at the Massachusetts Institute of Technology (MIT) in 1984 and the Award of Merit from the American Academy and Institute of Arts and Letters in 1987. He was the recipient of an honorary degree from Williams College (1984) as well as the New England Conference Annual Award for Greater Achievement (1987). In the 1990's, Gurney won the Elliot Norton Award (Boston, 1990), the Lucille Lortel Award (1994), and the American Community Theatre Award (1996). He also received an honorary degree from Buffalo State University in 1992.

He is a member of the Dramatists Guild (council) and the Writers Guild. His *Three People* was included in *The Best Short Plays of 1955-56*; *Turn of the Cen-*

tury appeared in *The Best Short Plays of 1957-58*; *The Love Course* was selected for *The Best Short Plays of 1970*; and *The Open Meeting* was anthologized in *Best American Short Plays, 1991-1992*.

BIOGRAPHY

Albert Ramsdell Gurney, Jr., nicknamed "Pete," was born in Buffalo, New York, on November 1, 1930, the son of Albert Ransdell Gurney, Sr., a dealer in real estate and insurance, and Marion Spaulding Gurney. The young Gurney grew up in the exclusive suburbia he depicts in his plays. From St. Paul's school, he went to Williams College, where he was graduated in 1952 with a B.A. degree in English literature. After graduation, he served three years (1952-1955) in the navy as an officer and then attended the Yale School of Drama, where he earned the M.F.A. degree in 1958. In 1984, he was awarded an honorary D.D.L. degree. In 1960, he began a long, distinguished career as teacher of literature and humanities at MIT.

In June, 1957, Gurney married Mary Forman Goodyear; they have four children: George, Amy, Evelyn, and Benjamin. They lived in Boston until 1983, when Gurney moved his family to New York to be near the theater, television, and publishers while he was on sabbatical from MIT. All this time he was concerned with the contrast between the values instilled in him as a youth and those of the world he was experiencing.

From early childhood, he had a passion for drama. He wrote his first play in kindergarten. His passion was fostered by his aunt, who liked to attend matinees but could find no one to go with her. It became Gurney's lot to go, and he enjoyed every minute of the saturation. He also liked to listen to dramas on the radio and through them learned the importance of sound to drama, especially the spoken word. He developed an accurate ear for the kinds of things certain kinds of people say. While at Williams College, he began his writing career by creating college revues. In the Navy, as special services officer, he wrote and produced revues on a grander scale. Finally, in drama school at Yale, his playwriting career began in earnest, and he published his first drama, the one-act play *Three People*, in 1956.

While teaching he had little time to write, but he always had writing on his mind. As he lectured and read, ideas for drama would come to him; during summer vacations, he would write. Following this routine, he managed to publish more than fifteen plays between the late 1960's and the early 1980's.

Gurney's first major success came in 1982 with *The Dining Room*. He continued to turn out commercially successful dramas throughout the 1980's, though critics found many of these plays to be somewhat slender. In a brief prolific period near the decade's end, Gurney wrote *The Cocktail Hour*, *Love Letters*, *The Old Boy*, and *The Snow Ball* (from his novel of 1984), all of which enjoyed success in New York as well as in the regional theater circuit. During a sabbatical from MIT, Gurney began adapting *Love Letters* for the screen.

In 1996 Gurney retired from his position as professor of American literature and humanities at MIT. Afterwards, he and his family divided their time between a home in Connecticut and an apartment in New York City.

ANALYSIS

A. R. Gurney, Jr., crafts his plays about the people he knows—WASPs. The setting of most of his plays is New England suburbia. The stage is never crowded with actors or furniture; rather, Gurney's sets suggest moods and situations. Often the audience become participants, and offstage actions, sounds, and characters are central to the play. Though writing with classical constraint, he is innovative in staging. In several plays, multiple scenes go on simultaneously. Music is also an integral part of many of his plays; Gurney deftly employs songs for atmosphere and tone. His plays are notable for their structure and polish; not a word is wasted.

THREE PEOPLE

Gurney's first published play, *Three People*, written while he was in the Yale School of Drama, deals with his major theme: freedom. Two of the three characters—a university professor and his wife—are sympathetically presented in their struggle to accept the fact that their child is mentally deficient. They struggle magnificently with their broken dreams. The

A. R. Gurney, Jr., in 1986. (AP/Wide World Photos)

tragedy of this tightly knit one-act, one-scene play is that the third character, the baby, gets very little consideration as a person. Gurney manages the pathos of the situation without being morbid or sentimental. The baby is never onstage. He is talked about and tended to, but he is never seen. Much dialogue is exchanged from the offstage nursery as the wife talks to her husband from the nursery. The characters are honestly and sympathetically drawn, each encased in a tragic plight from which there is no release.

THE BRIDAL DINNER

Gurney's first three-act play, *The Bridal Dinner*, is typical of his classical restraint of setting and time. All action takes place in one room in which a bridal dinner is held during an evening and a morning in June. The characters are also typical of Gurney: high livers in high society, concerned with money and status, acting out their lives of boredom. Gurney masterfully presents a play-within-a-play wherein the bride and groom look into themselves and their future. WASPish standards are humorously, satirically, and delightfully paraded before the bridal party and the audience. The play is full of telling vignettes and repartee as the young couple feel alone, isolated, apart— all the links broken. They recognize the empty ritual of the bridal dinner for what it is and discard symbolic relics of the past. The problem, ever-present in Gurney plays, is what to do next. Are they strong enough to cast off the old armor and face up to a new and challenging future? Where can they go from here? They feel wobbly, so they decide to dance. This parody of marriage in a "rotten world" has enough reality to make the caricature believable. As the characters themselves admit, it smacks of Thornton Wilder, Luigi Pirandello, and "the worst from Broadway"; still, it is delightful and thought-provoking. As in most of Gurney's plays, literary references abound, and clichés and old saws are subversively employed. Finally, reflecting Gurney's patriotic theme in the 1960's, the marriage assumes global scope with a vision of world peace through the marriage of nations in love. Gurney's wit saves the play from melodrama by posing the question, "But can she cook?"

THE DAVID SHOW

Gurney continued in this seriocomic vein in *The David Show*, in which he sets the biblical story of the coronation of King David in a modern television studio. This one-set, one-scene, five-character parody is good fantasy. The characters are catchy, if a bit overdrawn. David is portrayed as a Madison Avenue type who uses people for his benefit; Bathsheba, with her cliché-studded dialogue, is a combination of charm and clowning. She comes across as a true philistine, while Jonathan is a playboy seeking only "the good life." Gurney's characterization is vivid and entertaining, and the dialogue sparkles. Clichés are cleverly sprinkled throughout, and there is much witty wordplay. Undergirding the spoof is Gurney's usual seriousness. Problems of war, the good life, moral fiber, and ethnic groups are aired, until in contrast with the surface hilarity, David is forced to face up to the reality that Goliath is David himself: his own rotten soul looming larger than life. Though not always successful onstage, this satire laced with wit and underlying seriousness is good reading.

SCENES FROM AMERICAN LIFE

Scenes from American Life, as the title indicates, is a montage depicting the upper-middle-class society that Gurney knows so well. Like most of his plays, this one lends itself to easy production. The set is attractive, simple, and functional, with the action flowing around a burnished baby-grand piano. To achieve this feeling of flow, no curtain is used and few blackouts; one scene blends naturally into the next, with the actors setting up the stage and carrying on and off their props and costumes. Music plays an integral part in this drama, establishing the time and tone of each scene. Props, accessories, and costumes also help anchor the date of a particular scene.

The play is set in Buffalo; the time fluctuates from the early 1930's of the opening scene to the mid-1980's. One character, Snoozer, serves to unify the diverse vignettes. From the opening scene of his christening to the final scene, when, inebriated, he participates in the burning of a canoe, the play depicts the passing of an old order of Americanism. Four male actors and four female actors are all that are required for producing these vignettes. These eight characters may act various roles in the various scenes, with the stipulation that the same actor and actress play the father and mother in the first and last scenes. In the intermittent scenes, sons play fathers and mothers play daughters so as to keep the play from appearing to be about only one or two families. A sense of virtuosity prevails. Here is a kaleidoscope of scenes from the United States.

Here again, Gurney satirizes upper-middle-class society. The characters are self-centered, modish, pampered, misguided, opinionated, and bored. They speak in clichés and find their world disappearing. Like an unmoored boat, they float along. At times the satire is more biting than in Gurney's earlier plays, but the message is clear and the entertainment delightful.

The language, typical of these characters, helps reveal their plight. A toast to the Father, the Son, and the best gin ever smuggled across Niagara River is followed by chatter about a pusher and manners at meals. The characters' names underscore the satire. Snoozer earns his name by sleeping through everything; Grace, Snoozer's godmother, to the tune of "The Star Spangled Banner" boozily proposes a one-word toast to Snoozer, "responsibility." From the Depression days of Franklin D. Roosevelt to an apocalyptic vision of a fascist America in the 1980's (a decade in the future when the play was produced), Gurney depicts a vapid society that lacks any moral foundation.

In one of the drama's strongest scenes, a father takes his son, who is in trouble for draft evasion, out for a day's sailing. Quoting his own code of honor, which is anachronistic to the boy, the father tries to persuade his son to stand trial and go to prison. His son tells him off with one epithet. In another scene typical of Gurney's dramas, a Yale graduate dictates a letter to a classmate declaring that he will not contribute to the alumni animal fund; midway into the letter, however, he resorts to the usual clichés, sending his wife's regards and an enclosed check. Gurney's recurring theme of freedom and coercion is evident in a luncheon scene with a mother and daughter. The mother says that the daughter may do as she pleases, choosing between a coming-out party and a college education, yet in spite of the daughter's protests in favor of an education, the mother ultimately decides on the party.

CHILDREN

Not surprisingly, Gurney has often been compared to novelist and short-story writer John Cheever, the rueful chronicler of suburbia. Gurney's play *Children*, based on Cheever's story "Goodbye, My Brother," is another satire on the old gentry as they conduct themselves when they come face-to-face with the upheavals of the present. *Children* provides actors with a number of splendid roles, but, as in several other Gurney plays, the characters who motivate much of the action are never seen onstage. These include Pokey, scion of the genteel family at the center of the action, who stands ominously in the shadows offstage; his braless Jewish wife, who holds a doctoral degree; and their uninhibited child. Also unseen but significant to the action is the rich local builder, who once worked as a yard boy for the WASP family.

Set in a summer house on an island off the Northeast coast during a Fourth of July weekend in 1970, *Children* includes four characters who appear onstage: an affluent, attractive mother; her daughter, Barbara, a divorceé; her son, Randy; and his wife, Jane. Though a slight disruption threatens and slight violence erupts, the play ends in unrelieved, unenlightened stasis. The characters prefer withdrawing into their status quo, staying put, deeply embedded in the customary ground of their past. Here, as in *Scenes from American Life*, Gurney presents intelligent entertainment for a wide audience, offering an ironic portrait of a classic WASP family that is losing its identity in a changing America. Subversive forces are undermining what is eventually revealed as the hypocrisy of an entire way of life.

THE WAYSIDE MOTOR INN

The Wayside Motor Inn, like *Scenes from American Life*, is composed of scenes that flow into each other. Five separate subplots take place simultaneously in one room of a suburban motor lodge outside Boston during the late afternoon and early evening of a spring day in the late 1970's. Like other Gurney plays, *The Wayside Motor Inn* deals with decadent Americans. Each of the five plots dramatizes the plight

of WASP society, underscoring the characters' inability to escape to freedom. Such key words as "door," "escape," and "choose" hint at a choice, but the characters cannot bestir themselves to act decisively. They are not so much enthralled as self-entrapped. They and their language ring true to themselves and to life. They mirror, enlighten, and entertain.

A Willy Loman-type father confronts his Biff-like son to no avail, while a couple pondering divorce look out from the balcony at the world, then come back inside for a drink. A traveling salesperson bitterly chafes under the domination of the computerized world, while a young college couple can make love only when hyped up by dope and a hot tub. Another couple snap at each other between fits of sympathy, contempt, and boredom. The television in the background amplifies and extends the drama of ordinary life. These ten ordinary people find themselves at the wayside of their lives, wondering which turn to take. Their difficulties and conflicts are commonplace, but Gurney succeeds in giving them resonance by presenting them side by side, simultaneously, onstage, thereby making the ordinary seem somehow extraordinary. The diverse scenes flow into an organic whole, commenting on the dark undercurrents of modern life.

THE DINING ROOM

Gurney scored his greatest hit with *The Dining Room*. In this play, the dining room becomes a metaphor for the continuity of bourgeois values, challenged by the younger generation in the latter part of the twentieth century. The space of the dining room itself—and the changing use of the space as scenes from different time periods are going on simultaneously—dramatizes the ways in which these values have been distorted. Through a humorously poignant series of vignettes, Gurney dramatizes the changing role of the classical, formal dining room through the course of three generations of WASPs. The changes are bittersweet—in some ways inevitable, but lamentable—a combination of continuity and change. Like Gurney, the little boy in the play views his great aunt's Waterford crystal finger bowls with fascination, seeing in them the habits of a vanishing culture, a neurotic obsession with cleanliness that is associated with the guilt of the last stages of capitalism. In its combination of moral critique, satiric wit, and humane sympathy. *The Dining Room* epitomizes Gurney's contribution to contemporary American drama.

THE PERFECT PARTY

Gurney's work in the wake of *The Dining Room*'s success continued to explore the suburban WASP lifestyle and its decay. *The Perfect Party* centers on the efforts of a fiftyish college professor to host a social event that will rise to the level of great art; Gurney's Oscar Wilde-style repartee won wide praise (the critic John Simon, however, demurred that the playwright had written nothing more substantial than "a two-act play entirely in *New Yorker*-caption cartoons.")

SWEET SUE AND ANOTHER ANTIGONE

In *Sweet Sue*, Gurney experimented with the simultaneous onstage use of two actors for each of the two central roles, but the doubling of the characters struck most reviewers as little more than an unnecessary special effect. *Another Antigone* is notable chiefly for its portrait of yet another middle-aged scholar, Henry Harper, an uncompromising classics professor fighting a rearguard action against the decay of Western civilization. An idealistic anachronism, Harper is a moving figure emblematic of many of Gurney's characters, doomed to endure the extinction of a culture they cherish.

LATER LIFE

Gurney's 1993 comedy *Later Life* is again set in New England and centers on Austin, a divorced and WASPish Boston banker in his late middle age who one night unexpectedly meets an old woman friend. The woman, Ruth, whom Austin had met about thirty years before as a serviceman on the Italian island of Capri, happens to be present at a cocktail party that he attends. Ruth is still attractive and single, and the two almost spend the night together. Austin, however, acting on a presentiment that something bad is going to happen to him in the near future, kisses Ruth good-bye.

With the future now drawing nearer, the plot centers on the intriguing premonition that Austin felt and on whether the couple will this time grab the chance for happiness that is at their fingertips. *Later Life*, which is partly inspired by Henry James's *The Beast in the Jungle* (1903), once more demonstrates the playwright's talent for satirizing New England WASPs and his ability to bring his audience not only to laugh at his characters but also to sympathize with them.

SYLVIA

One of Gurney's most delightfully original works is *Sylvia*, in which a middle-aged financial analyst (Greg) brings home a stray dog that eventually comes between his wife and him. Sylvia is one of Gurney's most challenging and enjoyable female roles, a dog that is alternately melancholy, amorous, vulgar, aggressive, and devoted. To add another dimension to Sylvia's irrepressible body language is that Gurney has given her the ability to speak but only to one person when no one else is in the room. To the despair of Greg's much-put-upon wife, everyone and everything else in Greg's life diminishes in importance except Sylvia. This insightful canine comedy about mid-life crisis and mid-marital disillusionment is a source of joy for actors and audiences alike.

FAR EAST

In *Far East*, Gurney takes a more momentous turn. Set at a Japanese naval base in 1954, *Far East* concerns an innocent young naval officer from Milwaukee ("Sparky") who, in search of worldly experience, commences an affair with a Japanese waitress. Sparky's captain sees in the young officer a reminder of his own youth, while the captain's wife, lonely in her marriage, is gradually attracted to Sparky. The subplot of another young officer who is being blackmailed by his male lover serves as a foil to the emotionally charged triangle of Sparky, the captain and the captain's wife.

DARLENE AND THE GUEST LECTURER

From the serious to the dark comic and melodramatic, Gurney's next effort was an evening of two one-act plays, *Darlene* and *The Guest Lecturer*. First, a housewife (Angela) becomes obsessed with a threatening note for "Darlene" mysteriously left on her car, and in the second play, a professor's lecture on theater is interrupted by a voluble panel moderator whose intentions are strangely homicidal.

LABOR DAY

The versatile Gurney returned to lighthearted comedy with *Labor Day*, about which Gurney says, "life and art don't mix." Here a successful, delightfully irritable playwright (Joe) has written a play in which the characters are thinly veiled versions of his family members. When a pushy young director brings Joe offers from regional theater and possibly Broadway if major script changes could be made, Joe's family members intrusively fight among themselves and derail the discussions with fears about how they will be portrayed.

ANCESTRAL VOICES

Gurney returns to his more traditional setting, the upper crust of 1930's and 1940's society, in *Ancestral Voices*. A young boy serves as narrator and witness for his grandmother's shocking choice to leave her husband for his best friend, after which the boy tries to arrange a reconciliation between his grandparents. Although Gurney is deeply sympathetic to the play's grandmother, *Ancestral Voices* is suffused with a gossamer veil of nostalgia for a bygone era.

HUMAN EVENTS AND BUFFALO GAL

Two new Gurney comedies were produced in 2001. *Human Events* involves a witty insight into campus politics when a British impostor takes over the life, home, and family of a New England university humanities professor. *Buffalo Gal* deals with the repercussions when a famous actress returns to her hometown to play the lead in a local production of Anton Chekhov's *Vishnyovy sad* (pr., pb. 1904; *The Cherry Orchard*, 1908).

OTHER MAJOR WORKS

LONG FICTION: *The Gospel According to Joe*, 1974; *Entertaining Strangers*, 1977; *The Snow Ball*, 1984.

SCREENPLAY: *The House of Mirth*, 1972 (adaptation of Edith Wharton's novel).

TELEPLAYS: *O Youth and Beauty*, 1979 (based on a short story by John Cheever); *Love Letters*, 1999.

BIBLIOGRAPHY

Barnes, Clive. "Wasps, No Sting." *Post* (New York), May 6, 1991. The Playwrights Horizons, a tryout house for much good work in New York, presented *The Old Boy*, to the disdain of Barnes: "The whole cast goes flat out . . . but the play, for all its evident demonstration of skills, just goes flat." Good synopsis, however, of the play's themes and plot.

DiGaetani, John L. *A Search for a Postmodern Theater: Interviews with Contemporary Playwrights.* New York: Greenwood Press, 1991. In this valuable resource, Gurney offers his observations about his life, plays, and writing process.

Gurney, A. R. "Here's to Playwright A. R. Gurney." Interview by Daryl H. Miller. *Daily News* (Los Angeles), April 13, 1990. The Canon Theatre's production of *Love Letters* coincided with previews of *The Cocktail Hour* at the Doolittle Theatre in Hollywood. This biographical interview brings both plays, and Gurney's successful *The Dining Room*, into perspective. *The Cocktail Hour* "examines the differences between the new and the old WASP," Gurney remarks.

Rizzo, Frank. "A Gentle Man, a Civil Man, and Theater's Favorite Playwright WASP." *Courant* (Hartford, Conn.), February 10, 1991. Based on informal interviews during rehearsal breaks for the Hartford Stage Company's production of *The Snow Ball*, this piece discusses Gurney's involvement with the Dramatist Guild's dispute with the League of Resident Theatres (LORT), examines his WASP image, and reports his screenplay work for *Love Letters*.

Williams, Albert. "Gurney Cuts Loose—Sort Of." *American Theatre* 10, no. 10 (October, 1993): 12. This interview covers Gurney's play *Later Life* and his observations on the importance of touching young people through theater.

Winn, Steven. "*Letters* Notes Change in Star System." *San Francisco Examiner*, December 17, 1989. Praising the "deft and graceful script" of *Love Letters*, Winn describes the performance (here with John Rubinstein and Stockard Channing) as "a beautifully tooled vehicle for pure acting," unlike the big "ensemble" shows of Broadway, such as *Phantom of the Opera* and *Cats*.

Helen H. Naugle,
updated by Thomas J. Taylor
and Howard A. Kerner

H

PETER HACKS

Born: Breslau, Germany; March 21, 1928

OTHER LITERARY FORMS

Peter Hacks abandoned a career as a scholar and critic of German literature to devote himself to the writing of plays, for which he is best known; he has also written a large number of articles on the theory of drama. In addition to his works for and about the theater, Hacks has published a number of well-received children's books and has translated works from English, including plays by William Shakespeare and John Millington Synge. In 1994, Hacks published a volume of short stories, and in 2000, an expanded version of his collected poems appeared.

ACHIEVEMENTS

In his critical introduction to postwar German literature of 1970, Peter Demetz claimed for Peter Hacks the distinction of being Bertolt Brecht's most sophisticated disciple. Whether this title should go to Heiner Müller rather than to Hacks is still an open question. Müller and Hacks have been the leading dramatists of the East German theater, and both have been known as representatives of dialectic theater in the Brechtian tradition. Brecht provided the ideological and aesthetic basis for their development as dramatists. Both have continued this tradition in a most creative and even challenging manner. Müller can be called the better dialectician, while Hacks has had a greater talent for comedy. During the 1960's and early 1970's, Hacks's plays were among those most often performed on the stage in East and West Germany. Although Hacks also had his share of problems with the official cultural policies in East Germany during the 1960's, Müller has perhaps been more controversial during the 1970's and 1980's. Müller, however, exerted significant influence on the theater in East Germany and abroad, whereas Hacks's influence had begun to diminish after the late 1970's, both because of a lack of publications and productions and, in West Germany, because of his support of government policies in the expulsion of poet and singer Wolf Biermann from East Germany in 1976. Furthermore, the West German stage of the 1960's and 1970's saw the debuts of younger playwrights such as Peter Handke, Franz Xaver Kroetz, and Botho Strauss.

Inspired by Brecht's ideas of an epic, or non-Aristotelian, theater, Hacks developed his concepts of a dialectic theater for a socialist society in an important essay on realist drama, "Das realistische Theaterstück," published in 1957. With the advent of socialism, Hacks argued, class antagonisms, based on conflicting class interests, had disappeared. There remained, however, nonantagonistic contradictions that were to be employed for the benefit of socialist society. In Hacks's view, the dialectic dynamism of contradictions should provide the motivating force of socialist drama, supplanting the individual conflicts and clashes of personal interest that animate traditional bourgeois drama. Thus, "realism" is redefined: Reality is not a given, but rather is dialectically changeable—and therefore beautiful. In this new aesthetic, Hacks saw the promise of drama in a socialist society.

In addition to Brecht, the Marxist philosopher Ernst Bloch and his utopian philosophy of hope greatly influenced Hacks. In his book on the nature of imaginative literature, *Das Poetische: Ansätze zu einer postrevolutionären Dramaturgie* (1972), Hacks declares that the image of history, as conceived by the

aesthetic consciousness, is a "humane utopia" that does not exist in historical reality. It is to be understood as a "counter-design" to the world, existing in the past and in the future "perhaps only in remembrance and hope." Hacks suggests that the principal subject of modern literature is the relationship between utopia and reality; the only mode of perfection open to reality, he concludes, is to be found in perpetual striving, in utopian hope. Even in a socialist society, the individual is never so completely integrated as to be beyond improvement. It is the function of the theater, Hacks argues, to show this potential for growth.

In spite of these philosophical concerns, Hacks managed to write entertaining plays and attract large audiences in East and especially West Germany during the 1960's and early 1970's. His talent for comedy, combined with his highly developed skill in handling blank verse and his demand for a socialist classicism, account for his success as a dramatist during those decades. His later plays, based on dramas by Johann Wolfgang von Goethe, have been neglected by most theaters, except for Goethe anniversaries and memorials.

During the 1980's and 1990's, Hacks appeared to have diminished in popularity. Although he published a two-volume edition of his late plays in 1999, none of them was performed by a major stage, except for an adaptation of an operetta by Jacque Offenbach (*Orpheus in der Unterwelt*). His major dramatic achievements remain his early plays.

Biography

Peter Hacks was born in Breslau, Germany (now Wrocław, Poland), in 1928, into an upper-middle-class family, the son of a lawyer who was a member of the Social Democratic Party. He studied philosophy, sociology, German literature, and theater arts in Munich, receiving a Ph.D. in German literature in 1951 with a dissertation on nineteenth century German drama. He began writing radio drama and cabaret sketches, and in 1954, he won a prize for his first major drama, *Eröffnung des indischen Zeitalters*, which premiered in Munich in 1955. During the same year, Hacks decided to move to the German

Democratic Republic (GDR). There, he served as a dramaturgical assistant to Wolfgang Langhoff, director of the Deutsches Theater in Berlin, until 1963, when both Hacks and Langhoff were dismissed because of conflicts with the cultural policies of the government.

At the Bitterfeld Conference of 1959, which was arranged by the ruling state party to plan in detail the future of socialist literature, dialectic drama had been proscribed, and dramatists had been admonished to write more about the workers and their lives. Literature was to treat topics of national significance. Hacks had tried his hand at realist drama, as prescribed by the Bitterfeld Conference, by writing *Die Sorgen und die Macht*, a play about brown coal production. Its dialectics, however, proved to be in conflict with official cultural policies. The play's second production at the Deutsches Theater in Berlin was canceled in 1962, and both Hacks and Langhoff were criticized by the writers' union for misrepresenting conditions in the GDR.

With *Moritz Tassow*, Hacks continued to write drama in dialectical fashion, yet managed to avoid any major clashes with official cultural policies. A general trend of East German drama toward a new socialist classicism around 1968 proved to be favorable to Hacks, who could now apply his dialectics to classical myth, as in *Amphitryon* and *Omphale*, thereby avoiding conflicts with party doctrines. Similarly, his monodrama on Charlotte von Stein, Goethe's great love of the 1770's and 1780's, *Charlotte*, was a great stage success. During the early 1970's, Hacks experienced his greatest popularity in West Germany, after which, as noted above, his reputation there declined rapidly.

Hacks was a member of the East German branch of PEN, the international writers' organization, and after 1972, he was a member of East Germany's Academy of Arts.

Hacks isolated himself from his colleagues in the GDR when he supported the government in its action against Wolf Biermann, the dissident poet and singer who was denied re-entry into the GDR and lost his East German citizenship after a concert tour to West Germany in 1976. Even after the reunification of East

and West Germany in 1990, Hacks did not change his allegiance to GDR socialism.

ANALYSIS

Peter Hacks began with historical drama from a Marxist perspective. His early plays demonstrate the force of history through the characters of so-called great men, such as Christopher Columbus, modeled after Brecht's *Life of Galileo*, in *Eröffnung des indischen Zeitalters*, Duke Ernst of Swabia in *Das Volksbuch vom Herzog Ernst*, and Frederick II of Prussia in *Der Müller von Sanssouci*.

ERÖFFNUNG DES INDISCHEN ZEITALTERS

In *Eröffnung des indischen Zeitalters*, the discovery of America is seen as the historical event that energized the merchant middle class to evolve as the most powerful class of the future. Its ascent to power is achieved at the expense of the nobility and clergy, who prove to be unable to adapt to historic changes. Columbus is far from being a great man. Like Brecht's Galileo, he betrays his science. At the Spanish court, he is manipulated not by scientific discovery but by the imperialist and capitalist interests of the Spanish crown. Once a scientific discoverer and scholar, Columbus becomes a representative of the new bourgeois class. He does not feel compromised by his opportunism, until he sees the future of America: the rape of a continent and the enslavement of its natives in the name of historical progress.

DIE SCHLACHT BEI LOBOSITZ

In *Die Schlacht bei Lobositz*, Hacks presents the perspective of the little man—in this case, an eighteenth century Swiss citizen, kidnapped for service as a mercenary in the Prussian army. This unheroic hero deserts when he realizes that officers belong to a different class, a class that is not interested in the welfare of its charges. Even if an officer shows a humane attitude, this attitude is but a trick to keep the common soldier from deserting.

DIE SORGEN UND DIE MACHT

Die Sorgen und die Macht—inspired, as noted previously, by the Bitterfeld Conference of 1959—deals with the initial difficulties of brown coal production in the GDR. Criticizing the workers' petty bourgeois self-interest and the bureaucratic socialism of the party, the play projects a path toward the communism of the future. In spite of its socialist happy ending and its vision of "true communism," the play was severely criticized by the ruling party, and its production at a major theater in Berlin was canceled.

MORITZ TASSOW

In *Moritz Tassow*, a blank-verse comedy and parody of Goethe's classical drama *Torquato Tasso* (pb. 1790; English translation, 1827), Hacks continues to deal in dialectic fashion with the problems of building a socialist society in the GDR, in this particular case with the problems of land reform and the collectivization of farms. After the defeat of Nazi Germany, Moritz Tassow, a former swineherd, takes over the estate of the local Junker and establishes a farming commune. Current party policies, however, prescribe the division of the old estates into small, individual farms, although large communes may be more productive. While the members of the party insist on compliance with the party directives, Moritz Tassow holds on to his utopia. In the end, the representatives of the party prevail, and the land is subsequently divided among the farmhands. Yet Tassow has the satisfaction of knowing that he is ahead of his time. The land reform of 1945 was finally replaced in East Germany by the drive for collectivization of 1960. In 1945, however, Tassow must withdraw, like his Goethean model, from his clash with party functionaries, the men of action, and, like Goethe's protagonist, he retires to writing fiction, yet he continues to fight for his utopia against the courtiers of his age—that is, the party functionaries.

AMPHITRYON

In the two comedies, *Amphitryon* and *Omphale*, Hacks resorts to mythology to dramatize his concern for a humane utopia in socialist society. The Amphitryon plot, well-known to theater audiences through the treatment of Plautus, Molière, Heinrich von Kleist, and Jean Giraudoux, is changed insofar as Alkmene prefers the god to the human being, because Jupiter represents the utopian dimension of humankind. He is what people are supposed to be, and something beyond that, incorporating the humane utopia, whose essence consists of love and the striving toward perfection. The comedy lacks the tragic elements of the Kleistian version, affirming the potential of human growth and development toward perfection. Because Amphitryon fails to develop this potential, his wife, Alkmene, knowingly chooses the god over her husband; Jupiter achieves what her husband was meant to be. When Amphitryon argues that there are limits to human achievement—paradoxically, only a god is able to be a human being—Jupiter answers with the metaphor of border crossing (*Grenzüberschreitung*) that is so central to Bloch's philosophy of hope, saying that recognizing one's limits means transcending them. Amphitryon proves to be not totally uneducable; he and Alkmene experience through divine intervention their growth toward their humane utopia in spite of all their shortcomings.

OMPHALE

In Hacks's other blank-verse comedy *Omphale*, the exchange of male and female dress and attributes between Hercules and Omphale is presented as a positive event symbolizing their emancipation from the traditional stereotypes of male and female roles. Hercules becomes Omphale, and Omphale becomes Hercules, forming a new union on a higher level of human growth. This new synthesis, however, would merely be a short-lived private utopia if the two partners failed to establish contact with society: Individual love and growth become meaningless without social interaction. Hercules and Omphale must return to their former roles, he as a dragon slayer, and she as a mother of heroes, in order to restore their social standing. Their return is not a defeat; rather, it constitutes an enrichment of their former personalities. Hacks appears to be saying that although this Herculean feat of becoming a new human being is impossible to achieve, society is thereby set into motion in a direction that will lead to the humane utopia in the not too distant future.

CHARLOTTE

Hacks's outlook on human life and love is not as optimistic in *Charlotte*. With Charlotte von Stein, Goethe's great love of the 1770's and 1780's, as sole *dramatis persona*, this monodrama deals with the price of human suffering paid for great artistic achievements. While stirring Goethe's passion, Charlotte had challenged his intellect and inspired his creativity. In 1786, however, Goethe left her to seek new inspiration in Italy. The play opens after Goethe's hasty and secretive departure for Italy, with Charlotte explaining to her husband, playing a mute role in this drama, what it was that happened between her and the young poet and statesman. She tries to deny any transgressions on her part, calling Goethe a self-centered lout who adored her, but whose attention she discouraged all those years. She protests too much, however, betraying not only an erotic passion for Goethe but also resentment and bitterness for the price she had to pay for the self-centered development of a great poet. Not much, if anything, is left of the humane utopia of this great love relationship. Like so many of Hacks's dramas, it is a dialectic thesis play that presents, however, in contrast to the plays of his middle period from 1960 to 1970, a negative assessment not only of human relationships but also of art, including his own, and its inherent utopian function. This pessimism may be an explanation for the subsequent decline of Hacks's dramatic productivity.

OTHER MAJOR WORKS

SHORT FICTION: *Die Erzählungen*, 1994.

POETRY: *Die Gedichte*, 1988, expanded 2000.

NONFICTION: "Das realistische Theater," 1957; *Das Poetische: Ansätze zu einer postrevolutionären Dramaturgie*, 1972; *Die Massgaben der Kunst: Gesammelte Aufsätze 1959-1994*, 1977, revised 1996; *Schöne Wirtschaft: Ästhetisch-ökonomische Fragmente*, 1988; *Ascher gegen Jahn: Ein Freiheitskrieg*, 1991; *Zur Romantik*, 2001.

CHILDREN'S LITERATURE: *Das Windloch: Geschichten von Henriette und Onkel Titus*, 1956; *Das Turmverlies: Geschichten von Henriette und Onkel Titus*, 1962; *Flohmarkt: Gedichte für Kinder*, 1965; *Der Schuhu und die fliegende Prinzessin*, 1966; *Die Katze wäscht den Omnibus*, 1972; *Der Bär auf dem Försterball*, 1972 (*The Bear at the Hunter's Ball*, 1976); *Kathrinchen ging spazieren*, 1973; *Die Sonne*, 1974; *Das musikalische Nashorn*, 1978; *Leberecht am schiefen Fenster*, 1979; *Der Mann mit dem schwärzlichen Hintern*, 1980; *Jules Ratte: Oder, Selbstlernen macht schlau*, 1981.

BIBLIOGRAPHY

Demetz, Peter. *Postwar German Literature: A Critical Introduction*. New York: Pegasus, 1970. Survey of German literature between 1945 and 1970 with chapters on individual authors.

Huettich, H. G. *Theater in the Planned Society: Contemporary Drama in the German Democratic Republic in Its Historical, Political, and Cultural Context*. Chapel Hill: University of North Carolina, 1978. Monograph on theater and drama in the GDR until 1976.

Mitchell, Michael. *Peter Hacks: Theatre for a Socialist Society*. Glasgow: Scottish Papers in Germanic Studies, 1990. An examination of Hacks's plays and his political positions.

Scheid, Judith R. *"Enfant terrible" of Contemporary East German Drama: Peter Hacks in His Role as Adaptor and Innovator*. Bonn: Bouvier, 1977. Study of text adaptation and innovation in Hacks's plays through the 1970's.

Waidson, H. M. "Peter Hacks." In *Twentieth Century German Dramatists, 1919-1992*, edited by Wolfgang D. Elfe and James Hardin. Vol. 124 in *Dictionary of Literary Biography*. Detroit, Mich.: Gale Research, 1992. Survey article of Peter Hacks's plays through the 1980's.

Ehrhard Bahr

JESSICA HAGEDORN

Born: Manila, Philippines; 1949

PRINCIPAL DRAMA

Chiquita Banana, pb. 1972
Where the Mississippi Meets the Amazon, pr. 1977
   (with Thulani Davis and Ntozake Shange)
Mango Tango, pr. 1978
Tenement Lover: no palm trees/in new york city, pr.
   1981, pb. 1990
Holy Food, pr. 1988 (staged), pr. 1989 (radio play)
Teenytown, pr. 1990 (with Laurie Carlos and
   Robbie McCauley)
Black: Her Story, pr., pb. 1993
Airport Music, pr. 1994 (with Han Ong)
Silent Movie, pr. 1997 (as part of *The Square*)
Dogeaters, pr. 1998 (adaptation of her novel)

OTHER LITERARY FORMS

Jessica Hagedorn has published two novels, *Dogeaters* (1990), which was nominated for a National Book Award and translated into several languages, and *The Gangster of Love* (1996), and three collections containing short fiction and poetry: *Dangerous Music* (1975); *Pet Food and Tropical Apparitions* (1981), and *Danger and Beauty* (1993). Her poetry has been anthologized in a number of collections and published in several literary journals. In addition, she has published several short essays and is the editor of *Charlie Chan Is Dead: An Anthology of Contemporary Asian American Fiction* (1993). Hagedorn's nonfiction articles, interviews, and essays have appeared in the *New York Times Magazine, Harper's Bazaar, The Nation*, and *USA Weekend*. In collaboration with photojournalist Marissa Roth, Hagedorn published *Burning Heart: A Portrait of the Philippines* (1999). She wrote the screenplay for *Fresh Kill* (1994), an independent film directed and produced by Shu Lea Cheang. Other work with Cheang includes *Color Schemes* (1989) and *Those Fluttering Objects of Desire* (1992), both of which were screened at the Whitney Museum. Hagedorn also collaborated with John Woo on *The Pink Palace* (2000), a set of animated short films for Oxygen's *X-Chromosome* series.

ACHIEVEMENTS

Jessica Hagedorn's *Pet Food and Tropical Apparitions*, a multigenre novella, won the American Book Award in 1981, the year of the book's publication. Hagedorn received her first Macdowell Colony Fellowship in 1985, her second in 1986. Her third Macdowell fellowship, in 1988, supported her work on *Dogeaters*. In 1990, *Dogeaters* was awarded the American Book Award by the Before Columbus Foundation and was a finalist in the fiction category for the National Book Award that same year. In 1994, Hagedorn was awarded a Lila Wallace Reader's Digest Writers Award, and in 1995, she received a National Endowment for the Arts Creative Writing Fellowship. In 1996, her second novel, *Gangster of Love* was nominated for the Irish Times International Fiction Prize. Hagedorn held a Sundance Theatre Lab Fellowship in 1997 and a National Endowment for the Arts-Theatre Communications Group (NEA-TCG) Theatre Residency Fellowship in 1998.

BIOGRAPHY

Jessica Hagedorn was born in the Santa Mesa district of Manila in the Philippines in 1949 and spent her childhood in the midst of a family that considered literary and artistic activities to be a vital part of life. As a child, Hagedorn was influenced by her mother, an artist, and by her grandfather, a writer and political cartoonist, as well as by a cultural milieu that included American movies, Tagalog radio melodramas, and classic literature in the Western tradition. Hagedorn recalls attempting her first "novel" at the age of eight, writing "The End" on the last page of the little "books" she created. When she was thirteen, her parents divorced, and her artist mother moved to the United States with their three children and settled in San Francisco, where the young Hagedorn continued writing poetry and creating

Jessica Hagedorn (Nancy Wong)

Asian American. These influences, together with those of her childhood in Manila, ultimately led to the unique brand of performance writing for which Hagedorn is known.

Hagedorn very early took an interest in the performing arts; her first stage appearance—at sixteen—was at the Straight Theatre in San Francisco's Haight-Ashbury district. Instead of going to college, she decided to enter the two-year theater arts program at American Conservatory Theatre where she studied acting, as well as martial arts in addition to the more traditional mime and fencing activities common to acting programs.

For Hagedorn, the 1970's was significant to the evolution of the distinctive multigenre performance style for which she would become known. She discovered Latin American fiction, especially the works of Gabriel García Márquez, Manuel Puig, and Julio Cortázar. In 1975, she published her first literary collection, *Dangerous Music*, a compilation of poetry and prose fiction. Hagedorn, Thulani Davis, and Ntozake Shange formed The West Coast Gangster Choir, a rock-and-roll band for which Hagedorn was the lead singer and songwriter for a decade.

During the 1970's, she performed as one of the original cast members of Shange's *for colored girls who have considered suicide/when the rainbow is enuf* (pr., pb. 1975), an experimental performance piece incorporating dance and poetry. Her experience as a musician imbued her poetry with definitive rhythms and patterns; her theatrical work enhanced the already performative nature of that same poetry. The ultimate result was Hagedorn's brand of multimedia theater.

In 1977, Hagedorn collaborated with Davis and Shange on *Where the Mississippi Meets the Amazon*, a theatrical spectacle that blended music and poetry. After the piece was produced in 1978 by Joseph Papp at the Public Theatre in Manhattan, Hagedorn moved to New York and began a new career as a playwright and musician, renaming her band The Gangster Choir. Later that year, Hagedorn wrote and per-

comic books. When a family friend sent samples of Hagedorn's poetry to the poet Kenneth Rexroth, he became a mentor, giving her permission to sit in on his creative writing classes at San Francisco State University and taking her with his own daughter to poetry readings. Rexroth encouraged her to read widely and to continue writing and included her work in *Four Young Women*, a collection that he edited in 1973.

Growing up in the San Francisco of the 1960's, Hagedorn was immersed in the diversity of the city and inspired by the growing multicultural consciousness that pervaded both the literary and social environments. Among the authors whose work she read and now cites as influential are Amiri Baraka, Gabriel García Márquez, Bienvenido Santos, Stephane Mallarme, and Ishmael Reed. Through her involvement with San Francisco's Kearny Street Writers' Workshop, she deepened her awareness of and empathy with her own literary and historical heritage as an formed *Mango Tango*, which was also produced by Joseph Papp at the Public Theatre. In New York, she participated in the Basement Workshop and worked with the performance trio Thought Music.

In the 1980's, Hagedorn created several more pieces for the stage, including *Tenement Lover* in 1981, and *Holy Food*, which received a theater production in 1988 and a radio production in 1989. She collaborated with Laurie Carlos and Robbie McCauley on *Teenytown*, first produced at New York's Franklin Furnace in 1988. Also that year, *A Nun's Story*, a dance-theater piece, was broadcast on public television's *Alive from Off Center*.

Hagedorn's work entered a new phase in 1990 when she published *Dogeaters*, the novel that brought her mainstream fame and recognition. Like her poetry and theater pieces, the novel shunned straightforward narrative, relying on seemingly disparate elements—poetry, letters, news items, dialogue, excerpts from other books—embedded in a storyline to explore ethnic tensions, class divisions, corruption, and revolution in the context of political totalitarianism and postcolonial angst. That novel was followed by *Gangster of Love* in 1996. Despite the critical acclaim that her novels have brought her, she has not abandoned the theater. In 1994, Hagedorn and Han Ong produced *Airport Music*, and in 1998, the La Jolla Playhouse awarded Hagedorn a commission to write a play based on her novel, *Dogeaters*. The play was premiered at the Playhouse in the fall of 1998 and received a New York production at the Public Theatre in 2001.

Hagedorn worked with Angel Velasco Shaw on *Excuse Me . . . Are You Pilipino?* (2000), a feature documentary set in New York, San Francisco, and Hawaii. The film examines the unique strategies employed by Filipino Americans to create identity and community in an alien dominant culture. The work was supported by a 1999 production grant from the Jerome Foundation.

In addition to her work as a playwright, musician, and performance artist, Hagedorn has taught at Columbia University and New York University, both in New York City. She is an occasional commentator for the National Public Radio magazine *Crossroads*.

ANALYSIS

Jessica Hagedorn's entire body of work focuses on Filipino Americans' struggle to discover a place in a new culture without having to relinquish every element of the home culture. In her plays—as in her novels, essays, and poetry—Hagedorn explores a number of significant issues, among them the search for or formation of identity, the clash of cultures, and the problems inherent in an immigrant's attempts to fit into a new community. Although she is much better known as a novelist than as a dramatist, she has produced an interesting body of mixed-media and multimedia work for the stage, pieces that are closer to performance art than to the traditional play format.

Hagedorn's work defies simple categorization, instead straddling the boundaries between high and low culture, and crossing between and among genres. In theater circles and to theatergoing audiences, Hagedorn is best known in as a performance artist, and her plays are infused with distinctively performative elements drawn from music, dance, poetry slams, storytelling, and role playing. Except for the themes on which Hagedorn focuses—themes that surface in many American plays—her work has little in common with conventional American drama, even with contemporary ethnic drama. Instead, her pieces belong with the work of theater artists and innovators such as Karen Finley, John Leguizamo, Ping Chong, and Ntozake Shange.

TENEMENT LOVER

A multimedia theater piece, *Tenement Lover* incorporates film, dance, poetry, music, and narration with slides projected on a wall, a radio newscaster providing updates on a current political crisis, and a television that broadcasts throughout the piece. Focusing on the experiences of two immigrants, Bongbong, who never appears onstage, and Ludivinda, who watches television obsessively, the play uses dream visions, poems, letters, reflections, mime, dialogue, and monologue to dramatize the clash between a culture of origin and American culture (represented by New York), chronicling an immigrant's gradual assimilation into an alien environment that he initially finds to be impossibly confusing. Two actors playing several characters mime several tense encounters while a Narrator and a band provide commentary.

The subtitle, *no palm trees/in new york city*, immediately signals the play's focus on bifurcations, on the distance between cultures, on the difference between reality and dreams, on the divide between powerful nations and developing countries. A series of slides featuring scenes from the Philippines functions as a backdrop to the opening narration telling the story of Bongbong, twenty-nine years old and marooned in New York, homesick, jobless, taking comfort in letters to his artist friend, Frisquito. Bongbong's story is followed by that of Ludivinda, whose rambling monologue tells her tale of marriage to a marine who brought her from her home in the Philippines to a roach-infested New York tenement. Like Bongbong, she is homesick and unhappy, taking refuge in television. As the Narrator and the band members recount and enact the immigrants' stories, a blonde Sunbather in dark glasses appears and unrolls a length of barbed wire across the stage, neatly delineating her space from that of the rest of the world, emphasizing the distance between her and those who cannot afford leisurely vacations. As the Sunbather, on her side of the wire barrier, lolls languidly in her lounge chair beneath a beach umbrella, sipping a drink brought by an obsequious waiter, and clearly unconcerned with the rest of world on the other side of the barbed wire, Ludivinda watches television in her dreary apartment, a guerrilla fighter creeps out of the underbrush, slides of mountain tribes are projected on a backdrop, and a newscaster announces that Pope John Paul has publicly scolded Philippine president Marcos at a reception in the presidential palace.

The band performs songs that mirror the stage action. Singing "Sleazy Desire/New York Reggae" and "Tenement Lover," the band members paint a harsh picture of immigrant life, underscoring the displacement and alienation that characterize Bongbong's and Ludivinda's daily existence and commenting on the disparity between their fantasies of life in the United States and the realities they face daily. Ultimately, Bongbong does come to terms with his situation, but only after he has a dream in which he learns to fly but is still unable to catch Frisquito who flies still higher. Meanwhile, the Sunbather becomes aware of the guerrilla who has entered her space and begins to stalk her, and she backs away from him in terror and disappears offstage. The play ends with the band singing about "Ming the Merciless" described as "the asian nightmare/ the yellow peril." In a culture that identifies Asians with cartoon villains, Bongbong and Ludivinda will never fully assimilate; they will always be outsiders, they will forever be on the wrong side of any power relationship.

TEENYTOWN

Teenytown is a performance piece that incorporates poetry, songs, and dialogue written singly by Hagedorn, Laurie Carlos, and Robbie McCauley, as well as material cowritten by the three collaborators. Written specifically for performance by the three authors, Teenytown relies heavily on the specific talents and performance styles of those individuals. Through an episodic structure that borrows heavily from several forms of popular entertainment, the piece explores the pervasiveness of racism in popular entertainment and the media. Five actors (including the three authors) play several different characters, acting, singing, and dancing in front of television monitors showing vintage racist cartoons and films, as well as historic film footage of lynchings, police officers with dogs, and protest marches.

The first—and longer—portion of the piece, designed in the traditional format of the old-time minstrel show, explores the history of racism through a form of performance that is identified strongly with a racist past. Opening with the traditional song and dance, the three main performers—Hagedorn, Carlos, and McCauley—wielding makeshift "instruments" including a washboard, spoons, and cooking pots, transform themselves into a variety of characters: Dorothy Dandridge, Hazel Scott, standup comedians, Oprah Winfrey, a church choir, Stepin Fetchit clones, Shakespearean actors with strong ethnic accents, and torch singers. Their performances are punctuated by cameo appearances by a man and a woman who act the roles of black militant, janitor, rap artist, preacher, and tango dancer. After a scripted intermission, the second part opens with a radio play, moving into a send-up of the television talk show format to comment on contemporary manifestations of more globalized racism. Parodying the *Tonight Show*, the three major performers take on the personas of "Johnny," "Ed," and "Doc" in their white dinner jackets, black tuxedo pants, and wingtip shoes. Racist cartoons and films substitute for the commercials that interrupt jokes by Hagedorn, Carlos, and McCauley and guest performances by the man and woman. The piece ends with "Buck and Wing" described as "an original Aboriginal tap dance."

Hagedorn's contribution to *Teenytown* consists of two original pieces, "All Shook Up" and the title piece "Teenytown," as well as two collaboratively created segments, "Dog Eat Dog" and "Sex and Death." Like most of Hagedorn's other work, "All Shook Up" incorporates a staggering array of popular culture and geographical references, from Josephine Baker to Elvis and Otis Redding, Paris to Manila, and rednecks to gendarmes. Created for performances by a female trio, the piece's lyrics move in and out of four languages—English, French, Spanish, and Tagalog—evoking images of exile, difference, and exclusion and employing racial stereotypes to highlight the existence of racist attitudes in all cultures, even those in developing countries. Unlike "All Shook Up," "Teenytown" is not a song; rather, it is a parable spoken by the three major performers who underscore, with appropriate hand gestures, the narrative of a tiny place populated by tiny people who have tiny minds and even tinier aspirations and horizons.

Teenytown is autobiographical, very much in the tradition of performance art that is inextricably tied to specific writers/performers. Hagedorn and her two cowriters/performers deliberately chose to work in a format that allowed them to transcend time, genre, playwriting tradition, and theatrical expectations to create a piece that examines the impact of race on identity and memory, the tensions between a minority culture and the dominant culture in which the former is embedded, and the pervasiveness of power inequities in cultural structures.

DOGEATERS

Adapted from Hagedorn's award-winning novel by the same title, *Dogeaters* was first produced at the La Jolla Playhouse in California and later at the Public Theatre in New York City. The play, which has thirty-three characters played by fifteen actors, is set in the Philippines and presents events from the perspective of Rio Gonzaga, a Filipina American woman in Manila during the crucial year 1982, in the midst of the corrupt regime of President Ferdinand Marcos, although flashbacks take Rio to her thirteen-year-old self in the late 1950's. Dramatizing events in a country on the edge of revolution, *Dogeaters* explores the ways in which a single event affects the lives of seemingly unconnected people in different parts of the country. Hagedorn points out that although the play has parallels with actual historical events such as the 1983 assassination of former senator Benigno Aquino, her aim is not to provide a history lesson but to re-create the atmosphere of corruption and tension that pervaded the Philippines during a crucial period in its recent history.

Dogeaters (the title refers to a pejorative term used by American soldiers to refer to Filipinos) is driven by a double plot. Framing the political events in the play is the story of Rio Gonzaga who has returned to the Philippines to attend her grandmother's funeral. After an absence of many years, Rio is an outsider in the country of her birth, and her narrative is reminiscent, questioning, a coming to terms with her identity as a stranger.

A second plot, much broader and more complicated, revolves around Senator Domingo Avila, a vocal critic of the Marcos administration and a leader of the opposition party. Avila is gunned down in the lobby of a fashionable Manila hotel during Rio's visit, and the sole witness, an Afro-Filipino hustler named Joey Sands, is caught up in the political complications surrounding the assassination. Meanwhile, the Avila plot also dramatizes the transformation of Daisy Avila, the senator's daughter and a beauty queen, from a torture victim to a rebel with an outlaw gang in the mountains.

In addition to the already named characters above, Hagedorn has created a wildly varied and unconventional collection of characters: media personalities, military personnel, a corrupt general and his fanatically religious wife, Perlita the drag queen and night club owner, a gay hairdresser, a pimp, an American journalist, a wise grandmother, a nineteenth century French Jesuit, a cinema cashier and her boyfriend who wants to be a movie star, and political radicals turned rebels-on-the-run. Interacting with these flamboyant and sometimes cartoonish characters are two "real" persons: former Philippine first lady Imelda Marcos and German filmmaker Rainer Fassbinder. The array of eccentric personalities, not uncommon in Manila, allows Hagedorn to explore the ways in which a single dramatic event—the assassination—reverberates throughout all segments and all levels of a society, transforming the lives of unrelated individuals.

Events in the play are initially narrated by a pair of radio and television stars, Barbara Villanueva and Nestor Noralez, who represent not only the glamorous personalities who are deified in celebrity-driven Filipino popular culture but also the theatricality of the play's events. Principals in the longest-running Filipino soap opera, Barbara and Nestor function as the emcees for a series of complications that rival even the most far-fetched and convoluted soap-opera plot. Integral to the plot are such larger-than-life events as a showdown between two prominent and powerful men at a country club; the rape and torture of a beauty queen; a conversation between the narrators and a priest who has been dead for over a century; an interview between an American media representative and Imelda Marcos, who refuses to say anything that might be even remotely incriminating; and, of course, the assassination that connects both plots and the many subplots that make up the play. Settings are no less flamboyant: a trendy hotel, a gay disco, a club featuring live sex acts, and a talk show set. Rio Gonzaga functions as a secondary narrator, as a commentator on the events from the point of view of an outsider.

Dogeaters explores in some detail two themes that appear in Hagedorn's other work: the Americanization of popular culture and power relations. The United States becomes a pervasive influence, even a presence, not only through Rio Gonzaga, the Filipina American who has returned for a visit, but also in the person of Joey Sands, the son of a prostitute and an African American soldier. Moreover, Manila, in the play, is a city engaged in a cultural dialogue with the United States: American-style talk shows proliferate on television, people wear American brands, American films are popular, and images of America form the landscape of most people's dreams and fantasies. Hagedorn's other plays show immigrants' attempts not to lose their home cultures even as they are seduced by the charms of the American culture into which they try desperately to assimilate. *Dogeaters* makes it clear that Philippine culture has already partially succumbed to the force of a transplanted and very attractive American popular culture. Hagedorn also dramatizes the uses and abuses of power: political, social, cultural, and sexual power. Through the rape of Daisy Avila, several forms of power collide: the power of men over women, the military over civilians, and the political in-crowd over the dispossessed. Joey Sands also embodies a number of power collisions. As a prostitute, his mother has no power, while his father, an American, does; however, because his father is black, Joey lacks the cachet typically accorded to mestizos (individuals who are half Filipino and half Anglo American or European). In addition, Joey exists at the mercy of his only living kinsman, a ruffian pimp who controls Joey with drugs. Finally, because he witnesses the killing of Senator Avila, Joey inadvertently acquires the power of knowledge, thus coming to the attention of the even more powerful military who must destroy him.

OTHER MAJOR WORKS

LONG FICTION: *Dogeaters*, 1990; *The Gangster of Love*, 1996.

POETRY: *The Woman Who Thought She Was More than a Samba*, 1978; *Visions of a Daughter Foretold*, 1994.

SCREENPLAY: *Fresh Kill*, 1994.

EDITED TEXT: *Charlie Chan Is Dead: An Anthology of Contemporary Asian American Fiction*, 1993.

MISCELLANEOUS: *Dangerous Music*, 1975; *Pet Food and Tropical Apparitions*, 1981; *Danger and Beauty*, 1993.

BIBLIOGRAPHY

Bloom, Harold. "Jessica Hagedorn." In *Asian American Writers*, edited by Harold Bloom. Philadelphia: Chelsea House, 1997. A very brief biographical essay, covering the highlights of Hagedorn's life and career, introduces a sampling of critical extracts, most of which are disquisitions on *Dogeaters*, although one or two address Hagedorn's poetry. In one extract, Hagedorn herself writes about *Tenement Lover* and its place in Asian American writing.

Doyle, Jacqueline. "'A Love Letter to My Motherland': Maternal Discourses in Jessica Hagedorn's Dogeaters." *Hitting Critical Mass: A Journal of Asian American Cultural Criticism* 4, no. 2 (Summer, 1997): 1-25. Doyle comments on Hagedorn's portrayal of the "invention" of personal identities in the context of a Philippine culture whose colonial history is riddled with the omissions imposed by the Catholic Church and by Spain.

Hau, Caroline. "*Dogeaters*, Postmodernism and the 'Worlding' of the Philippines." In *Philippine Post-Colonial Studies: Essay on Language and Literature*. Quezon City: University of the Philippines Press, 1993. Hau's essay is a critique of Hagedorn's first novel, calling into question the fact that the work, which focuses on a turbulent and controversial period of Philippine history, is the creative production of an Asian *American* writer, generated with the support of *American* institutions and funding agencies, read by an *American* audience, and favorably reviewed by *American* critics.

Jenkins, Joyce. "Jessica Hagedorn: An Interview with a Filipina Novelist." In *The Asian Pacific American Heritage: A Companion to Literature and Arts*, edited by George J. Leonard. New York: Garland, 1999. Hagedorn remembers her early mentor, Kenneth Rexroth, and his influence on her poetry and her development as a multigenre artist. She discusses *Dogeaters* and the "language of place" and remarks on how her writing has changed over the years. She comments on other Filipino American writers and their contributions to contemporary American literature.

San Juan, Epifanio, Jr. "Mapping the Boundaries: The Filipino Writer in the U.S.A." *Journal of Ethnic Studies* 19:1 (1991). Somewhat unsettled by Hagedorn's refusal to identify clear boundaries between American culture and the Philippines, San Juan warns Hagedorn and other Filipino American writers that they might unwittingly be apologists for the United States and its materialistic culture by overemphasizing the Philippines' colonial past as they negotiate the shifting borders between postcolonialism and postmodernism.

E. D. Huntley

TAWFIQ AL-HAKIM

Born: Alexandria, Egypt; October 9, 1898
Died: Cairo, Egypt; July 26, 1987

PRINCIPAL DRAMA
Khatim Sulayman, pr. 1924
al-Marʾah al-jadidah, pr. 1926, pb. 1952
Ahl al-kahf, pb. 1933, pr. 1935 (*The People of the Cave*, 1989)
Shahrazad, pb. 1934, pr. 1966 (English translation, 1955)
Muhammad, pb. 1936 (partial English translation, 1955)
Nahr al-junun, pb. 1937 (*The River of Madness*, 1963)
Shajarat al-Hukm, pb. 1938
Piraksa: Aw, Mushkilat al-hukm, part 1, pb. 1939, part 2, pb. 1960
Salah al-mala ʾikah, pb. 1941 (*Angels' Prayer*, 1981)
Pijmalyun, pb. 1942, pr. 1953 (*Pygmalion*, 1961)

Sulayman al-hakim, pb. 1943 (*The Wisdom of Solomon*, 1981)

Himari qala li, pb. 1945 (short plays, one translated as *The Donkey Market*, 1981)

al-Malik Udib, pb. 1949 (*King Oedipus*, 1981)

Ughniyah al-mawt, pb. 1950, pr. 1956 (*The Song of Death*, 1973)

al-Aydi al-naʿimah, pb. 1954, pr. 1957 (*Tender Hands*, 1984)

Bayna al-harb wa-al-salam, pb. 1956 (*Between War and Peace*, 1984)

Rihlah ila al-ghad, pb. 1957 (*Voyage to Tomorrow*, 1984)

al-Sultan al-haʾir, pb. 1960, pr. 1961 (*The Sultan's Dilemma*, 1973)

Ya taliʿ al-shajarah, pr. c. 1961, pb. 1962 (*The Tree Climber*, 1966)

al-Taʿam li-kull fam, pb. 1963, pr. 1964 (*Food for the Millions*, 1984)

Shams al-Nahar, pr. 1964, pb. 1965 (*Princess Sunshine*, 1981)

Masir Sursar, pb. 1966, pr. 1969 (*Fate of a Cockroach*, 1973)

Kullu shayʾ fi mahallihi, pb. 1966 (*Not a Thing Out of Place*, 1973)

al-Wartah, pb. 1966 (*Incrimination*, 1984)

Ahl al-qamar, pb. 1969 (*Poet on the Moon*, 1984)

al-Dunya riwayah hazaliyah, pb. 1971, pr. 1972 (*The World Is a Comedy*, 1985)

Fate of a Cockroach: Four Plays of Freedom, pb. 1973

Plays, Prefaces, and Postscripts of Tawfiq al-Hakim, pb. 1981, 1984 (2 volumes; William M. Hutchins, translator)

OTHER LITERARY FORMS

In addition to drama, Tawfiq al-Hakim was active in a number of genres. Among his novels, written rather early in his career, *al-Qasr al-mashur* (1936; the enchanted palace) is notable as a collaborative effort composed with the distinguished man of letters Taha Husayn. His most celebrated work of long fiction, *Yawmiyat naʾib fi al-aryaf* (1937; *Maze of Justice*, 1947), draws on al-Hakim's experience as a legal functionary and deftly combines social commentary with satire. Other novels are significant as indications of al-Hakim's propensity to experiment with this form of fiction. At intervals during his career, al-Hakim wrote short stories, which are most readily accessible through the two-volume collection *Qisas*, published in 1949. He also published a number of essentially autobiographical works, of which *Sijn al-ʿumr* (1964; *The Prison of Life*, 1992) deserves particular mention; *Zahrat al-ʿumr* (1943; life in flower) is a compilation of letters, translated from the French, from al-Hakim's correspondence with those he met during his student days in Paris. Reflections on drama, art, and life are presented in works of literary criticism such as *Min al-burj al-ʿaji* (1941; from the ivory tower) and *Fann al-adab* (1952; the art of literature), as well as other studies. For a number of years, beginning in 1943, al-Hakim wrote columns for the influential newspapers *Akhbar al-yawm* (news of the day) and *al-Ahram* (the pyramids) of Cairo. His collection of political essays, *ʿAwdat al-waʿy* (1974; *The Return of Consciousness*, 1985), and a companion volume of documents published the next year, aroused criticism in some circles and wonderment in others, for their unfavorable commentary on the government of Egypt under President Gamal Abdel Nasser.

ACHIEVEMENTS

At the beginning of the twentieth century, drama in Egypt and the Arab world remained a derivative and largely secondary form of creative expression. Puppet and shadow plays were produced alongside adaptations drawn for the most part from French and Italian playwrights. Some innovations were introduced on the Egyptian stage with the production of works by Salim Khalil al-Naqqash, Yaʿqub Sannuʿ (James Sanua), and Ahmad Shawqi. After World War I, important new plays were written by Mahmud Taymur, and Najib al-Rihani's performances in comic roles also aroused interest in the theater. Nevertheless, with only an exiguous native tradition, Tawfiq al-Hakim came to the forefront of modern Egyptian dramatists with strikingly original depictions of time-honored Middle Eastern themes. His earlier work, particularly that beginning with *The People of the Cave*, achieved the fusion of regional themes with

European techniques. More than that, al-Hakim's work came to be classed as pioneering on at least three other fronts as well. He brought to the Egyptian and Arab stage unique and distinctive interpretations of Western works, notably versions of classical Greek drama. Many of his works have a surrealistic bent, suggesting analogies, which he has encouraged, with the Western Theater of the Absurd. He was also among the first Arab dramatists to write dialogue in colloquial language. Purists, who insisted on the use of classical Arabic, were outraged, but others have conceded that the effects may have heightened the contrasts between the timeless and the mundane that are integral concerns of al-Hakim's productions. His efforts to introduce idiomatic usage into the language of the stage were followed by those of other notable playwrights. This trend in itself marks the extent to which, largely as a result of al-Hakim's influence, drama has developed from the stylized, ritualistic forms that characterized the early Arab theater.

Notwithstanding the decidedly mixed reception accorded his works during the early phases of his career, al-Hakim received a number of awards and honors in his native country. In 1951 he was made director general of the Egyptian National Library, and three years later he became a member of the Academy of the Arabic Language in Cairo. He was awarded the cordon of the republic in 1958, and he served as Egypt's representative to UNESCO, in Paris, during the following two years. He received the State Literature Prize in 1961, and in 1963 a theater in Cairo was formally named for him. His position as the preeminent modern dramatist in the Arab world was underscored when a Tawfiq al-Hakim Festival was held at the University of Cairo in 1969. At that time he also presided over a Congress of Arab Dramatists that was held in the Egyptian capital. In 1974, he became president of his country's Story Writers' Club. Although personally at times he may have been inclined to overstate his own importance—during the early 1960's he announced his candidacy for the Nobel Prize in Literature—Tawfiq al-Hakim's stature was imposing among Middle Eastern playwrights, and on the international level his works are almost certainly the most widely recognized of any Arab dramatic productions.

BIOGRAPHY

For some time, the date of Tawfiq al-Hakim's birth was in doubt—in places the year 1902 was cited, but later October 9, 1898, was accepted as proved. It is certain that he was born in Alexandria, Egypt, of an Arab doctor and a mother who was descended from a family of Ottoman officials and army officers. Although his education moved forward slowly during his early years, al-Hakim evinced an early interest in dramatic storytelling. In 1915, he entered the Muhammad Ali Secondary School in Cairo, and he received the baccalaureate in 1921. His youth evidently was marred somewhat by difficult relations with his mother, and a brief, unrequited love affair did nothing to improve his attitude toward women. During the short-lived revolution of 1919, which was provoked by the exile of Saʿd Zaghlul, a prominent national leader, to Malta, al-Hakim was imprisoned for composing patriotic songs. His incarceration was brief and hardly unpleasant; at about that time he wrote his first play, a work that Cairo producers would not stage because of its defiantly anti-British standpoint.

For four years, until 1925, al-Hakim studied law at the state university in Cairo; increasingly it became evident that his proclivities, and his real calling, lay elsewhere. His further efforts at the writing of drama brought forth *al-Marʾah al-jadidah* (modern woman), which was composed in 1923 and produced on the stage three years later. Three other short plays, including *Khatim Sulayman* (the ring of Solomon), were produced in 1924, shortly after he had committed them to paper. In spite of an undistinguished academic record—he graduated third from last among those who were promoted in his class—he entered the Collège des Lois at the Sorbonne in Paris. At that time he was still guided in part by his father's wish that he should become a lawyer, and evidently he was otherwise undecided about which direction his career should take. During his student years in France—between 1925 and 1928—he spent much of his time reading, sightseeing, and absorbing as much European culture as possible. In addition to philosophy and narrative fiction, he delved at length into published drama and attended performances of major plays. It would seem that he was particularly fascinated by the works of Henrik Ibsen, George Bernard Shaw, and Luigi Pirandello. Classical Greek theater also left a lasting impression on him. The lack of an Arab dramatic tradition, which had troubled him during his first efforts in Egypt, was brought home to him more definitely; along the way, two love affairs, which turned out badly, added further poignancy to his outlook. In 1928, having passed all but one of his examinations, he returned to Egypt, ostensibly to commence work within the legal profession, but with his creative aspirations probably now foremost in his mind.

After an apprenticeship of one year in Alexandria, al-Hakim served as a public prosecutor in various rural communities between 1929 and 1934; he then became director of the investigation bureau of the Ministry of Education, and in 1939 he was appointed to a position in the Ministry of Social Affairs. In 1943 he left public service to devote himself entirely to writing. It may readily be inferred from his fictional and autobiographical works that he regarded government positions as sinecures, an attitude he also detected in those around him. The decisive event of his career as a playwright was the publication in 1933 of his *The People of the Cave*. His transfer from legal to bureaucratic responsibilities may have been a result of the uproar that greeted this work. Although Taha Husayn, a leading critic, and other men of letters praised its bold, unconventional approach, others castigated it for its use of informal, even ungrammatical, language. *Shahrazad* had already been published (in 1934) when an outcry broke out over the staged version of *The People of the Cave*; audiences rejected it as far too long and too far removed from the formal routines that they had come to expect from the theater. Typical of other dramatic works from this period are *Muhammad*, a lengthy treatment of episodes from the life of the Prophet, and other works set in classical times. In 1936, al-Hakim, on a visit to Europe, attended the Salzburg Theater Festival, and in 1938 he vacationed in the Alps, in an effort again to maintain cultural contacts abroad.

The next period of al-Hakim's creative life is sometimes associated with the title of his book *Min al-burj al-ʿaji*, which refers to the literary life as being led in an "ivory tower." To be sure, some of his writings expressed concern about Nazi ambitions during World War II; in a more general light, he also wrote about his fears for world peace during an age dominated by brute militarism and technology. Other works explored classical Greek themes or considered episodes from the Old Testament that are also part of Islamic lore. In 1946 he was married, and thereafter fathered a son and three daughters; critics later have tried to determine the effect his family life had on the obvious though sometimes playful misogyny of his literary efforts.

His reputation as a playwright detached from ideological concerns was reinforced during the period surrounding the Egyptian revolution of 1952 and the ultimate withdrawal of British forces from that country in 1956. In 1953, al-Hakim's version of Shaw's *Pygmalion* was staged at the Salzburg Theater Festival; in 1960, *The Sultan's Dilemma* was published simultaneously in Cairo and, in a French translation, in Paris. He was honored by President Gamal Abdel Nasser, who secured official awards for him and attended the production premiere of *Tender Hands* in 1957. The author thus had reason to believe that his renown and acceptance of his works were on the rise. His works were also produced in other Arab countries; some of them were successfully adapted for the cinema. Quite apart from experiments with language, he turned increasingly to futuristic, global concerns or to the bemused contemplation of the absurdities in everyday life. Students of the theater struggled to find political allusions in al-Hakim's later plays; some of them were set in remote historical periods and others took place in future ages.

In January, 1973, the dramatist became directly embroiled in public concerns; he presented President Anwar el-Sadat with a letter on behalf of forty-six writers, protesting the nation's indecisive stance against Israel. Although for a brief period publication and production of al-Hakim's work were suspended, in October of that year war broke out, and the aging author vociferously supported Egypt's military efforts. By 1974 a short treatise that al-Hakim had written that criticized the excesses and extravagances of the Nasser years was cleared for publication, in keeping with Sadat's efforts to chart a political course of his own. Although this work, *The Return of Conscious-*

ness, was denounced by Nasser's remaining supporters (who, among other questions, asked why al-Hakim had remained silent until four years after their leader's death), it became a best-seller for some time. In 1975, it was reported that a companion volume, which presented documents from the author's work, in its turn had become the most popular book in Egypt. Although he did not go further in his professed intention to open the political files from his country's recent past, al-Hakim remained an important and widely cited newspaper columnist. In line with the nation's foreign policy, at times he suggested that Egypt and Israel may serve as islands of security in the Middle East. He also edited and supervised the collection of the numerous dramatic writings and other works that he composed over the years. Moreover, as the senior representative of an important modern tradition in Arabic and Egyptian literature, his works have been reprinted and have been made available in many parts of the world. Translations of al-Hakim's writings exist in French, Spanish, Italian, German, Hebrew, Russian, and Japanese as well as other Middle Eastern languages; English language compilations of his major plays have also done much to increase his following.

ANALYSIS

Although Tawfiq al-Hakim's dramatic imagination ranged across at least three millennia of human experience, touching down at particularly evocative points along the way, some generalizations may be made about common features in much of his work. Characterization has been important, but something less than a vital issue in his efforts; for that matter some leading personages have been typecast as abstract categories, such as war and peace, while others have been significant not for their intrinsic qualities but as participants in seemingly irrational situations. Characters in the plays based on medieval themes might possibly be interchanged with others from similar works. The domestic dramas also feature some stock types who seem to appear under various names in works of this kind. The author never claimed to have developed a florid, polished style—indeed, he purposely avoided such tendencies—and his dialogue has a crisp, staccato ring that often serves to heighten dramatic

tension. There are, in many of his works, series of exclamations and interjections that, particularly in the absurdist dramas, merge with scenes taken up mainly with the exchange of questions. Even the most carefully constructed plays have been meant as much for the reader as for the theater audience. Although some works have enjoyed considerably more success on the stage than others, the structure of al-Hakim's major dramatic efforts has been determined more by his thematic concerns than by the requirements of actual production. Many plays have long sequences of brief scenes, or sometimes present lengthy acts alternating with short, abrupt transitional passages. On another level, regardless of whether, during his classical or his absurdist phases, al-Hakim resolved the perennial questions of love, art, guilt, and social division, his works have posed these issues in unusual and distinctively original variations. Although at times he complained that during thirty years he attempted to accomplish for the Arab theater what it had taken Western civilization two thousand years to achieve, the freshness of his works, and the extent to which he has realized the conjunction of diverse aesthetic and moral concerns, should signify the magnitude of Tawfiq al-Hakim's efforts within and indeed beyond the limits of the drama as he had found them.

The drama of al-Hakim displays a remarkable diversity of outlook, and his breadth of vision inspires respect mingled slightly with awe. His cosmopolitan standpoint, coupled with his relentless quest for the new and untried, was in evidence across the span of his career. He was extraordinarily prolific; one recent count yielded eighty-four titles of dramatic works that he has composed, quite apart from his writings in other genres. His plays have been set in historical periods from the times of King Solomon of the Old Testament, through the age of classical Greek drama, across early and medieval periods of Islamic history, on to modern times in Egypt, and beyond, into the space age. He depicted the rustic peasant landscapes of his native country, the courts of great monarchs from the past, and the cosmic scenery of new worlds to come. It may well be argued that his work is uneven, both in its technical execution and where depth of characterization is involved. It would seem that his penchant for the unexpected and the unusual at times may have affected the direction of his dramatic efforts; any facile attempt to devise categories for his works is doomed to frustration. Nevertheless, although even a chronological approach would be subject to anomalies and overlapping impulses may be observed in many areas, there are some broad elements of thematic continuity that may be discerned in the development of al-Hakim's repertory.

THE PEOPLE OF THE CAVE

The historical contexts for major early works were derived from Islamic religious and literary traditions. *The People of the Cave*, the work that in 1933 was hailed as heralding the onset of a new era in Arab drama and that elicited stormy protests on the part of subsequent audiences, deals with the Christian legend of the Seven Sleepers of Ephesus, which is also cited in the Qur'an. In this play, visions of the miraculous, hope, and despair are presented in a light that is broadly consonant with the convictions of Muslim believers, but without prejudice to the Christian values that are also affirmed by Islam.

SHAHRAZAD

Shahrazad was al-Hakim's effort to supply a continuation of *Alf layla wa-layla* (15 C.E.; *The Arabian Nights' Entertainment*, 1706-1708); when the fabled storyteller survives and marries the monarch from the tale, some poignant and revealing reflections on nature, beauty, and mortality are recorded.

MUHAMMAD

Muhammad, which serves as a sort of Muslim Passion play, is a sweeping pageant that was meant to demonstrate al-Hakim's belief that suitable dramatic forms could be found to evoke themes from the life of the Prophet. This play may also point to the author's contention that the drama is meant to be read as much as it is meant to be viewed: In one edition there are a prologue, three acts, and an epilogue, comprising, in all, ninety-five scenes.

THE RIVER OF MADNESS

Absolute power and helplessness are treated in plays taken from past epochs of Oriental despotism. In *The River of Madness*, a one-act production, a monarch's subjects drink mystical waters that render them impervious to his commands. At the end, the unnamed ruler also seeks wisdom in this form of supposed madness. It is not clear who is sane and who is not, or whence real authority springs.

THE WISDOM OF SOLOMON

For all of his powers, the biblical King Solomon is unable to win the favor of a beautiful woman, in one of al-Hakim's longer works, *The Wisdom of Solomon*. This effort, which draws on characters depicted in one of the author's earliest plays, *Khatim Sulayman*, opens when a jinni appears to a humble fisherman and informs him of his quarrel with the king. He hopes for reinstatement into Solomon's good graces. When the Queen of Sheba, the most beautiful of all women, is brought before the mighty monarch, Solomon in all of his glory is unable to win her favor. He is tempted to enlist the spirit, but is reluctant to summon unearthly powers. The queen remains demure as ever, and for all of his countless treasures and innumerable wives, the great ruler falls prey to the frailties of the flesh; he becomes old and dies. At the end, the jinni warns that love and power will provoke struggle on this earth for centuries and ages to come.

THE SULTAN'S DILEMMA

Themes of punishment and justice converge with concerns about past politics in some of the author's later plays. In *The Sultan's Dilemma*, which is set in late medieval Egypt, a man is sentenced to death for maintaining that the sultan is a slave; a lady intervenes on his behalf, demonstrates that the condemned man is indeed correct, and in the end the ruler's place before the people must be redeemed by a complicated process of manumission. By emphasizing the absurdities of a bygone political system (where in fact under the Mamluk Dynasty the loftiest as well as the lowliest positions were occupied by those who in a technical legal sense were held in bonded servitude), al-Hakim implies that authority and official dignity are transitory attributes that are real only to the extent that society accepts them.

PRINCESS SUNSHINE

Princess Sunshine has an unspecified medieval setting, during the reign of a certain Sultan Nu'man. He rules over an odd kingdom: Princes from all around are flogged to deter them from courting the princess; executions must be halted because the gallows rope has been stolen. Harmony is achieved, however, when the princess agrees to marry one of her suitors, even after she learns that he is actually a commoner and his real name is the unprepossessing Dindan.

PIRAKSA

Works that are borrowed from Western traditions exhibit another facet of al-Hakim's conception of the drama. Aristophanes was the original source for *Piraksa: Aw, Mushkilat al-hukm* (Praxagora: or, the difficulties of government). The Egyptian playwright's version turns out to be an exercise in political discourse. Some ludicrous problems arise when the protagonist of the title subjects ancient Athens to a form of feminist communism.

PYGMALION

Pygmalion, though suggested by George Bernard Shaw's work, also takes up classical concerns. A Cypriot Greek artist calls on the goddess Venus to endow one of his statues with life; when he falls in love with his creation, Pygmalion, the title character, fears that he will have to abandon sculpture. This work, published in 1942, highlights the conflicting demands of life, love, and art in a felicitous union of several disparate approaches to the drama.

KING OEDIPUS

A major work in al-Hakim's canon is *King Oedipus*, which is an adaptation of Sophocles' *Oedipus Tyrannus* (c. 429 B.C.E.; *Oedipus Tyrannus*, 1715). In this version, the tragic denouement takes place when the monarch learns that he is not of royal birth. He is driven by a zealous pursuit of the truth even beyond the doors that should not be opened. Curiosity is Oedipus's tragic flaw; when he learns that he was adopted, he is blinded. It is noteworthy here that, without introducing overt references to Islam, the pantheon of Greek gods from the original tragedy is replaced with suggestions of a monotheistic purpose. Countervailing concerns with predestination and free will arise when al-Hakim points to problems of divine intentions in this world.

TENDER HANDS

Contemporary social issues figure in many of al-Hakim's plays, sometimes in a bizarre, mocking sense; but a more straightforward presentation of these themes may be found in *Tender Hands*, which

concerns the place in society of university graduates who have more formal learning than practical training. Whether grammatical usage has any relevance to the management of an oil company is a problem that is no more readily resolved than the just division of household tasks for a prospective couple. Nevertheless, all ends happily when a marriage uniting two leading characters is secured.

HIMARI QALA LI

Whimsical and broadly comic themes have been pursued in several of al-Hakim's works; this is the case with *Himari qala li* (my donkey said to me). In this group of dramatic sketches, the author's donkey asks him questions about life's predicaments; in some sequences the roles of human and animal almost seem to be reversed, as ordinary logic appears inadequate to explain the anomalies of humankind's condition.

THE TREE CLIMBER

In some of his works, al-Hakim acknowledged the examples of European playwrights such as Bertolt Brecht, Samuel Beckett, and Eugène Ionesco; in 1962 he announced that his most recent play had an irrationalist inspiration, and some affinities with the Theater of the Absurd, in the introduction to one of his best-known works. *The Tree Climber* opens as a retired railway inspector is perplexed by the simultaneous disappearance of his wife and a female lizard that had lived under their orange tree. After police interrogation, and with the testimony of a bizarre dervish who appears at the train station, the old railwayman confesses to murder and claims that by burying his wife's body under the tree he had hoped to increase its yield of fruit. The lawmen begin digging, but they uncover nothing; the wife reappears later, and, when her husband questions her about her absence, he becomes enraged by her evasive answers. He strangles her, puts the body in the hole the police have left under the tree, and then is distracted by the mysterious dervish. During their conversation, the wife's body vanishes; in its place they find the body of the lizard, the man's talisman of good fortune.

THE FATE OF A COCKROACH AND NOT A THING OUT OF PLACE

Another notable effort in the same vein is *Fate of a Cockroach*, which commences with a satirical view of order and legitimacy in the insect world. The cockroach king takes precedence over the queen because his whiskers are longer, but the female talks of mobilizing her sex for a war against predatory ants. The two seem to agree, however, that their species is the most advanced on the planet. Unknown to them, a married couple is arguing about the equitable disbursement of household funds. The wife asks the husband to kill a cockroach in their bathtub; when first the man and then the woman begin instead to contemplate the insect in admiration, a doctor is called in. He cannot understand either one of them because he has never been married. For a certain time, the husband and the wife quarrel about rank and obedience in a way that recalls the argument between the cockroach king and queen; relations seem more strained than ever after the maid, in the course of her cleaning routine, drowns the insect without a second thought.

Not a Thing Out of Place is a brisk one-act piece that has villagers talking of melons that resemble human heads and a philosophically inclined donkey when they go off to join a local dance.

THE SONG OF DEATH AND INCRIMINATION

Themes of violence and guilt—notably those that elude any judicial resolution—are taken up in certain works. The one-act play *The Song of Death* deals with a blood vendetta between peasant families in Upper Egypt. A young university graduate is unable to persuade them that they would be better concerned with technological means to improve their living standards.

Although power, punishment, and the political order have been considered in plays set in earlier periods, an absurdist treatment of crime during modern times is presented in *Incrimination*. Here a law professor who has written learned treatises on criminal psychology, but has never met any lawbreakers, is introduced to some local gang members. When a policeman is shot to death during a jewel theft, the scholar agrees to defend his acquaintance from the underworld in court. By a strange transposition of the clues, however, the evidence in the end points to the professor. It would seem, then, that in the author's view guilt and innocence have no more fixed constancy than visual illusions.

VOYAGE TO TOMORROW

Voyage to Tomorrow begins with a crime story and ends with some of the ironic, futuristic twists that are notable in al-Hakim's later drama. A man who perpetrated murder while in the throes of romantic infatuation is allowed to participate in an experimental, and extremely hazardous, space flight; his companion is a fellow convict who had committed four murders for personal gain. Against all the odds they survive and return to Earth during a future age when all material wants are provided for and people routinely live several hundred years. This state, however, is actually a despotism wherein love and romance are regarded as unwanted, somehow subversive relics of the past. The first convict, after a brief flirtation with a sympathetic brunette, threatens to kill a security guard who tries to separate them. He comes close to committing murder again for the sake of a woman. Here the great themes of conscience and emotional commitment are interwoven with the author's visionary and speculative concerns.

ANGELS' PRAYER

A final grouping of al-Hakim's works might include those that deal with global issues. Here a question that is frequently posed is whether science will benefit humanity or assist in its mass destruction; this issue was taken up at intervals across much of al-Hakim's career. In his attitude toward World War II, and in his considerations on the advent of nuclear weapons and rivalries in space exploration, al-Hakim dealt with important developments in advance of many other Arab authors. The short play *Angels' Prayer* depicts an angel who comes to Earth. He finds a monk and a scientist quarreling over responsibility for the wayward path of the human race. The angel is later captured, tried, and executed at the behest of two tyrants who resemble Adolf Hitler and Benito Mussolini. When he returns to Heaven, still holding his apple of peace, which the dictators have vainly tried to take from him, he urges the other angels to pray for the inhabitants of Earth.

BETWEEN WAR AND PEACE AND
FOOD FOR THE MILLIONS

The one-act play *Between War and Peace* has an odd bit of personification: Characters named War and

Peace meet in the boudoir of a lady named Diplomacy, where their deliberations resemble the intrigues of a lovers' triangle.

Human issues in the nuclear age are examined in *Food for the Millions*. A scientific prodigy claims to have made a discovery more important than the atom bomb: Food can be produced at an infinitesimal fraction of its original cost, and families everywhere will be able to have it in abundance. Others compare this project to the fond dreams of science fiction, and it falls by the wayside when the youth and other family members learn that their mother, before remarrying, may have acted to hasten the death of their seriously ill father. Toward the end of the drama there are some homely but portentous musings on water stains that repeatedly appear on their apartment walls; these may be symbolic of guilt in the household that has not yet been expunged.

POET ON THE MOON

In one of his last plays, *Poet on the Moon*, al-Hakim describes a flight to the moon on which, in spite of some misgivings from the authorities, a poet is allowed to accompany two astronauts. When they arrive, the poet is the only one who can hear the voices of moon creatures, who warn against any attempt to remove precious or hitherto unknown minerals from their domain. On the return of the spacecraft to Earth, the creatures effect the mysterious transmutation of moon rocks into ordinary vitreous earth, thus averting any premature or unprincipled exploitation of outer space.

OTHER MAJOR WORKS

LONG FICTION: ʿAwdat al-ruh, 1933 (*Return of the Spirit*, 1990); *al-Qasr al-mashur*, 1936 (with Taha Husayn); *Yawmiyat naʾib fi al-aryaf*, 1937 (*Maze of Justice*, 1947); ʿUsfur min al-Sharq, 1938 (*Bird of the East*, 1966); *Raqisat al-maʿbad*, 1939; *al-Ribat al-muqaddas*, 1944.

SHORT FICTION: *Qisas*, 1949 (2 volumes); *Arini Allah*, 1953; *In the Tavern of Life and Other Stories*, 1998.

NONFICTION: *Tahta shams al-fikr*, 1938; *Tahta al-misbah al-akhdar*, 1941; *Min al-burj al-ʿaji*, 1941;

Zahrat al-ʿumr, 1943; *Fann al-adab*, 1952; *Sijn al-ʿumr*, 1964 (*The Prison of Life*, 1992); *Qalabuna al-masrahi*, 1967; ʿAwdat al-waʿy, 1974 (*The Return of Consciousness*, 1985); *Wathaʾiq fi tariq ʿAwdat al-waʿy*, 1975; *Nazarat fi al-din, al-thaqafah, al-mujtamaʿ*, 1979; *Mamalih dakhiliyah*, 1982.

BIBLIOGRAPHY

Badawi, M. M. *Modern Arabic Drama in Egypt.* Cambridge, England: Cambridge University Press, 1987. Badawi's study examines the state of Arabic drama in modern Egypt, touching on al-Hakim.

_____, ed. *Modern Arabic Literature.* Cambridge History of Arabic Literature. Cambridge, England: Cambridge University Press, 1992. This history of Arabic literature from the mid-nineteenth century to the late twentieth century contains a long section on al-Hakim as well as a description of many other major dramatists in Egypt and the Arabic world.

El-Enany, Rasheed. "Tawfiq al-Hakim and the West: A New Assessment of the Relationship." *British Journal of Middle Eastern Studies* 27, no. 2 (November, 2000): 165-175. An analysis of one of al-Hakim's early novels on the cultural clashes between the East and the West. Provides insights into the dramatist's views.

Long, Richard. *Tawfiq al Hakim: Playwright of Egypt.* London: Ithaca Press, 1979. A basic biography of al-Hakim that examines his life and works. Bibliography and index.

Starkey, Paul. *From the Ivory Tower: A Critical Analysis of Tawfiq al-Hakim.* Atlantic Highlands, N.J.: Ithaca Press, 1988. Starkey presents criticism and analysis of the works of al-Hakim.

_____. "Tawfiq al-Hakim." *African Writers.* Vol. 1. New York: Charles Scribner's Sons, 1997. A concise overview of the life and works of al-Hakim.

_____. "Tawfiq al-Hakim (1898-1987): Leading Playwright of the Arab World." *Theater Three* 6 (1989). A look at the life and works of al-Hakim two years after his death.

J. R. Broadus

WILLIS HALL

Born: Leeds, England; April 6, 1929

PRINCIPAL DRAMA

The Long and the Short and the Tall, pr. 1958, pb. 1959

A Glimpse of the Sea and Last Day in Dreamland, pr. 1959, pb. 1961

Billy Liar, pr., pb. 1960 (with Keith Waterhouse; adaptation of Waterhouse's novel)

Chin-Chin, pr. 1960 (adaptation of François Billetdoux's play)

A Glimpse of the Sea: Three Short Plays, pb. 1961 (includes *Last Day in Dreamland* and the teleplay *Return to the Sea*)

Celebration, pr., pb. 1961 (with Waterhouse)

England, Our England, pr. 1962, pb. 1964 (musical, with Waterhouse; music by Dudley Moore)

The Sponge Room, pr. 1962, pb. 1963 (one act, with Waterhouse)

Squat Betty, pr. 1962, pb. 1963 (one act, with Waterhouse)

Yer What?, pr. 1962 (revue, with others; music by Lance Mulcahy)

Come Laughing Home, pr. 1964 (with Waterhouse; originally as *They Called the Bastard Stephen*, pb. 1965)

Say Who You Are, pr. 1965, pb. 1966 (with Waterhouse)

Joey, Joey, pr. 1966 (musical, with Waterhouse; music by Ron Moody)

Whoops-a-Daisy, pr. 1968, pb. 1978 (with Waterhouse)

Who's Who, pr. 1971, pb. 1974 (with Waterhouse)

Saturday, Sunday, Monday, pr. 1973, pb. 1974 (with Waterhouse; adaptation of Eduardo De Filippo's play)

The Card, pr., pb. 1973 (musical, with Waterhouse; music and lyrics by Tony Hatch and Jackie Trent; adaptation of Arnold Bennett's novel)

Walk On, Walk On, pr. 1975, pb. 1976

Filumena, pr. 1977, pb. 1978 (with Waterhouse; adaptation of De Filippo's play)

The Wind in the Willows, pr. 1984, pb. 1986 (musical; music by Denis King; adaptation of Kenneth Grahame's story)

Treasure Island, pr. 1984, pb. 1986 (musical; music by King; adaptation of Robert Louis Stevenson's novel)

Lost Empires, pr. 1985 (musical, with Waterhouse; music by King; adaptation of J. B. Priestley's novel)

The Water Babies, pr., pb. 1987 (adaptation of Charles Kingsley's novel)

Budgie, pr. 1989 (musical, with Waterhouse)

Jane Eyre, pb. 1994 (adaptation of Charlotte Brontë's novel)

Mansfield Park, pb. 1994 (adaptation of Jane Austen's novel)

The Three Musketeers, pb. 1995 (adaptation of Alexandre Dumas's novel)

OTHER LITERARY FORMS

Willis Hall has become familiar to English audiences through a variety of media and genres. He and Keith Waterhouse, with whom he regularly collaborates, are highly regarded for their screenplays. Some of their more notable efforts are *Whistle Down the Wind* (1961) and *Billy Liar* (1963). With Wolf Mankowitz, Hall has adapted for the screen *The Long and the Short and the Tall* (1961). Hall has also worked extensively in television, writing for programs such as *The Fuzz* and *Secret Army*, coauthoring a half dozen other series with Waterhouse, and writing a number of television plays, often for children. Hall has written musicals (*England, Our England*, with music by Dudley Moore, was reviewed with great praise), books on sports, the text for a documentary, pantomimes, novels, award-winning adaptations of foreign drama, and scripts for television series. The sheer bulk of Hall's work and its rich variety testify to his artistic strength and durability.

ACHIEVEMENTS

It is difficult to find any single descriptive category or term under which Willis Hall's achievements as a dramatist will fit with accuracy. *The Long and the Short and the Tall* (commissioned by the Oxford Theatre Group for the Edinburgh Festival of 1958, and winner of the *Evening Standard* Drama Award for Best Play in 1959), associated him with the new drama appearing in the wake of John Osborne's *Look Back in Anger* (pr. 1956), and comparisons have often been made between Hall's Private Bamforth and Osborne's Jimmy Porter. At the same time, Hall's early collaborations with Keith Waterhouse have been considered in terms of regional realism as authentic representations of life in the North of England. Plays such as *Billy Liar* and *Celebration* reflect their authors' feel for the idiosyncrasies of regional language, serving as reminders that Hall and Waterhouse often draw with success on their shared Yorkshire background. These descriptions are somewhat helpful; yet with plays such as *The Sponge Room* or *Squat Betty* they plainly break down, since these are expressly nonrealistic plays. Such descriptions also do not apply well to later plays, such as *Say Who You Are* and *Who's Who*, which move away from realistic Northern themes and introduce elements of farce.

If Hall's work resists any single-phrase summary, this in itself is perhaps an indication of his achievement as a writer. He has directed his efforts toward a wide variety of literary ventures in a variety of genres, each demanding its own kind of discipline, and he has performed with some success in all of them. Further, his writings with Waterhouse represent the foremost dramatic collaboration in twentieth-century England, and both are admired for their professional competence and consistency. In addition to their own work, they have created successful adaptations of two plays by Eduardo De Filippo, *Saturday, Sunday, Monday*, which starred Sir Laurence Olivier and Joan Plowright, and *Filumena*, which enjoyed a two-year run in England. On his own, Hall has written and staged a successful adaptation of François Billetdoux's *Chin-Chin* (pr. 1960). Hall, then, has written on his own and in collaboration, for children and adults, for the stage and for the radio and screen.

While praising Hall's versatility and the range of his work, reviewers and critics have at times questioned its depth, and indeed it is difficult to avoid feeling that some of the plays are too light or are perhaps dominated by an adept dramatic technique that masks other and more profound limitations. One might say simply that the aims of the plays are sometimes modest but that they achieve those aims with delightful flair and insight and offer genuine rewards for their readers.

BIOGRAPHY

Willis Hall was born on April 6, 1929, in Leeds, England, the son of Walter and Gladys Hall, and was educated in Leeds at Cockburn High School. As a youth, he became friends with Keith Waterhouse, with whom he worked on a youth-club magazine and collaborated on a wide variety of projects for the stage, television, film, and radio. That friendship was interrupted in 1947 by Hall's five-year stint in the British Regular Army, during which time he served in the Far East as a radio playwright for Forces Radio. The military provided the background for Hall's first major stage success after his return to England, *The Long and the Short and the Tall*, which included Peter O'Toole and Robert Shaw in the cast. Hall resumed his friendship with Waterhouse, and together they adapted Waterhouse's novel *Billy Liar* for the stage in 1960, a highly successful production that established Albert Finney and Tom Courtenay, each of whom had a turn at the title role, as exceptionally gifted actors.

From that time on, Hall has occupied himself with a remarkably prolific and consistent literary life. With more than two dozen stage plays to his credit, some written with Waterhouse, Hall has successfully experimented in additional commercial forms. In addition to an active career writing and adapting for television, Hall has contributed *The A to Z of Soccer* (1970, with Michael Parkinson), the first of several soccer books in the 1970's. He has written much high-quality children's literature, including *Spooky Rhymes* (1987), *Dr. Jekyll and Mr. Hollins* (1988), *Henry Hollins and the Dinosaur* (1988), and *The Vampire's Holiday* (1991). He is an avid amateur magician and a member of several magic societies.

ANALYSIS

Many of Willis Hall's plays (including those he coauthored with Keith Waterhouse) concern the discrepancy between the real world and the world that people invent for themselves. Again and again one comes on figures who have created their own drama about the world and their own part in it, only to find that reality is an entirely different drama that proceeds indifferent to its characters. This theme lends itself to a variety of treatments. In a play such as *Billy Liar*, it can create a pathetic character whose imagination defends him from the world and masks his lack of courage, and who, when he sees beyond the veil of his own private fictions, knows that he is alone and insignificant. It can also produce the lighthearted farce of a play such as *Who's Who*, in which the distortions of reality create a complex series of mixups and mistaken identities culminating in comic disclosures, admissions, embarrassments, and reconciliations. In many of the plays, the imagination is a kind of obstacle to a character's growth, for it substitutes the satisfying (and effortless) vision of distant success and security for any real development.

THE LONG AND THE SHORT AND THE TALL

The Long and the Short and the Tall, Hall's first major success, is a realistic war drama about a small unit of British soldiers in the Malayan jungle, set during the Japanese advance on Singapore in 1942. It seems at first to have little to do with the themes or subjects of Hall's subsequent work, but much of the play's conflict grows out of the soldiers' storybook ideas about war, their visions of themselves as heroic and moral men defending the side of good—visions that are denied by the reality of the war as it quickly closes in on them. This theme is suggested in an early scene. As the men rest in a deserted store-hut in which nearly all the action takes place, Private Evans sits reading the serial story in an issue of *Ladies Companion and Home* (his mother sends it to him each week), a romantic tale about a second lieutenant who must leave his girl behind when he is posted overseas. The story takes its hero through a variety of exciting and fantastic adventures, the last installment having left him in the hands of some Bedouins who have bound and suspended him above a roaring fire.

Evans is puzzled, though, because the current issue finds the hero inexplicably escaped from the Bedouins and enjoying a honeymoon in Brighton with the girl he had left behind, who has waited faithfully for him. The events of the play contradict everything about this kind of story. The petulant Private Bamforth quickly questions the fidelity of Evans's own girl, taunting him with the suggestion that by now she has probably found a variety of substitutes for him. Bamforth also rejects the heroic ideal of the magazine story by describing his plans for a fast exit in the event of a Japanese invasion. Often, Bamforth's remarks have a disturbing edge of reality to them that deflates the *Ladies Companion and Home* image of war, and this is one reason that he is often at odds with his comrades, who still cling to that image. At the play's conclusion, that image is finally destroyed. Far from effecting any miraculous escape, the men are surrounded by the Japanese and killed, except for Corporal Johnstone, who is wounded and surrenders.

The romantic view of the war is attacked in the second act of the play by Sergeant Mitchem, in his speech on women. The context of that speech is important. The unit has captured a Japanese soldier, separated from his patrol, who has wandered into the hut, and in the initial struggle several of the men find that they are unable to kill the soldier when called on to do so, largely because they realize for the first time that war involves killing men very much like themselves. "He's human at least," Private Macleish later explains to Mitchem after the captured soldier has shown them a picture of his family. For Mitchem, however, the point is obvious: "What do you want for your money? Dracula?" He is annoyed by the naïve assumptions about war that the men have brought with them to battle, and he lays the blame on "bints," on women, who give a man a heroic image of himself in uniform as he heads gallantly off to war. "Few weeks after that," Mitchem concludes, "he's on his back with his feet in the air and a hole as big as your fist in his belly. And he's nothing." This remark might just as easily have come from Bamforth's mouth, for he shares with Mitchem an unflinching sense of the truth that lies covered by the men's self-deceiving fictions.

The Long and the Short and the Tall examines the nature of war, the ways in which it changes the moral relations between men, the almost unbearable demands that it makes on the human conscience. Hall demonstrated, in this play, his skill with dialogue and pace; he also demonstrated a subtlety in his handling of theme that often goes overlooked. At its heart, the play is a study of the fundamental human tendency to believe and act according to the stories we tell ourselves about life and the problems that arise when these stories are contradicted by the sometimes harsh facts of the world.

BILLY LIAR

In Billy Fisher, the main character of *Billy Liar*, this storytelling tendency is taken to an extreme. Billy is a conscious fabricator who deceives his family, his friends, his employers, and perhaps most of all himself, for reasons so obscure that one is tempted to agree with his friend Arthur in saying that Billy's condition is pathological.

Billy Liar is set in the industrial North of England, and the play's action describes the affairs of the Fishers, a lower-middle-class household whose father, Geoffrey Fisher, has recently lifted his family above his own working-class background through his success as a garage owner. The father is plainly expecting something of the same initiative from Billy, his nineteen-year-old son, but as one meets him in the opening moments of the play, he seems an unlikely successor to his father. He has risen late from bed and comes downstairs in his pajamas and an old raincoat. Billy is also pressured by his mother, Alice, and by her mother, Florence Boothroyd, who is living in the Fisher household and who habitually directs her remarks to the sideboard. The house is decorated in poor taste, and this contributes to the tense and oppressive atmosphere in which Billy is almost constantly derided by his father for being lazy and also for mismanaging his affairs. In some sense, it is understandable that Billy retreats into the worlds created by his imagination.

Billy is in a bad position from the very start of the play. His job with Shadrack and Duxbury, Funeral Furnishers, is in jeopardy because he has been absent on days when he was supposed to have been at work

(including the day on which the play takes place). He has also apparently been taking money from the firm and has failed to mail the company's Christmas calendars as requested. The calendars are crammed into a cupboard that Billy uses for his "private" things, but which he opens for Arthur when Arthur asks him about the calendars. In the cupboard, also, is a letter from Alice Fisher to the host of a radio show called "Housewives' Choice," asking him to play an old favorite for her. She concludes the letter with a postscript saying that her son also writes songs but that he probably will amount to little in that line because he lacks the training. She ends with a remark about the family being just "ordinary folk," and on reading this Billy abruptly tosses the letter back into the cupboard, denying the limitations his mother seems to be putting on his abilities. One senses in this scene that Billy's stories and fantasies are part of an effort to escape from the mediocrity of his life, an attempt to be something more than ordinary. One soon discovers, however, that he lacks the courage to make any significant break with his environment and that his only escape is to change his world by inventing it anew in his own mind. When Billy threatens to make some practical effort to change his life by quitting his job, Arthur recognizes the characteristic bravado that masks a deeper fear of change and he scoffs at Billy's threat by saying that he has heard it before.

At first, Billy's fictions strike one as wonderfully absurd, as flashes of life in a generally dull existence. He has apparently told his parents and others that his friend Arthur's mother is pregnant—a lie—and this story has gotten back to her. When Arthur's mother threatens to come and see Mr. Fisher about it, Billy complains to Arthur that she cannot do that, because Billy has since told his parents that she has had a miscarriage to prevent his own mother from delivering a present for the baby. This is good fun, but it suggests other more serious problems that will confront Billy later. Often his stories have significant effects on people around him, and his insensitivity to the problems he may be causing for others reveals a certain self-centeredness.

Billy also seems unaware of the problems he may be causing for himself when the real world breaks through his artifice. His stories have a way of turning on him, as, for example, in his relationships with women. He is expecting a visit in the afternoon from Barbara, a girl to whom he is supposedly engaged and whom he plans to try to seduce by dropping some "passion pills" in her drink. He also needs to convince her to return her engagement ring to him for a time because he needs it to give to another girl—Rita—to whom he is also engaged. The plan backfires when the passion pills prove worthless and Barbara refuses to give up the ring. When Rita suddenly appears at the Fishers' door demanding her engagement ring, there is an angry and embarrassing exchange among the saucy Rita, Barbara, and the astonished Mrs. Fisher. In this scene, Billy has lost control over events that his lies have set in motion. He is clearly to blame for the situation, and any comic element in it is overshadowed by his apparent indifference to the feelings of others and his inability to foresee the consequences of his actions.

Billy nevertheless wins a measure of sympathy in the play's conclusion, where we see him as a frustrated dreamer whose imagination is marvelously agile but who is unable to get beyond that agility to the more profound courage required by genuine growth and maturity. In the third act, he meets an old girlfriend, Liz, a much more levelheaded and insightful girl than the others, and with her Billy at least approaches self-recognition. By this time, his deceptions have landed him in a complicated mess that even involves a physical threat from Rita's brother, and Billy for the first time seems to sense that he has only himself to blame. His fantasies become visions of self-extinction, and he imagines going to London with Liz to lose himself, to become "invisible." Liz plainly shares his feelings, and they arrange to meet at the train station at midnight to run off to London. The vision, however, succumbs to reality, and the play closes with Billy's silent return to the house after his parents are in bed. Just why he cannot bring himself to go is left to the audience's judgment. Billy may realize that a life of invisibility is as much a lie as is the life that he is living now, or it may be that he is lured back by the prospect of manipulating the world in the hope that someday it may match his own

desires. In any case, the fertility of his imagination is inextricably tied to his frustrations and his lack of growth, and the play's ending leaves little hope for any immediate change in his life. The last line of the play, appropriately, is Rita's, shouting from outside the Fisher house that she will be back in the morning for her ring, her angry voice an emblem of the world outside Billy's imagination, demanding satisfaction.

LAST DAY IN DREAMLAND

Last Day in Dreamland is a shorter and less ambitious play than *Billy Liar*, but it illustrates how deftly Hall can establish atmosphere and mood and how, even in a short play, his attention to language can give solidity to a half dozen different characters. The play is related to *Billy Liar* in dealing with characters who seem trapped in an unsatisfying way of life, powerless to take the actions that might create some real change.

Like *Billy Liar*, too, *Last Day in Dreamland* is set in the North, but in a seaside town. It centers on the owner and operators of an amusement arcade during what turns out to be the last day of the season, though none of them knows this at the start. Still, they know that the end of the season is very near and that they will soon be out of work again until the next season comes around, and it is this atmosphere of melancholy anticipation that hangs over the action throughout, ironically heightened by the backdrop of festivity.

The play begins with a strong sense of pattern and repetition, a strong sense that each of these characters has been at his job for countless years, for they move about with a clear understanding of both their own responsibilities on the job and their relationships to the other workers. In his production notes to the play, Hall emphasizes its "group construction" and the importance of each actor's studying the parts of the others, because the mood of the action depends on a complete familiarity among the characters and on their displaying the sense that they have done all of this hundreds of times before. Tich Curtis's question about whether today is their last day is met with affectionate scorn by the manager and mechanic, Coppin, who has heard the same question for fourteen years from Curtis when the season comes to an end. Though he is young, George Fentrill is already noted by the others for claiming that each year at the arcade is his last, and each year Sailor Beeson seems to come closer to losing his job because of his tardiness. The repetition, the sameness, helps to give these figures identity, yet it is an identity that each of them might willingly forsake for a different life.

Coppin's history is representative of that of the others. One of the younger members of the crew, Harry Lomax, announces that he plans to leave and try his hand at lorry driving after this season, and Coppin responds by recalling his own youthful dreams. He had, he says, planned to open his own shop, repairing wirelesses, but like the others, Coppin's dream simply slipped away. "So what happened?" Lomax asks, and Coppin's response gives one some insight into his sympathies with the men who work under him:

Nothing. That's all—nothing. For years I talked about having that shop—the summers I've spent in here dreaming about that joint don't bear thinking about. So one day, before you know where you are, you're fifty-two and all you've got is a screwdriver, a fistful of loose change and six months' work a year.

In some ways, the speech recalls Sergeant Mitchem's in *The Long and the Short and the Tall*, because it breaks through the haze of dreams and fantasies to a level of reality that few of the characters are willing to face. In the end, Coppin's description of his own life proves to be true for the others; both Lomax and Fentrill hedge their plans to get away at the end of the season, and the audience is left with a strong sense—as in *Billy Liar*—that despite the dreams of the characters, a new season at the arcade will find all of them there, lacking the will to escape.

THE SPONGE ROOM

In other plays, Hall has allowed his form to echo these themes, so that while their characters avoid reality by arranging their own worlds of fantasy, the works become less realistic. This is true of plays such as *The Sponge Room* and *Who's Who*, which, as Hall and Waterhouse observe in their production notes, depend on a "mood of suspended disbelief in which the audience will be ready to go along with the incongruities of the plot while at the same time appreciating the basic truths about loneliness, fear and fantasy." *The Sponge Room* in particular puts the audience in a situation somewhat analogous to that of the characters: The young "lovers" are also suspending their disbelief by pretending to plan an intimate rendezvous, though neither really wants to carry it out. "The play is about three dreamers," say the authors, "who will never have the courage to carry out their dreams—for the dreams themselves are a substitute for courage."

WHO'S WHO

The later farce, *Who's Who*, is another example of this nonrealistic treatment. The play's two acts are divided by a discussion between the two actors playing Bernard White and Timothy Black in which they agree to reenact the events of the first act with some important changes in the scenario. In some ways, the play represents a comic flip side to *Billy Liar* in that Black, like Billy, runs his life on deception, but without the kind of consequences suffered by Billy. It is a highly stylized, artificial play, but, as in *The Sponge Room*, the technique seems curiously appropriate here, applied as it is to a work about that fundamental human drive to orchestrate the events of one's life and re-create a world according to one's desires.

The Sponge Room and *Who's Who* demonstrate the diversity of Hall's talents, and his longevity and consistency as a writer must in some degree be attributed to his skill for finding new and varied methods of handling his subjects. Though they depart from the earlier, more conventional techniques, they share with Hall's other plays the insight and feeling that make his art worth experiencing. It is an art full of sympathy for its characters, perhaps because Hall sees in the human urge to dream, to fantasize, to imagine a world and to believe in it, an impulse very much like the dramatist's.

OTHER MAJOR WORKS

LONG FICTION: *The Fuzz*, 1977 (novelization of television series).

SCREENPLAYS: *The Long and the Short and the Tall*, 1961 (with Wolf Mankowitz); *Whistle Down the Wind*, 1961 (with Keith Waterhouse); *The Valiant*, 1962 (with Waterhouse); *A Kind of Loving*, 1963 (with Waterhouse); *Billy Liar*, 1963 (with Waterhouse); *West Eleven*, pr. 1963 (with Waterhouse);

Man in the Middle, pr. 1963 (with Waterhouse); *Pretty Polly (A Matter of Innocence)*, 1967 (with Waterhouse); *Lock Up Your Daughters*, 1969 (with Waterhouse).

TELEPLAYS: *Air Mail from Cyprus*, 1958; *Return to the Sea*, 1960; *On the Night of the Murder*, 1962; *Happy Moorings*, 1963 (with Keith Waterhouse); *How Many Angels*, 1964 (with Waterhouse); *That Was the Week That Was*, 1964-1965; *The Ticket*, 1969; *The Railwayman's New Clothes*, 1971; *The Villa Maroc*, 1972; *They Don't All Open Men's Boutiques*, 1972; *Song at Twilight*, 1973; *Friendly Encounter*, 1974; *The Piano-Smashers of the Golden Sun*, 1974; *Illegal Approach*, 1974; *Midgley*, 1975; *Match-Fit*, 1976 (from Brian Glanville's story); *A Flash of Inspiration*, 1976; *Danedyke Mystery*, 1979 (from a work by Stephen Chance); *National Pelmet*, 1980; *Christmas Spirits*, 1981; *Stan's Last Game*, 1983; *Return of the Antelope*, 1986 (with Waterhouse).

NONFICTION: *The A to Z of Soccer*, 1970 (with Michael Parkinson); *The A to Z of Television*, 1971 (with Bob Monkhouse).

CHILDREN'S LITERATURE: *The Play of the Royal Astrologers*, 1958 (play); *The Gentle Knight*, 1964 (radio play); *Kidnapped at Christmas*, 1975 (play); *Christmas Crackers*, 1976 (play); *A Right Christmas Caper*, 1977 (play); *Worzel Gummidge*, 1980 (play,

with Keith Waterhouse); *The Inflatable Shop*, 1984 (novel); *Dragon Days*, 1984 (novel); *The Return of the Antelope*, 1985; *The Antelope Company Ashore*, 1986; *Spooky Rhymes*, 1987; *The Antelope Company at Large*, 1987; *Dr. Jekyll and Mr. Hollins*, 1988; *Henry Hollins and the Dinosaur*, 1988; *The Vampire's Holiday*, 1991; *The Vampire's Revenge*, 1993; *The Vampire's Christmas*, 1994; *The Vampire Hunt*, 1998; *Vampire Island*, 1999.

BIBLIOGRAPHY

Martin, Mick. "Timeless Appeal." Review of *Billy Liar*, by Willis Hall. *The Times Educational Supplement*, September 18, 1992, p. SS15. This review examines the National Theatre's Mobile production of Hall's *Billy Liar* and touches on the play's relevance for the contemporary world.

Matlaw, Myron. *Modern World Drama*. New York: E. P. Dutton, 1972. Although Hall has written a large number of plays, screenplays, teleplays, and children's books, little has been published about him and his work. This short entry mentions some of his plays and the influence of John Osborne on his work, and briefly traces his switch to light comedy.

Steven Reese,
updated by Thomas J. Taylor

PETER HANDKE

Born: Griffen, Austria; December 6, 1942

PRINCIPAL DRAMA

Publikumsbeschimpfung und andere Sprechstücke, pr., pb. 1966 (*Offending the Audience*, 1969)
Selbstbezichtigung, pr., pb. 1966 (*Self-Accusation*, 1969)
Weissagung, pr., pb. 1966 (*Prophecy*, 1976)
Hilferufe, pr. 1967 (*Calling for Help*, 1970)
Kaspar, pr., pb. 1968 (English translation, 1969)
Kaspar and Other Plays, pb. 1969

Das Mündel will Vormund sein, pr., pb. 1969 (*My Foot My Tutor*, 1970)
Quodlibet, pr. 1970 (English translation, 1976)
Der Ritt über den Bodensee, pr., pb. 1971 (*The Ride Across Lake Constance*, 1972)
Die Unvernünftigen sterben aus, pb. 1973 (*They Are Dying Out*, 1975)
The Ride Across Lake Constance and Other Plays, pb. 1976
Über die Dörfer, pr., pb. 1982 (*Among the Villages*, 1984)

*Das Spiel vom Fragen: Oder, Die reise zum
sonoren Land*, pr., pb. 1989 (*Voyage to the
Sonorous Land: Or, The Art of Asking*, 1996)

Die Stunde da wir nichts voneinander wussten, pr.,
pb. 1992 (*The Hour We Knew Nothing of Each
Other*, 1996)

*Zurüstungen zur Unsterblichkeit: Ein
Königsdrama*, pr., pb. 1997

*Die Fahrt im Einbaum: Oder, Das Stück zum Film
vom Krieg*, pr., pb. 1999

OTHER LITERARY FORMS

Although Peter Handke first achieved literary celebrity on the basis of his avant-garde plays, he is best known as a writer of fiction, having largely abandoned the theater early in his career. Most of Handke's novels are quite short (several are of novella length), and their language is highly concentrated. As critic June Schlueter notes, while Handke's awareness of the linguistic medium has remained constant, there has been a development in his fiction from an early emphasis on the limits of language and the failure of communication to an emphasis on the "redemptive power of poetic language."

In addition to his novels, Handke has published several books, which are often classified as nonfiction but which he himself regards as of a piece with his fiction. Among these are the much-praised novel *Wunschloses Unglück* (1972; *A Sorrow Beyond Dreams*, 1975), written in response to his mother's suicide, and *Das Gewicht der Welt* (1977; *The Weight of the World*, 1984). Handke has published a small number of short stories, essays, and several slim collections of poetry; he has also written radio plays and has written or co-written screenplays and otherwise collaborated on the making of several films. Since the 1980's, Handke has translated many works of French, Slovenian, English, and Greek writers, among them Marguerite Duras, Bruno Bayen, Aeschylus, and William Shakespeare's *The Winter's Tale* (pr. c. 1610-1611).

ACHIEVEMENTS

Despite his rather sparse output, Peter Handke is widely regarded as an important and influential contemporary dramatist. He became one of the first of the generation of German speakers born during World War II to achieve prominence. Unlike many other postwar German and Austrian writers, he does not hark back to the Nazi era, nor does he concern himself with "the past" in any usual way. At the same time, his plays do not follow the example of Bertolt Brecht, so pervasive in the postwar German theater: Handke's plays are not theatrical in the ways Brecht's are, nor do they have Brecht's scope. Rather, they seek to define language as act and language as power. Three of Handke's plays, *Offending the Audience*, *Kaspar*, and *The Ride Across Lake Constance*, have entered the international repertory; these works made him the most prominent German-language playwright of the 1970's. While Handke was awarded several notable honors and awards—for example, the Gerhart Hauptmann Prize in 1967 and the Schiller Prize in 1972—he refused or returned other prizes, including the Büchner Prize (won in 1973, returned in 1999) and the Kafka Prize (refused in 1979). He accepted the Salzburg Literature Prize in 1986.

Peter Handke (Jerry Bauer)

BIOGRAPHY

Peter Handke was born in Griffen, Austria, on December 6, 1942. With the exception of a four-year period from 1944 to 1948, when he lived in Berlin, Handke lived in the country in Southern Austria. In 1961, he entered the University of Graz to study law. The critic Nicholas Hern argues that this legal training influenced Handke's style: "Most of his plays . . . consist of a series of affirmative propositions each contained within one sentence which is usually a simple main clause on a main clause on a main clause plus one subordinate clause." While he was at the university, Handke published his work in *Manuskripts*, the university's literary review. From 1963 onward, he devoted himself to writing, and his first novel, *Die Hornissen* (1966; the hornets), appeared the year after he left the university.

This novel earned for Handke the chance to read at the prestigious Gruppe 47 conference in April of 1966, held that year at Princeton University. There he read from his second novel, *Der Hausierer* (1967; the peddler), and on the last day of the meeting he delivered a blistering attack on what he saw as the artistic failures of the group's older members. Handke argued that much German postwar writing was too realistic and descriptive and "failed to realize literature is made with language, not with the things that one describes with language."

This outburst and the success of his first play, *Offending the Audience*, at the Frankfurt "Experimenta" theater week in June of that year, brought Handke considerable media attention; since he affected a Beatles-like hairstyle and mirrored sunglasses, he was much photographed, interviewed, and read. In 1966, he married actress Libgart Schwarz and moved to Germany from Austria. Over the next seven years, he lived in Düsseldorf, Berlin, Paris, and Kronberg (outside Frankfurt). His daughter, Amina, was born in Berlin in 1969. That same year, he joined with ten other writers to form a cooperative publishing house, Verlag der Autors. In 1979, he returned with his daughter to Salzburg in his native Austria.

In the late 1990's, Handke reestablished himself as one of the enfants terribles of German literature by vociferously taking the side of the Serbs in the Bosnian and Kosovo conflicts, thus finding himself under attack from fellow writers, journalists, and politicians alike. Most of Handke's literary output in the late 1990's is a reflection of and a commentary on the events in the former Yugoslavia. As part of his condemnation of the North Atlantic Treaty Organization (NATO) attacks on Serbia, Handke returned the Georg Büchner Prize, including a substantial stipend, that the German government had awarded him in 1973, and formally renounced his membership in the Roman Catholic Church, which he accused of supporting what he called the genocide of the Serbian people. At the same time, he proudly accepted his elevation to the rank of Knight of Serbia.

ANALYSIS

Peter Handke calls his first three plays—*Offending the Audience*, *Self-Accusation*, and *Prophecy*—Sprechstücke (literally, speaking pieces). Both "speech" and "piece" are important, for Handke does away with such mundane dramatic considerations as plot and character, replacing them with activities and speakers. Thus, all three plays are made up of speech—pronounced word and rhetorical gesture—which is not involved in imitating an action. The plays examine the power and banality of public and private speech.

OFFENDING THE AUDIENCE

Offending the Audience, the first of these plays to be produced, appeared in 1966 at Frankfurt's Theater am Turm, a theater known for its dedication to the avant-garde. The play was accepted there only after it had been rejected by some sixty other more conservative theaters, and the avant-garde setting may have lessened the play's impact, for it depends on the assumptions and conventions of mainstream theater—a theater in which William Shakespeare, Friedrich Schiller, and more recently Brecht have been the mainstays of the repertory. The play also depends on the predictable reactions of the patrons of such a theater—middlebrow, middle-class, and conservatively dressed.

The audience enters a theater that appears set up for business as usual, complete with assiduous ushers and elegant programs. The usual routine occurs:

Doors close and lights dim. When the curtain opens, four speakers are revealed (usually, but not necessarily, two men and two women) on a bare stage. The four ignore the audience and insult one another. Their speeches overlap and blend until at last a formal pattern is established, which culminates in the four saying one word in unison. (Handke has left what they actually say here unscripted.) The four now face the audience and, after a pause, begin to address it directly. Handke has simply broken his text into paragraphs, presumably each one spoken by a different speaker. He has not assigned gestures or speeches, and the script can in no manner be construed as a dialogue among the speakers. Thus, the director has a free hand with the assignment of speeches and movements.

The direct address to the audience concerns four basic themes: the audience's expectations of the theater, the nature of the audience itself, the nature of theatrical illusion and its absence in the current piece, and, by extension, the roles the spectators play in society. These topics are not presented in a logical way but, rather, in a repetitive intertwining of single, declarative sentences. A short sample from Michael Roloff's translation conveys the flavor:

> The possibilities of theatre are not exploited here. The realm of possibilities is not exhausted. The theatre is not unbound. The theatre is bound. Fate is meant ironically here. We are not theatrical.

After some twenty minutes of this, the audience is told, "Before you leave you will be offended." They are then told why they are going to be offended. The piece ends with a decrescendo of silly and vulgar insults. At the end of the play, the curtain closes, only to open again as the four speakers take bows to recorded applause.

So described, one has difficulty seeing why this was a popular play. Handke demonstrates the power of convention by removing it from the context in which it usually exists. He goes further by discussing those same conventions while violating them. The play affirms the power of theater by pointing out that the conventions are mistaken for the reality. When theater imitates, it does so through a structure of conventional movement and language. Handke forces the audience to see how often it confuses the convention with the reality it purports to imitate.

SELF-ACCUSATION

Similar themes animate the two other *Sprechstücke*. *Self-Accusation* has two speakers—one male, one female—who in no sense carry on a dialogue. Rather, speaking alternately and together, they portray an Everyman who spells out the process of growing up civilized. Every sentence in the dialogue has "I" as its subject. Again a short quote will convey more than a description.

> I learned. I learned the words. I learned the verbs. I learned the difference between singular and plural. . . . I learned the adjectives. I learned the difference between mine and yours. I acquired vocabulary.

In this play, the processes of verbal, moral, and physical growth are intertwined by Handke's curiously declarative style. This style seems to imply that verbal growth is the controlling factor in shaping human life: Language civilizes at great cost and it creates our world.

KASPAR

This notion that language creates the individual's world also motivates Handke's first full-length play, *Kaspar*. This play has a historical antecedent. In Nuremberg in 1828, a boy, Kaspar Hauser, was discovered, who—as a result of abuse and sensory deprivation—could, at age sixteen, say only one sentence: "I want to become a horseman such as my father once was." Handke, however, does not write historical drama. He says in the play's introduction that his play "does not show how IT REALLY IS OR REALLY WAS with Kaspar Hauser. It shows how someone can be made to speak through speaking. The play could also be called *speech torture*."

The play, like the *Sprechstücke*, presents a speaker on what is obviously still a stage, although a much more cultured stage than in the earlier plays. This speaker, Kaspar, is costumed and heavily made up as a Chaplinesque clown. This clown interacts with the voices of four *Einsager*, a neologism that literally means "in-sayers" but implies indoctrinator. (Michael Roloff translates it as prompter.) Later, Kaspar is joined by six other Kaspars all identically made-up and costumed.

Handke lists sixteen stages through which Kaspar must pass, beginning with the question "Can Kaspar, the owner of one sentence, begin and begin to do something with his sentence?" and ending with "What is now Kaspar, Kaspar?" Handke has stressed his concern with identity and individuality by changing Kaspar's only sentence to "I want to be a person like someone else was once."

Basically three main movements constitute the play. Kaspar and the audience learn that his one sentence is inadequate. The *Einsager* teach Kaspar new sentences until he has mastered language. It is at this point that the identical Kaspars appear. Finally Kaspar discovers that by accepting the *Einsager*'s language he has lost his uniqueness and identity. As Kaspar says, "I was trapped from my first sentence."

Voices heard on the loudspeaker suggest all the voices of coercion one hears in growing up—parents' warnings, teachers' threats, government propaganda. By calling the speakers "in-sayers," Handke demonstrates how quickly humans internalize such voices. The audience is never fully certain where these prompters exist. Are they outside or inside Kaspar's head? Handke might argue that humankind cannot answer that question about its own consciousness and that this inability to answer is the point. Each human being is made up of others' speech that has been internalized.

As the play progresses, the action onstage and the verbal images in Kaspar's speech become increasingly more violent; indeed, there is the sense of a barely hidden threat throughout the play. By the end, Kaspar is left writhing on the ground to a shrill electronic noise, shouting over and over Othello's phrase, "Goats and monkeys."

Writer June Schlueter suggests that *Othello*, like *Kaspar*, is concerned with the "idiocy of language": Othello is led astray by Iago's lines, just as Kaspar is by the *Einsager*'s sentences. A significant difference between the two works, however, is the difference between Renaissance and modern concepts of language. Iago manipulates language to his own ends and violates the moral order by destroying the relation between the world of objects and events and the world of language. Kaspar's *Einsager* use a language that has only a tenuous and conventional relationship to the world of ideas and events. The play seems to argue that this is the only relationship language can have to reality.

INFLUENCE OF WITTGENSTEIN

In discussing Handke's ideas of language, nearly every critic mentions his countryman, the philosopher Ludwig Wittgenstein (1889-1951), and the group of linguists and philosophers known as the Vienna Circle, who flourished in the 1920's. Although Handke admits to having read Wittgenstein and some of the others, he has not explained the effect of this philosophy on his work, nor have critics satisfactorily suggested what this relationship might be.

Wittgenstein's first major work, "Logischphilosophische Abhandlung," (1921; best known by the bilingual German and English edition title of *Tractatus Logico-Philosophicus*, 1922, 1961), reveals similarities with Handke's understanding and use of language. The first is a stylistic similarity. Both writers use simple declarative sentences, frequently not connected by the usual linguistic connectors to what precedes or follows. In part, the style is a working out of Wittgenstein's dictum: "What can be said can be said clearly, and what cannot be said must be passed over in silence."

The concern with "what can be said" and "what cannot" seems common to both writers. Wittgenstein seeks to put a limit to philosophy, which he defines as "not a body of doctrine, but an activity." One "does philosophy," and its value lies in its doing. Similarly, Handke presents a definition of speech as an activity in which the nature, direction, and energy of the act are all more important than the content conveyed by the speech. That about which "we must remain silent" Wittgenstein calls "the mystical," by which he means not only the subjective religious feelings ordinarily associated with that term but also such normal areas of philosophic inquiry as ethics and aesthetics. Indeed he seems to put ontology (the question of existence) in the realm of the mystical: "It is not *how* things are in the world that is mystical, but *that* it exists."

The notion that humankind infers the existence of the world from language extends throughout Handke's work and even approaches the notion that humans create the world by speaking about it and by hearing elders speak about it. Drama has traditionally dealt with those subjective feelings and expressions about which Wittgenstein says humankind "must pass over in silence." In fact, Handke does pass over them in silence. The expressions of subjective feelings (and they are very rare) are offered as objective statements and have no value beyond themselves.

Thus, one becomes aware of a hole, an absence, in the middle of Handke's work. His dramas seem to be concerned with aesthetics, ethics, and identity—yet there is no language in them that discusses these issues; they are approached through silence. One could argue that Handke parodies a Wittgensteinian universe to show its inadequacies. A more consistent understanding of the plays, however, might be approached through another of Wittgenstein's ideas, the pictorial theory of language, which argues that language can picture reality and that propositions "show what they say." Further, he insists, "What can be shown, *cannot* be said."

This last proposition is extremely important in considering Handke's purpose. Instead of parodying Wittgenstein's universe, he displays its tragicomic nature. Because language is always inadequate, humankind is led to wildly comic errors and actions; because human beings can never speak about that which is most important, they are left alone and twitching at the end of the action.

During his later years, Wittgenstein rethought the *Tractatus Logico-Philosophicus* and challenged his own picture theory. He admitted that language arises out of specific social occasions, and, therefore, words need not always name objects. In his posthumously published *Philosophical Investigations* (1953), Wittgenstein developed the notion of language games and stressed that speech is an activity.

THE RIDE ACROSS LAKE CONSTANCE

Handke clearly likes to play language games, but for him, unlike Wittgenstein, they are never innocent. Handke's games are always zero-sum; there is a winner and loser, a master and servant, a speaker and lis-

tener. In this, Handke seems to participate in a major theme of German drama, the relation of the individual will to authority. His use of this theme creates a tragic paradox: Language, which enables human beings to conceive of freedom, is the principal force that prevents them from achieving it.

Handke's two full-length plays *The Ride Across Lake Constance* and *They Are Dying Out* explore this paradox and the power relations that it creates. Unlike Handke's earlier plays, *The Ride Across Lake Constance* has a real set—a kind of nineteenth century drawing room with a long double staircase leading into it. There are some suggestions that this may be a madhouse, but Handke, as usual, never specifies. What is apparent is that it is a set. Handke insists on the theatricality of the piece. He arbitrarily assigns the names of famous German actors to his characters, but he suggests that "the characters should bear the names of the actors playing the role . . . the actors are and play themselves at one and the same time." In an interview, Handke said that the play examines "poses" as they are used onstage and in life.

The title derives from a folktale in which the hero, lost in fog, crosses Lake Constance on very thin ice. When learning of his narrow escape, he dies of fright. "To ride on Lake Constance" is the German equivalent for the expression "skating on thin ice." Author Nicholas Hern suggests that the "thin ice" in the play is society itself and that the play explores what society means by the concepts of sense and madness.

This sense of the social definition of madness relates this play to the themes of power and domination in all Handke's work. The familiar images and apparatus of dominance fill the stage. One woman is sold a riding crop and later beaten, another seeks to dominate a man through temptation. Two men are shown in a clear master-servant relationship. Yet the audience feels neither threatened nor enraged by these relationships and acts because they appear as theatrical poses.

A typical first reaction to *The Ride Across Lake Constance* is befuddlement; New York theater critic Clive Barnes admitted that within the first two minutes of the play, he realized that he did not know what was going on. One suspects that Handke wants the audience to see that reality is a mental construction socially imposed and accepted and that madness reconstitutes the world in a socially unacceptable but no less valid way. Again language, sentences, and the place of objects deny the viewer the freedom to re-create reality except through madness.

THEY ARE DYING OUT

Handke's next play, *They Are Dying Out*, suggests that humankind's normal construction of the world is equally mad. Its protagonist, Herr Quitt, is a protean, laissez-faire capitalist of the sort who prompted Germany's economic recovery. Throughout the play, he sees into and seems to criticize capitalist society. As Schlueter points out, however, no critic has convincingly given a definition of Handke's politics; she adds that the play "stops considerably short of becoming a Marxist platform." The German title of the play means, literally, the irrational are dying out, and the play seems to be about irrationality. Quitt cannot reconcile his inner sensibilities with his social actions. When he denounces capitalism, another capitalist says, "It was just a game, wasn't it? Because in reality you are. . . ." Quitt cuts him off with, "Yes, but only in reality." This notion that one can choose the irrational world and that it is truer than the rational world motivates one strain of German Romantic thought, especially that of the poet Novalis.

Again, it is unclear where Handke stands. His hero commits suicide at the end of the play by beating his head against a rock to the sound of recorded belching. Is this the defeat of the poet by the modern world? Is it the ultimate image of the failure of civilization? Whatever it is, Handke believes that one cannot talk rationally about it. Handke can only offer the image. Thus Quitt, who is shown as a dominant force throughout the play, destroys himself in part because of society's dominion over him, because of the understanding that society drives human beings away from their true selves.

Because Handke is in this play more concerned with society than language, it is the first of his plays to have conventional characters and something approaching a plot. Narrative seems here to be the appropriate mode. This might suggest that Handke's ca-

reer as a dramatist began with an examination of language's inability to communicate, passed through an examination of how language forces people to construct reality, and concludes with the acknowledgment that language is only one of the forces that determine humankind. His work centers on force, attack, control, and humans' inability to protect themselves.

1990'S PLAYS

Handke's career as a dramatist began with an examination of language's inability to communicate and passed on to an examination of how language forces humans to construct reality. In the plays he wrote in the late 1990's responding to the Balkan conflict, *Zurüstungen zur Unsterblichkeit* (preparations for immortality) and *Die Fahrt im Einbaum* (the journey in the dug-out canoe, or the play about the film about the war), he arrives again at a position first articulated in *Kaspar*: Language is a tool of manipulation and indoctrination. The *Einsager*, the linguistic social engineers of his most famous play, turn into the chorus of the three journalists in *Die Fahrt im Einbaum*.

OTHER MAJOR WORKS

LONG FICTION: *Die Hornissen*, 1966; *Der Hausierer*, 1967; *Die Angst des Tormanns beim Elfmeter*, 1970 (*The Goalie's Anxiety at the Penalty Kick*, 1972); *Der kurze Brief zum langen Abschied*, 1972 (*Short Letter, Long Farewell*, 1974); *Wunschloses Unglück*, 1972 (*A Sorrow Beyond Dreams*, 1975); *Die Stunde der wahren Empfindung*, 1975 (*A Moment of True Feeling*, 1977); *Die linkshändige Frau*, 1976 (*The Left-Handed Woman*, 1978); *Langsame Heimkehr*, 1979 (*The Long Way Around*, 1985); *Die Lehre der Sainte-Victoire*, 1980 (*The Lesson of Mont Sainte-Victoire*, 1985); *Kindergeschichte*, 1981 (*Child Story*, 1985); *Der Chinese des Schmerzes*, 1983 (*Across*, 1986); *Slow Homecoming*, 1985 (includes *The Long Way Around*, *The Lesson of Mont Sainte-Victoire*, and *Child Story*); *Die Wiederholung*, 1986 (*Repetition*, 1988); *Die Abwesenheit: Ein Märchen*, 1987 (*Absence*, 1990); *Nachmittag eines Schriftstellers*, 1987 (*The Afternoon of a Writer*, 1989); *Mein Jahr in der Niemandsbucht: Ein Märchen aus den neuen Zeiten*, 1994 (*My Year in the No-Man's-Bay*, 1998); *In einer dunklen Nacht ging ich aus meinem stillen Haus*, 1997 (*On a Dark Night I Left My Silent House*, 2000); *Der Bildverlust: Oder, Durch die Sierra de Gredos*, 2002.

SHORT FICTION: *Begrüssung des Aufsichtsrats*, 1967.

POETRY: *Die Innenwelt der Aussenwelt der Innenwelt*, 1969 (*The Innerworld of the Outerworld of the Innerworld*, 1974); *Gedicht an die Dauer*, 1986.

SCREENPLAYS: *Chronik der laufenden Ereignisse*, 1971; *Der Himmel über Berlin*, 1987 (*Wings of Desire*, with Wim Wenders, 1987).

TELEPLAY: *Falsche Bewegung*, 1975.

NONFICTION: *Ich bin ein Bewohner des Elfenbeinturms*, 1972; *Als das Wünschen noch geholfen hat*, 1974; *Das Gewicht der Welt*, 1977 (journal; *The Weight of the World*, 1984); *Das Ende des Flanierens*, 1980; *Die Geschichte des Bleistifts*, 1982 (journal); *Phantasien der Wiederholung*, 1983 (journal); *Aber ich lebe nur von den Zwischenräumen*, 1987; *Versuch über die Müdigkeit*, 1989; *Versuch über die Jukebox*, 1990; *Versuch über den geglückten Tag*, 1991; *The Jukebox and Other Essays on Storytelling*, 1994 (translation of *Versuch über die Müdigkeit*, *Versuch über die Jukebox*, and *Versuch über den geglückten Tag*); *Eine winterliche Reise zu den Flüssen Donau, Save, Morawa and Drina: Oder, Gerechtigkeit für Serbien*, 1996 (*A Journey to the Rivers: Justice for Serbia*, 1997); *Am Felsfenster morgens: Und andere Ortszeiten 1982-1987*, 1998 (journal).

TRANSLATIONS: *Prometheus, gefesselt*, 1986 (of Aeschylus); *Das Wintermärchen*, 1991 (of William Shakespeare's *The Winter's Tale*).

BIBLIOGRAPHY

DeMeritt, Linda. *New Subjectivity and Prose Forms of Alienation: Peter Handke and Botho Strauss.* New York: Peter Lang, 1987. Examines the use of social psychology in German-language twentieth century literature by providing critical interpretation of Handke's and Strauss's prose works.

Firda, Richard A. *Peter Handke.* New York: Twayne, 1993. The most accessible and comprehensive introductory survey of Handke's work up to the early 1990's. Includes a good biography and a jargon-free overview of his major dramatic and prose works. Bibliography and index.

Hern, Nicholas. *Peter Handke.* New York: Ungarm, 1971. One of the first scholarly studies of Handke, particularly useful for a study of his early *Sprechstücke* plays.

Konzett, Matthias. *The Rhetoric of National Dissent in Thomas Bernhard, Peter Handke, and Elfriede Jelinek.* Rochester, N.Y.: Camden House, 2000. Examines the ways in which three authors expose state-directed consensus and harmonization that impede the development of multicultural awareness in modern-day Europe. Explores how Handke focuses on national suppression of post-ideological voices in the history telling of marginalized individuals.

Schlueter, June. *The Plays and Novels of Peter Handke.* Pittsburgh: University of Pittsburgh Press, 1983. Concentrates on the use of language in Handke's work. Useful as an update of the Hern book.

Sidney F. Parham,
updated by Franz G. Blaha

LORRAINE HANSBERRY

Born: Chicago, Illinois; May 19, 1930
Died: New York, New York; January 12, 1965

PRINCIPAL DRAMA
A Raisin in the Sun, pr., pb. 1959
The Sign in Sidney Brustein's Window, pr. 1964, pb. 1965

To Be Young, Gifted, and Black, pr. 1969, pb. 1971
Les Blancs, pr. 1970, pb. 1972
The Drinking Gourd, pb. 1972 (Robert Nemiroff, editor)
What Use Are Flowers?, pb. 1972 (Nemiroff, editor)
Les Blancs: The Collected Last Plays of Lorraine Hansberry, pb. 1972 (includes *Les Blancs*, *The Drinking Gourd*, and *What Use Are Flowers?*)

OTHER LITERARY FORMS

As a result of her involvement in the Civil Rights movement, Lorraine Hansberry wrote the narrative for *The Movement: Documentary of a Struggle for Equality* (1964), a book of photographs, for the Student Nonviolent Coordinating Committee (SNCC). Because she died at such a young age, Hansberry left much of her work unpublished, but her husband, Robert Nemiroff, the literary executor of her estate, edited and submitted some of it for publication and, in the case of *Les Blancs*, production. In addition, he arranged excerpts from Hansberry's various writings into a seven-and-a-half-hour radio program entitled *To Be Young, Gifted, and Black*, which was broadcast on radio station WBAI in 1967. This program was later adapted for the stage, opening at the Cherry Lane Theatre in New York on January 2, 1969, and becoming the longest running production of the 1968-1969 season. Many readers know Hansberry through the anthology of her writings edited by Nemiroff, *To Be Young, Gifted, and Black: Lorraine Hansberry in Her Own Words* (1969), a book that has enjoyed very wide circulation.

ACHIEVEMENTS

Lorraine Hansberry's career was very brief, only two of her plays being produced in her lifetime, yet she recorded some very impressive theatrical achievements. She was only twenty-nine when *A Raisin in the Sun* appeared on Broadway, and its great success earned for her recognition that continues to this day. When *A Raisin in the Sun* was voted best play of the year by the New York Drama Critics Circle, she became the first black person as well as the youngest person to win the award. In 1973, a musical adapted from *A Raisin in the Sun*, entitled *Raisin* (with libretto by Nemiroff), won a Tony Award as best musical of the year (1974). She was respected and befriended by such figures as Paul Robeson and James Baldwin, and she helped in an active way to further the work of the Civil Rights movement. Though her later work has received far less recognition than her first play, *A Raisin in the Sun* continues to enjoy a broad popularity.

BIOGRAPHY

Lorraine Vivian Hansberry was born on May 19, 1930, in the South Side of Chicago, the black section of the city. Her parents, Carl and Mamie Hansberry, were well-off. Her father was a United States deputy marshal for a time and then opened a successful real estate business in Chicago. Despite her family's affluence, they were forced by local covenants to live in the poor South Side. When Hansberry was eight years old, her father decided to test the legality of those covenants by buying a home in a white section of the city. Hansberry later recalled one incident that occurred shortly after the family's move to a white neighborhood: A mob gathered outside their home, and a brick, thrown through a window, barely missed her before embedding itself in a wall.

In order to stay in the house, to which he was not given clear title, Carl Hansberry instituted a civil rights suit against such restrictive covenants. When he lost in Illinois courts, he and the National Assocation for the Advancement of Colored People (NAACP) carried an appeal to the United States Supreme Court, which, on November 12, 1940, reversed the ruling of the Illinois supreme court and declared the local covenants illegal. Thus, Lorraine had a consciousness of the need to struggle for civil rights from a very young age. Her father, despite his legal victory, grew increasingly pessimistic about the prospects for change in the racial situation, and he finally decided to leave the country and retire in Mexico City. He had a stroke during a visit to Mexico, however, and died in 1945.

Hansberry's uncle, William Leo Hansberry, was also an important influence on her. A scholar of African history who taught at Howard University, his pupils included Nnamdi Azikewe, the first president of

Nigeria, and Kwame Nkrumah of Ghana. Indeed, William Leo Hansberry was such a significant figure in African studies that in 1963, the University of Nigeria named its College of African Studies at Nsakka after him. While Lorraine was growing up, she was frequently exposed to the perspectives of young African students who were invited to family dinners, and this exposure helped to shape many of the attitudes later found in her plays.

Lorraine, the youngest of four children, was encouraged to excel and was expected to succeed. After attending Englewood High School, she enrolled in the University of Wisconsin as a journalism student. She did not fare very well at the university, however, and felt restricted by the many requirements of the school. After two years, she left Wisconsin and enrolled in the New School for Social Research in New York, where she was permitted greater leeway in choosing courses.

Once in New York, Hansberry began writing for several periodicals, including *Freedom*, Paul Robe-

Lorraine Hansberry (Library of Congress)

son's monthly magazine. She quickly became a reporter and then an associate editor of the magazine. In New York, she met Robert Nemiroff, then a student at New York University, and they were married in June of 1953. By this time, Hansberry had decided to be a writer, and although the bulk of her energies went into writing, she did hold a variety of jobs during the next few years. When Nemiroff acquired a good position with music publisher Phil Rose, she quit working and began writing full-time.

Hansberry's first completed work was *A Raisin in the Sun*, which, after an initial struggle for financial backing, opened on Broadway at the Ethel Barrymore Theatre on March 11, 1959. The play, starring Sidney Poitier, Ruby Dee, Louis Gossett, Jr., and Claudia McNeil, was an enormous success, running for 530 performances, and in May, winning the New York Drama Critics Circle Award.

Soon thereafter, Hansberry and Nemiroff moved from their apartment in Greenwich Village to a home in Croton, New York, in order for Hansberry to have more privacy for her work. At the same time, her success made her a public figure, and she used her newfound fame to champion the causes of civil rights and African independence. She made important speeches in a variety of places and once confronted then Attorney General Robert Kennedy on the issue of civil rights.

It was not until 1964 that Hansberry produced another play, *The Sign in Sidney Brustein's Window*, and by that time she was seriously ill. The play opened at the Longacre Theatre on October 15, 1964, to generally good but unenthusiastic reviews, and Nemiroff had to struggle to keep it open, a number of times placing advertisements in newspapers asking for support, accepting financial support from friends and associates, and once accepting the proceeds from a spontaneous collection taken up by the audience when it was announced that without additional funds, the play would have to close. On this uncertain financial basis, production of the play continued from week to week.

Hansberry's life continued in much the same way. While the play struggled, she was in a hospital bed dying of cancer. She once lapsed into a coma and was not expected to recover, but for a brief time she did rally, recovering all of her faculties. Her strength gave out, however, and on January 12, 1965, she died. That night, the Longacre Theatre closed its doors in mourning, and *The Sign in Sidney Brustein's Window* closed after 101 performances.

ANALYSIS

Lorraine Hansberry claimed Sean O'Casey as one of the earliest and strongest influences on her work and cited his realistic portrayal of character as the source of strength in his plays. In *To Be Young, Gifted, and Black*, she praised O'Casey for describing

the human personality in its totality. O'Casey never fools you about the Irish . . . the Irish drunkard, the Irish braggart, the Irish liar . . . and the genuine heroism which must naturally emerge when you tell the truth about people. This . . . is the height of artistic perception . . . because when you believe people so completely . . . then you also believe them in their moments of heroic assertion: you don't doubt them.

In her three most significant plays, *A Raisin in the Sun*, *The Sign in Sidney Brustein's Window*, and *Les Blancs*, one can see Hansberry's devotion to the principles that she valued in O'Casey. First, she espoused realistic drama; second, she believed that the ordinary individual has a capacity for heroism; and finally, she believed that drama should reveal to the audience its own humanity and its own capacity for heroism.

Hansberry claimed that her work was realistic rather than naturalistic, explaining that

naturalism tends to take the world as it is and say: this is what it is . . . it is "true" because we see it every day in life . . . you simply photograph the garbage can. But in realism . . . the artist . . . imposes . . . not only what *is* but what is *possible* . . . because that is part of reality too.

For Hansberry, then, realism involved more than a photographic faithfulness to the real world. She sought to deliver a universal message but realized that "in order to create the universal you must pay very great attention to the specific. Universality . . . emerges from truthful identity of what is." This concern for realism was present from the very beginning of Hans-

berry's career and persists in her work, though she did occasionally depart from it in small ways, such as in the symbolic rather than literal presence of "The Woman" in *Les Blancs*, that character symbolizing the spirit of liberty and freedom that lives inside humanity.

Essential to Hansberry's vision of reality was the belief that the average person has within him or her the capacity for heroism. Hansberry believed that each human being is not only "dramatically interesting" but also a "creature of stature," and this is one of the most compelling features of her drama. Like O'Casey, Hansberry paints a full picture of each character, complete with flaws and weaknesses, yet she does not permit these flaws to hide the characters' "stature." Perhaps she expressed this idea best in *A Raisin in the Sun*, when Lena Younger berates her daughter Beneatha for condemning her brother, Walter Lee. Lena says, "When you start measuring somebody, measure him right, child, measure him right. Make sure you done taken into account what hills and valleys he come through before he got to wherever he is." For Hansberry, each character's life is marked by suffering, struggle, and weakness, yet in each case, the final word has not been written. Just as Beneatha's brother can rise from his degradation, just as Sidney (in *The Sign in Sidney Brustein's Window*) can overcome his ennui, so each of her characters possesses not only a story already written but also possibilities for growth, accomplishment, and heroism. Hansberry permits no stereotypes in her drama, opting instead for characters that present a mixture of positive and negative forces.

Hansberry's realistic style and her stress on the possibilities for heroism within each of her characters have everything to do with the purpose that she saw in drama. As James Baldwin observed, Hansberry made no bones about asserting that art has a purpose, that it contained "the energy that could change things." In *A Raisin in the Sun*, Hansberry describes a poor black family living in Chicago's South Side, her own childhood home, and through her realistic portrayal of their financial, emotional, and racial struggles, as well as in her depiction of their ability to prevail, she offers her audience a model of hope and perseverance and shows the commonality of human aspirations, regardless of color. In *The Sign in Sidney Brustein's Window*, she takes as her subject the disillusioned liberal Sidney Brustein, who has lost faith in the possibility of creating a better world. After all of his disillusionment, he realizes that despair is not an answer, that the only answer is hope despite all odds and logic, that change depends on his commitment to it. So too, in *Les Blancs*, Hansberry gives her audience a character, Tshembe Matoseh, who has a comfortable, pleasant, secure life and who seeks to avoid commitment to the cause of African independence, though he believes in the justness of that cause. He learns that change comes about only through commitment, and that such commitment often means the abandonment of personal comfort on behalf of something larger.

A RAISIN IN THE SUN

Hansberry's earliest play, *A Raisin in the Sun*, is also her finest and most successful work. The play is set in the South Side of Chicago, Hansberry's childhood home, and focuses on the events that transpire during a few days in the life of the Younger family, a family headed by Lena Younger, the mother; the other family members are her daughter, Beneatha, her son, Walter Lee, and his wife, Ruth, and son, Travis. The play focuses on the problem of what the family should do with ten thousand dollars that Lena receives as an insurance payment after the death of her husband, Walter Lee, Sr. The money seems a blessing at first, but the family is torn, disagreeing on how the money should be spent.

The play's title is taken from Langston Hughes's poem "Harlem" and calls attention to the dreams of the various characters, and the effects of having those dreams deferred. The set itself, fully realistic, emphasizes this theme from the first moment of the play. The furniture, once chosen with care, has been well cared for, yet it is drab, undistinguished, worn out from long years of service. The late Walter Lee, Sr., was a man of dreams, but he could never catch up with them, and he died, exhausted and wasted, worn out like the furniture, at an early age. His family is threatened with the same fate, but his insurance money holds out hope for the fulfillment of dreams.

Lena and Walter Lee, however, disagree about what to do with the money. Walter Lee hates his job as a chauffeur and plans to become his own man by opening a liquor store with some friends, but Lena instead makes a down payment on a house with one-third of the money, and plans to use another third to finance Beneatha's medical studies. After the two argue, Lena realizes that she has not permitted her son to be a man and has stifled him, just as the rest of the world has. In order to make up for the past, she entrusts him with the remaining two-thirds of the money, directing him to take Beneatha's portion and put it into a savings account for her, using the final third as he sees fit. Walter Lee, however, invests all the money in a foolhardy scheme and discovers shortly thereafter that one of his partners has bilked him of the money.

The house that Lena has purchased is in a white neighborhood, and a Mr. Lindner has approached the Youngers, offering to buy back the house—at a profit to the Youngers—because the members of the community do not want blacks living there. Walter Lee at first scornfully refuses Lindner's offer, but once he has lost all the money he is desperate to recoup his losses and calls Lindner, willing to sell the house. The family is horrified at how low Walter has sunk, but when Beneatha rejects him, claiming there is "nothing left to love" in him, Lena reminds her that "There is always something to love. And if you ain't learned that, you ain't learned nothing." Lena asks Beneatha, "You give him up for me? You wrote his epitaph too—like the rest of the world? Well, who give you the privilege?" The epitaph is indeed premature, for when Lindner arrives and Walter is forced to speak in his son's presence, Walter gains heroic stature by rejecting the offer, telling Lindner in simple, direct terms that they will move into their house because his father "earned it." It is a moment during which Walter comes into manhood, and if it has taken him a long while to do so, the moment is all the richer in heroism.

The theme of heroism found in an unlikely place is perhaps best conveyed through the symbol of Lena's plant. Throughout the play, Lena has tended a small, sickly plant that clings tenaciously to life despite the lack of sunlight in the apartment. Its environment is harsh, unfavorable, yet it clings to life anyway—somewhat like Walter, whose life should long ago have extinguished any trace of heroism in him. Hansberry gives her audience a message of hope.

Hansberry also reminds her audience of the common needs and aspirations of all humanity, and she does so without oversimplification. None of the characters in the play is a simple type, not even Lindner, who might easily have been presented as an incarnation of evil. Instead, Lindner is conveyed as a human being. When asked why she portrayed Lindner in this manner, Hansberry replied "I have treated Mr. Lindner as a human being merely because he is one; that does not make the meaning of his call less malignant, less sick." Here is where Hansberry calls her audience to action. She reminds the audience of what it is to be human and enjoins them to respect the dignity of all their fellows.

An interesting subtheme in the play, one that would be developed far more fully later in *Les Blancs*, is introduced by Joseph Asagai, an African student with a romantic interest in Beneatha. Some of the most moving speeches in the play belong to Asagai, and when Beneatha temporarily loses hope after Walter has lost all the money, Asagai reminds her of her ideals and the need to keep working toward improvement in the future. When Beneatha asks where it will all end, Asagai rejects the question, asking, "End? Who even spoke of an end? To life? To living?" Beneatha does not fully understand Asagai's argument at the time, but its meaning must be clear enough to the audience, who will see at the end of the play that Walter's victory is not an end, but rather one small, glorious advance. There will be other trials, other problems to overcome, but, as Asagai says, any other problem "will be the problem of another time."

THE SIGN IN SIDNEY BRUSTEIN'S WINDOW

Hansberry's second play, *The Sign in Sidney Brustein's Window*, never matched the success of her first, but it, too, uses a realistic format and was drawn from her own life. Instead of South Side Chicago, it is set in Greenwich Village, Hansberry's home during the early years of her marriage with Robert Nemiroff, and the central character is one who must have re-sembled many of Hansberry's friends. He is Sidney Brustein, a lapsed liberal, an intellectual, a former insurgent who has lost faith in his ability to bring about constructive change. As the play opens, Sidney moves from one project, a nightclub that failed, to another, the publication of a local newspaper, which Sidney insists will be apolitical. His motto at the opening of the play is "Presume no commitment, disavow all engagement, mock all great expectations. And above all else, avoid the impulse to correct." Sidney's past efforts have failed, and his lost faith is much the same as Beneatha's in *A Raisin in the Sun*.

The surrounding environment goes a long way toward explaining Sidney's cynicism. His wife, Iris, has been in psychoanalysis for two years, and her troubled soul threatens their marriage. Iris's older sister, Mavis, is anti-Semitic, and her other sister, Gloria, is a high-class call girl who masquerades as a model. Sidney's upstairs neighbor, David Ragin, is a homosexual playwright whose plays invariably assert "the isolation of the soul of man, the alienation of the human spirit, the desolation of all love, all possible communication." Organized crime controls politics in the neighborhood, and drug addiction is rampant; one of Sidney's employees at the defunct nightclub, Sal Peretti, died of addiction at the age of seventeen, despite Sidney's efforts to help him. Faced with these grim realities, Sidney longs to live in a high, wooded land, far from civilization, in a simpler, easier world.

The resultant atmosphere is one of disillusionment as characters lash out in anger while trying to protect themselves from pain. One of the targets of the intellectual barbs of the group is Mavis, an average, settled housewife who fusses over Iris and pretends to no intellectual stature. When the wit gets too pointed, though, Mavis cuts through the verbiage with a telling remark: "I was taught to believe that creativity and great intelligence ought to make one expansive and understanding. That if ordinary people . . . could not expect understanding from artists . . . then where indeed might we look for it at all." Only Sidney is moved by this remark; he is unable to maintain the pretense of cynicism, admitting, "I *care*. I care about it all. It takes too much energy *not* to care." Thus,

Sidney lets himself be drawn into another cause, the election of Wally O'Hara to public office as an independent, someone who will oppose the drug culture and gangster rule of the neighborhood.

As Sidney throws himself into this new cause, he uses his newspaper to further the campaign, and even puts a sign, "Vote for Wally O'Hara," in his window. Idealism seems to have won out, and indeed Wally wins the election, but Sidney is put to a severe test as Iris seems about to leave him, and it is discovered that Wally is on the payroll of the gangsters. Added to all this is Gloria's suicide in Sidney's bathroom. Her death brings Sidney to a moment of crisis, and when Wally O'Hara comes into the room to offer condolences and to warn against any hasty actions, Sidney achieves a clarity of vision that reveals his heroism. Sidney says,

> *This world*—this swirling, seething madness—which you ask us to accept, to maintain—has done this . . . maimed my friends . . . emptied these rooms and my very bed. And now it has taken my sister. *This* world. Therefore, to live, to breathe—I shall *have* to fight it.

When Wally accuses Sidney of being a fool, he agrees:

> A fool who believes that death is waste and love is sweet and that the earth turns and that men change every day . . . and that people wanna be better than they are . . . and that I hurt terribly today, and that hurt is desperation and desperation is energy and energy can *move* things.

In this moment, Sidney learns true commitment and his responsibility to make the world what it ought to be. The play closes with Iris and Sidney holding each other on the couch, Iris crying in pain, with Sidney enjoining her: "Yes . . . weep now, darling, weep. Let us both weep. That is the first thing: to let ourselves feel again . . . then, tomorrow, we shall make something strong of this sorrow."

As the curtain closes, the audience can scarcely fail to apply these closing words to themselves. Only if they permit themselves to feel the pain, Hansberry claims, will it be possible to do anything to ease that pain in the future. James Baldwin, referring to the play, said, "it is about nothing less than our responsibility to ourselves and to others," a consistent theme in Hansberry's drama. Again and again, she reminds the audience of their responsibility to act in behalf of a better future, and the basis for this message is her affirmative vision. Robert Nemiroff says that she found reason to hope "in the most unlikely place of all: the lives most of us lead today. Precisely, in short, where *we* cannot find it. It was the mark of her respect for us all."

LES BLANCS

Hansberry's last play of significance, *Les Blancs*, was not in finished form when she died and did not open onstage until November 15, 1970, at the Longacre Theatre, years after her death. Nemiroff completed and edited the text, though it is to a very large degree Hansberry's play. It was her least successful play, running for only forty-seven performances, but it did spark considerable controversy, garnering both extravagant praise and passionate denunciation. Some attacked the play as advocating racial warfare, while others claimed it was the best play of the year, incisive and compassionate. The play is set not in a locale drawn from Hansberry's own experience but in a place that long held her interest: Africa.

Les Blancs is Hansberry's most complex and difficult play. It takes as its subject white colonialism and various possible responses to it. At the center of the play are the members of the Matoseh family: Abioseh Senior, the father, who is not actually part of the play, having died before it opens, but who is important in that his whole life defined the various responses possible (acceptance, attempts at lawful change, rebellion); in addition, there are his sons, Abioseh, Eric, and, most important, Tshembe. Hansberry attempts to shed some light on the movement for African independence by showing the relationships of the Matosehs to the whites living in Africa. The whites of importance are Major Rice, the military commander of the colony; Charlie Morris, a reporter; Madame Neilsen, and her husband, Dr. Neilsen, a character never appearing onstage but one responsible for the presence of all the others.

Dr. Neilsen has for many years run a makeshift hospital in the jungle; he is cut in the mold of Albert Schweitzer, for he has dedicated his life to tending the medical ills of the natives. It is because of him that all the other doctors are there and because of him, too, that Charlie Morris is in Africa, for Charlie has come to write a story about the famous doctor.

Whereas Charlie comes to Africa for the first time, Tshembe and Abioseh are called back to Africa by the death of their father. Abioseh comes back a Catholic priest, having renounced his African heritage and embraced the culture and beliefs of the colonialists. Tshembe, too, has taken much from the colonial culture, including his education and a European bride. He has not, however, rejected his heritage, and he is sensitive to the injustice of the colonial system. Though he sees colonialism as evil, he does not want to commit himself to opposing it. He wants to return to his wife and child and lead a comfortable, secure life.

For both Charlie and Tshembe, the visit to Africa brings the unexpected, for they return in the midst of an uprising, called "terror" by the whites and "resistance" by the blacks. Charlie gradually learns the true nature of colonialism, and Tshembe, after great struggle, learns that he cannot avoid his obligation to oppose colonialism actively.

While Charlie waits for Dr. Neilsen to return from another village, he learns from Madame Neilsen that the doctor's efforts seem to be less and less appreciated. When Tshembe comes on the scene, Charlie is immediately interested in him and repeatedly tries to engage the former student of Madame Neilsen and the doctor in conversation, but they fail to understand each other. Tshembe will accept none of the assumptions that Charlie has brought with him to Africa: He rejects the efforts of Dr. Neilsen, however well-intentioned, as representing the guilty conscience of colonialism while perpetrating the system. He also rejects Charlie's confident assumption that the facilities are so backward because of the superstitions of the natives. Charlie, on the other hand, cannot understand how Tshembe can speak so bitterly against colonialism yet not do anything to oppose it. Tshembe explains that he is one of those "who see too much to take sides," but his position becomes increasingly untenable. He is approached by members of the resistance and is asked to lead them, at which point he learns that it was his father who conceived the move-

ment when it became clear that the colonialists, including Dr. Neilsen, saw themselves in the position of father rather than brother to the natives and would never give them freedom.

Still, Tshembe resists the commitment, but Charlie, as he leaves the scene, convinced now that the resistance is necessary, asks Tshembe, "Where are you running, man? Back to Europe? To watch the action on your telly?" Charlie reminds Tshembe that "we do what we can." Madame Neilsen herself makes Tshembe face the needs of his people. Tshembe by this time knows what his choice must be, but he is unable to make it. In his despair, he turns to Madame Neilsen, imploring her help. She tells him, "You have forgotten your geometry if you are despairing, Tshembe. I once taught you that a line goes into infinity unless it is bisected. Our country needs *warriors*, Tshembe Matoseh."

In the final scene of the play, Tshembe takes up arms against the colonialists, and Hansberry makes his decision all the more dramatic by having him kill his brother Abioseh, who has taken the colonial side. Yet, lest anyone misunderstand the agony of his choice, Hansberry ends the play with Tshembe on his knees before the bodies of those he has loved, committed but in agony, deeply engulfed by grief that such commitment is necessary.

Les Blancs is less an answer to the problem of colonialism than it is another expression of Hansberry's deep and abiding belief in the need for individual commitment, and in the ability of the individual, once committed, to bring about positive change for the future, even if that requires suffering in the present. Surely her commitment to her writing will guarantee her work an audience far into the future.

OTHER MAJOR WORKS

NONFICTION: *The Movement: Documentary of a Struggle for Equality*, 1964 (includes photographs); *To Be Young, Gifted, and Black: Lorraine Hansberry in Her Own Words*, 1969 (Robert Nemiroff, editor).

BIBLIOGRAPHY

Carter, Steven R. *Hansberry's Drama: Commitment amid Complexity*. Urbana: University of Illinois

Press, 1991. An examination of Hansberry's plays from the political standpoint. Bibliography and index.

Cheney, Anne. *Lorraine Hansberry*. New York: Twayne, 1994. A basic biography of Hansberry that examines her life and works. Bibliography and index.

Domina, Lynn. *Understanding "A Raisin in the Sun": A Student Casebook to Issues, Sources, and Historical Documents*. Westport, Conn.: Greenwood Press, 1998. A study that places Hansberry's works and life in context and examines her portrayal of African Americans in literature. Bibliography and index.

Effiong, Philip U. *In Search of a Model for African American Drama: A Study of Selected Plays by Lorraine Hansberry, Amiri Baraka, and Ntozake Shange.* Lanham, Md.: University Press of America, 2000. A study of the plays of three prominent African Americans, including Hansberry. Bibliography and index.

Kappel, Lawrence, ed. *Readings on "A Raisin in the Sun."* San Diego, Calif.: Greenhaven Press, 2001.

A collection of essays that deal with aspects of Hansberry's most famous work. Bibliography and index.

Keppel, Ben. *The Work of Democracy: Ralph Bunche, Kenneth B. Clark, Lorraine Hansberry, and the Cultural Politics of Race*. Cambridge, Mass.: Harvard University Press, 1995. Keppel examines race relations and the Civil Rights movement, including a discussion of Hansberry's role in the movement. Bibliography and index.

Leeson, Richard M. *Lorraine Hansberry: A Research and Production Sourcebook*. Westport, Conn.: Greenwood Press, 1997. This sourcebook focuses on Hansberry as a dramatist, examining her portrayal of African Americans in literature. Bibliography and index.

Scheader, Catherine. *Lorraine Hansberry: A Playwright and Voice of Justice*. Springfield, N.J.: Enslow, 1998. A biography that examines Hansberry's dual roles as civil rights advocate and dramatist. Bibliography and index.

Hugh Short,
updated by Katherine Lederer

THOMAS HARDY

Born: Higher Bockhampton, England; June 2, 1840
Died: Dorchester, England; January 11, 1928

PRINCIPAL DRAMA

The Dynasts: A Drama of the Napoleonic Wars, pb. 1903, 1906, 1908, 1910 (verse drama), pr. 1914 (abridged by Harley Granville-Barker)

The Famous Tragedy of the Queen of Cornwall, pr., pb. 1923 (one act)

OTHER LITERARY FORMS

Thomas Hardy is best known for his fiction. He was the author of fourteen novels, four collections of short stories containing more than forty tales, and several volumes of poetry containing some nine hundred poems, as well as a large assortment of nonfic-

tion prose, prefaces, and essays. His letters, diaries, notebooks, and private papers have survived, despite Hardy's intention that this material be destroyed. Several volumes of his correspondence have been published. In addition, there are two books of autobiography, *The Early Life of Thomas Hardy* (1928) and *The Later Years of Thomas Hardy* (1930), which Hardy dictated to his wife.

ACHIEVEMENTS

Although Thomas Hardy's achievements as a novelist and poet are widely recognized, his achievements as a playwright are less well-known. Hardy's training as an architect has been taken to explain his intricately plotted novels, and it might also be seen as the reason Hardy liked the conventions of dramatic structure. Hardy had a lifelong interest in drama and the theater, and it was his original literary ambition to be a playwright, although he did not produce any plays until near the end of his career and then wrote only two. Although he was sometimes tempted by London theatrical agents and friends to turn his talents to the stage, he largely resisted the lure of stagelights, being unwilling to compromise with the demands of actors and directors in the commercial theater, a position he explains in an essay, "Why I Don't Write Plays" (1892). Alternately fearful of the limitations and fascinated by the possibilities of drama, Hardy finally wrote his first "play," *The Dynasts*, which is something of a composite literary form. Intended for a mental rather than a real stage, it is epic in size and scope. This immense verse play, about which one might remark, as Samuel Johnson did of John Milton's *Paradise Lost* (1667, 1674), "none would wish it longer," has attracted some critical attention, but it has never drawn many readers from the general public. As a closet drama, it is a major artistic accomplishment, and it rivals Leo Tolstoy's *War and Peace* (1865, 1869) as a work that most vividly chronicles the defeat of Napoleon's dynastic ambitions. Hardy's hope of reviving interest in the verse drama, however, was not fulfilled with *The Dynasts* or with his second verse play, *The Famous Tragedy of the Queen of Cornwall*, which was conceived for actual stage production. The one-act *The Famous Tragedy of the Queen of Cornwall* was a coda to Hardy's brief career as a playwright; an extremely different type of poetic drama from *The Dynasts*, it shows what Hardy might have been able to do with stage conventions had he kept to his early ambition "to write a few fine plays."

BIOGRAPHY

Thomas Hardy was born on June 2, 1840, in a thatched-roof cottage at Higher Bockhampton, a village near the small city of Dorchester in the southern shire of Dorset—an area that was known as Wessex in ancient times and that has many historical associations with the Druids, the Celts, and the Romans. Hardy's father, a music-loving building contractor, was ambitious for young Thomas; thus, after he com-

Thomas Hardy (Library of Congress)

pleted his education through grammar school, Hardy was apprenticed at age sixteen to an architect. Whatever of his education did not pertain to his vocation he had to pick up on his own, and it was in this fashion that he continued to study Latin and Greek. He also began writing poetry during his late teens, imitating the style and substance of the dialect verses of the Reverend William Barnes, a local curate and poetaster.

Hardy's apprenticeship under the ecclesiastical architect John Hicks lasted until 1862, after which he went up to London at the age of twenty-one to study architecture further. Under the tutelage of John Blomfield, Hardy became proficient enough in his professional life to win a prize given by the Royal Institute of British Architects for an essay on the use of ancient building materials in modern architecture. Hardy's expository talent was further demonstrated in a sketch, "How I Built Myself a House," in *Chamber's Journal*. During this period, Hardy's life was somewhat inchoate. He began at this time, however, to become more deeply interested in literature, writing stories as well as poetry and availing himself of the cultural opportunities London provided. He used his free time to visit the British Museum and the art galleries and spent his evenings at King's College, studying French. The routine of work and study and the rigors of urban life placed a strain on Hardy's health, which had been delicate since his childhood, and after five years, he sought rustication, returning to Bockhampton to recover. While he was at home and employed only part-time with church restorations, he began to write his first novel, "The Poor Man and the Lady." He sent the manuscript to a publisher, but it was rejected because the story lacked plot and suspense. Despite this disappointment, Hardy was encouraged by the editor's praise, and he attempted a second novel, *Desperate Remedies*, which satisfied the requirement for plot ingenuity and was published anonymously in 1871. This book was quickly followed by *Under the Greenwood Tree* (1872) and *A Pair of Blue Eyes* (1872-1873); neither novel was a popular success, but both received positive notice from the reviewers.

At the time, Hardy was encouraged by the editor of *Cornhill Magazine* to write a serial novel. The result was Hardy's first popular and financial success, the pastoral novel *Far from the Madding Crowd* (1874). Success with this book enabled Hardy to marry Emma Lavinia Gifford in the same year. He also gave up his practice as an architect, for he was assured of an income from his writing. After a honeymoon trip to France, Hardy settled down at Max Gate, his home near Dorchester, where he spent the next twenty-five years writing stories and novels. Although he wrote continuously and preferred a retired life, Hardy was by no means a recluse. He made many friends in literary circles and was active on the London social scene as his reputation as a major writer grew. During these decades, when Hardy's creative productivity was at its peak, he published the five major novels that he came to call stories of "Character and Environment": *The Return of the Native* (1878), *The Mayor of Casterbridge* (1886), *Tess of the D'Urbervilles* (1891), and *Jude the Obscure* (1895).

Although Hardy's career as a writer was flourishing throughout the 1870's, the 1880's, and the 1890's, his marriage to Emma was not. The couple was childless, which put a strain on their relationship, and the evidence points to sexual difficulties between Hardy and his wife. Although Emma was a conventional helpmate as a wife, tending to Hardy's business affairs and making fair copies of his manuscripts, she was not a mate to him in the full sense. As the years passed, each was embittered against the other, and the difficulties of their marriage increased. Emma Hardy's death in 1912 was an occasion of mixed relief and bereavement for Hardy, but after two years of mourning he married, at age seventy-four, for a second time. His new wife was Florence Emily Dugdale, who was a longtime friend of the Hardys and had served as his secretary following Mrs. Hardy's death.

During the later years of his writing career, after the hostile reception of *Jude the Obscure* in 1895, Hardy turned again to poetry and worked primarily in this medium for the rest of his life, producing two experiments in drama—the epic drama in verse, *The Dynasts*, and a second verse play, *The Famous Tragedy of the Queen of Cornwall*.

Honors and recognition came to Hardy in abundance in his later years. He was awarded the Order of Merit by King Edward; his home of Max Gate was a shrine visited with veneration by the literati of the English-speaking world. Although Hardy had wished to be buried in his native Dorset, at his death in 1928, he was honored by the nation with a burial in the Poets' Corner of Westminster Abbey. His heart, however, was taken home, where it was interred in the village graveyard of his native heath.

ANALYSIS

It is not really surprising that Thomas Hardy should have turned his talents to the production of dramatic poetry. There are many indications of an early and lifelong interest in the drama—both folk and professional. Hardy enjoyed plays both in the study and on the stage, and he read widely among the classical Greek, Elizabethan, modern Continental, and modern English playwrights. He was a frequent playgoer in London and knew many theatrical people, among them Harley Granville-Barker, Sir James Barrie, George Bernard Shaw, and John Galsworthy. In fact, at one point in his life Hardy had thought of becoming a playwright himself, and as early as 1867, he was considering writing plays in blank verse but postponed this project after being discouraged by the realities of a stage production.

Hardy's interest in playwriting lay dormant for many years, but, having abandoned the writing of fiction, disgusted by the adverse critical reaction to his later novels, he turned to poetry and drama—his interest in the latter whetted by stage adaptations of *Far from the Madding Crowd* and *Tess of the D'Urbervilles*. Thus, near the end of the 1890's, Hardy plunged into the writing of a verse drama; "nothing could interfere with it," as he said, for it was intended for a "mental performance."

THE DYNASTS

Hardy's *The Dynasts* is, along with John Milton's *Samson Agonistes* (1671) and Percy Bysshe Shelley's *Prometheus Unbound* (1820), one of the longest closet dramas in English literature. This vast epic drama, consisting of nineteen acts and 130 scenes, traces the Napoleonic Wars from 1805 to 1815. On publication, *The Dynasts* was hailed as a major achievement, but subsequent generations have found the massive work more problematic. Indeed, while Hardy's novels continue to be read and are available in numerous editions in any bookstore, only Victorian scholars are likely to plough their way through the 10,553 lines of *The Dynasts*. As Hardy's importance as a novelist increases, his importance as a dramatic poet seems to be fading, despite pleading by some critics to justify *The Dynasts* categorically either as an epic or as a drama.

The Dynasts, which was published in three separate parts in 1903, 1906, and 1908, was initially untitled and was referred to simply as "A Drama of Kings." When all three parts of the completed work were published together in 1910, Hardy labeled it an epic drama and gave it the title by which it is now known. Hardy's title comes from a line on the last page of the final act: ". . . who hurlest Dynasts from their thrones?" As to his choice of this title, Hardy wrote, "it was the best and shortest inclusive one I

could think of to express the rulers of Europe in their desperate struggle to maintain their dynasties rather than to benefit their people."

The Dynasts required all of Hardy's skills as a writer. Written in a variety of verse forms, the drama tells an epic story with a cast of thousands. Hardy's forte as a novelist was his ability to tell a story with interest and suspense, and his talent with plot did not desert him here. *The Dynasts* relates a well-known story—the rise and fall of Napoleon—with vivid and fresh appeal. There are scenes of battle, of political intrigue, and of the ordinary life of the people that provide spectacle on the scale of the films of the late Cecil B. De Mille. Unlike previous closet dramas, such as Lord Byron's *Manfred* (pb. 1817), Shelley's *The Cenci* (pb. 1819), or Alfred, Lord Tennyson's *Harold* (pb. 1876), Hardy selected a recent historical event as his subject, as he did in his novels, in which the setting is generally only a few decades removed from the telling. In *The Dynasts*, the time of the action is 1805-1815. Whereas in his fiction Hardy was concerned with the fate of common people in the grips of an indifferent destiny, in the epic drama his concern was to show how princes and powerful men, who often seem to control the fate of the masses, are in turn moved and influenced by the same blind forces that govern the humblest of people.

Hardy's epic drama was the result of his lifelong interest in Napoleon's character and career, a subject that had attracted many other writers of his own and earlier generations. It was his intention to do more than dramatize the turbulent period of the Napoleonic Wars; Hardy's purpose was to show how the events that led up to the period of conflict had been shaped by blind causes rather than human will; the major premise underlying *The Dynasts* is that all human thought and action are predestined—an expression of the anthropomorphic force that Hardy called the "Immanent Will," rather than of Divine Providence. Although this was an advanced idea for 1904, it seems to make the drama passé to modern readers, who are not as concerned with questions of ultimate causation as were the post-Victorians.

The cast of characters in Hardy's drama, epic in proportions, is arranged on three levels: first, the celestial abstractions—the Will, the Ironies, the Spirit Sinister, the Shade of the Earth, and the Earth of the Years; next, the great historical figures—Napoleon, the Duke of Wellington, Lord Nelson, George III, William Pitt, the Younger, and the various kings, princes, and generals of Prussia, Austria, Spain, and Russia (these are the dynasts of Europe, all of whom are concerned only to maintain their rule); and finally, the ordinary people, the suffering masses who are puppets caught in the grip of political and historical forces beyond their control. Hardy makes these lower-class characters his collective protagonists, the heroes of the play. On the other hand, the conquerors and kings, the so-called dynasts, are cast as the antagonists, indifferent to the plight of the people and concerned only with expanding their borders; they side with Napoleon when he is up and combine against him when he is down. In the struggles on the human level among the dynasts and their nations, only England stands above the sordid schemes of the Continental kings as the British defy Napoleon's design for world conquest. Among the British generals, Wellington emerges as a worthy rival, whose tenacity will prove to be a match for Napoleon's brilliant strategies.

Of all the characters in the drama, Napoleon is by far the most interesting. He is a complex and evolving personality, whose career as depicted by Hardy is a working out of the Immanent Will in the history of the world. At first, Napoleon functions as an agent of order as he imposes his dream of a unified Europe on the chaos unleashed by the French Revolution. When he crowns himself emperor, however, his decline into egotistical megalomania begins. His march of conquest across Russia is undertaken only for selfish reasons, and from this point on, he is pursued by a Nemesis-like retribution for his overwhelming hubris. The human actions in *The Dynasts* culminate in Napoleon's defeat at Waterloo, the battle scenes being presented from a panoramic perspective to which only a motion picture could do justice in visual terms. Hardy's careful historical research, which included interviews with surviving veterans of the Battle of Waterloo, is particularly evident here as every battalion and regiment is cataloged in the best epic tradi-

tion. Hardy lavishes admiring detail on the exploits of the Scots Greys, the Black Watch, and the British Grenadiers as they hold the thin red line against the furious but futile charge of the French Imperial Guard.

As the numerous acts of the historical drama are played out, scenes are interspersed in which the spirits play their part, acting as symbols of abstract powers that are personified as actual characters. The Immanent Will influences events through its attendant spirits—the personified Pities, the Years, and the Ironies—but the Will itself, because it stands for the all-inclusive mind or ultimate reality of the universe, is never depicted. Its operation is keenly felt at numerous points in the drama when its human puppets, including Napoleon himself, act on impulses or instincts that they cannot resist.

The Pities, Years, and Ironies are indicative of human traits, attitudes, and perspectives. The Spirit of Pities symbolizes sympathy and altruism. The Spirit of Years stands for objective reason as time places distance between emotions and events. His outlook on human affairs is rationalistic and unsentimental. The Spirit of Pities, with all its compassion, is the obvious foil of the Spirit of Years, who has no feeling.

The debate between the spirits creates the effect of a Greek chorus and lends a traditional dramatic ingredient to the otherwise unique drama. Other allegorical characters, such as the Spirit Sinister, the Spirit of Rumor, and the Shade of Earth, enter the scene and attempt to interpret the meaning of the unfolding historical events. Their debate, however, is inconclusive, and though their final chorus ends with a weak note of optimism, on the hope that the current "rages of the ages shall be cancelled," to be followed by a future period when human reason will overcome selfish aggression and destructive impulses, it is clear that it will take ages of evolution to turn human instincts of passion into compassion. This evolutionary process, which Hardy termed "meliorism," was his faint but larger hope for humankind.

The foregoing summary can only suggest the total scope of Hardy's *The Dynasts*, which in volume exceeds all the other poetry that he wrote during his career. The work is no less than a poetic representation in dramatic terms of Hardy's personal philosophy and understanding of history. The magnitude of Hardy's poem, however, makes it difficult to come to terms with critically and even artistically. Though Hardy issued the caveat that *The Dynasts* was written for a "mental" staging, he agreed in 1914 to an abridged version that was adapted for a theater production by Granville-Barker, who cut the original to a tenth of its size. The operation was necessary to bring *The Dynasts* within the practical range of time for a theatrical performance because it is estimated that it would have required two entire days and nights of consecutive stage time to dramatize the whole text. As it was, Granville-Barker's abridgment was a strain on audiences and actors, and it caused some reviewers to conclude that *The Dynasts* was an "unplayable play." Its excessive length was not the only fault found with the stage version: The chopped-up plot lacked any sense of progression, and the play had no climax; even more debilitating was the replacement of Hardy's philosophical concerns with an overlay of patriotic sentiment that was devised by Granville-Barker to fit the nationalistic mood fostered in England by the outbreak of World War I.

THE FAMOUS TRAGEDY OF THE QUEEN OF CORNWALL

Hardy's final attempt at a dramatic work was a one-act play entitled *The Famous Tragedy of the Queen of Cornwall*, which was published in 1923. In this play, Hardy's aim was exactly opposite from the purpose of *The Dynasts*: Here, he aimed at concentration rather than expansiveness in his choice of plot, characters, and setting, as he consciously tried to observe the unities. His subject for this play is the tragic love story of Tristram and Iseult, whose story attracted a number of nineteenth century authors, most notably Tennyson, Matthew Arnold, and Algernon Charles Swinburne, who had all written versions of the ill-starred romance.

Hardy dedicated his one-act verse drama to the memory of Emma Gifford, his first wife, and the play has associations with the courtship that took place in the spring of 1870 when he and Emma visited King Arthur's castle, Tintagel, in Lyonnesse—a place he called "the region of dream and mystery." The leg-

ends associated with this area lingered in his mind for fifty years and led to the composition of *The Famous Tragedy of the Queen of Cornwall*, which he began in 1916 but did not finish until 1923.

Hardy develops the Tristram story in a unique way, though his basic conception of the romance depends on Sir Thomas Malory's *Le Morte d'Arthur* (1485). The use of the dramatic format forced Hardy to compress a good many details in his version. For example, to maintain unity of place, he has all the action take place at Tintagel. Furthermore, Hardy begins his drama immediately before the catastrophe, the events of his play taking place during the last hours of the lovers' lives. Moreover, Hardy adds several original details to the story of the doomed couple who are victims of the irresistible and fatal force of love. He employs a chorus (termed "chanters") and Merlin, the wizard, to provide necessary exposition at the start of the play. We learn that while King Mark has been away on a hunt, Queen Iseult has been called to come to Brittany by Tristram, her lover, who, she believes, is dying. She is prevented from seeing him by Iseult of the White Hands, Tristram's wife, who informs her falsely that he is dead. Queen Iseult returns to Lyonnesse thinking that her suspicious husband is none the wiser about her flight to Tristram's bedside; informants, however, have told Mark of her actions. In a subsequent scene, Tristram recovers and comes to Cornwall, traveling incognito, to see Iseult, who is gratified to learn that he is not dead. He lays bare his heart to her, saying that he has been forced into a miserable marriage with Iseult of the White Hands. Shortly thereafter, a strange ship arrives bringing Tristram's wife, who has followed him on discovering that he has returned to his former love.

In a poignant scene that was added by Hardy, the deserted wife and passionate mistress meet. It is clearly shown by this episode that the theme of the play is the tragedy of mismatched mates. Queen Iseult cannot love Mark, who is cruel by nature; she is compelled by a love potion to love Tristram. Tristram is loved by both women, but he is too weak to do what is right, his fate also having been sealed by the same love potion. Meanwhile, Mark discovers

Tristram's presence at the castle and, catching him in an embrace with Iseult, stabs him in the back with a dagger. The queen plucks the knife from the body of her dying lover and uses it to kill her husband. Then she leaps over the ledge of the castle and plunges to her death in the sea below, providing to the legendary story an ending that was entirely Hardy's own.

Whatever the intentions of this play, Hardy's revision of the legend created a great deal more sympathy for Iseult of the White Hands than had previous versions. Hardy was able to renew, in this, his last work, the old formula of tragedy that ruled so many of his own doomed pairs of lovers, from Eustacia Vye and Clem Yeobright in *The Return of the Native* to Jude Fawley and Sue Bridehead in *Jude the Obscure*—lovers whose destinies were shaped, like Tristram and Iseult's, by the dual compulsion of character and fate.

The Famous Tragedy of the Queen of Cornwall was Hardy's only work written expressly for the stage. It was first produced by the Hardy Players in Dorchester on November 21, 1923. There was also an operatic version produced in 1924, which Rutland Boughton scored. In writing *The Famous Tragedy of the Queen of Cornwall*, Hardy was perhaps trying to meet the objections of those critics who had indicted him for an inability to write a concentrated play in *The Dynasts*. In the case of this short poetic drama, Hardy proved that he could indeed create plays for the commercial theater. It is ironic in the best Hardyesque fashion that he succeeded at last with a genre that had been his first aspiration as a literary artist—the poetic drama.

OTHER MAJOR WORKS

LONG FICTION: *Desperate Remedies*, 1871; *Under the Greenwood Tree*, 1872; *A Pair of Blue Eyes*, 1872-1873; *Far from the Madding Crowd*, 1874; *The Hand of Ethelberta*, 1875-1876; *An Indiscretion in the Life of an Heiress*, 1878 (serial), 1934 (book); *The Return of the Native*, 1878; *The Trumpet-Major*, 1880; *A Laodicean*, 1880-1881; *Two on a Tower*, 1882; *The Mayor of Casterbridge*, 1886; *The Woodlanders*, 1886-1887; *Tess of the D'Urbervilles*, 1891; *Jude the Obscure*, 1895; *The Well-Beloved*, 1897.

SHORT FICTION: *Wessex Tales*, 1888; *A Group of Noble Dames*, 1891; *Life's Little Ironies*, 1894; *A Changed Man, The Waiting Supper, and Other Tales*, 1913; *The Complete Short Stories*, 1989 (Desmond Hawkins, editor).

POETRY: *Wessex Poems and Other Verses*, 1898; *Poems of the Past and Present*, 1901; *Time's Laughingstocks and Other Verses*, 1909; *Satires of Circumstance*, 1914; *Selected Poems of Thomas Hardy*, 1916; *Moments of Vision and Miscellaneous Verses*, 1917; *Late Lyrics and Earlier*, 1922; *Human Shows, Far Phantasies, Songs, and Trifles*, 1925; *Winter Words in Various Moods and Metres*, 1928; *Collected Poems of Thomas Hardy*, 1943; *The Complete Poetical Works*, 1982-1985 (3 volumes; Samuel Hynes, editor).

NONFICTION: *Life and Art*, 1925 (Ernest Brennecke, editor); *The Early Life of Thomas Hardy*, 1928; *The Later Years of Thomas Hardy*, 1930; *Personal Writings*, 1966 (Harold Orel, editor); *The Collected Letters of Thomas Hardy*, 1978-1988 (7 volumes; Richard Little Purdy and Michael Millgate, editors).

BIBLIOGRAPHY

Armstrong, Tim. *Haunted Hardy: Poetry, History, Memory.* New York: Palgrave, 2000. An attempt to elevate Hardy as poet within the Western tradition.

Gibson, James. *Thomas Hardy: A Literary Life.* Writers in Their Time series. New York: St. Martin's Press, 1996. A biography of Hardy that covers his life and works. Bibliography and index.

_____, ed. *Thomas Hardy: Interviews and Recollections.* New York: St. Martin's Press, 1999. A study that uses interviews and recollections to portray the life of Hardy. Bibliography and index.

Hands, Timothy. *Thomas Hardy.* New York: St. Martin's Press, 1995. A biography of Hardy that attempts to place his life and literary works within the framework of the society in which he lived.

Kramer, Dale, ed. *The Cambridge Companion to Thomas Hardy.* New York: Cambridge University Press, 1999. A comprehensive reference work dedicated to the literary work and life and times of Hardy. Bibliography and index.

Mallett, Phillip, ed. *The Achievement of Thomas Hardy.* New York: St. Martin's Press, 2000. A study of the literary achievements of Hardy that also examines his depiction of Wessex. Bibliography and index.

Maynard, Katherine Kearney. *Thomas Hardy's Tragic Poetry: The Lyrics and "The Dynasts."* Iowa City: University of Iowa Press, 1991. This study examines the question of tragic literature's vitality in a secular age and explores the philosophical underpinnings of Hardy's tragic vision in his lyric poetry and in *The Dynasts.* It also examines Hardy's efforts within the context of nineteenth century poetry.

Page, Norman, ed. *Oxford Reader's Companion to Hardy.* New York: Oxford University Press, 2000. An encyclopedia devoted to the life and literary works of Hardy. Bibliography.

Wilson, Keith. *Thomas Hardy on Stage.* New York: St. Martin's Press, 1995. An examination of Hardy's two plays and adaptations of his novels for the stage. Bibliography and index.

*Hallman B. Bryant,
updated by Genevieve Slomski*

DAVID HARE

Born: Bexhill, England; June 5, 1947

PRINCIPAL DRAMA

Inside Out, pr. 1968 (with Tony Bicat; adaptation of Franz Kafka's diaries)

How Brophy Made Good, pr. 1969, pb. 1971

What Happened to Blake?, pr. 1970

Slag, pr. 1970, pb. 1971

The Rules of the Game, pr. 1971 (adaptation of Luigi Pirandello's play)

Lay By, pr. 1971, pb. 1972 (with Howard Brenton, Brian Clark, Trevor Griffiths, Stephen Poliakoff, Hugh Stoddart, and Snoo Wilson)

Deathsheads, pr. 1971

England's Ireland, pr. 1972 (with others)

The Great Exhibition, pr., pb. 1972

Brassneck, pr. 1973, pb. 1974 (with Brenton)

Knuckle, pr., pb. 1974

Fanshen, pr. 1975, pb. 1976 (adaptation of William Hinton's book *Fanshen: A Documentary of Revolution in a Chinese Village*)

Teeth 'n' Smiles, pr. 1975, pb. 1976 (music by Nick Bicat, lyrics by Tony Bicat)

Plenty, pr., pb. 1978

A Map of the World, pr., pb. 1983

Pravda: A Fleet Street Comedy, pr., pb. 1985 (with Brenton)

The Bay at Nice, pr., pb. 1986

Wrecked Eggs, pr., pb. 1986

The Secret Rapture, pr., pb. 1988

Racing Demon, pr., pb. 1990

Murmuring Judges, pr. 1991

The Absence of War, pr., pb. 1993

Ivanov, pr. 1995, pb. 1997 (adaptation of Anton Chekhov's play)

Mother Courage and Her Children, pr., pb. 1995 (adaptation of Bertolt Brecht's *Mutter Courage und ihre Kinder*)

Skylight, pr., pb. 1995

Plays, pb. 1996-1997 (2 volumes)

Amy's View, pr. 1997, pb. 1998

The Blue Room, pr., pb. 1998 (adaptation of Arthur Schnitzler's *La Ronde*)

The Judas Kiss, pr., pb. 1998

Via Dolorosa, pb. 1998, pr. 1999

My Zinc Bed, pr., pb. 2000

Platonov, pr., pb. 2001 (adaptation of Chekhov's play)

The Breath of Life, pr. 2002

OTHER LITERARY FORMS

While continuing to work in the theater, David Hare turned to television in 1973 to write and produce *Man Above Men* for the British Broadcasting

Corporation (BBC), followed by *Licking Hitler*, which Hare authored and directed for the BBC in 1978, *Dreams of Leaving* (1980), and *Saigon: Year of the Cat* (1983). In 1985, Hare adapted his play *Plenty* for the motion-picture screen and also wrote and directed *Wetherby*, which some critics regarded as a better film than *Plenty*. *Wetherby* demonstrated that Hare could work effectively in the medium of film as a total artist. Other Hare films are *Paris by Night* (1988) and *Strapless* (1989). He directed the film of Wallace Shawn's *The Designated Mourner* in 1997.

ACHIEVEMENTS

David Hare has been identified as a socialist playwright, a committed artist whose concerns are predominantly moral and often satiric. His work reflects the stance of the "angry" writers of the 1950's carried forward into a second generation of "furious" playwrights, as Jack Kroll has aptly described them. Hare's English characters are shaped by the postwar realities of British life; some of them (such as Susan, the central character of *Plenty*) have not properly adjusted to a changing world, while others (such as Curly, the central character of *Knuckle*) have adjusted at the expense of becoming hardened and cynical or morally complacent. Hare has a genius for drawing strong, distinctive characters who often behave outrageously.

Although many of the plays are set in his native England, his concerns are global, as reflected by increasingly international and exotic settings for the later plays: New York, Leningrad, Saigon, India, and the People's Republic of China, for example. He has also extended his work from the stage to film and television. Hare has a unique talent for dramatizing people under pressure and confronted with crises—social, commercial, moral, revolutionary, and political. His scope is impressively broad, and his concerns in general involve issues of truth, honesty, and integrity. Indeed, the title of one of his most successful plays of the 1980's, *Pravda*, means "truth."

Hare has been favorably compared with Bertolt Brecht (for *Fanshen*, his documentary play about the Chinese Revolution, "the nearest any English contemporary writer has come to emulating Brecht," in the estimation of Michael Coveney) and Harold

David Hare in 1998. (AP/Wide World Photos)

Pinter, perhaps the most gifted playwright of the previous generation. Among younger talents, the volume and quality of his work may perhaps be matched by Tom Stoppard, but few others.

After the success of *Slag* in 1970, Hare won the *Evening Standard* Award for Most Promising Playwright. In 1974, *Knuckle* won for him the John Llewellyn Rhys Award. In 1979, the British Academy of Film and Television Arts voted *Licking Hitler* the Best Television Play of the Year. In 1985, the film *Wetherby*, which Hare both wrote and directed, won the Berlin Film Festival's Golden Bear Award. *The Secret Rapture* was named the best play for 1988 by *Drama Magazine*. Hare's awards also include the New York Drama Critics Circle Award (1983), the Olivier Award (1990 and 1995), and the London Theatre Critics' Award (1990).

BIOGRAPHY

David Hare was born in Bexhill, England, on June 5, 1947, the son of Clifford Theodore Rippon and the former Agnes Gillmour, his wife. Hare was first educated at Lancing College (among his classmates were future playwright Christopher Hampton and lyricist Tim Rice) before going on to Jesus College, Cambridge, where he earned a master's degree, with honors, in 1968. Hare began writing plays at the age of twenty-two. In 1970, his first full-length play, *Slag*, about three women teachers locked in a power struggle over a failing English boarding school, won for him the Most Promising Playwright Award granted by the *Evening Standard*, even though the play was not favorably received by some feminists, who considered the playwright to be sexist; others went so far as to call him a misogynist. *The New York Times* drama critic Clive Barnes described *Slag* as a metaphor for the decline of English society, following Hare's suggestion that the play was not so much about women as institutions. Also in 1970, Hare married Margaret Matheson, a marriage that produced three children before ending in divorce in 1980. In 1992, he married Nicole Farhi, a designer.

From the beginning of his theatrical career in 1968 when he cofounded the Portable Theatre (with Howard Brenton and Snoo Wilson), an experimental troupe that toured Great Britain, Hare demonstrated an interest in creative dramatic collaboration and in theatrical direction, as well as in writing plays. In 1969, Hare became literary manager of the Royal Court Theatre, and in 1970 he was appointed resident dramatist. (*Slag* was first produced at the Hampstead Theatre Club before being moved to the Royal Court.) After working at the Royal Court, Hare served as resident playwright at the Nottingham Playhouse, where his play *Brassneck* (written in collaboration with Howard Brenton), which traced corruption through three generations of a Midlands family, premiered in 1973. In 1974, Hare cofounded Joint Stock, another fringe company; *Fanshen* was done as a Joint Stock production in the city of Sheffield.

As a young man, Hare once worked for Pathé Pictorial and went on to write for television productions after having established himself as a successful playwright. *Saigon: Year of the Cat* was directed by Stephen Frears for Thames Television in 1983, for example, but his earlier award-winning teleplay, *Licking*

Hitler, Hare wrote and directed himself for the BBC in 1978. In 1985, his film *Wetherby*, which Hare also wrote and directed, earned the Golden Bear Award at the Berlin Film Festival and received a large measure of critical acclaim internationally. Hare wrote the screenplay adaptation of *Plenty*, one of his most successful plays, for a major motion picture that starred Meryl Streep, Charles Dance, and Sir John Gielgud and was directed by Fred Schepisi and released by Twentieth Century-Fox. Having earned a reputation as a sometimes controversial national playwright during the 1970's, Hare had established himself by the mid-1980's as a multifaceted writer and director of international scope and importance. After 1975, Hare began to write for the National Theatre which produced *Plenty*, *A Map of the World*, and *Pravda*, and beginning in 1984, Hare served as associate director of the National Theatre in London.

ANALYSIS

David Hare's creative work can be sorted into three categories: plays he wrote and directed himself, scripts written for film and television productions, and plays written in collaboration with Howard Brenton and others. In discussing Hare for the journal *Modern Drama*, C. W. E. Bigsby described the playwright as having been shaped by his times, the political turmoil and social upheaval of the student rebellions of 1968 and the growing dissent over Western policy in Southeast Asia. Bigsby also noted that 1968 was the year that "marked the beginnings of the theatrical fringe in London." Active in fringe theater from the beginning of his dramatic career, Hare became one of the architects of the fringe movement.

Early in his career, for example, Hare became interested in dramatic collaboration, which later led to successful partnerships with Howard Brenton— *Brassneck* in 1973 and *Pravda* in 1985. At the Royal Court Theatre in 1971, Hare instigated an experiment in group collaboration that resulted in the play *Lay By*, a group effort of seven writers (Trevor Griffiths, Brian Clark, Stephen Poliakoff, Hugh Stoddard, and Snoo Wilson, along with Brenton and Hare), stimulated by a *Sunday Times* feature by Ludovic Kennedy, concerning an ambiguous rape case that might have resulted in an erroneous conviction. The Royal Court rejected the play, but Hare's colleagues in the Portable Theatre Company mounted a production directed by Wilson in conjunction with the Traverse Theatre at the Edinburgh Festival Fringe. The Portable Theatre also produced another collective effort in which Hare was involved as a writer, *England's Ireland*, in 1972.

The rationale for the Portable Theatre was political. The idea was to have a touring company that would address working-class audiences, an "antagonistic theatre," as Brenton described it, designed for "people who have never seen the theatre before." The plays produced were intended to be controversial in nature (*Lay By* was an exercise in sexual politics, for example, reconstructing a rape and interspersing the reconstruction with a pornographic photo session) and to challenge conventional assumptions and the traditional forms and methods of the established theater.

Hare has a particular genius for designing ingeniously constructed, unpredictable plots and strong, ambiguous characters that defy immediate classification and interpretation. The male characters tend to be flawed, either because they are infirm of purpose and self-deceived, or because they are all too purposeful and self-assured, in some instances even brutal. In Hare's male characters, civilized behavior and even signals of basic decency can be signs of weakness. In *Pravda*, Andrew May's apparently "good" qualities (bourgeois ambition, a dedication to the work ethic, a capacity for moral outrage) are in fact merely the product of an unthinking liberal idealism, which easily gives way to his monstrous hatred for Le Roux and his absolute thirst for vengeance. Brock, the diplomat in *Plenty*, is also misled by his emotions.

"Decent" people are not survivors in the kind of world Hare imagines, a world that requires intellectual toughness for survival. The idealist, like the sympathetic Darwin of *Plenty*, cannot stand a chance when countered by the unfeeling pragmatists who operate the machinery of state. Hare's men, often dominated by career ambitions, gradually lose their integrity while serving the corrupt and corrupting establishment of government and big business. They give themselves to these enterprises and are trans-

formed into cogs in the machinery of state, disposable and interchangeable parts. The career diplomat Darwin of *Plenty*, for example, has given a lifetime of loyal service to the Foreign Office but is betrayed by his superiors during the Suez Crisis. Determined to speak his mind and tell the truth, an honorable course of action, he is crushed and his career ruined. This is the sort of career from which Susan extricates her husband, but Brock, lacking her perspective, can only regret the career loss and resent Susan's interference.

The male characters, then, are driven by ambition and the lure of professional success; their vision will be clouded and their integrity compromised. Brock is not a fool, but he will not conclude, as Susan apparently does, that a state bureau that will betray a career loyalist such as Darwin and make a scapegoat of him is not worthy of one's service. In *Pravda*, with its broad, satiric distortions, Andrew can be seen as a fool because his self-betrayal is expanded to farcical proportions. In a more restrained context, Andrew might be seen as a parallel figure to Brock. In the end, Andrew's integrity is compromised when he goes back to Le Roux to edit the sleaziest tabloid in England, but the man is so stupidly devoted to his profession that he hardly seems to care that he has lost his integrity and self-respect. Rebecca has attempted to clarify his decision and to explain the consequences, but to no avail. In a more subtle way, Susan performs a similar function for Brock in *Plenty*, but Brock is so ordinary, so average, and so typical in his ambition that audiences may miss the point.

Plenty may be mistaken for domestic melodrama (even though Susan is hardly a typical melodramatic heroine), but the movement is toward pathos and tragedy in the way men allow themselves to be transformed and corrupted into banality. The meaning of *Pravda* is the more easily recognized by its satiric approach and farcical distortions. Even so, Gavin Millar, in *Sight and Sound*, praised *Plenty* as "one of the few recent texts, in theatre or cinema, that undertakes an unpretentious but serious review of postwar Britain's decline."

THE GREAT EXHIBITION

In this context, Hare may be regarded as a social critic functioning as a practicing dramatist with a flair for satire. His play *The Great Exhibition* is a political satire treating a Labour member of Parliament, Charles Hammett, swept into office during the great Labour victory of 1965 and swept out of office when the Conservative Party returned to power in 1970. Peter Ansorge has called the play a parody of "middle-class playwrights who have turned to working-class communities both for inspiration and as an escape from the more subtle dilemmas of their own environment and class."

FANSHEN

Hare's interest in politics is also obvious in *Fanshen*, a play based on a book by William Hinton, an American who went to China "as a tractor technician," as Hare has described him, "both to observe and help the great land reform programmes of the late 1940's." Hare felt "an obligation to portray Chinese peasants" of the village of Log Bow "in a way which was adequate to their suffering" but was "not interested in portraying the scenes of violence and brutality which marked the landlords' regime and its overthrow." After seeing the play, Hinton objected to Hare's "liberal slant" and urged the playwright to revise the play so as to provide a clear Marxist emphasis, but Hare incorporated only a few of Hinton's list of 110 suggested emendations. *Fanshen* (the title is translated as "to turn the body," or, alternatively, "to turn over") was written for the Joint Stock Company in 1974 and opened in Sheffield before moving on to the ICA Terrace Theatre in London in April of 1975.

TEETH 'N' SMILES

As has been noted, Hare's artistic sensibilities were no doubt influenced by the events of 1968, and his early work suggests a theater of political commitment and protest, carried into the 1970's. His play *Teeth 'n' Smiles*, produced in 1975 at the Royal Court Theatre, has been called "a metaphor for British society" and "an elegy for the vanished visions of the late Sixties" because of the way it treats rock music and popular culture.

The action is set at Cambridge on June 9, 1969, and centers on a performance of a rock band for the May Ball of Jesus College. This concert proves to be a disaster when Maggie, the lead singer of the group, gets drunk, insults the audience, and is finally sent to

prison on a drug charge. The musicians regard their privileged audience with contempt: "Rich complacent self-loving self-regarding self-righteous phoney half-baked politically immature evil-minded little shits." Interviewed about the play by *Theatre Quarterly*, Hare claimed it was intended to question "whether we have any chance of changing ourselves."

In his survey *British Theatre Since 1955: A Reassessment* (1979), Ronald Hayman criticizes the play for setting up Cambridge as symbolizing a repressive capitalist system, concluding that "this kind of play bases its appeal on giving the audience a chance to believe that there is a common enemy which can be fought." Hare's targets in this play are self-delusion, class guilt, and class war, but the play mainly attacks the upscale educational establishment, represented by Cambridge (which Hare knew at firsthand), and has been regarded as an indictment of the detached university intellectuals.

KNUCKLE

The protagonist of *Knuckle*, which opened at London's Comedy Theatre in March of 1974, is far removed from the privileged setting of Cambridge. He is a tough-minded vulgarian who is pragmatic and cynical about the hypocrisy of his world and his own family. Curly Delafield has returned to his home in Guildford seeking information about the disappearance of his sister Sarah, who had worked as a nurse in a psychiatric hospital. Curly is a blunt and brutal man. He had not seen his sister in twelve years, but he is determined to discover what has happened to her.

Sarah's overcoat was found on the beach at Eastbourne, famous for a ghastly murder that was committed there in the spring of 1924. Apparently Sarah either committed suicide or was murdered. The play therefore involves a process of detection, as those close to Sarah, a journalist named Max, her friend Jenny, and her father, are subjected to Curly's relentless interrogation. The mystery of her disappearance is solved at the end, after a sordid story of scandal and blackmail has been brought to light.

Curly is extremely cynical, a man who has been involved in selling arms, and in this regard he resembles in his amoral outlook the character of Andrew Undershaft in George Bernard Shaw's play *Major*

Barbara (1905). Curly is habitually skeptical of men and their motives, including his own father. His view of the world is revealed by his motto: "Every man has his own gun. That's not a metaphor. That's a fact." In a mean world, Curly does not "pick fights" but merely provides weapons: "They're going to kill each other with or without my help," he claims. London is viewed as the corrupt center of a corrupt and fallen world, and the corruption has spread to Guildford. As Curly remarks at the end of the play, "In the mean square mile of the City of London they were making money. Back to my guns." Nearly everyone in this play is contaminated by money.

Knuckle is experimental in the way it mixes genres. The play develops as an apparent murder mystery, a whodunit that leaves open the possibility of suicide but turns out to be merely a parody of a conventional thriller. The sleuth Curly is like a stripped-down, plain-spoken Andrew Undershaft wearing a Mike Hammer mask, a very private eye. In fact, however, the play is an allegory of family betrayal, capitalist greed, and corruption. Hare's declared intention in writing it was "to subvert the form of the thriller to a serious end."

Curly is not a likable character because he is so cynical and so crude, but his character, shaped by the world that has molded it, is at least redeemed by his brutal honesty. He is not self-deluded, as so many of Hare's characters seem to be.

A MAP OF THE WORLD

One of Hare's most ambitious plays that attempts to take on human delusion on a global scale is *A Map of the World*, first performed at London's Lyttleton Theatre in January of 1983. The title comes from Oscar Wilde: "A map of the world that does not include Utopia is not worth even glancing at . . . ," and the central conflict is a philosophical argument between a Marxist idealist, Stephen Andrews, and a conservative "realist," an expatriate celebrity Indian writer named Victor Mehta; the two have been invited to address a UNESCO conference on world poverty in Bombay.

The play is complicated by the way it is framed, with the action shifting from the original confrontation to a filmed reconstruction being shot in London,

as the audience realizes when scene 1 gives way to scene 2. This polemical play has been criticized for being too experimental in its framework and conception and too ambitious in scope, taking on issues of artistic freedom, world poverty, Third World nationalism, political compromise, and the decline of Western civilization, in the midst of a rhetorical contest partly based on sexual jealousy. "Unarguably," Hare has confessed, "I was trying to do too many things at once, and although I have now directed three productions of the play, I cannot ever quite achieve the right balance between the different strands."

PLENTY

Hare describes *A Map of the World* as a "disputatious play" that intended "to sharpen up people's minds, to ask them to remember why they believe what they do." Perhaps this goal was better achieved in the earlier play, *Plenty*, despite the puzzlement over motivation evident in the reviews of the later film version. *Plenty* was one of Hare's most successful plays but also one of his most ambiguous. It was first performed at London's Lyttleton Theatre in 1978, starring Kate Nelligan as Susan Traherne, the protagonist, before going on to Broadway. In 1985, Hare reshaped the script for the motion picture adaptation. The film version rearranged the opening, starting the action at St. Benoît, France, in November of 1943, rather than in the Knightsbridge area of London in 1962, presumably to establish Susan's character from the start as a young Englishwoman serving the French Resistance behind enemy lines during World War II.

Thereafter, in general, the film follows the chronology of the play, which mainly concerns Susan's difficulty in adjusting to civilian and domestic life in England after the war in the time of "plenty" that was to follow. The play seems to document a movement from innocence to insanity, as Susan restlessly moves from one job to another and from one relationship to another, presumably trying to recapture the excitement she knew with her wartime lover, a British agent in France known only by his code name, Lazar. After a brief flirtation with a working-class lover named Mick, whom she had selected to father a child in a liaison that only proved frustrating to both of them, she

　　　　　　　　　　　　　　　　　　　　　　　　Critical Survey of Drama

agrees to marry a career diplomat, Raymond Brock, whose career she later destroys for no clearly explained reason.

With regard to Susan, Hare has written that he was struck by a statistic "that seventy-five percent of the women flown behind the lines for the Special Operations Executive were subsequently divorced after the war." The play, which dramatizes Susan's restlessness in this context, has been criticized for its failure to explain her motives. After all, Raymond Brock seems to be a decent character who sincerely cares for his disturbed wife. Hare describes him as a young man of "delightful ingenuousness" and has noted that it would be a mistake to play him as a fool. His character is blemished, however, by the corrupt institution he serves, the Foreign Office. In a less obvious way than Andrew May in *Pravda*, Brock is ruined by his professionalism and his dedication to an unworthy career.

On the surface, Susan may appear to be maladjusted and irrational. She expresses the need to "move on" several times during the course of the play, but at first glance it seems that she is only able to "move on" from one job to another or from one relationship to another. Psychologically, she does not seem to be able to "move on" from the excitement of love and life behind enemy lines during the war. When she is much later reunited with Lazar in England, she discovers that he has "moved on" to shabby domesticity and a life without joy or enthusiasm. The danger of "moving on" in the sense of adjusting to a changing commonplace world is that this could mean nothing more than accepting banal conformity.

Susan's character is vibrant because she resists that kind of commonplace adjustment. Hare has written that men "are predisposed to find Susan Traherne unsympathetic." The commonplace judgment likely to be made about Susan is that she is emotionally unstable, if not completely deranged. "It's a common criticism of my work," Hare notes in his postscript to the play, "that I write about women whom I find admirable, but whom the audience dislikes."

The case against Susan "makes itself, or is made by the other characters," Hare adds, but the character

is remarkable in her fierce independence and quite extraordinary in her behavior, which Hare believes should create "a balance of sympathy" throughout the play. Hare has written that he intended to show through Susan "the struggle of a heroine against a deceitful and emotionally stultified class." Her motives are submerged and complex, no doubt, but if that is a criticism of the character, it is one that could also be leveled at Hamlet. The mystery of motivation is not necessarily a flaw in a complex and enduring drama.

PRAVDA

Hare's most critically acclaimed play after *Plenty* was *Pravda*, a biting satire of farcical dimensions on the newspaper industry in Great Britain and the dangers of collusion between Whitehall and Fleet Street, between government and the press. *Pravda* was written with Hare's earlier collaborator Brenton and appears to be a not-so-thinly-veiled attack upon the brand of journalism represented by the Australian press tycoon Rupert Murdoch, who took over *The Times* of London, just as *Pravda*'s central character, Lambert Le Roux (from South Africa rather than Australia) takes over the most influential establishment in Brenton and Hare's fictional London, *The Victory*.

Pravda premiered at the National Theatre in 1985, with Anthony Hopkins gaining rave notices for his caricature of Le Roux. Murdoch was reportedly angered by the play. Trevor Nunn, enjoying the limelight of *Les Misérables* (1985), which he directed and adapted as a musical from Victor Hugo's novel, told *Newsweek* that Murdoch "was extremely incensed and sent out the word to get the National and the RSC [Royal Shakespeare Company, whose London home is the Barbican Arts Centre], the two subsidized theatres" in Great Britain. Nunn and Peter Hall, who was instrumental in creating the three-auditorium National Theatre complex on London's South Bank, were both disappointed that the government of Margaret Thatcher did not support the integrity of the National Theatre in the "totally corrupt campaign" (as Hall described it) that followed. When government subsidies to the arts were cut (threatening to close down the National's smallest experimental auditorium in the complex), the director of the National must have sensed political pressure nearly as bizarre and dangerous as what is imagined in the Brenton and Hare play.

Pravda shows Hare's skill as a gadfly, questioning not only journalistic ethics but the larger issue of truth in journalism as well. This "comedy of excess" (as Hare described it) concerns the monopolizing of newspapers in England by the ruthless Lambert Le Roux. The action opens with Le Roux's takeover of a provincial paper, the *Leicester Bystander*, hardly a paradigm for journalistic ethics even before Le Roux's bid. Moira Patterson, a local shop owner maligned by the newspaper by mistake, goes to the editorial offices to demand a retraction. The cynical editor, Harry Morrison, and his subordinate, Andrew May (soon to become the new editor-in-chief) tell her "we . . . don't publish corrections," because "what is printed must be true," and so "to print corrections is a kind of betrayal" of the public trust. May considers this perverse logic a matter of journalistic ethics.

This satiric introduction to an already corrupt world of journalism hardly inspires confidence in the *Leicester Bystander* and what it represents. The corruption of this provincial paper, however, pales in comparison to Andrew's later experiences as editor of *The Victory*, a national paper, a "paper for England."

Although billed as a comedy and often howlingly funny, *Pravda* is an extremely bitter satire that manages to strike out at corruption in high places and to spoof newspapers at all levels and television journalism as well. Besides *The Victory*, Le Roux owns a gutter tabloid (famous for its nudes) called *The Tide* and also attempts to take over a left-wing paper called *The Usurper* (shades of *The Guardian*?). Once in power, Le Roux fires underlings with the gleeful abandon of the Queen of Hearts in Lewis Carroll's *Alice's Adventures in Wonderland* (1865). A fired journalist from *The Victory* regrets most that he will never again appear on a television talk show called *Speak or Shut Up*. Now, he will have to "sit at home shouting at the television like ordinary people."

In his bluntness, Le Roux resembles the unsentimental Curly of *Knuckle*, blown up to monstrous proportions, a vindictive Citizen Kane running amok. There is no clever Hamlet to counter the villainy of this Claudius, as Hare's satire seems to be moving in the direction of tragedy. The tragic vision depends on a sense of justice, however, and finally all that appears in Hare's bitter satiric world is a sense of the absurd so total that railing against it is clearly pointless.

Andrew's wife, Rebecca, gives him a "leaked" document that indicates a breach of public trust by the Minister of Defence concerning the transport of plutonium in flasks that are demonstrably unsafe. When Andrew decides to print the story in *The Victory*, Le Roux fires him. When Andrew and other fired journalists from *The Victory* take over *The Usurper*, Le Roux and his subordinate trick them into running libelous stories about their former employer, then threaten Andrew with litigation and bankruptcy.

At the end, Andrew is humiliated into begging Le Roux's forgiveness and editing *The Tide* as a means of penance. Practicing journalism is more important to him, finally, than ethics, integrity, truth, or love. A muddled idealist not fully understanding his presumed convictions, Andrew deserves to become a lackey to the demoniac Le Roux, devoting his skill to purveying falsehood and smut, the foreman of what Le Roux calls his "foundry of lies."

Rebecca, who loves Andrew, is forced to abandon him after he succumbs to his bloodlust for revenge against Le Roux (his tragic flaw, if this play could be a tragedy) and after he finally sells his soul to the demon magnate who believes "No one tells the truth. Why single out newspapers?" Rebecca is the only character clever enough to see through Le Roux's deviousness, but she is powerless to take action against him. Otherwise, this bitter, satiric world is populated by mean-spirited, unscrupulous, dishonest people.

LATER PLAYS

Hare's later plays and films continued to advance his criticism of Tory society and Thatcherism. His films *Paris by Night* (starring Charlotte Rampling and Michael Gambon) and *Strapless* (starring Blair Brown, Bridget Fonda, and Bruno Ganz) extended his interest in conflicted women characters trying to resolve the contradictions in their lives. To prepare himself for *Paris by Night*, Hare attended the annual

Tory party conference in Blackpool to observe closely the "new Tory woman," as he described, in his introduction to the screenplay published by Faber and Faber in 1988, the new breed of women who entered conservative politics in Great Britain during the Thatcher years. Also in 1988, he created his most sympathetic woman character, Isobel Glass, for his play *The Secret Rapture*. Isobel is set in conflict with her sister, Marion French, who has become a Thatcherite junior minister and who believes that not to make money is "worse than stupid; it's irresponsible." The humanistic Isobel is saintly and is ultimately destroyed by the morally corrupt world that she inhabits.

RACING DEMON

Hare then began a trilogy of plays dealing with British institutions. The first play of the trilogy, *Racing Demon*, is about ecclesiastical betrayal and the Church of England and focuses on a well-meaning minister who lost his faith in God but found purpose in serving the needy. The minister's career, however, is threatened and ruined by his superiors for political reasons.

MURMURING JUDGES

Another play, *Murmuring Judges*, concerns the legal system. A note on the curtain of the Olivier Theatre explained the title: "In Scottish law, a form of contempt, meaning 'to speak ill of the judiciary' or 'to scandalize the court.'" Hare added in a note to the play, published by Faber and Faber, "It is still an offense in Scottish law."

The published text of *Murmuring Judges* begins with a quotation from Ogden Nash: "Professional people have no cares/ Whatever happens, they get theirs." The play is about moral corruption and compromise in the prison service (a young Irishman is jailed and brutalized unjustly) and about an idealistic woman lawyer who is taught a lesson about how justice operates in England. Hare therefore continued to write from a position of political outrage, satirizing and dramatizing the foibles of his time.

THE ABSENCE OF WAR

The third play in the trilogy, *The Absence of War*, combines the cinematic spectacle of *Murmuring Judges* with a simple plot line reminiscent of *Racing*

Demon. Based on the Labor Party and its attempt to win power in the general election of 1992, *The Absence of War* was the product of much research by Hare, who interviewed reporters, politicians, and their advisers. Dramatizing the workings of the British parliament and the electoral process, the play also includes a critique of the Labor Party and its failure to govern or unite English society.

AMY'S VIEW, THE JUDAS KISS, AND THE BLUE ROOM

After this trilogy, which questioned the Church of England, the British legal system, and, finally, the Labor Party, Hare turned to less overtly political plays. His next play, *Amy's View*, is a witty examination of the troubled relations of a stage actress and her daughter, from whose perspective the story is told. However, although this is a play centered on a personal relationship between two women, the narrative also is a metaphor for the political ups and downs of Britain in postwar society. *The Judas Kiss*, a short play written during the same period, is also a story of a personal relationship between two people, speculating on what might have happened behind closed doors between playwright Oscar Wilde and his lover Lord Alfred Douglas.

In 1997 Hare freely adapted Austrian dramatist Arthur Schnitzler's famous play, *Reigen* (pb. 1900, pr. 1920; *Hands Around*, 1920; also as *La Ronde*, 1959). Like the original, Hare's play explored the erotic drive as a ruthless and powerful force in modern life. Retitled *The Blue Room*, this production attracted much attention because of the nudity of its star character, which perhaps overshadowed the play's message.

SKYLIGHT

The most important play following the trilogy, however, is *Skylight*, which was first performed in England in 1995 and won the 1996 Olivier Award. *Skylight* was written with reference to the era in British life from 1979 to 1990, when Margaret Thatcher presided over a shift from a socialist economy to a free market society in England. The play concerns the possible reconciliation between two estranged lovers, whose lives diverged when Britain's old socialist economy unraveled. The break between the two principal characters, a teacher named Kyra and a businessman named Tom is also symbolic of divisions within English society itself. The prosperous Tom, who appreciates "the good life," is contrasted with Kyra, whose life of service and personal sacrifice has led to significant material discomfort. As in *Amy's View*, a close relationship between two people is blended with larger political and social themes—in this case the question is the sustainability of a society that has hopelessly divided itself into two separate political and philosophic camps. Like his other plays, *Skylight* continues Hare's exploration of social and political fragmentation in postwar Britain, and indicates the need for a new consensus that will allow for balance rather than dogged opposition.

VIA DOLOROSA

In 1997, the Royal Court Theatre sent Hare on a series of trips to the Middle East to gather material for a play on the conflicts in the region. Hare ended up writing not a play but a dramatic monologue titled *Via Dolorosa*, which he performed himself in London and New York, and which eventually became a television play. In the course of his monologue, Hare relates the views of more than thirty people from the region, including both Palestinians and Israelis. In addition to exploring the tensions in the Middle East, Hare also explores his own values and spiritual life, his own personal "via dolorosa." Hare ends by contrasting those in the Middle East, whose lives are passionately involved in issues of faith and politics, with the foundering convictions and commitments of British society. Like his previous work, *Via Dolorosa* takes a specific and situation and heightens it so that it can come to stand for a general and important political or moral situation.

MY ZINC BED

Hare continued to wed the personal and the political with *My Zinc Bed*, his first play of the twenty-first century. As with some of his other plays, this was already "in the air," inspired by the case of Audrey Kishline, the founder of a support group advocating moderation in contradistinction to Alcoholics Anonymous's (AA's) well-known policy of abstinence. In the play it is the character Victor who represents the Kishline perspective. An Internet entrepreneur and former communist, Victor, like Kishline, ends up driving while intoxicated and dying in a car crash. His opposite number is Paul, a poet, an alcoholic in recovery who subscribes to the principles of Alcoholics Anonymous. As in *Skylight*, this play once again opposes a prosperous businessman with someone who is more sensitive but less successful. The entrepreneurial Victor is contrasted with a humbled Paul, whose struggles with alcohol have led him to lose faith in Victor's libertarian philosophy of individual empowerment. Paul's sense of his own vulnerability and weakness has led him to depend on the AA system of support, which allows him to survive, albeit in a wounded, broken condition. Like *Skylight*, this play uses a highly charged personal situation and weds it to a substructure that is symbolic and abstract. The larger issues in this case concern the fall of communism, the rise of the Internet, and the adoption of a "new economy" moral philosophy associated once again with the Thatcher revolution. This ability to take the lives and feelings of specifically realized contemporary characters and to brilliantly indicate their relationship to larger social, political, or philosophical themes continues to make Hare one of Britain's most important playwrights.

OTHER MAJOR WORKS

SCREENPLAYS: *Plenty*, 1985 (adaptation of his play); *Wetherby*, 1985; *Paris by Night*, 1988; *Strapless*, 1989; *Damage*, 1992; *The Secret Rapture*, 1994 (adaptation of his play); *The Hours*, 2002 (adaptation of Michael Cunningham's novel).

TELEPLAYS: *Man Above Men*, 1973; *Licking Hitler*, 1978; *Dreams of Leaving*, 1980; *Saigon: Year of the Cat*, 1983; *Heading Home*, 1991.

NONFICTION: *Writing Left-Handed*, 1991; *Asking Around: Background to the David Hare Trilogy*, 1993; *Acting Up: A Diary*, 1999.

BIBLIOGRAPHY

Dean, Joan Fitzgerald. *David Hare*. Boston: Twayne, 1990. Survey of Hare's work up to *The Secret Rapture*, including films and plays for television. Provides background information about British political and social concerns as the context for

Hare's work for the benefit of American readers, and tracks the expanding scope of Hare's plays. Includes a chronology and extensive bibliography.

Donesky, Finlay. *David Hare: Moral and Historical Perspectives*. Westport, Conn.: Greenwood Press, 1996. Often contentious survey places Hare's plays in the social context of England and demonstrates how his characters move from identification with a moral consensus developed during World War II to a concern with spiritual issues during the ascendancy of Prime Minister Thatcher. Praises Hare for his sensitivity to the personal dimension and his ability to dramatize simultaneously a specific and universal moral perspective but is inclined to debunk Hare's reputation as a spokesperson for left-wing political dissent.

Gussow, Mel. "David Hare: Playwright as Provocateur." *The New York Times Magazine*, September 29, 1985, p. 42-47, 75-76. A substantial evaluation of Hare's career anticipating the opening of *A Map of the World* at New York's Public Theatre. Gussow concentrates on the controversial nature of Hare's works that polarize both audiences and critics because of the playwright's political concerns: "the collapse of the English empire, the debilitating effects of the class system, the myths of patriotism, the loss of personal freedom."

Hayman, Ronald. *British Theatre Since 1955: A Reassessment*. New York: Oxford University Press, 1979. Hayman covers Hare's early career; the influence of Raymond Williams, the Marxist don under whom Hare studied at Jesus College; the Portable Theatre; the Royal Court; and a number of plays, from *Teeth 'n' Smiles* to *Plenty*. An appendix surveys the plays produced year by year from 1955 to 1978. Chapter 3, "The Politics of Hatred," concentrates on Hare's work.

Homden, Carol. *The Plays of David Hare*. New York: Cambridge University Press, 1995. A consideration of Hare's work from the 1970's to the 1990's trilogy. Rejecting a strictly linear chronological approach, the plays and screenplays are discussed in overlapping strands, with particular attention to key themes in Hare's work, particularly his relationship with both the political left and the political right, and to the development of a "theatre of juxtaposition."

Oliva, Judy Lee. *David Hare: Theatricalizing Politics*. Ann Arbor, Mich.: UMI Research Press, 1990. Includes textual analyses of more than twenty plays, television scripts, and feature films, addressing both literary and performance issues. Chapters are divided into "Individual Concerns," "National Concerns," and "International Concerns," with special attention to how the plays' components produce Hare's perspective on social and political issues. Illustrated with photographs from productions directed by Hare, this study also includes a 1989 interview with the playwright.

Zeifman, Hersh, ed. *David Hare: A Casebook*. New York: Garland, 1994. A collection of essays by theater scholars largely on specific plays, plus an interview with Hare conducted in 1991. Topics discussed include the role of women in Hare's plays, relationship between his films and his work in theater, and the language of Hare's drama.

James M. Welsh,
updated by Margaret Boe Birns

LORENZ HART

Born: New York, New York; May 2, 1895
Died: New York, New York; November 22, 1943

PRINCIPAL DRAMA

Fly with Me, pr. 1920, pb. 1982 (lyrics; libretto by Milton Kroopf and Philip Leavitt; music by Richard Rodgers)

The Melody Man, pr. 1924 (libretto, with Rodgers
  and Herbert Fields)
The Garrick Gaieties, pr. 1925, pb. 1951 (lyrics;
  sketches by Sir Arthur Sullivan, Morrie
  Ryskind, and others; music by Rodgers)
Dearest Enemy, pr. 1925 (lyrics; libretto by Fields;
  music by Rodgers; based on Jean Gilbert's
  operetta *Die Frau im Hermelin*)
The Girl Friend, pr. 1926 (lyrics; libretto by Fields;
  music by Rodgers)
Peggy-Ann, pr. 1926 (lyrics; libretto by Fields;
  music by Rodgers)
A Connecticut Yankee, pr. 1927 (lyrics; libretto by
  Fields; music by Rodgers)
Chee-Chee, pr. 1928 (lyrics; libretto by Fields;
  music by Rodgers)
Present Arms, pr. 1928 (lyrics; libretto by Fields;
  music by Rodgers)
Jumbo, pr. 1935 (lyrics; libretto by Ben Hecht and
  Charles MacArthur; music by Rodgers)
On Your Toes, pr. 1936 (lyrics; libretto, with
  Rodgers and George Abbott; music by Rodgers)
Babes in Arms, pr. 1937, pb. 1951 (libretto, with
  Rodgers; music by Rodgers)
I'd Rather Be Right, pr., pb. 1937 (lyrics; libretto
  by George S. Kaufman and Moss Hart; music
  by Rodgers)
I Married an Angel, pr. 1938, pb. 1941 (libretto,
  with Rodgers; music by Rodgers; adaptation of
  James Vasarzy's play)
The Boys from Syracuse, pr. 1938, pb. 1965 (lyrics;
  libretto by Abbott; music by Rodgers)
Pal Joey, pr. 1940, pb. 1952 (lyrics; libretto by
  John O'Hara; music by Rodgers)
By Jupiter, pr. 1942, pb. 1951 (lyrics; libretto, with
  Rodgers; music by Rodgers; adaptation of
  Julian Thompson's play *The Warrior's
  Husband*)
The Complete Lyrics of Lorenz Hart, pb. 1986,
  expanded 1995

OTHER LITERARY FORMS

Lorenz Hart is known primarily as a lyricist. Although he collaborated on several librettos for stage
comedies, he wrote more than a thousand song lyrics

for those and twenty-four other stage comedies and
revues and for ten motion-picture musicals, of which
Love Me Tonight (1932) is representative. Hart also
translated plays, operettas (such as Jean Gilbert's *Die
Frau im Hermelin*), and lyrics (such as those to the
1934 motion picture *The Merry Widow*, often without
receiving credit).

ACHIEVEMENTS

Lorenz Hart played a major role in advancing musical theater from the level of vaudeville, revue, and
spectacle to that of musical drama. He was not the
first to take this step, nor did he take it alone, but he
was one of the pioneers in an era that included such
other musical-theater giants as George and Ira
Gershwin, Herbert and Dorothy Fields, George M.
Cohan, Irving Berlin, Arthur Schwartz and Howard
Dietz, Oscar Hammerstein II, Cole Porter, and Hart's
partner Richard Rodgers. In the early 1900's, W. S.
Gilbert and Sir Arthur Sullivan were writing their satiric light operas in England; Sigmund Romberg, Vincent Youmans, Victor Herbert, and Rudolf Friml
were writing operettas in the romantic Viennese tradition; and the team of Jerome Kern, Guy Bolton, and
P. G. Wodehouse had just begun to adapt these European forms to an American form influenced by
music-hall traditions. The satiric lyrics of Gilbert and
Wodehouse strongly influenced the young Hart, and
the stories that held these musicals together inspired
him to want musical comedies in which the songs
were closely integrated with the plots and characters.

When Hart and Richard Rodgers met, they found
that they shared this vision of the musical theater, and
their partnership thrived on their commitment to it.
Their attempt to integrate song and drama began in
the early shows, as with "Old Enough to Love," a
song for mature lovers in *Dearest Enemy*. It continued improving throughout their partnership to the
Amazon's defiant "Nobody's Heart" in *By Jupiter*. In
their early shows, the integration was not entirely
successful, but the partners learned quite a lot about
musical integration from their motion-picture experiences in the 1930's. When they returned to Broadway
from Hollywood, they began writing their own librett-
tos in which the songs could be inherent parts of the

action and dialogue. The epitome of Hart's achievement in integrating lyrics into drama is considered to be *Pal Joey*, with its character pieces, Joey's hypocritical "I Could Write a Book" and Vera's cynical "Bewitched, Bothered, and Bewildered."

In addition to their importance in integrating the music into the drama, Rodgers and Hart also pioneered the use of subjects and stories that had previously been disregarded for the musical theater. For example, *Dearest Enemy* was based on a historical incident of the Revolutionary War; *Peggy-Ann* was the first musical to use Freudian dream theories; *A Connecticut Yankee* used Mark Twain's satire on Yankeeism; *I'd Rather Be Right* was the first musical satire of in-office government officials; *The Boys from Syracuse* set a Shakespearean comedy (*The Comedy of Errors*, pr. c. 1592-1594) to music; and *Pal Joey* dealt with sleazy, small-time nightclub entertainers and criminals. Rodgers and Hart were determined to turn musical comedy away from the stock plots and characters of the early stage. *Pal Joey*, which was not well received at its introduction, is now considered to be the masterpiece that brought Broadway musicals to maturity. Its 1952 revival won the New York Drama Critics Circle Award for Best Musical and eleven out of sixteen Donaldson Awards.

Hart was equally concerned with breaking the "June, moon, soon" mold of the Tin Pan Alley rhyme. An avid reader, he had an understanding of rhyme theory and poetic rhythm that allowed him to write witty, subtle, complex lyrics that impressed nearly everyone who heard them. One has only to compare his "Manhattan" lyrics ("Manhattan" rhymed with "Staten," "Coney" with "baloney") with those of another song, "East Side, West Side" ("town," "down," "O'Rourke," "York") to see the difference. He had an excellent understanding of dialect and could range from the slangy in "The Girl Friend" to the archaic in "Thou Swell" through the romantic in "Isn't It Romantic" and the tender in "My Funny Valentine," from the ironic in "I Wish I Were in Love Again" to the satiric in "Dear Old Syracuse" and the impudent in "Girls, Girls, Girls." Hart may have been the first truly literate American lyricist; certainly he was the first to achieve equal credit with the composer for the

songwriting and to have his name, along with those of the author and composer, in lights on the theater marquee.

BIOGRAPHY

Lorenz Milton Hart was born in New York City on May 2, 1895, to Max Hart and Frieda Isenberg Hart. He had one brother, Theodore Van Wyck Hart, who also gained theatrical fame, as comic actor Teddy Hart. Lorenz Hart was educated at Columbia Grammar School, DeWitt Clinton, Weingart Institute, and Columbia University. In school, he belonged to literary societies and wrote for and edited the school papers.

Hart grew up in a highly literary environment. His mother, Frieda, had wanted to be an actress, and from the age of six, he was taken to the theater. He began to write poetry when he was six, and he wrote and performed skits and satires of plays he had seen both on and off Broadway. He loved the Gilbert and Sullivan and Kern-Bolton-Wodehouse musicals, but he never liked Herbert's "schmaltzy" music. At the Weingart Institute summer school, he belonged to the Weingart Literary Society and wrote articles for the literary magazine, often satires and humorous essays. In 1909, he became the editor of *The Weingart Review*. Also at Weingart, he acted in school dramas, farces, and minstrel shows. At fifteen, he began to attend Paradox Lake Camp, where he was active in weekly shows. He was nicknamed "Shakespeare" because he brought to camp a trunkload of books, including a fifteen-volume set of William Shakespeare's works, and performed Hamlet's soliloquy in one of the camp shows.

In 1917, Hart became the dramatic counselor at Brant Lake Camp; there he wrote comedy acts for small-time vaudeville shows. While he was there, Arthur Schwartz (who later composed "That's Entertainment" and "Dancing in the Dark") heard some of Hart's lyrics and took a job at Brant Lake Camp in order to meet Hart and work with him on camp productions. While working at Brant Lake in the summers, Hart also worked for United Plays, a reading and translating company associated with the Shubert theaters. Between 1920 and 1925, he translated and adapted French and German plays and Viennese operettas. Notably, he translated *Die Frau im Hermelin* by Jean Gilbert as "The Lady in Ermine," which was never published or produced but from which he adapted material to use in *Dearest Enemy*. He also is recognized to have done part of what is now the standard translation of Ferenc Molnár's *Liliom* (pr., pb. 1909; English translation, 1921), although he did not receive credit. Schwartz claims that Hart also wrote lyrics for three songs by Billy Rose for which he did not receive credit or royalties. Hart was working in both instances for salary, and his material became the property of the employer.

In 1919, he was introduced to Richard Rodgers by a friend who knew that Rodgers was looking for a lyricist. Hart was twenty-three, Rodgers sixteen. The two collaborated on a number of amateur shows. One of their early songs, "Any Old Place with You," was purchased by Lew Fields for *A Lonely Romeo* (pr. 1919); this was their first song performed on Broadway. While Hart (and later Rodgers, too) was at Columbia University, he and Rodgers collaborated on musicals produced in New York hotel ballrooms. These amateur university productions were often clever enough to attract theatergoers and critics; they provided excellent training for potential theatrical talent.

Rodgers and Hart created more than twenty-five musicals before becoming professionals. The partners were unable to sell any of their work to Broadway producers for about four years. Hart was continuing to translate and Rodgers was considering changing his career goal when Rodgers was offered the chance to write songs for *The Garrick Gaieties*, and he insisted on having Hart as lyricist. They were not paid for this work, but the show was on Broadway, produced by the Theatre Guild, and attended by professional critics. The show, intended for two performances, was so original and witty that it received rave notices and was extended for a six-month run. The hit of the show was the Rodgers and Hart song "Manhattan," which established their reputations on Broadway. Their first big success, however, was "My Heart Stood Still," which was written for the British show *One Dam Thing After Another* (pr. 1927). Its popularity preceded their return to the United States,

and the song was then introduced to Broadway in *A Connecticut Yankee*. After that hit production, with few exceptions, Rodgers and Hart's musicals enjoyed one success after another.

After the Crash of 1929 depressed Broadway production, the songwriting team worked in Hollywood periodically in the early 1930's. Their film experiences, particularly when working with Rouben Mamoulian, taught them much about enhancing their story with music and making songs a part of the dialogue. These were ideas that they had already used in such musical dramas as *A Connecticut Yankee*. Innovations in the use of song in the motion picture *Love Me Tonight* prompted improvements in the music of the great Rodgers and Hart Broadway shows of the late 1930's and early 1940's. Motion-picture production techniques, however, were frustrating to them, being so different from their ingrained Broadway techniques. They were unhappy with the long periods of inactivity enforced by studio contracts, with the arbitrary and unexpected rejection or substitution of songs, and with the cancellation of entire film projects deemed noncommercial. They missed their customary participation with their Broadway colleagues in other aspects of stage production: interpreting, staging, choreographing, revising, and directing. When they read "Whatever happened to Rodgers and Hart?" in the Los Angeles *Examiner*, they were convinced that they should return to Broadway.

Drinking had already become a problem for Hart. Indeed, when Hart began his collaboration with Rodgers at age twenty-three, Rodgers's mother had predicted that Hart would not live to be twenty-five. Hart grew up in a fun-loving family. His father had plenty of money most of the time, and the family lived in large New York apartments and had two maids, a chauffeur, and a footman. Max Hart enjoyed living well and indulging his sons. Although Frieda Hart was a good housekeeper, she never minded disruptions caused by her sons and their numerous friends, who made the home a center for games, parties, poetry readings, and dramatic and musical performances. From childhood, Hart developed a taste for high living, conviviality, and incessant activity. He inherited a small size: He was only five feet tall, and his brother was only two inches taller. Furthermore, his head was slightly large for his body, so that he had a somewhat dwarfish look. Although people said they did not notice his size and proportions because his personality was so charming, he remained sensitive about his appearance all of his life. Still, Rodgers recalled that Hart was actually handsome, with animated features and warm brown eyes. When he was young, his father unstintingly gave him money for dates and treating his friends, and it is possible that his father's largess taught him an unintended lesson—that he could gain love and friendship only by paying for them. Certainly he delighted throughout his life in picking up the check for whatever group he was with or even for everyone in the room.

Hart's friend Mel Shauer, however, believed that Hart's drinking was an attempt to quiet the incessant, restless activity of his brain. As boys, Hart and his friends joked that his vertical growth was held down by the size of his brain. He read voraciously, was fluent in three languages, loved conversation and entertaining, and kept constantly on the move, motoring, attending the theater, the opera, the ballet. George Balanchine, commenting about Hart's quick mind, said that whatever was needed on a show Hart would do in a moment, and then he would be off doing something else. He had a certain intuition about what techniques and what talents would work. He was described as "impish" and "puckish," and he might disappear in the middle of a conversation. He loved to tease and laughed easily and readily. His vocabulary was immense and expressive. As far as anyone knew, he never used a rhyming dictionary. He was a perfectionist about lyrics and shows.

Whatever the reason, Hart's drinking increased during the 1930's, although it did not yet interfere with his work. After he and Rodgers returned from Hollywood, they wrote the songs for eight of their greatest musicals. For four of these, they also coauthored the librettos. These were the years of *On Your Toes*, *Babes in Arms*, *I Married an Angel*, *The Boys from Syracuse*, and what is now considered Rodgers and Hart's masterpiece, *Pal Joey*. Hart, however, became increasingly undependable; he would disappear and be inaccessible for lengthening periods of time. Rodgers

sometimes had to track him down and stay with him to get a lyric written. Hart would not discipline himself to write until a rehearsal simply could not proceed until he did. Still, he would turn out brilliant lyrics under these adverse conditions.

By the onset of the 1940's, Hart's alcoholism was becoming a serious detriment to his work. After *By Jupiter*, Hart no longer wished to work with Rodgers, and he went to Mexico to avoid the pressure of doing *Oklahoma!* (pr. 1943) because he did not like the original play. When he returned, although in ill health, he was enthusiastic about working with Rodgers again on an adaptation of Henry Fielding's *Tom Jones* (1749), but he was unable to carry it out. Rodgers had already begun working with Oscar Hammerstein II. The former partners did collaborate on a 1943 revival of *A Connecticut Yankee*, and Hart's last song was "To Keep My Love Alive," a new one for that production. Its quality and critical acclaim proved that his lyric ability was still unimpaired. He developed pneumonia after attending the opening of the revival on November 17, and died at Doctors Hospital on November 22, 1943.

ANALYSIS

"Amusing, breezy, contagious, energetic, fresh, gay, impudent, joyful, sophisticated, unhackneyed, versatile, witty, youthful, zestful"—such are the critical reactions to the works of Rodgers and Hart. Perhaps Lorenz Hart's failure to grow up physically and emotionally, a failure that destroyed him personally, was also what gave his lyrics and plots those fun-loving qualities that contributed to his success professionally. Youthful vitality and wit are the first characteristics common to all the shows of Rodgers and Hart. Hart evidenced a satiric turn of mind from his earliest attempts at writing, and he kept it until his death; Rodgers commented that Hart "really didn't know how not to be clever." All their plots, those they wrote and those they set to music, were witty satires, in which Hart's irreverent lyrics could play their role.

Another characteristic of Rodgers and Hart's shows is their variety. Both partners believed in avoiding formulas, other people's or their own, and in never doing the same thing twice in a row—or twice at all, if possible. Subject matter for their shows includes anything from grand opera, the Depression, and long-distance bicycle racing to Freudian dreams, Chinese eunuchs, and Amazons. In the six librettos that they wrote themselves, there is a somewhat more consistent use of show business themes. Nevertheless, they made a deliberate policy of turning to a story quite different from whatever they had just completed, no matter how successful. For example, the political satire *I'd Rather Be Right* was followed by the fantasy *I Married an Angel*, which was followed in turn by the Shakespearean farce *The Boys from Syracuse*.

A third important characteristic of Rodgers and Hart's artistry was their effort to make the musical comedy a more completely integrated musical drama, in which the songs advanced the plot and portrayed character. As youngsters, both were impressed with the Kern-Bolton-Wodehouse musicals, in which the plots were not episodic or situational but were motivated by the characters, and the songs were not interludes but were part of the drama. Both writers wished to emulate and indeed surpass what they had admired. Their first Broadway comedy, *Dearest Enemy*, was such a drama, and the history of their songs and librettos is the history of improvements in song as drama.

DEAREST ENEMY

Dearest Enemy was based on an incident in U.S. history: Some ladies of New York entertained the officers of British general William Howe's staff with cakes and ale, enabling American forces to make a strategic retreat. The show was turned down by several producers who could not imagine the commercial success of a musical based on American history. Rodgers and Hart, however, could see the possibilities of an element of sexual enticement in the delay of the British, and the situation allowed them to counterplay a genuine love affair between a young American girl and a British officer against a strategic flirtation by an older woman. Two contrasting love songs were used to emphasize the differences between these relationships: "Here in My Arms" and "Old Enough to Love." Tired of the traditional love ballad, typically a stock love song with little appropriateness to the singer, the composers were looking for new ways to sing about

love. "Old Enough to Love" allowed two variations on the theme: First, it was a love song between mature adults rather than ingenues, and second, it ironically used a tender lyric as a medium for a harsher emotion. (The latter was a technique that Rodgers and Hart used again in many later shows.) Furthermore, Hart suited the dialect of each song to the character singing it. In translating "The Lady in Ermine" a few years earlier, he had researched the eighteenth century, and in writing *Dearest Enemy* he was able to draw on this research in creating dialogue and lyrics that suggested the period. *Dearest Enemy* was one of the first musical comedies to achieve such authenticity. In general, comedy had simply placed a modern story in period costumes and settings. Besides the period dialect, Hart also used simple, ingenuous language for the girl's song and more complex, sophisticated language for the woman's. Thus he began his adaptation of lyric to the portrayal of dramatic character. *Dearest Enemy* also introduced the type of spunky, resourceful females that typically populate Rodgers and Hart musicals.

PEGGY-ANN

Although *The Girl Friend* was one of Rodgers and Hart's most popular and profitable productions, it did not add a great deal to their growth as artists. *Peggy-Ann* was the next significant step in their career. Based on a popular play, *Tillie's Nightmare*, in which the heroine had a series of comic dreams, the Rodgers-Hart-Fields team reinterpreted the dreams as Freudian fantasies. It was one of the first musical comedies to use Freudian theory. It also made use of a non-Broadway, balletic style of dancing, which along with the music was an integral part of the dream action. The dream, in turn, constituted the main plot, for the frame story was simply a young girl's coming to terms through her fantasies with the unromantic realities of her everyday life. In accordance with the Freudian background, the songs featured sexual innuendo to a degree unusual for the time, as in "A Little Birdie Told Me So" and "A Tree in the Park."

CHEE-CHEE

Chee-Chee, Rodgers and Hart's worst flop, was nevertheless one of their most daring experiments. It was based on a story about a young Chinese man who is trying to avoid inheriting his father's office as Grand Eunuch; the subject of castration was even more daring than the Freudian content of *Peggy-Ann*. The comedy did not appeal widely to critics or audiences. Indeed, the satiric treatment of the subject impressed critics as tasteless and sophomoric, at best. This reception was vastly different from the raves Hart usually received for his witty words. Nevertheless, *Chee-Chee* integrated music and drama more completely than did any other Rodgers and Hart musical. So completely did the music become a part of the dialogue that only six songs had titles, compared with between ten and fifteen songs in most musicals. Most of the music consisted of snatches of songs and brief bits of musical dialogue interwoven in the progress of the plot. If the story of *Chee-Chee* had been more palatable to the public, it might have become one of Rodgers and Hart's most highly admired works, but even its failure taught the partners several important lessons: first, that music alone cannot make an unpopular subject acceptable; second, that having at least one and preferably more popular favorites among the songs is almost essential to the success of a musical comedy; third, that it is possible to achieve a nearly complete integration of music and drama; and, fourth, that they had not yet mastered that art. As a result of *Chee-Chee*'s failure, the next five Rodgers and Hart shows were far less venturesome. On the other hand, without the failure, the partners might not have been so receptive to some of the lessons that they learned from motion-picture techniques.

FILMS PROVIDE TECHNIQUES

The Depression took Rodgers and Hart to Hollywood, which was less affected by hard times than Broadway had been. They did not enjoy working on films, but they were impressed by the technique by which a song was made to seem a natural extension of the dialogue; they were to use this technique in many of their subsequent stage shows. In *Love Me Tonight*, they also adapted the musically accompanied preliminary dialogue into a form they called "rhythmic dialogue" or "musical dialogue," a form of nonmelodic singing that they used again, as did many other musical comedy writers. For example,

the technique was very useful in *My Fair Lady* (pr. 1956) and *Camelot* (pr. 1960) for Rex Harrison and Richard Burton, neither of whom had singing voices. A camera that moved about as a song was playing very likely gave Hart the idea for using the reprise to show character development. In *Love Me Tonight*, the camera moved across seven characters whistling or singing "Isn't It Romantic?" Three different sets of lyrics presented three different attitudes toward love. Hart had the reprise of "There's a Small Hotel" in *On Your Toes* serve a similar purpose. Later, he extended the technique to emphasize plot and character change. In *Pal Joey*, for example, Vera's reprise shows she is no longer "Bewitched, Bothered, and Bewildered." Another lesson came from Mamoulian, director of *Love Me Tonight*, who insisted that Rodgers write not only the songs but also all the background music, in order to achieve musical coherence throughout the film. What was true of musical coherence might also be true of literary coherence, and it was after this experience with Mamoulian that Rodgers and Hart began to write their own books. The ones they wrote themselves—the products of their fully matured talents—are accounted the best of their collaborations.

ON YOUR TOES

On Your Toes, the first of their books, did not have a very original plot, but it did bring together all that Rodgers and Hart had learned from their twenty-three years of collaboration. It was a fairly standard show-within-a-show plot, but it made ballet as well as song an essential part of the plot and characterization. The story concerns a former vaudeville dancer with classical yearnings, who becomes involved with a ballet company, fumbles traditional ballet in a comic travesty of classical dance forms, but finally introduces a jazz ballet in which his style succeeds very well. The ballet serves as the climax to the story, and not merely in the traditional "would-be star makes good" sense: In a confusion of identity, two gangsters are trying to shoot the hero, and at the conclusion of the jazz ballet performance, he signals the orchestra to continue playing so that he can keep on dancing and avoid being a stationary target for their guns. Meanwhile, his girlfriend calls the police, who arrive at the moment he becomes too exhausted to continue dancing. Thus, the satiric ballet, the jazz ballet, and the songs advance the plot and show the hero realizing his abilities.

BABES IN ARMS

Babes in Arms was a return to the type of joyous revue that had succeeded so well in the 1920's. There is not much to be said about the book, which Rodgers and Hart wrote this time without a collaborator. It is, however, notable that not one or two but five of their greatest songs came from this one show: "Where or When," "My Funny Valentine," "The Lady Is a Tramp," "Johnny One-Note," and "I Wish I Were in Love Again." Their songwriting skills had obviously reached an apex at this time, along with their dramatic skills.

I MARRIED AN ANGEL

I Married an Angel was a triumphantly witty account of an angel trying to adapt to the ways of this faulty world. In this show and in *By Jupiter*, all their dramatic and lyric skills came together in what are still among the most memorable productions of musical comedy entertainment.

PAL JOEY

It was *Pal Joey*, however, that made the greatest impact on the Broadway musical tradition. The idea of doing this cynical, gritty show instead of the usual lighthearted comedy was suggested to them by John O'Hara, who wrote the book, and Rodgers and Hart were quick to see its possibilities. *Pal Joey* concerns a small-time nightclub entertainer who aspires to greater success. He is a handsome but unscrupulous opportunist who lies and seduces his way nearly to the top. Through a liaison with Vera, a wealthy older woman who is willing to pay for sexual excitement, he acquires his own nightclub. On a threat of blackmail, however, she quickly becomes disenchanted and drops him. There are no likable characters in this story, with the exception of a girl whom Joey attracts at the beginning of the play but drops in favor of Vera's money. The satire in *Pal Joey* is bitter and disillusioned instead of gay and youthful, and the wit is found in the slangy dialogue and sharp repartee. The show songs are designed to be trite and shoddy, as one might expect in a low-class nightclub, and even the love songs are hypocritical mockeries of genuine love songs. Critical reception of *Pal Joey* was mixed. Some critics found it distasteful; others recognized it as excellent drama and a trailblazing departure from the Broadway traditions. The latter critical opinion was supported by the show's success. It had a long initial run and an even longer run on its revival in 1952, when it also won the New York Drama Critics Circle Award for Best Musical. As Rodgers observed, "The shoe . . . forced the musical comedy theatre to wear long pants for the first time."

Indeed, this witty observation perhaps best sums up Rodgers and Hart's contribution to the musical theater. Along with Ira Gershwin and Cole Porter, Hart set a new standard in musical comedy for poetic excellence, semantic and phonetic appropriateness, and perfect rhythmic phrasing of lines to his partner's music. Together, Rodgers and Hart, with their collaborators, dared to break the mold of musical theater tradition and open the way to the great musical dramas of the 1950's and 1960's.

BIBLIOGRAPHY

Green, Stanley. *The World of Musical Comedy*. 4th rev. ed. New York: DaCapo Press, 1980. The chapter "Rodgers and Hart" demonstrates how the two formed the first composer-lyricist team for which each man received equal recognition. Green provides standard biographies and traces the two artists' development, show by show. Index, illustrations, and a complete listing of musicals with credits and discography.

Hart, Dorothy. *Thou Swell, Thou Witty: The Life and Lyrics of Lorenz Hart*. New York: Harper and Row, 1976. A poignant biography by Hart's sister-in-law, lovingly but truthfully telling the story of Hart's tortured life. It includes several reminiscences by friends and associates such as Irving Berlin and Richard Rodgers. Contains the lyrics for more than ninety of Hart's songs, a complete listing of his plays and films with the songs he wrote for each, and numerous personal and theatrical photographs.

Lerner, Alan Jay. *The Musical Theatre: A Celebration*. New York: McGraw-Hill, 1986. Lerner provides biographical and critical information about Hart from the perspective of a friend in the business. Of special interest is his description of Hart's physical challenges and how they caused the melancholy and pessimism in his life and lyrics. Illustrations, bibliography, and index.

Marx, Samuel, and Jan Clayton. *Rodgers and Hart.* New York: G. P. Putnam's Sons, 1976. This popular, anecdotal double biography of Rodgers and Hart chronicles their lives, collaboration, and achievements. It contrasts Rodgers's storybook life with Hart's sad and troubled life and examines how those difficulties influenced their work. Illustrations and index.

Nolan, Frederick W. *Lorenz Hart: A Poet on Broadway.* New York: Oxford University Press, 1994. A biography of Hart that covers his life and work. Bibliography and index.

Secrest, Meryle. *Somewhere for Me: A Biography of Richard Rodgers.* New York: Random House, 2001. This biography of Rodgers covers his years of association with Hart. Bibliography and index.

Carol Croxton,
updated by Gerald S. Argetsinger

MOSS HART

Born: New York, New York; October 24, 1904
Died: Palm Springs, California; December 20, 1961

PRINCIPAL DRAMA

The Hold-up Man, pr. 1923
Jonica, pr. 1930 (with Dorothy Heyward)
Once in a Lifetime, pr., pb. 1930 (with George S. Kaufman)
Face the Music, pr. 1932 (libretto; music by Irving Berlin)
As Thousands Cheer, pr. 1933 (revue; music by Berlin)
The Great Waltz, pr. 1934
Merrily We Roll Along, pr., pb. 1934 (with Kaufman)
Jubilee, pr. 1935 (music by Cole Porter)
You Can't Take It with You, pr. 1936, pb. 1937 (with Kaufman)
I'd Rather Be Right, pr., pb. 1937 (with Kaufman; score by Richard Rodgers and Lorenz Hart)
The Fabulous Invalid, pr., pb. 1938 (with Kaufman)
The American Way, pr., pb. 1939 (with Kaufman)
The Man Who Came to Dinner, pr., pb. 1939 (with Kaufman)
George Washington Slept Here, pr., pb. 1940 (with Kaufman)

Lady in the Dark, pr., pb. 1941 (music by Kurt Weill)
Winged Victory, pr., pb. 1943
Christopher Blake, pr., pb. 1946
Light Up the Sky, pr. 1948, pb. 1949
The Climate of Eden, pr. 1952, pb. 1953 (adaptation of Edgar Mittelholzer's *Shadows Among Them*)

OTHER LITERARY FORMS

Moss Hart is known primarily for his plays. He also achieved success as a screenwriter; among his best-known screenplays are those for *Gentleman's Agreement* (1947) and *A Star Is Born* (1954). In 1959, Hart published his autobiography, *Act One*, which was made into a film in 1963, as were many of his plays. Finally, Hart published a handful of miscellaneous articles on theater subjects.

ACHIEVEMENTS

Moss Hart was one of the great comic playwrights of American drama. In works such as *Once in a Lifetime*, *You Can't Take It with You*, and *The Man Who Came to Dinner*, he gave the theater some of its most amusing moments. He was awarded the Roi Cooper Megrue Award in 1930 for *Once in a Lifetime* and in

1937, with George S. Kaufman, the Pulitzer Prize for *You Can't Take It with You.*

Because Hart's best works are his collaborations with Kaufman, his critical stature will always be obscured by that of the older, more famous dramatist. It would be a mistake, however, to think of Hart as simply Kaufman's collaborator. Kaufman worked with several partners in his career, including such talents as Ring Lardner, Alexander Woollcott, and Edna Ferber, but none of them produced such fine results with Kaufman as Hart did, nor were any of the Kaufman and Hart plays the work of one man more than the other. Theirs was a true collaboration, with each man contributing equally to the final product. Moreover, Hart's solo works, such as *Lady in the Dark,* with its innovative staging and probing of psychological conflicts, show that he could create significant drama on his own.

In addition to playwriting and screenwriting, Hart directed such plays as Alan Jay Lerner and Frederick

Moss Hart speaks at a press conference at the Savoy Hotel in London in 1958. (Hulton Archive by Getty Images)

Loewe's *Camelot* (pr. 1960) and *My Fair Lady* (pr. 1956); the latter won for Hart a Tony Award.

BIOGRAPHY

Moss Hart was born in the Bronx section of New York, the son of Barnett Hart, a cigar maker who was left without a trade when a cigar-making machine was developed. The family survived as best they could, but Hart's early life was dominated by a sense of poverty. The two most important influences in his childhood were his grandfather and his Aunt Kate. These impractical, domineering people, though a great drain on the family finances, were the only sources of color and vitality for the young Hart. Aunt Kate, an avid theatergoer, introduced Hart to the world of drama, which formed in his mind a desire to escape from his squalid surroundings via the glittering stage.

At the age of seventeen, Hart got his first theatrical job as office boy to Augustus Pitou, a touring-show producer known as "the King of the One-Night Stands." While reading plays that were submitted to Pitou, Hart began writing a play of his own, replete with the sentimental and hackneyed elements of those he had read. He presented the play to Pitou, who was enthusiastic about it and agreed to produce it. Entitled *The Hold-up Man,* it opened in Rochester in 1923 and flopped.

The failure of his first play also cost Hart his job. He worked as a director for little theater companies and as an actor, once playing the role of Smithers in Eugene O'Neill's *The Emperor Jones* (pr. 1920) to glowing reviews. He spent his summers as a social director in various resort camps. During this time, he still nursed a desire to write plays in the manner of O'Neill and George Bernard Shaw, but he learned that his talent lay not with serious drama but with light comedy. In the late 1920's, Hart began writing a comedy in the manner of his idol, the comedic writer George S. Kaufman, dealing with the advent of sound in motion pictures. Producer Sam Harris agreed to do the play only if Hart collaborated on it with Kaufman himself. The play, *Once in a Lifetime,* after dubious early showings and several major rewrites, was a smash hit and marked the beginning of one of the greatest writing teams in American drama. It also marked Hart's escape from the poverty of his early years. After reading the enthusiastic reviews of *Once in a Lifetime*, Hart moved his family from their Bronx apartment to rooms in the fashionable Edison Hotel.

In the following years, Hart wrote some of his best plays. These included musicals with Irving Berlin and Cole Porter and further collaborations with Kaufman, including their greatest works, *You Can't Take It with You* and *The Man Who Came to Dinner*. With the money from these plays, Hart was able to buy a large country estate in the Poconos, yet he found that success did not solve all of his problems. In 1934, he began seeing a psychiatrist and came to believe that he was too dependent on Kaufman. Finally, Hart, acting on the advice of his psychiatrist, broke off his collaboration with Kaufman, although the two remained friends.

Hart's first play after the break, *Lady in the Dark*, proved that he could write without Kaufman's support. He went on to write other successful plays but never with the popularity of his work with Kaufman. In 1945, he married actress Kitty Carlisle; they had two children. After World War II, Hart wrote some of his finest screenplays, including *Gentleman's Agreement* and *A Star Is Born*. Hart served as president of the Dramatists Guild from 1947 to 1955 and of the Authors League from 1955 to 1961. Hart also returned to directing, winning a Tony Award in 1957 for *My Fair Lady*. In 1961, he died of a heart attack.

Analysis

Those who approach the plays of Moss Hart as literary products to be analyzed and placed in some dramatic category will be disappointed. Hart wrote his plays to give pleasure to large crowds. He learned early in his career that his talent lay in witty light comedy rather than serious drama. Though his plays satirized every institution of the time, from the New Deal to the motion-picture industry, their prevailing tone is one of wild spoofing, not serious criticism. This is not to dismiss Hart as merely a pleasant hack. With Kaufman, he created some of America's funniest plays. Hart stayed within the limits of the popular theater, though he did try to extend those limits. As a

result, he created superior entertainment that continues to delight audiences even today.

Once in a Lifetime

A good example of the Kaufman and Hart comedy is their first collaboration, *Once in a Lifetime*. It concerns three down-and-out vaudeville actors: the likable-but-dumb straight man George Lewis; the tough, clever May Daniels; and the enterprising Jerry Hylands. They sell their act and travel to Hollywood in the first days of sound pictures to open an elocution school for movie actors, who must now be heard as well as seen. The school, operating in Glogauer Studios, is a failure, but when George repeats some unflattering comments on motion pictures in general and Glogauer in particular (comments that he has picked up from Lawrence Vail, a disgruntled playwright hired by Glogauer to turn out film scripts), he is taken by the producer to be an outspoken genius and is made studio supervisor. With Jerry and May as his assistants, George oversees the production of *Gingham and Orchids*, a movie that has the script of another film, a set only half-lit, and the noise of George incessantly cracking Indian nuts throughout the sound track. To everyone's surprise, the film becomes a financial and critical success, and George is the hero of the hour. Jerry and May, realizing that George does not need their guidance in order to get along in pictures, return to New York to get married.

There is scarcely any facet of Hollywood in the early 1930's that *Once in a Lifetime* does not ridicule, whether it is the "early De Mille" architecture, vapid movie columnists, temperamental German directors, or stars who cannot act. Many of the authors' opinions are put into the mouth of Lawrence Vail, a representative figure among the successful Broadway dramatists who went to Hollywood to write for the studios and then were given nothing to do. (Vail's part was played in the original run of *Once in a Lifetime* by Kaufman himself.) According to Vail, the film industry is "the most God-awful thing I have ever run into."

Given the topsy-turvy nature of movies, the success of George Lewis is perfectly logical. George takes everything at face value and therefore is perfect in a business that runs on hype. He is incompetent and thus is able to excel in a business that cannot tell the difference between a good film and a bad one. Ironically, Jerry and May decide to leave Hollywood, even though it was Jerry who suggested that they go there and May who came up with the elocution idea. Hart and Kaufman imply that intelligence has no value in pictures.

The major targets of the play's satire are stupidity and vanity, rather than the darker flaws revealed in such a work as Nathanael West's *The Day of the Locust* (1939). The only hint of such depths in *Once in a Lifetime* comes when Jerry denies any involvement with the making of *Gingham and Orchids* because the movie looks initially like a flop, but Jerry's duplicity is soon atoned for when he nobly tells off Glogauer and gets himself fired. Even Glogauer, though he is as inaccessible and arbitrary as an Eastern potentate, is not genuinely corrupt; he is simply a silly, vulgar little man puffed up with money. The play does not try to expose Hollywood as much as it tries to have fun at its expense. The film industry was not particularly offended by the play and even made it into a movie.

THE MAN WHO CAME TO DINNER

Another example of Kaufman and Hart's good-natured humor is *The Man Who Came to Dinner*. The main character, Sheridan Whiteside, was largely based on the authors' friend Alexander Woollcott, radio commentator, wit, and man of letters. Whiteside slips on a piece of ice on the doorstep of the Stanleys, a prominent family in Mesalia, Ohio, and fractures his hip. Convalescing for several weeks in the Stanleys' home, he turns their lives inside out. He does his radio broadcasts from the library, sends and receives messages from all over the world, and populates the house with murderers, penguins, and other exotic creatures. Worse, he encourages the Stanleys' son and daughter to direct their lives independently of their parents' wishes and blackmails Mr. Stanley into submitting. Whiteside also tries to break up and then restore the romance between his secretary, Maggie Cutler, and Burt Jefferson, a Mesalia reporter. Just as the play ends and Whiteside is leaving, he slips on the ice again and announces that he is suing Mr. Stanley for $350,000.

The comedy in *The Man Who Came to Dinner* is based on the fantastic characters that populate it, the greatest of whom is Whiteside. In fact, the personality of Whiteside, his eccentricities, his talent for insults and witty repartee, his scheming mind, and his carefully concealed streak of compassion dominate the play and win the audience to him in spite of his boorishness and his impositions on the Stanleys. Whiteside is supported in his comic antics by such figures as the nymphomaniac actress Lorraine Sheldon, the playwright Beverly Carlton (based on Noël Coward), and the movie clown Banjo (based on Harpo Marx). These figures are part of the great world in which Whiteside lives, the world of such figures as Mahatma Gandhi, Walt Disney, and H. G. Wells, all whom provide some of the play's fun.

YOU CAN'T TAKE IT WITH YOU

Hart and Kaufman's finest play is probably *You Can't Take It with You*, which to some extent resembles *The Man Who Came to Dinner*. Both plays portray the collision of a group of wild eccentrics with a respectable family. The eccentrics in *You Can't Take It with You* are Martin Vanderhof and his family. Martin, called Grandpa in the play, was once a businessman who felt that he was missing the fun of life. For thirty-five years, he has dedicated his life to enjoying himself, and his family has done likewise. While Grandpa collects snakes and attends commencements, his daughter Penny Sycamore writes plays; her husband, Paul, makes fireworks; their older daughter, Essie Carmichael, studies ballet with an expatriate Russian tutor; and Essie's husband, Ed, plays the xylophone and operates a small printing press. The only "normal" member of the group is Penny's younger daughter, Alice, a secretary for a Wall Street firm who has fallen in love with Tony Kirby, Jr., her boss's son. Even though she loves the members of her family, and even though Tony himself is charmed by them, Alice fears that their somewhat anarchistic lifestyle will clash with the values of the ultra-respectable Kirbys.

Alice's fears are justified when the Kirbys arrive for dinner on the night before they are expected. A drunken actress flirts with Mr. Kirby, Penny tells Mrs. Kirby that the Spiritualism in which she devoutly believes is fake, and Kolenkhov, the Russian dance instructor, wrestles with Mr. Kirby. At the evening's climax, federal agents, suspecting Ed of subversive activities, arrest everyone just as Paul's fireworks go off. Alice and Tony's wedding seems doomed until Grandpa explains his way of life to Mr. Kirby. According to Grandpa, the quest for material success and social acceptance should never be pursued at the cost of personal happiness. When Tony reminds his father that he once dreamed of being a trapeze artist and later a saxophone player, the elder Kirby becomes reconciled to the Vanderhofs' unusual ways and his son's refusal to follow in his footsteps, and he joins his future in-laws for dinner.

You Can't Take It with You contrasts two families who have in different ways achieved the American Dream. The Kirbys, through hard work, sobriety, and duty, have attained wealth and respectability. The cost of their success has been the sacrifice of their personal happiness. Mr. Kirby suffers from indigestion and regrets that he has lost his youthful ideals. Mrs. Kirby takes solace in the fashionable humbug of Spiritualism and, in a game of word-association, responds to "sex" with "Wall Street." Tony feels that his parents do not understand him and plans to leave his father's firm to become a bricklayer. Even Mr. Kirby's hobby of growing orchids has been taken up as a refuge from business cares and not for its own sake. His remarks concerning the orchids center on the time it takes to grow one, as the Kirbys' lives are, in general, centered on time and schedules.

The Vanderhofs are another side of the American Dream, the individualistic side of the Dream represented by Walden Pond. They do exactly as they like and live off the money from Grandpa's land. They have no desire to make money or to win other people's respect, only to be happy and to make others happy. Their hobbies are taken up spontaneously; Penny became a dramatist only because a typewriter was accidentally delivered to the house. Their meals are largely impromptu affairs. The house is shared by various people, including Donald, the boyfriend of their housekeeper Rheba, and Mr. De Pinna, who used to be their iceman. While the Kirbys live by the clock, time is not quite real to the Vanderhofs; when Alice asks the time, her family's replies are confused.

Like many radical individualists in American history, the Vanderhofs are at odds with the government. Not only is Ed thought to be a subversive, but also Grandpa is harassed for not paying his income tax. Mr. Kirby calls their way of life Communism, but it is really closer to the American ideals of life, liberty, and the pursuit of happiness than is his own way of life. The play does not really answer the arguments against living exactly as one pleases, nor is it meant to do so. What attracts the audience to the Vanderhofs is not the cogency of their arguments but the delight in seeing people do things that others would like to do and the charm with which the Vanderhofs succeed. In this sense, the play is an American pastoral presenting an idyllic world to relieve the frustrated Kirbys in the audience. Interestingly, *You Can't Take It with You* was not originally as successful in England as in the United States; perhaps its celebration of individualism was too extreme for English tastes.

LADY IN THE DARK

No survey of Moss Hart's work would be complete without notice of his solo plays, of which the best is *Lady in the Dark*. Lacking the slapstick situations and witty dialogue of his best work with Kaufman, the play examines the psychological state of Liza Elliot, editor of *Allure*, the most popular women's magazine in the country. Liza has reached the top of her profession yet is going through a psychological crisis. She undergoes analysis to find the cause of her problems, and her psychological states are dramatized in a series of fantasy sequences. In one sequence, Liza is a glamour girl adored by every man, even though in real life she tries to appear totally unglamorous. The fantasy ends when a man resembling Charley Johnson, the advertising manager, paints a portrait of Liza as she really appears.

As Liza's analysis continues, she realizes that her problems relate to a sense of inferiority as a woman, derived from an unconscious belief that she can never be as beautiful as her celebrated mother, who died when Liza was young. Therefore, Liza tries to make other women beautiful while remaining plain herself. Her lover, Kendall Nesbitt, is a married man for whom Liza does not have to compete. When Kendall gets a divorce, Liza does not wish to marry him. Similarly, she has a brief romance with Randy Curtis, an insecure movie star who looks to Liza as a mother figure rather than as a lover. Only when Liza understands her neurosis can she love the man who really loves her, Charley Johnson, who appears in her fantasies as her nemesis. Charley sees behind Liza's unfeminine pose and infuriates Liza until she realizes that he is the only man who can fulfill her needs as a woman.

Lady in the Dark, with its concern for psychological complexity, innovative dramatic techniques, and serious theme, was a marked departure from Hart's previous work, although similarities to the earlier plays exist. Like *Once in a Lifetime* and *You Can't Take It with You*, this play explores the somewhat dubious value of success. Hart comments in his autobiography, *Act One*, that, as sweet as success is, it does not bring personal happiness and indeed often makes unhappiness more noticeable and difficult to bear. Just as success has given no joy to Mr. Kirby, so it has given none to Liza, since it is largely a flight from her unconscious fears. Only when Liza faces these fears can she achieve happiness.

Hart's technique of alternating fantasy and reality in the play through the use of four revolving stages is a brilliant and innovative method for dramatizing what occurs in Liza's mind. Especially effective is the device of using people from the real world as characters in Liza's dreams. Thus, Charley Johnson exposes Liza's self-imposed plainness in her glamour fantasy, exactly as he destroys her unglamorous competent-executive image in reality. The technique's effectiveness is weakened, however, by having Dr. Brooks explain what the fantasies mean rather than having the audience interpret them on its own.

Lady in the Dark demonstrated that Hart could work alone as well as in collaboration and in serious drama as well as in comedy, yet it also proves that his real talent lay in comedy, for although the play received popular and critical praise, it does not have the bite or sparkle of *The Man Who Came to Dinner* or *You Can't Take It with You*. It is good serious drama but not superlative entertainment, and it

is for his or her superlative work that any artist should be remembered.

OTHER MAJOR WORKS

SCREENPLAYS: *Flesh*, 1932; *The Masquerader*, 1933; *Broadway Melody of 1936*, 1935; *Frankie and Johnny*, 1936; *Winged Victory*, 1944; *Gentleman's Agreement*, 1947; *Hans Christian Andersen*, 1952; *Prince of Players*, 1954; *A Star Is Born*, 1954.
NONFICTION: *Act One*, 1959.

BIBLIOGRAPHY

Bach, Steven. *Dazzler: The Life and Times of Moss Hart*. New York: Alfred A. Knopf, 2001. A biography that covers the personal and professional life and works of Hart. Includes portrayals of many of the people with whom Hart worked, including George S. Kaufman. Examines his marriage with Kitty Carlisle.

Goldstein, Malcolm. *George S. Kaufman: His Life, His Theater*. New York: Oxford University Press, 1979. In this standard work on the Broadway theater of the period, Goldstein gives an insightful portrait of Kaufman as a man and an artist. Offers an interesting account of the period of collaboration between Kaufman and Hart. Contains numerous illustrations.

Miller, Daryl H. "Like Father, Like Son? Sort Of, as He Stages Moss Hart's Plays, Son Chris Learns from His Late Legend of a Dad." *Los Angeles Times*, October 17, 1999, p. 50. Christopher Hart, son of Moss Hart and Kitty Carlisle Hart, discusses his father and the theater on the occasion of a staging of *You Can't Take It with You*.

Mordden, Ethan. *The American Theatre*. New York: Oxford University Press, 1981. This chronicle of the American stage from its beginnings to 1980 discusses Hart's 1936 play *You Can't Take It with You* in the context of the Broadway stage in the midst of the Depression years. According to the author, a major feature of American drama in the 1930's was its interpretations and affirmations of the democratic system.

Anthony Bernardo,
updated by Genevieve Slomski

GERHART HAUPTMANN

Born: Obersalzbrunn, Silesia (now Szczawno Zdrój,
Poland); November 15, 1862
Died: Agnetendorf, Germany (now Jagniatków,
Poland); June 6, 1946

PRINCIPAL DRAMA

Vor Sonnenaufgang, pr., pb. 1889 (*Before Dawn*,
1909)

Das Friedensfest, pr., pb. 1890 (*The Reconciliation*,
1910)

Einsame Menschen, pr., pb. 1891 (*Lonely Lives*,
1898)

Die Weber, pb. 1892, pr. 1893 (*The Weavers*, 1899)

Kollege Crampton, pr., pb. 1892 (*Colleague
Crampton*, 1929)

Der Biberpelz, pr., pb. 1893 (*The Beaver Coat*, 1912)

Hanneles Himmelfahrt, pr. 1893, pb. 1894 (*The
Assumption of Hannele*, 1894)

Florian Geyer, pr., pb. 1896 (English translation,
1929)

Die versunkene Glocke, pr., pb. 1896 (*The Sunken
Bell*, 1898)

Fuhrmann Henschel, pr., pb. 1898 (*Drayman
Henschel*, 1913)

Schluck und Jau, pr., pb. 1900 (*Schluck and Jau*,
1929)

Michael Kramer, pr., pb. 1900 (English translation,
1911)

Der rote Hahn, pr., pb. 1901 (*The Conflagration*,
1929)

Der arme Heinrich, pr., pb. 1902 (*Henry of Auë*,
1929)

Rose Bernd, pr., pb. 1903 (English translation,
1913)

Elga, pr., pb. 1905 (wr. 1896; English translation,
1906)

Und Pippa tanzt!, pr., pb. 1906 (*And Pippa
Dances!*, 1907)

Die Jungfern vom Bischofsberg, pr., pb. 1907 (*The
Maidens of the Mount*, 1929)

Kaiser Karls Geisl, pr., pb. 1908 (*Charlemagne's
Hostage*, 1915)

Griselda, pr., pb. 1909 (English translation, 1929)

Die Ratten, pr., pb. 1911 (*The Rats*, 1929)

Gabriel Schillings Flucht, pr., pb. 1912 (wr. 1905-
1906; *Gabriel Schilling's Flight*, 1929)

The Dramatic Works of Gerhart Hauptmann, pb.
1912-1929 (9 volumes)

Festspiel in deutschen Reimen, pr., pb. 1913
(*Commemoration Masque*, 1929)

Der Bogen des Odysseus, pr., pb. 1914 (*The Bow of
Odysseus*, 1917)

Winterballade, pr., pb. 1917 (*Winter Ballad*, 1929)

Der weisse Heiland, pr., pb. 1920 (*The White
Savior*, 1924)

Indipohdi, pb. 1920, pr. 1922 (English translation,
1925)

Peter Brauer, pr., pb. 1921 (wr. 1910)

Veland, pr., pb. 1925 (English translation, 1929)

Dorothea Angermann, pr., pb. 1926

Spuk: Oder, Die schwarze Maske und Hexenritt,
pr., pb. 1929

Die goldene Harfe, pr., pb. 1933

Hamlet in Wittenberg, pr., pb. 1935

Ulrich von Lichtenstein, pr., pb. 1939

Die Tochter der Kathedrale, pr., pb. 1939

Iphigenie in Delphi, pr. 1941, pb. 1942

Magnus Garbe, pb. 1942, pr. 1956 (wr. 1914-1915)

Iphigenie in Aulis, pr. 1943, pb. 1944

Agamemnons Tod, pr. 1946, pb. 1948

Die Finsternisse, pr., pb. 1947 (wr. 1937)

Elektra, pr. 1947, pb. 1948

Herbert Engelmann, pr., pb. 1952 (wr. 1924)

OTHER LITERARY FORMS

Gerhart Hauptmann was a versatile and prolific
author who wrote in every genre. In addition to his
plays, on which his reputation is chiefly based, he
wrote novels and stories, epic and lyric poetry, and
essays.

ACHIEVEMENTS

Gerhart Hauptmann became immediately famous
when his first play, *Before Dawn*, was produced in

Berlin in 1889. In his later years, he became a national figure, as the celebrations organized for his later birthdays demonstrate. He was praised as the greatest German writer, reaching his peak during the Weimar Republic. His plays were not only popular with the intelligentsia but also had a wide appeal.

Outside Germany, Hauptmann is known primarily for his realistic plays. He was awarded the Grillparzer Prize three times, in 1896, 1899, and 1905, and he was nominated for the Schiller Prize (Kaiser Wilhelm II refused to grant it to him because of what he perceived to be the revolutionary nature of Hauptmann's plays). Among the honorary doctorates that Hauptmann received were ones from Oxford in 1905, Leipzig in 1909, and Columbia University in 1932. In 1912, Hauptmann was awarded the Nobel Prize in Literature, followed in 1932 by the Goethe Prize—a sign of his solid international reputation.

BIOGRAPHY

Gerhart Johann Robert Hauptmann was born on November 15, 1862, in Obersalzbrunn, Silesia. His grandfather on his father's side had been a weaver in his youth and was later an innkeeper; his father, Robert Hauptmann, owned a hotel. Silesia forms the background and the inspiration for many of Hauptmann's works. He said that his works were rooted in his native soil and that he drew his strength as a writer from this region. Between 1874 and 1878, Hauptmann attended *Realschule* (high school) in Breslau, but he was a mediocre student. In the years following his graduation, he shifted from one possible vocation to another. In 1880, after working as an agricultural apprentice on an uncle's farm in Silesia, he enrolled in art school in Breslau, intending to become a sculptor. In 1882 and 1883, he studied at the University of Jena, where he heard lectures on history, philosophy, literature, and archaeology. He also heard lectures by the most important disciple of Charles Darwin in Germany, Ernst Haeckel, whose theories were important in Hauptmann's early plays.

In 1883, Hauptmann visited the Mediterranean and lived several months in Rome as a sculptor. Like Johann Wolfgang von Goethe, whom Hauptmann emulated, he was fascinated by the Mediterranean

world, and it had a strong impact on his writing. In 1884 and 1885, he studied for two semesters at the University of Berlin, during which time he attended many theatrical performances. Indeed, Hauptmann thought for a while that he would like to become an actor, but then decided to devote himself to writing. In 1885, he married Marie Thienemann and moved with her to Erkner, near Berlin, where they stayed until 1889. While there, Hauptmann became involved with writers in the naturalist movement, which was very strong in Germany at the time. In 1891, Hauptmann moved with his family to Schreiberhau in Silesia. Tensions began to arise between Hauptmann and Marie, and in 1894, she left with their children for the United States. Hauptmann followed to fetch his family back; although this trip ended in reconciliation, the tensions were not resolved. In 1901, Hauptmann moved to the "Wiesenstein," a house that he had had built in Agnetendorf in Silesia. Although he spent only a few months each year there, this was his

Gerhart Hauptmann (© The Nobel Foundation)

home for the remainder of his life. Hauptmann liked to spend the winter on the Italian Riviera, the spring and fall in the Southern Alps, and the summer on the Baltic island of Hiddensee. In 1904, Hauptmann divorced Marie and married Margarete Marschalk.

Hauptmann's visit to Greece in 1907 was a turning point in his life. Greece exerted a strong influence on his works, especially on his epic poetry. For the Goethe centenary in 1932, Hauptmann visited the United States once more to lecture on Goethe. During this visit, he was awarded an honorary doctorate at Columbia University and was received at the White House by President Herbert Hoover. Hauptmann's last years were filled with pessimism, a quality that pervades his works of this period. As the political situation in Germany worsened, Hauptmann increasingly withdrew from public life. Although he disapproved strongly of the Nazi regime, he made no public stand against it, and unlike many writers who chose exile when the Nazis gained power, Hauptmann remained in Germany. His apparent tolerance for the regime aroused scorn and led some of his friends to break off their friendship with him. The Nazis found it useful for a writer of his stature to remain in Germany; his presence seemed to give legitimacy to the regime (on Hauptmann's eightieth birthday, Adolf Hitler sent congratulations). Hauptmann did not leave his native Silesia when the Russians occupied it, but remained in Agnetendorf (now part of Poland), where he died on June 6, 1946.

ANALYSIS

Gerhart Hauptmann's great strength as a writer is his talent for portraying reality and for creating lifelike characters. Throughout his works, Hauptmann displayed more interest in characters than in language or plot. He was more concerned with human beings than he was with ideas. In his "Dramaturgie" (dramaturgy), he notes that the more complex the plot, the less important the characters. If the plot is simple, however, the characters can be richer. The protagonists of Hauptmann's early plays are often passive sufferers who are acted on by events beyond their control. Suffering is a central theme in Hauptmann's works, a suffering that is sometimes caused by social conditions but is often the result of simply being alive. Typical of all Hauptmann's plays is his deep compassion for those who are poor, oppressed, and suffering.

The plays that Hauptmann wrote early in his career are mostly realistic, often with close affinities to naturalism. In them, Hauptmann gives a critical portrait of German society before World War I. Gradually, he began to incorporate dreams, myths, and symbols into his realistic plays in an attempt to illuminate the inner life of his protagonists. As he developed as a playwright, he moved even further from the realism of his early work, although, in his later years, he occasionally returned to his realistic style. He began to draw his material from diverse sources, from legend; fairy tales; folklore; the supernatural; classical, Norse, and Aztec myths; and history. Some of his plays are symbolic and neoromantic, some are historical, and others concern the artist's conflict with society.

Throughout his life, Hauptmann was interested in William Shakespeare, Goethe, and Dante, and he often derived plots for his plays from these writers, as his Hamlet studies demonstrate. After his journey to Greece in 1907, Hauptmann wrote that when he was walking in the Greek countryside, he sensed the presence of the ancient gods. Fascinated more by the Dionysian than the Apollonian, he incorporated more classical allusions into his works. Greek mythology is prominent in several of his plays, including his last work, the *Atriden-Tetralogie* (the tetralogy of the Agamemnon legend), which is composed of *Iphigenie in Aulis*, *Agamemnons Tod*, *Elektra*, and *Iphigenie in Delphi*. Mysticism plays a frequent role in Hauptmann's works, a mysticism that is rooted in his native Silesia (the home of such mystics as Angelus Silesius and Jakob Böhme). Hauptmann's journey to Greece also gave him a new understanding of tragedy. He wrote that human sacrifice was the bloody root of tragedy. In Greece, he saw that tragedy consisted of "enmity, persecution, hatred and love, . . . fear, need, . . . villainy, murder, incest and slaughter."

Although Hauptmann preferred his later, more poetic, dramas, his early plays, up to *The Rats*, are the ones that are best known and most frequently performed. These are the works that made Hauptmann internationally famous. Hauptmann had a gift for portraying reality faithfully, for creating living, convincing characters. When he wrote poetic or symbolic drama, he lost contact with his Silesian roots, which often resulted in a weakening of his creativity. The verse in his later plays is often insipid (Hauptmann was more interested in character than in language) and does not compare with the vigor of the dialect used in his realistic plays (he noted that he wanted to give dignity back to dialect). It was his realistic plays that established his reputation as a writer.

Hauptmann's early plays were hailed as masterpieces of naturalism, the literary movement that developed in Europe in the second half of the nineteenth century. Naturalist authors tried to record reality faithfully. According to Arno Holz, one of the theorists of German naturalism, art had the tendency to become nature again. He formulated his theory thus: Art equals nature minus x, the x representing the ability of the author to represent reality. As this formula shows, Holz and the other naturalists tried to emulate scientific methodology in their writing. They strove for an objective portrayal of life and tried to avoid all subjectivity, which, they thought, falsified reality. Following Darwin, the naturalists perceived humankind to be determined by heredity and environment. In the drama, this belief resulted in passive heroes who succumbed helplessly to their predetermined fate. Because the naturalists believed that the environment was so important in shaping people, they tried to improve harsh social conditions. Their works were socially critical and focused on the problems of modern civilization, especially on the ugliness and poverty of life in the big cities. Most of the naturalists wrote literature that was politically committed, and many of them were socialists. In their works, the naturalists tried to avoid beauty because they thought that it did not truly reflect reality. (Hauptmann was, in fact, criticized for making the love scene between Helene and Loth in *Before Dawn* too beautiful. He defended himself by remarking that he could not help it if nature was also beautiful.)

The German naturalist movement produced much theory but few enduring creative works. Many of Hauptmann's concerns in his early plays show his close connection to naturalist circles. His social criticism, his depiction of poverty, his discussion of hereditary and environmental factors, all show his affinity with naturalism. Yet his plays are not naturalistic in the strict sense. Naturalist playwrights tried to present a "slice of life." They avoided conventional dramatic structure, monologue, and suspense because they thought these were unnatural; instead, they attempted to cut out a piece of "real" life to show on the stage. Hauptmann, however, was a craftsperson whose plays are carefully structured; his plays are far removed from the reportage favored by strict naturalists. Indeed, Hauptmann's critical distance from naturalism is particularly evident in one of his most naturalistic plays, *Before Dawn*. In this play, the protagonist, Alfred Loth, is a proponent of naturalistic views, yet Hauptmann treats both Loth and his theories critically.

BEFORE DAWN

Before Dawn, which is a social drama, was the second play (Henrik Ibsen's *Gengangere*, pb. 1881; *Ghosts*, 1885, was the first) to be performed at the Freie Bühne, the influential naturalist theater in Berlin. The production immediately made Hauptmann famous. Hauptmann had originally intended to call the play "Der Säemann" ("The Sower"), an allusion to the ideas of freedom that Loth sows, but Arno Holz encouraged him to change the title. In a letter to Hauptmann, Holz praised the play, calling it the best ever written in the German language. The premiere, on October 20, 1889, aroused fierce debate. Some, like Holz, praised the play for its depiction of social problems, while others attacked it for what they saw as its immorality. Such controversy typically surrounded many of Hauptmann's realistic plays.

As the play opens, Alfred Loth, who was modeled on Alfred Plötz, a social reformer and Utopian thinker who was a friend of Hauptmann, arrives in a Silesian mining village to investigate the terrible economic conditions of the coal miners. By chance, Loth's old friend Hoffmann has married into the Krause family. Like the other peasants in the region, the Krause family has suddenly become very rich because of the coal found on their land. Hauptmann gives a vivid portrait of the members of this family. The sudden wealth that the family has acquired has corrupted them. Krause's second wife commits adultery. Krause, a hopeless alcoholic, tries to seduce his daughter Helene when he is drunk. Helene's sister Martha, who is married to Hoffmann, is also an alcoholic. Her alcoholism has led to the death of her three-year-old son, and in the course of the play, she gives birth to another baby who is stillborn, again the result of her addiction. Hoffmann, the son-in-law, is a ruthless businessperson who has taken advantage of the naïve peasants to gain control of their coal. As long as it is to his advantage, Hoffmann is pleasant, but this pleasantness masks a basic brutality in his nature. When Hoffmann learns that Loth is going to be studying mining conditions in the area, he tries to persuade Loth to leave by offering him money. He does not want the conditions for which he is responsible exposed. Hoffmann also tries to seduce his sister-in-law Helene.

Loth's views on alcoholism and eugenics emerge during his first dinner at the Krause home. He talks about the devastating impact that alcohol has on modern life: He cites statistics from the United States about the deaths and suicides it causes and tells of the many wives and children who are forced into poorhouses because of alcoholism. Loth himself refuses to touch alcohol. The effects of alcohol, he says, are not limited to the present; they also undermine the health of future generations. Loth says that he has inherited healthy genes and is determined to pass these genes on to his future children. When he attacks alcohol so strongly, Loth has no inkling that the Krause family suffers from this very problem.

In a later conversation with Helene, Loth expresses his social beliefs. He attacks a system in which the workers who work long hours are poor and hungry while those who are rich live in comfort without having to work. According to Loth, the values of the state are completely perverted. As an example, he cites the state's attitude toward killing: In peacetime, it is a crime, while in war, it is a heroic deed. Loth wants to change society radically; he wants to abolish sickness and poverty and all other social ills. In his fight for better conditions, he is willing to make whatever sacrifices are needed in order to help those who are oppressed. In keeping with his progressive ideas, he is also strongly for the emancipation of women.

Helene, the only member of the Krause family who has escaped the corruption caused by sudden wealth, is captivated by Loth's ideas, and she encourages him in his work. She sees Loth as her savior and declares her love for him. The audience knows, however, that this relationship is doomed. Once Loth discovers that Helene's family suffers from alcoholism, he will not marry her because of his views on eugenics.

In the last act, Doctor Schimmelpfennig, who is also an old friend of Loth, tells Loth about the alcoholism in the family. Predictably, Loth flees from Helene, abandoning his work on the economic conditions of the miners. He is even too cowardly to explain his reasons for his flight in person—he leaves her a note instead. Loth's sudden departure destroys all hope that Helene had of escaping from the sordid conditions that surround her, and in despair she kills herself. Although Loth intends to help people, his theories blind him, and when a concrete situation faces him, he fails as a human being. The title of the play is ironic. The new day that Loth's theories of freedom could have brought into being does not dawn.

THE WEAVERS

The Weavers, Hauptmann's fourth play, made him famous throughout Europe. Although the play actually has no political bias (Hauptmann said that the play was social, not socialist), it was interpreted as revolutionary by the police and the conservative press, and the Berlin police banned public performances of the play for two years. When it was finally performed at the Deutsches Theater in Berlin, Kaiser Wilhelm II canceled his box there in protest. Vladimir Ilyich Lenin also saw the play as a revolutionary statement. Most of the Socialists who saw the play, however, were disappointed because there was no mention of class struggle and Hauptmann did not offer political solutions to the problems that he depicted. Instead, it seemed to them as though Hauptmann merely wanted to arouse pity for the weavers' plight. Hauptmann in fact said that he hoped to move the wealthy audience to pity the weavers.

The play concerns a revolutionary subject—the rising of the famished Silesian weavers in 1844 in protest against their economic conditions. The play was inspired in part by stories that Hauptmann heard from his father about his grandfather's experiences as a weaver in his youth. Hauptmann also read Alfred Zimmermann's *Blüte und Verfall des Leinengewerbes in Schlesien* (1885; growth and decline of the linen industry in Silesia), in which he found the revolutionary song "Das Blutgericht" that he used in the play. To make the play as authentic as possible, Hauptmann wanted to see for himself the region in which the weavers still lived. In the early part of 1891, he made two trips to the Eulengebirge in Silesia. He visited the homes of weavers, where he was moved by the workers' extreme poverty. Yet Hauptmann thought that the weavers had dignity and nobility, despite their poverty. The first version of the play, *De Waber*, was written in Silesian dialect. Hauptmann then wrote a second version in which he made the dialect more comprehensible for non-Silesian audiences.

The protagonist of the play (which is the first mass drama in the German language) is a whole class—the weavers. The play shows how the weavers suffer from economic conditions that are beyond their control: The manufacturers exploit them, and the more efficient weaving methods in the new factories result in an oversupply of linen and therefore depress the weavers' wages. This powerful social drama had an impact on many socially critical dramas in Germany in the twentieth century.

The play opens with a mass scene in which Hauptmann vividly depicts the weavers' misery. They are delivering the cloth that they have woven at home to the manufacturer Dreissiger. Their work has physically broken them: Their bodies are bent from leaning over the loom, and their eyesight is ruined from long hours of work in dark houses. All are hungry and worn out by the worries of their daily lives; all are despairing and embittered, especially the mothers who have starving children to feed. The weavers plead for advances on their meager wages, complain about their lot, and one young boy falls unconscious from lack of food. One weaver, Bäcker, protests against the pittance that they earn for their long hours of work—he calls it shabby charity, not wages—but he is thrown out. At the end of the act, Dreissiger de-

fends himself by declaring that he is not responsible for the weavers' poverty, and he promises to employ more weavers, albeit at even lower wages.

The second act takes place in the hut of the cottager Ansorge. Here Hauptmann shows how the poverty and despair he depicts in the first act affect one family, which represents all the weavers' families. The hut is dilapidated, there is no food, and the family members are emaciated and pale. Old mother Baumert wants to die. She cannot work because she is ill, and she believes herself to be a burden to her family. Moritz Jäger, who has just returned home from his military service, sees the conditions that the weavers are forced to endure, and he tries to persuade them to change their lot. He preaches rebellion, arguing that dogs in the cities live better than the weavers and that the manufacturers live a life of luxury from the profits that they make from the weavers. The revolutionary song that the weavers sing depicts life as torture. By singing the song, the weavers express their pent-up anger and despair. The song brings them together as a group and helps them to articulate emotions that they otherwise would not be able to express. It helps them to see the causes of their misery and convinces them that things must be changed.

The last three acts show how the rebellion develops. The third act depicts other classes who oppress the weavers, including the rich peasants and the foresters, and the fourth act shows the rebellion in progress. As the weavers gather angrily outside Dreissiger's house, where his friends have gathered to play whist, Dreissiger becomes afraid and flees with his family through a back door. When Pastor Kittelhaus goes out to talk with the weavers, he is mistreated. Once the weavers discover that Dreissiger has fled, they begin a frenzy of destruction and plunder. The last act takes place in the home of the weaver, old Hilse. In this act, Hauptmann contrasts two different courses of action: those who try to help themselves by fighting against their fate and old Hilse, who refuses to join in the rebellion, preferring instead to put his faith in God. At the end of the play, old Hilse is killed by a stray bullet while he sits at his loom. Ironically, the only one who does not take part in the rebellion dies.

Hauptmann shows both positions, involvement and noninvolvement, positively and negatively. Hauptmann treats the weavers, on the whole, sympathetically, showing compassion for their suffering, a compassion that is particularly evident when Luise, Hilse's daughter-in-law, justifies her reasons for supporting the rebellion. She is a mother who has been driven to fury by the poverty that has caused all of her children to die of hunger. Yet Hauptmann also criticizes the rebellion because it leads to excesses and plunder; he does not advocate rebellion as a course of action to effect social change. Despite the initial success of the rebellion, it is doomed. Rather than being an organized revolution, it is a spontaneous uprising that the soldiers will later crush.

Hauptmann also shows the negative and positive aspects of Hilse's position of noninvolvement. Hilse is deeply religious and absolutely moral and honest (when his granddaughter finds a silver spoon, taken during the plundering of Dreissiger's house, old Hilse makes her take it to the police, even though the family could sell it and buy much-needed food). He sets his hopes on the afterlife, believing that renunciation in this world will lead to rewards in Heaven. For him, as for mother Baumert, religion offers the consolation of a better life after death. Yet because Hilse is old and his life is basically finished, it is easier for him to accept suffering as his lot. Unlike his daughter-in-law Luise, who is concerned about the fate of her still unborn children, old Hilse does not look to the future. Hilse's social resignation, caused by his religious beliefs, is easily manipulated by the capitalists. Indeed, religion is one of the pillars of the state: Pastor Kittelhaus preaches obedience and acceptance of one's allotted place. In the hands of people such as Kittelhaus and Dreissiger, religion becomes perverted into an instrument of reaction.

The ending of the play is open. Hauptmann shows that Hilse and the weavers are both right and wrong, and he does not give any political solutions for their suffering (Hauptmann thought that drama was most effective when it was politically impartial). Instead, he gives a compassionate portrayal of poverty, of people driven by despair and bitterness to extremes. Although the play is not political, by depicting these events, Hauptmann indicts a society that tolerates the existence of such conditions.

ROSE BERND

Rose Bernd, like many of Hauptmann's works, is based on an actual event. In April, 1903, Hauptmann served as a member of the jury at the trial of Hedwig Otte, a young agricultural laborer, who was accused of infanticide and perjury. Hauptmann was convinced that the woman committed these deeds in a period of confusion and despair and therefore was not responsible for her actions. During the jury's deliberations, Hauptmann managed to convince others of his views, and the woman was acquitted. Originally, Hauptmann had intended to give a broad depiction of peasant life in the play, but then he decided to cut out anything that did not directly pertain to the play's central theme. The theme of a woman driven by desperation to murder her illegitimate child is a common theme in German literature. In this play, Hauptmann sets the well-known Gretchen theme (from Goethe's *Faust: Eine Tragödie*, pb. 1808, pb. 1833; *The Tragedy of Faust*, 1823, 1828) in a Silesian peasant milieu. This play is one of the strongest that Hauptmann ever wrote. In it, he describes the suffering of a woman whose ruin is caused by love.

Rose Bernd, the protagonist of the play, is a hardworking, faithful, proud, and passionate human being. Like most of Hauptmann's female characters, she follows her emotions rather than her mind. Since the death of her mother, Rose has been a mother to her younger sister. At the beginning of the play, Hauptmann stresses her joy, her sheer love of living. Like Rose, Flamm, a local landowner and magistrate with whom she is having an affair, is physical and sensual. She has no prospect of marrying Flamm because he has a wife who is an invalid. Rose tries to break off her affair with Flamm and marry the bookbinder August Keil, to whom she has been engaged for some time and whom her father wants her to marry. When she realizes that she is expecting Flamm's child, a quick marriage to Keil seems to her the only solution to her situation. Flamm, however, tries to delay the marriage. Other complications also arise. The machinist Streckmann finds out about Rose's affair with Flamm and blackmails her. When she goes to him to plead for mercy, he rapes her, and later claims in public that she offered herself to him. Keil and father Bernd overhear these remarks, and Keil fights with Streckmann, losing an eye in the fight. Bernd institutes legal proceedings against Streckmann. At the trial, Rose perjures herself, denying that she has slept with anyone because, as she tells Flamm's wife, she is ashamed.

Hauptmann describes Rose's growing isolation from everyone. Some try to help her. Mrs. Flamm guesses that Rose is pregnant and offers help, which Rose cannot accept because Flamm is the father of the child. Even when Mrs. Flamm discovers that her husband is the father, she is still willing to help. Keil also guesses the truth, but since he loves Rose, it does not matter to him; although he is ugly and physically weak, he has an inner beauty and humaneness. Others, however, refuse to help. Flamm deserts her in jealousy when he discovers that she has slept with Streckmann (he prefers to believe Streckmann's version of what happened, rather than Rose's). Father Bernd, who, like Keil, is deeply religious, thinks only of the shame that Rose has brought on her family—he has no sympathy for his distraught daughter but fears only that his own reputation in the community will suffer.

As the play progresses, Rose changes from a joyful person into one who is despairing and persecuted. She becomes entrapped in lies and deceit, which are utterly foreign to her otherwise open, honest nature. On her return from committing perjury in court, Rose goes into labor, delivers the child herself, and then, almost crazed with grief, kills the newborn baby, confesses, and is arrested. Throughout the play, Hauptmann compassionately and sensitively shows the conflicts and growing despair that destroy Rose's inner harmony and lead her to commit perjury and infanticide.

OTHER MAJOR WORKS

LONG FICTION: *Der Narr in Christo Emanuel Quint*, 1910 (*The Fool in Christ: Emanuel Quint*, 1911); *Die Insel der grossen Mutter*, 1924 (*The Island of the Great Mother*, 1925).

SHORT FICTION: *Fasching*, 1887; *Bahnwärter Thiel*, 1888 (*Flagman Thiel*, 1933); *Der Apostel*, 1890; *Lohengrin*, 1913; *Parsival*, 1914 (English translation, 1915); *Der Ketzer von Soana*, 1918 (*The Heretic of Soana*, 1923); *Phantom*, 1922 (English translation, 1922); *Der Schuss im Park*, 1941; *Das Märchen*, 1941; *Mignon*, 1947.

POETRY: *Anna*, 1921; *Die blaue Blume*, 1927; *Till Eulenspiegel*, 1927; *Der grosse Traum*, 1942; *Neue Gedichte*, 1946.

NONFICTION: *Griechischer Frühling*, 1908; *Um Volk und Geist*, 1932.

BIBLIOGRAPHY

Marshall, Alan. *The German Naturalists and Gerhart Hauptmann: Reception and Influence.* Frankfurt am Main: Peter Lang, 1982. A look at naturalism in Germany and the influence it had on Hauptmann's works. Bibliography.

Maurer, Warren R. *Gerhart Hauptmann.* Boston: Twayne, 1982. A basic biography of Hauptmann that provides information on his life and analysis of his works. Bibliography and index.

_____. *Understanding Gerhart Hauptmann.* Columbia: University of South Carolina Press, 1992. This biographical study of Hauptmann describes the German dramatist's life and provides insights into his works. Bibliography and index.

Mellen, Philip A. *Gerhart Hauptmann: Religious Syncretism and Eastern Religions.* New York: Peter Lang, 1984. An examination of the role of religion in the works of Hauptmann. Bibliography and index.

Osborne, John. *Gerhart Hauptmann and the Naturalist Drama.* Amsterdam: Harwood Academic, 1998. A look at the naturalist theater in Germany and Hauptmann's place within it. Bibliography and index.

Skrine, Peter N. *Hauptmann, Wedekind, and Schnitzler.* New York: St. Martin's Press, 1989. A look at twentieth century German drama, with emphasis on Hauptmann, Frank Wedekind, and Arthur Schnitzler. Bibliography.

Sprengel, Peter, and Philip Mellen, eds. *Hauptmann Research: New Directions.* New York: Peter Lang, 1986. A study providing critical analysis of the literary works of Hauptmann. Bibliography.

Jennifer Michaels

VÁCLAV HAVEL

Born: Prague, Czechoslovakia; October 5, 1936

PRINCIPAL DRAMA

Autostop, pr., pb. 1961 (with Ivan Vyskočil)
Zahradní slavnost, pr., pb. 1963 (*The Garden Party*, 1969)
Vyrozumění, pr. 1965, pb. 1966 (*The Memorandum*, 1967)
Ztížená možnost soustředění, pr., pb. 1968 (*The Increased Difficulty of Concentration*, 1969)
Spiklenci, pr. 1974, pb. 1977
Žebrácká opera, pr. 1975, pb. 1977 (adaptation of John Gay's comic opera; *The Beggar's Opera*, 1976)
Audience, pr. 1976, pb. 1977 (English translation, 1976)
Horský hotel, pb. 1976, pr. 1981
Vernisáž, pr. 1976, pb. 1977 (*Private View*, 1978; also as *Unveiling*)
Protest, pr. 1978 (English translation, 1980)
Largo desolato, pb. 1985 (English translation, 1987)
Pokouśení, pb. 1986 (*Temptation*, 1988)
Asanace, pb. 1987, pr. 1989 (*Redevelopment: Or, Slum Clearance*, 1990)
Selected Plays, 1963-1983, pb. 1992
The Garden Party and Other Plays, pb. 1993
Selected Plays, 1984-1987, pb. 1994

OTHER LITERARY FORMS

Known primarily as a playwright, Václav Havel has also written criticism and poetry, plays for radio and television, and essays. Some of his poems (*Antikódy*, 1966) and essays, as well as his first two plays, were published as *Protokoly* (1966). His radio play *Anděl Strážny* was broadcast in 1968, and his television play *Motýl na anténě* appeared in West Germany in 1975. Perhaps Havel's most important essay is "Moc bezmocnych" (1978; "The Power of the Powerless," 1983).

By far Havel's most significant nondramatic work, however, is *Dopisy Olze, 1979-1982* (1985; *Letters to Olga*, 1988), which was first published in a somewhat different version in German translation, in 1984, as *Briefe an Olga: Identität und Existenz—Betrachtungen aus dem Gefängnis*. (The Czech version was issued in Canada by an émigré publisher.) The title of this remarkable book is misleading: Written in prison, these are not personal letters but rather wide-ranging reflections, tracing the author's intellectual and spiritual experience but anchored in harsh realities.

Another noteworthy nondramatic work is *Dalkovy vyslech* (1986; *Disturbing the Peace: A Conversation with Karel Hvížďala and Václav Havel*, 1990). Hvížďala, a noted Czech journalist in exile, wanted to interview Havel on his thoughts at turning fifty, but the politics of the time made it impossible to meet face to face. To work around this, Hvížďala sent written questions for reply. Havel's first attempt, answering in writing, came out too stiff and essaylike. Hvížďala was looking for a more conversational approach, so Havel turned to a tape recorder to capture oral responses, which Hvížďala subsequently transcribed.

ACHIEVEMENTS

Václav Havel is the most important Czech playwright of the second half of the twentieth century, acclaimed both in his native land and abroad. His early plays, which established his international reputation, are, as he has modestly said, "plays about bureaucrats." They are, however, much more than that: They are about the mechanism of power, about the dehumanization built into the very institutions that are supposed to serve humanity, about the prison built by the desiccated language of bureaucracy. The fact that he is enthusiastically received in the West suggests that bureaucracy has a momentum of its own and may well be yet another Frankenstein-like offshoot of modernity, whatever its ideological underpinnings may be.

That his plays were allowed to be staged at all is attributable to the relative liberalization or demoralization of the communist control of the arts in Czechoslovakia during the 1960's. Neither the import nor the relevance of Havel's work diminished in the harsher climate of the 1970's and 1980's. As Markéta Goetz-Stankiewicz, the leading Western critic of the Czech theater, has suggested, not all Havel's work has received its due in a world that would benefit from his insight into the roots of the continuing crisis of modernity. His plays offer the sad wisdom of an art born of suffering, tempered by the ironic self-awareness and black humor that he has identified as essential to the "Central European climate."

Havel was honored in 1969 with the Austrian State Prize for European Literature. Twice, in 1968 and 1970, he received the Obie Award. However, Havel's crowning achievement in the post-Soviet era has been in the field of politics. Shortly after the nearly bloodless collapse of the communist regime in Czechoslovakia, he became the nation's first democratically elected president. After the peaceable dissolution of the nation into the Czech Republic and Slovakia, the Czechs elected for him their president. His political work has earned for him numerous political awards, including the Averell Harriman Democracy Award, the Raoul Wallenberg Human Rights Award, and the Statesman of the Year award. He has received honorary degrees from numerous colleges and universities, including an honorary degree of doctor of philosophy from York University, Toronto, Canada, in 1982.

Václav Havel (Miloš Fikejz)

BIOGRAPHY

Václav Havel was born October 5, 1936, the son of a wealthy restaurateur and entrepreneur, Václav M. Havel, himself the author of a voluminous autobiography. Some of Prague's architectural landmarks were built by Havel's father, and an uncle was the owner of Barrandov Studios, the center of Czech filmmaking. Such illustrious connections, decidedly nonproletarian, were held against the young Havel in communist Czechoslovakia, making him ineligible for any higher formal education well into the 1960's.

On the other hand, as he was to note later, this very handicap forced him to view the world "from below," as an outsider—a boon to any artist.

After finishing laboratory assistant training, Havel began working in a chemical laboratory, attending high school at night; he was graduated in 1954. Between 1955 and 1957, Havel attended courses at the Faculty of Economy of the Prague Technical College. This was followed by military service and, finally, his work in the theater in Prague: first at the Theater Na Zábradlí and, from 1960, at the Balustrade.

His knowledge of the theater is truly intimate: He entered it as a stagehand, gradually moving to lighting, then to an assistant directorship, and finally becoming the *dramaturg*—that is, the literary manager—of the theater at the Balustrade. When, in the changed atmosphere of political liberalization, he was allowed to study dramaturgy, he took advantage of the opportunity, although he was already a full-fledged playwright and a literary manager, graduating in 1967.

Between 1967 and 1969, Havel became active as the chairman of the Circle of Independent Writers. This, as well as his work at the Balustrade, was prohibited by the authorities in 1969, when his plays were banned and his publications withdrawn from libraries. Officially, he ceased to exist as a Czech playwright.

During the first half of the 1970's Havel worked as a laborer in a brewery. In January, 1977, he reappeared in the public eye as one of the signatories and chief spokespeople of Charter 77, the courageous manifesto of the human rights movement in Czechoslovakia. As a result, he was imprisoned between January and May, 1977. In the same year, he wrote an open letter to Gustav Husák, the president of Czechoslovakia, and was arrested in January, 1978. Finally, after yet another arrest, in May, 1979, he was sentenced to four and a half years in prison. He was released in 1983, in poor health.

After his release, Havel was subject to intense police surveillance, but he managed to continue meeting with other dissidents and discussing politics. In 1989, he was arrested once again for political activity and was briefly imprisoned. However, on November 17 of that year, events transpired to thrust Havel into the forefront of politics. This was the sudden collapse of communist power in Czechoslovakia, known as the Velvet Revolution (a name derived from the 1960's alternative band The Velvet Underground, but also suggesting softness and civility, as opposed to the coarse brutality of most revolutions). In ten days marked by an astonishing absence of violence, the communist government gave way to a new democratically elected government, and Havel was elected its first president.

Over the next several years, Havel presided over the successful privatization of the Czechoslovakian economy, as well as the "Velvet Divorce" in which the Czech Republic and Slovakia peaceably parted ways to become independent countries, resolving their differences through legal negotiation instead of bloodshed. Unlike other notable dissidents to become their nations' first post-communist leaders, such as Lech Walesa of Poland or Zviad Gamsakhurdia of the Republic of Georgia, Havel proved to have long-term staying power. Even so, by the turn of the millennium, growing dissatisfaction with his administration had led to serious questions as to whether he would continue to be reelected.

Havel's personal life was turbulent throughout the 1990's. He had recurring medical problems, at least partly the result of damage to his health during his years in prison, although his bout with lung cancer was attributed to his heavy smoking. After the loss of his wife, Olga, to cancer, he married a movie actress, Dagmar Veškrnová, a move that opened him to heavy criticism from his opponents.

ANALYSIS

Václav Havel's plays appear in hindsight as crystallizations of the ambiguous time of relative liberalization in a monolithic totalitarian society. This may perhaps also be the reason for their success in the West: Czechoslovakia then, and the West both then and now, seem to share the mood of relativism, uncertainty, and ambiguity characteristic of any transitional period. Although it is a matter of speculation whether Western society is actually evolving toward full-scale socialism, Czechoslovakia at the time of Havel's greatest successes (between 1963 and 1968) was without any doubt moving toward a less pervasive socialism, at least as it is defined there. The monolith was cracked; the totalitarian machinery was breaking down, though still operating by fits and starts. This created a peculiar atmosphere, exploited by Havel to great effect: What was formerly unquestionably true and clear was suddenly being questioned. The leaders themselves encouraged such questioning by admitting past mistakes that included staged trials and real executions. The followers, on the other hand, could no longer be sure that the present party line would not change shortly and were thus inhibited from acting aggressively on the party's behalf. There were indeed further changes and new revelations of misdeeds. Thus, the political situation acted as a destabilizing force, motivating people to question not only it but also everything else. This was an intense time of debate, of discoveries—and of defeats as well.

THE GARDEN PARTY

Some of the questions Havel asked in *The Garden Party* could be formulated thus: Is it possible to adjust to the constantly changing policy emanating from above? If so, after all the maneuvering, is the human being still the same as before he started on the tortuous path of adjustment?

The Pludek family, middle-class, solid, and old-fashioned, fears that Hugo, their son, will not be able to make a successful career for himself in the confusing contemporary world with its contradictory signals. The Pludeks, survivors of a bygone era, manage to get by relying on routine, fortified by clichés that they keep repeating, as if trying to anchor themselves in a reality that keeps dissolving around them. In Havel's dialogue, the meaning is hilariously stripped from these clichés and proverbs by deft substitutions, so that while they still resemble proverbial sayings (for such is the form and context in which they are found), their content has been decanted from them, leaving behind an exotic sediment at once both grotesque and absurd. The result is not only absurd but also humorous and vitally meaningful on a higher level: It is immaterial whether the Pludeks' proverbs make sense because even perfect proverbs are irrelevant in the unstable world in which they live.

Hugo surprises his parents when, during and after a garden party, he penetrates an institution, learns its peculiar bureaucratic language, and turns this newly acquired knowledge against the institution and its representatives. His success is unexpected and phenomenal, but so is the price that he has to pay: He becomes a convert to the absurd and thoroughly relativist jargon of the institution, a jargon designed to hide the meaning of one's ideas, for one's commitment cannot be questioned if it is not clear what exactly one stands for. Thus, Hugo becomes an expert Inaugurator and Liquidator at the same time. When liquidation is in, he liquidates, but quickly, on noticing the slightest shift of policy, he begins to inaugurate, and so on. Thus, although Hugo is successful, he is no longer the same Hugo—indeed, his parents at first do not even recognize him. The parents themselves, however, are not immune to the contagion of the debased language, and, after a long harangue by Hugo, they accept him.

It is not necessary to point to the political allusions, because the play of necessity operates on a level of abstraction that universalizes the plight of Hugo and his parents. This quality shows Havel a worthy follower of the great masters of the Theater of the Absurd, Samuel Beckett and Eugène Ionesco, whom Havel helped to stage at the Balustrade.

THE MEMORANDUM

The Memorandum is, if anything, a further and quite logical extension of Havel's concern for the debasement of language. Here he expresses this concern through the brilliant satiric device of an artificial language, Ptydepe, which the bureaucracy decides to employ for all communications.

The introduction of the new language strikes terror, not unlike an unexpected change of political line. The question Havel asks is: What happens to an otherwise loyal bureaucrat who knows nothing about the impending introduction of Ptydepe? Can he adjust? Finally, as in the previous play: What is the price of such an adjustment? Thus, some of the concerns with which Havel dealt in *The Garden Party* reappear but in high relief because of the striking effect of the artificial language with its unearthly and perverse sounds, designed to be impossible to learn, and even if learned, impossible to use. Here science makes its entrance, for Ptydepe is a scientifically designed, perfectly rational language. This beautifully implies the "scientifically" designed society of socialism, in which—so the State claims—all the imperfections are caused by the survival of "prescientific" attitudes.

Alas, the converts to the scientific and unnatural Ptydepe are not immune to sudden political change, and no sooner do they "learn" Ptydepe, than another language appears, called Chorukor, based on a diametrically opposed premise: While Ptydepe is based on the principle of maximum differentiation among words, with words increasing in length as their frequency decreases (the word for wombat, for example, is more than three hundred letters long), Chorukor is based on the notion that words with related meanings should sound the same as well, with only slight variations to distinguish them from one another.

The protagonist of *The Memorandum*, Josef Gross, is a humanist battling the opportunist responsible for the introduction of Ptydepe. When Gross's chance to put his humanistic ideals to the test comes, however, he fails, having already accepted Balass, the careerist, and Ptydepe. When Maria, a girl in whom Gross is genuinely interested, is fired by Balass, Gross does not act, for this would mean countermanding Balass's instructions and making himself vulnerable. Gross's breakdown is a tragedy that contrasts with the prodigious ability to adjust found in a man such as Balass—a type that seems to predominate in bureaucracies. It is perhaps on this level, that of the depiction of "organization man," that the play is of most interest to audiences in the West.

THE INCREASED DIFFICULTY OF CONCENTRATION

After the success of these early plays, Havel made a departure of sorts with *The Increased Difficulty of Concentration*. Gone is the focus on bureaucracy and office intrigue but not Havel's preoccupation with language. Can language survive ethical relativism? Is it possible to have more than one personality: professional and private, with the latter subdivided further into husband and lover?

The protagonist, Dr. Huml, is a social scientist, a victim of the routine forced on him by circumstance and by his own choices. His behavior, robotlike and lacking in human feeling, is echoed by his tautological writings. It is very fitting that Dr. Huml, an intellectual, a member of the elite, becomes by the end of the play an unwitting collaborator in the dehumanizing policies to which he ostensibly objects. His writings and indeed his very life have had an alienating, dehumanizing effect, and it is only just that he in turn should become a guinea pig for others.

THE EXPERIMENTAL PLAYS

Havel's *Spiklenci* (the conspirators), *The Beggar's Opera*, and *Horsky hotel* (mountain resort) are of uneven quality because of their experimental nature and have thus been accorded less attention than his earlier plays. To be fair, one has to stress that two vital elements of the theater, the staging and the reaction of the audience, were no longer available to him, with the exception of *The Beggar's Opera*. Havel himself is not quite sure about *Spiklenci*, in which he deals with multiple conspiracies, moving from office intrigue to the shadowy world of revolutionary dictators, generals, and prisoners. This is a somber and unreliable world in which loyalty changes as unpredictably as the party line (or official language) did before. Havel is making a point here about the importance of the individual in history. The events of conventional history—the demonstrations, government

policies, and so on—are alluded to but always remain incidental and unimportant. The real history is conspiratorial. The implications are astounding: The role of the masses is that of extras; the revolution itself is a deal struck among a gang of power-hungry little people with few, if any, redeeming features. Most ominously, the system of conspiracy neutralizes the good man and gives an unfair advantage to the ambitious clod, the darling of absolute power.

The Beggar's Opera, yet another version of John Gay's masterpiece *The Beggar's Opera* (pr., pb. 1728), suggests that competing establishments, competing centers of power, are essentially the same beneath their surface enmity, as are their victims: the weak, the innocent, the defenseless. The play deserves to be staged, but perhaps Bertolt Brecht's treatment in the 1920's casts such a spell that few dare to stage Havel's version, whatever its merit.

Horsky hotel is another matter. Here the problem lies in an experiment that involves, as before, the use of repetition, nonsense, and dislocation based on interchangeability of characters and consequent lack of plot, development, and structure. The play is difficult to read, but may be salvaged, as Markéta Goetz-Stankiewicz suggested, as a film script.

THE AUTOBIOGRAPHICAL PLAYS

Havel returned to the stage—in the West, if not in his own country—with three one-act plays: *Audience*, *Private View*, and *Protest*. The plays met with great acclaim in the New York production in 1983 and were well received in Europe, Canada, and Australia as well. The popularity of these linked autobiographical plays, which differ considerably from Havel's early work, is particularly interesting given their genesis: They were originally conceived and performed as private entertainments for Havel's friends in Prague.

All three plays deal with the problems of a playwright, Vaněk, who like Havel is not allowed to publish in his country. In *Audience*, a brewery foreman asks the laborer-playwright Vaněk to inform on himself, since the boss is tired of writing police reports about him. In *Private View*, several friends attempt to bribe Vaněk to give up and make his peace with the regime because surrender pays so well. In *Protest*, Vaněk is called by an old acquaintance who has since accommodated the authorities but who now has a favor to ask. Ultimately, Vaněk refuses to accept the byzantine rationalizations by which men and women excuse their failure to take a stand.

Hugo, Gross, Huml, and Vaněk's tempters have lost or are about to lose something precious. Havel never spells out exactly what it is they are in the process of losing. He only tells the reader how that loss occurs. That seems sufficient in a world little aware of the existence of values that are precious enough to be preserved at any price. Havel's oblique reminder of their existence is a minor triumph in a major struggle in which he has acquitted himself as a master of his art and a hero of his nation.

TEMPTATION

Following his 1978-1983 period of imprisonment, Havel wrote a new play, drawing on the story of Dr. Faustus. *Temptation* tells the story of Dr. Henry Foustka, a scientist in a research institute, who is involved in various experiments of an ethically questionable nature. He also habitually treats his staff in a dehumanizing fashion and makes a great show of the idea that they are producing and protecting the Truth, even as all of them are constantly involved in idle chatter.

The devil is represented by one Fistula, an informer, who seeks to draw Dr. Foustka into his circle by mentoring Foustka in his investigation of black magic. The main action of the play deals with how Foustka struggles to cling to his respectability after his temptation, until he finally realizes that he is ruined and will be punished. Foustka claims that his dabbling in sorcery was solely to discredit it as unscientific. Fistula turns out to be a double agent, and the devil is the pride of the system that uses science for its own ends, a criticism of Soviet-supported and controlled communism. However, the ending of the play is left ambiguous, and the audience is never told precisely what manner of punishment will befall Foustka, since his final immolation onstage is a highly symbolic scene, not to be taken literally.

In leaving Foustka's precise fate unspecified, Havel gives the play its greatest strength because he leaves it up to the reader put the pieces together and realize that while the individual parts may be true, they add up to a lie. Even truth can become demoniac if it is instrumentalized and robbed of its own life.

OTHER MAJOR WORKS

POETRY: *Antikódy*, 1966.
TELEPLAY: *Motýl na anténě*, 1975.
RADIO PLAY: *Anděl Strážný*, 1968.
NONFICTION: *Dopisy Olze, 1979-1982*, 1985 (*Letters to Olga*, 1988); *Dalkovy vyslech*, 1986 (*Disturbing the Peace: A Conversation with Karel Hvížďala and Václav Havel*, 1990); *Letni premitani*, 1991 (*Summer Meditations*, 1992); *Open Letters: Selected Prose, 1965-1990*, 1991 (Paul Wilson, editor); *Toward a Civil Society: Selected Speeches and Writings, 1990-1994*, 1994 (Wilson, editor); *The Art of the Impossible: Politics as Morality in Practice*, 1997.
MISCELLANEOUS: *Protokoly*, 1966; *O lidskou identitu*, 1984.

BIBLIOGRAPHY

Goetz-Stankiewicz, Marketa. *The Silenced Theatre: Czech Playwrights Without a Stage.* Toronto: University of Toronto Press, 1979. Examination of the situation of numerous dissident playwrights under the communist regime, including Havel.

Keane, John. *Václav Havel: A Political Tragedy in Six Acts.* New York: Basic Books, 2000. Although this biography focuses primarily on Havel's political activities, it includes extensive information on Havel's plays and how they reflect the development of his political concepts.

Kriseova, Eda. *Václav Havel: The Authorized Biography.* Translated by Caleb Crain. New York: St. Martin's Press, 1993. Officially authorized biography, using sources provided by Havel that may not be available to other biographers but may be slanted to soft pedal awkward or uncomfortable aspects of his career.

Symynkywicz, Jeffrey. *Václav Havel and the Velvet Revolution.* Parsippany, N.J.: Dillon Press, 1995. Although dealing primarily with Havel's role in the Velvet Revolution, also looks at the role of his plays in forming his reputation.

Peter Petro,
updated by Leigh Husband Kimmel

FRIEDRICH HEBBEL

Born: Wesselburen, Schleswig-Holstein (now in
  Germany); March 18, 1813
Died: Vienna, Austria; December 13, 1863

PRINCIPAL DRAMA

Judith, pr. 1840, pb. 1841 (English translation,
  1974)

Genoveva, pb. 1843, pr. 1849

Maria Magdalena, pb. 1844, pr. 1846 (English
  translation, 1935)

Julia, pb. 1848, pr. 1903

Herodes und Marianne, pr. 1849, pb. 1850 (*Herod
  and Marianne*, 1930)

Michel Angelo, pb. 1851, pr. 1861

Agnes Bernauer, pr. 1852, pb. 1856 (English
  translation, 1904)

Gyges und sein Ring, pb. 1855, pr. 1889 (*Gyges
  and His Ring*, 1914)

Der gehörnte Siegfried, pr. 1861, pb. 1862 (*The
  Horned Siegfried*, 1921)

Siegfrieds Tod, pr. 1861, pb. 1862 (*Siegfried's
  Death*, 1921)

Kriemhilds Rache, pr. 1861, pb. 1862 (*Kriemhild's
  Revenge*, 1921)

Die Nibelungen, pr. 1861, pb. 1862 (*The
  Niebelungs*, 1921; includes *The Horned
  Siegfried*, *Siegfried's Death*, and *Kriemhild's
  Revenge*)

Demetrius, pb. 1864, pr. 1869 (unfinished)

Three Plays, pb. 1914

OTHER LITERARY FORMS

Although Friedrich Hebbel is best known as the
leading German dramatist of the mid-nineteenth century, he also wrote outstanding poetry and literary
criticism. His poems have been issued in independent
editions and are part of the poetic canon in anthologies. In addition, Hebbel wrote essays on literary theory, including "Mein Wort über das Drama" (1843),
and the "Vorwort zu Maria Magdalena" (1844; the
preface to *Maria Magdalena*); a hexameter epic,
Mutter und Kind (1859); and finally, a number of

short stories, first published in various periodicals,
then in book form as *Erzählungen* (1855). Aside from
these literary "works" in the strict sense, Hebbel left
a journal, originally published in two volumes as
Tagebücher (1885-1887), and referred to by Wilhelm
Scherer as a "literary-historical monument of the first
order." Hebbel's letters also provide many fascinating
insights into his thought and times.

ACHIEVEMENTS

Starting in his own lifetime and continuing into
the present, Friedrich Hebbel has evoked contradictory responses from audiences, readers, and critics.
Arthur Schnitzler in a letter to Hugo von Hofmannsthal stated, "Hebbel probably was next to Goethe the
greatest mind the Germans had in this century." Yet
other authors, such as Adalbert Stifter, found his
works to be insignificant and weak. Lesser voices in
Hebbel's day also injected either adulation or venom
into their reviews. Articles showing objective, balanced assessments were indeed in the minority. In
part, Hebbel's personality may have been responsible
for the varied reception of his work. Never a member
of a literary circle or school, he was opposed by such
groups, especially the Young Germans. In spite of
these circumstances, Hebbel moved slowly from success to success in his own time, and today his dramas
are part of the repertoire of the German stage, although the popularity of specific plays seems to be
affected by the shifting concerns of the day. *Maria
Magdalena*, in which a woman is driven to suicide
when the dominant male value system leaves her no
other alternative, is the most frequently produced
Hebbel play.

Numerous authors have admitted, or are assumed
to have, various degrees of indebtedness to Hebbel,
including Gottfried Benn, Franz Kafka, and, among
playwrights, Henrik Ibsen and Bertolt Brecht. Translations of Hebbel's works have appeared in the common languages of Europe as well as in Chinese, Es-
peranto, Hebrew, Japanese, and Turkish. Scholarly
works about Hebbel number in the thousands.

BIOGRAPHY

Christian Friedrich Hebbel was born on March 18, 1813, in Wesselburen in the duchy of Schleswig-Holstein, then under Danish suzerainty. His father, a mason, never was able to lift his family out of poverty; in the wake of the Napoleonic Wars and Denmark's bankruptcy, repairs and odd jobs were the only work a mason could find. When his father died in 1827, young Hebbel became a messenger boy and later a scribe for J. J. Mohr, the parish mayor. He worked there for more than seven years and was never treated better than the domestics but was allowed to use Mohr's library. Hebbel read extensively and became acquainted with contemporary German literature and the philosophy of Gotthilf H. Schubert and Ludwig Feuerbach.

Area newspapers published Hebbel's early poems and stories, some of which elicited the attention of Amalie Schoppe, author of trivial but then popular novels. She arranged for Hebbel to come to Hamburg, where he was to prepare himself for entrance into a university. Perhaps too old and certainly too impatient for detailed remedial work, Hebbel went to Heidelberg a year later to study law. Soon convinced that jurisprudence could not hold his interest, he moved on to Munich in 1836, in the hope of earning a living as a freelance writer. In the next two and a half years, Hebbel experienced almost continuous hardship. He earned little and came to rely on the financial support of Elise Lensing, a woman nine years his senior, whom he had met in Hamburg. He continued his autodidactic studies and wrote some of his finest poems. In March, 1839, his financial condition forced him to return on foot to Hamburg, where he contracted a severe case of pneumonia. Thanks to the patient care of Elise Lensing, he survived, and that fall, he wrote *Judith*. It was performed during 1840 in Berlin and Hamburg, then published.

This literary success did not improve Hebbel's financial situation, however, and in November, 1842, he traveled to Copenhagen to seek appointment to the chair of aesthetics at Kiel University. Instead, in 1843, the King of Denmark awarded him a travel stipend for two years. Hebbel stopped briefly in Hamburg, left Elise half of the money, wrote "Mein Wort über das Drama" to refute a Danish professor's attacks on his dramatic theories, and moved on to Paris. There, he wrote *Maria Magdalena*, adding the preface as a result of discussions with Felix Bamberg, a Hegelian, who became a friend and was later the first editor of Hebbel's journals and letters.

In September, 1844, Hebbel moved on to Rome, then to Naples. No major works date from this time. This lack of creativity, combined with ill-health, depletion of funds, and the refusal of his application for an extension of the travel grant, caused Hebbel to enter a period of depression during which he abruptly broke off his relationship with Elise Lensing. In October, 1845, with barely enough money to get to Germany, Hebbel left Italy. Stopping over in Vienna, he was greeted by very favorable newspaper articles. Two Galician barons outfitted him with new clothes and introduced him to Viennese society. Among Hebbel's new acquaintances was Christine Enghaus, a leading actress of the Royal Burgtheater, who wanted to stage his *Judith*. The professional relationship turned into a personal one, culminating in marriage in May, 1846.

The resulting tranquillity in Hebbel's life freed his creative impulses. In the next seventeen years, he produced not only the above mentioned principal dramas and others, but also the epic *Mutter und Kind*—considered by some to be his "social manifesto"—for which he was awarded by the Tiedge Foundation. He also wrote and reworked poems for the 1857 collected edition, edited his stories, and contributed literary and critical pieces to various periodicals. His plays were performed throughout the Austro-Hungarian realm and in Germany, and recognition of his achievements came in many forms. He was awarded Bavaria's Maximilian Medal for Science and Art and the Falcon Medal by the grand duke of Saxony-Weimar. For his trilogy *The Niebelungs*, his last completed work, he received the coveted Schiller Prize, sponsored by the king of Prussia. Receiving notification of this honor while in the advanced stages of osteomalacia, an extreme softening of the bones of which he died a month later, Hebbel remarked that it was people's lot to have either the cup or the wine but never both. Rather than expressing self-pity, this comment reflects Hebbel's conviction that a person's life is fundamentally tragic.

ANALYSIS

Personal experience and keen observation led Friedrich Hebbel to note early in his journal that life is a struggle between the individual and the universe. He further noted that just as leaves that fall and decay stimulate plant growth the following season, so the life of an individual contributes to the progress of the universe, even though the leaf that falls or the human being that suffers cannot claim compensation. It was but a short step for Hebbel from such general dicta to their application in his literary theory. In Hebbel's view, any human being can be a tragic individual. Any person, asserting himself as an individual, disturbs the universe's equilibrium and thus evokes tragedy. The descriptive term *Pantragismus* ("pantragism") was coined by Arno Scheunert in his book *Der Pantragismus als System der Weltanschauung und Ästhetik Hebbels* (1930) to refer to Hebbel's worldview and his aesthetic system.

Given such a conceptual framework, it is no surprise that Hebbel wrote *Maria Magdalena*, the first genuine bourgeois tragedy in German literature. According to Aristotle, only individuals of high rank were fit subjects for tragedy. Under English influence, this axiom had been modified in mid-eighteenth century German letters by Gotthold Ephraim Lessing's *Emilia Galotti* (1772; English translation, 1786), and subsequently by the Sturm und Drang (storm and stress) playwrights. In both cases, however, tragedy developed out of a dubious interaction between the nobility and the commoners, who bore the consequences. In *Maria Magdalena*, tragedy ensues, as the result of a rigid value system, entirely from within lower-middle-class society.

Hebbel's notion that the individual who is freed temporarily from a nexus with the universe, of which he nevertheless remains a part, falls through self-assertion into *Masslosigkeit* (immoderation), led him to a revised concept of tragic guilt. Aristotle viewed the tragic hero as an individual not preeminently virtuous and just, whose misfortune is brought on him not by vice or depravity but by some error, resulting from poor judgment, ignorance, or a moral flaw. Aristotle's comments, originally descriptive, had long been tacitly accepted as proscriptive. In contrast, Hebbel argued in "Mein Wort über das Drama," that dramatic guilt does not arise from the direction of the human will but immediately from the act of willing itself. Individuation—the state of existing as an individual—implies universal metaphysical guilt. Self-assertion added to that leads to *Masslosigkeit*, eliciting tragedy. Hence, he concludes, it makes no difference whether a hero perishes in pursuit of a praiseworthy or reprehensible aim. In a journal entry of the same period, he adds that it is foolish to demand of the poet what even God does not offer: reconciliation and a leveling of dissonances. The poet, he claims, may let any character perish, but he must show simultaneously that his doom was unavoidable—that it, like death, was set a priori at birth.

JUDITH

Although these ideas were not committed to paper at the time *Judith* was written, they clearly apply to Hebbel's first play. Based on the account of the Jewish heroine in the Apocrypha, Hebbel altered the plot in some significant aspects to provide psychological veracity and a tragic outcome. Whereas the Apocryphal Judith is certain at all times that she acts in accord with God's will as she saves her people, Hebbel's heroine receives only ambivalent signs of divine approval. On her wedding night, for example, her husband sees something—a vision?—that moves him not to consummate the marriage, then or subsequently. He meets with an accident not long afterward, and his dying words, which might have shed light on his unusual behavior, break off inconclusively.

Her husband's behavior and various other incidents confirm Judith's resolve to trick Holofernes, slay him, and free her people from the death-dealing siege. When she meets Holofernes, however, she is so taken by his stature that she is unable to carry out her plan. In fact, she reveals it to him, speaking as an equal to the avowed enemy of her people. Completely unable to understand her unique personality, Holofernes rapes her. The physical abuse (Hebbel had purposely prepared for it with the virgin-widow motif), but even more so the psychological shock of being reduced to a "thing," together cause Judith to lose sight of her commission. When she beheads Holofernes in his sleep, she acts in personal revenge.

This switch of motives is taken by Judith as evidence that God has "dropped her," a fate prefigured in a dream. She is deeply despondent. As the play ends, her people celebrate the rout of the leaderless enemy, but Judith hopes for death. Hebbel endowed Judith with exemplary attributes, in part based on his source—that is, with piety, charity toward the unfortunate, and so on—yet circumstances force her into actions and reactions that make her a guiltless victim in the evolution of the world.

The notion that the world evolves by a process in which a status quo or a thesis is challenged by an antithesis, implying a tragic struggle and the doom of those involved in it, but leading to a synthesis further on, is a Hegelian notion. When Hebbel first embraced this view and saw one purpose of drama to be the depiction of such evolutionary change, he did not know that Georg Wilhelm Friedrich Hegel had preempted him. It is uncertain whether Hebbel arrived at the same view entirely on his own or unknowingly absorbed Hegelian thought through an intermediary in his wide-ranging autodidactic studies. At any rate, Hebbel enunciated his conviction that dramas ought to be set at historic turning points, as early as 1843 in "Mein Wort über das Drama," and noted subsequently in his journal his surprise that some of his ideas matched those of Hegel.

MARIA MAGDALENA

Just as in *Judith*, heathen polytheism and Judaic monotheism are the contending orders from which the characters derive their uniqueness, so in *Maria Magdalena*, Hebbel sets up an opposition between the older generation and the younger one. In modern terms it would be called a generation gap, but one that is not solely based on age difference. The title refers to the biblical Mary Magdalene, with the suggestion that Klara, the protagonist, is free of moral guilt. When her brother Karl is arrested on suspicion of theft, her father, Anton, a master cabinetmaker, swears that, should Klara also bring him shame, he will commit suicide. Klara's fiancé, Leonhard, having learned that the expected dowry will not materialize, uses the arrest as a pretext to break the engagement. Klara, finding herself pregnant, begs Leonhard to reconsider, but he answers in cynical sophisms. Confiding in a childhood friend, a young man recently returned from college studies, Klara is told that no man will be able to overlook the fact that she is carrying someone else's child. As she prepares to go to the well to drown herself, her brother returns, released from false arrest, but in his defiant mood (Karl wants to break with his father and go to sea) he fails to understand the thinly veiled allusions Klara makes to her death. Instead of stopping her, he even delivers the alibi she needs to make her suicide appear an accident; he asks for a glass of fresh water.

Lest it be argued that Klara, by having been intimate with her fiancé, assumes moral guilt or tragic guilt in the Aristotelian sense of "error of judgment," it must be pointed out that without Karl's false arrest, the entire chain of events leading inevitably to her death would not have been set in motion. As it is, Klara dies as a victim of a society with a long-established, inflexible moral code. The promise that a more tolerant society will evolve (the synthesis in the developmental process) is implicit in the final words of Klara's childhood friend, addressed to Master Anton, and in the latter's famous line which closes the play: "I don't understand the world anymore!"

HEROD AND MARIANNE

Herod and Marianne, based on the accounts of the historian Flavius Josephus, is set in Jerusalem before the birth of Jesus. Again Hebbel makes symbolic use of the timing. There are clear implications in the play that, under Christianity, humankind will not merely serve as a means toward someone's ends but will possess inherent value. Herod treats Marianne as if she has no purpose in life but to serve as his support; he behaves as if he owns her. The crisis between them, one of love and trust, is precipitated when intriguing parties groom Aristobulus, Marianne's brother, as a rival for the kingship. Herod has him drowned in what passes as a swimming accident. Though Marianne knows what he has done and even understands the political necessity of the act, Herod never admits it to her for fear of losing her. To reassure himself of her love, he tells her of a woman who refused rescue from a burning building because her husband had just died. Failing in this attempt to move her to pledge suicide should he not return from an imminent battle, he "places her under the sword"—that is, he arranges for someone to kill her as soon as his death is confirmed. When she finds out what he has done, he assumes that she gained the knowledge at the price of adultery and has her sentenced to death. Through a confidant, Titus, an impartial Roman officer, Herod later learns why she refused to defend herself. Again, Hebbel depicts in Marianne a character free of a moral flaw. She is everything Herod wants in a wife, yet he is too egocentric to recognize it. Their tragedies are that circumstances confront them that neither can control, given their basic personalities. To use Hebbel's terms, their individuation evokes tragedy.

AGNES BERNAUER

In *Agnes Bernauer*, the familiar elements of Hebbelian tragedy recur yet again. The play is set in the early fifteenth century in Germany at a time when the still powerful nobility began to feel the political ascendency of the bourgeoisie in the growing cities. Through skillful use of dialogue and action, Hebbel capitalizes on this thesis/antithesis relationship even before the main characters, Duke Ernst and Agnes, are introduced. In fact, the drama is unique in that the two opponents never meet face to face. After Duke Albrecht, the heir apparent, falls in love with and marries Agnes, a commoner, his father excludes him in favor of a nephew for the succession. When that nephew, a sickly boy, dies, Duke Ernst takes his passing as an oracle, an indication that God wants him to dissolve the *mésalliance* by executing Agnes, thus assuring Albrecht an unquestionable succession and avoiding civil war. In the dialogue, especially in a conversation between Duke Ernst and his counselor Preising, Hebbel establishes the salient facts: Agnes is innocent of any wrongdoing; to avoid general calamity, she must die nevertheless. Using traditional criteria, it might be said that Agnes's fate is indeed pathetic but not tragic, precisely because she lacks a tragic flaw in the Aristotelian sense. Hebbel rejected such a restriction, just as other dramatists disregarded Aristotle's insistence on the unities of time, place, and action.

GYGES AND HIS RING

Gyges and His Ring, exhibiting masterful diction in blank verse, is considered Hebbel's best play in purely poetic terms. Nevertheless, it seems to puzzle audiences and some critics because Gyges, the titular hero, is, on the surface at least, not a tragic figure; either Rhodope or Kandaules, and perhaps both of them, qualify for that designation. Indeed, Rhodope, the queen who clings to traditions, and King Kandaules, who sees no value in veils and rusty swords, represent thesis and antithesis in yet another clash between differing value systems. The basic plot, taken from Herodotus, has Kandaules arrange for his friend Gyges to see Rhodope, the most beautiful woman in the world, in her bedroom. When the queen, never before seen unveiled by any man but Kandaules, learns of this abuse, her upbringing demands atonement. In a carefully motivated plot development, Gyges slays Kandaules in a duel and consents to marry his widow. At the altar of Hestia, the goddess of fire, which in Rhodope's words, "consumes what she cannot refine," Rhodope, satisfied now that no one but her husbands saw her, commits suicide. The implication, especially in the final scene, is that Gyges as king will find the proper balance between tradition and innovation.

THE NIEBELUNGS

In *The Niebelungs*, a trilogy consisting of *The Horned Siegfried*, *Siegfried's Death*, and *Kriemhild's Revenge*, Hebbel created the most successful dramatic adaptation of the well-known German medieval epic, rivaled only (but in a different medium) by Richard Wagner's operatic tetralogy *Der Ring des Nibelungen* (1852). Staying remarkably true to his source, Hebbel reshapes the epic description into dramatic action, leaves out retarding elements, and above all subtly provides a deeper, more psychologically convincing motivation for the actions of the major characters. In *Siegfried's Death*, for example, while Hebbel employs all the circumstantial reasons—Brunhild's oath, the threat to King Gunther's honor, and so on—to lead up to Hagen's murder of Siegfried, he has Kriemhild confront him with yet another reason: jealousy. In the epic, external motivations play on Hagen's sense of feudal loyalty, while in Hebbel's drama, Hagen's actions arise out of a subconscious hate: the hatred of an ordinary man for a superman. (Hebbel himself used these terms in writing about the play to the literary historian Hermann Hettner.) Similarly, Kriemhild's obtaining the fateful knowledge about Siegfried's possession of Brunhild's belt is revealed in Hebbel's play through an oversight instead of vain boasting on her husband's part.

In *The Niebelungs* as in Hebbel's earlier plays, tragedy follows excessive self-assertion. This is true not only of Siegfried in *Siegfried's Death* and of Kriemhild in *Kriemhild's Revenge* but also of the supporting characters from Brunhild to Hagen. Kriemhild, originally gentle except in the provocation scene initiated by Brunhild, is still a passive character at the beginning of *Kriemhild's Revenge*. A mourning widow, she asks only that Hagen be brought to justice, but when that is denied, she begins to seek revenge. She marries an unloved second husband, Etzel (Attila), to use him to effect her design, and in so doing, Kriemhild enters on the path to her own destruction.

Following his conviction that tragedy should show humanity at evolutionary turning points, Hebbel set the trilogy in a time of transition, the change from the age of Germanic mythology to Christianity. Not merely grafted onto the plot but made part of it in dialogue and action, the clash of conflicting worldviews helps delineate the characters. With intuitive empathy Hebbel grasped the inherent greatness of the epic that set it apart from others of its time. It does not differentiate between laudable hero and despicable enemy but draws both in somber neutrality. Placed by circumstance into attitudes of animosity, both accept their fate to the end. This stoic acceptance appealed to Hebbel, who observed: "*Der Mensch hat freien Willen—d.h. er kann einwilligen ins Nothwendige.*" ("Man does have free will—i.e., he can accept the necessary.") Such was the worldview informing all Hebbel's works.

OTHER MAJOR WORKS
LONG FICTION: *Schnock: Ein niederländisches Gemälde*, 1848.
SHORT FICTION: *Erzählungen*, 1855.
POETRY: *Gedichte*, 1842; *Neue Gedichte*, 1848; *Gedichte von Friedrich Hebbel*, 1857; *Mutter und Kind*, 1859.
NONFICTION: *Tagebücher*, 1885-1887 (2 volumes).

BIBLIOGRAPHY
Flygt, Sten Gunnar. *Griedrich Hebbel*. New York: Twayne, 1968. A basic biography covering Hebbel's life and works.

Garland, Mary. *Hebbel's Prose Tragedies: An Investigation of the Aesthetic Aspect of Hebbel's Dramatic Language*. Cambridge, England: Cambridge University Press, 1973. A look at the literary style of Hebbel in his dramatic works. Bibliography.

Kofman, Sarah. *Freud and Fiction*. Boston: Northeastern University Press, 1991. A look at Hebbel's *Judith*, among other works, for the influence of Sigmund Freud. Bibliography and index.

Niven, William John. *The Reception of Friedrich Hebbel in Germany in the Era of National Socialism*. Stuttgart, Germany: H.-D. Heinz, 1984. An analysis of the appreciation for Hebbel during the period when National Socialism flourished in Germany. Bibliography.

U. Henry Gerlach

GUNNAR HEIBERG

Born: Christiania (now Oslo), Norway; November 18, 1857
Died: Oslo, Norway; February 22, 1929

PRINCIPAL DRAMA
Tante Ulrikke, pb. 1884, pr. 1901
Kong Midas, pr., pb. 1890

Kunstnere, pr., pb. 1893

Gerts have, pr., pb. 1894

Balkonen, pr., pb. 1894 (*The Balcony*, 1922)

Det store lod, pr., pb. 1895

Folkeraadet, pr., pb. 1897

Harald Svans mor, pr., pb. 1899

Kjælighet til næsten, pr., pb. 1902

Kjærlighedens tragedie, pr., pb. 1904 (*The Tragedy of Love*, 1921)

Jeg vil værge mit land, pr., pb. 1912

Paradesengen, pr., pb. 1913

OTHER LITERARY FORMS

Gunnar Heiberg combined a career as a journalist and theater critic with the writing of plays, for which he is best known. Many of his newspaper essays on political and cultural matters have enduring value.

ACHIEVEMENTS

Gunnar Heiberg is the chief Norwegian dramatist after Henrik Ibsen (1828-1906) and before Helge Krog (1889-1962). Although his œuvre, which spans the period from 1884 to 1913, earned for him the reputation as Norway's leading young playwright at the time, only three of his plays have survived the intervening years. The author's first drama, the satiric social comedy *Tante Ulrikke*, continues to delight modern audiences. In this work, Heiberg champions the ideals of social justice, the emancipation of women, and youthful radicalism as opposed to the narrow, Philistine concerns of the older generation. The drama's striking main character is modeled on Heiberg's aunt, the Norwegian suffragist Aasta Hansteen (1824-1908), who also inspired Lona Hessel in Henrik Ibsen's *Samfundets støtter* (pr., pb. 1877; *The Pillars of Society*, 1880). Both Hansteen's life and Heiberg's play remain an inspiration to progressive Norwegians.

Two other Heiberg plays that are still read and sometimes performed are the lyrical dramas *The Balcony* and *The Tragedy of Love*. Their timeless theme of erotic love continues to elicit interest. However, modern audiences find their highly stylized and rhetorical dialogue dated, and the primarily aesthetic concerns of their author seem foreign to readers and spectators who have been reared in the predominantly ethical and socially committed Scandinavian literary traditions.

BIOGRAPHY

Gunnar Edvard Rode Heiberg was born in Christiania (now Oslo) in 1857 into a family that belonged to the upper bourgeoisie, inasmuch as his father was a high government official. The boy followed the common path of young men of his class and prepared for his matriculation certificate, which he obtained in 1874. A student of law, he also developed literary interests and published his first works in 1878. These works, two long poems, attempt to rewrite the story of the Fall of Man in such a manner that Lucifer and Cain appear as the real heroes and to establish a rational basis for a view of life that could replace Christianity, which Heiberg, like his radical contemporaries, regarded as outdated.

Shortly after the publication of his poems, Heiberg left Norway and went to Rome, ostensibly for the purpose of studying art history. He hoped, however, that some distance from home would permit him to collect his thoughts and write a play. This proved not to be the case, and after his return to Christiania, he worked for some time as a journalist and theater critic for the daily newspaper *Dagbladet*. He continued to work on his ideas for a drama, however, and finished the manuscript of his first play, *Tante Ulrikke*, in 1883. It was published the following year, but its radical content made it unacceptable to Norway's main stage, the Christiania Theater.

Tante Ulrikke was, however, accepted by the National Stage of Bergen, Norway, but before it was produced, Heiberg withdrew it after his appointment as director of that theater. He undoubtedly felt a need to distance himself from this period of his authorship so that he could explore other artistic possibilities. After leaving his directorship in 1889, the actualization of these possibilities began to take place.

The greatest force to be reckoned with in Norwegian public debate at the time was the poet, dramatist, and novelist Bjørnstjerne Bjørnson, who had established himself as a champion of truth and virtue, particularly with regard to sexual matters. Heiberg, who felt some affinity with Bjørnson's critics, a group of young artists and intellectuals referred to as the Bohemians, published a play, *Kong Midas*, which was a direct attack on Bjørnson's conservative concept of truth and which many believed to be an attack on Bjørnson himself. The Christiania Theater refused to take the play, but it was performed by one of the popular stages in town, accompanied by much tumult.

Heiberg's real coming-of-age as a dramatist can be dated to 1894, when he published his most original play, *The Balcony*. His earlier dramas had been dependent on the realistic and naturalistic drama of the Scandinavian countries, especially with regard to form. *The Balcony*, on the other hand, is a stylized Symbolist portrayal of erotic love as a natural force. Continued in *The Tragedy of Love*, the discussion of the individual, not social, aspects of erotic love constitutes Heiberg's most original contribution to Norwegian literature.

Most of Heiberg's remaining life was spent in Christiania. Married to the actress Didi Tollefsen in 1885, he was divorced in 1896. Heiberg died in 1929.

ANALYSIS

Gunnar Heiberg was, above all, a dramatist of passion. In his first play, he passionately spoke in favor of the rights of oppressed workers and women. Later, he advocated the rights of passion itself. Although the public at large regards *Tante Ulrikke* as Heiberg's most important work, literary historians generally view *The Balcony* and *The Tragedy of Love* as his most significant contributions to Norwegian drama.

Norwegian literature in the 1870's and 1880's focused its attention on those aspects of society that needed reform. Both the novel and the drama had pointed to abuses of power, social hypocrisy, and the situation of women as issues that urgently needed to be addressed. The chief dogma of the literary theory of the day was, indeed, that the primary purpose of literature should be to subject social problems to debate. Heiberg's *Tante Ulrikke* fits this tradition well.

TANTE ULRIKKE

The title character of *Tante Ulrikke* is an older, unmarried woman whose brother-in-law, Professor Blom, is next in line to be named to the king's cabinet. Ulrikke's behavior is a threat to his future appointment, however, for she is a radical and feminist with Socialist sympathies. The conflict in the play is between her and Blom and his conservative friends, and a point of crisis is reached when Ulrikke declares that she will attend a Socialist meeting at which she intends to speak to the crowd about social and political issues. Blom and his friends consider having her declared insane, but this design is frustrated when Helene, Blom's daughter and Ulrikke's niece, states that she will accompany her aunt to the meeting. At the meeting, some students who have been sent there by one of Blom's friends subject Ulrikke to so much scorn and derision that Helene feels driven to defend her publicly. This is such a scandal that Helene has to leave the home of her parents to protect her father's political future.

Of particular interest is the dramatist's portrayal of the character Ulrikke. Lacking physical beauty, Ulrikke, by her own admission, fell in love with the great ideas of her time because no young man showed an interest in her. The drama vividly shows the price she has had to pay for her radicalism. She is ridiculed both publicly and privately and even has to carry a whip to defend herself when she walks the streets of Christiania. At the end of the play, when Helene sides with her and wants to live with her, Ulrikke attempts to dissuade her niece from following the path that she herself has chosen. Heiberg shows that Ulrikke has paid such a high price for her political involvement that she cannot bear the thought that her niece, whom she loves dearly, should have to endure the same kind of suffering.

THE BALCONY

Although *Tante Ulrikke* belongs squarely to the realistic and naturalistic traditions in Norwegian drama, *The Balcony* takes place in no identifiable social or geographical reality. The characters are stylized, lack individual history, and can scarcely be said to have much individuality at all. The play is in three acts. As the action begins, it is sunrise, and the drama's only female character, Julie, and her lover, Abel, are standing inside an open door to a balcony. They find it difficult to part even though they know that Julie's husband, Ressmann, an older man, is about to come home from work. When Ressmann does arrive, Abel first hides and then comes forth, stating that he has heard that Ressmann's house is for sale and that he might have an interest in buying it. While Ressmann is showing Abel the various rooms, he steps out on the balcony and jumps up and down to demonstrate that it is structurally sound, despite the fact that it has a visible crack. Ressmann's jumping causes the balcony to collapse, and he is killed. At the end of act 1, Julie and Abel are kneeling together, thanking God that they may now remain with each other. Heiberg shows that the power of love is such that a pair of lovers will go to any length to satisfy their desire for each other. Eros is an uncivilized and untamable force.

The second act takes place years later. Julie has not changed, but Abel has grown to the point that he has interests other than his love for Julie. He has gradually come to regard love as a dangerous force precisely because it does not allow itself to be civilized and because his devotion to love hinders his growth as an individual. When Abel explains his new perception of love to Julie, she voices no opposition to him. It is clear, however, that she does not share his understanding, and soon Abel is replaced by a man named Antonio, who relates to her in much the same way that Abel once did. He wins Julie because he is insistent and will allow absolutely nothing to stand in his way.

In the beginning of act 3, Abel, who has been away giving a lecture, surprises Julie with Antonio. It is night, and they are unaware of his presence. Abel has a pistol, which he contemplates using on Antonio. As it turns out, Abel proves too civilized to use the gun, but had he used it, it not only would have indicated that he was still in the grip of primitive eros but also would have brought Julie back to him. In the end, he leaves Julie with Antonio.

The Balcony expresses Heiberg's ambivalent attitude toward love. On one hand, the play is a celebration of the idea of physical love as an all-consuming force. On the other hand, Heiberg does not allow Abel to make the choice that would have brought Julie back to him. The demands of civilization must

also be met, and human beings are forever torn between natural demands and those of culture.

THE TRAGEDY OF LOVE

Heiberg continued his discussion of the power of eros in *The Tragedy of Love*. The conflict in this drama takes place within a traditional marriage, which made it necessary to give the play a more realistic form than that of *The Balcony*. Erling Druse, the male protagonist, is a forester by profession, and he loves his work as well as his wife, Karen. She, on the other hand, is completely swallowed up by her love for him and cannot think of anything but him.

The play has four acts. Having met earlier, Erling and Karen have agreed to have no contact with each other for a year, at the end of which time they are to meet at a mountain cabin to discuss the state of their feelings for each other. In act 1, which takes place in the cabin a year later, Erling wins Karen by refusing to accept her claim that she really does not love him. Erling's persistence awakens Karen's love, and by the beginning of act 2, they have married and are in the middle of their honeymoon in the German Alps. It is time for Erling to return to Norway to look after his life's work, but Karen wishes to go on to Paris. As Erling is unwilling to consent to this, she risks her life to save a child, stating that Erling's love is no longer sufficiently strong to make her feel fully alive; only the sensation of danger is able to fill this need in her.

The third act takes place two years later. Erling is happy with his peaceful existence, two very important aspects of which are his work as a forester and the home that Karen provides for him. She, on the other hand, has grown gradually more dissatisfied; she is jealous of Erling's work and unhappy about the fact that his love is not as ardent as it once was. Act 3 is taken up by a long conversation about love, which husband and wife have on the eve of one of Erling's trips to the forest. Karen tries to make Erling understand how she feels, but in his complacent everyday happiness, he is unable to see her point. Toward the end of the act, Karen tries to keep him from leaving for the forest, thinking that her ability to change his decision will evidence his love for her. She sends him conflicting messages, however, and the emotionally uncomplicated Erling leaves on his journey, thinking that he has actually catered to her will.

At the end of act 3, Karen receives a visit from the poet Hadeln, who has appeared on two other occasions earlier in the play. Hadeln is an embodiment of Karen's concept of the ideal man. She tells him about her frustration in her marriage and, in fact, invites Hadeln to seduce her. Hadeln, although in love with Karen, will not accept her invitation out of his respect for Erling and because of his regard for Karen's true happiness, which he sees in her marriage to Erling. In act 4, when Erling returns, the frustrated and even desperate Karen makes him think that she has actually made love to Hadeln, despite the latter's denial. While Hadeln is trying to explain Karen's desperate situation to Erling, Karen takes her own life.

Heiberg's main message is that two people are never really in love with each other at the same time and that genuine love leads to death. Karen's concept of love, which in many respects is close to Heiberg's own, is such that it can never lead to happiness. It does, however, make for interesting drama, and Heiberg will undoubtedly retain his reputation as one of Norway's foremost dramatists of passion.

BIBLIOGRAPHY

Longum, Leif. "In the Shadow of Ibsen: His Influence on Norwegian Drama and on Literary Attitudes." In *Norway: Review of National Literatures*, edited by Sverre Lyngstad. New York: Council on National Literature and Griffon House Publishers, 1983. Henrik Ibsen's influence on writers such as Heiberg is examined in this essay.

Mitchell, Phillip Marshall. *A History of Danish Literature*. 2d ed. New York: Kraus-Thomson Organization, 1971. This general history of Danish literature examines drama as well as other genres.

Naess, Harald S., ed. *A History of Norwegian Literature*. Lincoln: University of Nebraska Press, 1993. A general history of the development of literature in Norway, including drama.

Jan Sjåvik

JOHAN LUDVIG HEIBERG

Born: Copenhagen, Denmark; December 14, 1791
Died: Bonderup, Denmark; August 23, 1860

PRINCIPAL DRAMA

Kong Salomon og Jørgen Hattemager, pr., pb. 1825
Aprilsnarrene, pr., pb. 1826 (*The April Fools*, 1999)
Recensenten og dyret, pr., pb. 1826
Den otte og tyvende januar, pr., pb. 1826
Et eventyr i Rosenborg Have, pr., pb. 1827
De uadskillelige, pr., pb. 1827
Elverhøj, pr., pb. 1828
Nei, pr., pb. 1836 (*No*, 1999)
Fata Morgana, pr., pb. 1838
Syvsoverdag, pr., pb. 1840
Emilies hjertebanken, pr., pb. 1840
En sjæl efter døden, pr., pb. 1841 (*A Soul After Death*, 1991; verse play)

OTHER LITERARY FORMS

Johan Ludvig Heiberg wrote prolifically in all the various literary forms. He wrote nonfiction both as a journalist and as a scholar. His journalism spans the spectrum from politics to theatrical criticism. His scientific works reflect his multitude of interests. Heiberg wrote on Nordic mythology, on philosophy, and on linguistics; he also published both poetry and short stories.

ACHIEVEMENTS

Johan Ludvig Heiberg managed, in his own lifetime, to go from being considered an inferior dramatist whose works were in bad taste, empty, and silly to being *the* arbiter of taste and his country's most highly regarded and popular dramatist. He singlehandedly introduced the vaudeville as a dramatic form in Denmark, by way of the Royal Theatre in Copenhagen. After finishing his doctoral dissertation, Heiberg spent several years in France, where he first saw vaudeville on the stage. The French vaudeville can be described as lighthearted comedy spiced with popular tunes. He was enchanted, and when he returned to Copenhagen, he began to write his own vaudevilles. At first they were met with a dual response, unadulterated enthusiasm from the audience—Copenhagen saw its first ticket scalpers as a result of the popularity of Heiberg's vaudevilles—and icy contempt from critics and the intelligentsia.

Heiberg met his critics head-on. After repeatedly having read how empty and distasteful his plays were, how they were a menace to the tastes of unsuspecting and intellectually unsophisticated audiences, he answered in the form of a long article, "Om vaudevillen," in which he declared his program and denounced his critics as amateurs. The article was so well argued and convincing that the criticism virtually stopped. Heiberg had won.

Soon after Heiberg's first vaudevilles had appeared, and after he had successfully argued the merits of the vaudeville as a national dramatic form, vaudeville writers emerged from everywhere. In 1832, the highly regarded critic Christian Molbech wrote about Heiberg that he had created a theatrical form that was original, national, and the best in comic dramatic literature since the works of the great Ludvig Holberg. Heiberg had created a national comedy.

Heiberg went from honor to major honor. He was asked, in 1828, to write a play to be presented on the occasion of the marriage of Princess Vilhelmine, the daughter of King Frederik VI, to her cousin Prince Frederik. The result was *Elverhøj*. In 1829, Heiberg was named house poet at the Royal Theatre. In 1849, he was appointed director of the Royal Theatre.

Heiberg was influenced by such great European spirits of his day as Pedro Calderón de la Barca, whose work was the subject of Heiberg's doctoral dissertation, and the German philosopher Georg Wilhelm Friedrich Hegel. Heiberg was a formalist who believed that what one says is not as important as how one says it. He was also a Romantic in the sense that he was concerned less with expressing his ideas

clearly than with expressing them adorned with symbolism. The form was to be a hazy aesthetic mist through which the content was suggested rather than actually perceived.

After Heiberg's death in 1860, the great critic Georg Brandes wrote that when he, Brandes, grew up, Heiberg was the most influential person in the spiritual and artistic life of Copenhagen (and therefore Denmark). His Hegelian aesthetics were so dominant that he influenced not only how and what writers and other artists wrote and produced but also how members of the bourgeoisie—at least those who wanted to be considered *au courant*—decorated their homes. The final, and possibly strongest, measure of Heiberg's importance is that at the height of his stature in Danish intellectual life, an anti-Heiberg movement arose which vociferously expressed dissent from his reigning tastes and opinions.

BIOGRAPHY

That Johan Ludvig Heiberg became a writer whose major concerns were with artistic form rather than with content may have been the result of an

Johan Ludvig Heiberg (Kongelige Bibliotek)

event that occurred when he was only nine years old. In 1800, Peter Andreas Heiberg, Johan Ludvig Heiberg's father, was sent into exile by royal decree. The elder Heiberg was a passionate opponent of the Danish absolute monarchy and a caustic wit who used the relative freedom of expression to vent his republican views. In response to the elder Heiberg's writings, King Frederik VI introduced tight censorship and exiled the writer. When the elder Heiberg left Denmark to live the remainder of his life in Paris, he left his wife and young Johan Ludvig behind. One can assume that this had a profound impact on the young boy's outlook on the world.

Actually, Johan Ludvig Heiberg, who was born in Copenhagen on December 14, 1791, lived to see both the most stringent censorship that Denmark has had in its history and the total abolition of censorship when Denmark changed from an absolute to a constitutional monarchy in 1849. Yet he never became involved in the political tempest that raged during most of his productive years. Never identified with any particular political or social point of view, he stuck to his Hegelian aesthetics and a Romantic concern with the national heritage. If a political interest emerges from Heiberg's writings at all, it is a Hegelian one that focuses on the individual rather than on classes or social groups.

The young Heiberg was not much interested in school, probably because his childhood after his father's departure for Paris became a constant pilgrimage from home to home. His mother divorced his father and was remarried. The father was awarded the boy and placed him with various friends and relatives. Finally, at the age of twelve, the boy ran away from his adoptive parents to live with his mother. He seems, despite his initial lack of interest, to have gotten a sound education and passed his *artium* with flying colors.

After his exam came a period when Heiberg had to decide what his future should be. His main interests were writing and the theater, and, after two or three false starts involving law and medicine, he finally wrote his doctoral dissertation on aesthetics, specifically, the Spanish national drama, especially the dramatist Calderón de la Barca.

Heiberg traveled, as was customary, to the centers of European civilization. He was especially taken with Paris, where he lived for two years with his father. It was during this stay that he came to appreciate the vaudeville, which was extremely popular in the Parisian theaters featuring lighter fare. The vaudeville that he saw in Paris, and that he was to adapt into his own Danish national vaudeville, mixed the various performing arts: Comedies were interspersed with music and dance. The music usually took the form of popular arias or other popular music for which new lyrics were written.

Heiberg experienced financial difficulties throughout most of his life. His lack of funds forced him to leave Paris. He then tried desperately to get a professorship at the University of Copenhagen but had to settle for a position at the university in Kiel, Germany, where there was a large contingent of Danes. During his stay in Kiel, Heiberg traveled to Berlin, where he met and became friendly with Hegel. This was an important event in terms of Heiberg's intellectual outlook. He became a devout Hegelian, and indeed, everything he subsequently wrote was infused with the Hegelian dialectic.

Eventually Heiberg left Kiel and moved back to Copenhagen, where he began to write vaudevilles. These were produced by the Royal Theatre as fast as he could finish them. From 1825, when his first vaudeville, *Kong Salomon og Jørgen Hattemager*, was written and produced, Heiberg averaged one or two vaudevilles a year, and they invariably were produced immediately.

Heiberg wrote prolifically, not only for the theater but also as a scientist and, for many years, as the editor of the weekly paper *Flyvende Post*, on anything and everything. He managed, as already mentioned, to become first the royally appointed resident dramatist of the Royal Theatre, and, in 1849, the director of that institution. He died at the age of sixty-eight, on August 23, 1860.

ANALYSIS

Johan Ludvig Heiberg has come to be represented almost exclusively by *Elverhøj*, which is a weak and boring play, but even his best efforts, such as

Recensenten og dyret or *A Soul After Death*, are neither weighty nor universal enough to have anything but historical value. Heiberg was a major figure in his own time who created a national Danish Romantic drama and was an important intellectual force, but he has not been able to penetrate the time barrier and reach modern audiences as more than a voice from the past, a voice locked in the past.

Heiberg was a writer with a program. He wanted to create a Danish national comic drama; he wanted this drama to embody his ideas about the nature and function of art; and he wanted to infuse this drama with his Romantic vision of the world. The central themes in Heiberg's work are his ideas about the Romantic movement and his Hegelian convictions. For Heiberg, Romanticism meant, first and foremost, a focus on the national. He believed that each nation has its own unique "spirit" and that this spirit is a force, a raw energy. The spirit is expressed in such ancient sources as myths and folklore, and the task of the Romantic artist is to take the raw energy locked into the myth or folktale and give it an artistic/moral form. Heiberg perceived myths and folklore as embodiments of nature, but nature with a national imprint. The Romantic artist must transform nature into art, or rather, weave a thread intertwining nature and artistic form.

Heiberg regarded the drama as the ideal medium for his artistic creation, a conviction based on a rather unwieldy argument. Drama, he contended, is the most complete of the verbal arts; in turn, by intricate Hegelian dialectic, he argued that the verbal arts are the most sophisticated of all the arts. That lyric drama is the pinnacle of dramatic forms is established by another set of dialectic equations. Poetry, the most sophisticated of the verbal arts, has two primary modes, lyric and epic. Drama is both lyric and epic—that is, it embodies both poetic form, which is timeless, and a story, which is located in time. Heiberg's insistence on dialectic equations is both amusing and pathetic.

From a more practical point of view, Heiberg wanted to create a new dramatic art form, the Danish vaudeville, which he wanted to be different both from classical drama and from its contemporary forebears, French Opéra Comique (or song plays) and German plays with songs. Heiberg castigated both of the above as hodgepodges of drama, music, and dance in which the three performing arts are thrown together without taste or artistic merit. The songs and the dance in these theatrical forms were, Heiberg said, unmotivated interruptions of the action, and the action an unwelcome activity to be endured between musical numbers. He proposed to create a drama in which the three forms united to compose a synthetic whole. Most important, the music was to be incorporated into the action, growing naturally from it. In addition to this strong emphasis on form, his drama would be distinguished by a preoccupation with the Danish national character.

RECENSENTEN OG DYRET

When one reads Heiberg's plays, especially the best ones such as *Recensenten og dyret*, his program comes to life. To be sure, *Recensenten og dyret* is light fare, but it is witty, well constructed, and closely follows Heiberg's specifications for what a good vaudeville should be.

Recensenten og dyret is, like all of Heiberg's vaudevilles, a play about young love. Keiser and Viva love each other, but as Keiser is a young and penniless student, and Viva's father is in financial trouble caused by his vain ambitions to be a serious publisher, Pryssing, the father, refuses to let the young lovers marry. He has decided that he wants a son-in-law with money, one who can help him out of his economic distress.

The setting for the play is the Copenhagen amusement park, Bakken. For a paper he publishes, Pryssing has hired Torp, a sixty-year-old law student, to write reviews of everything from the circus to street-singers. Pryssing thinks that his paper will succeed if it has reviews. He and Viva come to Bakken, Pryssing to check on Torp, Viva to meet Keiser secretly.

Torp, because his pay from Pryssing is not merely low but also overdue, has devised the scheme of presenting an act of his own in a tent at Bakken. He wants to display an unusual animal that he has happened on and captured (thus the title, the critic and the animal). Pryssing is somewhat upset because this will mean an artistic event that will not be reviewed in his paper, but he is put at ease when Torp assures him that he will review his own act, too. Two other characters show up, Klatterup and Lederman. One is a writer (he writes social criticism for newspapers) and the other is a publisher. They are at Bakken because Pryssing owes them money, and they have heard that he is going to be there.

As the intrigue develops, young Keiser uses his quick wits to save Pryssing from his angry creditors. He has Torp give Pryssing the animal, which Pryssing, in turn, gives to Klatterup and Lederman in payment of his debt. In the end, when Pryssing has already given Keiser and Viva his consent, it is disclosed that the "unique" animal is merely an insect that has lost one of its legs. The audience who has gathered to see the animal is justifiably furious, and the representatives of greed, bourgeois stupidity, and self-righteousness, Pryssing, Torp, Lederman, and Klatterup, are the butt of the public's anger.

The themes of *Recensenten og dyret* are young love, greed, and literary and critical dilettantism. The major conflict is the typically Romantic one between nature and culture. Keiser and Viva, who are young and in love, embody nature as an invincible force. They also represent, because they symbolize nature, Danishness: If one is Danish, one should act Danish and not try to imitate foreigners. The older characters represent a dying social system based on unnaturalness, on greed, and on misunderstood and naïve artistic pretensions. Un-Danishness is represented by various characters who perform at Bakken. They are Italian, German, and French (important cultural influences in Denmark at the time). The older characters succumb to the charms of the Italian equestrienne; the other foreigners have equally "elevated" artistic pursuits. Clearly, the moral is that the two young people, representing nature and Danishness, have the moral right over the older generation, which finds its ideals in foreign dilettantes. There is a logic in nature (young love) that invariably overcomes all cultural constraints.

The form is light but witty and linguistically sophisticated. Heiberg shows great skill in the construction of his play. The songs are textbook examples of his theory on how to use music in vaudeville: They never intrude, but fit neatly and naturally into the ac-

tion and often have the character of dialogues and dramatic encounters. The more straightforward songs effectively set the mood, which is an important aspect of Heiberg's theory concerning the use of music in vaudeville. He deliberately uses light tunes that are already known to the audience, so that the tunes can help to set a mood without themselves becoming intrusive. *Recensenten og dyret* is probably Heiberg's most successful vaudeville in terms of his program for the creation of a Danish national vaudeville. Its principal drawback is that it seems to have been written, in part, as a polemic against particular individuals in his own day.

THE APRIL FOOLS

All the other vaudevilles that Heiberg wrote are variations on the same theme: A boy and girl are in love, and their parents or guardians oppose their love because of greed and because they are part of an old and dying system. In the end, romance and young, unbridled nature win out, and everybody is happy. *The April Fools* is no exception. It follows the pattern in every way. It is interesting, however, because it clearly exemplifies Heiberg's rather heavy-handed use of symbolism.

The April Fools is set in a girls' boarding school and depicts the love affair of Sigfried Møller and Constance, who are young adults, and the love affair of Hans Mortensen and Trine Rar, who are twelve-year-olds. The principal villains are Miss Bittermandel, the headmistress of the school and Constance's aunt and guardian, and Mr. Zierlich, one of the teachers in the school. He is an older man, to whom Miss Bittermandel has promised Constance in marriage.

The story is, in brief, that Miss Bittermandel is giving a party because it is her birthday, the first of April. Traditionally, the first of April is a day for playing practical jokes on people, and that is exactly what the young lovers do. Miss Bittermandel is desperately trying to keep Sigfried and Hans away from Constance and Trine, respectively. Her way of doing this is to keep them out of the school. On this particular first of April, they both manage to get into the school anyway. Sigfried gets in disguised as a giant basket of wine from a fictitious wine grocer; for his part, Hans throws a stone through a window, and when the servants come out to see who did it, he sneaks in behind them.

Through a series of mishaps, some orchestrated by Sigfried and Hans, and some not, the party ends as a total disaster, with Miss Bittermandel having to send all the parents and their daughters back home. Sigfried, however, manages to get his Constance, and Hans and Trine enjoy some time together. The final song contends that life is a school and that life is where real learning takes place.

The text of the last song refers to the play's central theme: That girls' schools are places where young ladies are taught a lot of silly nonsense and where snobbery for things foreign is taken beyond the absurd. As social criticism, *The April Fools* is less than convincing, but as good, sparkling, innocent fun, it is everything one could desire.

Heiberg's other usual themes—nature versus culture, Danishness versus foreignness, youth versus age, and the new order versus the old order—are also present. Nature is symbolized, as always in Heiberg, by the young lovers, by the quintessentially natural Mrs. Rar (Trine's mother), who owns a meat-and-game shop, by Sigfried's profession as a carpenter, and by Constance's love for nature and distaste for the city. The unnatural is symbolized by Miss Bittermandel's greed, by her desire to marry off a young girl such as Constance to the elderly Zierlich, and by the various foppish foreigners who teach at the school or offer their services as entertainers at the party. The most obvious symbols of unnaturalness are the silly things that the girls at the school are taught, such as dancing, piano playing, and sewing.

The opposition between Danish and foreign cultures is symbolized in the characters' names. This is generally true in Heiberg's plays, but it is especially obvious in *The April Fools*. All the good—that is, natural or Danish—characters have good Danish names that highlight a particular characteristic. Constance is constant and faithful, Sigfried is, as he explains to Constance, lest she or the audience miss the symbolism, a man who is a match for his name: He will "sieg," which means "win," and he will create "fried," or "peace," having convinced everybody of

the righteousness of his cause. Hans Mortensen is also a good Danish name, reeking of country and fertile farmland. Trine is his female equivalent, and Rar, as Trine and her mother are called and are, means "nice."

The other characters also are characterized by their names. Bittermandel means "bitter almond," while Zierlich means "finicky." There is a Swedish dancemaster, Tenneman (the symbolism lies in the fact that this, to Danes, is an obviously Swedish name), and there is Simon, who is a German-Jewish *avanturier*, which can be translated as "con man." The internal symbolic structure of the play is an intricate reticulum, evoking sympathy for the people and actions that symbolize romance, Danishness, naturalness, and the new Romantic social order, while ridiculing the representatives of the old order and of foreign affectation.

No

One of Heiberg's very last vaudevilles, *No*, is but a piece of frothy literary fluff. The story is the usual, young lovers who are kept from each other because of economic considerations that have nothing to do with them. This vaudeville was clearly influenced by the play *Nein* (1825), by the German dramatist Gustav Friedrich W. von Barneckow. The interesting twist on the usual theme is that the girl, Sophie, is forced, first by her lover, Hammer, and then by her guardian, Gamstrup, to answer "no," in Danish, "nei," to everything that is said to her.

Her guardian has decided that Sophie is to marry an old friend of his, the sacristan Link. Link is an older man, and Sophie is in love with Hammer, which is the source of the play's central conflict. Hammer, when told that a suitor is expected, tells Sophie that she must say "no" to whatever the suitor says. She manages so deftly that Link can say to Hammer that she is a brilliant conversationalist. She also manages to turn Link's proposal down. When Gamstrup finds out that his friend was met with a barrage of noes, he forces Sophie to repeat the success with Hammer. She does, in more ways than one. Not only does she answer no to everything he says without his noticing, but also she manages to make the sum of her negative answers a positive one: In saying no, she says yes. All ends well. Hammer suddenly comes into money, Link is happy to leave Copenhagen behind, and Gamstrup makes peace with Hammer.

No has even less substance than the other vaudevilles. It is simply a tour de force, a demonstration of its author's mastery of the form. Yet it is an empty shell. Where the early vaudevilles had some kind of moral and ideational content, *No* is pure form without content.

A Soul After Death

In 1841, which was an exceptionally productive year for Heiberg, he published a book of dramatic poems entitled *Nye digte*. One of these, *A Soul After Death*, has been praised as Heiberg's masterpiece of poetic elegance and acerbic wit. As the title suggests, this play is about the adventures of a dead man's soul. The soul in question was, on Earth, not the soul of simply any man, but that of a solid bourgeois citizen of Heiberg's Copenhagen. One is dealing here with tongue-in-cheek social criticism.

The drama is written in elegant and energetic verse. It follows the soul on his quest for a place in which he can spend eternity. His immediate inspiration is to head for Heaven, but there are complications. It turns out that having been a good, solid citizen who claims to be a Christian is not enough for the vigilant and inquisitive Saint Peter, who doles out the entry passes at Heaven's gate. Saint Peter wants proof that the soul really, profoundly believed in Jesus as humankind's savior. The soul falls seriously short of that ideal, as he has subscribed to the idea that God is beyond human understanding and that humans therefore do not have to waste time thinking about him. The soul is turned down and heads down the road to Elysium, where Aristophanes stands guard (the play has as one of its models Aristophanes' *Nephelai*, 423 B.C.E.; *The Clouds*, 1708). Again, the soul from Copenhagen is weighed and found too much of a solid citizen and too little of a sparkling spirit to spend eternity with the likes of Socrates. Aristophanes ends their conversation with the words, "Soul, go to Hell!"

The soul does go to Hell. What is more, he does not initially realize where he is and rather likes it. He likes it because it reminds him of the Copenhagen he

has recently left. This is Heiberg's witty point: Those who are punished by going to Hell are condemned to live exactly the life they left on Earth. Or, inversely, life in nineteenth century Copenhagen is Hell. In Hell, the soul meets Mephistopheles, who shows him around and points out all the nice features that will make the soul feel right at home.

Hell is a continuation of humdrum bourgeois emptiness on Earth. As Mephistopheles points out, "people yawn a lot in this country." This, however, is no problem for the soul; he is used to being bored. There is a minor crisis when the soul inquires what the name of the country is. He cannot understand why he, who was such a good and solid citizen, should be punished by going to Hell. Mephistopheles assuages his fears by saying that Hell is the right place for him and his likes, who were not good enough to go to Heaven and not bad enough to go to the lower regions of Hell, where souls are roasted over a slow fire and tormented in other inventive ways. In the end, the soul is content, convinced that he has indeed found the right place.

A Soul After Death gives Heiberg a chance to impale verbally certain types of people whom he detests. In Hell, the soul meets, among others, a poet who personally was bad, but whose work was good. The poet ended up in Hell, while his work went to Heaven. The soul also meets an actor who is so devoid of a personality or a conviction of his own that he sways with the dramatic breeze, back and forth between being good or bad depending on the character he currently is playing. It also gives Heiberg a chance to show the Copenhagen middle class in all its stolid, empty-headed complacency.

A Soul After Death is probably Heiberg's best piece of work in any genre. It displays technical virtuosity, genuine wit, and some well-argued social criticism. Yet it must be added that even this, the best of Heiberg's works, falls short of greatness. It is not quite amusing enough, not quite serious enough in its social criticism, not dazzling enough in its manipulation of ideas and literary forms to warrant permanent escape from oblivion. It has interest as a good example of ironic literature from its time and as a record of the intellectual and social currents of nineteenth century Copenhagen but not enough stature to stand on its own as a work of art.

ELVERHØJ

This last assessment is even more true of *Elverhøj*, the play that Heiberg wrote for the wedding of Prince Frederik and Princess Vilhelmine. This drama (as opposed to the vaudevilles), is in five long acts. It shares with the vaudevilles the themes of young lovers who cannot unite and the celebration of nature and national pride, but it adds to this layer of events in the "real" world a layer of events in the world of the elves (the title translates "hill of the elves"). *Elverhøj* features one of the great Danish kings, Christian IV, and his counterpart, the king of the elves. The latter does not appear, but the audience hears about him. The story is a repetition of all the stories in Heiberg's plays, with one major twist. An old saying in Denmark, so the characters in *Elverhøj* claim, states that no Danish king has dared cross the brook of Tryggevælde in the southeastern part of the island of Sjælland, because beyond the brook the kingdom of the elves begins. Christian IV, in the play, proves the myth wrong. He crosses the brook without incident and brings the despondent young lovers together by royal decree.

Elverhøj is not a very good play, but it is, surprisingly, the only one of Heiberg's plays that even today has a permanent place in the repertoire of the Royal Theatre in Copenhagen. This has less to do with the play's merits, however, than with ritual. It has become customary to perform *Elverhøj* (or at least one act of it) every time the Danish royal family makes an official visit to the Royal Theatre.

OTHER MAJOR WORKS

SHORT FICTION: *Noveller*, 1818-1819 (2 volumes).

POETRY: *Nye digte*, 1841.

NONFICTION: *Formenlehre der dänischen sprache*, 1823; *Om den menneskelige frihed*, 1824; "Om vaudevillen," 1826; *Nordische mythologie: Aus der Edda und Oehlenschlägers mythischen dichtungen*, 1827; "Om det materialistiske og idealistiske i Sproget," 1827; "Bretschneiders forsvar for rationalismen," 1830; *Om philosophiens betydning for den nuværende tid*, 1833; "Symbolik," 1834.

BIBLIOGRAPHY

Fenger, Henning. *The Heibergs*. New York: Twayne, 1971. The story of Johan Ludvig Heiberg and his family, covering the younger Heiberg's life and works. Bibliography.

Mitchell, P. M. *A History of Danish Literature*. 2d ed. New York: Kraus-Thomson Organization, 1971. An analysis of literature in Denmark, covering Heiberg and many other Danish writers. Bibliography.

Rossel, Sven H., ed. *A History of Danish Literature*. Lincoln: University of Nebraska Press, 1992. An overview of Danish literature that covers the development of drama. Bibliography and index.

Per Schelde Jacobsen

HERMAN HEIJERMANS

Born: Rotterdam, the Netherlands; December 3, 1864

Died: Zandvoort, the Netherlands; November 22, 1924

PRINCIPAL DRAMA

Dora Kremer, pr., pb. 1893

Ahasverus, pr., pb. 1893 (as Ivan Jelakowitch; English translation, 1929)

Ghetto, pr. 1898, pb. 1899 (English adaptation, 1899)

Het zevende gebod, pr. 1899, pb. 1900

Op hoop van zegen, pr. 1900, pb. 1901 (*The Good Hope*, 1912)

Het pantser, pr. 1901, pb. 1902

Ora et labora, pr. 1902, pb. 1903

Het kind, pr., pb. 1903 (as Samuel Falkland)

In de jonge Jan, pr., pb. 1903 (as Falkland; *A Case of Arson*, 1906)

Schakels, pr. 1903, pb. 1905 (*Links*, 1908)

Bloeimaand, pr. 1904, pb. 1905

Saltimbank, pb. 1904, pr. 1922 (English translation, 1923)

Allerzielen, pr. 1904, pb. 1905

Uitkomst, pr. 1907, pb. 1909

De meid, pr. 1908, pb. 1911 (*The Hired Girl*, 1917)

De opgaande zon, pr. 1908, pb. 1911 (*The Rising Sun*, 1917)

Glück auf!, pr., pb. 1911

Robert, Bertram & Comp., pr., pb. 1914 (adaptation of Gustav Raeder's German farce *Robert und Bertram: Oder, Die lustigen Vagabunden*)

Eva Bonheur, pr. 1917, pb. 1919 (*The Devil to Pay*, 1925)

Dageraad, pr. 1918, pb. 1920

De wijze kater, pr. 1918, pb. 1919 (*The Wise Tomcat*, 1937)

OTHER LITERARY FORMS

Herman Heijermans began his literary career by writing prose sketches under a variety of pseudonyms and became a journalist by writing theater criticism for *De telegraaf*, a newspaper that had been founded in Amsterdam. He won his first literary success with *'n Jodenstreek?* (a Jew's trick?), a novella about intermarriage, which appeared in 1892 in *De gids* (the guide), one of the most respected periodicals in the Netherlands.

During his literary career, Heijermans employed several pen names, the most famous of which was Samuel Falkland, which had originally belonged to his father. He affixed "Jr." to it and made it his own. With this pseudonym, he signed a series of vignettes and sketches of Amsterdam life that appeared weekly for twenty-one years, first in *De telegraaf* and later in *Algemeen handelsblad* (general journal of commerce). His "Falklandjes," as they came to be called, attracted a large audience that looked forward to each new sketch and, sometimes, a one-act play. When they were later published in book form, they filled eighteen volumes. As a writer of Dutch prose, Heijermans is also known for his autobiographical novel *Kamertjeszonde* (1898; sin in a furnished room); *Droomkoninkje* (1924; the little dream king), a novel

filled with the dreams and fantasies of childhood; and other sketches, novellas, and novels.

ACHIEVEMENTS

In the last decade of the nineteenth century, the Dutch drama emerged from the literary revolution known as *de Beweging van Tachtig* (the movement of the eighties) unchanged. The man who was to revive the Dutch drama and to become the greatest playwright of modern Holland was Herman Heijermans. He was aware not only of the vitalizing effect of the new literary movement in the Netherlands but also of the influence of such new dramatists as Henrik Ibsen, Leo Tolstoy, Gerhart Hauptmann, and Maurice Maeterlinck. Ibsen's *Samfundets støtter* (pr., pb. 1877; *The Pillars of Society*, 1880), *Et dukkehjem* (pr., pb. 1879; *A Doll's House*, 1880; also known as *A Doll House*), and *Vildanden* (pb. 1884; *The Wild Duck*, 1891) had already appeared on the Dutch stage when, in 1892, André Antoine toured the country with his Théâtre Libre and returned again in 1893 and 1894 with such plays as Ibsen's *Gengangere* (pb. 1881; *Ghosts*, 1885), Tolstoy's *Vlast tmy* (pb. 1887; *The Power of Darkness*, 1888), and Hauptmann's *Die Weber* (pb. 1892; *The Weavers*, 1899). In September, 1894, Lugné-Poë brought his company, L'Œuvre, to Amsterdam, with performances of Maeterlinck's *Pelléas et Mélisande* (1892; English translation, 1894) and Ibsen's *Rosmersholm* (pb. 1886; English translation, 1889) and *En folkefiende* (pb. 1882; *An Enemy of the People*, 1890). Heijermans was sensitive to the new ideas and points of view in the modern European theater, and he soon began to put them on the stage in his own country. Like many great dramatists, however, he does not fit neatly into the narrow definition of this or that movement in the drama, and he was never a member of any school or coterie.

For the next thirty years, apart from occasional interruptions, Heijermans devoted himself to his career in the Dutch theater, as dramatist, critic, director, and producer. Although he borrowed for his own purposes what seemed best to him from the new European drama, he put on the Dutch stage much that was his own and much that was native to Dutch soil. He had a keen insight into Dutch society, as well as into

Jewish life in Amsterdam. He was a sharp critic of the middle classes and never hesitated to attack hypocrisy. A foe of intolerance, he castigated it whether it came from Christians or Jews. His zeal for social reform, as well as the popularity of *The Good Hope*, one of his greatest plays, contributed to the passage of the Ships Act of 1909, which provided for better protection of the lives of sailors and fishermen.

Heijermans brought to the Dutch theater a mastery of dramatic technique and the ability to create characters on the stage. Even as he criticized and satirized, he could not help revealing his love for some of his characters, both working-class people and self-made middle-class businessmen. He had a gift, too, for portraying the comic, even eccentric, side of human nature and an understanding of the lonely, but cantankerous, so that he had a sure hand for comedy.

He is much more closely connected to Ibsen and Hauptmann than to Émile Zola, and to classify Heijermans as a naturalist would be a superficial criticism of him, as well as a misinterpretation of his work. The Dutch dramatist had too much of an interest in fantasy and in the imagination of the child, and some of his plays reveal neo-Romantic characteristics and even display a fairy-tale atmosphere. Although Heijermans did, indeed, speak out against middle-class marriage based on money and class, against exploitation of the toilers of the sea, the workers in the mines, and the tillers of the soil, against the dehumanizing effect of imprisonment, and against the immorality of businessmen, his humor, his interest in individual character, his optimistic love of life, and his pantheism make him less a naturalist than a realist. He observed the life and people of his native land, with all their strengths and weaknesses, and put them on the stage with all the skill and living warmth that Dutch painters had made famous two centuries before. Heijermans is, for many critics, the greatest dramatist modern Holland has produced. He is the only playwright since Joost van den Vondel who has won admiring recognition outside his own country.

BIOGRAPHY

Herman Heijermans was born in Rotterdam in 1864, the eldest son in a family of eleven children.

His father, Herman Heijermans, Sr., was a well-known and highly respected journalist, whose talents and professional career had a considerable influence on the life of his famous son. His mother, née Mathilde Spiers, was well educated and, unlike her husband, came from a wealthy family. Heijermans's formal schooling ended with his graduation from the Hogere Burgerschool, a secondary school equivalent to the European lycée or gymnasium and thus more advanced than the American high school. He was a good student, but although his father would have liked to send him to the university, it was all he could do to provide a solid basic education for each of his many children.

Heijermans had early shown an interest in writing, and before he was twenty, he had finished his first play, "Don Gables," a tragedy in blank verse. His father knew from his own experience, however, how difficult it was to earn a living as a journalist, and because he knew someone at an important Dutch bank, a position was soon found for his son. Not long afterward, young Heijermans went into the wholesale rag business, to which his fiancée's family contributed some money. He was not a very good businessman, an unfortunate side of his nature that turned up at several points later in his career. It was only by assuming some of the financial burden himself that his father was able to save him from the disgrace of bankruptcy. Nevertheless, Heijermans lost his standing in the community, people he had thought were his friends deserted him, his family was deeply disappointed by the sudden collapse of such a bright career, and his engagement came to an end.

In the meantime, he had not really given up his interest in writing, and his success as a journalist and a writer of sketches and stories enabled him to leave Rotterdam for Amsterdam. Heijermans was already at work on his first play, *Dora Kremer*, which was produced in Rotterdam. It was not as good as Ibsen's *A Doll's House*, from which he had borrowed a theme, but the young Dutch playwright blamed its failure on the audiences, who, he believed, lacked interest in the work of native dramatists. He had already written his effective one-act play *Ahasverus*, but he decided to have it produced under the Russian-sounding pseudonym Ivan Jelakowitch. This drama of the persecution of the Jews in Russia during the pogroms was a tremendous success and marked the beginning of Heijermans's fame as a dramatist.

He had lived with Marie Peers for some years, then he scandalized his family and neighbors by marrying her. He transformed the experiences of his early business career and of his life with Marie Peers into two full-length plays, *Ghetto*, in which he revealed his alienation from the Jews, and *Het zevende gebod* (the seventh commandment), in which he castigated the narrow-mindedness of tradition-bound Catholics. His greatest and most famous play is *The Good Hope*, in which he brought the figure of Kniertje to the Dutch stage as a tragic symbol of the cost of taking the fish out of the sea. It was a tribute to the mariners of a great seafaring nation, and during the decades following the play's premiere in 1900, it was performed, in several languages, in European countries, Russia, the United States, Israel, and Japan.

In 1907, Heijermans moved to Berlin, hoping to gain the copyright protection that was available under the Berne Convention, but not in the Netherlands. He remained there almost five years. During this period, many of his plays were produced in Berlin, and he wrote for the *Berliner Tageblatt* (Berlin daily newspaper), which also published his Falklandjes and serialized his novel *De roode flibustier* (1911; the red buccaneer). When the Nederlandsche Tooneelvereeniging (the Dutch Stage Society) collapsed at the end of 1912, Heijermans decided to leave Germany and return to the Netherlands, which had, meanwhile, joined the Berne Convention. The theatrical company had produced most of his plays, and together they had brought new glory to the Dutch theater. Unfortunately, he now became involved in the business side of the theater, and this made enormous demands on his energies, thus preventing him from pursuing his interests as a dramatist.

The marital relationship of Heijermans and his wife became strained during these years, and in 1918 he divorced her and married Annie Jurgens, a young actress with the theatrical company. His theatrical enterprises involved him in ever greater financial re-

sponsibilities, however, and instead of declaring the Dutch Stage Society bankrupt, as any prudent businessman might have done, he refused to take the step he had dreaded in his early years in business. When the financial disaster did come, he assumed all the outstanding obligations. In an effort to pay off these debts, he returned to journalism. He was soon turning out material with all his old speed and energy. In addition to *De telegraaf*, he contributed to several other newspapers, writing feuilletons, articles, detective stories, and novels.

He moved with his wife and family to Zandvoort and took a small room in Amsterdam, where he would go to work alone every day. In 1923, he began working at his literary career again, glad to be away from the nagging demands of business and once more hopeful and enthusiastic. Then pain and suffering intervened; he became seriously ill. In April, 1924, he underwent an operation for cancer of the mouth. After a period of temporary improvement, the wasting disease consumed him. He died shortly before his sixtieth birthday.

ANALYSIS

During his career as Holland's leading modern dramatist, Herman Heijermans produced more than twenty full-length plays and at least that many one-act plays, most of them of outstanding quality. His first play, *Dora Kremer*, showed his talent, but it was a weak drama, and the characters were not convincing. *Ahasverus*, the one-act play that followed, revealed the master hand of the born dramatist. He created a moving picture of the pious old Jew who refuses to give up his faith, in spite of the horrors of the Russian pogroms.

GHETTO

With *Ghetto*, a full-length "middle-class tragedy," Heijermans achieved the development promised by this first success. The play also reflects his early business experiences in Rotterdam, as well as his observations of Jewish life in Amsterdam. He was alienated from Judaism and attracted by socialism. There is thus much of the rebellious Heijermans in the play's young hero, Rafaël, but although he wanted to criticize the Jews unmercifully for the spiritual ghetto in which they had trapped themselves, he could not resist warm admiration for life and character wherever he found them.

The redeeming qualities of Rafaël's father, Sachel, and his father's sister, Esther, as well as what he himself called "the Jewish spirit," are fused in Rebbe Haëzer, who emerges as the only wholly admirable character in the play. The easygoing rabbi, continually sipping coffee, presents such a warm and glowing view of Jewish family life that the stubborn adherence of Sachel and Esther to the old ways seems more understandable, their characters more human. Rafaël appears as a romantic but vague hero when he comes up against the life-size figure of this genial, wise old man.

Het zevende gebod

In *Het zevende gebod*, Heijermans gave his ideas on middle-class and religious conservatism and on marriage based on property a setting more typical of Dutch national life than the one he had employed for *Ghetto*. This time the family is Catholic, but it is again the authoritarian father, with his blunt manners, who is the dominant figure in the play. A member of the agricultural middle class, Dobbe, Sr., abides by its most hypocritical conventions and is a symbol of the bourgeoisie that Heijermans despised. His relationship with his children has never been a loving and intimate one. Yet the younger generation, while romantic and idealistic, like the one in *Ghetto*, is not very convincing.

The Good Hope

With *The Good Hope*, Heijermans began a group of plays that were to portray the position of the worker in society. There is socialism in this play, too, but the setting of this "play of the sea" is not the home of a middle-class Dutch family, but of a fisherman's widow, Kniertje, in a village on the North Sea. She is a symbol of the people who earn their living from the sea. Yet it is not Heijermans's socialism that makes *The Good Hope* a great play, but the skill with which he has combined his message with the realistic portrayal of the people of a Dutch fishing village. It is the characters who make the doctrine credible, not the doctrine that makes the characters credible.

One cannot speak of a hero or heroine in *The Good Hope*, for all the fishermen and their people are heroes and heroines, but Kniertje is the central character about whom the play revolves, and it is she who, before the final curtain falls, stands on the stage as the symbol of her people. When the play begins, Kniertje has already lost her husband and two of her sons at sea. "I have my belly full of that waiting on the pier," she says. Kniertje is submissive yet courageous. It is not only resignation but also the courage to face the dangers of a hard life that are at the bottom of her attempts to persuade her son to go to sea, and she tells him that every trade has some element of danger. Her trust in God sustains her. There is no bitterness in her humble fortitude, and when she is reminded that her sons are out in the storm for the shipowner and his daughter, Kniertje adds, "And for us . . ." Yet it is this patient bravery and this firm faith in the goodness of God and humanity that, in the end, make of her such a tragic figure. When the sea has claimed her two remaining sons, she is left to depend on the crust of charity condescendingly granted by those very members of society who have exploited her. She stands for all the loyal women who wait at home in loneliness while their men risk their lives at sea and who must suffer in poverty if their men do not return.

Het pantser and Ora et labora

In 1901, Heijermans wrote the antimilitarist play *Het pantser* (the suit of armor), which belongs to the same group of plays as *The Good Hope* and *Ora et labora* (pray and work), "a play of the land" that portrays the peasants of Friesland locked in a harsh and unequal struggle to force a living from their soil. Their deeply ingrained traits of pride and stubbornness, or the alternative, submissiveness, are their only weapons against degradation. In *Het pantser*, Heijermans's message is so clear as to be heavy-handed, and he himself admitted that is was a "propaganda play." In *Ora et labora*, on the other hand, the didactic element is, if anything, too weak. In this drama, which also belongs to this group, the characters have not been developed effectively, and although the construction is excellent, the conflict involves not so much the characters as the environment.

BLOEIMAAND AND GLÜCK AUF!

Also connected with this group is *Bloeimaand* (May time), "a play of the city," which portrays the aged poor with great skill but which lacks a certain unity. Mention must also be made of *Glück auf!* (good luck!), "a play of the mines," which was based on a visit to a mine made by Heijermans while he was in Germany. Although individual scenes show his dramatic skill at its best, there is a certain weakness in the characters and structure.

LINKS

One of Heijermans's most interesting and effective plays is *Links*, which bore the ironic subtitle, "A Happy Play of the Family Fireside." The hero, Pancras Duif, a self-made middle-class businessman, dominates the play, with none of the faults of his class. He is no longer young, and when his children discover that he is thinking of remarrying, they scheme to protect their shares of his estate. It has been one of the dramatist's most popular plays.

OTHER MAJOR WORKS

LONG FICTION: *'n Jodenstreek?*, 1892; *Kamertjeszonde*, 1898; *Diamantstad*, 1904; *Gevleugelde daden*, 1905; *De roode flibustier*, 1911; *Droomkoninkje*, 1924; *Vuurvlindertje*, 1925; *Duczika*, 1926.

SHORT FICTION: *Interieurs*, 1897; *Sabbath*, 1903; *Schetsen*, 1903.

BIBLIOGRAPHY

Flaxman, Seymour Lawrence. *Herman Heijermans and His Dramas*. The Hague: Nijhoff, 1954. The classic biography of Heijermans in English. Focuses on his dramatic works. Bibliography.

Yoder, Hilda van Neck. *Dramatizations of Social Change: Herman Heijermans's Plays as Compared with Selected Dramas by Ibsen, Hauptmann, and Chekhov*. The Hague: Nijhoff, 1978. A comparison of Heijermans's dramas with those of Henrik Ibsen, Gerhart Hauptmann, and Anton Chekhov, with emphasis on presentation of social problems. Bibliography.

Young, Toby. "Gritty but Grotty." Review of *The Good Hope* by Herman Heijermans. *The Spectator*, November 17, 2001, p. 64. This review examines a revival of the political play *The Good Hope*, revised by Lee Hall and performed at the Cottesloe Theatre in London, finding it heavy on the political statement and light on dramatic development. The reviewer notes, however, that many in the audience enjoyed the play.

Seymour L. Flaxman

LILLIAN HELLMAN

Born: New Orleans, Louisiana; June 20, 1905
Died: Martha's Vineyard, Massachusetts; June 30, 1984

PRINCIPAL DRAMA

The Children's Hour, pr., pb. 1934
Days to Come, pr., pb. 1936
The Little Foxes, pr., pb. 1939
Watch on the Rhine, pr., pb. 1941
The Searching Wind, pr., pb. 1944
Another Part of the Forest, pr. 1946, pb. 1947
Montserrat, pr. 1949, pb. 1950 (adaptation of Emmanuel Robles' play)
The Autumn Garden, pr., pb. 1951
The Lark, pr. 1955, pb. 1956 (adaptation of Jean Anouilh's play *L'Alouette*)
Candide, pr. 1956, pb. 1957 (libretto; music by Leonard Bernstein, lyrics by Richard Wilbur, John Latouche, and Dorothy Parker; adaptation of Voltaire's novel)
Toys in the Attic, pr., pb. 1960
My Mother, My Father, and Me, pr., pb. 1963 (adaptation of Burt Blechman's novel *How Much?*)
The Collected Plays, pb. 1972

OTHER LITERARY FORMS

In addition to her original stage plays, Lillian Hellman published original screenplays, a collection of the letters of Anton Chekhov, her adaptations of two French plays (*Montserrat, L'Alouette*) and of an American novel (*How Much?*), an operetta adapted from Voltaire's *Candide: Ou, L'Optimisme* (1759; *Candide: Or, All for the Best,* 1759; also as *Candide: Or, The Optimist,* 1762; also as *Candide: Or, Optimism,* 1947), many uncollected articles, and several volumes of memoirs, the first two of which have received as much acclaim as her best plays.

ACHIEVEMENTS

Lillian Hellman was the most important American follower of Henrik Ibsen after Arthur Miller. Like Ibsen in his middle period, she wrote strong, well-made plays involving significant social issues. Like Ibsen, she created memorable female characters, some strong, some weak. Her most important female character, Regina Giddens of *The Little Foxes* and *Another Part of the Forest,* seems at least partially modeled on Ibsen's Hedda Gabler. Both Hellman and Ibsen were exceptional in depicting believable, memorable children. Like him, though more frequently, she used blackmail as a dramatic ploy. Her plays, like Ibsen's, can be strongly and tightly dramatic, and, like his, some, notably *The Little Foxes,* have a question ending: That is, one in which the eventual outcome for the major characters is left ironically uncertain.

Her last two original plays, however, recall Chekhov more than Ibsen in their depiction of feckless characters and, in one of the two, an apparent, though only apparent, plotlessness. She has been blamed for her employment of melodramatic plot elements, but her use of them is often valid and essential and does not interfere with accurate character analysis, convincing dramatic dialogue, and adroit handling of social issues. Hellman was, after Tennessee Williams, the most important dramatist writing primarily about the American South. Two of her plays, *Watch on the*

Lillian Hellman (Library of Congress)

Rhine and *Toys in the Attic,* won the New York Drama Critics Circle Award. Hellman received many other awards, including the Brandeis University Creative Arts Medal and the National Institute of Arts and Letters Gold Medal.

BIOGRAPHY

Lillian Florence Hellman was born in New Orleans of Jewish parents. Her father was also born in New Orleans, and her mother in Alabama, of a family long established there. Part of her mother's family moved to New York, and when Hellman was five years old, her parents moved there and commenced a routine of spending six months of each year in New York and six in New Orleans with her father's two unmarried sisters. As her memoirs make clear, Hellman's plays are strongly influenced by her Southern, urban background. Her mother's family was a source for the Hubbards in *The Little Foxes* and *Another Part of the Forest*; her paternal aunts, for the sisters in *Toys in the Attic*. All her original plays except the first two (*The Children's Hour* and *Days to Come*) are set in the South: in the Washington area, in Alabama towns, or in New Orleans. Hellman was graduated from high school in New York in 1922, attended New York University from 1922 to 1924, and briefly attended Columbia University in 1924, without completing a degree at either school. She worked for a time thereafter in New York and Hollywood in the areas of publishing, book reviewing, and reading manuscripts of plays and movie scenarios. In 1925, she married Arthur Kober; they were divorced in 1932. Two years later, her first play, *The Children's Hour*, was a tremendous hit, achieving a longer original run (691 performances) than any of her later plays. From that success until her last play in 1963, she was primarily a playwright and occasionally a scriptwriter, though she was never really happy in the theater.

Over the years, Hellman made various visits to Russia, to Civil War Spain, and elsewhere in Europe, including a very dangerous visit to Nazi Germany to take money to the underground at the request of a friend. For many years, she was the companion of the novelist Dashiell Hammett, though they lived together only sporadically. Congressional investigations of communism in the United States in the early 1950's caused serious trouble for both her and Hammett, though she denied having sufficiently consistent or deep political convictions to belong to any party. As a result of the investigations, Hellman and Hammett were both blacklisted in Hollywood, and she lost the home she owned and shared with Hammett in upstate New York, as well as various friends. Hammett was imprisoned. Soon after his release, he became ill, and Hellman took care of him until his death in 1961. In her later years, Hellman devoted herself to her four books of memoirs and taught at Harvard University, the Massachusetts Institute of Technology, and the University of California at Berkeley. She died on June 30, 1984, at Martha's Vineyard.

ANALYSIS

Beginning with her first play, *The Children's Hour*, Lillian Hellman's plays possessed certain dramatic characteristics: crisp, forceful, realistic dialogue; clear character construction and analysis; and a clear-cut plot line in the tradition of the well-made play, with fast movement and adroitly handled suspense that kept (and can still keep) audiences enthralled. Most of her plays can be called melodramatic, because of the suspense, because of the use of violence and of blackmail, and because of obvious authorial manipulation to achieve a neat conclusion. The plays are never, however, pure melodrama because pure melodrama would not include valid, well-drawn characters or significant themes.

THE CHILDREN'S HOUR

The Children's Hour, like many of Hellman's plays, concerns the destructive power of evil, its ability to erode human relationships and destroy lives. In this play, evil is manifested by a child's malicious lie and its repercussions in the lives of two women. The play, which was based on an actual lawsuit, the Great Drumsheugh Case, opens on a class in progress at a girls' boarding school in Massachusetts. The teacher, Lily Mortar, is the aunt of Martha Dobie, one of the two young women who own and operate the school. Presently, student Mary Tilford enters—very late for class—carrying a bunch of flowers with which she appeases the teacher. Then the other owner, Karen Wright, enters. Karen has lost her bracelet and asks one of the girls, Helen, if she has found it, an important issue in the play. Karen asks Mary where she got the flowers. Mary repeats her claim that she picked them. Karen, apparently recognizing them, says Mary got them out of the garbage pail and has been lying. Mary's response is, and continues to be, that the teachers are against her, that they never believe her, and that she is telling the truth. Karen grounds her for two weeks. Mary says her heart hurts and pretends to fall into a faint. She is carried to her room.

Martha enters, and she and Karen discuss Mary as a troublemaker, send for Karen's fiancé (Joe Cardin, who is a doctor and also Mary's cousin), discuss getting rid of Mrs. Mortar, and discuss Karen's plans to marry Joe as soon as school is out. Martha is clearly upset at the imminent marriage, although she likes Joe. She hates interference with a friendship that has gone on since college and hates the possibility that Karen might leave the school. Joe arrives and goes off to examine Mary.

At this point in the play, the audience cannot be sure of the meaning of Martha's jealousy, of whether Mary's feelings are in any sense justified, of whether the events thus far are more taut with emotion than what might be expected on a day-by-day basis in a girls' boarding school. Mrs. Mortar, deeply insulted at Martha's desire to get her away from the school and at her offer to send her to London and support her there, indirectly accuses her niece of homosexual feelings toward Karen. Mary's two roommates are caught eavesdropping. Joe has a friendly confrontation with Martha, who apologizes and falls into his arms, weeping. It is reasonably clear that she does not recognize her feelings for Karen as homosexual, if they are. Mary comes in, and it is clear that Joe considers her a troublemaker, as do the women. Then, as the adults leave and the audience sees Mary for the first time alone with other girls, her character becomes only too clear.

Indeed, one becomes more and more convinced that Mary's lies, her manipulation, her dictatorial attitude toward her schoolmates, and presently her outright blackmail of one of them and her cruelty to another represent more than mere naughtiness or adolescent confusion. Mary is psychotic, and dangerously so. Feeling no affection for anyone, she lives for manipulation and power. As soon as the teachers leave the room, she throws a cushion at the door and kicks a table. Apparently, her one genuine feeling other than hatred is the belief that the teachers hate her as much as she hates them. She tells her roommates that if she cannot go to the boat races (since she has been grounded), she will see to it that they do not go either. She forces a girl named Rosalie to do some work for her by hinting of knowledge that Rosalie stole the bracelet that Karen asked about earlier. She forces her roommates to report the conversation that they overheard, and while Mary certainly does not completely understand its import, she nevertheless recognizes it as a weapon she can use. She im-

mediately announces that she is going to walk out and go home, and by physical force, she makes one of the girls give her the money to get there. On this moment of tension, typical of a well-made play, act 1 closes.

The Children's Hour is unusual among Hellman's plays in that it does not all take place in one setting. Act 2 takes place in the living room of the home of Mary's grandmother in Boston. As scene 1 of the act opens, Mary arrives and is admitted by the maid, Agatha, who clearly does not trust her for an instant. Left alone while Agatha goes to fetch Mrs. Tilford, Mary tries with the aid of a mirror to make herself look sick. Mrs. Tilford enters, and Mary dashes into her arms, in tears. It soon becomes clear that Mrs. Tilford is an intelligent woman but that, unlike Agatha, she can be taken in by her granddaughter. It is an irony of the play, however, that she cannot be taken in easily. Had Mary been able to deceive her by simple lies, there would have been no play. Her usual tricks—tears, stories of being mistreated—do not work. Mrs. Tilford has supported Martha and Karen in their establishment of the school, has encouraged her friends to send their daughters there, and certainly trusts the schoolmistresses. Mary, therefore, begins to use the story she has heard secondhand, mentioning it at first vaguely and uncertainly, but then, as she sees that it is having an effect, more positively and specifically. Mrs. Tilford is deeply disturbed and obviously finds it difficult to believe that such a story could be invented. She starts to phone Karen but decides against it. She calls Joe and urgently asks him to come over. She calls a friend, perhaps one with a daughter or granddaughter at the school, asking her to come over as well. Scene 2 opens with Agatha telling Mary that Rosalie is coming to spend the night; a few moments later, Rosalie arrives. The audience learns, partly now and fully later, that Mrs. Tilford has communicated with the parents of all the girls and told them Mary's story, with the result that all the girls have been called home. Rosalie is spending the night with Mary because her mother is in New York.

These circumstances represent significant flaws in the structure of *The Children's Hour*, though they are not as noticeable in performance: First, it is difficult to believe that a woman of Mrs. Tilford's maturity and intelligence would take such drastic action on the basis of her granddaughter's word alone; second, it has to be Rosalie, among all the students, whose mother is out of town, or the play would simply grind to a halt. About the first, one might say in Hellman's defense that it would be emotionally and even intellectually difficult for Mrs. Tilford to believe that her granddaughter would have either the desire or the knowledge to invent such a lie; that to seek external verification of the story would be, even if it were true, almost surely fruitless; and that, given the time and place, it would have been irresponsible of her not to inform the other parents. Problems remain, even so. Surely Mrs. Tilford could have spoken with Joe first. True, Hellman arranges that Joe arrives late, on the plausible ground that he had to stop at a hospital, but would one more night have mattered so much? Doubtless, Mrs. Tilford's urgency is partly emotional, on the ground that most, if not all, of the girls have been at the school on her recommendation. This does not explain, however, her calm assurance later in the play that the story is true. She takes the logical attitude that Martha's, Karen's, and Joe's denials are meaningless, since they are to be expected regardless of whether the story is accurate. She is also a woman who, given her class, her money, and her intelligence, is not prone to being wrong. Perhaps one should regard her attitude as a typical Hellman irony: It is her very sense of responsibility that has made her act irresponsibly. Less defense can be offered for the presence of Rosalie. All one can say is that her presence is essential to the play, and that in a well-made play this represents perhaps the minimum of manipulation.

The scene develops very dramatically. Mary blackmails Rosalie into being prepared to support her lies if necessary. Joe arrives, and very soon he and his aunt are battling. Karen and Martha arrive, and the battle enlarges, with strong emotions on one side and calm assurance on the other. Mrs. Tilford is not even moved by the threat of a libel suit. Finally, Joe insists that Mary be questioned and, against Mrs. Tilford's wishes, brings Mary in. Mary, genuinely nervous, tells her story, making it more and more circumstantial, until finally the circumstances catch her in a lie. She has said that she has seen things through Karen's keyhole, and Karen announces that her door has no keyhole. Mary is therefore forced to say that it was Martha's room, not Karen's; Martha announces that she lives on a different floor, at the other end of the house, and, moreover, shares her room with Mrs. Mortar. Mrs. Tilford is severely shaken. Backed into a corner, Mary says that it was not she but Rosalie who saw them, and that she saw them because Karen's door was halfway open. Rosalie is summoned and at first denies the story, but when Mary makes it plain that she will, if necessary, expose Rosalie as a thief, Rosalie agrees that the story is true and collapses in tears. The curtain falls.

After so tense a moment, act 3 is almost anticlimactic. It opens on the same scene as act 1. Karen and Martha are alone in the house. They have lost their case; the townspeople are against them; they feel so persecuted that they refuse even to answer the phone; and they have not even dared to leave the house. In a rather surprising anticipation of Samuel Beckett and the Absurdists, Martha says that they are "waiting," with the implication that that is all they— or at any rate, she—will ever do. Martha hopes that Karen will escape through marrying Joe, but Karen seems doubtful. Mrs. Mortar, who had left when told to by Martha, unexpectedly enters, and the audience learns that she would have been the key witness at the trial, that she refused to return, and thus the case was lost. Her failure to return was owing to her reluctance to become involved in such a scandal. She returns now because she has run out of money, but Martha has no more to give her. She leaves the room, and Joe enters. He is planning for the marriage and for all three of them to leave together permanently, even though he would thus be giving up a promising career. Martha leaves, and in his words and attitude toward Karen it becomes clear that Joe is uncertain of the truth. Karen quietly denies any homosexual relationship, and he apparently accepts the denial, but it is uncertain whether his doubts have been laid to rest. Karen asks him to think things over for a day or two and make a decision. He reluctantly agrees and leaves, insisting that he will come back, though Karen is sure that he will not. Martha returns and, in a scene of high emotion, tells Karen that, though she had not previously been aware of it, the story that has been told about them was, at least so far as her feelings went, true. She loves Karen "that way." She leaves the room, and presently, a muffled shot is heard. Karen opens the door and sees that Martha has killed herself. Mrs. Mortar rushes in, sees what has happened, and expresses her remorse. The doorbell rings, and she answers it. It is Agatha. Mrs. Tilford is waiting in her car. Mrs. Mortar tries to keep her from coming in, but Karen allows her to enter, and Mrs. Mortar rushes out sobbing.

The final dialogue is between Karen and Mrs. Tilford. Mrs. Tilford has learned the truth. The bracelet was found among Rosalie's things, and Rosalie confessed. Apparently, Mary has confessed, too. The judge at the trial will arrange a public apology and explanation, and Mrs. Tilford will pay the amount of the damages and as much more as they will take. Karen announces Martha's death and expresses her bitter feelings toward Mrs. Tilford and her attempts to relieve her conscience through money. Gradually, however, Karen recognizes Mrs. Tilford's sincerity and sees that the old woman will be the greater sufferer because she has refused to commit Mary to an institution and will hence have to live permanently in her company and because Martha's suicide will inevitably burden her memory. Karen agrees to accept Mrs. Tilford's money. She disagrees with Mrs. Tilford's hope that she and Joe will marry. The two separate amicably, and Karen is left alone at the play's end.

Hellman expressed the feeling later that the final scene was unnecessary, that it was simply evidence of her personal compulsion to spell things out. Certainly none of her important later plays spells things out so thoroughly, but in *The Children's Hour*, the final scene provides desirable satisfaction for the audience. The only valid objection to the scene is that it raises a new possibility: Mrs. Tilford appears soon after Martha's suicide, rather than earlier, perhaps in time to prevent it. Once Martha's feelings are clear, however, it seems doubtful, given the time and circumstances,

that anything could have kept her alive, and Hellman properly leaves Karen with an uncertain future. Karen's belief in Joe's permanent defection may be wrong; it may not. The possibility of a happy outcome for her is a valid comfort to an audience after so much bitter emotion, but the certainty of a happy ending would be difficult to accept.

The play was in part a *succès de scandale* on Broadway, since open treatment of homosexuality was very unusual at the time. Hellman wrote the scenario for the first film version, *These Three* (1936), in which the homosexuality was changed to a traditional triangle. A later version restored both title and content.

THE LITTLE FOXES

The Little Foxes is, and almost surely will remain, Hellman's standard play. It represents significant advances in technique over *The Children's Hour* and is in various ways more typical of Hellman's overall production. First, it is set in the Deep South (small-town Alabama), as are three of Hellman's four most significant later plays. Second, the characters are more sharply distinguished and more deeply realized, and the dialogue is more individualized. Third, Hellman displays three significant qualities that are not fully realized in *The Children's Hour*: compassion, humor, and irony. Fourth, *The Little Foxes* displays more clearly a sociopolitical theme than does the earlier play: These are "the little foxes who spoil the vines" (a quotation from the Song of Solomon), whom Hellman sees as twentieth century capitalists in embryo.

The Little Foxes concentrates on a rapacious small-town Alabama family, the Hubbards, and on some of their victims. The year is 1900. As the play opens, Regina Giddens is giving a dinner party for a businessman from Chicago, William Marshall, with whom her brothers are negotiating to join them in opening one of the first cotton mills in the South. All the characters in the play are present except Regina's husband, Horace, the town banker, long confined at the Johns Hopkins Hospital with a bad heart. The remaining characters are Regina's brothers, Ben and Oscar Hubbard; Oscar's wife, Birdie, the last member of an aristocratic family impoverished by the Civil War; Oscar and Birdie's son, Leo; Horace and Regina's daughter, Alexandra; and the servants, Addie and Cal. Unlike the Hubbards, Birdie has cultural interests; she is a frightened woman, bullied by her husband. Ben is a jovial hypocrite whose hypocrisy has become so practiced that he is sometimes almost unaware of it. He and Regina are the dominant Hubbards. Oscar is relatively weak, obtuse, and blustery, while Leo is a lesser version of Oscar. Alexandra shares Birdie's cultural interests and seems not at all Hubbard-like. Regina herself is a handsome woman, a smooth and clever conniver, who takes in Marshall to a degree that Ben, for all his hypocrisy, cannot.

When the deal for the cotton mill has been struck, the young couple drive Marshall to the station to return to Chicago. The Hubbards are triumphant, looking forward to being rich. One problem remains: The three siblings are supposed to contribute equal sums to the mill project, enough to make them together the majority shareholders, but while Ben and Oscar are ready to put up their share, Regina must get hers from Horace, who has ignored all letters on the subject. In a piece of typical Hubbard trickery, Regina declares that Horace is holding out because he wants a larger share, and Ben finally agrees that he should have a larger share and that the difference will come out of Oscar's. Oscar is furious, but he is mollified by Regina's quite specious assurance that she will consider something that Oscar very much wants: a marriage between Leo and Alexandra. A plan is then made to send Alexandra, who is devoted to Horace, to bring him home.

Many modern plays, including several of Henrik Ibsen's, involve the return of someone long gone, but the return is almost always early in the play. In *The Little Foxes*, the audience must wait, with anticipation, for what Horace's return in the second act will bring. Before Horace's arrival, Oscar and Leo conceive a plan to steal eighty thousand dollars' worth of bonds from Horace's safety deposit box, to finance their venture. (If they can do this, they will not need Regina as a partner.) Horace then arrives, stiff and ill, accompanied by Alexandra, who has his heart medicine. During the course of the act, it becomes clear

that Horace and Regina are, and have been, at odds during most of their marriage, that Horace will not agree to finance the proposed project, and that he will not consent to a marriage between Alexandra and Leo. It is also clear that Regina will not be thwarted and that Horace is too physically frail to withstand her will.

In act 3, Horace, who has discovered the theft of the bonds, informs Regina about the crime and tells her that he will pretend that the theft was a loan. Moreover, he will change his will, leaving Regina the bonds and all his other property to Alexandra. Regina will thus lose the opportunity to invest in the business venture (because the partners will no longer need her money), and she will lose her inheritance from Horace. Furiously, she tells him that she married him only for money. He becomes distraught, reaches for his medicine, spills it, and asks her to get his new bottle. She simply stands there as he collapses and dies. Regina is now in a position to blackmail her brothers into assigning her a 75 percent interest in the mill, lest she prosecute them. Regina is triumphant; nevertheless, she now faces a life of loneliness because Alexandra has discovered her mother's treachery and will leave her.

The play ends with a question and is the better for it. If the ending represented a total and final triumph, it would emphasize the play's kinship to pure melodrama, and given the characters, an ending that had finality would be unlikely. Ben is too clear-sighted, too ironically aware, too psychologically healthy to give up. Alexandra's potential for fighting is probably small, but one cannot be sure. Moreover, the Hubbard siblings are more complex than a recital of the plot might make them seem. Ben retains an incompetent servant because she has always been in the family. Ben and Oscar both seem genuinely moved by Horace's death. Ben and Regina are both capable of viewing their own, and others', behavior ironically, and there is humor in some of their dialogue. Regina is frightened at what she has done, or rather not done. Wicked as the two may be, and much as they might remind one of nineteenth century melodramatic villains, they are human beings, complex enough to be believable.

The play, moreover, has other ironies that remove it from total melodrama. It is ironic that Leo should be Birdie's son and Alexandra Regina's daughter, because Leo is an extreme version of Oscar, and Alexandra has the outlook of Horace. For most of his life, however, Horace has been weak, yielding to his wife, as Birdie has to her husband. Birdie, for whom one is made to feel compassion, gains enough strength to tell Alexandra the truth, and Horace gains enough strength to stand up to Regina. These are highly individualized human beings, and the play is skillfully constructed, absorbing, and genuinely insightful.

WATCH ON THE RHINE

Like *The Little Foxes*, *Watch on the Rhine* contains murder and blackmail, but it is a very different kind of play, peopled with a very different set of characters. It takes place entirely in the living room of Fanny Farrelly, in her country mansion near Washington, D.C. Fanny is a wealthy, eccentric matriarch in her sixties, a character typical of comedy of manners: basically good-hearted, sparklingly alert, and accustomed to having her own way. The time of the play is the spring of 1940. Germany is Nazi-ruled, and there is war in Europe in which the United States has not yet become involved.

The pattern of the first two acts of the play consists of alternating conversation of three kinds: humorous and witty, at times gossipy, as is appropriate to comedy of manners; affectionate; and tense, either because of personally threatening political maneuvers or because of the triangle that is a subplot in the play. The shifts from one type to another can be sudden, but they are always appropriate. Tension can lapse into humor, or an unexpected remark can turn humor into tension.

The characters include, besides Fanny, the other permanent residents of the mansion: Fanny's son, David, a lawyer in his deceased father's firm in Washington, in his late thirties; Fanny's longtime companion Anise, a Frenchwoman; and one of the servants, Joseph. There are also two houseguests who have long overstayed their welcome, Marthe de Brancovis, the daughter of an old friend of Fanny, and her husband, Teck, a Romanian count. Fanny's daughter Sara, her husband Kurt Müller, a member of the anti-

Nazi underground and a German in exile, and their children arrive. The audience learns that Kurt has collected twenty-three thousand dollars to aid the resistance in Germany. In brief, Teck discovers the money and threatens to expose Kurt to the German embassy officials unless he is paid ten thousand dollars. Kurt is forced to kill Teck and flee the country, aided by Fanny, who during the course of the play has come to realize the Nazi threat and to be lifted above her own private concerns. The killing is presented, strangely, as an absence of the need to fight evil on all fronts, whether on a conventional battlefield or in one's own environment.

Watch on the Rhine is probably the best American play concerning World War II. It demonstrates that war is not limited to battlefronts and that the world is too small for anyone, anywhere, to be unaffected by large-scale violence. It demonstrates that such violence affects the cultured and the humane, whether they are poor, like Kurt, or wealthy, like Sara's family. The play is highly unusual in being a comedy of manners in which the central subject is war. In spite of the attempted blackmail and actual murder that figure prominently in its plot, it is among the least melodramatic of any of Hellman's plays, and to call the murder melodramatic has its own irony because this particular murder constitutes an act of war.

The characters in *Watch on the Rhine* are developed with clarity and depth. Fanny is a far more individualized portrait of a wealthy, dominant older woman than is Mrs. Tilford in *The Children's Hour*. Unlike Mary Tilford or Ben and Regina, Teck is a flaccid, unwilling villain. Unlike Birdie, Horace, and Alexandra, the good people are strong, and for the only time in all her plays, Hellman presents, in Kurt, an admirable hero and a marriage based on strong and permanent love. A believable presentation of either of these is indeed a rarity in modern drama. The children in *Watch on the Rhine* are more fully portrayed than those in *The Children's Hour*. The theme has universal validity; oppression is indeed a major issue throughout Hellman's plays. In *The Children's Hour*, it is oppression by the established rich, by a psychotic child, by established standards of behavior. In *The Little Foxes*, it is anticipated oppression on a broad scale by a rising class of capitalists, and actual oppression on a narrower scale by moneyed Southerners against blacks, poor whites, fallen aristocrats, and one another. *Watch on the Rhine* widens the range in dealing with oppression by Fascists and would-be Fascists. Blackmail itself, in all three plays, is a form of oppression. Later in Hellman's work, in *The Autumn Garden* and *Toys in the Attic*, she showed that even generosity and love can be forms of blackmail; those plays, like *Watch on the Rhine*, give the theme a universality that Hellman's first two successes lack. *The Little Foxes* will probably remain the most popular Hellman play in dramatic repertory, but *Watch on the Rhine* is certainly among her most effective.

OTHER MAJOR WORKS

SCREENPLAYS: *The Dark Angel*, 1935 (with Mordaunt Shairp); *These Three*, 1936; *Dead End*, 1937 (adaptation of Sidney Kingsley's play); *The Little Foxes*, 1941 (with Dorothy Parker, Arthur Kober, and Alan Campbell); *Watch on the Rhine*, 1943 (with Dashiell Hammett); *The North Star: A Motion Picture About Some Russian People*, 1943; *The Searching Wind*, 1946; *The Chase*, 1966.

NONFICTION: *An Unfinished Woman: A Memoir*, 1969; *Pentimento*, 1973; *Scoundrel Time*, 1976; *Maybe*, 1980; *Eating Together: Recipes and Recollections*, 1984 (with Peter Feibleman); *Conversations with Lillian Hellman*, 1986.

EDITED TEXTS: *The Selected Letters of Anton Chekhov*, 1955; *The Big Knockover: Selected Stories and Short Novels of Dashiell Hammett*, 1966.

BIBLIOGRAPHY

Feibleman, Peter. *Lily: Reminiscences of Lillian Hellman*. New York: William Morrow, 1988. The author, the son of old New Orleans friends of Hellman, became her close friend and companion in her last years, a relationship he describes in this book. His accounts of renovating the house on Martha's Vineyard inherited from Hellman were first published in his column in *Lear's* magazine. Contains a sadly riveting account of Hellman's illness. Some of the anecdotal accounts of their time together are in Hellman's section of *Eating Together*, a collection of Southern recipes selected by both writers, in page proof when she died in 1984.

Griffin, Alice, and Geraldine Thorsten. *Understanding Lillian Hellman*. Columbia: University of South Carolina Press, 1999. A study of Hellman's literary output, including *The Children's Hour*, *Another Part of the Forest*, *The Little Foxes*, *Watch on the Rhine*, *The Autumn Garden*, and *Toys in the Attic*. Bibliography and index.

Horn, Barbara Lee. *Lillian Hellman: A Research and Production Sourcebook*. Westport, Conn.: Greenwood Press, 1998. Provides criticism and interpretation of Hellman's dramatic works as well as plots and stage history. Bibliography and indexes.

Mahoney, Rosemary. *A Likely Story: One Summer with Lillian Hellman*. New York: Doubleday, 1998. A look at Hellman from her friend, Rosemary Mahoney.

Mellen, Joan. *Hellman and Hammett: The Legendary Passion of Lillian Hellman and Dashiell Hammett*. New York: HarperCollins, 1996. The story of Hellman's relationship with author Dashiell Hammett. Bibliography and index.

Rollyson, Carl. *Lillian Hellman: Her Legend and Her Legacy*. New York: St. Martin's Press, 1988. A readable and scholarly biography of Hellman. Photographs, bibliography, index.

Wright, William. *Lillian Hellman: The Image, the Woman*. New York: Simon and Schuster, 1986. A biography of Hellman that covers her life and works. Bibliography and index.

Jacob H. Adler,
updated by Katherine Lederer

BETH HENLEY

Born: Jackson, Mississippi; May 8, 1952

PRINCIPAL DRAMA

Am I Blue, pr. 1973, pb. 1982
Crimes of the Heart, pr. 1979, pb. 1982
The Miss Firecracker Contest, pr. 1980, pb. 1982
The Wake of Jamey Foster, pr., pb. 1982
The Debutante Ball, pr. 1985, pb. 1991
The Lucky Spot, pr. 1986, pb. 1987
Abundance, pr. 1990, pb. 1991
Beth Henley: Four Plays, pb. 1992
Monologues for Women, pb. 1992
Control Freaks, pr. 1992, pb. 2001
Signature, pr. 1995, pb. 2001
L-Play, pr. 1996, pb. 2001
Impossible Marriage, pr., pb. 1998
Family Week, pr. 2000
Beth Henley: Collected Plays, pb. 2000-2001
    (2 volumes)

OTHER LITERARY FORMS

In addition to her works for the stage, Beth Henley has written screenplays, including *Nobody's Fool* (1986); *True Stories* (1986), in collaboration with David Byrne and Stephen Tobolowsky; and the film versions of her plays *Crimes of the Heart* (1986), *The Miss Firecracker Contest* (1989), and *Come West with Me* (1998). She has also written the teleplays *Survival Guides* (1986) and *Trying Times* (1987), both with Budge Threlkeld.

ACHIEVEMENTS

Beth Henley is often compared to fiction writers Eudora Welty and Flannery O'Connor for her sympathetic portrayals of eccentric characters who lead deceptively simple lives in small southern communities. Her work has also been identified with the literary traditions of the grotesque and the absurd. Henley's unique achievement, however, is the intermingling of absurdism and realism. Her plays realistically capture the southern vernacular and take place in authentic southern settings, yet they also exaggerate the recog-

nizable and push the bizarre to extremes to reveal the underlying absurdity of the human condition. Henley's characters are rooted in her southern heritage, but the meaning of their experiences is not limited to time and place. Loss and renewal, the vulnerability of loving, and the frail but indomitable human spirit are among her recurring themes. Henley delivers these serious concerns, however, through unpredictable characters, outrageously witty dialogue, and offbeat humor. It is her insistence on the value of laughter in the face of adversity that places her within the tragicomic tradition of modern dramatic literature. Another of Henley's strengths is that she approaches her craft with a keen insight into what is stageworthy. This awareness, no doubt, is one of the reasons that her first full-length play, *Crimes of the Heart*, won the Pulitzer Prize in drama in 1981 with the distinction of being the first play to win the coveted award before appearing on Broadway. *Crimes of the Heart* also received the New York Drama Critics Circle Award in 1981, and in the same year, Henley captured the prestigious George Oppenheimer/ *Newsday* Playwriting Award. Experiments with style and theme during the 1990's led Henley away from her Southern characters and settings, however, these plays, including *Family Week*, have not received critical or popular acclaim.

BIOGRAPHY

The second of four daughters, Elizabeth (Becker) Henley was born May 8, 1952, in Jackson, Mississippi. Her parents, Charles Boyce and Elizabeth Josephine Becker, were reared in the neighboring communities of Hazlehurst and Brookhaven, locales that Henley adopted for two of her plays. Henley's father, an attorney, served in both houses of the Mississippi legislature. A shy child plagued with chronic attacks of asthma, Henley, often bedridden, entertained herself by reading play scripts that were in production at the New Stage Theatre in Jackson, where her mother, an amateur actress, regularly performed.

Beth Henley (AP/Wide World Photos)

Henley attended high school in Jackson. During her senior year, she took part in an acting workshop at the New Stage Theatre, an experience that influenced her decision to become an actress. Selecting drama as her major, Henley enrolled at Southern Methodist University in Dallas, Texas, in 1970. While a sophomore, she wrote her first play as an assignment for a playwriting class. The play, a one-act comedy titled *Am I Blue*, was produced at the university under a pseudonym in her senior year. After graduation from Southern Methodist University in 1974 with a bachelor of fine arts degree, Henley taught creative dramatics and acted for the Dallas Minority Repertory Theatre. She earned a livelihood at odd jobs as a waitress, file clerk, and photographer of children at a department store. In 1975, she received a teaching scholarship from the University of Illinois, where she taught acting classes while pursuing graduate studies in drama. In the summer of 1976, she acted in the *Great American People Show*, a historical pageant presented at the New Salem State Park.

Hoping to break into films as an actress, Henley moved to Los Angeles in the fall of 1976. Failing to get auditions for parts, Henley turned to writing screenplays as a creative outlet, but without an agent to represent her, the studios would not read her scripts. Thinking that stage plays would have a better chance of getting performed, especially in small theaters, Henley began working on a comedy (set in Hazlehurst, Mississippi) about a crisis in the lives of three sisters. With production costs in mind, she deliberately limited the play to six characters and one indoor set. She finished *Crimes of the Heart* in 1978 and submitted it to several regional theaters without success, but Henley's friend and fellow playwright Frederick Bailey had faith in the play. Without Henley's knowledge, he entered *Crimes of the Heart* in the annual drama competition of the Actors Theatre of Louisville, Kentucky, where it was selected as a cowinner for 1977-1978.

In February, 1979, the Actors Theatre produced the play as part of the company's annual Festival of New American Plays. The play was an immediate success. After productions in Maryland, Missouri, and California, *Crimes of the Heart* opened to full houses on Off-Broadway on December 21, 1980. The public's high regard for the play was matched by critical acclaim. In April, 1981, at the age of twenty-eight, Henley was awarded the Pulitzer Prize in Drama for *Crimes of the Heart*, the first woman so honored in twenty-three years. In the fall of 1981, after having been recognized by the New York Drama Critics Circle as the best American play of the season, *Crimes of the Heart* premiered on Broadway; it ran for 535 performances. Subsequent productions were staged in England, France, Israel, and Australia.

Meanwhile, Henley was writing a television pilot entitled "Morgan's Daughters" for Paramount Pictures and a screenplay called *The Moon Watcher* about a historical pageant set in Petersburg, Illinois. She also took a small role as a bag lady in Frederick Bailey's *No Scratch*, produced in Los Angeles in the summer of 1981. In January, 1982, the New York Repertory Company staged Henley's *Am I Blue* with two other one-acts under the collective title *Conflu-*

ence. Theater critics found weaknesses in the playwright's student effort but also acknowledged that the comedy showed the promise of her later work.

Within the next three years, two other comedies written before Henley won the Pulitzer Prize were produced in New York City. *The Wake of Jamey Foster* opened on Broadway on October 14, 1982, but closed after only twelve nights. Critics found the play, which was also set in Mississippi, too repetitious of *Crimes of the Heart.* Written before *The Wake of Jamey Foster, The Miss Firecracker Contest* was staged in New York in the spring of 1984. Again critics faulted the play for its similarity to her earlier works. Undaunted by these box-office failures, Henley kept writing for the stage. In the spring of 1985, the South Coast Repertory Theater in Costa Mesa, California, produced her next play *The Debutante Ball.* In the following year, Henley's *The Lucky Spot* (set in a dance hall in Pigeon, Louisiana, in 1934) premiered in New York City. Reviews of the play varied, but one critic considered *The Lucky Spot* to be Henley's best play since *Crimes of the Heart.* In 1990, *Abundance,* Henley's drama about two mail-order brides whose lives become entangled in the American West of the late nineteenth century, opened in New York City to mixed reviews. Later in the same year, the New York Stage and Film Company staged a workshop production of Henley's *Signature* in Poughkeepsie, New York, but the play was not produced until 1995. Set in Hollywood in the year 2052, Henley envisioned a ruined society in which everyone is obsessed with pursuing fame. Henley's *L-Play* continued a period of experimentation with style and theme. The play deals with six themes done in six different styles. *Impossible Marriage* marked Henley's return to Off-Broadway theater in 1998. The play is set in Savannah, Georgia, and tells of a young bride-to-be named Pandora whose upcoming wedding is opposed by nearly every other character, including her older, very pregnant sister, Floral (Holly Hunter). While Hunter received positive notices, the play was not a success. *Family Week* followed in 2000 and starred another Henley regular, Carol Kane. The play closed after only six performances. The darkly comic play explores issues of alcoholism, sexual abuse, and murder.

As a Pulitzer Prize winner, the playwright-actress also found herself in demand as a screenwriter. While continuing to write stage plays, Henley wrote the screenplay for the acclaimed film version of *Crimes of the Heart,* released in late 1986; the script for another film, *Nobody's Fool;* and a screenplay based on her drama *The Miss Firecracker Contest.* Henley also collaborated with David Byrne and Stephen Tobolowsky on the screenplay entitled *True Stories* and with Budge Threlkeld on two television scripts, *Survival Guides* and *Trying Times.* Henley lives in California with her son Patrick.

Henley's plays have reached audiences far beyond the regional theaters for which she first wrote, making her a significant contributor to American dramatic literature. Although the plays written after *Crimes of the Heart* have failed to bring her the critical praise she earned with that first full-length comedy, her dramatic output as a whole reveals a consistency in tone and theme unsurpassed by her American contemporaries.

ANALYSIS

While the plays of Beth Henley are well constructed and provide ample conflict and suspense, the playwright's keen sense of place and character and her humorous yet compassionate view of the human predicament most typify her work. Her plays are set most often in her home state of Mississippi, where the innocent façade of friendly small-town life belies the horror and lunacy within. The dark side of humanity—the unpredictable, the irrational, the abnormal—attracts Henley, and her plays abound with stories of sickness, disease, and perversions. Ironically, however, Henley creates comedy out of the grotesque and shapes endearing characters out of eccentricity.

Usually, Henley's plays depict the family in crisis joined by a close circle of friends and neighbors. From this basic situation, Henley makes her case for emotional survival. Guilt, despair, and loneliness are typical experiences of Henley's failed heroines, but each continues to search for some measure of happiness and often finds it, if only momentarily, in the community of others. Whereas Henley doggedly exposes human frailties, in the final analysis, her view is a charitable one and her plays are optimistic, although they offer no lasting resolutions to her characters' problems. The key to understanding Henley's optimism lies in the laughter that her plays evoke; laughter functions to undercut that which is horrifying in life and to render it less horrifying.

Henley's reputation as a major American playwright was established with three full-length plays, *Crimes of the Heart*, *The Miss Firecracker Contest*, and *The Wake of Jamey Foster*. These plays also best illustrate the qualities that shape her unusual talent: a uniquely comic but sad voice, a distinguishing preoccupation with the bizarre, and a gift for working out variations on the themes of loneliness, guilt, loss, and renewal.

CRIMES OF THE HEART

Set in Hazlehurst, Mississippi, five years after Hurricane Camille, *Crimes of the Heart* is about three sisters—Lenny, Meg, and Babe MaGrath. The immediate crisis is that the youngest sister, Babe, has shot her husband, Zackery Botrelle, who is the richest and most powerful man in the community. The plot is fairly easily resolved when Zackery recovers and his threat to confine Babe in a mental institution is thwarted. This, however, hardly accounts for the sisters' bizarre tale, which Henley unravels through exposition that is brilliantly interspersed with the main action.

Babe's trouble is only one more disaster among many that the MaGrath women have experienced, beginning with their father's desertion and their mother's suicide (she hanged herself and the family's cat). The mother's death left the sisters under the supervision of their grandfather, and now the care of the sick old man has fallen to Lenny, the oldest sister, because Babe married young and Meg escaped to California to pursue a singing career. Growing up in the shadow of their mother's inexplicable suicide and the notoriety it brought, each of the sisters suffers silently and alone. Meg was especially affected. Fearing to show pity as a sign of weakness, she tested herself as a youngster by staring at a book full of pictures of people with horrible skin diseases. Remarkably, Henley wrings laughter out of the MaGrath's misfortunes:

The sisters suspect that Mama MaGrath killed herself because she was having a bad day; Lenny's prospects for marriage are bleak because she has a deformed ovary; and Babe shoots Zackery because she does not like his looks. To Henley's credit, the laughter is never at the expense of her characters, and there is a kind of bizarre logic to their eccentric behavior that makes the incredible credible. After Babe attempts suicide twice (because she, too, is having a bad day), she learns why her mother hanged the cat: She was afraid to die alone.

THE MISS FIRECRACKER CONTEST

Of the same eccentric mold as the MaGrath women, twenty-four-year-old Carnelle Scott, the central character of *The Miss Firecracker Contest*, seeks to overcome her well-earned reputation as the town trollop by becoming Miss Firecracker at the annual Fourth of July celebration in her hometown of Brookhaven, Mississippi. Because Carnelle's determination to succeed is exceeded only by her lack of talent, the outcome is predictable. Carnelle loses (she comes in fifth in a field of five), but she manages to overcome her despondency over the loss and joins her friends to watch the fireworks display at the close of the play. Henley enlivens the simple plot with a number of very odd characters, all of whom, like Carnelle, seek redemption from their unhappy pasts. Delmount Williams, Carnelle's cousin, is a former mental patient who wants to be a philosopher; his sister Elain finds it easier to desert her husband and sons than to abandon her clock collection; and Carnelle's seamstress, Popeye Jackson, who learned her trade by making dresses for frogs, hears voices through her eyes. Henley's propensity for the grotesque is even more marked in *The Miss Firecracker Contest* than in *Crimes of the Heart*. Carnelle recalls a childhood bout with ringworm, the treatment for which was to shave her head and cover it with a disgusting ointment; Delmount's last job was scraping up dead dogs from county roads; and all fondly remember Ronelle Williams, Delmount and Elain's mother, who died looking like a hairy ape after having her cancerous pituitary gland replaced by one from a monkey. Although in *The Miss Firecracker Contest* Henley tries too hard to be amusing at times, her characters are distinctly drawn and believable despite their whimsicality.

THE WAKE OF JAMEY FOSTER

Henley pushes the morbid to extremes in *The Wake of Jamey Foster*, which is set at Easter time in Canton, Mississippi. The inevitability of death, an underlying theme in Henley's earlier work, is the central focus of this very black comedy in which Marshael Foster, the thirty-three-year-old widow of Jamey Foster, endures the embarrassment of holding the wake of her estranged husband in her home. Marshael faces the ordeal with anger and remorse; she has only recently filed for divorce because her alcoholic husband left her for another woman. The widow finds little comfort from the strange group of friends and relatives who gather to pay their last respects to Jamey, who is laid out in the cheapest pine box available and dressed in a bright yellow sports coat. Among the mourners are Marshael's brother, Leon Darnell, a turkey jerker in a chicken factory; the orphan Pixrose Wilson, Leon's betrothed, who is planning a career washing dogs; Collard Darnell, Marshael's promiscuous sister, whose whole life has been marred by a low score on an IQ test that she took when she was twelve years old; Jamey's brother, Wayne Foster, a successful banker, and his wife, Katie, who turn up their noses at the other guests; and Brocker Slade, a pig farmer who is in love with Marshael. Very little that is significant happens in the play. As the group waits for morning and Jamey's funeral, they eat, drink, play cards, and take pictures of the corpse, but mostly they talk about gruesome things that have happened to them or others they know: arson, brain damage, miscarriages, automobile accidents, the cow that kicked Jamey in the head and killed him, and exploding pigs. Although plot is subsumed by character and character borders on caricature, *The Wake of Jamey Foster* is both entertaining and convincingly human, especially in the solace the characters find in the calamities of others.

Henley's rise to prominence in the American theater is remarkable considering the regionalism that characterizes her work. The weaknesses of her plays, a penchant for telling tall tales that stretch credulity and a tendency to write gags that force laughter, are overcome by her gift for creating memorable characters. Whereas Henley's most important dramatic material is often confined to small Southern towns and the misfits who inhabit them, her humorous but sympathetic treatment of human foibles has a universality and originality that make her one of the most imaginative dramatists writing for the American theater.

OTHER MAJOR WORKS

SCREENPLAYS: *Nobody's Fool*, 1986; *Crimes of the Heart*, 1986 (adaptation of her play); *True Stories*, 1986 (with David Byrne and Stephen Tobolowsky); *Miss Firecracker*, 1989 (adaptation of her play); *Come West with Me*, 1998 (adaptation of her play *Abundance*); *The Shipping News*, 2002 (adaptation of E. Annie Proulx's novel)

TELEPLAYS: *Survival Guides*, 1986; *Trying Times*, 1987 (with Budge Threlkeld).

BIBLIOGRAPHY

Betsko, Kathleen, and Rachel Koenig, eds. *Interviews with Contemporary Women Playwrights*. New York: Beech Tree Books, 1987. In an interview, Henley discusses her individual development as an artist, themes, and dramaturgy; gives advice to new writers; and touches on feminist issues, especially the recurring question of a feminist aesthetic.

Bryer, Jackson R., ed. *The Playwright's Art: Conversations with Contemporary American Dramatists*. Brunswick, N.J.: Rutgers University Press, 1995. Chronicles Henley's contribution to contemporary Broadway, Off-Broadway, and regional theater in the United States. Henley discusses the creative process.

Haller, Scot. "Her First Play, Her First Pulitzer Prize." *Saturday Review* 8 (November, 1981): 40-44. Critiques the Off-Broadway production of *Crimes of the Heart* and attempts to account for Henley's idiosyncratic voice. Henley combines elements of the naturalistic play with characters from absurdist comedy and writes "with wit and compassion about good country people gone wrong or whacko." Some attention is given to Henley's biography.

Harbin, Billy J. "Familial Bonds in the Plays of Beth Henley." *Southern Quarterly* 25 (Spring, 1987): 81-94. Examines Henley's plays through *The Debutante Ball* but gives *Crimes of the Heart* the most attention. Recurring themes concern "the disintegration of traditional ideas, such as the breakup of families, the quest for emotional and spiritual fulfillment, and the repressive social forces within a small southern community."

Hargrove, Nancy D. "The Tragicomic Vision of Beth Henley's Drama." *Southern Quarterly* 22 (Summer, 1984): 54-70. Analyzes *Crimes of the Heart, The Miss Firecracker Contest*, and *The Wake of Jamey Foster* and finds that the plays "are essentially serious, although they are presented in the comic mode" and that the value of love, especially family love, is Henley's predominant theme. Hargrove's is the first scholarly article to examine Henley's work.

Jaehne, Karen. "Beth's Beauties." *Film Comment* 25 (May/June, 1989): 9-12. Highlights the film version of *The Miss Firecracker Contest* and quotes Henley extensively. Henley's plays analyze "the ways women conform to or rebel against standards of femininity." Although she likes to read tragedies, Henley says "in my own writing I can't see the situations I look at without laughing. I back into comedy. I can't help it."

Jones, John Griffin, ed. "Beth Henley." In *Mississippi Writers Talking*. Vol. 1. Jackson: University Press of Mississippi, 1982. Interviews Henley about her family background, education, and playwriting. Henley says that she likes to write about the South "because you can get away with making things more poetic." About the meaning of her plays, Henley confesses, "I don't think very thematically. I think more in terms of character and story."

McDonnell, Lisa J. "Diverse Similitude: Beth Henley and Marsha Norman." *Southern Quarterly* 25 (Spring, 1987): 95-104. Compares Henley's *Crimes of the Heart, The Miss Firecracker Contest*, and *The Wake of Jamey Foster* and Norman's *Getting Out* (pr. 1977, pb. 1979) and *'night, Mother* (pr. 1982, pb. 1983). Whereas both writers use the family as a framework and employ gothic humor, their plays differ remarkably in tone and style. Henley "writes comedy with serious dimensions, Norman, serious drama with comic overtones."

Simon, John. "Sisterhood Is Beautiful." Review of *Crimes of the Heart. New York* 14 (January 12, 1981): 42-43. Reviews the Off-Broadway production of *Crimes of the Heart*. Simon calls Henley "a new playwright of charm, warmth, style, unpretentiousness, and authentically individual vision." His analysis connects Henley's characters to those of Anton Chekhov, Flannery O'Connor, and Tennessee Williams. If Henley "errs in any way, it is in slightly artificial resolutions."

Ayne C. Durham,
updated by Rhona Justice-Malloy

JAMES ENE HENSHAW

Born: Calabar, Nigeria; August 29, 1924

PRINCIPAL DRAMA

This Is Our Chance, pr. 1948, pb. 1956
The Jewels of the Shrine, pr. 1952, pb. 1956 (one act)
A Man of Character, pb. 1956

This Is Our Chance: Plays from West Africa, pb. 1956 (includes *The Jewels of the Shrine* and *A Man of Character*; also as *The Jewels of the Shrine*, pb. 1956)
Children of the Goddess and Other Plays, pb. 1964 (includes *Companion for a Chief* and *Magic in the Blood*)

Medicine for Love: A Comedy in Three Acts, pb. 1964

Dinner for Promotion: A Comedy in Three Acts, pb. 1967

Enough Is Enough: A Play of the Nigerian Civil War, pr. 1975, pb. 1976

A Song to Mary Charles, Irish Sister of Charity, pr. 1981, pb. 1984

OTHER LITERARY FORMS

James Ene Henshaw is known only for his drama.

ACHIEVEMENTS

As one of the pioneering dramatists in Nigeria, James Ene Henshaw was also one of the first to be published outside West Africa. *This Is Our Chance*, which has undergone many reprintings, has been extremely popular in West Africa since its first production by the Association of Students of African Descent in Dublin in 1948. It has been staged by professional companies as well as school and amateur groups.

In 1952, Henshaw's dramatic talents were acknowledged when his play *The Jewels of the Shrine* won the Henry Carr Memorial Cup as the best one-act play in the All-Nigeria Festival of the Arts. Henshaw's reputation was enhanced when *A Man of Character* was mentioned in *Nigeria 10*, the tenth-anniversary commemorative publication in honor of Nigerian independence compiled by the Federal Military Government.

BIOGRAPHY

James Ene Ewa Henshaw was born in 1924 in Calabar, South Eastern Nigeria, West Africa, into a large family, the youngest of nine sons. His father was of royal ancestry, descended from the Efik lineage in Calabar, where in the days before independence his importance gave him a position within the colonial Nigerian Legislative Council, an august lawmaking body.

Having been brought up by his eldest brother, Lawrence Eken Richard Henshaw, following the death of their father, James Henshaw was encouraged to continue his schooling at the Sacred Heart Primary School in Calabar. He then went on to Christ the King College, a secondary school in Onitsha, a well-known commercial center in what was then the Eastern region (now known as Cross River State) of Nigeria.

Upon graduation from Christ the King College, Henshaw traveled abroad to Ireland and in 1943 enrolled as a medical student at the National University of Ireland in Dublin. He took bachelor of science and bachelor of medicine degrees and in 1949 qualified as a physician. In 1954, Henshaw had the opportunity to pursue a course for specialized training in cardiovascular diseases and was awarded the T.D.D. degree by the University of Wales.

Henshaw's professional practice as a physician began in earnest on his return to Nigeria in 1955, where he first served as a senior consultant in tuberculosis treatment for the government of Eastern Nigeria, in Port Harcourt, until 1978. From 1968 to 1972, he served as the First Controller of Medical Services in Cross River State. Thereafter he became medical consultant in thoracic medicine to the Ministry of Health at the chest clinic in his hometown, Calabar.

In 1973, Henshaw was appointed senior consultant on tuberculosis control at Rivers State, a post he held until 1978. He also participated in national programs connected with the medical profession in Nigeria and held membership in the National Council of Health (1968-1972) and the Nigerian Medical Council (1970-1972). In spite of his demanding professional commitments, Henshaw remained a family man. He married Caroline Nchelem Amadi in 1958; they had eight children.

ANALYSIS

James Ene Henshaw's influence, impact, and success as a dramatist in Nigeria stem from the fact that he is a very direct, matter-of-fact dramatic artist. Compared with such contemporary Nigerian writers as Wole Soyinka and John Pepper Clark-Bekederemo, Henshaw's work is less intellectually oriented. His plays are straightforward, not bookishly philosophical, and are written in simple language. Most of the works are aimed both at the adult reader and at schoolchildren. The beguiling simplicity of plot and style facilitates the staging of his plays, making him one of the most frequently produced playwrights in West Africa. He is also adept at stagecraft (although some critics have complained of implausibility in this regard), giving precise, detailed directions and analysis as to how his work is to be produced at every stage, whether for a school production or for adults.

Henshaw's dramatic philosophy contributes greatly to his popularity. His subject matter, which deals directly with African culture and traditions, focuses on major issues familiar to both his African and his Western audience. For this reason, Henshaw prefaces most of his plays, in the manner of George Bernard Shaw, with elaborate introductions that discuss thematic concerns and other ancillary matters connected with the work. Thus, both the foreign and African producer/reader are helped to see the proper perspective from which the work is to be approached, studied, analyzed, and evaluated. Henshaw himself views the function of his drama, in part, as providing a positive impact on his society. Joseph Bruchac believes that Henshaw's cardinal aim in writing is to forge, through the dramatic medium, a unity and understanding among Africans, who share closely related traditions and heritage, rather than "explaining the African to the non-African."

THIS IS OUR CHANCE

Most of Henshaw's early, short plays share two thematic threads: tradition and its conflict with modern life and the worldwide problems of corruption, crime, and materialism. *This Is Our Chance*, one of Henshaw's most popular plays, revolves around Kudaro, the Crown Princess; her father, Chief Damba; her mother, Ansa; her suitor, Prince Ndamu; her tutor, Bambulu; and other village folk whose offices bring them into the story. Set in the royal household and village-kingdom of Koloro and in the rival village of Udura, the play addresses the typically Henshawian preoccupation with the conflict between tradition and modernity and the need to assimilate the best of both African and Western cultures.

From the outset of the play, Chief Damba's obsession with tradition is clear: Tradition compels him to keep the fortune-teller at court, to forbid extravillage marriages, to opt for age-old customs instead of ex-

perimenting with new ideas. In Damba's opinion, Koloro's strict adherence to tradition is the key to the village's superiority. He will declare war on any village that threatens traditional values. Yet when the conflict of interest compels him to take his daughter's life—in eloping with Ndamu, the prince of the rival village, Udura, she has broken one of the most important tenets of Koloro tradition—Damba bends tradition to fit the circumstances, thereby opening new avenues for progress in his village.

Ajugo, Damba's prime minister, is a diehard protector of tradition, convinced that the old ways must never succumb to new ideas, no matter what the cost. Ajugo states categorically that matrimonial links outside the village of Koloro are punishable, in the case of the commoner, by banishment, and, in the case of royalty, by death. Damba, faced with the options of war, his daughter's death, or his own loss of life, must choose. Ajugo, ever faithful to tradition, prepares the hemlock for Damba's punishment. Damba's life is spared, however, by the sudden arrival of Princess Kudaro. Even though tradition now dictates Ajugo's death, the prime minister is spared and a new prime minister, Enusi, appointed. Ajugo remains the uncompromising custodian of the indigenous culture.

There is a dichotomy between those characters who favor modernity (Enusi, Bambulu, Princess Kudaro, Ansa, Ayi the maid, Udura's ambassador, and Prince Ndamu) and those who stand for tradition (Damba, Ajugo, and Chief Mboli of Udura). Princess Kudaro, having lived in the city while attending school, is at once sophisticated and down to earth. Although she is the Crown Princess, she frequently states how much she detests village life. Her elopement with Prince Ndamu is one of the greatest of village taboos. As a character, she represents progress. Princess Kudaro's elopement and the subsequent events, especially her use of Bambulu's antivenom serum, help to bring about peace between the perennially feuding villages.

The bombastic Bambulu, although a foreigner, wields great influence in the village. An accomplished scientist, educated in the Western tradition, and a good teacher, Bambulu the radical is always dressed in Western style. He refers to himself as the catalyst in the village. Under the cloak of teaching about vitamins, he succeeds in sowing the seeds of revolution, which undermine the traditional values of Koloro. He is opposed to the blind adherence to tradition that breeds ignorance, hatred, war, disease, bigotry, poverty, and backwardness. As an apostle of progress, good-neighborliness, and reconciliation, Bambulu is mainly responsible for introducing Western ideas and civilization to the village. With Chief Damba's support, he opens more schools and is given full autonomy to teach basic scientific skills, reading, and writing, as well as agriculture.

Chief Damba thus rises out of adversity and seizes the chance to bring peace, progress, and prosperity to his village. Enusi's metaphoric description of their tradition being a sword of Damocles ties in neatly with the problems raised by tradition in the village of Koloro.

A MAN OF CHARACTER

A Man of Character foreshadows in its thematic concerns many of the issues addressed in contemporary African writing. One of the most urgent of these is the problem of corruption. In the play, an honest, sincere, dedicated man—a man of character—who refuses to be corrupted in a corrupt society must suffer the consequences of his decision.

As in most Henshaw plays, with the exception of *Magic in the Blood*, when the protagonist runs into an intricate problem, he manages both to extricate and to vindicate himself. In this play, the serene, happy family life of Kobina and his wife, Ayodele, is disrupted by the negative influence of Ayodele's mercenary, domineering sister, Serinya, and her venal husband, Anosse. Kobina, a God-fearing man, refuses to be influenced by Anosse's offer of a bribe. His moral position is that West African society needs people of conscience and that appointments and promotions should be based on merit, not on nepotism or bribery. His refusal to enter into this system of institutionalized corruption breaks apart the family, since Serinya's values have influenced the once content Ayodele. Ayodele now desires a house of her own, new clothes, money for trips abroad, and security for their child, Ibitam. Kobina obviously cannot afford all of these

luxuries because his modest income is being used to educate his daughter. After a quarrel, Ayodele and Ibitam leave Kobina, whose misfortunes are compounded by the suspicious loss of five hundred pounds from his office safe. He becomes the prime suspect, and the onus of proof of innocence rests on him. In fact, Seboh, Kobina's servant, together with Seboh's crooked, vicious-looking brother, has engineered the entire plot. Seboh, who is referred to as the "stranger" in the play, attempts to blackmail Kobina and his associates (the lawyer Diyego, the magistrate Kopechi, and Sergeant Mbedu), but the judge's quick thinking neutralizes the stranger's malevolent plan. Seboh, the servant, filled with remorse, is apprehended by the police as he attempts to return the money. The two Seboh brothers are hauled off to prison, with the stranger's strong avowal to turn over a new leaf.

The series of coincidences in the play dilutes the plausibility of the plot somewhat because it is unlikely that all of Kobina's important associates would suddenly and simultaneously converge, uninvited, on his home. The moral preoccupations of the protagonist render him rather too saintly, even somewhat self-righteous, although his depression and subsequent drinking do indicate that he is indeed human and vulnerable.

As many critics have remarked, the language in the play is inflated and bookish; the characters hardly speak as typical Nigerians do. The ending, as in Henshaw's *Companion for a Chief*, *Children of the Goddess*, *Dinner for Promotion*, and *This Is Our Chance*, takes the form of a happy reconciliation. Equilibrium is restored. The moral lesson that *A Man of Character* teaches is the age-old adage that crime does not pay. The upright are vindicated, truth stands, and honesty is shown to be the best policy. The characters become wiser and more determined to continue living in an upright way.

MEDICINE FOR LOVE

Medicine for Love, subtitled *A Comedy in Three Acts*, is a humorous examination of politics, politicians, and political practices in modern West Africa. It also explores the concept of the African marriage system, examining the issue of traditional wives and arranged marriages—an ancient custom being forced on a modern city-dweller, Ewia Ekunyah. Henshaw, in his introduction to the piece, succinctly sums up these motifs: monogamy, polygamy, medicine men, tradition, and the African.

Ewia Ekunyah, the hero of the play and would-be politician, finds his life complicated by the unexpected arrival in the city of no less than three traditional wives, Bekin Wari, Ibiere Sua, and Nene Katsina, married to him through the agency of various relatives. According to tradition, these wives cannot be returned. Naturally, rivalry and suspicion are rampant among the three women and their assorted relatives, who resort to medicine for love in order to win Ewia Ekunyah's favor. The machinations begin when Ibiere Sua and Bekin Wari team up against Nene Katsina, the youngest, best educated, and most beautiful of the three. Apart from Nene Katsina, who displays the characteristics of good humor, romance, and seriousness, the women are eminently unsuitable as wives of a prospective politician. Auntie Dupeh, a dowager-duchess type, is too domineering and aggressive in trying to push Ewia's interests. Auntie Dupeh's imposition as chairperson of Ewia's political planning committee and her recommendation of Agatarata the medicine man as spiritual adviser destroy Ewia's political career.

The array of Ewia's dishonest advisers clearly indicates that the political policymakers active in urban affairs are no better than the candidates themselves. Mr. Joss, Ewia's political agent, using his Machiavellian expertise, spends eighty-one hundred pounds and manages to swindle the poor Ewia into selling his last house to finance the campaign. The Reverend Sanctus Kyei cannot, in times of trouble, give Ewia any sensible advice regarding Ewia's concrete, everyday problems; Agatarata's ignorance of the chemical composition of the ink that becomes invisible on Ewia's application form leads to Ewia's downfall. Henshaw touches here on the very delicate interconnection between Christianity, tradition, and politics. That a modern educated African politician such as Ewia Ekunyah thinks he can win an election or solve his marital entanglements through a juju priest or a Christian minister is preposterous and ironic; these services, in fact, cost Ewia the election.

Henshaw has given a comic look at the operation of politics in contemporary Africa. The fundamental concept of democracy does not seem to be fully understood by the politicians, who tend to think that the survival of the fittest, by any means, foul or fair, is a more appropriate tenet. Instead of honest people of integrity and dignity, there is a multiplicity of crooked, politically self-serving, corrupt candidates and political advisers. The unqualified Ewia resorts to bribery to edge out honest, sincere, and dedicated rivals such as Mr. Sonrillo.

There is no poetic justice in *Medicine for Love*. At the end, all characters, good or bad, gain: Ewia and Nene Katsina gain marital bliss; Auntie Dupeh marries a VIP, Kiudu Bonga; Bekin Wari marries Ewia Ekunya's secretary, Olu Ita, who finds a new job; and Ibiere Sua marries Dr. Sigismond Marsey. Finally, Papa Garuka marries Mama Ebunde, Ibiere Sua's mother. The matrimonial ceremony of the entire cast is presided over by the Reverend Kyei.

DINNER FOR PROMOTION

Dinner for Promotion, as the title implies, centers on the plans of Tikku and Seyil, two young and ambitious employees of Sipo Amalgamated, to get to the top. In the play, promotion depends on a sumptuous dinner for the Sipo family and on marrying the boss's daughter rather than on merit. *Dinner for Promotion* thus touches on the relationships between employer and employee, between friends, between parents and children, and between in-laws, and deals with the life of the young, educated urban group. Through *Dinner for Promotion*, Henshaw portrays the callous disregard for decency or ethical behavior or even loyalty among friends when personal interests are at stake.

Each character seems to have an ulterior motive. Tikku has his eye on Sharia, the boss's daughter, but his interest is purely selfish; he sees her only as a means for promotion. Seyil, not knowing Sharia's family connections, courts Sharia and takes the advice of Tikku to speak ill of Mr. Sipo, their employer. Naturally, Sharia takes offense as Seyil heaps insults on her father's head, then promptly walks into Tikku's waiting arms. Through a series of deceptive moves, Seyil plots Tikku's downfall both as suitor to

Sharia and as prospective executive in Sipo Amalgamated by sabotaging Tikku's "dinner for promotion," but his plans backfire. In spite of all this confusion and hostility, the ending of the play is typically amicable: The two sisters-in-law, Madam Pamphilia Sipo and Madam Una, are reconciled; Tikku and Sharia, blessed by their parents, are about to be married; Tikku does get his promotion and material gain; and even Seyil gains by being offered a much better job elsewhere. A form of equity reigns.

ENOUGH IS ENOUGH

Enough Is Enough is a contemporary drama set in a detention camp during the last weeks of the Nigerian Civil War. The play documents the incarceration and plight, both psychological and physical, of six detainees and their guards. Henshaw's introduction to the work concentrates on the personal attitudes and feelings of the detainees, the reactions of Nigerians to the war, and the complex human emotions that permeated the detainees' existence.

Set against the prison backdrop, *Enough Is Enough* centers on the notion of reconciliation, the woes and gloom of the war, and the role of charitable and relief organizations at that time. The outcry "genocide and pogrom," which became the Biafran slogan during the course of the war, is alluded to throughout the work.

Apart from Ufanko, Bisong, and the disembodied voice of Nwakego, the major characters enacting the drama are Peter Emeribe, a very important member of Parliament; the lawyer Linus Nosikeh; Dr. Dagogo, a politician and medical practitioner; and the arrogant Professor Ezuba, who apparently masterminded the rebellion against the revolution. The remaining characters—the Superintendent, the warder, Mother Cecilia, Sister Lucinda, Major Maxy, and others—serve to highlight the suffering and anguish of the main characters. Referred to as detainees, saboteurs, and criminals, the incarcerated men seem to have rebelled against those advocating war and secession. This rebellion is regarded as treason and is the cause of their detention.

Divided into four acts, each with a distinct thematic concern, *Enough Is Enough* gives a concrete insight into the ravages of war, which claims the lives of healthy, innocent, able-bodied people (sometimes civilians). Although all wars are destructive, this war is especially so: It is a civil war, with relatives killing one another, creating a generation of orphans and cripples.

Henshaw is here concerned with the brutal treatment of the detainees, the resultant psychological problems of both the long-term detainees and their guards, the economic difficulties, and ecological destruction. There is a general lack of trust, a lack of freedom to speak or even to remain silent, and a very real lack of decent food and water. The detainees are denied such amenities as radios and the right to receive visitors or uncensored mail. Everyone in the camp is vulnerable to the constant attacks from bombing and disease. Survival becomes a critical issue; the detainees, in spite of their former privileged positions, have had to resort to sordid, subservient practices to survive. Part of the irony of Peter Emeribe's case is that the warder is his former houseboy.

The psychological problems range from insanity to alcoholism. The Superintendent, for example, a brilliant zoologist in civilian life, unsure of his competence in his present position, ends up a nervous, alcoholic wreck. Dr. Dagogo becomes moody, embittered, and mentally unstable after four years of detention at Umudali camp. Ufanko has turned into a cynic, while Peter Emeribe burns with a strong sense of injustice. The lack of privacy and the constant harassment to which they are subject cause the prisoners, understandably, to lash out at one another. As for Professor Ezuba, his arrogance leads to the eventual destruction of most of the group. Treating the warders as a pack of ignorant, unqualified upstarts, he insults his captors without considering the consequences for his fellow prisoners, always reminding the world of his former importance. On the other side, the presence of Major Maxy—a mere child trying to behave as an adult soldier, a boy who, at the age of fourteen, functions as an undercover agent—points out the absurdity and unprepared nature of the revolutionaries. Ironically, Maxy, in contrast with his dead brothers, displays filial devotion by trying to protect his father.

One important motif present in this drama is that of peace and reconciliation. The war, having taken its impartial toll of destruction, ends with the signing of the Lagos peace treaty. Umudali Camp is disbanded, and some of the detainees are released. As a consequence of the personal vengeance of the Superintendent, however, the most vocal of the detainees are killed, although, unbeknown to them, the war has already been over for four days.

The play's title, *Enough Is Enough*, fittingly expresses a yearning for peace, unity, reconciliation, and a return to normal life; as the first voice in act 3 cries, "Let's waste no further time. Let's spill no further blood. Let's rebuild the nation anew." Dagogo poignantly replies that the fighting should cease because there has been enough of brother killing brother, of suffering, of dying from bullets, of hunger and disease—enough of everything connected with the war and the prisoners' detention. The emotional demands of such a painful, historical moment give this later play an uncharacteristic slant in the Henshaw canon. The language itself strikes a note of pathos and patriotism, while the imagery constantly reverts to horror and bestiality (references to vampires, lizards, boa constrictors, hawks) to underscore the reality of human suffering.

BIBLIOGRAPHY

Dathorne, O. R. *African Literature in the Twentieth Century.* Minneapolis: University of Minnesota Press, 1975. Under a chapter entitled "African Drama in French and English," Dathorne compares "social reality and the inner life" in the plays of Henshaw and others. Discusses *This Is Our Chance*, saying that the "title play describes a society that is fettered by an outmoded tradition but nevertheless aspires toward western values." The main character is discussed in terms of "tradition" versus "worn-out institutions."

Edet, Rosemary N. *The Resilence of Religious Tradition in the Dramas of Wole Soyinka and James Ene Henshaw.* Rome: R. Nkoyo Edet, 1984. An examination of the role of religion in the works of Henshaw and Soyinka. Includes bibliography.

Graham-White, Anthony. *The Drama of Black Africa.* New York: Samuel French, 1974. In the chapter entitled "Drama Seeking Independence," Graham-White places Henshaw with the transitional playwrights, between the British era and the stylistic changes after the independence movement. Graham-White notes that "Henshaw's plays have little artistic value, yet they are often performed in the schools and are popular there for their simple characterization and firm didacticism."

Ogunba, Oyin. "Modern Drama in West Africa." In *Perspectives on African Literature*, edited by Christopher Heywood. New York: Africana Publishing, 1971. Henshaw is placed with R. Sarif Easmon as a playwright whose motive is "as he himself has implied again and again, to make good citizens of his audience." Discusses *This Is Our Chance* and *Children of the Goddess* at some length.

Omobowale, Babatunde. "Ageing in Nigerian Literature: James Ene Henshaw's *The Jewels of the Shrine.*" *The Lancet* 354 (November, 1999): S21-S23. Omobowale offers a critique of *The Jewels of the Shrine* as well as a discussion of aging in Nigeria.

Taiwo, Oladele. *An Introduction to West African Literature.* 1967. Reprint. Walton-on-Thames, England: Nelson, 1981. Puts the work of Henshaw in place as the beginnings of Nigerian drama. Describes the one-act plays, "based on one aspect or other of African culture and tradition."

Kwaku Amoabeng and Carrol Lasker,
updated by Thomas J. Taylor

DUBOSE HEYWARD

Born: Charleston, South Carolina; August 31, 1885
Died: Tryon, North Carolina; June 16, 1940

PRINCIPAL DRAMA

An Artistic Triumph, pr. 1913
Porgy, pr., pb. 1927 (with Dorothy Heyward;
    adaptation of his novel)
Brass Ankle, pr., pb. 1931
Porgy and Bess, pr., pb. 1935 (libretto; music by
    George Gershwin; adaptation of *Porgy*)
Mamba's Daughters, pr., pb. 1939 (with Heyward;
    adaptation of his novel)

OTHER LITERARY FORMS

In addition to three plays and the libretto for *Porgy and Bess*, DuBose Heyward was the author of poetry, short stories, and novels. In his own time, he probably achieved more recognition as a novelist than as a playwright. In fact, his plays *Porgy* and *Mamba's Daughters* are dramatizations of his novels of the same titles, set in African American communities in and around Charleston, South Carolina. Heyward's final novel, *Star Spangled Virgin* (1939), also has African American characters, but it is set on St. Croix in the Virgin Islands. Heyward also wrote three novels featuring white characters. *Angel* (1926) is about the mountaineers of North Carolina's Blue Ridge Mountains. *Lost Morning* (1936), set in the Piedmont, deals with an artist trying to regain his artistic integrity. *Peter Ashley* (1932) is a historical novel set in Charleston at the beginning of the Civil War. *The Half Pint Flask* (1929), Heyward's best short story, was published separately as a book. Heyward also published volumes of poetry: *Carolina Chansons* (1922), *Skylines and Horizons* (1924), and *Jasbo Brown and Selected Poems* (1931).

ACHIEVEMENTS

DuBose Heyward, a famous writer in his own time, is a comparatively obscure figure today. His characters, however, have become part of the American folklore. People who have not heard of Hey-ward nevertheless do know Porgy, thanks primarily to the success of what has come to be thought of as George Gershwin's *Porgy and Bess*. It must be remembered, though, that Heyward wrote the libretto as well as many of the lyrics of *Porgy and Bess*. According to virtually all sources, he also helped shape all other aspects of the production of what was undeniably America's first folk opera. Through *Porgy and Bess*, *Mamba's Daughters*, and *Brass Ankle*, Heyward made at least two other contributions to American theater: Arguably, he was the first American playwright to treat African Americans as human beings in their own right, not as mere accessories to whites, and to portray them in this way in their own communities. Langston Hughes describes Heyward as one who saw "with his white eyes, wonderful poetic, human qualities in the inhabitants of Catfish Row." Heyward's plays with African American characters also hastened the acceptance of blacks as serious actors. Ethel Waters in *Mamba's Daughters*, for example, was the first African American actress ever to star on Broadway in a dramatic play.

BIOGRAPHY

Edwin DuBose Heyward was born in Charleston, South Carolina, into an old Charleston family. When he was two years old, his father was killed in an accident, and his mother began a struggle to support DuBose and his younger sister. Both of these events were to shape his work.

Heyward's writing, both his fiction and his plays, often portrays life in Charleston, most notably life in the black quarter. His contact with the African American community probably came principally from his employment as a checker on a steamship company wharf, where he developed an understanding and appreciation of the lives of the African American stevedores with whom he worked. Afterward, he became successful in the real estate and insurance businesses. He was to pursue this career until his decision to commit himself to full-time writing.

Three people, in particular, influenced Heyward's decision to commit himself to writing as a career. He developed friendships with John Bennett, a critic and author of children's books, and Hervey Allen, who was later to write *Anthony Adverse* (1933). From these friendships grew the founding of the Poetry Society of South Carolina and Heyward's serious involvement with writing. Heyward's marriage to Dorothy Hartzell Kuhns also influenced his commitment to a writing career. He met her at the McDowell Colony, a retreat founded by the composer Edward McDowell for the purpose of encouraging artistic achievement. A graduate of the Harvard School of Drama, Kuhns had a play produced in the fall of 1923, the year in which she and Heyward were married. For the rest of his life, she gave her husband en-

DuBose Heyward in 1931. (Library of Congress)

couragement and the benefit of her own expertise as a dramatist and collaborated with him on two successful Broadway dramas, *Porgy* and *Mamba's Daughters*, although she consistently claimed that his contribution was greater than hers.

Ira and George Gershwin were collaborators with Heyward for *Porgy and Bess*, first produced in 1935. Ironically, though the libretto and part of the lyrics are Heyward's, *Porgy and Bess* has come to be associated almost totally with the Gershwin name, as the opera has gone through numerous revivals over the years.

Heyward and Gershwin discussed yet another collaboration, a dramatization of Heyward's novel *Star Spangled Virgin*, but Heyward's death at the age of fifty-four ended those plans. Heyward died in Tryon, North Carolina, on June 16, 1940, and was buried in Saint Phillips Churchyard in Charleston.

ANALYSIS

DuBose Heyward's contributions to American drama are minor but nevertheless important. He was one of the first American dramatists to portray African Americans seriously and sympathetically. The use of African American music in his plays, as well as in the folk opera *Porgy and Bess*, helped create acceptance of black folk expression as an art form. His influence helped African American writers realize the value of their own culture and experience. Judged by the standards of a later generation, Heyward's dramatic portraits of the African American community are deeply flawed. The notion of "rhythm" as the defining characteristic of the black spirit is a notorious stereotype, all too representative of Heyward's baggage of cultural assumptions. Judged by the standards of their own time, however, Heyward's works were courageous, pioneering efforts, and they played a significant role in bringing the African American experience to the American stage.

Heyward's plays also provided access to the stage for African American performers. In fact, when *Porgy* was being cast, vaudeville performers had to be recruited and trained for their roles in a dramatic play because at that time there were no African American performers with experience in serious drama. The blues singer Ethel Waters, who played Hagar in *Mamba's Daughters*, was the first African American woman to star on Broadway in a dramatic play.

Despite the pioneering significance of Heyward's work, he had severe limitations as a dramatist. Virtually all of his critics point to his tendency to rely too heavily on melodrama and to a lack of character development. Many also believe that his critique of white society lacks depth. Nevertheless, Heyward provided the American theater with a positive treatment of an African American community and its inner spirit—a spirit to which Heyward referred as "rhythm." For him, "rhythm" was the spirit of a people close to their God and the earth and bound together in their community by suffering, hope, and joy.

PORGY

Porgy was Heyward's first play. Although Dorothy Heyward wrote a first draft of the play, she asserts that her role was minor, that the play versions of both *Porgy* and *Mamba's Daughters* were nine-tenths DuBose Heyward's. The basic plot of *Porgy*, well known because of *Porgy and Bess*, concerns a summer in Catfish Row, the black quarter in Charleston. The time is the 1920's (a change from the turn-of-the-century setting of the novel). Porgy, the central character, a crippled beggar, is drawn about the streets on a cart made from a soapbox and pulled by a goat.

The play centers on Porgy's brief time of happiness and love with Bess. Bess seeks protection and shelter from Porgy after her brutal lover, Crown, murders Robbins at the beginning of the play. Ostracized by the other women of Catfish Row, Bess slowly finds acceptance and a new life with Porgy. From the beginning, though, the couple's happiness is threatened by Sportin Life, a Harlem drug dealer, and by the possibility of Crown's return.

Their summer of love comes to an end when Crown, who is hiding on Kittiwah Island, brutally forces Bess to resume her relationship with him (she has come to the island on a holiday picnic with others from Catfish Row). Shortly afterward, during a great storm, Crown returns to the Row. Although people at first believe that he has died in the storm, he actually returns to the Row later that night, determined to

murder Porgy and take Bess back. Instead, he is killed by Porgy. The storm also orphans a baby whom Bess claims as her own, after the mother leaves it with her and then goes out into the storm.

Although Porgy is not charged with Crown's murder, he is taken to jail to identify the dead man. Terrified by having to identify the man he has murdered, Porgy tries to escape, urged on by Sportin Life. After the police have caught Porgy and taken him into custody, Sportin Life convinces the people of the Row and Bess that Porgy will be in jail for a year. In fact, Porgy is in jail for only a week and comes back happy, bringing money and presents for Bess and the baby and other friends. Joyfully, he searches for Bess and the baby, only to find that Sportin Life has lured her away with lies and a drug called "happy dust." As the play ends, Porgy drives his goat through the gate out of the Row on the way to New York to look for Bess.

The great achievement of *Porgy* (and the novel on which it was based) lies in Heyward's treatment of his African American hero and the black community of which he was a part. The play succeeds as theater, primarily through its use of music and group expression—through spirituals, chants, shouts, parading—and the crowd movements associated with all of these. Its saucer burial scene and hurricane scene are, in particular, made powerful through the use of spirituals to express emotion that could not be conveyed by words.

Although the play is powerful on the emotional level, it is marred by an excess of melodrama and, more seriously, a failure to provide the characters with adequate motivation. The audience is not prepared for Bess's crucial decision to leave Porgy and go with Sportin Life, whose character is never developed sufficiently to explain his actions. Even Porgy, the protagonist, is essentially a static character. In addition, in adapting his novel for the stage, Heyward minimized the element of racial conflict and added some incidents and characters that give to certain scenes in the play a condescending, minstrel-show quality. Yet the play does succeed, as an expression of "rhythm" and as a depiction of the significance and humanity of its black characters.

PORGY AND BESS

Porgy and Bess, the folk opera that made the Gershwins more famous than its librettist, succeeds in the same ways as the play on which it is based, and in some other ways as well. In comparison to that of *Porgy*, the plot of *Porgy and Bess* is simplified—some of the extraneous minstrel-show scenes are cut—but the songs and chants and "rhythm" of the play are retained and heightened, allowing the folk opera to profit "both by its escape from the play's clutter and the opportunity its songs provided for the characters to express their personal feelings," according to William H. Slavick. Indeed, there are critics who were disappointed with the oversimplification of the opera in comparison with the play from which it was taken, yet, as Slavick notes, *Porgy and Bess* was unique in realizing "the rhythms, color, music, movement, and passion" that bestow on it "more merit than vaudeville."

MAMBA'S DAUGHTERS

Mamba's Daughters, like *Porgy* and *Porgy and Bess*, derives much of its success from the use of music and songs. In fact, one of the characters, an African American singer named Lissa, transforms the expression of her people into art. The play's central character, however, is not Lissa, but her mother, Hagar. The play focuses on Hagar's loneliness and separation from the daughter whom she has her own mother, Mamba, rear while she is in prison. Men are Hagar's adversaries—the sailors who refuse to pay her for delivering wash, the white men who administer a mockery of justice, but above all Gilly Bluton, whose life she saves at the expense of her freedom, when she takes him to the hospital in Charleston after being forbidden to return to the city from the plantation to which she was sent. In return for this sacrifice, Bluton rapes Lissa and then blackmails her after she achieves some success. The play ends with Hagar protecting Lissa's name by murdering Bluton and then committing suicide.

Aside from the music in the play—Lissa's music and the song with which Hagar consoles herself—*Mamba's Daughters* derives its power from its focus on the suffering figure of Hagar, who is separated from the daughter whom she loves and for whom she sacrifices everything—even her life. The theme of love as a weapon against injustice, and the song through which Hagar (and Lissa) express their love and suffering, give the play its power. Its weakness lies in its overly melodramatic plot.

BRASS ANKLE

Unlike *Porgy*, *Porgy and Bess*, and *Mamba's Daughters*, *Brass Ankle* was unsuccessful on Broadway. Also unlike the previous works, *Brass Ankle* was a play from the start, and Heyward had no collaborator. The play is about interracial marriage and passing. The white protagonist, Larry Leamer, must confront the knowledge of his wife Ruth's African American ancestry when she bears him a dark-skinned son after previously bearing a blond daughter, June. The play fails primarily because Heyward resolves the conflict through Ruth protecting her husband from the truth by claiming, falsely, that she has taken a lover. Leamer then kills her and their son—and is thus not forced to come to terms with his knowledge of her race.

OTHER MAJOR WORKS

LONG FICTION: *Porgy*, 1925; *Angel*, 1926; *Mamba's Daughters*, 1929; *Peter Ashley*, 1932; *Lost Morning*, 1936; *Star Spangled Virgin*, 1939.

SHORT FICTION: *The Half Pint Flask*, 1929.

POETRY: *Carolina Chansons*, 1922; *Skylines and Horizons*, 1924; *Jasbo Brown and Selected Poems*, 1931.

BIBLIOGRAPHY

Alpert, Hollis. *The Life and Times of Porgy and Bess: The Story of an American Classic*. New York: Alfred A. Knopf, 1990. Alpert tells the interesting story—flavored with the spirit of the 1920's and 1930's—of how Heyward wrote *Porgy and Bess* as a novel, how his wife, Dorothy Hartzell Kuhns, turned it into a hit play, and, how, finally, George Gershwin presented his own version in 1935. Alpert describes the performances, recounts Gershwin's experiences with the Gullah language, and illustrates the volume with photographs.

Hutchisson, James M. *DuBose Heyward: A Charleston Gentleman and the World of Porgy and Bess*. Jackson: University Press of Mississippi, 2000.

Hutchisson describes the world in which Heyward lived—Charleston, North Carolina—and how it influenced his writing. He portrays him as a promoter of southern writing and a progressive interested in helping African Americans. Bibliography and index.

Slavick, William H. *DuBose Heyward*. Boston: Twayne, 1981. Slavick is excellent at depicting the Charleston world in which Heyward flourished. The cultural history is presented in "A Charleston Gentleman and the World of Letters,"

and the Charleston ambience is described in "The Irony of Freedom in Charleston: *Porgy*." The dramatization of *Mamba's Daughters* is analyzed in "The Rhythms of Charleston: *Mamba's Daughters*."

Watson, Charles S. *The History of Southern Drama*. Lexington: University Press of Kentucky, 1997. Watson devotes a chapter to a discussion of Heyward in his history of drama in the South.

Doris Walters,
updated by Frank Day

JOHN HEYWOOD

Born: London(?), England; c. 1497
Died: Louvain(?), Spanish Netherlands; October, 1578

PRINCIPAL DRAMA

The Play of Love, pr. c. 1528-1529, pb. 1533

Witty and Witless, wr. c. 1533, pb. 1846 (abridged), 1909 (also known as *A Dialogue on Wit and Folly*)

The Pardoner and the Friar, pb. 1533 (possibly based on *Farce nouvelle d'un pardonneur, d'un triacleur, et d'une tavernière*)

Johan Johan the Husband, Tyb His Wife, and Sir Johan the Priest, pb. 1533 (commonly known as *Johan Johan*; adaptation of *Farce nouvelle et fort joyeuse du pasté*)

The Play of the Weather, pb. 1533

Gentleness and Nobility, pb. 1535 (attributed to Heywood)

The Playe of the Foure P.P.: A Newe and a Very Mery Enterlude of a Palmer, a Pardoner, a Potycary, a Pedler, pb. 1541-1547 (commonly known as *The Four P.P.*; possibly based on *Farce nouvelle d'un pardonneur, d'un triacleur, et d'une tavernière*)

The Dramatic Writings of John Heywood, pb. 1905 (John S. Farmer, editor)

OTHER LITERARY FORMS

In his own time, John Heywood was best known for his published collections of epigrams, not for his plays, even though the dramas were printed earlier. His first published poetic work was *A Dialogue of Proverbs* (1546), a versified discussion of marriage incorporating more than twelve hundred proverbs. Heywood's reputation was made by his several collections of original versified epigrams, six hundred in all, published beginning 1550 and collected in his *Works* in 1562; these quips and anecdotes, ranging from two to scores of lines apiece, are sometimes turgid, but they often shine with the wit for which Heywood was famous. He also wrote short occasional poems, songs and ballads, and a lengthy and obscure verse allegory, *The Spider and the Fly* (1556).

ACHIEVEMENTS

John Heywood was one of the first writers of secular English drama who portrayed not abstractions but individual persons as characters. Most early Tudor plays represented Bible stories or saints' legends, or dramatized the conflict of such allegorical characters as Wisdom and Treason. Heywood's interludes portray husbands, pardoners, scholars, and fools; while most are unnamed types, each is individualized deftly and many have more than one dimension of character. Although Heywood's three disputation plays are heavy with choplogic, his three farces retain their vigor and interest. In plotting, character drawing, and versifying, Heywood was far more skilled, at his best, than were other Tudor playwrights. It must be said, however, that Heywood's direct influence on later dramatists seems to have been small. The flowering of Elizabethan comedy, some fifty years after his interludes were published, developed without evident influence from his plays.

BIOGRAPHY

The two hallmarks of John Heywood's life were his ready wit and his loyal Catholicism. Through a long life and drastic swings in religious opinion at the English court, he kept in royal favor by his wit until finally, as an old man, he was driven into exile for his faith. His birth, parentage, and early life are obscure. He was born about 1497, possibly in London; he may have been the son of a lawyer, William Heywood, sometime of Coventry. He may have spent some time at Oxford; the early historian of Oxford, Anthony Wood, claimed that Heywood had been a short time at Broadgates Hall but that "the crabbedness of logic not suiting with his airy genie, he retired to his native place, and became noted to all witty men, especially to Sir Thomas More (with whom he was very familiar)."

Heywood certainly became an intimate of the Humanist circle centered on More, and it is probably no coincidence that Heywood first appears as a salaried appointee at the court of King Henry VIII in the summer of 1519, at about the time that More resigned as under sheriff to concentrate on his duties as privy councillor. Heywood's position at court, at first, was as "singer" and "player on the virginals" (an early keyboard instrument). His skills were appreciated by King Henry, himself an accomplished musician, and were rewarded with grants of money and leases on land in addition to his quarterly stipend. The exact time when Heywood became involved with dramatic activities at court is unknown, but it seems likely that his six extant plays were written in the 1520's. He was later renowned for his varied skills as an entertainer. John Bale, for example, wrote in 1557 that Heywood "was accomplished in the arts of music and

John Heywood (Hulton Archive by Getty Images)

poesy in his own tongue, and ingenious without great learning; he spent much time in conducting merry dances after banquets and in presenting pageants, plays, masques, and other 'disports.'" In 1528, he received a life annuity of ten pounds and may have left the court; on January 20, 1530, he was admitted to the London company of mercers and appointed to the office of measurer of linen cloths.

Sometime during the period 1523-1529, Heywood married Eliza Rastell, daughter of the Humanist author and printer John Rastell. Eliza's mother was a sister of Sir Thomas More, and thus Heywood by his marriage cemented his relationship to the More circle at the time More was approaching his zenith at court as chancellor. In 1533, Eliza's brother, William Rastell, published four of Heywood's plays. These interludes and the poet's epigrams reflect at many points the Humanists' social ideas, critical temper, and harsh clerical satire. The circle was soon to be split, however, divided by the rise of Protestantism in England.

In 1532, More resigned the chancellorship, and in 1535, he was executed for his Catholicism. The Rastell family was torn by the controversy; Heywood's father-in-law converted to Protestantism, while the son, William Rastell, remained loyal to the old faith. Heywood likewise retained his Catholic sympathies, and near the end of Henry's reign, the dramatist became involved in a Catholic plot against Archbishop Cranmer that nearly cost him his life. The plot was discovered and several participants were executed. Heywood himself was condemned and his property ordered forfeit, but he "escaped hanging with his mirth," according to the 1596 report of John Harington, since King Henry was "truly persuaded that a man that wrote so pleasant and harmless verses, could not have any harmful conceit against his proceedings." Heywood read a public recantation in London on July 6, 1544.

Not only were Heywood's properties restored to him after his public humbling, but also he was reinstated at court. At the request of none other than Archbishop Thomas Cranmer, he wrote an interlude, "The Parts of Man," of which only fourteen lines survive, recorded in the manuscript autobiography of Thomas Whythorne, the dramatist's secretary from 1545 to 1548. When the Catholic queen Mary Tudor came to the throne in 1553, Heywood's prospects brightened, for he had been faithful to her through her years of eclipse after her mother's divorce from Henry VIII. In 1534, he had written her a flattering poem, and in 1538, "with his Children" he presented a play before her. Later, he delivered an oration at her coronation and penned a fulsome poem about her marriage. She rewarded him with a higher annuity and more gifts of land. Soon, however, it became obvious that the Protestant Elizabeth would succeed Mary, who was in ill health, and only five days before Mary's death, Heywood resigned his annuity and Mary granted him a forty-year lease on the substantial Bolmer manor in Yorkshire. Mary apparently wanted to protect Heywood from possible loss of income under her successor.

Under the new queen, Heywood managed for some time to remain active at court. In 1559, he aided in presenting a play for Elizabeth at Nonesuch during her summer "progress" or tour. Matters became increasingly difficult for Catholics in England, however, and on July 20, 1564, Heywood and his son Ellis fled to the Low Countries. Heywood lived for some time in Malines, then was granted a place at the Jesuit college of his son Ellis at Antwerp. When in 1578 the college was overrun by a Protestant mob, he barely escaped along with the Jesuits to Louvain. It was probably there that, late in 1578, more than eighty years of age, he died. Even on his deathbed, Heywood retained his wit; when his confessor kept intoning "The flesh is frail," the master epigrammatist twitted him: "You seem to be blaming God for not making me a fish." Heywood's career spanned the Tudor age: Linked to Erasmus by wit and to More by marriage, he survived at four Tudor monarchs' courts by his gifts as poet and dramatist; his son Jasper translated three tragedies of Seneca, and his daughter was the mother of the poet John Donne.

ANALYSIS

The six plays of John Heywood's canon fall naturally into two groups: three debate plays, rhetorical disputations on set topics, and three farces, which include considerable argumentation but also feature rudimentary plots and lively onstage action. Heywood's reputation as a dramatist rests on six plays, though he is known to have written others, along with masques at court, and he has sometimes been credited with the authorship of the two-part interlude *Gentleness and Nobility* (pb. 1535), by John Rastell. Heywood's accomplishment was that he detached the interlude from its dependency on allegorical figures and introduced flesh-and-blood people into his simple plots; in his farces, Heywood created vivid characters whose interests and passions the audience shares even while it laughs at them. His plays benefit from his wide metrical range and considerable skills as a versifier; he makes good use, too, of his extensive proverb lore and of his famous facility with the quick quip. Despite the long passages of tedious dispute in some of the plays, at its best Heywood's dramatic dialogue sparkles with vivid homely diction, lively rhythms, and clever rhymes.

WITTY AND WITLESS

Of the farces, the simplest is *Witty and Witless*, with only three characters. In the play, John and James debate the latter's paradoxical proposition that it is "better to be a fool, than a wise man." James triumphs by showing that the Witless and the Witty equally suffer bodily pain, that Witless suffers lesser mental pain, and that Witless, being innocent, is sure of the supreme pleasure—salvation. At this point, a third interlocutor, Jerome, intervenes; he upbraids John for yielding and proceeds to overturn all three conclusions. He ends in a terse sermon showing that good deeds affect heavenly rewards proportionally—an anti-Lutheran view that at the time would have pleased Henry VIII, who in 1521 was named Defender of the Faith for his anti-Lutheran writing. Heywood's debate is in the ironic Humanist tradition of Erasmus's *Moriæ Encomium* (1511; *The Praise of Folly*, 1549); it also is indebted to a French farce, *Dyalogue du fol et du sage*, but goes beyond this source, which ends with the victory of the fool, to make a pious nonironic ending.

THE PLAY OF LOVE

A considerable step up from this play in rhetorical complexity is *The Play of Love*, a disputation in which two pairs of debaters consider the pains and pleasures of love. This play may have been produced about 1528-1529 for a Christmas revel before an Inns of Court audience who would have followed the legalistic arguments with interest. The four characters make up the possible permutations of love pairings. Lover Not Loved begins by asserting that of all pains, his is the worst. Beloved Not Loving, a woman, challenges him with a claim that her pain from incessant and unwelcome wooing is worse. After fruitless argument, they go off to find an arbitrator. Meanwhile the joyful Lover Loved enters with a song and declares that "The highest pleasure man can obtain,/ Is to be a lover beloved again." He in turn is challenged by the cocky, taunting Vice named Neither Lover Nor Loved, who avers that a lover is always torn by some passion but that he, being passionless, lives in quiet. When Lover Loved goes to find an indifferent judge of their dispute, the Vice relates to the audience his own love experience, in which he and a sweet damsel deceived each other; this story provides plausible mo-

tivation (unusual for a Vice character) for his mocking attitude toward all love. Each pair of disputants chooses the other as judges, with the result that both disputes end, anticlimactically, in a tie: Lover Not Loved and Beloved Not Loving are judged to suffer equal pains, while Lover Loved and Neither Lover Nor Loved enjoy equivalent pleasures. While the arguments are tedious, the play has its moment of excitement: At one point, the Vice runs in "among the audience with a high copper tank on his head full of squibs fired crying . . . fire! fire!" His prank has a purpose: He tells Lover Loved that his mistress has been burned, and the Lover's misery amply proves the Vice's contention that lovers are anxiety-ridden.

THE PLAY OF THE WEATHER

The third of the debate plays, *The Play of the Weather*, has the largest cast among Heywood's dramas, with ten characters. Heywood makes an entertaining play from the most trifling of subjects: complaints about the weather. When the great god Jupiter resolves to hear and redress grievances about the weather, eight characters representing a cross section of social types come in turn to make their conflicting pleas; in the end, Jupiter decides the issue in the only possible way: He will continue the weather "even as it was." Heywood enlivens this unpromising material in two ways: He arranges for lively antitheses between pairs of petitioners, and he selects as Jupiter's "cryer" (and the play's chief character) a Vice named Merry Report, whose quips and mocks enliven each episode. The successive pairs of petitioners make directly opposed requests; the Gentleman, for example, wants fair weather for hunting, while the Ranger desires terrific storms to level trees for his prerogative of windfall. Some pairs are set off by simultaneous appearance; the preening, fashion-conscious Gentlewoman is disdained for her vanity by the coarse, robust Launder. The final complainant, a masterpiece of economical characterization, is the boy, "the least that can play," who comically mistakes the jaunty Merry Report for "master God" and then petitions for frost and snow, for all of his "pleasure is in catching of birds,/ And making of snow-balls and throwing the same." The boy's artless egotism highlights the selfishness of all the petitioners.

Though the ostensible topic is commonplace, the real subject of *The Play of the Weather* is social strife among competing interests and the need for a strong ruler to keep the peace. Particularly under the threat of religious innovation, Heywood is suggesting, England needs a powerful monarch to maintain the harmony of the ancient commonwealth.

THE PARDONER AND THE FRIAR

Quite different from the *débat* plays are Heywood's three farces. These represent Heywood's most distinctive dramatic contribution, yet they are mostly derivative of French originals, two in part and the third substantially. Like any farce, these three feature fast-moving verbal and physical strife, single-line plots, and an absence of theme or idea; they are designed to dissolve all tensions in laughter. All three plays sharply satirize one or more clerics, or, as Francis Kirkman put it in his 1671 playlist, Heywood "makes notable work with the then Clergy."

The simplest and probably earliest of the three, *The Pardoner and the Friar*, is little more than an extended quarrel between two itinerant preachers. The supposed setting is a parish church, with the dramatic audience as congregation, where the two title characters have come to raise money for their respective brotherhood or almshouse. The Friar begins first. While he prays before his sermon, the Pardoner displays his papal bulls and holy relics. Like Geoffrey Chaucer's pardoner in *The Canterbury Tales* (1387-1400), this pardoner carries a collection of ludicrous relics that includes such treasures as Saint Michael's brain-pan, the arm of Saint Sunday, and "the great toe of the Holy Trinity." When the Friar begins preaching, the Pardoner refuses to yield the floor, so the two harangue in tandem, in rapid line-by-line alternation, pausing occasionally to rail at one another. Finally they fall to hair-pulling, scratching, and biting just as the parish priest, scandalized, rushes in to part them, calling on Neighbor Pratt the constable for assistance. The two charlatans, facing a night in the stocks, thrash their captors and make their escape. The basic situation of the flyting between two itinerants may derive from the short French play *Farce nouvelle d'un pardonneur, d'un triacleur, et d'une tavernière* (a new farce of a pardoner, an apothecary,

and a tavern-girl); the similarities are, however, slight and perhaps coincidental.

THE FOUR P.P.

The Four P.P. exhibits a lively lying contest among a Pardoner, a Palmer, and a Potyecary, with a Pedler as judge. (This play may also be indebted to the French farce mentioned above.) After considerable quarreling, the Pardoner tells a coarse tall tale of a remarkable cure, topping it with an exotic story of a woman rescued from Hell. Both stories make sport of women; when the Potyecary in reaction swears he never knew "any one woman out of patience," the three others involuntarily exclaim at his monstrous lie and the Pedler immediately awards him the prize. Lest we take the satire of corrupt churchmen too much to heart, the play ends, somewhat incongruously, with the Pedler's advice that we should "judge the best" of clerics and receive them "as the church doth judge or take them." The Palmer follows, speaking for the author, with an apology and disavowal of "all that hath scaped us here by negligence." The apology seems needless; the play's satire is light and harmless enough.

JOHAN JOHAN THE HUSBAND, TYB HIS WIFE, AND SIR JOHAN THE PRIEST

Heywood's most entertaining play is a vigorous domestic farce, *Johan Johan the Husband, Tyb His Wife, and Sir Johan the Priest*. This play has by far the most complicated plot, the most developed characterization, and the liveliest dialogue in the Heywood canon. Most of the credit, however, is not Heywood's, for his play is a fairly close translation of a French original, *Farce nouvelle et fort joyeuse du pasté* (a new and merry farce of a pie). At many points the translation is phrase-for-phrase; in other sections, Heywood shows originality and often improves on the French version. The story is simple enough: A husband vows to beat his wayward wife, but she easily outfaces him, sends him to fetch her lover the Priest, and dallies with the lover, eating a meat pie while poor Johan Johan is kept busy at the fire warming wax to fix a leaky bucket. Tyb the Wife snickers to Sir Johan about her cuckolded mate, who "chafeth the wax" and "for his life, dareth not look hitherward." She gloats over her "pretty jape" of making "her husband her ape." Poor Johan Johan complains that "the smoke putteth out my eyes two: I burn my face . . ./ And yet I dare not say one word" as his wife and her paramour eat his pie and taunt him. Finally his rage spills out and he beats the two of them soundly and drives them out of the house. From this simple situation, Heywood's version develops considerable human interest; the husband's vacillation between boastful manliness and sniveling servility is the mainspring of the action. He is caught in repeated ironies: He goes at his wife's bidding to fetch her lover to dine because he hopes the Priest will quell their strife; he has to beg the apparently reluctant Sir Johan to accept his invitation; he watches, famished, while the guest eats up his share of a pie; and he drives wife and lover from the house at the end, only to run after them in fear of what the pair may be up to at the Priest's house. Apart from its picture of a corrupt cleric, the play makes no statement and has no moral; it is simply good fun.

OTHER MAJOR WORKS

POETRY: *A Dialogue of Proverbs*, 1546, 1963 (Rudolph E. Habenicht, editor); *The Spider and the Fly*, 1556.

MISCELLANEOUS: *Works*, 1562 (epigrams and poems); *Works and Miscellaneous Short Poems*, 1956 (Burton A. Milligan, editor).

BIBLIOGRAPHY

Bolwell, Robert George Whitney. *The Life and Works of John Heywood.* New York: AMS Press, 1966. A biography of Heywood that covers his life and works. Bibliography.

De la Bère, Rupert. *John Heywood, Entertainer.* 1937. Reprint. Folcroft, Pa.: Folcroft Library Editions, 1970. Presents an analysis of four of Heywood's plays: *Witty and Witless, Johan Johan the Husband, Tyb His Wife, and Sir Johan the Priest, The Pardoner and the Friar,* and *The Four P.P.* Bibliography.

Farmer, John Stephen, ed. *The Dramatic Writings of John Heywood.* 1905. Reprint. New York: Barnes & Noble, 1966. This work examines the plays *Witty and Witless, Johan Johan the Husband, Tyb His Wife, and Sir Johan the Priest, The Pardoner and the Friar, The Play of the Weather, The Play of Love,* and *The Four P.P.*

Johnson, Robert Carl. *John Heywood.* New York: Twayne, 1970. In this basic biography, Johnson characterizes Heywood the dramatist as "a man of his age who consciously looked backward and to his contemporaries, both in England and on the Continent." Bibliography.

Walker, Greg. *The Politics of Performance in Early Renaissance Drama.* New York: Cambridge University Press, 1998. A look at politics in literature in sixteenth century Great Britain. Writers examined include Heywood, Nicholas Udall, and Thomas Norton. Bibliography and index.

William M. Baillie,
updated by Frank Day

THOMAS HEYWOOD

Born: Lincolnshire, England; c. 1573
Died: London, England; August, 1641

PRINCIPAL DRAMA

The Four Prentices of London, pr. c. 1594, pb. 1615
Edward IV, Parts I and II, pr. 1599, pb. 1600
The Royal King and the Loyal Subject, pr. c. 1602, pb. 1637
A Woman Killed with Kindness, pr. 1603, pb. 1607
The Wise Woman of Hogsdon, pr. c. 1604, pb. 1638
If You Know Not Me, You Know Nobody: Or, The Troubles of Queen Elizabeth, Part I, pr., pb. 1605, *Part II*, pr. 1605, pb. 1606

Fortune by Land and Sea, pr. c. 1607, pb. 1655

The Rape of Lucrece, pb. 1608, pr. before 1611

The Fair Maid of the West: Or, A Girl Worth Gold, Part I, pr. before 1610, pb. 1631, *Part II*, pr. c. 1630, pb. 1631

The Golden Age: Or, The Lives of Jupiter and Saturn, pr. before 1611, pb. 1611

The Silver Age, pr. 1612, pb. 1613

The Brazen Age, pr., pb. 1613

The Iron Age, Parts I and II, pr. c. 1613, pb. 1632

The Captives: Or, The Lost Recovered, pr. 1624, pb. 1885

A Maidenhead Well Lost, pr. c. 1625-1634, pb. 1634

The English Traveler, pr. c. 1627, pb. 1633

London's Jus Honorarium, pr., pb. 1631 (masque)

Londini Artium et Scientiarum Scaturigo, pr., pb. 1632 (masque)

Londini Emporia: Or, London's Mercatura, pr., pb. 1633 (masque)

The Late Lancashire Witches, pr., pb. 1634 (with Richard Brome)

A Challenge for Beauty, pr. c. 1634, pb. 1636

Love's Mistress, pr. 1634, pb. 1636

Londini Sinus Salutis: Or, London's Harbour of Health and Happiness, pr., pb. 1635 (masque)

Londini Speculum: Or, London's Mirror, pr., pb. 1637 (masque)

Porta Pietatis, pr., pb. 1638 (masque)

Londini Status Pacatus: Or, London's Peaceable Estate, pr., pb. 1639 (masque)

The Dramatic Works of Thomas Heywood, pb. 1874

OTHER LITERARY FORMS

Thomas Heywood was as prolific in other forms of writing as he was in the drama. Very little of his other work, however, has any particular literary merit. The long poem *Troia Britannica* (1609) was based on material that Heywood had earlier put into dramatic form, but the poetry is generally considered to be poor, Heywood having never shown a particular flair for verse. *An Apology for Actors* (1612), on the other hand, is an excellent critical work that defends the Jacobean stage on didactic grounds. Because Heywood so often used women as the protagonists of his plays, his *Gunaikeion: Or, Nine Books of Various*

History Concerning Women, Inscribed by the Nine Muses (1624) is of interest to the modern reader because it suggests even further the degree to which Heywood was interested in the nature of women and their sufferings. None of these works, however, can lay claim to the merit of Heywood's best plays, and they have received little critical attention.

ACHIEVEMENTS

In 1633, Thomas Heywood claimed to have written either all or most of some 220 plays, in addition to his volumes of poetry and prose. Yet only *A Woman Killed with Kindness* is well known or anthologized with any regularity. To measure Heywood's significance in such terms would be to ignore the impact he had on the theater of his day and particularly on the development of the theater since the Restoration, both in England and in Europe. Heywood was the first English playwright to demonstrate consistently the potential of the sentimental drama, particularly the domestic tragedy, to produce effective theater. Restoration writers such as Nicholas Rowe and Thomas Otway followed Heywood's use of the female protagonist in their "she-tragedies," and George Lillo in *The London Merchant: Or, The History of George Barnwell* (pr., pb. 1731) employed the middle-class ethic of *A Woman Killed with Kindness* and *The English Traveler* to effect a similar pathos. Gotthold Ephraim Lessing, Friedrich Schiller, and Denis Diderot also saw the potential of the sentimental drama as Heywood had used it, although they were more directly influenced by the Restoration dramatists. In Heywood, one can find the beginning of a type of drama that has had a profound impact on Western dramatic literature. Although he did not have the dramatic and artistic talents of those who developed his forms, his plays solidly established the notion that pathos built on a foundation of basically bourgeois morality has both popular appeal and literary merit.

BIOGRAPHY

The facts of Thomas Heywood's early life are scarce. Heywood was apparently born sometime in 1573 to the Reverend Robert Heywood and his wife, Elizabeth. Probably a Cambridge graduate, Robert

Heywood migrated before Thomas's birth from Cheshire to Lincolnshire, where he served as rector first at Rothwell and then at Ashby-cum-Fenley. Thomas was one of eleven children; there is, however, no record of any dealings between him and his siblings after he arrived in London.

The Heywoods were, it would seem, a family of gentility, evidenced by the application of Heywood's Uncle Edmund for a grant of arms. At sixteen or seventeen, Heywood entered Emmanuel College, Cambridge, a stronghold of Puritanism, which may explain the moral thrust in much of his writing, particularly in the pamphlets of his later career. His college work ended early, however, when his father died in 1593. At this point, Heywood, like so many young men with talent and a bit of learning but no degree, accepted the challenges of the London stage and began his career as an actor.

In 1593, Heywood was hired by Philip Henslowe as an actor for the Admiral's Men. Heywood, however, turned his hand very quickly to writing, sharing in the revision of works being done by the company. Among these may have been, in 1599, *The Siege of London*.

Around 1600, Heywood began writing for Derby's Men, although the specifics of his relationship with this company are relatively obscure. *Edward IV* was produced by Derby's Men before Heywood broke the connection in 1601, when he became an actor-sharer with Worcester's Men and entered the service of Queen Anne, under the auspices of Henslowe. This new association connected Heywood with Henry Chettle, Thomas Dekker, Wentworth Smith, and John Webster. By this time, as A. M. Clark notes, Heywood was financially well off as a result of his hasty writing, which, according to Clark, was "fatal to [the] literary quality" of his scripts but which "did not greatly diminish their price." Whatever effect Heywood's mercenary spirit may generally have had on his work, he did in 1603 write *A Woman Killed with Kindness*, the play on which his reputation rests.

A successful actor-sharer and playwright in 1603, Heywood married Ann Butler on June 13, with whom he had six children. Although no record of Ann Heywood's death has been found, Heywood apparently married Jane Span in 1632.

In 1608, after fifteen years of increasing success as a dramatist, Heywood turned his energies to other forms of literary achievement. His decision was probably spurred by the financial problems the theater experienced because of a new outbreak of the plague in London. More to the point, however, Heywood had always envisioned himself as a literary figure whose talent had been absorbed by his efforts to earn a living rather than achieve recognition as a poet. In 1609, he published *Troia Britannica*, certainly his best effort at poetry. Yet, whatever its merits, *Troia Britannica* is not as accomplished a piece as his series known as *The Ages* (*The Golden Age*, *The Silver Age*, *The Brazen Age*, and *The Iron Age*), his dramatizations of basically the same material. In 1612, Heywood published his major piece of criticism, *An Apology for Actors*, which defended on didactic grounds the London theater. This work remains a major piece of criticism, its value being enhanced by the fact that it was written by a major figure of the Jacobean theater.

For approximately the next ten years, Heywood had his finger in a number of activities but produced very little himself. In 1619, he joined the Lady Elizabeth's Men when the Queen's Company split. His new troupe produced *The Captives* just before he moved in 1625 to Queen Henrietta's Company, for which he wrote *The Fair Maid of the West, Part II*, which enjoyed a successful Christmas performance at court. Again, Heywood's interests began to turn from the stage, although he did write *The English Traveler*, *The Late Lancashire Witches*, and his last play, either *A Challenge for Beauty* or *Love's Mistress* (the dates are somewhat uncertain), all of which were performed by the Lady Elizabeth's Men.

In 1631, Heywood began a series of city pageants that displayed his limited abilities with the masque. At the same time, he published a number of didactic journalistic pieces, such as the pamphlet *Philocothonista: Or, The Drunkard, Open, Dissected, Anatomized* (1635), a treatise against the abuses of drinking. His *A Curtain Lecture* (1636) celebrates the value of marriage and further glorifies the domestic virtues that Heywood championed throughout his career. All these works, however, have little to recommend them other than their support of our understanding of the changes in thought that Heywood experienced as he grew older.

When Heywood was buried at the Church of St. James, Clerkenwell, on August 16, 1641, he had had his hand in the writing of more than two hundred plays that had appeared between the years 1592 and 1641.

ANALYSIS

In an age that produced William Shakespeare, Ben Jonson, and Christopher Marlowe, Thomas Heywood achieved a popular success on the stage that very likely dimmed even that of the masters. He was extremely popular in the pit with an audience that sought entertainment more than enlightenment. Critic A. M. Clark has said that Heywood "was the journeyman-playwright *par excellence*, with a facility, not unlike the knack of a skilled artisan, with a dramatic insight that never altogether failed him, and without the vagaries and transcendences of a conscious literature." Heywood's plays presented characters and plots with which his audience could identify. That Heywood was able to present such middle-class characters, speaking naturally and responding to their conflicts with a morality consistent with their station in life, is not surprising, nor is it necessarily commendable. That he was able to do it and, within such strict boundaries, still produce effective scripts, always with dramatic and sometimes with literary quality, is more than commendable. As a result, Heywood became, in a genuine sense, the founder of the middle-class drama.

Heywood's plots were often borrowed from the chapbook literature that was popular during the early seventeenth century, and those that were not were framed as if they had been. Thus, his settings and actions were familiar to theatergoers. *The Wise Woman of Hogsdon*, for example, follows from the interest of his contemporaries in witches—an interest on which Heywood later capitalized in *The Late Lancashire Witches*—and the play effectively uses the comic potential in the fraud of such persons as the Wise Woman proves to be. Such con artists were familiar to Heywood's audience; thus, the Wise Woman's various in-

trigues were of considerable interest. *The Fair Maid of the West*, although spiced with a certain amount of romance, also demonstrates this sense of immediacy. The audience would have found themselves quite at home during the tavern scenes or laughing with recognition at the clown Clem, who, with typical English decorum, takes himself a bit too seriously for his own good. The central plots of *A Woman Killed with Kindness* and *The English Traveler*, however, best demonstrate this point. Such accounts of infidelity and lovers' intrigues were common in the popular literature of the day, materials that certainly would have been familiar to Heywood's audience. They are, moreover, stories of characters from the middle class.

It is in fact the characters more than the plots in Heywood's plays that do the most to break down barriers between the playwright and his audience. In *A Woman Killed with Kindness*, Frankford, though a member of the landed gentry, is not a member of the nobility. His grief is not that brought on by the peculiar circumstances of lofty birth but, rather, the kind of sorrow that anyone in the audience might experience. Anne's sin, moreover, is not one she commits because of some gruesome sense of fate. Hers is the weakness of human nature—again, a weakness shared with the audience. Bess, the heroine of *The Fair Maid of the West*, despite her excessive virtues, would have greatly pleased the audience, as she was a tavern mistress, a member of their own plebeian class. These few examples well illustrate the generalization that the characters of Heywood's plays, at least the better works, held up a mirror to early seventeenth century life.

To depict the experiences of such middle-class characters confronting what were generally the conflicts of the middle class, Heywood used what could well be regarded as pedestrian language. Poetry was the appropriate language for Shakespeare's noble characters, just as Heywood's prose and simple diction are completely in line with the thematic structure of his plays. His characters are lower in stature than are Shakespeare's; his themes are domestic. For his characters to speak in lofty tones would be out of place, and Heywood was enough of a dramatist to realize that his characters should use language and express sentiments appropriate to their station in life and the conflicts they faced.

THE FAIR MAID OF THE WEST

Clark has labeled *The Fair Maid of the West* the "quintessence of popular literature," referring primarily to its excellent fusion of romantic elements with those of the domestic comedy. Heywood's success in combining these seemingly disparate elements also makes this his best comedy, containing characters from the domestic mode and plot from the romantic. Both work well to illustrate a theme basic to the Heywood canon: that fidelity, chastity, and married love are virtues that ennoble men and women of the middle class.

Bess Bridges, the heroine of *The Fair Maid of the West*, is reputed to be unmatched in virtue as well as in beauty, making the tavern where she works a popular gathering place for a lively crowd of suitors, including the gallant Spencer, who in her defense kills the overbearing Carroll and is forced to flee to Fayal to avoid being arrested. There he is wounded and, thinking that he will die, sends Goodlack to entrust his entire estate to Bess if she has remained faithful to him. She has, and after hearing that her love is dead, she sets out to Fayal to see his grave. While on the sea, she purges it of Spanish pirates until she is reunited with and married to Spencer at the court of Mullisheg.

This summary illustrates the romantic aspects of the play. It includes voyages on the high seas, suggestive of the many chronicles of travel that were popular at the time. Bess takes on heroic if improbable stature as she captures ships that have been terrorizing the English merchant fleet. Thus, the play rings with patriotism such as would have been applauded by an audience who had within recent memory seen the defeat of the Spanish Armada. The settings shift from the tavern at Fay, in the domestic comedy tradition, to the court of Mullisheg, in the realm of romance. Yet throughout, the basic theme of the play is that the fundamental chastity of simple characters such as Bess and the faithfulness to love characteristic of Spencer are ennobling—that it is virtue, not birth, which confers true nobility.

In one sense, all Heywood's plays, including the comedies, are concerned with the nobility of virtue,

particularly the virtue of fidelity. In Heywood's terms, this virtue alone could ennoble even the most lowly characters on the social scale. *The Fair Maid of the West* treats this theme in various ways. First, there is the chastity that distinguishes Bess from the beginning. There is, moreover, the faithful love that she and Spencer share and that finally overcomes all the problems they face. There is, as well, the conversion of the two schemers Roughman and Goodlack, effected by Bess's virtue. Under her influence, these two become her true friends and loyal companions in her search for Spencer. Mullisheg, the pagan, serves as the final yardstick by which these characters, particularly Bess, can be measured. Despite his non-Christian frame of reference, he is so overcome with Bess's morality and her nobility of spirit that he ensures her marriage to Spencer and, despite his own loss, rewards all the characters in her entourage.

In *The Fair Maid of the West*, Heywood masks his seriousness of purpose, one that dominates all his plays, with comedy and occasionally with sheer farce. He was well aware that audiences came to the theater more for entertainment than for enlightenment, but he demonstrates that they could well appreciate homily and entertainment together if the playwright suitably fused the two.

THE WISE WOMAN OF HOGSDON

The Wise Woman of Hogsdon is perhaps Heywood's best example of what can legitimately be called domestic comedy. Lacking the ornamentation of romance elements that spice the action of *The Fair Maid of the West*, the play points up Heywood's place as a link in the chain that connects Renaissance and Restoration comedy. His role in linking the domestic tragedy of the two periods is well known, but too often his role in connecting the comedy of the two periods goes unacknowledged.

The action of *The Wise Woman of Hogsdon* revolves around the antics of the rake Young Chartley, who has deserted Luce from the city, has contracted to marry Luce from the country, and has left his marriage bed to pursue the lovely Gratiana, the daughter of Sir Harry. These intrigues are complicated even further when the country Luce contracts the Wise Woman, whom Young Chartley has insulted, to handle the wedding arrangements. To avenge herself on Young Chartley, the Wise Woman mixes wedding partners. All is finally resolved when Young Chartley, who does in fact end up married to Luce from the city, repents, and all the others are satisfied with the mates they have been left holding.

The Wise Woman of Hogsdon is an acknowledgment of the virtues of chastity, fidelity, and married love. Here Heywood's recurring theme is treated within a completely comic framework. Here, moreover, the content is purely middle-class, suggesting strongly the notion that these virtues glorify even the common folk. Two other aspects from the play demonstrate further the fact that Heywood was directing his homily chiefly at a middle-class audience. First, the Wise Woman herself is a character drawn from contemporary life; she is a fraud and a charlatan akin to the witches, alchemists, and other con artists who were constantly being exposed both in the courts and in the popular literature of the day. Her antics are precisely what Heywood's audience would have expected from her; her duping of Young Chartley and the others would have been much to their appreciation. One scene in particular demonstrates Heywood's awareness of his audience. In the combat between Sir Boniface and Sencer, disguised as Sir Timothy, in which the Latin of the farcical schoolmaster is used by Sencer as a weapon against him, Heywood is clearly painting a comic picture of the pedants, the pretenders to learning, who in their own way were seen by the middle-class audience as even more absurd than con artists such as the Wise Woman. This is low comedy perhaps, but the scene works well to illustrate the folly not only of Sir Boniface but of the pretentious Sir Harry as well.

The gulling of Sir Boniface is reminiscent of the slapstick humor that Jonson fell into in plays such as *The Alchemist* (pr. 1610), as when Face and Subtle dupe the Puritans. The overall style of the play, however, is much more in line with the works of Sir George Etherege and William Wycherley; its action is not unlike that of Etheredge's *The Man of Mode: Or, Sir Fopling Flutter* (pr., pb. 1676) or Wycherley's *The Country Wife* (pr., pb. 1675). Young Chartley, too, reminds one a great deal of Horner and Dorimant, whose quests for women trap them in a web of comic intrigue. For Heywood, however, there is a stronger moral bent at the denouement, not the essentially immoral conclusion typical of Wycherley or the amorality typical of Etherege. Young Chartley is penitent, and all the lovers are satisfied that they have ended up with the partners they should have. No character is totally humiliated. Even the con artists of the play have used their talents to ensure a proper resolution to the basic conflict. Thus, whatever this play may have in common with Restoration comedy, its morality sharply distinguishes it from the masterpieces of that licentious period.

A WOMAN KILLED WITH KINDNESS

A Woman Killed with Kindness is generally regarded as Heywood's masterpiece, and it has ensured him of a lasting place in the history of English literature. It is a sentimental or domestic tragedy constructed, like his other works, to appeal to a popular audience. The play has, moreover, a subplot that causes many of the same distractions caused by the secondary action in works such as *The English Traveler*. There is, however, one significant difference between this play and Heywood's lesser-known works. In *A Woman Killed with Kindness*, the poet in Heywood shines. His language, although appropriate to his domestic framework and therefore still somewhat pedestrian, is used so well to express meaning consistent with the theme and the characters of the work that there is a harmony between language and sentiment that is characteristic only of great literature.

The central plot of *A Woman Killed with Kindness* begins with the marriage of Frankford and Anne, a marriage viewed by their friends as the perfect union. Frankford, however, takes Wendoll into his home, only to have his friend tempt Anne to infidelity. On discovering her adultery, Frankford banishes Anne to a secluded cottage on their estate. Anne refuses to eat and soon lies on her deathbed. Frankford, however, comes to her and forgives her, reinstating her to her position as wife and mother.

A Woman Killed with Kindness is Heywood's best statement of his constant theme: the ennobling grace of married love and fidelity. In this work, however, the statement is enhanced by an explicitly Christian sentiment. Frankford overcomes his initial rage and his desire to kill Anne and Wendoll, determined that he will not destroy two souls that Christ died to save. In this way, the revenge tragedy motif so characteristic of Renaissance theater is shattered by Christian sentiment. His punishment of Anne, suggested by the title of the work, is also characteristic of his goodness, as is his final forgiveness of her. Such is Frankford's virtue that scholars generally refer to him as the ultimate Christian hero.

While the goodness of Frankford accounts in part for the overwhelming sentimentality of the play, the genuine repentance of Anne and Wendoll adds significantly to the final pathos. They accept the tortures of their guilt and do not at any point try to justify their actions. Anne dies—Heywood's morality would not have allowed otherwise—but there is beauty in her death, the beauty of justice matched by forgiveness.

What makes *A Woman Killed with Kindness* a superior work, recognized as such even by those critics who do not accept the possibility of domestic tragedy and do not call Heywood's work a tragedy, is the language. The play's powerful fusion of language and sentiment is particularly clear in the scene in which Frankford confronts Anne about her infidelity. With a series of short questions, pointedly delivered, he asks her what failings as a husband he had demonstrated that would make her turn from him. She denies there being any, until at last Frankford explodes with a declaration of innocence from such failings that demonstrates well the grief he feels. This whole scene is built on the assumption that the marital vows are sacred and that Frankford's faithfulness as a husband should preclude such treachery by his wife.

Of all Heywood's plays, *A Woman Killed with Kindness* has had the most lasting interest to scholars; more important, the play has had an enormous impact on dramatic literature. Writers interested in the possibilities of sentimental tragedy have taken it as their model; Diderot referred explicitly to the success of *A Woman Killed with Kindness* as justifying the writing of domestic tragedy. Though the bulk of his work has been forgotten, Heywood has achieved a permanent place in the history of drama.

OTHER MAJOR WORKS

POETRY: *Troia Britannica*, 1609; *The Hierarchy of the Blessed Angels*, 1635.

NONFICTION: *Oenone and Paris*, 1594; *An Apology for Actors*, 1612; *Gunaikeion: Or, Nine Books of Various History Concerning Women, Inscribed by the Nine Muses*, 1624; *England's Elizabeth, Her Life and Troubles During Her Minority from the Cradle to the Crown*, 1632; *Philocothonista: Or, The Drunkard, Open, Dissected, Anatomized*, 1635; *A Curtain Lecture*, 1636; *The Exemplary Lives and Memorable Acts of Nine of the Most Worthy Women of the World: Three Jews, Three Gentiles, Three Christians*, 1640; *The Life of Merlin, Surnamed Ambrosius*, 1641.

BIBLIOGRAPHY

Baines, Barbara J. *Thomas Heywood*. Boston: Twayne, 1984. A basic biography of Heywood, covering his life and works. Bibliography and index.

Johnson, Marilyn L. *Images of Women in the Works of Thomas Heywood*. Salzburg: Institut für Englishche Spraceh und Literatur, Universität Salzburg, 1974. An examination of Heywood's works, with emphasis on his portrayal of women. Bibliography.

McLuskie, Kathleen. *Dekker and Heywood: Professional Dramatists*. New York: St. Martin's Press, 1993. An analysis of English drama, particularly the life and works of Heywood and Thomas Dekker.

Wentworth, Michael D. *Thomas Heywood: A Reference Guide*. Boston: G. K. Hall, 1986. A bibliography of Heywood's works and writings about him. Index.

_____. "Thomas Heywood's *A Woman Killed with Kindness* as Domestic Morality." In *Traditions and Innovations: Essays on British Literature of the Middle Ages and the Renaissance*, edited by David G. Allen and Robert A. White. Newark: University of Delaware Press, 1990. Wentworth shows how *A Woman Killed with Kindness* can be "described as a repentance play or a domestic morality" descended from medieval morality plays such as *Everyman*.

Gerald W. Morton,
updated by Frank Day

ROLF HOCHHUTH

Born: Eschwege, Germany; April 1, 1931

PRINCIPAL DRAMA

Der Stellvertreter: Ein Christliches Trauerspiel,
pr., pb. 1963 (*The Representative*, 1963; also
known as *The Deputy*)

Soldaten: Nekrolog auf Genf, pr., pb. 1967
(*Soldiers: An Obituary for Geneva*, 1968)

Guerillas: Tragödie in fünf Akten, pr., pb. 1970

Tod eines Jägers, pr. 1970, pb. 1976

Die Hebamme, pb. 1971, pr. 1972

Dramen, pb. 1972

Lysistrate und die Nato, pb. 1973, pr. 1974

Juristen, pb. 1979, pr. 1980

Ärztinnen, pr., pb. 1980

Judith: Trauerspiel, pr., pb. 1984

Unbefleckte Empfängnis: Ein Kreidekreis, pb.
1988, pr. 1989

Sommer 14: Ein Totentanz, pb. 1989, pr. 1990

Alle Dramen, pb. 1991

*Wessis in Weimar: Szenen aus einem besetzten
Land*, pr., pb. 1993

Effis Nacht: Monolog, pb. 1996, pr. 1998

Das Recht auf Arbeit, pb. 2000

Hitlers Dr. Faust, pb. 2000, pr. 2001

Nachtmusik, pb. 2000, pr. 2001 (*Mozart's
Nachtmusik*, 2001)

OTHER LITERARY FORMS

Rolf Hochhuth is foremost a dramatist. That he
achieved world renown with his first drama, *The
Deputy*—a play that condemns Pope Pius XII for tol-
erating the extermination of the Jews in Nazi death
camps during World War II by not speaking out publicly—tends to overshadow Hochhuth's admittedly
more modest accomplishments in the fields of poetry,
fiction, and the essay.

The moral fervor that is evident in *The Deputy* and
in subsequent plays also infuses his collection of essays *Krieg und Klassenkrieg* (1971; war and class
war). In these essays, Hochhuth drew attention to
phenomena that were supposedly no longer existent

in the West German welfare state: poverty, lack of
housing, job-related accidents, and a high incidence
of disease among certain segments of the population.
Not surprisingly, politicians and other establishment
figures reacted harshly. Despite the employment of
Marxist vocabulary in his first major essay collection,
Hochhuth is not advocating the radical and sudden
upheaval of society in the hope of achieving the ideal
state. Rather, he points out the ills of society in copiously documented writings that too often elicit invec-
tive instead of factual analysis.

In *Tell '38* (1979; English translation, 1984), his
acceptance speech on being awarded the Basel Art
Prize in 1976, Hochhuth returned to the Nazi past
that he had first explored in *The Deputy*. In a similar
vein, the writer paid tribute to members of the German student resistance movement in *Räuber-Rede:
Drei deutsche Vorwürfe: Schiller, Lessing, Geschwister Scholl* (1982; a lecture on robbers: three German subjects).

The title of Hochhuth's essay collection *Einsprüche! Zur Geschichte, Politik und Literatur* (2001; in-
terventions: On history, politics, and literature) indicates both his motivation for writing, that is, to
intervene in public affairs as well as the—rather
broadly defined—areas he considers his province as a
writer. Frequently, Hochhuth focuses on extraordinary historical individuals, for example, in the volume of essays *Täter und Denker* (1987; doers and
thinkers). In *Und Brecht sah das Tragische nicht*
(1996; Brecht did not perceive the tragic), Hochhuth
faulted playwright Bertolt Brecht for ignoring the
tragic dimension in his dramas. In his lectures on
poetics, *Die Geburt der Tragödie aus dem Krieg:
Frankfurter Poetik-Vorlesungen* (2001; the birth of
tragedy out of war), Hochhuth alludes to philosopher
Friedrich Nietzsche and posits in a far-reaching historical survey that drama is the offspring of politics
and war.

Hochhuth's novel *Die Berliner Antigone* (1963;
the Berlin Antigone) presents a Sophoclean heroine
who appears in modern guise in Berlin during World

War II and accepts the death penalty for burying her brother, who had been executed by the Nazis. His *Eine Liebe in Deutschland* (1978; *A German Love Story*, 1980) delves even more deeply into the Nazi past by unearthing a shocking, though not atypical, occurrence: the love story of a German woman and a Polish prisoner of war that ended when the incident was reported to the authorities.

The narrative *Alan Turing* (1987) features the British mathematician by the same name who, during World War II, was instrumental in breaking the code of the encoding machine used by the German military and thereby contributed significantly to the eventual victory of the allies. In *Julia: Oder, der Weg zur Macht* (1994; *Julia: or the way to power*), Hochhuth deals with another victim of history (and historiography), Julia, daughter of Roman emperor Augustus.

ACHIEVEMENTS

When on February 20, 1963, *The Deputy* premiered in West Berlin, neither the play's famed director, Erwin Piscator, nor its then completely unknown author could have anticipated the full extent of the violent, international controversy in which it soon became engulfed. In fact, the critic Eric Bentley claimed in *The Storm over The Deputy* (1964) that the uproar was "almost the largest storm ever raised by a play in the whole history of the drama."

In this five-act play, Rolf Hochhuth contrasts the fictitious protagonist Riccardo, a young and idealistic Italian Jesuit priest, with Pope Pius XII. After Riccardo has learned in Berlin that the extermination of European Jews is taking place in Auschwitz on a grand scale, he becomes convinced that only an unequivocal appeal by the pope to the Nazi leaders can halt the mass slaughter. When Riccardo confronts the pope and begs him to exercise his moral authority, the latter places political considerations above humanitarian and Christian values. Riccardo then takes it on himself to set an example; he joins the Roman Jews, who have been arrested virtually under the pope's nose, on their transport to Auschwitz, where he dies a martyr's death.

Underlying Hochhuth's condemnation of the pope's failure to act is a concept of history that en-

dows the individual with a high degree of autonomy and the ability to influence historical processes. The dramaturgy that pits Riccardo against the pope is ultimately derived from Friedrich Schiller's historical drama of conscience rather than from Bertolt Brecht's sociologically oriented epic theater; the wealth of documentary material has been fashioned into a drama with a traditional structure, albeit a sprawling one, that relies essentially on elements of the illusionist stage.

In his second drama, *Soldiers*, Hochhuth tackled another controversial issue harking back to World War II: Winston Churchill's responsibility for the indiscriminate bombing of German population centers. The furor over Hochhuth's alleged character assassination of Churchill obscured one of the dramatist's vital concerns: the adoption of an international agreement that would outlaw the bombing of urban areas predominantly inhabited by civilians. In his subsequent plays, Hochhuth turned to topical, current events with varying degrees of success.

There remains a seeming paradox in the reception of Hochhuth's plays: Whereas theater critics tend to dwell on the real or imagined flaws of Hochhuth's works—such as the traditional dramaturgy that derives from an outmoded concept of the individual's place in the historical process, the portrayal of largely one-dimensional characters, the employment of sensational or melodramatic elements, the excessive documentation—audiences have been quite receptive to Hochhuth's dramas. Moreover, as the furor over *The Deputy* amply demonstrates, Hochhuth's plays have stimulated public debate, resulting in a reexamination of the past in the light of the present and, in some instances, actually influencing current events. Although Hochhuth will be remembered for his role in the development of documentary theater, it is perhaps his uncompromising stance as an outspoken public figure and moralist of radical convictions that ensures the dramatist a place of significance among those writers who emerged in the 1960's and who have continued to shape the literary scene as well as the theater for four decades or so.

Since 1962, Hochhuth has received a number of literary prizes, among them that dedicated to Hans and Sophie Scholl, members of a Munich student resistance movement against Hitler, who were executed. In 2001, in recognition of his endeavors to creatively preserve and further develop the German language that he sees as threatened by the encroachment of (American) English, he was awarded the newly established prize named after Jacob Grimm, one of the Grimm brothers.

BIOGRAPHY

Rolf Hochhuth was born on April 1, 1931, the offspring of a family that had established ancient roots in Eschwege, a small town in Hesse that was, before reunification of the two postwar German states in 1990, situated in close proximity to the border separating the Federal Republic and the German Democratic Republic. In 1948, Hochhuth—who, because of his youth, had missed military service in World War II—left secondary school to become a bookseller's apprentice, a vocation in which he could indulge his appetite for reading and writing. The novelist Thomas Mann, whom in 1975 Hochhuth vehemently defended against attempts to minimize Mann's political commitment during the latter's exile in the United States, became his favorite author.

From 1950 to 1955, Hochhuth worked as a bookstore employee in several West German cities and audited classes at the universities of Munich and Heidelberg. In 1955, he became an editor for the Bertelsmann book club; he edited the German classics as well as modern writers, among them the nineteenth century humorist Wilhelm Busch, an edition of whose works sold a million copies within a few weeks. In his editing activities, Hochhuth often collaborated with Marianne Heinemann, a friend from Eschwege, whom he married in 1957 and from whom he was divorced in 1972. Hochhuth was married again—to Dana Pavic, a Yugoslavian medical student—in 1975.

In 1959, Hochhuth spent a sabbatical in Rome, where he engaged in archival research at the Vatican. *The Deputy*, the play that resulted from these studies, was accepted by a publisher in 1961; however, fearing an adverse reaction from the Catholic Church, the publisher reneged on the contract. Another publisher

was willing to assume the risk of publication; in addition, one of the pioneers of the political theater of the 1920's, Erwin Piscator, agreed to produce the play.

The royalties from *The Deputy* afforded Hochhuth the means to establish himself as a freelance writer in Basel, Switzerland, subsequently his principal place of residence. The uproar that followed *The Deputy* set the tone for the reception of Hochhuth's later works as well; the writer's vilification by the chancellor of the Federal Republic in 1965 was followed by numerous lawsuits that were brought against him—particularly in England—as a consequence of the publication and production of *Soldiers*, Hochhuth's play about Churchill, in 1967. *A German Love Story* not only stirred up violent emotions but also achieved direct results in the political sphere by forcing a prominent politician with a Nazi past to withdraw from office. Hence the comparative uneventfulness of Hochhuth's life assumes a different dimension when one takes into account the reactions to his works—which, by virtue of their author's propensity for both controversial and topical issues, agitate public opinion beyond the confines of the theater and the literary scene.

Another major theater scandal erupted when Hochhuth's play *Wessis in Weimar: Szenen aus einem besetzten Land* (1993; West Germans in Weimar: Scenes from an occupied country) was produced at the Berliner Ensemble, the (East) Berlin theater company that had served as a cultural beacon under the direction of Brecht—from 1949/1950 until his death in 1956—and his successors. Critics attacked the play's tendentiousness because of its one-sided indictment of the practices of the Treuhand, a trust that had been set up to administer and dispose of the industrial plants that were formerly owned by the defunct East German state. However, Hochhuth protested what he considered the mutilation of his play by the director. To become independent from the assumed arbitrariness of directors, he sought to establish a theater in which dramatists were in control of most matters, including the staging of plays. Although his plans ultimately did not materialize, he achieved a success of sorts. In 1996, a foundation that he had created assumed ownership of the Theater am

Schiffbauerdamm, home of the Berliner Ensemble. Although the theater was leased to the city of Berlin, Hochhuth was guaranteed the right to produce his own plays. In view of the increased significance that the capital of the "Berlin Republic" is likely to assume in both the political and cultural realms, Hochhuth's tenacity and perseverance have resulted in obtaining a prestigious venue for the production of his plays in one of Germany's premiere theaters.

ANALYSIS

There is a consensus among critics that Rolf Hochhuth is to be taken seriously as playwright because of the moral fervor with which he confronts significant issues. At the same time, critics have been reluctant to proclaim Hochhuth a major dramatist, pointing to the artistic shortcomings of his plays. Whatever the final verdict on his drama—whether, that is, Hochhuth's plays endure as dramatic literature—he has undeniably contributed to the program of moral revaluation that distinguishes postwar German literature. Like his contemporary Günter Grass, he has not reserved his criticism for the Nazis and those who made their rise possible. He has also been unsparing in his criticism of the Western democracies. As a platform for provocative expression of moral and political viewpoints, his theater is a resounding success.

THE DEPUTY

Both his strengths and his weaknesses are evident in *The Deputy*, his first drama. The time of action in the first act is 1942. The Jesuit Riccardo, who has been transferred to the nuncio's office in Berlin, is almost immediately confronted with an explosive revelation by the SS officer Gerstein—who, unlike Riccardo, is a historical figure. Gerstein informs the nuncio about the mass killings of Jews in Auschwitz by means of gas. In contrast to the ambivalent attitude displayed by the nuncio, Riccardo decides to act; he assures Gerstein that this information will induce the pope to issue a formal protest that will stop the murders. Unlike Gerstein, whose conscience has forced him to reveal the terrible secret about Auschwitz and who has to hide his horror and revulsion in order not to betray himself, Eichmann and

other Nazi functionaries chat jovially about the "final solution" of the Jewish problem while they relax by drinking beer and bowling.

In the second act, Riccardo has returned to Rome; his conversation with his father, the pope's trusted adviser in financial matters, indicates that it will be difficult to persuade the pope to speak out against the systematic killing of the Jews. Political considerations are of prime importance. Hitler's setbacks on the eastern front have weakened his position as a bulwark against Joseph Stalin and communism, and moral condemnation on the part of the pope might further diminish Hitler's strength. Another high church official essentially agrees with this assessment. Both Riccardo's father and the cardinal aver that the pope's heart is with the innocent victims; however, they are not sanguine about the prospects of the pope's intervention. Both men see in Riccardo a dangerous idealist who, in his complete disregard for realpolitik, is able to do harm to the interests of the Church.

In the third act, Riccardo is joined by Gerstein. The former has almost given up hope that the pope will intervene forcefully. In desperation, he proposes to a Jesuit general, who has been actively engaged in assisting Jews, to murder the pope and to blame the SS on the grounds that they considered the pope a protector of the Jews. Riccardo's plan is regarded as completely unacceptable by the Jesuit general. At the end of act 3, the SS and their Italian collaborators arrest the Roman Jews, among them converts to Catholicism who live within earshot of the Vatican. The officer in charge, reminded by Gerstein that Hitler does not want any complications in his relations with the pope, is reluctant to proceed with the deportation of the Jews, but in the absence of any unequivocal statement by the pope he follows orders. Hochhuth uses this scene as an effective demonstration of his insistently promoted thesis: that by speaking out, the pope could indeed have stopped the transport of Jews to Auschwitz and their subsequent deaths.

The fourth act shows a pope who does not seriously entertain the notion of condemning Hitler's crimes; rather, he thinks and acts like a functionary of the institutional church, whose sphere of influence and material possessions he has to protect against the onslaught of communism. Humanitarian concerns, Hochhuth provocatively asserts, decidedly take second place in the pope's scheme of things. Thus Riccardo's mission is bound to fail. The pope's declaration of compassion for innocent victims regardless of their nationality, religion, or race is formulated in such nonspecific terms that Riccardo perceives it to be an authorization for Hitler to continue his persecution of the Jews unhampered by the Catholic Church. In a gesture of defiance and desperate protest, Riccardo pins the yellow star, which Jews were forced to wear as an identifying mark, to his cassock. In the pope's stead, Riccardo will act as the true deputy of Christ by sharing the Jews' suffering.

The figure of Riccardo has thus been designed as the embodiment of pure humanity, the dramaturgical function of which is to call attention to the pope's failure to follow his calling. The drama that compels the protagonist to accept the consequences of his idealistic humanitarianism, however, does not end with the fourth act. Just as Riccardo is profoundly good, so the nameless Doctor, who has been introduced in the first act, is profoundly evil. The realm of this satanic figure is, appropriately, the inferno of Auschwitz, the setting of the fifth act. Several critics took exception to the figure of the Doctor. They argued that he was less a fully developed character than evil incarnate, a figure of almost mythological dimensions that seemed out of place in a drama professing to hew to documented history. In addition, these critics claimed, the final encounter between the Doctor and Riccardo in the concentration camp seemed to suggest a view of the world that was simplistically divided into good and evil.

The fifth act in particular presents other problems. Hochhuth himself remarked in one of his stage directions—which, in conjunction with the interspersed playwright's comments, contribute to the play's unwieldiness—that naturalistic devices were insufficient to depict Auschwitz onstage. Yet Hochhuth does use acoustical and optical means that are clearly derived from the naturalistic-illusionist theater. At the same time, he transcends naturalism by means of introducing such figures as the Doctor, whose sordid love affairs, however, tend to diminish his stature as the embodiment of evil. Neither pure documentary drama in the vein of Peter Weiss's *Die Ermittlung* (pr., pb. 1965; *The Investigation*, 1966) nor unadulterated Brechtian epic theater, *The Deputy* contains a somewhat bewildering mixture of styles, but its impact—especially in presenting persuasive evidence of the pope's silence in the face of the Holocaust—is undeniable.

SOLDIERS

In *Soldiers*, which probes the ethics of massive air raids on civilians, Hochhuth employs the device of a play-within-a-play. A former Royal Air Force pilot, Dorland, a modern Everyman burdened with guilt for the destruction of Dresden, rehearses a three-act play in front of Coventry Cathedral, which was destroyed by the German Luftwaffe. The central figure of this inner play is Churchill, who rejects the humanitarian arguments of the bishop of Chichester and decides in favor of the indiscriminate bombing of German cities. Although Churchill violates the dictates of morality on at least two counts—by ordering the saturation bombing and by planning the "accidental" death of General Sikorski, premier of the Polish government-in-exile in London—Hochhuth does not unequivocally condemn the British prime minister. Unlike Pius XII in *The Deputy*, Churchill emerges as a tragic hero who is faced with an insoluble moral dilemma and with whom the reader or spectator can sympathize. Nevertheless, the play aroused controversy, particularly in England, where its production was temporarily prohibited—an event anticipated by Hochhuth in the concluding section of the frame play. Apart from the more intricate structure, it is this portrayal of a complex moral dilemma rather than a clear choice between good and evil that distinguishes *Soldiers* from *The Deputy*.

GUERILLAS

Although Hochhuth was not a partisan of the student protest movement of the late 1960's, *Guerillas* may be called a product of the revolutionary unrest that gripped many young people at that time, much of the impetus of which was derived from the Vietnam War. There is, however, a Hochhuthian twist; the revolution depicted in the play is carried out by an individual rather than by the masses. Unlike the coups that lead to military or other dictatorships, the revolution from within the establishment that is being planned by United States Senator Nicolson is intended to achieve social justice and true democracy. Hochhuth's attempt to anticipate conceivable, if far-fetched, historical developments suffers from abstract polemics that tend to accentuate the weaknesses of a plot relying heavily on effects ordinarily to be found in detective and adventure stories.

DIE HEBAMME AND LYSISTRATE UND DIE NATO

If the hope for a truly democratic society is not met in *Guerillas*—Nicolson is murdered, but his designated successor will carry on—the female protagonists in the comedies *Die Hebamme* (the midwife) and *Lysistrate und die Nato* (Lysistrata and NATO) are successful in achieving their altruistic goals by waging limited war with their respective establishments. Although both women are Hochhuthian heroines in that they essentially act as individuals to effect changes for the better, they employ cunning—a means germane to the genre of comedy. The midwife dupes both the elected officials of a small West German town and the military bureaucracy in order to obtain decent housing for the socially disadvantaged under her care; the modern-day Lysistrata persuades the women of a fictitious Greek island to practice the time-honored antiwar ploy suggested by Aristophanes—that is, the withholding of sexual favors until their husbands agree not to lease their land to the military for the establishment of a United States base.

TOD EINES JÄGERS

In Hochhuth's second "American" play, *Tod eines Jägers* (death of a hunter), the main character, Ernest Hemingway, before committing suicide, reflects in an extended monologue on the moral obligations of the privileged individual—including the artist and writer—to fight and speak out against social and political ills. He attributes his inability to continue writing to his failure to have become engaged in socially relevant causes. He thereby serves as an example of Hochhuth's conviction of the decisive role of the individual in the historical process; in addition, Hemingway appears as a representative of the American dream and its destructive tendencies.

JURISTEN

In a slightly different vein, the three-act drama *Juristen* (jurists), which premiered simultaneously at three West German stages, indicts an entire profession, that is, the military judges who sentenced thousands of German soldiers to death during World War II for often trivial incidents. They were usually able to continue their careers in West Germany without ever having had to justify their verdicts. The accusations against the establishment that turns a blind eye to the crimes of the Nazi era are articulated by a representative of the younger generation. Despite the seriousness of its accusatory stance, the play suffers from the incorporation of a surfeit of contemporaneous issues.

ÄRZTINNEN

Similarly, in *Ärztinnen* (female doctors), Hochhuth again takes on errant professionals by exposing the dubious connections between the pharmaceutical industry and those physicians who use their patients as guinea pigs via prescribing insufficiently tested medication. Motivated by righteous indignation, Hochhuth occasionally overshoots the mark by indulging in sensationalism rather than in enlightening the spectators/readers about the genuine social ills he presents on stage.

JUDITH

Both *Judith* and *Unbefleckte Empfängnis* (immaculate conception) pertain to the type of Hochhuthian topical play that combines documentary and fictional elements. In the former play, Hochhuth resorted to the Judith in the Old Testament who served as a model for her two successors: a Russian woman who kills a high Nazi functionary during World War II (in the prologue), and a radical American female pacifist who wants to prevent the unfettered proliferation of weapons of mass destruction by assassinating the American president during the presidency of Ronald Reagan. Although Hochhuth did not explicitly endorse assassinations as a means to a political end, he wanted to stimulate debate about one of his favorite topics: the moral responsibility of the individual in the face of life-threatening political developments and the potential consequences of such responsibility.

UNBEFLECKTE EMPFÄNGNIS

The biblical connection in *Unbefleckte Empfängnis* as suggested by the play's title and subtitle, *Ein Kreidekreis* (a chalk circle), is rather tenuous. Nor does the drama bear any resemblance to Brecht's well-known reinterpretation of the biblical story via a Chinese source, *Der kaukasische Kreidekreis* (1944-1945; *The Caucasian Chalk Circle*, 1948). With regard to the chalk circle, the child is not claimed by two "mothers." Rather, both the surrogate mother, in whose womb a fertilized egg has been implanted and who gives birth to a child, and the natural mother, the donor of the egg, fight against societal prejudice and legal restrictions that prevent childless couples from having children via modern reproductive methods.

SOMMER 14: EIN TOTENTANZ

In *Sommer 14: Ein Totentanz* (summer, 1914: a dance of death), Hochhuth turned to a fateful moment in history, the eve of World War I. In contrast to his usual method of featuring individual protagonists, the playwright introduced the central figures of the European powers, such as the German and Austrian emperors and the king of England, in thirteen scenes. Hochhuth wanted to demonstrate that the outbreak of war was not inevitable but could have been prevented by courageous and enlightened actions on the part of those in power. As it is, only ever-present death, portrayed as an allegorical figure, is the inevitable consequence of misguided calculations and decisions on the part of statesmen and their ilk.

WESSIS IN WEIMAR

Wessis in Weimar may be considered Hochhuth's response to German reunification, a historical event that he views from an unrelentingly bleak perspective by adopting the viewpoint of parts of the East German populace as well as West German leftist intellectuals. The latter blamed the economically straitened circumstances in East Germany on the "takeover" by the Federal Republic rather than on the decade-long mismanagement of the former German Democratic Republic. The dichotomous perception of victims (East Germans) and oppressors/exploiters (West Germans), buttressed by wealth of documentary evidence

(in the printed version of the play), brings into sharp focus particularly the economic disparities between the two parts of unified Germany, but it tends to skirt the complexity of issues addressed in favor of a one-side interpretation.

EFFIS NACHT

Hochhuth's desire to do justice to maligned or downtrodden figures is also evident in *Effis Nacht* (Effi's night). Nineteenth century novelist Theodor Fontane had the aristocratic, adulterous heroine of his novel *Effi Briest* die at an early age; in contrast—and in accordance with the biography of Effi Briest's real-life model—Hochhuth showed her as a ninety-year-old woman who, disowned by her family and impoverished, made her living as a nurse. During one night in 1943, she sits by the bedside of a dying soldier, an event that reminds her of the agonizing death of her lover, shot in a duel with her husband, and leads to her general recapitulation of as well as reflection on her life. In her monologue, she is overwhelmed by her individual guilt feelings about the death of her lover but also by the collective guilt about not having resisted Nazism more forcefully. Despite Hochhuth's emphasis on personal responsibility, history appears to be a force that is impervious to well-intentioned human endeavor.

MOZART'S NACHTMUSIK

In a further attempt to set the historical record straight, the playwright investigated the circumstances surrounding Mozart's death in 1791. In *Mozart's Nachtmusik*, a play for three actors, he posits that Mozart was poisoned by a minor bureaucrat whose wife had been the composer's mistress. The lack of compelling dramatic moments detracts from Hochhuth's dubious hypothesis. Also, in ignoring Mozart's genius and his creativity, the play appears to deal with a marginal aspect of the composer's biography.

HITLERS DR. FAUST

Conversely, *Hitlers Dr. Faust* (Hitler's Dr. Faustus) addresses a topic of general significance, that is, scientists' responsibility when faced with the consequences and applications of their research. The rocket engineer Hermann Oberth is Dr. Faustus, who concludes a pact with the devil by putting his research and his practical know-how at Nazi leader Adolf Hitler's disposal. He is supported by his student Wernher von Braun, who, after World War II, was instrumental in developing the rocket program in the United States. Oberth is not depicted in entirely negative terms, however. Although he supports the war efforts of a criminal regime, he has visions of a better future for humankind via scientific discoveries. Hochhuth thus offers a somewhat differentiated portrait that avoids oversimplification.

OTHER MAJOR WORKS

LONG FICTION: *Die Berliner Antigone*, 1963; *Zwischenspiel in Baden-Baden*, 1974; *Eine Liebe in Deutschland*, 1978 (*A German Love Story*, 1980); *Atlantik Novelle: Erzählungen*, 1985; *Julia: Oder, der Weg zur Macht*, 1994.

NONFICTION: *Krieg und Klassenkrieg*, 1971; *Tell '38*, 1979 (English translation, 1984); *Schwarze Segel: Essays und Gedichte*, 1985; *Täter und Denker: Profile und Probleme Von Cäsar bis Jünger*, 1987; *Was Hier Europa? Reden, Gedichte, Essays*, 1987; *Von Syrakus aus gesehen, gedacht, erzählt*, 1991; *Tell gegen Hitler: Historische Studien*, 1992; *Und Brecht sah das Tragische nicht*, 1996; *Einsprüche! Zur Geschichte, Politik und Literatur*, 2001; *Die Geburt der Tragödie aus dem Krieg: Frankfurter Poetik-Vorlesungen*, 2001.

EDITED TEXTS: *Sämtliche Werke und eine Auswahl der Skizzen und Gemälde*, 1959 (of works by Wilhelm Busch); *Liebe in unserer Zeit: 32 Erzählungen*, 1961; *Am grauen Meer: Gesammelte Werke*, 1962 (of works by Theodor Storm); *Die grossen Meister*, 1966; *Kaiser Zeiten: Bilder einer Epoche*, 1973 (of works by Oskar and Gustav Tellgmann); *Räuber-Rede: Drei deutsche Vorwürfe, Schiller, Lessing, Geschwister Scholl*, 1982; *Alan Turing: Erzählungen*, 1987.

MISCELLANEOUS: *Panik im Mai: Sämtliche Gedichte und Erählungen*, 1991; *Alle Erzählungen, Gedichte und Romane*, 2001; *Zwischen Sylt und Wilhelmstrasse: Essays, Gedichte, Reden*, 2001.

BIBLIOGRAPHY

Bentley, Eric, ed. *The Storm over The Deputy*. New York: Grove, 1964. A useful compilation of reviews of the play, editorials, and comments by literary critics and philosophers. Bibliography.

Bosmajian, Hamida. *Metaphors of Evil: Contemporary German Literature and the Shadow of Nazism*. Iowa City: University of Iowa Press, 1979. The volume includes a valid comparison of *The Deputy* and Peter Weiss's *The Investigation* in terms of coming to grips with Nazism.

Durzak, Manfred. "American Mythologies: Rolf Hochhuth's Plays *Guerillas*, *Tod eines Jägers*, and *Judith*." In *Amerika! New Images in German Literature*, edited by Heinz D. Osterle. New York: Peter Lang, 1989. A cogent discussion of Hochhuth's three "American" plays that sees them as projections of Hochhuth's ambivalent attitude toward the United States.

Hinck, Walter, ed. *Rolf Hochhuth: Eingriff in die Zeitgeschichte*. Reinbeck bei Hamburg: Rowohlt, 1981. A substantive collection of essays by literary critics, including one on *Ärztinnen*. In German.

Hoffmeister, Reinhart, ed. *Rolf Hochhuth: Dokumente zur politischen Wirkung*. Munich: Kindler Verlag, 1980. A comprehensive collection of reviews of and comments on Hochhuth's works, including *Juristen*. In German.

Rennison, Lucinda. "'Was von Bismarck übrigblieb . . .'Rolf Hochhuth and the German Question." In *The New Germany: Literature and Society After Unification*, edited by Osman Durrani, Colin Good, and Kevin Hilliard. Sheffield, England: Sheffield Academic Press, 1995. A detailed examination of Hochhuth's position with regard to Germany from his emergence as a writer in the 1960's to the postunification period.

Sanchez, Jose M. "The Search for the Historical Pius." *America* 186, no. 5 (February 18, 2002): 8-11. An examination of the controversy surrounding the role of the Catholic Church, particularly Pope Pius XII, during the Holocaust. Mentions *The Deputy* as one of the earliest sources of the debate.

Schmidt, Dolores B., and Earl R. Schmidt, eds. *The Deputy Reader: Studies in Moral Responsibility*. Glenview, Ill.: Scott, Foresman, 1965. This useful compilation of essays, not all of which address *The Deputy*, seeks to establish the historical, literary and critical perspectives from which the play may be viewed.

Taëni, Rainer. *Rolf Hochhuth*. Translated by R. W. Last. London, Wolff, 1977. A succinct survey of Hochhuth's life, work, and politics that focuses

especially on the plays, including *Tod eines Jägers*.

Ward, Margaret E. *Rolf Hochhuth*. Boston: Twayne, 1977. A sound, general survey of Hochhuth's works, including *Tod eines Jägers*.

Siegfried Mews,
updated by Siegfried Mews

FRITZ HOCHWÄLDER

Born: Vienna, Austria; May 28, 1911
Died: Zurich, Switzerland; October 20, 1986

PRINCIPAL DRAMA

Jehr, pr. 1933
Liebe in Florenz: Oder, Der unziemliche Neugier, pr. 1936, pb. 1979
Esther, wr. 1940, pb. 1948
Das heilige Experiment, pr. 1943, pb. 1947 (*The Strong Are Lonely*, 1954)
Der Flüchtling, pr. 1945, pb. 1955 (based on a scenario by Georg Kaiser)
Hôtel du Commerce, pr. 1946, pb. 1954
Meier Helmbrecht, pr. 1947, pb. 1956
Der öffentliche Ankläger, pr. 1948, pb. 1954 (*The Public Prosecutor*, 1958)
Virginia, pr. 1951
Donadieu, pr., pb. 1953 (based on Conrad Ferdinand Meyer's ballad "Die Fusse im Feuer")
Die Herberge, pb. 1956, pr. 1957
Der Unschuldige, pr., pb. 1958
Donnerstag, pr., pb. 1959
1003, pr., pb. 1964 (English translation, 1998)
Der Himbeerpflücker, televised, staged, pr., pb. 1965 (*The Raspberry Picker*, 1970)
Der Befehl, televised and pb. 1967, staged 1968 (*The Order*, 1970, also as *Orders*, 1998)
Lazaretti: Oder, Der Säbeltiger, pr., pb. 1975 (*Lazaretti: Or, The Saber-Toothed Tiger*, 1980)
The Public Prosecutor and Other Plays, pb. 1980
Die Prinzessin von Chimay, pb. 1982
Der verschwundene Mond, pb. 1985
Die Bürgschaft, pb. 1985
The Holy Experiment and Other Plays, pb. 1998

OTHER LITERARY FORMS

The only writing Fritz Hochwälder did outside his dramatic works is contained in his book *Im Wechsel der Zeit: Autobiographische Skizzen und Essays* (1980), a collection of autobiographical sketches and essays on the theater written between 1949 and 1979.

ACHIEVEMENTS

In the preface of the first English volume of Fritz Hochwälder's dramas, *The Public Prosecutor*, theater critic Martin Esslin wrote that the enduring value of Hochwälder's work will be increasingly recognized in the future and that his best plays will rightfully survive in the permanent repertoire of world drama. Other critics have not always been as generous—for example, at premiere performances of *Donnerstag* and *Lazaretti* in Hochwälder's native Austria, at the Salzburg festivals. Nevertheless, as is evidenced by the many productions of his plays and his numerous Austrian literary awards, Hochwälder was probably the best-known Austrian dramatist between the years 1945 and 1970.

The prestigious Burgtheater of Vienna has staged three premieres and four other productions, while Switzerland and Germany have hosted others. Translations of his plays have spread throughout Western Europe, Eastern Europe, the Middle East, and North and South America. There were four hundred performances of *The Strong Are Lonely* in Paris alone.

Hochwälder was the recipient of several literary honors: the Literature Prize of the city of Vienna in 1955, the Grillparzer Prize from the Viennese Academy of Sciences in 1956, the Anton Wildgans Prize in 1963, the bestowal of the title of Professor from the president of Austria in 1964, the State Prize for Literature in 1966, the Austrian medal of honor for Art and Science in 1971, the Ring of Honor from the city of Vienna in 1972, and the Drama Prize in 1982 from the Swiss section of the Society of Authors and Playwrights, an award that is usually granted to French-speaking authors.

Although Hochwälder attained a certain amount of literary acclaim, his dramas have suffered from a dearth of interest and analysis. There is, nevertheless, no doubt about the forcefulness of his message, applicable at the personal, political, or social level, that man is capable of the worst evils and therefore must cultivate vigilance to keep that evil in check.

BIOGRAPHY

Fritz Hochwälder was born May 28, 1911, in Vienna, Austria. He was the only child of a poor Jewish family that lived in a modest apartment at Westbahnstrasse 3. His father worked as an interior wall decorator and his mother managed a small antique shop. The first influence on his literary life, however, did not come from his family, but rather from a third-grade teacher who told stories and took the class to afternoon productions at the Raimund-theater. Ferdinand Raimund's plays *Das Mädchen aus der Feenwelt: Oder, Der Bauer als Millionär* (1826; *The Maid from Fairyland: Or, The Peasant as Millionaire*, 1962) and *Der Verschwender* (1834; *The Spendthrift*, 1949) made a lasting impression on the young Hochwälder, and he later considered Raimund's *Der Alpenkönig und der Menschenfeind* (1828; *Mountain King and Misanthrope*, 1962) to be one of the twelve best dramas of world theater.

During his Viennese years, Hochwälder was also influenced by a youth group in which he met others with a similar interest in literature, among them Richard Thieberger, who later translated Hochwälder's

plays into French. At this time, literature was only a hobby for Hochwälder. He had begun his apprenticeship as an upholsterer and decorator in 1929, and he passed the master's test in 1936. He opened his own one-man shop, but soon, like most of his contemporaries, he was out of work. During this period of worldwide depression, he had to survive on meager financial aid from the state and goulash handed out across the street from the state opera house.

Despite the poverty, the fall of the monarchy, and the revolutionary upheaval, Hochwälder always felt at home in Vienna. Had someone suggested that he would spend most of his life in another country, Hochwälder would have ridiculed the idea. What made him decide to leave his beloved Vienna was the annexation of Austria in 1938 and persecution by the Nazis. The twenty-seven-year-old tried to persuade his parents to accompany him, but because of their age and unaware of the dangers of staying under Nazi rule, they preferred to remain. With the borders to Switzerland closed, Hochwälder daringly swam across the Rhine with his papers and possessions tied to his back. His parents were never heard from again.

In Zurich, as an immigrant with few job possibilities and as a young man who had already written a few plays, he began to write in earnest. With the help of friends who provided him in the early years with a place to live, he wrote *The Strong Are Lonely*, the play that perhaps more than any other made him known. It premiered in Biel/Solothurn, Switzerland, on March 24, 1943, and was a success with both the public and the press. The newspaper predicted that the play would achieve artistic recognition in the free world. Yet only after the postwar Austrian premiere in 1947 (arranged by Hochwälder's friend Franz Theodor Csokor for the Burgtheater) and the subsequent 1952 Paris production did this prediction come true.

Georg Kaiser, another dramatist living in Swiss exile, became in the last two years of his life a close friend and consultant to Hochwälder. *Der Flüchtling* was based on an outline by Kaiser and, bearing the mark of Kaiser in its character types, tightly knit plot, and theme of moral regeneration, became one of Hochwälder's most performed plays. Although this play dealt with the recent war, most of Hochwälder's important plays up to 1953 had distant historical settings: *The Strong Are Lonely* is set in seventeenth century Paraguay; *Meier Helmbrecht*, in the Middle Ages; *The Public Prosecutor*, during the French Revolution; and *Donadieu*, in seventeenth century France.

In 1954, thinking that the historical drama no longer appealed so much to modern audiences, Hochwälder wrote about modern settings. He considered *Die Herberge*, a dramatic legend of an unjust world, to be a turning point in his life and work; he decided to write about what interested him rather than be a commercial writer, mass-producing for profit. His experiments with an allegorical, fanciful world in *Donnerstag* and *1003* were not as successful. In his next two dramas of the mid-1960's, *The Raspberry Picker* and *The Order*, he returned to conventional plot structure, examining the mentality of those who supported the Nazis and warning that all people are capable of such crimes. Ten years later, he repeated the warning about what the potential evil in man can do, that terror as an answer to terror can eventually annihilate humankind.

After the fairy-tale play *Der verschwundene Mond*, inspired by his rediscovery of the poetry of Jakob Haringer (1898-1948), Hochwälder returned in 1985 to writing plays with historical settings. *Die Prinzessin von Chimay* deals with murder committed during the French Revolution. The stage directions prescribe scenes and clothing exactly according to the period. *Die Bürgschaft*, a satiric historical treatment of the tyrant Dionysius, is meant to be staged as a timeless political *commedia dell'arte* in modern costume.

ANALYSIS

Fritz Hochwälder was one of the few contemporary dramatists who employed the traditional dramatic techniques of Aristotelian theater almost exclusively. The prevalent literary philosophy of the postwar era was that the traditional theater is passé because it is unable to stimulate social improvement or critical thought, as the epic theater, the Theater of the Absurd, and other varieties of modern theater have supposedly done. What concerned Hochwälder

more than this theoretical controversy, however, was the practical condition of the German theater: He compared it to a tubercular patient, outwardly suntanned and blooming with life, but on the inside a moribund creature hastening to the grave. Generous subsidies to the theater by the cities and states suggest cultural vigor, yet the theater is dying because it has intellectualized the drama instead of encouraging vital, absorbing plays. Hochwälder's own stated aim was to write well-constructed plays that audiences will appreciate—plays that deliver a message that audiences will understand, not plays that modern critics will endorse merely because of theatrical innovation and sophisticated intellectualism.

It is evident from his own statements about his dramas and from the plays themselves that Hochwälder used theater as an entertainer and moralist. The prevailing influence of theater as entertainment comes from the Viennese *Volkstheater*, and the dominant influence of Hochwälder's message stems from World War II, especially the Nazi experience.

The Viennese theater tradition influenced him to present metaphysical truths through the senses rather than through the mind, by means of intellectual discourse. He believed that by combining spectacle and truth, his theater would be meaningful to all classes of people. In practice, his dramas for the most part adhere to his theoretical intention. His plays feature tightly knit plots with straightforward action, unity of time, place, and action, and folksy dialogue. There are character types, such as the miser Kavolius, the schemer Fouquier, and the academician Galgotzy, but most of the characters, such as the Provincial, Pomfrit, Mittermayer, and Lazaretti, are realistically developed. A major character often has a *Hanswurst* counterpart who is a servant or who is subordinate in rank or intellect. These exaggerated figures, such as Birnstrudl, Krott, and Damboritz, exemplify Viennese qualities of comedy and farce. Not evident in the plays, however—even those labeled comedies—is the quality of fun and lightness.

A recurring message in Hochwälder's plays is that, because of the basic evilness of man, he is a potential murderer and must therefore always be on his guard against his own impulses, exercising personal responsibility to keep them in check. He cannot excuse himself by saying that he has merely followed orders, or that society, the times, or the circumstances are at fault, or that injustice in the world has made him the way he is. The characters in the play who have been irresponsible must usually pay the grim consequences, and those who are not guilty must beware lest the same happens to them. Even with the presence of evil and injustice, man is often capable of learning, of changing, and of achieving a kind of enlightenment or salvation. Nevertheless, there are dilemmas, resulting from the natural evil in man, that are not resolved in the plays. To try to produce heaven on earth (as in *The Strong Are Lonely*) will yield a hell. To try to fight terror with terror (as in *Lazaretti*) will bring destruction. Hochwälder believed that neither religion nor the state has the answer, nor do his dramas; consequently, the individual must grope for the solution himself, aware that his most formidable foe is himself.

THE STRONG ARE LONELY

The Strong Are Lonely, Hochwälder's first success, is a good example of both his theater and his message. In this play, as well in his other historical dramas, he was concerned with giving life to themes rather than biography or history. According to Hochwälder, the play portrays the eternal problems of mankind, the questions about social justice and the kingdom of God on earth.

This seventeen-character, five-act play of the classical tradition takes place in a Jesuit school in Buenos Aires in 1767. The Jesuits are trying to establish a spiritual kingdom and a social-welfare state for the Indians of Paraguay. The state is becoming so economically and militarily powerful that Spain has commanded an immediate political dissolution and an abandonment by the Jesuit founders. Should the Father Provincial, the leader of this missionary project, disobey and continue his work, providing for the spiritual and material needs of the oppressed Indians, or must he obey Spain and his religious superiors in Rome, knowing that if he does this, the Indians will be subject to further colonial exploitation?

In regard to the Indians, the play is predictable: They are unable to preserve a permanent utopia for themselves and, as a result of the Jesuits' eventual departure, they become prey to the colonialists. Because they are portrayed as naïve, unquestioning followers whose only desire is a heaven in which there will be no lack of earthly or spiritual goods, they will necessarily be losers, regardless of the Father Provincial's decision; whether they are under the Jesuits or under the colonialists, they will lose personal freedom and autonomy.

What is not so predictable and what makes this play dramatic theater is the Father Provincial's internal strife when faced with opposing commands. Suspense is felt until he reluctantly reverses his first, instinctive decision to fight for the Indians and gives in to the secular command of Spain and the religious obedience to the Church—contrary to his better judgment and his conscience. The only one to refuse the Father Provincial's new order to surrender to the Spaniards is the Jesuit ex-soldier Oros, who believes that religious authority is no longer binding when a sin is commanded. Oros intends to fight to the death defending the poor and weak. The moment of personal enlightenment for Father Provincial occurs when he is shot while attempting to quell the uprising led by Oros. As he is dying, he sees that he cannot solve his personal dilemma, that to fight force with force is futile; he hopes that the kingdom of God he feels in himself will live on in others.

HISTORICAL DRAMAS

After *The Strong Are Lonely*, Hochwälder wrote three more important historical plays: *Meier Helmbrecht*, *The Public Prosecutor*, and *Donadieu*. In the historical dramas, he seemed less interested in directly criticizing maladies of the recent war than in presenting timeless truths, objectified by historical garb and meant for all theatergoers regardless of time or geography. In fact, he once went so far as to say that there are no burning current issues in these plays.

In *Meier Helmbrecht*, the title character must stand trial because his son was a robber-knight. He pleads his innocence, saying that he cannot be held responsible because he was powerless to do anything. He did provide a horse for his son, but he was afraid of him. Finally, however, Helmbrecht acknowledges and confesses his guilt, a guilt that includes neglect, weakness, permissiveness, and cowardice. The general message of the parable seems to be that everyone shares in evil and guilt through sins of commission or omission; the play's specific message may refer to the guilt that Germany and Austria must bear for their part in the atrocities of World War II.

Fouquier, the prosecutor in *The Public Prosecutor*, is also irresponsible but is more guilty because of his ruthlessness. To preserve his own life and position, he is ready to serve a terrorist government, even if it means sending innocent people to the guillotine. Through his own guile, he unwittingly prepares a case against himself; he is condemned and sent to the same death that he has arranged for so many others. The play ends in a struggle for power and forebodes even further terror and the downfall of yet another tyrant.

Donadieu poses the timeless questions of revenge and retribution, and the resolution is more optimistic than those of the former two plays. The Huguenot Donadieu's immediate response to the discovery of his wife's murderer is to take the matter into his own hands. In a moment of enlightenment, however, Donadieu overrides his desire for revenge, realizing that it would precipitate further persecution. He entrusts retribution to divine justice.

DIE HERBERGE

Hochwälder considered *Die Herberge* a turning point in his life and work. He wanted to be creative and experiment with forms of drama other than the classical—in part because the classical historical play did not seem popular among modern audiences, and he wanted to keep entertainment in the theater. On the other hand, he did not want to be a commercial writer whose aim is mere profit. He was still willing to probe the conscience of his audience; in fact, he seemed more intent on criticizing modern society than on entertaining it. *Die Herberge* presents the contemporary world, where injustice is rampant and where everyone is tested and found guilty. Each character typifies a certain kind of sin. Kavolius, the innkeeper and father of Staschia, whose sin is greed, represents the bourgeois burgher who already has money and whose only desire is to obtain more. He is willing to sacrifice principles for money—and, what is worse, his own daughter. Anyone, including the moneylender and extortionist Berullis, can marry her as long as he has money. The comic policeman is also guilty of greed, wanting to drive the beggar out of town lest the villagers will have to feed him over the winter months. The other comic figure, the coffin maker, hoping for a quick execution of the thief so that he can get some drinking money, is similarly greedy. The most outrageous example of greed, however, is Berullis, who robbed Jurgis's father many years before.

Staschia, less guilty than her father, nevertheless shares in the general guilt of the world. Her fault is untruthfulness. Not wanting to hurt anyone, she lies to cover up Jurgis's theft of Berullis's money and the half-wit Andusz' lustful attack against her. Andusz also lies to protect himself, but his guilt stems from a previous murder and his uncontrollable lust. The judge is guilty of setting up his own principle of man-made order to rule people in the absence of justice; since there is no justice, it is better that ten should die rather than that one guilty man should go free. The judge finds the hobo Schimke guilty of the theft, simply because he was found asleep in the barn with the stolen gold next to him. In a noble gesture, trying to avert an injustice, Jurgis admits that he took the money in the hope that with it he would be able to marry Staschia.

The hobo, the only character without guilt, thinks that God's justice lives in man's heart like a seed in fruit. Hochwälder implies that the seed of justice exists in man's heart and that, even if others will continue to perpetrate and perpetuate injustice, justice will at times be observable outside man's heart in the darkness of the world.

DER UNSCHULDIGE

In the ironically titled play *Der Unschuldige* (the guiltless one), all the characters are guilty. Erdmann's wife, his daughter, his neighbor, and the ambitious judge are guilty of false accusations; having based their judgment on circumstantial evidence after finding a skeleton in Erdmann's rose garden, they accuse him of being a murderer. Although proven innocent of murder, Erdmann is nevertheless guilty of tyranny over his wife, daughter, and servants. His enlightenment allows him to see himself as he really is: not the perfect man who expects to be adored by his family, but a weakling who in anger could have killed a man whom he hated.

DONNERSTAG

In *Donnerstag*, Hochwälder was more concerned with modern man's materialistic life than with his guilt. *Donnerstag* is a mystery play, an allegory that is set in an imaginative world of the Faustian, Everyman, and the Austrian *Zaubertheater* traditions. Hochwälder's Everyman, Pomfrit—a successful architect—is an allegorical figure for one who has become king of all creation yet possesses within himself nothing more than dissatisfaction, unrest, and despair. These woes plague Pomfrit, even though in his pursuit of happiness he has been a Freemason, Methodist, Socialist, reactionary, drunk, European, world citizen, nihilist, and existentialist. Even when death approaches after a heart attack, his previous soulless existence prevents him from believing in God. He does not confess to having been a mass murderer (as some have suspected), but only to being a fool. In a moment of despair, he seems to opt for the Devil. There is, however, a hint of hope in the minor character of Estrella, a simple ragpicker whose love for Pomfrit is symbolic of the human capacity for unselfish love. Pomfrit's final humble prayer to the God in whom he cannot believe suggests a chance for himself or for others to attain future salvation.

THE RASPBERRY PICKER AND THE ORDER

In the plays *The Raspberry Picker* and *The Order*, Hochwälder left the imaginary world to treat the real world of World War II. The setting is twenty years after the war has ended, but the effect of the war is present in the hearts of individuals and communities.

The Raspberry Picker exposes an entire Austrian village that has benefited economically from a concentration camp and still recalls the good old days, especially the fond memory of one Nazi hero. He was called the Raspberry Picker because he shot down prisoners while they were picking raspberries. When a stranger registers at a local inn, he is mistaken for the famous Nazi; in actuality, he is no more than a petty thief. The villagers, happy about this triumphant return and proud of their hero, are willing to help him escape the country. After discovering that the stranger is a mere thief and a Jew rather than the famous murderer, the people become outraged. Later, when reading about the capture of the real Raspberry Picker and his subsequent suicide in jail, they drink to his memory.

In the more serious and less satiric *The Order*, Hochwälder psychologically probes the personal guilt of a man's war crime. Mittermayer, a satisfied citizen and competent police inspector, is confronted with a past deed far removed from his consciousness: a murder he had committed twenty years ago, during the war. He eventually recognizes his weak yet vicious nature, which caused him to follow blindly the commands of his superior officers during the war and which even now turns violent under the influence of alcohol. Unable to cope with this revelation and perhaps trying to expiate his offenses, Mittermayer chooses a way out: He chases a gangster outside his own police jurisdiction and permits himself to be shot by the hoodlum.

In both *The Raspberry Picker* and *The Order*, Hochwälder condemns leaders, followers, and fence sitters alike for their irresponsible actions during and after the war. At the same time, he is warning that everyone is capable of similar crimes under similar circumstances and must therefore control the beast within; unfavorable historical conditions do not absolve personal or collective guilt.

LAZARETTI

An even greater peril to society than the Nazis is nuclear terrorism. The thesis of *Lazaretti* is that if man continues to be corrupt and irresponsible, he will use the ultimate weapon of terror, the nuclear bomb. He will then become like the saber-toothed tiger of the play's subtitle, which was doomed to extinction because of its overgrown fangs—the very armament that was supposed to protect it. The dramatic action of the play, however, is not centered on this warning, but rather on the personal conflicts of two writers. Professor Camenisch is worried about his lack of inspiration to complete a book he is writing, and the publishers are pressuring him. His boyhood friend Lazaretti, now a famous writer and lecturer, seeks refuge because he believes that he is being persecuted. Lazaretti claims that a gang is trying to drive him insane to prevent him from publishing his latest manuscript, which tells how to eliminate terrorists. As an idealist, his intentions are good, but the consequences could be disastrous; the book could result in a growing spiral of international nuclear terror. His plan is to kill all potential aggressors immediately by establishing an international secret society, a conspiracy of young idealists from all countries. They will be cold-blooded, daring, unscrupulous, and merciless in the service of mankind. Camenisch finally has his friend committed to an asylum and solves his own problem of nonproductivity by publishing Lazaretti's work as his own.

The pessimistic dimension of this play is that nobody is really enlightened; today's society—its elite humanists as well as its idealistic youth—can only resort to terror as an answer to terror. A minuscule trace of hope is provided by the play's sole female character, the secretary Rouzha, because she abandons all the characters to preserve her faith in humankind. Even with this desperate message, Hochwälder is an entertainer as well as a moralist: The love triangle, the comic characters of an overzealous servant and a classicist neighbor, the dramatic swings in the moods and sanity of Lazaretti, the intrigue, and the uncertain outcome make this play as much entertaining melodrama as serious social commentary—consistent with Hochwälder's belief that, in order to reach the largest number of people, a warning must be cloaked in entertainment.

DER VERSCHWUNDENE MOND

Der verschwundene Mond (the vanishing moon) is very different from Hochwälder's other dramas because it is not a warning about society or the theater, but rather a literary legacy, a meditation on the essence of poetry. The author even considered this fairy-tale play his best work, inasmuch as it is pure poetry, something he wanted to express for personal satisfaction. A first version was typed in 1951. Then, after thirty years of gestation and a rediscovery of the work and life of the wandering poet Jakob Haringer, Hochwälder was inspired to complete it. The main character, Gustave, modeled after Haringer, is a poet and an isolated yet content hobo who envies no one's power or riches. He is unlike his former academic associates and his rich friend who writes for fame and money. He possesses something more wonderful: the power to take the moon out of the sky.

A beautiful woman persuades him to sell the moon so that he can make himself more presentable to her with the profits. French mobsters direct Gustave to their boss, who already has everything else and is still unhappy, but he dies of a heart attack while negotiating a deal with Gustave. Then a rich American entrepreneur offers to purchase the moon. Spending the money for new clothes and entrance into her bordello, Gustave discovers that the woman is a whore: For this, he stole the moon. He acquires the money to repurchase the moon from a successful writer friend, who realizes that Gustave had something that he himself has never possessed: the gift of writing literature. While searching in vain for the American, Gustave finds the love of a poor flower girl. She insists that all they need is each other, but he knows that without the moon there is no poetry, no love, no life. He gives her the money. Later, Gustave is found dead on his bench, but the moon is shining once again.

Unlike the dramatic conflicts of other Hochwälder plays, this work of admiration for Jakob Haringer generates a mood of love and melancholy reminiscent of lyric poetry. The moon is a metaphor for the gift of poetry; it may not be stolen, sold for money, or hoarded for exclusive personal use. It must be shared by all, but only the unfettered poet will have access to it. Free of material possessions, removed from the evils of everyday life, the poet is able to live a just life, dreaming and writing. Similarities can be seen between the life and work of Hochwälder and that of the poet Haringer, who unwillingly became a vagabond, who sank into anonymity after having been honored by literary prizes, and who, despite it all, retained the gift of poetry.

OTHER MAJOR WORKS

NONFICTION: *Im Wechsel der Zeit: Autobiographische Skizzen und Essays*, 1980.

BIBLIOGRAPHY

Demetz, P. *Postwar German Literature: A Critical Introduction*. New York: Pegasus, 1970. Gives history and criticism of mid-twentieth century literature, providing a context for the contemporaries and genres of Hochwälder.

Finlay, Frank, ed. *Centre Stage: Contemporary Drama in Austria*. Amsterdam: Rodopi, 1999. Examines the contributions to Austrian theater by many playwrights not previously studied, including Hochwälder, Wolfgang Bauer, Thomas Bernhard, Elias Canetti, and Peter Handke. Focus is on the themes, forms, and concerns of Austria's contemporary playwrights.

Robertson, Ritchie. *Theatre and Performance in Austria: From Mozart to Jelinek*. Edinburgh: Edinburgh University Press, 1993. In providing a wide-ranging account of Austria's theater, one of the defining features of the country's culture, Robertson offers a context to Hochwälder's development as a playwright.

Schmitt, J. "The Theatre of Fritz Hochwälder: Its Background and Development," in *Modern Austrian Literature* 2, no. 1 (1978). Traces the development of Hochwälder as a dramatist and explores his techniques and themes.

James Schmitt

HUGO VON HOFMANNSTHAL

Born: Vienna, Austro-Hungarian Empire; February 1, 1874

Died: Rodaun, Austria; July 15, 1929

PRINCIPAL DRAMA

Gestern, pb. 1891

Der Tor und der Tod, pb. 1894, pr. 1898 (*Death and the Fool*, 1913)

Das kleine Welttheater, pb. 1897 (*The Little Theater of the World*, 1961)

Der weisse Fächer, pb. 1898 (*The White Fan*, 1909)

Die Frau im Fenster, pr., pb. 1898 (*Madonna Dianora*, 1916)

Der Abenteurer und die Sängerin, pr., pb. 1899 (*The Adventurer and the Singer*, 1917)

Die Hochzeit der Sobeide, pr., pb. 1899 (*The Marriage of Sobeide*, 1913)

Theater in Versen, pb. 1899

Der Kaiser und die Hexe, pb. 1900, pr. 1926 (*The Emperor and the Witch*, 1961)

Elektra, pr. 1903, pb. 1904 (*Electra*, 1908)

Das gerettete Venedig, pr., pb. 1905 (*Venice Preserved*, 1915)

Kleine Dramen, pb. 1906

Ödipus und die Sphinx, pr., pb. 1906 (*Oedipus and the Sphinx*, 1968)

Vorspiele, pb. 1908

Christinas Heimreise, pr. 1910, pb. 1920 (*Christina's Journey Home*, 1916)

König Ödipus, pr., pb. 1910

Alkestis, pb. 1911

Der Rosenkavalier, pr., pb. 1911 (libretto; *The Cavalier of the Rose*, 1912; also known as *The Rose Bearer*)

Jedermann, pr., pb. 1911 (*Everyman*, 1917)

Ariadne auf Naxos, pr., pb. 1912 (libretto; *Ariadne on Naxos*, 1922)

Der Bürger als Edelmann, pr., pb. 1918

Die Frau ohne Schatten, pr., pb. 1919 (libretto; *The Woman Without a Shadow*, 1957)

Dame Kobold, pr., pb. 1920

Der Schwierige, pb. 1920, pr. 1921 (*The Difficult Man*, 1963)

Florindo, pr. 1921

Das Salzburger Grosse Welttheater, pr., pb. 1922 (*The Salzburg Great Theatre of the World*, 1958)

Der Unbestechliche, pr. 1923, pb. 1956

Der Turm, pb. 1925, pr. 1948 (*The Tower*, 1963)

Die ägyptische Helena, pr., pb. 1928 (libretto; *Helen in Egypt*, 1963)

Das Bergwerk zu Folun, pb. 1933 (*The Mine at Falun*, 1933)

Arabella, pr., pb. 1933 (libretto; English translation, 1955)

Dramatische Entwürfe, pb. 1936

Silvia im "Stern," pb. 1959

OTHER LITERARY FORMS

In addition to drama, Hugo von Hofmannsthal's works include several novellas, a large number of poems, and essays on literary, philosophical, and political topics, as well as translations into German of Greek, French, and Spanish dramas. Autobiographical reflections, including the crucial self-interpretation entitled *Ad me ipsum* (1930), as well as Hofmannsthal's extensive correspondence, fictitious letters, and fictitious dialogues, are published in the fifteen-volume *Gesammelte Werke in Einzelausgaben* (1945-1959).

ACHIEVEMENTS

The name Hugo von Hofmannsthal means many things to many people. Some see his achievement primarily in the depth of his philosophical poems and in the formal perfection of those poems. Others know him as the cofounder (with Max Reinhardt) of the Salzburg Festival, for which he created *Everyman*, a modern version of the old morality play, and *The Salzburg Great Theatre of the World*. Many music lovers know only Hofmannsthal the librettist, who wrote the texts for Richard Strauss's operas *The Cavalier of the Rose*, *Arabella*, and several others. Still others appreciate primarily his comic genius, both as an original playwright and as an adapter of comedies by Molière and Pedro Calderón de la Barca. The truth is that Hofmannsthal excelled in all the above mentioned literary spheres and was one of the foremost poets and dramatists of the twentieth century.

BIOGRAPHY

Hugo Laurenz August Hofmann Elder von Hofmannsthal was born on February 1, 1874, in Vienna. His father was a bank manager. During the last quarter of the nineteenth century, there was considerable social unrest in the Austro-Hungarian Empire, but Hofmannsthal enjoyed a sheltered and carefree childhood and youth. From an early age, he was exposed to the theater, to opera, and to other forms of art. From 1884 to 1892, he attended the prestigious Wiener Akademisches Gymnasium (academic high school). He was a brilliant student, particularly in languages and literature. At the age of twelve, he had read the German classics (Johann Wolfgang von Goethe, Friedrich Schiller, Heinrich von Kleist, and Franz Grillparzer). Three years later, he was acquainted with the works of Homer, Voltaire, Dante, William Shakespeare, George Gordon, Lord Byron, and Robert Browning, all of which he read in the original languages. In 1890, he published his first poems under the nom de plume "Loris." This pseudonym became known rapidly in the literary circles of Vienna, particularly in the famous Café Griensteidl. When Hofmannsthal was eventually introduced to the influential critic Hermann Bahr, the latter was astounded to meet a seventeen-year-old youth; given the intellectual maturity of Loris's writings, he had expected to encounter a man in his forties.

Hofmannsthal's precocious maturity was based primarily on reading, not on real, "lived" experiences. The accumulation of his vicarious experiences and their transmutation into literature eventually led to a human and artistic crisis. In his famous "Ein Brief" ("The Letter of Lord Chandos"), he described how the "presumptuousness of his intellect" had given way to dejection and feebleness, how he had lost the ability to speak and think coherently because he had lost faith in language itself. In this seminal work, half-story, half-essay, Hofmannsthal renounced lyric poetry.

From 1892 to 1894, Hofmannsthal studied law, and from 1895 to 1897, he studied Romance philology, both at the University of Vienna. In 1899, he earned his Ph.D. with a dissertation on the use of language by the poets of the *Pléiade*. From 1900 to 1901, he worked on a second dissertation (on Victor Hugo) with the aim of becoming a university professor. He abandoned this idea shortly afterward, however, and devoted the rest of his life to literature, to

Hugo von Hofmannsthal

writing, editing, and translating. In 1901, he married Gertrud Schlesinger, and he purchased a house at Rodaun, near Vienna, where he continued to live until his death in 1929.

Hofmannsthal's studies were interrupted by periods of military service, and when World War I broke out, he entered the Austrian army with the rank of an officer but was quickly reassigned to administrative duties at the Ministry of War in Vienna. The war inspired in Hofmannsthal a feeling of "Austrianness," of patriotism, which resulted in a series of essays on Austrian (as differentiated from German) culture. He also edited a series of specifically Austrian literary, philosophical, and political texts, collectively entitled *Die österreichische Bibliothek* (1915-1917; the Austrian library).

The collapse of the Austro-Hungarian Empire in 1918 had a devastating emotional effect on Hofmannsthal. He felt as though the soil in which he was rooted had been washed away. In his view, the bond

between the political and the cultural spheres had been cut, and he felt that traditional spiritual and intellectual values had been lost. During the last years of his life, he was increasingly worried about political and social conditions in Europe and Asia; he looked into the future with despair. The poet's son Franz committed suicide on July 13, 1929. Two days later, Hugo von Hofmannsthal died of a heart attack.

ANALYSIS

At least a limited overview of Hugo von Hofmannsthal's dramatic œuvre can be obtained from a detailed analysis of three plays. Two of these plays, although chronologically quite far apart, demonstrate the author's continuous concern with the question of human existence. They are *Death and the Fool* and *The Tower*. The third play, *The Difficult Man*, is a prime example of Hofmannsthal's genius for comedy.

DEATH AND THE FOOL

Hofmannsthal called *Death and the Fool* "a small one-act, very sad play." The playlet is a work of great beauty, consisting of some six hundred verses in iambic pentameter, abounding in alliteration and in subtle allusions to works of art and to mythology. *Death and the Fool* is also one of the most important examples of Hofmannsthal's concern with the concept of preexistence. He viewed human existence on three planes. The first plane is that of preexistence, a state of visionary knowledge and insight into events and actions without their actual occurrence. A person who is in this "glorious, but dangerous state" is granted insight or foresight, but at the same time he or she is deprived of real experiences and is separated from the rest of humanity.

Such is the case with Claudio, the protagonist of *Death and the Fool*, whose very name suggests that he is shut off from others. During the opening monologue, Claudio is sitting by the window of his ornate study contemplating a vista of the world. The world he sees is populated by active, living people who experience sorrows, joys, fears, ecstasies—in short, the whole range of human emotions. Claudio, on the other hand, has always understood, analyzed, and categorized these emotions; he has even pretended to feel them, but in fact he never has. Works of art (such as the painting of Mona Lisa hanging in his study) have provided surrogate experiences, but he has never had any real ones.

Claudio's musing is interrupted by a haunting violin solo played by Death. This is not, however, the traditional figure of death found in the medieval dances of death; in Hofmannsthal's play, Death introduces himself as a relative of Dionysos, the Greek god of wine, and of Venus, the Roman goddess of love. Nevertheless, the ominous purpose of Death's visit is clear to Claudio, who protests, ever more passionately, that he has not yet lived, that he has never been really involved with or committed to another human being, that he has not even known the difference between good and evil. As he protests that he is now ready to live, to have experiences, to be faithful to other humans, Death summons the three people who have loved Claudio most during his earthly existence, those who have suffered the most from his lack of feeling: his mother, his sweetheart, and his friend. The increasing intensity of their reproaches, ranging from his mother's gentleness to his friend's bitter accusations, produces a strong dramatic tension that culminates in Claudio's final passionate outburst in which he curses his gift for preexistential insights and vicarious experiences. The play ends with a Dionysian affirmation of life by Claudio, who feels that his entire life has been compressed into the hour of his death.

Claudio's statement echoes several similar ones in Hofmannsthal's other writings, particularly in *Ad me ipsum*. Having realized the dangers of preexistence, Hofmannsthal strove to attain "existence": He turned toward the active life. In his private sphere, this meant marriage and fatherhood, and in his art it meant writing plays that were more accessible to a large audiences than were his poems and verse plays.

THE DIFFICULT MAN

The Difficult Man is Hofmannsthal's only play that takes place in contemporary Vienna. The principal characters are members of the Austrian aristocracy who have survived World War I. The protagonist (the "difficult man" of the title) is Count Hans Karl Bühl, aged thirty-nine, whose essence almost defies

description: In some ways, he is simple, like a child, and yet he is highly complex. He is truthful and highly sensitive to the confusions that arise every time he opens his mouth. Because of his profound distrust of language, he prefers to remain silent, but the entire plot of the comedy depends on his having to speak, to convey important messages to other characters.

During the afternoon before a big party in the house of Count Altenwyl, Hans Karl has a series of conversations in his own house. He has declined an invitation to the party but is persuaded by his older sister, Crescence, to attend after all, in order to ask for the hand of Helen Altenwyl on behalf of his nephew Stani (Crescence's son). From the conversation between Hans Karl and Crescence, the audience learns that Helen has been in love with Hans Karl and probably still is, but he denies that he is in any way attached to her. Hans Karl's decision to attend the party is also motivated by his wish to speak to Antoinette Hechingen, with whom he had had a brief affair two years earlier. During the war, he had become a friend of Count Hechingen, and he now wishes to reconcile Antoinette to her husband. During the party (act 2), Hans Karl has two important conversations, one with Antoinette and one with Helen. At the conclusion of the party (act 3), there occurs the crucial conversation between Helen and Hans Karl that culminates in their engagement.

Throughout the play, Hans Karl is the pivotal figure around whom everything revolves and with whom most of the play's other characters interact. Both the comedy and the serious implications of the play arise from the fact that none of the many other characters, except Helen (and Hans Karl's faithful servant, Lukas), understands Hans Karl's "difficult" personality, and they invariably draw the wrong conclusions from his words and actions. The dramatic structure of the play is not complex: Serious scenes are invariably followed by comical ones, until the final ritualistic embrace provides comedy's traditional affirmation of life through marriage and the promise of procreation.

The three serious conversations in the play reveal the mature poet's views on the central issues of man's life in society. During the encounter with Antoinette, Hans Karl at first asserts a grateful acceptance of beautiful, if fleeting, moments and warns her against seeking permanence in such necessarily transient pleasures. According to him, human relationships, particularly relationships between men and women, are haphazard, and "everyone could live with everyone else if chance so decreed." This reality, however, is so difficult to accept that humanity had to invent the institution of marriage, which "transforms the accidental and the impure into necessity and permanence." In his attempt to lead Antoinette back to her husband, Hans Karl describes what a man's love for a woman means: "That a man loves a woman he can demonstrate only through . . . one single thing on earth: Through permanence, through constancy." Elaborating on the idea of "necessity," he says that wherever it exists between men and women, "there is a drawing together, and pardon and reconciliation and staying together. And there may be children, and there is a marriage and sanctity in spite of everything." The irony of Hans Karl's words at this point is that, on a conscious level, he means to apply them to Antoinette and her husband, but on a subconscious level he is speaking about Helen and himself, a fact that is intuitively perceived by Antoinette. Their conversation ends with a halfhearted promise by Antoinette that she will try to live with her husband, provided that Hans Karl will visit her often to encourage her.

In spite of a few intervening scenes, Hans Karls's statements on love and marriage have prepared the audience for his first important conversation with Helen. It is a tender and delicate encounter between two sophisticated and sensitive people who are in love with each other but are prevented by social conventions and their own psyches from admitting this fact. Ostensibly, Hans Karl wants to speak to Helen about his nephew Stani, who wants to marry her, but their conversation is curiously muted, and Stani is mentioned only in passing. Eventually Hans Karl says that Helen should marry "a good, noble human being—and a [real] man." He believes that he himself does not have these qualities and rises, as if to terminate the conversation. Helen feels that he is trying to say good-bye to her forever and quickly tells him

about a sort of *déjà vu* experience: She feels that in her thoughts, she and Hans Karl once stood in a similar setting, with the same music being played in the background, and he said farewell to her. This prompts him to tell her of an experience during the war when he thought he would die, and, for thirty seconds, he had a vision of his entire life, and she was his wife: "Not my future wife. That is the strange thing. Simply my wife. As a *fait accompli*." As Helen grows ever more agitated, Hans Karl presents a Claudio-like interpretation of his vision: "In a chosen moment it was to be impressed on my mind what the happiness looks like that I forfeited." He goes on to tell her how he had a vision of her marriage but did not know to whom she was married. At this point, he realizes that she is so upset that she is close to collapsing. He apologizes for "all his confused talk" and bids her farewell. She also says good-bye, and they try to shake hands, but their hands do not meet. A pompous "Famous Man" and Crescence provide comic relief as Hans Karl rushes offstage. When Helen almost collapses into Crescence's arms, Crescence once more misunderstands the situation, believing that Helen has agreed to marry her son Stani.

In the third act, there occurs an excellent example of a psychological process that Hofmannsthal called "allomatism"—that is, the transformation of one character through the influence of another. Hans Karl has left the party. Helen totally discards all social conventions as she prepares to leave her father's house so that she can look for Hans Karl. She hands a letter addressed to her father to an old manservant and asks him to stay with her father when he reads it. At this moment, Hans Karl reenters the vestibule. During the ensuing conversation, Helen has the leading role; she has an uncanny air of authority and of psychic power about her as she explains Hans Karl's own self to him: "Your will, your self . . . turned you around when you were alone and led you back to me. . . ." Then she becomes unabashedly a woman in love, as she lays claim to him and at the same time gives herself to him. Helen's psychic strength, her intellect, and her charm are thus able to release Hans Karl from his preexistential "difficultness" and to lead him into existence.

To varying degrees, Hofmannsthal's serious dramas continued to deal with the problem of preexistence versus existence. In order to combat the deterioration of political, social, and moral values so prevalent in Europe during the first quarter of the twentieth century, and in order to fill a spiritual void, he wrote a number of religious dramas. Their heroes leave the plane of preexistence and enter the second (temporal) plane of existence. Having entered the second plane, they lose their claim to the first one, but if their activity is of an extraordinary quality, they transcend the temporal plane and attain the third plane, that of the "superego," which encompasses all the knowledge and insight of preexistence, as well as the actual experiences of temporal life.

In Hofmannsthal's earlier religious dramas, the evils of contemporary society are represented by allegorical, universal figures. For example, the ruthlessness of modern capitalism is exemplified by Everyman in the play of that title, and the mindless brutality of revolution is embodied in the Beggar in *The Salzburg Great Theatre of the World*. In these religious dramas, the protagonists eventually reach a point at which they transcend their human limitations, attaining the superego. Their attainment of the superego invariably results from their acceptance of Christian ethical standards. Because of the allegorical quality of these plays, the protagonist's attainment of his superego must always be extended to suggest some sort of salvation for man, for contemporary society.

THE TOWER

Toward the end of his life, Hofmannsthal no longer considered this optimistic solution acceptable. This change in his *Weltanschauung* had a profound effect on the final version of his tragedy *The Tower*. The author's main concern in this play is again preexistence, or rather, the fate that befalls humans once they leave preexistence and pass into "real life." This fate is portrayed as a ruthless and anonymous power that crushes the individual. Hofmannsthal described his intentions regarding the theme of the drama in the following manner: "To portray the truly merciless elements of our reality into which the soul passes from a dark, mythical realm." The span of temporal life through which the protagonist, Prince Sigismund, must pass presents Hofmannsthal with the opportunity to portray the evils of society with utter realism, while the figures who perpetrate these evils are again drawn as allegorical, universal figures.

The Tower may be divided into three parts, corresponding to Sigismund's three stages of existence. The first part concerns his confinement in the tower (preexistence), the second part deals with his temporal life until his renunciation of worldly power, and the third part relates the remainder of his temporal life, during which his soul has already attained the superego. Throughout the play, society and the evil forces dominating it are juxtaposed with the purity of Sigismund.

It is noteworthy that during the first part, Sigismund's preexistence is represented as a painful confinement from which he yearns to be released. The tower, whose symbolic value changes throughout the play, is at this point a prison situated at the very frontier of the realm. Sigismund is a captive there, not only physically but also spiritually. The geographic remoteness of the tower from the king's court symbolizes Sigismund's spiritual remoteness from the rest of humanity.

In the course of the play, Sigismund comes to recognize both the necessity for engagement and the futility of any temporal programs—especially political programs—that seek to alter fundamentally the lot of humankind. In the final scenes of the revised version of *The Tower*, Hofmannsthal concedes the possibility of salvation for exceptional individuals, but he presents the rest of humanity as so evil as to be beyond redemption.

Having the doubtful benefit of hindsight, today's reader is awed by the prophetic quality of Hofmannsthal's vision, grounded in his early diagnosis of the self-imposed isolation of the artist. In his attempt to come to grips with the realities of the modern world, Hofmannsthal rejected aestheticism, yet he ended by investing such despairing faith as he possessed in his notion of a spiritual elite, an aristocracy of the soul.

OTHER MAJOR WORKS

LONG FICTION: *Andreas: Oder, Die Vereinigten,* 1932 (*Andreas: Or, The United,* 1936).

SHORT FICTION: *Reitergeschichte,* 1899 (*Cavalry Patrol,* 1939); *Erlebnis des Marschalls von Bassompierre,* 1900 (*An Episode in the Life of the Marshal de Bassompierre,* 1952); *Das Märchen 672: Nacht, und andere Erzählungen,* 1905 (*Tale of the Merchant's Son and His Servants,* 1969); *Lucidor,* 1910 (English translation, 1922); *Drei Erzählungen,* 1927; *Das erzählerische Work,* 1969.

POETRY: *Ausgewählte Gedichte,* 1903; *Die gesammelten Gedichte,* 1907 (*The Lyrical Poems of Hugo von Hofmannsthal,* 1918); *Loris,* 1930; *Nachlese der Gedichte,* 1934; *Gedichte und lyrische Dramen,* 1946 (*Poems and Verse Plays,* 1961).

NONFICTION: *Gespräch über Gedichte,* 1904; *Unterhaltungen über literarische Gegenstände,* 1904; *Die Briefe des Zurückgekehrten,* 1907; *Der Dichter und diese Zeit,* 1907 (*The Poet and His Time,* 1955); *Wege und die Begegnungen,* 1913; *Reden und Aufsätze,* 1921; *Buch der Freunde,* 1922 (*The Book of Friends,* 1952); *Augenblicke in Griechenland,* 1924 (*Moments in Greece,* 1952); *Früheste Prosastücke,* 1926; *Richard Strauss und Hugo von Hofmannsthal: Briefwechsel,* 1926 (*Correspondence of Richard Strauss and Hugo von Hofmannsthal,* 1927); *Ad me ipsum,* 1930; *Loris: Die Prosa des jungen Hugo von Hofmannsthal,* 1930; *Die Berührung der Sphären,* 1931; *Festspiele in Salzburg,* 1938; *Briefwechsel zwischen George und Hofmannsthal,* 1938 (letters); *Selected Prose,* 1952; *Selected Essays,* 1955.

EDITED TEXTS: *Deutsche Erzähler,* 1912 (4 volumes); *Die österreichische Bibliothek,* 1915-1917 (26 volumes); *Deutsches Epigramme,* 1923 (2 volumes); *Schillers Selbstcharakteristik,* 1926.

MISCELLANEOUS: *Gesammelte Werke in Einzelausgaben,* 1945-1959 (15 volumes); *Selected Writings of Hugo von Hofmannsthal,* 1952-1963 (3 volumes); *Hofmannsthal: Gesammelte Werke,* 1979 (10 volumes).

BIBLIOGRAPHY

Beniston, Judith. *Welttheater: Hofmannsthal, Richard von Kralik, and the Revival of Catholic Drama in Austria, 1890-1934.* Leeds, England: W. S. Maney, 1998. This study of Catholic drama in Austria compares and contrasts the works of Hofmannsthal and Richard von Kralik. Bibliography and index.

Bennett, Benjamin. *Hugo von Hofmannsthal: The Theaters of Consciousness.* New York: Cambridge University Press, 1988. A critical analysis and interpretation of Hofmannsthal's literary works. Bibliography and index.

Del Caro, Adiran. *Hugo von Hofmannsthal: Poets and the Language of Life.* Baton Rouge: Louisiana State University Press, 1993. An examination of the works of Hofmannsthal, particularly his poetry, that sheds light on his dramatic works. Bibliography and index.

Joyce, Douglas A. *Hugo von Hofmannsthal's Der Schwierige: A Fifty-Year Theater History.* Columbia, S.C.: Camden House, 1993. This study examines the stage history of Hofmannsthal's *The Difficult Man.* Bibliography.

Michael, Nancy C. *Elektra and Her Sisters: Three Female Characters in Schnitzler, Freud, and Hofmannsthal.* New York: Peter Lang, 2001. This study examines the role of Elektra and other women characters in Hofmannsthal's *Electra* and in the writings of Arthur Schnitzler and Sigmund Freud. Bibliography and index.

Vilain, Robert. *The Poetry of Hugo von Hofmannsthal and French Symbolism.* New York: Oxford University Press, 2000. This study examines the relationship between Symbolism and the works of Hofmannsthal. Bibliography and indexes.

Yates, W. E. *Schnitzler, Hofmannsthal, and the Austrian Theatre.* New Haven, Conn.: Yale University Press, 1992. An examination of the Austrian theater in the early twentieth century, with emphasis on Hofmannsthal and Arthur Schnitzler.

Franz P. Haberl

LUDVIG HOLBERG

Born: Bergen, Norway; December 3, 1684
Died: Copenhagen, Denmark; January 28, 1754

PRINCIPAL DRAMA

Den Politiske kandstøber, pr. 1722, pb. 1723 (*The
    Political Tinker*, 1914)
Den Vægelsindede, pr. 1722, pb. 1724 (*The
    Weathercock*, 1912)
Jean de France: Eller, Hans Frandsen, pr. 1722,
    pb. 1731 (*Jean de France*, 1990)
Jeppe paa Bjerget, pr. 1722, pb. 1723 (*Jeppe of the
    Hill*, 1906)
Mester Gert Westphaler, pr. 1722, pb. 1723 (*The
    Loquacious Barber*, 1903)
Den ellefte junii, pr. 1723, pb. 1724
Barselstuen, pr. 1723, pb. 1731
Erasmus Montanus, wr. 1723, pb. 1731 (English
    translation, 1885)
Comoedier, pb. 1723-1725 (3 volumes)
Det arabiske pulver, pr., pb. 1724 (*The Arabian
    Powder*, 1950)
Julestuen, pr., pb. 1724 (*The Christmas Party*, 1950)
Mascarade, pr., pb. 1724 (*Masquerade*, 1946)
Ulysses von Ithacia, pr. 1724, pb. 1725
Henrich og Pernille, pr. 1724, pb. 1731 (*Henry and
    Pernilla*, 1912)
Diderich Menschen-Skræk, pr. 1724, pb. 1731
    (*Diderich the Terrible*, 1950)
Kilde-reysen, pr. 1724, pb. 1725 (*The Healing
    Spring*, 1957)
Melampe, pr. 1724, pb. 1725
Jacob von Tyboe, pb. 1725
Uden hoved og hale, pb. 1725
Den stundesløse, pr. 1726, pb. 1731 (*The Fussy
    Man*, 1946)
Den pantsatte bonde-dreng, pr. 1727, pb. 1731
    (*The Peasant in Pawn*, 1950)
Den danske comoedies liigbegiængelse, pr. 1727,
    pb. 1746 (*The Burial of Danish Comedy*, 1990)
Hexerie: Eller, Blind alarm, pb. 1731, pr. 1750
Det lykkelige skibbrudd, pb. 1731, pr. 1747
Pernilles korte frøiken-stand, pb. 1731, pr. 1747

(*Pernille's Brief Experience as a Lady*, 1990)
De usynlige, pb. 1731, pr. 1747 (*The Masked
    Ladies*, 1946)
Den honette ambition, pb. 1731, pr. 1747
Plutus, pr. 1751, pb. 1753
Abracadabra, pr. 1752, pb. 1753-1754
Den forvandlede brudgom, pb. 1753, pr. 1882 (*The
    Changed Bridegroom*, 1950)
Don Ranudo de Colibrados, pb. 1754
Philosophus udi egen indbildning, pr., pb. 1754
Republiquen: Eller, Det gemene beste, pr., pb. 1754
Sganarels reyse til det philosophiske land, pb. 1754
    (*Sganarel's Journey to the Land of the
    Philosophers*, 1950)
Three Comedies by Ludvig Holberg, pb. 1912
Comedies by Holberg, pb. 1914
Four Plays by Holberg, pb. 1946
Seven One-Act Plays, pb. 1950
Three Comedies, pb. 1957
Jeppe of the Hill and Other Comedies, pb. 1990

OTHER LITERARY FORMS

Although he is regarded today mainly as an author
of comedies, Ludvig Holberg spent only two short
periods of his life writing in that genre. A man of the
Enlightenment, he wrote extensively in history, biography, law, and moral philosophy. Among his many
works of nonfiction is an important autobiography. In
addition, he is one of the most prolific essayists in
both Danish and Norwegian literature.

Closer to his comic authorship are his novel
Nicolai Klimii iter Subterraneum (1741; *Journey to
the World Underground*, 1742), his satires, and his
long mock-heroic poem *Peder Paars* (1722; English
translation, 1962), which narrates the woefully unheroic journey of a merchant and his clerk from the
town of Kallundborg to that of Aarhus, where the
merchant is to visit his fiancée.

ACHIEVEMENTS

Ludvig Holberg stands as the originator of modern Danish and Norwegian literature. He not only in-

troduced the essay as a genre in Denmark and Norway and established a native comic tradition but also created a literature for a new public. Earlier writers had addressed a select group of state officials, particularly pastors, who possessed the education and knowledge necessary to appreciate their writing, while Holberg appealed to a bourgeoisie that was growing rapidly both in numbers and in influence. His contemporary success as a writer can be explained with reference to that fact.

His later success, however, depends entirely on the intrinsic quality of his art. Holberg is still considered Denmark's greatest dramatist, and in Norwegian literature he is eclipsed only by Henrik Ibsen. His comedies continue to be performed regularly in both his native land and in his adopted country. More than half of them have been translated into English, as have *Peder Paars* and a number of Holberg's prose works.

BIOGRAPHY

Ludvig Holberg was born on December 3, 1684, to Christen Nielsen Holberg and Karen Lem. His father was of peasant stock but had worked his way from the rank of private to that of lieutenant colonel in the army. His mother came from a clerical family including several educated men.

Holberg's father died when the boy was two years old, and his mother passed away in 1695. The child, who had attended the German school for boys and the grammar school in Bergen, was sent to live with his mother's country cousin. In 1698, he returned to Bergen, where his uncle and guardian, the merchant Peder Lem, took him into his family, and Holberg grew up in Bergen amidst the enterprising burghers of the city.

He returned to the grammar school, but a fire in 1702 reduced it and most of Bergen to ashes. Members of the senior class were sent to Copenhagen, where Holberg matriculated at the university. He soon came back to Norway, however, and found a position as tutor and spiritual assistant in the home of the rural dean at Voss, northeast of Bergen. Returning to Copenhagen in the fall of 1703, he passed his theological examinations in April of 1704.

At the age of eighteen Holberg had gained control of a small inheritance, which he converted to cash to finance travel abroad. He spent a year in Holland and then returned to Norway, having run out of funds. He spent the winter as a tutor in the city of Kristiansand, and the following spring he traveled to England in the company of a fellow graduate in theology.

He returned to Copenhagen in 1708, having spent his time in Oxford and London. After another year as a tutor, during which part of his duty was to accompany a young man on a journey to Germany, he was given lodging at Borch's College and was thus free to pursue his scholarly interests. The result was his first book, *Introduction til de fornemste europæiske rigers historier* (1711; introduction to the principal kingdoms of Europe).

Holberg's ambitions at this time were most likely directed toward a career at the University of Copenhagen. By 1711, he applied to the king for censors to be appointed to examine a work of history that he was contemplating, and about 1714 he applied for a professorship, probably on the strength of a historical work that was never published in the form it then had. He received a promise of the next available professorship, but the position of *adjunctus professor philosophiae*, in fact an academic promotion, carried no salary. It did, however, put Holberg in a position of risking the loss of his present support, and he decided to guard against this danger by doing some study abroad.

He remained abroad for two years, traveling in Germany, France, and Italy. On his return home in 1716, he oversaw the publication of his second book, *Moralske kierne: Eller, Introduction til naturens og folke-rettens kundskab* (introduction to the natural law and the law of nations). The following year, he was finally given the promised professorship, which unfortunately turned out to be in metaphysics, a discipline that Holberg despised. In 1720, however, he advanced to the professorship in Latin literature, which was more to his liking.

About the same time, the desire for creative writing awoke in him. Inspired by a quarrel in which he had employed satiric devices to make his point, Holberg produced several satires and a large mock-heroic epic titled *Peder Paars*. From this work it was only a short distance to the writing of comedies. Holberg, who learned much from the plays of Molière, embarked on playwriting in 1722, when a theater in the vernacular was being established in Copenhagen, and during the next several years, the neophyte dramatist produced more than twenty comedies.

The development of the thriving new Danish theater came to a halt in 1730, when a Pietist king, Christian VI, ascended to the throne. The clergy actively labored in opposition to theatrical performances, and in 1731 a royal declaration expressed strong disapproval of anyone associated with the writing or performance of comedies. This led Holberg to return to his scholarly pursuits, and he produced a number of large historical works. His renewed interest in history was perhaps also a function of his having been made professor of that subject in 1730.

Nevertheless, Holberg was not able to leave creative writing completely behind. In 1741, he published his *Journey to the World Underground*, a Latin romance that, by telling about the protagonist's discovery of a world inside the earth, enabled its author to expose countless contemporary follies. The book created a stir and was almost banned, for its message of tolerance was not appreciated by the king and his circle of Pietist advisers.

The struggle for tolerance was continued in *Moralske tanker* (1744; moral thoughts and epistles). After the death of the king in 1746, however, the theater was revived, and Holberg was again free to write comedies, but his later plays are more philosophical and less amusing than the early ones.

His frugal habits and the sale of his books had enabled Holberg to amass a considerable fortune, which was safely invested in real estate. Because Holberg had no heirs, he wanted his wealth to be used for the public good. The reestablishment of a school for young noblemen, Sorø Academy, presented an opportunity for the wise disposition of his property, which at the same time was designated the Barony of Holberg. Through the donation Holberg also was given considerable say in the academy's curriculum.

Holberg died on January 28, 1754. He remained busy planning new editions of his works and selling his books to the end of his life.

ANALYSIS

Ludvig Holberg grew up among the burghers of Bergen, representatives of a class that at that time was starting to come into its own. The scholar and dramatist shared their basic values, and in his comedies he catered to their tastes. Holberg was also a man of considerable learning, and as such he never doubted his competence as a judge of good and evil and prudence and folly. His background in the emerging bourgeoisie and his position as an intellectual leader combine to explain the form of his comedies.

The typical Holberg comedy is constructed according to the rule of Horace, in that it attempts to instruct the audience at the same time that it entertains. The comedy is centered on a character who has one dominating weakness, and around this figure are placed both schemers and innocent characters who suffer because of the central figure's follies. The characters onstage are also typical of the people in the audience, for although people are basically rational beings, they are also afflicted with all manner of caprices, obsessions, and strange notions. By holding up a mirror in which the audience can get a clear view of itself, Holberg attempts to remove some of this folly and strengthen the rule of reason.

THE POLITICAL TINKER

Holberg's first play, *The Political Tinker*, has struck a later age as antidemocratic, in that its central character, a Hamburg pewterer named Herman von Bremen, is soundly thrashed by the author for his desire to become involved in political life. His basic fault is that he neglects his work in order to read books about politics and engage in useless discussions with equally silly companions. Herman also possesses a considerable amount of pride, however, and it can be argued that he is punished for this rather than for his wish to influence life in the society in which he lives. There is indeed little desire for true understanding to be detected in Herman von Bremen; his "politics" is a means to satisfy his vanity and desire for power rather than the expression of a genuine wish to be of service to his fellow citizens.

Those who suffer most from Herman's folly are his wife Geske, his daughter Engelke, and Antonius, a young man who wishes to marry Engelke. Geske must watch Herman destroy both his reputation as a reliable craftsperson and the family finances, while Antonius and Engelke cannot get married because of the father's desire to get a son-in-law who is as interested in politics as himself. The schemers in the play are two men, Abrahams and Sanderus, who inform Herman that he has been elected mayor by the city council. This is according to a plan supported by some of the councilmen, who are annoyed at Herman's criticism of city politics.

As soon as Herman believes that he has been elected mayor, his vanity and lust for power take complete control of him. Much comedy results from his attempts to imitate his social superiors as well as from the way that his wife and servants cope with his elevated standing. Herman changes his last name to Bremenfeld, Geske is no longer permitted to get up at sunrise and has to acquire a lapdog, and the servant Henrich takes advantage of the situation by soliciting bribes from visitors to the "mayor."

Herman soon gets his just reward. According to the plan, he is presented with a number of difficult problems, and he discovers that he is totally unfit for his job. In the end, he regrets ever having wanted to be mayor and is immensely relieved when the truth of the matter is revealed to him. He swears never to read another book about politics, promises to do his work as he did before, and welcomes Antonius as his son-in-law.

The Political Tinker is, in the final analysis, not only a play about a political eccentric but also a discussion of the opposition between appearance and reality, what a person thinks he is and what he really is, and what happens when a person is robbed of his illusions. As such it is a play of universal interest.

JEPPE OF THE HILL

The basic motif in *The Political Tinker* is the age-old story of the man who is lifted up from a lowly station to a position of prominence for a short period of time. The same motif is employed in *Jeppe of the Hill*, but while Herman von Bremen is a German burgher, Jeppe is a Danish peasant. He is also a drunkard who squanders his family's meager substance. He is henpecked by his wife, Nille, and is made a cuckold by the local sexton.

Holberg borrowed the plot of *Jeppe of the Hill* from the German Jesuit Jacob Bidermann's fictitious travel memoir *Utopia* (1640). While Jeppe is drunk and asleep, he is found by the local baron and his men and, for sport, is placed in the baron's bed. When awake, he is made to believe that he is the baron. The power is too much for him, however, and he begins to behave in a most tyrannical fashion. He attempts to take indecent liberties with the wife of the bailiff of the estate, and knowing that the bailiff cheats his lord, he wants to punish him by hanging the bailiff, his wife, and his seven children. When he gets drunk again, he is placed where he was found, after which he is accused of having entered the manor unlawfully and is condemned to die by poisoning and subsequent hanging. Strung from the gallows with the rope fastened under his arms, he is found by his wife, Nille, who believes that he is dead and who now regrets having treated him so harshly during his life. Jeppe awakens and asks for a drink, however, and this removes all traces of sympathy from his wife. Against her wishes, he is given his life back by the same mock court of law that had condemned him to death in the first place. Shortly thereafter he is informed that his experiences are not real, but only a joke played as a diversion for the baron.

Holberg's aristocratic attitude is revealed by the fact that he lets the play's main character be used deliberately by his social betters. As in *The Political Tinker*, the moral of *Jeppe of the Hill* is that one should not aspire to change one's lot in life. Even more damaging, however, is the fact that the play's representatives of the upper class seem also to represent Holberg's concept of reason's rule over ignorance and folly. It is true that Jeppe is an ignorant peasant, but it must also be remembered that the sins for which he is being punished are the result of the baron's men having duped him in the first place.

A present-day audience will view Jeppe as both a comic and a tragic figure. The enduring appeal of the play resides in the fact that Jeppe, the prototype of a subjugated man, displays true humanity in the midst of degeneration. Caught in a static and rigid society, trapped in an unfair economic system and condemned to a frustrating marriage, there indeed seems to be no exit for him.

ERASMUS MONTANUS

Like *Jeppe of the Hill*, *Erasmus Montanus* takes place in a small Danish village. Rasmus Berg, the son of a prosperous farmer, is returning home after the completion of his studies at the University of Copenhagen, and the play shows how he relates to the milieu in which he has his origin. The comedy can be viewed both as a satire on the young candidate, who in the manner of the learned has Latinized his name and taken on what Holberg considered the silly habits of academic life, and as an attack on the ignorance and superstitions so common among the rural population.

The local society is represented by an ignorant sexton named Peer, Jesper, the stupid bailiff representing the local landlord, Erasmus's parents, Jeppe and Nille, Erasmus's brother Jacob, Erasmus's fiancée Lisbed, Lisbed's stubborn father Jeronimus, and Jeronimus's wife, Magdelone. The most admirable character here is Jacob, who possesses an abundance of sound practical sense.

Erasmus also has his share of human follies, however. He has acquired the trappings of a university education but none of its substance. Arguing for the sake of argument only, he soon offends his future father-in-law by maintaining that Earth is round rather than flat. This is perceived by Jeronimus as an atheistic doctrine, and he therefore refuses to allow Erasmus marry his daughter. Erasmus's dilemma is now the following: He may maintain what he objectively knows to be true, namely that Earth is round, and lose the girl he loves, or he may assent to Jeronimus's error and marry Lisbed. This might make Erasmus look like a martyr for the cause of truth, but this he is not. The reason that he is unwilling to agree with his father-in-law is not that he loves truth but that he is afraid his reputation at the university will suffer.

Erasmus's dominating weakness is thus the old sin of pride. The people who suffer because of him are first his parents, who are being made a laughingstock because of their son's actions, and second his fiancé, who desperately wants to marry him. The conflict is resolved only by the aid of an outsider, a lieutenant who tricks Erasmus into enlisting in the army. When the learned young man has been subjected to military drills and whipped into humility, he is more than willing to admit that Earth is flat. By recanting, he is able both to get out of the military and to marry Lisbed, and everybody is happy. By the end of the play, Erasmus also appears to have learned the difference between empty academic form and the substance that ought to be the essence of academic study. This distinction was important to Holberg, who, above all, was a practical man. As in *The Political Tinker* and *The Fussy Man*, the victory over folly leads to the triumph of romantic love.

THE FUSSY MAN

Like Herman von Bremen in *The Political Tinker*, Vielgeschrey in *The Fussy Man* causes a number of people, above all his daughter Leonora and her beloved Leander, to suffer from his caprices. Vielgeschrey believes that he has a host of things to do and not enough time to accomplish them; the reason is that he is unable to concentrate on one matter and get it out of the way. In reality he is no busier than most people. He already has four clerks to help him in his business but believes that he also needs an accountant, and he therefore wants to force his daughter to marry one. The man whom he has in mind, Peder Erichsen, wants Leonora only for her money. Vielgeschrey's housekeeper, Magdelone, also suffers from his inability to bring anything to its conclusion, for she, being forty years old and unmarried, has been promised by her master that he will find her a husband.

The schemer in this play is Vielgeschrey's servant girl Pernille, who allies herself with the old trickster Oldfux in order to save Leonora and Leander, satisfy Magdelone, teach Peder Erichsen a lesson, and, if possible, cause Vielgeschrey to develop some much-needed concentration by showing him where his behavior may lead. By carefully taking advantage of Vielgeschrey's inability to concentrate and by further confusing him, Pernille manages to get Leonora married to Leander, whom Vielgeschrey believes to be

Peder Erichsen, while Peder Erichsen marries Magdelone, whom he believes to be Leonora. When the victims of the trickery become aware of what has happened, Vielgeschrey is persuaded by his brother Leonard to forgive his daughter and son-in-law, while Peder Erichsen willingly settles for Magdelone as soon as he learns that she has three thousand dollars in the bank. It does not become clear, however, whether Vielgeschrey has learned anything from his experience.

Vielgeschrey, like Herman von Bremen, Jeppe, and Erasmus, has been instructed throughout the play by having had to suffer the consequences of his foolishness. As a man of the Enlightenment, Holberg was above all concerned with strengthening the rule of reason. By exposing the nature and consequences of its opposite, folly, he created comedies that have had enduring value for generations of readers and spectators.

OTHER MAJOR WORKS

LONG FICTION: *Nicolai Klimii iter subterraneum*, 1741 (*Journey to the World Underground*, 1742).

POETRY: *Peder Paars*, 1722 (English translation, 1962); *Hans Mickelsens fire skæmte-digte samt Zille Hansdotters forsvarsskrift for kvindekønnet*, 1722; *Metamorphosis: Eller, Forvandlinger*, 1726.

NONFICTION: *Introduction til de fornemste europæiske rigers historier*, 1711; *Moralske kierne: Eller, Introduction til naturens og folke-rettens kundskab*, 1716; *Ludovici Holbergii ad virum perillustrem: Epistola prima*, 1728 (*Memoirs*, 1827); *Dannemarks og Norges beskrivelse*, 1729; *Dannemarks riges historie*, 1732-1735; *Opuscula latina*, 1737; *Den berømmelige norske handel-stad Bergens beskrivelse*, 1737; *Almindelig kirke-historie*, 1738; *Adskillige store helte og berommelige mænds·* *sammenlignende historie*, 1739; *Den jødiske historie fra verdens begyndelse fortsat til disse tider*, 1742; *Tredie selvbiografiske epistola*, 1743; *Moralske tanker*, 1744; *Adskillige heltinders og navnkundige damers sammenlignende historie*, 1745; *Epistler I-IV*, 1748-1750 (*Epistles I-IV*, 1955); *Moralske fabler*, 1751; *Epistler V*, 1754 (*Epistles V*, 1955); *Moral Reflections and Epistles*, 1991.

BIBLIOGRAPHY

Anderson, Jens K. *Conflicting Values in Holberg's Comedies: Literary Tradition or Social Teaching?* Minneapolis: Center for Nordic Studies, University of Minnesota, 1991. This study examines the comedies of Holberg, with emphasis on the values that he portrays in them. Bibliography.

Argetsinger, Gerald S. *Ludvig Holberg's Comedies.* Carbondale: Southern Illinois University Press, 1983. A critical analysis and interpretation of Holberg's comedic dramas. Bibliography and index.

Billeskov Jansen, F. J. *Ludvig Holberg.* New York: Twayne, 1974. A basic biography of Holberg that covers his life and works. Bibliography.

Housgaard, Jens. *Ludvig Holberg: The Playwright and His Age up to 1730.* Odense, Denmark: Odense University Press, 1993. A study of the works of Holberg and a description of the times in which he lived. Bibliography and index.

Rossel, Sven Hakon, ed. *Ludvig Holberg: A European Writer: A Study in Influence and Reception.* Atlanta, Ga.: Rodopi, 1994. An examination of Holberg's works, with particular emphasis on his critical reception and influence on other writers. Bibliography and index.

Jan Sjåvik

ISRAEL HOROVITZ

Born: Wakefield, Massachusetts; March 31, 1939

PRINCIPAL DRAMA

The Comeback, pr. 1958

The Death of Bernard the Believer, pr. 1960

This Play Is About Me, pr. 1961

The Hanging of Emmanuel, pr. 1962

The Killer Dove, pr. 1963

Hop, Skip and Jump, pr. 1963

The Simon Street Harvest, 1964

Line, pr. 1967, pb. 1968 (one act)

It's Called the Sugar Plum, pr. 1967, pb. 1968 (one act)

The Indian Wants the Bronx, pr., pb. 1968 (one act)

Rats, pr., pb. 1968 (one act)

Acrobats, pr. 1968, pb. 1971

Morning, pr. 1968 (as *Chiaroscuro*), pb. 1969 (one act)

The Honest-to-God Schnozzola, pr. 1968, pb. 1971

Leader, pr. 1969, pb. 1970

Clair-Obscur, pr. 1970, pb. 1972

Dr. Hero, pr. 1971 (as *Hero*), pr. 1972 (revision of *Dr. Hero*), pb. 1973

Shooting Gallery, pr. 1971, pb. 1973

Alfred the Great, pr. 1972, pb. 1974

Our Father's Failing, pr. 1973, pb. 1979

Spared, pr. 1974, pb. 1975 (one act)

Hopscotch, pr. 1974, pb. 1977

Turnstile, pr. 1974

Uncle Snake: An Independence Day Pageant, pr. 1975, pb. 1976

The Primary English Class, pr. 1975, pb. 1976

Stage Directions, pr. 1976, pb. 1977

The Reason We Eat, pr. 1976

Alfred Dies, pr. 1976, pb. 1979

The Former One-on-One Basketball Champion, pr. 1977, pb. 1982

The 75th, pr., pb. 1977

The Lounge Player, pr. 1977

Man with Bags, pr., pb. 1977 (adaptation of a translation of Eugène Ionesco's play)

Mackerel, pr. 1978, pb. 1979

A Christmas Carol: Scrooge and Marley, pr. 1978, pb. 1979 (adaptation of Charles Dickens' story)

The Widow's Blind Date, pr. 1978, pb. 1982

The Wakefield Plays, pb. 1979 (includes the Alfred Trilogy—*Alfred the Great, Our Father's Failing, Alfred Dies*—and the Quannapowitt Quartet—*Hopscotch, The 75th, Stage Directions, Spared*)

Park Your Car in the Harvard Yard, pr. 1980, pb. 1993

Sunday Runners in the Rain, pr. 1980

The Good Parts, pr. 1982, pb. 1983

The Great Labor Day Classic and The Former One-on-One Basketball Champion, pb. 1982

A Rosen by Any Other Name, pr. 1986, pb. 1987 (based on the book *A Good Place to Come From* by Morley Torgov)

Today, I Am a Fountain Pen, pr. 1986, pb. 1987 (based on *A Good Place to Come From*)

North Shore Fish, pr. 1986, pb. 1989

The Chopin Playoffs, pb. 1987 (based on *A Good Place to Come From*)

Semper Fi, pr. 1987

Year of the Duck, pr. 1987, pb. 1988

Faith, Hope, and Charity, pr., pb. 1989 (with Terrence McNally and Leonard Melfi)

Henry Lumper, pr. 1989, pb. 1990

Strong-Man's Weak Child, pr. 1990, pb. 1995

Fighting Over Beverley, pr. 1993, pb. 1994

Collected Works, pb. 1994-1998 (*Volume 1: Sixteen Short Plays; Volume 2: New England Blue, Plays of Working-Class Life; Volume 3: The Primary English Class and Six New Plays; Volume 4: Two Trilogies*)

Unexpected Tenderness pb. 1994

Captains and Courage, pr. 1996, pb. 1999 (adaptation of Rudyard Kipling's *Captains Courageous*)

My Old Lady, pr. 1996, pb. 1997

Lebensraum, pr. 1996, pb. 1999

One Under, pr., pb. 1997

OTHER LITERARY FORMS

The relish with which Israel Horovitz approaches language has found its way into two novels, *Cappella* (1973) and *Nobody Loves Me* (1975), and a book of poetry, *Spider Poems and Other Writings* (1973). None of these works, however, has approached the effectiveness of his drama. *Cappella* does show a dramatist's flair for vivid monologue, but the Samuel Beckett-like stream of consciousness that pervades much of the novel is rather irritating and often impenetrable. Not surprisingly, it is Horovitz's work in film that comes closest to the level of his stage works. His first produced film script, *The Strawberry Statement* (1970), based on the book by James Simon Kunen, conveyed the atmosphere of the Columbia University student riots in the late 1960's with shrewd social and psychological observations. His next major screenplay was the frankly autobiographical *Author! Author!* (1982), one of his most humane and least ironic works. It depicts the problems of a playwright whose second wife leaves him for another man and who must then deal with five children as well as the preparation for his first Broadway play, entitled *The Reason We Eat* (one of Horovitz's own, lesser-known plays). Ivan Travalian's life and work mirror Horovitz's quite closely, but Horovitz can view his own experience with much humor, giving some satiric insights into theater production. The screenplay is filled as well with a great deal of warmth and love between Ivan and the five children (four of whom are not even biologically his). Horovitz has also written a number of plays for television, sometimes with a social message (*VD Blues*, concerning venereal disease, in 1972; *Play for Trees*, on the importance of saving trees, in 1969). His television adaptation of Herman Melville's *Bartleby the Scrivener* (1977) effectively captured the gloom and poignancy of the original. In 1978, Horovitz wrote a cycle of plays for television called *Growing Up Jewish in Sault Ste. Marie*, adaptations of Morley Torgov's novel *A Nice Place to Come From*. Also, Horovitz has contributed to a number of periodicals, most notably as a lively, refreshing, and personal art critic for *Crafts Horizons* from 1968 to 1970.

ACHIEVEMENTS

Israel Horovitz early staked out his claim to a share in the Samuel Beckett-Eugène Ionesco tradition of modern absurdity. He dramatizes the alienation of characters trapped in their own realities, often at cross-purposes, unable to communicate. Horovitz examines the violent roots of much human interaction. In his plays, submerged fears and hostilities rise to the surface and take concrete shape in often senseless acts of aggression.

Horovitz is a master of modern metropolitan malaise, yet he has also exposed the decay at work in small-town New England, setting most of his later plays either in Wakefield or Gloucester, Massachusetts. A native of Wakefield, Horovitz has returned to it in a series of plays, linked by related characters, similar themes and moods, and even repeated lines. Through these Wakefield plays, he portrays the constriction, pettiness, and desperation of life in a small town, where people are trapped for generations and where those who have escaped return only to be caught up in the same power struggles.

Horovitz's stark view of contemporary human relationships assures him a significant position in the history of Off-Broadway, a theater tradition given to intense engagement of the audience in ways diverging from the more familiar and comfortable realistic tradition of Broadway (and London's West End). Although, as a consequence, most of his plays have gone unreviewed by the national press, his work has been translated into more than twenty languages, and theaters across the United States and around the world are continually performing his plays. His keen vision earned for him Obie Awards for both *The Indian Wants the Bronx* and *The Honest-to-God Schnozzola*, both of which have also been otherwise honored, while awards have also gone to *Line*, *Rats*, and *It's Called the Sugar Plum*. As one of the creators of sketches for the television special *VD Blues*, he received an Emmy Award, and his script for *The Strawberry Statement* won for him the Cannes Film Festival Prix du Jury. Other awards and honors include an American Academy Award, a Rockefeller Fellowship, the Vernon Rice Award, a Drama Desk Award, a National Endowment for the Arts Fellowship, and a

Fulbright Fellowship. In 1980, he founded and became the producer and artistic director of the Gloucester Stage Company in his hometown of Gloucester, Massachusetts. He often directs his own plays at his own and other theaters; *Strong-Man's Weak Child* was produced in Los Angeles under his direction in 1991.

Horovitz's plays and performances have had an impact on the world of drama, films, and television, particularly in regard to acting: Many important and successful actors and actresses received their big break in Horovitz's plays. In the first New York City production of a Horovitz play—*Line*, produced by Ellen Stewart at Cafè La Mama in 1967—John Cazale got his first break, playing Dolan. Ann Wedgeworth played Molly. Because the actor playing Stephen left at the last minute to star in a television pilot, Horovitz was forced to play the part. Horovitz was nervous and got the first line of the play wrong. He yelled out "Line!" when the first line was supposed to be "Is this a line?" The stage manager, Bonnie Frindel Morris, yelled out the correct line; the audience approved, not realizing that it was a correction, but instead thinking that the play was self-conscious and perhaps avant-garde; thus began Horovitz's debut. Horovitz was later replaced by another unknown actor, who thus got his big break—Richard Dreyfuss. Dreyfuss also appeared in Horovitz's *Rats*. *Line*, appearing at the Thirteenth Street Repertory Theater, became the longest running Off-Broadway play of all time. *It's Called the Sugar Plum* initially starred Marsha Mason, who was then replaced by Jill Clayburgh, both of whom were unknown at the time. When *The Indian Wants the Bronx* was first staged, Horovitz selected a janitor who was trying to break into the acting profession (Al Pacino) to play the role of Murph, but the producer refused. Horovitz insisted passionately that Pacino, who at the time was not a member of Actors Equity, get the role, which he finally did. Cazale played opposite Pacino as Joey. For *The Indian Wants the Bronx*, Pacino won an Obie for Best Actor, Cazale for Distinguished Actor, and Horovitz for Best Play. The play was instrumental in making Horovitz's career a success. Scott Glenn made a name for himself as Bobby in *Rats*, Jill Eikenberry as Margy in *The Widow's Blind Date*, Hervé Villéchaize as Coffee in

Israel Horovitz at his Greenwich Village townhouse in 1986.
(AP/Wide World Photos)

The Honest-to-God Schnozzola, and Swoosie Kurtz as Elsa and Lenny Barker as Will in *Hopscotch*.

BIOGRAPHY

Israel Horovitz was born in Wakefield, Massachusetts, a town of more than twenty thousand people not far from Boston. Its impact on him is clear in much of his later work—notably *The Wakefield Plays* and *The Widow's Blind Date*, with their evocation of a stifling small-town atmosphere. Although one source, *Contemporary Authors* (1978), says that his father, Julius Charles Horovitz, was a lawyer, a 1982 interview in *New York* indicates that his father was a truck driver. Bright but lower-middle-class, Horovitz did not attend college. When asked in 1972 to teach playwriting at City College of New York, he listed on his employment form, "Harvard, B.A." for his college education. When this falsification was discovered, Horovitz lost the job. Comparison of various biographical sketches in his published works and other sources reveals a number of discrepancies.

Horovitz's first play, *The Comeback*, was written when Horovitz was seventeen and was produced in Boston in 1958, when he was nineteen. He continued to write and to have plays produced throughout the early 1960's. During this period, he was a fellow in playwriting at the Royal Academy of Dramatic Art and was honored as the first American to be selected as playwright-in-residence with the Royal Shakespeare Company's Aldwych Theatre, in 1965. It was not until *Line*, in 1967, however, that his work was produced in New York, by Ellen Stewart's Café La Mama, an important force in the theater scene of the 1960's. For the next two or three years, Horovitz's work was much produced and much discussed, but a hiatus came in his New York work in the early 1970's, and thereafter his work enjoyed only rare major productions there. Instead, he offered world premieres of his work to major regional theaters in Chicago, Los Angeles, and other cities, especially those in New England.

Although Horovitz early supported himself by working in an advertising agency (an experience he was able to use in *Dr. Hero*), he soon began making a satisfactory income from his writing, not only because of his early plays' striking successes but also because of his prolific output. He has written more than thirty-five plays, many of them unpublished.

Horovitz is very much a man of the theater. During the early and mid-1960's, he stage-managed in and around New York; he has directed a number of his plays; and he has even acted in several of them, sometimes replacing an actor at the last moment. He is active in groups that develop new plays and playwrights, and he has taught playwriting at New York University as well as at other locations.

Horovitz's family life was revealed to audiences across the country in the 1982 film *Author! Author!*, and although certain details were changed, the spirit of the script is accurate. The film's title character has been once divorced and has custody of a son from that marriage. As the film begins, he is in the middle of a separation from his second wife, who has brought into their marriage four children from three previous marriages. Horovitz, on the other hand, was first married in 1959—to Elaine Abber—and divorced in 1960; he was married to Doris Keefe in 1960 and had three children with her, divorcing in 1972; he then married Gillian Adams, an Englishwoman sharing his love of running. Adams is a former British National Marathon champion; they have twin sons born in 1986.

ANALYSIS

In *En attendant Godot* (pb. 1952, pr. 1953; *Waiting for Godot*, 1954), Samuel Beckett created an indelible image of modern humanity: two bums cut off from any reality other than their immediate present and each other. The image of two men bound together in a mutually dependent but uncomfortable relationship was central also in Beckett's next play, *Fin de partie: Suivi de Acte sans paroles* (pr., pb. 1957; *Endgame: A Play in One Act, Followed by Act Without Words: A Mime for One Player*, 1958). The tradition continues in the work of Israel Horovitz. In his plays, the most characteristic relationship is not that of man and woman, as in Tennessee Williams and Edward Albee, nor that of parent and child, as in Eugene O'Neill and Arthur Miller. Rather, it is the relationship of two men, generally equals in age, intelligence, and social class but bound by mutual insecurity, the unrelenting need each has for reinforcement of his masculinity and his own sense of identity. Though considered friends, the two men share a deep undercurrent of hostility based on an insecurity related to both work and sex.

Such relationships in Horovitz's work, however, are not homosexual in any sense. In fact, in contrast to Lanford Wilson—who, in a 1984 issue of *The Advocate*, said, "Since 10 percent of the population is gay, then every tenth character is going to be also"—Horovitz portrays virtually no homosexuality in his work beyond the transvestite in *The Honest-to-God Schnozzola*, with whom two American executives engage in sex under the impression that the transvestite is really a woman. The disgust and shame that they feel, like the feeling of Murph in *The Indian Wants the Bronx* when he makes his friend Joey take back a joking suggestion that Murph likes men, are evidence of a fear of homosexuality underlying this kind of relationship.

THE INDIAN WANTS THE BRONX

Because of this fear, the men in Horovitz's plays find any expression of affection difficult. A moment of tenderness may occur—even in that most tension-fraught of Horovitz's plays, *The Indian Wants the Bronx*—but it is only a moment, and the "true" masculine stance, hard and aggressive, is bound to return with greater force. When Joey is left by himself at the bus stop with the non-English-speaking man from India, he begins to make friends, instead of merely taunting him, as he and Murph had been doing before. He begins confiding in the Indian, though the Indian can understand only the emotions Joey's face and voice reveal. Joey's anxiety leads the Indian to comfort him with a hug, which Joey accepts as fatherly affection. Yet Joey's propensity for violence, along with the language barrier, betrays this moment: He takes out his knife to show as a cherished possession, but the Indian interprets this act as a threat, and when the Indian begins to move surreptitiously away, Joey believes that he is going to Murph to reveal what Joey had told him in confidence. Thus, the Indian's attempted escape provokes Joey to hit him and triggers the increasing hostility that culminates in Murph's wounding the Indian's hand.

The play, Horovitz's best known and certainly one of his most powerful, is filled with ironies. Like most of Horovitz's work, it explores failed connections: Joey and Murph are friends, yet their friendship is marred by taunts and insults, signs of a constant quest to make the other seem inferior; the Indian is trying to reach his son, and here are two men in their early twenties whom he could reach (one of whom he does reach, for a moment), yet they finally offer him only hostility and bloodshed. The mutual misinterpretation from which Joey and the Indian suffer results in the exact opposite of what each of them actually wants. Most important, the knife that instigates the misunderstanding and resulting violence is actually being shown by Joey in mockery—it and another like it were given to Joey and Murph as Christ-mas presents by a girlfriend, even though Murph had been arrested for stabbing someone. Joey is not a truly violent person—much less so than Murph is—but his need to prove himself the equal of Murph, to assert his manhood, outweighs his decent instincts. Murph, too, is acting out imagined male behavior rather than his real emotional responses. Both young men, living basically aimless lives with no real hope for escape, are essentially dispossessed and seek a bogus manhood in tough behavior and aggressive action.

RATS

Compassion, in this postmodern world, simply does not pay. Jebbie, one of the title figures in the one-act *Rats*, has been enjoying a blissful coexistence with a human baby, whom he protects rather than attacks, when his territory is invaded by a younger rat, Bobby. Bobby has idolized Jebbie, and he feels betrayed when he sees that the older rat, a hero to numerous rats before him, is keeping company with the enemy. When Bobby tries to get a piece of the action (a piece of baby's flesh), Jebbie stops him—in fact strangling him in order to do so. All should therefore be well—but the baby becomes upset and yells to its parents that there are rats, thus ensuring Jebbie's death. Jebbie's compassion for the human infant is largely a matter of self-protection, a kind of middle-aged complacence and gratitude for being free from worry, struggle, and "the rat race." This desire for peace and comfort, like Joey's deprecation of violence and desire for sympathetic human contact, results ironically in a return to violence and, in Jebbie's case, to his own defeat. An ironic god is looking down and laughing at the intentions that never quite work out, and Horovitz is right there with him, finding as a touchstone these words of Beckett, which he has quoted in his film script *Author! Author!*: "The highest laugh is the laugh which laughs at that which is unhappy."

OUR FATHER'S FAILING

There is certainly plenty of unhappiness in Horovitz's plays—especially the insecurity reflected in constant one-upmanship, whether involving rats, street punks, the working class (in *The Widow's Blind Date*), the professional class (*The Good Parts*), old men in a rest home (*Our Father's Failing*), or the corporate world (*The Honest-to-God Schnozzola*, *Dr. Hero*). Some of Horovitz's funniest dialogue comes from the banter between male friends as each tries to come out on top by putting the other down. Sam and Pa, two centenarians sharing their declining years in a home for the aged (or the insane) in *Our Father's Failing*, provide the most memorable scenes in Horovitz's Alfred Trilogy, part of his longer series entitled *The Wakefield Plays*. Constantly mocking each other, cutting in on each other's jokes (far too familiar to them), and mishearing or misinterpreting each other, they provide a hilarious image of old age and the undying competition between two men whose lives have overlapped for decades. Their competition is not without its sardonic side, for it is based on secret on secret, what they are keeping from others as well as what one is keeping from the other. The long-concealed violence is bound to erupt at last, and it does, with serious repercussions. Such grim consequences—the dissolution of a lifelong friendship, disillusionment regarding other people, and the destruction of several lives—seem inevitable when competition, rather than cooperation, is the prime motivator.

Competition does produce interesting drama, and at his best, Horovitz exploits this potential to the full, dramatizing conflict through superbly observed dialogue that is often inarticulate, ungrammatical, and fragmentary, but also sharp and believable. Characters interrupt one another, stumble and hesitate, repeat themselves, very rarely engaging in typical stage rhetoric. Horovitz has clearly listened to people and their often inconsequential talk and has re-created such talk for his very ordinary characters. Through their talk, their numerous conflicts emerge.

LINE

Although competition is a major factor in many of Israel Horovitz's plays, perhaps the theme is most apparent in his drama *Line*. In this play, five characters compete to be first on line. It is unclear—and irrelevant—what the line is for specifically. One character remarks that the line is for a baseball game, while another claims that he believes the line is for a movie. Fleming, the stiff and foolish character who initially holds the first place on line, has been waiting all night even though he has no idea what the line is for. Flem-

ing, Stephen, Molly, Dolan, and Arnall then compete with reckless abandon to hold the first place on line. The voluptuous Molly even has sex with Dolan and Stephen (symbolized by dance) in her effort to pass them on line. She expresses willingness to have sex with Fleming as well, but he is too slow and thus misses his opportunity. Stephen ends up eating the line (tape), which Molly extracts from his mouth with a kiss. The characters strive to obtain their piece of the line, and they are willing to kill to garner their share. Horovitz's point concerns the competitive nature of human beings, how they are overly ambitious and consequently argue and fight over insignificant and irrelevant matters. The playwright never mentions—and the characters never discover or care about—what the line signifies because the line is extraneous; the five characters compete for first place on the line simply because it is their nature to be competitive, aggressive, and violent.

THE WIDOW'S BLIND DATE

Because much of his work deals with men's relationships to one another, and heterosexual men specifically, a major instigator of conflict and competition is the opposite sex: Friends become rivals for a woman's attentions. *The Good Parts*, for example, presents this rivalry comically, and *The Widow's Blind Date* treats the same theme with great seriousness. Here the motivating sexual rivalry is complex, rooted in the past, about twelve years before the time of the play, when George and Archie, the principal male characters, and several high school friends gang-raped Margie, now a widow, who, as the play begins, has returned to Wakefield, Massachusetts, from a sophisticated intellectual life in New York.

Margie, who has tried to forget the whole rape experience, has returned to be with her dying brother, a friend of George and Archie, and she asks Archie over for dinner, though they have not seen each other for years. George resents the attention that Archie receives from her, and Archie, recalling the distant past, resents the terrible experience of his first (and only) sexual intercourse with the girl whom he had secretly loved, when he went second in the gang-rape after George had coolly taken Margie's virginity. That the past endures is made explicit when Archie kills

George by pushing him against a sharp object that, years before, had almost killed another man with whom Archie had fought. Before Margie leaves, she tells Archie that her revenge is still not finished. In return for her gang-rape, she has destroyed not only a friendship but two men's lives.

It is generally difficult in a Horovitz play to label one character the villain because most of his characters have unappealing traits and are often to be viewed as victims, but in *The Widow's Blind Date*, it is difficult at the end to see Margie as anything but a villain. The increasing tension and violence in the two acts of the play suddenly appear as part of a revenge plot, and it is this widow—like a black widow spider—who is responsible for one man's death and the other's inevitable arrest.

Such characterizations of women are frequent in Horovitz's work. His women exist solely in relation to men; they are often motivated by a desire to get back at a man (or several men) for some sexual injustice in the past. In turn, the men in Horovitz's plays are often motivated by resentment against women, though without this same need to get back at them; they are apparently content merely to feel oppressed by women.

VIOLENCE

The resentment, conflict, and hostility pervading Horovitz's work find their inevitable result in some act of violence, or several, most frequently as the conclusion to the play—George's death in *The Widow's Blind Date*, the stabbing of the Indian's hand in *The Indian Wants the Bronx*, the shootings ending two of the Alfred plays, a hideous self-brutalization in *Stage Directions*. Horovitz's purpose is to provoke a strong reaction from his audience rather than allow them to sit back and let the play wash over them.

This provocative approach, largely a result of the influence of Edward Albee's *The Zoo Story* (pr. 1959, pb. 1960), was effective in the 1960's, when Horovitz began his career, as Albee did, Off-Broadway. A quarter-century after *The Zoo Story*, however, and nearly two decades after *The Indian Wants the Bronx*—not to mention films such as *Bonnie and Clyde* (1967), or the work of Sam Peckinpah and Francis Ford Coppola—such violence, in and of itself, is not sufficient to make a play powerful. David

Rabe and Sam Shepard, in plays such as *Streamers* (pr. 1976, pb. 1977), *In the Boom Boom Room* (pr. 1974, pb. 1975), *Curse of the Starving Class* (pb. 1976, pr. 1977), and *True West* (pr. 1980, pb. 1981), can revivify the use of violence by giving it mythic or sociological resonance, but the violence in *The Wakefield Plays*, for example, is both predictable and inadequately prepared for by emotional involvement with the characters. Horovitz's work is more potent when presenting instead the psychic violence people inflict on one another.

A Rosen by Any Other Name examines the effects of such psychic violence on a Jewish Canadian family during World War II. Barney Rosen, the family's father, seeks to change the family name to Royal in order to ward off anti-Semitism. Stanley, Barney's adolescent son, is mortified by his father's efforts and by his own approaching Bar Mitzvah, but he nevertheless finds a way to outwit his father and keep his own name. *North Shore Fish*, a social realist look at the day-to-day operations of a fish-packing plant, depicts a foreman who uses the power of his position to extort sexual favors from his female employees.

Horovitz is too much a realist—absurdist though he may be—to show his audiences a world where destructive competition does not prevail, yet he is capable of evoking real warmth and love, most notably in his screenplay *Author! Author!*, which depicts father-child relationships in a manner both touching and credible. Thus, his sardonic vision of the world is leavened with compassion.

LEBENSRAUM

Horovitz's last several plays have not garnered the success of his earlier plays such as *The Indian Wants the Bronx* and *Line*. Of his latest plays, the only success has been *Lebensraum*, and the others have not received major productions. *Lebensraum* appeared in an Off-Broadway production in October, 1997, and was published in 1999. *Lebensraum* (German for "living space") originated from Horovitz's decision to come to terms with his phobia of Germans. Beginning at the age of five, the playwright experienced a fear that Nazi soldiers would invade his house and murder him and his family. When he finally visited Germany, Horovitz confronted his fear and began asking questions about how Germans felt about Jews. He was appalled to discover that many people in Germany today have never interacted with—or even met—Jews. Consequently, Horovitz constructed a play in which the German chancellor decided that in order to appease the terrible sense of guilt that German citizens have inherited because of the atrocities of their parents and grandparents, six million Jews from around the world would be invited to Germany to live and be awarded immediate citizenship. The play focuses on the reaction to and the results of Chancellor Stroiber's experiment. In an effort to be unique in respect to the significant and special subject matter—the Holocaust—Horovitz includes only two actors and one actress to play the parts—all forty-two of them. In a series of vignettes, Horovitz shifts back and forth between characters. The result is mixed because although the style of the play is unique, the drama can become confusing to an audience because the actors and actress are constantly changing the roles that they play.

The violence in the play manifests the bitter feelings that might exist if such an experiment indeed took place. Horovitz portrays the bitterness of German citizens, who express anger over the guilt with which they feel that they have been unfairly saddled. Jews around the world experience various emotions, including suspicion, disbelief, and bitterness. Dock worker Mike Linsky, a nonreligious Jew, sees the experiment as a source of hope and a brighter future. He moves his family to Germany, against their wishes, and finds instant success and even becomes a celebrity. However, his success is at the expense of German dock workers, who become very upset and violent because he takes one of their jobs and then, when placed in a supervisory role, hires only Jews. In the most poignant scene, Maximillian Zylberstein returns to Germany and, in particular, to the Krebs home, where he visits and becomes the caretaker for the old woman (Uta Krebs) who, decades before, informed on his family to the Nazis. Zylberstein had wanted for years to murder the woman, now a senseless invalid, but instead, he punishes her by urinating on her carpet and devoting his time to telling her how she has ruined his life and the lives of others, such as Tanta

Elke. Zylberstein's punishment of Krebs is powerful to some extent but also impotent. The Stroiber experiment turns out to be a failure because the resentment and suspicion that exist between Germans and Jews have failed to subside.

OTHER MAJOR WORKS

LONG FICTION: *Cappella*, 1973; *Nobody Loves Me*, 1975.

POETRY: *Spider Poems and Other Writings*, 1973.

SCREENPLAYS: *The Strawberry Statement*, 1970 (adaptation of James Simon Kunen's book); *Alfredo*, 1970; *Believe in Me*, 1970; *Machine Gun McCain*, 1970; *Acrobats*, 1972 (adaptation of his play); *Author! Author!*, 1982; *A Man in Love*, 1987; *Sunshine*, 1994.

TELEPLAYS: *Play for Trees*, 1969; *VD Blues*, 1972 (as *Play for Germs*, pb. 1973); *The Making and Breaking of Splinters Braun*, 1975; *Start to Finish*, 1975; *Bartleby the Scrivener*, 1977 (adaptation of Herman Melville's story); *Growing Up Jewish in Sault Ste. Marie*, 1978 (adaptations of Morley Torgov's novel *A Nice Place to Come From*); *James Dean*, 2001.

BIBLIOGRAPHY

Cohn, Ruby. *New American Dramatists: 1960-1990*. 1982. 2d ed. New York: St. Martin's Press, 1991. In this update of the 1982 edition, Cohn places Horovitz with Jack Gelber, Jean-Claude van Itallie, Megan Terry, and Maria Irene Fornes as "actor-activated" playwrights because Horovitz was active in the Royal Academy of Dramatic Arts (RADA) and because, working closely with actors, he often wrote plays that became vehicles for the actors' rise to stardom.

DiGaetani, John L. *A Search for a Postmodern Theater: Interviews with Contemporary Playwrights*. New York: Greenwood, 1991. Horovitz speaks affectionately of his theater, the Gloucester Stage Company. With prompting, he runs through his repertory, citing his favorite plays and summarizing the themes. *Year of the Duck*, which "got almost no notice in New York," dramatizes some of his own theaiter experiences in the guise of a rehearsal of Henrik Ibsen's *The Wild Duck* (pr., pb. 1884).

Haedicke, Susan C. "Doing the Dirty Work: Gendered Versions of Working Class Women in Sarah Daniels' *The Gut Girls* and Israel Horovitz's *North Shore Fish*." *Journal of Dramatic Theory and Criticism* 8, no. 2 (1994): 77-88. Haedicke compares the Horovitz play with that of Sarah Daniels and mentions that although Horovitz's drama is clearly sympathetic to women, the playwright portrays the women and provides their dialogue from a male perspective.

Horovitz, Israel. "Tragedy." In *Playwrights, Lyricists, Composers on Theater*, edited by Otis L. Guernsey, Jr. New York: Dodd, Mead, 1974. This excerpt from *The Dramatists Guild Quarterly* describes stage tragedy as "grand fiction" that "can take its audience to the outer limits of human possibility." Although Horovitz's work is not discussed here, this piece, especially in the middle section on tragedy in the modern theater, is revealing of Horovitz's use of "the opposition of conflicting goods."

Kane, Leslie, ed. *Israel Horovitz: A Collection of Critical Essays*. Westport, Conn.: Greenwood, 1994. Kane's book is unquestionably the best source available on Horovitz criticism. The book contains a wide variety of topics, including violence and homosexuality, the influence of Samuel Beckett, and ethnicity. Kane provides an informative interview that she conducted with Horovitz, as well as an excellent essay that she wrote on the author's *The Widow's Blind Date*.

Miller, Daryl H. "Horovitz Pledges Stronger Allegiance." *Daily News* (Los Angeles), June 4, 1990. Fine-tuning his script of *Strong-Man's Weak Child* at the Los Angeles Theatre Center, Horovitz discusses the play's setting in Gloucester and the rest of the nine-play series used "to represent the contemporary American experience." Normally premiered in Gloucester, these plays represent an ongoing statement of Horovitz's view of life.

Raidy, William A. "Tireless Energy." *Star-Ledger* (Newark, N.J.), December 1, 1991. Comparing the "tireless marathon runner" (Horovitz's hobby for many years was running) with the playwright's prolific career, Raidy places him in the Gloucester environment, which Horovitz says is "a metaphor for life on this earth." Good personal glimpses of the playwright, plus comments on his friendship with Samuel Beckett.

Rosenberg, Scott. "Coming of Age—with a Twist." *San Francisco Examiner*, January 14, 1992. *A Rosen by Any Other Name*, being produced at the Mountain View Center for the Performing Arts, is the springboard for this review, which examines Horovitz's moral: "If your heritage is under attack, the last thing you should do is deny it." Notes the "wry humor rather than soapbox rhetoric" of the piece.

Scott Giantvalley,
updated by Thomas J. Taylor,
Robert McClenaghan, and Eric Sterling

ÖDÖN VON HORVÁTH

Born: Fiume, Italy (now Rijeka, Yugoslavia); December 9, 1901
Died: Paris, France; June 1, 1938

PRINCIPAL DRAMA

Das Buch der Tänze, pb. 1922, pr. 1926
Revolte auf Côte 3018, pr. 1927
Die Bergbahn, pb. 1927, pr. 1929 (revision of his *Revolte auf Côte 3018*)
Sladek der schwarze Reichswehrmann, pr., pb. 1929 (*Sladek*, 2000)
Italienische Nacht, pb. 1930, pr. 1931 (*Italian Night*, 2000)
Geschichten aus dem Wiener Wald, pr., pb. 1931 (*Tales from the Vienna Woods*, 1977)
Kasimir und Karoline, pr., pb. 1932
Die Unbekannte aus der Seine, wr. 1933, pr. 1949

Glaube Liebe Hoffnung: Ein Kleiner Totentanz,
   pb. 1933, pr. 1936 (*Faith, Hope, and Charity: A
   Little Dance of Death in Five Acts*, 1989)
Himmelwärts, pb. 1934, pr. 1937
Hin und Her, pr., pb. 1934
Mit dem Kopf durch die Wand, pr., pb. 1935
Don Juan kommt aus dem Krieg, wr. 1936, pr. 1952
   (*Don Juan Comes Back from the War*, 1978)
Figaro lässt sich scheiden, pr., pb. 1937 (*Figaro
   Gets Divorced*, 1991)
Ein Dorf ohne Männer, pr., pb. 1937
Pompeji, wr. 1937, pr. 1959
Plays One, pb. 2000
Plays Two, pb. 2000

OTHER LITERARY FORMS

Ödön von Horváth wrote a number of prose pieces
and sketches as well as three short novels: *Der ewige
Spiesser* (1930), *Jugend ohne Gott* (1938; *Youth
Without God*, 1938), and *Ein kind unserer Zeit* (1938;
A Child of Our Time, 1938).

ACHIEVEMENTS

A passionate social moralist with a keen sense of
satire and irony, Ödön von Horváth was considered
an undesirable individual by Adolf Hitler's National
Socialists and his work was on the Nazi index of
banned books. He was extremely critical of the hypocrisy and falsity that he saw in the middle-class
society around him (especially with regard to issues
such as the societal mistreatment of workers, sexuality, and the often exploitative relations between
men and women), and it became the expressed intention of his writing to "unmask the false consciousness" (*Demaskierung des Bewusstseins*) or the self-
delusion that veiled such injustices in the minds of
those who perpetrated them. He accomplished this
with great skill and success. Equipped with an ear
for the speech and language habits of the German/
Austrian middle and lower-middle classes as well as
a keen psychological insight into human motivations,
Horváth exposed the often vicious and cunning motives behind the beautiful and noble sentiments expressed in the words of everyday conversation, and he
did so with a sly and devastating sense of humor.

In order to appreciate the full achievement of Horváth's dramatic art, one must realize that his major
works stand within two important traditions in Ger-
man-Austrian culture. First, he revitalized and modified in his plays the nineteenth century Viennese genre
of the *Volksstück*, or popular folk play, which used the
linguistic expressions and dialect of the people. These
pieces were often rather sentimental and trite, but in
the hands of more skilled writers such as Johann
Nestroy and Ludwig Anzengruber, they contained elements of satire and social criticism. Second, Horváth's writings should also be seen within the larger
context of the twentieth century philosophical and
aesthetic movement of language criticism (also centered in Vienna), most prominently associated with the
drama critic turned philosopher Fritz Mauthner, the
poet and playwright Hugo von Hofmannsthal, and the
well-known philosopher Ludwig Wittgenstein. The
thought of these individuals evidences not only a profound skepticism concerning the ability of language to
reflect reality accurately but also a suspicion that linguistic forms are themselves a major component of
human perception and may even falsify the reality that
one does perceive. Horváth's *Volksstück* draw on both
of these traditions, focusing on ordinary, lower-middle-
class people and on the ways in which their use of
language (which Horváth labeled *Bildungsjargon*)—
in the form of pretentious clichés, trite proverbs, and
popular sentimental platitudes—shapes and distorts
their perception of themselves and of others. Voicing
the most tired romantic clichés or the most idealistic
sentiments, his characters—particularly the males—
often perform vicious and egotistic acts that reveal
the hypocrisy and emptiness of their words. The
ironic and satiric thrust of Horváth's writing consists
in this unmasking of the false consciousness of his
figures. His intention as a dramatist is essentially a
moral one: He seeks to create a society in which honesty and sincerity—not falsity and duplicity—are the
guidelines for human relationships.

Horváth's most important plays were written during the last years of the Weimar Republic, before Hitler's rise to power. They present great psychological
insight into the social and spiritual malaise that
plagued that society and that, in part at least, allowed

the advent of National Socialism and the horrors that it subsequently unleashed. Horváth is thus of great significance as both a chronicler of a pivotal period in European history and a moral commentator on the human spirit. Although his plays were well received during his lifetime, there was little scholarly attention to his work until the 1960's and 1970's. He has been an influence on the modern Austrian writer Peter Handke and on writers of the contemporary *Volksstück* such as Martin Sperr and Franz Xaver Kroetz.

BIOGRAPHY

Ödön von Horváth was born in 1901 to upper-middle-class parents, the son of a diplomat. Because of the father's occupation, the family moved frequently during Horváth's early years, and he resided in various cities in the Austro-Hungarian Empire and in Germany, such as Belgrade, Budapest, Munich, and Vienna. In 1919, he attended the University of Munich for several semesters, and in 1924 he moved to Berlin, where his early plays met with some success and he gained a reputation as a talented dramatist. Performances of his work also began to attract the vigorous protests of the National Socialists in the late 1920's. In 1931—on the recommendation of the well-known playwright Carl Zuckmayer—Horváth was awarded the coveted Kleist Prize. He left·Germany in 1933, after Hitler's election, and moved to Budapest and then to Vienna. When Austria joined the Nazi Reich in 1938, Horváth went into exile in Paris. On June 1, 1938, he met a bizarre and untimely death: He sought shelter under a tree on the Champs-Élysées during a thunderstorm and was killed by a falling branch. He is buried in Paris.

ANALYSIS

Ödön von Horváth's corrosive wit, his skeptical treatment of language, and his awareness (before the feminist revolution) of feminist issues make him a valuable resource for playwrights in the late twentieth century, many of whom see in his works a prescient expression of their own concerns.

ITALIAN NIGHT

Horváth's most successful plays were his *Volksstück* written between 1930 and 1932. His first major

work in this style, the satiric comedy *Italian Night*, received highly positive reviews from liberal theater critics and was roundly condemned in the Nazi press. The text consists of seven scenes without traditional act divisions. Set in a provincial small town in Southern Germany (Bavaria) around 1930, the play satirizes the political climate of the time. A group (which includes the town's mayor) of democratic supporters of the Weimar Republic are planning a big party—a festive "Italian Night"—at their local pub. Much to their chagrin, they learn in the first scene that the enterprising owner of the restaurant has also rented the place for that afternoon to the town's group of National Socialists, who are celebrating a solemn "German Day" with a nationalistic parade and nighttime military maneuvers. As the play opens, the mayor's group is playing cards in the pub and discussing their evening's events. One of their members, a politically intense young man named Martin, angrily reveals the plans of the Nazi group and suggests that they should take more aggressive action. The mayor responds with an impressive sounding but vague and pretentious answer about how the reactionary elements lack any real ideological basis. This is a good example of *Bildungsjargon*, a seemingly educated but actually meaningless use of language that masks the mayor's basic lack of concern. The Weimar supporters do not seem to regard the National Socialists as a genuine threat. The mayor and the others have little interest in politics and are really concerned only with eating, drinking, and having a good time. Horváth comments satirically here not only on the political complacency of the German middle classes at the time—a fact that would lead a few years later to the collapse of the Weimar government and the takeover of the Hitler regime—but also on the extent to which politics (or all social behavior for that matter) is linked to basic and unconscious psychological drives and desires (eros/pleasure in its broadest Freudian sense). The theme of the political versus the erotic is prominent throughout the play. Karl, another militant younger member of the group, cannot, for example, separate his political commitment from his attraction to the opposite sex. Horváth thus also takes up the pervasive theme of male-female relationships. This theme is apparent in the first scene, in the mayor's crass comments about his wife.

The second scene opens with two women watching members of the National Socialist group parade past in their military uniforms. The older of the two women is greatly impressed by the spectacle—with an erotic fascination—and she voices worn-out political clichés concerning Germany and World War I. The younger woman, Leni, then meets Karl, who asks her to accompany him to the party that night. Karl is later confronted by Martin, who considers Leni to be politically uncommitted. Karl tries to mask his erotic intentions by suggesting that she is sympathetic to their cause. He then attempts to excuse himself by claiming that Martin, as a laborer, cannot understand his individualistic and artistic nature, which compels him to seek erotic adventure as aesthetic stimulation. Karl's words are a virtual listing of trite and sentimentalized bourgeois notions of the artistic personality. In this dialogue, Horváth ironically exposes the falsity of Karl's reasoning. His idealized and romantic notions mask the more elemental erotic drives that motivate his actions. At the end of this scene, Horváth makes the psychological implications of the play explicit by having Betz, one of Martin's group, discuss Sigmund Freud and the relationship of desire, aggression, and social behavior.

The themes of the interaction of men and women and the interrelationship of politics and the erotic are continued in the third scene. Martin meets his girlfriend Anna in the park. Concerned solely with his duty as a political leader, he treats her brusquely, rejecting her attempts at affection. After Martin leaves, Karl learns from Anna that Martin intends for her to have a sexual encounter with one of the Nazis so that he can gather information about the type of weapons they carry, making her, as Karl aptly expresses it, into a kind of political prostitute. Horváth points in satiric fashion to what he sees as the fundamental exploitation that often underlies the relationship of the middle-class couple. Conditioned to feel inferior and worthless, the woman accepts such treatment and continues to idolize the man. This type of relationship is a frequent theme in Horváth's plays. Anna sees nothing wrong in Martin's request and feels gratitude that he has "elevated" her. Karl then meets Leni, and they have a discussion about politics. Leni is not at all interested in political issues and is concerned only with marriage. Karl voices a number of trite (but unfortunately, in view of German history, somewhat accurate) notions concerning the traditional German apathy toward politics, seeking to give the impression that he is interested in more than the merely sexual. In the end, however, his desire for Leni wins over his political scruples.

The fourth scene opens with several of Martin's group painting the statue of the state leader red in an attempt to infuriate the National Socialists. Meanwhile, Anna has met one of the Nazi group, and they stroll through the park. The man voices the conservative ideology of the Fascists. In one of the most comic passages of the play, he decries Jewish socialism and its "materialist" philosophy while simultaneously attempting to molest Anna. With such a humorous juxtaposition, Horváth reveals the discrepancy between language and action that is characteristic of so-called civilized behavior. When the Nazi suddenly sees the defiled statue, he is so incensed that he finally stops molesting Anna.

In the fifth scene, the National Socialists celebrate their "German Day," and Horváth satirically rehearses the standard Nazi rhetoric about Germany's enemies (the French, the English, and the Bolsheviks). After the National Socialists leave, the Weimar supporters enter with their "Italian Night." As a protest gesture, Martin and his group refuse to dance. Karl, however, is finally "persuaded" by Leni. Again there is an instance of the discrepancy between words and behavior that is so characteristic of Horváth's ironic "unmasking" of the false consciousness in his characters: Karl speaks to Leni of having given his word to Martin and the others that he would not dance—and a man's "word of honor" is a sacred thing—but at the same time, he is fondling her with his hand, and soon he unconsciously begins to dance with her. The dialogue between the mayor and his wife, Adele, reveals the often cruel suppression of women within the middle-class family structure as well as the hypocrisy of its social behavior. The mayor tries to present the image to others that he is a loving and concerned husband while he viciously seeks to silence his protesting wife. He attempts to mask the violence of his behavior by citing a famous quote about women from the philosopher Friedrich Nietzsche. (This is another good example of Horváth's use of the *Bildungsjargon* of the middle classes.) The evening ends in a hostile debate between Martin and the mayor over the Weimar group's lack of response to the threat of the National Socialists. The issues involved, although treated in a humorous manner, are serious indeed. In a prophetic fashion, Horváth focuses precisely on the apathy and blithe lack of concern that characterized the Weimar democratic parties' response to the rise of Fascism in Germany during the late 1920's and early 1930's.

In the sixth scene, Martin learns from Anna, who has been intimate with one of the Nazis, that they are planning to disrupt the "Italian Night" party and beat up the Weimar group because of the defiled statue in the park. Although he tries to mask his emotions with socialist rhetoric, Martin is somewhat jealous that Anna has had an affair with another man. Karl is asked to leave the group of younger radicals because of his lack of political commitment. The final scene of the play begins with the mayor and his fellows playing cards at the pub after the party has dispersed. Again the mayor reveals his true self in his callous treatment of his wife. She voices the truth about him when she declares that although he publicly proclaims sympathy with the proletariat and the worker, he has exploited her at home for the thirty years of their marriage. (Horváth's female characters are often the true voices of reason and humanity in his plays.) Ironically, the mayor's wife saves him at the end when the Nazis enter the restaurant, planning to assault him and his friends. She chases them out, and they leave as Martin and his group approach. The play ends on a comic note—one that particularly irked the Nazi press—but as with all Horváth's plays, one is left with a disquieting sense that all is not as right as it seems.

TALES FROM THE VIENNA WOODS

Tales from the Vienna Woods is the most famous of Horváth's *Volksstück*. It consists of three parts made up of individual scenes. The premiere performance in Berlin featured the young actor Peter Lorre and received excellent press reviews. In this play, set in Vienna and the surrounding area around 1930, Horváth satirizes the mentality of the Austrian lower-middle classes. The action opens with strains of a Johann Strauss waltz, which suggests the kitsch, sentimental sensibility of the characters. (Horváth uses such music throughout the play as a means of ironic commentary.) Alfred has brought his new girlfriend, Valerie, to meet his mother and grandmother, who live out in the country. Their conversation, however, centers not on love but on money and whether this will be a financially profitable marriage opportunity. The economic situation in Europe was very poor at the time Horváth wrote the play; recession and unemployment were felt by everyone, especially the lower-middle classes. Thus, in the opening scene, Horváth suggests a theme similar to that seen in *Italian Night*: One's crasser instincts often overcome one's presumably more noble sentiments.

The next scene shifts to the lower-middle-class district of Vienna and features the two rather crude butchers Oskar and Havlitschek. The latter's comment concerning one of the store's female customers again raises Horváth's theme of violence and the exploitation of women. Marianne, who helps run her father's doll store, enters the scene. She is a kind young woman. Oskar is planning their engagement and asks her for a kiss, though in his coarseness he bites her (again a suggestion of suppressed violence). The two talk to each other, as do all the characters, in meaningless clichés, which Horváth accentuates by periodically inserting the word "silence" in the stage directions. These pauses in the dialogue are intended to reveal the emptiness in the minds of the speakers.

Alfred comes to visit Valerie, who owns a small tobacco shop on the street. He sees Marianne, and the two seem very attracted to each other. He then purposely begins an argument with Valerie. The next scene is of a picnic on the Danube that is to celebrate the engagement of Oskar and Marianne. Alfred ends his relationship with Valerie and begins talking with Marianne. Speaking of marriage, he asserts that the financial independence of the husband and the financial dependence of the wife are "natural laws" or a matter of "fate." With these trite and yet very commonly accepted notions, he confuses the natural, biological differences between men and women with the social roles that are the product of specific historical and sociological developments. Horváth's goal is for the audience to realize the difference as well as the fact that such social roles can be changed. In this respect, his drama is very close to that of his German contemporary, Bertolt Brecht, whose works are intended to make the audience aware that circumstances can be altered, that mutual exploitation is not an inevitable consequence of human nature but a result of social conditions.

The theme of the exploitation of women is also continued in this episode when Oskar practices his judo holds on Marianne, and in the clichéd speech given by Marianne's father about his deceased wife. He shows his own egocentric feelings and seems to have had little empathy for her problems. He then tries to seduce Valerie. With the figure of Erich, the visiting student from Germany, Horváth also satirizes the rigid Prussian mentality, so different from the more relaxed attitudes of the Austrians. In the next scene, the picnic continues. Alfred and Marianne speak in sentimental and romantic clichés about love, and he kisses her. The first part ends with Marianne breaking her engagement to Oskar.

The second part begins with a misogynistic conversation between Oskar and Havlitschek. In the second scene, the audience learns that Marianne and Alfred have lived together for a year, that they have a child, and that Alfred is unemployed; Marianne supports them both by working in her father's store. Alfred's treatment of her is crude and manipulative. In the course of the third scene, in which Alfred and a friend are playing cards, it becomes clear that the relationship has gone sour and that they are extremely poor; their child is with Alfred's mother in the country. Because Marianne is interested in dance and gymnastics, the friend suggests that she try to get a job dancing in an "elegant establishment" owned by his acquaintance. This is a euphemism for a nightclub in which there is nude dancing. In the next scene, Marianne, unaware of what kind of job it really is, tries out and is accepted. That Alfred would permit

such a thing indicates his callous attitude and suggests again Horváth's theme of male mistreatment of women. During the fifth scene, Alfred visits his mother and grandmother, who are resentful of having to take care of his child without payment. They tell him to move to France, where economic conditions are better. The sixth scene is set back in Vienna; Alfred meets Valerie, from whom he tries to borrow money. The next scene shows Marianne going to church to confess her "wrongdoings," and here Horváth illustrates the cruelty and repression that can be a part of rigid religious doctrine: The priest demands that Marianne show contrition for having borne her child out of wedlock, but because of her strong love for the child, she is unable to regret its birth, and she is sent away without absolution.

The third part takes place during the annual Austrian celebration of the year's wine harvest, a time of celebration and festivity. Horváth satirizes in the first scene the sentimentalized nostalgia of the Viennese for their city and culture. The drunken revelers sing all the clichéd songs about their "beloved Vienna." They all then decide to go to Maxim's, unaware that this is the disreputable nightclub where Marianne performs in a nude revue. In this nightclub episode, Horváth gives another example of the pretentiousness with which society often tries to mask its baser motives and desires. Although the show is a crass exploitation of female nudity, the nightclub announcer introduces it with ceremonious allusions to Johann Wolfgang von Goethe. During the proceedings, Marianne appears and is recognized by her father, Valerie, and the others. When she tries to explain, she is denounced for her "shameful" behavior and labeled a "whore." That she has acted out of poverty and desperation is not considered in the hypocritical condemnations of her father and the others. Marianne's options in life are slowly being eliminated, and the tragic conclusion of the play becomes apparent. The second scene shows Alfred again with his mother and grandmother, from whom he tries to borrow money for the second time. They have a violent argument, and he leaves. Marianne's child, Leopold, is ill, and Alfred's mother reveals that the grandmother has left his window open at night. With such an example of blatant cruelty, Horváth shows the depths to which human beings can fall in their greed and lust for revenge. In the third scene, one of the drunken customers in the nightclub has accused Marianne of stealing money, and she has been arrested and is in jail. Alfred and Oskar commiserate with each other and express a hypocritical feeling of pity for Marianne. Seeing an economic advantage to be gained, Alfred begins to court Valerie again. The motives for the characters' behavior are so transparent that the situation becomes humorous; it is through this painful humor that Horváth seeks to bring awareness to the audience. The final scene of the play has Marianne visiting Alfred's mother and grandmother, where she learns that her child has died. The tragedy completely crushes her spirit. Oskar, who will now marry her, leads her offstage. The portrait of the Austrian lower-middle classes that Horváth gives in *Tales from the Vienna Woods* is one of viciousness, greed, and pettiness masked by stupidity, pretentiousness, and sentimentality.

Faith, Hope, and Charity

Faith, Hope, and Charity is another of Horváth's central *Volksstück*. The scheduled premiere in 1933 in Berlin was forbidden by the National Socialists, and it was finally produced in Vienna in 1936. The play's subtitle means "a little dance of death in five parts." It begins with Elizabeth, the impoverished heroine, who goes to the Anatomical Institute in the mistaken belief that she can sell her body in advance for the use of science. She tells one of the attendants that she needs the money in order to purchase a special working permit. The scene is an ironic commentary on the poverty and desperation experienced by the lower-middle classes during the economic crisis of the late 1920's and early 1930's in Germany and Austria.

In the second part, Elizabeth is at her job in a store specializing in ladies' undergarments. Her boss criticizes her poor sales record. One of the Institute employees, who has lent Elizabeth the money she needed, enters and claims that she deceived him when she said that her father was a customs inspector. It is then revealed that she did not need the money for a work permit but rather for the court fine that she had to pay when she was arrested for not having had

the proper working permit. Because of this arrest record, she is fired from her job. The irony of the situation is clear, and it becomes apparent that Horváth is criticizing the stupidity and inhumanity of the bureaucracy that condemns Elizabeth. In the third part, she is at the Welfare office and has spent fourteen days in jail. She meets a policeman named Alfons, and their conversation is another listing of tired expressions and clichés that mask their sexual interest in each other. An older woman advises her that she should marry so that she can achieve a measure of security. The position of women in a largely male-dominated society again becomes a major theme in this work. Horváth's portrayal of men is, as in the other plays, rather negative; as Elizabeth says earlier, all men are crass egotists.

The fourth part takes place in Elizabeth's room. She and Alfons have obviously slept together. Alfons's words suggest an attitude toward women that is typical of the lower-middle-class male, as in his comment that he values a woman who is dependent on him more than one who is not. The chief inspector of the vice squad comes to check on Elizabeth's source of income. Worried about his career as a policeman, Alfons denounces her. In the last part, the attendants from the Anatomical Institute as well as Alfons and some other policemen are together when someone yells that a woman has thrown herself into the river in a suicide attempt. A man rescues her, and it is Elizabeth. The crass attitude of the men is suggested by the fact that her rescuer is interested only in getting his picture in the newspaper and getting some attention for his firm. The men try to give Elizabeth courage to go on living but merely recite trite platitudes about life and hope. When she recognizes that one of the policemen is Alfons, she becomes enraged and denounces him for the cad and egotist that he is. The intensity of her emotions is such that her heart gives out and she dies; the men react with indifference.

Other major works

LONG FICTION: *Der ewige Spiesser*, 1930; *Jugend ohne Gott*, 1938 (*Youth Without God*, 1938); *Ein Kind unserer Zeit*, 1938 (*A Child of Our Time*, 1938).

BIBLIOGRAPHY

Balme, Christopher B. *The Reformation of Comedy: Genre Critique in the Comedies of Ödön von Horváth*. Dunedin, New Zealand: Department of German, University of Otago, 1985. A study of the comedies of Horváth.

Bance, Alan, and Ian Huish, eds. *Ödön von Horváth, Fifty Years On: Horváth Symposium, London, 1988*. London: Institute of Germanic Studies, 1988. A collection of essays in English and German on Horváth's life and works. Bibliography.

Beardsworth, Robert. *From Virgin to Witch: The Male Mythology of the Female Unmasked in the Works of Ödön von Horváth*. Stuttgart, Germany: H.-D. Heinz, 1991. An examination of the women characters in the works of Horváth.

Carstens, Belinda Horton. *Prostitution in the Works of Ödön von Horváth*. Stuttgart, Germany: H.-D. Heinz, 1982. A study of Horváth's dramas, with the emphasis on his treatment of prostitution. Bibliography and index.

Gussow, Mel. "Examing the Dark Flower that Was Weimar Culture." *New York Times Current Events Edition*, October 23, 1991, p. C17. An account of the Classics in Context festival, on Weimar culture, at the Actors Theater of Louisville in Louisville, Kentucky, in October, 1991. Contains an overview of the works of Horváth and Bertolt Brecht.

Hampton, Christopher. *Tales from Hollywood*. Boston: Faber and Faber, 1983. An examination of the drama of Horváth.

Thomas Barry

BRONSON HOWARD

Born: Detroit, Michigan; October 7, 1842
Died: Avon-by-the-Sea, New Jersey; August 4, 1908

PRINCIPAL DRAMA

Saratoga: Or, Pistols for Seven, pr. 1870, pb. c. 1870 (also known as *Brighton*)
Diamonds, pr. 1872
Hurricanes, wr. 1873, pr. 1878, pb. 1941
Moorcroft: Or, The Double Wedding, pr. 1874
Old Love Letters, pr. 1878, pb. 1897
The Banker's Daughter, pr., pb. 1878 (revised; originally as *Lillian's Last Love*, pr. 1873)
Wives, pr. 1879 (adaptation of Molière's plays *The School for Husbands* and *The School for Wives*)
Knave and Queen, wr. 1882(?), pb. 1941 (with Sir Charles L. Young)
Young Mrs. Winthrop, pr. 1882, pb. c. 1899
One of Our Girls, pr. 1885, pb. 1897
Baron Rudolph, pr. 1887, pb. 1941 (with David Belasco)
The Henrietta, pr. 1887, pb. 1901 (revised by Winchell Smith and Victor Mapes as *The New Henrietta*, pr. 1913)
Met by Chance, pr. 1887
Shenandoah, pr. 1888, pb. 1897
Aristocracy, pr. 1892, pb. 1898
Peter Stuyvesant, pr. 1899 (with Brander Matthews)
The Banker's Daughter and Other Plays, pb. 1941

OTHER LITERARY FORMS

Bronson Howard is remembered primarily as a dramatist. Given his place as the first American to make a profession of writing plays, his comments on playwriting and the theater in America are important for the student of American dramatic literature. In 1906, for example, he surveyed, in New York's *Sunday Magazine*, the accomplishments of American playwrights and their critics after 1890 in an essay entitled "The American Drama." He commented on the art of acting in "Our Schools for the Stage," which appeared in *Century Magazine* in 1900. In one of the most revealing contemporary articles on late nineteenth century American dramatists—"American Playwrights on the American Drama," appearing in *Harper's Weekly* on February 2, 1889—Howard described his own approach to drama. Howard was a man of very definite opinions, and his most significant explanation of his theory of the "laws of dramatic composition" was first given as a lecture before the Shakespeare Club at Harvard College in March, 1886. This speech, in which he discussed at some length the origin and development of his play *The Banker's Daughter*, was repeated for the Nineteenth Century Club in New York in December, 1889, and was printed by the American Dramatists Club in New York and published as *The Autobiography of a Play* in 1914. This volume also included "Trash on the Stage and the Lost Dramatists of America," in which

Bronson Howard (Courtesy of the New York Public Library)

Howard outlined his approach to the theater and expressed his optimism regarding the future of American drama.

ACHIEVEMENTS

Bronson Howard's most significant achievement was his ability to earn a living by writing plays. Before Howard, many Americans—including William Dunlap, John Howard Payne, Robert Montgomery Bird, Nathaniel Bannister, Cornelius Mathews, George H. Boker, Epes Sargent, and Nathaniel Parker Willis—had written plays, some of which were better than Howard's. Although these earlier writers were professionals in the sense that they made money by writing plays, they were unable to sustain themselves with the income from their plays alone.

There is neither an extensive nor an impressive body of dramatic theory from pre-twentieth century American dramatists. Before Howard's lecture "The Laws of Dramatic Composition," commentary on dramatic theory was often scattered, slight, and haphazard. Basing his observations on one of his own plays, *The Banker's Daughter*, Howard outlined certain laws of dramatic construction that are significant in the history of dramatic theory in the United States, in particular illuminating those practices that made the melodramas of late nineteenth century America among the best that have been written. For Howard, the laws of dramatic composition were derived from an understanding of the sympathies of the audience as well as from the expected actions and motives of characters. To follow these laws, he believed, the dramatist had only to use common sense—to remain in touch with human nature. An audience will accept as "satisfactory" an occurrence that is, in a sense, deserved. For example, while an audience will accept the death of a good person in a tragedy, this acceptance will not be forthcoming in an ordinary play. Here, the death must be deserved or the audience will not be satisfied. Further, if a character is evil, the audience will not be satisfied unless that character is punished.

Howard's understanding of the importance of American business during the late nineteenth century and his ability to portray this characteristic of society effectively in his plays is both evidence of his insight and an achievement that distinguishes his work. His first work to explore the world of business, and, in fact, the first in its genre, was *Young Mrs. Winthrop*, a play in which business affairs consume the time and energies of the title character's husband, whose neglect of his society-minded wife threatens their life together. *The Henrietta*, considered by some critics to be his most successful play, reflects the stressful life of Wall Street financiers.

A creator of popular social melodramas on both the American stage and the English stage, Howard also left his mark on the future of professional American dramatists as the founder, in 1891, of the American Dramatists Club, later the Society of American Dramatists and Composers, the forerunner of the Dramatists Guild. Concerned with promoting a sense of community among dramatists, Howard used his prestige as the first president of the club to bring into existence an amendment to copyright laws that threatened severe punishment for any individual who attempted to steal the work of a playwright.

BIOGRAPHY

Bronson Howard was the son of Charles Howard, a merchant in Detroit, Michigan, whose grandfather, Seabury Howard, fought for the English in the French and Indian War and against them in the American Revolution. After a public school education in Detroit, Howard attended an eastern preparatory school, intending to go on to Yale University. Instead, after suffering from eye problems, he returned to Detroit, where he began his writing career with a series of humorous sketches for the *Detroit Free Press*. In 1864, the *Detroit Free Press* published his first play, *Fantine*, a dramatization of a portion of Victor Hugo's *Les Misérables* (1862; English translation, 1862).

Howard's interest in writing plays made him aware of the need to know and to understand the commercial theater, and he moved to New York in 1865. Although he continued to write plays, his innocence of the demands of his chosen profession rendered his early efforts fit only for the fireplace. He persisted, however, until he learned the accepted the-

ater conventions of his day, eventually evolving his own principles of dramaturgy. As he studied his craft, he attended theatrical performances, observed the society around him in New York, and made his living by writing for the New York *Tribune* and *Evening Post*.

One of the major problems facing American dramatists of this period was the dual demand placed on them: to satisfy the immediate theater audience while also providing dialogue that could be enjoyed by a literate public. Before Howard, American literary dramatists had generally eschewed the theatrical techniques that brought people into the theaters, while the actor-playwrights gave little thought to anything but the action on the stage. As a consequence of this split, there were few fully satisfactory American plays. Although Howard started as a journalist writing plays, he soon learned that plays were to be seen and must present interesting spectacles to the eye. At the same time, he was aware of the importance of the written word, particularly of dialogue that would reflect the interests of society.

Like all successful dramatists, Howard realized that his work would have to be judged not wholly as literature but according to the laws of the theater. Indeed, he objected to the publication of his plays and felt a slight contempt for literary people such as William Dean Howells, resenting their assumption that a true American drama might be realized only through their efforts. Late in his life, he went so far as to argue that drama should be absolutely divorced from literature, and he insisted on being called a "dramatist" rather than a "literary man."

Howard's first success in the theater came with the production in 1870 of a farce entitled *Saratoga*, which ran for 101 nights in Augustin Daly's Fifth Avenue Theatre. Two years later, Daly opened another Howard play, *Diamonds*, a comedy of manners which dealt with New York society. *Moorcroft*, also produced by Daly, was not particularly successful, but by this time *Saratoga* had been transferred to English circumstance by Frank Marshall and produced at the Court Theatre as *Brighton*, with Charles Wyndham in the leading role of Bob Sackett. *Brighton* had considerable success on London stages and gave Howard the beginning of a fine reputation that brought him much pleasure during his visits to England. His marriage to Charles Wyndham's sister helped sustain his English popularity. Five of Howard's plays eventually found responsive English audiences, and he was recognized during his lifetime as the first American playwright with a substantial reputation in Great Britain.

Howard's best-remembered play, *The Banker's Daughter*, first produced in 1873 as *Lillian's Last Love*, gained prestige after Howard's 1886 account of its development in his lecture *The Autobiography of a Play*. It was still being produced in 1914. A dozen years after he first came to New York, Howard was an established playwright. *Young Mrs. Winthrop* appeared in 1882; *One of Our Girls*, which stressed the international contrast in social life that was being exploited by Howells and Henry James, opened in 1885 and ran for two hundred nights. In *The Henrietta*, Howard satirized life on the stock exchange, and in *Shenandoah* he provided an exciting sentimental melodrama about love during the Civil War.

Howard wrote fewer plays in his later years. He lessened his stature in the eyes of historians of the drama by writing for the Theatrical Syndicate, an association of businessmen, formed in 1896, which for years controlled most New York theaters and many theaters in other large towns and which gradually exerted a stranglehold over entertainment in the United States. With audiences, however, he remained popular. Howard was one of the first American playwrights to make a fortune in his profession. A kind and honorable man, wholly without pretense, he enjoyed a long and productive career as a dramatist. When he died on August 4, 1908, at his home in Avon-by-the-Sea, New Jersey, he was widely acknowledged as the dean of American dramatists.

ANALYSIS

Bronson Howard came into the theater at an opportune time—a time when American rather than English actors and managers were beginning to control American theaters and were looking for American playwrights. As a writer-journalist rather than an actor or manager, Howard tried new approaches in order to learn about the theater. His subsequent comments reveal that literary dramatists and elitist critics tried his patience. This was a transition period—Howard's life in the theater—and when it was over, the writing of drama in the United States had undergone a change. Clyde Fitch was making a fortune in New York and elsewhere; Langdon Mitchell and William Vaughn Moody were successful playwrights, while Rachel Crothers and Edward Sheldon were about to appear on the scene. During that transitional period, other dramatists added to the development of an American drama, but no one matched Howard's accomplishments in social melodrama, dramatic theory, and service to American playwrights.

Howard's career as a dramatist developed during that period in American drama when playwrights were turning from dramatizing farcical representations of a stereotyped society, portrayed only in the most obvious ways, to a social comedy in which manners might be clearly distinguished. Earlier, the American theater had been dominated by spectacles and amusements created either by a star actor or actress or by the ingenuity of a theater manager and his stage carpenter. The Civil War cast a shadow over the American theater, but amid the struggle of social reconstruction, the dramatic arts bounced back with astonishing vigor, strengthened by the nationalism of Andrew Jackson's years, stimulated by the social and intellectual revolutions sparked by Karl Marx and Charles Darwin, and tempered by the sorrows of war. By the time Howard stopped writing, the United States had changed, both forcibly and by choice. American society, challenged by the strains on it, developed its own unique and distinctive character, and the United States was recognized as a nation among nations.

To match these changes, American dramatists needed to create a drama that could both amuse and stimulate the emotions and thoughts of the human mind. Howard was a major factor in the development of this American drama—as it grew from amusement to art.

Although Howard collaborated on at least three plays—*Baron Rudolph* with David Belasco, *Knave and Queen* with Sir Charles L. Young, and *Peter Stuyvesant* with Brander Matthews—and adapted

Molière's *L'École des maris* (pr., pb. 1661, verse play; *The School for Husbands*, 1732) and *L'École des femmes* (pr. 1662, verse play; *The School for Wives*, 1732) as *Wives*, he is remembered primarily for the originality of his plots and for his sensitivity and insight into American society. Although he was limited by the conventions and requirements of the theater of his time, he was deeply interested in dramatic theory and was particularly concerned with questions of dramatic structure. A well-constructed play, for Howard, was a "satisfactory" play—a play that is satisfactory to the audience. Believing that American and English audiences would not accept the death of a heroine in a play, Howard changed the ending of his original version of *The Banker's Daughter*. He made other changes in this play—changes that he claimed were founded on his "laws of dramatic composition." One of these laws, based on Howard's theory of what will satisfy an audience, is that those who do wrong (for example, a wife who has soiled her moral character) must always die before the final curtain falls. Similarly, and for the same reason, a love triangle must always bring disaster.

THE BANKER'S DAUGHTER

In the original version of *The Banker's Daughter*, Lillian Westbrook has married an older and wealthy man, John Strebelow, in order to save her father from financial ruin and also as a result of a quarrel with Harold Routledge. Five years later, now living in Paris with her husband and child, Lillian again meets Harold but remains faithful to her husband. The situation is then complicated by the Count de Carojac, who loves Lillian and who forces a duel with Harold. The supposed death of her old lover causes Lillian to reveal her passion and tell Strebelow that she never loved him. As a result, Strebelow takes the child away, and Lillian dies of a broken heart. The revised work shows the influence of Howard's theories of dramaturgy. First, because she has remained faithful, Lillian cannot be allowed to die in the last act, but because a love triangle cannot go unresolved, either Strebelow or Routledge must die. Howard chose Routledge, who is killed in the duel with the Count. Lillian now needs to recognize her own moral strength and save herself through this recognition

rather than depend on her child for that renewed strength. Finally, Strebelow needs to become a much stronger character, the hero of the play, in fact, and an appropriate mate for a mature Lillian, who now recognizes her own love for him.

YOUNG MRS. WINTHROP

By the third quarter of the nineteenth century, American society had been strongly affected by the industrial advances that had helped the North win the Civil War and by the so-called Robber Barons, notorious for their lifestyle of "conspicuous waste." Howard recognized the growing influence of the businessman in American society, and he foresaw the social pressures that would result. Howard's first play to reveal a conscious use of the social-economic movement against a background of fashionable society was *Young Mrs. Winthrop*. In this play, Howard dramatized the conflict between the world of business and the domestic sphere. The play enjoyed an initial run of 180 performances, and reviews hailed it as a great American dramatic work; indeed, many consider it to be Howard's most important play, if only because it was the first of its kind. Douglas and Constance Winthrop, businessman and society wife, no longer find joy in their married life. When a gossip, Mrs. Chetwyn, arouses Mrs. Winthrop's suspicions concerning Mr. Winthrop's fidelity, Mrs. Winthrop attends a society ball in opposition to the wishes of her husband. Circumstances promote ready suspicions, but Howard added melodrama to social comedy by having the Winthrops' child fall ill and die while they are away. Although the early action is enlivened by the careless and amusing Mrs. Chetwyn, the parents' grief in the later stages of the play threatens to overwhelm the initial premise. Mr. and Mrs. Winthrop part, only to be reunited in the final act as Howard superimposes his moral opinion on the problems that can confront the businessman in American society.

THE HENRIETTA

In *Young Mrs. Winthrop*, Howard portrayed a businessperson but did not present the details of the business world. He would do this most explicitly in *The Henrietta*, which more recent critics have called the first of the American business plays. Linking New

York society and the world of finance, Howard created a stage sermon on the vices of commercial gambling and the worship of money. Taking its title from the fictitious Henrietta Railroad, the control of which is the main issue in the melodramatic plot, the play dramatizes the financial rivalry between a father and his son. Nicholas Vanalstyne is known as "the Napoleon of Wall Street." His son, Nicholas Vanalstyne, Jr., is equally unscrupulous and is monomaniacally concerned with wrenching control of the financial empire from his father—he is even capable of robbing the company safe. To both men, business is "health, religion, friendship, love—everything." Through the activities of a second Vanalstyne son, Bertie, a satiric portrait of the club man of this period, Howard showed that other side of society that looked askance at the feverish and frequently sordid life of moneygrubbers such as the Vanalstynes. The success of young Nicholas is short-lived, and Bertie eventually saves the day for his father and wins the heroine. In addition, while the villainous son dies of a heart attack, Bertie continues his successful operation on the stock exchange, basing his decisions on the flip of a coin. Popular on the American stage for a number of years, *The Henrietta* was revised by Winchell Smith and Victor Mapes in 1913 as *The New Henrietta*. Changed to meet new theater conventions and modern thought, the play was surprisingly successful.

ONE OF OUR GIRLS

As the international comedy of manners became a strong social theme for American writers, Howard began to plumb its possibilities in his plays. His first such work, *One of Our Girls*, illustrates his mastery of the international theme. *One of Our Girls* ran for two hundred nights after its opening. The action of the play takes place in Paris, where the Fonblanque family is arranging the marriage of their daughter Julie to the Comte de Crebillon, known as a scoundrel and as a fine duelist. Opposed to this situation is Fonblanque's niece, Kate Shipley, the forthright and confident daughter of an American millionaire, who not only would not tolerate this arranged marriage of her cousin but also finds no good qualities in the Comte. The complications include a British army captain who falls in love with Kate, and Julie's lover,

Henri Saint-Hilaire, but these are finally resolved through the good sense and actions of Kate. Julie is united with her lover; Kate and the Captain have a promising future; and the Comte, having confessed that he killed his first wife, is proved to be a villain. Strong melodramatic action is present in the duel in which Henri is wounded and in the scene in which Kate protects Julie and allows herself to be caught in an embarrassing situation with Henri. Kate's American speech patterns provide some humor, as do the chatter of the gossips and the witticisms of the doctor. The main subject of the play, however, is the contrasting pictures of French and American marriage customs.

ARISTOCRACY

Howard tried again but failed to dramatize an international contrast in *Met by Chance*, in which part of the action takes place in the Adirondack Mountains. In *Aristocracy*, however, he effectually combined his interests in international society and the business world. The hero is Jefferson Stockton, a California capitalist and millionaire whose power and self-confidence precede him into every room. When his young wife reveals her social ambitions, he knows exactly how to satisfy them. Millionaires, he explains to her, are graded according to years and grandfathers, and in New York the newly rich man who thinks himself impressive is a fool. As he once ordered ten thousand tons of iron in New York, he will now order about five tons of good society for his wife, but it must be done carefully. The way to enter New York society is to take a house in London, and this Stockton does—after a few farcical episodes in London among the money-hunting European nobility. Although the caricatures of the financier and of the society he encounters weaken the overall effect of the social melodrama, the play has an interesting basic idea, and it held the stage for a respectable run.

OTHER MAJOR WORKS

NONFICTION: "American Playwrights on the American Drama," 1889; "Our Schools for the Stage," 1900; "The American Drama," 1906; *The Autobiography of a Play*, 1914.

BIBLIOGRAPHY

Frerer, Lloyd Anton. *Bronson Howard, Dean of American Dramatists*. Lewiston, N.Y.: Edwin Mellen Press, 2001. A biography of Howard that examines his life and the times in which he lived in addition to his dramatic works. Bibliography and index.

Mason, Jeffrey D. *Melodrama and the Myth of America*. Bloomington: Indiana University Press, 1999. Mason examines five nineteenth century melodramas, including Howard's *Shenandoah*, to demonstrate how dramatists interpreted history for their audiences. He argues that the melodramas presented reassuring myths about the past.

Meserve, Walter J. "Comedy and Social Drama: Caricature, Comedy, and Thesis Plays." In *The Revels History of Drama in English, 1865-1920*. Vol. 8. London: Methuen, 1977. A brief introduction to Howard as the first professional American playwright. Meserve focuses on Howard's depiction of businessmen and describes his "Laws of Dramatic Composition." Howard pioneered the awareness of the new social, middle class in the United States.

Vaughn, Jack A. *Early American Dramatists*. New York: Frederick Ungar, 1981. A brief biography and introduction to the major plays. Contrasts Howard's early comedies with his later social dramas, focusing on *The Henrietta* and *Shenandoah*.

Walter J. Meserve,
updated by Gerald S. Argetsinger

SIDNEY HOWARD

Born: Oakland, California; June 26, 1891
Died: Tyringham, Massachusetts; August 23, 1939

PRINCIPAL DRAMA

Swords, pr., pb. 1921
Casanova, pb. 1921, pr. 1923 (adaptation of Lorenzo de Azertis' play)
S.S. Tenacity, pr. 1922, pb. 1929 (adaptation of Charles Vildrac's play *Le Paquebot Tenacity*)
Bewitched, pr. 1924 (with Edward Sheldon)
They Knew What They Wanted, pr. 1924, pb. 1925
Lucky Sam McCarver, pr. 1925, pb. 1926
The Last Night of Don Juan, pr. 1925 (adaptation of Edmond Rostand's play *La Dernière Nuit de Don Juan*)
Morals, pr. 1925 (with Charles Recht; adaptation of Ludwig Thoma's play)
Ned McCobb's Daughter, pr., pb. 1926
The Silver Cord, pr. 1926, pb. 1927
Salvation, pr. 1928 (with Charles MacArthur)
Olympia, pr., pb. 1928 (adaptation of Ferenc Molnár's play)
Half Gods, pr. 1929, pb. 1930
The Late Christopher Bean, pr. 1932, pb. 1933 (adapted from René Fauchois' play *Prenez garde à la peinture*)
Alien Corn, pr., pb. 1933
Yellow Jack, pr., pb. 1934 (with Paul de Kruif; based on de Kruif's book *Microbe Hunters*)
Dodsworth, pr., pb. 1934 (adaptation of Sinclair Lewis's novel)
Paths of Glory, pr., pb. 1935 (adaptation of Humphrey Cobb's novel)
The Ghost of Yankee Doodle, pr. 1937, pb. 1938
Madame, Will You Walk?, pr. 1953, pb. 1955

OTHER LITERARY FORMS

Although best known for his plays, Sidney Howard also translated and adapted a number of works. In his early years, Howard worked as a literary editor and wrote, with Robert Dunn, a collection of articles on strikebreaking agencies entitled *The Labor Spy* (1921). In 1924, he published four stories under the single title *Three Flights Up*. Like Robert E. Sherwood and Clifford Odets, Howard devoted much of his time to writing screenplays, primarily for Samuel Goldwyn's studio. With Wallace Smith, he wrote the script for *Bulldog Drummond* (1929), based on stories by the British writer H. C. McNeile, who wrote under the pen name "Sapper." Howard also adapted two novels by Sinclair Lewis, *Arrowsmith* (1925) in 1931 and *Dodsworth* (1929) in 1936, to the screen. For his 1939 film adaptation of Margaret Mitchell's *Gone with the Wind* (1936), Howard won an Academy Award.

ACHIEVEMENTS

Although Sidney Howard contributed little that was unique to American drama, his reputation rests chiefly on his ability to focus on limited, narrow subjects and, in the process, to reveal something essential about the human condition. He created a number of substantial and effective plays, characterized by sound craftsmanship, honesty, and skill. In limiting himself to dramatizing concrete, specific situations, he created sharp, telling vignettes about particular people in varied yet specific settings.

Howard's achievements are seen in his expert characterization and in his emphasis on social perspective, which helped his plays transcend the limitations of contemporary drama. In 1925, his efforts were recognized; he was awarded the Pulitzer Prize for *They Knew What They Wanted*.

BIOGRAPHY

Sidney Coe Howard was the son of John Lawrence Howard and Helen Louise Coe. His paternal grandfather, born of English parents, had emigrated from Antrim, Ireland, in 1848 and had settled in Philadelphia. After attending public schools in Oakland, California, Howard was graduated from the University of California in 1915 and then attended George Pierce Baker's Workshop 47 at Harvard University. During this time, Howard began his early collaborative efforts with Edward Sheldon, who had a great influence on the development of American drama. In 1916, Howard received a master of arts degree from Harvard.

World War I interrupted Howard's creative career. Inducted into the service in 1916, he served first as an ambulance driver in France and in the Balkans and then as a captain and fighter pilot in the newly formed Air Service. In 1919, Howard joined the editorial staff of the old humor magazine *Life* in New York. Three years later, he became the literary editor of *Life* and was writing and adapting plays. In 1921, he married Clare Eames, an actress, and they had a child, Clare Jenness Howard.

Howard's determined interest in the daily lives of people led him to work in 1923 as a special investigative reporter and fiction writer for *The New Republic* and *International Magazine*. Before settling into the style of social drama that eventually brought him success, Howard wrote his first play, *Swords*, which failed, and collaborated with Sheldon on *Bewitched*.

Following Howard's recognition as a playwright for *They Knew What They Wanted*, he continued over the next five years to write or translate and adapt several plays. Three of these, *Dodsworth*, *Paths of Glory*, and *The Late Christopher Bean*, are among his best contributions to American drama.

Lucky Sam McCarver opened at the Playhouse Theatre in New York on October 21, 1925, and capitalized on the spectacle of affluent life among New York's socialites. The play is an ironic statement on that society and those who aspire to it. *Ned McCobb's Daughter* and *The Silver Cord* both came to New York theaters in 1926. With its well-drawn characters, *The Silver Cord* is one of the outstanding social-thesis plays in American drama. Neither *Salvation* nor *Half Gods* was successful, and after 1929 Howard concentrated on writing screenplays. During the last ten years of his life, Howard continued to write for the stage and achieved moderate success with his adaptation of *The Late Christopher Bean* and with *Alien Corn*. Active in theater affairs, Howard served from 1935 to 1937 as president of the Dramatists Guild, and in 1938—along with Sherwood, S. N. Behrman, Maxwell Anderson, and Elmer Rice—he formed the Playwrights' Producing Company, organized to produce their plays without interference from commercial producers.

In 1930, following the death of Clare Eames, by that time his former wife, Howard married Leopoldine Blaine Damrosch, the daughter of musician Walter Damrosch. They had two children: a daughter, Sidney Damrosch Howard, and a son, Walter Damrosch Howard. Sidney Howard died on August 23, 1939, as a result of a tractor accident on his Massachusetts farm.

ANALYSIS

Sidney Howard was neither an innovator in dramatic form nor a particularly profound writer, and he readily admitted these facts. He was content to "get a kind of glamour around reality," to dare less and achieve more. He was nevertheless a substantial playwright of considerable theatrical skill and imagination who stepped into the ongoing stream of social drama in America and produced at least two major plays in that genre.

THEY KNEW WHAT THEY WANTED

Despite a tendency toward preachiness, *They Knew What They Wanted* is an important play for its humanity and for its insight into social morality. A modern version of Dante's story of the love of Paolo and Francesca, it demonstrated Howard's ability to write a compact, effective play.

Tony, a sixty-year-old Italian winegrower, proposes by mail to Amy, a young waitress, whom he has seen once and admired. They correspond, and Amy asks for a photograph of him. Instead, he sends one of Joe, his handsome young hired hand. On his way to the station to pick up Amy, Tony has an automobile accident and is injured. When Amy arrives at the house, she mistakes Joe for Tony, and on discovering that Tony is to be her husband, she is shocked. After the wedding party, Amy, miserable, is left alone with Joe, and they make love. The discovery three months later that Amy is pregnant, Tony's resultant anger, his struggle with his pride, and his final acceptance of and triumph over the trouble, as well as the resolution for all three characters of this dilemma, make up the heart of the play. All three characters, in the end, know and get what they want, and all are, in the end, satisfied.

In Tony, Howard created his most successful character. The most appealing and most real figure in the play, Tony is also the one most able to deal with the exigencies of the world. He discovers that he can ac-

cept Amy's child, love Amy, and find joy in his new family. He becomes not the most miserable of men but a "most happy fella." The other two characters make similar discoveries: Amy discovers that she really cares for Tony and wants to be his wife, and Joe finds that he really values his freedom. The play ends satisfactorily, for the characters and for the audience.

THE SILVER CORD

The Silver Cord, although it also suffers from preachment, has a profound effect on audiences, delving into a deep and often hidden layer of human emotion. Mrs. Phelps, a domineering mother, is in a struggle to possess the love of her two sons and to exclude from their affections the women whom they love. She successfully destroys the love of Robert and his fiancée, Hester, but fails to break up the marriage of her older son, David, and Christina, a more determined woman than Hester and more of a match for Mrs. Phelps. Howard expresses his antipathy toward filial duty grounded on pathological dependence through Christina, who says, "An embryological accident is no ground for honour," and through Hester, who says of children, "Have 'em. Love 'em. And then leave 'em be."

The play dramatizes this conflict—between a "professional" mother and an independent and ambitious wife. Both deserve some sympathy even as each struggles desperately for the fulfillment of her own selfish needs. Christina, however, is not morally disfigured, as is Mrs. Phelps. Christina's concern for her own career is balanced by her more healthy concern for the life of her unborn child and for the freedom to live that she knows is necessary for her own happiness and for David's.

Mrs. Phelps is singularly diabolical, and this makes her a very interesting character; she stalks her sons like prey, weakening their other loyalties with innuendo and crafty appeals for sympathy, then pouncing when these loyalties have been sufficiently worn down. The play is marred, however, by too much weakness in the sons, by the lack of any real dramatic discovery on Christina's part, by the lack of credibility in David's late and undermotivated decision to leave in the end, and, finally, by the playwright's preachiness. By the end of the play, the audience is satisfied: Christina has defeated the villainess after an intense battle, she has helped to free innocent Hester, and she has gained her own personal objective. Christina, however, seems a bit too much like Mrs. Phelps for comfort, and David may well be merely stepping out of one trap and into another. As a social drama with a Freudian thesis, however—the level on which the play was most generally understood—it was successful and powerfully dramatic on the stage.

LUCKY SAM MCCARVER AND NED MCCOBB'S DAUGHTER

During the 1920's, Howard adapted several plays and wrote several more. Both *Lucky Sam McCarver* and *Ned McCobb's Daughter*—one a theatrical failure and the other a success—show elements of the social drama at which Howard excelled. Each is concerned with a strong character who faces a series of frustrating social situations and who reacts powerfully to those conditions and frustrations.

Lucky Sam McCarver starts as an analysis of cold, materialistic Sam McCarver but is more effective as the story of a woman who desperately wants love from a man who has only money to give. Sam, who is hardened in his worship of money, frankly uses his wife and her name and sees nothing beyond his growing empire. Having lost human compassion and the ability to feel, he can only think and contrive; in Howard's world, which is essentially a world of action and feeling rather than thought, Sam has no value.

Unlike the comedy *Ned McCobb's Daughter*, in which social conditions provide the background for Carrie to show her superiority of character and her Yankee determination, *Lucky Sam McCarver* is an unhappy social drama about irresponsible people: a frustrated woman and a materialistic man who will always be "disappointed in the universe." Howard's characters usually know what they want, but Howard invariably controls their destinies. Although he frequently tempers his moral judgments with true mercy, within his definitions of right and wrong he is completely conventional in meting out rewards and punishments, emphasizing his preference for a "satisfactory" ending to a play.

YELLOW JACK

In the 1930's, Howard wrote and adapted several plays, bringing his total output to more than twenty-five plays. Worthy of mention is *Yellow Jack*, written with Paul de Kruif and based on de Kruif's book *Microbe Hunters* (1926). Although not a popular success when first staged, it has been frequently revived. Set in and around an army barracks near Havana, Cuba, it follows Major Walter Reed and his colleagues' fight to isolate the cause of yellow fever, quietly tracing the events and highlighting the nobility of the characters involved in the enterprise and the sacrifices they made. Again, Howard keeps the focus of the play narrow, allowing no extraneous "love interest" or other episodes to interfere with the progress of the action.

CHARACTER DEVELOPMENT

Howard found his greatest success in creating social drama from a mixture of realism, melodrama, and comedy. His major interest in his plays, however, was his characters. Psychological interpretation of character is an essential part of his best plays. More exuberant than thoughtful, he was frequently satisfied to have his characters simply react emotionally to strong stimuli.

In *They Knew What They Wanted*, for example, Tony tells Amy: "What you have done is mistake in da head, not in da heart." For Howard, emotion is more important than intellect. Similarly, Christina in *The Silver Cord* at first relies on reason to resolve her difficulties with Mrs. Phelps, but her attempts fail; intellect is not enough.

Although he generally followed an established trend in American drama, Howard, in his best plays, created strong, compelling characters, interacting in situations that allowed his drama to transcend the limitations of the merely personal. The individualistic, life-affirming spirit of his work was a welcome addition to the social drama of the 1920's.

OTHER MAJOR WORKS

SHORT FICTION: *Three Flights Up*, 1924.

SCREENPLAYS: *Bulldog Drummond*, 1929 (with Wallace Smith; based on stories by H. C. McNeile); *Arrowsmith*, 1931 (based on Sinclair Lewis's novel);

Dodsworth, 1936 (based on Lewis's novel); *Gone with the Wind*, 1939 (based on Margaret Mitchell's novel).

NONFICTION: *The Labor Spy*, 1921 (with Robert Dunn).

BIBLIOGRAPHY

Bonin, Jane F. *Major Themes in Prize-Winning American Drama*. Metuchen, N.J.: Scarecrow Press, 1975. This insightful analysis of Howard's plays shows that he was interested in staging the self-made man and the success ethic as well as depicting women in various roles in marriage and society. Marriages are grim, yet American women are pragmatic; they need a husband for security, no matter how intelligent and strong they might be.

Leff, Leonard J. "*Gone with the Wind* and Hollywood's Racial Politics." *Atlantic Monthly* 284, no. 6 (December, 1999) 106-114. Discusses producer David O. Selznick's efforts to remain true to Margaret Mitchell's novel, adapted for the screen by Howard, while improving the portrayal of African Americans in the film.

White, Sydney Howard. *Sidney Howard*. Boston: Twayne, 1977. This well-conceived monograph offers a biographical and critical survey of the early essays and stories as well as of the major stage plays and screenplays. Quotations from letters, articles, and reviews help to shape the final evaluation of Howard's corpus. The endnotes present information on performances. The chronological table and the bibliography are useful.

Walter J. Meserve,
updated by Irene Gnarra

TINA HOWE

Born: New York, New York; November 21, 1937

PRINCIPAL DRAMA

Closing Time, pr. 1959
The Nest, pr. 1969
Birth and After Birth, wr. 1973, pb. 1977, revised
    pr. 1995
Museum, pr. 1976, pb. 1979
The Art of Dining, pr. 1979, pb. 1980
Appearances, pr. 1982 (one act)
Painting Churches, pr. 1983, pb. 1984
Three Plays, pb. 1984
Coastal Disturbances, pr. 1986, pb. 1987
Approaching Zanzibar, pr., pb. 1989
Coastal Disturbances: Four Plays, pb. 1989
One Shoe Off, pr., pb. 1993
Approaching Zanzibar and Other Plays, pb. 1995
Pride's Crossing, pr. 1997, pb. 1998
Rembrandt's Gift, pr. 2002

OTHER LITERARY FORMS
Tina Howe is known primarily for her plays.

ACHIEVEMENTS
Tina Howe has earned distinction as one of the leading American dramatists of the commercial theater, and she has received some of the highest awards for playwriting. In 1983, largely in response to her most studied and successful play, *Painting Churches*, she captured an Obie Award for Distinguished Playwriting, the Rosamond Gilder Award for Outstanding Creative Achievement in Theatre, and a Rockefeller Playwright-in-Residence Fellowship. In addition to the Outer Critics Circle John Gassner Award for Outstanding New American Playwright in 1984, she has received two National Endowment for the Arts Fellowships, a Guggenheim Fellowship, an American of Arts and Letters Award in Literature, a Tony nomination for Best Play (*Coastal Disturbances*), and an honorary degree from Bowdoin Col-

lege. *Pride's Crossing* was a finalist for the Pulitzer Prize in Drama and in 1998 received the New York Drama Critics Circle Award for best play.

BIOGRAPHY

Tina Howe, reared in New York City, was born into an aristocratic and celebrated family. Her grandfather, Mark Antony DeWolfe Howe, was a renowned poet and Pulitzer Prize recipient. Her father, Quincy Howe, was an eminent radio and television broadcaster, and her mother, Mary, was a painter. After attending private schools in New York, Howe went to Sarah Lawrence College in Bronxville, New York, where she received a baccalaureate degree in 1959. Howe tried her hand at playwriting during her undergraduate studies and had a play produced (*Closing Time*) at Sarah Lawrence College, with Howe directing and Jane Alexander, Howe's classmate, starring in the production. She did not seriously consider becoming a dramatist, however, until the year after her graduation, when she traveled to Paris and had the opportunity to meet aspiring young writers and, more important, to see various experimental, absurdist theater productions, in particular Eugène Ionesco's *La Cantatrice chauve* (pr. 1950; *The Bald Soprano*, 1956) and *Rhinocéros* (pr., pb. 1959; *Rhinoceros*, 1959). This experience was a turning point for Howe, for the absurdist dramas appealed to her own antic, comic spirit, and these plays would later influence her dramaturgical style. She returned to New York, married writer Norman Levy in 1961, and taught high school English in Maine, where she also served as drama coach for the school's club. This position helped her learn her craft, for the rigors of writing one-act plays for the club's production season helped her gain the discipline and focus that she needed as a writer. During the late 1960's and early 1970's, Howe and Levy took various teaching positions at colleges in Chicago, Madison, and Albany. Howe continued to write plays, with *The Nest* receiving a professional production. In 1973, the couple settled in New York City with their two children. In 1983 Howe began working as an adjunct professor of playwriting at New York University and in 1990 became a visiting professor at Hunter College.

ANALYSIS

Tina Howe is not only one of the most prominent female playwrights from a new generation of American dramatists who emerged during the second women's movement but also represents a group of dramatists whose works characterize the postmodern theater movement that began in the early 1970's. Her plays blend traditional domestic drama with the experimental techniques that deploy considerable theatricality. On the surface, they appear naturalistic, slice-of-life comedies, but she injects an element of Surrealism throughout her plays by inserting unexpected, outrageous actions: the frenetic destruction of artworks, an old lady jumping on a trampoline. Like the absurdists, Howe focuses on existential issues, but she lacks their darkness and nihilism, preferring that her characters, and the audience, laugh at life's reversals and accept them with valor and courage. Her language can be, at turns, everyday conversation with dialogue overlapping, or elegantly poetic arias and soliloquies. Through comedy, Howe probes the most basic of human emotions, forces laughter and compassion for those who suffer agonies familiar to all, and reminds viewers that life is full of both tragic and comic events. She celebrates life's everyday, ordinary events—the sunsets, the family vacation, the reunion with relatives—those special ephemeral moments that can be captured perhaps on canvas or with a photograph but can never be relived. Between birth and death is life in process. Howe reminds the audience to live it to the fullest.

Howe's plays are remarkable for their absurdist depiction of life and their female perspective. Her playwriting style closely allies her with the absurdists, to whom she admits her indebtedness. In particular, she borrowed the absurdists' use of surreal details, incongruous actions, bizarre situations, and farcical characters, for these devices suited her interest in exploring the passions, drives, fears, and anxieties that lie below the surface in all persons. As a result, her plays are, on the one hand, wildly comic, replete with pratfalls, sight gags, and much physical and verbal comedy, and yet, on the other hand, are rueful and poignant, exposing the emotional pain of characters who battle life's unavoidable tragedies and suffering. This tragicomic view of life has sparked comparisons between Howe and Russian playwright Anton Chekhov, specifically for Howe's ability to capture "the same edgy surface of false hilarity, the same unutterable sadness beneath it, and the indomitable valor beneath both." Howe presents her absurdist view of life from the female perspective: The central protagonists of her plays are women, and it is through their experiences that Howe explores such universal concerns as the ravages of time, the ineluctable human process of deterioration, the basal anxieties over death, and the human need to find meaning and permanence in an ephemeral world.

THE NEST AND BIRTH AND AFTER BIRTH

Howe's first two comedies, *The Nest* and *Birth and After Birth*, are her most overtly feminist and absurdist plays. In these works, Howe draws biting satirical portraits of women as they struggle to find autonomy in a world demanding that they live according to the traditional roles of wives and mothers. *The Nest* depicts a trio of young women battling one another for the prize of an ideal husband, and the inanity of their actions culminates in a highly charged, symbolic moment, when one of the women

Tina Howe (© Miriam Berkley)

removes all of her clothes and dives into a seven-foot-tall wedding cake. *The Nest* was panned by critics and closed after one performance. *Birth and After Birth* looks at women's choices concerning childbirth. Through Sandy, mother of a four-year-old son with behavioral problems (played by an adult actor), who grows increasingly disillusioned and enraged over the demands that her family places on her, Howe shows the physical and emotional toll that child rearing takes on women and attacks the myth that marriage and motherhood fulfill women's lives. On the opposite pole, Mia, a married anthropologist with no children, fears the physical pain of childbirth, and although she has tried to find personal fulfillment through her job, she feels inadequate as a woman because she has no children. With this play, Howe said she wanted "to show how threatening women on either side of the fence can be to each other." The play implies as well that women, regardless of their choices regarding marriage and children, continue both to define and to judge themselves according to the myths of motherhood and family life. *Birth and After Birth* has proved so incendiary that Howe has had difficulty getting it staged.

A NEW APPROACH

After the failure of these two plays, Howe made a conscious effort to alter her playwriting style. She took note of the successful Broadway plays at the time and concluded that audiences wanted escape, so she set out to find settings that had not been used onstage before, something that audiences would find novel. More important, she decided to tone down her feminist voice by couching it in less threatening dramatic terms. As a result, Howe took women out of their domestic arena, placed them in such exotic and unlikely locales as museums, restaurants, and beaches, and made her central protagonists women artists. When Howe hit on this idea and wrote her first successful play (*Museum*) as a result of her new writing strategy, she knew that she had hit her stride: "I had found my niche at last. I would write about women as artists, eschew the slippery ground of courtship and domesticity and move up to a loftier plane." Her later plays are still full of comic exuberance, zany characters, and outrageous situations, but her female characters, in the main, now seek their creative and intellectual potential through nontraditional roles, most particularly as artists.

MUSEUM

As the play's title suggests, *Museum* takes place in a museum gallery with three modernist exhibits: five life-size, clothed figures hanging from a twenty-five-foot clothesline and a basket of clothespins on the floor, a series of sculptures made from animal bones and feathers displayed on pedestals, and a group of three, totally white paintings along one wall. *Museum* has no traditional plot; it is a collage of conversations by some forty gallery visitors who meander about studying the exhibits, some expressing their disgust and confusion over such abstract drivel, others completely enthralled and postulating the meaning of each work and the purpose of art in general. The climax of the action occurs when Tink Solheim, a friend of Agnes Vaag (the sculptor of the animal-bone exhibit) begins frantically to search for the special secret that Agnes said was hidden in one of the sculptures. Tink finds a hidden switch, and when she turns it, the lights dim, floodlight illuminates the statue, and music by Johann Sebastian Bach swells out from a hidden speaker. The crowd stands entranced for several minutes, experiencing a communal epiphany. This spiritual awakening leads to pandemonium, as the play concludes with the gallery visitors running about in a frenzy, ripping apart the exhibits, and stealing parts of them in their desire to own at least a small part of something artistic, spiritual, and eternal.

THE ART OF DINING

The communal and spiritual experience brought about by a woman's work of art in *Museum* has its parallel in Howe's next play, *The Art of Dining*. The artist in this play is Ellen, a gourmet chef and partner with her husband in a trendy restaurant. Where people coveted art in *Museum*, in this comedy they wish literally to devour it. Starving diners from the surrounding area come to the restaurant to feast voraciously on Ellen's famous culinary masterpieces. The symbol of spiritual starvation in the previous play is made more literal in *The Art of Dining*, and, similar to the finale of *Museum*, Howe brings all the visitors together in one communal, ritual moment brought

about by the female creator. Everyone huddles together to feast on Ellen's complementary dessert. The symbolism of this closing moment of shared community is articulated by one of the diners, Elizabeth Colt, a young anorexic novelist, who stands apart as the diners eat with gusto and explains that centuries ago people gathered together in a shared celebration to enjoy the feast. Through their collective communion brought about by Ellen's gift, this group of strangers comes together in one common humanity, "purified of their collective civilization and private grief."

PAINTING CHURCHES

Painting Churches, Howe's most successful comedy, returns to the world of the artist. It explores parent-child relationships, children's need to gain parental acceptance and approval, and, especially, the larger and more serious issues of life's inevitable process toward deterioration and the ultimate movement toward death. In this play, Mags Church, an impressionist painter, visits home after a long absence to paint a portrait of her aged parents before their imminent move from their Boston family home and just prior to her first solo show in a famous art gallery. Mags needs her parents' recognition of her creative genius (something they have never given her), and she hopes that her portrait of them will gain their respect for her as an artist and an adult. Once home, however, Mags sees the debilitating effects of time on her parents; her father, Gardner, once a renowned poet, is now addled, and her mother, Fanny, has been reduced to a life of taking care of her senile husband. Mags must face the shattering reality that all children encounter: Her parents are nearing death. After some difficulty getting her parents to sit still long enough to pose, Mags finally finishes her portrait, and it is this gift to her parents that brings all three together in a celebratory moment at the end of the play. When Fanny and Gardner look at their portrait, they compare it to one of Pierre-Auguste Renoir's works, and eventually they envision themselves as figures in a Renoir café scene with couples dancing. A Chopin waltz begins to play, and they start to dance about the room, oblivious to Mags, who stands watching them, her eyes filled with tears. Through Mags's painting, her parents have been rejuvenated, if only for a moment, for in effect they have been transformed into the painting. For a brief, magical moment, time stands still. Mags has locked her parents in time, capturing and immortalizing them by her portrait. Although her parents will soon die, they will continue to live not only in her memory but also forever on her canvas.

COASTAL DISTURBANCES

Coastal Disturbances includes various short scenes that form a collage, a series of impressions about love from different points of view, from an elderly couple who have withstood infidelities and other marital tragedies to a young couple caught up in sexual infatuation. The play's heroine, Holly, is a professional photographer who has come to a private beach in Massachusetts for a two-week vacation to take photographs and to forget a disastrous affair with her agent-boyfriend in New York. Holly becomes enamored of a compassionate and lovable lifeguard, but when her former boyfriend tracks her down and begs a reconciliation, she capitulates to his charm. Although Howe is concerned with the passage of time, which is made quite visible by the ever-changing and gorgeous sunrises and sunsets on the beach, she does not explore this theme as vividly and dramatically as in *Painting Churches*. *Coastal Disturbances* is atypical of Howe's work; it is a love story that attempts to teach that forgiveness, compassion, and tenderness can calm any emotional disturbance and heal the heart.

APPROACHING ZANZIBAR

With *Approaching Zanzibar*, Howe returns to her previous preoccupations with life's ephemerality, death, art, and rebirth. The Blossom family (husband Wally, wife Charlotte, and two children, Turner and Pony) take a cross-country trek from Hastings, New York, to Taos, New Mexico, to visit Charlotte's dying aunt, Olivia. On this two-week trip, the Blossoms enjoy a typical vacation, camping out, fishing, visiting relatives, and meeting some interesting strangers. At every turn, however, the realities of life's brevity and ultimate closure through death form a palpable background. Not only is the trip itself a metaphor for the journey of life with its end in death (symbolized by

Olivia), but also, throughout, characters make repeated references to the passage of time and the loss of youth and its promise of a future. Charlotte is menopausal, and her anguish over her inability to have more children causes her nightmares about abandoned babies. Wally, once a famous composer, lost his creative energy when his parents' deaths the year earlier traumatized him, forcing him to confront his own mortality. Howe underscores her theme of the inexorable cycle of life (birth, death, rebirth) not only through dialogue with numerous allusions to evolution and reincarnation but also through the Blossom children. Although Charlotte and Wally face midlife, their children are their source of hope and touch with immortality. Turner is a musical prodigy with great promise of carrying on his father's talent. Pony possesses the most miraculous and powerful counter to death, her potential progeny. The celebration of the female's ability to create life and rejuvenate her species as the ultimate defense against death forms the play's closing tableau: Pony, alone at Olivia's bedside, rejuvenates the dying woman; soon the two hold hands and begin jumping on Olivia's bed (a trampoline) while crying out "Paradise." All the others rush into the room, freeze at the sight of them leaping into the air, and then gather around the bed to join their euphoric shouts of "Paradise." Here again, Howe ends her play in a highly charged, theatrical moment of spiritual communion, an affirmation of life, nurturing, and humanity, with the female at its core.

PRIDE'S CROSSING

In *Pride's Crossing*, Howe wanted fictionally to allow an elderly maiden aunt of hers, a "dutiful Boston daughter" who never rebelled against social mores, to express anger over what she had missed. *Pride's Crossing* explores a powerful woman's passage through a life marred by social constraints. The play's main protagonist is ninety-year-old Mabel Tidings Bigelow, who in her twenties was the first woman to swim across the English Channel. In the course of the play Mabel's memories take shape and we see the younger Mabel at ages ranging from ten to sixty. The usually rebellious young woman's family were part of a proper Bostonian upper class, and her ties to that society cost her the one great—but socially unacceptable—love of her life; she married an alcoholic Boston Protestant instead of the Jewish doctor who truly loved her. The younger Mabel's athleticism and physical strength contrast with the lost potential of the feisty but aged woman who still clings to social niceties and has lost her physical power. In the end, *Pride's Crossing* expresses the passion of the old woman who looks back and sees the consequences of doing what she thought was right, rather than taking the plunge and following her heart.

BIBLIOGRAPHY

Backes, Nancy. "Body Art: Hunger and Satiation in the Plays of Tina Howe." In *Making a Spectacle*, edited by Lynda Hart. Ann Arbor: University of Michigan Press, 1989. Women writers' use of food has become a major area of research, and this essay adds to that body of scholarship by incisively examining Howe's abundant use of food imagery relative to cultural inscriptions about women's bodies, self-image, self-control, and nurturing.

Barlow, Judith E. "The Art of Tina Howe." In *Feminine Focus*, edited by Enoch Brater. Oxford, England: Oxford University Press, 1989. Barlow discusses one of the central motifs in Howe's plays, the importance of art in daily life. Barlow pays particular attention to Howe's use of women as artists, and her insightful comments clarify Howe's interest in celebrating the unique and powerful creativity of women artists.

_____. "Tina Howe." In *Speaking on Stage: Interviews with Contemporary American Playwrights*. Edited by Philip C. Kolin and Colby H. Kullman. Tuscaloosa: University of Alabama Press, 1996. Howe discusses writing comedic plays and the recurring themes in her work.

Betsko, Kathleen, and Rachel Koening. *Interviews with Contemporary Women Playwrights*. New York: Beech Tree Books, 1987. Howe's interview contains a range of biographical information on her, including her writing habits, her view on the arts, her absurdist roots, and her thematic concerns from *The Nest* to *Painting Churches*.

DiGaetani, John L. *A Search for a Postmodern Theater: Interviews with Contemporary Playwrights*. Westport, Conn.: Greenwood Press, 1991. In this interview, Howe discusses her indebtedness to the absurdist playwrights, her concerns as a feminist writer, and autobiographical aspects of her plays and characters. Contains a photograph of Howe.

Howe, Tina. "Antic Vision." *American Theatre* 2 (September, 1985): 12, 14. Although numerous published interviews with Howe provide firsthand information from the playwright, this essay by Howe, written after the success of *Painting Churches*, offers the most insight into her views about comical playwriting, her feminist vision, and her aesthetic voice. Contains photographs from production scenes of *Painting Churches* and *The Art of Dining*.

_____. "Women's Work: White Gloves or Bare Hands?" *American Theatre* 15 (September, 1998): 7. Excerpts from a keynote speech given at the November, 1997, Women's Project Conference. Howe talks about critical responses to her early plays and being both a writer and mother.

Kachur, B. A. "Women Playwrights on Broadway: Henley, Howe, Norman, and Wasserstein." In *Contemporary American Theatre*, edited by Bruce King. New York: St. Martin's Press, 1991. This chapter on four prominent women playwrights includes information on Howe's metadramatic techniques and her feminist perspective, particularly her use of women both as central protagonists and as artists.

Swarns, Rachel L. "New Play, and Old Questions, About Women." *New York Times*, December 7, 1997, Section 2, p. 4. Howe discusses the struggle to find acceptance for women playwrights and feminist topics on Broadway. Other women playwrights and producers offer their perspectives.

Wetzsteon, Ross. "The Mad, Mad World of Tina Howe." *New York* 16 (November 28, 1983): 58. Wetzsteon surveys Howe's plays through *Painting Churches*, discusses biographical details, and provides a brief analysis of Howe's playwriting style and themes.

B. A. Kachur,
updated by Maureen Puffer-Rothenberg